Child Development

Child Development

Laura E. Berk
Illinois State University

Allyn and Bacon
Boston   London   Sydney   Toronto

In loving memory of my parents
Sofie and Philip Eisenberg

 Copyright © 1989, by Allyn and Bacon
A Division of Simon & Schuster
160 Gould Street, Needham Heights, Massachusetts, 02194

Library of Congress Cataloging-in-Publication Data

Berk, Laura E.
    Child development.

    Bibliography: p.
    Includes index.
    1. Child development.   I. Title.
HQ767.9.B464   1989   649′.1   88-7740
ISBN 0-205-11715-5

Managing Editor: Mylan Jaixen
Series Editor: John-Paul Lenney
Developmental Editor: Leslie G. Goldberg
Series Editorial Assistant: Susan S. Brody
Cover Administrator: Linda Dickinson
Composition Buyer: Linda Cox
Manufacturing Buyer: Bill Alberti
Editorial-Production Administrator: Rowena Dores
Text Designer: Glenna Collett
Photo Researcher: Jennifer Ralph/Picture Research Consultancy

Printed in the United States of America.

10   9   8   7   6   5   4   3   2   1   93   92   91   90   89   88

About the Author

Laura E. Berk is Professor of Psychology at Illinois State University, where she has taught child development to undergraduate and graduate students for nearly two decades. She received her Bachelor's degree from the University of California, Berkeley, and her Masters and Doctoral degrees from the University of Chicago. She was visiting scholar at Cornell University in 1975–1976 and at the University of California, Los Angeles, in 1982–1983. She has published extensively on effects of school environments on children's development, and more recently, on the relationship between children's language and thought. Her research on children's private speech is currently funded by the National Institute of Child Health and Human Development. She is consulting editor for *Young Children,* journal of the National Association for the Education of Young Children.

Brief Contents

Detailed Contents

Preface

For many years, I have taught courses in child development to students with diverse college majors, future goals, interests, and needs. Some are students in my own academic department, psychology, while many others come from other child-related fields, such as education, home economics, sociology, anthropology, and biology, to name just a few. Each semester, the professional aspirations of my students have proved to be as varied as their fields of study. Many look toward careers in applied work with children — teaching, caregiving, nursing, counseling, social work, school psychology, and program administration. A few plan to teach child development at the college level, and some want to do research. Most hope someday to have children of their own, and a number are already parents who come with a desire to better understand the development of their own youngsters. And almost all my students arrive with a deep curiosity about how they themselves developed from tiny infants into the complex adults they are today.

Finding a textbook that meets the instructional needs of the course as well as the needs of students is a challenging task. I wanted a book that was intellectually stimulating; that provided depth as well as breadth of coverage; that did not oversimplify the complexities of child development; that captured the preciousness, beauty, and wonderment of childhood; and that did all this in a clear, approachable, and engaging writing style. It is my goal, in writing this book, to meet all of these needs.

PHILOSOPHICAL ORIENTATION

My own professional and personal history — as student, teacher, researcher, and parent — shaped the basic approach of this book. I believe that a text must communicate six essential ingredients for students to emerge from a course in child development with a thorough understanding of the field. Each is emphasized in every chapter of this book, and together they form the philosophical orientation of the text:

1. An appreciation of the diverse array of theoretical perspectives in the field and of the strengths and shortcomings of each. This text takes an eclectic approach to describing and explaining child development. In each topical domain, a variety of theoretical perspectives are presented and critiqued. If one or two have emerged as especially prominent in a particular area, I indicate why, in terms of the theory's broad explanatory power. Moreover, I show how each new theory highlights previously overlooked aspects of development, and I argue that only knowledge of multiple theories can do justice to the complexities of childhood and the course of human development. Consideration of contrasting theories also serves as the context for an evenhanded analysis of many controversial issues throughout the text.

2. A sense of the history of child development as a field of study and of the impact of historical trends on current theories. Throughout this book, I emphasize that the modern field of child development is the culmination of a long history — of changes in cultural values, changes in philosophical thinking about children, and scientific progress. A thorough understanding of the current status of the field depends on an appreciation of this history. The first chapter presents an overview of child study, from its philosophical origins in earlier centuries to the current refinement of theories and empirical methods. In each succeeding topical chapter, I describe how theories build upon earlier contributions and are related to cultural belief systems of their times. Thus the text provides students with a broad perspective on the emergence of child study and with a sense of its progress.

3. An understanding of both the sequence of child development and the processes that underlie it. This book provides students with a description of the organized sequence of child development, along with a discussion of processes of change. An understanding of process — how multiple biological and environmental factors produce developmental change — has been the focus of most research during the last few decades. Accordingly, the text discussion reflects this emphasis. But new information about the timetable of development has also emerged in recent years. In virtually all developmental domains, the young child has proved to be a far more competent being than was believed to be the case in decades past. I give thorough attention to recent evidence on the timing and sequence of development, and its implications for developmental process, throughout the text.

4. An appreciation of basic research designs and methodologies used to investigate child development and of the strengths and weaknesses of each. The continued existence of child development theories depends on scientific verification. To rationally evaluate theories, students need a firm grounding in basic research design and methodology. I devote an entire chapter to a description and critique of research strategies. In each topical chapter, numerous research studies are discussed in sufficient detail for students to use what they have learned to critically evaluate the findings, conclusions, and theoretical implications of research.

5. A sense of the interdependency of all aspects of development — physical, cognitive, emotional, and social. The basic organization of this text is topical — an approach that permits a continuous, more coherent, and deeper discussion of each aspect of development than is possible with the alternative age-period organization used in many other textbooks. At the same time, a wealth of current research reveals that the separate domains of development are interdependent; they mutually influence one another. In every chapter, an integrated approach to child development is emphasized. Students are shown how physical, cognitive, emotional, and social development are interwoven. In many instances, they are referred back to sections in earlier topical chapters that enhance their understanding of relationships among the various components of development.

6. An appreciation of the interrelatedness of theory, research, and applications. Throughout this book, I illustrate the vital connections that exist among theory, research, and applications. I show how major research methods have been stimulated by, and are intimately related to, dominant theories — for example, how the clinical (case study) method emerged from psychoanalysis; controlled laboratory investigations from behaviorism; naturalistic observation from ethology and ecology; and the clinical interview from Piagetian theory. In addition, I emphasize that theories of child development, and the research generated by them, provide an essential foundation for sound, effective interventions aimed at improving the welfare and treatment of children. The linkage between theory, research, and applications is reinforced in every chapter by an organizational format that presents theoretical perspectives first, followed by an analysis of the research stimulated by them. Then practical applications and social policies are discussed in light of theories and research findings.

OVERVIEW OF CONTENT

This text is divided into 5 parts and 15 chapters, each of which develops the six themes described above. The salient features of each part and chapter are summarized below.

Part I. Theory and Research in Child Development. This section offers a unified overview of the history of the field, modern theories, and dominant research methods. **Chapter 1** introduces students to the importance of theories as organizing frameworks for understanding the child and traces the evolution of views of childhood from medieval to modern times. Separate sections on behaviorism and social learning theory, the ecology of human development, ethology, Piaget's cognitive-developmental theory, information processing, social cognition, the study of emotions, and cross-cultural research provide an overview of the current status of the field. Child development is depicted as an interdisciplinary endeavor that draws from psychology as well as from a variety of applied fields, including education, home economics, medicine, and social service. The chapter concludes with a consideration of the recent interest of child development specialists in the design of broad social policies to better the lives of children. **Chapter 2** is devoted to a consideration of strategies for conducting scientifically sound research. Common research methods, as well as general and developmental research designs, are explained and critiqued. The chapter closes with a discussion of special ethical concerns in doing research on children.

Part II. Developmental Foundations. A trio of chapters introduces students to the foundations of development. **Chapter 3** combines a discussion of genetic mechanisms and prenatal and perinatal environmental influences into a single, integrated analysis of these earliest determinants of development. A special, concluding section discusses the various ways in which behavioral geneticists and child development specialists conceive of the relationship between heredity and environment, as a prelude to revisiting the nature-nurture controversy in subsequent chapters of the book. **Chapter 4** is devoted to a discussion of the burgeoning literature on infancy. Research on neonatal reflexes, states, and learning capacities is reviewed, followed by a consideration of motor and perceptual development during the first two years of life. The chapter closes with the question of whether infancy is a critical period in which certain experiences must occur to assure a healthy, normal course of child development. **Chapter 5** addresses physical growth. The orderly, asynchronous nature of physical development is described, followed by a special section on development of the brain. The intimate connection between physical and psychological development is emphasized. The chapter concludes with an in-depth consideration of factors affecting physical growth — heredity, nutrition, disease, climate and season, and affection and stimulation.

Part III. Cognitive and Language Development. Four chapters summarize the diverse theoretical perspectives and wealth of research on cognitive and language development. The first, **Chapter 6**, is devoted to a comprehensive description and critique of Piaget's theory. Although Piaget's work has recently been questioned, no other single individual has contributed more to our understanding of child development. Students are offered a thorough grounding in Piagetian theory as a prerequisite for understanding areas of child study addressed in subsequent chapters, such as language development, social cognition, emotional development, and moral reasoning. **Chapter 7** provides an introduction to information processing, the leading current approach to the study of children's thinking. Major general as well as developmental models of the information processing system are reviewed, along with research on sensory and attentional processing, memory strategies, reconstructive processing, metacognition, and problem solving. Special attention is given to new evidence on very young children, in addition to the more extensive literature on middle childhood and adolescence. Educational applications of research are discussed throughout the chapter, which concludes with a critique of the information processing approach to cognitive development. **Chapter 8** presents the psychometric perspective on children's intellectual growth, which serves as the basis for the wide variety of mental tests available for the assessment of children. The chapter provides an overview of the intelligence testing movement and discusses a variety of controversial issues and research findings, including the stability and predictability of IQ, the origins of racial/ethnic and socioeconomic differences in IQ, the extent to which individual differences in intelligence are heritable, and cultural bias in the tests. A concluding section moves beyond IQ to a discussion of creativity. **Chapter 9** offers a comprehensive introduction to language development, including a review of nativist, environmentalist, and interactionist theories. The development of four basic components of language — phonology, semantics, grammar, and pragmatics — is described, along with a consideration of the more controversial question of how children master their native tongue with such rapidity during the preschool years. The chapter also addresses such controversial questions as, Can apes learn language? Is there a critical period for language learning? Does early bilingualism interfere with or enhance cognitive development?

Part IV. Personality and Social Development. Coverage of personality and social development is divided into four chapters. **Chapter 10**, covering emotional development, provides an overview of current theory and research on children's expression and recognition of discrete emotions. Special attention is given to new findings on complex emotions (shame, guilt, envy, and pride), empathy, and emotional development beyond the period of infancy. The second section of the chapter is devoted to temperament and development. It includes current research on the stability and heritability of temperamental traits and the implications of temperament for cognitive and social development. The chapter concludes with a review of theory and research on infant-mother attachment. The impact of infant temperament on the attachment bond, fathers as attachment figures, and effects of maternal employment and day care on attachment security are among the special issues discussed. **Chapter 11** offers an overview of the development of social cognition. The discussion is organized into three sections: children's understanding of self, other people, and relationships between people. Among the topics included are the development of self-esteem, achievement-related attributions, person perception, friendship, and social problem solving. **Chapter 12** addresses moral development and self-control. It includes a review and critique of psychoanalytic, behaviorist, and cognitive-developmental approaches to children's morality. Child-rearing practices that foster moral internalization, cross-cultural research on moral reasoning, and the controversial issue of whether sex differences exist in moral understanding are among the special features of this chapter. **Chapter 13** focuses on the development of sex differences and sex roles. Biological and environmental influences on sex-role adoption, the development of sex-role identity, and sex differences in cognitive abilities and personality attributes are reviewed. The chapter also includes an applied section on raising non-sex-stereotyped children.

Part V. Contexts for Development. A major current emphasis in child development research concerns the importance of environmental contexts for children's development. A final pair of chapters examines four highly influential developmental contexts — family, peers, media, and schooling. **Chapter 14** considers the family from both ethological and social systems perspectives. The reciprocal, bidirectional nature of parent-child interaction, as well as the significance of linkages between family and community for optimal family functioning and child development, is discussed. The impact of current changes in the American family is covered in the central portion of the chapter, which concludes with a discussion of the need for strong national social policies to support the American family in its child-rearing role. In **Chapter 15**, the social systems approach is carried over to other salient contexts for development. In the section on peer relations, the development of peer sociability, peer popularity, peer groups, and peers as socialization agents are the major topics. The second major section addresses the impact of television and computers on various aspects of social and cognitive development. A concluding section on schooling discusses a variety of research findings and controversial issues, such as teacher expectations for children's academic performance, mainstreaming, school desegregation, the current crisis in the quality of American education, and cross-national research on school achievement.

SPECIAL FEATURES

Writing Style. In writing this book, I made a concerted effort to adopt a prose style that is both engaging and scholarly. I aimed for clear, precise exposition that facilitates student interest and understanding. Throughout the text, to encourage critical thinking about the material, I use an interactive approach that poses student-directed questions. My intent is to offer students a model of good writing and, at the same time, prepare them for reading more advanced, original source material.

Boxes. Boxed presentations reflect two major themes. *Theory, research, and applications* boxes (which are set off with a blue rule) illustrate the interrelatedness of these three basic elements of child study. *Contemporary issues* boxes (which are set off with a purple rule) focus on current controversies and summarize cutting-edge research. The content of each box has been carefully selected to expand on important points in the text discussion and is clearly tied to the chapter narrative.

Part Opening Outlines and Chapter Introductions. Outlines of the major divisions in each chapter, along with an overview of chapter content in each introduction, provide students with helpful previews of what they are about to read.

Tables and Illustrations. Tables distributed throughout the book succinctly summarize and elaborate on text discussion, and colorful, easy-to-interpret graphs and illustrations depict research methods and findings.

Photos. Four-color and black-and-white photographs distributed throughout the text have been carefully selected to illustrate important points in text discussion. The photos and accompanying captions teach students about development, rather than serving as mere adornments on the page.

Chapter Summaries. Especially comprehensive, well-organized summaries appear at the end of each chapter, reminding students of the major discussion points and reinforcing their learning.

Footnotes. Footnotes help students understand the interdependencies among domains of development by reminding them of earlier presented text material and encouraging them to turn back for review.

Important Terms and Concepts. Terms and concepts that make up the basic vocabulary of the field appear in boldface type. They are also listed at the end of each chapter, to assist students with reviewing chapter content. A secondary set of important terms is italicized throughout the text discussion.

Glossary. A glossary of 450 terms is provided at the end of the book. It includes items appearing in boldface type, as well as a large selection of italicized terms. Students can access the text page on which each glossary item is introduced by looking it up in the index.

Reference List. The text contains an extensive list of reference citations, including historically important as well as current sources. The up-to-date nature of the text is reflected in the inclusion of over 1,300 references published during the 1980s, including more than 200 that appeared since 1986. The citation list is comprehensive enough for students to use as a primary basis for research papers and projects.

TEXT SUPPLEMENTS

A set of carefully prepared supplements accompanies this text. In collaboration with Ellen Potter of the University of South Carolina at Columbia, I have written an instructor's manual that includes chapter overviews, learning objectives, lecture topics, classroom activities, suggestions for supplementary readings, and a comprehensive listing of available media materials. In addition, a set of transparencies is available. Amye Warren-Leubecker of the University of Tennessee at Chattanooga has prepared a test bank of 2,000 well-written multiple choice questions, each of which is page-referenced to chapter content and classified according to type (factual, applied, or conceptual). The test bank is available in both hard copy and computerized formats. Toni Campbell of San Jose State University has written a student guide that offers learning objectives, chapter reviews, self-tests, and critical thinking exercises that enhance student mastery of material.

As part of Allyn and Bacon's Inside Psych series, a media presentation entitled Children's Private Speech is available as a supplement to the book. It comes in a choice of two formats: a series of 80 slides, accompanied by an audiocassette, or a VHS videotape. The presentation describes the contrasting theories of Piaget and Vygotsky on the significance of children's private speech, summarizes recent research on the topic (including my own), and discusses educational implications of current findings. An instructor's guide that contains discussion questions and multiple choice test questions is enclosed.

ACKNOWLEDGMENTS

The dedicated contributions of a great many individuals helped make this book a reality. An impressive cast of 33 reviewers provided many helpful suggestions, constructive criticisms, and much encouragement and enthusiasm for the project as it progressed. I am grateful to each one of them:

Dana W. Birnbaum
University of Maine at Orono

Kathryn N. Black
Purdue University

Cathryn L. Booth
University of Washington

Sam Boyd
University of Central Arkansas

Celia A. Brownell
University of Pittsburgh

Toni A. Campbell
San Jose State University

Beth Casey
Boston College

John Condry
Cornell University

James L. Dannemiller
University of Wisconsin, Madison

Darlene DeSantis
West Chester University

Elizabeth J. Hrncir
University of Virginia

Kenneth Hill
Saint Mary's University, Halifax

Alice S. Honig
Syracuse University

Mareile Koenig
George Washington University Hospital

Gary W. Ladd
Purdue University

Frank Laycock
Oberlin College

Robert S. Marvin
University of Virginia

Carolyn J. Mebert
University of New Hampshire

Gary B. Melton
University of Nebraska-Lincoln

Mary Evelyn Moore
Indiana University at Bloomington

Larry Nucci
University of Illinois at Chicago

Carol Pandey
Pierce College, Los Angeles

Thomas S. Parish
Kansas State University

B. Kay Pasley
Colorado State University

Ellen F. Potter
University of South Carolina at Columbia

Kathleen Preston
Humboldt State University

Maria D. Sera
The University of Iowa

Beth Shapiro
Emory University

Gregory J. Smith
Dickinson College

Harold Stevenson
The University of Michigan

Ross A. Thompson
University of Nebraska-Lincoln

Barbara J. Tinsley
University of Illinois at Urbana-Champaign

Kim F. Townley
University of Kentucky

I am also grateful to several of my colleagues at Illinois State University who willingly read chapters and offered feedback and consultation in areas of their expertise. They are Raymond Bergner, Barbara Goebel, Elmer Lemke, Leonard Schmaltz, and Mark Swerdlik. Felissa Cohen of the Department of Medical Surgical Nursing, University of Illinois Medical School, provided helpful consultation on Chapter 3. A special thank you is extended to Benjamin Moore, Clinical Director of The Baby Fold, Normal, Illinois, for his interest in the development of this project and the inspiration of his dedicated work with children.

Many students contributed in important ways to the content and quality of the text. Among them are Kelly Maxwell, who read chapters from the student's perspective and provided astute, detailed commentaries on each emerging draft. Janet Kuebli served as my graduate assistant during the final year in which I wrote. She provided invaluable assistance with revisions and updating of research described in the book. Jennifer Bivens, Christine Mitchell, Laura Norris, and Rose Schwager helped obtain permissions for use of copyrighted material and assisted with preparation of the glossary and index.

An indispensable part of the development and realization of this book were the publishing staff at Allyn and Bacon. John-Paul Lenney, Psychology Editor, worked closely with me through every phase of the project. His high standards of quality, keen sensitivity to the needs of students, and continuous support and encouragement strengthened my own efforts; his commitment to an aesthetically pleasing as well as scholarly, well-written text is responsible for the distinctive beauty of this volume. Rowena Dores, Production Administrator, worked with tireless dedication and meticulous attention to accuracy and detail on the complex, time-consuming tasks that transformed my typescript copy into a finished textbook. Leslie Goldberg, Developmental Editor, arranged for and synthesized manuscript reviews, provided helpful advice on design and inclusion of illustrations, and wrote many of the photo captions. Susan Brody, Editorial Assistant, handled the final set of manuscript reviews, coordinated the preparation of text supplements, and graciously took care of a wide variety of pressing, last-minute details. Diana Gibney and Daniel Otis copyedited the manuscript and offered a wealth of helpful suggestions for tightening and polishing the writing. Jennifer Ralph selected the appealing photos that so aptly illustrate many points in the text discussion. Glenna Collett is responsible for the book's artistic design and for its effective layout.

A final word of gratitude goes to my husband and children, whose love, patience, and understanding enabled me to be wife, mother, teacher, researcher, and text writer at the same time. My sons, David and Peter, have provided me with many valuable lessons in child development over the past decade and a half. During the years in which I wrote, both crossed the dividing line between childhood and adolescence and were an important impetus for the attention I have given to adolescent development throughout the text. David and Peter eagerly tracked my progress ("Are you *still* on that chapter?"), and I thank them for their expressions of pride in having a mom who wrote a book. My husband, Ken, willingly helped make room for this project in our family life and communicated his belief in its importance in a great many unspoken, caring ways.

Laura E. Berk

Child Development

PART I

Theory and Research in Child Development

Writing to Father, by Jonathan Eastman Johnson.
Museum of Fine Arts, Boston. Bequest of Maxim Karolik.

CHAPTER 1

History, Theory, and Method

Child development is a field of study devoted to the understanding of all facets of human growth and change from conception into adolescence. It is part of a larger discipline known as **developmental psychology,** which encompasses the study of all changes that human beings experience throughout the entire life span. In fact, no branch of psychology is broader in scope than the study of development, for every facet of the individual—physical, mental, social, and emotional—changes over time. Great diversity characterizes the interests and concerns of the thousands of investigators who study child development. But all child development researchers have a single goal in common: the desire to describe and identify those factors that influence the dramatic changes that occur in young people during the first decade and a half of life.

The field of child development poses many questions about children that you may have wondered about yourself:

How do human beings grow before they are born, and what can be done to assure a healthy newborn baby?

Can infants "make sense" of their complex perceptual world at birth? What do they already understand about their surroundings, and what must they learn over time?

How do children become such amazingly effective users of their complex language system during the first few years of life? Is it harder or easier for young children to learn a second language than it is for older children and adults?

Where do individual differences in intelligence and personality come from? Does heredity play a role in whether children are bright or dull, active or passive,

3

sociable or shy? What aspects of children's home environments make a difference?

Why do most babies begin to show a strong affectional tie to their mothers in the second half of the first year? Do infants who do not become attached to a familiar caregiver show impaired development in later life?

What kinds of child-rearing practices promote the development of academically motivated, socially competent youngsters? Should parents try to be permissive or strict with their children, or should they aim for something in between?

Look at these questions, and you will see that they are not just of scientific and intellectual interest. Each is of practical importance as well. In fact, scientific curiosity about what makes children the way they are is not the only factor that led child development to become the exciting field of study it is today. Knowledge about development has also been stimulated by social pressures to better the lives of children. For example, the growth of public education in the early part of the twentieth century led to a demand for scientific knowledge about what and how to teach children of different ages. The interest of pediatricians in improving children's health and preventing disease required a systematic understanding of physical growth and nutrition. The social service profession's desire to alleviate children's fears, anxieties, and behavior problems required comprehensive knowledge about personality and social development. And parents have continually sought advice from child development specialists about child-rearing techniques and experiences that would promote the optimum growth of their child.

Our current vast storehouse of information about child development grew through the combined efforts of people from many fields of study. Because of the need for solutions to everyday problems concerning children, academic psychologists joined forces in research endeavors with professionals from a variety of applied disciplines, including education, home economics, medicine, and social service, to name just a few. Today, child development is a melting pot of contributions stimulated by both intellectual and practical concerns. Its body of knowledge is not only scientifically significant, but also relevant and useful.

THE ROLE OF THEORY

Before scientific study of the child, questions about children were answered by turning to common sense, opinion, and belief. Efforts at systematic study of children began to flourish in the early part of the twentieth century. These activities led to the construction of **theories** of child development, to which professionals and parents could turn for both understanding and practical guidance. Although there have been many scientific and philosophical definitions, for our purposes we can think of a theory as an orderly, integrated set of statements that explains and predicts behavior. As we shall see later on, child development theories, like the garden variety speculations and convictions mothers exchange across the backyard fence, are heavily influenced by the cultural values and belief systems of their times. But theories differ in an important way from mere opinion and belief in that their continued existence depends on scientific verification. Such verification takes place when the assumptions of the theory are tested by means of a fair set of methods and procedures that are agreed upon by the scientific community.

In the field of child development there are many theories with dramatically opposing assumptions about the nature of the child and the course of human development. In reading this chapter you will soon see that basic to some theories is the idea that children are passive reactors to environmental stimuli, whereas other theories view children as active contributors to their own development. Some theories maintain that children and adults respond to the world in much the same way; others assume that children are qualitatively different from adults and must be understood on their own terms. Finally, some theories regard genetic influences as most important in development, others stress the environment, while still a third group strikes a balance between the two.

The study of child development provides no single, ultimate truth. Instead, it offers a smorgasbord of explanations about how the child grows, forcing us to pick and choose, leaving us uncomfortable and unsure about our current convictions, and motivating us to seek additional knowledge as the basis for our choices (Scarr, 1985). The field of child development should not be considered deficient because it has no single, all-encompassing theory. The child's behavior is too complex and multifaceted for any single theory to adequately explain all its aspects. Moreover, the existence of multiple theories, though demanding flexibility and tolerance of ambiguity from students of child development, leads to advances in knowledge. Theoretical variety stimulates new research aimed at affirming, contradicting, or reconciling available perspectives. Multiple theories also serve as organizing frameworks and guides for what is important to observe about the child, and they provide a systematic, rational basis for practical action.

Theories as Guides to Observing the Child

Imagine yourself as a forerunner in the field of child development, confronted with investigating the child's growth and behavior for the first time, with little in the way of established precedents to guide you. Faced with the child who is your object of study, what will you observe? Perhaps you can think of many possibilities — relationships with parents, siblings, and peers; school performance; thought processes; language and communicative abilities; eating habits; play preferences; and motor coordination, to name only a few. There is an infinite range of possible aspects to select for study. One solution to your problem might be to observe everything about the child, but should you try this, you would probably find yourself overwhelmed by a multitude of observations and measurements. These discrete, unintegrated facts about the child would seem meaningless and trivial because you would have no organizing framework for guiding and interpreting your observations.

Theories are essential tools for advancing knowledge because they tell us what aspects of child behavior are important to observe, at least for the moment, and why they are important. In addition, theories provide us with an explanation of how facts about the child fit together. Thomas (1985) likens them to camera lenses through which we view the child, highlighting, organizing, and patterning certain observations while filtering out many others. Thus, theories provide orderly, meaningful direction to our research efforts. Carrying our camera analogy a step further, the benefits of multiple child development theories discussed earlier become even clearer. New theories can serve as eye openers in the quest for knowledge about the child, causing us to attend to new or previously overlooked facts so that we "see" things differently than we did before. Adherence to only a single theory can be obstructive; it may blind us to the existence of new facts that do not fit with currently held beliefs.

Theories as Rational Guides to Practical Action

For the researcher, theories provide essential frameworks for generating new knowledge. Increasing our understanding of the developing child is a worthwhile goal in itself. In addition, the more we *understand* about development, the better we will know *what to do* in our efforts to improve the welfare and treatment of children. When understanding precedes action, coherent plans replace floundering and groping attempts at solution (see Box 1-1).

The diffusion of child development knowledge to practitioners and the general public over the course of this century has already had a profound impact on the modern child's experiences. For example, research findings indicating negative consequences from using punishment to discipline children have led to an emphasis on positive motivational techniques in both child-rearing and educational practice. Years of research on the importance of mother-infant attachment has influenced the relationships of mothers and, more recently, fathers and substitute caregivers to very young children.

Scientists involved in child development have, over the last decade, been increasingly drawn into government planning for children. A new emphasis, *child development and social policy,* has recently emerged, consciously concerned with how to translate theory and research into practical situations. These efforts range from the development of government policies that promote children's welfare to finding ways to help individual parents do a better job of raising children. In view of such advances, dissemination and application of child development knowledge may, in the longer perspective, be regarded as one of the more significant achievements of the twentieth century (Senn, 1975; Stevenson & Siegel, 1984).

FOCUS ON THEORY, RESEARCH, AND APPLICATIONS

Box 1.1
Illustrating the Relationship of Theory to Practice

A theoretical understanding of children's development, and especially, knowledge of multiple theories, is vitally important for professionals who work on a day-to-day basis with children. To illustrate this point, let's consider a familiar problem for teachers of young children. Suppose we imagine three nursery school children, all exhibiting destructive behavior in the form of throwing toys and blocks. The behaviors we observe look very much the same for all three children, but in searching for facts about their origins and development, we arrive at three strikingly different pictures:

Ann—The Conditioned Child. This child has a warm and stimulating home life, but her well-meaning, child-centered parents inadvertently provide attention and rewards after she behaves destructively. When Ann misbe-

haves, her mother frequently offers her treats or distracts her with pleasurable activities. Her unacceptable behavior has been *learned,* according to the principles of *operant conditioning.*

Michael—The Emotional Child. This child's home environment is emotionally tense and unhappy. His parents quarrel and engage in demeaning criticism, of one another and of him. Michael's behavior is a manifestation of emotional stress, confusion, and anxiety. Like Ann's, some of his disruptiveness may have been reinforced, but its initial appearance was an anticipation of rejection by teachers and peers based upon the rejection he had already experienced at home.

Janet—The Unsocialized Child. Janet does not know how to use the blocks. She comes from an underprivileged background where there are few toys, and her preoccupied mother seldom has time to play with her or to provide

instruction on how to use materials appropriately.

Choice of appropriate intervention strategies depends on an understanding of the origins of each child's behavior. Theories help us order and analyze facts about the child so that we can detect these origins.

Behaviorist theory helps us understand development, and consequently appropriate treatment, for Ann. This child clearly has a faulty conditioning history. Understanding this history suggests an appropriate intervention: If Ann's parents change their responses to her so that desirable behaviors are reinforced and pleasant outcomes no longer follow as consequences of destructive behavior, then Ann's unacceptable behavior will decrease in frequency and eventually disappear. Rearranging reinforcement contingencies is a tried-and-true procedure that stems from behaviorist theory. It seems unnecessary to consider Ann's feelings or state of mind. An analysis of past reinforcements provides a full appreciation of

The modern science of child development is the culmination of centuries of change in Western cultural values, philosophical thinking about children, and scientific progress. The current structure of the field has deep roots extending far back into the past. In the sections that follow, we consider major historical influences, beginning with those preceding scientific study of the child, that linger on as important forces in current theory and research.

Early Views of Childhood

Medieval Times. In medieval times, little importance was placed upon childhood as a separate phase of the life cycle. The idea so commonly accepted today, that the child's nature is unique and to be distinguished from youth and adulthood, did not exist then. Instead, children were regarded as miniature, already-formed adults, a view that is called **preformationism.** Like early beliefs regarding the Solar System in which the Earth was thought to be at the center and the Sun to revolve about it, children were first understood from an egocentric viewpoint; that is, adults assumed that the forms and functions of children were very much the same as their own. This attitude is reflected in the language of medieval times, in that the word *child* did not

---

the origins of her behavior and leads directly to treatment methods that work.

Emotional stress and feelings of rejection underlie the behavior of Michael. If behaviorist procedures are used, the disruptive behavior would very likely disappear, but the emotional tensions would still be there, and they would probably be manifested in new ways. While behaviorist theory ignores internal feelings and states of mind, psychoanalytic theory calls attention to the importance of the child's emotional health. This approach tells us that opportunities to express unmanageable fears and anxieties, sympathetic acknowledgment of the child's feelings by adults, and reassurance regarding parental affection would alleviate emotional stress and decrease Michael's need to engage in destructive behavior.

Janet is inadequately socialized. In trying to change her behavior, we could wait for destructive acts to occur and then try to modify them by removing events that seem to reinforce them, but this seems need-

less and inefficient. Lacking early social training about appropriate use of the toys, Janet could profit from direct teaching strategies, such as those suggested by social learning theory. Although social learning theory accepts the conditioning principles of traditional behaviorism, it also emphasizes that children can learn rapidly by simply observing the behaviors of others. Modeling, involving observation and imitation of acceptable behaviors by adults and peers, as well as direct instruction, seems most appropriate for Janet.

The behaviors of Ann, Michael, and Janet look identical, but their origins are strikingly different. Yet each of the theories of development mentioned above focuses on one developmental path, while de-emphasizing or ignoring the others. Strict adherence to one theory runs the risk of using intervention procedures in circumstances where they are unsuitable. Applying reinforcement procedures to Michael would leave troubled feelings untended, while for Janet, it would permit undesirable behaviors to

continue longer than necessary. Alternatively, using psychoanalytic procedures with Ann would prolong behaviors that her parents unknowingly rewarded and that did not originate from inner tensions and anxieties.

Children come in great diversity and in far more complex mixtures than are represented by the examples described above. In contrast, theories are summaries, organizations, and constructions of reality. By its very nature, a theory cannot represent and explain everything; theories tend to come in pure types. A theoretical perspective is vitally important as a systematic, rational basis for practical action. At the same time, only knowledge of multiple theories can do justice to the complexity of childhood and safeguard the quality of children's experiences.

Source: Katz, 1972.

The idea of childhood as a unique, distinct period in life is a relatively new concept. As reflected in this painting, during medieval times children were viewed as miniature adults. (The Bettmann Archive)

have the very specific meaning that we now give to it. Instead, it was used indiscriminately to refer to sons, lads, and young men. In medieval art, children were depicted in dress and expression as immature adults. Due to their fragility and dependence, infants were not regarded as recognizable members of society, but children mixed with adults as soon as they were capable of leaving their mothers and nannies. Special toys and games were not devised to occupy and fascinate children, but were used by all people. Even age, so important an aspect of modern personal identity, our marker of progress toward maturity and status, and a fact about the self that today's children are able to recite almost as soon as they can talk, was unimportant in medieval custom and usage. People did not refer to it in everyday discourse, and age was not recorded in family and civil records until the fifteenth and sixteenth centuries (Aries, 1962).

The Sixteenth and Seventeenth Centuries. By the sixteenth century, a revised conception of childhood sprang from religious ideas—in particular, the Protestant conception of original sin. According to this view, the child was regarded as a fragile creature of God who needed to be safeguarded, but who also needed to be reformed. Born evil and stubborn, children had to be led away from their devilish ways, and it was necessary to take them in hand, beat down their obstreperous wills, and begin to civilize them toward a destiny of virtue and salvation. Schools, in which boys of the middle classes were separated from the corrupt world of older youth and adults, prolonged the period of childhood beyond infancy. However, girls and children of the lower classes were excluded, their limited childhood still the same as it was in medieval times (Aries, 1962; Suransky, 1982).

Harsh, authoritarian, and restrictive child-rearing practices were applied as the most efficient means for transforming the depraved child. Infants were tightly swaddled, and children's clothing was heavily corseted to hold them in adultlike postures. Moral training was an essential feature of schooling, as demonstrated by the text of the *New England Primer,* originally published in Puritan America in 1687. *"A — In Adam's fall we sinned all"* served as the child's first introduction to reading and the alphabet. Pictures of schools showed the rod or birch, and disobedient pupils were routinely beaten by their schoolmasters. The child had no autonomy and was expected to behave like a little adult.

While these attitudes represented the prevailing philosophical dictates of Puritan child rearing, it is important to note that they may not have been typical of the actual day-to-day practices of many Puritan parents who, influenced by love and affection for their children, probably deviated from strict authoritarian child-rearing modes. Recent historical evidence suggests that with their own children, New England parents and ministers were reluctant to exercise extremely repressive measures, preferring instead to adopt a more moderate balance between discipline and indulgence, severity and permissiveness (Moran & Vinovskis, 1986).

Early Philosophies of Childhood. The seventeenth-century Enlightenment brought new philosophies of reason and fostered ideals of human dignity and respect. Revised conceptions of childhood appeared that had a tremendous humanizing influence on how children were regarded.

The writings of John Locke (1632–1704), a leading philosopher during this Age of Reason, served as an important forerunner of twentieth-century behaviorist theory. Locke conceived of the child as **tabula rasa.** Translated from Latin, this means blank slate or white piece of paper. He championed *nurture,* not *nature;* if some people were better than others, it was due to more favorable circumstances. Children were not basically evil. They were, to begin with, nothing at all, and their characters could be shaped by all kinds of experiences during the course of growing up. In *Some Thoughts Concerning Education* (1690/1892), Locke described the parent as a rational tutor who could mold the child in any way she wished, through the use of associations, repetitions, imitation, rewards, and punishments. These elements of child training later became important in modern behaviorist theory. Locke was ahead of his time in recommending to parents child-rearing practices whose soundness was eventually fully validated by twentieth-century empirical research (e.g., Parke, 1977). For example, he suggested careful use of rewards and punishments and advocated that parents not reward children with money or sweets, but rather with praise and approval. Locke also expressed opposition to physical punishment, because it only works when the rod is in sight, does not foster self-control, and establishes unfavorable associations: "The child repeatedly beaten in school cannot look upon books and teachers without experiencing fear and anger." Locke's philosophical view heralded a change from punitiveness and brutality toward kindness and compassion for children.

In the eighteenth century, the child was dressed more comfortably, babies were not swaddled, and corporal punishment declined. A new, natural theory of childhood was expressed by a French philosopher of the Enlightenment, Jean-Jacques Rousseau (1712–1778). Children, Rousseau thought, were not blank slates and empty con-

This drawing of "The Five Senses," published in an elementary reader in 1744, reflects the new, humane attitudes toward children that developed during the Enlightenment. The illustration depicts children learning through direct experience, with gentle, understanding teachers looking on.

tainers to be filled by adult instruction. Instead, they were **noble savages**, naturally endowed with a sense of right and wrong and with an innate plan for orderly, healthy growth. In his book *Emile* (1762/1955), Rousseau described the development of a fictitious boy whose upbringing took place according to nature's plan. Unlike Locke, Rousseau had little faith in the capacity of the social environment to raise a healthy individual. He thought that children's innate moral sense and unique modes of thinking and feeling would only be obstructed by adult training and restriction. Rousseau's was a child-centered, permissive philosophy. The adult should be responsive to the child's expressed needs at each of four stages of development: infancy, childhood, late childhood, and adolescence.

Rousseau's philosophy is thought of as the first truly developmental position (Crain, 1980). It embodies two vitally important concepts that are found in modern developmental theories. The first is the concept of **stage** of development. Stages are qualitatively distinct organizations of behavior and thought at particular periods of growth. The second is the concept of **maturation,** which refers to a naturally unfolding, genetically predetermined pattern of growth. If you accept the notion that children mature through a sequence of stages, then they cannot be preformed, miniature adults. Rather, they are assumed to be unique and different from adults, and their development is responsive to their own inner promptings. Rousseau's philosophy foreshadowed important twentieth-century developmental ideas, such as Arnold Gesell's maturational theory and Jean Piaget's stage theory of cognitive development, which we shall review shortly. Perhaps it is not mere coincidence that Piaget spent the major part of his research career at the Rousseau Institute at the University of Geneva.

Darwin — Scientific Father of Child Development

In the mid-nineteenth century, Charles Darwin, a British naturalist, joined a scientific expedition in which he traveled to distant parts of the world, making careful observations of fossils and animal and plant life. Darwin observed the infinite variation among species and that within a species, no two members were exactly alike. From these observations, he constructed his theory of evolution, reported in his famous volume, *The Origin of Species,* published in 1859.

The theory emphasized two related principles of evolution — *natural selection* and *survival of the fittest.* Darwin explained that certain species were selected by nature to survive in particular parts of the world because they possessed characteristics that fit with, or were adapted to, their surroundings. Others died off because their traits were not well-suited to their environments. Reproduction and survival within a species followed a pattern that facilitated the evolution of that species. The individual members that best met the survival requirements of their environment were the ones that lived long enough to reproduce and transmit their more favorable characteristics to future generations. Others, along with their less favorable traits, died out. Darwin observed that the earliest forms of embryos of many species were strikingly alike in appearance and characteristics. He concluded that all species were descended from a few common ancestors and that the human species, like animals, had gradually evolved over millions of years according to the process of natural selection.

In Darwin's earliest writings, it was the emergence of physical characteristics that promoted survival. Later he came to believe that the behaviors of particular species also had survival value (Darwin, 1871/1936), an idea that influenced many child development theories of the twentieth century. For example, it is present in Sigmund Freud's psychosexual theory, for Freud believed that development culminates in mature heterosexual behavior and family life, which assures the birth and survival of the next generation. As we shall see shortly, evolutionary ideas also underlie the work of G. Stanley Hall (1904) and Arnold Gesell (1952/1972), whose maturational theories of predetermined growth depended in part on the (no longer accepted) belief that *ontogeny recapitulates phylogeny* — the development of the growing child (ontogeny) parallels the evolution of the human species (phylogeny). While the theories of Hall, Gesell, and Freud are now considered to be largely of historical importance in the study of child development, Darwin's influence nevertheless remains alive in contemporary theories. For example, Piaget's theory is centrally concerned with how children's developing cognitions enable them to achieve a successively better adaptive fit between behavior and environmental demands. A strong Darwinian impact is present in modern ethological theory. Ethological researchers compare children's behaviors with those of animal species, and study those social behaviors that ensure survival, such as mother-infant attachment (Ainsworth, 1973; Bowlby, 1969).

Beginnings of Empirical Child Study

The Baby Biographies. The first attempts to study the child directly occurred in the late nineteenth and early twentieth centuries in the form of biographical records of a single child's behavior. There were dozens of these diaries, recorded by isolated individuals who worked without precedents or established procedures. These biographical accounts involved day-by-day narrative descriptions of the sequential growth of an infant or young child who was generally related or well known to the observer. For example, a famous one published by Charles Darwin in 1877 was an account of the development of his young son. Although these records contained some astute observations, these first empirical students of child development were eventually criticized for emotional investment in their subjects of study, naive and unobjective recording of behavioral anecdotes, absence of theoretical direction, and unwarranted interpretations of what they saw (Frank, 1943). This mixture of insights and shortcomings is evident in the following excerpts from one diary record published in 1900, Milicent Shinn's *The Biography of a Baby,* in which Shinn recorded and reflected on the growth of her young niece during her first year of life:

Charles Darwin's (1809–1882) belief that the physical and behavioral characteristics of each species have survival value influenced many important twentieth century theories of child development. (North Wind Picture Archives)

> In the nineteenth week, she seemed to act once from something like a definite memory. Her grandfather entered the room while she was in her bath, and her usual joyous up and down movement of arms at sight of him produced a novel and fascinating splashing. Next day the baby splashed without suggestion, and again the next, looking up to my face and smiling; and after that no one could teach her anything about splashing. Yet even this was probably not really memory, but an association formed by a single vivid occurrence. (p. 139)

> Mothers do not like to think that the baby is at first an automaton; and they would be quite right in objecting if that meant that he was a mere machine. He is an automaton in the sense that he has practically neither thought, wish, nor will; but he is a living, conscious automaton, and that makes all the difference in the world. And it would be a bold psychologist who should try to say what germ of thought and will is there, and an automaton with such a capacity is a more wonderful creature than the wise, thinking, willing baby of nursery tradition would be. . . . (p. 37)

Although the biographies have often been upheld as examples of how *not* to do research on children, we must keep in mind that their authors were like explorers first setting foot on alien soil. When a field is new, we cannot expect the methods of study to be completely formulated. Furthermore, the biographical approach did have certain advantages. Direct recording and description offered potential for preserving the richness and complexity of children's behavior, the subtle relationship of momentary behavior to its environmental context, and the continuity of behavior over time (Wright, 1960). The legacy of the baby biographies lives on in contemporary methods of naturalistic observation and in longitudinal research design, in which the development of individual children is followed over time. The baby biographies also provide us with a perspective of progress. We can see where we began and how far we have come in our attempts to study the child scientifically.

The Normative Period and Testing. G. Stanley Hall (1844–1924), one of the most influential psychologists of the early twentieth century, is generally regarded as the founder of the child study movement (Dixon & Lerner, 1984). Profoundly influenced by Darwin, Hall devised a theory of evolutionary recapitulation in which he argued that the development of the child repeated the history of the species (Hall, 1904). Today his theory is all but forgotten. However, one of Hall's lasting contributions was his attempt to give child psychology something more than philosophic content by increasing the scientific nature of research on children.

Hall's effort to collect a sound body of objective facts regarding children's development launched the normative approach to child study. In a **normative study**, quantitative measurements of children's behavior are taken, and age-related averages are computed to chart the course of development. The normative approach dominated child development research until the middle of the twentieth century (Thomas, 1985). Bent on creating objective instruments that would permit the scientific measurement of children's traits and capacities, Hall constructed elaborate questionnaires and arranged to have them distributed to thousands of schoolchildren who were asked almost everything that they could possibly tell about themselves—interests, fears, imaginary playmates, dreams, play, friendships, and more. Because there was no theoretical framework to give meaning to the questions, and because casual data collection procedures left the characteristics of samples unknown, the findings of Hall's studies were of little value. But his normative approach did take hold, and it provided the direction for several succeeding decades of research (Sears, 1975; Ross, 1972). The result was a large body of descriptive facts about children's behavior and characteristics at different ages, but little information about process—the how and why of development. Yet the child's development had to be described before it could be understood, and the normative tradition became the basis for more sophisticated research that followed later.

One of Hall's students was Arnold Gesell (1880–1961). Like Hall, Gesell based his theory on heredity and evolutionary recapitulation, and he thought that maturation was the regulating force in children's development. Although Gesell acknowledged that environmental factors could produce minor deflections and modifications in children's behavior, he believed that development largely followed a genetically set, predetermined path. Environment, from Gesell's perspective, had very little to do with affecting the overall sequence and rate of children's growth (Gesell, 1933).

Gesell devoted a major portion of his career to collecting detailed normative information on the behavior of infants and children. His schedules of infant development were particularly complete and comprehensive, and they continue to serve as the basis for many items included in modern-day tests of infant intelligence (Knobloch, Stevens, & Malone, 1980). However, because of massive cultural changes occurring since the 1930s and 1940s, some of Gesell's original normative observations of children are no longer typical and have had to be updated. Elkind (1974), in describing child development for parents and teachers, revised them, and the Gesell Institute recently conducted new normative appraisals on a more socioeconomically diverse sample of preschool children than Gesell studied 40 years earlier (Ames et al., 1978).

Gesell's contribution also exemplifies one of the first efforts to make theory and research meaningful to parents. He wrote for the layperson, providing age-related, typical descriptions of children's motor achievements, social behaviors, and personality characteristics, in an attempt to relieve parental anxieties by providing parents with information about what to expect at each age (Gesell & Ilg, 1943/1949; 1946/1949). If, as Gesell believed, the timetable of child development is the product of millions of years of evolution, then children are inherently knowledgeable about their needs. His child-rearing advice, in the tradition of Rousseau, was a permissive approach that advocated sensitivity and responsiveness to the child's cues.

While the general value of Gesell's extensive body of normative information survived, his maturational theory was eventually dismissed by those who believed more strongly in the importance of experience. The infusion of behaviorism into American child psychology, with its heavy emphasis on the role of environment in shaping developmental outcomes, eventually overshadowed Gesell's contributions.

Another student of Hall's was Lewis Terman (1877–1956). In 1916, at Stanford University, he published the first widely used intelligence test for children in the United States—the Stanford-Binet Intelligence Scale. It was a revision of the work of Alfred Binet and his colleague Theodore Simon in Paris. In the early 1900s, Binet and Simon were given the task of devising a test to identify retarded children in the Paris school system who required placement in special classes. Thus, the measure of intelligence they developed, and which eventually provided the impetus for objective testing and measurement in the United States, grew out of practical educational concerns. Previous attempts to create a useful intelligence test had met with little success; however, Binet approached the task with a well-developed, sophisticated theory that guided the selection of test items. In contrast to earlier conceptions of intelligence, which stressed sensitivity to physical stimuli (Galton, 1883; Cattell, 1890), Binet viewed intelligent thought as good judgment involving planning and critical reflection. Binet and Simon (1916) wrote:

> Judgment, otherwise called good sense, practical sense, initiative, is the faculty of adapting one's self to circumstances. To judge well, to comprehend well, to reason well, these are the essential activities of intelligence. A person may be a moron or an imbecile if he is lacking in judgment; but with good judgment he can never be either. Indeed the rest of intellectual faculties seem of little importance in comparison with judgment. (pp. 42–43)

Because of its sound theory and careful construction, the Binet test was successful in discriminating among children who varied in school achievement, and it became the primary yardstick for measuring children's intelligence for decades to come. It underwent several revisions, the most recent appearing in 1986.

Using the Binet test, Terman initiated the first, and the longest lasting, longitudinal study, the purpose of which was to chart the development of highly intelligent children. In 1921, about 1,500 children with IQs above 135 were selected, and they were followed from childhood well into mature adulthood. The research performed a great practical service in dispelling the then commonly held belief that gifted children were odd and freakish—physically weak, susceptible to insanity, one-sided in their abilities, and socially maladjusted. The subjects were found to be socially better adjusted, emotionally more stable, and healthier than the rest of the population. In adulthood, they showed extraordinary professional accomplishment (Terman, 1925; Terman & Oden, 1959).

Terman's work provided both an educationally useful instrument and a clear demonstration that intelligence tests incorporated into research could help with an understanding of children's development. The mental testing movement was in motion. Not only were many new intelligence tests devised, but the measurement techniques used in intelligence testing were soon applied to the objective assessment of children's personality as well. The study and understanding of intellectual differences among children who vary in such characteristics as sex, birth order, family background, and schooling became a major focus for research. Intelligence tests also rose quickly to the forefront of the scientific controversy over nature versus nurture that has continued over the course of this century.

Contributions from Practitioners

In the 1930s and 1940s, a growing suspicion of the usefulness of norms for understanding the individual case arose among pediatricians and child guidance professionals who had daily contact with the living, growing child. Diminished faith in the normative approach led these professionals to seek alternative conceptions of health and adjustment that took into account the unique life histories of individual children.

Pediatrics. Pediatricians started out with an interest in norms, because they needed a body of representative information about the physical development of children as a basis for pinpointing deviations from normality. However, from direct contact with individual children, they quickly became aware that even in bodily dimensions and physical capacities practically no child fell at the norm (Frank, 1943). With tremendous strides made in treating acute illness and childhood diseases, some pediatricians turned toward a concern for the overall development of the well child and helping parents rear children with behavior problems. Parents turned to pediatricians for advice, and several exceptional practitioners provided it on a national scale by authoring best-selling books, such as Benjamin Spock's influential *Baby and Child Care* (first edition, 1946; recent edition, Spock & Rothenberg, 1985), which sold millions of copies, and more recently, T. Berry Brazelton's (1974; 1983) popular volumes for parents of infants and young children.

The interest of pediatricians in child rearing and child care lay the foundation for important collaborative efforts between child development specialists and pediatricians. Mutual interchange between these two fields has had an important payoff in the recent emergence of a new field called *developmental pediatrics,* which integrates physical and psychological assessment of children, traditional health care, and parental guidance. Special contributions of developmental pediatricians to the field of child development include instruments for assessing the overall developmental status of newborn infants that permit very early diagnosis of neurological impairments (Brazelton, 1984). Another growing specialty within developmental pediatrics concerns the other end of the child development continuum: adolescent health. For many years, the unique physical and psychological changes taking place during adolescence were all but ignored by the medical field. Today, pediatricians recognize that a number of modern teenage problems, including pregnancy, suicide, and drug abuse, are conditions that demand a combination of both psychological and medical intervention (Hamburg, 1985).

Child Guidance and the Psychoanalytic Approach. Historically, children identified as problem cases were brought to child guidance professionals, many of whom were psychiatrists and social workers. Behavioral misconduct, school failure, and difficulties in parental and peer relations could not be understood and dealt with in the context of the normative tests and measurements that had become prevalent during the early part of the twentieth century. While the normative movement had answered the question, "What are children like?," child guidance clinicians had to address the question, "How and why did children become the way they are?" as a prerequisite for diagnosing and treating their difficulties. They turned for answers to Sigmund Freud's (1856–1939) **psychoanalytic theory** because of its emphasis on understanding the unique developmental history of each child.

Freud's Theory. Freud, a Viennese physician and neurologist, encountered patients in his practice with a variety of nervous symptoms, such as hallucinations, fears, and physical paralyses, that appeared to have no physical basis. Seeking a cure for these troubled adults, Freud became intrigued with the work of his colleague Joseph Breuer, who found that symptoms could be alleviated by encouraging patients to talk freely about painful events of their childhood past that had been forgotten or repressed. Freud adopted this "talking cure" and carefully examined the recollections of his patients. Startling the straight-laced Victorian society in which he lived, Freud concluded that infants and young children were sexual beings, and the way they were permitted to express their impulses lay at the heart of their adult behavior. Using adult remembrances, Freud constructed his *psychosexual* theory of development, emphasizing that how parents manage their youngster's sexual and aggressive drives in early childhood is crucial for healthy personality development.

In Freud's theory, three portions of the personality—the id, ego, and superego—

Sigmund Freud's (1856–1939) psychosexual theory was the first child development theory to focus on the importance of early experience for later development. (Culver Pictures, Inc.)

become integrated with one another during a sequence of five stages of development. The **id**, the largest agency of the mind, is inherited and present at birth. It is the seat of basic biological needs and desires. Because the id seeks to satisfy its impulses head on, without delay, babies soon experience frustration as tensions mount until the drives can be satisfied in the real world. The **ego** emerges in early infancy to assure that the id's desires are satisfied in accordance with reality. Using its mental powers of attending to the environment and storing up experiences in memory, the ego moderates and redirects the id's urgent demands so that they are discharged on appropriate objects and at acceptable times and places. At the end of early childhood, the **superego,** or seat of conscience, appears. It contains the values and dictates of society and is often in conflict with the id's desires. The superego develops from children's social interactions with their parents, in whom is vested the task of helping children harness their biological impulses. Once the superego is formed, the ego is faced with the increasingly complicated task of mediating among the demands of the id, external reality, and the repressive dictates of conscience (Freud, 1923/1974).

Freud (1938/1973) believed that over the course of childhood, sexual impulses shift their place of expression from the oral to the anal to the genital regions of the body. In each stage of development, parents walk a fine line between permitting too much or too little gratification of their child's basic needs. Either circumstance can result in fixation of psychic energies at a particular stage, for too much satisfaction makes the child unwilling to move on to a more mature level of behavior, while too little leads the child to continually seek gratification of the frustrated drive. Here is a brief account of Freud's stages of development:

1. **The oral stage** (birth–1 year). In this stage, the id focuses on obtaining sensual pleasure through the oral zone of the body, and the newly emerging ego directs the baby's sucking activities toward breast or bottle to satisfy urgent pangs of hunger and for pleasurable oral stimulation. If oral needs are not gratified appropriately during infancy, the individual is likely to discharge them through such obsessive habits as thumb sucking, fingernail biting, and pencil chewing in childhood and overeating and smoking later in life.

2. **The anal stage** (1–3 years). Pleasure is now derived from the anal and urethral areas of the body, and the young toddler and preschooler enjoy retaining and expelling urine and feces at will. At this stage, the ego must learn to postpone pleasurable release to an appropriate time and place, and toilet training becomes a major issue between parent and child. If parents insist children be trained before they are physiologically ready or make too few demands, conflicts over anal control may become evident later on in the form of obsessive punctuality, orderliness, and cleanliness, or the alternative extreme of messiness and disorder.

3. **The phallic stage** (3–6 years). The focus of id impulses transfers to the genitals, and the child now derives pleasure from genital stimulation. During this stage, Freud's famous *Oedipal conflict* takes place. The young boy feels a sexual desire for his mother, but eventually represses this urge out of fear that his father will punish him for his unacceptable desires. To retain his parents' love and approval, the boy *identifies* with, or adopts, his father's characteristics and social values. Becoming like the father also serves as a means of vicariously enjoying the adult's power and pleasures. Freud believed that a similar *Electra conflict* takes place for girls that leads them to identify with their mothers. With the resolution of the Oedipal conflict, the superego is formed, and the relations among id, ego, and superego established at this time determine the individual's basic personality orientation.

4. **The latency stage** (6 years–puberty). During this stage, sexual instincts lie repressed and dormant. The child works on solidifying the superego by playing and identifying with same-sex children and assimilating social values from adults beyond the family.

5. **The genital stage** (post-puberty). Maturation of sexual functions at puberty causes the sexual drive of the earlier phallic stage to be reactivated, but now it can be gratified through love relationships outside the family. If development has proceeded appropriately during the early stages, it culminates at this time in marriage, mature genital sexuality, and the birth and rearing of children.

Freud's theory highlighted the importance of family relationships for children's development and provided a framework for understanding their emotional problems. In addition, it was the first theory of child development to emphasize the importance of early experience for later development. Nevertheless, Freud's perspective was eventually criticized by many child development specialists. First, the theory over-emphasized the importance of erogenous zones and sexual feelings in development. It failed to recognize that developmental tasks of a social and intellectual nature also prepare children for adulthood, and that important ones are dealt with beyond the early childhood years. Second, because it was based on the problems of sexually repressed, middle-class adults, many critics thought Freud's theory would not apply to child development in cultures that differ from nineteenth-century Victorian society. Finally, another reason that Freud's ideas were called into question was that he never really studied children directly.

Erik Erikson's Expansion of Freud's Theory. Several of Freud's contemporaries and followers took what was useful from his theory and stretched and rearranged it in ways that improved upon his vision. The most important of these neo-Freudians for the field of child development is Erik Erikson. Erikson's interest in children began with his work as teacher of the sons and daughters of Freud's psychoanalytic circle in Vienna. Although he originally intended to become an artist, Erikson was captivated by Freud's ideas. Eventually he graduated from the Vienna Psychoanalytic Institute, having developed a deep concern for the development, treatment, and education of children. The European upheaval of World War II brought Erikson to the United States in the early 1930s, where he made major advances in psychoanalytic theory by building upon Freud's work. In 1950, Erikson's most important contributions were published in *Childhood and Society,* which is still among the books most widely read by psychologists today.

Although Erikson accepted Freud's basic psychosexual framework, he provided an expanded picture of the tasks of development at each stage. He emphasized the *psychosocial* outcomes of development — how each Freudian stage contributes to the development of a unique personality and at the same time helps the individual become an active, contributing member of society. A series of basic psychological conflicts, each of which is resolved along a continuum from positive to negative outcomes, characterizes the course of development. As shown in Table 1.1, Erikson's first five stages parallel Freud's stages. However, Erikson did not regard important developmental tasks as occurring only in early childhood. Instead, he believed that significant psychosocial problems are addressed at all stages of life and was one of the first to recognize the life-span nature of development. Finally, unlike Freud, Erikson emphasized that normal development at each stage must be understood in relation to the child's unique life situation and cultural context. Here is a brief description of each of Erikson's stages:

1. **Basic trust versus mistrust** (birth–1 year). Based upon warm, responsive maternal care and pleasurable sensations while feeding, the infant gains a sense of trust, or confidence, that people who care for him are predictable, good, and gratifying. Mistrust of others is promoted when the infant has to wait too long for comfort and is handled harshly and insensitively.

2. **Autonomy versus shame and doubt** (birth–3 years). During this stage of achieving muscular control and exercising new exploratory skills of walking, climb-

Erik Erikson (1902–) expanded Freud's stages of development and was one of the first theorists to address development throughout the life-span. (Harvard University)

Table 1.1. The Relationship Between Freud's and Erikson's Stages

PERIOD OF DEVELOPMENT	FREUD'S PSYCHOSEXUAL STAGES	ERIKSON'S PSYCHOSOCIAL STAGES
Birth–1 year	Oral Stage	Basic Trust versus Mistrust
1–3 years	Anal Stage	Autonomy versus Shame and Doubt
3–6 years	Phallic Stage	Initiative versus Guilt
6 years–puberty	Latency Stage	Industry versus Inferiority
Adolescence	Genital Stage	Identity versus Identity Diffusion
Young adulthood		Intimacy versus Isolation
Middle adulthood		Generativity versus Stagnation
Old age		Ego Integrity versus Despair

ing, and manipulating, the child develops mental powers of choosing and deciding. Autonomy is fostered when parents offer guided opportunities for free choice and do not overly restrict, force, or shame the child.

3. **Initiative versus guilt** (3–6 years). Through make-believe play, children learn about the roles and institutions of society and gain insight into what kind of person they can become. Initiative, involving a sense of ambition and social responsibility, develops when parents support their child's emerging sense of purpose and direction. The danger at this stage is that parental demands for self-control will lead to overcontrol, or too much guilt.

4. **Industry versus inferiority** (6 years–puberty). This is the school age, during which the child develops an industrious capacity for productive work, cooperative participation with others, and pride in doing things well. Inferiority, the sense that one will never be good at anything, develops when children's experiences at school, in the peer group, and with parents do not foster feelings of competence and mastery.

5. **Identity versus identity diffusion** (adolescence). This is a culminating stage that marks the transition between childhood and adulthood. In it, the tasks of the

According to Erikson, these school-age children have already developed a sense of initiative and have some insight into what kinds of people they can become. They now display an industrious capacity for work and cooperative participation. (Richard Hutchings)

earlier stages become integrated into a lasting sense of identity. Past and present experiences, along with expectations for the future, are brought together into a coherent sense of who one is and one's place in society. The negative outcome, identity diffusion, is marked by confusion about one's sexual, occupational, and self-definition.

6. **Intimacy versus isolation** (young adulthood). Once a sense of personal identity is achieved, young people turn toward the task of establishing meaningful intimate relationships with other people. Although important relationships with members of the opposite sex are established at this time, close friendships with members of the same sex also occur. Both enhance the individual's sense of identity and provide gratifying feelings of connectedness to others. Young adults who experience negative outcomes at this stage are unable to establish close relationships. They cannot risk the possibility of rejection or disagreement and remain isolated from others.

7. **Generativity versus stagnation** (middle adulthood). Generativity means giving of oneself to the next generation, a task accomplished through child rearing, caring for other people, and productive work. The person who fails to contribute in one or more of these ways to the continuation of society feels a sense of stagnation, boredom, and absence of meaningful accomplishment.

8. **Ego integrity versus despair** (old age). In this final stage, individuals look back on the kind of person they have been and what they have accomplished over their lifetime. Integrity results from the feeling that life was worth living as it happened, and with it, death is not threatening. Old people who are dissatisfied with their life course feel a sense of despair that time is too short to correct its shortcomings, and they fear death.

All psychoanalytic theorists accept the *clinical method* as the most effective technique for gathering information about a child's development and emotional health. Sometimes referred to as the case study approach, the clinical method combines interview material obtained from the child, family members, and others who know the child well; results on psychological tests; and observations of the child in a clinic setting, and sometimes in everyday contexts as well. The information gathered is synthesized into a description of the unique personality functioning of the individual child so that the practitioner can better understand the child's problems and come up with effective ways to solve them. Because data obtained through the clinical method are often selective and subjective in nature, it is risky to rely on them for conclusions about children in general. Nevertheless, clinical records serve as rich sources of ideas about child development that can be tested systematically using other procedures.

Currently, psychoanalytic theory is not in the mainstream of child development research. There are various speculations as to why this is the case. Psychoanalytic theory may have become isolated from the rest of the field because it was so strongly committed to the clinical method that it failed to acknowledge the importance of findings about child development that accrued from other approaches (Sears, 1975). In addition, many psychoanalytic concepts, such as the unconscious, infantile sexuality, and the Oedipal conflict, seemed so vague that it was difficult to test them and impossible to prove or disprove them empirically (Nagel, 1959; Schultz, 1975).

Despite its shortcomings, psychoanalytic theory provided a tremendous stimulus to research on many aspects of child development, including mother-infant attachment, aggression, sibling and peer relationships, child-rearing practices, moral development, sex-role development, and adolescent identity. When academic psychology first became interested in children's behavior, it looked to the richness of Freudian theory for problems to study. Also, the clinical method was applied to the study of areas other than personality. For example, we shall see later on that it was adopted and modified by Piaget, who used a flexible, open-ended means of questioning children to investigate their developing cognitions.

THE INFLUENCE OF ACADEMIC PSYCHOLOGY
AND THE RISE OF MODERN THEORY AND METHOD

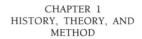

Behaviorism

In the late 1930s and 1940s, child study was profoundly influenced by a perspective that differed radically from psychoanalysis: **behaviorist theory,** a tradition consistent with Locke's tabula rasa. Behaviorism originated in several preceding decades of research by academic psychologists, beginning with the work of John B. Watson (1878–1958). Watson advocated an objective science of psychology. Directly observable events — stimuli and behavioral responses — should be the focus of study, not fuzzy internal constructs of the mind.

Impressed with the work of Ivan Pavlov in the Soviet Union, who taught dogs to salivate at the sound of a buzzer by pairing it with the presentation of food, Watson performed an historic experiment in which he applied Pavlov's principles of **classical conditioning** to children's behavior. Albert, a 9-month-old baby, was taught to fear a neutral stimulus — a furry white rat — after Watson presented it several times in the company of a loud obnoxious sound. Little Albert, who initially reached out eagerly to touch the soft white object, soon cried vehemently and turned his head away at the mere sight of it (Watson & Raynor, 1920).

Watson regarded environment as the supreme force in child development and thought that a child could be molded in any direction adults desired if they carefully controlled stimulus-response associations. To that end, he applied conditioning theory to child rearing. In *Psychological Care of Infant and Child,* Watson (1928) recommended that parents withhold cuddling and affection to prevent spoiling and dependent behavior. He wrote:

> There is a sensible way of treating children. Treat them as though they were young adults. . . . Let your behavior always be objective and kindly firm. Never hug and kiss them, never let them sit on your lap. If you must, kiss them once on the forehead when you say goodnight. Shake hands with them in the morning. Give them a pat on the head if they have made an extraordinarily good job of a difficult task. (pp. 81–82)

In place of warmth and love, Watson advised parents to use efficient procedures to promote children's learning of desirable habits. His regimen of scientific child management was to begin in early infancy with rigidly scheduled feedings and introduction to the potty chair at the vastly premature age of 1 to 3 months![1] Even in his own time, Watson's advice was controversial — adhered to by some as symbolizing a scientific approach to child rearing, but considered cold, rigid, and extreme by others. Today we know that Watson's child-rearing advice is much too harsh and insensitive to children's needs and capacities to promote healthy child development.

With Watson's behaviorism, an American experimental child psychology was born. Learning became its key element, and biological factors (such as those emphasized by Gesell and Freud) were important only in that they provided a basic foundation for learned responses. Following Watson, American behaviorism underwent several lines of development. The first was Clark Hull's (1884–1952) *drive reduction theory.* According to this view, the organism continually acts to satisfy physiological needs and reduce states of tension. As *primary drives* of hunger, thirst, and sex are satisfied, a wide variety of stimuli associated with them become *secondary,* or learned *drives.* For example, a Hullian theorist believes that infants will seek the closeness and attention of adults who have given them food, or that children will agree to wash dishes to get their allowance because money has been paired with the purchase of ice cream, candy bars, and soft drinks, which are pleasurable reducers of primary drives indeed!

---

[1] Modern child development specialists recommend that toilet training begin sometime between 18 months and 3 years of age, depending on the child's readiness.

John B. Watson (1878–1958) was the founder of behaviorism, a theory that led to the emergence of experimental child psychology.
(Culver Pictures, Inc.)

Another variant of behaviorism that emerged was B. F. Skinner's **operant conditioning** theory. Skinner rejected Hull's idea that primary drive reduction was the only way to get an organism to learn. He observed that animals and people will continue to behave in ways that lead to pleasant outcomes of *all* kinds, and they will stop responding in ways that lead to unpleasant outcomes. According to Skinner, a child's behavior can be increased if it is followed by any one of a wide variety of *reinforcers* besides food and drink, such as praise, a friendly smile, or a new toy; and it can be decreased by such *punishments* as withdrawal of privileges, parental disapproval, or being sent to be alone in one's room. Skinner applied his principles of operant conditioning to the child rearing of his young daughter. For example, she was toilet trained on a potty chair that played "The Blue Danube" waltz every time she urinated into it (Skinner, 1979). As a result of Skinner's work, operant conditioning became a broadly applied behaviorist learning paradigm in child psychology.

Social Learning Theory

Perhaps you have already noticed that Freud's focus on gratification of biological needs resembles Hull's emphasis on drive reduction as the basis for learning. Although psychoanalytic and behaviorist theory had little else in common, beginning in the 1930s this basic similarity led to a vigorous effort by researchers to take those psychoanalytic predictions that seemed testable, translate them into learning theory terms, and subject them to rigorous experimental verification. For example, Freudian theory predicted that intense frustration of the child's basic desires would lead to anxiety and maladaptive behavior such as aggression. Learning theorists adopted this frustration-aggression hypothesis and studied it thoroughly. Children's aggressive responses were related to the degree of frustration experienced and to rewards and punishments for aggressive behavior (Dollard et al., 1939). With such investigations, the field of child development entered the scientifically controlled environment of the laboratory, and a new **social learning theory** of childhood emerged. Social learning theorists accepted the principles of conditioning and reinforcement identified by the behaviorists who came before them. But they also built upon these principles, offering expanded views of how children and adults acquire new responses. After World War II, social learning theory became one of the dominant forces in child development research. Several theoretical varieties emerged.

Robert Sears led the way in constructing a social learning theory of personality development. In the tradition of Hull, his focus was on child behaviors learned due to association with primary drive reduction. Prompt feeding, as well as satisfaction of other infant dependency needs, was seen as the basis for all later social learning. Gradually it led, by means of association, to such secondary drives as the desire to obtain physical closeness, attention, and approval from the parent. This desire for closeness, attention, and approval provided the parent with a powerful tool for teaching the rules of social life. Parental controls eventually became secondary drives also. Children enacted them, leading to self-control and conscience. In Sears's theory, the manner in which parents satisfy their children's needs for food, warmth, and affection is vitally important for their development. Therefore, Sears's research focused heavily on parents' child-rearing practices — their nurturance, punitiveness, and methods of discipline — as predictors of children's aggression, dependency behavior, and self-control (Sears, Maccoby, & Levin, 1957; Sears, Rau, & Alpert, 1965).

Other social learning theorists set out to show that observational learning and imitation are powerful tools for childhood socialization. Albert Bandura (Bandura & Walters, 1963; Bandura, 1977) is responsible for an extensive line of laboratory investigations demonstrating that observational learning, often referred to as **modeling,** is the basis for a wide variety of children's learned behaviors, such as aggression, prosocial behavior, and sex typing. Bandura recognized that from an early age, children acquire many of their responses simply by watching and listening to others

B. F. Skinner (1904–) rejected primary drive reduction as the basis for all learning. He developed an alternative learning paradigm, operant conditioning, that has been broadly applied in the field of child development. (Harvard University)

around them, without direct rewards and punishments. What makes children want to imitate the behaviors of certain models? Research by Bandura and his followers has shown that children are drawn to models who are warm and powerful and who possess desirable objects and other characteristics. By acting like these models, children hope to obtain their valued resources for themselves sometime in the future. Bandura's work continues to influence much research on children's social development. However, like recent changes occurring in the field of child development as a whole, it has become more cognitive, acknowledging that children's abilities to listen, remember, and abstract general rules from complex sets of observed behaviors affect their imitation and learning (Bandura, 1986).

Behaviorism and social learning theory have had a major impact on applied work with children. *Behavior modification* refers to a set of practical procedures that combines reinforcement, modeling, and the manipulation of situational cues to eliminate children's undesirable behaviors and increase their adoption of socially acceptable responses. These principles have largely been used with children who have behavior problems, but they are also effective in dealing with relatively common problems of childhood. For example, Bandura (1967) showed that watching a peer play comfortably and pleasurably with a dog can help children who are afraid of dogs overcome their fears. Reinforcement and modeling have been used to teach social skills to those children who have few friends because they lack effective social behaviors (Asher, Odden, & Gottman, 1976).

Naturalistic Studies and the Ecology of Human Development

While a great many psychologists embraced the laboratory in the middle part of this century, others had serious reservations about it as an appropriate context for studying child development. Urie Bronfenbrenner, a contemporary leader of theory and research in *ecology of human development,* suggested that an overemphasis on laboratory research had caused developmental psychology to become ". . . the science of strange behavior of children in strange situations with strange adults for the briefest possible periods of time" (1977, p. 513). A new breed of psychologists began to advocate the study of children in their natural environments. Laboratory research, while scientifically *rigorous,* was not necessarily *relevant,* that is, generalizable to the everyday contexts in which children were living their lives and growing up.

In the late 1940s, Roger Barker began research that led to the emergence of a field of study called **ecological psychology.** Its basic premise is that natural environments are a major source of influence on human behavior—a source overlooked when psychologists installed the individual in the artificial environments of laboratory and clinic. Research demonstrating the explanatory power of the environment involved the observation of young children in natural settings. Ecological psychologists recorded children's behavior as it happened, and the method of naturalistic observation, first introduced by the baby biographers decades before, was refined into a major tool for gathering information about children's development.

Barker used the concept of the **behavior setting** as a way to analyze the environment so that its impact on children's behavior could be understood. A behavior setting has both spatial boundaries and a set of typical behaviors, such as a classroom surrounded by four walls in which teachers instruct and children learn, or a park playground, marked off by a sandy area and bounded by a fence, where children climb, swing, and run. Behavior settings can be large or small—an entire school or the block play corner of a classroom. Settings can be compared in terms of the child behaviors occurring within them and encouraged by them.

Many (but not all) ecological studies focused on the impact of school settings. An early investigation was Barker and Gump's *Big School, Small School* (1964). The findings showed that pupils attending small as opposed to large high schools received an enhanced extracurricular experience. A greater percentage of them felt a responsibility to become involved in activities, actually participated, and held positions of leadership and responsibility. In small schools there were fewer outsiders, that is, pupils on the fringe who did not participate at all.

Other ecological studies have compared such environments as open versus traditional classrooms, day care versus home-rearing experiences, and different housing arrangements, such as living in high-rise versus low-rise buildings. Results on the latter topic provide a vivid illustration of the usefulness of ecological research for the design of safe and healthy rearing environments for children. For example, apartment noise increases as one moves from higher to lower floors in high-rise city buildings. Children living for four or more years on lower floors have poorer auditory discrimination skills and read less well than those living on the upper floors (Cohen, Glass, & Singer, 1973). However, living on the higher floors of high-rise housing contributes to social isolation, health-related complaints, family tensions, and an increase in child abuse (Fanning, 1967; Gump, 1975; Parke & Collmer, 1975). Upper-floor residences hamper family members' easy access to environmental escape values in the form of playgrounds and the out-of-doors.

Urie Bronfenbrenner (1977, 1979) has expanded Barker's conception of environmental influences. In Bronfenbrenner's theory of the ecology of human development, the environment is envisioned as a series of nested environmental structures that extend beyond the immediate setting (see Figure 1.1). Each layer of the environment

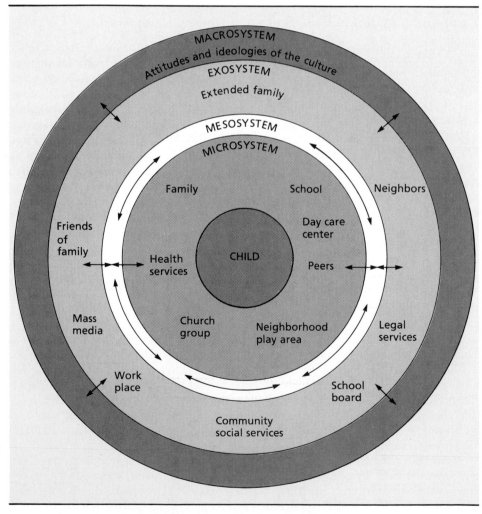

Figure 1.1. Bronfenbrenner's ecological model of the environment as a series of nested structures. The microsystem refers to relations between the child and the immediate environment; the mesosystem to connections among the child's immediate settings; the exosystem to social settings that affect but do not contain the child; and the macrosystem to the overarching ideology of the culture. *(Adapted from* The Child: Development in a Social Context, *edited by C. B. Kopp and J. B. Krakow. ©1982, Addison-Wesley Publishing Co., Reading, Massachusetts. P. 648. Reprinted with permission.)*

is regarded as having a powerful effect on children's development. The innermost level is called the **microsystem,** which refers to the activities, roles, and relationships in the child's immediate surroundings. Traditionally, psychologists have focused on the study of two-person, or *dyadic relationships,* such as a mother's or teacher's effect upon a child, when examining events at the microsystem level. Bronfenbrenner points out that not only do adult agents affect children's behavior, but children are also influential in affecting the behavior of adults. In other words, all dyadic relationships are bidirectional and reciprocal. Today, much more research in child development recognizes the impact of children's characteristics on the reactions they receive from others. Also, dyadic interaction is indirectly influenced by the presence of *third parties* within the microsystem. When other individuals present in the setting are supportive, the quality of dyadic exchange is enhanced. For example, when fathers give mothers encouragement in their caregiving role, mothers are more effective in feeding their babies. In contrast, high marital tension and conflict is associated with inept infant feeding (Pedersen, 1976). Bronfenbrenner points out that child development within the microsystem must be understood in terms of these complex, interacting relationships.

At the second level of Bronfenbrenner's model is the **mesosystem.** It refers to relationships among microsystem settings such as home, school, neighborhood, and child care center. Bronfenbrenner believes that child development is facilitated by interconnections among these settings. For example, a child's ability to learn to read may depend not just on learning activities that take place in the first grade, but also on the extent to which those activities carry over and are encouraged in the home environment. A mother's interaction with her child may be affected by the child's relationships with caregivers in a day care center, and vice versa. Mother-child and caregiver-child relationships are each likely to be supportive and consistent with one another to the extent that there are links, in the form of mutual visits and exchange of information, between the home and center. Furthermore, as children get older, they establish their own supportive links with a variety of settings, as a recent study described in Box 1.2 reveals.

The **exosystem** refers to social settings that do not actually contain children, but that nevertheless affect their experiences in immediate settings. Exosystems can be formal, such as the parent's workplace and organizational memberships or health and welfare services available in the community. They can also be informal, such as parents' social networks — friends and extended family members who provide advice and support for child rearing. Bronfenbrenner emphasizes the importance of goals and activities within the exosystem that support actions on behalf of the developing child. For example, flexible work schedules, paid maternity and paternity leave, and sick leave for parents whose children are ill are ways that work environments can help parents in their parenting roles and, indirectly, enhance child development. Research also demonstrates the potentially negative impact of a breakdown in exosystem activities. Families who are socially isolated, that is, who have few personal or community-based relationships on which to rely, and families affected by unemployment, show an increased incidence of child abuse (Parke & Collmer, 1975; Starr, 1979).

Finally, the outermost level of Bronfenbrenner's model is the **macrosystem.** It is not a specific environmental context. Instead, it refers to the overarching ideology, values, laws, regulations, rules, and customs of a particular culture. The priority given by the macrosystem to children's developmental needs is especially crucial in determining their experiences and interactions within the lower levels of the environmental structure. For example, child abuse is likely to be prevalent in cultures that positively sanction violence and physical force. In addition, where countries place a priority on developing high-quality standards for child care and allocate public monies to ensure that those standards are met, children are likely to experience positive, stimulating interactions with peers and adults in day care centers.

Box 1.2
The Neighborhood Walk: Sources of Support in Middle Childhood

Theory. In an unusual study, Brenda Bryant (1985) examined the importance of children's everyday environments for their social and emotional development during middle childhood. Bryant's consideration of children's environmental sources of support is at the mesosystem level of Bronfenbrenner's ecological model. She predicted that a *network* of supports would be more important for development than any single environmental factor alone. To examine this network, a broad range of environmental contexts were identified. Some included children's contacts with people who were members of peer, parent, and grandparent generations, and even pets. Others involved special environments, such as places to go off by oneself, formally sponsored organizations (scouting, 4-H, church, or synagogue), and informal, unsponsored meeting places (a backyard fort or neighbor's home).

Research. To assess children's environmental supports, a unique interviewing procedure called "the neighborhood walk" was used. Seven- and 10-year-old children each walked around their neighborhood with an investigator and reported on important aspects of their personal and social worlds — friends, relatives, neighbors, clubs, organizations, and places to go off alone. By walking in areas pertaining to particular interview questions, children were able to use concrete cues to make their answers more accurate and complete. A variety of measures of social and emotional functioning were also used. They included assessments of how children think and feel about themselves and other people as well as measures of their social skills.

Bryant's findings showed that children's networks of social support change with age. Ten-year-olds had more complex and expanded social networks than 7-year-olds. For example, older children felt that adults of their parents' and grandparents' generations were more salient in their lives, and they more often viewed pets as special friends. An important part of development during middle childhood seems to involve building such bridges from immediate family to extended family and community resources.

Consistent with Bronfenbrenner's concept of the mesosystem, children's networks of support predicted socioemotional functioning better than did single sources of support. However, the relationship of environmental supports to development was complex, and it depended upon such factors as the child's age and family size. For example, several aspects of support (intimate talks with pets and with members of the grandparent generation, visits to mother's workplace, and involvement in formally sponsored organizations) were related to more positive socioemotional functioning for 10-year-olds, but not for 7-year-olds. Bryant suggested that either 10-year-olds use environmental supports more effectively than younger children, or by age 10 the supports have had more time to take effect. For children from large families, interaction with adults and intimate involvement with those of the grandparent generation were positively related to children's empathy, or ability to understand and respond to the feelings of others. In contrast, opportunities for independence from the nuclear family were more important for children from small families. Those who had more places to go off to by themselves and more informal meeting places (a treehouse, fort, or neighbor's garage) showed greater tolerance of individual differences among people. These findings suggest that in small families where adult involvement with children is fairly intense, an occasional opportunity to break away from it leads to enhanced socioemotional functioning. In large families, adult involvement with children is not as intense, and supplementary relationships with other adults in the community are more important.

Applications. Middle childhood can be described as a period when children develop more elaborate environmental supports for development that extend beyond the family. Bryant's research shows that children's own social networks and community ties, not just those of their parents, have important implications for their social and emotional functioning. Relationships with older adults of the grandparent generation and with pets were found to be particularly supportive, perhaps because both offer unconditional acceptance of the child's feelings and opportunities to explore and acknowledge those feelings. Bryant believes that it is vitally important to foster children's informal ties to kin and community during middle childhood.

In middle childhood, children's social networks extend beyond the immediate family, and the support and friendship of loving grandparents becomes especially important. (Nancy Sheehan)

Bronfenbrenner calls for more research on the complex interrelationships among different parts of the environment. He recommends *ecological experiments,* or experiments of nature, as ideal ways to understand the impact of the environment on the developing child. In an ecological experiment, the investigator actually intervenes in the natural environment, changes it, and looks to see what effects the intervention has on the individual. Ecological experiments can be conducted at any level of Bronfenbrenner's model. At the level of the exosystem, providing socially isolated parents of abused children with supports in the form of parent groups, where they can discuss child-rearing problems and experience gratifying social relationships, is an example. Ecological experiments at the overarching level of the macrosystem, where established values and social policies are restructured in directions that are more favorable to children's development, are considered by Bronfenbrenner to be especially important.

Ethology

Another theoretical perspective that emphasizes the relevance of environmental contexts to behavior is **ethology.** It began to be applied to research on children in the 1960s and 1970s and continues to be prevalent today. Ethology is concerned with understanding the adaptive, or survival, value of behavior and its evolutionary history. The origins of ethology can be traced to the work of Charles Darwin; its modern foundations were laid by two European zoologists, Konrad Lorenz and Niko Tinbergen. Watching the behaviors of diverse animal species in their natural habitats, Lorenz and Tinbergen observed a number of built-in behavior patterns that seemed to promote survival. The most well-known of them is **imprinting,** the early following behavior of certain baby birds that assures that the young will stay close to the mother and be fed and protected from predators. Imprinting occurs during an early, restricted time period of development. If during this time the mother is not present, but an object that resembles her in important features is, such as a squatting, quacking adult or a moving milk bottle, young ducklings may imprint on it instead (Lorenz, 1952). Observations of imprinting led to a major theoretical concept that has since been widely applied in developmental psychology: the *critical period.* It refers to a limited time span during which the organism is biologically prepared to acquire certain new behaviors but requires the support of an appropriately stimulating environment for normal development to occur. Many investigators have conducted studies to find out if complex cognitive and social behaviors of human beings must be acquired during restricted time periods, and we shall discuss their findings in subsequent chapters of this book.

Inspired by observations of imprinting, John Bowlby (1969) applied ethological theory to the understanding of the human mother-infant relationship. Bowlby argued that attachment behaviors of infants to their mothers, in the form of smiling, babbling, grasping, and crying, were built-in social signals that encouraged the mother to approach the infant. They could best be understood from an evolutionary perspective, as behaviors that had evolved because they favored survival of the young. By promoting proximity to the mother, attachment behaviors assured that the infant would be adequately fed and protected from danger. According to Bowlby, the development of attachment in humans begins with a set of instinctive behaviors and gradually evolves into a true attachment relationship in which the primary caregiver is highly preferred as a source of comfort and social interaction. Infant characteristics, cognitive development, and sensitive, responsive caregiving combine with one another to support the entire process. Notice how this ethological view of attachment, with its focus on innate infant signals, differs sharply from the social learning explanation of the baby's desire for physical closeness to the mother as a secondary drive based on feeding (Bowlby, 1969).

Observations by ethologists of a wide variety of animal behaviors have recently

According to the ethological perspective, nonverbal cues and facial expressions signal dominant and submissive behavior among children, much as they do among primates. (Richard Hutchings)

stimulated ethological investigations of dominance hierarchies, aggression, play, cooperation, and nonverbal communication among human children. Results of these studies provide us with a stark reminder that our evolutionary ancestry is retained in many of our everyday social behaviors. For example, Strayer and Strayer (1976) recorded naturally occurring conflicts among a group of preschool children and found evidence of a rigid and stable dominance hierarchy similar to that which exists in nonhuman primate groups. The low frequency of counterattacks in children's conflicts suggests that the adaptive value of the dominance hierarchy is to reduce aggression within the group, just as it does in other primates. Other studies have identified specific nonverbal cues in human children that seem to signal dominance and submission. When elementary school children engage in behaviors that lead to reduced body stature, such as slumping the shoulders, bowing the head, kneeling, or shoe tying, aggressive activity subsides (Ginsburg, Pollman, & Wauson, 1977). Zivin (1977) observed a facial expression, involving raised eyebrows and chin combined with a direct stare toward another child's eyes. When used in competitive encounters between children, the child who displays it almost always wins. The facial expression is similar to dominance-related threat stares in nonhuman primates.

The research methodology of ethology begins with naturalistic observation. To understand the evolutionary and adaptive significance of behavior, it must first be observed in its natural context (Jones, 1972; McGrew, 1972). Then ethologists may conduct laboratory investigations in which the specific environmental eliciting conditions for behaviors are studied. Harry Harlow's research, which compares the behavior of monkeys reared under a variety of conditions — in isolation, with various types of surrogate mothers, and with peers — is an example of the latter type of investigation (Suomi & Harlow, 1978). Another powerful laboratory procedure that has been employed to study attachment in human infants is Mary Ainsworth's *Strange Situation*. Infants' responses to a series of brief separations from and reunions with their mothers are observed. On the basis of the pattern of the babies' reactions, the security of the attachment bond is assessed (Ainsworth et al., 1978).

The ethological perspective in child development is an excellent example of how developmental psychology has borrowed from other disciplines. Research efforts emphasize the genetic and biological bases of behavior, but learning, because it lends flexibility and greater environmental adaptiveness to behavior, is also considered important. Since ethologists believe behavior can best be understood in terms of its adaptive value, they are interested in a full understanding of environmental contexts, including their physical, interpersonal, and cultural aspects. Thus, the interests of ethologists are broad; they aim to understand the entire organism—environment system (Miller, 1983).

Ethological research is of practical as well as theoretical significance. Social changes over the last two decades, such as the rise in single-parent families and in use of substitute child care as mothers enter the labor force in increasing numbers, have led to dramatic changes in the early environments of children. Ethological theory can help us understand which aspects of the environment are essential to maintain, and what kinds of changes are likely to strain the adaptive resources of the infant and young child.

Piaget's Cognitive-Developmental Theory

If there is any single individual who has had more influence on the modern field of child development than any other, it is the Swiss psychologist Jean Piaget (1896–1980). In the United States, Piaget's work was not given much attention until the 1960s, although American psychologists had been aware of it since 1930. A major reason for the delay was that his theory and methods of studying children were so very much at odds with the behaviorist tradition that dominated American psychology during the middle of the twentieth century.

Recall from our earlier description of behaviorism and social learning theory that the child was considered to be a passive organism whose responses were shaped by environmental stimuli. Behaviorists, such as Watson and Skinner, did not speculate about internal mental processes. Thinking could be reduced to simple connections between stimuli and responses, and the course of development was *quantitative,* consisting of a gradual increase in the number and strength of such connections with age. In contrast, Piaget did not think that knowledge was bestowed upon a passive child. He believed that children construct it actively as they manipulate and explore their world.

Piaget's view of cognitive development was greatly influenced by his early training in biology. Central to his theory is the biological concept of *adaptation* (Piaget, 1971). Just as the structures of the body are adapted to fit with the environment, so the structures of the mind develop over the course of infancy and childhood to achieve a better and better adaptive fit with external reality. In early childhood, children's understanding of reality is very different from that of adults. For example, preschoolers think that a quantity of liquid changes when it is poured into a differently shaped container and that dreams are real objects visible to other people. Such cognitive understandings change as a result of the child's constant efforts to achieve an *equilibrium,* or balance, between internal structures and the demands of the external world.

Piaget believed that the child traverses a series of four broad stages of development, each characterized by a qualitatively different organization of cognitive structures. During the *sensorimotor stage* of infancy, the structures are sensorimotor action patterns derived from the reflexes of the newborn infant. These action patterns are devoted to recognizing objects and events and acting on the world through the senses. Sensorimotor behaviors gradually become internalized and representational during the *preoperational stage* of the preschool years. Preschoolers' new symbolic capacities are most evident in the rapid advances they make in language acquisition. In the *concrete operational stage,* internalized mental structures become the more organized and accurate thinking of the elementary school child, who can think about concrete problems in a logical fashion. For example, during this stage children understand that the weight of a round ball of clay remains the same even after it is flattened like a pancake and that a quantity of liquid is unchanged after it is poured from a tall, narrow container into a short, wide one. Finally, in the *formal operational stage* of adolescence, the structures become the abstract, logically organized system of adult intelligence. When faced with a complex problem, the adolescent speculates about all possible solutions before trying them out systematically in the real world, much like a scientist experimenting in the laboratory. Piaget (1966) thought that little could be done by adults to deliberately teach, train, or accelerate the child's movement through these stages. Instead, children had to act directly upon experience and initiate their own cognitive transformations. However, the availability of a rich and stimulating environment was still considered important as a general context for developmental change.

Piaget used research methods that were designed to uncover the child's unique construction of reality. To study infants, he carefully observed his own three children and showed an intuitive genius for arranging situations that revealed the infant's understanding of actions and objects in the surrounding world. Piaget's small number of infant subjects and anecdotal approach to recording observations were criticized by American experimental psychologists, but his general findings on infancy have since been replicated using more rigorous procedures. With older children, he used the method of the *clinical interview* (Piaget, 1926/1930). Unlike a test, where the form of the question is the same for all children and the examiner's interest is in whether the child's answer is right or wrong, the clinical interview is flexible and open-ended. Verbal probes are used in which questions are varied and rephrased to give children the widest possible latitude in displaying what they know and to assure that children's responses are truly representative of the quality of their thinking. Here is an excerpt from a clinical interview in which Piaget tried to find out about a young child's understanding of dreams (the child's name and age in years and months are given at the beginning):

> METR (5:9): "Where does the dream come from?—*I think you sleep so well that you dream. — Does it come from us or from outside?—From outside. —* What do we dream with?—*I don't know.* — With the hands? . . . With nothing?—*Yes, with nothing.* — When you are in bed and you dream, where is the dream?—*In my bed, under the blanket. I don't really know. If it was in my stomach, the bones would be in the way and I shouldn't see it.* — Is the dream there when you sleep?—*Yes, it is in the bed beside me.*" We tried suggestion: "Is the dream in your head?—*It is I that am in the dream: it isn't in my head. When you dream, you don't know you are in the bed. You know you are walking. You are in the dream. You are in bed, but you don't know you are.* — Can two people have the same dream?—*There are never two dreams* (alike)!—Where do dreams come from?—*I don't know. They happen.* — Where?—*In the room and then afterward they come up to the children. They come by themselves.* — You see the dream when you are in the room, but if I were in the room, too, should I see it?—*No, grownups don't ever dream.* — Can two people ever have the same dream?—*No, never.* — When the dream is in the room, is it near you?—*Yes, there!* (pointing to 30 cms. in front of his eyes)." (Piaget, 1926/1930, pp. 97–98).

Piaget's clinical interviewing approach has been criticized because it is not applied in the same way to all children. However, the method reflects the central core of Piaget's theory in that it is a systematic effort to understand and explore the child's point of view and to avoid an adult-centered interpretation of responses.

Piaget's cognitive-developmental perspective has stimulated more research on children's development than any other single theory. Nevertheless, recent research has raised questions about the accuracy of his stages of development. Some investigators have concluded that the quality of children's thinking at each stage forms a far less unified whole than Piaget assumed, and that the maturity of children's cognitions may depend on the child's familiarity with the elements of the task and the particular kind of knowledge sampled (Mandler, 1983). Furthermore, many studies have shown that children's performance on Piagetian tasks can be improved with training, raising questions about his conclusion that little can be done in the way of direct teaching and intervention to foster the child's developmental progress (Gelman & Baillargeon, 1983).

Despite these challenges, Piaget convinced many developmental psychologists that children are active learners from the very beginning and that their minds are inhabited by rich structures of knowledge. Piaget's emphasis on an active and adaptive organism has been especially influential in the recent expansion of research on infant development, including perceptual, motor, cognitive, and social competencies.

Practically speaking, Piaget's theory encouraged the development of educational philosophies and programs that emphasize children's discovery learning and direct experimentation with the environment. His work also stimulated the development of new intelligence tests designed to assess the child in terms of Piagetian stage-related milestones. In Chapter 6 we will consider Piaget's theory in greater detail.

CURRENT AND FUTURE DIRECTIONS

New ways to think about and study the child are constantly emerging — questioning, building upon, and enhancing the discoveries of earlier theories. Today, a burst of fresh approaches and research emphases — information processing, social cognition, a renewal of enthusiasm for studying children's emotions, and cross-cultural investigations — are broadening our understanding of children's development.

Information Processing

Developmental psychologists had become disenchanted with the behaviorist perspective as a complete account of children's learning and disappointed in their attempts to fully validate Piaget's stage theory. They turned to the field of cognitive psychology as a whole for new ways to understand the development of children's thinking. Today, the leading approach for studying children's cognition is **information processing.** Influenced by research in adult cognition, psycholinguistics, and computer science, information processing is not so much a unified theory as it is a general approach in which the human being is viewed as a system through which information flows. Between presentation to the senses at *input* and behavioral responses at *output,* information is actively transformed, coded, and organized.

Information processing is often thought of as a field of scripts, frames, and flowcharts. An example of this kind of representation is Atkinson and Shiffrin's flowchart of the memory system, shown in Figure 1.2. From input to output, internal control processes, or mental strategies, act on information to register it, store it in memory, and make it useful for generating responses (Shiffrin & Atkinson, 1969). The use of such computer-like analogies does not mean that psychologists believe that the human information processing system is identical to that of a computer. Rather, they believe that because human beings program computers, important insights into how people think can be obtained from computer processes.

Several lines of research were especially influential in the current embrace of information processing by developmental psychologists. First, the popularity of the computer metaphor for human problem solving may be traced to important advances that were made in the field of computer science following World War II. Parallels between the symbol-manipulating ability of the human mind and computers encouraged psychologists to borrow both terminology and orientation from the computer

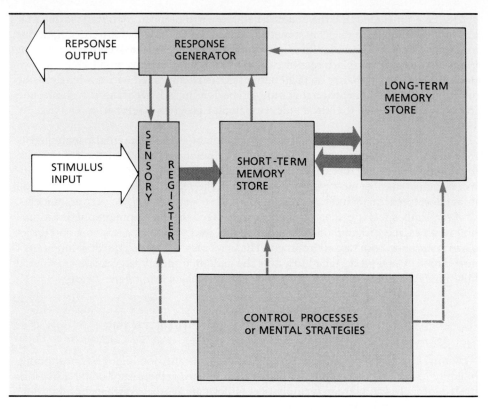

Figure 1.2. Atkinson and Shiffrin's model of the information processing system. Stimulus input flows through the sensory register, short-term memory store, and long-term memory store. Mental strategies act on and transform it before a response is generated. *(From R. M. Shiffrin & R. C. Atkinson 1969, "Storage and Retrieval Processes in Long-term Memory."* Psychological Review, 76, 180. *Copyright 1969 by the American Psychological Association. Adapted by permission of the authors.)*

field to serve as the basis for new theories of cognitive functioning. At the same time, other useful concepts and applications arose from technological leaps in the communications industry as well as in the discipline of human engineering, which addresses the interaction of people with complex machines.

Of no less consequence were the ground-breaking discoveries of linguist Noam Chomsky (1957) that children comprehend and produce novel utterances they have never heard before. Chomsky argued that children are *rule-oriented* in their acquisition of language. His idea that children use internal rules that must be inferred from the language they hear (input) and the language they produce (output) is consistent with an information processing framework. By the 1960s, Chomsky's work had sparked a tremendous upsurge in developmental studies of children's language. Psychologists' excitement over new evidence for the rule-governed aspects of language caused them to search for corresponding rules and strategies in children's thinking and problem solving.

Today, the information processing approach in child development encompasses a wide variety of research activities, including studies of children's attention, memory, comprehension, language, and problem solving. There is no assumption of stages of development. Rather, because the processes studied apply to all ages but may be present to a lesser extent in children, the developmental viewpoint is largely one of quantitative increase rather than qualitative change (Ault, 1983).

The methods used are mostly experimental and laboratory-based, such as reaction times to examine the temporal course of information flow, children's verbal reports to describe the strategies they use to remember and solve problems, and eye movements to determine how infants and young children process visual information. However, besides tasks that require subjects to learn discrete bits of information like nonsense syllables and separate words and pictures, researchers also use tasks that emphasize meaningful, potentially organizable material, such as picture sequences, sentences, and stories.

The information processing approach has begun to provide important practical implications for children's education. Successful learning is more likely if the tasks required of children are within their perceptual, memory, and problem-solving capabilities. Already, there is a trend in information processing to study educationally important domains of learning, such as reading, arithmetic, and scientific problem solving, in which children's performances are described, and factors that give them difficulty are identified (Glaser, 1982; Siegler, 1983).

Social Cognition

So far, information processing has not had much impact on our understanding of social and personality development. However, another area has evolved within the last two decades that has led to substantial advances in our understanding of these two topics. It is called the development of **social cognition.** In earlier theories, such as psychoanalytic and social learning, the child was not described as a *thinking social* being. Now social and cognitive development are being brought together.

Research in social cognition examines how children think and reason about themselves and their social world, how thinking and reasoning about the self and social relationships develop, and how these processes are related to social behaviors. Like information processing, there is no single unified theory, but rather an approach that emphasizes children's active efforts to make sense out of their social experiences. A major influence has been Piaget's theory. His stages of cognitive development have led to stage theories of children's conceptions of friendship, authority relations (Damon, 1977), and moral understanding (Kohlberg, 1969; 1976). In all of these theories, the development of *perspective-taking*—children's capacity to understand what another person is thinking and feeling—is central and believed to underlie a variety of positive social behaviors, such as cooperativeness, kindness, helpfulness, friendliness, and generosity (Selman & Byrne, 1974; Selman, 1980).

The interest developmental psychologists have in social cognition has also been stimulated by work in the mainstream of academic social psychology, especially *attribution* theory, which focuses on how people understand the causes of their own and others' behavior. Attribution theory has been applied to research on how children interpret their successes and failures in achievement situations. For example, children can attribute their successes to ability (being smart or good at something) or to effort (trying hard). Such attributions have been found to originate in part from children's social experiences with teachers and parents, and they predict how hard children are willing to try again at a given activity and whether they expect to succeed in the future (Dweck, 1983).

Since the research topics are diverse, a variety of methods have been employed to study children's social cognition. The Piagetian clinical interview is often used to probe for children's social understanding—for example, what children of different ages mean by a "best friend." Children have also been presented with a variety of tasks in the laboratory, such as perspective-taking problems in which they must describe another person's point of view. Sometimes children are observed in the natural environment interacting with one another, and their social behaviors and statements are used to infer their social knowledge.

Research in social cognition also has important practical implications. Children's attributions as to why they succeed and fail are of concern to educators, and children profit from interventions designed to help them change attributions that lead to self-defeating behaviors in learning situations (Dweck, 1975; 1986). Programs that train children in perspective-taking, and others that provide experiences in social problem solving, such as how to gain entry into peer play groups and sustain positive interactions with agemates, have been developed for children who have interpersonal problems (Asher & Renshaw, 1981; Chandler, 1973; Shantz, 1983).

The Study of Emotions

Although cognitive psychology dominated child development research during the middle part of this century and continues to be vigorously influential today, a rebirth of interest in children's emotions has occurred over the last decade, and it shows every indication of gathering additional momentum in the future. Once the impact of the psychoanalytic perspective began to recede during the 1950s and 1960s, emotions were no longer credited with playing a central role in children's development. Instead, they were treated as mere by-products of cognitive processing. For example, smiling and laughter were regarded as indications of children's delight at being able to process a new stimulus, and fear was thought to be produced by events so different from those to which the young child was accustomed that cognitive processing was disrupted, producing anxiety and withdrawal (Kagan, Kearsley, & Zelazo, 1978; McCall & McGhee, 1977). Although these cognitive explanations of emotional reactions proved to be partially correct, they failed to account for many emotional phenomena. For example, cognitive theorists could not explain why infants' fear of strangers varies depending on whether they sit close to their mothers or some distance away, and why children's repeated encounters with certain familiar events and persons continue to elicit positive responses rather than disinterest and boredom. The deficiencies of the cognitive perspective, coupled with the discovery during the 1970s of innovative laboratory methods that permitted psychologists to study emotional reactions more accurately than was previously possible, touched off a new theoretical perspective on the development of emotions called the **organizational approach.**

The organizational approach has much in common with ethology in the way it emphasizes the adaptive role of emotions in promoting survival of the organism. In addition, it regards emotions as centrally important in all facets of human behavior. While cognition does affect emotional reactions, organizational theorists regard the relationship between emotions and cognition as reciprocal. Emotions play a major role in determining what we perceive and remember and how we interpret events in the surrounding world. Moreover, emotions powerfully affect social interaction. For example, infants' and children's smiles elicit positive emotional reactions from their caregivers, and the exchange of smiles draws adults and children closer to one another and encourages them to continue their pleasurable interaction. Emotional reactions also affect physiological processes and physical health, as illustrated by cases of children who fail to grow normally because they lack the experience of warm, caring parenting (Gagan, 1984; Vietze et al., 1980).

Over the past two decades, organizational theorists have generated a large body of research on the development of a variety of emotional reactions, such as happiness, interest, surprise, anger, fear, and sadness. Developmental psychologists have also been interested in studying *temperament,* or individual differences in style of emotional responding. Assessments of children's temperamental styles, such as sociability, activity level, and irritability, are usually derived from parental reports of children's typical emotional reactions or from ratings made by other adults familiar with the child. In some instances, direct observation in the home or laboratory as well as physiological measures of emotional arousal have also been employed. Researchers are investigating the long-term stability of temperamental characteristics, the origins of temperament in both heredity and child-rearing practices, and the extent to which early temperament is predictive of adult personality.

Cross-Cultural Research

Another current trend in child development research is an increase in *cross-cultural studies*. Investigations that make comparisons across cultures, and between ethnic and social class groups within cultures, provide insight into whether developmental sequences are universal and characteristic of all children or limited to particular environmental circumstances. Cross-cultural research also aids child development specialists in untangling the respective contributions of biological and environmental factors to the timing and the order of appearance of children's behaviors.

A variety of aspects of children's development have been investigated cross-culturally, including physical, motor, cognitive, social, and personality development (Adler, 1982; Monroe, Monroe, & Whiting, 1981). Researchers have moved away from examining broad cultural influences on development—for example, whether children in one culture as opposed to another are more advanced in motor development or do better on intellectual tasks. This approach can lead investigators to conclude incorrectly that one culture is superior in enhancing development while another promotes developmental deficiencies. In addition, it does not help us understand the specific experiences that contribute to cross-cultural differences in children's behavior.

Currently, more research is examining the relationship of *context-specific* practices to children's performance. When cross-cultural researchers moved beyond the presentation of laboratory tasks to the observation of children's everyday activities, they noticed that children who had difficulty performing certain skills in artificial situations often demonstrated surprisingly sophisticated competencies in natural contexts. The familiarity of materials and meaningfulness of the task to members of the culture has a great deal to do with how advanced children's performance will be. For example, when asked to copy two-dimensional figures, Zambian children do better when they can make the form out of strips of wire, an activity that is a frequent part of their daily experience. English children do better with paper and pencil (Serpell, 1979). African babies have been observed to be more advanced in infant motor development than American babies in that they sit up and walk at an earlier age. However, a close look at the child-rearing practices within those African cultures where this motor precocity is observed reveals that African parents deliberately teach these sitting and walking skills. Before babies can support themselves, sitting is encouraged by propping babies in holes in the ground and using rolled blankets to keep them upright. Walking is promoted from earliest infancy by frequently bouncing babies on their feet (Super, 1981). Results of studies like these reveal that the development of children's skills and behavior is related to the specific activities that are familiar and well-practiced in their culture. There are strengths in every culture that are not present in others because children adapt to the demands of their culture through the practice of particular activities (Laboratory of Comparative Human Cognition, 1983).

A major contribution of cross-cultural research has been the demonstration that cultures select different contexts for children's learning. Social interactions surrounding materials, tasks, and goals lead to the mastery of knowledge that is essential for success in a particular culture. The field of child development has again borrowed heavily from another discipline, anthropology, to achieve this understanding. A cross-cultural perspective reminds us that the great majority of child development specialists reside in the United States, and our usual subjects of study comprise only a small minority of humankind. We cannot assume that the developmental sequences observed in our own children are "natural" or that the environments that foster them are "ideal" without looking around the world (Heron & Kroeger, 1981).

SUMMARY OF MAJOR THEORETICAL PERSPECTIVES

The history of child study is a chronicle of contrasting themes of childhood and child development. Major theories and approaches we have discussed, along with their dominant methods and representative applications, are summarized in Table 1.2.

Three *metatheoretical issues,* or larger questions about the nature of the child and developmental change, which we mentioned at the beginning of this chapter, emerge from comparisons of the theories. Because these metatheoretical issues help us summarize basic similarities and differences among the major theories, we consider them in greater detail below:

1. *Are children active organisms who play a major role in determining the course of their own development, or are they passive recipients of environmental inputs?* This issue contrasts the **organismic model** of child development, represented by maturational, psychoanalytic, and cognitive-developmental theories, with the **mechanistic model,** represented by behaviorist and social learning theories.

Organismic theorists posit the existence of organizing structures internal to the child that underlie and exert control over development. The organismic model holds that children are active and purposeful contributors to their own development. The environment facilitates growth, but it does not play a causal role.

In contrast, the mechanistic view focuses on relationships between environmental input and behavioral output. The model is called mechanistic because children's behavior is likened to the workings of a machine. Change is initiated by the environment, which actively impinges upon the child who is a passive reactor. Development

Table 1.2. Summary of Major Theories, Methods, and Practical Applications

MAJOR THEORIES AND APPROACHES	VIEWS OF CHILD DEVELOPMENT	DOMINANT METHODS	REPRESENTATIVE APPLICATIONS
Maturational theory (Hall, Gesell)	Predetermined maturational unfolding of behavior	Normative study using questionnaires, observations	Child-rearing advice
Psychoanalytic theory (Freud, Erikson)	Qualitatively distinct series of psychosexual and psychosocial stages	Clinical method	Child-rearing advice; treatment of children with emotional problems
Behaviorism and social learning theory (Watson, Skinner, Sears, Bandura)	Quantitative increase in learned responses due to reinforcement and modeling	Laboratory study	Behavior modification to eliminate children's undesirable behaviors and increase the adoption of socially acceptable responses
Ecological theory (Barker, Bronfenbrenner)	Environmental contexts as sources of influence on children's development. Social interaction as a bidirectional, reciprocal process	Naturalistic observation	Design of environments to enhance development
Ethological theory (Bowlby, Ainsworth, Harlow)	Evolutionary origins and adaptive value of child behavior. Existence of built-in behavior patterns and social signals that promote survival	Naturalistic observation, follow-up laboratory study	Interventions that promote secure mother-infant attachment
Piaget's cognitive-developmental theory	Cognitive structures change through a sequence of qualitatively distinct stages. The child actively adapts to the environment	Infant observation, clinical interview	Educational programs emphasizing discovery learning; stage-based assessments of intelligence
Information processing	Quantitative increase in knowledge and active use of information-processing strategies	Laboratory study	Matching learning tasks to children's processing abilities; improving children's learning and problem-solving strategies
Social cognition	Social understanding changes through qualitatively distinct stages. Children actively think about their social world	Clinical interview, laboratory tasks, and naturalistic observation	Training in perspective-taking and social problem solving for children with interpersonal problems
Organizational approach to emotions	Adaptive value of emotions. Emotions as central forces in all human behavior	Naturalistic observation, laboratory study	Using knowledge about the role of emotions to optimize cognitive and social development as well as physical health

is treated as a predictable, manageable consequence of learning, based on fundamental principles of conditioning and modeling.

2. *Is child development a matter of quantitative or qualitative change?* The quantitative position suggests that development is a linear, cumulative process that proceeds in gradual, continuous increments. Differences between the immature and mature organism are assumed to be merely a matter of amount or complexity of behavior, and children can be described and understood on the same basis as adults. Behaviorist theory, social learning theory, and the information processing approach share this view. In contrast, stage theories of development—psychoanalytic, cognitive-developmental, and social cognition—assume that children have unique, qualitatively distinct ways of thinking, feeling, and responding to the world that must be understood on their own terms. Development is a discontinuous rather than continuous process in which fundamentally new and different modes of behavior emerge following periodic revisions and reorganizations in underlying structures.

3. *Are genetic or environmental factors the most important determinants of child development and behavior?* This is the age-old nature-nurture controversy. Almost all theories have at least given lip service to both sides, but nevertheless a few have taken extreme positions. For example, in Gesell's maturational theory, inherited potential for growth is of paramount importance, while the child's experiences are supreme in behaviorist and social learning theories.

Some theories, especially the more recent ones, steer a middle course on these controversial issues. The thinking of many major theorists has moderated, and they recognize the importance of both sides. For example, on the nature-nurture issue, psychoanalytic theory, cognitive-developmental theory, and social cognition all recognize biological foundations by positing universal, maturationally determined sequences of stages. However, the child's experiences during each stage are regarded as essential for developmental progress. The importance of both maturation and experience can also be seen in the ethological concept of critical period, where nature determines timing and nurture influences how well the needs of the individual will be met during a particular phase of development. Finally, both mechanistic and organismic perspectives are combined in the information processing approach. An input-output, machinelike model coexists with active processing strategies going on within the organism.

CHILD DEVELOPMENT AS A RAPIDLY CHANGING FIELD

Six "Great Handbooks" summarizing theory, methods, and research findings in the field of child development have been published during the last 60 years. The most recent, appearing in 1983, reveals that child development in the latter part of the twentieth century is still seeking theoretical direction, continuously questioning and refining old methods, and confronting more directly than ever before the complexity of the child's development (Kessen, 1983). The latest *Handbook of Child Psychology* contains four volumes and over 4,000 pages. There are new chapters on such topics as play, logical thinking, schooling, information processing, social cognition, and emotional development. Three chapters are devoted to language development (as opposed to one in the 1970 Handbook), and an entire volume is given over to the burgeoning research literature on infant development. The 1983 Handbook reflects the use of diverse methods and varied settings to study the child. The scientific respectability of research on children no longer rests so exclusively on laboratory investigations as it did a few decades ago.

The field of child development continues to be influenced by pressing unresolved

As more mothers of young children enter the labor force, child development specialists are becoming increasingly concerned about the effects of day care on children's development. (Nancy Sheehan)

problems faced by today's children. High infant mortality rates, poor health care for pregnant women and children, teenage pregnancy, widespread child abuse, rising rates of divorce, developmental risks of poverty, and increased demand for substitute child care as women enter the labor force are pervasive national concerns. The need to incorporate lessons from scientific theory and research into our efforts to solve these problems is now recognized, as solutions must be based on good theories of what the child is like and how development occurs (DeLone, 1982). For this reason, child development specialists are no longer exclusively confined to academic settings. They have entered the arena of public policy, and their theoretical principles and methods of study have benefited, in turn, from the stimulus of direct experience with the realities of children's lives (Zigler & Finn-Stevenson, 1988).

During the last 25 years, a wide range of social programs aimed at improving children's development have been implemented. One of the most well known is Project Head Start, a federally funded preschool intervention and early education program aimed at preventing the ill effects of poverty. Initiated in 1965, thousands of Head Start programs currently exist throughout the United States, and child development experts have been continuously involved in program design, implementation, and evaluation. In the 1970s and 1980s, Head Start inspired academic researchers to study the importance of early experience and the benefits of early intervention. Their investigations showed that an essential ingredient of successful programs is parent involvement and participation, and that good programs can lead to gains in children's motivation to learn and their school performance during the elementary school years. Such findings have had a major practical impact. They have helped improve the design of early childhood interventions and have been instrumental in bringing about recent increases in federal funding for Head Start (Brown, 1985). Project Head Start illustrates how pressing social problems can stimulate child development research, and the research, in turn, can influence programs and policies for children.

This reciprocity between theory, research, and the applied needs of children is a major driving force behind the ever-changing, continuously evolving field of child development. It also offers child development specialists unique opportunities to contribute in significant ways to the improvement of human life.

CHAPTER SUMMARY

1. Child development is the study of human growth and change from conception into adolescence. Its knowledge base is unique in having been stimulated by both scientific curiosity and social pressures to better the lives of children. Theories of child development lend structure and organization to this knowledge base, provide frameworks from which to generate

new knowledge, and offer practical guides for improving the welfare and treatment of children.

2. Modern theories of child development are the result of centuries of change in cultural values, philosophical thinking, and scientific progress. In medieval times, children were

viewed as miniature, preformed adults. By the sixteenth and seventeenth centuries, childhood began to be regarded as a distinct phase of the life cycle, but the Protestant conception of original sin led to a harsh, authoritarian philosophy of child rearing. The Enlightenment brought new philosophies and more humane child treatment. Locke's tabula rasa furnished the philosophical basis for modern behaviorism, while Rousseau's natural philosophy of childhood foreshadowed the developmental concepts of maturation and stage. In the nineteenth century, Darwin's theory of evolution provided the scientific foundation for empirical child study and influenced many twentieth-century theories.

3. Efforts to study the child empirically began with the baby biographies. Although methodologically naive, they served as forerunners of naturalistic observation and longitudinal research. From the early normative period emerged Gesell's maturational theory, a large body of descriptive facts about child development, and the Stanford-Binet Intelligence Scale, the first widely used intelligence test for children. Some professionals sought alternatives to the normative approach that would take into account the unique life histories of individual children. Child guidance professionals turned to psychoanalysis—Freud's psychosexual and Erikson's psychosocial theories—for help in understanding and treating children with problems. With the tremendous strides being made in treating childhood diseases, pediatricians devoted greater attention to the overall development of the well child. They provided parents with child-rearing advice and made special contributions to the field of child development in the areas of newborn behavioral assessment and adolescent health.

4. In the 1930s and 1940s, academic psychology began to influence modern child study. From behaviorism came social learning theories of childhood, efforts to convert psychoanalytic predictions to behaviorist principles, controlled laboratory studies, and practical procedures for modifying children's

behavior. Ecological theories, in which natural environmental contexts were seen as major influences on children's development, emerged in part as a reaction to contrived laboratory investigations. Developmental psychologists turned toward ethological theory to understand the adaptive or survival value of children's behavior and its origins in the evolutionary history of the human species. Burgeoning interest in Piaget's theory during the 1960s stimulated a cognitive revolution in child development. The strong cognitive flavor of current research is apparent in the approaches of information processing and social cognition. Interest in the central role children's emotions play in their development has been revitalized. The recent rise in cross-cultural studies is helping to untangle the respective contributions of biological and environmental factors to children's development.

5. Three controversial questions about the nature of the child and the course of development emerge from comparisons of major child development theories: (1) Are children active beings who shape the course of their own development, or are they passive, reactive organisms controlled by environmental inputs? (2) Is development a linear, continuous process in which children think, feel, and behave in much the same way as adults, or is it a discontinuous, stage-wise process in which children have their own qualitatively distinct ways of organizing experience and responding to the world? (3) Are genetic or environmental factors most important in determining the course of development? While some theories take extreme positions on these issues, others incorporate elements from both sides.

6. Reciprocity between theory, research, and the applied needs of children stimulates the field of child development to move rapidly forward. In the last 25 years, social programs aimed at alleviating pressing problems faced by today's children have attracted academic researchers, and their findings have, in turn, had an impact on programs and policies.

IMPORTANT TERMS AND CONCEPTS

child development
developmental psychology
theory
preformationism
tabula rasa
noble savage
stage
maturation
normative study
psychoanalytic theory
id
ego
superego
oral stage
anal stage

phallic stage
latency stage
genital stage
basic trust versus mistrust
autonomy versus shame and doubt
initiative versus guilt
industry versus inferiority
identity versus identity diffusion
intimacy versus isolation
generativity versus stagnation
ego integrity versus despair
behaviorist theory
classical conditioning
operant conditioning
social learning theory

modeling
ecological psychology
behavior setting
microsystem
mesosystem
exosystem
macrosystem
ethology
imprinting
information processing
social cognition
organizational approach to emotional
    development
organismic model
mechanistic model

Bubbles, by Amy B. Atkinson.
By courtesy of the City of Manchester Art Galleries.

CHAPTER 2
Research Strategies

In Chapter 1, we discussed the relationship of theory to child development research. We saw how theories structure the research process by identifying important questions to ask about the child and preferred methods for collecting data. We also saw how theories guide the interpretation of research findings and their application to real-life circumstances and practices with children. In fact, research usually begins with a prediction about behavior, or what we call an **hypothesis,** drawn directly from a theory. Think back to the diverse array of child development theories that we reviewed in Chapter 1. A myriad of hypotheses can be drawn from any one of them, which, once tested, would reflect back on the accuracy of the theory.

Sometimes research pits an hypothesis taken from one theory against an hypothesis taken from another. For example, a maturationist would predict that parental training will have little effect on the age at which children take their first steps or say their first words, while a behaviorist would speculate that these skills can be accelerated through systematic reinforcement. At other times, research tests predictions drawn from a single theory. For example, an ecologist would hypothesize that providing isolated, divorced mothers with social supports will increase their sensitivity and patience with children. An ethologist would speculate that a tape recording of a baby's cry will stimulate strong physiological arousal in mothers who hear it. When little or no theory exists in an area of child development, rather than making a specific prediction, the researcher starts with a question, such as: "Are children reaching puberty earlier and growing taller than they did a generation ago?" "Do first-grade girls learn to read more easily and quickly than first-grade boys?"

But theories, hypotheses, and research questions are only the beginning of the many activities that culminate in sound information about child development. Conducting research according to scientifically accepted procedures involves many important steps and choices. Investigators must work out the particulars of which subjects and how many will be asked to participate. Then they must decide what the subjects will be asked to do, and when, where, and how many times each will need to be seen. Finally, they must examine relationships and draw conclusions from their data.

This chapter is devoted to a close look at the steps of the research process. We begin by considering why an appreciation of research strategies is important — not just for researchers who are immersed in the research enterprise, but also for students who want to understand child development and practitioners who work directly with children. Next we consider two vital research concepts — validity and reliability — that help scientists evaluate the accuracy of their procedures and, ultimately, the trustworthiness of the conclusions they draw from a research study. Our discussion then turns to the strengths and weaknesses of a variety of research strategies commonly used to study children. Deciding on an appropriate research strategy involves two main tasks. The first task involves selecting one or more *research methods*, the specific activities individuals participate in as subjects in a study, such as taking tests, filling out questionnaires, responding to interviews, or being observed, and where those activities will take place — in the laboratory or in the natural environment. The second task involves choosing a *research design*, or an overall plan for the study that will permit the best possible test of the researcher's question. You have probably already heard of some common research designs. Correlational and experimental designs are two broadly applied strategies in psychological research of all kinds, and we will discuss them in this chapter. But research in child development is often complicated by the fact that age differences in behavior are of central interest. Longitudinal and cross-sectional designs are two *developmental* research strategies that permit investigators to examine age-related changes. As we discuss these designs later on in this chapter, you will see that drawing conclusions about age differences presents investigators with special problems, and innovative modifications of developmental designs have been devised to overcome some of these difficulties.

In the final portion of this chapter, we consider ethical issues involved in doing research on children. Research on any subjects, whether animal or human, must meet certain ethical standards that protect participants from harmful and unnecessarily stressful treatment. But extra precautions must be taken to ensure that children's rights to humane treatment are not violated in the course of a research study.

WHY KNOW ABOUT RESEARCH STRATEGIES?

Researchers in the field of child development need to understand scientific procedures for studying human behavior in order to assure as accurate a representation of child development as possible. But students of child development and practitioners who work with children in applied settings might ask why they, too, should know about research strategies. Why not leave these matters to research specialists and concentrate on what is already known about the child and how this knowledge can be applied?

There are several reasons. First, students who want to understand child development, and people who work directly with children, must be wise and critical consumers of knowledge, not naive sponges who indiscriminately soak up facts about the child. As we saw in Chapter 1, the field of child development is full of many contrasting theories, findings, and conclusions. Therefore, a basic appreciation of research strategies becomes important as a rational means through which accurate, useful information can be separated from misleading and erroneous results. Without an understanding of the research process, you must depend on authorities to tell you about the worth of child development information, not on your own well-reasoned judgments.

Researchers' questions and investigative plans benefit from the astute insights of practitioners, who have a rich background of direct experience with children. (Blair Seitz/Photo Researchers, Inc.)

Second, ideally, researchers and practitioners should be partners in the quest for knowledge about the child. The researcher needs to find out about behavior in the everyday environments in which teachers, caregivers, social workers, and others deal with children. In addition, research questions and plans often benefit from the astute insights and suggestions of practitioners. When this partnership happens, research findings are generally more relevant and useful in our search for new ways to enhance children's development. But for researchers and practitioners to work fruitfully together, they must try to understand each other's goals and activities. Part of this mutual understanding involves a shared appreciation of accepted research strategies.

Finally, sometimes practitioners are in a position to carry out small-scale research studies to answer practical questions about the children with whom they work. At other times they may have to provide systematic information on how well their goals for children are being realized in order to justify continued support for their programs and activities. Under these circumstances, a basic understanding of research strategies is essential practical knowledge.

RELIABILITY AND VALIDITY: KEYS TO SCIENTIFICALLY SOUND RESEARCH

Two essential concepts — reliability and validity — must be kept in mind during each step of the research process to assure that a study provides a trustworthy answer to an hypothesis or research question. **Reliability** refers to the consistency or repeatability of measures of subjects' behavior. **Validity** refers to how accurately the measures reflect what the investigator intended to measure in the first place. Let's discuss each of these important criteria for scientifically sound research, first as they apply to the methods researchers use to collect information on their subjects, and second as they apply to the overall findings and conclusions of a research study.

Suppose you go into a classroom and record the number of times a child behaves in a helpful and cooperative fashion toward others, but your research partner, in simultaneously observing the same child, comes up with a very different set of measurements. Or you ask a group of children some questions about their interests, but a week later when you question them again, their answers are very different. To be *reliable,* observations of children cannot be unique to a single observer; people must agree on what they see. And a test, questionnaire, or interview, when given again within a short period of time (before subjects can reasonably be expected to change or develop in their responses), must yield similar results on both occasions. If a method turns out to be unreliable, it tells us that we did not manage the conditions of observation or testing carefully enough. In observational studies, the behaviors of interest may have been so poorly defined, and the observers so casually trained, that they could not record children's behavior consistently from moment to moment (Anastasi, 1982). With tests and interviews, perhaps instructions to subjects were vague, questions were not phrased clearly, or the content of the instrument did not engage the interest and attention of the research participants. Any one of these factors could have caused our measures to be so unreliable that they would be useless for answering our research questions.

Investigators estimate the reliability of the information they collect in different ways. In observational research, they need to know the extent to which observers agree about the behavior they see. In other words, if two or more people apply the same observational method, will they come up with essentially the same codes and scores? A typical approach for answering this question is to have pairs of observers record the same behavior sequences independently and examine the extent to which their judgments of subjects' activities and behaviors agree. With tests and questionnaires, reliability can be demonstrated by finding out how similar children's responses are when the test is retaken, or children's scores can be compared on different forms of the same test. If necessary, reliability can also be determined in a single test administration by comparing children's scores on different halves of the test.

Research methods are *valid* if they yield measurements of those subject characteristics that they were intended to measure in the first place. Perhaps you have already noticed from the discussion presented above that reliability is absolutely essential for valid research techniques. Methods that are implemented carelessly, unevenly, and inconsistently cannot possibly represent what an investigator originally intended to study. But reliability is not sufficient by itself to ensure that a research strategy will accurately reflect an investigator's goals. Investigators must go further to assure that their methods are valid indicators of their research intentions, and they generally do so in a number of different ways. They may carefully scrutinize the content of tests and observation instruments to see if they provide thorough coverage of the behaviors of interest. For example, a test intended to measure fifth-grade children's knowledge of arithmetic would not be valid if it contained only addition, and no subtraction, multiplication, or division problems (Miller, 1987). Another approach to validity is to see how effective a method is in predicting behavior in other situations that we would reasonably expect it to predict. For example, if scores on an arithmetic test are valid, we might expect them to be related to how well children do on their arithmetic assignments in school, or even to how quickly and accurately they can make change in a game of Monopoly.

Aside from their relevance to research methods, the concepts of reliability and validity can be applied more broadly to the overall findings and conclusions of research studies (Achenbach, 1978). An investigator's findings are reliable if **replication** is possible — that is, if the investigation, when carried out again with a new group of subjects, yields the same findings. Replication studies give investigators important information about the consistency of research findings, and they take place far too seldom in psychological research.

Two special kinds of validity are important for the accuracy of research findings and conclusions. The first is called **internal validity,** which applies to factors within the context of the study itself (Miller, 1987). To assess internal validity, investigators must look carefully at every aspect of their research procedures and ask, "Have my results really come about for the reasons I hypothesized, or can they be attributed to some other factor in my research design?" To assure internal validity, each of the methods chosen by the researcher must be reliable and valid, in ways that we have discussed above. But beyond the choice of trustworthy methods, if during any phase of the research process the investigator permits factors unrelated to the hypothesis to influence subjects' behavior, then internal validity is in doubt, and the study cannot be considered a fair test of the investigator's theory. There are many factors that researchers must be on guard against to make sure that a study is internally valid, but as an illustration of some of the most important ones, let's look at an example of a hypothetical investigation.

Suppose a researcher predicts that attending open classrooms, where children are offered plenty of free choice in learning activities, causes elementary school children to be more creative thinkers than children enrolled in traditional classrooms, where teachers structure and assign most of the learning experiences. But what if parents who choose to send their youngsters to the open schools happen to encourage autonomy and freedom of expression more often than parents of traditional school children? In this case, *children's background characteristics* are a threat to the internal validity, or accuracy, of the study's conclusions, because we cannot tell if parental encouragement or school experiences (or both) are responsible for differences in children's creativity scores. In addition, imagine that our researcher arrives at the classrooms to give the creativity test on a day when many pupils are home with the flu, and several who take the test in the traditional school are not feeling well and do poorly. If this happens, an *inadequate sample size* can account for the results. The number of children tested is so small to begin with that when a few subjects respond atypically, the findings are severely distorted. Finally, suppose our investigator believes so zealously in the superiority of open schooling that he inadvertently gives children in the open school more time to complete the creativity test than he does those in the traditional school. This time, *researcher bias* — subtle efforts on the part of the investigator to obtain the results he desires — taints the outcome. This last example shows how researchers, if they do not take special precautions, can contaminate their own results. In most studies, it is wise to have people who have no knowledge of the investigator's hypotheses, or who at least have little personal investment in them, collect the data. Throughout this chapter, we shall encounter additional examples of "extraneous" influences that can jeopardize the internal validity of a research study. When investigators cannot take steps to reduce the impact of these factors, they need to qualify the conclusions they draw by indicating that more than one possible explanation may account for their findings.

A second type of validity that applies to the overall accuracy of findings and conclusions is **external validity.** It refers to whether results can be generalized to

In studying the benefits of open classrooms, where children are granted freedom to learn on their own, researchers must take into account the unique family backgrounds of children in their samples. (Michal Heron)

other groups of children and situations where the same findings are expected to prevail. Investigators may limit this kind of validity by using *biased samples*—for example, children of only one sex, or subjects of a single social class or ethnic background—so that results are applicable only to restricted groups of children. External validity is also reduced when researchers assume their findings have meaning in everyday contexts but conduct the investigation in contrived, artificial situations that induce children to behave in ways that do not represent their usual behaviors (Achenbach, 1978; Bracht & Glass, 1968). However, we should keep in mind that some kinds of behaviors, like infant perceptual abilities, can be investigated only in the laboratory. For example, if we want to know whether infants can perceive colors, we need precision instruments that permit control of brightness and wavelength in order to measure their responses with scientific accuracy. Moreover, there is no reason for us to suspect that infants' color perception in the laboratory would be very different from their responses in everyday contexts (Seitz, 1988). But in the case of many cognitive and social behaviors, children's responses may differ substantially between strange and familiar places. In these instances, researchers can determine the external validity of their findings by conducting **cross-validation studies** in

---

FOCUS ON THEORY, RESEARCH, AND APPLICATIONS

Box 2.1
"Don't Forget to Take the Cupcakes Out of the Oven": A Study of Children's Prospective Memory

How well do laboratory studies of children's memory inform us about their memory performance in the everyday world? To find out, Stephen Ceci and Urie Bronfenbrenner (1985) conducted a cross-validation study in which they observed children in the laboratory as well as in the familiar context of their own homes.

Theory. Most research on memory is concerned with *retrospective* memory, or recalling information learned in the past. However, in daily life, an important part of remembering is *prospective*. Children must learn to attend to future events, such as catching the morning bus on time, turning off the sprinklers in the front yard, or taking one's spelling book to reading class on Fridays. To remember to do something in the future, children often use external retrieval cues, such as setting the kitchen buzzer for when it's time to leave or placing the spelling book in a conspicuous place on Friday mornings. Ceci and Bronfenbrenner decided to examine another

approach for remembering future events, which they called *strategic time-monitoring*. If there is something you need to remember to do very soon, strategic time-monitoring is an efficient memory strategy that permits less frequent clock-checking during the waiting period so you can turn your attention to other activities.

Strategic time-monitoring consists of three phases: (1) an early calibration phase, in which individuals engage in frequent clock-checking to synchronize their "psychological clocks" with the passage of real clock time; (2) an intermediate phase, in which there is reduced clock-checking along with freedom to pursue other activities; and (3) a scalloping phase, in which clock-checking increases sharply as the time limit approaches. If children are using strategic time-monitoring, it should be reflected in a U-shaped distribution of clock-checking over time. This is in contrast to an alternative memory strategy, *anxious time-monitoring*, in which the person's need to maintain greater vigilance should be revealed in a constantly rising rate of clock-checking during the waiting period, and more clock-checking overall.

Strange and unfamiliar environments induce anxiety in children, and anxiety interferes with efficient memory processing. Therefore, Ceci

and Bronfenbrenner hypothesized that when children have to remember a future event, they will be more likely to show anxious time-monitoring in the laboratory and strategic time-monitor-

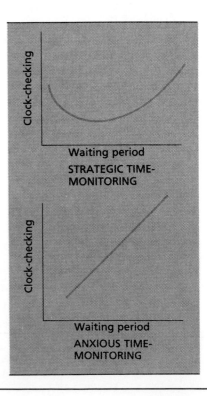

Waiting period
STRATEGIC TIME-MONITORING

Waiting period
ANXIOUS TIME-MONITORING

which they try to replicate their results in new situations or with different samples of children. Refer to Box 2.1 for an interesting example of cross-validation research.

In the following sections of this chapter, we consider a diverse array of methods and designs from which investigators may choose as they plan a research study. As you read about the strengths and weaknesses of each of these research strategies, note how matters of internal and external validity are continually at the heart of investigators' efforts to choose wisely from among available research alternatives.

COMMON RESEARCH METHODS USED TO STUDY CHILDREN

Below we consider the researcher's choice of a basic approach to gathering information about children. Commonly used methods in the field of child development include systematic observation, self-report techniques (such as questionnaires and interviews), and clinical or case studies of the behavior and development of a single child.

---

ing in the comfortable and familiar environments of their own homes. Memory strategies should also change with age. Older children, because they are more advanced in cognitive development, should show more strategic time-monitoring than younger children. Also, Ceci and Bronfenbrenner expected differences in memory performance between boys and girls, depending upon the sex-typed nature of the task children were asked to perform. If the task is sex-appropriate — baking cupcakes for girls, charging a motorcycle battery for boys — children should be more likely to respond with anxious clock-watching because of an especially strong desire to do well.

Research. Nearly 100 children, half 10-year-olds and half 14-year-olds, half boys and half girls, were each offered $5 either to bake cupcakes or to charge a motorcycle battery. Half of the children did the baking or charging in their own homes, the other half in the laboratory. Children asked to bake cupcakes were told to put them in the oven at a certain time and remove them exactly 30 minutes later. Those charging the battery were asked to remove the cables after the battery had charged for 30 minutes. To make sure that an attractive activity was available while children waited, a Pac Man video

machine was placed in an adjoining room. An observer pretending to read a magazine recorded children's clock-checking behavior during the waiting period.

Ceci and Bronfenbrenner took special precautions to protect the internal validity of their study. They ruled out family socioeconomic status and living in a single-parent household as alternative explanations for their findings by making sure these characteristics were equally distributed across children's age and sex groups. They also checked their data carefully to assure that interest and success in playing Pac Man was not the factor responsible for clock-checking behavior. Furthermore, reliability was determined by seeing if different observers watching the same child were able to record clock-checking behavior in the same way. Also, none of the observers knew the purpose of the study until after it had been completed.

As predicted, the investigators found that strategic time-monitoring was more pronounced in the home, while anxious time-monitoring was more prevalent in the laboratory. Apparently, many children took special precautions in the laboratory to ensure that they would live up to adult expectations. Interestingly, all age, sex, and task differences in clock-

watching occurred *only* in the laboratory. For example, 14-year-olds spent less time clock-watching and made greater use of strategic time-monitoring than 10-year-olds while in the lab, but no age-related differences in behavior occurred in the home environment. The expected sex differences occurred only for older boys and, again, just in the lab, where these boys were more anxious and less efficient clock-checkers when asked to disconnect a battery than when requested to bake cupcakes. These findings indicate that laboratory settings may bring out differences among children and tasks that do not necessarily occur in the natural environment.

Applications. Ceci and Bronfenbrenner's results indicate that children as young as 10 years of age are able to use a complex, sophisticated strategy to remember future events and that they are more likely to do so in the familiar environment of their own home than in an unfamiliar laboratory setting. Their study shows that we cannot assume that children's performances in contrived, unfamiliar contexts are a valid indication of the cognitive competencies that prevail in their everyday activities.

Systematic observation involves observing and recording behavior as it happens. Observations of the behavior of children, and of the adults who figure importantly into their development, can be made in different ways. One approach is to go into the field or natural environment and collect observations of the behavior of interest, a method called **naturalistic observation.** Recall from Chapter 1 that this method is especially useful for testing hypotheses generated by the theoretical perspectives of ecological psychology and ethology, but social cognitive theorists, investigators interested in emotional development, and individuals of a variety of other theoretical persuasions use it as well.

A study by Barrett and Yarrow (1977) provides a good example of the application of naturalistic observation to the study of children's social development. Observing 5- to 8-year-old children at a summer camp, the researchers recorded the number of times each child provided another person with physical or emotional support, in the form of comforting, sharing, helping, or expressing sympathy. In addition, they noted the occurrence of cues from other people nearby, such as a tearful playmate, that indicated a need for comfort or assistance. The great strength of naturalistic observation in studies like this one is that investigators can see directly the everyday behaviors they hope to explain (Miller, 1987).

However, Barrett and Yarrow's research also highlights an important weakness of naturalistic observation: not all children have the same opportunity to display a particular behavior in everyday life. In their investigation, some children happened to be exposed to more cues for positive social behaviors than others, and for this reason they showed higher rates of helpful and comforting actions. Barrett and Yarrow adjusted for this problem in the way they scored each child's responses. But the usual way researchers deal with this difficulty is by making **structured observations** in a laboratory. In this approach, the investigator sets up a cue for the behavior of interest, and because every subject is exposed to it in the same way, each has equal opportunity to manifest the response. In one recent study, researchers made structured observations of children's helping behaviors by having an adult "accidentally" spill a box of stars in a laboratory and recording how each participating child reacted (Stanhope, Bell, & Parker-Cohen, 1987). Structured observations permit investigators to exert more control over the research situation. In addition, the method is particularly useful for evoking behaviors that researchers rarely have an opportunity to see in everyday life. For example, in one study, the investigators wanted to know how preschoolers react emotionally to arguing and bickering among family members. Having little or no chance to watch families argue in real-life settings, they set up a laboratory to resemble a homelike atmosphere, brought in pairs of preschoolers to play with one another, and had two adults speak angrily in the background (Cummings, Iannotti, & Zahn-Waxler, 1985). Of course, the great disadvantage of structured observations, as you already know from the study described in Box 2.1, is that children do not always behave in the laboratory as they do in everyday life.

The particular procedures that investigators use to collect systematic observations may vary considerably from one study to another, depending on the nature of the research problem posed. Some investigators may choose to use a **specimen record,** a description of the subject's entire stream of behavior, in which everything that is said and done for a specified time period is recorded (Wright, 1967). In one recent study, a researcher wanted to find out how sensitive, responsive, and verbally stimulating caregivers were when they interacted with preschool children in day care centers (Berk, 1985a). In this case, everything each caregiver said and did, and even the amount of time she spent away from the children taking coffee breaks and talking on the phone, was important. In other studies, information on only one or a few kinds of behavior is needed, and it is not necessary to preserve the entire behavior stream. In these instances, researchers may choose more efficient observation procedures. One approach is to do an **event sampling,** in which the observer records all instances of a particular behavior of interest during a specified time period and leaves the rest out of the record. For example, in an observational study of children's antisocial behavior, every episode of physical aggression during a one-hour observation period of each child could be noted. Another approach is **time sampling.** In this procedure, the investigator records whether or not certain behaviors occur during a sample of short time intervals. First, a checklist of the behaviors of interest is prepared. Then the observer divides up the entire observation period into a series of brief time segments. For example, a half-hour observation period might be divided into 120 fifteen-second intervals. The observer collects data by alternately watching the child for an interval and then checking off behaviors during the next interval, repeating this process until the entire observation period is complete. Whether an investigator chooses event sampling or time sampling as the basis for collecting observations depends on the goals of the research as well as on how convenient the procedure is to use in a particular setting (Miller, 1987).

A major problem in collecting systematic observations is the influence of the observer on the behavior to be observed. The presence of a watchful unfamiliar individual may cause children and adults who are targets of the observation to change their behavior in unnatural ways. For children below the age of 7 or 8, observer influence is generally limited to the first session or two in which the strange adult is present in the setting. Young children cannot "stop being themselves" for very long, and they quickly get used to an observer's presence. Older children and adults are more likely to be affected, and their manner of responding is usually biased in a positive, socially desirable direction, which the investigator can take as an indication of the best behavior that they typically display under the circumstances. However, not all older subjects will conceal socially undesirable behavior while being observed.

By making structured observations in a laboratory, researchers can ensure that all subjects have the same opportunity to display the behavior of interest in a research study. However, subjects may not respond in the laboratory as they do in everyday life. (Mimi Forsyth/Monkmeyer Press Photo Service)

In a number of studies, parents who had developed severely maladaptive patterns of family interaction continued to engage in harsh methods of disciplining their children, including physical punishment, even when they were well aware that an observer was watching and recording their behavior (Reid, Taplin, & Lorber, 1981).

There are a number of ways that researchers can minimize the behavioral distortion introduced by placing an observer in the same environment as research subjects. Adaptation periods are helpful. In these, observers make frequent visits to the research setting so that subjects have a chance to get used to their presence. Another approach is to have individuals who are typically a part of the child's natural environment do the observing. In several recent studies, parents have been trained to record children's behavior, a procedure that has the advantage of reducing observer influence and permitting information to be gathered on behaviors that occur so infrequently that researchers would have to remain in the natural setting for a very long time to obtain enough data themselves. In one such study, mothers kept diary records of each episode in which their infants showed evidence of recall memory (Ashmead & Perlmutter, 1980). The information obtained provided important new insights into the emergence of memory capacities during the first year of life.

Several decades ago, most naturalistic observations were recorded by jotting down notes on a pad of paper. This was a cumbersome technique, and information was missed in instances in which investigators tried to capture a complete account of each subject's behavior. Today, sophisticated equipment and recording devices are available to increase the efficiency and accuracy of observational research. Tape recorders with mouthpieces that muffle the sound of an observer's voice enable investigators to dictate on-the-spot descriptions of subjects' activities. Cordless microphones attached to children's collars permit researchers to pick up verbal data that are not easily heard by even the most astute observer, such as soft-spoken conversations with peers and adults (Tizard et al., 1980). Videotaping is often used to capture a complete record of subjects' behavior in the laboratory, and it can sometimes be used effectively in natural settings if the equipment is placed in an inconspicuous location so that subjects are neither distracted nor made to feel self-conscious by its presence.

Systematic observation provides invaluable information on how children and adults actually behave, but the records that result generally tell us little about the thinking and reasoning that lie behind their behavior. For this kind of information, researchers must turn to another type of method — self-report techniques.

Self-reports: Interviews and Questionnaires

Self-reports are instruments that ask subjects to answer questions of various kinds so that information can be obtained on their perceptions, thoughts, feelings, attitudes, beliefs, abilities, and past behaviors. They include relatively unstructured clinical interviews, the method used by Piaget to assess the quality of children's thinking, as well as highly structured interviews, questionnaires, and tests.

Turn back to page 28 in Chapter 1 to study the sample **clinical interview** in which Piaget questioned a young child about his understanding of dreams. Notice how the child is encouraged to follow his own train of thought, and the investigator prompts only enough to get a full picture of the child's thinking on the topic. Piaget's use of the clinical interview to study children's cognition is the method's most well-known application, but it has been applied to the study of other areas of child development as well. For example, Sears, Maccoby, and Levin (1957) conducted one of the most comprehensive studies of child-rearing practices and young children's behavior that has been completed to date. Mothers were questioned about a wide range of topics, including their handling of weaning, feeding problems, aggression, dependency, exploration, and more. Although a basic set of questions was given to each mother, an open-ended format was used, and participants were free to respond at any length and in any way they wished. In addition, follow-up probes were used in which what was asked and how the question was worded varied from mother to mother, depending on her initial response. Taken together, Piaget's and Sears, Maccoby, and Levin's research highlight two major strengths of the clinical interviewing procedure. The first is that it permits subjects to display their thoughts in terms that come as close as possible to the way they think about events in everyday life. The second is the breadth and scope of information yielded by the clinical interview in a relatively brief period of time. For example, in a session that lasted about 2 hours, Sears, Maccoby, and Levin obtained a wide range of child-rearing information from each mother, much more than could be captured in the same amount of time by making observations of parent-child interaction.

A major weakness of the clinical interview has to do with the accuracy with which subjects report their own thoughts, feelings, and behaviors. Some interviewers tend to probe too little, so that a full understanding of the subject's point of view is not revealed, and biased responses can result. At the opposite extreme, some interviewers press, prompt, and suggest too much. Under these conditions many young children, desiring to please the adult, may make up answers that really do not represent their way of thinking. Furthermore, the clinical interview depends on children's verbal ability and expressiveness, and there is a danger that the capacities of subjects who have difficulty putting their thoughts into words will not be adequately reflected by the method. However, a skillful interviewer knows how to minimize these problems by wording questions carefully, and by being sensitive to cues that indicate that a child may not have clearly understood a question or may need extra time to feel comfortable in the situation.

Interviews in which adults are asked about their child-rearing practices and the behaviors of their youngsters are known to be subject to distortion, particularly under certain conditions. When parents are asked to recall events that happened during an earlier period in the child's life, they often give responses that depict their child in glowing terms. In cases where it has been possible to compare recall of early events with information obtained at the same time the events actually occurred, mothers have been found to report faster development, fewer childhood problems, and child-rearing practices more in line with contemporary expert advice than that found in the records of actual behaviors (Robbins, 1963; Yarrow, Campbell, & Burton, 1970). In addition, most parents find it difficult to recall specific instances of early events, although they can report general tendencies more readily — the child as "fussy" versus "easy to manage," or their disciplinary approach as "permissive" versus "strict." But strictness to one parent may register as permissiveness to another, and parents may have very different subjective definitions of these general terms, causing their retrospective accounts to be inconsistent and virtually useless as predictors of children's later behaviors (Maccoby & Martin, 1983). It is now recommended that parent interviews focus on obtaining concurrent, not retrospective, information, and that parents be asked for specific practices and behaviors, not just global judgments and interpretations.

We already mentioned in Chapter 1 that the clinical interview has been subject to criticism because of its nonstandardized administration procedures. When questions are phrased differently for each subject, variations in responses may be due to the manner of interviewing rather than to real differences in the way subjects think about a certain topic. **Structured interviews** and **questionnaires,** in which each participant is asked an identical set of questions, can eliminate this difficulty. In addition, their administration and scoring procedures are much more efficient. For example, when using a questionnaire, a researcher can obtain written responses from an entire class of children or group of parents simultaneously. Furthermore, when these instruments make use of multiple choice, yes-no, or true-false formats, as is done in many tests, the responses can be tabulated quickly by machine. However, while these approaches gain in impartiality and efficiency, they do not yield the same depth of information about the subject's perspective as does a clinical interview. In addition, they are not immune to inaccurate reporting, although investigators can minimize this effect by telling subjects that their answers will be recorded anonymously and by phrasing questions in nonevaluative ways. In addition, when asking for opinions and beliefs, researchers can remind subjects that there are no right or wrong answers.

The Clinical Method

In Chapter 1, we discussed the **clinical method** (sometimes called the case study approach) as an outgrowth of psychoanalytic theory, which stresses the importance of understanding the unique individual child. Recall that the clinical method synthesizes a wide range of data about one subject, including interview material, test scores, and observations. The aim is to obtain as complete a picture of that child's psychological functioning and the experiences that led up to it as possible. Clinical studies are generally carried out on children who have emotional problems, but the approach is used with normal, well-adjusted youngsters as well (e.g., Coles, 1977). The method yields case narratives that are rich in descriptive detail and that frequently offer important insights into the processes of development. We shall discuss the findings of a number of well-known clinical studies in subsequent chapters of this book. One example is the case of Genie, a child isolated in the back room of a house from the time she was 20 months old until she was an adolescent of 13 (Curtiss, 1977). Her story sheds important light on whether there is a critical period for early language learning.

The clinical method, like all others, has its drawbacks. Collection and recording of information are often unsystematic and subjective, and investigators cannot assume that conclusions generalize to anyone other than the particular child studied. Therefore, the insights drawn from clinical investigations need to be tested further, using other research strategies.

Table 2.1 provides a summary of the strengths and weaknesses of each of the research methods discussed above. Now we turn to a consideration of research designs — general investigative plans that permit researchers to use the data obtained from the various methods to test hypotheses and answer research questions.

RESEARCH DESIGNS

In deciding on a research design, investigators choose a way of setting up a study that enables them to identify relationships among events and behaviors and the causes of those relationships with the greatest certainty possible. There are two main types of research designs: correlational and experimental.

Correlational Design

In a **correlational design,** the investigator gathers information on already existing groups of individuals, generally in natural life circumstances, and no effort is made to manipulate or intervene in the subjects' experiences in any way. Once the data are obtained, relationships among various pieces of information can be examined, but the correlational design does not permit exact determination of the causes of those relationships. Suppose we want answers to such questions as: Does structure and organization in the home make a difference in children's school performance? Does attending a day care center promote children's friendliness with peers? Do mothers' styles of interacting and disciplining children have any bearing on children's intelligence? In these and many other instances, although we can observe and measure the events of interest, it is very difficult, if not impossible, to deliberately arrange, manipulate, and control them. Consequently, if we find in a correlational study that maternal interaction style does relate to children's intelligence, we would not know for sure if maternal behavior was actually responsible for the intellectual differences among the children. In fact, the reverse direction of causality is certainly possible. The behaviors of highly intelligent children may be so attractive and inviting that they cause mothers to interact more favorably. Or a third variable that we did not even think about studying, such as amount of noise and distraction in the home, may be causing both the quality of maternal interaction and children's intelligence to change simultaneously in a particular direction.

Researchers often examine relationships among variables in correlational investigations, and in other types of research designs as well, by using a **correlation coefficient** (other statistical approaches to examining relationships are also available). We shall encounter the correlation coefficient many times in discussing the findings of research throughout this book, so let's look at what it is and how it is interpreted. A correlation coefficient provides a numerical estimate of how two measures, or variables, are associated with one another. It can range in value from $+1.00$ to -1.00. The magnitude of the number gives an indication of the strength of the relationship. A zero correlation indicates no systematic association, but the closer the value is to $+1.00$ or -1.00, the stronger the relationship that exists. The sign of the number ($+$ or $-$) refers to the direction of the relationship. If the sign is positive ($+$), this means that as one measure of performance *increases,* the other also *increases.* If the sign is negative ($-$), then this indicates that as one measure *increases* the other *decreases.*

Let's take several examples to illustrate how a correlation coefficient works. In one study, a researcher found that a measure of maternal attentiveness at 11 months of age was positively correlated with infant mental test scores during the second year of life at $+.60$. This is a moderately high correlation, which indicates that the more

Table 2.1. Strengths and Weaknesses of Common Research Methods

METHOD	DESCRIPTION	STRENGTHS	WEAKNESSES
Naturalistic observation	Observations of behavior taken in natural environments	Observations are applicable to children's everyday lives and experiences	Conditions under which children are observed cannot be controlled and may not be the same for all children
Structured observation	Behavior of interest recorded in a laboratory situation designed to evoke it	Offers a standardized observation situation for all children	Observations may not be typical of the way children behave in everyday life
Clinical interview	Flexible, open-ended interviewing procedure in which the investigator obtains a complete account of the subject's train of thought	Provides a full picture of each subject's perceptions, thoughts, and feelings about an experience or event. Great breadth and depth of information can be obtained in a limited time period	Subjects may report information in a selective, distorted fashion. Nonstandardized administration procedures make comparisons of subjects' responses difficult
Structured interview and questionnaire	Self-report instruments in which each subject is asked the same questions in the same way	Standardized method of asking questions permits comparisons of subjects' responses and efficient administration and scoring	Does not yield the same depth of information as a clinical interview. Responses still subject to inaccurate reporting
Clinical method (Case study)	Synthesis of interview, test, and observational data to yield a full picture of an individual child's development and psychological functioning	Provides rich, descriptive insights into processes of development	Collection of information often unsystematic and subjective. Conclusions cannot be applied to individuals other than the subject child

Does a rich, supportive home environment bear any relationship to a child's performance in school? A correlational design can be used to answer this question, but it does not enable researchers to determine the precise cause of their findings. (Richard Hutchings)

attentive the mothers were to their babies in infancy, the better their youngsters did on an intelligence test as toddlers several months later (Clarke-Stewart, 1973). In another similar study, a researcher reported that uninvolved behavior on the part of mothers—the extent to which they ignored their 10-month-old-infants' bids for attention—was negatively correlated with children's willingness to comply with parental demands one year later, at $-.46$ for boys and $-.36$ for girls (Martin, 1981). These moderate correlations reveal that the more the mothers ignored their babies, the less cooperative their children were during the second year of life. Although in both of these investigations the researchers suspected that maternal behavior played a causal role in affecting children's mental test performance and compliance, in neither could they really be sure about what caused the variables of interest to be associated with one another.

Let's take just one more example to illustrate the usefulness of correlational research. This time, the researchers asked preschoolers and their parents to indicate how much time the children spent watching television and the kinds of programs they viewed. The findings revealed a correlation of $+.33$ between time spent watching action-oriented television shows with high violent content and children's display of aggression during play periods at nursery school (Singer & Singer, 1981). Once again, we cannot conclude from the evidence that watching violent TV caused these children to behave aggressively, for it can just as easily be argued that children who are inherently aggressive prefer to watch violent TV. But television viewing is a factor that investigators *can* manipulate and control to some degree, and the identification of a relationship between violent TV and aggressive behavior in a correlational study suggests that it would be worthwhile to try to track down its cause with a more sensitive research strategy. We shall see in the section that follows that a number of investigators have pursued the causal basis of the television-aggression connection using more powerful experimental procedures.

Experimental Designs

In contrast to correlational studies, **experimental designs** permit precise determination of cause and effect relationships. In an experiment, the events and behaviors of interest are divided into two types: independent and dependent variables. The **inde-**

pendent variable is the one anticipated by the investigator, on the basis of an hypothesis or research question, to cause changes in another variable. The **dependent variable** is the one that the investigator expects will be influenced by the independent variable. In an experimental design, inferences about cause and effect relationships are possible because the investigator directly controls or manipulates changes in the independent variable. This is done by assigning subjects to two or more treatment conditions and then comparing the performance of the different treatment groups on measures of the dependent variable. For example, if an investigator wants to know whether watching violent television programs (independent variable) causes aggressive behavior (dependent variable), an experiment could be designed in which some children are deliberately exposed to violent films and others to alternative treatments, followed by a comparison of the groups based on a measure of their aggressiveness.

A classic laboratory experiment aimed at answering this very question was carried out by Bandura and his associates in the early 1960s (Bandura, Ross, & Ross, 1963). Nearly a hundred preschoolers were assigned to one of three treatment conditions — an adult model portraying aggression on film, an aggressive cartoon character, and a real-life aggressive adult model — and a control group experiencing no treatment. In the three treatment conditions, children watched adult and cartoon models repeatedly punch a Bobo doll on the nose, hit it with a mallet, toss it into the air, and kick it harshly. Afterward, children from all four conditions were brought individually into a playroom and given an opportunity to use a variety of toys. Some were designed to stimulate aggressive behavior, while others were chosen for their nonaggressive play possibilities. Bandura found that children in all three experimental treatments engaged in far more aggressive play with the toys than control children, and many of their behaviors were exact replicas of the model's aggressive responses. Furthermore, film-mediated models were just as effective as live adult models in promoting a variety of aggressive behaviors.

In experimental studies, investigators must take special precautions to control for

In a classic experiment by Bandura, some preschoolers watched an aggressive model punch, kick, and hit a Bobo doll, while others received no treatment. Then each child was given an opportunity to play with toys. Those who observed an aggressive model displayed far more aggressive behavior in the playroom than did children in the no treatment condition. (Albert Bandura)

unknown characteristics of subjects that could reduce the validity of their research findings. In Bandura's study, if a greater number of children who had learned prior to the experiment to behave in hostile and antagonistic ways happened to end up in one of the treatment groups, we could not tell if the independent variable or children's background characteristics were responsible for the obtained differences in aggressive behavior. **Random assignment** of subjects to different conditions offers protection against this problem. By using an evenhanded procedure, such as drawing numbers out of a hat or flipping a coin, the experimenter increases the chances that children's characteristics will be equally distributed across experimental groups. Bandura took even more stringent precautions to make sure that his results would not be contaminated by children's background characteristics. Before the study, nursery school teachers were asked to rate each child on aggressive attributes. Then a **matching** procedure was used in which equal numbers of children having high and low aggressive tendencies were randomly assigned to each of the four conditions. Matching assures equal distribution of certain subject characteristics across experimental groups. They are matched, or deliberately made equivalent, on subject qualities that have an especially strong chance of distorting the results.

Like Bandura's study, most experiments are conducted in laboratories, because laboratory conditions enable researchers to achieve the maximum possible control over the treatments to which subjects are exposed. Consequently, the strength of laboratory experiments resides in their high internal validity, but this is often obtained at some sacrifice to external validity. The ideal solution to this problem is to do ecological experiments, or experiments in the field, as a complement to laboratory investigations. In **field experiments,** investigators capitalize on rare opportunities to assign subjects to different treatments in natural settings. In the case of Bandura's laboratory experiment, we are able to conclude that filmed aggression *can* cause children to behave more aggressively, but *does* it do so when children are exposed to violent television fare in everyday life?

A field experiment conducted by Friedrich and Stein (1973) helps answer this question. They began their research by hypothesizing that if television programs can cause children to imitate antisocial and aggressive responses, then the opposite may also be true. Perhaps programs with the right kind of content can teach socially desirable behaviors, such as cooperation, sharing, sympathy, and self-control. Consequently, they designed a study to investigate both the positive and negative outcomes of children's television programming. Over 90 children enrolled in a summer nursery school session were randomly assigned to watch one of three types of TV shows each day for a period of 4 weeks: aggressive cartoons ("Batman" and "Superman"), a prosocial program ("Mister Rogers' Neighborhood"), and neutral films that had neither aggressive nor prosocial content (e.g., farm and animal scenes). The investigators had groups of children come to a small room near their nursery school classroom to watch the films for a half hour period each day. Before, during, and after the children experienced the treatments, their aggressive and prosocial free play behaviors in the nursery school were observed and recorded. To study the effects of the different viewing conditions, children's behavior before watching the programs was compared to their behavior during and after television viewing.

Friedrich and Stein found that television treatments had a dramatic influence on children's behavior. Children who watched aggressive films showed a decline in tolerance of delay (being able to wait for materials or adult attention) and rule obedience in the classroom. Interpersonal aggression, such as hitting, teasing, name-calling, tattling, and yelling at others, increased as well, but only for those who were above average in aggressive behavior to begin with. In contrast, children exposed to prosocial programming displayed higher levels of task persistence, rule obedience, and tolerance of delay. Positive interpersonal behavior (cooperating with, helping, comforting, and verbalizing feelings to others) also increased, but only for children in the sample who came from low-income families.

Friedrich and Stein's field experiment extends Bandura's earlier work by showing that imitation of film-mediated aggression does occur in everyday life, although it suggests that this effect may be limited to children who are high in aggression to begin with. The study also reveals that television has as much potential for helping children learn positive social behavior as it has for teaching aggression and violence.

We have already indicated that in the case of many hypotheses and research questions, investigators cannot randomly assign subjects and manipulate conditions, as Bandura and Friedrich and Stein were able to do. However, in many instances they can select naturally occurring treatments, such as different school environments, day care centers, and preschool programs, in which children's backgrounds and prior experiences are as similar as possible. Studies of existing variations in children's experiences are sometimes referred to as **natural experiments,** because investigators try to find situations that at least approximate the controlled conditions of a true experiment. In this way, they rule out as best as they can alternative explanations for their treatment effects. Despite such efforts, researchers conducting natural experiments are unable to achieve the precision and rigor of true experimental research (Achenbach, 1978; Campbell & Stanley, 1966). An example of this kind of study is described in Box 2.2 on page 56.

Designs for Studying Development

Developmental psychologists are unique among researchers in requiring information about the way their subjects change over time. Longitudinal and cross-sectional designs are *developmental* research strategies. In each, age comparisons form the basis of the research plan.

The Longitudinal Design. In a **longitudinal design,** one sample of children is observed repeatedly at different ages, and changes are noted as they mature. The time period spanned may be relatively short — a few months to several years — or it may be very long — a decade or even a lifetime. In the 1920s and 1930s, several longitudinal studies were initiated in which samples of infants were followed through childhood, adolescence, and well into the adult years. Important examples are the Fels Institute Study, begun in 1929 in Yellow Springs, Ohio, and two investigations carried out at the University of California at Berkeley, the Berkeley Growth Study and the Guidance Study, both initiated in 1928 (Kagan, 1964). The investigators of each major study hoped that collection of a massive data base on a group of individuals over a long period of time would provide important insights into the course and continuity of development. Therefore, they obtained repeated measurements on a wide range of experiences, characteristics, and behaviors, including physical growth, intelligence, personality, child-rearing practices, and more. We shall use findings from these classic studies to illustrate the unique kinds of information about development that can only be obtained from a longitudinal design.

Advantages of the Longitudinal Design. A major strength of the longitudinal design is that it permits researchers to examine developmental changes in various attributes for each individual in the sample. By tracking the performance of each subject over time, investigators can identify common patterns of development as well as individual differences in the paths children follow to maturity (Wohlwill, 1973).

Data gathered from the Fels and Berkeley studies on changes in children's mental test performance illustrate the value of this kind of information. During the early part of this century, it was commonly assumed that intelligence was a largely inherited capacity that remained fairly constant over time. The Berkeley and Fels studies offered the first challenge to this idea, for many children followed over childhood and adolescence showed marked changes in their intelligence test scores. Of the 222

Box 2.2
Sex-Typed Social Behaviors in Traditional and Open Schools: A Natural Experiment

Theory. An extensive body of research on children's peer preferences indicates that by the preschool years, children prefer playmates of the same sex. But what happens when school environments are designed to deliberately minimize sex-typed play and peer associations? Barbara Bianchi and Roger Bakeman (1978) conducted a natural experiment to answer this question. They hypothesized that if social learning theory is correct in asserting that modeling contributes to sex-typed play preferences, then school environments that hold less extreme views of acceptable sex-role conduct should be able to modify them.

Research. Bianchi and Bakeman observed over 50 children between 4 and 6 years of age, half enrolled in a traditional kindergarten and half in an open classroom school. The philosophies and consequent learning activities of the two school environments were markedly different. The traditional school stressed children's acquisition of conventional values and standards of conduct, including established sex roles and sex-typed activities. In contrast, the goal of the open school was to respond to children on the basis of their unique characteristics, and sex-typed expectations about children's interests, abilities, and personalities were consciously avoided. In the open school, both male and female teachers translated this philosophy into classroom practice by modeling a wide range of activities and roles for children.

Observations of children in both schools were made during free play by using a time-sampling technique. Over a 6-day period, observers repeatedly worked through a list of the children in each classroom, recording how often each child played with other children as well as the number of times their playmates were all of the same sex.

In line with expectations, the findings showed that traditional school pupils largely played in a sex-segregated fashion, while open school boys and girls could frequently be seen playing together (see Figure 2.1). In fact, the majority of open school pupils spent more than half their time in mixed-sex play activities, and both boys and girls were equally affected.

Bianchi and Bakeman's results suggest that school environments can modify children's sex-typed social behaviors. However, because the study was limited to comparisons of intact, already existing groups of children, the authors were careful to point out that factors other than schooling may have been responsible for the findings. Parents of the open school children had made a conscious decision to send their children to the open school, so it is possible that parental and school attitudes were highly similar in this investigation. The natural experiment does not permit us to rule out the likelihood that the observed school differences were merely a reflection of modeling and reinforcement patterns implemented by parents at home.

Applications. Despite ambiguity regarding the causes of school differences in social behavior, Bianchi and Bakeman's study does indicate that young children's same-sex peer associations can be modified by the environments to which children are exposed. The results suggest that teachers think carefully about the social experiences encouraged by their classroom environments. Providing children with a broader range of social opportunities, like those observed by Bianchi and Bakeman in the open school, may have an important impact on the development of less sex-stereotyped attitudes and behavior.

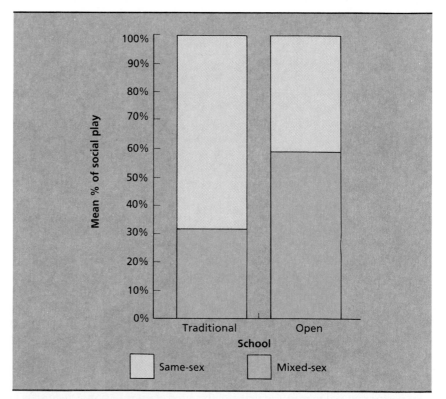

Figure 2.1. Same-sex and mixed-sex social play in a traditional and open school in the Bianchi and Bakeman (1978) study. Pupils attending an open school played far more often than traditional school pupils with children of the opposite sex. *(Adapted from Bianchi & Bakeman, 1978.)*

children tested repeatedly as part of the Berkeley Guidance Study, 85 percent showed changes of 10 or more IQ points, and a third showed changes of more than 20 IQ points, between 6 and 18 years of age (Honzik, Macfarlane, & Allen, 1948). In the Fels Study, the changes were even more dramatic. Among 80 children studied, the average shift between 2½ and 17 years of age was 28.5 points (McCall, Appelbaum, & Hogarty, 1973; Sontag, Baker, & Nelson, 1958). Furthermore, those children who changed radically in test performance usually showed patterns of change that were orderly and predictable, not random, haphazard fluctuations. As illustrated in Fig 2.2, some had steadily increasing scores, while others had steadily decreasing performances over childhood and adolescence.

The existence of these stable patterns of change raises provocative questions about the factors responsible for them. A second strength of the longitudinal design is that investigators can compare age changes in different aspects of behavior to see if the timing of change in one is similar to the timing of change in another (Wohlwill, 1973). When correspondences are identified, they often lead to valuable insights into why certain changes occur. For example, the Berkeley investigators carefully examined the information they had collected on children's emotional and physical health and compared it to changes in children's IQ scores. The results revealed that emotional factors and illness closely paralleled major shifts in intellectual performance. For example, Case 567, whose increase in IQ is shown in Figure 2.2, experienced improved health and emotional well-being at the same time as she showed an upward shift in the test scores. The researchers wrote:

> The early preschool history of this girl (the period of her lowest scores) was characterized by the critical illnesses of her mother and brother and the emotional and financial strain that these entailed. Further, the girl . . . was very shy and reserved. At 6½ years she had pneumonia. From ten on, she had many supports in her life—music, athletic success, summer camps, the honor roll at school. Eighteen years marks her first year in college and away from home and her first really completely satisfying social life. (Honzik, Macfarlane, & Allen, 1948, p. 314)

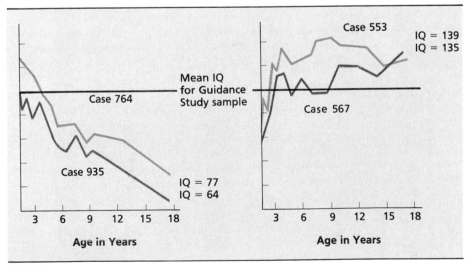

Figure 2.2. Individual patterns of change in intelligence test scores for four children in the Berkeley Guidance Study sample. Cases 935 and 764 showed age-related declines in performance, while Cases 567 and 553 showed gradual gains. The overall magnitude of change for each of these subjects was between 70 and 79 IQ points. *(From M. P. Honzik, J. W. Macfarlane, & L. Allen, 1948, "The Stability of Mental Test Performance Between Two and Eighteen Years," Journal of Experimental Education, 17, 319. Adapted by permission.)*

In contrast, the IQ of Case 935 dropped steadily over time. Although she experienced an early satisfying home life, serious emotional and economic stress characterized her family in middle childhood, and she experienced repeated school failure during her elementary school years. The Berkeley investigators reported that emotional adjustment, physical health, and changes in intelligence test scores varied in tandem for a substantial number of children in their sample. Although we cannot conclude for sure that variations in emotional and physical health cause changes in children's IQ scores, the existence of these associations presents a serious challenge to the traditional assumption that IQ scores are largely a reflection of hereditary endowment and are only minimally influenced by environmental factors.

A final advantage of the longitudinal design is that it permits investigators to examine relationships between early and later events and behaviors (Wohlwill, 1973). For example, to increase our understanding of factors that contribute to development, researchers can look at the extent to which early experiences with parents, siblings, peers, and teachers are related to children's emerging characteristics. They can also see if children with particular personality attributes in childhood retain those characteristics in adult life. In fact, the Fels Study investigators tried to answer this very question. Using extensive observational and interview data gathered during middle childhood, they rated each of their subjects on a variety of personality characteristics. Later, when the subjects were in their twenties, they returned to the Fels Institute, and their interview responses as young adults were rated on these same characteristics. The two sets of ratings were then correlated with one another. The results showed that many of the attributes exhibited by children between 6 and 10 years of age were fairly good predictors of what they were like as young adults. However, as Figure 2.3 shows, when separate correlations were obtained for males and females, several relationships varied with the child's sex. Girls showed greater stability for passive and dependent behavior, while boys showed greater stability for

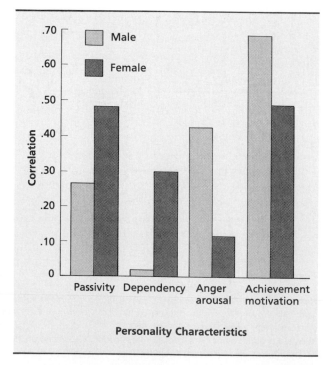

Figure 2.3. Correlations between child (6–10 years of age) and adult personality characteristics among the Fels longitudinal sample. Passivity and dependency proved to be more stable for girls, while anger arousal and achievement motivation were more stable for boys. *(From J. Kagan & H. A. Moss, 1962,* Birth to Maturity, *New York: John Wiley & Sons, p. 267. Adapted by permission.)*

anger arousal (a measure of aggression) and achievement motivation. The investigators concluded that sex-role expectations probably play a central role in the maintenance of these personality dispositions (Kagan & Moss, 1962). Because passivity and dependency are regarded as typically "feminine" characteristics, parents may encourage them among girls and not among boys, whereas the reverse is probably true for aggression and, to a lesser extent, for achievement. Later on, in Chapter 13, when we discuss what is currently known about sex-role development, we shall see that a great deal of new research supports the validity of this interpretation.

Problems in Conducting Longitudinal Research. Despite their many strengths, longitudinal investigations confront investigators with a wide variety of obstacles and problems. There are practical difficulties, such as obtaining adequate financial support and waiting the many years that it takes for meaningful results to accrue in a long-term study. But beyond these drawbacks, many threats to internal and external validity plague longitudinal investigations, which can create serious difficulties for the meaningfulness of the findings.

Biased sampling is a prevalent problem in longitudinal research. People who willingly participate in a study that requires them to be continually observed and tested over many years are likely to have unique characteristics, and we cannot easily generalize from them to the rest of the population. In the Fels and Berkeley Growth studies, the families who volunteered to participate were better educated and socioeconomically more advantaged than average, and they probably had a unique appreciation for the scientific value of the study. Furthermore, longitudinal samples generally become more biased as the research proceeds because of **subject attrition.** Some people may move or drop out of the study for other reasons, and the ones who remain are likely to be different from the ones who do not continue. To minimize this problem, participants are sometimes chosen on the basis of their long-term availability as residents in a particular community. But in view of the mobility of so many American families, this criterion for subject selection only reduces the generalizability of longitudinal findings still further.

The very experience of being repeatedly interviewed, observed, and tested can also threaten the validity of a longitudinal study. If the measures concern attitudes, feelings, or moral judgments, **subject reactivity** may pose problems. Participants may gradually be alerted to their own thoughts and feelings, think about them, and revise them in a way that has little to do with age-related change (Nunnally, 1982). In addition, with repeated testing, subjects may become "test-wise," and their performance may improve as the result of better test-taking skills and increased familiarity with the test. Investigators can check for such **practice effects** by introducing new children into the testing program and comparing their scores with those of longitudinal subjects of the same age who have experienced repeated testing. If longitudinal subjects obtain higher scores, then practice effects may be operating. In addition, longitudinal researchers can carefully examine the developmental trends of children in their sample to see if they are consistent with the influence of practice effects. When children who are studied longitudinally show a wide variety of developmental profiles, including the steady increases and declines over many years that we described for the Fels and Berkeley children, then we know that the findings cannot simply be due to repeated assessments.

The most widely discussed threat to the validity of longitudinal investigations is **cultural-historical change,** or what are commonly called **cohort effects.** Longitudinal studies examine the growth and development of cohorts, or children born in the same historical era who are influenced by a particular set of cultural conditions. Findings based on one cohort may not be universal and generalizable to children growing up at other points in time. For example, children's intelligence test performance may be affected by differences in the quality of public schooling from one decade to another or by generational changes in parental values regarding the importance of stimulating children's intellectual abilities. A longitudinal study of social development would probably result in different findings if children were observed during the Vietnam War of the 1960s and 1970s, around the time of World War II, or during the Great Depression of the 1930s (see Box 2.3).

Finally, changes occurring within the field of child development may create problems for longitudinal studies that last many years. Theories and dominant methods for studying children are constantly changing, and those that originally inspired a longitudinal study may become dated and obsolete (Nunnally, 1982). For this reason, as well as others mentioned above, many recent longitudinal studies are short-term, spanning only a few months or years in a child's life, and investigators are spared some of the formidable obstacles that threaten longitudinal findings that cover an extended period from childhood to maturity.

The Cross-Sectional Design. The sheer length of time that it takes for many behaviors to change, even in limited longitudinal studies, has led researchers to turn toward another strategy for studying development. In the **cross-sectional design,** groups of children of different ages are studied at the same point in time. For example, we could choose a group of 5-year-olds, a group of 10-year-olds, and a group of 15-year-olds and compare their responses. In cross-sectional studies, researchers do not have to worry about many of the difficulties that plague the longitudinal design. When participants have to be measured only once, it is much easier to obtain representative samples, and investigators do not need to be concerned about subjects dropping out of the study, practice effects, or theoretical transformations in the field of child development that might make the research obsolete by the time it is complete. However, when researchers choose the more convenient cross-sectional shortcut, they are short-changed in the kind of information they can obtain about development.

FOCUS ON THEORY, RESEARCH, AND APPLICATIONS

Box 2.3
Cultural-Historical Influences on Children's Development: Children of the Great Depression

Theory. Economic disaster, wars, and periods of social ferment can produce major reorientations in people's lives. It follows that sweeping social and historical change may uniquely shape the course of children's development. Glen Elder (1974) took advantage of variations in the extent to which families experienced economic deprivation during the Great Depression of the 1930s to study its consequences for children's development.

Research. To examine the impact of the Great Depression, Elder capitalized on the extensive research archives of the Oakland Growth Study, a longitudinal investigation begun in the early 1930s and originally intended to chart the growth and development of 167 children as they made the transition between late childhood and adolescence. The research was eventually extended over several decades, to cover long-term development well into the adult years. Elder subdivided the longitudinal sample into those whose childhoods were marked by severe economic deprivation and hardship during the depression years and those whose youth was relatively free of economic strain. Then he compared the two groups on a wide range of information, including ratings of family relations, social behaviors, and personal attributes.

The findings showed that unusual responsibilities were placed on children from deprived families as their parents' roles and responsibilities changed. Mothers entered the labor force, fathers sought work outside the immediate community, and the emotional stress of economic hardship led to a rising rate of parental separation, divorce, and illness. In response, children experienced an accelerated entry into the adult world as they were challenged to take on many of the burdens of family maintenance. The nature of these new responsibilities depended on the child's sex, with girls assuming more domestic responsibilities and boys seeking part-time jobs outside the home during the teenage years. These changes in children's lives had major consequences for their future aspirations. Girls' early immersion in domestic responsibilities led their interests to be largely centered around home and family and decreased their aspirations to enter careers. The experience of economic insecurity during childhood exposed many boys to the realities of self-support, convinced them that economic resources could not be taken for granted, and fostered an early commitment to occupational roles and career choices.

Relationships also changed in economically deprived families. Unemployment led fathers to lose status in the family, and mothers became increasingly prominent in family affairs. This reversal of traditional sex

Evidence about change at the level at which it actually occurs—the individual—is not available. Instead, the study of development is limited to comparisons of the average performance of different age groups of children.

Furthermore, to conclude from a cross-sectional study that a true age-related change has occurred, researchers must make a special, sometimes unwarranted assumption: that the behavior of the younger subjects reflects how the older subjects behaved at an earlier age. In cross-sectional investigations that cover a large age range, this assumption is especially risky, because the separate age groups contain individuals born in widely separated years. Differences found between 10-year-old cohorts who were born in 1979 and 20-year-old cohorts who were born in 1969 may not really represent age-related changes. Instead, they may be due to unique cultural and historical experiences associated with the different time periods in which the age groups were growing up. Thus, the validity of cross-sectional studies can also be threatened by cultural-historical change, and cross-sectional research is likely to suffer from fewest problems if the age range sampled is fairly narrow.

Despite these limitations, the cross-sectional design is an efficient strategy for identifying developmental trends, and results from such studies frequently lead to fruitful speculations about the reasons for age-related changes. A cross-sectional study by Loney (1974) serves as a good example. Loney wanted to find out if hyperactive boys, whose behavior is characterized by impulsiveness, inattentiveness, and overactivity, differ from normal agemates in the development of intelligence and self-esteem during middle childhood. To find out, she obtained intelligence test scores and teacher ratings of self-esteem on hyperactive and normal boys enrolled in second- and fifth-grade classrooms. The results, displayed in Figure 2.4, show that the scores of both types of boys were similar in second grade, but at fifth grade hyperactive boys' self-esteem and intelligence were considerably below the performance of their nor-

roles was distressing for many families, and it tended to provoke dissension and conflict. Fathers became explosive, punitive, and arbitrary in their behaviors toward children (Elder, Liker, & Cross, 1984). In response, children became more self-conscious, emotionally sensitive, and moody, and they admired their fathers less. Boys especially turned toward peers and adults outside the family as substitute sources of emotional support during a time when their parents' ability to provide it was impaired. Economic hardship seemed to increase fathers' rejecting and nonsupportive behavior toward daughters in particular, perhaps because girls' closeness to home and greater involvement in household affairs made them readily available targets of family discord and tension. Also, fathers may have been particularly resentful toward daughters as family power and status were given over to females during the period of economic misfortune (Elder, Nguyen, & Caspi, 1985).

The impact of the depression continued to be apparent in family and work patterns as Elder's sample of children entered adulthood. Girls who grew up in economically deprived households remained strongly committed to domestic life as adults, and many married at a relatively early age. As a result, their educational goals were restricted, and fewer entered college. Twenty-five years after the depression, commitment to family life continued to be stronger for them than for women with nondeprived upbringings. Men reared in deprived homes had an especially intense desire for occupational security, and they changed jobs less frequently during adulthood than did those from nondeprived backgrounds. Those from middle-class families showed higher adult occupational attainment than their nondeprived counterparts did, perhaps because of their early vocational focus and a strong sense of responsibility and commitment acquired early in life. Finally, the chance to bear and rear

children was particularly important to men from deprived backgrounds. For those who had experienced the failure of economic security, children may have been viewed as the most rewarding and enduring benefit of their adult lives.

Applications. Elder's study is a forceful illustration of how cultural-historical factors can have a long-term impact on the course of human development. History is always in the making, and families by necessity must absorb the changes wrought by the press of external events. When practitioners intervene in order to help children overcome adjustment difficulties and reach their developmental potential, they must take into account the larger social pressures that affect family life and, in turn, the adaptations children make.

mal counterparts. Loney suggested that hyperactive boys' poor self-control probably leads to negative reactions from teachers and repeated failure in school. Between second and fifth grade, these experiences may lower the child's self-esteem and motivation, which, in turn, may depress their intelligence test performance. Loney's study does not offer definite proof for this explanation, but it highlights some thought-provoking developmental trends that deserve to be followed up in subsequent research.

Improving Developmental Designs. In order to overcome some of the limitations of longitudinal and cross-sectional designs, several new approaches for studying development have been devised. One of them, called the **longitudinal-sequential design,** is depicted in Figure 2.5. It is called a sequential design because it is composed of a sequence of samples, each of which is followed longitudinally for a number of years (Schaie & Hertzog, 1982). In the example shown here, three samples of children born in different years have been selected. Each group is followed longitudinally during 1988, 1989, and 1990. Because the design includes several different samples that are followed over time, it actually combines longitudinal and cross-sectional strategies (Achenbach, 1978).

The new design has several advantages. First, it enables investigators to find out if cultural-historical effects are operating by making a *time-lag comparison.* This entails comparing the samples born in different years with one another when they have reached the same age. Using the example shown in Figure 2.5, we can compare the behaviors of the three samples of children when they are each 7 years of age. Because the ages of the three groups of children are identical, any differences we find among them can be attributed to cultural-historical influences associated with their different birth years. Second, it is possible to do both longitudinal and cross-sectional comparisons among the samples of children. Thus, the design permits us to find out if age-related changes can be replicated using the two different developmental approaches. Third, the design is efficient, in that it enables us to obtain information over a fairly long period of development in less time than it takes the development to occur. In our example, it takes only 2 years, from 1988 to 1990, to carry out the study. However, as long as there are no cultural-historical influences to contaminate our age-related findings, we have obtained information about development over a 4-year period, from 5 to 9 years of age (Achenbach, 1978).

A final point about developmental research designs is in order. Perhaps you noticed that all of the examples of longitudinal and cross-sectional research discussed in the sections above provide only correlational, and not causal, inferences about

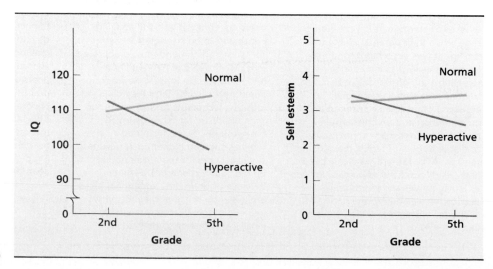

Figure 2.4. Cross-sectional changes in intelligence and self-esteem among hyperactive and normal boys in the Loney (1974) study. In comparison to their normal counterparts, hyperactive boys showed age-related declines in IQ and self-esteem. *(Adapted from Loney, 1974.)*

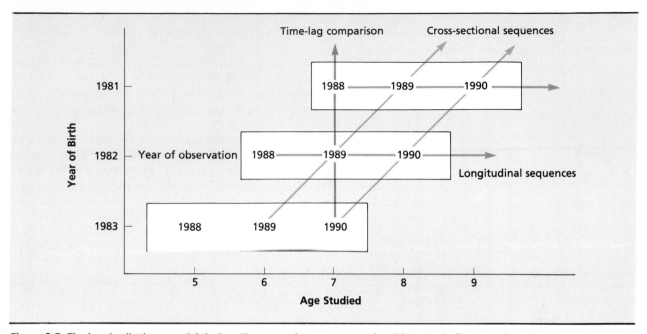

Figure 2.5. The longitudinal-sequential design. Three samples of children born in 1981, 1982, and 1983, respectively, are observed longitudinally in the years 1988 to 1990. The design permits both longitudinal and cross-sectional comparisons. In addition, a time-lag comparison allows the investigator to assess cultural-historical effects. *(Adapted with permission of The Free Press, a Division of Macmillan, Inc., from Research in Developmental Psychology: Concepts, Strategies, Methods, by Thomas M. Achenbach. Copyright © 1978 by The Free Press.)*

development. Yet ideally, causal information is desirable, both for verifying theories of child development and for coming up with ways to improve children's experiences in order to help them reach their full developmental potential. If we find that children's experiences and later behavior are related in a developmental design, in some instances we can explore the causal relationship between them by experimentally manipulating the early experience in a subsequent study. If, as a result, children's development is enhanced, this would provide strong evidence for a causal relationship between the early experience and later behavior. Today, research that combines an experimental strategy with either a longitudinal or a cross-sectional approach appears with increasing frequency in the research literature. Such designs are a vital force in helping child development specialists move beyond the mere identification of correlated variables toward a causal account of factors responsible for developmental change.

In the sections above, we have discussed a wide variety of research designs commonly used in the field of child development, and we have seen that each offers investigators both advantages and disadvantages. To help you review and compare the various designs, Table 2.2 provides a brief, descriptive summary of each, along with its major strengths and weaknesses.

ETHICS IN RESEARCH WITH CHILDREN

In any study, investigators must address fundamental questions about whether or not the research presents ethical risks to the subjects involved. Research into human behavior creates ethical issues because, unfortunately, the quest for scientific knowledge can sometimes be turned to manipulative and exploitative purposes as well. When children are research participants, the ethical considerations are especially complex. Children are more vulnerable than adults to physical and psychological harm, and immaturity makes it difficult or impossible for children to evaluate for themselves what participation in research may mean. For these reasons, special ethical guidelines for research involving children have been developed by the federal government, by funding agencies, and by research-oriented associations, such as the American Psychological Association (1968) and the Society for Research in Child Development (1975). A summary of children's basic research rights drawn from these guidelines is presented in Table 2.3.

Most studies in which children are observed, questioned, or tested present little potential for harm. However, occasionally investigators find it difficult to study important topics, such as reactions to divorce or death of a parent, without asking anxiety-provoking questions and exposing children to some stress. Virtually every committee that has worked on developing ethical principles for research has concluded that the conflicts raised by such studies cannot be resolved with simple right or

Table 2.2. Strengths and Weaknesses of Common Research Designs

DESIGN	DESCRIPTION	STRENGTHS	WEAKNESSES
GENERAL DESIGNS			
Correlational design	Obtains information on existing groups of individuals without researcher intervention	Enables study of relationships among variables in many natural life circumstances	Does not permit determination of cause-and-effect relationships among variables
Experimental design	Investigator manipulates changes in an independent variable and looks at what effect this has on a dependent variable. Requires random assignment of subjects to treatment conditions	Permits determination of cause-and-effect relationships between variables	Often limited to laboratory studies. Findings may not generalize to the real world
Field experiment	Experimental design involving random assignment of subjects to treatments in natural settings	Permits generalization of experimental findings to the real world	Control over treatment generally weaker than in a laboratory experiment
Natural experiment	Comparison of intact real world treatments to which subjects cannot be randomly assigned	Allows study of many naturally occurring variables not subject to experimenter manipulation	Observed differences may be due to variables other than the treatment
DEVELOPMENTAL DESIGNS			
Longitudinal design	A group of subjects is observed repeatedly at different ages	Permits study of individual developmental trends and relationships between early and later events and behaviors	Age-related changes subject to distortion if biased sampling, subject attrition, subject reactivity, practice effects, or cultural-historical change occurs
Cross-sectional design	Groups of subjects of different ages are observed at a single point in time	More convenient and efficient than the longitudinal design	Does not permit study of individual developmental trends. Age differences subject to distortion by cultural-historical effects
Longitudinal-sequential design	Several groups of children born in different years are followed longitudinally over the same time span	Provides both longitudinal and cross-sectional comparisons. Time-lag comparison reveals cultural-historical effects	Subject to same problems as longitudinal and cross-sectional designs, but the design itself helps illuminate difficulties

Table 2.3. Children's Research Rights

65

CHAPTER 2
RESEARCH STRATEGIES

Protection from Harm. Children have the right to be protected from physical or psychological harm in research. If in doubt about the harmful effects of research, investigators should seek the opinion of others. When harm seems possible, investigators should find other means for obtaining the desired information or abandon the research.

Informed Consent. Informed consent of parents as well as others who act on the child's behalf (such as school officials) should be obtained for any research involving children, preferably in writing. All research participants, including children, have the right to have explained to them all aspects of the research that may affect their willingness to participate in language appropriate to their level of understanding. Adults and children should be free to discontinue participation in research at any time.

Privacy. Children have the right to concealment of their identity on all information collected in the course of research. They also have this right with respect to written reports and in any informal discussions about the research.

Knowledge of Results. Children have the right to be informed of the results of research in terms that are appropriate to their understanding.

Beneficial Treatments. If experimental treatments believed to be beneficial are under investigation, children in control groups have the right to alternative beneficial treatments if they are available.

Sources: American Psychological Association, Division on Developmental Psychology, 1968; Society for Research in Child Development, Ethical Interest Group, 1975.

wrong answers, and the ultimate responsibility for the ethical integrity of research resides with the investigator. However, researchers are advised or, in the case of federally funded research, required to seek advice from others, and **institutional review boards** exist in colleges, universities, and other research-oriented organizations for this purpose. These review boards evaluate research studies on the basis of a **risks versus benefits ratio.** This involves weighing the costs of the research to the individual participant in terms of time, stress, and inconvenience against its value for advancing knowledge and increasing our capacity to better children's conditions of life (Cooke, 1982). The general ethical question that must be asked about every research study is whether there is any negative impact on the safety and welfare of participants that the worth of the research findings really does not justify. If so, priority should always be given to the research participant.

The ethical principle of **informed consent** requires special interpretation when research participants are children, for children's competence and freedom to make choices regarding their own participation must be taken into account. Parental consent is meant to protect the safety of children whose ability to make this choice is not yet fully mature. Besides parental consent, agreement of other parties who act on children's behalf, such as institutional officials when research is conducted in schools, day care centers, or hospitals, should be obtained. Furthermore, researchers should seek the agreement of children as soon as they begin to develop some ability to understand verbal explanations and can express their own feelings. Children's ability to make such judgments varies tremendously. Infants and preverbal toddlers certainly cannot make reasoned judgments, and parental consent should be the deciding factor. By the time children enter the preschool years, they have some capacity to understand investigators' explanations if they are conveyed concretely, in terms that refer to the immediate situation and the child's recent experiences. Therefore, in addition to obtaining parental consent, investigators should provide preschool children with simple explanations, such as "We want to find out more about how children play, how they solve problems, what they think about these questions" (Ferguson, 1978, p. 118). Federal guidelines indicate that informed consent of children 7 years of age and older should be obtained in addition to parental consent (National Commission for the Protection of Human Subjects, 1977). Around the age of 7, changes in children's thinking permit them to better understand simple scientific principles, the perspectives of others, and the consequences of their behavior for those around them. Researchers should respect and enhance these new capacities by providing school-age children with a full explanation of research activities in everyday language that children can understand, and they should seek prior consent for research participation from the children themselves, even after parents have already given their permission (Ferguson, 1978; Cooke, 1982).

Finally, young children rely on a basic faith in the trustworthiness of adults for feeling secure in unfamiliar situations. Therefore, it is possible for some types of research activities to be particularly disturbing to them. Virtually all ethical guidelines advise that special precautions be taken in the use of deception and concealment, as occurs in studies in which researchers give children false feedback about their performance, observe them surreptitiously behind one-way mirrors, or do not tell children the truth regarding what the research is all about. When these kinds of procedures are used with adults, **debriefing,** in which a full account and justification of the activities is provided by the experimenter, occurs after the research session is over. Debriefing should also take place with children, but it does not always work as well. Despite explanations, children may still come away from the research situation thinking that some adults do not tell the truth and with their basic faith in adults undermined. Ethical standards permit deception in research with children if investigators satisfy institutional review boards that such practices are necessary. Nevertheless, since deception may have serious emotional consequences for children, many psychologists take the position that its use is always unethical, and that investigators should use their ingenuity to come up with alternative research procedures when children are involved (Ferguson, 1978; Cooke, 1982).

CHAPTER SUMMARY

1. Research generally begins with an hypothesis, or prediction about behavior drawn from a theory. In areas where there is little or no existing theory, it starts with a research question. Based on the hypothesis or question, the researcher chooses a research strategy. In addition to deciding which subjects and how many will be involved, the investigator selects research methods (specific activities each subject will participate in) and a research design (overall plan for the study).

2. Reliability and validity are two important concepts that help investigators determine if their research strategy produces accurate and meaningful information. A research method is reliable if it produces consistent, repeatable results. A method is valid if, after examining its content and relationships with other measures of behavior, the investigator finds that it reflects what it was intended to measure. Two special kinds of validity refer to the accuracy of the researcher's overall findings and conclusions. The internal validity of a study is jeopardized if factors unrelated to the researcher's hypothesis serve as alternative explanations for the results. External validity refers to the generalizability of research findings. It is compromised when investigators use biased samples or conduct research in contrived, artificial situations while assuming that the findings generalize to the real world.

3. Commonly used research methods in child development include systematic observation, self-report measures such as questionnaires and interviews, and the clinical or case study method. Observations can be made in natural settings or in controlled, laboratory environments where investigators deliberately set up cues to elicit behaviors of interest. In addition, depending on the researcher's purpose, observations can preserve the entire behavior stream of the subject, or they can be limited to one or a few behaviors, as in event sampling and time sampling. Self-report methods can be flexible and open-ended like the clinical interview, which yields a full picture of each subject's thoughts and feelings. Or structured interviews and questionnaires can be given, which permit easy comparison of subjects' responses and efficient administration and scoring. When investigators desire an in-depth understanding of a single child, they can employ the clinical method, in which a wide range of interview, test, and observational information is synthesized into a description of the subject's development and psychological functioning.

4. Two basic kinds of research designs are correlational and experimental. Correlational studies examine relationships between variables as they happen to occur, without the researcher's intervention. The correlational approach does not permit determination of the precise causal links between

variables, but its use is justified when investigators find it difficult or impossible to control the variables of interest. In contrast, experimental designs permit precise determination of cause and effect relationships. In a typical experiment, researchers manipulate an independent variable by exposing groups of subjects to two or more treatment conditions. Then they see what effect this has on changes in a dependent variable. Random assignment and matching are techniques used in experiments to assure that characteristics of subjects do not contaminate the findings. To achieve high degrees of control, most experiments are conducted in laboratories. Thus, their strength is the achievement of high internal validity, but this is often obtained at some expense to external validity. Researchers have tried to improve the external validity of experimental findings by conducting field experiments, in which they manipulate treatment conditions in the real world. When this is impossible, they resort to natural experiments, in which already existing, naturally occurring treatments are compared with one another. However, natural experiments cannot achieve the precision and control of true experimental designs.

5. Longitudinal and cross-sectional designs are uniquely suited for studying human development. The longitudinal approach, in which a sample of children is observed repeatedly at different ages, is the most powerful developmental design. It permits the study of individual developmental trends, relationships among changes in different aspects of behavior, and relationships among early and later events and behaviors. Investigators face a variety of problems in conducting longitudinal research, including biased samples, subject reactivity, practice effects, cultural-historical change (cohort effects), and outdated theories and methods in long-term studies.

6. The cross-sectional design, in which groups of children of different ages are observed at a single point in time, provides an expedient approach to the study of development. However, the developmental information available is restricted to comparisons of the average performance of different age groups. In addition, cross-sectional studies that span a wide age range are threatened by the effects of cultural-historical change. To deal with some of the limitations of longitudinal and cross-sectional designs, new approaches for studying development, such as the longitudinal-sequential design, have been devised. In addition, experimental procedures can be combined with longitudinal or cross-sectional designs to examine causal influences on development.

7. Research involving children raises special ethical concerns. Because of their immaturity, children are more vulnerable to harm and cannot always make informed choices about research participation. Ethical guidelines for research and institutional review boards help assure that children's research rights are protected. As soon as children are old enough to understand the researcher's verbal explanations, investigators should seek consent for research participation from children themselves, in addition to informed parental consent. The use of deception in research with children is especially risky, as it may leave emotional scars and undermine children's basic faith in the trustworthiness of adults.

IMPORTANT TERMS AND CONCEPTS

hypothesis
reliability
validity
replication
internal validity
external validity
cross-validation study
naturalistic observation
structured observation
specimen record
event sampling
time sampling
clinical interview

structured interview
questionnaire
clinical method
correlational design
correlation coefficient
experimental designs
independent variable
dependent variable
random assignment
matching
field experiment
natural experiment
longitudinal design

biased sampling
subject attrition
subject reactivity
practice effects
cultural-historical change (cohort effects)
cross-sectional design
longitudinal-sequential design
institutional review board
risks versus benefits ratio
informed consent
debriefing

PART II

Developmental Foundations

The De Vegh Twins (1975), by Alice Neel.
Collection of Gerald S. Fineberg.

CHAPTER 3

Biological Foundations, Prenatal Development, and Birth

In this chapter, we consider the beginnings of development. In a brief nine-month period, a tiny, one-celled fertilized ovum miraculously unfolds into a newborn infant equipped with complex physical and behavioral characteristics specially suited for life outside the womb. Because nature has prepared the human infant for survival, all healthy newborns possess many characteristics in common. At the same time, a glance around the hospital nursery reveals that the newborn's individuality and uniqueness are evident soon after birth. Excited relatives looking for family resemblances find that one infant shows combined features of both parents, another resembles only one of the parents, while a third bears characteristics with no similarity to either parent. These visibly apparent differences, referred to as **phenotypes,** depend in part on genetic, or **genotype** differences among children. In this chapter, we consider basic genetic principles of transmission that underlie important individual differences in appearance and behavior.

Then we trace development during the most rapid phase of growth, the prenatal period, in which complex transactions between heredity and environment begin to shape the course of future development. The prenatal environment is far more constant than the world the infant will encounter after birth, but it is nevertheless an environment that can have major consequences for the child's physical and behavioral characteristics. Our discussion considers environmental supports necessary for normal intrauterine development as well as damaging environmental influences having irrevocable consequences for the future of the unborn child. Then we turn to the drama of birth and a consideration of developmental risks for infants born prematurely, before prenatal growth is complete.

Finally, we take a look ahead. This earliest period of development introduces us to the operation of two basic determinants of development: heredity and environment.

We discuss how psychologists think about and study the relationship between heredity and environment as they continue to moderate the child's emerging characteristics during infancy and childhood.

GENETIC FOUNDATIONS

Genetics is the science of heredity, of how traits are passed from one generation to another. The study of genetic mechanisms of transmission began over a century ago, with the famous genetic crossings between varieties of garden peas made by the Austrian monk, Gregor Mendel. Conducting experiments in which he recorded the number of times the immediate and remote offspring of white- and pink-flowered plants had white or pink flowers, Mendel was able to come up with important generalizations about heredity. Mendel inferred the presence of genes, factors controlling each of the traits he studied. In recent years, more knowledge has accumulated about the biochemical and molecular makeup of genetic material. While peas and humans may seem completely unrelated, the transmission of heredity conforms to the same basic principles among diverse forms of life, and knowledge of lower forms has greatly clarified our understanding of the genetics of the human species.

The Genetic Code

The human organism is made up of trillions of independent units called cells. Inside each cell is a control center or nucleus, which contains, among other things, **chromosomes,** the bearers of our genetic fate. When cells are chemically stained and viewed through a powerful microscope, the chromosomes, or "colored bodies," are visible as rodlike structures in the nucleus. Chromosomes store and transmit genetic information, control how the cells are made, and play an important role in determining the individual's development and characteristics. The number of chromosomes varies from species to species—48 for the chimpanzee, 64 for the horse, 40 for the mouse, and 46 for the human being. Chromosomes come in duplicates, or what are called **homologous pairs** (an exception is the XY pair in males, which we shall discuss later). Each pair member corresponds to the other in size, shape, and genetic functions, with one inherited from the mother and one from the father. Therefore, in humans, we speak of 23 *pairs* of chromosomes residing in each human cell (see Figure 3.1).

Chromosomes contain long, double-stranded molecules of a chemical substance called **deoxyribonucleic acid,** or **DNA.** In the early 1950s, Watson and Crick's (1953) discovery of the chemical architecture of the DNA molecule unlocked the genetic code. As shown in Figure 3.2, DNA has a "double helix" structure that resembles a twisted ladder. The sides of the ladder are two threads wound around each other made up of alternating sugar and phosphate molecules. Each rung consists of a pair of chemical bases attached to the sugar units and joined together between the two sides of the ladder. The pairings of bases across the rungs are very specific. Whenever the base adenine (A) appears on one side, thymine (T) is joined to it on the other, and whenever cytosine (C) appears, guanine (G) is its complement. While the bases occur in fixed association across the rungs of the ladder, they can occur in any order along its sides, and it is the sequence of bases along the length of the molecule, written in an alphabet of four letters—A, T, G, and C—that provides specific genetic instructions. **Genes** are segments of DNA along the length of the molecule. Genes can be of different lengths—perhaps a thousand to several thousand ladder rungs long —and each gene differs from the next because of its unique sequence of base pairs. Thus, each new organism begins life with a set of hereditary instructions built in to the structure of its DNA that determines what kind of organism it is and many of its unique characteristics.

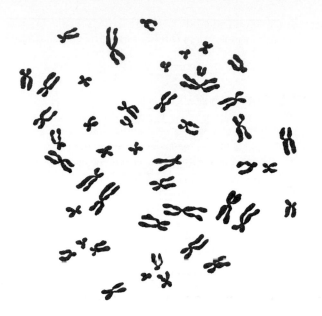

Figure 3.1. Human chromosomes. *Above,* a *karyotype,* or photograph of human chromosomes from a white blood cell. *Below,* the chromosomes have been assembled in pairs and ordered according to decreasing size. Note the 23rd pair, XY. The cell donor is a male. *(From E. Frankel, 1979,* DNA: The Ladder of Life, *New York: McGraw-Hill. P. 16. Reprinted by permission.)*

DNA accomplishes its task by sending instructions for making a rich assortment of proteins to the cytoplasm, the area surrounding the nucleus of the cell. Proteins, which trigger chemical reactions throughout the body, are the foundation upon which the characteristics and capacities of each new individual are built.

Cell Duplication

A unique feature of DNA, one that distinguishes it from all other molecules, is that it has the ability to duplicate itself. In the growth and development of organisms, the precise mechanism of cell duplication that keeps the genetic code and the number of chromosomes constant from cell to cell is called **mitosis.** In mitosis, the DNA ladder splits down the middle so that the pairs of bases forming the rungs are separated, but each side of the ladder remains intact (see Figure 3.2). Each base is now free to pick up a new complementary mate from the cytoplasm of the cell. The newly attached bases are in precisely the same order as the old ones, and two new DNA ladders, each

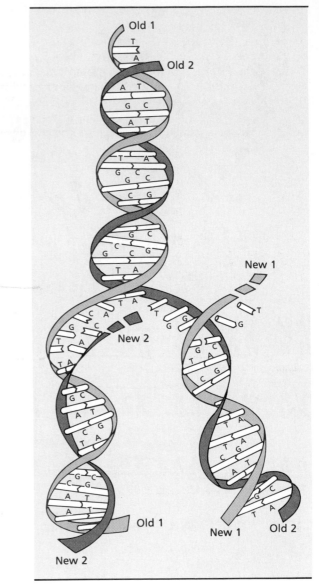

Figure 3.2. DNA's double helix structure. Here the DNA ladder is shown splitting down the middle and duplicating itself. *(From E. Frankel, 1979, DNA: The Ladder of Life, New York: McGraw-Hill. P. 54. Reprinted by permission.)*

containing one new side and one old side of the previous chain, are produced. At the level of chromosomes, mitosis involves each chromosome duplicating itself. As a result, each new cell contains an exact copy of the original chromosomes and thus, the identical genetic material. The special ability of DNA to duplicate itself makes it possible for the one-celled fertilized ovum to develop into a complex human being composed of trillions of cells.

The Sex Cells

The new individual is created by the union of two special cells, a sperm and an ovum, which are referred to as **gametes.** Gametes are unique in that they contain only 23 single chromosomes, half as many as a regular body cell, and they are formed through a special process of cell division called **meiosis.**

Meiosis takes place according to the sequence of steps displayed in Figure 3.3. First, homologous chromosomes pair up within the original cell, and each member of the pair replicates itself. Then the paired and duplicated chromosomes align themselves at the middle of the cell. While there, a special event called **crossing over** takes place, in which the pair members break at one or more points along their length and exchange corresponding segments, so that genes from one chromosome are replaced by genes from another. Then the two chromosomes in a pair separate and are pulled to opposite poles of the cell. However, chance governs which of the chromosomes from a homologous pair will gather with others and eventually end up in the same gamete. Finally, in the last phase of meiosis, each pair member separates from its partner and becomes part of a gamete containing 23 chromosomes. In the male, the meiotic process results in the formation of four gametes, or sperm cells, from the original cell. In the female, the end product is slightly different in that it results in only one unfertilized ovum; the leftover cellular material soon degenerates. When the sperm and ovum unite at fertilization to form the beginning of the new individual, the cell that results, called a **zygote,** will again have 46 chromosomes.

The process of meiosis assures that a constant quantity of genetic material will be transmitted from one generation to the next. In addition, it also acts to increase the

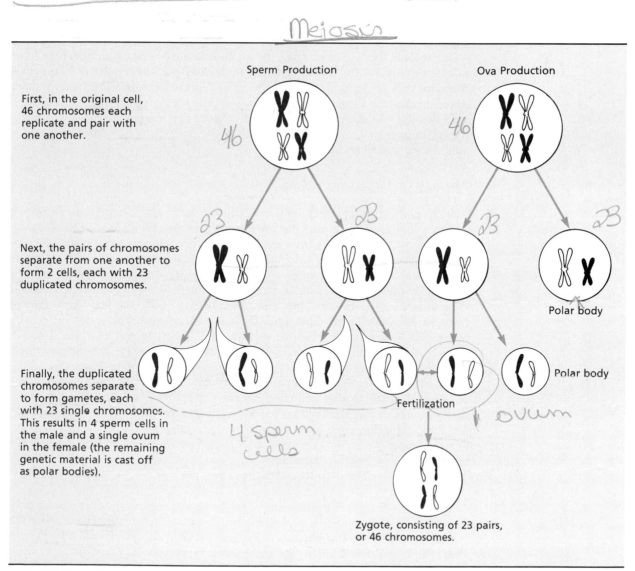

Figure 3.3. The cell division process of meiosis, leading to gamete formation. Original cells are depicted with 2 rather than the full complement of 23 chromosome pairs.

genetic variability among offspring. Crossing over and independent assortment of the members of chromosome pairs assure that no two gametes will ever be genetically identical (except for identical twins, which result when a zygote duplicates itself, and two genetically identical individuals develop). While half the new individual's genes are drawn from the mother and half from the father, each offspring receives a different selection of genes from each parent. Thus, meiosis explains why siblings differ from one another in appearance and characteristics, although they also share features in common, since their genotype is the result of selection from a common pool of parental genes.

The genetic variation produced by meiosis is important in an evolutionary sense. Certain combinations of genes enable individuals to adapt better to the environment. When these individuals reproduce, their favorable genetic makeup has the opportunity to undergo further modifications, and some new genetic combinations may prove even better suited to the environment than the original ones. In addition, environments also undergo change, and the greater the genetic variability present among members of a species, the greater the chances that some will be able to cope with new environmental conditions. Thus, the genetic variability that results from the meiotic production of sex cells is essential for evolutionary progress and the survival of a species.

In the male, the cells from which the sperm arise are produced continuously, from puberty onward. In the female, gamete production is more restricted. The ovum-producing cells are formed and enter the early stages of meiosis before birth, and the female is born with all her potential gametes already present in her ovaries. Still, there is no shortage of female reproductive cells. About one million are present at birth, 300,000 remain at age 7, and approximately 350 to 450 will mature during a woman's childbearing years (Rothwell, 1977).

Patterns of Genetic Inheritance

Using special microscopic techniques, the pairs of chromosomes can be distinguished from one another. The 22 pairs that are homologous are called **autosomes,** and they are numbered by geneticists from longest to shortest (refer back to Figure 3.1). The 23rd pair is made up of the **sex chromosomes.** In females, this pair is called XX, while in males it is called XY. The single X is a relatively long chromosome, while the Y is short and carries very little genetic material. In gamete formation in males, the X and Y chromosomes separate into different sperm cells, while in the female all gametes carry an X chromosome. Therefore, the sex of the individual is determined by whether an X-bearing or Y-bearing sperm fertilizes the egg. In fact, scientists have recently isolated a single gene on the Y chromosome that triggers male sexual development. When this gene is absent, the fetus that develops is female (Page et al., 1987).

Two forms of each gene occur at the same locus, or place, on the autosomes, one inherited from the mother and one from the father. Each is called an *allele.* If the alleles from both parents are alike, the new individual is said to be **homozygous** and will display the inherited trait. If the alleles are different, the individual is called **heterozygous.** Under heterozygous circumstances, the way that the two alleles interact with one another determines the phenotypic trait that the individual will display, and there are a number of different possibilities.

Dominant-Recessive Relationships. Under many heterozygous conditions, only one of the alleles becomes phenotypically apparent. It is termed **dominant,** while the second allele whose influence does not appear in the phenotype is called **recessive.** Hair color is an example of this dominant-recessive pattern of inheritance. The allele for dark hair is known to be dominant (we can represent it with a capital H), while the one for blond hair is recessive (symbolized by a small h). Individuals who inherit a homozygous pair of dominant alleles (HH) or a heterozygous pair (Hh) will display

Heredity manifests itself in many visible human characteristics; sometimes the resemblance between parent and offspring is striking. (Fredrik D. Bodin)

the same dark-haired phenotype even though their genotypes are different. Blond hair can only result when the individual inherits the combination of two recessive alleles (hh).

A list of some of the human characteristics that operate according to the dominant-recessive mode of inheritance is given in Table 3-1. As you can see by examining the table, many serious disease conditions are the product of two recessive genes. Although the homozygous combination of harmful alleles is rare, many of the conditions that result are strongly associated with mental retardation (Kopp, 1983; Moser, 1975). Among the most frequently occurring of such disorders is *phenylketonuria, or PKU*. PKU is an especially good example of genetic transmission, since it shows that inheritance of unfavorable genes does not necessarily mean the resulting condition is permanent and unmodifiable. For PKU, we know the specific biochemical consequences of recessive gene inheritance. Consequently, we can use this information to intervene with the environment in order to prevent the most serious aspects of the disease.

PKU occurs about once in every 8,000 births (March of Dimes, 1983). Inheritance of two autosomal recessive alleles (pp) affects the way that the body metabolizes proteins contained in many foods, such as cow's milk and meat. Infants born with PKU lack an enzyme (phenylalanine hydroxylase) that converts a potentially harmful amino acid contained in proteins (phenylalanine) into a harmless by-product (tyrosine). In the absence of this enzyme, a toxic excess of phenylalanine quickly accumulates and damages the central nervous system. By 3 to 5 months of age, untreated PKU infants begin to lose interest in their surroundings, and by one year of age, they are permanently mentally retarded.

Table 3.1. Examples of Dominant and Recessive Characteristics and Diseases

DOMINANT	RECESSIVE
Dark hair	Blond hair
Curly hair	Straight hair
Facial dimples	No dimples
Normal hearing	Some forms of congenital deafness
Normal vision	Nearsightedness
Farsightedness	Normal vision
Normal vision	Congenital eye cataracts
Normal color vision	Red-green color blindness
Normally pigmented skin	Albinism
Type A blood	Type O blood
Type B blood	Type O blood
Rh positive blood	Rh negative blood
Normal respiratory and gastrointestinal functioning	Cystic fibrosis
Normal blood-clotting factors	Hemophilia
Normal protein metabolism	Phenylketonuria (PKU)
Normal red blood cells	Sickle cell anemia
Normal central nervous system development	Tay-Sachs disease
Huntington's chorea	Normal central nervous system functioning in adulthood

Sources: McKusick, 1983; Stanbury, Wyngaarden, & Fredrickson, 1983.

Note: Many normal characteristics previously thought to be governed by the single gene dominant-recessive mode of inheritance, such as eye color, are now regarded by geneticists as polygenetically determined (due to multiple genes). For the characteristics listed here, there still seems to be fairly common agreement that the simple dominant-recessive relationship holds.

Most states require that every newborn be tested for PKU shortly after birth. If PKU is diagnosed, treatment involves placing the baby on a diet low in phenylalanine and monitoring the concentration of this substance in the bloodstream to make sure that it never reaches toxic levels. Children receiving this dietary treatment show near-normal levels of intelligence (Dobson et al., 1976), and the most harmful effects of the disorder are averted. Children with PKU are frequently taken off the special diet by 5 or 6 years of age, when many physicians believe that the central nervous system is sufficiently mature to resist the effects of phenylalaline. However, others disagree and recommend lifetime dietary maintenance, because of declines seen in the intelligence test scores of some children who stopped the diet at school age (Cohen, 1984).

There is another reason for long-term dietary intervention. If a woman who had PKU as a child but stopped the diet becomes pregnant, her baby is likely to be born retarded. Toxic levels of phenylalanine in the mother's bloodstream enter the baby's circulatory system before birth and interfere with the development of the central nervous system. In this case, the unborn child may not have inherited the disorder but will nevertheless bear its effects because of a damaging intrauterine environment provided by the PKU mother. Retardation can be prevented if the mother goes back on a low-phenylalanine diet before and during pregnancy (Levy, Kaplan, & Erickson, 1982).

In dominant-recessive autosomal inheritance, if we know the genetic makeup of the parents, we can predict the proportion of offspring in a family who are likely to manifest the recessive trait or be heterozygous carriers of it. Figure 3.4 shows one hypothetical example for PKU. Note that in order for a child to inherit the condition, a recessive allele (p) must be carried and transmitted by each parent. One good reason for cultural and legal prohibitions against marriages between close blood relatives is that related parents have an increased risk of inheriting the same damaging recessive allele from a common ancestor and passing it along to their offspring. Recessive disorders like PKU are more common among children born to parents who are first or second cousins (Reed, 1975).

Co-dominance. In the case of a few characteristics attributable to single gene inheritance, the dominant-recessive pattern of expression does not hold completely. There are some heterozygous allele combinations in which it is possible for both alleles to be expressed in the individual's phenotype. This is called **co-dominance.** ABO blood typing provides an illustration. Three possible alleles — A, B, and O — can be inherited in any paired combination, and three heterozygous combinations are possible: AO, BO, and AB. When paired with O, the A and B alleles will determine the phenotype, and the usual dominant-recessive mode of expression holds. But when both A and B alleles are inherited, the result is the combined phenotypic expression known as type AB blood, in which both A and B antigens are present.

Sickle cell anemia, a blood disorder that afflicts 1 out of every 500 black Americans, is another instance of single gene inheritance in which co-dominance, or the phenotypic expression of both heterozygous alleles, applies. However, in the case of the sickle cell trait, special circumstances in the environment are responsible for triggering co-dominant expression in heterozygous individuals. Thus, the sickle cell genetic disorder is an illustration of the subtle interaction of hereditary and environmental factors that can contribute to phenotypic results. Sickle cell anemia occurs when a person inherits a pair of recessive alleles leading the red blood cells to contain hemoglobin molecules of an abnormal type (hemoglobin gives red blood cells their color and carries oxygen to body tissues). The defective hemoglobin causes the usually round red blood cells to assume a sickle shape, a response that is especially acute under low oxygen environmental conditions. The sickled cells clog the blood vessels, interfere with the flow of blood, and interrupt the delivery of oxygen to body tissues. Organs whose demand for oxygen is particularly great — brain, kidney, liver, heart, spleen, and muscles — are most affected. Individuals afflicted with the disorder suffer severe attacks involving intense pain, swelling, and tissue damage (Pearson & Diamond, 1971). Persons inheriting the pair of recessive alleles generally die in the first two decades of life; few live past age 40. Heterozygous individuals are protected from the disease under a broad range of normal environmental conditions. However, when they are exposed to oxygen deprivation — for example, at high altitudes or after

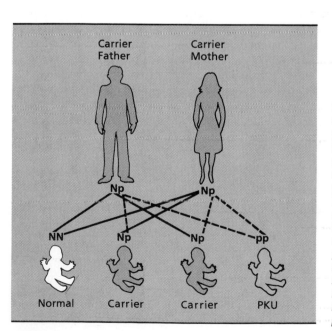

Figure 3.4. Dominant-recessive mode of inheritance, as illustrated by PKU. When both parents are heterozygous carriers of the recessive allele, we can predict that 25 percent of their offspring will be normal, 50 percent will be carriers, and 25 percent will be afflicted with PKU. *(From March of Dimes, 1983, PKU [Genetic Series, Public Health Education Information Sheet], White Plains, NY: March of Dimes Birth Defects Foundation. Reprinted by permission.)*

intense physical exertion—the single recessive allele asserts itself, and hetero-zygotes experience mild sickling attacks accompanied by painful swelling and fa-tigue. Thus, under specific environmental circumstances, the otherwise dominant allele does not completely overcome the effects of the sickle cell gene, and the combined, or co-dominant effects of both alleles are apparent in a less severe and temporary form of the illness.

Natural Selection, Mutation, and Unfavorable Genes. Inheritance of unfavorable genes decreases the chances that afflicted individuals will reproduce and pass them on to their offspring. Why, then, do some harmful alleles continue to survive? In some instances, natural selection provides the answer. In the case of the sickle cell trait, research has shown that African heterozygous carriers are more resistant to malaria than individuals with two genes for normal red blood cells. In malaria-ridden regions of the world, these carriers survived and reproduced more frequently than others, leading the gene to be transmitted to their offspring and maintained in the population. However, the frequency of the sickle cell gene can be expected to gradually decrease over generations, as it confers no special survival advantage in malaria-free environ-ments such as the United States (Reed, 1975).

Perhaps you are also asking yourself, "How do genes with unfavorable conse-quences for the individual come to be present in the gene pool in the first place?" The answer is **mutation,** which refers to a sudden but permanent change in genetic material. A mutation can involve large amounts of genetic material, as is the case in the chromosomal abnormalities we will discuss later on in this chapter, or it may affect only one or two alleles. Mutations can occur spontaneously, or they can be provoked by hazardous environmental agents, such as agricultural and industrial chemicals that enter the food supply or are present in the air we breathe (Paigen, 1982). For many years radiation has been known to cause mutation. Large dosages are more mutagenic than the same amount received in low dosages over time, and a few studies show a relationship between increased exposure of mothers to radiation before conception and chromosomal defects in their children. Other studies have found chromosomal abnormalities to be higher among the offspring of fathers who are exposed to high levels of radiation in their occupations (Schrag & Dixon, 1985).

Not all mutations are due to environmental toxins. As we mentioned above, there are also random, spontaneous mutations. Many of those that are known are harmful, but others are necessary and desirable from an evolutionary perspective, as they contribute to the genetic variation available in a population, thereby helping it adapt to unexpected environmental challenges and survive. In humans, little is known about favorable mutations. Scientists seldom go looking for the mutagenic origins of exceptional talents and physical characteristics. Instead, they are far more concerned with identifying and eliminating unfavorable mutations that threaten the healthy development and adaptability of the organism.

X-Linked Inheritance. Recessive disorders like PKU and sickle cell anemia are caused by the inheritance of homozygous pairs of alleles on the autosomes, and both males and females have an equal chance of being affected. When a recessive charac-teristic is carried on the X chromosome, a special **X-linked** pattern of **inheritance** applies. Males (XY) are more likely to be affected than females (XX) because the male sex chromosomes are not homologous. In females, any X-linked recessive allele has a reasonable chance of being suppressed by a dominant allele on the other X chromo-some. Males have only one X chromosome, and there are no complementary alleles on the Y to dominate or soften the effects of those on the X. This leads the genes carried by the X to be expressed in the male phenotype when they are present in only a single copy, regardless of whether they have dominant or recessive consequences for fe-males. Red-green color blindness is one example of a frequently occurring X-linked recessive trait. Its phenotypic appearance is twice as great for Caucasian males (8 out of 100) as it is for females (4 out of 100).

Hemophilia, a disorder in which the blood fails to clot normally, was one of the earliest known instances of an X-linked recessive disease, appearing relatively frequently in the royal families of Europe. In the general population, it occurs about once in every 4,000 to 7,000 male births (the disease seldom occurs in females). Hemophilia may become evident shortly after birth if the male infant is circumcised, or it may be recognized later in the first year in a baby who seems to bruise easily or who bleeds excessively after an accidental fall. The major problem in hemophilia is internal bleeding into the joints and muscles that, if not stopped, can lead to deformity, loss of function, and even death. However, with improved medical treatment, bleeding is often preventable, and the life span of afflicted males has increased so that many of them live long enough to reproduce. Provided he marries a woman without the recessive gene, none of the sons of a hemophiliac male will manifest the disease because they inherit his Y chromosome. However, all daughters will be carriers of the disease since they receive his X chromosome, and their sons will have a 50-percent chance of inheriting the disease.

A wide variety of X-linked recessive disorders with increased prevalence in males have been identified — blood-clotting deficiencies, metabolic diseases, one form of diabetes, and one form of muscular dystrophy, to name just a few (McKusick, 1983). In addition, many sex differences in development and behavior reveal the male to be at a general disadvantage. The rate of spontaneous abortion, stillbirths, and infant and childhood mortality is greater for males, and males also show a higher incidence of learning disabilities, behavior disorders, and mental retardation than do females. It is possible that these sex differences may have their origins in the genetic code. The female, with two X chromosomes, benefits from a greater variety of genetic material, while the male's single rather than double dose of X-linked genes contributes to his disadvantage (Singer, Westphal, & Niswander, 1968). However, nature seems to make an adjustment for the greater male vulnerability. About 106 boys are born for every 100 girls, and judging from miscarriage and abortion statistics, a still greater number of boys appear to be conceived (Childs, 1965; Rugh & Shettles, 1971).

Pleiotropism and Modifier Genes. So far, we have considered only one-to-one relationships between genes and phenotypic attributes. However, it is possible for a single gene to affect more than one characteristic. This is known as **pleiotropism,** and the recessive gene responsible for PKU provides an example. Untreated PKU children differ from normal children not only in intelligence, but also in hair color. Hair pigment is formed from the protein tyrosine, and the blond coloring of PKU victims is due to their inability to metabolize phenylalanine into tyrosine.

It is also possible for some genes to modify the phenotypic expression of other genes by either enhancing or diluting their effects. Due to the influence of **modifier genes** on the two recessive alleles for PKU, children differ from one another in the degree to which abnormally high levels of phenylalanine accumulate in their tissues, and they also differ in the extent to which they respond to dietary treatment. Other genetic diseases, such as hemophilia and cystic fibrosis (see Table 3.1), also vary in severity, and modifier genes are thought to be responsible.

Polygenic Inheritance. There are over 1,000 characteristics believed to be inherited according to the rules of dominant-recessive genetic transmission described above (McKusick, 1983). In most of these instances, people either display a particular phenotypic trait or they do not. Such relatively cut-and-dried individual differences are much easier to trace to their genetic origins than characteristics that vary continuously among people. Many physical and behavioral characteristics of interest to child development specialists, such as height, weight, intelligence, and personality, are of the latter type. People are not just tall or short, bright or dull, outgoing or shy. Instead, they show various gradations between these extremes. For continuous characteristics like these, an uncomplicated, single-gene model of inheritance is not valid. Instead, **polygenic inheritance** is more likely (Cavalli-Sforza, 1977). More than one gene, and perhaps a great many, affect the characteristic in question, and the rules of genetic transmission are complex, as yet unspecified, and may never be precisely known. Therefore, scientists have had to study the influence of polygenic inheritance on many important human characteristics indirectly. In the last part of this chapter, we will discuss ways that have been used to infer the influence of heredity on behavior when knowledge of specific genetic influences is unavailable.

Finally, heredity is certainly not the only explanation for most human characteristics. We have already seen how, even in the case of traits attributable to a single gene, the environment can make an important difference in the phenotypic outcome. The severe retardation associated with PKU does not occur in nutritional environments low in phenylalanine, and sickle cell heterozygotes do not become ill as long as environments provide adequate oxygen. Almost all characteristics are the result of the combined influence of heredity and environment, and developmental psychologists have been interested in achieving a better understanding of how heredity and environment work together to influence the development of many human attributes. We will explore some of their ideas regarding the complex interplay of nature and nurture a little later on.

CHROMOSOMAL ABNORMALITIES

In addition to the inheritance of recessive genes, chromosomal abnormalities are a principal cause of serious developmental problems. Most chromosomal defects are thought to be the result of imperfect meiosis during gamete formation, in which a part of a chromosome may break off, or two chromosomes do not separate properly from one another. Since chromosomal errors involve far more DNA than problems associated with a single gene locus, they usually produce disorders that display a wide variety of physical as well as mental symptoms, with depressed intellectual functioning being one common outcome. However, as will be apparent when we discuss some of the more frequent chromosomal abnormalities below, the phenotypic results of inheriting a particular disorder are not completely clear-cut. Aside from the affected chromosomes, thousands of other genes also act on the individual's development, and each affected person is exposed to unique environmental influences from conception on. These factors can minimize or intensify the chromosomal condition.

Down Syndrome

The most common chromosomal abnormality is *Down syndrome*, which occurs in about 1 out of every 660 live births. Down syndrome is due to one of several different types of chromosomal mistakes. In over 90 percent of the cases, it results from a failure of the 21st pair of chromosomes to separate during meiosis. Therefore, two in one gamete join with a single 21st chromosome in the other gamete, and the result is three rather than the normal two when the gametes unite to form the zygote. In other less frequently occurring forms, a broken piece of a 21st chromosome may be joined to the 21st pair, or a piece can be attached to a variety of other chromosomes. In the latter instances, the phenotype can vary from one that is practically normal to one that bears the typical characteristics of Down syndrome, depending on how much extra genetic material is present (Rosenberg & Pettegrew, 1983).

Down syndrome children have a variety of seemingly unrelated defects. These include distinct physical features—a short stocky build, flattened face, protruding

Although most Down syndrome children show severe intellectual impairment, those who experience a stimulating, responsive home environment make better developmental progress. (Ray Solomon/ Monkmeyer Press Photo Service)

tongue, almond-shaped eyes, and an unusual crease running across the palm of the hand. In addition, Down syndrome infants are often born with such congenital[1] problems as heart defects, malformations of the intestinal tract, eye cataracts, and others, and their facial deformities often lead to breathing and feeding difficulties in infancy. Because of medical advances, early mortality of Down syndrome children due to heart defects and respiratory infections has been reduced, but it is still common. About 30 percent die by age 1 and 50 percent by age 4, with the rest living until middle adulthood (Cohen, 1984). The behavioral consequences of Down syndrome include mental retardation, poorly articulated speech, limited vocabulary, and slow motor development. These deficits become increasingly apparent with age, as Down syndrome children show a progressive slowing down in development from infancy onward in comparison to normal children (Kopp, 1983). Although they vary somewhat in the extent of this decline, most show severe impairment. They generally fall within an IQ range of 20 to 50, and only about 5 percent eventually learn to read.

Typically, children with Down syndrome have been described as friendly, easygoing, and placid in disposition (Smith & Wilson, 1973). However, recent research suggests that as a group, they are more variable in personality characteristics than this stereotype suggests. Parent ratings indicate that they show the same range of basic temperaments as normal children (Bridges & Cicchetti, 1982; Gunn & Berry, 1985). Some are passive and easy to please, while others are overactive, prone to angry outbursts, and difficult to manage. Other evidence suggests that Down syndrome babies are less emotionally expressive in social interaction than their normal counterparts. They smile less readily and show poor eye-to-eye contact, and parents may have to play a more assertive role in getting these infants to become actively engaged in their surroundings (Cardoso-Martins & Mervis, 1985). However, when parents make this effort, their children show better developmental progress. In one study, researchers found that those mothers who actively stimulated, played with, and were sensitively responsive to their Down syndrome 2-year-olds had children who scored higher in social responsiveness and play maturity (Crawley & Spiker,

---

[1] The term *congenital* refers to any malformations that have their origins during the early weeks of prenatal life when the organs of the body are being formed. The concept is used rather broadly. It includes defects that are due to hereditary influences, prenatal environmental influences, or both factors.

1983). In addition, Down syndrome infants enrolled in early and long-term intervention programs providing intellectual, social, and motor stimulation show more optimal development (Bricker, Carlson, & Schwarz, 1981). In one of these programs, infants who were intensively tutored from birth to 3 years of age obtained intelligence test scores that averaged 85, substantially higher than untreated children (Rynders, as reported by Scarr-Salapatek, 1975). These findings show that even though Down syndrome is genetic in origin, environmental factors play an important role in how well these children develop.

The incidence of Down syndrome rises dramatically with maternal age, from 1 in about 1,900 births for mothers of 20 years of age to 1 in 12 for mothers age 49 (Hook & Chambers, 1977). The unfertilized ovum released by the older mother has remained in the early stages of meiosis for over three or four decades, ever since her own prenatal period of development. Geneticists believe that the condition is caused by a weakening or deterioration of the cell structures necessary for the proper separation of chromosomes in meiosis. Recently, paternal age has also been implicated as a cause of Down syndrome, with fathers over 40 years of age showing a strongly increased risk of having offspring with the disorder (Hook, 1980; Stene, Stene, & Stengel-Rutkowski, 1981).

Abnormalities of the Sex Chromosomes

Although there are other disorders of the autosomal chromosomes besides Down syndrome, they generally disrupt normal development so severely that they account for about 50 percent of spontaneous abortions, and affected individuals rarely survive beyond early childhood. In contrast, there seems to be greater tolerance for deviations involving the sex chromosomes. The shortness of the Y means that relatively little genetic material is involved, and geneticists think that additional X chromosomes may be largely inactivated early in development (Cohen, 1984). This may explain why in most instances the problems shown by individuals with sex chromosome abnormalities are milder than those involving the autosomes. Many times the disorders go unrecognized until the adolescent years when, in a number of the deviations, pubertal development is delayed. The most common disorders involve the presence of an extra chromosome (either X or Y) or the absence of one X in females.

Turner Syndrome. That both X chromosomes are needed for the normal physical development of females is shown by *Turner syndrome,* in which the second X chromosome or part of it is missing (the disorder is symbolized as XO). The estimated incidence of Turner syndrome is 1 in every 2,500 to 8,000 live births. Phenotypically, these individuals are females, but the ovaries usually do not develop during the prenatal period. Therefore, sex hormone levels are low, secondary sexual characteristics and menstruation generally do not appear at puberty, and afflicted girls remain childlike in physical appearance. Other features include short stature (usually below 57 inches) and a webbed neck, and heart abnormalities are present at birth in 25 percent of the cases. If Turner syndrome is diagnosed early enough, hormones can be administered in childhood to stimulate physical growth, and at puberty to induce breast development and vaginal maturation (Cohen, 1984).

Unlike other chromosomal abnormalities, general intelligence is not impaired by this disorder. In fact, the majority of individuals with Turner syndrome seem to show above-average educational attainment. In one study, 80 percent of those surveyed were reported to have finished college (Hall et al., 1982), and in another, they were found to have performed better than their chromosomally normal sisters in school (Nielsen, Nyborg, & Dahl, 1977). However, despite their overall normal intelligence, there is evidence that girls with Turner syndrome have specific cognitive deficits in spatial perception and orientation. Such children have trouble telling right from left, copying geometric designs, and constructing "mental maps" that help them find their way from one place to another in the real world. Problems with spatial perception are also reflected in the difficulties that many Turner syndrome girls have with handwriting in the early elementary school years. By the time they reach high school, it is not surprising that they begin to avoid courses like geometry and those that demand drawing skills (Pennington et al., 1982).

Turner syndrome girls often experience difficulties in relationships with peers and have been described as socially immature and unassertive (McCauley, Ito, & Kay, 1986). Although their social difficulties could stem from reactions of others to their physical appearance, a recent study showed that in comparison to short-stature controls, Turner syndrome youngsters had difficulty discriminating and interpreting emotional cues from facial expressions (McCauley et al., 1987). The ability to process facial affect is another area of cognitive weakness that may underlie the social problems of these children.

Girls with Turner syndrome usually have a typical feminine gender identity. In childhood, they show the same feminine interests and play preferences as genetically normal girls. In one medical clinic specializing in treatment of Turner syndrome, more than half of the adult patients were married (Hall et al., 1982). However, most are sterile and cannot bear children.

Triple X Syndrome. In contrast to Turner syndrome where the afflicted child is missing an X, in *triple X syndrome (XXX)*, the opposite is the case: an extra X is present. Triple X disorder occurs far more frequently than Turner syndrome, about once in every 850 to 1,250 births, but most of the time it goes unnoticed because it produces no consistent pattern of physical anomalies. Afflicted girls are usually no different in appearance from normal children, except for a greater tendency toward tallness. They show typical development of sexual organs and characteristics, and in adulthood they can bear children (Cohen, 1984).

Intellectual deficits related to Turner syndrome involve spatial and not verbal abilities, but the reverse is the case for triple X. When compared to normal female siblings and agemates, the verbal intelligence of triple X girls is consistently low, and they show delays in speech and language development. School performance in spelling and arithmetic, which depend heavily on verbal memory skills, is particularly affected (Pennington et al., 1982).

Information on the intellectual abilities of children with sex chromosome abnormalities is of particular interest to child development specialists because it can provide insights into biological factors affecting the development of intelligence among normal boys and girls. The verbal deficits found among triple X females are highly similar to those found in XXY boys, who also have an extra X chromosome. Although there are a variety of speculations about why the additional X is related to depression of verbal skills, one popular hypothesis has to do with the relationship of the extra X to rate of physical maturation and brain hemispheric specialization. According to Waber (1976), slow physical maturation is necessary to provide maximum opportunity for the development of the right hemisphere of the brain, where spatial abilities are housed for most individuals. In contrast, fast growth is thought to accentuate early development of verbal abilities in the left hemisphere and to suppress the emergence of right hemispheric spatial skills. The evidence on physical growth of children with sex chromosome abnormalities is consistent with this idea. Despite their ultimately shorter stature, Turner syndrome girls, who do better verbally, have been found to mature physically at a more rapid rate than extra-X children (XXX and XXY), whose stronger mental performance is in spatial ability tasks (Rovet & Netley, 1983). Waber believes that this hypothesis may account for sex differences in mental abilities in the general population, since girls (who mature faster) are advantaged in verbal abilities and boys (who mature more slowly) do better at spatial skills. However, as we shall see later on in Chapter 13, evidence in support of this notion among normal children is mixed and controversial, and additional research is needed to confirm it.

Klinefelter's Syndrome. The inheritance of an extra X chromosome in boys, called *Klinefelter's syndrome,* occurs once in every 500 to 1,000 births. Most XXY boys are not identified until puberty, when incomplete development of the secondary sex characteristics is evident, but hormone therapy can be instituted to remedy this problem. XXY boys are tall, and many of them are also likely to be overweight, to have a body fat distribution resembling that of females, and to show poor muscle development. Nevertheless, they show masculine interests and activities in childhood, develop a normal male gender identity, and as adults most of them marry (although the additional X chromosome almost always results in sterility). Like triple X girls, XXY boys show delays in language development and poorer verbal skills. Otherwise, their only distinguishing behavioral features are a tendency toward shyness, timidity, and low self-esteem — difficulties that probably result from the reactions of others to their physical characteristics. XXY boys have been found to experience problems in relating to peers, particularly around the time of adolescence (Bancroft, Axworthy, & Ratcliffe, 1982). In addition, some parents may communicate disappointment to their son that he is awkward and not athletically inclined. Thus, the personality characteristics associated with Klinefelter's syndrome are best understood as the joint product of constitutional and environmental factors.

XYY Syndrome. This is the most controversial and highly publicized of chromosomal disorders. In the 1960s, it was first suggested that *XYY syndrome* was associated with aggression and antisocial behavior. Although this soon became a widespread popular belief, by the end of the decade scientists had begun to recognize that XYY individuals were being unfairly stigmatized. Early studies concluding that XYY males were dangerous included observations of only a few cases, and they were based on highly select groups of individuals housed in prisons and mental institutions (Hook, 1973). Carefully conducted follow-up research showed that although the incidence of XYYs in penal institutions was greater than their frequency in the general population, these individuals were not among the most violent and physically aggressive inmates. In fact, their crimes were generally less serious than those of many XY prisoners.

In studies of noninstitutionalized XYYs, deviant and aggressive behavior is not a common finding (Jarvik, Klodin, & Matsuyama, 1973; Schaivi et al., 1984). The presence of a Y chromosome may be responsible for increased aggression in males when compared to females. However, normal men vary widely in their aggressive tendencies, so it is reasonable to expect very similar individual differences among XYYs.

Contrary to popular opinion, the most frequent characteristics of XYY males are not violence and criminality, but above-average height, large teeth, and in some cases severe acne. Development of sexual characteristics and fertility are normal. The combined results of nine longitudinal studies in which 59 XYY boys were followed through childhood indicated that their intelligence test performance was not depressed and that the incidence of behavior problems among them was no different from XY controls (Stewart, 1982). Thus, the general belief that below-average intellectual functioning is part of the XYY "syndrome" is not correct. Like the mistaken association of XYY with aggression, it is the unfortunate result of investigations limited to small numbers of XYY men who happen to be found in penal institutions (Witkin et al., 1976).

Fragile X Syndrome. Fragile sites on chromosomes are special spots where abnormal gaps and breaks occur. Recently, the identification of a fragile site in a special place on the X chromosome has been associated with mental retardation as well as with a collection of mild facial deformities, such as large ears and a prominent jaw. *Fragile X syndrome* seems to operate according to X-linked patterns of genetic transmission, so it offers one concrete genetic explanation for why more males than females are mentally retarded. Males who inherit the fragile site generally display its phenotypic effects, while most females have a normal X chromosome to reduce or overcome its consequences. The disorder is estimated to be responsible for 30 to 50 percent of the cases of mental retardation that show X-linked modes of inheritance and to occur with a frequency of nearly 1 in 1,000 male births. It currently ranks second only to Down syndrome as a major chromosomal cause of mental retardation (Carpenter, Leichtman, & Say, 1982). Preliminary research also suggests that it may be associated with infantile autism, a serious emotional disorder of early childhood involving bizarre self-stimulating behavior and delayed or absent language and communication (Brown, Friedman, & Jenkins, 1982).

GENETIC COUNSELING AND PRENATAL DIAGNOSIS

In the past, many couples with genetic disorders in their families chose not to bear a child at all rather than take the risk of giving birth to an abnormal baby. Today, the availability of **genetic counseling** along with advances in prenatal diagnosis help people make informed decisions about the risks involved in conceiving a child or carrying a particular pregnancy to term.

Genetic counselors are persons trained in genetics, interpretation of individual and family histories, and psychological counseling techniques. They help people understand their chances of bearing a child with a genetic disorder and assist them in choosing the best course of action in view of the risks and life goals of those involved. Individuals most likely to seek or be referred for genetic counseling are those who have a history of genetic disorders in their family, have already given birth to an abnormal child, or have experienced reproductive problems such as repeated miscarriages and stillbirths. The genetic counselor interviews the couple and prepares a *pedigree,* a pictorial representation of the family history in which affected relatives are identified and their relationship to others is made clear. The pedigree is examined for *consanguinity*, the extent to which the couple is genetically related through descent from a common ancestor within the last few generations. Consanguinity increases the chances of the homozygous pairing of recessive genes and, therefore, of having offspring with genetic disorders. The pedigree is also used to determine modes of inheritance and to calculate the odds that parents may bear an abnormal child, using the same basic principles of genetic transmission that we discussed earlier. For some genetic disorders, such as hemophilia, Tay-Sachs disease, and sickle cell anemia, whether or not parents are carriers can be directly determined through chromosomal or biochemical analyses. In others, such as cystic fibrosis and Huntington's chorea, this is not yet possible. However, research efforts of geneticists have recently brought them closer to the identification of DNA sequences linked to these diseases, so it may soon be possible to identify individuals at risk and even treat the disorders before their devastating symptoms appear (Clark & Hager, 1986; Pines, 1984).

When all the relevant information is assembled and explained, the genetic counselor helps people consider appropriate options—"taking a chance" and conceiving a child, adoption, artificial insemination, or (as discussed in Box 3.1) new techniques involving test tube fertilization and embryo transfer (Cohen, 1984; Harper, 1981). If individuals who are at risk do decide to have a child, a variety of **prenatal diagnostic methods** are available that permit early detection of some fetal problems that formerly could not be identified prior to birth. Besides a family history of genetic problems, a common reason for prenatal testing is the age of the mother, since women over 35 have an increased chance of bearing children with genetic abnormalities.

The most widely applied technique for diagnosing chromosomal defects prenatally is *amniocentesis*. A hollow needle is inserted through the abdominal wall to obtain a sample of amniotic fluid, and fetal cells are extracted and cultured for chromosomal studies. A major limitation of amniocentesis is that the test cannot be done until sufficient amniotic fluid is available, at 15 to 16 weeks gestation. Since

Box 3.1
Test Tube Fertilization:
A New Frontier

In vitro fertilization refers to the mating of ovum and sperm in a laboratory dish. In 1978, the first test tube baby, Louise Brown, was born to a British couple who spent more than a decade trying to conceive a child. Currently, the demand for the new reproductive technology has become so great that in vitro fertilization clinics have sprung up all around the world and hundreds of test tube babies have been born.

In the method used to create Louise, hormones stimulate the ripening of reproductive cells in the mother's ovaries. Then they are extracted through a delicate surgical process and placed in a dish of nutrients, to which sperm are added. Once an ovum is fertilized and begins to divide into several cells, it is injected into the mother's uterus where, hopefully, it will grow and develop.

In vitro fertilization is a last resort for many couples who have tried unsuccessfully to have a child. It has been used most often to treat infertility in women whose fallopian tubes are blocked or scarred and cannot be surgically repaired. While only 20 percent of couples who try in vitro fertilization successfully achieve a pregnancy, the results have been encouraging enough so that the method is currently being expanded to treat a variety of reproductive problems. When husband or wife cannot supply an adequate sperm or ovum, a donor's can be used. By "mixing and matching" the cells of donors and recipients, pregnancies can be brought about in instances where the gamete-producing organs of either husband or wife do not function or where one of them is known to carry a genetic disease. In the most controversial variations of the new technology, "surrogate mothers" can be used to bear a couple's child if the mother has experienced repeated spontaneous abortions. Or, fertilized ova can be frozen and stored in embryo banks early in marriage for use at some future time, allowing childbearing by older mothers without increased risk of genetic defects such as Down syndrome. The creation of embryo banks also makes possible "embryo adoption" if genetic parents are willing to provide sterile couples with frozen embryos.

Although in vitro techniques offer new hope to couples who would otherwise remain childless, public reaction to them has been mixed. The procedures raise many sensitive ethical questions, and some believe they mark the beginning of a Brave New World come true. Doctors wish to do research on human in vitro embryos in hopes of improving the chances of successful pregnancies. They also believe such research may eventually lead to ways of detecting and repairing genetic defects during the earliest possible stages of development. Nevertheless, the in vitro field is so politically and ethically sensitive that a ban on federal funding to support research has existed since 1975. In response to the ban, doctors argue that they are obliged to provide the best possible medical treatment to individuals with all kinds of afflictions, and that the cloud of suspicion hanging over in vitro research works against people with infertility.

Sources: Gold, 1985; Grobstein, Flower, & Mendeloff, 1983.

several more weeks are required to culture the cells, the decision to terminate pregnancy must be delayed until 18 weeks gestation or later. *Chorionic villi biopsy* is a relatively new approach that may soon replace amniocentesis, for it can be performed by 6 to 8 weeks gestation, and results are available immediately. In this procedure, a small plug of tissue is removed from the end of one or more chorionic villi, the hairlike projections on the membrane surrounding the embryo. The cells obtained are then subjected to chromosomal analysis. In both amniocentesis and chorionic villi biopsy, *ultrasound* is used to guide the extraction of fetal material. High-frequency sound waves are beamed at the uterus, and their reflection is translated into a picture that reveals the size, shape, and placement of the fetus. Ultrasound is also used to support another technique called *fetoscopy*. Between 18 and 22 weeks gestation, a small tube with a light source at one end can be inserted into the uterus to inspect the fetus for malformations of the limbs and face. In addition, fetoscopy allows a sample of fetal blood from the placenta or umbilical cord to be obtained, permitting prenatal diagnosis of such disorders as hemophilia and sickle cell anemia. Besides its combination with other prenatal diagnostic techniques, ultrasound is frequently used by itself to estimate gestational age, monitor fetal growth, and detect gross structural abnormalities (Kolata, 1983b).

Technological advances in prenatal diagnosis have led to remarkable developments in fetal medicine. Today, some medical problems can be treated before birth. For example, drug therapy has been introduced to treat some genetically transmitted metabolic defects, and surgery in utero has been performed to correct such problems as urinary tract obstructions and neural defects (Kolata, 1983a). Medical and surgical interventions like these promise new hope for fetuses that otherwise would have little or no chance of survival.

If prenatal diagnosis reveals the fetus to have an abnormal condition that cannot be corrected, parents are faced with the very difficult choice of whether or not to have an abortion. The decision to terminate a pregnancy is anguishing for virtually all who have to make it. Parents must deal with the emotional shock of the news and make a decision within a very short period of time. If they choose to have an abortion, they face the grief that comes with having lost a wanted child, worries about future pregnancies, and ambivalence and guilt about the abortion itself. Fortunately, 95 percent of fetuses examined through prenatal diagnosis are perfectly normal (Borg & Lasker, 1981). Because modern medicine makes such tests possible, many individuals whose age or family history would have caused them to avoid pregnancy entirely are now able to have healthy children.

PRENATAL DEVELOPMENT

The sperm and ovum that will unite to form the new individual are uniquely suited for the task of reproduction. The ovum is a tiny sphere, measuring 1/175 of an inch in diameter, that is as barely visible to the naked eye as a dot the size of the period at the end of this sentence. Nevertheless, in its microscopic world it is a giant. It has been estimated that enough ova to populate the world would fit in a top hat. In contrast, the sperm are much tinier, measuring but 1/500 of an inch. The world's population of sperm would fill only a thimble. In the middle of a woman's menstrual cycle, the ovum matures. Surrounded by thousands of nurse cells that will nourish it along its path, the ovum ruptures from the ovary and is drawn into one of the two fallopian tubes, long, thin structures that convey the ovum from the ovaries to the uterus (see Figure 3.5). The ruptured ovarian follicle or cavity, now known as the *corpus luteum*, begins to secrete hormones that prepare the lining of the uterus for implantation of a fertilized ovum. If pregnancy does not occur, the corpus luteum shrinks, and the lining of the uterus is discarded in two weeks with menstruation (Rugh & Shettles, 1971).

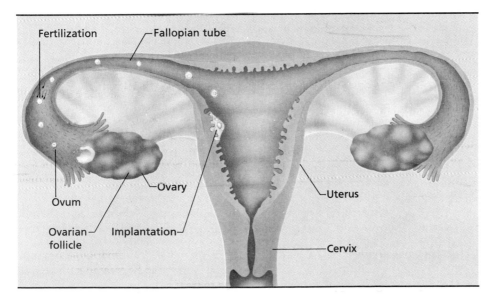

Fertilization   Fallopian tube

Ovum

Ovary

Ovarian   Implantation
follicle

Uterus

Cervix

Figure 3.5. Journey of the ovum toward the uterus after its release from the ovarian follicle.

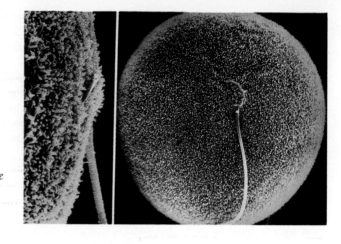

Fertilization occurs when sperm and ovum unite in the fallopian tube. (D. W. Fawcett/D. Phillips/Photo Researchers)

The sperm are produced in profuse numbers, at a rate of 300 million a day. In the final process of maturation, they develop a tail permitting them to swim long distances, upstream through the female reproductive tract and into the fallopian tube where fertilization takes place. The journey is arduous. Of the 360 million sperm released in a single ejaculation, only a hundred or so reach the vicinity of the ovum, if one happens to be there. The sperm have an average life of 48 hours and therefore can lie in wait for the ovum for up to two days, while the ovum survives for up to 24 hours. Thus, the maximum fertile period during each monthly cycle is about 72 hours long (Nilsson, 1977).

Timing of intercourse during this 72-hour period affects the chances that parents will conceive a boy or a girl. Recall that males produce sperm bearing either an X (female) or a Y (male) chromosome. Besides chromosomal makeup, the two types of sperm also differ in size, speed, and hardiness. The smaller, more compact Y sperm move faster but are less resistant to the acidity of the female reproductive tract prior to ovulation. The larger, less delicate X sperm travel more slowly, but they are better able to withstand the acidity of the reproductive environment. Intercourse a day or more in advance of ovulation leads the less resistant Y-bearing sperm to be eliminated in large numbers. As a result, a greater proportion of the X variety lie in wait as the egg is released, increasing the odds of conceiving a girl. In contrast, intercourse at or near the moment of ovulation is more likely to produce a boy. Around the time the ovum is released, the reproductive tract becomes more alkaline. This enhances the survival rate of the Y-bearing sperm, which move swiftly toward the egg (Shettles, 1970).

As far back as the time of Aristotle, husbands and wives have wanted to preselect the sex of their offspring. Today, new techniques for pinpointing the time of ovulation enable couples to increase their chances of conceiving a child of the preferred sex (Shettles & Rorvik, 1984). However, dissemination of information about these methods by representatives of the scientific community has provoked serious moral debate. According to the most recent survey evidence available, more people prefer their firstborn child to be a boy (Coombs, 1977). Critics of sex selection methods worry that this pro-male bias could lead to a serious imbalance in the ratio of male to female births. Proponents respond that because many people wish their second child to be a girl, a balanced ratio of males to females would ensue. They also argue that use of the techniques would increase the chances that a child born of either sex will be a desired child. The ethical controversy will undoubtedly continue as scientific methods for controlling the sex of offspring undergo further refinement and become more widely known.

With fertilization and the formation of the zygote, the story of prenatal development begins to unfold. Although prenatal growth is a continuous, 9-month process, the dramatic changes that transform the one-celled zygote into a complex, differentiated organism comprised of trillions of cells are best understood in terms of three periods of development: the period of the zygote (sometimes called the germinal period), the period of the embryo, and the period of the fetus. These distinctions are useful in two ways: (1) for organizing individual growth and (2) for understanding the impact of environmental agents on the developing person.

The Period of the Zygote

This period lasts approximately 2 weeks, from fertilization until the first tiny mass of cells attaches itself to the wall of the uterus and becomes deeply embedded in the uterine lining. Thirty-six hours after fertilization, the zygote has undergone its first cell duplication by the process of mitosis. Occasionally the first two cells produced separate completely and give rise to two individuals, called **identical** or **monozygotic twins** because they develop from a single zygote and have identical genetic blueprints. **Fraternal** or **dizygotic twins** are the result of the ripening and release of two ova from the mother's ovaries. If each is fertilized, two offspring develop who are genetically no more alike than ordinary siblings.

While the first cell division of the zygote takes many hours, each successive one occurs with increasing rapidity. By the end of the fourth day, 60 to 70 cells exist, and they have begun to differentiate into separate structures. The mass of cells, now known as a *blastocyst,* begins to form a hollow sphere around a fluid-filled cavity. An inner cell mass projecting into the cavity forms the *embryonic disk,* which will become the new individual. The rest of the cells will provide protective covering. Seven to 9 days after conception, the blastocyst bores into the uterine lining. Engulfed by the mother's nourishing blood, the cell mass begins to grow at a much more astounding rate. At first, the protective outer layers grow more rapidly than the embryonic disk. An inner membrane, the *amnion,* is formed, which encases the baby in amniotic fluid, helping to keep the temperature of the prenatal environment constant and cushioning the organism against any jolt the mother might suffer. Additional protection is provided by an outer membrane, called the *chorion,* which, along with its fingerlike villi, has appeared by the end of the second week (Moore, 1983). A *yolk sac* emerges and begins to produce blood cells for the embryo until its liver, spleen, and bone marrow are mature enough to take over this process independently. By the second month, the yolk sac is no longer needed and disappears.

As soon as implantation takes place, the **placenta** begins to form as chorionic villi burrow into the uterine wall. The villi rupture uterine capillaries, and maternal blood is freed to circulate in spaces around the villi. In each villus are blood vessels that send nutrients and oxygen to the embryo and take away waste products to be excreted by the mother. A semipermeable placental membrane forms through which these substances are exchanged but which, at the same time, keeps the maternal and fetal blood from directly mixing with one another. The placenta is connected to the developing organism by the **umbilical cord** (in the period of the zygote it first appears as a primitive body stalk). The umbilical cord contains one vein that delivers blood loaded with nutrients and two arteries that remove waste products, and during the course of pregnancy it grows to a length of from 1 to 3 feet. The force and volume of blood flowing through the cord keeps it taut, much like a garden hose, so that it seldom tangles or forms knots while the developing baby, like a spacewalking astronaut, floats freely in its fluid-filled chamber (Rugh & Shettles, 1971).

By the end of the period of the zygote, the primitive organism has already found food and shelter by submerging itself in the uterine lining. Though it does not yet resemble a human being, it has begun to grow and differentiate in earnest. These momentous beginnings take place before all but the most sensitive mother even knows that she is pregnant.

The Period of the Embryo

From implantation to 8 weeks gestation, the developing organism is called an **embryo.** During this brief 6 weeks, the most rapid and dramatic changes in prenatal development take place. In the embryonic period, the groundwork for all of the bodily structures and internal systems is laid down, and at the conclusion of this phase, the organism is human in form and shows signs of beginning movements.

By the middle of the first month, the embryonic disk folds over to form three layers of cells — the *ectoderm,* from which will emerge the nervous system, outer skin, hair and sweat glands; the *mesoderm,* which will form the deeper layers of skin, the muscles, skeleton, circulatory system, and a variety of internal organs and connective tissue; and the *endoderm,* which will differentiate into the digestive system, lungs, urinary tract, and internal glands. Thus, the three layers give rise to all of the tissues and organs of the body. At first, the emphasis is on development of the nervous system, although other organs begin to form at the same time. The ectoderm folds over to form a neural tube or primitive spinal cord, the top of which swells to form a brain, and nerve fibers begin to emerge along with the rudiments of the embryo's eyes. While the nervous system is developing, a primitive heart begins to pump blood around the embryo's circulatory system, and the beginnings of basic muscles, vertebrae, ribs, and digestive organs appear. At the end of the first month, the curled embryo consists of millions of intricately organized groups of cells with specific functions, although it is only a fourth of an inch long. Most of this length is taken up by the head and upper region of the body, since the brain and heart develop sooner than the other organs. A rudimentary tail (an extension of the spinal column) and primitive gill arches (like those found in fish and tadpoles) are present as vestiges of our primordial past, but they soon disappear.

In the second month, growth and differentiation continue rapidly. The eyes, ears, nasal organs, and jaw form, so that the face is clearly human and no longer resembles the embryos of a variety of other developing species. Protruding buds gradually become arms, legs, fingers, and toes. Internal organs are more distinct: the intestines grow, the heart develops separate chambers, the kidneys and genital and eliminative passages appear, and the liver takes over the manufacture of blood cells so that the yolk sac is no longer needed. The head continues to enlarge, and a distinct neck is formed. Skeletal growth and changing bodily proportions lead the embryo's posture to be more upright. By the end of the second month, the major muscle groups have developed, and some movements are possible, although they are still too light to be felt by the mother. Although only an inch long and one-seventh of an ounce in weight, the developing organism is now human in form. Growth in size must occur and details must be perfected, but everything is present that will be found in the newborn infant, and the threshold has been crossed between embryo and fetus (Nilsson, 1977; Rugh & Shettles, 1971).

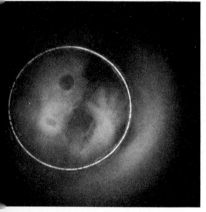

This embryo, which is approximately six weeks old, has developed the protruding buds that will become arms, legs, fingers, and toes. (Alexander Tsiaras/Science Source/Photo Researchers)

The Period of the Fetus

Lasting until the end of pregnancy, this longest prenatal phase is the "growth and finishing period" for the new organism. Now called a **fetus,** the organism has already safely formed many of its vital parts. As a result, by the beginning of the third month it is far less vulnerable than it was as an embryo to the effects of damaging environmental influences, such as drugs, disease, and radiation. In addition, the organism is now larger in size, so it takes far greater doses of some toxic agents to injure the fetal constitution than it did in the earlier months. As shown in Figure 3.6, the rate of body growth during the fetal period is extraordinary, especially from the ninth to the twentieth week (Moore, 1983).

In the third month the newly differentiated organs, muscles, and nervous system start to become organized and interconnected. The brain signals, and in response the

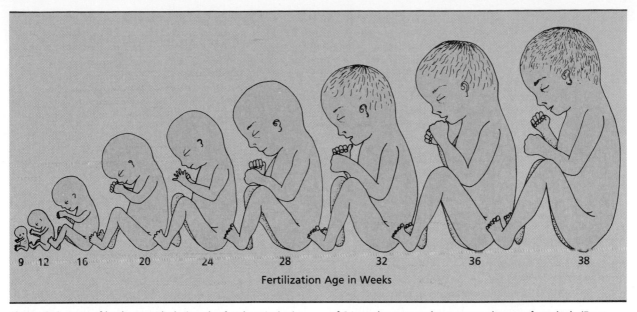

Figure 3.6. Rate of body growth during the fetal period. The drawings are about one-fifth actual size. The average duration of pregnancy is 38 weeks from fertilization. Premature infants of 24 weeks or more have some chance of survival. *(From K. L. Moore, 1983,* Before We Are Born *(2nd ed.), Philadelphia: Saunders. P. 68. Reprinted by permission.)*

fetus kicks, bends its arms, forms a fist, curls its toes, and grimaces by squinting, frowning, and opening its mouth. The primitive lungs begin to expand and contract in an early rehearsal of breathing movements. The external genitalia become increasingly refined, so that the sex of the baby is distinguishable externally by the twelfth week. Finishing touches appear — fingernails, toenails, hair follicles, tooth buds, and eyelids that open and close. The fetal heartbeat is now stronger and can be heard through a stethoscope.

Prenatal development is often divided into three trimesters. At the end of the third month the first trimester is complete.

The Second Trimester. By the middle of the second trimester, between 17 and 20 weeks of age, the fetus has lengthened sufficiently so that its movement — at first a tiny flutter and later a firm kick or turn of the entire body — can be felt by the mother. The body of the fetus is now covered with a white cheeselike substance called *vernix,*

At about 20 weeks, this fetus looks distinctly human and can move about within the uterus. (Petit Format/Nestle/ Science Source/Photo Researchers)

which protects the skin from chapping and hardening as a result of the long months spent bathing in the amniotic fluid. A white, downy hair covering called *lanugo* appears over the entire body and helps the vernix stick to the skin. By the end of the second trimester almost all the fetal organs are so well developed that one might wonder why the 1½-pound infant, if born prematurely, cannot yet survive. The reason is that the lungs, although structurally formed, are still quite immature, and the central nervous system has not yet developed to the point where it can control breathing movements and body temperature (Moore, 1983).

The Third Trimester. This final trimester of development differs from the previous six months in that now the fetus, if born prematurely, has a chance for survival — a probability that improves with each successive day that the baby remains in the uterus. If born between the seventh and eighth months, breathing would still be a problem and oxygen assistance necessary, not because the respiratory center of the brain is poorly developed, but because the alveoli (tiny air sacs) in the lungs are not yet ready to inflate and exchange oxygen for carbon dioxide.

The brain makes tremendous strides during this final phase of fetal development. The cortex, seat of human intelligence, enlarges, and its convolutions, wrinkles, and crevices continue to form. At the same time, the fetus becomes increasingly responsive to external stimuli — the sudden whir of the electric mixer, the vibrating washing machine, the sound of the mother's voice. In one clever study, newborns were found to recognize and prefer unique auditory stimulation to which they were exposed in the last few weeks before birth. A researcher had mothers-to-be read Dr. Seuss's lively poem "The Cat in the Hat" to their unborn children twice a day for the last 6 weeks of their pregnancies. When the babies were born, they were given a nipple to suck on, an activity that permitted them to control the sound on a tape recorder. One pattern of sucking activated a tape of the mother reading "The Cat in the Hat," while another produced the mother's rendition of a different rhyming story. The babies quickly varied their sucking to get "The Cat in the Hat." They had apparently learned to prefer it while still in the womb (DeCasper & Fifer, as reported by Kolata, 1984).

During the last trimester the fetus gains 5 pounds and grows 7 inches. As a result, the rapidly enlarging baby now finds it difficult to move about in the confines of the uterus and becomes increasingly less active as the end of the prenatal phase approaches. In the eighth month, a layer of fat begins to be deposited under the skin to assist with temperature regulation after birth, and in the last month the baby acquires antibodies from the mother's blood, granting it temporary protection from illnesses that could be dangerous to the newborn (its own immune system does not function effectively until several months after birth). In the final weeks, most babies assume an upside-down position, partly due to the shape of the uterus and because the baby's head is heavier than its feet. Growth starts to slow as the placenta begins to degenerate rather than develop further, and birth is imminent (Moore, 1983).

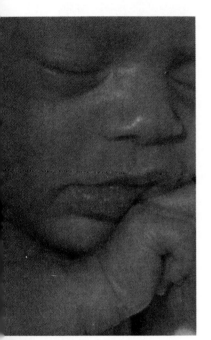

This fetus looks like a sleeping newborn. During the final weeks of gestation, a layer of fat is laid down in preparation for life outside the warm, protective womb. (Petit Format/Nestle/Science Source/Photo Researchers)

PRENATAL ENVIRONMENTAL INFLUENCES

Teratogens

In the first half of this century, it was commonly believed that the unborn child, safely cradled in the mother's uterus and surrounded by her protective body, was completely shielded from the adversities of the environment, and all deviations from normal development were attributed to the genes. However, the increasing medical use of X-rays in the 1920s and 1930s led to a growing realization that the structures and functions of the fetus could be profoundly damaged by environmental agents. In the 1940s, it was established that maternal rubella (German measles) during the first 3 months of pregnancy was associated with a variety of physical defects in the newborn infant. The 1960s brought the shocking demonstration that a tranquilizer called thalidomide, made available with the best intentions for benefit of the mother, could have disastrous consequences for the unborn child (Wilson, 1973).

The term **teratogen** refers to environmental agents that cause damage during the prenatal period. The modern science of teratology has revealed that the consequences of toxic environmental agents for the unborn child are complex and varied. Effects depend on such factors as amount and length of exposure, combination with other teratogenic and environmental agents, and the genetic constitution of the mother and fetus, which affects their ability to withstand the harmful influence. The developmental impact of teratogenic agents is further complicated by the fact that, whereas physical deformities are easy enough to notice, important behavioral consequences may be harder to identify, not be evident until later in development, or may occur as the indirect result of physical damage. For example, a gross anatomical defect resulting from the mother's ingestion of drugs during the prenatal period will undoubtedly affect parent-child interaction, peer relations, and exploration of the environment during childhood. These, in turn, can have consequences for a broad range of cognitive, social, and emotional behaviors (Stechler & Halton, 1982).

In addition, the effects of teratogenic influences depend on the age of the embryo or fetus at the time of exposure. We can best understand this if we conceive of the prenatal phase of development as a sequence of carefully timed **critical periods,** or moments when bodily structures are developing most rapidly and are therefore acutely sensitive to both facilitating and disruptive environmental influences. Figure 3.7 provides a schematic summary of prenatal critical periods. It shows that they vary from one organ or tissue to another, depending on timing and duration of development. Some structures, such as the brain and eye, have long critical periods that extend throughout the embryonic and fetal stages of growth, while others, such as the limbs and palate, are of more restricted duration. Figure 3.7 also indicates that some general statements can be made about the effect of teratogens during prenatal growth. During the period of the zygote, before implantation, the organism is rarely influenced by teratogens. When it is, the primitive mass of cells is so completely affected that the result is usually death and spontaneous abortion. The embryonic period of development is the time of maximum susceptibility to environmental influences. During this period the foundations for all essential body systems are rapidly emerging, and teratogens generally produce gross structural abnormalities. The fetal period involves growth toward the size and bodily proportions of the newborn infant, along with some completion of body systems. When teratogenic agents interfere, the result is often minor structural alterations, although some organs, such as the central nervous system and genitals, can still be strongly affected. Now let's consider what is known about a variety of teratogenic agents.

Drugs. Almost any agent dissolved in the mother's bloodstream can pass to the developing organism, although the placenta offers some protection by slowing the transfer of substances so that the maternal system has a chance to break them down and reduce their concentration (Wilson, 1973). A tragic lesson was learned from the drug thalidomide, an over-the-counter sedative widely available in Canada and Europe in the early 1960s that is now regarded as a classic example of a teratogenic agent. Thalidomide showed that the human embryo can be extraordinarily sensitive to a substance that reveals little or no harmful effects when given to human adults or test animals typically employed in teratogenic research. When ingested by mothers between the 21st and 36th days after conception, thalidomide produced gross deformities of the embryo's arms, legs, and ears (Heinonen, Slone, & Shapiro, 1977). The coincidence of thousands of infants born with these malformations and the widespread distribution of thalidomide in Europe led to the discovery of its teratogenic effects.

Despite the bitter lesson of thalidomide, pregnant women continue to take a wide variety of drugs, including aspirin, sleeping pills, caffeine, vitamins, iron, and more. In one study it was found that 65 percent took self-prescribed drugs, and when physi-

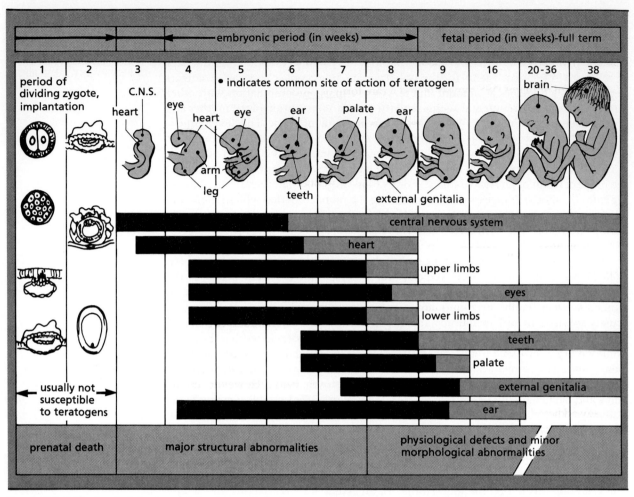

Figure 3.7. Critical periods in prenatal development. Each organ or structure has a critical period during which its development may be disturbed. Black indicates highly sensitive periods; pink indicates periods that are less sensitive to teratogens. *(From K. L. Moore, 1983, Before We Are Born (2nd ed.), Philadelphia: Saunders. P. 111. Reprinted by permission.)*

cian-prescribed medications were also considered, the total number of drugs taken by mothers during pregnancy ranged from 3 to 29, with an average of 10.3 (Hill, 1973). Among commonly used drugs, aspirin has been linked to a variety of physical deformities in the embryo, and caffeine has been associated with prematurity, spontaneous abortion, and early induction of labor (Collins, 1981; Rosenberg et al., 1982). However, the findings on these and many other drugs are actually ambiguous. Because mothers often take multiple drugs, it is difficult to evaluate their independent effects, and dosage level is highly relevant. As a result, we know little that is definite about the prenatal consequences of a wide variety of over-the-counter medications.

Hormones. During normal prenatal development, the organism secretes hormones that affect the development of the reproductive system. The presence of androgens (male sex hormones) influences the development of the male structures, while its absence leads to the emergence of female reproductive organs. Irregularities and imbalances in the quantities of hormones available prenatally lead to structural abnormalities of the genital organs as well as other defects. For example, exposure of the embryo to oral contraceptives, which may occur in the early weeks when the mother is not aware she is pregnant, has been associated with cardiovascular problems and limb deformities.

Between 1945 and 1970, a synthetic estrogen, diethylstilbestrol (DES), was widely used to prevent miscarriages in women who had a history of spontaneous abortion. As the female offspring of these mothers reached adolescence, the relationship between prenatal DES exposure and a rare form of cancer of the vagina became apparent. It was later discovered that DES causes abnormal development of the vaginal cells during the prenatal period. In one study, 70 percent of female neonates exposed to DES were found to have the abnormal cells, in comparison to only 4 percent of unexposed infants (Johnson et al., 1979). Although it is estimated that there may be millions of DES-exposed daughters, only a small number—1 out of every 700 to 7,000—eventually develop cancer (Orenberg, 1981). However, the long-term impact of the hormone is also manifested in other ways. When DES daughters bear children themselves, their pregnancies are significantly more likely to lead to spontaneous abortion (Barnes et al., 1980). In addition, DES-exposed sons are not left unaffected. Research shows that they are subject to a variety of genital abnormalities as well as an increased risk of testicular cancer (Herbst, 1981; Stenchever et al., 1981; Stillman, 1982).

Narcotics. Cocaine and marijuana severely damage the offspring of pregnant animals, but the human evidence on these agents is not yet clear (Samuels & Samuels, 1986). In contrast, infants of heroin addicted mothers are known to be at risk for a wide variety of problems, including premature birth, physical malformations, respiratory distress, and increased mortality at birth. Substitute use of methadone reduces the incidence of many of these complications (Cushner, 1981). However, infants exposed prenatally to either heroin or methadone become, like their mothers, physiologically addicted, and they exhibit withdrawal symptoms at birth, including tremors, vomiting, fever, and a shrill cry (Zelson, Lee, & Casalino, 1973). The symptoms disappear in the first few months of life, but in the meantime these mothers are likely to have a very difficult time coping with the jittery and irritable behavior of their babies, especially since the mothers have many problems of their own (Stechler & Halton, 1982).

Smoking. While the prevalence of smoking among men has recently declined from 53 to 38 percent, it has remained unchanged among women, at 30 percent, and the number of women identified as heavy smokers has increased (Merritt, 1981). There is now abundant evidence that maternal smoking is related to a variety of serious consequences for the fetus and newborn child, including decreased birth weight and size (prenatal growth retardation), a higher incidence of spontaneous abortion, and increased death rate in the period surrounding birth. Cigarette smoking has also been linked to cleft lip and palate as well as other congenital malformations (U.S. Department of Health and Human Services, 1980), although these associations are controversial and remain to be confirmed (Finnegan, 1985)

In addition, newborn babies of smoking mothers show slight behavioral differences when compared to those of nonsmoking mothers in that they seem less responsive to the surrounding environment. For example, they will turn to the sound of an auditory stimulus (such as the jingle of a bell) more slowly, and they will *habituate,* or stop responding to it more rapidly than the average infant (Picone et al., 1980). Infants of smoking mothers also cry more during neonatal examinations (Woodson et al., 1980). As we mentioned earlier, behavioral deficits like these can negatively influence the adjustment of newborn babies to their physical and social surroundings and may be the beginning of a spiraling incidence of problems extending into childhood. In one study, 4-year-old children of mothers who smoked during pregnancy showed poorer attention to a picture recognition task than did controls (Streissguth et al., 1984). A long-term follow-up of children born to mothers who smoked over ten cigarettes a day revealed that they scored lower on intelligence and achievement measures during the elementary school years, and they also remained slightly shorter in stature (Butler & Goldstein, 1973). However, a more recent investigation was unable to replicate these findings (Lefkowitz, 1981), and lasting consequences of maternal smoking are still uncertain.

Why do unfavorable outcomes appear in babies of mothers who smoke? Studies of maternal blood supply and placental functioning show that smoking reduces the amount of oxygen that is available to the fetus. Because of increased tissue demands for oxygen, smoking leads to a rise in maternal blood pressure and fetal heart rate. However, these physiological adjustments by both mother and infant are not powerful enough to overcome the toxic effects of nicotine. Examination of the placentas of mothers who smoke reveals structural abnormalities and reduced maternal blood flow, problems believed to cause the prenatal growth retardation and increased mortality experienced by their babies (Cushner, 1981).

The more cigarettes smoked by a mother during pregnancy, the greater the chance of adverse outcomes for the fetus. But smoking mothers gain less weight during pregnancy than their nonsmoking counterparts, and the decreased weight gain is also correlated with the number of cigarettes smoked. Because smoking and maternal weight gain are related to one another, some investigators have suggested that mothers who smoke may not eat very well, and inadequate nutrition may be the real cause of the prenatal problems associated with smoking, rather than the smoking itself. However, the results of one study in which data on over 50,000 births were examined suggest that tobacco is, in fact, a causal agent. At every level of maternal weight gain between 5 and 40 pounds, smoking was strongly associated with an increased incidence of fetal growth retardation (Meyer, 1978). After reviewing the findings of hundreds of investigations, the United States Surgeon General concluded that ". . . maternal smoking directly retards the rate of fetal growth and increases the risk of spontaneous abortion, of fetal death, and of neonatal death in otherwise normal infants" (U.S. Department of Health, Education and Welfare, 1979, p. ix).

Alcohol. A specific cluster of abnormalities appearing frequently in the offspring of alcohol-abusing mothers was described and named *fetal alcohol syndrome (FAS)* by Jones and his collaborators in 1973. Since then, numerous research studies have confirmed that heavy prenatal alcohol consumption produces a severe and complex set of handicaps for children. Among the distinguishing features of this disorder are prenatal and postnatal growth retardation and a particular pattern of facial abnormalities, including widely spaced eyes, short eyelid openings, a small up-turned nose, thin upper lip, and minor ear deformities. Sometimes affected children show a variety of other physical problems as well, including cleft lip and palate and defects of the skeleton and internal organs (Hill & Stern, 1979). The fetal brain seems to be highly sensitive to damage from alcohol. Microcephaly (a small, underdeveloped brain) occurs in 80 percent of children with FAS, and most are mentally retarded, with average intelligence test scores of about 65 or 70. Behavior problems appear in infancy, and they persist into childhood, the most common of which are irritability and hyperactivity (Aronson et al., 1985).

A number of research studies reveal that children with the most severely affected physical features are also those who show the lowest intelligence test scores, findings that strongly suggest that alcohol underlies both sets of handicaps (Iosub et al., 1981). Also, the risk of abnormalities is twice as great in heavy as opposed to moderate drinkers. Many alcoholic mothers are heavy smokers and have drug histories, and their nutritional intake is often inadequate. However, when these prenatal factors are separated from alcohol and controlled in animal research, alcohol remains a powerful teratogenic agent (Streissguth et al., 1980).

How much alcohol consumption is safe during pregnancy? Is it all right to have just one drink, either on a daily basis or every once in a while? Answers to these questions are not yet clear, and so far no minimum safe level of prenatal alcohol consumption has been established. For this reason, the United States Surgeon General has advised pregnant women to abstain from alcohol entirely and to be conscious of the alcohol content in food and drugs (Surgeon General's Advisory on Alcohol and Pregnancy, 1981).

Radiation. In addition to its mutagenic consequences discussed earlier in this chapter, high doses of radiation have been associated with severe damage to the developing embryo and fetus, including spontaneous abortion, microcephaly, and gross structural malformations, particularly of the skeleton, genitals, and eyes. For a variety of medical reasons, approximately 1 percent of all pregnant women are given X-rays during their first trimester of pregnancy, often without knowledge of the fact that they are actually pregnant (Mossman & Hill, 1982). Since the dosage levels are low, the specific hazards of X-rays are still unsettled, but no amount of radiation can really be considered safe. Even if the child appears normal at birth, the possibility of problems developing later on is not ruled out. Researchers believe that low-level radiation increases the risk of childhood cancer and that it may damage developing brain cells that will not be replaced (Brent, 1983; Fabrikant, 1983).

Environmental Pollution. Pollution of the air we breathe, the water we drink, and the food we eat involves risk for people in general, and also for the fetus. The number of potentially dangerous chemicals in the environment is astounding. Roughly 100,000 are in common use in the United States, and 1,000 additional ones are introduced each year. The teratogenic impact on the human organism of only a small fraction of them is known, although many more have been found to cross the placenta and to cause major birth defects in animals. Mercury, lead, and dioxins (highly toxic chemicals frequently found in herbicides, fertilizers, and wood preservatives) are established teratogens that cause increased rates of spontaneous abortion and structural abnormalities. Of those chemicals that commonly pollute the air, carbon monoxide is thought to present one of the greatest hazards. In some urban areas and near some industrial plants, it reaches blood concentration levels comparable to the effect of smoking a package of cigarettes a day (Longo, 1980).

In view of the sensitivity of the human fetus to these agents, pregnant women should do what they can to avoid exposure to all hazardous chemicals. Although the control of pollution in the larger environment rests in the hands of legislators and environmental engineers, women can still do a great deal to assure healthier immediate surroundings for their unborn infants. Those in occupations involving exposure to toxic chemicals should switch assignments or stop work early in pregnancy. A pregnant mother who decides to refinish baby furniture in her garage comes into contact with chemical levels thousands of times greater than is considered occupationally

Some environmental agents that damage the developing fetus have been traced to toxic waste dumps and other sources of environmental pollution. (Environmental Protection Agency)

safe by the federal government. When she permits her garden to be sprayed with pesticides, she may be exposed to higher chemical concentrations than most farmworkers (Samuels & Samuels, 1986).

Maternal Disease. Most diseases that cause prenatal defects are viruses, probably because the majority of other disease-producing microorganisms are so toxic to the embryo that they usually cause spontaneous abortion rather than malformations. Viral infections occur in about 5 percent of all pregnancies. Although most exert no effect, a few can cause serious damage and pose a significant danger to the child before birth.

Mothers contracting rubella (3-day, or German measles) during the first trimester of pregnancy often give birth to babies with heart and eye defects and who suffer from permanent hearing loss. Recently, central nervous system damage and a variety of other physical abnormalities have been added to this "congenital rubella syndrome" (Sever, 1982). The virus clearly operates according to the critical period principle. The risk of eye and heart malformations is greatest in the first 8 weeks of pregnancy, while deafness is most likely to result if the mother contracts the illness between 5 and 15 weeks (see Figure 3.7). The consequences of infection during the last two trimesters of pregnancy are not clear, although there are some reports of minor physical defects. Since development of the rubella vaccine in 1966, the number of prenatal cases in the United States has dropped dramatically. Still, 25 to 30 percent of women of childbearing age lack the rubella antibody, and some pregnant women who contract the disease do not recognize that they have it, since it can occur without the usually expected rash (Cohen, 1984).

The harmful impact of other common viruses is summarized in Table 3.2. The developing organism is particularly sensitive to the family of herpes viruses, for which there is no vaccine or treatment. Cytomegalovirus, a form of herpes that affects

Table 3.2. Effects of Some Infectious Diseases During Pregnancy

| | EFFECTS | | |
DISEASE	INCREASED SPONTANEOUS ABORTION	PHYSICAL MALFORMATIONS	PREMATURITY OR PRENATAL GROWTH RETARDATION
Viral			
Cytomegalovirus	+	+	+
Rubella	+	+	+
Chicken pox	0	+	+
Herpes simplex 2	+	+	+
Mumps	+	?	0
Rubeola (red measles)	+	0	+
Bacterial			
Syphilis	+	+	?
Tuberculosis	+	?	+
Parasitic			
Malaria	+	0	+
Toxoplasmosis	+	+	+

+ = established finding   0 = no present evidence   ? = possible effect which is not clearly established

From *Clinical Genetics in Nursing Practice* (p. 16) by F. L. Cohen, 1984, Philadelphia: Lippincott. Reprinted by permission.

the salivary glands and may remain latent for years, only to be reactivated during pregnancy, is said to be the most frequent cause of fetal infection, invading 0.3 to 0.5 percent of all fetuses and 1 to 2 percent of infants during the birth process. Herpes simplex 2, one of the most common sexually transmitted diseases in the United States, can also infect the fetus either prenatally or during birth. The herpes viruses are associated with a wide variety of congenital malformations. Because they attack the central nervous system, the long-term consequences for child development, including mental retardation and learning problems during the school years, are only beginning to be appreciated (Samuels & Samuels, 1986).

Also listed in Table 3.2 are several bacterial and parasitic infections. Among the most common is toxoplasmosis, acquired from eating raw or undercooked meat or from contact with infected cats. Toxoplasmosis has been linked to eye and central nervous system damage during the first trimester (Marcus, 1983). In view of what we now know about the disease, advice to pregnant women that they not eat red meat, or that they avoid direct contact with cats, should not be dismissed as an old wives' tale.

A relatively new illness that is rapidly spreading among certain groups of the American population is acquired immune deficiency syndrome (AIDS). Recent research reveals that, like other viruses, the AIDS virus can be transmitted across the placental barrier to the fetus, and offspring of mothers who carry the virus are at serious risk for contracting the disease. You can read more about the prenatal transmission of AIDS in Box 3.2.

FOCUS ON CONTEMPORARY ISSUES

Box 3.2
AIDS and Prenatal Development

AIDS is a relatively new viral disease that is rapidly increasing among certain sectors of the American population. The AIDS virus ravages the immune system. Afflicted individuals eventually die of a variety of intractable illnesses that invade and destroy the body. Groups at high risk for contracting AIDS are male homosexuals and bisexuals, intravenous drug abusers, and heterosexual partners of these individuals. Transfer of body fluids from one person to another, either directly or through use of contaminated needles, must take place in order for the disease to spread.

According to the U.S. Centers for Disease Control, more than 50,000 cases of AIDS were diagnosed in the United States between 1981 and 1988. Of these, approximately 1 percent were children under 13 years, several hundred of whom were infants.

A growing body of evidence points to intrauterine infection as the major cause of AIDS in infancy. Afflicted babies are often born to drug-abusing women who soon develop symptoms of the disease themselves. Since AIDS has an extended incubation period of up to 5 years in adults, expectant mothers carrying the virus usually are not aware at the time of their pregnancies that they can transmit the illness to their offspring.

In contrast to adults, AIDS seems to have a relatively short incubation period in infants. The average age at which symptoms appear in babies for whom prenatal transmission is suspected is 6 months. Weight loss, chronic fever, and diarrhea appear, as well as a number of infectious illnesses. Affected infants rarely survive more than 5 to 8 months after symptom onset (Minkoff et al., 1987).

Recent research suggests that, like other intrauterine viral infections, AIDS may cause serious malformations in the developing embryo and fetus. A pattern of congenital abnormalities has been linked to prenatal AIDS infection, including microcephaly and a set of facial deformities involving a prominent boxlike forehead, widely spaced and obliquely positioned eyes, thickened lips, and other distortions.

Those infants who manifest more of these abnormalities show an earlier onset of AIDS symptoms during the first year of life, suggesting to researchers that the defects are caused by early intrauterine transfer of the AIDS virus. Babies with AIDS often have mothers who are drug abusers and in poor health, so it is possible that the anomalies could have resulted from other agents. However, the pattern of deformities differs from that of fetal alcohol syndrome and from the consequences of other drugs and diseases known to cause prenatal damage (Marion et al., 1986).

A great deal remains to be learned about prenatal transmission of AIDS and the course of the illness in infants and children. At present, the exact risk of fetal infection from pregnant women who carry the virus is not known. In addition, AIDS is difficult to diagnose in infancy, and it can be confused with other diseases. These circumstances make its prenatal consequences especially difficult to study.

Other Maternal Factors

Emotional Stress. A large number of studies have demonstrated that women who report severe and prolonged anxiety just before or during pregnancy experience more medical complications and give birth to more infants with abnormalities than women who do not. Emotional stress has been associated with increased incidence of spontaneous abortion, labor difficulties, prematurity, low birth weight, newborn respiratory difficulties, and physical deformities such as cleft palate and infantile pyloric stenosis, a defect involving tightening of the infant's stomach outlet due to an enlarged muscle that must be treated surgically (McDonald, 1963; Norbeck & Tilden, 1983; Revill & Dodge, 1978).

Medical research has led to increased understanding of the specific mechanisms by which stress can affect the developing baby. Anxiety activates the autonomic nervous system, which stimulates the release of adrenal hormones into the mother's bloodstream. The hormones cause large amounts of blood to be diverted to parts of the body involved in a defensive response — the brain, the heart, and the voluntary muscles in the arms, legs, and trunk. Blood flow to other organs, including the uterus, is diminished. Stress hormones also cross the placenta, so that whenever the mother is under stress, the baby is under stress as well. Fetal heart rate rises and activity level of the fetus increases several hundred percent when mothers are under intense anxiety (Sontag, 1944). These are predictable responses on the part of the developing organism to the stimulant hormones released into its bloodstream and to the inadequate oxygen supply resulting from reduced maternal blood flow. Stress has also been associated with low weight gain in pregnant mothers (Picone et al., 1982). Such mothers do not eat less. Rather, the physiological consequences of their intense anxiety reduce the utilization of food by their bodies, and this, in turn, may be responsible for the low birth weights of many of their infants. Some researchers believe that prolonged exposure to stress hormones during the prenatal period is responsible for the increased irritability, restlessness, and digestive disturbances observed in infants born to anxious mothers. However, the quality of maternal interaction with the baby during the period after birth may be just as important in causing these difficulties (Sameroff & Chandler, 1975). Intense stress experienced in utero may have lifelong consequences for the ability of the developing person to cope with stress. A long-term follow-up of infants born to mothers who experienced the trauma of their husbands' death during pregnancy revealed a higher incidence of psychiatric disorders by the time the offspring reached adulthood, in comparison to a control group whose mothers experienced the same loss during the first year after birth (Huttunen & Niskanen, 1978).

It is important to note that high stress experienced during pregnancy does not always lead to negative prenatal outcomes. The problems mentioned above are greatly reduced when mothers have ready access to supportive social relationships. One study showed that among women experiencing severe life stress during pregnancy, those who reported that they had other people on whom they could count for help had a complication rate of only 33 percent, as compared to 91 percent for those who had few or no social supports (Nuckolls, Cassel & Kaplan, 1972). These results suggest that finding ways to strengthen supportive social ties during pregnancy can have a strong preventative impact on prenatal complications. In this regard, the father's behavior is probably just as important as efforts on the part of the mother to reduce the stressful experiences to which she is exposed. His support, understanding, and awareness of what is important in the pregnant mother's lifestyle can lead to beneficial outcomes for both the expectant mother and the newborn infant.

Nutrition. At one time it was commonly believed that under conditions of inadequate nutrition, the growing fetus, like a parasite, would take whatever it needed from its mother's body, and only the mother would suffer. The parasite theory was proved wrong when enough evidence had accumulated from research on both animals and humans to demonstrate that the offspring of mothers with poor diets had higher prematurity and mortality rates, an increased incidence of congenital malformations, lower birth weights, and reduced head circumferences (Burke et al., 1943; Jeans, Smith, & Stearns, 1955; Kaplan, 1972; Montagu, 1962).

The critical period principle seems to operate with nutrition as it does with other environmental agents, in that the type of damage depends on the period of prenatal development during which malnutrition occurs. In a study of the pregnancy outcomes of women who experienced severe famine conditions in Holland during World War II, mothers subjected to the peak of the famine during their third trimester had babies with low birth weights and reduced head circumferences. When the famine coincided with the first trimester of pregnancy, there was no effect on infant size, although a higher incidence of congenital malformations and infant deaths due to disorders of the central nervous system occurred (Stein et al., 1975). Even though radical developmental changes take place during the embryonic period, the organism is so small that it does not require much nutritional energy; however, very severe malnutrition during this time can cause structural damage. Undernutrition appears to have its greatest effect on fetal growth when it occurs late in pregnancy. Cells are increasing rapidly in number and size, and a maternal diet high in all the basic nutrients is necessary for optimal development.

Prenatal malnutrition has especially severe consequences for the development of the central nervous system. Animal studies show that prenatal brain growth is retarded due to a reduction in the number and size of brain cells and inadequate myelinization (formation of the fatty sheath on nerve fibers that facilitates the transmission of nerve impulses). Again, the effect of malnutrition depends on the phase of brain growth at the time of insufficient food intake. In one study in which the diets of rats were restricted, malnutrition during the period in which the brain was growing most rapidly caused a reduction in the number of brain cells. Even when the animals were subsequently fed nutritious diets, they did not recover. Malnutrition during a later phase led to a reduction in cell size, but with improved diets recovery was possible (Winick & Noble, 1966). The direct consequences of poor nutrition for human brain development are very difficult to demonstrate, because researchers cannot deliberately subject pregnant women and young infants to poor diets. However, autopsies of children who died of malnutrition in the first few years of life indicate that the human brain is similarly affected. Such children show a dramatic reduction in number of brain cells, and the weight deficits of their brains are sometimes as high as 36 percent. The greater the nutritional deficiency, the greater the loss in brain weight, especially if the malnutrition occurred during the last 3 months of gestation or the first 3 months of postnatal life (Naeye, Blanc, & Paul, 1973; Parekh et al., 1970; Winick, Rosso, & Waterlow, 1970).

The mental and behavioral effects of prenatal malnutrition include intellectual deficits and learning problems that become increasingly apparent with development. In addition, nutritionally deprived infants are apathetic, unresponsive to environmental stimulation, and irritable when aroused, and they have an abnormal, high-pitched cry that may be particularly distressing to their caregivers (Zeskind & Lester, 1981).

Prevention or recovery from the effects of malnutrition is thought to be possible only if adequate feeding is resumed early in development, while cell production is still taking place in the brain. We will see later on, in Chapter 5, that the human brain undergoes rapid cell duplication during gestation and into the second year of postnatal life. Studies show that providing inadequately nourished women with dietary supplements during pregnancy is successful in reducing prenatal and infant mortality rates (Toverud, Stearns, & Macy, 1950). The consequences of maternal dietary supplements for children's intellectual and behavioral development are harder to investigate. Malnutrition is highest among low socioeconomic sectors of the world's population, and it is difficult to separate inadequate nutrition from the host of other high-risk prenatal and postnatal environmental factors to which children of poverty are exposed. However, several studies suggest that prenatal dietary enrichment leads to improved motor development in infancy (Herrera et al., 1980; Joos et al., 1983), higher intelligence test scores at age 3 (Harrell, Woodyard, & Gates, 1955), and greater social involvement, affect expression, and interest in the environment during middle childhood (Barrett, Radke-Yarrow, & Klein, 1982).

After birth, intervention with prenatally malnourished infants may require more than just dietary enrichment. Investigators believe that the lethargic and irritable dispositions of these babies may lead parents to withdraw from them and be less supportive and sensitive in caregiving. A self-perpetuating system is formed in which disturbed social experiences compound the behavioral and intellectual deficits of fetal malnutrition (Lester, 1979). In one successful intervention effort aimed at breaking this apathetic infant — nonsupportive caregiver feedback system, malnourished babies from low-income families were, from earliest infancy, provided with a highly stimulating and responsive day care environment, in addition to an enriched diet. By 15 months of age, their intellectual performance was equivalent to that of adequately nourished youngsters of the same socioeconomic background, and it far surpassed the scores of infants who had received only dietary supplements (Zeskind & Ramey, 1978; 1981).

Maternal Age. The number of older mothers giving birth has risen in recent years. Today, many women are choosing to delay motherhood until their careers are well underway. Still others decide to have second families after divorce and remarriage, while some have their children later on after being treated for infertility. What risks do mothers take when they bear children at a more mature age? The most significant one was discussed earlier: an increased likelihood of giving birth to a Down syndrome baby. Because of the older mother's greater susceptibility to chromosomal abnormalities, women over 35 also experience a higher rate of spontaneous abortion.

For many years, aging of the mother's reproductive organs was also thought to make her more susceptible to a variety of pregnancy and birth complications, including longer labors, higher rates of infant mortality, congenital deformities, and low birth weight infants. However, the assumption that advanced maternal age causes these problems has recently been questioned. New studies indicate that when mothers who have major medical problems are eliminated from the samples under study, women over age 35 do not show a greater incidence of any of these complications in comparison to their younger counterparts (Grimes & Gross, 1981; Stein, 1983). Therefore, as long as women are in good health, having a child at an older age poses few risks to the mother and her developing infant.

Teenage mothers have also been reported to experience an increased incidence of pregnancy and delivery complications, and it has been conjectured that immaturity of the very young mother's reproductive organs may be responsible. However, like the findings on older mothers, a number of studies now show that teenage mothers are not at risk because of physiological immaturity. Rather, many of them do not seek or have access to prenatal medical care and come from low-income backgrounds where nutrition and general health status are more likely to be inadequate. Studies that have taken socioeconomic status and prenatal care into account report few if any differences in pregnancy outcomes between teenagers and women between 20 and 30 years of age (Mednick, Baker, & Sutton-Smith, 1979; Roosa, 1984; Rothenberg & Varga, 1981). Offspring of teenage mothers are at serious risk for developmental problems in infancy and childhood because adolescent pregnancy is associated with poverty and lack of psychological readiness for the responsibility of raising a child.

Parity. Parity refers to the number of children to whom a mother has given birth. Many women are surprised to find that length of labor is less than half as long with subsequent deliveries as it is with the first. Additional use seems to "break in" the uterus, but can repeated pregnancy also lead to "overuse" and damaging consequences for the developing child? Bearing a great many children has generally been thought to magnify the number of pregnancy complications and birth defects in later offspring, but a study of the relationship of number of prior pregnancies to a wide range of problems in over 50,000 births showed no such effect (Heinonen, Slone, & Shapiro, 1977). In instances in which parity does seem to be related to problems, they are not caused by a wearing down of the reproductive organs due to overuse, but rather by the cumulative effects of poor health or long-term exposure to damaging environmental agents. For example, when alcoholic mothers have had several children, the youngest offspring have been found to be most affected, largely because years of alcohol abuse leads to progressive deterioration of the mother's internal organs (Iosub et al., 1981).

CHILDBIRTH

The 9-month period of gestation culminates in labor, a complex series of events that physically separate the mother and baby from one another. The hard work of labor consists of muscular contractions that open the lower part of the uterus so that the baby can be pushed down the birth canal and out into the external world. Labor naturally divides into the following three stages (see Figure 3.8):

1. *Dilation and effacement of the cervix.* This is the longest stage of labor, lasting, on the average, 12 to 14 hours with a first baby and 4 to 6 hours with subsequent births. Contractions cause the cervix, or bottom of the uterus, to thin and widen so that the baby can enter the birth canal. The contractions gradually become more intense and closely spaced over the course of this initial stage, but they take place quite automatically, and there is nothing the mother can do to actively speed up the process.

2. *Expulsion of the fetus.* This is a much shorter stage than the first, lasting about 50 minutes in a first delivery and 20 minutes in later births. The baby is moved into and down the birth canal and is finally born. During this stage, if the mother is not medicated, she will feel a reflexive urge to squeeze and push with her abdominal muscles. It is the mother's pushing combined with further contractions of the uterus that force the baby down and out.

3. *Expulsion of the placenta.* In this final stage, which lasts about 5 to 10 minutes, the placenta detaches from the uterine wall, and a few contractions and pushes by the mother cause it to be expelled from the birth canal (Samuels & Samuels, 1986).

These events that thrust the baby from the warm, dark, protective womb toward independent physical existence in a cold, brightly lit external world may strike you as a traumatic and perilous ordeal. The fetus is, after all, squeezed through the birth canal for many hours, during which time its head is subjected to considerable pressure. Furthermore, constriction of the placenta and umbilical cord during the contractions causes all infants to experience periodic oxygen deprivation. In response to the trauma of labor, the infant produces extraordinarily high levels of stress hormones. We have discussed how, during the prenatal period, the physiological effects of maternal stress can threaten the organism's development. In contrast, production of stress hormones by the fetus during the birth process has positive, highly adaptive consequences. Stress hormones help the baby withstand oxygen deprivation during labor by ensuring that a rich supply of blood is delivered to the brain and heart. In addition, they help the infant breathe effectively when first separated from the

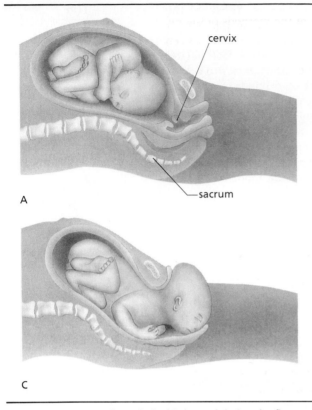

cervix

sacrum

A

B

C

D

Figure 3.8. Progress through the birth canal during the first two stages of labor. Stage 1. *(A)* Before contractions commence, the baby still floats freely in the uterus. *(B)* Uterine contractions cause the cervix to thin and widen in anticipation of the baby's entry into the birth canal. Stage 2. *(C)* Uterine contractions combine with the mother's reflexive pushing to force the baby down the birth canal, and the head appears for the first time. *(D)* Near the end of Stage 2, the shoulders emerge and are followed quickly by the rest of the baby's body. After the baby is born, Stage 3, the final stage of labor, is completed when the placenta is expelled.

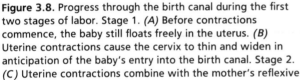

mother by dilating the bronchial tubes, facilitating the absorption of liquid from the lungs, and preparing the alveoli (air sacs) for taking in oxygen and releasing carbon dioxide. Because high levels of stress hormones also arouse the infant into alertness at birth, researchers believe that they may facilitate the neonate's readiness to interact with the environment and promote attachment between mother and child (Lager-crantz & Slotkin, 1986).

Infants who have difficulty meeting the survival demands of the external world must be given special assistance immediately. To quickly assess the infant's physical condition at birth, physicians use the **Apgar Scale** (Apgar, 1953), which provides a rating from 0 to 2 on each of five characteristics at 1 minute and 5 minutes after birth (see Table 3.3). An Apgar score of 7 or better indicates that the infant is in good physical condition. If the score is between 4 and 6, the infant requires special help in establishing breathing and other vital signs, while if the score is 3 or below, the baby is in serious danger, and emergency medical attention is needed.

Prepared Childbirth

A wide variety of prepared, or natural childbirth techniques have become popular over the last several decades, as many expectant parents want to make the birth of their baby as gratifying and fulfilling an experience as possible. Physicians favor these methods because they want to avoid the use of anesthesia, which might endanger the newborn infant, and at the same time make the mother as comfortable as possible. Most prepared childbirth techniques incorporate aspects of the methods of the English obstetrician Grantly Dick-Read (1959) or the French physician Ferdinand Lamaze (1958). All of them teach what to expect during childbirth, as well as relaxation and breathing exercises to counteract pain and increase the amount of oxygen available to the baby. They also offer support to mothers by permitting husbands or another sympathetic and responsive companion to be present during labor and delivery.

Although there is little systematic research on natural childbirth, results of a field experiment conducted in Guatemala indicate that social support is probably an especially important part of the success of these techniques. In a hospital in which patients were routinely prevented from having friends and relatives with them during childbirth, some mothers were randomly assigned a supportive companion who stayed with them throughout labor, talking to them, holding their hands, and rubbing their backs to promote relaxation and relieve discomfort. These mothers showed a lower incidence of birth complications, and their labors lasted less than half as long as those assigned to a control group who experienced no supportive companionship. In addition, observations of the mothers interacting with their newborn infants in the first hour after delivery indicated that those in the experimental group were more likely to respond to their babies by talking to them, smiling at them, and stroking them (Sosa et al., 1980).

Labor and Delivery Medication

When natural childbirth techniques are successful in reducing the stress and pain experienced by the mother, they also lessen or eliminate entirely the need for obstetric medication. Like other drugs, anesthesia administered during labor crosses the placenta, and research indicates that it produces a depressed state in newborn infants that may last for several days. Attentiveness to sights and sounds in the environment as well as motor movements decrease in affected babies, and such infants also suck poorly during feedings and are more irritable (Brackbill, 1979; Stechler & Halton, 1982). The baby's depressed condition affects the early mother-infant reciprocal relationship. A recent study found that obstetrically medicated mothers engaged in less smiling and touching of their babies and that this effect persisted throughout the

Table 3.3. The Apgar Scale

SIGN	SCORE		
	0	1	2
Heart rate	No heartbeat	Under 100 beats per minute	100 to 140 beats per minute
Respiratory effort	No breathing for 60 seconds	Irregular, shallow breathing	Strong breathing and crying
Reflex irritability	No response	Weak reflexive response	Strong reflexive response (sneezing, coughing, and grimacing)
Muscle tone	Completely flaccid	Weak flexion of arms and legs	Strong flexion of arms and legs
Color	Blue body and extremities	Body pink with blue extremities	Body and extremities completely pink

CHAPTER 3
BIOLOGICAL
FOUNDATIONS, PRENATAL
DEVELOPMENT, AND BIRTH

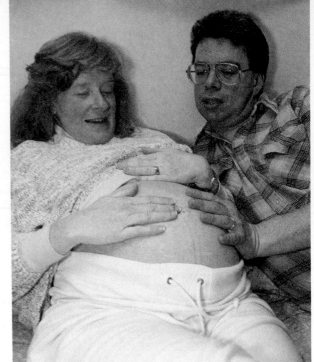

In prepared or natural childbirth, the support of an involved, sympathetic companion is especially important. Here an expectant mother and father delight in feeling the movements of their soon-to-be-born baby. (Robert Brenner/PhotoEdit)

first month of postpartum life (Hollenbeck, Gewirtz, & Sefris, 1984). However, longer-lasting effects of obstetrical medication are controversial and still unproved (Kolata, 1979).

Some form of anesthesia is used in a great many births in the United States (Brackbill, 1979), but in most instances it is mild and administered quite late in delivery (Kolata, 1979). Since obstetric drugs can be helpful in easing long labors and difficult births so that they proceed more smoothly, it is not practical to try to eliminate them entirely. Nevertheless, the negative impact of obstetric medications on early infant behavior and maternal caregiving is well-documented, supporting the current trend in the medical profession toward restrained and limited use.

Leboyer "Gentle Birth"

Natural childbirth techniques are introduced to lessen the discomfort of the mother. **Leboyer "gentle birth"** delivery, on the other hand, focuses on easing the stress and trauma of birth for the infant. The method is named for its originator, Frederick Leboyer, a French obstetrician. He regarded conventional delivery room practices, which thrust the baby into a room full of bright lights, startling noises, and cold temperatures, as a violent and terrifying assault on the infant's senses. The Leboyer approach tries to make the baby's entry into the world as peaceful and soothing as possible. The delivery room is warmed, and the intensity of sound and light is reduced. Immediately after birth, the baby is placed skin-to-skin against the mother's abdomen. The baby is then given a warm water bath and a gentle massage (Leboyer, 1975).

Leboyer believes that lasting benefits for children's physical and psychological development accrue from his birthing method, but to date little evidence exists to support this claim. In one study, mothers randomly assigned to Leboyer as opposed to conventional delivery gave birth to infants who did show more periods of quiet alertness during the first few days. However, Leboyer babies were not less irritable, and their mothers did not perceive them more favorably or interact with them differently than did mothers of conventionally delivered infants (Sorrells-Jones, 1983). Furthermore, long-term follow-ups during the first year of life of Leboyer and comparison babies show no differences between the two in behavioral dispositions or developmental milestones (Sorrells-Jones, 1983; Maziade et al., 1986).

Despite the absence of support for enhanced development, Leboyer's method has encouraged American hospitals to modify birthing practices to take into account the physical comfort of the newborn infant. No evidence exists to suggest that Leboyer delivery is in any way harmful, and it is still possible that it has as yet unknown benefits for some mother-infant pairs.

Perinatal[2] Complications

The great majority of births take place quite normally and result in healthy newborn infants. However, sometimes the mother's labor is long and drawn out, or serious complications occur that strain the adaptive mechanisms of the infant and result in medical emergencies. Abnormal separation of the placenta before the baby is born and breech births (where the buttocks or feet emerge first and both the umbilical cord and the infant's head have an increased chance of being compressed) are situations in which damage due to **anoxia,** or lack of oxygen, may occur. In addition, premature labor is one of the most significant complications of pregnancy. When infants are born too soon, they are at greater risk for a variety of physical and behavioral problems of development.

Anoxia. Although all infants experience some oxygen deprivation during labor and delivery, a small percentage are subjected to high levels of anoxia when they fail to breathe spontaneously within a minute or two after birth, greatly reducing the oxygen supply to the brain. Prolonged suspension of breathing is called *apnea,* which can occur if there is delay between the time the baby is no longer receiving oxygen through the umbilical cord and when it starts to breathe on its own. Newborns can survive periods of apnea longer than adults, but there is risk of brain damage if breathing is suspended for more than three minutes (Stechler & Halton, 1982).

Severe anoxia may occur during labor if the umbilical cord is squeezed or if excessive pressure is applied to the baby's head, as may happen in a breech birth or when forceps are used in a difficult delivery to assist the baby out of the birth canal. Rh blood incompatibility is another cause of perinatal anoxia. If the mother's blood is Rh negative (lacking Rh antigens), and she carries an Rh positive baby, it is possible for the infant's antigens to cross the placenta and enter the mother's bloodstream. When this happens, she produces antibodies against the infant's cells that are different from her own. The antibodies may travel back into the baby's system and lead to *erythroblastosis,* a condition in which the baby's red blood cells are destroyed and the oxygen supply to the fetus is reduced. The exchange of blood that leads to erythroblastosis is most likely to occur during labor and delivery, although it can occur earlier. Since it takes time for the mother's system to produce Rh antibodies, firstborn children are rarely affected, but the danger increases with successive offspring. Fortunately, erythroblastosis can be prevented by giving the mother an injection of a substance called RhoGam after the birth of each Rh positive baby to prevent the buildup of antibodies in the mother's system. However, sometimes errors are made in maternal blood typing, and her production of antibodies is not controlled. In these cases, if the baby is in danger, it is possible to perform blood transfusions immediately after birth or, if necessary, even before the baby is born (Simkin, Whalley, & Keppler, 1984).

Results of a major longitudinal study of over 100 anoxic newborns revealed sensorimotor impairments during the first few days of life, which were greatest for infants experiencing the most severe oxygen deprivation (Graham et al., 1957).

---

[2] The perinatal period begins with the onset of labor and ends with the expulsion of the baby from the birth canal and the cutting of the umbilical cord.

Studied again during the preschool years, the anoxic infants continued to show behavioral deficits. They scored lower on intelligence tests than control children, and parents as well as researchers rated their personalities less favorably (Graham et al., 1962). However, by age seven the intellectual differences between anoxic children and controls had largely disappeared, and only scattered differences remained in personality (Corah et al., 1965). Evidence from this study, as well as a substantial number of other investigations, indicates that although deficits persist through the first few years of life, by school age there are few differences between infants who have suffered from anoxia at birth and those who have not (Stechler & Halton, 1982).

It is surprising that so many studies find that the trauma of perinatal oxygen deprivation has no permanent, long-term consequences for children's development. Some investigators believe that in order for lasting effects to occur, anoxia has to be extremely profound, and inadequate child-rearing environments must combine with it to promote poor intellectual and personality functioning (Sameroff & Chandler, 1975). Many severely retarded individuals are known to have histories of perinatal anoxia. In instances of permanent developmental impairment, the oxygen deprivation during birth was probably especially acute, and it may have occurred because of earlier damage to the central nervous or respiratory system during the prenatal period, then becoming one of a number of contributing factors to developmental deviation. It is also possible that some anoxic damage may remain latent for years, only to surface in later childhood or adolescence. Furthermore, it may not be detected at all in cases where it amounts to the difference between what would have been an intellectually gifted but is now an average child (Towbin, 1978).

The growing concern about the serious consequences of perinatal anoxia is a major factor that has led to the widespread use of electronic *fetal monitoring devices* during labor. The monitors pick up unusual changes in the baby's heart rate that indicate fetal distress due to lack of oxygen. Two types are now in common use. The most popular is an external device that uses ultrasound to provide continuous detection of the infant's heartbeat and remains strapped to the mother's abdomen throughout labor. The other type, a more accurate method, uses an internal lead that is inserted through the cervix and placed just under the baby's scalp. At present, fetal monitoring is regarded as a safe medical procedure that picks up 95 percent of babies who are in true fetal distress. A large study of 16,000 deliveries concluded that among mothers who have experienced serious pregnancy complications, fetal monitoring saves an estimated 109 lives per 1,000 births (Neutra, 1978). However, there is controversy over the generalized use of monitoring devices. Among mothers who experience healthy and uncomplicated pregnancies, fetal monitoring does not reduce the rate of infant mortality. Moreover, there is concern that fetal monitoring mistakenly identifies fetal distress in many normal babies, since it is associated with a higher than average incidence of Caesarean deliveries. For this reason, when heart rate monitors suggest distress, many doctors now look for additional confirmation by analyzing the oxygen content of a blood sample taken from the scalp of the fetus before they decide on emergency action. Fetal monitoring devices have been the target of additional controversy, since many women desire as natural a birth experience as possible and feel that the devices are intrusive, uncomfortable, and may interfere with the normal course of labor. While strong advocates of the technology feel that it should be used routinely to enhance the chances for healthy outcomes in all births, other medical experts believe that the devices are unnecessary in the great majority of labors and need only be used with high-risk mothers (Samuels & Samuels, 1986).

Preterm and Low Birth Weight Infants. The term premature has traditionally been used to refer to infants born 3 weeks or more before the end of a full gestational period or to babies weighing less than 2,500 grams (5½ pounds). Several decades of research on premature infants has revealed that they show high mortality rates and are at risk for developmental problems. Birth weight is a strong predictor of long-term developmental outcomes. A substantial number of infants below 1,500 grams (3.3 pounds) experience developmental difficulties that are not overcome later, an effect that becomes more pronounced the less the baby weighs. However, many premature babies—even some who weigh only a couple of pounds—fare reasonably well (Britton, Fitzhardinge, & Ashby, 1981), and developmental psychologists and pediatricians now believe that the category of "prematurity" is too global to help us fully understand the factors affecting outcomes for these infants. Currently, low birth weight babies are divided into two groups. The first consists of **preterm,** or short-gestation infants who are born several weeks or more before their due date. Although small in size, their weight may still be appropriate for their gestational age. The second group includes infants who are called **small for dates.** These babies are born below their expected weight when their gestational age is taken into account. Some of them are full term, while others are preterm infants who are especially underweight.

Until recently, most investigators interested in prematurity failed to make these distinctions, and the samples of infants studied were very heterogeneous. Though all low birth weight infants are developmentally at risk, a review of the few studies in which infants have been separated into subgroups suggests that small for dates infants are somewhat more disadvantaged in terms of long-term outcomes than are preterm babies. In childhood, they have lower intelligence test scores, and they seem to experience more educational and behavior problems. However, the outcomes for both groups vary with socioeconomic conditions, and those who fare best come from supportive home environments (Francis-Williams & Davies, 1974; Kopp & Parmelee, 1979). Small for dates babies are considered prenatally growth retarded, and many are thought to have experienced inadequate prenatal nutrition, because of their mother's diet, faulty functioning of the placenta, or other factors. Nutritional deprivation, which we discussed earlier, is a serious problem, and it may help to explain the poorer developmental prognosis of the small for dates baby in comparison to the preterm infant.

The largest body of research exists for infants labeled preterm, regardless of the relationship between their gestational age and weight (Kopp, 1983). Twins are usually born about 3 weeks preterm, and because of restricted space inside the uterus they gain less weight than singletons after the 20th week of pregnancy. Otherwise, preterm births are more prevalent among women from low socioeconomic backgrounds and are probably caused by many factors, including poor maternal health, drug use and smoking during pregnancy, lack of prenatal care, or a uterus that is insufficient for carrying a baby to term. The number of preterm infants showing serious developmental consequences is markedly reduced today because of improved hospital techniques for feeding, controlling body temperature, and monitoring the physiological status of these very tiny infants. Nevertheless, preterm babies are still highly vulnerable infants who are subject to later intellectual deficits and school difficulties. These negative outcomes seem to have something to do with family rearing conditions, since they occur more often among preterm infants from low socioeconomic status homes (Kopp & Parmelee, 1979).

In an effort to understand the origins of later developmental problems, researchers have amassed an extensive literature on the early characteristics and experiences of preterm infants. Results of these studies indicate that low gestational age is associated with infant behavior that is more variable and less competent than that of full-term newborns (Ferrari et al., 1983). For example, preterm babies are less alert and responsive and more difficult to feed than full-term infants, and they show poorer motor coordination, less well organized sleep patterns, and hyper-responsiveness to sounds (Bench & Parker, 1971; Brown & Bakeman, 1980; DiVitto & Goldberg, 1979; Dreyfus-Brisac, 1970; Howard et al., 1976). In addition, at birth they look quite different from babies of full gestational age. Scrawny, thin-skinned, and still covered with hairy lanugo on their shoulders and backs, preterms are regarded by most people as far less attractive and appealing than their round-faced, chubby full-term counterparts (Maier et al., 1984; Stern & Hildebrandt, 1986).

The appearance and behavioral disorganization of preterm infants create strains for parents that may adversely affect their relationship with the baby. An added factor is that parents are initially separated from and have infrequent early contacts with preterm infants, a circumstance that may interfere with maternal attachment. In one study, observations were made of parents interacting with their preterm babies after hospital discharge. During feedings, parents less often held them close, touched, and talked to them than they did full-term infants (Goldberg, Brachfeld, & DiVitto, 1980). Developmental differences between most preterm and full-term babies diminish over the course of the first year of life, but preterms who are sickly at birth continue to be more irritable and less responsive to their environment for many months. When their poorly adapted behaviors are combined with parents who have difficulty coping because they are young, impoverished, uneducated, or lacking in social supports, unfavorable developmental outcomes are likely to occur. Research shows that sick preterms tend to be responded to by parents with more intrusive and controlling behaviors by the middle of the first year of life. Parents probably use more interfering touches, verbal commands, and criticisms in an effort to obtain a higher level of response from an infant who is, to begin with, passive, slowly developing, and not a very rewarding social partner (Beckwith & Cohen, 1980). Some parents may accelerate these intrusive efforts in the face of continuing ungratifying and irritable infant behavior, and this may explain why preterm infants as a group have been found to be especially susceptible to child abuse (Kennell, Voos, & Klaus, 1979; Parke & Collmer, 1975).

By the school years, most preterm infants catch up in development and show intelligence test scores that are within normal range. Shifts in performance during the preschool years are associated with the quality of early caregiving, and nonsupportive caregiver-infant relationships characterize those who, in the long run, fare least well (Cohen & Parmelee, 1983). In view of these findings, intervention programs directed at improving caregiver-infant interaction should help preterm babies make a successful recovery.

A variety of intervention efforts have been tried with preterm babies. Some treat the infant side of the relationship by providing increased stimulation to ameliorate the baby's initially passive, poorly organized behavior. In a number of these interventions, newborns are picked up and stroked, rocked in suspended hammocks, or placed on waterbeds to overcome the effects of confinement to a stimulus-deprived incubator. Sometimes visual or auditory stimulation (for example, an attractive mobile or the soothing sound of the mother's voice) accompanies the extra handling and rocking. In general, these stimulus enrichment programs have been successful in leading to increased weight gain, more predictable sleep patterns, and improved visual alertness and motor maturation during the early postnatal period (Cornell & Gottfried, 1976; Schaefer, Hatcher, & Bargelow, 1980). Touch seems to be an especially important form of intervention for preterm infants. In animal research, tactile stimulation has been found to release certain brain chemicals that support physical growth, and these effects are believed to hold for humans as well (Schanberg & Field, 1987). In one recent study, long-term benefits accrued for preterm infants whose backs, legs, and necks were gently massaged each day in the hospital. They not only gained weight faster, but were advantaged over infants not receiving the tactile stimulation in mental and motor ability at 8 and 12 months of age (Field et al., 1986).

Other intervention programs have focused on the maternal side of the relationship by providing training to mothers who are at risk for poor parenting skills. In one such program, Field and her collaborators (1980) taught low-income teenage mothers to provide age-appropriate stimulation to their preterm infants, educated them about developmental milestones, and provided interaction coaching aimed at fostering a positive mother-infant relationship. In comparison to controls, mothers receiving the intervention had more desirable child-rearing attitudes, rated their infants' temperaments as less difficult, and were more verbally responsive and emotionally involved with their babies. At 4 months of age, their infants had greater weight and length measurements, and at 8 months, they had higher mental scores.

UNDERSTANDING REPRODUCTIVE RISK

Throughout this chapter, we have discussed how biological risks can interfere with the development of the child at conception and during the prenatal and perinatal periods. We have emphasized that developmental outcomes can vary from severely damaging to near normal, depending on the type and timing of influence. Pasamanick and Knobloch (1966) refer to this variation in severity of biological insults as the **continuum of reproductive casualty.** In general, the earlier the insult, the greater the damage to the developing organism. However, we have also shown that even when the nature of the early biological trauma is known, definite predictions about the ultimate course of growth and development are still not possible. For just about any biological assault, the outcomes vary from child to child. In fact, the evidence on certain insults, especially those that occur late in pregnancy or during labor and delivery, suggests that many children eventually overcome initial handicaps and, by middle childhood, adapt successfully to their environments (Kopp, 1983).

Sameroff and Chandler (1975) point out that successful prediction of long-range developmental outcomes cannot be made on the basis of the continuum of reproductive casualty alone, for reproductive risk is affected by an equally important **continuum of caretaking casualty.** Caretaking can vary from severe abuse and neglect to stimulating, sensitive, and supportive parenting. In many instances, it can perpetuate or break the relationship between early trauma and later disorders. Long-range predictions of how a child will fare are only possible if *both* reproductive and caretaking history are taken into account.

The results of a major longitudinal study conducted in Hawaii provide a clear demonstration of how the continua of reproductive and caretaking casualty work together. In 1955, 670 infants born on the island of Kauai were rated as having experienced mild, moderate, or severe perinatal complications and then matched, on the basis of socioeconomic status and race, with infants who had uncomplicated births. In childhood, their family environments were rated on extent of emotional support and educational stimulation. By age 10, early developmental differences between children with various degrees of perinatal stress and those with no stress had become less pronounced. Any persisting effects were found largely among a very small group of children who had experienced the most severe complications. At age 18, this group had 10 times the incidence of mental retardation, 5 times the number of mental health problems, and 2 times the number of physical handicaps as the remainder of the children studied. Among mild to moderately stressed children, quality of the caretaking environment was the best predictor of later developmental deficits. Homes rated low in family stability and in educational stimulation produced lasting behavior and learning problems. Among homes rated high, the consequences of perinatal complications were less and less evident as the child matured (Werner & Smith, 1979; 1982).

In summarizing the joint effects of the continua of reproductive and caretaking casualty, Sameroff and Chandler (1975) state, "When the child's vulnerability is heightened through massive reproductive trauma, only an extremely supportive environment can help to restore the normal integrative growth process. . . . On the other extreme, a highly disordered caretaking setting might convert the most sturdy and integrated of children into a caretaking casualty" (pp. 235–236). For the great majority of children who have experienced reproductive risk, familial and socioeconomic characteristics of the caretaking environment provide the most potent predictors of long-term developmental outcomes.

HEREDITY, ENVIRONMENT, AND BEHAVIOR:
A LOOK AHEAD

Most infants emerge from the prenatal period of development unscathed. Born healthy and vigorous, as developing members of the human species they soon begin to show great variation in characteristics and abilities. Some are outgoing and sociable, others are incessantly curious explorers of their physical environment, while still others are quiet, shy, and reserved. By school age, one child shows a penchant for arithmetic, another loves to read, while a third excels at music or athletics. *Behavioral geneticists* are scientists interested in discovering the sources of this great diversity in human behavior and characteristics. We have already seen that they are only now beginning to understand the genetic and environmental events preceding birth that assure a healthy, intact organism or that place limits on the individual's developing potential. How, then, do they unravel the hereditary and environmental roots of the complex characteristics and behaviors that emerge after birth, and that are the focus of the remaining chapters in this book?

All behavioral geneticists acknowledge that *both* heredity and environment are indispensable for the development of any behavior. There is no real controversy on this point, because the organism can only develop through the joint action of genetic information and environmental contexts that allow this information to be expressed (Scarr & Kidd, 1983). No child can learn to talk without being exposed to verbal communication or learn to read without access to written media and instruction in how to decipher the printed word. However, for polygenic traits like intelligence and personality, scientists are a very long way from direct knowledge of the specific genes responsible for individual differences and the biochemical mechanisms through which they exert their effect. They must study the relationship of genetic factors to these behaviors indirectly, and there exists an unresolved nature-nurture controversy because scientists do not agree on how heredity and environment influence these complex characteristics.

Some believe that it is both useful and possible to answer the question of *how much* each factor contributes to differences among children. To find out if one factor is more important than the other, behavioral geneticists use special research methods to separate individual differences into their hereditary and environmental components. In doing so, they try to tell which factor plays the major role. A second group of scientists regards the question of which factor is more important as neither useful nor answerable. These individuals believe that heredity and environment do not make separate contributions to human behavior. Instead, they are interdependent, and the nature and extent of influence of one factor depends upon the contribution of the other. Because these scientists see development as a complex interaction of nature and nurture, they think that the real question we need to explore is *how* heredity and environment depend upon one another and work together (Anastasi, 1958; Lerner, 1986). Let's consider each of these two positions in turn.

The Question of "How Much?"

Behavioral geneticists use **heritability estimates** to measure the extent to which variation among individuals in complex behaviors can be attributed to genetic factors. Investigators have obtained heritabilities for intelligence and a variety of personality characteristics. We will review their findings in greater detail in later chapters that are devoted to these topics, while providing only a brief overview of the issues involved in estimating heritability here. Heritability estimates are obtained from **kinship studies,** investigations in which individuals within a family who have different degrees of genetic relationship to one another are compared. The most common type of kinship study compares identical twins, who, because they develop from a single zygote,

Because they share the same genetic makeup, identical twins are a fascinating and common subject in studies of the heritability of behavior (Porterfield/Chickering/ Photo Researchers)

share all of their genes in common, with fraternal twins, who are genetically no more alike than ordinary siblings. The assumption made in these comparisons is that if individuals who are of greater genetic similarity to one another also resemble each other more closely in behavior, then the behavior must be at least partly genetically determined.

Findings from kinship studies on the heritability of intelligence provide one of the most controversial sets of data in psychology. While some experts claim a high degree of genetic determination, others take the position that there is no convincing evidence that genetic factors have anything to do with individual differences in intelligence. Currently, most behavioral geneticists support a moderate role for heredity. There are many studies that have compared the resemblance in intelligence of identical and fraternal twins. When they are compiled, correlations between the intelligence test scores of identical twins are consistently higher than those for fraternal twins. In one summary of over 30 such investigations, the mean correlation for intelligence was .86 for identicals and .60 for fraternals (Bouchard & McGue, 1981). Using special statistical procedures, behavioral geneticists compare the two correlations to arrive at a heritability index, ranging from 0 to 1.00, which refers to the proportion of differences among individuals in behavior that can be explained by their genetic differences (Plomin, DeFries, & McClearn, 1980). Depending on the particular twin studies used to calculate heritability, the values for intelligence range from .30 to .70. Scarr and Kidd (1983) suggest that a likely value is probably about .50. Other kinship comparisons — for example, between identical twins and ordinary siblings or siblings and half-siblings — also support a moderate heritability of about this magnitude. In addition, the measured intelligence of adopted children consistently shows a stronger correlation with the scores of their biological parents than with those of their adoptive parents, offering further evidence that heredity plays an important role (Scarr & Weinberg, 1983; Skodak & Skeels, 1949).

Heritability indices have also been computed for a wide variety of personality characteristics. Heredity seems to play some role in personality. Nevertheless, these estimates are generally lower than those that have been obtained for intelligence (Scarr & Kidd, 1983).

Although heritability estimates derived from kinship studies provide evidence that genetic factors make important contributions to individual differences, they are limited statistics, and questions have been raised about their validity. A heritability index is heavily influenced by the range of environments to which kinship pairs have been exposed. For example, pairs of identical twins raised together under highly similar conditions have more strongly correlated intelligence test scores than those reared apart in very different environments. When the former are used to compute heritability estimates, the higher correlation causes the contribution of heredity to be overestimated. To remedy this difficulty, researchers try to compute heritabilities on pairs of twins who have been reared apart in foster or adoptive homes. But few separated twin pairs are available for study, and when they are, social service agencies often place them in advantaged home environments that are similar in many ways. These problems suggest a major concern about the heritability measure. The range of home environments to which most twin pairs are exposed is far more restricted than the variety of home environments found in the general population, and this makes it difficult to generalize heritability estimates to the population as a whole (Bronfenbrenner, 1972; Scarr & Kidd, 1983).

Another criticism of heritability estimates is that subtle environmental pressures may contribute to the substantially greater correlations between pairs of identical than fraternal twins. Knowing that identical twins are genetically the same, perhaps parents simply expect them to behave more similarly and therefore treat them more alike than fraternals, thereby increasing their behavioral similarity over what it would have been if rearing conditions like those experienced by most siblings prevailed. The idea that parents pressure identical twins to be more alike than fraternals seems plausible, although some research argues against it. In one study, Lytton (1977) carefully observed the interactions of mothers with their 2-year-old twin sons. He found that, although parents of identical twins did behave more similarly toward their children than parents of fraternals, they only did so in response to the identical twins' more similar behaviors. Parent-initiated behaviors that were not contingent on the child's actions did not differ between identical and fraternal twin pairs. In addition, twins whose zygosity has been misclassified (identicals who were thought to be fraternals, and fraternals who were thought to be identicals) show behavioral similarities more in line with their actual twin status than their perceived status (Scarr, 1968; Scarr & Carter-Saltzman, 1979). These findings suggest that parental treatment of twins is not based on knowledge of their genetic similarity.

Heritability estimates are controversial because they can easily be misapplied. For example, high heritabilities obtained from kinship studies have been used to suggest that racial differences in intelligence, such as the generally poorer performance of blacks in comparison to whites in the United States, have a genetic basis (Jensen, 1969; 1973). As we shall see in greater detail in Chapter 8, heritability estimates offer no direct evidence about genetically determined intellectual differences between the races, and the hypothesis that heredity is responsible for the black-white intelligence gap has been disproved. Research shows that when black and white children are raised in similar environments, they do not differ in performance on intelligence tests (Scarr & Weinberg, 1976; 1983).

Perhaps the most serious criticism leveled at heritability estimates has to do with their usefulness. While they are interesting statistics that tell us heredity is undoubtedly involved in the determination of complex behaviors like intelligence and personality, they give us no information on how these behaviors develop. Nor do they tell us how children might respond when exposed to novel child-rearing or educational environments that are designed to help them develop as far as possible. Behavioral geneticists respond to these criticisms by arguing that their efforts can be regarded as a first step. Once they have sufficient evidence to indicate that genetic factors underlie important individual differences in behavior, they can then begin to ask about the specific genes involved, the biochemical pathways through which the genes exert their influence, and how these pathways are modified by environmental factors.

The Question of "How?"

117

CHAPTER 3
BIOLOGICAL
FOUNDATIONS, PRENATAL
DEVELOPMENT, AND BIRTH

According to the concept of interaction, heredity and environment do not influence behavior independently of one another. Instead, behavior is the result of a dynamic interplay between these two fundamental sources of development. How do heredity and environment interact? Several important concepts shed light on this complex question.

The first is the concept of **range of reaction** (Gottesman, 1963). According to this idea, there is no simple, one-to-one correspondence between our genes and the characteristics we develop. Instead, each person's genotype establishes its own upper and lower boundaries for development because each responds uniquely to a given range of environmental conditions. Range of reaction applies to any phenotypic characteristic. In Figure 3.9 it is illustrated for intelligence. The figure depicts reaction ranges for three hypothetical children. As environments vary from extremely impoverished to highly stimulating and enriched, child A's intelligence test score changes dramatically, child B's only moderately, and child C's hardly at all. Reaction range assumes a complex interdependency between heredity and environment. First, it shows that when environments vary, a single genotype will produce different phenotypes. At the same time, identical environments do not have the same effect on all genotypes. A poor environment will result in a lower phenotypic intelligence for child C than for child A, while an advantaged environment will elevate child A's performance far above what is possible for child C. Second, different genotypes can lead to identical phenotypes when combined with appropriate environmental conditions. For example, children who show the same intelligence test score arrive there through distinct genetic and environmental routes. A score of 100 may be the result of a disadvantaged environment for a child with a favorable genotype, but a superior home and special schooling may produce the same score for a child with a less favorable genotype. Thus, different children vary in their range of possible responses to different environments, and unique genotype-environment combinations are responsible for both similarities and differences in human behavior.

The concept of **canalization** (Waddington, 1957), provides another view of how heredity and environment interact. A behavior that is strongly canalized follows a genetically predetermined growth path, and only strong environmental forces can

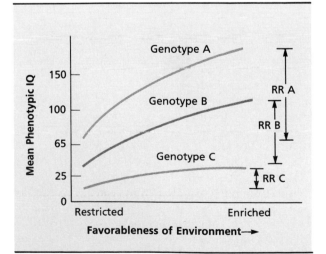

Figure 3.9. Intellectual ranges of reaction (RR) for three hypothetical children in environments that vary from unstimulating to highly enriched. *(From I. I. Gottesman, 1963, "Genetic Aspects of Intelligent Behavior." In N. R. Ellis [Ed.],* Handbook of Mental Deficiency, *New York: McGraw-Hill. P. 255. Adapted by permission.)*

deflect it from one or a few possible outcomes. Waddington's "developmental land-scape," shown in Figure 3.10, is a pictorial representation of this concept. A ball, representing the developing phenotype, rolls down a tilted surface toward its final end state at the bottom edge. The surface is grooved by a number of possible paths or channels of development. Early on, the ball can easily be diverted by an environmental push into one groove as opposed to another. But once it has rolled into a channel, it becomes increasingly difficult for the environment to redirect its course. Strongly canalized behaviors have channels that are relatively deep, and their course of development is not easily modified by the environment. Infant sensorimotor development is said to be strongly canalized, as all normal human infants suck on objects, smile, roll over, and eventually crawl and walk, and only extreme environmental conditions can modify these behaviors or cause them not to appear. Intelligence and personality are less strongly canalized characteristics that are more modifiable (Scarr-Salapatek, 1975). However, the developmental landscape also shows that over time, even weakly canalized characteristics like these become entrenched in a groove, and they become increasingly less subject to environmental modification after the early years of life. The concept of canalization shows that the often-heard statement, "Heredity sets the limits, within which environment determines the eventual outcome" is only partly true. The environment also sets limits by deflecting the phenotype into a particular channel, and early environmental forces affect the extent to which later experiences have an opportunity to modify the course of development. Can you think of examples from our discussion of prenatal development that illustrate this idea?

There is still another way in which heredity and environment are interdependent. Scarr and McCartney (1983) point out that a major problem in trying to separate genetic and environmental factors is that they are often correlated with one another. In other words, our genetic predispositions have some influence on the environments to which we are exposed (Plomin, DeFries, & Loehlin, 1977; Plomin, 1986). The way this happens changes with development. At younger ages, two types of genetic-environmental correlation are common. The first is called *passive correlation,* because the child has no control over it. Early on, parents provide rearing environments that are compatible with their own genotypes, and since they share genes in common with their offspring, the environments are also likely to be congruent with their children's genetic predispositions. For example, parents who enjoy reading offer their children a home environment rich in books, magazines, and encouragement to read, and their children are likely to become good readers for both genetic and environmental reasons. The second type of genetic-environmental correlation is *evocative.* Children

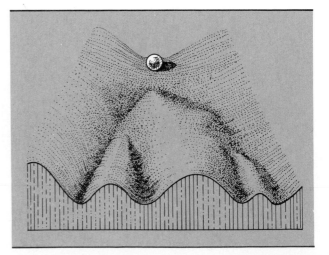

Figure 3.10. Waddington's developmental landscape, a pictorial illustration of the concept of canalization. *(From C. H. Waddington, 1957,* The Strategy of the Genes, *London: Allen & Unwin. P. 29. Reprinted by permission.)*

evoke responses from others that are influenced by the children's genotypes, and these responses act to strengthen their original predispositions. For example, an active, gregarious infant is likely to receive more social stimulation from those around her than a quiet, passive baby, and a conscientious, attentive preschooler probably receives more positive interactions from parents than an inattentive, distractible child. At older ages, *active* genotype-environmental correlation occurs. As children extend their experiences beyond the immediate family setting and are granted the freedom to make more of their own choices, they play an increasingly active role in seeking out environments that are compatible with their genetic inclinations. The well-coordinated, muscular child spends more time in after-school sports, the musically inclined child enrolls in the school orchestra and practices his violin, while the intellectually curious child is a well-known patron at the local library and reads avidly during her spare time. Scarr and McCartney refer to this tendency of individuals to actively choose environments that are compatible with their genetic predispositions as **niche-picking.** Infants and young children cannot do much niche-picking, because their exposure to environments is largely controlled by adults, but older children and adolescents are able to create their own environments to a much greater extent. Scarr and McCartney's niche-picking idea helps explain why pairs of identical twins reared apart during childhood and later reunited often find, to their great surprise, that they have similar hobbies, food preferences, friendship choices, and vocations. It also helps us understand some curious longitudinal findings from kinship studies that reveal declining similarities between fraternal twins and between adopted siblings from infancy to adolescence (Bouchard, 1981; Scarr & Weinberg, 1983). According to Scarr and McCartney, the relative influence of heredity and environment is not constant, but changes over the course of development. With age, genetic inclinations become increasingly important in determining the environments we experience and choose for ourselves.

A major reason that child development specialists have been interested in the nature-nurture issue is that they want to find ways to improve environments in order to help children realize their genetic potential. The concepts of range of reaction, canalization, and niche-picking remind us that the development of individual differences is best understood as a series of complex transactions between nature and nurture. When a characteristic is strongly determined by heredity, this does not mean that it cannot be modified. However, children are not infinitely malleable. The effectiveness of any attempt to enhance development depends upon the characteristics we want to change, the genetic makeup of the individual child, and the timing and strength of the environmental intervention.

CHAPTER SUMMARY

1. Development begins at conception, with the joining of sperm and ovum into the one-celled zygote. Within the cell nucleus are 23 pairs of chromosomes, and beaded along their length are the genes, segments of DNA that make us distinctly human and play an important role in the development of our unique characteristics. Through the process of cell duplication known as mitosis, the zygote develops into a complex human being composed of trillions of cells, each of which contains a duplicate of the original genetic information. The gametes—sperm and ovum—that merge to form the zygote are produced by a special process known as meiosis. By assuring that each offspring receives a unique complement of genes from each parent, meiosis promotes genetic variability important for evolutionary progress and survival of the species.

2. Except for the male's XY pair, the two members of each pair of chromosomes have identical genetic functions, and two forms of each gene occur at the same place along their length. Dominant-recessive and co-dominant relationships are basic patterns of genetic transmission that apply to traits governed by a single gene. Because most deleterious genes are recessive, they have a reduced likelihood of becoming phenotypically apparent. However, when recessive disorders are carried on the X chromosome, males are more likely to be affected because there are no complementary genes on the Y to overcome the effects of those on the X. Unfavorable genes arise from mutations, which can be provoked by hazardous environmental agents, such as radiation or environmental pollutants. Other mutations occur spontaneously and are not

necessarily detrimental. They are important in an evolutionary sense in that they contribute to genetic diversity and help a population survive.

3. Most relationships between genes and phenotypic attributes are not simple and one-to-one. Even when characteristics are attributable to a single gene, modifier genes can affect the eventual outcome. In addition, characteristics of major interest to developmental psychologists, such as intelligence and personality, are polygenic (influenced by the interaction of many genes), and the specific rules of genetic transmission are complex, as yet unspecified, and may never be known.

4. Chromosomal abnormalities can cause serious developmental problems, but the outcomes for any single disorder are not clear-cut and depend upon a host of additional genetic and environmental factors. Down syndrome is an autosomal disorder that results in physical defects and severe intellectual impairment. However, sensitive, responsive parenting and early intervention have been shown to make an important difference in how well Down syndrome children develop. Most disorders of the sex chromosomes are milder than autosomal abnormalities. Studies of the intellectual abilities of children with Turner, triple X, and Klinefelter's syndrome are beginning to provide important insights into biological factors affecting the development of intelligence among normal children. The most controversial and well-publicized of chromosomal disorders is XYY syndrome. Contrary to popular belief, research shows that XYY males are not prone to violence, criminality, and below average intellectual functioning. Fragile X syndrome, a disorder involving gaps and breaks in a special spot on the X chromosome, has recently been identified as a major cause of mental retardation.

5. Genetic counseling and prenatal diagnosis can help predict whether or not individuals will give birth to a baby with a chromosomal disorder or other genetic defect. Genetic counselors gather information on family history and help couples at risk decide whether to conceive a child or consider other options, such as adoption, artificial insemination, or test tube fertilization and embryo transfer. New techniques of prenatal diagnosis now make it possible to examine the condition of the developing organism early in pregnancy.

6. Prenatal development is usually divided into three phases. The period of the zygote lasts approximately 2 weeks, from fertilization until the first tiny mass of cells attaches itself to the uterine wall. The embryonic period extends from 2 to 8 weeks gestation. During this time, the foundations for all bodily systems are laid down, and at the end of this phase the organism is human in form and shows signs of beginning movement. The period of the fetus lasts until the end of pregnancy and involves a dramatic increase in body size and the completion of organs and structures.

7. Teratogens are environmental agents that cause damage during the prenatal period of development. Their specific effects are complex and depend upon a variety of factors, including timing, amount and length of exposure, combination with other environmental agents, and the genetic makeup of the mother and fetus, which affects their ability to withstand the harmful influence. Although teratogens can be harmful throughout pregnancy, the developing organism is especially sensitive to their damaging effects during the embryonic period, since all essential bodily structures are rapidly emerging during this time. Drugs, hormones, narcotic agents, alcohol, radiation, environmental pollution, and infectious diseases are teratogens that pose a significant danger to the child before birth.

8. Other maternal factors can also complicate prenatal development. Severe emotional stress has been linked to pregnancy and birth complications, but supportive social relationships can be helpful in reducing negative outcomes for mothers exposed to high life stress. Prenatal malnutrition can interfere with the development of the central nervous system, especially when it occurs late in pregnancy. Affected infants show a reduction in brain weight and number of brain cells, and intellectual deficits and learning problems become increasingly apparent as they mature. Although maternal age and parity were once thought to be major causes of pregnancy complications, recent research suggests that this is not the case. Instead, poor health status, inadequate prenatal care, and environmental risk factors associated with poverty are related to an increased incidence of prenatal problems in women of all ages.

9. Childbirth takes place in three stages, beginning with muscular contractions that open the lower part of the uterus so that the baby can be pushed down the birth canal and ending with delivery of the placenta. During labor, the infant produces high levels of stress hormones, which help it withstand oxygen deprivation and arouse it into alertness at birth. Natural childbirth techniques reduce stress and pain for the mother and lessen or eliminate entirely the need for obstetric medication, which can produce a depressed state in the newborn infant. Birth complications, such as anoxia, preterm delivery, and low birth weight, affect the adjustment and behavior of the newborn infant and lead to slower development during the early years of life. However, as long as reproductive risks are not too severe and children are raised in supportive home environments, their effects are not permanent and usually disappear by middle childhood.

10. Scientists have begun to achieve a fuller understanding of the genetic and environmental events preceding birth that assure a healthy organism or place limits on the child's developing potential. However, unraveling the genetic and environmental roots of complex characteristics emerging after birth, such as intelligence and personality, is especially difficult. Behavioral geneticists are a long way from direct knowledge of the specific genes responsible for individual differences in these behaviors, and they must investigate the contribution of heredity indirectly. Some believe that it is useful and possible to determine "how much" genetic factors contribute to individual differences by computing heritability estimates from kinship comparisons. While heritabilities show that genetic factors play an important role in the devel-

opment of intelligence and personality, they are limited statistics that can easily be misapplied. Other scientists think that separating individual differences into hereditary and environmental components is neither useful nor valid. They believe that the important question we need to answer is "how" heredity and environment depend upon one another and work together. The concepts of range of reaction, canalization, and niche-picking remind us that development is best understood as a complex series of transactions between nature and nurture.

IMPORTANT TERMS AND CONCEPTS

phenotypes
genotypes
chromosomes
homologous pairs
deoxyribonucleic acid (DNA)
genes
mitosis
gametes
meiosis
crossing over
zygote
autosomes
sex chromosomes
homozygous
heterozygous
dominant

recessive
co-dominance
mutation
X-linked inheritance
pleiotropism
modifier genes
polygenic inheritance
genetic counseling
prenatal diagnosis
identical (monozygotic) twins
fraternal (dizygotic) twins
placenta
umbilical cord
embryo
fetus

teratogen
critical period
parity
Apgar Scale
Leboyer "gentle birth"
anoxia
preterm
small for dates
continuum of reproductive casualty
continuum of caretaking casualty
heritability estimates
kinship studies
range of reaction
canalization
niche-picking

The Cradle, by Berthe Morisot. Cliché des Musées Nationaux-Paris.

CHAPTER 4
Infancy

Infancy refers to the period of development that begins at birth and ends at about 18 months to 2 years of age, with early language use. Though it comprises only 2 percent of the life span, it is one of the most remarkable and busiest times of development. The newborn baby enters the world with a surprisingly sophisticated set of perceptual and motor abilities, a repertoire of behaviors for interacting with people, and a capacity to learn that is put to use immediately after birth. By the end of infancy, the small child is a sociable, self-assertive, purposeful being who walks on her own, has developed refined manual skills, and is prepared to acquire the most unique of human abilities —language.

Since the 1960s, there has been a burgeoning interest on the part of psychologists in how such vast changes can take place during a period of development so brief in duration. An explosion of research over the last 25 years now offers answers to such questions as: What capacities are present in the infant from the very beginning? Which must wait to mature with the passage of time? And which ones must be learned as the result of constant exchanges between infants and their physical and social world?

Psychologists have been especially interested in infancy because the basic foundations for human skills and cognitive processes are laid down at this time. Study of the young infant offers an ideal opportunity to investigate the roots of complex human abilities. Also, because infancy is a formative period of development, information about the first 2 years of life generates important knowledge about early experiences essential for normal development, as well as those that are likely to maximize the development of each child.

Our view of the infant has changed drastically over the course of this century. At one time, the newborn baby was considered a passive, incompetent organism whose world was, in the words of turn-of-the-century psychologist William James, a "blooming, buzzing confusion." Recently developed methods and equipment enabling psychologists to test the newborn infant's capacities have permitted a very different picture of the young baby to emerge. It is now well accepted that infants are, from the outset, skilled, competent beings who engage in active efforts to organize their world. In this chapter, we explore the infant's remarkable organizing capabilities — early reflexive behavior, learning mechanisms, motor skills, and sensory and perceptual functioning. Throughout our discussion we will see how research on infant development adds to our practical understanding of environmental factors necessary to support the dramatic developmental changes that take place during these first 2 years of life.

THE ORGANIZED NEWBORN

Although excited new parents may be inclined to disagree, the newborn infant is a homely looking creature. At birth, the average baby is 7½ pounds in weight and 20 inches long, and consistent with sex differences that prevail later on, male infants are slightly heavier and larger than females. Infants' bodily proportions, which are markedly different from those of older children and adults, contribute to their strange and unflattering appearance. Head and eyes are disproportionately large in comparison to the pot-bellied trunk and bow-legged lower portion of the body. In addition, the pressure of passing through the narrow birth canal usually causes the baby's head to be molded and misshapen, and the newborn's skin is generally red, wrinkled, and "parboiled" in appearance. At first glance, this odd-looking little newcomer appears vulnerable and helpless, and naive parents may assume that their infant can do nothing but eat and sleep. However, these casual impressions are wrong. The neonate's[1] active capabilities are evident in a set of innate reflexes that enable the baby to adapt to the environment; an organized sleeping-waking cycle; distinct, clearly communicable cries that summon the caregiver; and the capacity to learn, which babies exercise as soon as they emerge from the womb.

Early Reflexes

Reflexes are the newborn infant's most obvious organized patterns of behavior. Dozens of neonatal reflexes have been identified, including reactions of the head, mouth, hands, feet, and entire body. The major ones are presented and described in Table 4.1 (see page 126). As you examine this table you will see that the ability to react to environmental stimulation with motor responses is a built-in property of the infant's nervous system (Touwen, 1984).

Some reflexes are thought to have survival value. For example, if we had to teach young infants the complex motor reactions involved in sucking, the human species would be unlikely to survive for a single generation! (Kessen, 1967). Other reflexes seem to be vestiges of our primate past. They probably had survival value at some time during the evolutionary history of our species, but they no longer seem to serve an adaptive purpose. For example, the Moro or "embracing" reflex is believed to represent a primitive tendency on the part of the infant to clasp and cling to its mother. If the baby were holding on to the surface of the mother and happened to lose support, the Moro reflex would immediately cause the infant to embrace and, in cooperation with the grasp reflex, regain its hold on the mother's body (Prechtl, 1958). In fact, the grasp reflex is so strong during the first week of life that infants are able to use it to support their entire weight (Kessen, Haith, & Salapatek, 1970). Another purpose of neonatal reflexes is to protect the infant from unwanted stimula-

---

[1] The term *neonate* is used to refer to infants from birth through the first month of life.

tion. The optical blink reflex helps shield the baby from intense bright light, while the withdrawal reflex is a response to unpleasant tactile stimulation. Organized reflexive behavior also plays a role in the control of infant distress. As any new mother who remembers to bring along a pacifier while on an outing with her young infant is aware, sucking will inhibit the mass, uncoordinated motor activity of a fussy neonate almost immediately (Kessen, 1967).

Most neonatal reflexes disappear during the first 6 months of life. Experts in infant development believe that this is due to a gradual increase in voluntary control as the cortex of the brain gains influence over behavior and suppresses subcortical reflexive responses (Touwen, 1984). However, opinions differ about the role that the reflexes play in the development of voluntary action. Do infant reflexes simply wane before voluntary behavior appears? Or, can the beginnings of human complexity be found in these early reactions, and do the reflexes play a facilitating role in organizing voluntary motor abilities (Sheppard & Mysak, 1984)?

The fact that immediately after birth babies begin to adapt their reflex actions to new and varying conditions in the environment suggests that many reflexes form the basis for and are gradually incorporated into more complex, purposeful behaviors. An experiment by Sameroff (1968) on sucking behavior illustrates how newborn infants modify reflexive responses adaptively. Infant sucking can be analyzed into two basic, alternating components: suctioning and expression. In the usual sucking response, delivery of milk occurs after suctioning (not after expression), but in a special experimental condition Sameroff arranged a nipple in such a way that delivery of milk actually followed expression (and not suctioning). When newborns were given milk each time they expressed, in just a few minutes the amount of suctioning began to decrease, and expression increased. Infants were also able to adapt the level of their expression pressure, depending upon how much was required to get the milk.

Infants suck in an organized and patterned fashion involving bursts of sucks separated by pauses, a type of sucking behavior that is unique to the human species. The function of these pauses has long been a mystery, as infants are quite capable of sucking without pause when milk flows very rapidly from the nipple. In a study of neonatal feeding, Kaye and Wells (1980) concluded that this burst-pause pattern is an evolved behavior that serves the adaptive function of helping parents and babies establish satisfying interaction with one another as soon as possible. The investigators observed that most mothers jiggle their babies during the pause, expressing the belief that this "wakes the baby up" and leads to a resumption of sucking. In response, neonates soon learn to anticipate and wait for their mother's jiggle before continuing to suck. As a result, mothers and babies build an early pattern of interaction that fits the turn-taking characteristics of the human dialogue, and neonates, even with their limited reflexive capacities, participate as active, cooperative partners.

Additional research reveals similar complexity and variability for other reflexive behaviors. For example, different sequences of finger flexion appear in the palmar grasp reflex, depending upon how the palm of the infant's hand is stimulated (Touwen, 1978). Also, some reflexes that appear rather purposeless may be related to later voluntary behavior in subtle ways. The tonic neck reflex is believed to pave the way for visually guided reaching, because it channels the infant's attention toward the hand and, by gradual stages, to active approach and manipulation of objects (Knobloch & Pasamanick, 1974). The ready adaptability of the newborn's reflexes to the demands of the environment has obvious survival value, and it seems clear that a number of neonatal reflexes facilitate the development of complex voluntary behaviors that emerge later on (Kessen, 1967).

Some reflexes that resemble later motor behaviors drop out in early infancy, and the motor functions involved are renewed later on in development. An example is the walking reflex. When newborn infants are held under the arms, and their feet are permitted to touch a flat surface, they lift one foot after another in a walking response.

Table 4.1. Major Neonatal Reflexes

REFLEX	FORM OF STIMULATION	RESPONSE	DEVELOPMENTAL COURSE	SIGNIFICANCE
Optical or acoustic blink	Bright light shined suddenly at infant's eyes, or hand clap 30 cm from infant's head	Quick closure of eyelids	Permanent	Protection from strong stimulation. Absent in some infants with impaired visual or auditory systems
Tonic neck reflex	Turn head to one side while infant lies awake on back	Infant assumes a "fencing posture." Arm is extended on side toward which head is turned. Opposite arm is flexed with the hand resting near or in the head-chest region	Characteristic of the first 12 weeks, but is not consistently present. Fades by the 16th week	If constantly present, may indicate neurological dysfunction
Biceps reflex	Tap on tendon of the biceps muscle in the elbow area	Short contraction of the biceps muscle	Brisker in the first 2 days of life than later	Absent in depressed infants or in cases of congenital muscular disease
Knee jerk	Tap on tendon just below the knee	Quick extension of the knee	More pronounced during first 2 days of life than later	Absent or difficult to obtain in depressed infants or in cases of congenital muscular disease
Palmar grasp reflex	Place finger into infant's hand and press against palmar surface	Spontaneous grasp of examiner's finger	Less intense during first 2 days of life than later. Disappears at 3 to 4 months of age	Absent or difficult to obtain in depressed infants. Facilitated by sucking movements
Babinski reflex	Stroke the sole of infant's foot, from toes toward heel	Extension of big toe and spreading of smaller toes	Disappears between 8 months and 1 year	Absent in infants with defects of the lower spinal cord

At first glance, the walking reflex seems to have little adaptive value, as neonates are a very long way from being able to support their own weight or balance well enough to walk alone. However, Zelazo, Zelazo, and Kolb (1972) conjectured that the walking reflex, like others described earlier, may facilitate later complex motor behavior. They speculated that the reason the reflex drops out so early, at the end of the second month, is that it is rarely exercised. In an experiment in which this idea was tested, infants given daily stimulation of the walking reflex from the second through the eighth week of life showed a strong increase in walking movements (see Figure 4.1). In contrast, walking motions remained at a low level and gradually became sluggish and poorly executed among control group infants receiving either daily passive exercise (movement of their arms and legs in a pumping motion while they lay on their backs) or no exercise at all. Also, babies who received reflexive stimulation walked on their own over one month earlier than infants in the two control conditions. These findings suggest that the mechanism responsible for walking movements in the neonate is "used" again by the brain at a later age (Touwen, 1978).

Exactly how does neonatal stimulation contribute to earlier emergence and refinement of the walking response? There are different answers to this question. Zelazo (1983) believes that exercising the walking reflex facilitates the emergence of voluntary cortical control over the behavior at the end of the first year. However, research

Table 4.1. Major Neonatal Reflexes (Continued)

REFLEX	FORM OF STIMULATION	RESPONSE	DEVELOPMENTAL COURSE	SIGNIFICANCE
Withdrawal reflex	Prick soles of foot with a pin	Withdrawal, with flexion of foot, knee, and hip	Constantly present during the first 10 days. Weaker thereafter	Protection from unpleasant tactile stimulation. Absent in infants with defects of the lower spinal cord. Weakened by breech birth and sciatic nerve damage
Rooting reflex	Tickle skin at one corner of mouth	Head turns toward source of stimulation. Infant tries to suck the stimulating finger	Less vigorous during the first 2 days. Most readily elicited in infants 1 to 2 weeks old. Disappears by 3 weeks as it becomes a voluntary head-turning response	Assists baby in finding the nipple. Absent in depressed infants
Sucking reflex	Place index finger 3 to 4 cm into mouth	Rhythmic sucking of finger	Less intense and regular during the first 3 to 4 days	Permits feeding. Weak or absent in depressed infants
Moro reflex	Body supported horizontally by examiner, and the head is allowed to drop a few cms, or a sudden loud sound or bang on the surface supporting the infant	Back arches, baby extends legs and throws arms outward and then in toward the midline of the body, as if to grab on for support	Disappears by the middle of the first year	An absent or weak Moro indicates serious disturbances of the central nervous system
Walking reflex	Hold infant under arms, permit bare feet to touch a flat surface	Infant lifts one foot after another in walking response	Generally disappears by 8 weeks. Retained longer in babies who are lighter in weight and if the reflex is exercised	May be absent in infants born by breech presentation and in depressed infants

Sources: Prechtl & Beintema, 1965; Knobloch & Pasamanick, 1974.

by Thelen suggests a much more direct explanation. She showed that babies who gained the most weight during the first month of life took the fewest reflexive steps at 4 weeks of age. In addition, neonatal stepping movements increased when babies' legs were submerged under water (Thelen, Fisher, & Ridley-Johnson, 1984). On the basis of this evidence, Thelen proposed that the walking reflex drops out because early infant weight gain is not matched by a comparable gain in muscle strength that permits babies to lift their increasingly heavy legs. Reflexive walking movements simply lie dormant until improved muscle strength allows them to be displayed again at the end of the first year. But the baby given an opportunity to exercise the walking reflex builds leg strength early, in much the same way that exercise leads an athlete to gain in muscle power. Such babies are strong enough to retain the reflexive stepping movements over the first year, and their greater leg strength also permits them to stand and walk at an earlier age (Thelen, 1983).

Aside from their adaptive value, neonatal reflexes provide a window through which the pediatrician can assess the intactness of the infant's neurological system. In babies who are brain damaged, reflexes may be weak or absent, or in some cases they may be exaggerated and overly stereotyped (Touwen, 1984). Brain damage may also be indicated when a number of reflexes persist past the point in development when they normally disappear.

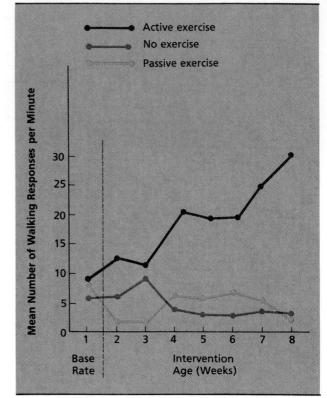

Figure 4.1. Mean number of walking responses for the experimental and control groups during the first 8 weeks of life in the Zelazo, Zelazo, and Kolb (1972) study. *(From P. R. Zelazo, N. A. Zelazo, & S. Kolb, 1972, " 'Walking' in the Newborn," Science, 176, 314–315. Copyright 1972 by the AAAS. Reprinted by permission.)*

Newborn States

Newborn babies spend their days in various gradations of sleep and wakefulness. Observing a sample of healthy newborns, Wolff (1966) identified seven different neonatal states, as follows:

1. Regular Sleep. The infant is at full rest and shows little or no diffuse motor activity. The eyelids are closed, no spontaneous eye movements occur, and the facial muscles are in repose. The rate and depth of respiration are even and regular.

2. Periodic Sleep. This state is intermediate between regular and irregular sleep. The infant shows slightly more motor activity than in regular sleep. Respiratory movements are periodic; bursts of rapid, shallow breathing alternate with bursts of deep, slow respiration.

3. Irregular Sleep. Motor activity is greater than in periodic sleep and varies from gentle limb movements to occasional stirring. Facial grimaces and mouthing occur, and occasional rapid eye movements can be observed through the eyelids. The rate and depth of respiration are irregular, and breathing occurs at a generally faster pace than it does in regular sleep.

4. Drowsiness. In this state, the infant is either falling asleep or waking up. The baby is less active than in periodic or irregular sleep, but more active than in regular sleep. Eyes open and close intermittently. When open, they have a glazed appearance and are poorly focused. When the infant is waking up, spurts of gross motor activity tend to occur. Respiration is usually even but somewhat quicker than during regular sleep.

5. Alert Inactivity. The infant is relatively inactive, with eyes open, attentive, and focused. Respiration is constant in frequency and depth.

6. Waking Activity. The infant shows frequent bursts of diffuse motor activity of the limbs, trunk, and head. The face may be relaxed, or tense and wrinkled as if the infant is about to cry, and respiration is very irregular.

7. Crying. Crying is accompanied by diffuse, vigorous motor activity.

Using these state classifications or very similar ones (e.g., Brown, 1964; Prechtl, 1965), researchers have recorded the amount of time young infants spend at different levels of arousal. In the first month after birth, infants sleep most of the time — on the average, about 16 to 20 hours per day — with frequent, alternating periods of sleep and wakefulness evenly distributed across the day and night. To the great relief of their fatigued parents, within a few weeks babies begin to show more organized and consolidated patterns of sleeping and waking. By 4½ to 6 weeks of age, fewer periods of longer duration occur, and they have also become diurnally organized, with wakeful states occurring during the day and sleep states at night. Also, as the infant gets older, sleep and wakeful periods of similar duration become coordinated with one another. By 6 months of age, the longest sleep period immediately follows the longest waking period, an association that adds to the organization and predictability of the baby's daily cycle (Coons & Guilleminault, 1984).

Although the timing, duration, and relationship between states gradually becomes more patterned and regular for all infants, virtually all investigators who have mapped these daily rhythms report striking individual differences among babies in how they spend their days. Variations among infants in time spent asleep and awake are likely to affect parents' attitudes and behavior toward their babies in significant ways. Infants who sleep for long periods of time at an early age influence the amount of rest their parents receive and the energies they have available to engage in sensitive, responsive caregiving. Babies who cry a great deal require that parents try harder to calm and soothe them, and if these efforts are not successful, parents' feelings of competence and attitudes toward their infants may be adversely affected. Infants who spend a great deal of time in an attentive and focused state are likely to receive more social stimulation from their parents. For example, when newborn infants are brought to their mothers in the hospital for a feeding, mothers are far more likely to greet their infants if they arrive in a quiet, attentive state than if they are delivered crying or asleep (Levy, 1958). Also, since the alert, focused state provides infants with greater opportunities to explore their environment, babies who favor it may be advantaged in terms of future development. In one study, male infants who spent more time in an awake, alert, and nonirritable state at 1 month of age were more attentive to visual stimuli when tested at 3½ months than their fussier or drowsier counterparts (Moss & Robson, 1970). The fact that an alert, quiet baby functions in an optimal manner for gaining visual experience may have implications for later cognitive competence. In a longitudinal investigation of the development of preterm infants, male babies who showed the most sustained attention to objects at 8 months of age had somewhat higher mental test scores when seen again at the age of 2 (Kopp & Vaughn, 1982).

Besides their concern with overall changes in infant sleep-waking patterns, psychologists have been interested in studying the organization of behavior *within* particular states, because such knowledge contributes to our understanding of both normal and pathological development. We now turn to a more detailed consideration of the two most extreme infant behavioral states: sleeping and crying.

Sleep. It is now generally accepted that sleep is not one unitary state. Instead, it is comprised of at least two distinct states that correspond to Wolff's (1966) classification, presented above, of irregular and regular sleep. Most investigators refer to these two basic sleep states as **REM** and **NREM** sleep, because a distinguishing feature of irregular sleep is the occurrence of rapid eye movements (REM), whereas in regular sleep they are absent. The two states also differ from one another in overall physiological organization, as revealed by electroencephalograph brain wave recordings (EEG), polygraph records of heart rate and respiration, and direct observation of motor activity.

We are used to thinking of sleep as a time of rest, recovery, and reversal of fatigue. However, the characteristics of REM sleep indicate that this simple, commonly accepted explanation of why we sleep is far from complete, especially where the young infant is concerned. During REM sleep, the brain and portions of the body are intensely active. Electrical brain wave activity, as measured by the EEG, is remarkably similar to that of the waking state, and heart rate, blood pressure, and respiration are uneven and slightly accelerated. In addition to the darting of the eyes beneath the lids, slight but continuous body movements occur. Sleeping neonates can be seen grimacing, whimpering, smiling, and engaging in twitches of the face and extremities, behaviors that suggest that this state signifies something other than restful repose! In contrast, NREM sleep is essentially devoid of muscular activity. Except for an occasional twitch, the infant is generally passive and motionless, and heart rate, respiratory rhythms, and EEG activity are slow and regular (Anders, 1978; Dittrichova, Brichacek, & Tautermannova, 1982; Roffwarg, Muzio, & Dement, 1966).

Like older children and adults, neonates demonstrate a structurally organized, alternating REM-NREM sleep cycle, but this organization changes substantially with age. As shown in Figure 4.2, infants spend far more time in REM sleep than do adults. REM comprises 20 percent of the average adult's sleep, but it consumes 50 percent of the newborn infant's sleep time. In fact, because neonates spend so much of their day asleep, the REM state accounts for about a third of their entire existence! Between the newborn period and young adulthood, REM sleep diminishes 80 percent, from a total of 8 hours to 1 hour and 40 minutes. In comparison, NREM sleep hardly seems to change at all. From infancy to adulthood, it declines only 25 percent, from 8 to 6 hours. These statistics indicate that the great sleep requirement of infancy is largely a need for REM sleep (Roffwarg, Muzio, & Dement, 1966).

Another difference between the sleep of infants and adults concerns the sequence of REM and NREM cycles. Adults do not enter REM sleep until 70 to 100 minutes after sleep onset, but newborn infants routinely begin sleep with REM activity. The transition to NREM sleep onset occurs at 7 to 9 weeks of age, at about the same time that

Figure 4.2. Developmental changes in total amount and percentage of REM sleep, NREM sleep, and the waking state from birth to old age. *(From H. P. Roffwarg, J. N. Muzio, & W. C. Dement, "Ontogenetic Development of the Human Sleep-Dream Cycle, Science, 152, 608. Copyright 1966 by the AAAS. Revised from original publication by the authors in 1969 on the basis of additional data.)*

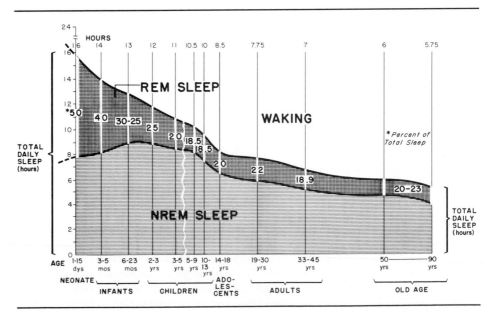

infants establish diurnally organized sleep and wakefulness periods (Kligman, Smyrl, & Emde, 1975). These simultaneous changes suggest that around 2 months of age, infants are beginning to move from the more primitive state organization of the newborn to a more mature sleep-wakefulness pattern (Berg & Berg, 1979).

According to **autostimulation theory,** REM sleep offers intense stimulation to the central nervous system, turned on from within the organism. In adults, REM sleep is associated with dreaming. Adults seem to interpret REM stimulation as if it were a set of perceptions impinging on the central nervous system from the outside. Babies probably do not dream, at least not in the same way as do children and adults. However, young infants are believed to have an especially great need for the stimulation of REM sleep because they spend relatively little time in an alert, conscious state. REM sleep seems to be a way in which the immature organism naturally compensates for unavailable activity. Sleep researchers believe that such stimulation is vitally important for the growth of the central nervous system and that, without it, the structures of the brain may be impaired (Roffwarg, Muzio, & Dement, 1966). The autostimulation function of REM sleep fits with research indicating that when newborn babies are encouraged to spend more time awake, their subsequent REM sleep is reduced in quantity, while their NREM sleep remains unchanged (Anders & Roffwarg, 1973; Boismier, 1977). In preterm infants, whose capacity to take advantage of external stimulation is especially limited, the percentage of sleep devoted to the REM state is particularly great — 58 percent at 36 to 38 weeks gestation; 67 percent at 33 to 35 weeks gestation; and a dramatic 80 percent in one infant of 30 weeks gestation (Roffwarg, Muzio, & Dement, 1966).

Because the normal sleep behavior of the neonate is organized and patterned, sleep studies are useful in the newborn period for identifying central nervous system dysfunction. Several investigations have found evidence of disturbances in REM-NREM cycling in infants who are brain damaged, premature, or who have been identified as high risk because of prenatal or perinatal complications (Dreyfus-Brisac, 1970; Prechtl, Theorell, & Blair, 1973; Theorell, Prechtl, & Vos, 1974).

Crying. Crying is the first way that infants communicate with their surrounding world. At delivery, a lusty cry signals the doctor that the baby has filled her lungs with air and begun to breathe, and it informs caregivers of the baby's need for food, comfort, and stimulation. Careful analyses reveal that the cry of the newborn infant is a complex, physically and emotionally expressive behavior. Wolff (1969) identified four different patterns of crying in young infants: (1) The *basic cry,* which is usually associated with hunger but has a fundamental rhythmic pattern into which all infant cries eventually resolve; (2) the *anger cry;* (3) the *pain cry;* and (4) the *attention cry,* which develops later than the other types, at about the third week after birth.

A crying baby stimulates strong feelings in just about anyone within earshot. In several studies, heart rate and skin conductance measures were taken on adults while they listened to sound recordings of infant cries. The crying response induced intense physiological arousal in both mothers and fathers (Boukydis & Burgess, 1982, Frodi et al., 1978), as well as in adults of both sexes who have no children (Freudenberg, Driscoll, & Stern, 1978; Murray, 1985). The powerful effect of the infant's cry is probably biologically programmed in all human beings to make sure that babies receive the necessary care and protection to survive. First-time parents respond to their infants' cries with somewhat more arousal than do parents who already have one or more children. Mothers and fathers of a first baby probably have a greater investment in learning to interpret infant cries than the seasoned parent of several children (Boukydis & Burgess, 1982).

Parents quickly become aware of and respond to differences in infant cries. Although they are not always completely correct in interpreting the meaning of the cry, experience in caregiving improves their accuracy (Green, Jones, & Gustafson, 1987; Zeskind & Lester, 1978). In addition, parents are somewhat better at distinguishing the cries of their own baby than those of a strange infant (Wiesenfeld, Malatesta, & DeLoache, 1981).

Observing maternal responses to crying infants of less than 6 months of age, Wolff (1969) found that mothers do not react to the hunger, anger, and attention cries in fixed ways. For example, in response to the basic hunger cry, mothers may or may not come immediately, and when they do, some may try feeding, while others may change the infant's diaper first. The anger cry leads mothers to stop and check on the baby, but they do not seem alarmed or unduly concerned, and some react with tolerant amusement at this early expression of indignation and rage in the tiny new being.

Only the pain cry produces a characteristic and very dramatic response. Wolff (1969) played tape-recorded pain cries to mothers of their out-of-sight infants. They immediately rushed into the room, anxious and worried. Although the mothers rightly expressed annoyance at the investigator's deception, they were relieved to find their infants intact and uninjured. In a study in which parents were played recordings of both anger and pain cries, they rated the pain cry as more unpleasant and as causing more tension. It also produced greater physiological arousal, as measured by skin conductance and heart rate responses (Wiesenfeld, Malatesta, & DeLoache, 1981). An intense emotional reaction and stereotyped response to the pain cry even seem to occur in adults who are not parents of the crying baby. Among the Zhun/twasi hunting and gathering people of Africa, an observed instance of the pain cry caused everyone in the village to orient in the direction of the sound, and a dozen concerned adults immediately jumped up and approached the crying child. In contrast, hunger cries of Zhun/twasi infants produce no reaction at all in anyone but the mother or substitute caregiver (Konner, 1972). By eliciting strong emotional arousal and a fixed reaction in all adults, the pain cry is an adaptive mechanism that assures that an infant in danger will quickly get help.

Events that cause newborn infants to cry are largely physical and physiological. Hunger is, of course, a common cause, but young infants may also cry in response to temperature change, being undressed, or when startled by loud, sudden sounds. An infant's state is an important factor in influencing whether he will cry in response to visual or auditory stimuli. Babies who, when alert and inactive, regard their mother's face, a colorful object, or the sound of a toy horn with interest and pleasure may react to the same events with a sudden burst of tears during a state of mild discomfort and diffuse activity (Tennes et al., 1972; Wolff, 1969). The reaction may be the result of momentary overstimulation, since it lessens with age as infants become better able to tolerate more sensory input and turn away when there is too much (Sroufe, 1979). Newborn crying can also be induced by the sound of another crying baby. Infants less than 1 day old cry when exposed to a recording of another infant's cry, a reaction that may indicate the presence of an inborn distress response to the experience of distress in others. Interestingly, a tape recording of the infant's own cry has the opposite effect. It causes a crying baby to stop crying, and it does not induce crying in a calm infant. Newborns seem to be able to make the fine distinction between their own cry and that of another baby, although exactly how this distinction is made is not yet known (Martin & Clark, 1982).

Fortunately, there are ways to soothe a crying infant. Observing the techniques that mothers used to calm their babies at the beginning and end of the first year, Bell and Ainsworth (1972) found, in agreement with other investigators (Brown, 1964; Wolff, 1969), that picking up the baby and providing close physical contact is the most frequent maternal intervention, and also the most successful. As shown in Figure 4.3, it soothed crying infants in over 80 percent of the instances in which it was observed. More specifically, lifting the crying baby to the shoulder, a method that involves at least three dimensions of stimulation — physical contact, motion, and the upright posture — is the technique that works the best. It not only encourages infants to stop crying, but also causes them to become quietly alert and visually attentive to

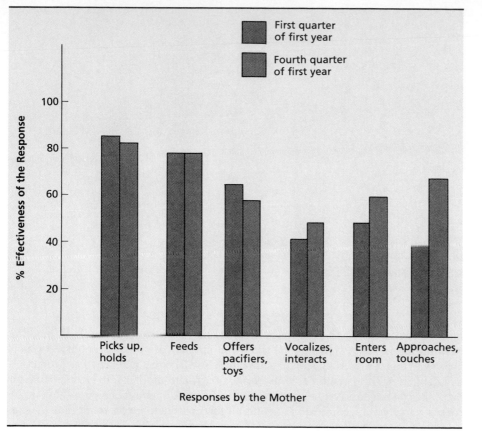

Figure 4.3. Effectiveness of various maternal responses to crying in the first and fourth quarters of the first year in the Bell and Ainsworth (1972) study. *(From S. M. Bell & M. D. S. Ainsworth, 1972, "Infant Crying and Maternal Responsiveness."* Child Development, *43, 1182. © The Society for Research in Child Development, Inc.)*

the environment. Other methods that offer tactile or motion stimulation, such as touching infants while they lie in their cribs or picking them up and holding them in a horizontal position, do not work as well (Korner & Thoman, 1972). Not surprisingly, Figure 4.3 also shows that feeding the baby is another highly successful soothing technique. In fact, any other method is bound to be just a temporary stop-gap if the crying baby is hungry. Additional soothing methods mothers use are offering their infants pacifiers and toys and talking to them. Although these are less successful than picking the baby up, they still work about 40 to 60 percent of the time. Rhythmic rocking and swaddling (wrapping babies so their limbs are restricted) are also effective soothing techniques (Brown, 1964; Gordon & Foss, 1966). Whereas very young infants tend to require holding if they are to be soothed, the older 1-year-old seems content with other techniques that do not necessarily bring the mother and baby into close physical contact (Bell & Ainsworth, 1972).

How quickly and how often should a mother respond to her infant's cries? Will reacting promptly and consistently strengthen crying behavior and produce a demanding, miniature tyrant, or will it give infants a sense of confidence that their needs will be met and, over time, reduce their tendency to fuss and complain? Available answers to this question are controversial and conflicting. In a widely publicized study, Bell and Ainsworth (1972) concluded that responding consistently to a young baby's cries will not lead to dependency and spoiling. They found that mothers who delayed or failed to respond had babies who engaged in more frequent and persistent crying in the latter part of the first year. In addition, by 1 year of age these infants were less mature in their communicative behaviors. They had developed fewer noncrying modes of expressing their needs and desires, such as facial expressions, bodily gestures, and vocalizations. Bell and Ainsworth used *ethological theory* to interpret their

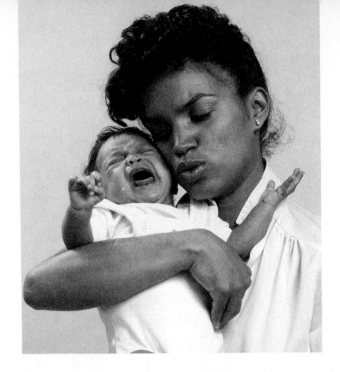

To soothe a crying infant, a mother often talks softly while holding her child closely. (Lew Merrim/ Monkmeyer Press Photo Service)

findings. According to this perspective, crying is viewed as the earliest possible proximity-promoting, signaling behavior in infants. Maternal responsiveness is adaptive in that it assures the infant's basic needs will be met and provides protection from danger. At the same time, it also brings baby and mother into close proximity where she can be sensitively responsive to a wide range of infant behaviors and, in the process, can encourage her baby to communicate through means other than crying.

Other investigators disagree with Bell and Ainsworth's (1972) findings and conclusions. Gewirtz and Boyd (1977a; 1977b) criticized their results on methodological grounds and, instead, adhered to a *behaviorist* position. From this point of view, consistently responding to a crying infant rewards the crying response and results in a whiny, demanding child. A cross-cultural study of several child-rearing environments in Israel provides support for this position. Infants of Bedouin tribespeople, among whom there is an explicit norm never to let babies fuss and cry, were compared with home-reared babies as well as with infants raised together in institutional and kibbutz[2] settings. In agreement with behaviorist theory, Bedouin babies (whose mothers rush to them at the first whimper) fussed and cried the most throughout the first year of life, followed by infants reared in homes, where there is greater opportunity to respond promptly to a crying baby than there is in institutional and kibbutz environments in which children are cared for in groups (Landau, 1982).

These contrasting theories and findings indicate that there is no simple, easy formula for how parents should respond to their infant's cries. The conditions under which babies cry are complex, and parents must make reasoned choices about what to do based on a variety of factors, including culturally accepted practices, the specific circumstances evoking the cry, its intensity, and the general context in which the cry occurs — for example, in the privacy of the parents' own home, while having dinner at a restaurant, or while visiting the household of friends or relatives. Certainly no one would suggest that a mother prolong the discomfort of a hungry baby or ignore her infant's urgent cry of pain. However, the communicative intent of infant cries changes over the course of the first year to include more psychologically based desires, such as demands for attention and expressions of impatience and frustration. As infants get older and cry less often for purely physical reasons, both ethological and behaviorist

---

[2] A kibbutz is an Israeli agricultural settlement in which children are reared together in children's houses, freeing both parents for full participation in the economic life of the community.

theory would probably agree that one way parents can lessen their babies' need to cry is to encourage them to choose other more mature ways of communicating their desires.

The fact that newborn babies produce typical cries has led investigators to search for abnormal patterns of infant crying. Spectrographic analyses indicate that the pitch of the baby's cry is a fundamental indicator of central nervous system distress. The cries of brain-damaged infants are especially shrill and piercing (Wolff, 1969). Newborns who have experienced prenatal and perinatal complications also tend to have high-pitched cries. In addition, they require more stimulation to elicit a crying response than control infants, and their cries are of shorter duration (Zeskind & Lester, 1978; 1981). The nature of the high-risk infant's cry has implications for the caregiver-infant relationship. Parents perceive tape recordings of such cries as especially noxious and describe them as "sick and urgent" (Zeskind & Lester, 1981; Frodi et al., 1978). The cry of the high-risk infant may, in some cases, be so unpleasant to parents that it does not induce the care necessary to facilitate recovery of the baby and leads to further difficulties for an already stressed infant. In infant child abuse cases, a high-pitched, grating cry is sometimes mentioned as a causal factor (Parke & Collmer, 1975; Frodi, 1985).

Neonatal Assessment

A variety of instruments are available for assessing the overall behavioral status of the infant during the newborn period. The most widely used is Brazelton's (1984) **Neonatal Behavioral Assessment Scale (NBAS).** It provides a general overview of the newborn infant's behavioral repertoire, including reflexes, responsiveness to a variety of environmental stimuli, state changes, and soothability.

Neonatal assessment is useful for a variety of reasons. When scores are combined with information from a physical examination, all but a very few cases of neurological impairment can be diagnosed within the first few weeks of life (Amiel-Tison, 1985). The NBAS has also been useful for describing the effects of prenatal and perinatal risk factors on infant behavior. In fact, a special adaptation of the scale has been developed for use with preterm infants (Als et al., 1980).

Neonatal assessment can help determine how infant behavior contributes to later development. Several studies show that NBAS scores bear some relationship to later developmental outcomes. Infants classified as "worrisome" on the NBAS have been found to be somewhat less responsive to caregivers in feeding and play situations at 6 months of age, and NBAS scores are modestly associated with mental test performance at 9 months (Vaughn et al., 1980) and social competence at age 3 (Bakeman & Brown, 1980). Because neonatal behavior is thought to affect the way parents respond to their infants, and because parental responsiveness, in turn, contributes to later behavior, additional research using the NBAS is likely to be helpful in clarifying the course of early development (Horowitz & Linn, 1982).

Research with the NBAS has also highlighted cultural differences in neonatal behavior. For example, assessments of Chinese-American newborns reveal that they are better at self-quieting and are more easily soothed than Caucasian-American infants (Freedman & Freedman, 1969). Cross-cultural research provides a means for understanding how behavioral differences at birth may contribute to maternal practices and, eventually, to developmental outcomes that are culturally adaptive. In one study, assessments of a group of Zambian babies who were undernourished and dehydrated at birth revealed low scores in responsiveness to their physical and social environment on the first day of life. However, by the tenth day the Zambian infants had obtained high scores on alertness, social interest, and soothability. The rapid recovery of these babies was attributed to the way Zambian mothers carry their infants about all day on their hips, thereby providing them with a rich variety of

Similar to women in the Zambian culture, Senegalese mothers carry their babies about all day, providing close physical contact and a rich variety of stimulation. (Arlene Bloom)

visual, auditory, and tactile experiences. This maternal practice also fits with Zambian cultural expectations for early physical and social development (Brazelton, Koslowski, & Tronick, 1976). In another study, neonatal assessments of Zinacanteco Indian babies of southern Mexico revealed them to be quieter and less demanding at birth than Caucasian infants. By swaddling, maintaining close physical contact, and nursing the infant at the earliest sign of restlessness, the Indian mothers encouraged their babies' moderate state behavior. The soothing child-rearing practices of this small society of Mayan descendants seemed well adapted to the culture's strong emphasis on conformity and compliance and, at the same time, complemented the quiet, placid behavior of the Indian babies (Brazelton, Robey, & Collier, 1969).

Although the NBAS is used largely for research, it has also been used in a practical way, to educate parents about infant capabilities and to sensitize them to their baby's individual characteristics (Widmayer & Field, 1980). In some hospitals, portions of the NBAS are done in the presence of parents as part of programs aimed at teaching them about their infants (Horowitz & Linn, 1982).

Learning in the Newborn

Learning refers to changes in behavior over time as the result of experience. Investigators have been interested in finding out how early infants are able to engage in certain types of learning. They have sought answers to the following questions: To what extent are newborn babies capable of profiting from experience? Are some kinds of experiences more effective in modifying infant behavior than others?

Most research directed at answering these questions has involved the application of two basic learning paradigms: classical and operant conditioning. Conditioning studies investigate how learning builds upon the baby's repertoire of reflexes through the direct association of environmental stimuli with infant responses. However, the ability of infants to profit from experience is not limited to these two basic forms of learning. As we shall see, very young infants also learn through their remarkable capacity to imitate and remember events in the surrounding world.

Classical Conditioning. **Classical conditioning** involves learning a new association between a neutral stimulus and a stimulus that reliably elicits a reflexive response. In other words, control of the response is transferred to a new stimulus that did not evoke it in the first place. You may know the famous experiment of Ivan Pavlov, the Russian psychologist who first identified the components of the classical conditioning paradigm. At the beginning of Pavlov's experiment, the taste of food powder automatically caused a dog to salivate, but a neutral stimulus, the sound of a bell, did not. After several repeated pairings of the bell with the food powder, Pavlov's dog learned to salivate at the sound of the bell alone.

The key steps in classical conditioning are as follows:

1. Before learning takes place, an **unconditioned stimulus (UCS)** must reliably elicit a reflexive, or **unconditioned response (UCR),** while a neutral, or **conditioned stimulus (CS)** does not.

UCS ⟶ UCR
Food powder   Salivation

CS   (does not elicit salivation)
Bell

2. To produce learning, the CS and UCS are presented in close temporal sequence. Optimally, the CS is presented just before the UCS.

CS
Bell
UCS ⟶ UCR
Food powder   Salivation

3. To find out if learning occurred, the CS presented by itself must produce the reflexive response, which, if it occurs, is now called a **conditioned response (CR).**

CS ⟶ CR
Bell   Salivation

Of course, if the CS is presented by itself enough times without further presentations of the UCS, eventually the CR will cease to occur. This is referred to as **extinction.** The occurrence of responses to the CS during the extinction phase of a classical conditioning experiment is the main indicator that learning has taken place.

Demonstration of classical conditioning in the neonate is problematic for several reasons. First, the infant's state can easily interfere with learning. Ideally, a state of alert wakefulness is best for conditioning, but babies frequently drift in and out of drowsiness or fall asleep during the various phases of an experiment. Second, elaborate controls are necessary in research designs to make sure that changes in infant behavior are truly the result of classical conditioning and do not occur for other reasons. When the UCR in question is a very pervasive neonatal behavior, such as sucking, investigators must take special precautions to make sure that spontaneous responding is not mistaken for conditioning.

Despite careful controls, efforts to classically condition newborn infants have not met with uniform success. The positive findings of some studies have not been replicated (Wenger, 1936; Wickens & Wickens, 1940). In others, so many CS-UCS pairings were required for learning to be demonstrated that it appeared that newborn infants could only be classically conditioned with difficulty (Papousek, 1967; Papousek & Bernstein, 1969). In fact, classical conditioning has almost completely disappeared from the infancy research literature, probably because investigators found the phenomenon so hard to demonstrate in young infants (Olson & Sherman, 1983).

The most successful attempts to classically condition newborns involve CS-UCS pairings that have biological significance for the human infant. In these cases, the organism seems "prepared" to form the association, and learning is more easily demonstrated. In one study that obtained classical conditioning in infants as early as 2 hours after birth, the investigators chose tactile stimulation as the CS. Touch is a natural means of mother-infant communication that may help babies predict biologically significant everyday events, such as when nursing is about to occur. Experimental group infants were offered a sugar water solution as the UCS, with resultant sucking as the UCR. Just before delivery of the sugar water, the babies' foreheads were stroked (CS). When the CS was presented alone during extinction, the experimental group showed a much higher incidence of sucking (CR) than did control group babies (Blass, Ganchrow, & Steiner, 1984).

In general, efforts to classically condition newborn infants show that some CS-UCS combinations produce conditioning, while others do not. Clearly, there are constraints on infant learning (Olson & Sherman, 1983). After an extensive review of many conditioning studies, Sameroff and Cavanaugh (1979) concluded that it would be a mistake to assume from the results of these investigations that babies are merely passive subjects of environmental contingencies. To the contrary, processes intrinsic to the infant play an important role in determining which associations will be classically conditioned. At the very least, the adaptive significance of what is to be learned, as well as the state of the infant at the time of conditioning, are major influences on the range of associations that infants will make.

Operant Conditioning. In **operant conditioning,** a spontaneously emitted behavior is followed by an outcome that changes the probability that the behavior will occur again. Outcomes that increase the occurrence of a behavior are called **reinforcers,** whereas those that decrease the occurrence of the behavior are called **punishments.** In contrast to classical conditioning where the subject's behavior has no effect on the sequence of events, in operant conditioning the subject's response determines whether reinforcers or punishments will follow it (Sameroff & Cavanaugh, 1979).

Unlike classical conditioning, operant conditioning of young infants has been demonstrated in a wide variety of studies. Because the newborn lacks voluntary control over many behaviors, successful operant conditioning has been limited to sucking and head-turning responses, with many types of stimuli serving as reinforcers. These studies show that neonates are competent beings who can control environmental events with the limited range of behaviors that they have (Appleton, Clifton, & Goldberg, 1975). For example, very young infants will vary their sucking patterns according to the sweetness of the fluid they receive. When water is delivered after a sugar solution, newborns display their apparent aversion for the water by dramatically reducing their rate of sucking (Kobre & Lipsitt, 1972; Lipsitt & Werner, 1981). Newborns also quickly learn to turn their heads to the side when this response is followed by a sugar water reinforcer (Siqueland & Lipsitt, 1966).

Stimulus variety and change are just as effective as food in reinforcing the behavior of the young infant. Researchers have created special environments for infants in which visual or auditory feedback is made contingent on the baby's rate of sucking on a nonnutritive nipple. Newborns as young as 3 weeks of age will suck faster when their sucking behavior controls the appearance and brightness of a visual display, and young infants will also increase their sucking when music, speech sounds, and human voices serve as reinforcers (Eimas et al., 1971; Siqueland & DeLucia, 1969). Because stimuli from such a wide variety of sensory modalities can modify infant behavior, the operant conditioning paradigm has become a powerful research tool for clarifying the infant's perceptual preferences and abilities.

As infants get older, successful operant conditioning expands to include a wider range of infant behaviors and environmental events. In several studies, special mobiles have been hung over the cribs of 2-month-old infants. By making small head movements on a pressure-sensitive pillow (Watson & Ramey, 1972) or by kicking a foot that is connected to the mobile by means of a long silk cord (Rovee & Rovee, 1969), babies can, through their own activity, make the mobile shake or turn. In both of these studies, infants receiving contingent visual stimulation from the mobile showed a dramatic increase in response rate in comparison to controls who received either noncontingent stimulation or who were exposed to a mobile that would not move at all. Studies like these show that infants quickly develop active modes of controlling the world around them and that they are motivated to repeat those behaviors that lead to interesting effects in the surrounding environment. Because the operant conditioning label is generally taken to reflect the traditional behaviorist position of an infant passively responding to environmental contingencies, Sameroff and Cavanaugh (1979) prefer the term *action-consequence learning* to describe the *active* efforts of infants to explore and control their surroundings. See Box 4.1 for an intriguing account of how the emergence of these active learning efforts may be related to a major cause of infant mortality: *sudden infant death syndrome.*

Like classical conditioning, there are constraints on the extent to which infants can be operantly conditioned, since they will not learn to associate any stimulus with any response. Social responses, like infant vocalization, are more easily conditioned by social reinforcers, such as a game of peek-a-boo, than they are by nonsocial reinforcers (Ramey & Watson, 1972; Weisberg, 1963). In contrast, nonsocial re-

---

FOCUS ON CONTEMPORARY ISSUES

Box 4.1
The Mysterious Tragedy of Sudden Infant Death Syndrome

In *sudden infant death syndrome (SIDS)*, a baby stops breathing, usually during the night, and dies silently without apparent cause. SIDS takes the lives of as many as 8,000 babies annually in the United States, and it is responsible for more deaths among infants between 10 days and 1 year of age than any other cause. The tragedy is especially difficult for parents to bear because of the absence of definite answers as to why SIDS occurs. As a result, many parents blame themselves. In the last two decades, more information has come to light about the characteristics of SIDS victims, and promising hypotheses about the causes of SIDS are being followed up with new research.

Several studies indicate that babies who succumb to SIDS show biological vulnerabilities from the very beginning. Birth records and early pediatric examinations of victims reveal lower Apgar scores, respiratory abnormalities, flaccid muscle tone, and poor visual performance in terms of ability to focus on objects (Anderson-Huntington & Rosenblith, 1976; Lipsitt, Sturner, & Burke, 1979). Abnormal fluctuations in heart rate and respiratory activity as well as disturbances of sleeping and waking states throughout the night are also thought to be involved (Gordon et al., 1984; Harper et al., 1981; Sadeh et al., 1987). At the time of death, many SIDS babies are reported to have a mild respiratory infection, a circumstance that seems to heighten the chances of respiratory failure in the already vulnerable baby (Guilleminault, Boeddiker, & Schwab, 1982).

Lewis Lipsitt (1982) believes that the biological fragility of SIDS infants makes it difficult for them to benefit from experience in ways that would prepare them to respond defensively if their survival is threatened—for example, when respiration is suddenly interrupted. According to Lipsitt, SIDS infants may suffer from a basic learning disability in the first few months of life. In the period between 2 and 4 months of age, when the incidence of SIDS reaches its peak, infant reflexes diminish and are supplanted by voluntary "learned responses." If babies have not acquired critical defensive behaviors to replace protective reflexes that have disappeared, their survival may be in jeopardy. Lipsitt believes that respiratory inadequacy, general lethargy, and visual inattentiveness at birth may lead the SIDS infant to engage the environment less well and to experience fewer opportunities for learning than infants not born under such risk conditions. When a respiratory threat occurs, appropriate voluntary behaviors may not have been learned in time to supplant the defensive reflex that wanes between 2 and 4 months of age, leading to oxygen deprivation and death.

On the basis of biological indicators, it is possible to identify infants who may be potential victims of this tragic syndrome. Lipsitt's hypothesis about the origins of SIDS suggests that in addition to monitoring physiological signs, intervention programs may need to provide infants with special help in the acquisition of life-saving defensive responses.

sponses, like kicking or touching an object in front of the infant, are best learned when the reinforcer consists of nonsocial visual and auditory stimuli. As with classical conditioning, there appear to be operant connections that the infant is especially "prepared" to learn (Sameroff & Cavanaugh, 1979).

Habituation and Memory. **Habituation** refers to the gradual waning of response when subjects are exposed to repetitive stimulation. Provided the repetitive stimulus is mild or only moderately intense, responses of human infants will decrease in strength, sometimes to the point of complete disappearance, even though the initial presentation of the stimulus may have produced strong reactions, such as a marked startle, intense looking, and a change in heart rate. Once the infant's behavior has waned, presentation of a new stimulus will cause the baby's response to **dishabituate,** or return to its original level. This habituation-dishabituation sequence indicates that the infant has stored some information about the repeatedly exposed stimulus in memory and then recognizes that the new stimulus is different from the old.

Let's take an example in order to examine this important paradigm for studying infant memory more closely. In one investigation, Fagan and Singer (1979) used the habituation-dishabituation sequence to find out if 5- to 6-month-old infants could discriminate between two similar photographs: one of a baby's face and another of a bald-headed man. As shown in Figure 4.4, during phase 1 of the study (habituation phase), infant subjects were presented with a baby picture and allowed to look at it for a short period of time. The researchers measured visual fixation to be sure that the infants had studied the photo. In phase 2 (dishabituation phase), the infants were shown the same baby picture, but now it was presented simultaneously with a picture of a bald-headed man. During this part of the procedure, the investigators kept careful track of which photo the infants looked at most. Because subjects paid more attention, or dishabituated, to the bald-headed man as opposed to the baby, the researchers concluded that infants both remembered the baby's face and identified the picture of the man as something new and different.

A large number of habituation studies demonstrate that infants several months old

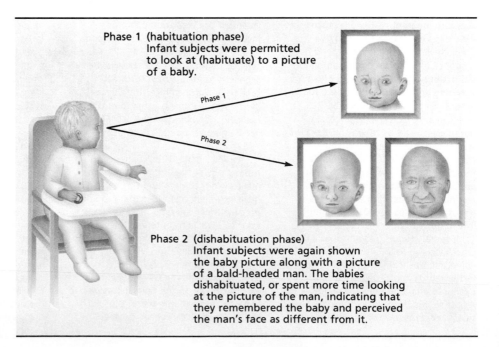

Phase 1 (habituation phase)
Infant subjects were permitted to look at (habituate) to a picture of a baby.

Phase 1

Phase 2

Phase 2 (dishabituation phase)
Infant subjects were again shown the baby picture along with a picture of a bald-headed man. The babies dishabituated, or spent more time looking at the picture of the man, indicating that they remembered the baby and perceived the man's face as different from it.

Figure 4.4. Example of the habituation-dishabituation paradigm, as applied in the Fagan and Singer (1979) study. *(Adapted from J. F. Fagan III & L. T. Singer, 1979.)*

remember visual stimuli to which they have been exposed. Can this ability be found even earlier, during the first few weeks of life? Although the first studies of habituation in the neonate did not find evidence of recognition memory, subsequent investigations showed that if infants were given a long time to study the initial stimulus and the stimulus patterns employed were widely different from one another, the ability to remember aspects of the environment could be detected from birth on. In fact, Werner and Siqueland (1978) even found evidence of memory for a visual stimulus in 6-day-old infants born 5 weeks preterm. They had babies suck on a nonnutritive nipple to bring a checkerboard pattern into focus (in the same way as was done in the operant conditioning studies we discussed earlier). After 5 minutes of study time, the babies habituated to the repeated target in that their sucking declined. When a new checkerboard was introduced that differed from the original on a variety of dimensions — size, number of pattern elements, color, and brightness — an immediate rise in sucking frequency showed that the infants retained sufficient memory of the first checkerboard to differentiate it from the new pattern. Werner and Siqueland's study shows that even preterm babies can remember some things they have seen when visual patterns are highly distinct. However, because they require an especially long exposure to the initial stimulus in order to demonstrate the habituation-dishabituation sequence, their memory processing seems to be slower than that of full-term infants (Rose, 1980).

As infants get older, they can make successively finer distinctions among stimuli in a habituation-dishabituation paradigm, and from 5 months on they require only 5 to 10 seconds of study time for immediate recognition. When the older infant is given more time to examine the first stimulus, recognition that two visual patterns are different will persist over delays of several minutes between presentation of the stimuli, even in the face of potential interference from other stimuli to which the infant may be exposed during the delay (Fagan, 1971; 1977).

Habituation can also be used to test how long an infant's memory of a single stimulus lasts. Infants can be exposed to a stimulus pattern until they habituate. Then they can be exposed to the same pattern again at a later time. If habituation takes place more rapidly on the second occasion, this indicates that infants must recognize they have seen the pattern before. Using this method, studies show that by 3 months of age infants remember a visual stimulus for as long as 24 hours (Martin, 1975). As they increase in age over the first year, they retain information for progressively longer times — up to several days or, in the case of very familiar stimuli such as the human face, even weeks (Fagan, 1973).

Individual differences among infants in visual recognition memory seem to be linked to later intelligence. Research shows that the extent to which infants dishabituate to novel stimuli during the first few months of life is moderately correlated with intellectual performance during the preschool years (Lewis & Brooks-Gunn, 1981; Fagan & McGrath, 1981). In addition, infants expected to show depressed intelligence in later life, such as Down syndrome babies, differ from normals in habituation and recovery to visual stimuli (Cohen, 1981). These findings suggest that the study of early infant memory may provide important insights into basic processes underlying human intelligence (Fagan, 1984).

Although most habituation studies have been concerned with the visual modality, neonates have been shown to habituate to auditory and olfactory stimuli as well (Bartoshuk, 1962; Engen & Lipsitt, 1965). Besides enhancing our understanding of infant memory, habituation research provides much information about the perceptual world of infants. As we shall see later on, it has become an important method for determining what babies can perceive, and for charting the course of perceptual development (Fagan, 1984).

In the discussion above, we referred to the young infant's memory as *recognition memory*. By this we mean an infant's ability to recognize a previously observed stimulus when it reappears (through habituating to it more quickly the second time around), or that two stimuli presented successively are different from one another (as in the habituation-dishabituation paradigm). We have not discussed *productive memory,* which involves the ability to recall something that is not present. There is evidence that by 1 year of age infants have some capacity for productive memory, since they spontaneously imitate games such as peek-a-boo and recall the locations of familiar objects (Nelson, 1984). However, productive memory depends heavily on mental representation and language, abilities that are more fully developed after 2 years of age (Piaget, 1968), and it is usually examined through verbal recall. We shall take up productive memory in Chapter 7 when we consider the memory capacities of the verbal child.

Imitation. If you have had the opportunity to spend time with infants, you may have noticed the extent to which babies in the first year of life tend to **imitate,** or copy, the behavior of others. Adults capitalize on this tendency when they amuse infants by playing imitative games with them, such as pat-a-cake and peek a boo. Babies take great pleasure in these activities and respond with smiles, gleeful vocalizations, and excited motor activity.

According to major theorists of infant development, imitative behaviors are not expected to appear before the end of the first year, and they are assumed to be beyond the cognitive competence of younger infants (Bayley, 1969; Gesell & Thompson, 1938; Piaget, 1945/1951a). Nevertheless, several studies report that newborn babies have the capacity to engage in rudimentary imitation of a visual model. These investigations are controversial because, if they are correct, they indicate that neonates are far more sophisticated in their ability to process environmental stimuli than was previously believed to be the case. Imitation as a powerful strategy for learning may be the starting point, rather than the culmination, of infant development.

Meltzoff and Moore (1977) conducted one of the first systematic investigations of neonatal imitation. Their study touched off a hot debate about whether newborn infants can imitate facial and manual gestures demonstrated by adults. Infants between 12 and 21 days of age were presented with four different gestures to imitate. Three of them were facial gestures (tongue protrusion, mouth opening, and lip protrusion), and one was a manual gesture (sequential finger movements). By showing that infants frequently exhibited the same gesture in response to the modeled behavior of an adult, Meltzoff and Moore claimed that neonates were capable of imitating all of these behaviors. In another study of neonatal imitation, Field and her collaborators (1982) reported that 2-day-old infants imitated happy, sad, and surprised facial expressions of an adult model. In both of these studies, the investigators concluded that newborn babies come into the world with a sophisticated ability to translate a wide variety of modeled behaviors they see into equivalent motor responses. Convincing photographic records offer further support for this conclusion (see Figure 4.5).

Claims that newborn infants can imitate the gestures of other human beings seem so extraordinary that it is not surprising they have been disputed. Anisfeld (1979) carefully studied Meltzoff and Moore's data and showed that although infants did exhibit behaviors that matched those of the model, many responses also occurred that did not match. For example, when an adult engaged in lip protrusions, the incidence of infant lip protrusions was high, but tongue protrusion and hand opening also occurred with great frequency. In addition, several studies have failed to replicate the findings on neonatal imitation (e.g., Hayes & Watson, 1981; McKenzie & Over, 1983). In two investigations that did find some evidence of imitation in infants under 6 weeks of age, the ability of young babies to imitate was much more limited than it was in Meltzoff and Moore's and Field's research. Among a variety of modeled behaviors, tongue protrusion was the only one that elicited imitation, and infant responses were partial and incomplete versions of the modeled action, not well formed copies (Abravanel & Sigafoos, 1984; Kaitz et al., 1988).

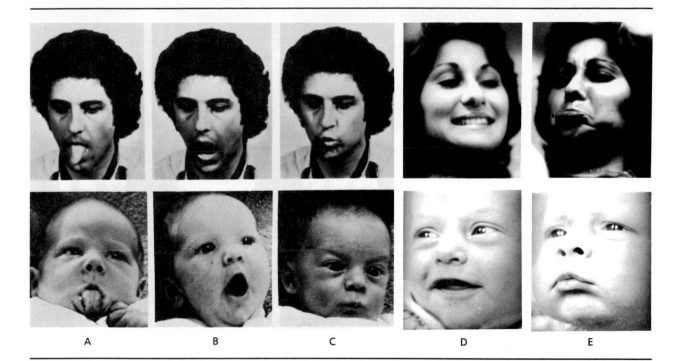

Figure 4.5. Photographs from two studies of neonatal imitation. Photographs from the Meltzoff and Moore (1977) study show 2- to 3-week-old infants imitating tongue protrusion *(A)*, mouth opening *(B)*, and lip protrusion *(C)* by an adult experimenter. In photographs from the Field et al. (1981) study, 2-day-old infants imitate happy *(D)* and sad *(E)* adult facial expressions. *(From T. M. Field et al., 1982, "Discrimination and Imitation of Facial Expressions by Neonates," Science, 218, 180 [Copyright 1977 by the AAAS]; A. N. Meltzoff & M. K. Moore, 1977, "Imitation of Facial and Manual Gestures by Human Neonates," Science, 198, 75 [Copyright 1977 by the AAAS].)*

Meltzoff and Moore (1983) have responded to skeptics of neonatal imitative abilities by providing their own replication of their original findings. They argue that investigations failing to find evidence for neonatal imitation were poorly controlled in that they did not use special laboratory procedures designed to keep the baby's attention on the model. In a review of research on infant imitation, Harris (1983) concluded that although the research is mixed, the weight of the evidence indicates that neonates *can* engage in some imitation, but the capacity is not fully developed, and imitative abilities undergo considerable change over the first 2 years of life. Imitation in newborn babies is restricted to a limited number of actions, such as tongue protrusion, that are common responses within the neonate's repertoire of behavior. Later on, as infants make strides in the development of skilled motor action, they are able to imitate increasingly complex and unfamiliar sequences of behavior, and in the latter part of the first year their ability to imitate becomes less approximate and far more exact (Kaye & Marcus, 1981). Finally, deferred imitation — the ability to replicate the behavior of a model hours or days after it is first observed — is a complex cognitive achievement that does not emerge until the second year of life, and we shall discuss how it develops in a later chapter.

However basic and elemental, the capacity to engage in imitation provides newborn infants with another powerful mechanism for learning. Imitation is a way to get young infants to express desirable behaviors, and once they are demonstrated, adults can encourage and reinforce them further. Later on in the first year, when infants are able to reproduce unfamiliar actions, imitation is an important way in which new responses are incorporated into the baby's behavioral repertoire (Rosenblith & Sims-Knight, 1985). Imitation also plays an important role in infant social development. Adults take great pleasure in a baby who imitates their facial gestures and actions, and as infants and adults trade imitative responses back and forth, both enjoy the interaction (Lipsitt & Werner, 1981). Such imitative interchanges are common in infancy and probably serve as an important ingredient in the development of mother-infant attachment.

MOTOR DEVELOPMENT IN INFANCY

Virtually all parents of young infants eagerly anticipate their baby's achievement of new motor skills. Baby books are filled with proud notations, and parents are quick to inform friends and relatives as soon as the infant holds her head up, reaches for objects, sits by herself, and walks alone. Parental enthusiasm for these motor accomplishments is not at all misplaced, for they are, indeed, milestones of development. With each additional skill, babies gain control over their bodies and the environment in a new way. Infants who are able to sit alone are granted an entirely different perspective on the world than are those who spend much of their day on their backs or stomachs. Coordinated reaching opens up a whole new avenue for exploration of objects, and when babies can move about, their opportunities for independent exploration and manipulation are multiplied. No longer are they restricted to their immediate locale and to objects that others place before them. As new ways of controlling the environment are achieved, motor development provides the infant with a growing sense of competence and mastery, and it contributes in important ways to the infant's perceptual and cognitive understanding of the world (Appleton, Clifton, & Goldberg, 1975).

Babies' emerging motor competencies also have a powerful effect on their social relationships. For example, the appearance of crawling leads parents to restrict the infant's activities in ways that were previously unnecessary when the baby, placed on a blanket, would stay there! New motor skills, such as pointing at and showing toys, enable infants to communicate more effectively with others. In response, parents place less emphasis on physical caregiving in the second half of the first year and engage in more game-playing and verbal requests with their babies, and these new ways of interacting provide further encouragement for infants' rapidly expanding motor abilities. Modifications in motor skills and in the infant's social environment are mutually supportive. Changes in one promote and sustain the changes that occur in the other (Green, Gustafson, & West, 1980).

The Organization and Sequence of Motor Development

Designers of tests to measure infant development rely heavily on motor skills because they are the most obvious and clearly visible accomplishments of infancy. Table 4.2 provides the average ages at which a variety of motor skills are achieved, as well as the age range during which the great majority of infants accomplish each skill, based on a major infant test, the Bayley Scales of Infant Development (Bayley, 1969). Whereas most infants adhere fairly closely to the sequence of motor skills given in the table, the age ranges indicate that there are substantial individual differences among normal babies in the rate at which motor development proceeds. In addition to individual differences, there is another reason to consider age averages for infant motor skills with caution. Like height and weight (which we will discuss in Chapter 5), motor development seems to be subject to a **secular trend,** in that infants achieve these milestones earlier today than they did half a century ago (Appleton, Clifton, & Goldberg, 1975; Harriman & Lukosius, 1982). A variety of factors could be responsible for this gradual acceleration in infant motor progress, including better nutrition, health care, and changing ways of rearing infants.

Table 4.2. Milestones of Infant Motor Development

MOTOR SKILL	AVERAGE AGE ACHIEVED	AGE RANGE WITHIN WHICH ACHIEVED BY MOST INFANTS
Holds head erect and steady when held upright	7 weeks	3 weeks – 4 months
When prone, elevates self by arms	2 months	3 weeks – 5 months
Rolls from side to back	2 months	3 weeks – 5 months
Rolls from back to side	4½ months	2 – 7 months
Grasps cube	3 months 3 weeks	2 – 7 months
Sits alone, good coordination	7 months	5 – 9 months
Pulls to stand	8 months	5 – 12 months
Uses neat pincer grasp	9 months	7 – 10 months
Plays pat-a-cake	9 months 3 weeks	7 – 15 months
Stands alone	11 months	9 – 16 months
Walks alone	11 months 3 weeks	9 – 17 months

Source: N. Bayley (1969).

Look carefully at Table 4.2 once more, and you will see that there is organization and direction to the infant's motor achievements. Two well-known patterns of motor development are reflected in the order of the entries. First, motor control of the head comes before control of the arms and trunk, and control of the arms and trunk is achieved before control of the legs. This head-to-foot sequence is called the **cephalo-caudal trend** of development. Second, motor functioning proceeds from the center of the body outward, in that head and arm control are achieved before coordination of the hands and fingers. This is the **proximo-distal trend** of development. It is interesting that physical growth during the prenatal period, as well as during infancy and childhood, follows these same trends. Because motor control shows the same directional course as early physical development, it is thought that the cephalo-caudal and proximo-distal patterns are genetically preprogrammed, maturational phenomena (Shirley, 1933).

Infant motor skills can be divided into two broad classes: (1) postural and gross motor accomplishments; and (2) fine motor skills. In each, mastery of behavior is sequential and builds upon prior accomplishments. In gross motor development, control of the head and upper chest contribute to the ability to sit with support, and crawling and standing to the ability to walk alone. The way in which simple motor acts are eventually combined and integrated into complex behaviors is even more evident in the development of fine motor skills. As we will see later on when we discuss the special significance of visually guided reaching, the component acts of grasping, looking, and arm movements at first emerge independently, and then they are coordinated with one another to achieve successful reaching. Once this is accomplished, reaching is available as a separate element to be combined with other skills in even more complex activities, such as stacking blocks and putting objects in containers (Appleton, Clifton, & Goldberg, 1975).

Maturation versus Experience and Motor Skills

We have described the organized, sequential quality of motor development and noted its profound impact on other areas of development, but the question still remains: What processes explain the emergence of motor skills?

The research of early investigators of the 1930s and 1940s led them to conclude that motor skills were under the control of biological maturation and that experience had little to do with the timing or form into which motor behaviors were cast. For example, Gesell (1929) conducted a famous study of a pair of identical twins in which one was given early practice at stair climbing and fine motor manipulation of cubes and the other was not. Without intensive practice, the untrained twin quickly caught up with the trained twin after exposure to the stairs and the cubes at a more mature age. In another investigation, Dennis and Dennis (1940) studied age of walking among the Hopi Indians, some of whom bound their infants to cradle boards, while others, influenced by Western ways, had given up this practice. Despite severe restriction of movement among the cradle board infants throughout the first year of life, both groups of infants walked unaided at precisely the same age—around 15 months. However, these studies were deliberately designed to decide between two extreme theories of development, and little attention was paid to subtle experiences that could have influenced the motor skills in question. For example, in Gesell's study, unknown aspects of the untrained twin's natural, everyday experiences, such as opportunities to climb on furniture, could have facilitated stair climbing, and in the Dennises' investigation of infant walking, constant exposure to the upright posture on the cradle board could have compensated for early movement deprivation among the Hopi babies (Bower, 1982).

It is now recognized that both maturation and experience influence the course of motor development. In fact, later in his career, after observing infants reared under extremely deprived conditions in Iranian institutions, Dennis (1960) recognized the vital importance of early postural experience and a generally stimulating environment for the emergence of motor skills. Iranian infants who were reared from the first month of life in an extremely deprived institution where they spent their days lying on their backs in cribs showed severe retardation in the appearance of gross motor skills, such as sitting, creeping, and walking. When the infants finally did begin to move about (which for the great majority was not until after 2 years of age), the constant experience of lying on their backs in early infancy led most of them to scoot about in a sitting position rather than crawl on their hands and knees the way that family-reared babies do. The early experience of these institutionalized infants changed not only their rate of motor development but the form into which it was cast. Dennis pointed out that the preference for scooting may have had the effect of further retarding the institutionalized infants' motor progress. Babies who scoot encounter furniture and objects with their feet, not their hands, and they are unlikely to pull themselves to a standing position in preparation for walking.

Research on babies born blind also indicates how experience affects the development of motor skills. Blind infants show a marked delay in locomotion in that they do not begin to creep, on the average, until 13 months of age, or walk until 19 months. After carefully observing their motor development, Fraiberg (1977) concluded that the absence of external stimulation normally provided by vision causes this delay. Sighted infants exhibit visually guided reaching between 3 and 4 months of age, but without vision, blind infants must depend on sound to localize the whereabouts of objects. Blind babies do not try to reach for and obtain a sounding object until the end of the first year of life, and until they do, they cannot be coaxed into moving from one place to another. Actually, sighted babies placed in darkness also do not reach for objects they can only hear but cannot see until the end of the first year (Wishart, Bower, & Dunkeld, 1978). Apparently, sound does not begin to function as a reliable clue to the whereabouts of objects until much later than vision. As a result, blind babies come to understand only relatively late in development that there is a world of tantalizing objects out there to be explored. Until "reaching on sound" has been achieved, they are not motivated to engage in self-initiated efforts to move about.

Without the advantage of sight as an early means for locating and responding to people and objects, blind babies tend to be passive, lethargic infants who do not evoke

Dennis and Dennis (1940) found that confinement to the cradle board did not impede the development of walking in Indian babies and concluded that the emergence of motor skills was largely under maturational control. Later studies revealed that both maturation and experience influence the course of motor development. (Leonard Lee Rue III/Photo Researchers)

responsive caregiving from their parents. Consequently, besides visual deprivation, many blind babies are also deprived of the tactile and sound stimulation that comes from being picked up, talked to, and played with frequently by their caregivers. Recognizing that blind infants require special stimulation of their intact senses for optimal development, Fraiberg (1977) developed an intervention program that provided them with experiences in which sound and touch were deliberately integrated. Parents were encouraged to talk to their blind baby when approaching, holding, and feeding the infant, and play experiences with objects that made sounds as the infant touched and manipulated them were provided. Fraiberg reasoned that everything done to facilitate "reaching on sound" would have the effect of motivating self-initiated movement at an earlier age. Indeed, this seemed to be the case, because infants participating in the intervention program showed much earlier achievement of locomotor milestones than a comparison sample receiving no intervention. Fraiberg's research on blind infants helps us appreciate how easy it is to ". . . overlook, in observing the sighted child, the contribution of vision to his eager, self-confident adventuring" (p. 217).

Fine Motor Development: The Special Case of Visually Guided Reaching

The ability to extend the hand and touch or grasp an object is a major advance in exploration and manipulation of the environment, and its perfection is believed to play an important role in infant cognitive development (Piaget, 1936/1952). Therefore, investigators have gone beyond merely identifying when visually guided reaching emerges to carefully charting its developmental course.

The development of reaching provides an excellent example of how motor development in infancy proceeds from diffuse, gross motor activity to skilled mastery of fine motor movements. Even newborns exhibit primitive reaching behavior. Placed upright in an infant seat, neonates direct their arms in the general vicinity of an object dangled before them, but their movements are not well coordinated, and they are rarely successful at contacting it. In fact, the newborn's primitive reaching movements have been called *prereaching*, as they resemble swipes or swings. Unlike older infants, neonates cannot carefully guide their hands with their eyes, and if they miss the object, they are unable to correct their error (Hofsten, 1982). Like the neonatal reflexes we discussed earlier, prereaching eventually drops out. It decreases abruptly around 7 weeks of age, and at about 3 months, visually guided reaching appears (Hofsten, 1984).

The reaching behavior of infants of a few months of age is far more accurate and successful than that of the neonate, as now infants use their eyes to guide the movements of their arms and hands, and as a result, imprecise movements and misses of the object can be compensated for and corrected (Bushnell, 1985). At first, visually guided reaching is limited and inflexible. The 3-month-old only contacts objects offered on the same side as the reaching hand. Reaching for objects at the midline and on the opposite side of the body develops gradually. By 4½ months, infants can successfully obtain objects in all three positions. This expansion in the range of visually guided manual skills greatly increases the variety of interactions the infant can have with the environment. Reaching to the midline is a preliminary step toward coordinated exploration of objects with both hands, and reaching across to the opposite side permits infants to grasp a second object when the hand on the same side is already occupied (Provine & Westerman, 1979).

Over the course of the first year, infants also improve the nature of their grasp so that they can adapt to objects of different sizes and characteristics. When the palmar grasp reflex weakens, it is replaced by primitive swiping at objects, and then by the **ulnar grasp,** a clumsy motion in which the fingers close against the palm. Soon, infants begin to use wrist movements and hand rotations to adjust to the way that objects are presented to them, and by the end of the first year, they use their thumb

Using an ulnar grasp, this 7-month-old baby clumsily grasps objects between her fingers and palm. (Gloria Karlson)

and forefinger opposably in a well-coordinated **pincer grasp** (Halverson, 1931). The opposable thumb is present in many primates, but only humans have the ability for thumb and index finger opposition (Bower, 1982).

Once the pincer grasp appears, infants begin to engage in far more refined and elaborate manipulation of objects, such as picking up raisins and blades of grass, turning knobs, manipulating latches, and opening small boxes. By 8 to 11 months of age, reaching and grasping are so well practiced that they are executed smoothly and effortlessly, and infants no longer need to monitor the movements of their arms and hands with their eyes to be successful. The decreased need for visual guidance is of major developmental significance, because the infant's attention is released from executing the motor skill itself and can be used for integrating events occurring before and after obtaining the object. The perfection of reaching attained at the end of the first year is thought to pave the way toward new cognitive advances, such as those described by Piaget, who indicated that infants first begin to search for hidden objects at this time (Bushnell, 1985).

Experience plays an important role in the development of visually guided reaching, as indicated by the results of a well-known study carried out by White and Held (1966), which is described in Box 4.2. White and Held's findings do not imply that parents must make a deliberate effort to teach their babies to reach, as almost all home environments offer sufficiently varied stimulation to assure that visually guided reaching will emerge quite adequately on its own. However, the study does suggest that some forms of infant stimulation — in particular, those that overwhelm the baby by providing too much all at once — can undermine the optimal emergence of important infant skills.

PERCEPTUAL CAPACITIES

In this section, we explore infants' sensitivity to touch, taste, smell, sound, and visual stimulation. Research on perceptual capacities of infants has largely addressed two questions: (1) What can infants perceive with their senses at birth; and (2) how do these capacities change over the first few months of life? Psychologists have been interested in answers to these questions for a number of reasons. One is the relevance

Box 4.2
The Role of Experience in the Development of Visually Guided Reaching

Theory. Burton White and Richard Held (1966) conducted an experiment with institutionalized infants that is renowned for having clarified the important role that experience plays in the emergence of visually guided reaching. Research with animals shows that a visually stimulating environment and opportunities for self-initiated movement are essential for the development of early sensorimotor skills. Animals deprived of visual stimulation (Riesen, 1966) or the opportunity to act on the environment through their own movements (Held & Hein, 1963) do not develop normally. White and Held reasoned from this evidence that enriching the environments of infants who ordinarily spend their early months under stimulus-deprived conditions and whose opportunities for active movement are restricted should have a facilitating effect on the development of early motor skills, such as visually guided reaching. Furthermore, providing infants with various types of enrichment should enhance our understanding of the consequences of different rearing conditions for early infant development.

Research. White and Held modified the early experiences of two groups of institutionalized infants who would have otherwise spent their days lying on their backs in a visually bland environment. In the massively enriched group, infants from 1 to 4 months of age were continuously exposed to an elaborate, multicolored mobile hung above their cribs, and patterned sheets and crib bumpers were substituted for the usual white ones. These changes were designed to encourage visual

attentiveness and, in so doing, to accelerate the appearance of swiping and visually guided reaching. In the moderately enriched group, infants were initially provided with a far simpler form of stimulation. Between 1 and 2 months of age, two pacifiers with red and white patterned disks attached to them were hung on their crib rails. Later on, between 2 and 4 months, the quantity of environmental enrichment was augmented by exposing the infants to the same elaborate mobile and crib bumpers that had been provided to the massively enriched group at an earlier age.

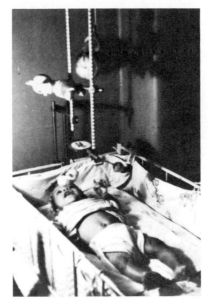

In the White and Held study, visually guided reaching emerged earlier when institutionalized infants were exposed to multi-colored mobiles than when they were left in a stimulus-deprived environment. However, massive enrichment in early infancy was not as beneficial as a moderate amount of stimulation. (Burton L. White)

White and Held confirmed their prediction that a visually stimulating environment has a dramatic effect on the emergence of early motor skills. Both the massively and moderately enriched groups mastered reaching for objects about a month and a half to two months earlier than control group babies exposed to the usual deprived institutional conditions. However, the investigators did not find that more stimulation was necessarily better! The moderately enriched infants were the ones who exhibited swiping and reaching for objects the earliest. Furthermore, during their first month of exposure to the mobile, massively enriched babies were the least attentive to their surroundings. They tended to look away from the mobile and crib bumpers, and they expressed their discomfort at being overwhelmed by so much stimulation by crying a great deal. At 2½ months of age, when they had matured sufficiently to handle a more complex environment, attentiveness to the mobile increased, and a month later, visually guided reaching emerged.

Applications. White and Held's study shows that a stimulating environment providing infants with ample opportunity to visually explore and touch objects has a major impact on the development of visual attention and fine motor skills. However, exposing very young babies to too many objects, designs, and patterns can cause discomfort and lead them to withdraw from their surroundings. In the more effective of White and Held's two enrichment conditions, highly complex visual stimulation was reserved for an older age. These findings suggest that environments that best facilitate infant development offer babies experiences that are adjusted to their capacity to handle and profit from stimulation.

of information on infant perception to the age-old nature-nurture controversy. Is an adultlike, organized perceptual world given to the infant at birth, or must it be gradually acquired through experience? As we shall soon see, infants exhibit a remarkable constellation of perceptual preferences and capacities from the very beginning. However, modifications and improvements occur as the result of both maturation and experience, and, therefore, an appropriate resolution to the nature-nurture debate seems, once again, to lie somewhere in between the two extremes. A second reason psychologists are interested in infant perceptual abilities is that they shed light on other areas of development. For example, visual and auditory capacities, which enable us to interact with other human beings, are basic to an understanding of social development. Through the auditory sense language is learned. Moreover, perceptual development serves as the foundation for understanding cognitive development, since knowledge about the world is first gathered through the senses.

Research on infant perception is especially challenging, since babies are unable to verbally describe their experiences. Therefore, the nature of the infant's perceptual world must be inferred from the repertoire of responses that infants do have. Fortunately, in investigating the behavioral competence of the young infant, researchers can make use of a variety of infant behaviors that change in response to environmental stimulation — looking, sucking, head turning, facial expressions, and startle responses, to name just a few. Advances in research technology also permit physiological indicators, such as changes in respiration and heart rate, to be used. To find out what babies perceive, researchers have also capitalized on the newborn infant's ability to learn. Habituation studies have been widely employed as a way to find out whether or not infants can discriminate among certain stimuli, and operant conditioning procedures, in which an effort is made to train infants to respond differently to one stimulus as opposed to another, are also sometimes used.

Tactile Sensitivity

As we will see in Chapter 10, the sense of touch is especially important for early emotional development. Therefore, it is not surprising that the variety of sensations possible through the skin appear quite early in prenatal life and are well developed by the time of birth. Responsiveness to touch in the area of the mouth is present by 7½ weeks gestation. Sensitivity in the oral and genital areas and on the palms of the hands and soles of the feet matures first, followed by other regions of the body. Reactions to temperature change also appear prenatally, and both the fetus and neonate are more sensitive to stimuli that are colder than body temperature than to those that are warmer (Humphrey, 1978). In addition, the newborn infant responds to pain, as reports of infant fussing and crying during circumcision, generally performed without anesthesia in the first few days of life, indicate (Anders & Chalemian, 1974).

Research employing the habituation-dishabituation paradigm reveals that newborns can discriminate between different touch stimuli, such as a brush stroke across the mouth and one across the ear (Kisilevsky & Muir, 1984). However, little information exists on the refinement of tactile sensitivity over the course of infancy. Habituation studies appear to be a promising approach for discovering more about the neonate's responsiveness to touch, and how it changes with development.

Taste

The taste buds are structurally mature long before birth (Bradley, 1972), and a variety of studies indicate that neonates can discriminate among the four basic tastes of sweet, sour, bitter, and salty. When permitted to suck for a sugar solution as opposed to water, newborn infants show an immediate rise in heart rate, and their typical burst-pause pattern of sucking changes. They begin to suck more continuously with fewer pauses, and their overall rate of sucking slows down. Researchers believe these changes indicate that infants prefer the taste of sweetness and modify their sucking in such a way as to savor the taste of their favorite food (Crook & Lipsitt, 1976; Lipsitt et al., 1976). Sucking bursts to salt solutions are shorter than those to sugar, suggesting that newborns react negatively to salty tastes (Crook, 1978). Research has not shown that infants vary their sucking in response to other taste qualities, but studies of changes in facial expressions indicate that neonates within the first few hours after birth differentiate among sweet, sour, and bitter solutions. Sweet stimulation promotes facial relaxation and an expression resembling a smile, sour stimulation pursing of the lips, and bitter stimulation a distinct archlike mouth opening, whereas water induces swallowing with no facial reaction. Since these same facial responses have been found in anencephalic infants (born with only a brain stem and no cortex), it is thought that they operate at a very primitive, reflexive level. Facial expressions are a basic form of human communication, and all infants seem to come into the world with a built in, nonverbal ability to communicate their taste preferences to others (Steiner, 1979).

Only limited evidence exists on developmental changes in taste perception from infancy to childhood. Some studies suggest that by the preschool years, children react positively to salty tastes, and that a trend away from preference for sweetness occurs in later childhood. The food environments to which infants and young children are exposed may contribute in important ways to changes in taste preferences, but their impact on taste perception still remains to be studied (Cowart, 1981).

Smell

Like taste receptors, the olfactory apparatus is well developed at birth, and newborn infants are able to detect and differentiate among odors. Given a sufficiently strong stimulus, even preterm infants as young as 28 weeks gestation respond to an unpleasant odor by increasing their general activity level and pattern of respiration (Sarnat, 1978). The strength of an odor stimulus needed to produce a response in newborn babies declines over the first few days of life, suggesting that the sense of smell becomes increasingly sensitive during this time (Lipsitt, Engen, & Kaye, 1963).

The ability of newborns to discriminate among odors has been demonstrated using the habituation-dishabituation paradigm (Engen, Lipsitt, & Kaye, 1963). Also, neonates show expected facial reactions to food odors judged by adults as pleasant or unpleasant. For example, the smell of bananas or chocolate provokes a relaxed, pleasant facial response in newborn babies, whereas rotten eggs leads to arching of the lips, turning down of the corners of the mouth, spitting, and salivation (Steiner, 1979). The fact that distinct facial responses resembling the reactions of adults appear so early in life indicates that at least some odor preferences are innate. Neonates also exhibit a surprising ability to respond to the location of an odor and, if it is unpleasant, to defend themselves accordingly. When a whiff of ammonia is presented to one side of the baby's nostrils, infants less than 6 days old quickly turn their heads in the opposite direction (Reiser, Yonas, & Wikner, 1976).

In lower mammals, the sense of smell is one of the most important for survival, and it plays an important role in eating, avoidance of predators, and mother-infant attachment. Though smell is a less well developed sense in human beings, vestiges of its evolutionary survival function may still be present in the human neonate. In a study in which newborn babies were simultaneously exposed to the odor of their own mother's breast pad and that of a strange mother, they turned significantly more often in the direction of the odor of their own mother by 6 days of age (MacFarlane, 1975). This olfactory recognition occurs in breast-fed babies who experience skin-to-skin contact with their mothers. Bottle-fed newborns are unable to detect a difference between their mother's axillary (underarm) odor and that of an unfamiliar woman (Cernoch & Porter, 1985). These findings indicate that smell is among the earliest senses through which human infants recognize and express their preference for the familiar caregiver.

Anatomical development of the ear begins early during the embryonic period and is nearly complete at the time of birth. However, some additional structural maturation of the middle and inner portions occurs during infancy, and the outer ear continues to enlarge in size until puberty (Acredolo & Hake, 1982).

At birth, infants are able to hear a wide variety of sounds, although responsiveness to them is selective. For example, babies react with greater activity level to complex sounds composed of a variety of frequencies (e.g., noises, voices) than to pure tones (Bench et al., 1976). Their sensitivity to pitch and loudness, particularly at low frequencies, is not as keen as that of an adult (Morrongiello & Clifton, 1984), but it improves markedly over the first few days of life and continues to do so throughout the first year (Hoversten & Moncur, 1969). However, during infancy it does not quite reach the level of an adult's sensitivity (Olsho, 1984; Sinnott, Pisoni, & Aslin, 1983; Trehub, Schneider, & Endman, 1980).

Responsiveness to sound provides support for the infant's visual exploration of the environment. Babies as young as 3 days of age will turn their eyes and head in the general direction of a sound, a response that increases the chances that they will notice and attend to visual changes. However, precise localization of sound sources is not present at birth and only gradually improves over the first half year of life (Bower, 1982; Field et al., 1980). In addition, neonates have difficulty localizing auditory stimuli under complex conditions in which more than one sound is present. The ability to selectively attend to one sound while suppressing interfering auditory stimulation is a sophisticated capacity that seems to depend upon maturation of the auditory cortex, and it does not appear until about 5 months of age (Morrongiello, Clifton, & Kulig, 1982; Clifton et al., 1981).

Psychologists have been especially interested in the infant's responsiveness to a particular set of sounds — those characterizing human speech. Language is a uniquely human attribute. Even though it does not emerge until the end of infancy, researchers have wanted to know the extent to which babies enter the world already prepared to understand and use it.

Newborns are particularly responsive to auditory stimuli within the frequency range of the human voice, and they show a special sensitivity to the sound patterns of human speech — findings that support the existence of a biological foundation for language acquisition. In addition, a large number of habituation studies reveal that newborn infants are able to make fine-grained distinctions among a wide variety of speech sounds — "ba" and "ga," "ma" and "na," and the short vowel sounds "a" and "i," to name only a few (Eimas et al., 1971; Eimas & Tartter, 1979). In fact, there are only a very few speech discriminations that young infants are *not* capable of detecting, and their ability to perceive speech sounds is more perfect than that of adults. In one study, infants between 1 and 4 months of age from English-speaking families discriminated sounds not found in the English language, whereas English-speaking adults found the same distinctions difficult to make (Trehub, 1976). Babies seem to come into the world prepared to respond to the speech sounds of any human language, although over the course of the first year, exposure to a single language starts to limit the sounds to which babies are sensitive (Werker & Tees, 1984).

Newborns prefer to listen to high-pitched, expressive voices with rising intonation patterns (Sullivan & Horowitz, 1983; Turnure, 1971), and by 3 days of age they demonstrate a preference for their own mother's voice, in that they will suck on a nipple to hear it more often than they will to hear the voice of a strange female (DeCasper & Fifer, 1980). Infants' special responsiveness to maternal speech undoubtedly plays an important role in encouraging mothers to talk to babies who are not yet verbal themselves. As mothers and infants are increasingly drawn together in reciprocal interaction, both early language acquisition and the emotional bond between mother and infant are simultaneously facilitated.

It is not surprising that more research has been done on the development of vision than on any other perceptual system. More than any other sense, humans depend on vision for active exploration of the environment. Long before coordinated reaching and crawling are possible, infants scan the environment, track moving objects, and bring sources of sound into sight. How mature are the visual capacities of newborn infants? Is their world fashioned like the adult's reality — a world of distinct, recognizable objects in which such features as brightness, color, pattern, and depth can be distinguished — or do these visual competencies have to mature or be learned over the course of time?

The visual apparatus is less well developed at birth than any other sensory system. The *retina* is the portion of the eye that captures light and transforms it into nerve signals that are transmitted to the brain. The *fovea,* the area at the center of the retina where visual images are focused most sharply, contains visual receptors that are not as mature nor as densely packed in the neonate as they are in adults. In addition, the muscles controlling the shape of the *lens,* that part of the eye that enables us to adjust our focus to various distances of objects, are weak at birth. For a long time, investigators believed that during the first month of the infant's life, ability to focus was limited to objects at a fixed distance of 19 centimeters (7½ inches) in front of the eyes (Haynes, White, & Held, 1965). It is now known that this is incorrect. Neonates can adjust the focus of the lens over a much wider range of distances, although not as effectively as adults. However, they rarely make full use of the focusing ability that they have. This is because the neonate's **visual acuity,** or fineness of discrimination, is severely restricted. Applying the same parameters eye doctors use to describe our own visual acuity, researchers estimate that newborn infants perceive objects at a distance of 20 feet about as clearly as adults do at 440 to 800 feet (Appleton, Clifton, & Goldberg, 1975). Furthermore, unlike adults, young infants see *equally unclearly* across a wide range of distances. As a result, there are no visual cues available to help them notice that an image near or far can be sharpened by refocusing the lens (Banks, 1980).

The infant's visual system matures rapidly over the first few months of life. The ability to focus on objects at different distances approximates that of the adult by about 3 months of age (Banks, 1980). Visual acuity develops over a somewhat longer period of time. It can be estimated by determining the narrowest distance between a series of stripes that the infant can detect visually. At 10 inches from the eye, newborns distinguish a striped stimulus from an unpatterned surface only if the stripes are at least ⅛ of an inch in width. By 6 months of age, they can discriminate much narrower stripes, those that are ¹⁄₆₄ of an inch wide, indicating that their acuity is comparable to that of an adult with 20/100 vision (Fantz, Ordy, & Udelf, 1962). During the second half of the first year, visual acuity improves even more. It is supported by continuous structural maturation of the fovea, which reaches adultlike status at about 11 months of age (Abramov et al., 1982). The optic nerve and visual cortex also undergo development during the first year of life, and both myelinization and developing connections between nerve cells contribute to the infant's gradually improved visual capacities (Banks & Salapatek, 1983).

Scanning and Tracking. Evidence on the scanning behavior of newborn infants indicates that they are, from the outset, active, organized visual explorers of the environment. The eye movements that adults use to explore the visual field are called **saccades.** A saccade is a rapid, accurate motion that goes smoothly from a starting point to a visual target, bringing it from the periphery to the center of the field of vision so that it can be inspected more carefully. Although they are somewhat slower than those of adults, saccadic eye movements do exist in newborns. Apparently, this basic mechanism for responding to visual information does not have to be learned, and it quickly improves in speed and accuracy during the first few months of life (Salapatek, 1975; Haith, 1980).

Once newborn infants bring a target to the center of the visual field, they begin to explore it, but the nature of their visual exploration changes markedly in the first 2 months of life. When scanning a simple figure or an outline shape, infants in the first month of life show very restricted visual exploration, in that they tend to look only at a single feature, such as one corner of a triangle. However, by 2 months of age they scan more broadly, covering the entire perimeter of the shape (see Figure 4.6). Complex stimuli having internal features, such as the eyes and mouth of the human face, are treated similarly. One-month-olds show eye fixations that are limited to the external boundaries of the visual target, and they are captured by a single feature or limited set of features, such as the hairline or chin. At about 2 months of age, infants shift from restricted scanning of the external border of a complex stimulus to a thorough examination of its internal features (Bushnell, Gerry, & Burt, 1983; Salapatek, 1975). However, if the internal features are made very salient — for example, by embedding a bull's-eye target or a checkerboard within a square or circle — even 1-month-olds will notice and inspect them (Ganon & Swartz, 1980). Apparently, visual scanning by the neonate is governed by high contrast and salience, and only by 2 months of age does the infant seem to take into account the entire configuration of a stimulus, including less salient, fine-grained features and details.

When adults track a moving target, they use **smooth pursuit eye movements,** which are much slower and more sustained than saccadic eye movements, enabling the individual to hold fixation on the moving stimulus. Newborns are sensitive to the motion of objects and track moving stimuli, but their eye movements while following a moving stimulus are jerky and uncontrolled (Kremenitzer et al., 1979). Smooth

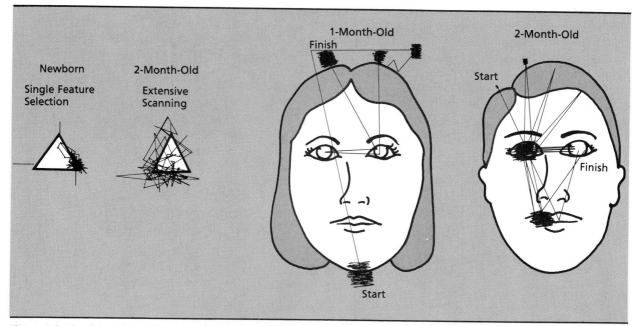

Figure 4.6. Visual scanning of simple and complex targets by young infants. When scanning a simple triangle, newborns focus only on a single feature, whereas 2-month-olds scan the entire shape. When targets are complex and have internal features, such as the human face, 1-month-olds limit their scanning to single features on the perimeter of the stimulus, whereas 2-month-olds examine the internal features. *(From P. Salapatek, 1975, "Pattern Perception in Early Infancy." In L. B. Cohen & P. Salapatek [Eds.], Infant Perception: From Sensation to Cognition. New York: Academic Press. Pp. 195, 201. Reprinted by permission.)*

and it continues to show gradual improvement during the first 6 months of life. The accuracy of infant smooth pursuit has been found to increase over successive trials in laboratory studies, indicating that it seems to develop, at least in part, as the result of practice and experience (Aslin, 1981).

Brightness and Color. Young infants are attracted to bright objects, such as lights, and based on the length of time they spend looking at lights of different brightness, they prefer those of medium intensity to ones that are very bright or dim (Hershenson, 1964). The extent to which infants discriminate between lights of different brightness can be determined by testing for whether they can distinguish a bar of light from its background. By 2 months of age, infants can discriminate between lights of different brightness almost as well as adults (Peeples & Teller, 1975).

Color perception is very difficult to investigate in infants. Colors differ from one another in brightness, and because the relationship between brightness and color is believed to be different for infants and adults, it is impossible to be sure that pairs of colors are equated for brightness in research involving infants. Investigators have tried to surmount this problem in a number of ways. One is to present pairs of colors repeatedly so that sometimes the first color is brighter than the second, and sometimes the second is brighter than the first. Under these conditions, if infants consistently look longer at one color as opposed to another, then their response cannot be based on brightness, and they must be able to perceive color (Cohen, DeLoache, & Strauss, 1979). Research studies using this technique have found that by 2 months of age, infants can discriminate among colors. Much less is known about color vision in infants less than 2 months of age. Color vision may not be complete at birth. In one of the few investigations of newborns' color perception, 1- to 5-day-old babies were able to discriminate gray from green, red, and yellow, but they could not differentiate gray from blue (Adams, Maurer, & Davis, 1986).

By 4 months of age, infants' looking times at colors spanning the width of the spectrum show a remarkable resemblance to adult ratings of color preferences, with reds and blues capturing their gaze to a greater extent than greens and yellows. These findings suggest, rather surprisingly, that certain color preferences are not cultural but are determined biologically, since it is highly unlikely that babies of this age are taught or otherwise influenced to prefer certain colors over others (Bornstein, 1975).

Depth Perception. Depth perception — the process by which we gauge the distance of objects from one another and from ourselves — is important for understanding the spatial layout of the environment and for guiding motor activity. We live in a three-dimensional world, but the surface of the retina onto which visual images of the environment are projected is two-dimensional. Therefore, we must depend on a variety of visual cues for converting this two-dimensional representation into a three-dimensional image of reality. Research on the development of depth perception has largely been aimed at answering two questions: Do very young infants have a perceptual appreciation of depth? How does sensitivity to various perceptual cues for depth develop during the first few months of life?

Early studies of depth perception used a famous apparatus called the **visual cliff** (see Figure 4.7). Developed by Gibson and Walk (1960), it consisted of a table covered by glass, at the center of which was a platform. On one side of the platform (the shallow side), a checkerboard pattern was placed just under the surface of the glass, whereas on the other (the deep side), the checkerboard was positioned several feet beneath the glass. Infants were placed on the platform, and their mothers were asked to coax them to crawl across both the deep and shallow sides by calling to them and holding out a toy. Using this technique, Walk and Gibson (1961) found that although

Figure 4.7. The visual cliff. By refusing to cross the deep side and showing a preference for the shallow surface, this infant demonstrates the ability to perceive depth. (*William Vandivert*/Scientific American)

infants between 6 and 14 months could easily be enticed to cross the shallow side, all but a very few avoided the deep side. At least by the time they are able to crawl, most infants discriminate deep from shallow surfaces and behave in such a way as to avoid potentially dangerous drop-offs.

The Gibson and Walk research demonstrates that infants can distinguish surfaces of different depths as soon as they are able to move about independently, but it does not tell us whether they can do so earlier. In a later study, younger, pre-mobile infants were placed face down on both sides of the visual cliff, and changes in their heart rates were recorded. Babies 1½ to 3 months old responded with a significant drop in heart rate on the deep side, but relatively little change on the shallow side, indicating that the two sides of the cliff *can* be discriminated by very young infants. However, the infants did not respond to depth with the fear and avoidance reactions that are typical of older infants. In fact, they fussed and cried *less* on the deep side than they did on the shallow (Campos, Langer, & Krowitz, 1970). It is possible that pre-mobile infants' reactions to the two sides of the visual cliff are based on something other than depth.

Therefore, recent investigators have turned toward the study of infants' responses to particular depth cues as a means for clarifying when depth perception first appears and how it develops. Three basic cues for depth are available to human beings: binocular, pictorial, and kinetic. Let's discuss each of them in turn.

Binocular Cues. **Binocular depth cues** arise from the fact that the eyes of humans are separated, so each receives a slightly different view of the visual field. The mature visual system blends these two views together into a single image, but it also registers the difference between them in order to provide strong cues for three-dimensionality, an ability that is called *stereopsis.* The infant's responsiveness to stereoscopic cues can be tested using a method similar to a 3-D movie. Two overlapping images are projected before the infant, and goggles worn by the baby allow one image to reach one eye and the other to reach the other eye. If infants are capable of stereopsis, they see an organized stereoscopic form that they track with their eyes, instead of a randomly distributed series of dots or elements. Using this method, research shows that responsiveness to stereoscopic cues is absent in 10-week-old infants, but shows gradual improvement between 3 and 6 months of age (Fox et al., 1979).

Another way of testing for whether infants use binocular cues for depth is to observe the way they reach toward a stereoscopic display of an object. If they adjust their reach to the distance of the object, they must be able to use stereoscopic cues. Bower (1971; 1972) reported that infants as young as 7 days of age use their capacity for primitive, pre-reaching motions to reach for stereoscopic displays, but other investigators have not been able to replicate this finding (Dodwell, Muir, & DiFranco, 1976; Ruff & Halton, 1977). Reaching behavior is better developed and a more reliable indicator of stereopsis in older babies. By 3 to 5 months of age, infants seem to adjust their reach in accordance with the distance of an object when responding to a stereoscopic display (Field, 1977).

Pictorial Cues. Human beings also depend on **pictorial depth cues,** of the kind that are used by artists to create the impression of three-dimensionality in a painting. Examples are linear perspective, texture gradients (nearby textured surfaces appear more fine grained than more distant surfaces), the interposition of objects (an object partially hidden by another object is perceived to be farther away), and shading (variations in lighting across the surface of an object give the impression of three-dimensionality). Because all of these cues can be distinguished using only a single eye, they are called *monocular depth cues.*

Yonas and his colleagues have investigated infants' sensitivity to a variety of pictorial depth cues by seeing if babies are guided by them in reaching for objects. In one recent study, they showed that 7-month-olds, but not 5-month-olds, could use *texture gradients* and *linear perspective* as cues for depth. They presented infants with the display shown in Figure 4.8. The two ducks, one suspended lower than the other, were equal in size and distance from the infant, but texture gradients and linear perspective in the background combined to create the illusion of two objects resting at different distances on a horizontal surface receding in depth. When viewing this display with one eye covered (monocular viewing condition), the older infants were more likely to reach for the nearer-appearing toy. With both eyes uncovered (binocular condition), there was no difference in 7-month-olds' reaching preference. These outcomes imply that in the monocular condition, 7-month-olds perceived the two objects' relative distances on the basis of textural and linear cues. The absence of a difference in preferential reaching between the two conditions for 5-month-olds suggests that the younger infants were not sensitive to these pictorial depth cues (Yonas et al., 1986).

Sensitivity to *interposition* also emerges by the middle of the first year. When

Figure 4.8. Test of infant's ability to perceive relative distance from pictorial cues in the Yonas et al. (1986) study. *A* provides side view of an apparatus in which two toy ducks — equal in size and in distance from the infant — are placed in front of a background combining texture gradient and linear perspective cues to depth. Preferential reaching is recorded under both a binocular viewing condition (as above) and a monocular viewing condition. *B* shows the experimental display as viewed by an infant who can perceive distance based on these cues. *(Adapted from Yonas et al., 1986. Photo courtesy of Albert Yonas, University of Minnesota.)*

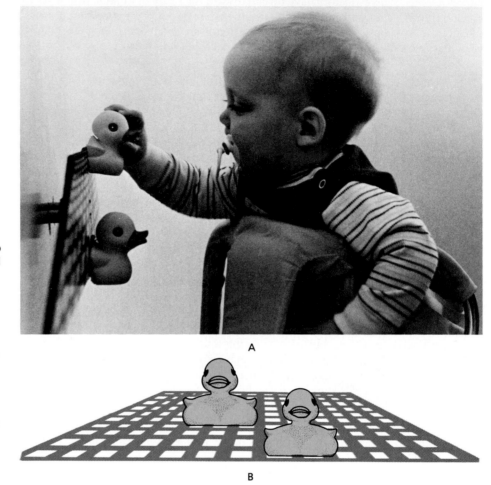

A

B

7-month-old infants are presented with the three stimuli depicted in Figure 4.9, they reach consistently for the perceptually "nearer" part of stimulus A, but they show no reaching preferences toward B and C. Five-month-olds are not responsive to interposition. They show no reaching preferences toward any particular part of the three stimuli (Granrud & Yonas, 1984).

Finally, babies also show sensitivity to *shading* at 7 months of age, as they will reach preferentially for a photograph of a convex over a concave surface (see Figure 4.10). Because of its shading, the convex area resembles a protruding sphere, and 7-month-olds, like adults, perceive it as closer to them than a concave shaded surface (Granrud, Yonas, & Opland, 1985).

A consistent finding in each of Yonas's studies is that 7-month-olds respond to pictorial depth cues, whereas 5-month-olds do not. The use of pictorial cues seems to emerge around the middle of the first year of life, somewhat later than infants' sensitivity to binocular depth information (Yonas & Granrud, 1985).

Kinetic Cues. **Kinetic depth cues** result from changes in retinal images created by movements of the infant's head or body, or by moving objects in the environment. When an object approaches us, its retinal image expands, and when it recedes, the image gradually shrinks. The cue for depth in this instance is the changing size of the object. The way infants respond to objects loomed at their faces is a commonly used indication of their sensitivity to kinetic depth cues. Early "looming" studies suggested that even newborns respond defensively to an object moving directly toward them by rotating their heads upward, widening their eyes, and raising their hands between the object and their faces (Bower, Broughton, & Moore, 1971). However, these findings have not been replicated (Yonas, Pettersen, & Lockman, 1979), and more controlled research indicates that infants do not respond defensively to an approaching object until between 3 and 4 months of age. However, by this time, the response is quite specific. It only occurs to an image expanding in such a way as to indicate to the baby that the object is approaching at a constant rate of speed, and not to one that appears to be slowing down as it moves toward the infant (Yonas et al., 1980).

In addition to providing a pictorial cue, the texture gradients of objects can also serve as a kinetic cue for depth. As objects move closer to the eye, their texture appears more detailed to us. To find out if infants use the texture of objects as a kinetic depth cue, Carroll and Gibson (1981) tested 3-month-old babies to see if they could distinguish an approaching object from an approaching aperture, or opening of the same shape. Infants avoided the approaching object more than they did the aperture, suggesting that 3-month-olds do rely on changes in texture as a means for judging the distance of objects from themselves.

Response to kinetic cues appears to be the earliest form of depth perception to develop in infants, as it is present by 3 months of age. However, it is still possible that some cues for depth operate even earlier, but are simply not apparent because infants do not reliably exhibit the motor responses that indicate them (Banks & Salapatek, 1983).

You may have noticed from our discussion that research on depth perception has largely been aimed at describing the ages at which various infant capacities first appear. Little information is available on factors that influence the infant's developing appreciation of depth. An exception is some intriguing research, summarized in Box 4.3, that indicates that the age at which infants first begin to crawl has a profound influence on how they respond when coaxed by their mothers to cross the deep side of the visual cliff.

Pattern Perception. Early research by Fantz (1961; 1963) indicated that even newborn infants prefer to look at some visual patterns as opposed to others. Fantz measured infants' preferences for the six different stimuli shown in Figure 4.11 and found that babies from birth to 6 months of age fixated longer on patterned as opposed to plain targets. This basic finding of an early preference for patterned stimuli gave rise to a massive research literature on the specific features of patterns to which infants are sensitive at various ages. In addition, the preference exhibited by Fantz's subjects for the pattern of the human face led subsequent investigators to pursue the

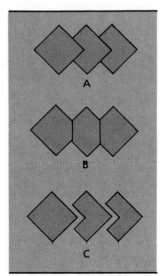

Figure 4.9. Interposition displays presented to 5- and 7-month-old infants in the Granrud and Yonas (1984) study. Seven-month-olds showed a reaching preference for the apparently "nearer" area of stimulus A. *(From C. E. Granrud & A. Yonas, 1984, "Infants' Perception of Pictorially Specified Interposition,"* Journal of Experimental Child Psychology, 37, 500–511. *Reprinted by permission.)*

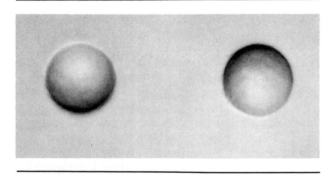

Figure 4.10. Convex and concave surfaces depicted by shading in the Granrud, Yonas, and Opland (1985) study. *(From C. E. Granrud, A. Yonas, & E. A. Opland, 1985, "Infants' Sensitivity to the Depth Cue of Shading,"* Perception and Psychophysics, 37, *416. Reprinted by permission.)*

Box 4.3
Maturation, Experience, and Avoidance of the Drop-Off on the Visual Cliff

Theory. In Gibson and Walk's research on the visual cliff, most infants refused to cross the deep side, but nevertheless a few did. To explain the unusual behavior of these babies, some developmental psychologists have taken a maturational position. They claim that avoidance of the deep side of the cliff matures with age, independent of early locomotor experience. Others emphasize the role of experience and maintain that practice in independent movement facilitates the emergence of the avoidance response. Several attempts to decipher the relative importance of maturation and experience in visual cliff behavior have been made.

Research. Nancy Rader and her colleagues (Rader, Bausano, & Richards, 1980; Richards & Rader, 1981) concluded that a special visual program controlled by maturation governs infants' avoidance of the visual cliff. Results from two experiments showed that babies who began crawling at earlier ages were more likely to cross the deep side than later crawlers, regardless of amount of prior crawling experience. Rader conjectured that infants who begin crawling early, before the ability to use visual depth information matures, rely on tactile rather than visual cues to guide their crawling movements. However, among late crawlers, the capacity to

use visual information emerges just before or at about the same time as crawling. For these babies, visual cues supersede tactile cues for guiding performance on the visual cliff, and they avoid the drop-off.

Rader also reasoned that if experience in independent movement is important for the development of the depth response, then the opportunity to use a walker, as well as to practice crawling, should be related to visual cliff avoidance. To investigate this question, infants between 4½ and 8½ months of age were given daily practice sessions in using a walker over several weeks to several months. Then they were tested on the visual cliff, both crawling and in the walker. Prior experience either in crawling or in practice with the walker failed to predict avoidance of the deep side. In addition, while many of the infants avoided the deep side when permitted to crawl, when tested in the walker almost none of them did! Rader concluded that visual cues that ordinarily guide babies' crawling movements are disrupted when they move about in an artificial locomotion device.

Contrary evidence comes from Bennett Bertenthal and his associates (Bertenthal & Campos, 1987; Bertenthal, Campos, & Barrett, 1984) who argue that maturational factors alone are not sufficient for explaining avoidance of heights. In one study, groups of pre-crawling infants were given many hours of artificial locomotor practice in walkers, while another group did not receive this experience. When held over the deep side of the cliff, the "walker" babies showed

heart rate accelerations (which the investigators took as an indication of avoidance); their "non-walker" counterparts did not.

In another investigation that directly refuted Rader's findings, visual cliff performance was tested as a function of both age when infants began crawling and duration of crawling experience. Results indicated that at each crawling-onset age, 35 percent of the infants avoided crossing the deep side if they had only 11 days of locomotor experience, but 75 percent refused to cross if they had 41 days of crawling experience. The researchers concluded that infants who do not avoid the drop-off are "tenderfoot" crawlers who have had insufficient self-locomotor experience.

Applications. The relative importance of maturation and experience in visual cliff performance remains unresolved. Until additional research unravels this complicated issue, what advice should be given to parents whose youngsters are just beginning to crawl? The old adage, "Better safe than sorry," applies. Parents of precocious crawlers often describe their babies as "fearless daredevils" who crawl about while looking elsewhere than at the surface ahead of them. Whether their failure to avoid drop-offs is a consequence of an immature visual program or too little experience, parents would do well to take special safety precautions when infants are near common household drop-offs, such as staircases, or when they are placed in walkers.

---

question of whether there is an innate tendency on the part of infants to recognize and respond to the human facial configuration.

Sensitivity to Pattern Features. Research that followed Fantz's early work showed that as infants get older, they prefer increasingly complex visual patterns. For example, when infants of 3, 8, and 14 weeks of age were exposed to black and white checkerboard patterns, younger infants looked longest at the one composed of only a few large squares, whereas older infants preferred checkerboards having many smaller squares (Brennan, Ames, & Moore, 1966). Checkerboards differ from one another in a variety of specific pattern features. The most obvious are the number and size of their pattern elements, but they also vary in amount of contour — the quantity

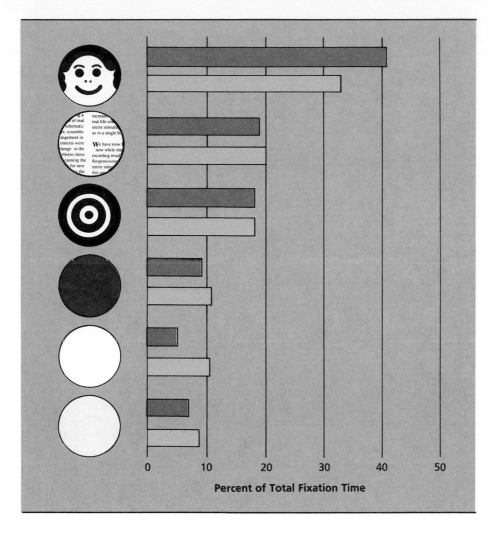

Figure 4.11. Fantz's (1961) findings on infant pattern perception. Preference for patterned stimuli was demonstrated by recording the extent to which infants looked at a face, newsprint, a bull's eye, and plain red, white, and yellow circles. The purple bars show the results for infants from 2 to 3 months of age, the blue bars for infants between 3 and 6 months of age. Even newborns showed pattern preferences similar to these. *(From R. Fantz, 1961, ''The Origin of Form Perception,''* Scientific American, 204, *72. Copyright © [1961] by Scientific American, Inc. All rights reserved.)*

of black-white transitions in the stimulus pattern (checkerboards with small squares have more contour than those with large squares). Other pattern stimuli differ in a myriad of additional features—curved versus straight lines, connected versus disconnected elements, vertical versus horizontal orientation, whether or not the pattern is organized about a central focus (as in a bull's-eye), to name only a few. Researchers have found it extremely difficult to sort out which of these features are most important to infants of different ages, because changing one feature in a pattern (e.g., number of elements) often leads to changes in other features (e.g., amount of contour). In general, studies that have tried to determine the pattern features that are most salient to younger versus older infants have found that newborns prefer large rather than small and circular rather than straight elements, vertically as opposed to horizontally oriented figures (Pipp & Haith, 1984), sharp as opposed to blurred edges, and figures with a greater amount of contour (e.g., a square as opposed to a line). By 2 months of age, some of these preferences change. Patterns that have a greater number of small elements, lines that are straight rather than curved, and edges that are more subtle and muted in contrast begin to consume more looking time (Cohen, DeLoache, & Strauss, 1979; Fantz, Fagan, & Miranda, 1975).

In the early months of life, infants respond to a variety of features that have to do with the separate parts of a pattern, but it is not until 5 months of age that they begin to integrate the separate elements, responding to a pattern as a complex, unified whole. Complicated habituation studies reveal that 4-month-old infants shown a compound stimulus, such as a cross inside a circle, respond to the configuration as two separate elements (cross and circle), whereas by 5 months of age infants perceive the two elements as a single, integrated figure (cross within a circle) (Cohen, De-Loache, & Strauss, 1979).

Currently, most investigators believe that maturation of the visual system is largely responsible for the infant's developing preference for increasingly complex patterns. As we saw earlier, both visual acuity and scanning behavior improve during the first few months of life, and these changes support the infant's exploration of complex stimuli (Pipp & Haith, 1984). Also, direct examination of the visual cortex in animals, along with indirect research on humans, reveals that neural receptors in the visual cortex are prewired to respond to very specific pattern stimuli, such as vertical, horizontal, and curved lines. Improvements in the sensitivity and organization of these receptors during the first few months of life are thought to play a major part in the infant's changing pattern preferences (Acredolo & Hake, 1982; Cohen, DeLoache, & Strauss, 1979).

Perception of the Human Face. If it existed, an innate capacity on the part of neonates to recognize and respond to the configuration of the human face would undoubtedly promote survival and be adaptive in an evolutionary sense. Although Fantz (1961) claimed that newborns prefer the regular configuration of the human face to patterns of equal complexity, such as scrambled facial features, this finding has not been replicated (e.g., Haaf, 1974; Koopman & Ames, 1968). Neither the orientation nor arrangement of facial features in a stimulus pattern influences the attention of infants under 2 months of age, largely because, as we indicated earlier, 1-month-old infants do not scan the internal features of a stimulus. By 2 months of age, when scanning is more mature, infants do prefer a schematic face over scrambled arrangements. At this age, they seem to recognize how the features of the human face are arranged, and they can generalize that knowledge to pictorial representations (Maurer & Barrera, 1981). However, the infant's emerging recognition of faces does not seem to be a built-in perceptual capacity. Instead, it seems to follow the same general course of development as other aspects of visual perception (Cohen, De-Loache, & Strauss, 1979).

By 3 months of age, infants are capable of making subtle discriminations among the internal features of faces. For example, 3-month-olds are able to distinguish between photos of strangers, even when the faces are judged by adults to be moderately similar to one another (Barrera & Maurer, 1981a). Also at 3 months of age, babies recognize their mother's face in a photo, as they will initially look longer at it than the face of a stranger (Barrera & Maurer, 1981b).

By 5 months of age, infants become capable of noticing the **invariant features** that make a human face unique. In other words, they recognize a particular configuration of eyes, nose, and mouth as stable, even when it appears in a new context. This awareness of the invariant, unchanging aspects of facial configurations is evident in 5-month-old infants' ability to recognize a new photo of a person they had previously seen in a different pose (Fagan, 1976) and to generalize from a real face to a color photograph of the same person (Dirks & Gibson, 1977). Also, around 7 months, infants recognize the same facial expression (happiness) in a photograph when it is demonstrated by different people (Caron, Caron, & Myers, 1982). These findings indicate that by the middle of the first year, infants seem to notice a number of basic structures that distinguish one face or expression from another and that remain constant over a variety of contexts.

The development of facial perception during the first few months of life contributes to the infant's ability to recognize and respond to the expressive behavior of others. One of the earliest infant behaviors elicited by the human face is the smile, a response that is important in the affectional bond that infants and caregivers build

The human face is a fascinating object of sensory exploration for young babies. (Gloria Karlson)

with one another during the first year of life. By the middle of the second month of life infants start to smile in response to a wide range of visual stimulation, especially high-contrast patterns that are perceptually attractive to them. These include the visual configuration of the human face (Bower, 1982). At 2 months, internal features of the human face become important in eliciting smiling — at first the eyes (a high-contrast feature), followed by the mouth and other elements (Kagan, 1971). At 3 months, when infants are able to recognize familiar facial configurations, smiling starts to become more selective in that it occurs more often in response to familiar than unfamiliar people. By this age, smiling is also truly social, for the infant seems to smile to get others to smile back (Gewirtz & Gewirtz, 1968). The baby's social smile is rewarding to caregivers; it draws them closer to the infant and encourages them to continue the pleasurable interaction, and as a result, babies respond by smiling all the more (Wahler, 1967). Thus, the visual abilities underlying infants' perception of the human face contribute in important ways to their recognition of familiar people, and to the formation of their earliest social relationships.

Object Perception. Research on pattern perception deals only with two-dimensional stimuli, but as adults we perceive a world made up of stable, three-dimensional objects. To what extent is the visual world of infants organized into coherent, independently existing objects, in the same way as our own?

Size and Shape Constancy. As we move around the environment and look at objects, the retinal images associated with them undergo constant changes in size and shape. To recognize objects as stable and unchanging, we must translate these varying retinal images into a single representation. An object far away from us casts a very small image on the retina in comparison to when it is up close, but we do not regard the same object as gigantic when near and toy-sized when far away. This ability to perceive the size of an object as constant, despite changes in its retinal image size, is called **size constancy.** Perception of an object's shape as stable, despite changes in the shape projected on the retina, is called **shape constancy.**

Although early research indicated that size constancy is present in infants as young as 6 weeks of age (Bower, 1964), subsequent attempts to replicate these results were not successful (McKenzie & Day, 1972; 1976). Recent research indicates that size constancy does not emerge until some time between 4 and 6 months of age. In a study in which infants were first habituated to a large mannequin and then tested to see whether they perceived it as equivalent to a mannequin of the same size, but a different distance away, McKenzie, Tootell, and Day (1980) obtained evidence for size constancy in 6- to 8-month-old babies, as well as some 4-month-olds. As illustrated in Figure 4.12, the infants regarded a mannequin whose real size was identical to the original stimulus as perceptually equivalent, even when its retinal image size was not the same. Size constancy seems to require some appreciation of depth and the third dimension. As we saw earlier, between 4 and 6 months of age, infants begin to respond to several new depth cues, and at about this time visually guided reaching also appears. These capacities probably contribute to the emergence of size constancy at this time (Aslin, 1987).

Shape constancy can also be tested using the habituation-dishabituation paradigm. Slater and Morison (1985) looked for evidence of shape constancy in newborns. Babies who were 6 hours to 6 days old were first habituated to one of two stimuli: a square or a trapezoidal shape that was presented in a sequence of different slants to the eye. In the next part of the experiment, the square and the trapezoid were paired together, only both were at slants other than those presented during the initial habituation phase. Dishabituation in all subjects proved to be greatest to the novel shape, indicating that newborns were able to extract the constant, real shape of the stimulus during the habituation phase and then respond to the novel shape. The findings of Slater and Morison's study suggest that shape constancy is an innate, organizing perceptual ability that is there at birth. It is interesting that shape constancy is present long before the emergence of controlled reaching and grasping, which permit babies to actively rotate objects and, in the process, view them from many different angles.

Perception of Objects as Distinct, Bounded Wholes. The achievement of perceptual constancies in the first few months of life does not give us a complete picture of the extent to which infants perceive a world of structured, independent objects like our

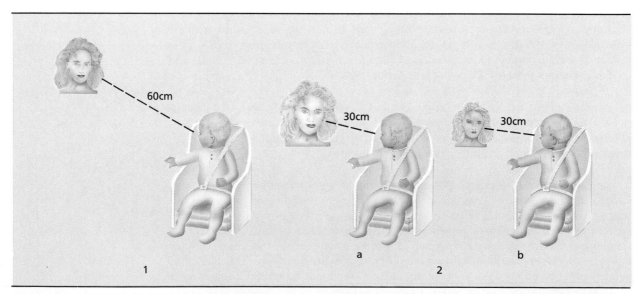

Figure 4.12. Testing infants for size constancy in the McKenzie, Tootell, and Day (1980) study. The procedure illustrated above is a simplified version of the one used by the investigators. 1. Infants were first habituated to a large mannequin head 60 cm from their eyes. 2. Then they were tested to see if they would dishabituate to the same size mannequin 30 cm away (a); or a smaller mannequin 30 cm away (b). Infants dishabituated to 2b, indicating that they regard objects of the same actual size presented at different distances from their eyes (1 and 2a) as perceptually equivalent.

own. Adults can distinguish a single object from surrounding objects and surfaces by looking for a regular shape and uniform texture and color. Observations by Piaget (1936/1952) of his 6-month-old son Laurent first suggested that young infants do not use these same cues. Piaget offered Laurent a small, attractive object dangling in the air, and Laurent eagerly grabbed it, but as soon as it was placed on top of a bigger object such as a book or a pillow, Laurent would no longer reach for it. Instead, he reached for the larger, supporting object. Laurent's behavior indicated that he did not perceive the boundary between the two objects created by their different sizes, shapes, and textures. As long as one object was adjacent to the other one, Laurent responded to them as if they were a single unit.

Recent carefully controlled studies support the results of Piaget's informal observations, and they also indicate that it is the *movement* of objects relative to one another and to their background that gradually enables infants to construct a visual world of independent objects as we know it. In one study, 5-month-old babies were shown two box-shaped objects, a smaller one in front of a larger one. In some presentations, the objects touched each other, whereas in others they were spatially separated. Also, sometimes the objects were stationary, and at other times they moved either independently or together. As long as the objects were touching one another or moved together in the same direction, infants reached for the two boxes as a whole and treated them as a single unit. When they were separated or moved in opposite directions, infants behaved as if the objects were distinct, independent units, and they reached only for the nearer one (Hofsten & Spelke, 1985). These findings suggest that the relative motions of surfaces help infants organize their visual environment into a world of separately existing objects. When an object moves across a background, its various features remain in the same relationship to one another and move together. Such movement helps the infant differentiate the object from other units in the visual field. The study described above, as well as others (Kellman & Spelke, 1983; Spelke, 1985), indicates that during the first 5 months of life, motion seems to exert a stronger effect on the infant's perception of an object as a bounded whole than do stationary cues, such as pattern, texture, and color. By the middle of the first year, stationary cues start to become more important as a basis for identifying objects as distinct and separate units (Bower, 1974).

Summary of Visual Development During Infancy. Recent research has led to an exciting and significant expansion of our understanding of infant visual development. To help you notice relationships among the emergence of the various visual capacities we have discussed, Figure 4.13 provides an overview of visual development during the first 7 months of life. The figure shows that age 2 months is clearly a turning point in infant visual competence, a finding that investigators attribute to rapid maturation of the visual system during the first 2 months after birth. However, experience also contributes to the development of visual abilities during the first year. According to two major theorists of perceptual development, James and Eleanor Gibson, infants become increasingly skilled observers as the result of repeated exposure to environmental stimulation. Over the course of the first year, they gradually learn to detect stable features of the environment in a constantly changing perceptual world. For example, in our discussion of pattern perception, we observed that infants first notice the invariant features that distinguish faces from non-faces, and then they go on to make more subtle distinctions between the invariant features of particular faces and different facial expressions. The detection of size constancy and the features that identify an object as a single, bounded unit are additional examples of the baby's gradually emerging ability to detect permanence and stability in a continually changing flux of stimulation. The general progression of development shown in Figure 4.13 reflects the young infant's impressive capacity to search for order in a complex perceptual world, an ability that becomes increasingly fine-tuned with development (Gibson, 1970; Gibson, 1979).

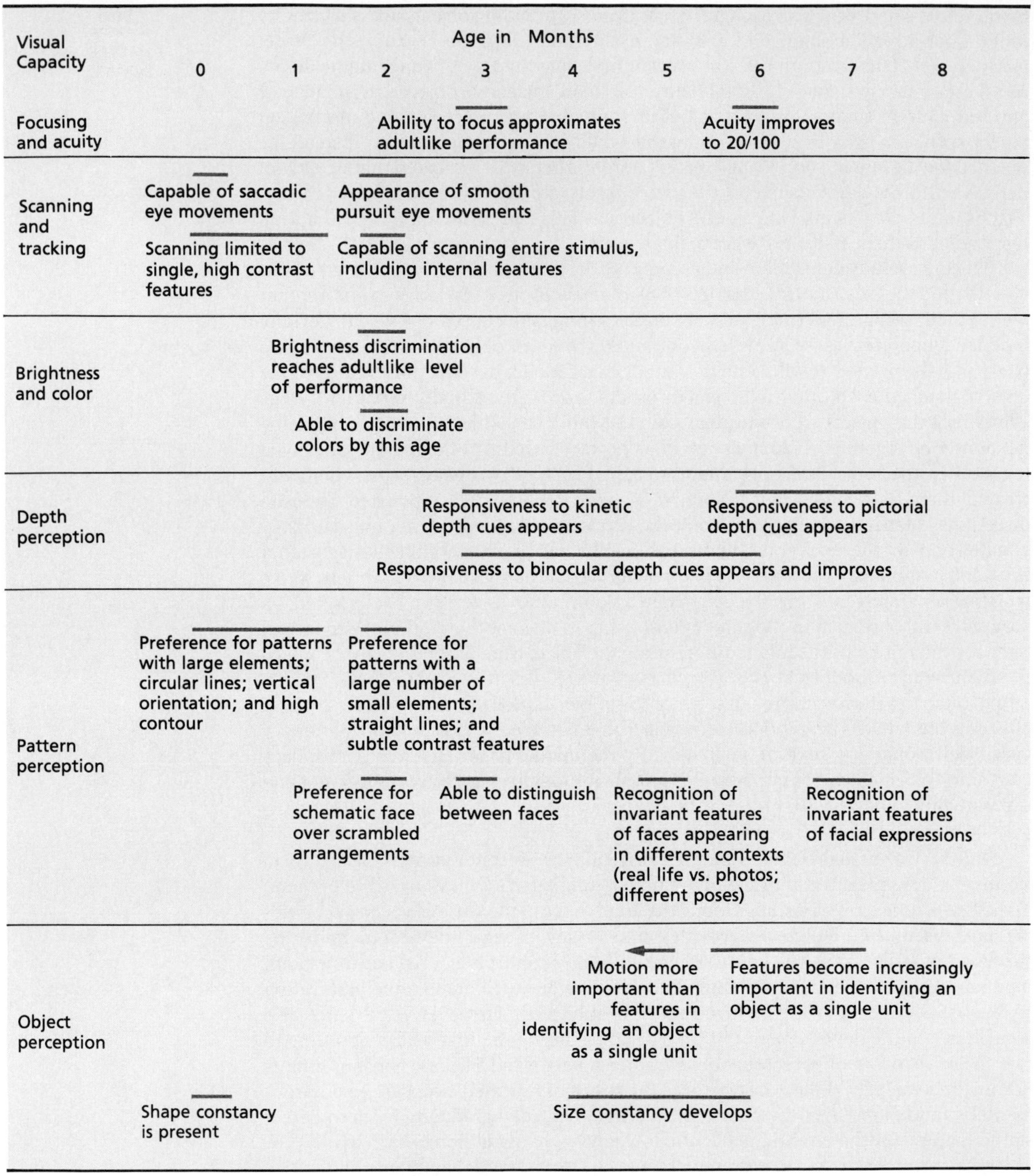

Figure 4.13. Emergence of visual capacities in infancy.

Visual Capacity	Age in Months
	0 1 2 3 4 5 6 7 8

Focusing and acuity
- Ability to focus approximates adultlike performance (at ~2–3 months)
- Acuity improves to 20/100 (at ~6 months)

Scanning and tracking
- Capable of saccadic eye movements (at ~0–1 months)
- Appearance of smooth pursuit eye movements (at ~2 months)
- Scanning limited to single, high contrast features (at ~0–1 months)
- Capable of scanning entire stimulus, including internal features (at ~2 months)

Brightness and color
- Brightness discrimination reaches adultlike level of performance (at ~2 months)
- Able to discriminate colors by this age (at ~2 months)

Depth perception
- Responsiveness to kinetic depth cues appears (at ~3 months)
- Responsiveness to pictorial depth cues appears (at ~6 months)
- Responsiveness to binocular depth cues appears and improves (at ~3–5 months)

Pattern perception
- Preference for patterns with large elements; circular lines; vertical orientation; and high contour (at ~0–1 months)
- Preference for patterns with a large number of small elements; straight lines; and subtle contrast features (at ~2 months)
- Preference for schematic face over scrambled arrangements (at ~1 month)
- Able to distinguish between faces (at ~2 months)
- Recognition of invariant features of faces appearing in different contexts (real life vs. photos; different poses) (at ~3 months)
- Recognition of invariant features of facial expressions (at ~5 months)

Object perception
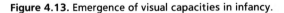
- Motion more important than features in identifying an object as a single unit (at ~4 months)
- Features become increasingly important in identifying an object as a single unit (at ~5 months)
- Shape constancy is present (at ~0 months)
- Size constancy develops (at ~4–6 months)

Intermodal Coordination: Bringing the Senses Together

So far we have discussed the infant's sensory systems one by one, but most events we perceive are **intermodal,** in that they make information available to more than one sensory system at a time. For example, we know that the shape of an object is the same whether we see it or touch it, that movements of lips are correlated with the sound of a voice, and that dropping a rigid object such as a block or a spoon on a hard surface will make a sharp, banging sound. As adults, we take information offered to more than one sensory modality at a time and perceive it as an integrated unit. Also, based on information picked up in one modality, we develop certain expectations about what we will perceive in another. For example, we expect an object with a smooth, curved surface that we *feel* to *look* round, and we expect to *hear* a voice in synchrony with lip movements that we *see*.

The emergence of intermodal coordination has been a long-debated topic in developmental psychology. Some investigators believe that human beings begin life with sensory modalities that are entirely independent, and over time they gradually learn intermodal coordination as the result of experiencing the repeated association of one sensory impression with another. Others believe that the detection of intermodal commonalities is a fundamental characteristic of the human perceptual system and that it is available from the start, without benefit of learned correlations. To decide between these two points of view, researchers have examined the extent to which young infants are able to appreciate the intermodal nature of perceived events.

Recent research suggests that intersensory connections are not learned and that instead, young infants are innately wired to put such information together. As early as 4 months of age, infants coordinate auditory and visual information for unusual events where it is highly unlikely that they could have learned the association. In one study, babies were shown two films side by side, one depicting two blocks banging and the other, two sponges being squashed together. At the same time, the appropriate sound track for only one of the films — either a sharp, banging noise or a soft, squashing sound — could be heard. Infants looked at the film appropriate to the sound track, indicating that they were able to detect a common rhythmic and temporal structure in both the seen movement and the sound of the objects and put them together (Bahrick, 1983). In another study, the images of two films were superimposed on one another while a sound track appropriate to only one of them was played. Using the habituation-dishabituation paradigm, investigators found that 4-month-old infants were able to attend to the appropriate complex visual event while ignoring the other one superimposed on it (Bahrick, Walker, & Neisser, 1981). These results provide especially convincing support for the view that visual-auditory integration is not learned, since it is highly unlikely that infants have had experience with such superimposed visual displays in everyday life.

Babies can also translate tactile information into visual information, an ability that has been demonstrated as early as 1 month of age. Meltzoff and Borton (1979) gave infants a pacifier to suck on with either a smooth surface or a surface with nubs on it. After exploring the pacifier in their mouths, the infants were presented with two similar-shaped objects for visual inspection. They preferred to look at the shape that they had sucked, indicating that neonates can recognize intermodal matches without months of prior experience in simultaneous tactile-visual exploration. In fact, the ability of newborn babies to turn in the general direction of a sound and to engage in primitive reaching toward objects suggests that a natural tendency to combine information across modalities is present from birth on. A captivating sight or sound seems to elicit total orientation of all of the neonate's sensory receptors, and infants appear to engage in multimodal exploration of their world from the very beginning (Bower, 1982).

EARLY DEPRIVATION AND ENRICHMENT: IS INFANCY A CRITICAL PERIOD OF DEVELOPMENT?

Throughout this chapter, we have discussed how certain experiences affect the development of perceptual and motor functions during infancy. In view of the findings on early experience that we have already reported, it is not surprising that a variety of investigations have found that attentive, warm, stimulating caregiving that is responsive to infants' self-initiated efforts promotes active exploration of the environment and early achievement of developmental milestones. In one investigation, mothers who frequently demonstrated, pointed, named, or positioned toys so that they were conveniently within the baby's reach had infants who spent more time manipulating objects and who played more maturely and competently (Belsky, Goode, & Most, 1980). In another study, the extent to which mothers initiated interactions, responded to their babies' vocalizations, and provided infants with appropriate play materials was positively related to mental performance during the second year of life (Bradley, Caldwell, & Elardo, 1979). In both of these investigations, the authors were careful to point out that the relationship between early experience and infant competence is bidirectional and reciprocal. Sensitive, responsive caregiving leads to active, exploratory, mature babies who, in turn, are more likely to evoke stimulating behaviors from parents. As a result, such infants profit from experience even more.

The powerful effect of early experience on infant development is even more apparent when we consider how infants develop in settings in which they are deprived of the quantity and quality of stimulation that is generally available in normal homes. We have already seen that infants reared in deprived institutions are severely retarded in motor development (Dennis, 1960). They also show fewer exploratory responses to objects, engage in stereotyped, immature play behaviors, and are fearful in new situations in which opportunities are available for them to play and explore (Collard, 1971). After only a few months, infants reared in underprivileged institutions show a level of mental development that is far below that of their home-reared peers (Dennis & Najarian, 1957).

Although these studies reveal that variations in early experience have a profound impact on infant development, they do not tell us if infancy is a **critical period** of development. That is, if infants do not experience rich and varied stimulation of their senses and opportunities for active exploration in the first year or two of life, will there be *permanent* deficits in development from which they cannot recover later on? This question has been of special interest to developmental psychologists ever since the 1940s, when several researchers observed institutionalized infants and suggested that the consequences of rearing babies under such extremely deprived conditions were both dire and irrevocable (Spitz, 1945; Goldfarb, 1945).

For ethical reasons, we cannot conduct experiments in which we deliberately deprive human infants of normal rearing environments and wait to observe the long-term consequences. However, a number of natural experiments in which children were the unfortunate victims of deprived conditions in early infancy but were later exposed to stimulating and sensitive care provide the best available test of whether human infancy is a critical period of development. These studies allow us to examine the long-lasting effects of early deprivation without the contaminating influence of later deprivation. If the critical period hypothesis is correct, then the effects of deprivation during infancy should persist, even when children are moved to enriched settings where efforts are made to help them recover from unsatisfactory early experiences.

In a classic study of this kind, Skodak and Skeels (1945; 1949) investigated the consequences of transferring 13 orphanage infants whose development was extremely delayed to an institution for the retarded at an average age of 19 months. The retarded adult residents eagerly welcomed the children into their wards, played with them, talked to them, took great pride in their new accomplishments, and even competed with one another to see whose baby was developing the fastest! The average intelligence score of the children when they were transferred was 64, but after a stay of one to two years, they showed dramatic gains ranging from 7 to 58 points, with a mean performance of 96. Eleven of the children were eventually adopted, and a follow-up after 2½ years in their adoptive homes revealed their average intelligence to be 101. As adults, half completed high school, 4 attended

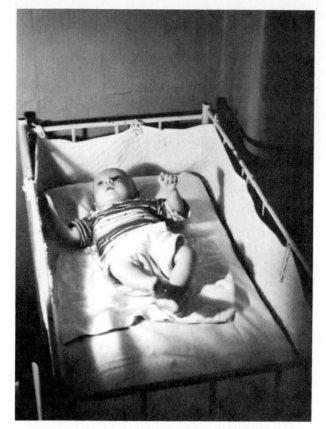

A deprived institutional environment can significantly delay an infant's development. However, if conditions improve, infants usually overcome the effects of early deprivation. (Burton L. White)

college, and 1 eventually earned a Ph.D. at a major university. All were self-supporting in skilled jobs, 11 married, and 9 became parents. Skodak and Skeels contrasted the development of these transferred infants with a group of 12 children who remained at the original orphanage. Their initial intelligence was higher (mean of 87) than those who had been placed with the retarded adults, but their subsequent performance was markedly inferior. By 2½ years of age, they had lost an average of 26 points. By adulthood, only half of the contrast group had completed the third grade. Five continued to reside in institutions, 5 of the 6 who worked held unskilled jobs, and 1 had died. Only two eventually married (Skeels, 1966).

The Skodak and Skeels research demonstrates quite dramatically that the effects of early deprivation can be overcome if children are provided with a more stimulating environment at an early age. Although their work has been subjected to intense methodological criticism (e.g., Longstreth, 1981), a number of other studies are in agreement with the conclusion that the development of deprived infants shows striking improvement when the quality of their rearing environments improves. In one remarkable investigation, Dennis (1973) studied the effects of child rearing in a Lebanese institution called the Creche where infants received adequate physical care, but lay in their cribs through most of the first year and received practically no stimulation and individual attention from caregivers. As Dennis wrote:

> (The caretakers) could place the nipple of a filled bottle in an infant's mouth while he lay in his crib, but they often failed to replace it if he lost the nipple. . . . When food was given by spoon to a 2- or 3-year-old, little consideration was given to the child's rate of eating, or to whether or not he liked the food. If he was slow, or if he protested, he was force-fed. . . . (The caretakers) did not talk to a child whom they were

dressing, changing, feeding, or bathing, and did not respond to the infrequent vocalizations of the child. . . . There were toys such as balls and stuffed animals at the Creche. These were sometimes placed in "play pens." They were routinely picked up and dropped over-board or thrown out by the infants and were not returned by the attendants. . . . Probably the most serious deprivation of the Creche children came from the lack of responsiveness to individual needs on the part of their caretakers. They were not cruel; they were only indifferent, ignorant, and apathetic. . . . There were about 10 children to each attendant on duty. (p. 19–20)

Extreme retardation in motor and language development was the result. Many babies did not sit up until 1 year of age or walk until well into the preschool years, and their average intelligence test score between 1 and 6 years was 53. Dennis took advantage of the fact that in 1956, adoption was legalized in Lebanon, and children of a variety of ages left the Creche and entered normal home environments. By comparing children who were adopted early (before 2 years of age) to those who were adopted later, Dennis was able to obtain a more definitive answer to the question of whether a responsive and stimulating environment during the first 2 years of life is critical for later development. The findings indicated that children adopted before age 2 overcame their initial retardation, gaining an average of almost 50 IQ points and achieving an intelligence test score of about 100 within 2 years' time. In contrast, those adopted later, although they gained steadily in intelligence over the period of childhood, never fully recovered from their earlier retardation. After spending from 6 to 8 years with their adoptive families, their scores were in the high 70s. Dennis concluded that environmental improvement by age 2 is necessary for complete recovery of deprived infants.

Research by Kagan on Indian children raised in an isolated farming village in northern Guatemala offers additional support for the conclusion that environmentally produced retardation during infancy, if remedied early, is not permanent and unchangeable. Infants in this small Guatemalan community spend their first year of life confined to the dark interior of their homes. During the first 6 months, they lie swaddled in hanging cradles with their faces covered, and sensory experience is reduced to a minimum. Tested at 1 year of age, the infants look passive and withdrawn, and they are several months behind American children in development. However, by the middle of the second year of life, they are permitted to roam outside their dark houses, and they encounter a greater variety of stimulation in the surrounding world. As a result, they gradually improve in intellectual performance over the course of childhood. By early adolescence, they appear active, alert, and sociable, and their performance on basic tests of memory and reasoning is comparable to the scores of Indian children residing in a nearby modern village, and to a comparison group of American children (Kagan & Klein, 1973; Kagan, 1976). However, the deprived Indian children do not do as well as their Indian or American peers on more complex intellectual tasks, and at 11 years of age they are still behind in academic skills such as reading, writing, and arithmetic (Kagan, 1976; Kagan et al., 1979). Unfortunately, Kagan's research does not tell us exactly why, despite improved circumstances beginning in the second year of life, the Indian children continue to show certain intellectual deficits. However, it is quite likely that underprivileged aspects of the small Indian community continue to exert an influence into the childhood years.

Taken together, research on early deprivation and enrichment indicates that the critical period concept is too strict a notion to apply to psychological development during the first two years of life. The evidence shows that babies are remarkably resilient beings who can withstand serious deprivation without being ruined or permanently stunted later on. However, much of the evidence that we have reviewed is consistent with a modified notion that considers infancy to be a **sensitive phase** of development. A sensitive phase is a time that is optimal for certain developmental functions to emerge, only its boundaries are less well defined than those of a critical period. It is possible for development to occur later on, but it is harder to induce it at that time. The research we have considered fits the conclusion that a sensitive phase of infant development may end somewhere around 2 years of age. The sensitive phase concept is consistent with the idea that massive enrichment may overcome the developmental deficits of children exposed to deprived rearing conditions beyond the age of 2. However, the extent to which this is possible awaits further research, and therefore treatment of poorly developing babies should not be postponed until some indefinite time in the future.

Unfortunately, most infants raised in underprivileged settings are likely to continue to be affected by the same disadvantaged conditions during their childhood years. Intervention programs that try to break this pattern as early as possible, by teaching caregivers about infant development and by training them to engage in attentive and stimulating behaviors with infants, have been shown to be markedly successful and to have lasting benefits (Andrews et al., 1982; Hunt et al., 1976). One of the most important outcomes of such interventions is that passive, apathetic babies become active, alert, exploratory beings with the capacity to evoke positive interactions from caregivers and to initiate stimulating play for themselves (Pines, 1979).

Research on early deprivation and enrichment also indicates that there are individual differences in how easily children recover from impoverished rearing conditions. Some are more responsive and resilient than others. Reports exist on several children who made dramatic recoveries in a very brief period of time, even though systematic treatment did not begin until as late as 5 or 6 years of age (Davis, 1947; Koluchova, 1972), whereas a few others barely changed at all, despite much earlier improvement in their environmental conditions. The existence of these cases suggests that, in addition to the timing and quality of intervention, the long-term consequences of early deprivation depend on infant constitutional factors. To help us understand what kinds of interventions work best with particular children, the joint effects of these variables need to be investigated (Gardner, Karmel, & Dowd, 1985).

Finally, there is currently a popular trend toward "educating" babies in infancy, even when no early biological or environmental handicaps are evident. The rationale for such efforts is that even if infants are healthy, reared in sensitive, responsive environments, and not obviously in need of intervention, more stimulation can only make things better. As a result, in recent years expensive early learning centers have sprung up around the United States where infants under a year of age are trained with letter and number flash cards and slightly older toddlers grapple with a full curriculum of art, music, gym, reading, math, French, and more. There is no evidence to date that such programs offer methods for raising babies that are superior to the natural inclinations of sensitive, caring parents, or that they are actually successful in transforming normal infants into smarter, better "super babies." Even if such evidence were available, infants growing up in stimulating and responsive family settings develop quite well without being pushed beyond what is appropriate for their current capacities, and programs designed to "hot house" or "jump start" them may actually pose serious risks to their development. As we saw in Box 4.2, more stimulation is not necessarily better for babies, and it can be harmful. Trying to stuff infants with knowledge for which they are not ready may cause them to withdraw and turn away, ultimately threatening their spontaneous interest and pleasure in learning. The first 2 years of life are a time when infants learn to use their bodies, make sense out of their perceptual world, and relate to people — learning that proceeds quite well without a deliberate adult lesson plan. Programs promising precocity that continue over many months subtract from the time babies have available for these vitally important developmental tasks. In addition, when they promise but do not produce young geniuses, such programs are likely to lead to disappointed parents who view their children as failures at a very tender age (White, 1985). Thus, they rob infants of a psychologically healthy start on the long road to maturity, and they deprive parents of relaxed, pleasurable participation in their infant's early growth.

CHAPTER SUMMARY

1. At one time considered passive, incompetent organisms whose world was a "blooming, buzzing confusion," infants are now viewed as active, competent beings who begin life with remarkable skills for relating to their physical and social worlds. The neonate's most obvious organized patterns of behavior are innate reflexes that enable the baby to adapt to the environment. A number of reflexes have survival value, while others provide the foundation for more complex motor behaviors that emerge later on.

2. The neonate has an organized sleeping-waking cycle that becomes increasingly patterned and predictable over the first 6 months of life. The newborn infant's sleep is also organized. It is comprised of at least two distinct states: REM and NREM sleep. However, infants spend far more time in the active, REM phase than do adults. According to autostimulation theory, REM sleep is a way in which the central nervous system compensates for unavailable activity. During infancy, REM sleep provides the brain with internal stimulation necessary for normal growth and development.

3. Newborn infants begin life with a set of distinct, clearly communicable cries that summon the caregiver. A crying baby stimulates strong physiological arousal in all human adults, and the pain cry produces an especially dramatic and immediate reaction. These responses are probably biologically programmed to assure that babies receive the necessary care and protection to survive. Events that cause a young infant to cry are largely physical and physiological, while older infants use the cry to express more psychologically based desires. Ethological and behaviorist theories disagree on how promptly and consistently caregivers should respond to infant cries. However, both positions seem to agree that parents can lessen older babies' need to cry by encouraging them to use more mature ways of communicating their desires.

4. Newborn infants demonstrate a remarkable capacity to learn. Neonates can be classically conditioned when CS-UCS pairings are of biological significance to the organism. Operant conditioning has been demonstrated in a wide variety of investigations. Habituation studies reveal the neonate's impressive ability to recognize and remember events they have seen before and to distinguish one stimulus event from another. Newborn babies also seem to have a rudimentary ability to imitate certain gestures of adults.

5. Infants' rapidly emerging motor competencies contribute to their perceptual and cognitive understanding of the world. Motor development appears to be subject to a secular trend, as infants achieve motor milestones earlier today than they did a half century ago. The sequence of motor achievements proceeds according to two maturationally determined patterns of development: the cephalo-caudal and proximo-distal trends. However, experience also has a profound effect on motor development, as shown by research on infants raised in deprived institutions and studies of blind infants. Visually guided reaching is gradually perfected over the course of the first year and plays a major role in infants' exploration and manipulation of the environment.

6. Infants exhibit a remarkable constellation of perceptual capacities from the very beginning. The senses of touch, taste, and smell are well developed at birth. In addition, neonates can hear a wide variety of sounds, and their sensitivity to pitch and loudness, as well as their ability to localize sounds, gradually improves over the first year of life. Newborns are particularly responsive to auditory stimuli within the frequency range of the human voice, and they can distinguish among a wide variety of speech sounds.

7. Infant visual capacities have received more research attention than any other sense. The visual apparatus is not fully developed at birth, but visual acuity as well as the ability to focus on objects rapidly matures over the first few months of life. Newborn infants are active visual explorers of their environment. From birth on, they use saccadic eye movements to explore the visual field, and smooth pursuit eye movements for tracking moving stimuli appear at 2 months and improve over the first half year. By 2 months, infants also discriminate between lights of different brightness as well as adults, and they can distinguish colors.

8. Research on depth perception using the visual cliff indicates that around the time infants are able to crawl they can discriminate between deep and shallow surfaces. The visual cliff studies have not clarified when infants respond to particular depth cues, but recent investigations show that responsiveness to kinetic cues appears first, at 3 months, followed by binocular cues between 3 and 6 months of age. Perception of pictorial depth cues emerges last, around 6 or 7 months of age.

9. As infants get older, they prefer increasingly complex patterns, a developmental trend that has been attributed to rapid maturation of the visual system over the first few months of life. Perception of the human face follows the same general course of development as do other aspects of visual perception, with single, high-contrast features on the periphery of a stimulus capturing the attention of the 1-month-old, and scanning of internal features appearing by 2 months of age. At 3 months, infants are capable of discriminating between different faces, and at 5 months they begin to notice the invariant features that make a particular human face unique.

10. Infants gradually build a visual world made up of stable, three-dimensional objects over the first 6 months of life. Shape constancy is present at birth, while size constancy does not appear until 4 to 6 months of age. The movement of objects relative to one another and to their backgrounds gradually enables infants to perceive objects as unique and independent of one another. Objects adjacent to one another or moving together in the same direction are treated as a single unit by infants under 6 months of age. By the middle of the first year, distinct shapes, textures, and colors of objects play a

more important role in the infant's identification of them as separate, independent wholes.

11. Young infants have a remarkable, built-in ability for intermodal perception. The fact that newborn babies look in the general direction of a sound source and engage in primitive reaching toward objects that they see suggests that a natural tendency to combine and integrate information across perceptual modalities exists from birth on.

12. Attentive, warm, stimulating caregiving that is responsive to the baby's self-initiated efforts is vitally important for development during infancy. However, infants are resilient and can recover from inadequate early rearing conditions if they are placed in stimulating, responsive environments by 2 years of age. Rather than being a critical period of development, infancy is a sensitive phase during which a variety of developmental milestones emerge easily and optimally. Children can compensate for inadequate development during infancy at a later time, but it is harder to do so, and recovery may not be complete.

IMPORTANT TERMS AND CONCEPTS

REM sleep
NREM sleep
autostimulation theory
Neonatal Behavioral Assessment
  Scale (NBAS)
classical conditioning
unconditioned stimulus (UCS)
unconditioned response (UCR)
conditioned stimulus (CS)
conditioned response (CR)
extinction
operant conditioning

reinforcers
punishment
habituation
dishabituation
imitation
secular trend in motor development
cephalo-caudal trend
proximo-distal trend
ulnar grasp
pincer grasp
visual acuity
saccades

smooth pursuit eye movements
visual cliff
binocular depth cues
pictorial depth cues
kinetic depth cues
invariant features
size constancy
shape constancy
intermodal coordination
critical period
sensitive phase

Children at Shore, by Edward Potthast.
Collection of Dr. Spencer H. Gross, Pamela B. Gross, and Lawrence E. Gross.

CHAPTER 5
Physical Growth

$\mathbf{A}$s time passes during the first two decades of life, the child's body changes continuously and dramatically, until it reaches the mature adult state. Think, for a moment, about the vast physical differences between a newborn infant and a full-grown young adult. From birth to maturity, the average individual's height is multiplied more than threefold, and weight increases as much as fifteen- to twentyfold. The top-heavy, chubby infant, whose head represents a quarter of the body's total length, is gradually transformed into the better proportioned young child, and eventually into the longer, broader, more muscular adult, whose head now consumes only a seventh of the body's total length. As we examine the physical changes that take place from infancy through childhood, you will quickly see that the story of physical growth is not just a matter of becoming taller and larger. Physical development involves a highly complex series of changes in bodily size, proportion, and composition — changes that proceed according to a carefully regulated and controlled growth plan. In this chapter, we describe the general course of human growth, and we consider fundamental biological knowledge about what regulates and controls it. We also discuss the impact of heredity as well as a variety of important environmental influences nutrition, disease, climate, seasonal changes, and familial and socioeconomic factors — on physical development. A special section of this chapter is devoted to maturation of the brain, the seat of human intelligence and adaptive functioning. We consider how its complex structure is generated during early growth, and how development depends on precise interaction between the environment and developing nerve cells.

Although a basic overall plan for growth is shared by all members of the human species, there are marked individual differences among children in the rate at which physical growth proceeds. These differences exist to some degree at all ages, but they are most evident at *puberty*, a period of rapid physical change leading to an adult-sized body and sexual maturity at the time of adolescence. Try to arrange a time to observe a group of 12-year-old girls or 14-year-old boys. You will see that obvious differences in progress toward maturity exist among them. These individual differences have important consequences for social and emotional adjustment. In this chapter, we take up the interplay and connectedness between physical and psychological development. We also address sex differences in physical growth, and the extent to which they mediate the development of body strength, motor skills, and athletic ability.

Finally, in several sections of this chapter, we consider disorders of physical growth that appear over the span of child development — failure to thrive in infants, deprivation dwarfism in children, childhood obesity, and anorexia nervosa during the adolescent years. These special problems illustrate the way in which physical growth is a prime indicator of the child's physical and mental health, and they emphasize the intimate relationship that exists between the physical and psychological domains of child development.

THE COURSE OF PHYSICAL GROWTH

Compared to other animals, primates (including human beings) experience an extended period of postnatal growth. Consider, for example, the mouse or the rat, traditional subjects in psychological experiments when circumstances prevail against the use of human subjects. In mice and rats, the interval between birth and puberty is only a matter of weeks, and it comprises only 1 to 2 percent of the life span, despite the fact that baby rodents are born at an earlier point in the course of physical development than are human infants. In chimpanzees, who are closest to humans in the evolutionary hierarchy of primates, the time between birth and puberty is extended to about 7 years, consuming about one sixth of the life span. This expansion of the period of physical immaturity appears to be a special evolutionary step taken by primates, and it is even more exaggerated in human beings, who devote about one fifth of their total years to growth and development (Napier, 1970). Evolutionary reasons for the long period of human growth are not hard to find. Prolonged immaturity leads to increased dependency of the human child on parents and other agents of socialization. In so doing, it provides added time for the acquisition of cultural knowledge, skills, and behavior patterns — time that is vital for the human child to learn to live in a complex physical and social world. In the words of anthropologist Weston La Barre (1954), "Biologically, it takes more time to become human. Obviously, too, it is the human brain and human learning which gain particular advantages by this biological slow-down" (p. 153).

Growth Curves and Changes in Overall Body Size

To parents of young children, the most obvious signs of physical growth are changes in the external dimensions of the body as a whole. During infancy, these changes are rapid. In the first 3 months of life, infants gain an average of 2 pounds per month. By 5 months of age, their birth weight has doubled, by the end of the first year it has tripled, and at 2 years of age it has quadrupled. Height undergoes similar dramatic gains during infancy. At the end of the first year of life, the infant's length is 50 percent greater than it was at birth, and by 2 years of age it is 75 percent greater. In comparison, bodily growth during the preschool and elementary school years is slow and steady. Increments in height average about 2 inches per year and weight about 5 pounds per year until the ninth or tenth birthday. Adolescence follows and is marked by a sharp acceleration in rate of growth. Large increases in height and weight are accompanied by sexual maturity, which is then followed by a deceleration in growth as human beings reach their mature adult stature.

Investigators of physical growth describe these age-related changes in postnatal height and weight using two types of growth curves. The first, shown in Figure 5.1, is a **distance curve.** It records the height and weight of an individual child, or the average height and weight obtained on a group of children, for each age level. It is called a distance curve because it indicates typical yearly progress toward maturity, or the average distance traveled at each age along the general path of growth. Besides serving as a useful set of growth standards, a number of interesting facts about children's growth can be obtained from these curves. Since data for boys and girls are plotted separately, we can discover some things about sex differences in growth progress. During infancy and childhood, boys and girls are very similar, with the typical girl just slightly shorter and lighter than the typical boy at all ages prior to adolescence. Shortly after 11 years of age, the girl becomes taller and heavier for a time, because, on the average, her adolescent growth spurt takes place 2 years earlier than the boy's. However, this advantage is short lived, for at age 14 she is surpassed in height by the typical boy, whose adolescent growth spurt has now started, while hers is almost finished. Growth in stature is complete for most girls by 16 years of age, and for boys by 17½ (Tanner, 1978b).

Distance curves also indicate something about prediction of growth. Look again at the curves in Figure 5.1, and you will see that the average girl has attained 50 percent of her mature height by 1¾ years of age, and the average boy the same by 2 years of age. By the end of the second year of life, a child's height becomes a reasonably good predictor of mature adult stature. Therefore, by doubling the height attained by girls

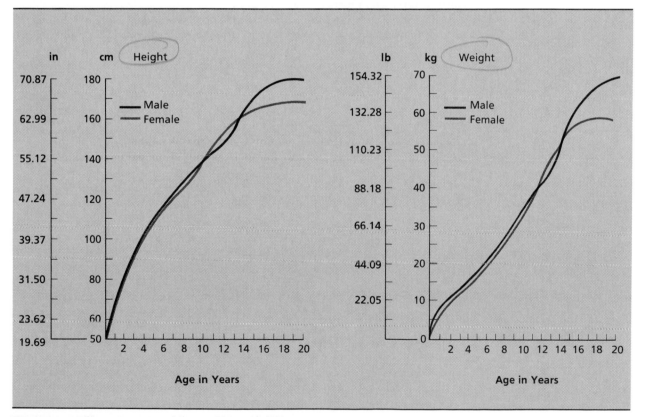

Figure 5.1. Height and weight distance curves for boys and girls, drawn from longitudinal measurements on approximately 175 individuals. *(From R. M. Malina, 1975,* Growth and Development: The First Twenty Years in Man. *P. 19. Minneapolis: Burgess. Adapted by permission.)*

and boys at these ages, we can obtain a rough estimate of how tall they will be as adults (Tanner, 1978b).

A second kind of growth curve is the **velocity curve,** depicted in Figure 5.2. It plots the absolute amount of growth that takes place at each yearly interval. Velocity curves are much better than distance curves at clarifying the exact timing of growth spurts, and Figure 5.2 makes plain some growth facts we have already mentioned. Two large spurts in general body growth take place during human postnatal development — one during the first year of life and the other at adolescence. Notice how the figure clearly reveals that the adolescent spurt takes place, on the average, 2 years earlier for girls than it does for boys.

The growth curves for height and weight shown in Figures 5.1 and 5.2 are often referred to as general growth curves, as most of the external body dimensions, as well as a number of internal organs such as the liver, spleen, and kidney, grow in a similar manner — rapid growth during infancy, slow, steady growth during middle childhood, rapid growth once more during adolescence, and slowing and cessation of growth during late adolescence. However, there are exceptions to this pattern. Among them are the brain and skull, the reproductive organs, and lymphoid tissues located throughout the body. As depicted in Figure 5.3, the brain and skull show very rapid growth early in life, so rapid that the brain attains 70 percent of its adult size by age 3 and 95 percent by age 7. The genital curve is characterized by a slight rise early in life, followed by a latent period throughout childhood, and then a very rapid growth spurt at adolescence. The lymphoid curve is unique in that it rises rapidly in infancy and early childhood to a peak just before adolescence, after which time the amount of lymphoid tissue decreases into adulthood. This path of development is adaptive, in that the lymph system plays a central role in the body's defense against infection and is also believed to influence nutritional absorption (Shields, 1972). Figure 5.3 illustrates the orderly, but asynchronous nature of postnatal growth. Various systems of the body have their own carefully timed, unique patterns of maturation (Malina, 1975).

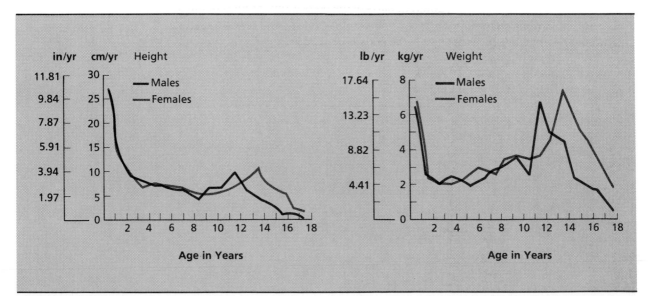

Figure 5.2. Height and weight velocity curves for boys and girls, drawn from longitudinal measurements on approximately 175 individuals. *(From R. M. Malina, 1975,* Growth and Development: The First Twenty Years in Man. *P. 20. Minneapolis: Burgess. Adapted by permission.)*

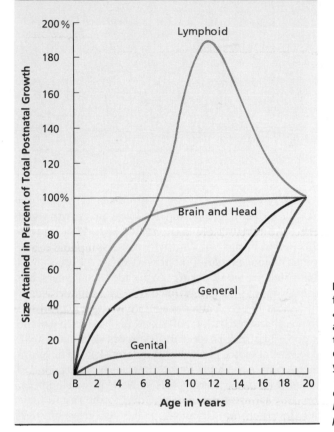

Figure 5.3. Growth curves of four different organ systems and tissues of the body. All are distance curves plotted in terms of percentage of change from birth to 20 years. *(From J. M. Tanner, 1962,* Growth at Adolescence *[2nd ed.], Oxford: Blackwell. P. 11. Reprinted by permission.)*

Changes in Body Proportions

As the child's overall size increases, different parts of the body grow at different rates, and body proportions change accordingly. For example, during the prenatal period and throughout infancy, the upper part of the body is better developed than the lower limbs, but this imbalance is gradually corrected because the legs lengthen at a faster rate than the trunk over the course of childhood. Perhaps you recognize this pattern of growth as the familiar *cephalo-caudal trend* we discussed in Chapter 4. You can see it depicted visually in the change in body proportions represented in Figure 5.4. Note that the ratio of leg length to total height is less than 1 : 4 in the early prenatal period, 1 : 3 at birth, and then rises to 1 : 2 by adulthood.

Physical growth during infancy and childhood also conforms to the *proximo-distal trend,* since it begins near the center axis of the body and moves outward, with the upper arms growing before the lower arms before the hands. However, exceptions to the basic cephalo-caudal and proximo-distal patterns begin to appear just before puberty. During this time, growth starts to proceed in the reverse direction, with the hands and feet enlarging before the dramatic adolescent rise in overall body growth. Also, during the late preadolescent period and the beginning of the adolescent growth spurt, leg length reaches a peak first. It is followed by additional growth in the length of the torso and trunk and, finally, by expansion of the breadth of the shoulders and chest. This pattern of physical development explains why young adolescents stop growing out of their shoes and trousers before they stop growing out of their jackets, and why parents, after doing a double-take of their rapidly transforming youngsters, often describe them as "all legs." It also helps us understand why early adolescence is

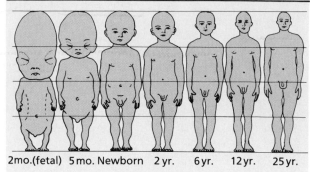

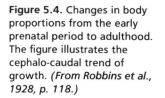

Figure 5.4. Changes in body proportions from the early prenatal period to adulthood. The figure illustrates the cephalo-caudal trend of growth. *(From Robbins et al., 1928, p. 118.)*

2mo.(fetal) 5mo. Newborn 2 yr. 6 yr. 12 yr. 25 yr.

often regarded as an "awkward" phase. During the period of adolescent growth when trunk length starts to change, the body's center of gravity shifts, causing new problems of balance. As a result, this period brings with it a temporary awkwardness in gross motor skills, but it seldom lasts longer than 6 months (Tanner, 1978b).

Sex differences in body proportions are small during the preadolescent years, but at adolescence, differences begin to appear that are typical of young adults. One of the most obvious physical differences between the sexes is the broadening of the shoulders relative to the hips that is characteristic of males, and the broadening of the hips relative to the shoulders and waist that is typical of females (Malina, 1975). These differences are the result of the influence of sex hormones on skeletal development during adolescence. Cartilage cells in the hip joints are specialized to respond to the rise in female sex hormones (estrogens) during this period of development, whereas in the shoulder region they are specialized to respond to the rise in male hormones (androgens, especially testosterone). Of course, males also grow substantially larger than females. This sex difference in eventual body size is partly due to boys' delayed pubertal growth spurt in comparison to girls', as boys have 2 additional years in which to continue their pre-adolescent growth before embarking on their adolescent spurt. Boys' later adolescent spurt also has important implications for sex differences in body proportions. Boys' legs are proportionately longer than girls' because of boys' added preadolescent growth time. As we mentioned earlier, during the last part of preadolescence the legs grow faster than the trunk of the body (Tanner, 1978b).

Sex differences in body build and proportions evolved over the history of our species because of their adaptive value. The widening of the female's hips provides room for the uterus and fetus to grow and a large enough pelvic opening so that a baby can be born. Broad shoulders, a muscular body, and long legs that contribute to running speed lead the male body to be adapted for tasks of heavy work, fighting, and hunting. Although these abilities are of limited importance in technologically advanced cultures where many strenuous tasks are accomplished with the aid of machines, the physical characteristics that support them continue to exist.

Changes in Body Composition

Major changes in the fat and muscular composition of the body take place with development. A large percentage of the body's fat lies immediately beneath the skin and can be measured with special calipers that indicate skin-fold thickness. Subcutaneous fat begins to appear in the last few weeks of prenatal life and gradually increases until it reaches a peak at about 9 months of age. Thereafter, it decreases until about 6 to 8 years of age, when it begins to rise again. Thus, newborn infants quickly fill out into round, plump babies over the course of the first year. Then, beginning in the second year of life, children start to become more angular and slender, a trend that continues into the school years. Girls have slightly more total fat at birth than do boys, a difference that becomes greater over the course of childhood and is especially marked after 8 years of age. Although both sexes show increases in fat on the trunk of the body until adulthood, girls accumulate fat at a substantially greater rate than boys. In addition, girls continue to add limb fat during adolescence, whereas the limb fat of boys generally decreases at this time (Tanner & Whitehouse, 1975).

Muscle tissue grows according to a very different early pattern than fat, accumulating very slowly and gradually at a decelerating rate throughout infancy and childhood. Then it undergoes a marked acceleration at adolescence (Tanner, 1978a). Although both sexes gain in muscle at puberty, the increase is much greater for males than it is for females. Adolescent boys develop larger hearts, larger skeletal muscles, and a greater vital capacity of the lungs than do girls. In addition, the number of red blood cells, and therefore the amount of hemoglobin available to carry oxygen from the lungs to the muscles, increases in boys at adolescence, but it remains unchanged in girls (Tanner, 1962). Since adolescent boys have a greater capacity for carrying oxygen through their bloodstream, this gives them greater power to neutralize the chemical products of muscular exercise. The combined result of all of these changes is that gains of boys in muscle strength at adolescence are substantial and far outstrip those of girls, whose increases trail off earlier and at a much lower level (Jones, 1971). Boys' muscle strength shows its largest rise in the latter part of pubertal growth (Stolz & Stolz, 1971), a pattern of gain that plays a major role in their steady increase in athletic performance throughout the teenage years. When adolescent boys and girls were compared on a series of basic athletic skills, such as distance throw, broad jump, and 50-yard dash, girls' performance increased up to age 14 and then leveled off, whereas boys' performance continued to improve through their 17th year (Espenschade, 1971). However, it is also the case that girls receive far less encouragement and social approval for athletic accomplishment throughout childhood than do boys, a factor that dampens the development of physical skills in many girls and exaggerates the differences that do exist between the sexes (Thomas & French, 1985).

Skeletal Growth

Because children of the same age differ in their rates of growth, a variety of methods for estimating their progress toward physical maturity have been devised. These estimates are useful to researchers studying the causes and consequences of individual differences in physical growth. They also provide a rough estimate of children's chronological age in areas of the world where birth dates are not customarily recorded. One type of maturity estimate involves an assessment of the state of development of the primary and secondary sexual characteristics. This is an excellent indicator of maturity status, but it is only useful during the adolescent years. The best method for assessing growth maturation is **skeletal age,** because the development of the skeleton spans the entire period of physical growth and is related to the percentage of growth completed at any age (Tanner et al., 1983).

The forerunners of bones appear as cartilage early in prenatal life and start to be replaced by bone in the sixth week of gestation, a process that continues until individuals are in their 20s. Each bone in the body begins as a primary center of **ossification** (place where cartilage hardens into bone) from which it enlarges and takes on a basic shape. Shortly before birth, secondary centers of ossification begin to appear called **epiphyses** (see Figure 5.5). In the long bones, the epiphyses generally emerge at the two extreme ends of the bone. Immediately beneath each epiphysis is a growth plate where cartilage cells divide and proliferate and over the course of time are converted into bone. Thus, long bones extend their length by growing inward from each end. As growth nears completion, the growth plate gradually gets thinner and eventually disappears. When this occurs, no more growth of the bone is possible. New epiphyses appear in various parts of the skeleton until puberty. The individual

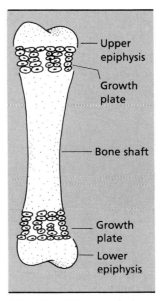

Figure 5.5. Diagram of a long bone showing growth plates beneath upper and lower epiphyses. *(From J. M. Tanner, 1978,* Fetus into Man, *Cambridge: Harvard University Press. P. 33. Reprinted by permission.)*

has approximately 400 at birth, and twice that number by the beginning of adolescence (Delecki, 1985).

Skeletal age can be estimated by X-raying the bones of the body and seeing how many epiphyses there are and to what extent they are not yet fused (see Figure 5.6). The X-rays are compared to norms established for bone maturity based on large numbers of children. Such estimates show that girls exceed boys in skeletal maturity throughout development. During the prenatal period, girls are already about 3 weeks ahead of boys in skeletal growth. At birth, the difference amounts to about 4 to 6 weeks, and by puberty it has increased to 2 years. Girls have been found to be ahead in the development of other organ systems as well. Their greater physiological maturity beginning in prenatal life may be partly responsible for their superior resilience in the face of environmental stressors, and for the lower infant and early childhood mortality rates that exist for girls in comparison to boys (Tanner, 1978b).

Pediatricians are concerned with another aspect of skeletal growth when they routinely measure the head circumference of babies from birth until 2 years of age. The pattern of development of the skull is very different from the rest of the skeleton. Its growth is rapid during the first 2 years of life, and its size is nearly complete by 6 years of age, although slight increases continue to occur through adolescence. At birth, the bones of the cranial vault are separated by six gaps, or "soft spots," filled with fibrous tissue called **fontanels** (see Figure 5.7). The gaps allow the bones to slide over one another to some degree as the relatively large head of the baby passes through the narrow birth canal. The largest gap, the anterior fontanel, can easily be felt at the top of a baby's skull, as it is slightly more than an inch across. It gradually shrinks and is filled in during the second year of life. The other fontanels are smaller and close more quickly. As the cranial bones come in contact with one another, they form sutures, or seams, which permit continued skull expansion as the brain enlarges in size. The sutures disappear completely after puberty, when skull growth ceases entirely (Delecki, 1985).

Besides increasing in length, the bones of the skeleton also grow in width, a process that takes place without the intervention of cartilage. Much like a tree

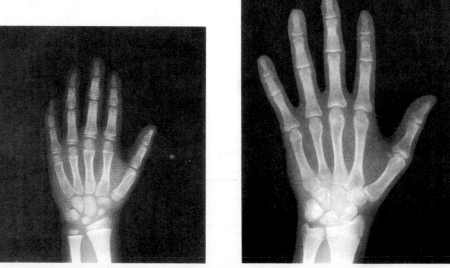

Figure 5.6. X-rays of the hand of a girl at two chronological ages, showing different degrees of skeletal maturity. Note the difference in ossification of the wrist bones and fusion of the epiphyses on the long bones of the forearm. *(From J. M. Tanner, R. H. Whitehouse, N. Cameron, W. A. Marshall, M. J. R. Healey, & H. Goldstein, 1983,* Assessment of Skeletal Maturity and Prediction of Adult Height *[TW2 method, 2nd ed.], Academic Press, Inc. [London, Ltd.]. P. 86. Reprinted by permission.)*

6½ Years   14½ Years

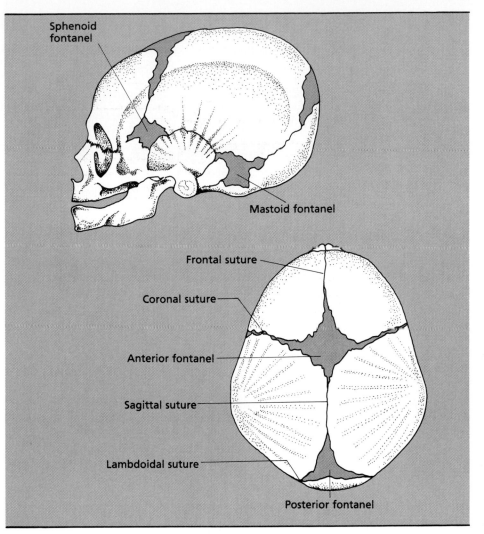

Sphenoid fontanel

Mastoid fontanel

Frontal suture

Coronal suture

Anterior fontanel

Sagittal suture

Lambdoidal suture

Posterior fontanel

Figure 5.7. The skull at birth, showing the fontanels and sutures. *(From J. Delecki, "Principles of Growth and Development." In P. M. Hill [Ed.],* Human Growth and Development Throughout Life. *Copyright © 1985 by John Wiley & Sons, Inc. Reprinted by permission of John Wiley & Sons, Inc.)*

expanding in girth, new layers are deposited as the result of cell duplication just under the surface of the bone. The bones of the skull and the face actually grow in this manner. Small increases in the width of the long bones of the body continue to take place throughout the life span (Tanner, 1978b).

Puberty: The Physical Transition to Adulthood

Puberty is the time of development in which individuals become sexually mature and capable of producing offspring. It is also the period of greatest sex differentiation since early intrauterine life. As we have already seen, dramatic changes in size, proportion, and muscular and fat composition of the body take place during this phase of development. In addition, the reproductive organs mature, and the secondary sex characteristics develop. Although the sequence of physical changes occurring at adolescence is fairly uniform among children, timing and speed of maturation differ substantially from individual to individual (see Figure 5.8). As we shall soon see, both the physical events of puberty and the individual differences that occur in rate of physical maturation have important implications for adolescent social and emotional development.

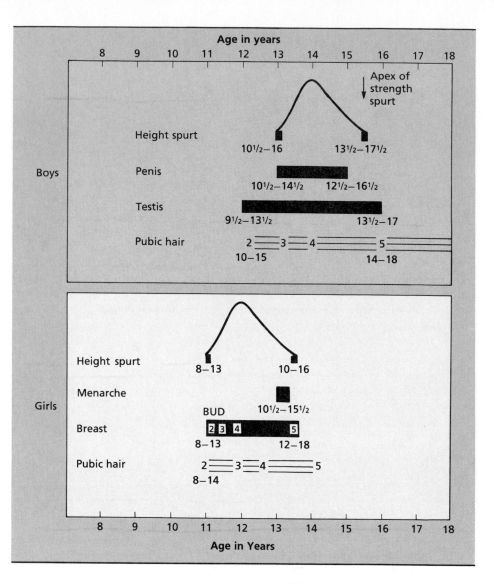

Figure 5.8. Range of ages for onset and completion of pubertal changes in boys and girls. To show the extent of individual variability, the beginning and completion of most changes are marked with a range of chronological ages. Pubic hair and breast development are rated on scales of 2 (initial signs) to 5 (completed growth). Note especially the relationship of the height spurt to other pubertal changes. It occurs earlier in the sequence of events for girls than it does for boys. *(From J. M. Tanner, 1962, Growth at Adolescence [2nd ed.], Oxford: Blackwell. Pp. 30, 36. Adapted by permission. Age ranges from Faust, 1977, and Tanner, 1978b.)*

Pubertal Development in Girls. Although **menarche,** or first menstrual period, is generally regarded as the major sign that puberty has arrived in girls, it actually occurs fairly late in the sequence of pubertal events. The first signs of female puberty are the budding of the breasts and the beginning of the growth spurt—the swift increase in height and weight and expansion of the pelvis that we discussed earlier in this chapter. The average age at which these early signs appear in European and North American girls is around 11, but the range extends from 8 to 13. The first appearance of pubic hair generally occurs slightly later than the budding of the breasts, usually between the 11th and 12th birthdays (Tanner, 1978b).

Menarche typically happens around the 13th birthday, although, again, the age range is large, extending from as early as 10½ to as late as 15½ years of age. By the time the girl has experienced her first menstrual period, her rapid gain in body size is starting to taper off, and the growth spurt is nearly over. The average girl adds almost 8 inches of total height during puberty, with only about 2 of these occurring after menarche. In the year following the appearance of menstruation, pubic hair and breast development are completed, and underarm hair appears. Although a 3-year time line for female pubertal growth is the norm, not all girls adhere to it. Some pass far more rapidly through the phases of puberty, taking as little time as a year and a half to complete them, while others require an extended period, lasting as long as 5 years (Marshall & Tanner, 1969).

Age of menarche is closely synchronized with the attainment of an appropriate level of skeletal maturity. In other words, when we examine the order in which pubertal changes occur in girls, it appears that menarche does not initiate, but follows, the girl's physical growing up (refer again to Figure 5.8). This sequence of events has clear adaptive value. It makes sense from a biological standpoint to delay menarche until an appropriate physical and pelvic size is attained to permit the successful bearing of children. Higher rates of stillbirths and obstetric complications occur among women who are short in stature and who have small pelvic dimensions (Ellison, 1982).

Menarche is generally taken as the sign that a girl has reached sexual maturity. It does mark a mature state of uterine development, but in many girls there is a period of 12 to 18 months following the first menstruation in which mature ova are not yet produced. However, this temporary period of sterility cannot be counted on (Tanner, 1978b). Pregnancies resulting from early sexual activity among adolescents are on the rise, and many babies are currently being born to mothers younger than 15 years of age. As indicated by the information presented in Box 5.1, teenage pregnancy is a major American problem in which the development of both young adolescent girls and their newborn infants is seriously at risk.

Pubertal Development in Boys. The first signs of puberty in boys are the enlargement of the testes, accompanied by modifications in the texture and color of the scrotum. These changes begin to appear, on the average, in the middle of the 11th year, although the growth of the testes does not show a steep rise until much later, around 14 years of age. Pubic hair first appears in boys around 12½, about the same time that the penis begins to enlarge in size. The penis is fully developed around age

Since the growth spurt for boys occurs later than it does for girls, females generally tower over their male peers during early adolescence. (Paul Conklin/Monkmeyer Press Photo Service)

14½, but there are wide individual differences, and in some boys this occurs as early as 12½, whereas in others it happens as late as 16½ (Tanner, 1978a; 1978b).

Refer once more to Figure 5.8, and you will see that the spurt in height occurs much later in the sequence of pubertal events for boys than it does for girls. It begins about 1 year after the initial enlargement of the testes, but it does not reach its maximum peak until a year later, at about 14 years of age. Around this time, the growth of pubertal hair is complete, and soon after underarm hair appears. Male facial and body hair emerges slightly after the peak growth spurt, but it progresses very slowly and does not reach completion until several years after puberty is over. Another landmark of male physical maturity is the deepening of the voice, an event that results from the enlargement of the larynx and lengthening of the vocal cords. Voice change also occurs late in the sequence of pubertal events, just after the peak spurt in general body growth (Tanner, 1978b).

At the same time as the penis is growing, the prostate gland and the seminal vesicles enlarge, and about a year later, around the age of 15, **spermarche,** the first spontaneous ejaculation of seminal fluid, occurs. The first fluid produced generally contains few viable sperm, so that, like adolescent females, males may have an initial

---

FOCUS ON CONTEMPORARY ISSUES

Box 5.1
Teenage Pregnancy: A Growing National Concern

Each year, more than a million American teenagers become pregnant, 4 out of 5 of them unmarried, and some 30,000 of them under the age of 15 (Mecklenburg & Thompson, 1983; Wallis, 1985). The United States leads nearly all other developed nations in the incidence of teenage pregnancy, making it a pervasive national problem (Jones et al., 1985). Not all adolescents who conceive give birth to a baby; in fact, teenagers account for one third of the legal abortions performed each year in the United States, and 13 percent of adolescent pregnancies end in miscarriage. Nevertheless, the number of out-of-wedlock births to mothers under 20 years of age rose from under 100,000 in 1960 to over 250,000 in the 1980s. Increased social acceptance of a young single mother raising a baby has probably contributed to the decline in placing such infants up for adoption. One survey reported that 93 percent of unmarried women between 15 and 19 years of age reside with their infants (Baldwin, 1983).

When a baby is born to a teenage girl, it imposes lasting hardships on two generations — both adolescent parent and child. Teenage mothers are many times as likely as older women

with young children to be poor, and a high proportion of adolescent births occur among members of America's low-income minority groups. Although those who receive adequate prenatal care and nutrition are not at greater obstetric risk than adult women of the same socioeconomic background, adolescent mothers (and fathers as well) suffer severe developmental disadvantages as the result of childbearing. For example, early pregnancy is educationally disruptive. Only 50 percent of girls who give birth before the age of 18 complete high school, as compared with 96 percent of those who postpone childbearing. Both teenage mothers and fathers are likely to be on welfare, and if they are employed, their educational background limits them to unsatisfying, low-paid jobs (Elster & Panzarine, 1983; Osofsky & Osofsky, 1983).

Why does teenage pregnancy occur? In part, it is due to pervasive sexual activity among adolescents, coupled with inadequate sexual knowledge and lack of easy access to contraception. A 1982 survey found that 20 percent of 15-year-old girls admitted to having already had sexual intercourse, as did nearly 33 percent of 16-year-olds and 43 percent of 17-year-olds (Kantner & Zelnik, as cited by Wallis, 1985). Even when school courses in sex education exist, many adolescent girls and boys continue to

misunderstand reproductive facts or to believe that pregnancy "can't happen to me." However, when earlier and better sex education programs are coupled with efforts to help teenagers obtain contraceptives, the pregnancy rate drops sharply (Kreipe, 1983; Elster & Panzarine, 1983).

The roots of teenage pregnancy are not limited to matters of sex education and birth control availability. Succumbing to peer pressure for premarital sex occurs more often among adolescents who feel alienated from their immediate family. Pregnant teenagers report less affection, less communication, and fewer demands and expectations made of them by parents than do their nonpregnant counterparts. Strong, trusting parent-child relationships seem to be effective insulators against premature parenthood (Olson & Worobey, 1984). In fact, one study found that when sex information is provided openly and freely by parents rather than obtained from peers, teenagers are more restrictive in their sexual behavior (Lewis, 1973).

Adolescent pregnancy also repeats itself from generation to generation. A recent estimate indicated that 82 percent of girls who give birth at age 15 or younger are daughters of teenage mothers. Generally they are from poverty families, and having little sense of a promising future, they period of reduced fertility (Tanner, 1978b). It is possible that spermarche may be as psychologically significant a pubertal event for boys as menarche is for girls (Gaddis & Brooks-Gunn, 1985), an issue that we address in the next section.

The Psychological Impact of Pubertal Events. How do adolescent boys and girls adapt to the massive physical changes that occur during puberty? Most research aimed at answering this question has focused on girls and deals with reactions to the first menstrual period. Other pubertal changes are far more gradual and take place over a period of months or years, providing the adolescent girl with at least some time to get used to them. In contrast, menarche is unique in that it happens suddenly and without warning. The fact that it is the most discrete marker of female physical maturity is probably the reason that it has consumed the lion's share of research attention (Greif & Ulman, 1982). However, the singular focus of research on the psychological meaning of menstruation has limited our understanding of other pubertal events. Also, no studies have looked at differences across social class and ethnic groups, and to date we know very little about the psychological significance of puberty for boys (Brooks-Gunn, 1984).

---

imagine that a baby will fill the void in their lives (Wallis, 1985).

The process of becoming a parent constitutes a major life transition that brings with it stress and disequilibrium for any individual, but for adolescents it is especially difficult. They must accept the responsibilities of parenting before they have established a clear sense of direction for their own lives, a circumstance that can create serious disruptions for both teenage parent and child. Research addressing the adequacy of adolescent girls as mothers has reported them to be less verbal, less nurturing, more impatient, and more prone to punish their children than controls (Lawrence, 1983). Also, the younger the teenage mother, the more limited her capacity to cope with the simultaneous stresses of adolescence and motherhood, and the less effective her parenting behaviors. In one study, mothers in the mid-adolescent years were seen engaging in aggressive actions, such as pulling and pinching their newborn infants — behaviors that are the early precursors of the high levels of child abuse known to be experienced by the offspring of teenage parents (Lawrence et al., 1981). In another study, the younger the adolescent mother, the less she engaged in the typical maternal behaviors of touching, speaking to her infant in a gentle high-pitched voice, and holding her baby close (McAnarney, Lawrence, & Aten, 1979). In view of these findings, it is not surprising that children of adolescents have been found to score low on intellectual measures, to achieve poorly in school, and to be disruptive socially (Kinard & Klerman, 1983; Lawrence, 1983). Still, how well an adolescent fares as a mother varies considerably. Outcomes are more positive when teenage mothers return to school immediately after giving birth and continue to reside in their parents' homes, where child care responsibilities can be shared with mature, experienced caregivers (Sahler, 1983).

Few adolescents under the age of 18 are ready for parenthood. In view of the magnitude of the teenage pregnancy problem in the United States, there is an overwhelming need for public programs to assist young people in avoiding unwanted pregnancies, and for interventions that offer health and medical services, educational and vocational counseling, child care, and training in parenting skills for adolescent mothers and fathers.

Most pregnant teenagers are not fully mature in their own right. As a result, they are often overwhelmed by the responsibilities of parenthood. (Ed Lettau/Photo Researchers)

Originally, reactions to menarche were studied retrospectively in samples of women being treated for emotional difficulties. Because these subjects tended to remember their experiences as traumatic and upsetting, puberty came to be viewed as a period of inevitable crisis and negative emotion (Brooks-Gunn, 1984). However, recent investigations, in which adolescents have been asked to report their feelings and experiences directly, indicate that girls' reactions to their first menstrual period are not singularly unfavorable. The most common response is "surprise," undoubtedly provoked by the sudden nature of the event. In addition, the majority of girls report a mixture of positive and negative emotions — "excited and pleased" as well as "scared and upset" (Petersen, 1983; Ruble & Brooks-Gunn, 1982; Whisnant & Zegans, 1975). Whether their feelings lean more in the positive or negative direction depends on a number of factors, including prior knowledge and support from family members, both of which are influenced by social and cultural attitudes toward physical maturation and sexuality (Greif & Ulman, 1982).

For girls who have no advance information about menstruation, its onset can be quite traumatic. Both those who are early and those who are unprepared report more negative experiences. Of course, it is difficult to untangle the separate effects of these two variables, as being early is positively correlated with not being prepared. Nevertheless, the absence of prior knowledge seems to have long-term negative consequences. Adults and adolescent girls who remember being unprepared report more severe physical symptoms, more unfavorable attitudes about menstruation, and more embarrassment and self-consciousness (Koff, Rierdan, & Sheingold, 1982; Ruble & Brooks-Gunn, 1982). Fortunately, the percentage of girls with no advance preparation is much smaller today than it used to be several decades ago. In the 1950s, up to 50 percent of all girls were given no prior information (Shainess, 1961), whereas by the 1970s, only 5 to 10 percent were uninformed. This shift is probably due to greater openness on the part of modern parents to discussing sexual matters with their youngsters. Currently, almost all girls acquire some information from their mothers (Brooks-Gunn & Ruble, 1980). Also, the recent widespread addition of health education classes to children's school subjects makes it likely that today's girls have at least heard about menstruation, even in instances in which their mothers have been reluctant to discuss it (Brooks-Gunn & Ruble, 1983).

The family environment also makes a difference in how girls respond to menstruation. In a study in which adolescent girls were asked about family communication, those who reported that their fathers were not told about their first menstruation, or who did not know if their fathers were told, described more negative attitudes and severe menstrual symptoms than those who stated that their fathers knew. Whether or not fathers are told may say something about family attitudes toward physical and sexual matters, which may be one of the most important factors in encouraging more positive emotional reactions to menarche among adolescent girls (Brooks-Gunn & Ruble, 1980).

Very little information exists on boys' attitudes and feelings about spermarche. One older study reported that almost all boys reacted to their first ejaculation in negative terms (Shipman, 1971). However, like the findings of early research on menarche, these results are probably related to boys' lack of preparation and understanding of the event, as only 15 percent of the sample understood the concept of ejaculation prior to its occurrence. In a recent investigation, Gaddis and Brooks-Gunn (1985) found that, like girls' reactions to menstruation, boys' responses to spermarche were not intensely negative, and most reported mixed feelings. All had some advance knowledge about ejaculation, but in contrast to girls, most of whom talk with their mothers and learn about menarche at school, very few of the boys in this study received information from others, and most obtained it from reading material.

Both boys and girls behave quite secretively about spermarche and menarche when it comes to telling their peers. Girls tell far fewer friends than they anticipated they would tell before their first menstruation had occurred, and only a fourth tell anyone besides their mothers. However, girls' reluctance to talk about menarche is temporary and lasts only about 6 months. By then, almost all have talked to their peers and know that some of their friends are also menstruating (Danza, 1983; Ruble & Brooks-Gunn, 1982; Brooks-Gunn et al., 1986). Far fewer boys ever tell anyone about spermarche. In the Gaddis and Brooks-Gunn (1985) study described above, the small minority of boys who eventually did confide in someone were those who had been given prior explanatory information by an adult male, and they told only that one person. None talked to their friends about the experience. Thus, spermarche, in contrast to menarche, is rarely discussed with others either before or after the experience, yet research has shown that information transmitted by parents and friends leads to better acceptance and adjustment to the physical changes of puberty (Brooks-Gunn et al., 1986). In this regard, girls seem to be provided with far more social support than boys, a finding that has important implications for the expansion and improvement of health education curricula in the schools.

The experience of puberty takes place in the larger context of the cultural attitudes and values of the society in which young pubescent boys and girls live. In many primitive cultures, puberty is recognized as a crucial time in the adolescent's physical, psychological, and social development. It is openly acknowledged through ceremonial rituals that mark the young individual's entry into the adult world. In contrast, in our society, little formal recognition is granted to the advent of puberty. There are no special customs to mark it, and no obvious changes in social status follow it.[1] Although school health programs provide information about some of the physical changes, the topic of puberty is generally approached from the standpoint of hygiene rather than as a recognized maturational milestone (Greif & Ulman, 1982). Yet

[1] An exception is the Jewish *bar* or *bat mitzvah* ceremony, a religious rite of passage that takes place for a boy at age 13 and a girl at age 12. On that day, the young person comes before the congregation to chant a section of the Torah (Five Books of Moses) in Hebrew and is publicly acknowledged as a new member of the adult Jewish community.

In many primitive cultures like the Warusha tribe of Africa, puberty is recognized through ceremonies that involve face painting and circumcision rituals. (George Holton/Photo Researchers)

research indicates that menarche is an emotionally charged event that relates to a girl's emerging identity as a woman, her newly acquired ability to reproduce, and her changing relationships with others. Although boys remain under-researched, it is likely that puberty has a similarly profound significance for them. As Whisnant and Zegans (1975) point out, because puberty brings with it many new psychological adjustments, there is a need for us to develop ". . . a more socially and culturally appropriate substitute to serve the emotional function that more primitive societies have met with familial and social rituals" (p. 814).

The Importance of Early Versus Late Maturation. Think back to your late elementary school and junior high school days. Were you early, late, or about on time in physical maturation with respect to your peers? Research suggests that maturational timing makes an important difference in social and emotional adjustment, since having physical characteristics that help one gain social acceptance from others can be very comforting to young adolescent boys and girls.

The well-known Berkeley longitudinal studies, to which you were introduced in Chapter 2, first explored the relationship of early versus late maturation to adolescent adjustment. Findings indicated that early-maturing boys have a special advantage relative to late maturers in many aspects of social and emotional functioning. They were seen as relaxed, independent, self-confident, and physically attractive by both adults and peers. Socially poised and popular with their agemates, early-maturing boys held a high proportion of positions of leadership in school, and they also tended to be athletic stars. In comparison, late-maturing boys were not well liked, and peers and adults viewed them as anxious and attention seeking in behavior (Clausen, 1975; Jones, 1965; Jones & Bayley, 1950). The differences in adjustment between early- and late-maturing boys were long lasting, as they were still present when the subjects reached adulthood (Clausen, 1975).

In contrast, the Berkeley studies showed that early-maturing girls were not socially advantaged. They scored below average in popularity, appeared withdrawn and lacking in self-confidence, and held few positions of leadership. Instead, their late-maturing counterparts were especially well off. Late-maturing girls were regarded as physically attractive, buoyant, sociable, and poised by peers and adults, and they held more positions of prestige and leadership at school (Jones & Mussen, 1958). However, the consequences of being an early versus late maturer were not as long lasting for girls as they were for boys. Negative outcomes associated with being an early maturer weakened between sixth and eighth grade as other girls caught up in physical status and the peer group as a whole developed heterosexual interests (Faust, 1960). By the time female subjects reached adulthood, early differences associated with rate of maturation were nonexistent (Peskin, 1973).

The research on maturational timing described above was largely completed in the 1950s and 1960s, but current evidence indicates that the same differences continue to be true of adolescents today. Recent studies also help explain why the consequences of maturational timing are so consistent and pervasive. Two factors seem especially important. First, early and late maturers have body types that match ideal standards of physical beauty to different degrees. Second, at adolescence, it is especially important to "fit in" physically with one's peers. Let's discuss each of these factors in turn.

Flip through the pages of your favorite popular magazine, and take a look at the figures of men and women portrayed in the ads. You will see convincing evidence for our society's current view of a physically attractive female as exceptionally thin and long-legged and an attractive male as tall, broad-shouldered, and muscular. The female image portrayed throughout the media is a prepubertal shape that tends to favor late-developing girls. Due to delayed closing of the epiphyses at the growth points of the long bones, the late-maturing girl has a longer time to grow. As a result, she is more long-legged than her early-maturing agemate (Faust, 1983). In addition, early-maturing children of both sexes are generally heavier and stockier than late-maturing children (Malina, 1975), a circumstance that conflicts with the female lithesome ideal but is consistent with the value of male physical robustness.

Recent evidence suggests that a preference for physical attractiveness, at least in terms of facial features, begins in infancy (Langlois et al., 1987). By the preschool years, children have acquired cultural ideals of physical beauty through exposure to media and the preferences of others around them (Styczynski & Langlois, 1977). By fifth grade, children apply these standards of physical appearance consistently (Cavior & Lombardi, 1973). As early and late maturers bring different physical characteristics to social situations, others begin to react to them in terms of accepted standards of physical beauty. This feedback strongly affects how comfortable and satisfied adolescents are with their physical selves, and ultimately, their social and emotional well-being (Lerner, 1985).

A consistent finding of many studies is that early-developing girls have less positive body images (view their physical appearance as less personally satisfying) than their on-time and late-maturing agemates. Among boys, the opposite is the case. Early maturation is linked to a positive body image, while late maturation is associated with dissatisfaction with the physical self (Blyth et al., 1981; Blyth, Simmons, & Zakin, 1985; Brooks-Gunn, 1984; Brooks-Gunn & Ruble, 1983; Tobin-Richards, Boxer, & Petersen, 1983). Both male and female adolescents who have physical characteristics seen by themselves and others as less attractive are less well liked by peers and have a lower sense of self-esteem (Langlois & Stephan, 1981; Lerner & Brackney, 1978). Thus, the adoption of society's "beauty is best" stereotype seems to be an important mediating factor in the adjustment of early- and late-maturing boys and girls.

A second way of explaining differences in adjustment between early and late maturers is in terms of their physical status in relation to the rest of their peer group. From this perspective, since early-maturing boys are about as physically mature as the average girl of the same age, and late-maturing girls are about as mature as the average boy, these groups of adolescents should experience few problems as the result of maturational timing. However, because girls who mature early do so much earlier than the rest of their peers, and boys who mature late do so much later, it is these two groups that are most likely to experience difficulties as the result of being different from their agemates. This analysis is certainly consistent with the evidence on maturational timing effects that we have already described, and additional support for it comes from results indicating that adolescents are most comfortable interacting with peers who match their own level of biological maturity. For example, individuals who are in the same stage of physical development are regarded as preferred companions and as closer friends by adolescent girls (Brooks-Gunn et al., 1986, Magnusson, Stattin, & Allen, 1986). But because few agemates of the same biological status are available to early-maturing girls, many of them seek older companions, who may influence them in ways that promote school behavior problems as well as lower academic performance — difficulties that are more prevalent among early-maturing girls. However, these problems generally disappear as agemates catch up in physical development and as early-maturing girls merge with the majority in terms of their physical status (Simmons, Blyth, & McKinney, 1983; Magnusson, Stattin, & Allen, 1985).

The fact that adolescents easily incorporate and apply socially transmitted ideals of physical attractiveness and are sensitive to peer pressures suggests that the difficulties they experience with respect to maturational timing can be affected by the social contexts to which they are exposed. Indeed, several studies reveal this to be the case. For example, Blyth, Simmons, and their colleagues (Blyth, Simmons, & Zakin, 1985; Simmons et al., 1979) found that sixth-grade, early-maturing girls had more positive body images when they attended kindergarten through sixth-grade (K–6) rather than kindergarten through eighth-grade (K–8) schools. Despite the scarcity of other children who were just as physically mature, early-maturing girls in K–6 schools were relieved of pressures from older adolescents to adopt behaviors for which they were not yet ready, particularly in dating and sexual activity. However, the same school context was not as advantageous for on-time maturing girls. They fared better in self-esteem if they attended K–8 environments, where they were not faced with making the transition to a new school (between sixth and seventh grade) at the same time as they experienced the physical changes of puberty. Additional research indicates that simultaneous physical and social changes in an early adolescent's life are stressful for both boys and girls. They not only have a negative impact on self-esteem, but on grade-point average and extracurricular participation as well (Simmons et al., 1987).

The standards and expectations of special social contexts can also modify maturational timing effects. For example, in a study of girls enrolled in dance company schools, on-time maturers had poorer body images, rated themselves as heavy (although they were thin by usual standards), and were less emotionally healthy than their counterparts in non-dance environments. Because the dance world places an especially strong value on a thin, petite feminine form, it favors girls who are late maturers, and in such schools delayed passage through the physical changes of puberty is normative rather than unique (Brooks-Gunn & Warren, 1985). Taken together, the results of the studies described above demonstrate that the effects of maturational timing can only be fully understood as a complex interplay among the biological changes of puberty, the social contexts to which adolescents are exposed, and the psychological aspects of development.

An additional example of the way in which biological, social, and psychological factors interact during adolescence is provided by a serious emotional and growth disturbance of adolescence called *anorexia nervosa.* It most commonly affects girls who have special difficulties accepting the physical changes of puberty and the new behavioral expectations that go along with a more grown-up appearance. Described in Box 5.2, anorexia nervosa also shows that a complete understanding of adolescent emotional adjustment must take into account a variety of factors: cultural values, family contexts, pubertal changes, and psychological characteristics of the young adolescent girl.

The Endocrinology of Growth

The vast physical changes that take place at puberty, as well as the growth that occurs earlier in development, are influenced and controlled by the endocrine glands of the body. These glands manufacture chemical agents known as *hormones,* substances secreted by specialized cells in one organ or part of the body that pass to and influence cells in another. Because there are particular receptors in our body cells that respond to some hormones and not to others, the action of each hormone is unique and highly specific. Dozens of hormones play specialized roles in the control of human growth. The most important ones are released from the anterior portion of the *pituitary gland,* located at the base of the brain near the *hypothalamus,* an important central nervous system structure that initiates and regulates pituitary secretions. The hypothalamus and the pituitary are connected to one another by a special system of blood vessels that enables stimuli coming from the hypothalamus to activate the pituitary. When this happens, pituitary hormones are released into the bloodstream, and they either act directly on body tissues to produce growth, or they stimulate the release of other hormones from endocrine glands located elsewhere in the body. These, in turn, affect various aspects of physical maturation and skeletal maturity.

Five hormones released by the pituitary play important roles in physical growth. Their concentration in the body is tightly regulated to make sure that children will not under- or over-grow. When these hormones reach a certain level, a feedback and balancing mechanism causes the hypothalamus to reduce or switch off its order for

Box 5.2
Anorexia Nervosa: Self-Inflicted
Adolescent Starvation

Anorexia nervosa is a tragic physical and psychological disorder in which adolescents starve themselves because of an aversion to food or weight gain. Its incidence is on the rise; some estimates indicate that it afflicts as many as half a million Americans. Ninety-five percent of victims are females, most falling between the ages of 12 and 25. The symptoms include body weight loss as great as 25 percent or more and amenorrhea, or cessation of menstrual periods. Victims take on a painfully thin appearance, and the serious malnutrition that accompanies the disorder leads to a cluster of additional physical effects, including brittle, discolored nails, pale skin, fine dark hairs appearing all over the body, and extreme sensitivity to cold. Anorectics show a constant preoccupation with food coupled with a persistent determination not to eat. Most lose weight by following a stringent, self-imposed diet, but a few also achieve it through *bulimia,* an accompanying disorder involving eating binges followed by intestinal purges in which the individual vomits or ingests large doses of laxatives. Anorectics deny their hunger and extreme physical fatigue by combining dieting with strenuous physical exercise. Most have such a distorted perception of the physical condition of their own bodies that they continue to regard themselves as fat, even after they have become grotesquely emaciated (Gilbert & DeBlassie, 1984).

Anorexia nervosa is the result of a complex combination of cultural, familial, and psychological conditions.

The American societal preoccupation with thinness seems to be one factor that contributes to the anorectic's compulsion to lose weight. But while almost all adolescent girls go on diets at one time or another, anorectics persist in their efforts to lose weight long after they have attained the cultural ideal of slimness. Many are perfectionists who have very high standards for their own behavior and performance. Conscientious, well-behaved, and excelling academically, most patients presented few problems at home or school before the appearance of their anorectic behavior.

However, psychologists who have studied the interaction of parents with their anorectic daughters have identified family problems surrounding issues of adolescent autonomy that may play a role in precipitating the compulsive dieting. The parents often appear controlling and overprotective and do not seem to recognize their daughter as an individual in her own right. Having compliantly accepted the values of her parents and fulfilled all their hopes and expectations for a model daughter, the anorectic girl has developed little in the way of an independent sense of self. As a result, she meets adolescent physical and social changes with anxiety and lack of self-confidence, and she responds by avoiding them through self-starvation and changing her bodily appearance to a much younger, prepubescent image (Bruch, 1978; Leon et al., 1985; Minuchin, Rosman, & Baker, 1978). The strange eating habits and excessive jogging and calisthenics of anorectics lead to social isolation and estrangement from family and friends, a circumstance that compounds feelings of loneliness, insecurity, and inadequacy. Yet attempts on the part of others to intervene in the anorectic's rigid, compulsive regime are met with angry and desperate resistance (Gilbert & DeBlassie, 1984).

When anorexia nervosa is prolonged and severe, it becomes a life-threatening illness. Mortality rates are estimated to be about 5 percent of those who are afflicted with the disorder (Romeo, 1986). Because the roots of anorexia nervosa are in individual and family problems, family therapy, in which efforts are made to change family members' interaction patterns and expectations of one another, is the most successful treatment, with 85 percent of cases showing full recovery (Bemis, 1978). Behavior modification programs, in which hospitalized anorectics who gain weight are rewarded with praise, social contact, and opportunities for exercise, are less successful as the sole treatment approach because they do not deal with underlying family dynamics. However, behavior modification has proved to be a useful adjunct to family therapy (Gilbert & DeBlassie, 1984). Since anorexia nervosa involves extreme body image distortion in the form of overestimation of body size, another supplementary treatment involves repeatedly confronting the anorectic girl with her self-image in mirrors, photographs, and on videotape in order to induce a more realistic physical self-appraisal. Also, some therapists try to provide patients with insights into social factors that have led them to value their bodies only in terms of how well they meet culturally accepted standards of physical beauty (Bemis, 1978). Early identification of victims of anorexia nervosa is crucial, permitting treatment to begin before the development of irreversible medical complications and the needless loss of a young life.

---

new production (an exception is growth hormone [GH], produced continuously throughout life, which we shall discuss shortly) (Tanner, 1978b). Figure 5.9 diagrams the way in which the hypothalamus, pituitary, and other endocrine glands work together to influence physical growth. You may want to refer to this chart as we briefly discuss each of the major endocrine influences below.

Growth hormone (GH) affects cell duplication of almost all body tissues, except the central nervous system and possibly the adrenal glands and gonads. While GH

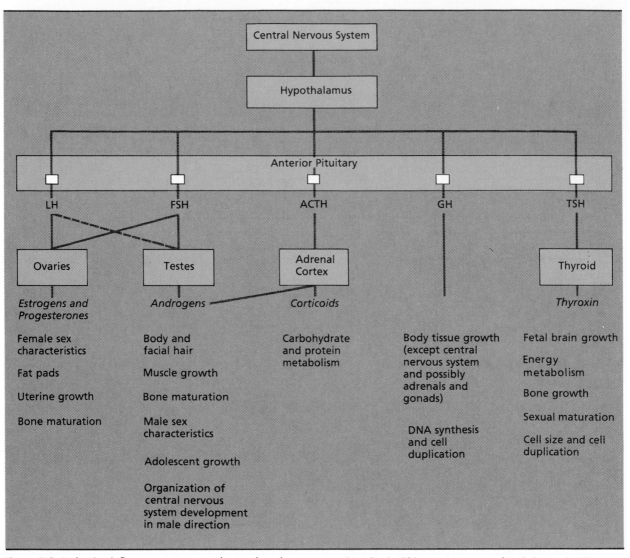

Figure 5.9. Endocrine influences on postnatal growth and development. *(Adapted with permission of Macmillan Publishing Company from* Children: Development and Relationships *[3rd ed.] by M. S. Smart and R. C. Smart. P. 500. Copyright © 1977, 1972, 1967, Macmillan Publishing Company.)*

does not seem to be crucial for fetal growth, it is necessary for normal growth from birth to adulthood. Children who lack it end up about 4 feet 4 inches tall (130 cm) at maturity, although they are normal in physical proportions and healthy in all other respects. When treated with injections of GH extracted from human pituitary glands, such children show catch-up growth and then begin to grow at a normal rate, although the extent to which they attain their genetically expected height depends on initiating treatment early, before the skeletal growth centers are very mature (D'Ercole & Underwood, 1986). At puberty, GH must be present in its full amount for the sex hormones to exert their full impact on body growth. In its absence, the height spurt in children of both sexes is only about two thirds of normal, and the broadening of the hips in girls and expansion of the shoulders in boys is also reduced (Tanner, 1978b).

Four other important pituitary hormones cause endocrine glands located in different parts of the body to release hormones that directly affect physical growth. **Thyroid stimulating hormone (TSH)** stimulates the release into the bloodstream of *thyroxin,* produced by the thyroid gland. Early thyroid deficiency causes mental retardation, because thyroxin is necessary for proper development of the nerve cells of the brain. Infants born with thyroid deficiency must be treated with synthetic thyroxin at once. At older ages, children with insufficient thyroxin show delayed growth and slow skeletal maturity, but the central nervous system is no longer affected because the most rapid period of brain growth is complete. With early treatment, such children catch up in body growth and eventually reach normal adult size (Tanner, 1978b).

Adrenocorticotropic hormone (ACTH) stimulates the adrenal cortex (the outer part of the adrenal glands located on top of each kidney) to produce *corticoids,* which regulate the body's protein and carbohydrate metabolism, and also *androgens.* During childhood, the rate of androgen secretion is low, but at puberty it increases to levels higher than occur in adults. In girls, androgens are largely responsible for the adolescent growth spurt and for the growth and maintenance of underarm and pubic hair. In boys, adrenal androgens play a lesser role, as skeletal growth and the appearance of secondary sex characteristics are mainly influenced by the androgen hormone *testosterone,* which is secreted from the testes.

Follicle stimulating hormone (FSH) and **luteinizing hormone (LH)** are two additional hormones released by the pituitary. Their concentrations in the bloodstream rise at the beginning of puberty, causing the ovaries and testes to release hormones that affect the growth and sexual changes of adolescence. In females, FSH initiates the production of *estrogens,* which influence maturation of the breasts, uterus, and vagina and cause the pelvis to broaden (Malina, 1975). FSH and LH also work together in cyclical fashion to control the menstrual cycle. FSH initiates the ripening of the ovum, and when it is mature, LH causes the ovary to release it and produce the hormone *progesterone.* Progesterone, in combination with estrogen, causes the lining of the uterus to thicken into a receptive state for implantation should the ovum be fertilized. If it is not, estrogen and progesterone levels decline, the uterus sheds its lining, and the menstrual cycle starts again. In males, FSH causes the testes to produce sperm, and LH stimulates testicular production of androgens, which bring about the maturation of male sexual characteristics, muscle growth, and large increase in body size.

Exactly what provokes the rise in pituitary hormones leading to the onset of puberty, as well as the role that hormones play in early versus late maturation of boys and girls, is not yet fully understood. As we mentioned earlier in this chapter, skeletal age is the best predictor of menarche, and some investigators believe that overall changes in body size (in terms of both height and weight) and increases in the ratio of body fat to lean body mass influence the pituitary secretions that initiate and maintain menstruation in females (Frisch & McArthur, 1974; Frisch, 1983). In support of this idea, it is now well established that high levels of exercise as well as low nutritional intake, both of which reduce the percentage of body fat, affect female menstrual periods. For example, girls who begin serious athletic training at young ages experience a greatly delayed menarche, sometimes as late as 18 or 20 years of age (Frisch, Wyshak, & Vincent, 1980; Frisch et al., 1981), a finding that helps explain the high proportion of late-maturing girls in the dance company schools that we discussed earlier. However, skeletal maturity and body composition show no relationship to other changes that occur at puberty, such as first enlargement of breast tissue or testes (Tanner, 1978b), and the underlying causes of these aspects of adolescent growth are still obscure.

Secular Trends in Physical Growth

Secular trends in human growth are changes in physical development that occur from one generation to another. Over the course of the last century, children in modern industrialized countries have been getting larger and growing to maturity more quickly. The occurrence of secular increases in height and weight has been documented in nearly all European nations, in Japan, and among black and white American children. In these countries, it has spanned all socioeconomic groups, although the generational changes in body size have been greater among economically privileged than underprivileged sectors of the population (Roche, 1979).

The secular difference in body size appears early in life and becomes greater over the course of childhood. For example, the average American 1-year-old boy of 1960 was approximately 1.6 inches taller and 3.5 pounds heavier than his agemate of 1880, the 6-year-old was 3.1 inches taller and 6 pounds heavier, and the 15-year-old was approximately 5.4 inches taller and 33 pounds heavier. Thereafter, from mid-adolescence until mature body size is attained, the secular difference diminishes, so that the difference in height between 20-year-old males in 1880 and 1960 is just over an inch, whereas the difference in weight is about 16 pounds. The fact that secular differences are greatest at the time of puberty and then begin to contract indicates that the size disparities among children of different generations are, to a large extent, differences in rate of maturation. Today, children mature earlier than they did several generations ago. For example, boys now reach their full height by age 17 or 18, whereas 50 years ago they continued to grow until age 25 or 26. This acceleration of physical growth across generations is most evident in the secular reduction that has occurred in age of menarche. From 1880 to 1960, menarche advanced about 3 months per decade (Tanner, 1962; 1978b). Of course, human beings will not keep on growing larger and maturing earlier indefinitely, as we cannot exceed the genetic limitations of our species. There is some evidence that secular change has slowed or ceased entirely in some developed countries, such as England, Japan, Norway, and the United States, although it continues in others (Roche, 1979). Also, the secular increases that we have described above are not worldwide. For example, they have not occurred in some areas of Mexico (Himes & Malina, 1975). Furthermore, in parts of India, Chile, and Africa that have been stricken by poverty, famine, or disease, there is evidence of a secular decrease in adult stature (Kenntner, 1969; Tobias, 1975).

Although it is possible for the genetic make-up of populations to change over the course of generations due to migration and variations in mating patterns, human biologists do not think that hereditary changes play a major role in the recent secular trends in physical growth (Roche, 1979). Instead, better environmental circumstances are regarded as the most important explanatory factors. Generally improved nutrition no doubt plays a major role. In addition, improved health care, sanitation,

The small stature of children who lived during the nineteenth century was partly due to the hard labor that many endured in factories. (International Museum of Photography at George Eastman House)

and the reduction or complete elimination of many diseases have not only led many more children to survive since the nineteenth century, but have also permitted them to experience fewer organic insults. As a result, today's children are more capable of utilizing available nutrients to support their full potential for growth. The end of child labor in industrialized countries around the early part of the twentieth century is also thought to have contributed to secular gains. Factory boys in England in the 1800s were shorter than other English boys (Tanner, 1968). Moreover, research conducted in Japan suggests that children living under poor nutritional circumstances and exposed to hard labor experience premature closure of the epiphyses of the long bones and, for this reason, end up shorter in stature (Kato & Ishiko, 1966). Finally, the general trend toward smaller families over the course of this century is a significant factor in secular change. Children from small families are somewhat larger and mature earlier than those from large families, particularly among individuals of low socioeconomic status. It may be that other important environmental influences, such as improved nutrition and better health care, are mediated through family size (Malina, 1979). We will discuss the impact of these factors on physical growth in greater detail in the last part of this chapter.

Secular trends in physical growth have consequences as well as causes. As Malina (1979) points out, the secular trend toward earlier menarche has contributed to the rise in teenage pregnancies (although sociocultural conditions, such as those discussed earlier in Box 5.1, are just as important). In addition, some nutritional changes, such as the widespread availability of processed foods and beverages high in refined sugar content, may be contributing to a secular trend toward excessive fatness and obesity. Secular changes also highlight the need for updated charts and reference data on children's physical growth for use by pediatricians and child psychologists (Roche, 1979).

DEVELOPMENT OF THE BRAIN

The human brain is the most complicated organ in the body, and it also ranks as the most elaborate living structure that exists on earth today. In absolute size it is not the largest brain in the animal kingdom (the brains of elephants and whales are far larger), and it does not rank first in terms of brain weight to body weight (on this score dolphins outrank us). But it is, without question, the most successful brain in achieving adaptive control over the environment (Suomi, 1982).

The mature human brain is composed of 10 to 20 billion **neurons,** or nerve cells, many of them having thousands of direct connections with other neurons. Although it is highly unlikely that the pattern of connections established among neurons is precisely the same in any two individuals, the basic structure and organization of the brain is fairly constant from one person to another. Furthermore, like the growth of other body structures, the development of the brain takes place according to an orderly, sequential plan.

The human brain is divided into three major parts: the *forebrain* (the major structure of which is the **cerebral cortex,** containing the "higher brain centers"); the *midbrain* (top of the brain stem, housing part of the visual and auditory systems as well as structures that relay signals between other parts of the brain); and the *hindbrain* (containing, among other structures, the cerebellum, which serves important functions in the maintenance of balance and motor coordination). It is the massive cortical areas of the forebrain that make the human central nervous system unique among all other species of mammals. The human cortex is much larger and far more structurally complex than that of even the most advanced apes. This is especially true of its *association regions,* areas of the cortex that are regarded as "thought centers" and whose capabilities surpass the brains of any other living being (Suomi, 1982).

The human brain achieves its peak velocity of growth earlier than other organs of the body. At birth, it is nearer to its adult size than any other structure, except perhaps the eye (Tanner, 1978b). However, when the growth curves of various parts of the brain are examined separately, the cerebral cortex once again distinguishes itself. The cortex undergoes greater structural change after birth than any other part of the central nervous system. Because of this, its patterns of neural connections are believed to be much more susceptible to the influence of postnatal environmental events than any other brain structure (Suomi, 1982). But to appreciate how experience can affect the developing brain, it is necessary to understand the basic progression of brain maturation. Some of the principles by which the brain develops are best understood at the level of single nerve cells and interconnected neurons, while others are best appreciated in a more general context, at the larger level of different areas of the cerebral cortex.

Neuronal Development

As shown in Figure 5.10, a neuron contains a cell body, at the center of which is a nucleus. The cell body sends out fibers filled with cytoplasm. One, called an *axon,* is a long fiber that conducts messages away from the cell body. Others are branchlike fibers called *dendrites,* which carry impulses to the cell body from other neurons. Neurons are not tightly packed together like the cells of most other tissues of the body. There are tiny gaps, or **synapses**, between them where axons and dendritic fibers come close to one another, but they do not touch. Information transmitted by a neuron travels electrically from the cell body along the axon to the synapse, where it is transformed into a chemical message that crosses the synapse, after which it is carried along a dendrite to the body of another cell.

Neurons are not the only cellular residents of the brain. About half the volume of the brain is occupied by **glial cells**, which do not carry messages (Tanner, 1978b). Glial cells help regulate neuronal metabolism, but their most important function is **myelinization**, a process whereby the axons in the developing brain become surrounded by an insulating fatty sheath that promotes efficient conduction of nerve impulses. As we shall see shortly, the proliferation of neurons takes place during a short and finite period of early brain maturation, but glial cells continue to multiply throughout life (Spreen et al., 1984).

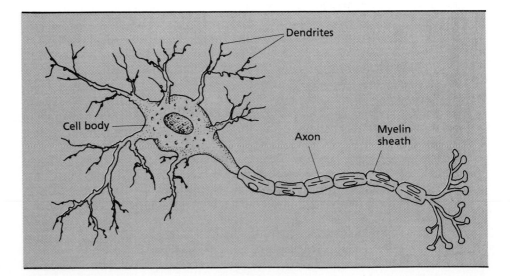

Figure 5.10. Principal structures of the neuron.

The basic story of brain development concerns how the cells of the nervous system mature and form their complex and intricate communication system. Each neuron passes through three developmental steps: cell proliferation, cell migration, and cell differentiation (Nowakowski, 1987). The *proliferation*, or production, of neurons takes place inside the primitive neural tube of the embryo by the process of cell duplication known as mitosis, which we discussed in Chapter 3. Once formed, neural cells must *migrate* from the initial site of proliferation to their permanent locations where they aggregate together to form the major parts of the brain (Moore, 1983). When the neurons arrive at their permanent locations, they turn and orient their primitive axons in the general direction toward which they will eventually extend. By 8 to 10 weeks gestation, the region from which the cortex will develop has been formed in this way, and by 6 months gestation, the proliferation of cortical neurons is complete; no more will be produced in the individual's lifetime. The precise location and orientation of each neuron and the direction of its axonal and dendritic growth is thought to be genetically determined (Suomi, 1982, Spreen et al., 1984), but the next phase of neuronal growth — the formation and maintenance of synaptic connections between neurons — is another matter, as we shall see below.

After arriving at their final destinations and orienting in the proper direction, cortical neurons begin a period of vigorous growth and *differentiation,* gradually extending the tips of their axons farther and farther away from the cell body and expanding and elaborating their dendrites into an intricate system of branches. Where an axon meets an appropriate dendrite from another neuron, a synapse is formed.

Because the growing neuron requires additional space in which to extend its axon and dendrites, many surrounding neurons atrophy and die when synaptic junctures are formed. Thus, the peak period of development in any brain area is also marked by the greatest rate of cell death, a fact that seems rather surprising since neurons, unlike other cells of the body, do not continue to replenish themselves over the life span of the individual. Fortunately, the embryonic neural tube produces far more cells than the brain will ever need, and in the process of making synaptic contacts, excess neurons degenerate (Suomi, 1982).

Neurobiologists believe that, in contrast to cell location and orientation, the formation of specific synapses in the brain may not be under genetic control, because the number of neurons in the brain and the possible combinations among them are so vast as to be well beyond the quantity of information that can be physically carried by the human genes (Spreen et al., 1984). Instead, the development of connections between neurons seems to be partly a matter of chemical offerings made by dendrites to appropriately receptive axons, and partly a matter of random contacts between neurons in the same vicinity (Wolff, 1981). Whether a particular neuron will survive or die off early in development depends, first of all, on whether it is successful at establishing synaptic connections with other neurons. Once it is successful, another factor becomes crucially important: stimulation. Neurons that are stimulated continue to flourish by growing new dendritic branches and forming myelin sheaths around their axons, increasing the probability that they will form new synapses and continue to receive stimulation in the future. Those that are seldom stimulated soon begin to degenerate. Thus, because the location and orientation of neurons is genetically determined, but the maintenance of synaptic connections is a matter of adequate stimulation, the growth of the brain is influenced by both hereditary and environmental factors (Suomi, 1982). The phases of neuronal development described above also indicate that appropriate environmental input to the brain is especially important when the establishment of neuronal connections and myelinization are at a peak.

Glial cells proliferate at different times than neurons. There are relatively few in the early stages of central nervous system development, but they multiply and mature at a dramatic pace from the fourth month of fetal life into the second year of postnatal life, after which their rate of duplication slows down. Whereas substantial increases

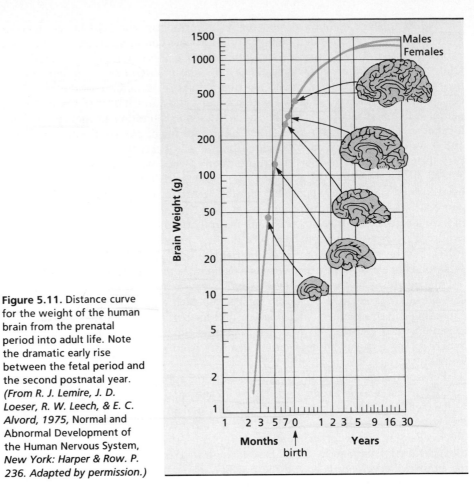

Figure 5.11. Distance curve for the weight of the human brain from the prenatal period into adult life. Note the dramatic early rise between the fetal period and the second postnatal year. *(From R. J. Lemire, J. D. Loeser, R. W. Leech, & E. C. Alvord, 1975,* Normal and Abnormal Development of the Human Nervous System, *New York: Harper & Row. P. 236. Adapted by permission.)*

in connectivity between neurons can take place with little increase in brain weight, the formation of myelin causes the brain to gain rapidly in overall size and weight. Therefore, glial cell production is largely responsible for the growth curve of the brain depicted in Figure 5.11 (Spreen et al., 1984).

As we will see when we discuss the development of the cerebral cortex below, various regions of the brain myelinate at different times and in a definite sequence. For some areas, the peak period of myelinization is before birth, whereas for others it is afterwards. Researchers have attempted to correlate such myelinization cycles with the emergence of specific abilities, such as language (e.g., Jacobson, 1975). In most cases, functional activity of an area of the brain seems to follow myelinization. However, it may occur without it, and in the adult nervous system some unmyelinated neurons have been found to conduct impulses (Spreen et al., 1984).

Development of the Cerebral Cortex

The cerebral cortex is the largest and most important structure of the human brain, containing the greatest number of neurons and synapses and accounting for the highly developed intelligence of our species. At maturity, it surrounds the rest of the brain, somewhat like a half-shelled walnut. The cerebral cortex is divided into two separate hemispheres, each of which contains several different lobes (see Figure 5.12). These are further divided into different regions. Some are *primary areas*— *motor regions* that give direct orders to the skeletal muscle system of the body,

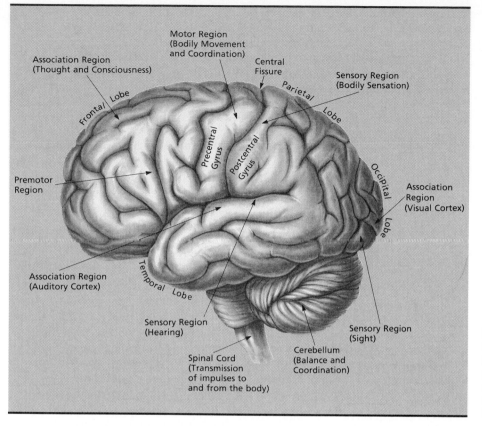

Figure 5.12. A lateral view of the left side of the human brain, showing the major structures. The locations of different functional areas of the cerebral cortex are identified.

premotor regions that provide information to motor regions, and *sensory regions* that receive direct input from the sense organs. *Secondary areas* are made up of *association or "thought" regions,* which are integrative systems having extensive connections to other parts of the brain and through which primary impulses can be combined with other impulses.

At birth, these different regions of the cortex are not fully developed, and they mature at different rates. If we look at the general order in which the regions of the cortex develop, we see that it corresponds to the order in which various capacities emerge in the growing infant and young child. Among the primary areas, the most advanced is the motor region of the precentral gyrus (see Figure 5.12) whose cells initiate gross body movements; within it, the nerve cells controlling movements of the head, arms, and upper trunk mature ahead of those controlling the legs. (Do you recognize a familiar developmental trend?) Sensory regions are the next to mature. Within them, nerve fibers mediating touch in the postcentral gyrus mature first, followed by vision in the occipital lobe, and then the primary auditory area in the temporal lobe (Tanner, 1978b)—a sequence of development that helps explain the variations in maturity levels of the infant's sensory systems, which we discussed in Chapter 4.

The newborn infant is primarily a reflexive, sensorimotor being, because the only regions functioning in the cortex at birth are the motor and sensory regions. Premotor regions begin to function as the infant starts to gain voluntary control over motor behavior, but the last areas of the cortex to develop and myelinate are the association regions. From about 2 months of age on, the association regions begin to function, and they continue their growth for years, some of them well into the second and third decades of life (Gibson, 1977; Suomi, 1982; Spreen et al., 1984). Being the last to emerge and having the most extended period of development, the association regions are the areas of the cortex with the greatest long-term sensitivity to environmental influences (Goldman & Rakic, 1979).

The *corpus callosum,* a large bundle of neural fibers that connects the two hemispheres, is not completely formed at birth and matures relatively slowly in comparison to other parts of the brain. In humans, myelinization of the corpus callosum does not begin until the end of the first year. By 4 years of age, its growth is fairly advanced, although it continues to develop into the second decade of life (Spreen et al., 1984). Efficient communication among different areas of the brain is important in the development of uniquely human abilities. However, most research on central nervous system maturation has concentrated on the emergence of separate brain subsystems. Increased knowledge about the growth of neural connections that link them together is likely to be of special value in enhancing our understanding of the development of complex, integrative human abilities, such as language, abstract thinking, and creativity and invention.

Lateralization of the Cortex

Few topics concerning the brain have stimulated as much interest as **lateralization,** or specialization of functions between the human cerebral hemispheres. Although they look very similar, the two hemispheres of the adult brain are not mirror images of one another. Some tasks are done predominantly by one side, and some by the other. For example, each hemisphere receives sensory input from and controls only one side of the body (the one that is opposite to it). In addition, in most individuals, the left hemisphere governs the processing of verbal information, whereas the right hemisphere plays the major role in processing spatial information, nonspeech sounds, and emotions (this pattern may be reversed in left-handed people, or it is possible that the brains of some left-handers are less clearly lateralized than those of right-handers). Developmental psychologists have been interested in whether lateralized hemispheric organization exists from the very beginning, or whether it emerges over the course of childhood. In addition, since sex differences in cognitive abilities exist in the verbal and spatial domains, the question arises as to whether some aspect of the development of cerebral lateralization may help to explain them.

Research findings support both the view that lateralization develops during childhood and the position that it is an inherent property of brain-behavior relations at birth. One way to investigate the development of lateralization is to study individuals who, as the result of damage to areas of the cortex controlling verbal functions, are afflicted with acquired *aphasia,* a condition in which there is difficulty in either comprehending or producing speech. Based on cases of brain-damaged young children who showed full recovery from aphasia, Lenneberg (1967) suggested that from birth to 2 years of age, the cerebral hemispheres of the brain have equal potential for processing language and other lateralized functions. That is, below the age of 2, if the speech centers in the left hemisphere are injured, comparable areas in the right hemisphere quickly take over functioning. Lenneberg reported that the ability of the brain to recover from aphasia seems to decrease from 2 years of age until puberty, suggesting that during this period of development the left hemisphere gradually assumes increasing importance as the seat of human language ability. However, a recent review by Satz and Bullard-Bates (1981) of many research studies indicates that the risk of permanent aphasia due to brain damage is very similar in adults and in children after the first year of life. According to these investigations, lateralized functioning of the brain is established earlier than Lenneberg speculated, and its development is not as gradual over the course of childhood as Lenneberg's original case studies indicated (Spreen et al., 1984).

In fact, there is some evidence from research on infants that the cerebral hemispheres may be programmed from the start for specialized functions. In anatomical studies of fetal brains, parts of the left temporal lobe have consistently been found to be larger than the same areas in the right hemisphere (Wada, Clark, & Hamm, 1975). When recordings are made of brain electrical activity, newborn infants show a greater amplitude of response to speech sounds in the left temporal hemisphere than they do in the right (Molfese, 1977; Molfese & Molfese, 1979).

Little is known about when certain right-brain functions, such as spatial abilities and the processing of information with emotional content, lateralize. In one study, Saxby and Bryden (1984) found that kindergarten, fourth-, and eighth-grade children showed a left ear (right brain) advantage for matching verbal messages in terms of their emotional tone, and a right ear (left brain) advantage for matching them in terms of their verbal content. No differences between age groups appeared, suggesting that the brain specializes early in childhood for processing stimuli that are emotional in nature.

Are there sex differences in brain lateralization, and if so, how do they develop? One reason that psychologists have been interested in answering this question is to help explain why females tend to excel in verbal rather than spatial tasks, whereas the opposite is true for males. Also, the study of sex differences in lateralization may someday be helpful in understanding disorders of the higher cortical functions. For example, childhood language disabilities, such as stuttering, reading problems, and aphasia, are three times more prevalent among boys than they are among girls (Hier & Kaplan, 1980). Unfortunately, as we shall see later on in Chapter 13, the literature on sex differences in brain lateralization is inconclusive. All that can be stated definitely at this time is that *both* males and females tend to be left hemispherically specialized for language functions and right hemispherically specialized for spatial functions. There are few hard biological explanations for why sex differences in cognitive abilities exist.

Brain Growth Spurts and Critical Periods of Development

In Chapter 3, we pointed out that an important critical period in the development of the central nervous system occurs during the third trimester of pregnancy, a time when axonal and dendritic growth and multiplication of glial cells are taking place at an astounding pace. We showed how damaging environmental influences during this period — in particular, malnutrition — can lead to a permanent loss in brain weight and reduction in number of brain cells. The validity of the critical period concept is well established for prenatal growth when the major organ systems of the body are forming. But because important neurological structures continue to mature after birth, the concept is also thought to apply to anatomical development and functioning of the human brain during postnatal life.

The importance of stimulation during periods in which cortical structures are growing most rapidly has been amply demonstrated in experimental studies of baby animals exposed to extreme forms of sensory deprivation. For example, there seems to be a critical period during which suitable visual experiences must occur if the visual cortex is to develop and function normally. Light deprivation for as brief a period as 3 to 4 days can cause severe degenerative changes in the visual cortex of a 4-week-old kitten. If the kitten's eye is sutured closed for as long as 2 months, the cortical damage is permanent (Hubel & Wiesel, 1970). Animal research also suggests that severe stimulus deprivation has an effect on the general growth of the brain, as comparisons of pet-reared animals with animals reared in isolation reveal the brain of the pet to be heavier and thicker, especially in certain cortical lobes (Bennett et al., 1964).

Because we cannot ethically expose human children to such experiments, investigators interested in identifying postnatal critical periods for human brain growth have had to rely on less direct evidence. Dobbing and Sands (1973) studied the anatomical development of the brains of children and adults who had either suffered accidental deaths or died from conditions in which there was no damage to the central nervous system. They identified two early growth spurts, one involving rapid multiplication of glial cells from mid-pregnancy to 18 months of age, and the other involving rapid myelinization beginning at about 18 months and continuing into the third and fourth years of life. Epstein (1974a; 1974b; 1980) identified a different set of brain growth spurts occurring intermittently throughout childhood and into adolescence, based on velocity curves for brain weight and skull circumference as well as developmental changes in the electrical activity of the cortex. He indicated that the spurts were correlated with peaks in children's mental test performance, based on longitudinal evidence. However, the existence of such brain-mind growth spurts has been seriously challenged (Marsh, 1985). In addition, exactly how the development of the human brain is environmentally facilitated or disrupted during such spurts is not known. If we had such information, it would have major implications for child rearing and educational practices. We would know which times during development environmental enrichment would be most effective, and during which periods we should be especially careful to protect the brain of the growing child from potentially damaging environmental influences.

FACTORS AFFECTING PHYSICAL GROWTH

Physical growth, like other human characteristics, is the result of the continuous and complex interaction of heredity and environment. In the following sections, we consider genetic as well as environmental influences on physical growth. A variety of facets of the environment are known to impinge on physical development — the human-made environment (nutrition), the natural environment (climate and disease), and the social environment (stimulation and affection versus deprivation and emotional neglect).

Heredity

Heredity plays a role in the determination of both body size and rate of physical maturation. Studies of the heritability of growth show that identical twins generally resemble each other in height and weight far more closely than do fraternals. However, the extent of resemblance varies with the period of development in which the twins are measured. At birth, differences in the lengths and weights of identical twins are actually greater than those of fraternals. This is because sharing of the same placenta frequently results in one identical twin occupying a more favorable position in the uterus and obtaining greater quantities of nourishment. However, by a few months after birth, this growth disparity begins to disappear. Unless the intrauterine disadvantage was extreme, the smaller twin recovers and returns to her genetically determined growth path (Wilson, 1976). The increasing resemblance of identical twins' body size over the first few months of life illustrates a genetic concept that we first discussed in Chapter 3: *canalization,* or the tendency to swing back to a particular channel or trajectory of growth after having been deflected off course. As long as environmental influences are not too severe, this tendency persists throughout the entire period of physical growth, and it is often referred to as **catch-up growth** (Tanner, 1978b).

When environmental circumstances are adequate, individual differences in the linear dimensions of the body — height and length of the long bones — are largely determined by heredity. Comparisons of parents with their biological offspring indicate that genetic influences on breadth and circumference measures also exist, but they are less strong (Susanne, 1975). Also, contrary to the popular belief that the physical dimensions of girls are closer to their mothers' and those of boys to their fathers', parents actually make equal genetic contributions to the overall body dimensions of their children. For example, when elementary school children are grouped according to their parents' height combinations, offspring of two tall parents are clearly the tallest, while those of two short parents are the shortest. Other parent combinations produce children of intermediate stature (Malina, Harper, & Holman, 1970).

Hereditary influences on rate of maturation are revealed most obviously by twin resemblance in timing of menarche. Identical twins generally reach menarche within a month or two of each other, whereas fraternal twins differ, on the average, by about 12 months. Again, parents seem to exert equal genetic influence on tempo of growth, as an early-maturing girl is equally likely to have a mother who matured early as she is to have a father who matured early. Also, genetic influences on rate of maturation are present throughout childhood and adolescence, as the same family resemblances that apply to menarche hold for skeletal maturity at all ages (Tanner, 1978b).

Nutrition

Nutritional status covers a broad spectrum, ranging from extreme undernutrition to ideal nutrition to overnutrition. Both undernutrition and overnutrition are forms of malnutrition—an abnormal condition of the body that results from either a deficiency or an excess of essential nutrients (Tanner, 1978b). A list of essential human nutrients is provided in Table 5.1. It shows the many substances we must regularly ingest for normal growth and maintenance of the body. Proteins, fats, and carbohydrates are the three basic components of the diet. Each serves different functions with respect to physical development. Proteins are essential for growth, maintenance, and repair of body tissues; carbohydrates supply the primary fuel to meet the energy requirements of the body; and fats contribute to energy reserves and insulate the body against heat loss. The human body also needs minerals, such as calcium for bone tissue, iron for hemoglobin, iodine for thyroid functioning, and vitamins, such as A for

Table 5.1. Essential Human Nutrients

Carbohydrate

Fat

Protein

Water

Minerals

Calcium	Iron	Cobalt
Phosphorus	Zinc	Chromium
Potassium	Selenium	Fluorine
Sulfur	Manganese	Silicon
Sodium	Copper	Vanadium
Chlorine	Iodine	Nickel
Magnesium	Molybdenum	Tin

Vitamins

A	Riboflavin
D	Niacin
E	Pyroxidine
K	Pantothenic acid
Ascorbic acid	Folacin
Thiamin	B_{12}

Biotin

Source: F. E. Johnston. 1980, "The Causes of Malnutrition." In L. S. Greene & F. E. Johnston (Eds.), *Social and Biological Predictors of Nutritional Status, Physical Growth, and Neurological Development,* New York: Academic Press. Reprinted by permission.

sight and D for bone growth. As it stands, the list of essential nutrients is impressive, yet it is probably not exhaustive, as some substances are not included because they are not yet established as essential for humans (Johnston, 1980; Tanner, 1978b).

Undernutrition. In developing nations where food resources are limited and population is on the rise, the most common nutritional problem is *protein-calorie undernutrition*. In some countries of the world, it afflicts more than 30 percent of the child population, and it therefore ranks as one of the most serious problems confronting the human species today (Johnston, 1980). When it is severe, protein-calorie undernutrition results in the prevalence of two dietary diseases—marasmus and kwashiorkor.

Marasmus is a condition of general starvation that usually makes its appearance in the first year of life. It is due to a diet that is low in all essential nutrients, including both protein and calories. The disease usually occurs when, due to extreme maternal malnutrition, breast milk is insufficient for the growing baby, and supplementary feeding is inadequate (Suskind, 1977). A condition of emaciation ensues—severe weight loss, muscular atrophy, and a decrease in subcutaneous fat.

In contrast to marasmus, **kwashiorkor** is not the result of general starvation. It is due to an unbalanced diet, one that is very low in protein. It commonly occurs between the ages of 1 and 3 after weaning, in areas of the world where protein resources are scarce and young children are provided with diets that are minimally adequate in terms of calories but consist almost entirely of starch. The stricken child shows a wasted condition of the body, accompanied by swelling of the face and limbs, skin rash, and an enlarged, fatty liver leading to a swollen abdomen.

When such severe forms of malnutrition occur for prolonged periods during the early years of life, growth is permanently stunted. Affected children show retarded physical development, and they grow to be smaller in all bodily dimensions than their better-nourished counterparts (Stoch et al., 1982; Galler, Ramsey, & Solimano, 1985a). Information about the direct effects of postnatal malnutrition on the anatomy of the developing brain is more limited for humans than for animals. However, several studies indicate that children who are severely malnourished during the first few years of life show deviant electrical brain wave recordings and a drastic reduction in speed of motor nerve conduction—findings that suggest interference with myelinization (Barnet et al., 1978; Engsner & Woldemariam, 1974; Malina, 1980). A 20-year study of the development of a group of grossly marasmic children revealed that nutritional intervention resulted in some catch-up growth in height, but the children failed to catch up in head circumference, suggesting permanent effects of severe malnutrition on the overall weight of the brain (Stoch et al., 1982).

Longitudinal studies of the development of severely undernourished children reveal wide-ranging cognitive and socioemotional problems in middle childhood and adolescence, including depressed intelligence, poor fine motor performance, and unfavorable classroom behavior in terms of attentiveness and social skills (Galler, Ramsey, & Solimano, 1985b; Galler et al., 1984; Stoch et al., 1982). These difficulties persist even when dietary supplementation and medical intervention took place during the preschool years. When early undernutrition is only mild to moderate, long-term intellectual deficits are less strong, but impaired ability to pay attention and reduced social responsiveness are still evident during the school years (Barrett, Radke-Yarrow, & Klein, 1982).

Since undernutrition of infants and children almost invariably occurs in combination with conditions of social deprivation and poverty, it is usually difficult to know whether behavioral deficits are the result of malnutrition alone, associated social circumstances, or both. Some studies have tried to isolate the influence of protein-calorie malnutrition on behavioral development by comparing malnourished children with sibling controls who were raised in the same family environment but who did not have a history of dietary insufficiency. In such studies, although both groups

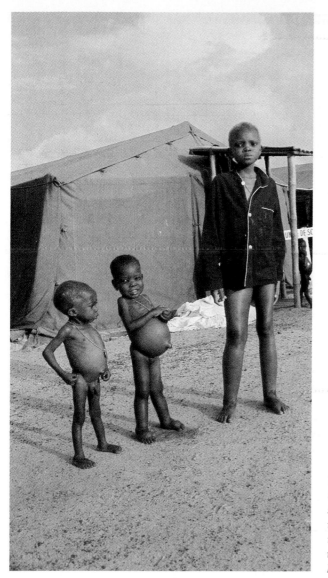

The swollen abdomens of these children are a classic symptom of kwashiorkor, a nutritional condition that results from a diet very low in protein. (Dourdin/Photo Researchers)

of children show depressed intellectual functioning, the deficit is greater for children who were malnourished in early childhood, suggesting that malnutrition contributes to low cognitive functioning beyond the influence of social and familial factors (Evans et al., 1980; Richardson & Birch, 1973).

Still, as we indicated in Chapter 3, the long-term consequences of malnutrition are probably the result of complex, bidirectional influences. The passivity and irritability of chronically undernourished children limits their ability to evoke sensitive, stimulating caregiving, thereby contributing to the development of abnormal patterns of social interaction and depressed intellectual functioning. To successfully break this cycle, interventions must improve the environmental situation of the family as well as the child's nutritional status. In addition, prevention programs that provide food supplements and medical care to at-risk mothers and children before the effects of malnutrition run their course are vitally important (Birns & Noyes, 1984). Another effective preventative of infant protein-calorie malnutrition is breast feeding. To find out more about its nutritional role in infancy, refer to Box 5.3. Interestingly, breast feeding may also help prevent childhood obesity, a growing problem in industrialized nations that we take up in the next section.

Box 5.3
The Nutritional Importance of Breast Feeding

The decision by a mother to breast-feed or bottle-feed her baby is influenced by many social, economic, and maternal factors. As long as infants are well nourished, there are no differences in psychological development between breast- and bottle-fed babies. However, breast feeding does have nutritional consequences, and these vary according to the environment in which the mother-infant pair lives.

In developing countries, bottle-fed babies are smaller and less viable than breast-fed babies in the first 6 months of life. This is because bottle feeding in many poverty-stricken areas of the world involves low-grade nutrients (such as rice or sugar water, crushed bananas, or highly dilute cow's or goat's milk) that are insufficient for satisfying the requirements of a growing infant. Human breast milk is ideally suited to the nutritional needs of the human baby, and its composition is highly resistant to inadequate maternal nutrition. When mothers are malnourished, breast milk is reduced in volume more than it is in nutritional makeup. In addition, antibodies transmitted from mother to infant via breast milk assist in the immune response of the baby, and breast-fed babies throughout the world experience fewer respiratory and gastrointestinal infections than bottle-fed babies

during the first year of life. In fact, bottle feeding in developing countries often increases the danger of infection and disease, as sanitation is poor and sterilization lacking (Stini et al., 1980).

In contrast to less affluent nations, in industrialized countries it is the bottle-fed baby who grows faster, adding extra muscle and fat tissue during the first 9 months of life. Recently, some investigators have speculated that cow's milk formula, artificially blended so that it is as high in fat as breast milk, but higher in protein and sugar, may result in overfeeding of infants. In addition, whereas breast milk serves as a nutritionally complete diet until the baby is 6 months old, bottle feeding necessitates the early introduction of solid foods (by about 3 months of age), which contributes further to early rapid weight gain. The stimulation of early growth in excess of what breast feeding would ordinarily produce is thought to be one factor, among others, that leads to a tendency toward obesity in childhood and later life (Kramer et al., 1985; Stini et al., 1980).

In breast feeding, the frequency and size of the meal is largely baby-controlled, whereas in bottle feeding it tends to be more mother-controlled. Breast-fed babies are more likely to be fed on demand and bottle-fed babies on schedule. Also, in breast-fed babies, the quantity of milk intake is correlated with the interval between meals in that larger meals are associated with longer intervals and smaller meals with shorter intervals. Bottle-fed babies

tend to receive the same amount of milk regardless of the feeding interval. Wright and Crow (1982) suggest that the infant who establishes early self-control over the frequency of meals and the course of the feed is more likely to become an adult whose food intake is determined by internal physiological signals of hunger rather than external cues, such as the quantity offered, the taste of the food, and the context in which feeding occurs, as is the case with overweight individuals.

The hypothesized connection between bottle feeding and later obesity requires further study, but there is no dispute over the fact that human breast milk is the product of long-term natural selection for uniquely human needs. When compared to the natural milk of other mammalian species, it is proportionally higher in fat and sugar and lower in protein. The greater fat content suits the needs of a rapidly myelinating central nervous system early in life, while the lower protein content fits with a prolonged period of physical growth in comparison to other mammals. Human beings have an extended period of childhood dependency during which a tremendous amount of learning takes place. To facilitate this learning, central nervous system development is emphasized early, while muscle growth is postponed for later, and the composition of human milk reflects these adaptive priorities (Stini et al., 1980).

Overnutrition. Overweight and **obesity**[2] are prevalent nutritional disorders in the United States today, posing significant health risks in terms of heart disease, hypertension, and diabetes, and leading to serious psychological and social consequences. Recent statistics indicate that from 25 to 45 percent of American adults suffer from overnutrition, and in spite of the many and varied approaches to weight reduction available, adult efforts to sustain weight loss generally fail (Grinker, 1981).

Obese children have a high probability of becoming obese adults, with 80 percent or more retaining their overweight status in later years (Abraham, Collins, & Nordsieck, 1971; Knittle, 1972; Rim & Rim, 1976). In fact, obesity can be detected by 2 years of age in a substantial number of cases. One survey revealed that 36 percent of those who exceeded the 90th percentile in weight as infants became overweight

[2] Obesity is generally defined as a greater-than-20-percent increment over average body weight, standardized for age, sex, and stature (Grinker, 1981).

adults, compared to 14 percent for average and lightweight infants (Charney et al., 1976). Another study showed that among nearly 500 cases of childhood obesity, at least half had become overweight by age 2 (Mossberg, 1948). These findings suggest that the first few years of life are very important for establishing lifelong patterns of overnutrition. Treatment of overnutrition in childhood is likely to be more successful than treatment instituted in adulthood, when factors responsible for the problem are well established and difficult to modify.

Not every child is equally at risk for overweight. Fat children tend to have fat parents, a relationship that reflects both hereditary and environmental components. Heredity clearly plays some role, because the weights of adopted children correlate more strongly with those of their biological than adoptive parents (Stunkard & Sorenson, as reported by Kolata, 1986). But there is also reason to believe that environment contributes importantly to a person's weight. For example, socioeconomic status and obesity are consistently related in industrialized nations, with a higher incidence of overweight occurring among low-income individuals (Stunkard, d'Aquili, & Filion, 1972; Stunkard, 1975)

Researchers have examined early growth patterns for clues about the origins of obesity. The evidence indicates that rapidity of weight gain during the first year of life predicts overweight during the school years (Eid, 1970; Heald & Hollander, 1965; Taitz, 1971). Animal research shows that excessive fat storage early in development leads to an overabundance of fat cells, which act to support and maintain the overweight condition. It is possible, although not yet proven, that this same biological factor may operate in the development of human obesity, with maladaptive eating patterns setting it in motion.

Obese individuals are more responsive to external stimuli associated with eating — taste, sight, smell, and time of day — and less responsive to internal hunger cues than are normal-weight individuals (Schachter & Rodin, 1974). This heightened responsiveness to food-related cues is already present in overweight elementary

Obese children often have psychological and social problems; they also have a high probability of becoming obese adults. (John Running/Stock, Boston)

school children and may develop even earlier (Constanzo & Woody, 1979; Ballard et al., 1980). Overweight people also eat faster and chew their food less thoroughly than their average-weight and thin counterparts, a behavior pattern that appears in overweight children as early as 18 months of age (Drabman et al., 1979).

Although the exact cause of the eating patterns of overweight children and adults is not known, a number of investigators believe they are learned early in life. Some mothers interpret almost all the expressed needs of their infants as a desire for food. As a result, they anxiously overfeed their babies and fail to help them learn to distinguish hunger from other physical and emotional discomforts (Weil, 1975). Bruch (1970) reported that parents of obese children frequently employ food as a reward as well as to relieve anxiety. When food is used to reinforce the performance of desirable behaviors (e.g., "Pick up your toys, and then you can have a cookie"), the child's desire for the presented food, as well as for other foods that are similar to it, is significantly enhanced (Birch, Zimmerman, & Hind, 1980; Birch, 1981). In families where rewarding children with food happens often, eating acquires important emotional significance beyond the reduction of hunger, a situation that may contribute to the overweight child's heightened responsiveness to food cues.

Overweight children do not just eat more; they are less physically active than their normal-weight peers. A causal relationship between inactivity and obesity is difficult to establish, but some investigators believe that activity level is at least as important as food intake in the development of obesity. One intriguing hypothesis is that the increase in obesity in the United States over the past 20 years is in part a function of television viewing. Using survey data acquired in the early and mid-1970s by the National Center for Health Statistics, Dietz (as reported in Kolata, 1986) found that next to prior obesity, television viewing was the strongest predictor of subsequent obesity in children, a relationship that held even when a variety of controls were introduced. Television watching is certainly a highly sedentary activity, and children tend to eat when they watch. In addition, while viewing they are repeatedly exposed to televised food ads, the overwhelming majority of which are for high-calorie foods containing large amounts of sugar and fat and few beneficial nutrients (Mauro & Feins, 1977).

Unfortunately, physical attractiveness is related to likability, and the psychological and social consequences of childhood obesity are especially severe. Both children and adults hold highly negative stereotypes of overweight children and rate them as less likable than children with a wide variety of physical disabilities (Richardson et al., 1961). As early as kindergarten, chubby children receive fewer positive nominations from their peers than do average-build children (Lerner & Gellert, 1969; Lerner & Schroeder, 1971), and negative traits assigned by peers to fat children increase with age (Lerner & Korn, 1972; Brenner & Hinsdale, 1978). Children even report that they would stand farther away when interacting with a chubby child than they would with an average-build partner (Lerner, Karabenick, & Meisels, 1975; Lerner, Venning, & Knapp, 1975). Peers also show negative attitudes toward and increase their personal distance from very thin children, but not nearly to the extent they do when a child is overweight.

Among treatments for obese children, behavior modification programs seem to work the best (Epstein & Wing, 1983; Wheeler & Hess, 1976). Therapists analyze the stimuli and rewards surrounding excess eating to arrive at a more suitable eating pattern. For example, tempting high-calorie foods may be eliminated from the household, smaller portions served at meals, television viewing curtailed, and planned opportunities for exercise integrated into daily activities. Programs that involve the entire family rather than just the overweight child are the most successful, as parental eating and exercise habits serve as influential models for children. Also, parental cooperation and support are especially important in the long-term maintenance of children's weight loss (Epstein et al., 1981). Because overnutrition is very difficult to change once it is firmly established, investigators have emphasized the need for early identification, as well as prevention, through such means as nutrition education in schools and widespread pro-nutritional media campaigns (Peterson et al., 1984).

Disease

In adequately nourished children, ordinary childhood illnesses, such as measles, chicken pox, and the common cold, have no effect on physical growth, except for minor and temporary weight fluctuations. However, in mildly or severely undernourished children, disease interacts with malnutrition in a vicious, bidirectional spiral in which one contributes to and enhances the detrimental effects of the other, and the consequences for physical growth are compounded.

Evidence on the relationship between illness and physical growth is best obtained from longitudinal studies in which children's health and growth histories are tracked over time. When such information is gathered in industrialized countries, illness and growth are unrelated, but in developing nations where a large portion of the population lives in poverty, common childhood ailments are clearly associated with poor physical growth (Martorell, 1980). In these countries, infectious diseases such as measles and chicken pox, which typically do not occur until after age 3, appear at much earlier ages, often afflicting children under 2 and taking the form of severe illnesses (Eveleth & Tanner, 1976). This is because poor diets have the effect of depressing the body's immune system, making children far more susceptible to disease (Salomon, Mata, & Gordon, 1968). The vulnerability of undernourished children to infection is clearly shown by the fact that immunizations containing live disease agents (such as smallpox, polio, and the diphtheria-pertussis-tetanus combination) often lead to substantial weight loss, especially among malnourished infants. They have little or no growth impact on the well-nourished baby (Kielman, 1977).

Disease, in turn, is a major cause of malnutrition and, through it, affects physical growth. Illness influences nutritional status by reducing children's appetite and limiting the absorption of nutrients. A variety of diseases affect nutrient metabolism, especially protein utilization, which is essential for growth. Also, parasitic diseases, such as tapeworm and malaria, draw significant quantities of nutrients for their own needs, subtracting further from what would otherwise have been available to the child (Beisel, 1977).

In developing countries, gastrointestinal infections are widespread. They increase among children around the time of weaning, when pathogenic organisms are introduced in supplementary foods. By affecting nutrient absorption, chronic gastrointestinal illnesses can have a substantial impact on physical growth. Studies by Martorell (1980) reveal that 7-year-olds growing up in poverty-stricken Guatemalan villages who had been relatively free from gastrointestinal infections since birth were nearly 1½ inches taller and 3½ pounds heavier than their frequently ill peers. This is a large difference, since all of the Guatemalan children were quite small to begin with — 5 inches shorter and 11 pounds lighter, on the average, than well-nourished children in the United States.

Climate and Season

Differences in body builds of peoples around the world are related to climate. Long, thin physiques are more typical in hot, tropical regions and short, stocky builds in cold, arctic areas. These differences are already apparent in childhood, and they are believed to be the result of evolutionary adaptation to climatic conditions over many generations. The long limbs and greater body surface area of central African peoples facilitate heat loss, while the short, compact bodies of the Eskimos aid in heat conservation (Malina, 1975).

The long, tall bodies of Africans who live in hot climates contrast sharply with the short, stocky builds of cold-dwelling Eskimos. (Left, Terence O. Mathew/ Photo Researchers; Right, Leonard Lee Rue III from National Audubon Society/ Photo Researchers)

Seasonal variation exerts considerable influence on velocity of growth in temperate regions of the world. Western European and American children grow faster in height in spring and summer than in fall and winter, with maximum growth occurring from March to July and minimum growth from September to February (Marshall, 1971). The exact cause of these seasonal variations is not known. Since temporal variations in growth rates of blind children are similar to those of sighted children except for the fact that they are not synchronized with season of the year, it is possible that seasonal growth patterns are mediated by some aspect of visual light perception (Marshall, 1975).

Affection and Stimulation

That parental affection and stimulation are vital for normal physical growth has been known since the thirteenth century, when Frederick II, King of Two Sicilies, tried to determine which of the world's languages was the true natural language of the human species. He took a group of newborn infants away from their mothers and isolated them on an island with wet nurses, who were instructed not to speak to the babies. The king's experiment was a failure. All of the infants died, "for they could not live without the petting and the joyful faces and loving words of their foster mothers" (Gardner, 1972, p. 76). Today, failure to thrive and deprivation dwarfism are recognized growth disorders believed to result from lack of maternal attention and affection.

Failure to thrive is a term applied to infants who show growth retardation, with no additional organic signs or obvious nutritional deprivation to account for it. Present in the majority of cases by 18 months of age, its most striking physical feature is a substantial reduction in weight. The loss of both fat and muscle tissue leads the baby to take on an emaciated, wasted appearance. The behavior of infants with failure to thrive also provides a strong clue to its diagnosis. Along with passivity and apathy toward the physical environment, they show an unusual, apprehensive watchfulness of adults, exhibit little smiling and vocalization, and do not react with cuddliness to being picked up (Leonard, Rhymes, & Solnit, 1966; Oates, 1984).

Deprivation dwarfism appears at later ages than failure to thrive. It is generally diagnosed between 2 and 15 years of age. Short stature is its most striking feature, but children's weight is usually in proportion to their height, and they do not present a picture of malnutrition. Children with deprivation dwarfism often show abnormally low levels of growth hormone, and their skeletal ages are immature. It is now believed that the disorder occurs because emotional deprivation affects hypothalamic-pituitary communication, decreasing growth hormone secretions and thereby inhibiting growth. When affected children are removed from their emotionally inadequate environments, their growth hormone levels quickly return to normal, and they grow rapidly. However, if treatment is delayed until late in development, the dwarfism can be permanent (Oates, Peacock, & Forrest, 1985).

The families of children with both failure to thrive and deprivation dwarfism are characterized by adverse social factors and non-nurturant communication. However, the conditions surrounding failure to thrive have been studied more intensively. Mothers of these infants take little pleasure in interacting with their babies and seem cold, impatient, and hostile. Examining videotapes of mothers and their failure-to-thrive infants engaged in feeding and play activities, Haynes and her colleagues (1983) found the mothers to be either overly intrusive or disengaged. They appeared insensitive to their baby's initiatives — arbitrarily removing toys, offering food efficiently but mechanically, and reprimanding and ridiculing the baby. The infants protected themselves from these negative behaviors by turning their heads away and avoiding the mother's gaze. In another study, the breakdown in mother-infant interaction leading to failure to thrive was already evident in the first few days after birth. Mothers whose infants later developed the disorder spent less time looking at their newborn babies and terminated interaction with them more quickly than did mothers of controls, and feeding problems were evident soon after delivery (Vietze et al., 1980). When treated early, through intensive family intervention or placement in a caring foster home, failure-to-thrive infants show quick catch-up growth. But if the problem is not corrected in infancy, some children remain small and show lasting intellectual and behavioral difficulties (Altemeier et al., 1984; Oates, 1984).

Maternal nurturing difficulties associated with growth disorders are often grounded in poverty and family disorganization. Job instability, chronic unemployment, and crowded living conditions place parents under severe stress. With their own emotional resources depleted, parents have little available energy to meet the psychological needs of their children. However, failure to thrive and deprivation dwarfism do not occur exclusively among the poor; the syndromes also appear in economically advantaged families where marital discord or other pressures cause parents to behave in non-nurturant and destructive ways toward their children (Gagan, 1984).

The study of growth disorders permits us to see important influences on physical development that are not readily apparent when we observe the healthy, normally growing child. In the case of failure to thrive and deprivation dwarfism, we become consciously aware of the intimate connection between sensitive, loving care and how children grow.

CHAPTER SUMMARY

1. Compared to other species, human beings experience a prolonged period of physical growth, providing ample time for human children to learn to live in a complex physical and social world. Physical growth follows an orderly, predictable pattern of development. Overall body growth is rapid during infancy, slow and steady during middle childhood, and rapid again during adolescence. Many, but not all, tissues and organs follow this progression. Human growth is asyn-

chronous, with various parts of the body having their own unique timetable of maturation.

2. Major changes in body proportions as well as in muscular and fat composition take place with development. Although all individuals adhere closely to the same sequence of physical growth, there are individual differences in rate of maturation. Determination of skeletal age by X-raying the bones of the body and examining the extent of ossification of bone growth centers is the best available method for assessing a child's progress toward physical maturity.

3. Sex differences in growth are relatively small during the preadolescent years. Girls are ahead of boys in skeletal age, whereas boys are slightly larger in overall body size. At puberty, obvious sex differences emerge. Girls reach puberty, on the average, 2 years earlier than boys. They develop physical characteristics, including a broad pelvic frame and extra fatty tissue, that are uniquely suited for carrying and bearing offspring. Boys' later pubertal growth spurt is partly responsible for the fact that they grow taller and have legs that are proportionately longer than girls'. Males also gain far more muscle tissue than females, and as a result, adolescent boys outperform girls in a wide range of athletic skills.

4. The adolescent growth spurt occurs earlier in the sequence of pubertal events for girls, with growth in height mostly complete by the time the girl experiences menarche. How girls react to first menstruation depends on a number of factors, including prior knowledge and family supports. The little information available on boys' reactions to spermarche indicates that it may be of comparable emotional importance.

5. The timing of pubertal maturation influences adolescent social and emotional adjustment. Early-maturing boys and late-maturing girls, who have body types that tend to match cultural standards of physical attractiveness, are advantaged. In contrast, early-maturing girls and late-maturing boys, who fit in least well with their agemates in physical status, experience social and emotional difficulties. Social contexts, such as the grade makeup of school environments, can modify maturational timing effects.

6. Physical growth is influenced and controlled by hormones released from the endocrine glands of the body. The hypothalamus initiates and regulates five important hormonal secretions from the pituitary gland. These either act directly on tissues to produce growth, or they stimulate the release of other hormones from endocrine glands located elsewhere in the body. Without early medical intervention, failure of the child's endocrine system to produce normal levels of hormones leads to serious growth problems.

7. Secular trends in physical growth have occurred over the last century in modern industrialized nations, with children growing larger and reaching maturity more quickly. Attributed to better nutrition, health care, and the end of child labor in the early part of this century, secular gains now appear to be leveling off. Secular increases in growth do not occur in all countries. In some developing nations stricken by poverty, famine, and disease, secular decreases have been found.

8. The human brain, the most complicated organ of the body, achieves its peak period of growth earlier than other organs. However, like the rest of the body, its growth is asynchronous. The cerebral cortex, seat of human intelligence, is the last part of the brain to stop growing. As a result, the cortex is more susceptible to postnatal environmental influences than any other brain structure. By 6 months gestational age, the production of neurons is complete. Their migration and orientation are under genetic control, but once neurons form synaptic connections with one another, stimulation determines which neurons will survive and which will die off. Thus, to develop normally, the brain requires appropriate environmental input during periods in which the establishment of neuronal connections is at a peak. Glial cells, which play an important role in myelinization of the nervous system, continue to multiply long after the production of neurons is complete, and they are largely responsible for the postnatal gains of the brain in size and weight.

9. Sensory and motor regions of the cortex are the first to mature postnatally, while association regions are the last to stop growing, with some continuing their growth well into the second and third decades of life. The cortex is a lateralized organ. For most individuals, processing of verbal information is concentrated in the left hemisphere and spatial information, nonspeech sounds, and emotions in the right hemisphere. There is evidence that this specialized organization of brain functions is already present in newborn infants, but research also lends support to the hypothesis that lateralization increases during the early postnatal period.

10. The course of physical growth is influenced by the continuous and complex interplay of heredity and environment. Heredity is important in determining the linear dimensions of the body and, to a lesser extent, breadth and circumference measures. Fathers and mothers make equal genetic contributions to the overall bodily dimensions and rate of physical maturation of their offspring. A variety of environmental factors are known to affect physical growth. The importance of nutrition is tragically evident in the dietary diseases of marasmus and kwashiorkor, which affect large numbers of children in developing countries. In industrialized nations, overweight and obesity are serious nutritional problems that are related to maladaptive eating patterns and physical underactivity during childhood. Disease interacts with undernutrition to affect physical growth, with each factor contributing to and enhancing the detrimental effects of the other. Differences in body builds are related to climate, as long, thin physiques are typical in hot, tropical regions and short, stocky builds in arctic areas of the world. In temperate climates, children grow faster in the summer than in the winter months of the year. Finally, failure to thrive and deprivation dwarfism are two growth disorders that illustrate the importance of adequate parental stimulation and affection for normal physical development.

IMPORTANT TERMS AND CONCEPTS

distance curve
velocity curve
skeletal age
ossification
epiphyses
fontanels
menarche
spermarche
growth hormone (GH)

thyroid stimulating hormone (TSH)
adrenocorticotropic hormone (ACTH)
follicle stimulating hormone (FSH)
luteinizing hormone (LH)
secular trends in physical growth
neurons
cerebral cortex
synapses
glial cells

myelinization
lateralization
catch-up growth
marasmus
kwashiorkor
obesity
failure to thrive
deprivation dwarfism

PART III

Cognitive and Language Development

Baby Reaching for an Apple, by Mary Cassatt.
Virginia Museum of Fine Arts, Richmond.

CHAPTER 6

Cognitive Development: A Piagetian Perspective

Cognition refers to the inner processes and products of the human mind that lead to "knowing." It includes all human mental activity: remembering, relating, classifying, symbolizing, imagining, problem solving, creating, and even fantasizing and dreaming. Indeed, we could easily enlarge upon this list; there is no clear place at which to limit a definition of human cognition, because mental processes make their way into virtually everything that human beings do (Flavell, 1985).

Among the great contributions of the eminent Swiss psychologist Jean Piaget was a theory of development in which human cognition is viewed as a broad, complex phenomenon made up of diverse components that emerge in a richly interwoven, organized fashion. Piaget's view of cognitive development stands as one of the two dominant positions on the nature of human thinking in the field of developmental psychology, the other being information processing, which we will take up in Chapter 7.

This chapter is devoted to highlighting Piaget's theoretical and empirical work. Piaget conceived of human cognition as a network of mental structures created by an active organism striving to make sense out of a complex external world. The Piagetian perspective of an active child with a mind inhabited by rich structures of knowledge was a revolutionary point of view at the time that it first reached the shores of the United States in the middle of the twentieth century. It represented a radical departure from the then dominant behaviorist position, which steered clear of any internal constructs of mind and conceived of the child as a passive entity shaped and molded from without. By the 1960s, Piaget's ideas were embraced by American psychologists and educators with enthusiasm. The power of his theoretical concepts, the large array of problem solving tasks he devised to mark the landmarks of children's cognitive development, and the relevance of his ideas for the education of children made his work especially attractive.

Over the last three decades, many research studies have been aimed at replicating and extending Piaget's research. In recent years, the results of these investigations have raised questions about the validity of core aspects of his theory. Currently, there is considerable debate among developmental psychologists about the adequacy and correctness of Piaget's ideas. As we review his work, we will pause at various points along the way to represent both new research that verifies Piaget's original conclusions and findings that indicate a need for revisions of his ideas. It is possible that someday Piaget's theory may be set aside in favor of an improved alternative. However, almost all developmental psychologists, including Piaget's staunchest critics, agree that without his contributions, we would not have progressed as quickly and as far as we have in our understanding of children's thinking.

JEAN PIAGET: A BIOGRAPHICAL SKETCH

Jean Piaget was born in 1896 in Neuchatel, Switzerland. He was an intellectually precocious child who turned to the serious study of nature at an early age. Captivated by birds, fossils, and the marine inhabitants of the lakes of Switzerland, by age 10 Piaget had published his first paper. As a young adolescent, he devoted his after-school hours to assisting the director of the Museum of Natural History in Neuchatel, who was a specialist in mollusks. Piaget became so interested in mollusks that by the age of 15 he had published several papers on them, and his expertise was widely known among Swiss naturalists (Piaget, 1952a). Piaget's fascination with how the shell structures of the mollusk adapt to variations in the animal's habitat had a profound impact on the way that he eventually saw the development of thinking. He came to view the gradual refinement of children's mental structures as a special form of biological activity, and as part of the overall process by which human beings successively achieve a better adaptive fit with their environmental surroundings.

Influenced by his godfather, Piaget became intensely interested in philosophy, especially in the subdiscipline called *epistemology*, which is concerned with the analysis of knowledge and the understanding of various forms of knowing. The combination of his early exposure to biology and philosophy led him, by his late teens, to become interested in biological explanations of the origins of knowledge.

After completing his bachelor's degree at age 18 and doctorate at age 21 in the natural sciences, Piaget turned to psychology for empirical methods, and very soon to the study of children. These interests brought him first to Zurich, where he studied and worked in the clinic of the well-known psychoanalyst Bleuler. There he discovered the clinical method of psychoanalysis, a technique that was to have a profound influence on the way Piaget studied children.

A year later, when Piaget went to work in the Paris laboratory of Alfred Binet (creator of the first successful intelligence test for children), he quickly saw the importance of the **clinical interview**[1] for understanding the thought processes of children. Asked to adapt English intelligence tests for use with French schoolchildren, Piaget was fascinated by children's wrong answers to the test questions and the reasons for them, as their mistakes seemed to follow predictable patterns related to age. He began to interview his subjects in a flexible, open-ended conversational style in which he followed a child's line of thought by permitting an initial explanation to determine the next question he would ask (Piaget, 1952a). As Piaget's work became widely known, he was criticized by American psychologists for adhering to this method, for it violated the widely held research canon that procedures be applied in an identical, standardized fashion to every subject (Flavell, 1963). Yet it was this very

---

[1] An example of a clinical interview conducted by Piaget is given on page 28 of Chapter 1. You may wish to read it again to refresh your memory of this method for investigating children's thinking.

Through careful observations of children, as well as clinical interviews with them, Jean Piaget (1896–1980) developed his comprehensive theory of cognitive development. (Yves Debraine/Black Star)

approach that made it possible for Piaget to investigate the underlying processes of children's thought.

In 1921, Piaget became Director of Research at the Rousseau Institute in Geneva, a center for the study of child psychology. For the remainder of his career, he devoted his research activities to investigating the logic of children's thought. Through these efforts, Piaget became increasingly convinced of the differences between the thinking of children and adults. He began to think of cognitive development in terms of *stages*—movement through a sequence of qualitatively different reorganizations of thought over the course of childhood (Ginsburg & Opper, 1979).

In the late 1920s and 1930s, Piaget made careful observations of his three infant children. As the result of this work, he described cognitive development during the sensorimotor stage and noted how the thinking of childhood and adolescence is prepared by the infant's sensorimotor activity (Piaget, 1936/1952b; 1937/1954). He concluded that cognitive development can only proceed when infants and children act directly on the environment. It was through *action*—manipulating objects and moving in space—that Piaget viewed cognitive structures as being created and transformed. In comparison to other European and American theorists, he de-emphasized the role of language as a primary source of cognitive development. The infant studies also motivated Piaget to revise his clinical interviewing methods, and he began to provide children and adolescents with tasks in which they both acted on objects and engaged in conversation with an examiner about them (Piaget, 1952a).

In the early 1940s, Piaget published his work on children's understanding of physical quantities. The development of *conservation* during middle childhood— how children gradually come to recognize that certain physical attributes of an object, like its substance and weight, do not vary when the object changes shape—is one of the most well known aspects of his research. During this period, Piaget also did work on children's understanding of number, and at the suggestion of Albert Einstein, who had come to know Piaget's work, he extended the study of children's logical thinking to their understanding of such physical concepts as distance, time, and speed (Ginsburg & Opper, 1979).

During the 1940s and 1950s, Piaget devoted his energies to the educational implications of his theory (e.g., Piaget, 1951b) and the study of adolescent thought (Inhelder & Piaget, 1955/1958). Then his attention turned toward philosophical concerns, and he wrote about the implications of his research for epistemological problems in the sciences (Ginsburg & Opper, 1979; Piaget, 1952a; Piaget, 1970a). The sheer volume of publications that span the 60 years of his career is overwhelming — scores of books and hundreds of articles. At his death in 1980, Piaget's work was being extended by researchers around the world, and despite criticisms and revisions of his ideas about how thinking develops, psychologists and educators continue to recognize the tremendous importance of his theoretical and empirical contributions.

PIAGET'S THEORY OF COGNITIVE DEVELOPMENT

In his comprehensive theory of cognitive development, Piaget viewed the development of thinking as a special case of biological growth in general. Just as the body of each species has physical structures that enable it to adapt to its environmental habitat, so the mind builds mental structures over the course of development that enable it to achieve a progressively better and better adaptive fit with experience. In the development of these structures, the mind of the child is intensely active. It selects, interprets, and reorganizes experience in terms of its currently existing mental structures, and it also modifies these structures so that they take into account a broader range of experiences and more subtle and detailed aspects of the environment over time. Thus, for Piaget, cognitive development is the story of how each of us actively discovers the nature of reality. Each child's mental reality is very much his or her own unique construction, but since all human beings possess the same basic biological apparatus for acting on and interpreting experience, the course of development of mental structures is the same for all individuals.

Because Piaget believed that children are active in determining their own cognitive growth, he viewed the emergence of more mature modes of thinking as self-motivated. He believed that we do not have to use external rewards, such as praise, grades, or gifts, to get children to learn. The motivation to make sense out of experience, to create and transform mental structures, is built into the child to begin with. In this respect, Piaget's approach stands in sharp contrast to behaviorist interpretations of development. His radical view of children as playing a crucial role in their own learning is a major reason that his theory was very slow to be studied and accepted in the United States.

Since Piaget viewed developmental changes in thinking as *qualitative*, his ideas are also different from the mental testing approach that has long dominated the investigation of children's intelligence in the United States. Intelligence tests have largely been concerned with *quantitative* changes — how much of a particular mental skill, such as memory or comprehension of information, children possess at different ages, and whether their performance at early ages can predict performance at later ages. Piaget was not concerned with these issues (although his theory has served as the basis for the construction of some new intelligence tests, as we shall see in Chapter 8). Instead, he focused on the description of cognitive structures that underlie intelligent behavior and the identification of discrete stages through which the structures are transformed during childhood (Brainerd, 1978). He also specified a common set of processes, or functions, that are responsible for all cognitive changes. Thus, the structures describe *what* changes, and the functions explain *how* developmental change takes place in Piaget's system.

Key Concepts: Cognitive Contents, Structures, and Functions

Since Piagetian cognitive structures and functions are mental phenomena and not directly observable, they must be inferred from cognitive **contents,** the specific intellectual acts that infants and children can be seen engaging in at any stage of development. As infants manipulate and experiment with objects, or as children solve problems and demonstrate reasoning skills, they provide raw behavioral data that can be interpreted for structural and functional properties.

Structures are organized properties of intelligence that change with age. They are inferred from, but they also underlie and determine the nature of behavioral content. For example, in a child who judges, after water is poured from a tall, thin glass into a short, wide container, that the container has less liquid in it because it is shorter, we witness behavioral content, and from it we infer that the child's cognitive structures are organized in such a way that the surface appearance of things dominates, and successive states of objects (a certain amount of water first in one place and then in another) remain unrelated to one another in any logical fashion. This knowledge of the nature of the child's structures then allows us to predict what the child may do when given the opportunity to display cognitive content in other situations.

Schemes. Specific cognitive structures are usually referred to as **schemes.** Piaget maintained that all schemes are spontaneously applied and exercised, and children have a natural tendency to use them repeatedly. This is evident, for example, in the infant's repetitious application of the sensorimotor scheme of grasping to a wide variety of objects and the 2-year-old's tireless exercise of new representational schemes in demanding that a story be read over and over again. Piaget believed that the spontaneous repetition of schemes assures that development will take place. As schemes are applied, they come into contact with new information, and children modify them to incorporate new and diverse experiences. To explain how schemes change, Piaget identified two important intellectual **functions:** adaptation and organization. The fundamental properties of these functions remain the same throughout life, despite the wide variety of schemes that they create.

Adaptation. **Adaptation** involves building schemes through direct interaction with the environment. It is comprised of two simultaneous but complementary processes: **assimilation** and **accommodation.** These two concepts provide an excellent illustration of the biological flavor of Piaget's theory, for they are taken directly from principles of biological growth (Piaget, 1936/1952b). In the biological incorporation of foodstuffs, we *assimilate* edible materials and make them like ourselves. At the same time, we also *accommodate* to them, for we must open our mouths to receive the food, chew some foods more thoroughly than others, and adapt our digestive processes to the physical and chemical properties of each food, or digestion cannot take place.

A similar process takes place on the level of intellectual adaptation. When we assimilate, we interpret the external world in terms of our current schemes, or presently available ways of thinking about things. For example, the infant who puts a variety of objects in her mouth is assimilating them all into a primitive, sensorimotor sucking scheme, and the preschooler who sees her first camel at the zoo and calls it a "horse" has sifted through her collection of schemes until she arrives at one that will incorporate the object. In this case, the stimulus of camel is assimilated into the pre-existing representational scheme of horse. In accommodation, the schemes are revised to take into account newly apprehended properties of the environment. For example, the infant who begins to suck differently on the edge of a blanket than on a nipple has started to modify the sucking scheme, and the preschooler who calls a camel a "lumpy horse" has noticed that certain properties of the camel are not just like horses and has revised and differentiated the horse scheme accordingly.

We have referred to assimilation and accommodation as distinct and separate activities, but Piaget really thought of them as inseparable aspects of adaptation that always work together. That is, in every interchange with the environment, the mind interprets information using its existing cognitive structures, and it also changes and refines its structures to achieve a better adaptive fit with experience. Nevertheless, the balance between assimilation and accommodation does vary from one time to another. Since assimilation accounts for the exercise of current schemes and accommodation for their modification, during periods in which the child is largely preoccupied with using recently formed schemes, assimilation predominates over accommodation. During periods of rapid change and development, accommodation prevails over assimilation.

Piaget used the term **equilibration,** which refers to continuous movement between states of cognitive *equilibrium* and *disequilibrium,* to describe the way in which assimilation and accommodation work together in varying balances to produce cognitive change. The term equilibrium implies a steady, comfortable cognitive state. It refers to a condition in which individuals use already-formed schemes to interpret reality; in this state, the balance of their cognitive activity is toward assimilation rather than accommodation. But in the process of exercising schemes, individuals notice new information that calls for intelligent behavior beyond the level of their current structures. This produces a state of disequilibrium, or cognitive discomfort, in which individuals shift away from assimilation toward accommodation as they try to resolve the discrepancy between the environment and their present schemes. Once they have successfully modified their schemes, they can use the newly formed structures to assimilate reality. As they do so, they reach a new, more stable level of cognitive equilibrium as the breadth of experiences to which their schemes can be applied expands (Brainerd, 1978). The process of equilibrating takes place continually during development, repeating itself at ever higher levels of cognitive maturity.

Organization. Adaptation leads to cognitive change as the result of direct contact between structures and the environment. However, Piaget was careful to point out that cognitive structures are not static and unchanging even in the absence of environmental stimulation. **Organization,** an additional cognitive function, goes on internally quite apart from the individual's interaction with the environment. Once structures reach a true state of equilibrium, they form an orderly, integrated whole, show a high degree of interdependence, and are part of a strong total system. Piaget believed that this is achieved through organization, the constant internal integration and rearrangement of schemes with one another, and he regarded organization as a vital source of cognitive progress (Piaget, 1936/1952b; Flavell, 1963).

The Piagetian Notion of Stage

Piaget viewed the major changes that take place in the structure of thought as a series of stages. Each stage groups together similar qualitative changes in a variety of schemes that occur during the same period of development (Tanner & Inhelder, 1956). The stages are assumed by Piaget to be *invariant;* that is, they emerge in a fixed order for all children, and there can be no skipping of stages. Piaget's invariant stage sequence reveals that his theory has a strong maturational component. The order of stages is regarded as a genetic given for all human beings, but the age at which a given stage appears may vary considerably from child to child. Piaget cautioned his readers not to use age as an indicator of stage of development, because many factors — both hereditary and environmental — affect the speed with which children move through the stages (Piaget, 1926/1928). In fact, he viewed both maturation and experience as making joint and inseparable contributions to development, for children cannot mature through his sequence of stages without opportunities to exercise their schemes in a rich and varied external world.

Piaget acknowledged that not all individuals achieve the final stages of development. For example, Piaget's collaborator Inhelder (1944) reported arrested stage development in mentally retarded subjects. More recently, Weisz and Zigler (1979) found that retarded individuals follow the same sequence of Piagetian stages as do nonretarded persons, differing only in the slow rate at which they progress and in the lower ultimate stage ceiling that they attain. As we will see later on when we discuss the highest stage of formal operations, attainment of the most advanced forms of logical reasoning is strongly dependent on extensive experience in specific content areas. Thus, a particular individual may not reach formal operations in all situations (Flavell, 1963).

A final important feature of Piaget's stages is that they are *hierarchically related* to one another. That is, the structures of the early stages are not lost forever once children advance to a new stage. Instead, they are absorbed and integrated into the later stages. For example, crawling infants have developed a rudimentary sensorimotor map of their immediate surroundings, and they use it to move quickly and efficiently from one place to another, making detours and avoiding obstacles. Years later, these sensorimotor action patterns become incorporated into representational schemes, as school-age children imagine spatial relationships and draw simple maps of their surroundings (Flavell, 1963; Piaget, Inhelder, & Szeminska, 1948/1960).

PIAGET'S STAGES OF DEVELOPMENT

Piaget referred to his stages as sensorimotor, preoperational, concrete operational, and formal operational. To orient you to the complex cognitive changes that occur during these four periods of development, a brief overview is provided below. Then we will embark on a detailed consideration of each stage.

The **sensorimotor stage** spans the age range of infancy, from birth to about 2 years. During this period, infants "think" by acting on the world with their eyes, ears, hands, and other sensorimotor equipment; they cannot carry out many activities "inside their heads." These sensorimotor action patterns become increasingly complex and flexible over the first two years of life. During the **preoperational stage,** which extends from approximately 2 to 7 years, children represent their earlier sensorimotor structures internally, and as a result they acquire "thought." However, their thinking is unsophisticated and lacks the rigorous, logical properties of the two remaining stages. The **concrete operational stage** begins around age 7 and ends at about age 11. During this period children's reasoning takes on logical characteristics, and a systematic, rational cognitive framework is applied to the world of concrete objects. When thought processes take on this orderly, logical character, Piaget calls them **operations,** but operational thinking at this stage falls short of adult intelligence in that it is not yet abstract. The **formal operational stage,** which begins around age 11 and is fully achieved by age 15, brings with it the capacity for abstraction. This permits adolescents to reason beyond a world of concrete reality to a world of possibilities, and to operate logically on symbols and information that do not necessarily have counterparts in the real world (Flavell, 1963; Brainerd, 1978).

The Sensorimotor Stage (Birth – 2 Years)

Compared to the cognitive characteristics of older children and adults, infants are far simpler beings, but the difference between the newborn baby and 2-year-old child is so vast that Piaget's description of the sensorimotor period ranks among his most complex and multifaceted statements on the development of intelligence. Unlike the neonate whose adaptations to the environment are limited and reflexive, the child of late infancy and the early preschool years can solve practical, everyday problems in planful ways and can represent reality in terms of symbols in speech, gesture, and play (Flavell, 1985). Given these enormous changes, it is no surprise that Piaget's sensorimotor stage is comprised of six separate substages.

The fact that Piaget's infant observations were based on the very limited sample of his own children caused many psychologists to question the validity of his sensorimotor stage. Although subsequent research has confirmed Piaget's general sequence of sensorimotor development (Corman & Escalona, 1969; Užgiris, 1973; Užgiris & Hunt, 1975), some investigators have recently raised questions about Piaget's interpretation of infant intellectual phenomena (Harris, 1983). It is now generally agreed that Piaget underestimated the young infant's intellectual competence (Gibson & Spelke, 1983). In the sections below, we first describe the development of sensorimotor intelligence as Piaget saw it, noting research that is supportive of his observations. Then we consider controversies and differences of opinion that presently surround Piaget's description of this first stage.

Major Intellectual Achievements of the Sensorimotor Stage. The sensorimotor period results in several landmark intellectual achievements. One of the most important is **object permanence,** the understanding that objects in the environment have a permanent existence that is independent of the infant's interaction with them. Think for a moment about your own understanding of objects. You know that when an object is out of sight it has not miraculously evaporated. You also know that an object's behavior is independent of your contact with it. While an object is out of sight, you know it can change locations, and that if you look for it again, it may be where you last saw it, or it may have moved or been moved by someone else. This multifaceted understanding of the nature of objects, which is basic to a coherent mental life, develops gradually over the first 2 years of life.

During the sensorimotor period, infants also develop the capacity for **intentional,** or **goal-directed behavior.** At the beginning of the sensorimotor stage, the baby's actions are not planful and goal directed. Instead, they have a random, hit-or-miss quality to them — for example, *accidentally* bringing thumb to mouth and latching on, or *happening* to kick the mobile, which then yields an interesting visual and auditory effect. But by about 8 months of age, infants have had enough practice with a variety of sensorimotor schemes that they are able to combine them together intentionally in the solution of simple sensorimotor problems. Thus, the sensorimotor period shows an evolution from unintentional behavior to purposeful activity.

Two important cognitive capacities, *play* and *imitation,* make their first appearance over the course of the sensorimotor period. These capacities serve as important mechanisms for solidifying old schemes and acquiring new ones. Play, pure self-expressive activity involving the exercise of schemes, was regarded by Piaget as placing its heaviest accent on assimilation, for play involves applying already-acquired schemes just for the pleasure and fun of doing so.[2] In contrast, imitation, the modeling or copying of behaviors not yet in the child's repertoire, is accommodation in its purest form. When infants and young children imitate, they put all their effort into modifying their behaviors to fit with what they perceive in the environment. Piaget believed that what infants and children choose to play at and are capable of imitating provide excellent indicators of their advancing intellectual achievements.

The Circular Reaction: Basic Sensorimotor Learning Mechanism. Before infants can play, imitate, or engage in intentional behavior, they must have some means for adapting to environmental demands and building schemes. Piaget referred to the earliest and most basic sensorimotor learning mechanism as the **circular reaction.** It consists of stumbling accidentally on a new experience that results from the infant's own activity. The reaction is "circular," because the infant then tries to repeat this

---

[2] There are many different definitions of play in the child development literature. Some emphasize the intrinsically motivated nature of children's activity, others children's active engagement with the environment, and still others the pleasurable emotional state that accompanies play behavior (Rubin, Fein, & Vandenberg, 1983). All of these characteristics fit very well with Piaget's definition of play. However, as we will see later on in this chapter, some theorists believe that play goes well beyond the practice of previously learned skills and increases children's repertoire of responses to the environment. They believe that Piaget underestimated the power of play in children's cognitive development.

new chance adaptation again and again. Through a series of such repetitions, a new response becomes strengthened and consolidated into a firmly established scheme. The circular reaction, like play and imitation, adapts over the course of the sensorimotor period to reflect major advances in infant intellectual capacities. Circular reactions change from *primary,* or centered around the infant's own body, to *secondary,* directed outward toward manipulation of objects, to *tertiary,* concerned with exploration and pursuit of novel effects in the surrounding world. We will illustrate these shifts as we trace sensorimotor development below, but you can see from this basic description that infant intellectual activity becomes less self-centered, less rigid, and more outer-directed, flexible, and exploratory over the first 2 years of life.

Sensorimotor Egocentrism. Central to Piaget's theory is the concept of *egocentrism* — young children's inability to distinguish their own cognitive perspectives from the perspectives of others. **Sensorimotor egocentrism** involves an absence of the understanding that objects exist independently of one's own actions and that the self is an object in a world of objects. At birth, the baby is a totally egocentric being, but sensorimotor egocentrism gradually declines as infants become aware that objects are permanent, external entities and that their own actions are separate from the objects themselves. Piaget's concept of infant egocentrism will become clearer to you as we describe his six sensorimotor substages below.

The Six Sensorimotor Substages. The major qualitative transformations in sensorimotor intelligence that take place during the first 2 years of life are as follows:

Substage 1: Reflexive Schemes (Birth – 1 Month). Because the newborn infant's behavioral repertoire consists of little more than neonatal reflexes, Piaget treated this stage briefly. Nevertheless, he regarded the baby's reflexive adaptations as the building blocks of sensorimotor intelligence. Although some reflexes like the Moro and Babinski (which we discussed in Chapter 4) never become cognitively relevant, others such as sucking, grasping, and eye movements begin to change as the result of repeated exercise and application to objects and external events. During this first substage, infants were regarded by Piaget as completely egocentric. Although equipped with innate responses, they have no understanding of a world of objects existing separately from the self (Flavell, 1963; Flavell, 1985; Piaget, 1936/1952b).

Substage 2: Primary Circular Reactions: The First Learned Adaptations (1 – 4 Months). By repeating chance behaviors that lead to satisfying results, infants develop some simple motor habits, such as sucking their thumbs, sticking out their tongues, and opening and closing their hands. In addition, infants of this stage start to vary their behaviors more clearly in response to environmental demands, as, for example, when they open their mouths differently depending on whether they are offered a nipple or a spoon. The improved coordination of actions with experience is also evident in the 2-month-old's limited ability to anticipate events — for example, when the baby displays anticipatory sucking movements in preparation for feeding. Still, the sensorimotor schemes of substage 2 are very limited in that they are primarily centered around the infant's own body and motivated by basic physiological needs. As yet, infants do not seem very concerned with the results that their actions lead to in the surrounding world. Therefore, the infant of a few months of age is still a very egocentric being.

By the end of this substage, visually guided reaching appears, and it plays a major role in turning infants' attention outward toward objects and in extricating them from the egocentrism of early infancy. Also, during substage 2, Piaget believed that infants show the first glimmerings of the capacity to imitate others, but it is limited to copying someone else's imitation of their own actions. However, as we discussed in Chapter 4, recent evidence suggests that even newborn infants have a rudimentary capacity to

As infants move through Piaget's sensorimotor stage, they imitate increasingly complex gestures of adult models. (Robert Brenner/ PhotoEdit)

imitate facial gestures of adults, and imitation seems to be one of the areas in which Piaget underestimated the young baby's sensorimotor competence. Finally, substage 2 infants can also be seen exercising some of their simple motor habits playfully, for they will smile as they repeat a newly developed action, as if for the sake of pure assimilatory pleasure.

Substage 3: Secondary Circular Reactions: Making Interesting Sights Last (4–8 Months). Now infants begin to perform events that are more definitely oriented to objects and events outside their own bodies. Using the secondary circular reaction, they try to maintain through repetition interesting changes in the environment that are produced by their own actions. Piaget described numerous examples of secondary circular reactions, most involving manual activity, such as pulling, striking, swinging, and rubbing. The following example illustrates the gradual evolution of the sensorimotor scheme of "hitting" in Piaget's 4-month-old son Laurent.

> At 4 months, 7 days, [Laurent] looks at a letter opener tangled in the strings of a doll hung in front of him. He tries to grasp (a scheme he already knows) the doll or the letter opener but each time, his attempts only result in his knocking the objects (so they swing out of his reach). He then looks at them with interest and starts over again. The next day, the same reaction. . . . but after trying to grasp the letter opener and failing each time, he then only sketches out his grasping gesture, and so simply keeps knocking one end of the object. The next day Laurent tries to grasp a doll hanging in front of him; but he only manages to make it swing. . . . Then he shakes his whole body, waving his arms (another scheme he already knows). But in so doing he hits the doll by accident; then he starts over on purpose, a number of times. . . . At 4 months 15 days, with another doll hung in front of him, Laurent tries to grasp it, then shakes himself to make it swing, knocks it accidentally, and then tries simply to hit it. . . . At 4 months 18 days, Laurent hits my hands without trying to grasp them, but he started by simply waving his arms around, and only afterwards went on to hit my hands. The next day, finally, Laurent immediately hits a doll hung in front of him. The scheme is now completely differentiated. (Piaget, 1936/1952b, pp. 167–168)[3]

[3] Quotations from Piaget, 1936/1952b, are reprinted by permission of International Universities Press, Inc.

Although they are a great cognitive advance over the previous stage, secondary circular reactions are limited in that they involve simple and undifferentiated connections between actions and objects. Infants do not yet really explore the objects that give rise to their pleasurable experiences. Instead, they simply repeat a newly acquired action with respect to an object over and over again. Therefore, substage 3 infants are still egocentric and have little understanding of objects as existing independently of their own actions. In addition, their behavior is not yet goal-directed and intentional, for new adaptations are limited to those that occur initially by chance and are then added to the baby's repertoire through circular repetition.

Notice how similar the example of Laurent's secondary circular reaction is to the evidence presented in Chapter 4 on operant conditioning of early infant behaviors. From this perspective, Laurent's hitting scheme is a conditioned response, and the visual effect it produces on the objects hung above his crib serves as a reinforcer. Infant operant conditioning research shows that the frequency of newborn babies' responses like sucking and head turning increases rapidly when they lead to interesting sensory stimuli, such as sounds and patterned visual displays. Therefore, some version of substage 3 behavior seems to appear earlier than Piaget indicated, and as with imitation, Piaget seems to have underestimated the young infant's capacity to engage in secondary circular reactions.

According to Piaget, infants of substage 3 show slightly more advanced imitative abilities, in that they will spontaneously imitate behaviors of a model. However, they can only imitate behaviors that are already within their own behavioral repertoire, not those that are novel and as yet unpracticed. Piaget also believed that substage 3 infants could only imitate behaviors that they could see or hear themselves produce. These include vocalizations and manual gestures, but not facial expressions, as babies cannot see their own faces. However, once again, the latter conclusion is at variance with the research on neonatal imitation that we described in Chapter 4.

Substage 4: Coordination of Secondary Circular Reactions and Their Application to New Situations (8 – 12 Months). In substage 4, the externally oriented schemes of the previous stage are combined with one another to bring about new action sequences that are intentional and goal-directed. The clearest example of this new capacity is provided by Piaget's object-hiding tasks, in which he shows the infant an attractive object and then hides it behind his hand, under a cloth cover, or beneath a cup. Infants of this stage are able to set aside the obstacle and retrieve the object. In doing so, they coordinate two earlier established schemes, one serving as the means (pushing aside the obstacle) and the other serving as the goal (grasping the object). Piaget regarded such means-end behaviors as the first truly intelligent actions and the sensorimotor foundation for all later problem solving.

The fact that infants of substage 4 will manually search for and retrieve an object that they see someone else hide beneath a cover also indicates that they have achieved some appreciation of the continued existence of objects when they are spirited out of sight. However, Piaget believed that infants' understanding of object permanence is still limited at this stage. If a hidden object is moved to a new location, Piaget claimed that infants will search for it only in the first place in which it was hidden. Therefore, Piaget concluded, infants really do not have a clear image of the object as continuing to exist beneath the cover.

Infants of this stage can better anticipate signs of impending events that are not connected with their own immediate behavior than they could before. For example, when the baby's mother puts on her coat and turns toward the door, the infant may begin to cry in anticipation of her departure. This heightened concern with events in the outside world is in keeping with the gradual decline in egocentrism that takes place over the sensorimotor period.

Substage 4 also brings advances in imitative abilities, as babies now imitate behaviors that are to some degree different from those that they customarily perform.

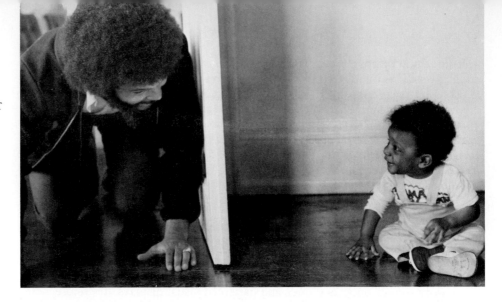

As infants master the nuances of object permanence, they delight in hiding-and-finding games such as peekaboo. (Alice Kandell/Photo Researchers)

Infants do this by searching through their current repertoire of schemes that are similar to the model's action and making deliberate modifications to approximate the new behavior. Thus, imitation, like means-end behavior, becomes intentional during this stage, but it is limited because infants are only able to imitate new actions that are very similar to their current schemes (Piaget, 1945/1951a).

Finally, during substage 4, play expands to include practicing the means in babies' newly acquired means-end action sequences. Piaget described an example in which one of his children began by pushing an obstacle aside to obtain a toy but ended up by ignoring the toy and, instead, pushing aside the obstacle (Piaget's hand or a piece of cardboard) again and again for fun (Piaget, 1945/1951a).

Substage 5: Tertiary Circular Reactions: The Discovery of New Means Through Active Experimentation (12 – 18 Months). The essence of intelligence at substage 5 is a purposeful, trial-and-error exploration of the properties of objects through acting on them in new and different ways. Presented with an object, the baby who is capable of tertiary circular reactions still stumbles on new and intriguing consequences by accident, but in attempting to recapture them, *repeats with variation,* trying this, then that, and then another action pattern on the object in a deliberately experimental and exploratory approach. A typical example is the way babies of this stage experiment with the dropping of objects. Substage 5 infants' vigorous experimental orientation makes them far more effective sensorimotor problem solvers, and through overt trial-and-error variations in behavior, they discover *new means to ends.* For example, they can figure out how to fit objects into container openings and how to tilt a long stick in order to draw it through the bars of their playpen.

According to Piaget, infants' new experimental approach to the world also permits a more advanced notion of object permanence. Now they will search in successive locations for a hidden toy. In addition, the exploratory strategies of substage 5 enable babies to imitate behaviors that are much more unfamiliar than those of the previous stage. Infants of substage 5 can be seen exercising their more advanced sensorimotor schemes in play when, for example, they bang blocks together in different ways. Because babies of this stage can vary their actions with respect to external objects and events, Piaget believed that they clearly distinguish themselves and their own actions from the world around them and that sensorimotor egocentrism disappears.

Substage 6: Invention of New Means Through Mental Combinations (18 Months – 2 Years). Substage 5 is the last truly *sensorimotor* stage, for substage 6 brings with it the ability to make the first primitive internal representations of reality. Infants can now solve problems through internal, symbolic means instead of through a series of trial-and-error, overt explorations. One indication of infants' new ability to represent sensorimotor actions and events, rather than just perform them, is that now they arrive at solutions to sensorimotor problems suddenly. Piaget infers from this that they go through a covert process that involves representing actions and experimenting with them internally. Faced with her doll carriage stuck against the wall, Piaget's daughter Lucienne, had she been in substage 5, would have pushed, pulled, and bumped it until she finally managed to reorient it in a new direction. Notice how she handles the problem differently below:

> At (1 year, 6 months, and 23 days) for the first time Lucienne plays with a doll carriage. . . . She rolls it over the carpet by pushing it. When she comes against a wall, she pulls, walking backward. But as this position is not convenient for her, she pauses and without hesitation, goes to the other side to push the carriage again. She therefore found the procedure in one attempt, apparently through analogy to other situations but without training, apprenticeship, or chance. (Piaget, 1936/1952b, p. 338)

With the capacity to represent reality internally, infants arrive at the understanding that objects can move or be moved when out of sight. Now they can solve object-hiding tasks involving invisible displacements. If a toy is hidden in a box, the box is placed under a cover, and, while out of the baby's sight, the toy is dumped out of the box, the substage 6 infant will search in each possible hiding place and eventually find the toy under the blanket. Younger babies are baffled and confused by this situation.

Representation also brings with it a major advance in imitative ability: the capacity for **deferred imitation,** or the ability to imitate the behavior of models not present in the immediate perceptual field. Deferred imitation shows how new representational capacities enable infants to remember past experiences when no current signs of them are present. A famous and amusing example is Piaget's daughter Jacqueline's delayed imitation of the temper tantrum of another baby:

> At (1 year, 4 months, and 3 days) Jacqueline had a visit from a little boy of (1 year 6 months) . . . who, in the course of the afternoon got into a terrible temper. He screamed as he tried to get out of a playpen and pushed it backwards, stamping his feet. Jacqueline stood watching him in amazement. . . . The next day, she herself screamed in her playpen and tried to move it, stamping her foot lightly several times in succession. (Piaget, 1936/1952b, p. 63)

Piaget concluded that Jacqueline's imitation of the little boy's tantrum must have involved a stored representation, since it followed more than half a day after the original encounter. In a recent experiment, Meltzoff (1988) showed that infants as young as 9 months of age can reproduce an experimenter's simple action with an unfamiliar toy even when their first opportunity to engage in imitation is delayed for 24 hours. This new finding suggests that the young infant's capacity for deferred imitation emerges considerably earlier than Piaget believed.

Finally, the ability to represent reality leads to a major change in the nature of play. At the end of the sensorimotor period young children can engage in **make-believe play** in which they reenact familiar activities, as when they pretend to eat, go to sleep, or drive a car. At this point, children's representational abilities are still rudimentary and unpracticed, but mental symbolism improves dramatically during the ensuing preoperational stage.

Summary of Sensorimotor Development. Piaget's six sensorimotor substages detail the enormous cognitive changes that take place during the brief interval between birth and 2 years of age. As the result of opportunities to act directly on the environment, the reflexive and egocentric schemes of the neonate are transformed

Table 6.1. Summary of Intellectual Development During the Sensorimotor Stage

SENSORIMOTOR SUBSTAGE	TYPICAL ADAPTIVE BEHAVIORS	OBJECT PERMANENCE	IMITATION	PLAY
1. Reflexive schemes (birth–1 month)	Neonatal reflexes	None	None according to Piaget, but recent evidence disputes this (see Chapter 4)	None
2. Primary circular reactions (1–4 months)	Simple motor habits centered around the infant's own body	None	Rudimentary ability to imitate. Believed by Piaget to be limited to copying of another person's imitation of the infant's own behavior	Beginnings of playful exercise of schemes for their own sake
3. Secondary circular reactions (4–8 months)	Actions oriented toward recapturing interesting effects in the external world	Ability to retrieve a partially hidden object	Spontaneous imitation of the behavior of a model, but only if the behavior is currently within the infant's repertoire	Same as previous substage
4. Coordination of secondary circular reactions (8–12 months)	Combination of two object-directed actions, one serving as the means and the other as the end in a goal-directed action sequence	Ability to retrieve a hidden object from the first location in which it is hidden	Imitation of behaviors slightly different from those the infant usually performs	Playful exercise of "means" in means-end behavior sequences
5. Tertiary circular reactions (12–18 months)	Exploration of the properties of objects by acting on them in varied ways	Ability to search in successive locations for a hidden toy	Imitation of unfamiliar behaviors of a model	More varied and less repetitive sensorimotor play
6. Mental combinations (18 months–2 years)	Internal representation of sensorimotor objects and events	Ability to solve object-hiding tasks involving invisible displacements	Deferred imitation. However, new evidence suggests it may appear as early as substage 4	First appearance of make-believe play

into the more versatile intellectual structures of the young preschool child. Table 6.1 provides an overview of the major intellectual accomplishments of this early period of development.

New Research on Sensorimotor Intelligence. During the past 20 years, many researchers have reinvestigated the accomplishments of Piaget's sensorimotor stage. Although the general sequence of development has survived quite well, a number of recent studies, such as those mentioned earlier on neonatal imitation and operant conditioning, show that infants attain some sensorimotor milestones earlier than Piaget believed. Piaget's underestimation of infant cognitive capacities is partly the result of the fact that he did not have the sophisticated experimental techniques that are available to modern researchers (Flavell, 1985). Currently, most studies of sensorimotor intelligence concern the development of object permanence. These investigations indicate that when researchers rely on assessments of infants' perception and memory instead of their willingness to engage in active search, object permanence shows up earlier than Piaget believed.

One such approach to studying object permanence used the habituation-dishabituation paradigm discussed in Chapter 4. In an intriguing set of experiments, Baillargeon and her colleagues (Baillargeon, 1987; Baillargeon, Spelke, and Wasserman, 1985) found evidence for object permanence in 4½- and even some 3½-month-old infants—months earlier than Piaget concluded it developed! First, infants were habituated to a screen that moved back and forth like a drawbridge through a 180-degree arc. Then a yellow box was placed behind the screen, and two test events were presented. The first was a *possible event,* in which the screen slowly moved up from a flat position until it rested against the box, where it stopped and then returned to its original position. The second was an *impossible event,* in which the screen began as before but then miraculously continued its movement as if the box were no longer there. It completed a full 180-degree arc before reversing direction, returning to its initial position, and revealing the box standing intact (see Figure 6.1). The findings showed that the infants looked longer, as though surprised, at the impossible event. Apparently early-substage 3 and some late-substage 2 babies can understand that an object continues to exist when it is hidden from view.

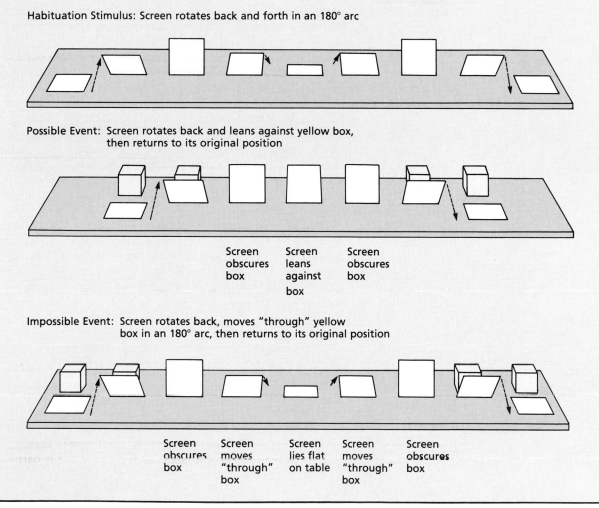

Habituation Stimulus: Screen rotates back and forth in an 180° arc

Possible Event: Screen rotates back and leans against yellow box, then returns to its original position

Screen obscures box | Screen leans against box | Screen obscures box

Impossible Event: Screen rotates back, moves "through" yellow box in an 180° arc, then returns to its original position

Screen obscures box | Screen moves "through" box | Screen lies flat on table | Screen moves "through" box | Screen obscures box

Figure 6.1. Schematic diagram of the habituation stimulus and the possible and impossible events used in the Baillargeon, Spelke, and Wasserman (1985) study. The habituation-dishabituation paradigm predicts that infants should look longer at the possible event, which depicts a novel, shorter screen movement compared to the original habituation stimulus. But subjects looked longer at the impossible event, as if with surprise, indicating their understanding of object permanence. *(From R. Baillargeon, E. S. Spelke, & S. Wasserman, 1985, "Object Permanence in Five-Month-Old Infants," Cognition, 20, 196. Adapted by permission.)*

If Baillargeon, Spelke, and Wasserman are correct that infants as young as 3½ months of age have some understanding of object permanence, then what explains the absence of active search behavior in young babies (who are quite capable of visually guided reaching) when they are confronted with toys hidden under blankets or concealed in the palm of an adult's hand? One explanation is that, just as Piaget suggested, they cannot yet coordinate separate actions into means-end sequences. As a result, what they *know* about object permanence is not yet *evident* in their motor activities. Support for this interpretation comes from observations of Užgiris (1973) that infants do not spontaneously search for hidden objects until they can engage in combined action sequences — pushing and pulling objects, and putting them in and taking them out of containers.

That infants attain object permanence early, but depend on the emergence of means-end action sequences to display it in their behavior, still does not explain why Piaget found that babies make errors in their first active efforts to find a hidden object. Remember that in Piaget's substage 4, infants tend to look for an object in the first place (A) in which it is hidden. If it is moved to a new location (B), many infants search again at A and are perplexed when this does not yield the object. If infants understand that an object still exists when it is hidden and are capable of the means-end action sequences necessary for retrieving objects, why does this AB search error occur?

One possible answer is provided in a recent study by Bjork and Cummings (1984). They concluded that infants make AB search errors because they have trouble remembering an object's new location when it is hidden in more than one place. Bjork and Cummings presented infants with a hiding task in which there were more than two possible hiding locations. As shown in Figure 6.2, the experimenter hid a toy in only the far right or far left holes of an oblong block with five holes. On B hiding trials, half of the infants made errors, but in contrast to Piaget's results, none of these was an A-returning error! Instead, infants tended to search in the holes nearest to B, as if they remembered the approximate, but not the exact hiding place. Bjork and Cummings's finding indicates that substage 4 search errors are not the result of an object permanence problem, and a recent review of other similar studies confirms this conclusion (Wellman, Cross, & Bartsch, 1987).

The evidence we have reviewed suggests that Piaget's interpretation of infants' initial efforts to search for hidden objects requires revision. However, Piaget seems to be correct that object permanence problems involving invisible displacements, which require the infant to internally represent the behavior of a hidden object, are rarely error-free until 18 months of age (Wishart & Bower, 1982). And despite some discrepancies in timing of development, recent research on the development of

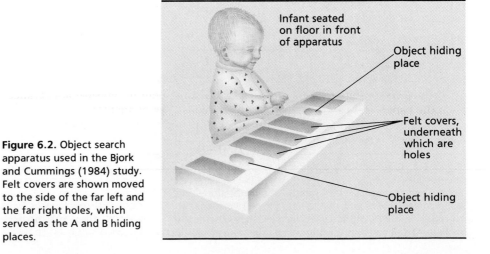

Figure 6.2. Object search apparatus used in the Bjork and Cummings (1984) study. Felt covers are shown moved to the side of the far left and the far right holes, which served as the A and B hiding places.

Infant seated
on floor in front
of apparatus

Object hiding
place

Felt covers,
underneath
which are
holes

Object hiding
place

imitation and play during infancy fits quite well with Piaget's overall developmental sequence and is consistent with the main tenets of his theory (Belsky & Most, 1981; Kaye & Marcus, 1981; McCall, Eichorn, & Hogarty, 1977).

The Preoperational Stage (2–7 Years)

Symbolic Activity. As children move from the sensorimotor to the preoperational stage, one of the most obvious changes is the extraordinarily rapid increase in symbolic activity. Around the age of 2, tremendous strides in language development occur. But children's new symbolic capacity actually makes use of a variety of representational media in addition to language, including deferred imitation, make-believe play, and mental images of actions and events. By detaching thought from action, mental symbolism permits thought to be faster and more freely mobile than it was during the sensorimotor stage. Now the child is able to transcend the confines of immediate time and space and represent several events simultaneously, rather than having to deal with them in a successive, step-by-step, action-oriented fashion (Piaget & Inhelder, 1967/1969).

Language. Piaget acknowledged that language is the most versatile of the human being's symbolic mechanisms, but he de-emphasized its role in cognitive development. According to Piaget, because thought in the form of sensorimotor intelligence begins long before language does, thought is not just a by-product of language. Instead, sensorimotor activity provides the cognitive foundations that make the very use of language possible, just as it makes possible deferred imitation and make-believe play. In agreement with Piaget's view of the primacy of sensorimotor activity, research shows that children's first words in the early part of the second year of life are initially not truly symbolic, in that they are tied to actions and objects in the immediate present. For example, the baby only says "ball" when she kicks and throws her red rubber ball. When a child begins to use words in place of things or actions that have taken place but are not there at the moment, then the true symbolic function has emerged. Also, research on language acquisition reveals that the first words that babies use have a strong sensorimotor basis. That is, the objects and events for which they stand are things that infants act upon (such as ball or cup), actions that they perform or see others perform (bye-bye, all gone), or things that act themselves and therefore have salient perceptual properties (car, doggie). Thus, the words that children learn first reflect their sensorimotor mode of structuring the world (Nelson, 1973).

Additional evidence for the view that language is a matter of learning how to represent what the child already knows on a sensorimotor plane comes from investigations demonstrating that before infants acquire language, they already have a prelinguistic knowledge of conceptual categories. In one such study, Ross (1980) presented babies of 12, 18, and 24 months of age with a series of toy objects one at a time that belonged to the same category, such as food items (e.g., hot dog, piece of bread, slice of salami). The infants habituated to the objects by decreasing their looking and touching of them over trials, suggesting that they regarded them as similar objects, despite the obvious diversity among them in physical appearance. Then the babies were shown a pair of objects consisting of another member of the same category (a round green apple) and a member of a different category (a round green chair). Even the 12-month-olds touched and looked longest at the member of the novel category, providing additional support for their capacity to group together and discriminate objects on a categorical basis. This ability could not have been based on language, as 12-month-olds have not yet learned such words as hotdog and salami! Instead, it must have been based on their wide-ranging sensorimotor experience with a great many objects. These results, as well as the findings of other infant categorization studies (Sherman, 1985; Younger, 1985), support Piaget's contention that

". . . language development largely follows on the heels of cognitive development, rather than the other way around" (Flavell, 1985, p. 31). However, once the child is capable of representation through language, it facilitates thought by releasing it from its sensorimotor ties to the here-and-now. Much later on in development, language becomes indispensable for abstract cognitive endeavor.

Make-Believe Play. Make-believe play provides a further example of the emergence of representational skills during the preoperational stage. Like language, it grows prodigiously over the course of the preschool years. In fact, it is largely confined to this age period. Young infants are not capable of it, and children older than 6 or 7 years of age have largely given it up in favor of other forms of play, like organized games, sports, and hobbies (Fein, 1979; Flavell, 1985). See Box 6.1 for more information on how make-believe play reflects the development of the symbolic function and the role that it plays in the cognitive development of the preschool child.

FOCUS ON THEORY, RESEARCH, AND APPLICATIONS

Box 6.1
The Development of Make-Believe Play During the Preschool Years

Theory. The appearance of **make-believe play** at the end of the second year of life marks one of the most significant cognitive achievements of the early childhood years. Piaget regarded the role of play in cognitive development as one of strengthening and consolidating newly acquired symbolic skills. Subsequent investigators have suggested that play involves more than the practice of already-acquired schemes and contributes positively to new cognitive achievements (Bruner, Jolly, & Sylva, 1976; Sutton-Smith, 1966; Rubin & Pepler, 1982). What does recent research say about how make-believe play consolidates and contributes to cognitive development during the preschool years?

Research. According to Greta Fein (1979), careful observation of young children at play reveals several strands of symbolic mastery that reflect as well as contribute to cognitive development. First, during play, behavior becomes increasingly detached from real-life situations and the motivational conditions usually associated with them. For example, the child who pretends to go to sleep does so in places other than bed and when she is not really tired. In time, children show that

they are consciously aware that they are pretending and are able to step back and forth between make-believe and reality, as when they pause to tell a playmate what to do next. Recent investigators believe that practice in stepping in and out of play may help children grasp the conceptual distinction between appearance and reality (Flavell, Green, & Flavell, 1986; Golumb & Cornelius, 1977).

Second, as children get older their use of symbols in play gradually becomes less dependent on objects in the immediate stimulus field and relies more heavily on internal representations of those objects (Elder & Pederson, 1978; Fein, 1975; Watson & Fischer, 1977; Ungerer et al., 1981). Research shows that the use of less realistic toys increases over the preschool years and that a greater variety of fantasy themes are evoked by nonrealistic than realistic play materials (Pulaski, 1970). When play objects are used in novel ways, they encourage the discovery of new relationships and may enhance children's ability to think flexibly and creatively (Feitelson & Ross, 1973).

Finally, the way in which the "child as self" participates in make-believe play changes with development. When symbolic play first appears in the latter part of the second year, children are both agents and recipients of pretend actions; for example, they pretend to feed or wash themselves. A short time later, other objects become recipients, as when the child pretends to feed or

wash a doll. Around 2 years of age, objects can be used as active agents, and the child becomes a detached participant who makes a doll feed itself or a parent doll feed a baby doll. The increased flexibility of pretend roles that children are able to assume is also evident in the emergence of **sociodramatic play,** the make-believe play with others that first appears at about 2½ years of age. By 5 years, children collectively create and manage intricate roles and complex plots. For sociodramatic play to be successful, all the players must understand the object substitutions, roles, and play themes. Looked at in this way, it is not surprising that sociodramatic play has been found to enhance children's perspective-taking abilities. When children are provided with special opportunities to engage in it (e.g., encouragement to act out "Little Red Riding Hood" or "The Three Billy Goats Gruff"), their capacity to understand the feelings, needs, and preferences of others increases (Saltz & Johnson, 1974). They also improve in general intellectual performance as measured by standardized tests (Saltz, Dixon, & Johnson, 1977).

Applications. Make-believe play is an important activity during early childhood. Research demonstrating its benefits serves as ample justification for play as a central part of early childhood and kindergarten programs and the daily life of the preschool child.

Pictorial Representation. Children's drawings are another important vehicle of symbolic expression. Even the scrawls of the 1½- or 2-year-old, which seem at first glance to be little more than indecipherable tangles of lines, are often "experiments in representation" (Winner, 1986, pp. 25–26). At first, children's artful representation is gestural and motoric rather than pictorial. For example, one toddler took her crayon and hopped it around the page, explaining as she made a series of dots, "Rabbit goes hop-hop." Although the marks did not resemble a rabbit, the child had symbolized one with the motion of the marker. By age 3, children's scribbles start to become pictures. Initially, this happens after they make a gestural motion with the crayon, notice that they have drawn a recognizable shape, and then decide to label it. In one case, a 2-year-old child made some random marks on a page and then, realizing the resemblance between his scribbles and noodles, named the creation "chicken pie and noodles" (Winner, 1986).

A major milestone in children's artistic development occurs when they begin to use lines to represent the boundaries of objects. This enables them to draw their first picture of a person by age 3 or 4. The tadpole image shown in Figure 6.3 is a universal one in which the limitations of the preschooler's fine motor skills reduce the figure down to the simplest form that still communicates that it is human (Gardner, 1980; Golumb, 1974; Winner, 1986). Unlike many adults, young children do not demand that a drawing be realistic. But as they get older, their fine motor control improves, and they learn to desire greater realism. As a result, they begin to create more complex, differentiated drawings, like the one shown in Figure 6.3 made by a 6-year-

Figure 6.3. Examples of young children's drawings. The universal tadpole-like shape that children use to draw their first picture of a person is shown on the left. The tadpole soon becomes an anchor for greater detail, as arms, fingers, toes, and facial features sprout from the basic shape. By the end of the preschool years, children produce more complex, differentiated pictures, like the one on the right drawn by a 6- year-old child. *(Tadpole drawings from* Artful Scribbles: The Significance of Children's Drawings, *p. 64, by Howard Gardner. Copyright © 1980 by Howard Gardner. Reprinted by permission of Basic Books, Inc., Publishers. Six-year-old's picture from E. Winner [August 1986], "Where Pelicans Kiss Seals," Psychology Today, 20, 35. Reprinted by permission.)*

old child. Still, children of this age are not very particular about mirroring reality in their pictures. There are perceptual distortions, which help to make their work fanciful and inventive. Accomplished artists, who also try to represent reality freely, must often work hard to do deliberately what they did without effort as 5- and 6-year-olds (Winner, 1986).

Aside from the development of representation, most of the cognitive characteristics of the preoperational stage are stated by Piaget in negative terms. That is, Piaget largely described what preschool children *cannot,* as opposed to what they *can,* understand. The very name of the stage—*pre*operational—indicates that Piaget compared the preschooler to the older, cognitively more capable concrete operational child and, as a result, discovered little of a positive nature about the younger child's thinking. As we shall see when we discuss new research on preschool thought, Piaget underestimated the cognitive competencies of early childhood. But first, let's describe the deficiencies of preoperational thought from Piaget's point of view.

Limitations of Preoperational Thought. For Piaget, mental operations—internal representations of actions that obey logical rules—are where cognitive development is going. In the preoperational stage, children are not capable of operations. Instead, their representational thinking is rigid, inflexible, and strongly influenced by the effects of momentary experience. As a result, preoperational reasoning is considered by Piaget to be prelogical and intuitive rather than rational, and when judged by adult standards, it often appears distorted and incorrect.

The most pervasive characteristic of this stage, and the one from which all other deficiencies of thought emanate, is **preoperational egocentrism.** Remember that sensorimotor egocentrism gradually disappeared over the first 2 years of life. But now, with the acquisition of the new symbolic function, egocentrism reappears in a different form. Preoperational children are egocentric with respect to their symbolic viewpoints. That is, they are unaware of points of view other than their own, and they think everyone experiences the world in the same way as they do (Piaget, 1950).

Piaget believed that egocentrism is responsible for young children's belief that inanimate objects have lifelike qualities—in other words, that objects have thoughts, wishes, feelings, and intentions, just like the self. He called this **animistic thinking** (Piaget, 1926/1930). The 3-year-old who charmingly explains that the sun is angry at the clouds and has chased them away is demonstrating this kind of reasoning.

But Piaget's most compelling demonstration of preoperational egocentrism involves a task called the *three mountains problem* (Piaget & Inhelder, 1948/1956). A child stands on one side of a table and views a display of three mountains of different heights. Then a small doll is placed at various locations around the display, and the child must choose from photographs what the display looks like from the doll's perspective. Below the age of 6 or 7, most children select the photo that shows the display from their own position.

Piaget believed that egocentrism was largely responsible for the rigidity and illogical nature of young children's thinking. Thought that proceeds so strongly from a single point of view prevents children from accommodating, or adjusting their schemes in accordance with feedback from the physical and social world. Egocentric thinking is also not reflective thought, which critically examines, rethinks, and restructures an aspect of the environment. Young children, believing so strongly that their own symbolic perspective is universal, cannot think reflectively and are not even motivated to do so.

To appreciate some of the other cognitive deficiencies that Piaget believed were characteristic of the preoperational stage, you must understand some of the tasks he presented to children that require logical operations for successful performance. An important set of tasks is the conservation problems. Recall that **conservation** refers to the idea that certain physical attributes of an object remain the same even though its outward appearance changes. A typical example is the conservation of liquid problem we mentioned earlier in this chapter. The child is presented with two identical tall glasses of water and asked to agree that they contain equal amounts of liquid. Then the appearance of the water in one glass (but not its amount) is transformed by pouring it into a short wide container. The child is asked once more if the amount of liquid is still the same, or if it has changed. Preoperational children think that the quantity of liquid has changed when it is poured into a differently shaped container. When asked to explain the reasoning behind their answer, they often respond in ways like this: "There is less now because the water is way down here" (i.e., its level is so low in the short wide container), or "There is more water now because it is all spread out." There are many types of Piagetian conservation tasks in addition to conservation of liquid. You will find others illustrated in Figure 6.4.

The inability of children at the preoperational stage to conserve highlights several related aspects of their thinking. First, their understanding of reality is **perception-bound.** They are easily distracted by the concrete, perceptual appearance of objects (it *looks* like there is less water in the short wide container, and so there *must be* less water). Second, their thinking is "centered," or characterized by **centration.** Preoperational children focus their attention on one detail of a situation to the neglect of other important features (Inhelder, 1960). In the case of the conservation of liquid problem, the nonconserver centers on the height of the water level in the two containers, failing to take account of the fact that all changes in height of the liquid are compensated for by changes in width (or vice versa). Third, preoperational children focus on successive states of a situation rather than on dynamic transformations between them. In the conservation of liquid problem, they seem to treat the initial and final states of the water as completely unrelated events. An even more dramatic illustration of this tendency to focus on **states versus transformations** is provided by another problem that Piaget presents to children. A bar is allowed to fall freely from a vertical, upright position to a horizontal one, and after watching it do so the child is asked either to draw its movement or to select from a group of illustrations one that depicts what happened. Young children fail to draw or select an illustration that represents the intermediate positions of the bar. As shown in Figure 6.5, they focus only on its beginning and ending states, ignoring the transformations that take place in between (Flavell, 1963).

Being perception bound, centered, and focused on states rather than transformations are preoperational characteristics that reflect Piaget's view of the preschool child as a limited, one-dimensional processor of information. But the most important illogical feature of preoperational thought is its *irreversibility*. **Reversibility,** the opposite of this concept, characterizes every logical operation. It refers to the ability to mentally go through a series of reasonings or transformations in a problem and then reverse direction and return to the starting point. In the case of the conservation of liquid problem, the preoperational child fails to see how the existence of the same amount of liquid is assured by imagining the liquid being poured back into its original container.

Reversible thinking is flexible, organized, and logical. Because preoperational children are not capable of it, their reasoning about events often consists of collections of logically disconnected facts and contradictions. Instead of *inductive* (proceeding from particular to general) or *deductive* (proceeding from general to particular), Piaget referred to young children's causal explanations as **transductive reasoning** (proceeding from particular to particular). That is, in providing explanations they simply link together two events that happened to occur close in time and space, as if one caused the other. Sometimes this leads to a correct conclusion, as when Piaget's daughter said at 2½ years of age, "Daddy's getting hot water, so he's going to shave" (Piaget, 1945/1951a, pp. 230–231). At other times, it leads to some rather fantastic connections, as illustrated in the following interview that Piaget conducted with a young child on the topic of why the clouds move:

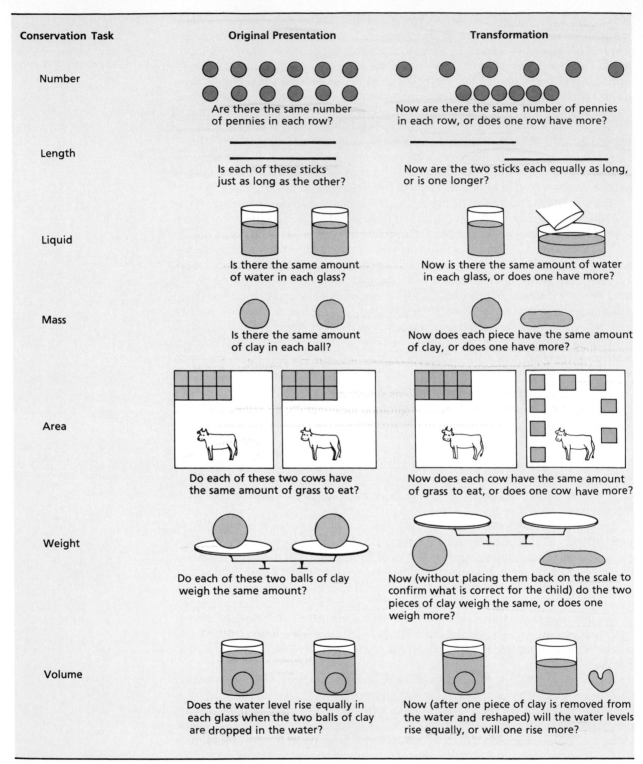

Figure 6.4. Some Piagetian conservation tasks. They are achieved successively over the concrete operational period. Number, length, liquid, and mass are acquired some time between 6 and 7 years of age; area and weight between 8 and 10 years; and volume between 10 and 12 years.

"You have already seen the clouds moving along? What makes them move? — *When we move along, they move along too.* — Can *you* make them move? — *Everybody can, when they walk.* — When I walk and you are still, do they move? — *Yes.* — And at night, when everyone is asleep, do they move? — *Yes.* — But you tell me that they move when somebody walks. — *They always move. The cats, when they walk, and then the dogs, they make the clouds move along.*" (Piaget, 1927/1929, p. 62)

Because they are not yet capable of logical operations, preoperational children have difficulty organizing objects into hierarchies of classes and subclasses based on similarities and differences among them. In fact, early in the preoperational stage, children do not seem to classify objects systematically at all. For example, when given paper cutouts of different shapes and colors and asked to put the things together that belong with one another, 2- and 3-year-olds simply arrange the objects into a large circle or square. They may label the configuration meaningfully by calling it a house or a truck, but they pay no attention to the attributes of the cutouts. Between 4 and 6 years of age, children begin to classify on the basis of the attributes of the cutouts, but their strategies are unsystematic. They may begin by putting all the circles together, but they quickly lose track of the dimension on which they began to sort. Late in the preoperational period, children classify systematically on the basis of attributes, but they appear unable to deal with hierarchies of classes, as Piaget illustrated with his famous **class inclusion** problem. Children are shown a set of objects, such as 16 flowers, most of which are yellow and a few of which are blue (see Figure 6.6). Asked whether there are *more yellow flowers* or *more flowers*, preoperational children re-

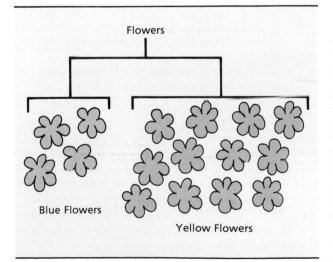

Flowers

Blue Flowers

Yellow Flowers

Figure 6.6. Example of a Piagetian class inclusion problem. Children are shown 16 flowers, 4 of which are blue and 12 of which are yellow. Asked whether there are more yellow flowers or more flowers, the preoperational child responds, "More yellow flowers," failing to take account of the fact that both yellow and blue flowers are embedded in the superordinate category of "flowers." In contrast, the concrete operational child understands class inclusion.

spond quite confidently, "More yellow flowers!" Their approach to the problem shows a tendency to center on the overriding perceptual attribute of color and an inability to think reversibly by moving from the whole class (flowers) to the parts (yellow and blue) and back again (Flavell, 1963; Phillips, 1975).

Just as they have difficulty with classification, very young preoperational children also have trouble with *seriation,* the systematic arrangement of a set of objects according to some quantitative characteristic, such as length. The 2- and 3-year-old cannot arrange 10 sticks in order from shortest to longest. Later, preoperational children can arrange a set of concrete objects in a series, but Piaget concluded that they cannot seriate mentally, a logical operation called **transitivity.** For example, Piaget regarded preschoolers as incapable of making the mental inference that stick A is longer than stick C from information that A is longer than B and B is longer than C (see Figure 6.7) (Piaget & Inhelder, 1948/1956; Piaget, Inhelder, & Szeminska, 1948/1960).

Finally, tricked by perceptual features of objects and events, preoperational children of 3 or 4 years of age have not yet attained **identity constancy.** In other words, they do not realize that qualitative characteristics of individuals, such as their sex or species (e.g., dog or cat), are permanent, despite changes in the way they appear. Making use of a trained black cat named Maynard, DeVries (1969) looked at the gradual development of identity constancy. Masks resembling a dog or rabbit's head were placed on Maynard, and children between the ages of 3 and 6 were questioned about what they thought the animal was. Then Maynard was unmasked, and the children were questioned again. The youngest subjects showed no identity constancy; the animal changed species whenever the mask was fitted or removed. At an intermediate age, children believed that Maynard's name changed when he wore a mask, but not his species. By 5 and 6 years of age, they understood that Maynard's identity always remained the same, despite alterations in his appearance.

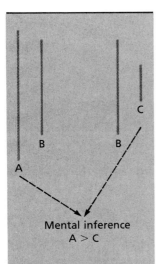

Figure 6.7. Example of a problem that requires children to make transitive inferences. After being shown a pair of sticks in which A > B, followed by a second pair in which B > C, the preoperational child cannot make the mental inference that A > C. In contrast, the concrete operational child is able to do so.

Summary of the Preoperational Stage. How can we pull the diverse cognitive characteristics of the preoperational stage together into a succinct, unified description of what Piaget believed the preoperational child to be like? Flavell (1963), a well-known Piagetian scholar, indicates that Piaget viewed all of the traits we have mentioned as expressions of a single, underlying cognitive orientation. He suggests that we could select any single preoperational characteristic and show how it implies several others; taken together, the attributes point to a view of preoperational thought as

. . . bear(ing) the impress of its sensory-motor origins. . . . It is extremely concrete . . . slow and static, concerned more with immobile, eye-catching configurations than with more subtle, less obvious components . . . it is unconcerned with proof or logical justification and, in general, unaware of the effect of its communications on others. In short, in more respects than not, it resembles sensory-motor action which has simply been transposed to a new arena of operation. (Flavell, 1963, p. 162)

New Research on Preoperational Thought. The results of many investigations carried out during the last two decades indicate that under optimal conditions, preschoolers are far more competent, logical thinkers than Piaget recognized. Piaget's failure to acknowledge the positive thought capabilities of young children can be attributed in large measure to the tasks he used to investigate their cognitions. In many instances, they contained unfamiliar elements or too many pieces of information for a young child to assimilate. As a result, the responses of preschoolers did not fully reflect their abilities. Also, as Gelman (1979) suggests, Piaget and his followers overlooked naturally occurring instances of preschoolers' reasoning that did not fit very well with his definition of preoperational thought. Let's look at some examples that illustrate these points.

Egocentrism and Animism. Are young children really so egocentric that they believe that an observer standing in a different location sees the same thing that they see? Children's responses to Piaget's three mountains task suggest that the answer is "yes," but more recent studies say "no." New investigations indicate that the age at which children demonstrate nonegocentric perspective-taking is heavily influenced by such task variables as the nature of the test display and the type of response required of the child. For example, Borke (1975) presented 3- and 4-year-olds with scenes containing familiar toy objects. Children's ability to recognize how a scene looks from a doll's vantage point was assessed by having them rotate an exact replica of the scene on a turntable until the doll's view was in front of them. Under these conditions, preschool children could assess the doll's perspective quite well.

Nonegocentric responses also appear in young children's everyday interactions with people around them. When showing a picture to an adult, children as young as 2 will turn it so it is oriented to the adult's perspective (Lemperers, Flavell, & Flavell, 1977). Gelman and Shatz (1978) observed that 4-year-olds use shorter, simpler utterances when talking to 2-year-old children than when talking to adults. In addition, their speech to adults includes hedges and expressions of uncertainty about factual information, indicating that they are aware that adults are better informed than they are. Thus, in communicating with others, children are clearly able to take the needs and capacities of listeners into account, something that they would not be able to do if they were staunchly egocentric (Gelman, 1979).

Piaget concluded that young children's egocentrism is responsible for their tendency to attribute lifelike characteristics to inanimate objects. But recent studies show that, because Piaget asked children about unfamiliar objects such as the clouds, sun, and moon, he overestimated their tendency to think in an animistic fashion (Bullock, 1985; Dolgin & Behrend, 1984). When Dolgin and Behrend (1984) questioned 3- to 9-year-olds about a large number of items varying in familiarity, all the children rarely attributed inappropriate characteristics to very typical animates (e.g., a human baby or adult) or inanimates (immobile objects such as rocks). They did make more errors on items that were less typical. Inanimate objects that were both self-moving and animate-appearing, such as cars and airplanes, yielded an especially large number of mistakes from young children. Apparently, self-movement is a very potent animistic characteristic for preschoolers, so much so that, when it occurs in objects they know little about, they may presume that other animistic properties (e.g., being able to think, feel pain, and misbehave) are there as well. But such animistic responses do not result from a generalized belief on the part of children that inanimate objects are alive. Rather, they result from incomplete knowledge about the properties of some objects with which children have had limited experience.

Illogical Characteristics of Thought. A host of studies have reexamined the question of whether the collection of illogical characteristics that Piaget ascribed to preschool children really reflects their cognitive capacities. Like the studies on egocentrism and animism reported above, these investigations show that when traditional Piagetian tasks are simplified and children are asked about objects and events with which they are very familiar, preschoolers display unexpected cognitive competencies.

For example, Anderson and Cuneo (1978; Cuneo, 1980) reexamined the question of whether preoperational children's thinking is *centered*. Preschoolers were asked to rate how happy a very hungry child would be to get different cookies to eat. The stimuli consisted of rectangular cookies whose height and width varied systematically. Children as young as 3 simultaneously took into account both height and width in judging the desirability of the cookies. They showed no evidence of centering on one relevant dimension to the neglect of the other.

Research by Markman (1979a) raises questions about the extent to which preschool children are *perception-bound* in their approach to conservation problems and suggests that the phrasing of an examiner's questions can have a profound effect on how well children perform. Markman gave children standard number conservation problems using small toy items, such as plastic soldiers. For children in one condition, she called them "soldiers," a term that focuses on the individual elements. For those in another condition, she referred to them as an "army," a term that emphasizes the whole group, or collectivity of items (e.g., "What's more, my army, your army, or are they both the same?"). Four-year-old children performed much better in the collectivity condition. Apparently, referring to objects as a collection enables young children to transcend the influence of misleading perceptual cues in conservation of number problems.

When asked to reason about everyday event sequences, preschoolers do not focus on *states* to the neglect of *transformations* of objects. Gelman, Bullock, and Meck (1980) showed 3- and 4-year-old children "picture stories" depicting familiar and unfamiliar event sequences (see Figure 6.8) in which one of the three items in each sequence was omitted. When asked to fill in the missing position from three choice cards, both 3- and 4-year-olds made few errors when dealing with either type of event sequence. In a related study, Gelman and her colleagues presented children of this age with story sequences in which the middle items were always missing and asked them to choose the absent component from four choice cards (refer again to Figure 6.8). The investigators found that 80 percent of the 3-year-olds and 90 percent of the 4-year-olds could pick cards appropriate for both left-right and right-left "readings" of stories. Contrary to Piaget's characterization of preoperational thought as *irreversible,* children were able to represent simple event sequences reversibly.

Gelman and Baillargeon (1983) believe the results of such studies indicate that preschool children show the rudiments of logical operational abilities long before the onset of Piaget's concrete operational stage. They acknowledge that preschool children's ability to reason logically is not as well developed as that of the elementary school child, for they do fail standard Piagetian tasks of conservation, class inclusion, and seriation. But when the number of elements in tasks is scaled down (e.g., when a conservation of number task contains only three elements instead of six or seven),

Figure 6.8. Stimuli used by Gelman, Bullock, and Meck (1980) to find out whether preschool children understand basic object transformations and can represent them reversibly. For the picture sequences on the left, children filled in a missing picture to show that they understood transformations of objects. Some sequences depicted familiar events (e.g., a cup breaking), whereas others showed unfamiliar events (e.g., sewing up a cut banana or writing on an apple). In the sequences on the right, young children's understanding of reversibility was tested. The middle items were missing, and children had to enter components that reversed the effects of one another. *(From R. Gelman, M. Bullock, & E. Meck, 1980, "Preschoolers' Understanding of Simple Object Transformations,"* Child Development, 51, 692, 693. © *The Society for Research in Child Development, Inc. Adapted by permission.)*

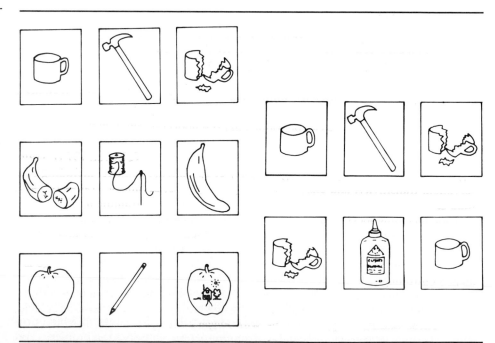

preschoolers perform quite successfully (Gelman, 1972). Such findings suggest that like other Piagetian tasks, traditional conservation problems mask the preschool child's logical competencies. One recent study showed that many 5-year-olds who pass a standard conservation of number task will spontaneously count or match the items in each row before giving a conserving response (Fuson, Secada, & Hall, 1983). Three- and 4-year-olds may be able to count and match rows of three items, but having to do so with seven is beyond their capacity. Under such circumstances, they may fall back on less mature, perceptual strategies for handling the task, and their ability to approach the problem logically will not be evident because of the complexity of the conservation task set before them.

However, a cautious approach to this explanation of young children's failure on standard conservation problems is appropriate, for not everyone agrees with it. Halford and Boyle (1985) recently argued that scaling down conservation of number tasks for young children so that they contain a countable number of elements means that they are no longer true conservation problems! A child who is capable of logical operations should be able to *mentally reverse* a transformation in a conservation problem without counting or matching. Halford and Boyle agree with Piaget that 3- and 4-year-olds do not really understand conservation.

But if we combine Halford and Boyle's argument with the research described above on preschool children's positive cognitive achievements, we obtain a clearer understanding of how children do emerge from the preoperational stage with a flexible capacity for manipulating reality internally and logically. The development of logical operations is a gradual process in which children use increasingly sophisticated mental as opposed to perceptual approaches to solving problems. Siegler (1981; Siegler & Robinson, 1982) indicates that in the case of conservation of number, the youngest preschool children rely on their perceptions of which row is longer in almost all cases—for both large and small arrays of items. But soon they start to solve conservation of number problems containing very few items using empirical strategies—by counting or pairing objects in the two rows. Later on, they extend these strategies to problems with larger numbers of items. Eventually they develop a mental understanding that number remains the same after a transformation as long as nothing is added or taken away, and they no longer need to rely on outside verification. This model of conservation acquisition shows preschool children passing through several phases of understanding. In doing so, it acknowledges preschoolers' positive cognitive accomplishments in a way that Piaget did not, but it is still consistent with Piaget's conclusion that a true, mental understanding of the principle of conservation is not present until the early school years.

Training Logical Operational Abilities. That the attainment of logical operations is a gradual acquisition helps explain why many studies show that more mature performance on Piagetian tasks can be trained in preschool children. It makes sense that children who possess part of a capacity are more likely to benefit from training than those who possess no understanding at all (Inhelder, Sinclair, & Bovet, 1974). Training has been successful in inducing a variety of operational abilities, including conservation, transitivity, and class inclusion (Beilin, 1978; Bryant & Trabasso, 1971; Judd & Mervis, 1979; Murray, 1978). In addition, a variety of training methods seem to work, including social interaction of nonconservers with more capable peers; adult instruction in which contradictions in children's logic are pointed out and correct explanations given; and training that helps children remember the component parts of the problem. However, training is not equally effective for all children. Age is a major controlling factor (Beilin, 1980). Three-year-olds, for example, can be trained, but they do not improve as much as 4- and 5-year-olds, and the effects of training young preschool children rarely generalize to unfamiliar tasks (Siegler, 1981; Field, 1981). These findings suggest, in line with Piaget's theory, that children with the simplest available cognitive structures will try to accommodate to new information, but they cannot do so as successfully as older children who possess more developed operational schemes.

Taken together, recent research on preoperational thought indicates that preschool children have the beginnings of a variety of logical structures that help them understand and predict their world. Although they still have a great deal of developing to do, the younger child's mind is considerably more coherent and organized than Piaget indicated it was (Flavell, 1985).

The Concrete Operational Stage (7–11 Years)

Operational Thinking. Piaget viewed concrete operations as a major turning point in cognitive development. When children attain this stage, their thought bears a much closer resemblance to that of adults than to the younger sensorimotor and preoperational child (Piaget & Inhelder, 1967/1969). According to Piaget, concrete operational reasoning is flexible, organized, and logical. This advance is evident in the school-age child's performance on a wide variety of problems that involve operational thinking—conservation, transitivity, and hierarchical classification, and, in addition, problems that require the child to reason about spatial relationships among objects. We will see as we discuss these achievements in the sections that follow that children do not grasp them all at once. Rather, they are mastered in a gradual, sequential fashion over the middle childhood years.

The Horizontal Décalage. For Piaget, conservation was the single most important cognitive achievement at the concrete operational stage, for it provides unequivocal evidence of the presence of mental operations (Brainerd, 1978). The conservation tasks depicted in Figure 6.4 are achieved one by one during the concrete operational stage. Piaget used the term **horizontal décalage**[4] to refer to the sequential mastery of concepts across different content areas within a single stage (Brainerd, 1978). In the case of conservation, he predicted that concrete operational children will always conserve number (which can be empirically verified) before they conserve length, mass, and liquid, and this pattern of development has been documented in several follow-up investigations (Brainerd & Brainerd, 1972; Gruen & Vore, 1972). Another horizontal décalage is the achievement of conservation of liquid and mass before weight, and conservation of weight before volume (Brainerd, 1978). Užgiris (1964) tested this sequence in children from first through sixth grade and found that 93 percent of them conformed to this order.

Horizontal décalages have been discovered in other cognitive contents at the concrete operational stage. Piaget assumed that there was parallel development in transitivity, number conservation, and class inclusion, which he grouped together as *logico-arithmetic operations* (Brainerd, 1978). Although he believed they were all achieved at about the same time in the early elementary school years, several recent investigations reveal that transitivity tests are passed first (during the late preschool years), then conservation of number (during the early elementary school period), and finally class inclusion (late elementary school years) (Achenbach & Weisz, 1975; Brainerd, 1974; Winer & Kronberg, 1974). Piaget thought that the mastery of these operations was closely tied to the elementary school child's increased facility with quantitative and numerical tasks, but recent research contradicts this assumption. As shown in Box 6.2, preschool children demonstrate some surprising numerical skills. Still, most of what people come to know about mathematics is acquired after early childhood, and elementary school children do have a more quantitative, measurement-oriented approach to many tasks and problems than do preschoolers (Flavell, 1985).

---

[4] Décalage is a name Piaget used to refer to a progression of development that is uniform, or invariant, for all children. Vertical décalage refers to development through the four major Piagetian stages, while horizontal décalage is development that takes place within a single stage and is the result of efforts by the child to apply newly attained structures to a variety of content areas.

Box 6.2
Young Children's Understanding of Number: More Than Meets the Eye

Theory. Because Piaget was interested in how children reason about number without counting in the number conservation task, he missed what early counting behavior reveals about very young children's appreciation of number concepts. After conducting extensive research on preschoolers' counting behaviors, Rachel Gelman and C. R. Gallistel (1986) concluded that although preschool children are not as numerically competent as older children, they clearly have some quantitative ability. Gelman and Gallistel's remarkable findings on what preschoolers do and do not understand about *how to count, what to count,* and *basic arithmetic operations* are summarized below.

Research. As long as they work with a small set of items, children as young as 2½ understand the basic principles of *how to count.* Preschoolers often use unique names for numbers in counting, but these are applied systematically and are always drawn from one of two ordered verbal lists: count words and the alphabet. For example, a preschooler can be seen counting a 3-item array by reciting "2, 6, 10" or "A, B, C." Gelman and Gallistel believe the lists are initially used idiosyncratically because children have not yet memorized the socially accepted order of number labels. However, even 2-year-olds will use as many verbal tags as there are items to be counted, assign the tags in a stable order to the array of items, and respond to the question, "How many?" by giving the last tag applied. When preschool children make errors in counting, they tend to run over or under by only one tag. That their errors are not extreme is an indication that they have an implicit understanding of

counting principles. As they spontaneously exercise their counting abilities, preschoolers gradually adopt conventional counting labels by accommodating to the feedback of parents, teachers, and older children.

Young children also have a very broad and flexible conception of *what to count.* Although some investigators used to think that the rigid, "perception-bound" preschooler would only count collections of identical objects (things of the same color or same item type), Gelman and Gallistel's research shows that they are quite willing to count heterogeneous sets, and variations in color, size, and type of toy have little effect on their counting accuracy.

Finally, counting seems to serve as the basis for development of the ability to engage in simple *arithmetic operations.* That is, the numerical reasoning involved in addition and subtraction at first depends on the counting process. With small set sizes of three or four items, even 3- and 4-year-old children demonstrate an understanding of addition and subtraction. The following 3-year-old child's behavior is a typical demonstration of how preschoolers rely on counting to solve simple addition problems:

Father: How much is two and three?

3-year-old son: [Holding up his right hand he counts] *One, two, three. That's three.* [Keeping three fingers on his right hand upright, he holds up a closed left hand and raises two fingers, one after the other.] *That's two.* [Then he puts together the fingers that are upright and counts them.] *One, two, three, four, five.* (Gelman & Gallistel, 1986, p. 170)

According to Gelman and Gallistel, young children's arithmetic reasoning gradually moves from the ability to manipulate specified, countable items to the more advanced capacity required by Piaget's number conservation task in which the child under-

stands that an *uncounted* array of items, when rearranged, retains the same quantity. Although the preschool child lacks this latter ability, Piaget was wrong to equate failure to conserve with an inability to reason numerically. Preschool children clearly have coherent number concepts at a very early age, long before they are able to pass Piaget's traditional conservation problem.

Applications. Gelman and Gallistel's work reveals that when permitted to exercise their own spontaneous counting strategies, all children come to count correctly at their own initiative. Their findings suggest that adults refrain from overcorrecting preschoolers' idiosyncratic number labels. Forcing children to count conventionally or to deal with large arrays of items before they are ready is likely to overload their memories, cause frustration, and transform their intrinsically systematic counting behavior into random, disorganized responding. Sometimes children err in their application of counting principles, but errors are not an indication that children do not know how to count. They merely suggest a need for more practice to perfect the counting skill. Pointing, touching objects, using fingers, and counting out loud are strategies that all young children rely on to successfully apply their early number concepts, and adults should not discourage children from using them. According to Vygotsky's theory of private speech (discussed at the end of this chapter), a child's tendency to count out loud can be taken as an indication of the difficulty of a particular numerical task and the demands that it places on the young child's attention. As counting and arithmetic operations become well practiced and routinized, children naturally stop counting out loud and begin to use more efficient, internalized counting procedures.

Spatial Operations. In addition to logico-arithmetic operations, the concrete operational child masters some *spatial operations.* These are geometrical in nature, for they deal with the *distance* of objects from each other, as well as with *projective concepts,* which tell us about the spatial relationships of objects to one another.

The conservation paradigm provides a good example of the new understanding of distance that is attained at the concrete operational stage. Between two small toy trees standing apart from one another on a table an examiner places a block or thick piece of cardboard. The child is asked whether the trees are still the same distance apart. Preoperational children believe that the distance has changed — in other words, that a filled-up space does not have the same value as an empty space.

According to Piaget (1946/1969; 1946/1970b), operational thinking permits children to integrate the spatial dimension of distance with other physical dimensions, such as time and speed. However, the understanding of such relationships is only gradually achieved over the course of the elementary school years and seems to form yet another horizontal décalage. Piaget found repeatedly that elementary school children first recognize the *positive* relationship that exists between distance and speed (e.g., in a given amount of time, a bunny can travel *farther* down a road than a skunk if the bunny runs *faster*) and between distance and duration (e.g., at a given speed, a bunny can travel *farther* down a road than a skunk if the bunny runs for a *longer* period of time). Only later on do they understand the *inverse* relationship that exists between duration and speed (e.g., for a given distance, a bunny will travel for a *shorter* period of time than a skunk if the bunny runs *faster*). In a recent study of children's appreciation of the relationships between these variables, Acredolo, Adams, and Schmid (1984) reported results in agreement with Piaget's findings. Elementary school children were told several versions of a story in which a bunny and a skunk raided a garden of cabbages. When frightened by a barking dog, the animals ran down a road and out of the garden. In telling the story, the examiner gave the child bits of information about two of the dimensions of interest (e.g., the bunny ran just as fast as the skunk but the bunny ran farther) and asked the child to determine the third piece of information (in this case, whether the bunny and skunk ran for an equally long period of time or whether one ran longer). As shown in Figure 6.9, from first grade on, children performed at a high level when asked to coordinate distance and speed, and almost as well when asked to coordinate distance and duration. But just as Piaget predicted, recognition of the inverse relationship between speed and duration was a later acquisition, emerging around the middle of the elementary school years.

Piaget investigated children's projective understanding of space by having them

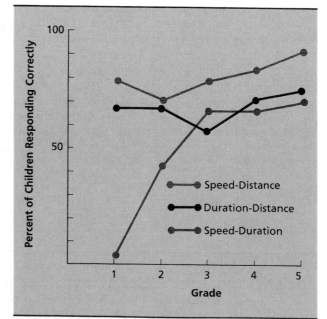

Figure 6.9. Elementary school children's understanding of the relationships between distance, time, and speed in the Acredolo, Adams, and Schmid (1984) study. In agreement with Piaget's work, the speed-distance and duration-distance relationships were understood before the speed-duration relationship. *(From C. Acredolo, A. Adams, & J. Schmid, 1984, "On the Understanding of the Relationships Between Speed, Duration, and Distance,"* Child Development, 55, *2156.* © *The Society for Research in Child Development, Inc. Reprinted by permission.)*

produce representations of large-scale environments — spaces too big to be seen all at once so that the locations of objects and routes of movement within the space have to be mentally constructed. Recent investigators refer to these mental constructions of environmental space as **cognitive maps.** In one study, Piaget had children reconstruct the vicinity in which they lived by building a scene using toy objects to represent buildings, parks, bridges, and rivers. He also asked them to draw maps showing how they get from home to school or to other familiar landmarks. Successful performance on such tasks requires advanced perspective-taking skills. Children must coordinate and integrate successive perceptions of an environment, since all parts of the space to be represented cannot be viewed at the same time and from a single vantage point. In reconstructing a familiar environment, children below the age of 7 could not arrange the placement of landmarks in terms of an organized spatial whole. Instead, landmarks remained unrelated to other landmarks and were poorly integrated with routes of movement through the setting (Piaget & Inhelder, 1948/1956; Piaget, Inhelder, & Szeminska, 1948/1960).

An extensive body of follow-up studies on children's cognitive maps of large scale spaces lends support to Piaget's assumption that the nature of children's spatial representations undergoes important developmental changes from the preschool through the elementary school years. Taken together, the research suggests a specific developmental sequence. Preschool children's spatial reconstructions focus on separate landmarks. Their representation of the locations of landmarks relative to one another is fragmented and disconnected. During the early elementary school years, *landmark knowledge* becomes subordinate to *route knowledge*. Children begin to represent landmarks in terms of an organized sequence along a route of travel, but the relationship of different routes to one another within a large-scale space is not well coordinated. Finally, over the course of the elementary school years, *configurational knowledge* of the environment emerges and improves. Children are able to form an overall representation of a large-scale space in which various landmarks and routes are spatially coordinated with one another, something like a survey map (Siegel, 1981; Newcombe, 1982). However, we must be cautious about interpreting this developmental progression as solely the result of the elementary school child's greater logical competence. Even adults, when introduced to a new environment, initially form fragmented spatial representations that are heavily dependent on landmarks. As they become familiar with the setting, their sketch maps become more organized and accurate (Evans, Marrero, & Butler, 1981). It is possible that the restricted range and variety of travel permitted to young children plays a significant role in their limited spatial representations. In support of this conjecture, one study showed that preschoolers and kindergartners could produce well-organized maps of their own homes, but their ability to represent unfamiliar settings was much more limited (Hart, 1979).

Limitations of Concrete Operational Thought. Although thinking is much more adultlike than it was earlier, the stage of concrete operations suffers from one important limitation. Elementary school children can only think in an organized, logical fashion when dealing with concrete, tangible information they can directly perceive. Their mental operations do not work when applied to information that is abstract and hypothetical. A good illustration of this limitation comes from solutions of concrete operational children to problems involving transitivity. During the stage of concrete operations, children can easily make the mental inference that if stick A is longer than stick B and stick B is longer than stick C, then A is longer than C. However, if they are asked to deal with an entirely hypothetical version of the problem, such as "Susan is taller than Sally and Sally is taller than Mary. Who is the tallest?", they have great difficulty. It is not until around age 11 or 12 that this type of transitivity problem is easily solved. We will see more examples of the "concreteness" of concrete operational thinking shortly when we compare it to formal operational thought.

Extensions and Applications of Concrete Operations: Children's Understanding of Humor. New logical capacities that emerge during the concrete operational stage have been helpful in explaining changes in children's appreciation of humor during middle childhood. Humor depends on cognitive surprise, incongruity, and discrepancy from the expected. A Piagetian model of humor comprehension would suggest that joke material moderately divergent from the child's current cognitive structures is likely to be regarded as most interesting and funniest (Brodzinsky & Rightmyer, 1980).

Elementary school children's logical operational abilities enable them to understand jokes that are beyond the comprehension of the preschool child. In fact, if you observe a group of preschoolers for examples of what they find amusing, you will see that their humor reflects their recent preoperational mastery of the symbolic function. Endless play with words and calling objects by names that the child knows to be incorrect are sources of great delight to children below the age of 6. School-age children no longer find such wordplay funny. Instead, their humor begins to resemble that of adults. For example, exchanges of riddles and puns that require an understanding of the double meanings of words are common social pastimes among elementary school children:

"Hey, did you take a bath?" "No! Why, is one missing?"

"Order! Order in the court!" "Ham and cheese on rye, your honor."

Preoperational children may laugh at these jokes because they are nonsensical, but they cannot explain what is funny about them. In contrast, concrete operational children's capacity to reverse their thinking and go back and forth between several different meanings of key words permits them to understand that a joke or riddle can have two possible interpretations, a usual one and an unusual one, the latter of which is funny because it is incongruous (Shultz & Pilon, 1973; Shultz & Horibe, 1974; Sutton-Smith, 1975). In fact, children can be given a riddle with two possible answers, as follows:

"Why did the old man tiptoe past the medicine cabinet?"
Serious answer: "Because he dropped a glass and did not want to cut his foot."
Joking answer: "Because he didn't want to wake up the sleeping pills."

Under these conditions, preschool children will choose the serious and joking answers with equal frequency. They show no awareness of the double meaning on which the riddle depends. By age 7, children begin to choose the joking answer more often, and they improve in their ability to do so over the elementary school years (McGhee, 1974).

In comparison to elementary school children, adolescents are able to understand more sophisticated and abstract humor (Couturier, Mansfield, & Gallagher, 1981). In addition, they tend to favor anecdotes and spontaneous wit over the memorized jokes that are preferred by younger children. Aside from these differences, once logical operations have been attained, the nature of humor appreciation remains essentially the same from middle childhood into adult life (McGhee, 1979).

Concrete operational capacities have also been used to explain elementary school children's more mature understanding of a very serious topic — the concept of death. Refer to Box 6.3 to find out how this concept changes from early to middle childhood, as well as how successful Piagetian theory has been in accounting for this change.

The Formal Operational Stage (11–15 Years)

The concrete operational approach to solving problems is rational and logical, but it does not deal with possibilities — that is, potential relationships that are not easily detected in the real world or that might not exist in it at all. Beginning somewhere around 11 years of age and becoming fully developed at about age 15, the capacity for abstract thinking appears. At the formal operational stage, adolescents become capable of reasoning in a manner like that of the scientist searching for solutions in the laboratory. Concrete operational children can only "operate on reality," but formal operational adolescents "operate on operations." It is in this sense that their thinking is truly abstract, for they can derive new, more general logical rules through internal

---

FOCUS ON THEORY, RESEARCH, AND APPLICATIONS

Box 6.3
The Development of Children's Understanding of Death

Children's understanding of death is the focus of a rapidly growing empirical literature. In a review of many studies, Mark Speece and Sandor Brent (1984) came to some general conclusions about how the concept of death changes with age, and whether the transition from preoperational to concrete operational reasoning helps to explain its development.

Theory. Children's understanding of death is an extension of their growing appreciation of the difference between animate and inanimate objects. A mature concept of death contains three components: (1) *permanence:* the understanding that once a living thing dies, it cannot be brought to life again; (2) *nonfunctionality:* the understanding that all life-defining functions cease at death; and (3) *universality:* an appreciation of the fact that all living things eventually die. Many investigators have expressed the belief that concrete operational children's ability to classify, understand transformations, and take the perspective of others underlies a mature understanding of death. If this is true, then an appreciation of the three components of the death concept should appear in the early elementary school years and be associated with successful performance on concrete operational tasks.

Research. To find out about children's understanding of death, most researchers ask children such questions as, "What is death?" "Can a dead person come back to life?" "Can a dead person think, talk, dream, or feel?" "Does everybody die?" "Will you die?" According to Speece and Brent, a large number of studies confirm that a mature understanding of death is achieved around the age of

7, at about the same time that children make the transition from preoperational to concrete operational thought.

Before children understand that death is permanent, they believe that dead things can return to life spontaneously as the result of magic, wishing, thinking, praying, or medical intervention. In addition, many young children regard death as a sleep from which people wake up or a trip from which they return. Young children also view dead things as retaining some functional capacities, and they realize certain functions cease at death before they understand that other ones do. For example, children are more likely to attribute continued cognitive functioning to the dead (e.g., thinking and dreaming) than physiological functioning (e.g., heart beating and breathing). They first seem to understand nonfunctionality in terms of its most visible aspects. Only later do they recognize that more subtle aspects of functioning also end with death. Before children understand that death is a universal experience, they believe that certain people do not die. People they exclude from dying are those with whom they have close emotional ties, such as family members and teachers, or who are like themselves—other children. Some evidence exists that children understand that others will die before they appreciate that they themselves will die. When they finally grasp that they too will eventually die, they believe that it will be in the very remote future (which is, of course, true for most children), but they do not seem to appreciate the idea that their own death could occur at any time.

Although a mature understanding of death does appear in the early elementary school years, Speece and Brent express skepticism about how adequately the Piagetian transition to concrete operations explains it. A close examination of the research literature reveals that the linkage between

performance on Piagetian tasks and children's understanding of death is inconsistent from study to study. Also, although 7 is the usual age at which the death concept is adultlike, many studies still report wide individual differences. Speece and Brent believe that children's direct experiences with death may exert as powerful an influence on their understanding as their stage of cognitive development. For example, some research shows that children find it far more difficult to understand the permanence and universality of plant death than human and animal death. Most children have witnessed the revival of wilted plants after they are watered, but they have not seen any comparable kind of event in the death of people or animals. Speece and Brent conclude that the cognitive-developmental basis of children's understanding of death requires much more in the way of empirical confirmation.

Applications. Children's ideas about the nature of death change with age, and these differences are important when the death of a relative or a pet places an adult in the position of explaining to a child what has happened. Explanations likely to facilitate children's understanding are ones that are simple, direct, draw from the child's concrete experiences, and provide factual information. Since children sometimes have magical answers to questions about death, adults who provide explanations can have children explain back to them what has been told, so that opportunities are available to correct distortions and misperceptions (Koocher, 1974). Some investigators believe that providing children with the opportunity to talk about death leads them to worry less about it. If so, then open and honest discussions with children contribute to both their cognitive appreciation of the concept and their emotional well-being.

reflection and manipulation of ideas. Concrete props and things are no longer required as contents of thought (Brainerd, 1978; Inhelder & Piaget, 1955/1958; Flavell, 1985). The major cognitive achievements of the formal operational stage are spelled out in more detail below, along with some examples.

Abstract, Scientific Thinking. According to Piaget, there are two major characteristics of thought that separate the formal operational adolescent from the concrete operational child. The first is called **hypothetico-deductive reasoning.** It refers to the way in which formal operational problem-solving strategies differ from those that are available to the younger child. When faced with a problem, the adolescent comes up with a *general theory* that includes all of the possible factors that may affect the outcome, *deduces* from it specific *hypotheses* that may obtain in the situation, and then systematically tests these hypotheses by seeing which ones do in fact occur in the real world. Thus, adolescent problem-solving strategies begin with possibility and proceed from there to reality, whereas concrete operational children begin with reality, but when the most obvious relationships are not verified in the situation, they are incapable of thinking of other alternatives and cannot solve the problem.

Adolescent performance on Piaget's famous *pendulum problem* illustrates this new hypothetico-deductive approach. Provided with strings of different lengths, objects of different weights to attach to the strings, and a bar from which to hang the strings, subjects are asked to figure out what makes a pendulum swing more rapidly in one case than another. Faced with this problem, formal operational subjects come up with four possible hypotheses: the length of the string, the weight of the objects hung on them, how high the object is raised before it is released, and how forceful a push the object is given. Then, by varying one factor at a time while holding all the others constant, they try out each of the various possibilities systematically, eventually discovering that only the length of the string makes a difference. In contrast, concrete operational children experiment with the pendulum, but their methods are unsystematic, and they cannot separate out the effects of relevant variables. For example, they may test for the effect of string length without simultaneously holding weight constant. In addition, they fail to notice the potential influence of variables that are not immediately suggested by the concrete materials of the task — the height and forcefulness with which the pendulum is released.

The second important characteristic of formal operational thought is that it is **propositional** in nature. Adolescents can focus on verbal assertions and evaluate

During the stage of formal operations, adolescents solve problems by generating all of the possible hypotheses that could occur in a situation. Then they systematically test their predictions to see which ones apply in the real world. (David R. Frazier Photolibrary)

their internal, logical validity without making reference to real-world circumstances. In contrast, concrete operational children can only evaluate the logic of statements by considering them against concrete, perceptible evidence. A study by Osherson and Markman (1975) illustrates this difference. A pile of poker chips was placed on a table, and an examiner indicated that some statements would be made about the chips and the subject was to respond to each statement as true, false, or uncertain. In one condition, a chip was concealed in the hand of the experimenter, who then said, "Either the chip in my hand is green or it is not green," or "The chip in my hand is green and it is not green." In another condition, the experimenter held up either a red or a green chip and made the same statements. Elementary school children focused on the concrete properties of the poker chips in the examiner's hand rather than on the purely logical characteristics of the statements. As a result, they replied that they were uncertain to both statements when the chip was hidden from view; and when it was visible, they judged both statements to be true if the chip was green and false if it was red. In contrast, adolescents were able to evaluate the logic of the statements as propositions. They were able to appreciate the fact that the "either-or" statement is always true and that the "and" statement is always false, regardless of any available empirical evidence.

The formal operational thinker is able to reason not only about single propositions, but also about relationships that hold between two or more propositions and how one proposition might imply or contradict another. Also, propositional statements do not have to refer to real objects and events at all, and they do not need to be factually correct assertions. Because the essence of formal operational reasoning is that it is no longer restricted to extrapolations of external reality, Piaget believed that language plays a far more central role in thinking at this stage than it did earlier. The abstract mental abilities of which the adolescent is capable rest on the capacity to use language-based systems of representation that are entirely divorced from concrete reality, such as those that exist in higher mathematics, and on the capacity to formulate language-based conjectures that deal with abstract concepts, such as "What is truth?" "What is justice?" "How are freedom and democracy related?" (Brainerd, 1978).

Adolescent Idealism and Egocentrism. Given these new abstract powers of logical reasoning, it is not surprising that adolescents spend a good deal of time thinking about and constructing grand systems that have to do with religion, ethics, and other philosophical questions. The ability of adolescents and young adults to reason about the way things could be, instead of confining themselves to the way that they are, leads them to be idealists and social reformers. However, because of their limited life experience, their theories are often naive and unsophisticated. Piaget believed that the insistence of adolescents that reality submit itself completely to their idealistic constructions marks the appearance of a new form of egocentrism. In **formal operational egocentrism,** the adolescent rigidly insists that it is only through the implementation of their grand idealistic systems that the world can become a better place to live. Gradually, as the result of efforts to implement their hypotheses, adolescents refine and adjust them to take account of the fact that many realities of human behavior do not conform to abstract ideals and systems of logic (Inhelder & Piaget, 1955/1958).

Elkind (1976; 1981) describes a second type of egocentrism that results from the adolescent's new abstract reasoning powers — in particular, the ability to imagine what others may be thinking. It is called the *imaginary audience*, and it refers to the belief that others are as concerned with and critical of the adolescent's behavior as adolescents are themselves. As Elkind puts it:

> When adolescents begin thinking about other people's thinking, they often assume that other people are thinking about them. They become, as a matter of fact, convinced

that others are as concerned with them and their appearance as they are with themselves. Hence the "self consciousness" so characteristic of young adolescents has to be attributed, in part at least, to the appearance of formal operations. While the physical and physiological transformations undergone by the adolescent play a part in this self consciousness, its cognitive determination must also be recognized. (Elkind, 1976, p. 101)

In a recent study, Gray and Hudson (1984) reported that adolescents' preoccupation with an imaginary audience increases during the transition from concrete to formal operations and then declines as formal operational abilities become better established. Nevertheless, some developmental psychologists reject the assumption that the imaginary audience actually results from egocentrism—a formal operational inability to distinguish between the abstract perspectives of self and others. They prefer to view it as an outgrowth of advances in perspective-taking during the adolescent years that cause young people to be increasingly concerned with what others think of them (Lapsley, 1985; Lapsley et al., 1986).

New Research on Formal Operational Thought. Investigators conducting follow-up research on formal operational thought have asked some of the same questions that have been posed about the cognitive achievements of earlier stages: Is there evidence that formal operations appear earlier in development than expected, and can they be trained in children who, according to Piaget's stage theory, should not yet be capable of formal operational reasoning?

A number of studies show that even early elementary school children are capable of understanding some forms of propositional logic (Ennis, 1971; Kodroff & Roberge, 1975; Paris, 1973; Taplin, Staudenmayer, & Taddonio, 1974). For example, they can handle if . . . then statements of implication, and even deal with more than one premise at a time, as long as the premises are stated in the affirmative. For example, Brainerd (1970) found that 8-year-olds could draw a correct conclusion when given the following problem:

Premise 1: If Jack washes the dishes, then his father will be very pleased.
Premise 2: If Jack's father is very pleased, then Jack gets 50¢.
Premise 3: Jack washes the dishes.
Conclusion: Jack gets 50¢.

However, when some of the premises are stated in the negative, elementary school children have great difficulty and usually draw erroneous conclusions, as is the case with the following problem:

Premise 1: If there is a knife, then there is a fork.
Premise 2: There is not a knife.
Erroneous Conclusion: There is not a fork. (Kodroff & Roberge, 1975)

But adolescents and adults also experience difficulty with this kind of problem and frequently come up with incorrect conclusions! Therefore, these findings raise important questions about Piaget's theory. They suggest that some propositional reasoning abilities identified by Piaget as formal operational appear much earlier than Piaget thought they could. They also indicate that many adolescents and adults may not be fully formal operational, as they do not differ very much from younger children in some of their spontaneous reasoning abilities. These are major concerns about the validity of Piaget's stage of formal operations, and we consider them in light of additional evidence below.

Can formal operational abilities be trained in concrete operational children? There is evidence that training does lead to improved performance on formal operational tasks, such as the pendulum problem and conservation of volume[5] (Brainerd & Allen,

---

[5] Piaget identified conservation of volume as a formal operational task (see Figure 6.4), as it involves understanding proportional relationships among length, width, and depth. Concrete operational children have difficulty separating out the relevant variables in this problem.

1971; Siegler, Liebert, & Liebert, 1973). However, the effects of training last longer and generalize far more easily to new tasks when subjects are adolescents and college students who do not spontaneously display formal thinking rather than elementary school children (Greenbowe et al., 1981; Kuhn, Ho, & Adams, 1979). Formal operational training research leads to conclusions like those we discussed earlier with regard to the training of preschool children on concrete operational tasks. Concrete operational children show the beginnings of more complex, abstract reasoning skills; their capacities are greater than Piaget believed them to be, but they are not as cognitively competent as adolescents and adults. The glimmerings of formal operational structures are first invoked among elementary school children on simple tasks, like the affirmative propositional reasoning problems illustrated above. Gradually they become more generalized, better integrated with other competencies, and more solidified and stable (Flavell, 1985).

If the beginnings of formal thinking are present at an early age, then why is it that many college students, and adults in general, do not spontaneously manifest the reasoning abilities required by Piaget's formal operational tasks (Keating, 1980; Kuhn, 1979; Neimark, 1975)? One interpretation is that many people never reach Piaget's highest stage of development. However, Kuhn and her collaborators (1979) suggest that this conclusion is not correct for most individuals—at least for people who are of average intelligence and above (Weisz & Zigler, 1979). The fact that adolescents and college students manifest formal operational abilities very quickly and at a high level after training indicates that they do not lack abstract reasoning competencies. Instead, it seems that people are most likely to display formal operational thinking in situations and contexts in which they have had extensive experience. This interpretation is supported by DeLisi and Staudt's (1980) finding that college students show formal operational reasoning in accordance with their college majors. If specific experiences and areas of specialization make a difference in the maturity of thought that individuals display, then assumptions made about formal operational competence based on single tasks and small samples of behavior are likely to be very misleading. Formal operational abilities have not been found in a number of preliterate cultures, but lack of schooling and urban experience, rather than absence of cognitive competency, probably explains these findings as well (Glick, 1975).

PIAGET'S WORK ON LANGUAGE AND THOUGHT

Throughout our discussion of Piaget's stages, we have noted important controversies and new findings that suggest that Piaget's theory is not entirely correct. Recall that unlike many of his contemporaries, Piaget de-emphasized the importance of language as a primary source of cognitive development. Yet another controversy arose early in Piaget's career over this idea. A major challenge came from a creative young Russian psychologist, Lev Semanovich Vygotsky (1896–1934), whose research was unknown in the United States until its translation into English in the 1960s. Since then, Vygotsky's work has steadily gained in stature within the field of child development.

Piaget's Studies of Egocentric Speech

The work reported in Piaget's first book, *The Language and Thought of the Child* (Piaget, 1923/1926), includes some of the most well-known and highly debated of his research (Lloyd, 1983). A major Piagetian theoretical construct—egocentrism—was first formulated in these early studies as Piaget saw evidence for it in children's spontaneous use of language. Because Piaget believed that young children's language was influenced by their underlying cognitive orientation, he looked for evidence of the quality of their cognitive structures and the logic of their thinking in their verbal utterances. Carefully observing the speech of children enrolled in the kindergarten at the Rousseau Institute in Geneva, Piaget reported that from a third to a half of the utterances of children below the age of 7 could be classified as **egocentric speech** — speech either not directly addressed to another individual or not expressed in such a way that others could easily understand its meaning. When children use egocentric speech, no attempt is made to adapt the utterance so that it communicates a message clearly to another person. In fact, often children do not even seem to care whether others nearby are really listening!

Piaget observed instances in which children mimicked the verbalizations of other nearby people, carried on verbal *monologues* in which they talked out loud at great length while involved in a solitary activity, or engaged in *collective monologues* in which two or more children in a group spoke, but their verbal utterances were not meaningful and reciprocal responses to one another. By calling such speech egocentric, Piaget expressed his view that it was an indication of the young child's cognitive immaturity. Young children, Piaget interpreted, engage in egocentric speech because they cannot take into account the perspectives of others. For this reason their talk is often "talk for self," and when they speak they merely run off their own thought sequences in whatever preexisting form they happen to occur, regardless of whether it is meaningful or understandable to a listener.

According to Piaget, increasing cognitive maturity and social experiences with peers eventually bring an end to egocentric thinking. Through arguments and disagreements with agemates, children are repeatedly confronted with evidence that others hold viewpoints different from their own. As children become less self-centered and more logical between the ages of 4 and 7, Piaget believed that egocentric speech declines and is gradually replaced by socialized speech involving the capacity to take the perspective of others and engage in real social exchange of ideas.

Vygotsky: Challenges to Piaget's Ideas

As Piaget's work on language and thought spread to other European countries and to the United States, child psychologists and educators began to challenge his ideas based on their own observations of children (Berk, 1985). But the most powerful objection came from Vygotsky, who disagreed with Piaget's idea that young children's language is largely egocentric and nonsocial, and that egocentric speech plays no useful role in the cognitive life of the child.

Vygotsky pointed out that the monologues noticed by Piaget actually occur most often in certain situations, a fact that he believed provided an important clue to their significance. When children engage in tasks in which they encounter obstacles and difficulties, the incidence of such speech nearly doubles. Under these circumstances, what children seem to do is to try to solve problems by talking to themselves:

> "Where's the pencil? I need a blue pencil. Never mind, I'll draw with a red one and wet it with water; it will become dark and look like blue." (Vygotsky, 1934/1962, p. 16)

Such speech, Vygotsky believed, was indeed quite communicative. Vygotsky regarded it as *communication with the self* for the purpose of self-guidance and self-direction.

In sharp contrast to Piaget, Vygotsky thought that language, even in the very youngest children, was inherently social, and that the speech-to-self that Piaget called egocentric actually had its origins in early social communication. As children's ability to use language to communicate with others develops, the quantity and complexity of their self-communication also expands, and it becomes increasingly effective in helping them plan, organize, and execute their actions as they go about daily activities. According to Vygotsky, children's speech-to-self does not disappear with age, as Piaget suggested. Instead, it gradually goes underground and becomes internalized as silent, inner speech — the continuous verbal dialogue that each of us carries on with ourselves and that we use to guide our behavior in everyday situations.

According to Vygotsky, private speech serves a self-guiding function. It helps children plan and organize their own behavior, especially when faced with difficult tasks. (Nancy Sheehan)

The differences between Piaget's and Vygotsky's theories are summarized in Table 6.2. Over the last two decades, a number of research studies have been carried out to determine which of these two approaches is correct. Almost all of the findings have sided with Vygotsky, and as a result, most researchers now call the phenomenon **private speech** instead of egocentric speech. It is now well documented that the majority of children's private utterances serve a self-guiding function, and that children use more private speech when tasks are difficult, after they make errors, or when they are confused about how to proceed (Berk, 1984; Deutsch & Stein, 1972; Dickie, 1973; Kohlberg, Yaeger, & Hjertholm, 1968). In addition, recent studies refute Piaget's conclusion that children who engage in high rates of private speech are not adept at social communication. To the contrary, preschoolers who "talk to themselves" a great deal engage in high rates of social participation and are more socially competent than those who use little private speech. This finding supports Vygotsky's claim that such speech originates in and grows out of early experiences in social communication (Kohlberg, Yaeger, & Hjertholm, 1968; Berk, 1984; 1985). Furthermore, recent evidence suggests that bright, cognitively advanced children use more private speech at earlier ages, a result that conflicts with Piaget's assumption that it is an indication of the young child's cognitive immaturity (Berk, 1986a; Berner, 1971; Kleiman, 1974; Kohlberg, Yaeger, & Hjertholm, 1968).

Vygotsky believed that all higher mental functions have social origins and appear, at first, on an interpersonal plane, between individuals, before they exist on an intrapsychic plane, within the individual (Vygotsky, 1930–1935/1978; Wertsch, 1986). He stressed the central role of social communication in the development of children's thinking by conceiving of children's learning as taking place within the **zone of proximal development**. Tasks within a child's zone of proximal develop-

Table 6.2. Differences Between Piaget's and Vygotsky's Theories of Egocentric or Private Speech

	PIAGET	VYGOTSKY
Developmental significance	Represents an inability to take the perspective of another and engage in truly relational and reciprocal communication	Represents externalized thought; its function is to communicate with the self for the purpose of self-guidance and self-direction
Course of development	Declines with age	Increases at younger ages and then gradually loses its audible quality to become internal thought
Relationship to social speech	Negative; least socially competent and least cognitively mature children use more egocentric speech	Positive; most socially competent and most cognitively mature young children use more private speech
Relationship to environmental contexts	———	Increases with task difficulty. Private speech serves a helpful self-guiding function in situations where more cognitive effort is needed to reach a solution

Source: L. E. Berk, 1984, ''Development of Private Speech Among Low-Income Appalachian Children,'' *Developmental Psychology, 20,* 272. Copyright 1984 by the American Psychological Association. Reprinted by permission of the author.

ment are ones that are too difficult to be done alone, but they can be accomplished with the verbal guidance and assistance of adults or other more skilled children. Then children can take the language of these verbal instructions, make it part of their private speech, and use this speech to organize their own independent efforts in the same way (Berk, 1986b). Vygotsky's suggestion that communication, and with it culture and social life, has a profound effect on how children think has recently captured the attention of American developmental psychologists.

It is important to keep in mind that Piaget certainly did not ignore the importance of social interaction for cognitive development, but his emphasis was very different from Vygotsky's. Piaget did not think that verbal guidance of adults was a major instrument of cognitive change, but he did stress the importance of interaction with peers. Peers, he believed, were more likely than adults to challenge children's egocentric beliefs and cause them to become aware of different points of view (Piaget, 1927/1929). There is good evidence that arguments and disagreements with peers do facilitate the development of children's thinking (Kerwin & Day, 1985). But so does the help and guidance of an adult (or more capable peer) on tasks too difficult for the child to do alone (Brown et al., 1983). So Piaget and Vygotsky really emphasized different facets of children's social experience, both of which contribute to cognitive development.

In conclusion, recent evidence on children's private speech stands as another important challenge to Piaget's assumption that the young child is egocentric. Nevertheless, Piaget's concept of egocentrism continues to influence new research. It has served as the inspiration for investigations of the development of children's perspective-taking skills, which we will discuss in Chapter 11. Recent studies show that the ability to take the perspective of others is not absent in preschool children and then suddenly present during the school years. Instead, it develops gradually over childhood and adolescence, becoming increasingly refined and more abstract.

Clarity, Correctness, and Completeness

We have seen that Piaget's theory of cognitive development has been the subject of intense critical scrutiny in recent years. Taken together, the wealth of accumulated research reveals that it has a number of important shortcomings. Flavell (1982a; 1982b) summarizes these as problems of clarity, correctness, and completeness.

Some of Piaget's ideas about cognitive development are not very clearly spelled out. Concepts like adaptation, organization, and equilibration are fuzzy and imprecise ideas, and it is not always clear exactly what they refer to in the child's cognitive activities. As an example of this problem, at the beginning of this chapter, we indicated that Piaget considered children's cognitive structures to be characterized by *organization*. That is, he assumed that the structures of each stage are strongly interdependent and form a coherent, integrated whole. But we do not always know in what way Piaget understood the diverse achievements of each stage—take, for example, conservation, transitivity, class inclusion, and the variety of spatial concepts identified with concrete operations—to be bound together by a single, underlying form of thought.

Throughout this chapter, we have indicated that a number of Piaget's ideas about development are now considered either incorrect or only partially correct. For example, infants achieve a number of sensorimotor milestones at earlier ages than Piaget anticipated. Preschool children are not egocentric in their thinking when tasks are simplified and made relevant to their everyday experiences. The fact that both preoperational and concrete operational children can be trained to exhibit more mature modes of thinking indicates that Piaget's assumption that they must act directly on the environment in order to revise their cognitive structures is too narrow a notion of how learning takes place. Cognitive development is not always self-generating, and left to their own devices, children may not necessarily notice important conflicting elements in a situation and come up with an improved interpretation of experience. Current evidence indicates that, in contrast to what Piaget believed, "there is no single, overarching process or principle sufficient to describe how all cognitive-developmental advances are made" (Flavell, 1985, p. 290).

Piaget's theory of development is also regarded as incomplete. Whereas logical structures are undoubtedly an important part of human mental life, investigators have begun to question whether they are the general, underlying basis of all human thought that Piaget believed them to be. Developmental psychologists now think that the Piagetian model cannot account for the complexity and variety of human thought phenomena (Flavell, 1985; Legendre-Bergeron & Laveault, 1983). Other equally important cognitive accomplishments in such areas as attention, memory, communication, and creativity have been identified, and we will discuss them in subsequent chapters.

Of all the questions that have been raised about the validity of Piaget's theory, the one that is most hotly debated is the question of whether cognitive development really does advance through a series of broad, qualitatively distinct stages. We take up this issue in the section below.

Are There Stages of Cognitive Development?

The type of developmental pattern emphasized by Piaget is one in which the child acquires a set of unique, interrelated cognitive abilities during a circumscribed time period that, taken together, form a major stage. Recently, this idea has come under heavy attack. Stages, in the strict Piagetian sense of the word, are *discontinuous* developmental entities. If they exist, children must display distinct competencies that they were not capable of at an earlier point in time. But throughout this chapter we have presented evidence that indicates that most cognitive changes proceed slowly and gradually; very few abilities are absent during one period of development and then suddenly present at another. Also, there seem to be few periods of developmental quiescence and equilibrium. Instead, if you look at what is happening in any one of Piaget's stages, the child seems to be constantly in the process of modifying structures and acquiring new competencies.

These difficulties have led some investigators to completely discard the notion of stage as an adequate account of how cognitive development takes place. For example, Gelman and Baillargeon (1983) favor a view that rejects the existence of stages and broadly applicable cognitive structures. Instead, children are seen as gradually working out their understanding of each type of task and domain of knowledge separately, and their thought processes are regarded as basically the same at all ages; they are just present to a greater or lesser extent. These assumptions — that cognitive development is *continuous* and that children's performance is context-specific — form the basis of the major current alternative to Piaget's theory: the information processing approach, which we take up next in Chapter 7.

Although some theorists have dismissed the idea of stage, it is important to keep in mind that whether cognitive stages do or do not exist is as yet an unsettled issue. A number of cognitive-developmental theorists think the stage notion continues to be valid, even though Piaget's strict definition of the term requires modification. For example, Flavell (1982a) argues for a more dynamic, less tightly knit concept of stage, one in which certain competencies take a long time rather than a short time to achieve. From this point of view, a stage simply refers to an extended period of related developmental changes. Flavell retains the stage idea because he finds it difficult to accept the notion that the child's cognitive acquisitions are so completely variable across tasks and situations as to have no coherence and unique identity. As he indicates, "Perhaps what the field needs is another genius like Piaget to show us how, and to what extent, all those cognitive-developmental strands within the growing child are really knotted together" (Flavell, 1985, p. 297).

PIAGET'S APPLIED LEGACY: IMPLICATIONS FOR EDUCATION

Piagetian ideas not only have been a mainstream force in American developmental psychology but also have had an impact on the design of educational programs for children, especially at the preschool and early elementary school levels. A number of educational principles derived from Piaget's theory have served as the foundation for a wide variety of Piagetian-based curricula that have sprung up around the United States over the past several decades. These principles include:

1. *A focus on the process of children's thinking, not just its products.* In addition to the correctness of children's answers, teachers must understand the processes children use to get to the answer. Learning experiences that enhance development build on children's current level of cognitive functioning, and only when teachers appreciate children's methods of arriving at particular conclusions are they in a position to provide such experiences.

2. *Recognition of the crucial role of children's self-initiated, active involvement in the activities of the classroom.* In a Piagetian classroom, the presentation of ready-made knowledge by teachers is de-emphasized, and children are encouraged to find out for themselves through spontaneous interaction with the environment. Instead of teaching didactically, teachers arrange situations that stimulate cognitive conflict and disequilibrium. These experiences offer children opportunities for direct physical

In a Piagetian classroom, children are encouraged to explore the environment. They learn from interacting with each other and with the physical world. (Alan Oddie/PhotoEdit)

commerce with their world, and they also promote social interaction with peers so that limited, one-sided mental structures can be challenged through contact with the viewpoints of others.

3. *A de-emphasis on teaching efforts aimed at making children adultlike in their thinking.* Piaget referred to the question, "How can we speed up development?" as the "American question." Among the many countries he visited, psychologists and educators in the United States seemed most interested in what techniques could be used to accelerate children's progress through the stages. Piagetian-based educational programs accept his firm belief that premature teaching may be worse than no teaching at all, because it leads to superficial acceptance of adult formulas rather than true cognitive understanding (Johnson & Hooper, 1982). In fact, some Piagetian concepts, like the horizontal décalage, underscore the idea that there is a certain advantage to slow development. It allows children to broaden and consolidate the achievements of one stage so a firm, solid foundation exists as a basis for effective transition to the next.

4. *Acceptance of individual differences in developmental progress.* Piaget's theory assumes that all children go through the same stage-wise sequence of development, but they do so at different rates. Therefore, teachers must make a special effort to arrange classroom activities that are appropriate for individuals and small groups of children, rather than for the total class group (Ginsburg & Opper, 1979). In addition, since individual differences in development are expected, assessment of children's educational progress should be made in terms of each child's own previous course of development, rather than against normative standards provided by the performance of same-age peers (Gray, 1978).

Criticisms have been made of Piagetian educational applications. Since much of Piaget's work has involved the investigation of mathematical and scientific concepts, some claim that his educational recommendations are only useful for teaching these subjects, and that they are less relevant to other areas, such as language arts (Roberts, 1984). Also, Piaget's insistence on the primacy of children's physical interaction with the environment is no longer fully accepted, even by sympathetic educators who have devoted great effort to implementing his ideas in classrooms (Hooper & DeFrain, 1980). Other theoretical approaches, such as the Vygotskian position, show that young children can and do use language-based routes to knowledge. But despite these shortcomings, perhaps the most powerful legacy of Piaget's lifelong effort to understand how children's cognition develops has been to provide educators with new ways of observing, understanding, and enhancing the thought processes of children and to offer strong theoretical justification for less traditional, more child oriented approaches to classroom teaching and learning.

CHAPTER SUMMARY

1. Influenced by his early background in biology, Piaget viewed cognitive development as an adaptive process. As infants and children act directly on the environment, their mental structures evolve through a series of stages in which they achieve a better and better adaptive fit with external reality. Piaget's conception of an active, thinking organism with a mind inhabited by rich structures of knowledge introduced American psychology to a radically new view of the nature of the child.

2. According to Piaget, children pass through four stages of development: (1) the sensorimotor stage; (2) the preoperational stage; (3) the concrete operational stage; and (4) the formal operational stage. The stages form an invariant maturational sequence and are hierarchically related. Structures, or schemes, undergo qualitative transformations as children move from one stage to another. The functions of organization and adaptation, with its two complementary processes of assimilation and accommodation, explain how change in structures takes place.

3. During the six substages of the sensorimotor period, the neonate's reflexive, sensorimotor action patterns gradually become more flexible and refined. The sensorimotor stage brings with it the attainment of object permanence; the appearance of goal-directed, intentional behavior; and the beginnings of imitation and play. Before infants have developed these capacities, they use the circular reaction to build and consolidate schemes. The egocentrism that Piaget ascribed to the very young infant diminishes and disappears as sensorimotor schemes become less self-centered and more outer-directed and as infants gradually master the permanence of objects. Although Piaget's general sequence of sensorimotor development has been supported, new studies reveal that infants attain some sensorimotor milestones, such as imitation, secondary circular reactions, and object permanence, earlier than Piaget expected.

4. Aside from the rapid increase in use of symbolic schemes, Piaget described preoperational children in terms of their cognitive deficiencies rather than their strengths. The most pervasive deficit of this stage is preoperational egocentrism, which Piaget regarded as largely responsible for the rigidity and illogical nature of young children's thought. Preoperational thinking is described as animistic, perception-bound, centered, irreversible, and focused on states rather than dynamic transformations of objects. In addition, preoperational children reason transductively as opposed to inductively or deductively. Because of these cognitive inadequacies, they fail to pass a wide variety of Piagetian tasks, including conservation, class inclusion, and transitivity.

5. Children of the preoperational stage are not as cognitively inept as Piaget made them out to be. When preschool children are given problems that are scaled down in complexity or that contain familiar items, their performance appears more mature. In addition, preoperational children can be trained on Piagetian tasks. These findings suggest that young children have preparatory structures for logical reasoning that were not recognized by Piaget.

6. At the concrete operational stage, children can think in terms of logical, reversible mental operations. The ability of elementary school children to pass Piagetian conservation, class inclusion, and transitivity problems provides evidence for the emergence of logical structures. Piaget recognized that some concrete operational abilities are achieved earlier than others, and he used the term horizontal décalage to refer to the gradual, orderly acquisition of logical concepts. During the concrete operational stage, children master a variety of spatial operations. However, concrete operational thought is limited in that children can only reason logically when dealing with concrete, tangible information. They cannot think abstractly.

7. At the stage of formal operations, the capacity for abstract, scientific reasoning appears. Formal operational thinking employs hypothetico-deductive reasoning and is propositional in nature. Piaget believed that language-based systems of representation play a more central role in the development of cognitive structures at this stage than they did earlier. At first, the capacity for abstract reasoning produces new forms of egocentrism, but these decline with increased life experience and as formal operational thinking becomes better established. New studies of formal thought indicate that the glimmerings of abstract reasoning are present at earlier ages than Piaget expected and that formal thinking tends to emerge in contexts in which individuals have had extensive background and experience.

8. In his early work, Piaget viewed egocentric speech as

an indication of preschool children's inability to take the perspective of others and engage in truly relational and reciprocal communication. A powerful objection to Piaget's interpretation came from Vygotsky. He viewed egocentric speech as serving a positive, self-guiding, and self-communicative function and believed that it is eventually internalized as inner, verbal thought. Recent research supports Vygotsky's interpretation rather than Piaget's. Today, child psychologists do not think the young child is as egocentric as Piaget believed.

9. Piaget's theory has been the focus of intense critical scrutiny in recent years. Currently, the most hotly debated question is whether or not cognitive development can be organized into a series of stages. Some investigators reject Piaget's notion of stage, while others retain the idea but argue for a modified, less tightly knit stage concept than was originally specified by Piaget. Piaget's theory has had a lasting impact on the design of educational programs for young children.

IMPORTANT TERMS AND CONCEPTS

clinical interview
contents
structures
schemes
functions
adaptation
assimilation
accommodation
equilibration
organization
sensorimotor stage
preoperational stage
concrete operational stage
operations

formal operational stage
object permanence
intentional, goal-directed behavior
circular reaction
sensorimotor egocentrism
deferred imitation
make-believe play
sociodramatic play
preoperational egocentrism
animistic thinking
conservation
perception-bound
centration
states versus transformations

reversibility
transductive reasoning
class inclusion
transitivity
identity constancy
horizontal décalage
cognitive maps
hypothetico-deductive reasoning
propositional thinking
formal operational egocentrism
egocentric speech
private speech
zone of proximal development

Two Young Girls at the Piano, by Pierre Auguste Renoir.
The Metropolitan Museum of Art, Robert Lehman Collection, 1975. (1975.1.201)

CHAPTER 7

Cognitive Development: An Information Processing Perspective

The information processing view of cognition arrived on the scene of child development in part as a reaction to the inadequacies of Piaget's theory. Unlike the Piagetian view, information processing does not provide a single, unified theory of children's thinking. Instead, it is an approach adhered to by developmental psychologists studying a variety of aspects of cognition, from perceptual, attentional, and memory processes to complex problem solving. Their combined goal is to find out how children and adults operate internally on different kinds of information, coding, transforming, and organizing it as it makes its way through the cognitive system.

This chapter provides an overview of the information processing perspective. First we review its history and major models of the human mental apparatus. Next we discuss the development of three basic operations that enter into all of human thinking: perception, attention, and memory. We also consider how children's growing knowledge of the world and awareness of their own mental activities affect these basic operations. Then we review one current effort to combine all of the various components of information processing into a general, integrative theory of problem solving that captures the development of children's thinking as a whole. Our discussion concludes with an evaluation of the strengths and weaknesses of the information processing approach as a framework for understanding cognitive development. Finally, throughout this chapter we point out the relevance of a great many research findings for the education of children.

THE INFORMATION PROCESSING APPROACH

Most information processing theorists have in common a view of the human mind as a complex, symbol-manipulating system through which information flows, operating much like a digital computer. Information from the environment is *encoded,* or taken in by the system and stored in symbolic, representational form. Then a variety of internal processes actively operate on the information, *recoding* it, or revising its symbolic structure if its form proves to be initially inadequate, and *decoding* it, or deciphering and interpreting its meaning by comparing and combining it with other previously stored information. Thus, while inside the system, information is manipulated and transformed in ways that permit the storage and generation of new representations. When these cognitive operations are completed, output in the form of a behavioral performance, a final solution to a task or problem, is generated.

Consider this brief description of the information processing view of mental functioning, and perhaps you already see that the computer analogue as a device for understanding cognition has a number of attractive features. It shares with the other major competing approach to cognitive development, Piagetian theory, the now commonly agreed upon view of the human organism as an active interpreter and processor of information. But beyond this, the computer model offers theoretical exactitude and precision in a way that many vague, wholistic Piagetian concepts do not. Information processing psychologists use the computer metaphor to help them articulate the precise series of cognitive operations that children and adults execute while performing a particular cognitive task. In fact, the major objective of information processing research is to provide a detailed understanding of what the human cognitive system actually does when faced with a task or problem. Information processing theorists want to know exactly what the mind does first and what it does next. Some try to map the "odyssey of information flow" (Flavell, 1985, p. 76) so precisely and in such detail that the same mental operations can actually be programmed into and run on a computer. Then such computer simulations can be used to make predictions about how children and adults will respond when exposed to particular task conditions and stimulus inputs (e.g., Klahr & Wallace, 1976). Other information processing theorists do not rely on computer simulations to test their ideas, but all of them hold in common a strong commitment to explicit, precisely articulated models of cognitive functioning that can be subjected to direct, empirical verification (Flavell, 1985; Kuhn, 1988).

Besides a growing disillusionment with the adequacy and precision of Piaget's theory, several other trends and influences led information processing to rise to the forefront of the field of child psychology and to be regarded as "*the* leading strategy for the study of cognitive development" (Siegler, 1983a, p. 129). In the section that follows, we consider the history of this burgeoning new emphasis in developmental psychology.

A Short History

Behaviorist Foundations. Historically, American psychologists have always had a special affinity for precise and clearly testable models of human behavior. The forerunner of the current preoccupation of information processing with explicitness and precision was *behaviorist theory*—a popular approach to the understanding of children's thinking into the 1960s. But "thinking," if we take the word, as it is usually taken, to refer to *internal* processes and products of mind, was not thinking at all to traditional behaviorists. They believed that only observable responses of the organism were proper objects of scientific study. Development was merely the progressive shaping of independent acts by environmental stimuli that served as reinforcers. Since all behavior was regarded as under the control of external stimulus events, a **black box model** of learning and cognitive functioning prevailed in which research focused on the stimuli that impinged upon the organism and the responses that emerged. Trying to explain behavior through the inner workings of the black box—by postulating internal, unobservable constructs of mind—was regarded by strict behaviorists as unnecessary and fruitless. Symbolic mental structures like *concepts*, representational labels that stand for the common features of a diverse set of objects, were not regarded by behaviorists as phenomena that had any real existence inside the child's head. Instead, a concept, like "dog" or "cat," was viewed as a verbal label the child had learned, through external reinforcement, to use in the presence of a class of objects with a particular set of stimulus properties, such as fur, four legs, claws, and a tail.

Originally, behaviorists had little interest in children as important subjects of study in their own right. Children were not regarded as unique beings; instead, their behavior was assumed to be governed by the same mechanisms of stimulus-response association as the behavior of all other animal organisms. But when, in the 1960s, behaviorists began to study the responses of children of different ages more carefully than they had before, learning as the gradual accumulation of discrete responses by an essentially passive organism could not account for what they saw.

A major turning point in the willingness of behaviorally oriented child psychologists to speculate about what may be going on inside the black box came from a series of classic studies of children's concept formation, involving **reversal and nonreversal learning,** by the Kendlers (Kendler & Kendler, 1962; 1975). Figure 7.1 shows the kind of experimental situation that the Kendlers used with children. The stimuli presented, in this case cups, differed on two conceptual dimensions — size and color. Children were first rewarded for responding to one dimension, size; that is, they were reinforced for choosing large as opposed to small cups. The other dimension, color, was irrelevant. After learning this first discrimination, they were forced to shift to a new response in one of two ways. In a *reversal shift,* they responded to the same dimension on which they were trained (size), but their choice had to be reversed; they

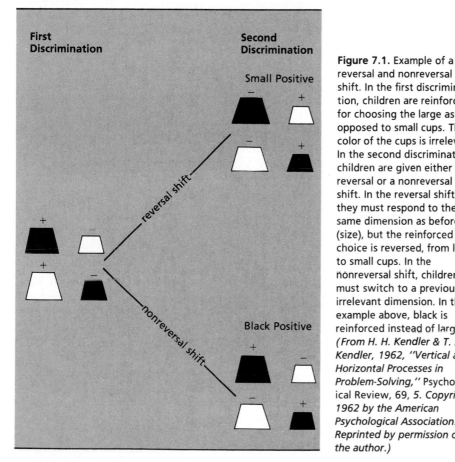

Figure 7.1. Example of a reversal and nonreversal shift. In the first discrimination, children are reinforced for choosing the large as opposed to small cups. The color of the cups is irrelevant. In the second discrimination, children are given either a reversal or a nonreversal shift. In the reversal shift, they must respond to the same dimension as before (size), but the reinforced choice is reversed, from large to small cups. In the nonreversal shift, children must switch to a previously irrelevant dimension. In the example above, black is reinforced instead of large. *(From H. H. Kendler & T. S. Kendler, 1962, "Vertical and Horizontal Processes in Problem-Solving,"* Psychological Review, 69, 5. *Copyright 1962 by the American Psychological Association. Reprinted by permission of the author.)*

had to learn to pick the small cup instead of the large one. In a *nonreversal shift,* the previously irrelevant dimension, color, became relevant; in our example, black was reinforced as opposed to white.

A traditional behaviorist who assumes that concept learning consists of direct connections of external stimuli to overt responses would predict that the nonreversal shift would be learned more quickly than the reversal shift. In the nonreversal shift, only two of the originally established discrete connections must be relearned, whereas in the reversal shift all four must be changed. The Kendlers found that this prediction worked for children under the age of 6, who learned the nonreversal shift faster. But for subjects over the age of 6, the reversal shift was consistently easier, even though it involved reestablishment of a greater number of stimulus-response connections. The inability of traditional behaviorist theory to account for how more-mature children, as well as adults, behaved on these problems led the Kendlers to develop a new, modified behaviorist position called **mediational theory.** What the older subject seemed to be learning in the first phase of this problem was a covert, mediational response — an internal *strategy* for dealing with the task, such as, "It's the size of the cup that matters, not the color." Once constructed, this internal

---

FOCUS ON THEORY, RESEARCH, AND APPLICATIONS

Box 7.1
When Reinforcement
Undermines Performance: The
Overjustification Hypothesis

Theory. Many parents are well aware that reinforcing children with extrinsic rewards, such as money, stickers, or special privileges, for engaging in activities that they are not interested in, or even happen to dislike, increases their engagement in those activities (e.g., Danner & Lonkey, 1981; McLoyd, 1979). An effective way to get children to wash the dishes or clean a messy room is to offer them an attractive reward for doing so. However, research offers an important exception to the behaviorist prediction that pairing an activity with a reinforcer will always increase the child's performance of the activity. The use of extrinsic rewards to reinforce children for activities that are intrinsically rewarding to them — that they like to do for their own sake — can have a detrimental effect on their subsequent interest in the task. Psychologists call this the **overjustification hypothesis.** Providing rewards for engaging in an intrinsically interesting activity overjustifies the activity by leading children to think that it is only worth doing when it results in an extrinsic goal. The overjustification hypothesis emphasizes that it

is the *information conveyed* by an extrinsic reward that determines whether the child will continue to engage in the behavior. In other words, children make cognitive sense out of reinforcers and the circumstances under which adults dispense them, just as they process all kinds of other information in the environment.

Research. Mark Lepper, David Greene, and Richard Nisbett (1973) conducted a formative study of the overjustification hypothesis. They selected preschool children who showed high intrinsic interest in drawing during free play time at school and escorted them to a different setting in which they were asked to draw pictures under one of three conditions. In the *expected reward condition,* children were shown a "Good Player" certificate and told that they could win it by drawing additional pictures. In the *unexpected reward condition,* children were asked if they would draw some pictures without any mention of the extrinsic reward. Then they were unexpectedly presented with the same certificate after finishing their pictures. Finally, in the *control condition,* children were simply asked to make drawings without any promise or offer of a tangible reward.

Observations of the children in their preschool classrooms several weeks later supported the overjustifca-

tion hypothesis. As shown in Figure 7.2, children in the expected reward condition showed much less interest in drawing after the experimental treatment than they did before it. In contrast, those in the other two treatments showed no significant change in interest. The results revealed that when a reward is made contingent on an already-desirable activity, subsequent intrinsic motivation to engage in the activity is undermined.

Follow-up studies have shown that the effect of extrinsic rewards on children's later intrinsic motivation is actually quite complex. The kind of information carried by the reward is quite important. *Task-contingent rewards* administered for simply working at an activity, like those in the study described above, consistently undermine children's spontaneous interest. In contrast, *performance-contingent rewards* that inform children about their competence at the activity do not undermine intrinsic motivation and in some cases may enhance it by increasing children's sense of mastery and self-esteem (Boggiano and Ruble, 1979; Pallak et al., 1982; Swann & Pittman, 1977).

Applications. Intrinsic motivation is a child-rearing and educational goal worth fostering, since it is associated with pleasure derived from the learning process itself, mastery of representation of the common features of the test stimuli controlled the choice of responses. The nonreversal shift took longer for the mediating subject to establish because not only the overt responses, but also the internal representation used to organize and direct the subject's behavior ("Now it's the color of the cup that's important, not its size") had to be changed.

As we will see later on in this chapter, a great deal of recent information processing research on children's cognitive strategies, internal techniques used to encode and interpret stimulus information from the environment, agrees with the Kendlers' finding that young children are far less effective cognitive mediators of environmental inputs than are older children and adults. But the important point about the Kendler research for now is that it revealed that constructs making reference to mental processes were the *only* route to an adequate explanation of the observed behavior of children. Without assuming the existence of internal mechanisms of thought, the difference between younger and older subjects' performances simply could not be understood (Kuhn, 1988).

Today, conditioning studies of children's learning have nearly disappeared from the research literature. As indicated by investigations like those described in Box 7.1,

challenging tasks, and high levels of task involvement and persistence (Gottfried, 1985). An important practical issue is how to use rewards in ways that will maintain and enhance intrinsic motivation. The suggestion derived from studies of the overjustification hypothesis is that rewards will not undermine intrinsic interest if they are administered in a manner that supports children's feelings of competence and self-worth.

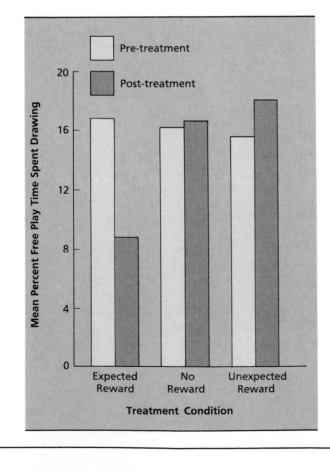

Figure 7.2. Mean intrinsic interest in drawing before and after experimental treatments in the Lepper, Greene, and Nisbett (1973) study. (*From "Intrinsic and Extrinsic Motivation in Children: Detrimental Effects of Superfluous Social Controls" by M. R. Lepper. In W. A. Collins [Ed.], 1980,* Minnesota Symposia on Child Psychology, 14 *[p. 174]. Hillsdale, NJ: Erlbaum. Copyright 1980 by Lawrence Erlbaum Associates. Reprinted by permission.*)

reinforcement, the basic operant conditioning explanation for cognitive performance, is now regarded by most child psychologists as theoretically inadequate. Since the 1960s it has produced little in the way of new, testable ideas about children's learning (Stevenson, 1983). Even the behaviorist school of social learning theory, which stresses observational learning and imitation in addition to reinforcement as basic learning mechanisms, has had to incorporate more cognitive explanations into its accounts of how models affect children's behavior (Bandura, 1986). For example, in an early study, Bandura found that elementary school children who were asked to describe the actions of a model in words — that is, engage in active verbal representation of what they saw — imitated more of the model's actions than children who either sat passively or counted to themselves while they watched, a mental activity that prevented them from internally representing the model's behavior (Bandura, Grusec, & Menlove, 1967).

Compared to modern information processing models of human thinking, the behaviorist verbal mediation approach, in which the possession of a relevant word like "big" or "black" intervenes between an environmental event and an overt response, is a substantial oversimplification of the complex manner in which human beings use symbolic activity to guide their subsequent behavior. But the more elaborate and detailed models of information processing, which try to specify what goes on inside the black box between stimulus and response, can be viewed as sophisticated modern descendants of the behaviorist mediational idea (Brown et al., 1983).

Influences from Cognitive Psychology and Linguistics. The growing commitment of child development researchers to information processing was strengthened by trends in adult experimental psychology. By the 1940s and 1950s, many experimental psychologists had become disenchanted with behaviorism as a viable approach for understanding adult learning and saw the necessity of studying underlying cognitive events (Miller, 1983). In addition, in the late 1950s the ground-breaking work of linguist Noam Chomsky made psychologists patently aware of young children's remarkable ability to comprehend and produce novel language utterances they had never heard before. In between input and output, children appeared to operate in a rule-oriented fashion on linguistic information. Chomsky's work was yet another influence legitimizing complex cognitive activity as a necessary focus of inquiry in developmental psychology (Siegler, 1983a).

The Computer Metaphor. The fields of computer science and cybernetics were major forces in the emergence of information processing as well. The computer-inspired representation of the human mind retained the features of precision and explicitness that had made behaviorism so attractive, but it also provided a more adequate conception of human mental functioning. Both human beings and computers could be thought of as complex, symbol-manipulating systems able to deal with difficult tasks and problems. Since computers were made by human beings, they were invaluable tools in the quest to specify and understand the various components of human symbol manipulation (Newell & Simon, 1972; Siegler, 1983a). Thus, the computer metaphor was used to help analyze thinking into a series of separate internal processes that operated individually on stimulus information and then combined with one another sequentially to generate a final performance. As a result, frames and flowcharts began to be employed to represent the human mental apparatus.

Major Models of the Information Processing System

Atkinson and Shiffrin's Store Model. The most influential of the computer-like conceptualizations of mental functioning is Atkinson and Shiffrin's **store model** of the information processing system (Atkinson & Shiffrin, 1968; Shiffrin & Atkinson,

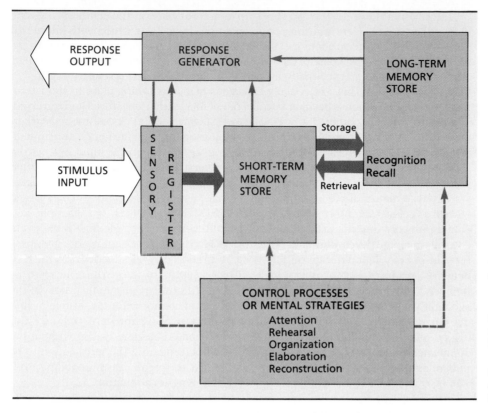

Figure 7.3. Atkinson and Shiffrin's store model of the information processing system. Solid lines indicate paths of information transfer. Dashed lines indicate connections that permit comparison of information residing in different parts of the system; they also indicate paths along which control signals may be sent to activate information transfer. *(From R. M. Shiffrin & R. C. Atkinson, 1969, "Storage and Retrieval Processes in Long-Term Memory."* Psychological Review, 76, 180. Copyright 1969 by the American Psychological Association. Adapted by permission of the authors.)*

1969). Depicted in Figure 7.3, it is called a store model because information is viewed as being held, or stored, in three parts of the system for processing. The three parts — the sensory store, the short-term memory store, and the long-term memory store — correspond to the *hardware* of the system. Atkinson and Shiffrin regard them as inborn and constant across all individuals. All three stores are limited in the speed with which they can process information. In addition, the sensory register and the short-term store are limited in capacity. They can only hold on to a finite quantity of new information, and it can only be retained for a brief period of time before it fades away entirely.

Besides these structural units, the model includes **control processes,** which are like the *software* of the system. Control processes are cognitive strategies that help people increase the efficiency and capacity of the storage bins. For example, given a list of numbers to learn, a standard memory span task that is often used to determine the limits of short-term memory, you can repeat the first ones to yourself while awaiting delivery of the remaining ones, operating on your limited processing space in a fashion that enables more information to be retained than if you used no strategies at all. According to Atkinson and Shiffrin, control processes are not innate; they are learned, and individuals differ from one another in how well they use them.

Look at Figure 7.3 again, and notice how information from the environment moves through the system sequentially. First, it enters the **sensory store.** Here, auditory and visual information are represented rather literally and held very briefly, generally for not more than a few seconds, while being initially processed and transferred to the short-term store. Control processes can be used to influence the workings of the sensory store. For example, people can deploy their attention selectively, screening out information from sensory modalities that are unimportant at the moment, and within a single modality, they can heighten their attention to particular stimuli.

Information flows next to the **short-term memory store,** the central processing unit of the system. Here information is operated on and combined with additional material from long-term memory, the largest processing receptacle containing the accumulated knowledge base of the system. The short-term store is the conscious part of memory. People are not really aware of the activities of the sensory register or long-term store, but they are actively conscious of events taking place in short-term memory as information is brought into and out of focal attention, stored and retrieved, and compared and combined in various ways (Siegler, 1983a). As mentioned earlier, the short-term store is limited in capacity. The sensory register, although also limited, can take in a wide panorama of information at once, but when the input reaches the short-term store, a bottleneck occurs. Only a very limited number of information units can be held there simultaneously. The capacity constraint of the short-term store is not a matter of physical units of material. Instead, it is a matter of *meaningful* pieces, or *chunks,* of information (Miller, 1956; Murdock, 1961). For example, you would probably find the task of holding the following list of single-digit numbers in short-term memory very difficult: 101212323434545. But try chunking or combining them into three-digit numbers, as follows: 101 212 323 434 545. Notice how the task becomes much easier, for only 5 instead of 15 pieces of information need to be retained. But even with chunking, once the limited number of memory slots in the short-term store is occupied, either new information cannot enter the system or, if it does, it will push out existing information. Information in short-term memory also decays quickly. It will be lost within 15 to 30 seconds (Siegler, 1983a) without the application of control processes, such as *rehearsal* (repeating the information to be remembered). The longer the material is maintained, the greater the probability that it will be transferred to the permanent storage bin, long-term memory.

Atkinson and Shiffrin indicate that besides rehearsal, other important control processes have an even greater effect on the permanent retention of information. For example, look at the string of three-digit numbers above once more. Do you see a pattern among them that makes them easier to remember? If so, you employed the control strategy of *organization;* you recoded the material into a new, more tightly organized form that enabled you to retain it more easily. Perhaps you also noticed that one or more of the three-digit numbers was the same as a familiar house number or the first three digits of your phone number. If in trying to remember the numbers you thought of one or more of the chunks in ways like this, you were using a control strategy called *elaboration.* You linked the material to already-existing information in long-term memory, thereby greatly increasing the probability that the new information would be incorporated into the permanent storage bin.

Atkinson and Shiffrin believe that once information enters the **long-term memory store,** the memory traces are permanent. Also, unlike the sensory and short-term stores, the capacity of long-term memory is assumed to be limitless. Inability to remember information stored in long-term memory is considered a problem in *retrieval,* or getting information back from the system. To aid retrieval, control processes dominate the activities of the long-term store, organizing and elaborating on each bit of material, interconnecting it with many other pieces of information, and filing it according to a master plan contingent on contents, very much like a "library shelving system which is based upon the contents of the books" (Atkinson & Shiffrin, 1968, p. 181). Then, if the information is needed at some time in the future, it can be retrieved by following the same strategic plan that was used to store it in the first place.

A considerable amount of research lends support to Atkinson and Shiffrin's store model (Siegler, 1983a). For example, the distinction between short- and long-term memory is supported by the well-known **serial position effect** that occurs in memory tasks involving lists of items. When people are presented with a set of words, numbers, or pictures to remember, immediate recall of a particular item is related to its serial position in the list. If an item occurs in the middle of the sequence, it is less likely to be remembered than if it occurs at the beginning or the end. The advantage of being at the beginning of the list is called the *primacy effect,* whereas the advantage of being at the end is termed the *recency effect.* However, research shows that over time, items at the end of a list will decay from memory, while those at the beginning will continue to be retained (Craik, 1970). The reason, investigators believe, is that those learned last are only held temporarily in short-term memory, while those learned first have had sufficient time to transfer to the permanent memory bank of the long-term store.

In a recent study, Cornell and Bergstrom (1983) demonstrated this very same effect in children as young as 7 months of age. Babies were presented with a list of three photos of women's faces. Then the infants were each assigned to a condition in which the photo that had occupied either the first, middle, or last position in the list was paired with a completely new photo. Memory for the original photo was inferred if infants dishabituated, or spent more time attending to the new picture. As shown in Figure 7.4, when tested immediately after the list presentation, the traditional primacy and recency effects occurred; looking time allocated to the novel face was greatest in serial positions 1 and 3 and least in serial position 2. But when tested after delays of 1 and 5 minutes, recognition of the photo in serial position 3 disappeared. Cornell and Bergstrom's study is consistent with Atkinson and Shiffrin's assumption that the existence of separate short- and long-term memory stores is fundamental to the human information processing system.

Despite such evidence, other findings have led some investigators to reject the memory store model of information processing. For example, the capacity limits of the sensory and short-term stores have been found to be highly variable. Depending on the study, estimates of the retention period for auditory sensory information range from 130 milliseconds to 5 seconds, and for visual information from 250 milliseconds to 25 seconds. Similarly, the capacity of the short-term store, although once thought to be limited to 7 slots (Miller, 1956; Murdock, 1961), actually ranges from 2 to 20

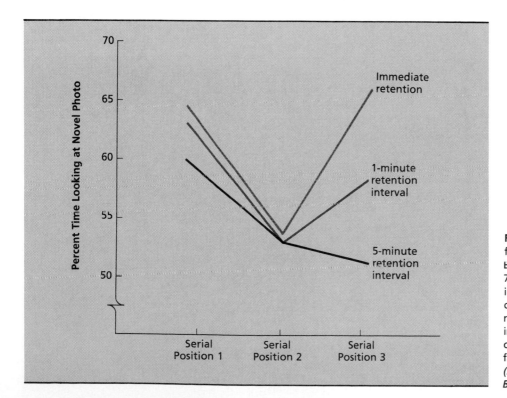

Figure 7.4. Serial position findings in the Cornell and Bergstrom (1983) study of 7-month-old infants. In the immediate retention condition, both primacy and recency effects occurred, but in the delayed retention conditions, recency effects faded and disappeared. *(Adapted from Cornell & Bergstrom, 1983.)*

chunks (Siegler, 1983a). Thus, the existence of separate information stores is called into question by the fact that the capacity parameters of the basic units are slippery and elusive. As a result, some information processing theorists have turned toward a levels of processing approach.

The Levels of Processing Model. The **levels of processing model** abandons the idea of a series of containers with fixed limits on how much information can be grasped at once. Instead, it assumes that retention of information is a function of the depth to which an incoming stimulus is analyzed by the system. For example, a written word can be encoded at a very superficial level, according to its perceptual features (e.g., whether it is printed in capital versus small letters). At a slightly deeper level, it can be encoded according to its phonemic characteristics, or how it sounds. Encoding at this intermediate level is akin to the memory strategy of rehearsal, in which the word is repeated over and over again to oneself. At the deepest level of analysis, the word could be encoded according to its meaning, or its *semantic* features. Here the strategies of organization and elaboration lead the incoming stimulus to be subjected to more extensive cognitive processing (Craik & Lockhart, 1972). In the levels of processing model, control processes or strategies are emphasized. Information that is processed at a very superficial level quickly decays and is soon forgotten, whereas information processed meaningfully and linked with other knowledge is retained for a longer period of time (Craik & Tulving, 1975). Thus, the major interest of the depth of processing theorist is in the various cognitive activities that people engage in that lead them to process information more or less effectively, at deeper versus shallower levels of analysis.

According to the levels of processing view, our limited capacity to handle a large number of stimulus inputs simultaneously is not the result of a fixed store or limited-size memory container. Instead, the limit is imposed by the extent to which we are able to distribute our attention across several activities at once. In this model, the limited-slot idea of short-term memory is replaced by the notion of attention as a limited resource pool from which our information processing activities draw. Attention is demanded by an activity depending on how automatic and well learned the

Once cognitive operations become automatic, they demand little or no attentional resources, and children can engage in several activities at once. For example, this child talks on the phone while writing down a message. (Paul Conklin)

cognitive operations required by the task happen to be. Unskilled subjects must allocate more of their attentional resources, and as a result, attention is drawn away from other operations that they otherwise would be able to engage in at the same time. In contrast, automatic cognitive operations demand little or no attentional capacity, and their execution is not affected by the presence of other tasks occurring simultaneously (Klatzky, 1984). For example, consider the difference between the novice bicycle rider, who is entirely engrossed in controlling the pedals, maintaining balance, and steering, with no attentional resources left over to devote to any other incoming information, and the practiced bicyclist who negotiates easily around the neighborhood, delivers papers, chews gum, and carries on a conversation with a nearby rider, all at the same time.

Questions About Development Raised by the Store and Levels of Processing Models. When applied to development, the two models described above emphasize somewhat different features. The store approach suggests that both the *hardware* of the system, the basic storage capacity of the information processing containers, and the *software,* or deployment of control processes affecting the speed and efficiency with which the system operates, may change with age. In other words, what develops may be both a bigger computer and a wider range of effective programs, or strategies. In contrast, the levels of processing approach suggests that all developmental changes have to do with the *software,* or functioning of the system, and that many operations become less capacity-consuming as the result of years of practice and experience with strategies, which eventually lead to more skillful deployment of the available space (Siegler, 1983a).

What is it that increases with age — the structural hardware, the functional software, or both? The evidence we will review throughout this chapter indicates that without a doubt, functional capacity — the use of control processes — does change with age. Children gradually acquire a variety of strategies for allocating space within the limited-capacity systems that they have, and they learn how to supplement their limited systems with external aids to processing, employing calendars, directories, notebooks, libraries, and even computers to enhance their ability to retain information. It has been difficult for researchers to find out if structural constraints on the system also change with age, but recent evidence seems to indicate that the basic hardware does not change much (Flavell, 1985). In two studies, developmental changes in memory span, the commonly used measure of the capacity of the short-term store, were completely explained by changes in the speed at which children and adults were able to process information. Adults' memory spans are twice as large as those of children of 5 or 6 years of age, but adults are also able to rehearse words and digits more quickly than children. Case, Kurland, and Goldberg (1982) gave college students numbers in a foreign language that they could repeat no faster than 6-year-olds can repeat English numbers. Under these conditions the memory span differences between children and adults completely disappeared. Similarly, Hulme and his colleagues (1984) found that young children who were able to repeat words in a list just as fast as older children and adults remembered an equal number of items. These findings suggest that developmental changes in capacity are the result of changes in acquisition strategies, and that the structural size of the information processing system is fairly constant from early childhood to adulthood.

In an innovative theory that reinterprets Piaget's stage sequence within an information processing framework, Case (1978; 1985) builds on the levels of processing assumption that development consists of better strategy deployment within a system that has a constant processing capacity from early childhood on. Case pictures development as a matter of increases in a computer-like construct he calls mental space, or **M-space.** It refers to the maximum number of schemes that the individual is able to apply simultaneously at any given time (Case, 1972). Piagetian schemes, in Case's theory, constitute the child's mental strategies. As schemes are repeatedly

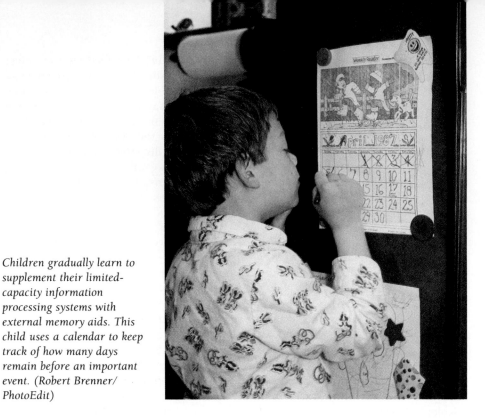

Children gradually learn to supplement their limited-capacity information processing systems with external memory aids. This child uses a calendar to keep track of how many days remain before an important event. (Robert Brenner/ PhotoEdit)

practiced, they become more automatic and require less attentional capacity, freeing up extra M-space for the child to work on combining and consolidating old schemes and generating new ones. Thus, Case views Piaget's stages as a series of increasingly powerful strategies, each of which is a modified but more effective version of previous ones.

Think back for a moment to the various Piagetian tasks we discussed in Chapter 6. In line with Case's theory, a notable feature of them is that at each successive stage of development, a greater number of items must be held in memory and combined with one another to reach a correct solution. In fact, preliminary support for Case's theory comes from evidence that shows a positive correlation between children's memory span and their ability to pass concrete and formal operational tasks (Case, 1977; 1978). Case preserves Piaget's idea that the mental structures of each stage build on and transform the structures of the earlier ones. But his approach is different from Piaget's in regarding the basis of cognitive development as an increase in working memory that results from the practice and routinization of earlier prerequisite schemes.

In summary, the distinguishing features of the levels of processing approach, when compared with the store model, are a focus on allocation of attention as the important factor leading to our limited ability to handle information and a more fluid emphasis on levels of processing rather than on rigid, finite-capacity stores. In addition, the two models differ in how they regard development. The store model allows for both storage capacity and control processes to change with age, whereas the levels of processing approach regards development as limited to more effective deployment of strategies. With regard to this controversy, current evidence leans toward the levels of processing view.

Models of Higher-Order Processing. Other important information processing models place less emphasis on discrete strategies people use to represent and transform information and more on how the system functions in terms of whole programs of information processing. An example is Newell and Simon's (1972) effort to develop a general theory of human problem solving by simulating on the computer the strategies used by human beings to solve a wide variety of problems. Writing programs that represent procedures employed by different people to accomplish a wide variety of logical tasks — from winning a chess game to solving a math problem — the investigators looked for similarities across individuals and situations in an effort to develop a broadly applicable description of human problem solving.

Research on children inspired by such frameworks has proceeded at a far slower pace than the study of the strategies they use to encode and retain discrete pieces of information. However, investigations of how children deal with complex tasks and problems are beginning to appear. In the course of this chapter, we will see several efforts to study children's ability to systematically monitor and regulate their own progress toward task goals and use rule-governed approaches to solve problems.

Despite the different emphases of the various models described above, all information processing theorists agree that memory is critically important to what we usually regard as high-level, cognitive processing. Mental activities that enable us to acquire new knowledge and retrieve it when it is needed are indispensable in tasks involving concept formation, reasoning, and problem solving. Since all thinking involves memory, the bulk of developmental research from the information processing approach has stressed how the ability to remember changes with age. Because many investigators continue to find the demarcations useful, we will retain Atkinson and Shiffrin's fundamental distinctions between the sensory register and short-term and long-term memory throughout our discussion, even though some theorists have completely abandoned them. In the following sections, we consider how sensory functioning, deployment of attention, short-term memory, and long-term memory change with age.

SENSORY PROCESSING

Differentiation Theory

The major perspective on the processing of sensory information is the theory of Eleanor and James Gibson, to which you were introduced in Chapter 4. In that chapter we showed that as the result of central nervous system maturation and repeated exposure to stimulation during the first few months of life, infants become increasingly skilled at detecting stable features of the environment in a complex flux of stimulation. The Gibsons' perspective on perceptual development is referred to as **differentiation theory,** because it views changes in sensory processing as a matter of being able to detect increasingly fine-grained and subtle differences that exist among objects and patterns with age (Gibson, 1970; Gibson, 1979). We introduce the Gibsons' approach more formally here, for it is an important perspective on how stimulation is dealt with at the sensory level, and it applies not only to infants, but also to older children as well.

According to the Gibsons, the organism has a natural tendency to search the environment for *invariant features,* any stable aspect of a stimulus that distinguishes it from its background or from other stimulus objects (Gibson, 1970; Gibson, 1979). The detection of invariant features is an adaptive process, for it reduces ambiguity and uncertainty for the organism by creating order and continuity out of an initially chaotic and fluctuating sensory world. For the young infant, the initial sensory processing task is largely one of locating objects and establishing a stable organization of space. Thus, as we saw in Chapter 4, infants scan the environment, track moving stimuli, bring sources of sound into sight, and gradually respond to a variety of depth cues that assist them in understanding the spatial layout of their environment. Once infants can locate objects in space, they concentrate on sorting them out according to their invariant features (Gibson, 1970). For example, in Chapter 4, we showed how infants first notice the features that distinguish human faces from non-faces, and then go on to make more subtle discriminations between the features of particular faces.

During childhood, the process of differentiation, of detecting the detailed, fine structure of stimuli, continues (Gibson & Spelke, 1983). In fact, Eleanor Gibson (1970) shows how perceptual differentiation is relevant to the way young children go about distinguishing written symbols from one another as they learn to read. Among animal species, only human beings are able to master the fine-grained identification of written symbols well, and it is a peak perceptual achievement.

Applications of Differentiation Theory to Learning to Read

According to Gibson (1970), the process of discriminating alphabet letters from one another is initially a matter of detecting the invariant features of letters as a set of items. Once letters are distinguished from non-letters, children begin to discriminate each letter by its unique pattern of features within the set. By the late preschool years, most children can distinguish numbers and letters from scribbling and pictures, even though they cannot yet identify very many individual letters and numbers.

Gibson and her colleagues (Gibson, Schapiro, & Yonas, 1968) looked at how children tackle the perceptual task of discriminating individual letters by showing them pairs of letters, asking them to indicate whether they were the same or different, and noting how long it took them to make each judgment. Using this information, the investigators constructed tree-like "confusion matrices" that indicated which letters are most often confused with one another. One of these matrices, shown in Figure 7.5, illustrates how children progressively discriminate letters by their invariant features. First they distinguish the set of curved from straight-line letters. Then, within the curved set, round letters are split from the P and R. Finally, within the straight-line set, square letters are distinguished from diagonals.

Gibson's finding that distinguishing among letters with diagonal lines is a difficult task for preschool and early elementary school children fits with other research results (Gibson et al., 1962; Rudel & Teuber, 1963). Rudel and Teuber (1963) gave 3- to 8-year-old children pairs of forms to discriminate, as shown in Figure 7.6. All of

According to Gibson, the early phase of learning to read involves increasingly fine-grained detection of the invariant features of graphic forms. (Mary Kate Denny/ PhotoEdit)

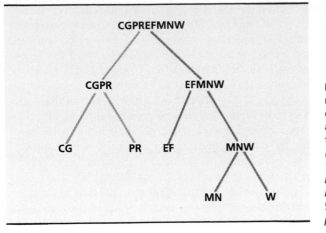

Figure 7.5. A "confusion matrix" indicating how children discriminate among a group of letters according to their distinctive features. *(From E. J. Gibson, 1970, "The Development of Perception as an Adaptive Process."* American Scientist, *58, 106. Reprinted by permission.)*

them easily discriminated the first and third pairs, involving vertical versus horizontal and right-side-up versus upside-down comparisons. However, practically no children younger than 6½ could tell the difference between the two diagonals in the second pair. In addition, the right-left discrimination in the fourth pair was quite difficult.

Does this last comparison remind you of the problems young children have in discriminating certain letters, such as b and d, that are left-right mirror images of one another? Until 7 or 8 years of age, children reverse such letters frequently in their handwriting. In a recent study, Casey (1986) showed that young children who confuse left-right mirror images and cannot be trained to make this discrimination failed to attend to the invariant features of such stimulus pairs. In other words, they did not visually search the stimuli systematically enough to notice the subtle difference between them. But one of the reasons that young children do not attend to diagonal and mirror-image perceptual distinctions may be that up until the time they learn to read, they do not find it especially useful to notice them. In contrast, vertical versus horizontal and upside-down versus right-side-up discriminations are required by many natural experiences in which objects assume an upright orientation against flat surfaces and have to be placed right-side-up to be used effectively. Casey presents convincing evidence that the tendency to tune in to mirror-image differences, as well as adhere to a left-right order of information flow, depends at least in part on experience with reading materials. Thus, the very activity of learning to read has the effect of increasing the variety of perceptual cues to which children respond.

For several decades, a "great debate" has waged among psychologists and educators about how to teach children to read. The controversy has centered around whether to use a *whole word method,* sometimes called the "look-say" approach because children are taught to read by naming whole printed words, or a *basic skills method,* often referred to as the phonics approach because it emphasizes rules for decoding graphic symbols into sounds. The whole word method places heavy emphasis on extracting meaning from the printed page. Its proponents criticize the basic skills approach for fragmenting the reading process, overloading the young child's memory with too many rules, and de-emphasizing meaning and comprehension (which is, after all, the basic goal of reading). In reply, basic skills advocates point out that reading must, in the final analysis, involve an appreciation of the rules by which graphic symbols are translated into sounds, for otherwise young readers cannot decode new words that they have never seen before. However, as Williams (1979) notes, perhaps the real debate is not over which method to use, but at what point to use each and with what emphasis, for research does not show a clear-cut superiority for either one.

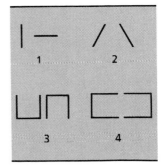

Figure 7.6. Pairs of forms 3- to 8-year-old children were asked to discriminate in the Rudel and Teuber (1963) study. *(From R. G. Rudel & H. L. Teuber, 1963, "Discrimination of Direction of Line in Children."* Journal of Comparative and Physiological Psychology, 56, *893. Copyright 1963 by the American Psychological Association. Reprinted by permission of the APA.)*

Eleanor Gibson's recommendations for helping children develop effective reading skills include elements of both these methods. Early on, parents can create home environments that foster children's appreciation that meaning is derived from the printed page and that also encourage the perceptual learning necessary for sorting out the invariant features of written symbols. When parents read a great deal themselves, they serve as models for children, who then begin to view the activity as an interesting and enjoyable one that they want to do, too. Reading to children shows them that meaningful ideas are extracted from written symbols, and young children's penchant for having the same story read over and over again until they know it by heart provides an ideal circumstance for them to discover the distinctive relationships between the sounds they hear and the letters on the page (Gibson & Levin, 1975).

Gibson believes that when children get to school, formal instruction in reading should relate to the invariant features of the graphic display. Teaching children to notice the common as well as distinctive features of words helps prevent confusions that frequently occur among such words as "soon" and "seen," or "chin" and "chat." Toward the end of the elementary school years, children develop enough knowledge of the structure of printed symbols that the difference between good and poor readers no longer lies in decoding skills but in comprehension (Gibson & Levin, 1975; Williams, 1979). Differentiation theory is most helpful in increasing our understanding of how children go about the perceptual phase of the reading process, and we shall discuss other aspects of reading that depend on additional components of the information processing system in later sections of this chapter.

When parents read to their young children, they help them understand that the ability to decipher written symbols opens up a fascinating new world of stories, facts, and ideas. (Mimi Forsyth/Monkmeyer Press Photo Service)

Enrichment Theory

While differentiation theory is the most widely accepted approach to sensory processing, it is not the only available viewpoint. In differentiation theory, stable aspects of stimuli in the environment — their invariant features — impose order on the child's internal perceptual world. Development is a matter of becoming better at noticing the structure that already exists in external stimuli. In contrast, **enrichment theory** of perception places the locus of perceptual organization inside the individual. From this point of view, perception involves using internal cognitive schemes to interpret incoming stimulus information. As schemes are refined and elaborated over the course of development, perceptual intake from the environment is enriched accordingly. As you probably noticed from this brief description, in viewing perception as largely a matter of mental interpretation of stimulus events, enrichment theory is strongly Piagetian in its orientation, although some information processing theorists subscribe to it as well (e.g., Neisser, 1967). The enrichment position helps remind us of the fine line that exists between perception and cognition. In addition, when we consider both differentiation and enrichment positions together, we are provided with a more complete picture. Both the nature of the stimulus material and the individual's mental approach to the world are influential during each phase of information processing. This is a point to which we will return a number of times in the course of this chapter.

ATTENTIONAL PROCESSES

Attentional processes are of fundamental importance in human thinking, for attention determines the sources of information that will be considered in any task or problem. When attentional processes are operating at their best, the individual picks up aspects of the stimulus environment that have optimal utility for the task at hand, and as a result task performance is more efficient and economical (Gibson & Rader, 1979). Attentional processing develops in a number of ways over the course of childhood. We can better understand these changes by organizing them according to three dimensions that are fundamental to successful deployment of attention: control, planfulness, and adaptability.

Control

As children get older, they become better able to consciously and deliberately focus their attention on just those aspects of a situation that are relevant to their task goals, and their performance is less disrupted by the presence of irrelevant information. A common way in which this increasing control or channeling of attention is studied is to introduce irrelevant stimuli into an experimental task and to monitor the performance of children and adults to see how well they can attend to the central task. A large number of studies of this type show that young children are more distractible than older children and adults; they have considerably greater difficulty inhibiting responses to irrelevant stimulation (Lane & Pearson, 1982).

In some cases, researchers have introduced irrelevant input that resembles the background events that are continuously present in children's everyday learning environments, such as classrooms. In one study, Higgins and Turnure (1984) presented preschool and second- and sixth-grade children with visual discrimination tasks. On each trial, two stimuli were presented, and children had to choose the stimulus of the correct shape and color by pressing a button as quickly as possible. Subjects did the task under one of three extraneous input conditions: in a quiet room (no extraneous input), or with background music played either softly or loudly. The music impaired the performance of younger children, who made more errors and frequently glanced away from the task when it was present. In contrast, the louder the music, the more it facilitated the performance of the older children! The sixth graders were able to actively overcome the background noise by becoming more attentive and acutely focused on the task. However, turning up the radio probably does not result in improved information processing by older children on all types of tasks, even when it is associated with greater attentional effort. In the case of complex tasks, such as comprehension of written text, a great deal of background noise may produce decrements in performance.

In other studies, the irrelevant information is not background stimulation. Instead, it is an intrinsic part of the task itself. Investigations of **incidental learning** are of this type. Since attentional resources are limited, the more people focus their attention on the relevant aspects of a task, the less they remember about incidental or irrelevant aspects. If older children are more selective in channeling their attention than younger children, when asked to remember a particular set of information embedded in a large stimulus array, they should retain a greater number of central items and fewer incidental ones. In an early study of this kind, Maccoby and Hagen (1965) presented third-, fifth-, and seventh-grade subjects with a set of distinctively colored cards with pictures of common objects on them. The cards were shown one by one and then placed face-down in a row in front of the child. The central task involved remembering the location in the row at which each color had been placed. The incidental task, given unexpectedly after a series of trials on the central task, was to match the objects with the colored background on which they appeared. Maccoby and Hagen found that central task performance improved steadily with age. Incidental learning improved slightly until fifth grade and then decreased sharply by seventh grade (see Figure 7.7).

A variety of subsequent studies report results that are consistent with Maccoby and Hagen's finding of an increase in incidental learning until age 11 and a steep decline thereafter (Hagen & Hale, 1973; Hagen & Stanovich, 1977). The increasing part of this developmental curve probably results from general improvement in information processing capacity with age. With the same amount of attention allocated to the incidental stimuli, older children simply remember more of them. But

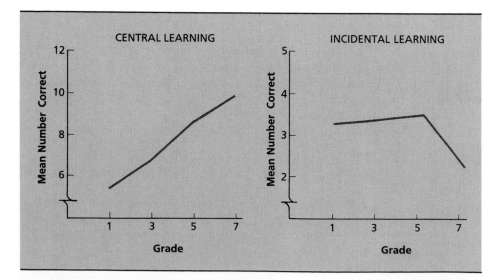

Figure 7.7. Age changes in central and incidental learning in the Maccoby and Hagen (1965) study. *(From E. E. Maccoby & J. W. Hagen, 1965, "Effects of Distraction upon Central Versus Incidental Recall: Developmental Trends,"* Journal of Experimental Child Psychology, 2, *285. Adapted by permission.)*

after age 11, children seem much better at actively and effortfully keeping their attention from being drawn to irrelevant aspects of the task stimuli. In contrast, the attentional approach of preschool and early elementary school children is more playful, exploratory, and easily captured by momentarily salient and attractive features of situations (Lane & Pearson, 1982; Vliestra, 1982; Wright & Vliestra, 1975).

Planfulness

In comparison to preschoolers, older children's deployment of attention is more planful. For example, when they know in advance that a specific kind of information is coming their way, they are primed and pretuned to search for it efficiently and economically (Brown & DeLoache, 1978; Flavell, 1985). Pick, Christy, and Frankel (1972) showed second and sixth graders pairs of wooden animals that varied in size, color, and shape and asked them to press either a "yes" or "no" button as quickly as possible to indicate whether the items were the same or different. In one condition, children were told beforehand which aspect of each pair to compare; the experimenter said "color" or "animal" (shape) before displaying the stimuli. In a second condition, children were informed after the stimulus presentation what dimension they were to use in making the comparison. The older children were faster on both tasks, but there was a much greater difference between the two age groups in the first condition. When the basis of judgment was announced ahead of time, the sixth graders were far more effective in pretuning themselves to seek out a particular kind of information.

Studies of children's visual scanning also reveal more planful, efficient, task-directed pickup of information with age. By carefully tracking their eye movements, Vurpillot (1968) studied how children scan pairs of stimuli, such as the houses depicted in Figure 7.8, to determine if they are the same or different. Children's scan paths became increasingly thorough and exhaustive between the ages of 4 and 9. Preschool children based their judgments on only a limited portion of the available information; they did not examine all features of the stimuli, and those they did examine were not studied systematically. As a result, preschoolers frequently judged pairs of houses that were different to be the same. In contrast, 6- to 9-year-olds used a comprehensive strategy of comparing the details of the houses window to window.

The studies reported above place the beginnings of well organized, planful search behavior on laboratory tasks in the early to mid-elementary school years. However, strategic search routines are evident as early as the preschool years when investigators move out of the laboratory and study children in natural environments. In one of the few studies of its kind, Wellman, Somerville, and Haake (1979) looked at how 3- to 5-year-old children searched for an object that was lost in a familiar playground. The child was taken through the setting by an experimenter, who stopped at each of eight locations along the way to play a game (see Figure 7.9). In the third location the experimenter took the child's picture, but by the seventh, the camera was missing. The child completed the path to the eighth location and was then asked to search for the camera. Children of all ages tended to search first in the third area where the picture was taken. When the camera could not be found there, most of the 3-year-olds gave up and did not search at a second location. Those who did tended to search outside the "critical area" (the path between location 3 where the picture was taken and location 7 where the camera was first discovered missing). In contrast, older preschool children were more likely to confine their search to the critical area and to search the possible locations sequentially and comprehensively. These findings, as well as several other naturalistic studies of young children's search behavior (Haake, Somerville, & Wellman, 1980; Anooshian, Hartman, & Scharf, 1982), indicate that a tendency to search planfully, systematically, and exhaustively in familiar environments develops over the preschool years.

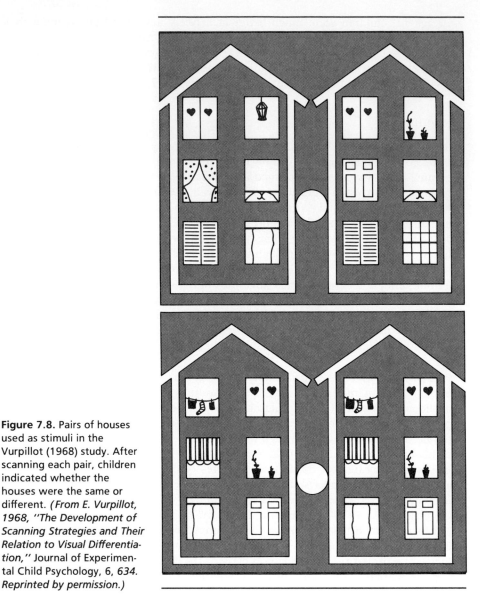

Figure 7.8. Pairs of houses used as stimuli in the Vurpillot (1968) study. After scanning each pair, children indicated whether the houses were the same or different. *(From E. Vurpillot, 1968, "The Development of Scanning Strategies and Their Relation to Visual Differentiation,"* Journal of Experimental Child Psychology, 6, *634. Reprinted by permission.)*

Adaptability

Children's increased attentional control and planfulness serve as essential ingredients in the emergence of greater attentional adaptability with age. An adaptable attentional system adjusts itself flexibly and efficiently to the momentary requirements of tasks and problems.

The ability to shift attention in accordance with task demands improves steadily over the course of childhood. Using the pairs of wooden animals from the Pick, Christy, and Frankel (1972) investigation described earlier, Pick and Frankel (1974) conducted a follow-up study in which they told all of their second- and sixth-grade subjects ahead of time which dimension (size, shape, or color) was relevant to the same-different judgment of each animal pair. However, in one condition, the experimenter varied the basis of judgment randomly over a series of trials, whereas in the other condition, each type of judgment was made repeatedly for a block of trials. Second graders' reaction times were especially slow when the feature to be judged

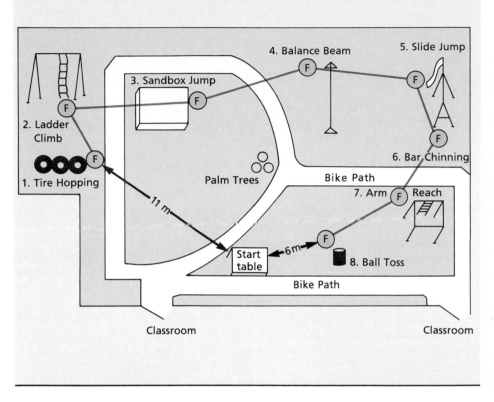

Figure 7.9. Layout of the playground in the Wellman, Somerville, and Haake (1979) study. The figure shows the games the children played at the eight locations. Each location was marked by a flag ⓕ that displayed a picture of the activity performed there. Red yarn stretched between the flags defined the path from location 1 to 8. Thus, children could easily retrace their steps during the search phase of the study. *(From H. M. Wellman, S. C. Somerville, & R. J. Haake, 1979, "Development of Search Procedures in Real-Life Spatial Environments,"* Developmental Psychology, 15, 532. *Copyright 1979 by the American Psychological Association. Reprinted by permission of the author.)*

switched unpredictably from one trial to the next. In contrast, the older sixth graders' response latencies changed very little. They were better able to rapidly vary their attentional focus when they needed to search for different information on each trial.

Older children do not just flexibly shift their attention in response to task demands; they also shift in response to increments in their own learning. In preparing for a test, the good student makes adaptive decisions about which portions of the material have been mastered and need no further attention and which ones must still be reviewed, and the proficient athlete or musician knows how to allocate attention between perfecting old skills and learning new ones. With age, children become more adept at these adaptive attentional strategies. In one investigation, elementary school pupils and college students were given lists of pictures to learn. On each trial but the first, they were allowed to select half of the items for additional study. First graders' choices did not follow any systematic pattern, but by third grade, children showed a strong tendency to choose items they had missed on previous recall attempts for further consideration (Masur, McIntyre, & Flavell, 1973). When children are presented with the task of mastering more intricate material, such as prose passages, their ability to allocate attention based on previous mastery continues to develop into the college years (Brown, Smiley, & Lawton, 1978), indicating that the age at which adaptive attentional strategies emerge is partly a function of task complexity.

In summary, research on the development of children's attentional processes indicates that attention becomes more deliberate and focused, patterned and integrated, as well as flexible and adaptive with age. The older child maintains an attentional strategy if it continues to work, changes it when it is inappropriate, and depending on momentary task demands, is capable of enacting a diversity of attentional sets and plans (Flavell, 1985; Hagen & Wilson, 1982). Despite these trends, a surprisingly large minority of children, most of them boys, experience serious difficulties in the development of controlled, planful attention during middle childhood. See Box 7.2 for a discussion of the special behavioral and learning problems of these **attention deficit-hyperactivity disordered** children.

SHORT-TERM MEMORY

Strategies for Storing Information

As attentional processes change with age, so do memory strategies, the intentional, voluntary acts that people engage in to store and retain information. As we shall see in the sections below, strategies commonly used by adults to keep information in short-term memory and to facilitate its transfer to the long-term, permanent store are not effectively employed during the early childhood years. But around the time that children enter elementary school, they become better at generating strategies for remembering. In fact, memory development during middle childhood has largely been characterized as the attainment of proficient use of memory strategies (Fabricus & Wellman, 1984).

    Rehearsal. Children below the age of 5 or 6 are less likely than older children and adults to **rehearse,** or repeat to themselves, information that they are trying to memorize. In an early study that demonstrated that young children rarely rehearse, Keeney, Canizzo, and Flavell (1967) presented 6- and 10-year-olds with pictures of objects to remember. To determine whether the children rehearsed, a space helmet was used to cover their eyes, but it permitted the experimenter to observe any lip movements they made. Very few of the 6-year-olds moved their lips, but almost all of the 10-year-olds did. Those children who used rehearsal recalled far more of the objects.

    Why do young children fail to rehearse? Is the problem simply a **production deficiency,** a failure to produce spontaneously an already-available strategy that would work quite well if only the young child would choose to rely on it? Or is it a **control deficiency,** an inability to skillfully implement a particular strategy even when it is used? Many investigations have been directed at answering these questions. Taken together, research indicates that both strategy production and control difficulties are responsible for the younger child's poorer performance on memory tasks.

    Studies in which young children have been trained to use rehearsal underline the importance of an early production deficiency. When nonrehearsing children are taught to rehearse, their recall improves substantially. However, when later given an opportunity to use rehearsal without prompting, most trained children abandon the strategy (Hagen, Hargrove, & Ross, 1973; Keeney, Canizzo, & Flavell, 1967). Thus, young children can be instructed to rehearse, but they fail to generate the strategy independently in new situations or to maintain it over time.

    When children first start to use rehearsal spontaneously, control deficiencies are evident. Their first rehearsal efforts differ in quality and effectiveness from those of older individuals. In a study that investigated how children of different ages go about rehearsing, 8-, 11-, and 13-year-olds were asked to rehearse aloud each word in a list of to-be-remembered items. The 8-year-olds rehearsed the items in isolation. For example, after being given the word cat, they would say, "Cat, cat, cat." In contrast, older children combined previously presented words in the list with the newest item. They would say, "Desk, man, yard, cat, cat," rehearsing items together as a set. When children used this approach, it substantially increased the serial position primacy effect; in other words, the combined rehearsal strategy resulted in the storage of much more information in long-term memory (Ornstein, Naus, & Liberty, 1975). In general, young children rehearse passively and piecemeal, verbalizing stimulus names only when the items to which they refer are perceptually present, whereas older children repeat several to-be-remembered words together at each opportunity (Garrity, 1975; Hagen, Jongeward, & Kail, 1975). Second-grade piecemeal rehearsers can be taught to use the more effective approach (Ornstein, Naus, & Stone, 1977). However, they require more time to execute the strategy and the extra support of having continuous visual access to all the items in a list for training to be very effective (Ornstein et al., 1985).

FOCUS ON CONTEMPORARY ISSUES

Box 7.2
Attention Deficit-Hyperactivity Disordered Children

Just about everyone has, at one time or another, encountered a child whose poorly controlled behavior and extreme distractibility immediately conjure up the term *hyperactive*. Such children often act impulsively without thinking, have difficulty focusing on a single task for more than a few minutes, and find it especially hard to wait patiently for a desired event. In addition, some approach what they do with excessive motor activity. Recently, the American Psychiatric Association (1987) introduced the term *attention deficit-hyperactivity disorder* to describe these youngsters. Between 3 and 15 percent of school-age children have the disorder, most of them boys. Their behavior quickly leads to social friction, academic failure, and low self-esteem. Parents and teachers easily become impatient when a hyperactive child repeatedly fails to listen to directions, talks out of turn, and cannot concentrate long enough to finish a task. Peers also notice the disruptive, off-task behavior and respond to it with annoyance and rejection (Klein & Young, 1979).

Attentional difficulties are the fundamental problem area for these children. Research indicates that they do poorly on laboratory tasks requiring controlled, planful, and sustained attention. For example, in one study, a series of numbers were projected on a screen, and the child's job was to push a button when a 4 appeared, but only

if it was preceded by a 6. In comparison to controls, hyperactive boys pressed the button much more often when they were not supposed to (Rapoport et al., 1980). These youngsters also show performance deficits on tasks similar to Vurpillot's houses (see Figure 7.8) that require them to engage in exhaustive search of a set of stimuli (Douglas, 1980). Longitudinal research indicates that although some outgrow these difficulties, most hyperactive children continue to have problems concentrating and finding friends into their adolescent and adult years (Weiss et al., 1971; 1979).

Attention deficit-hyperactivity disorder does not seem to have one single cause. Instead, it has been linked to genetic as well as a variety of environmental factors. Some evidence indicates that restlessness and school difficulties are more similar for identical than fraternal twins (O'Connor et al., 1980). However, these findings are inconclusive, for genetically identical siblings may also have been exposed to more similar environments. A higher proportion of hyperactive children than normal children come from homes characterized by marital instability and parental distress (Whalen, 1983). Other evidence indicates that high levels of exposure to lead, an environmental pollutant, is strongly related to impulsivity and distractibility (Needleman et al., 1979). Food additives have also been implicated as a cause, but the relationship has not been proven (Conners et al., 1976; Whalen, 1983). A common belief is that excessive dietary intake of sugar contributes to

hyperactivity, but recent research indicates that it does not play a major role (Milich & Pelham, 1986).

Currently, the major treatment approach to attention deficit-hyperactivity disorder is stimulant medication, which has been found to reduce overactivity and improve attention and academic performance (Douglas & Peters, 1979; Douglas et al., 1986; Whalen, 1983). However, dosage must be carefully regulated; if it is too high, learning will be impaired, despite the fact that activity level is reduced (Sprague & Sleator, 1975). Some psychologists believe that the basic problem experienced by hyperactive children is that they are chronically underaroused; that is, normal levels of stimulation are not sufficient to engage their interest and attention. Therefore, if a task is overly familiar or repetitive, hyperactive children begin to seek stimulation elsewhere, by attending to irrelevant features and engaging in high rates of motor activity. Stimulant drug therapy is thought to be helpful because it has an arousing and alerting effect on the central nervous system. As a result, it decreases the child's need to engage in task-irrelevant, self-stimulating behavior (Zentall & Zentall, 1983). However, because drug treatment by itself does not eliminate all of these children's difficulties, it is often supplemented with other treatments, including modeling of appropriate academic and social behaviors and teaching children to use verbal self-instructions to plan and order their task-related activity (Douglas, 1980).

The preschool child's failure to use rehearsal, and the young elementary school child's less effective deployment of it, indicates that the development of rehearsal skill is a gradual process; efficiency is reached only after much time and practice. The ability to recognize and repeat stimulus names rapidly and to keep track of where one is and is going in a rehearsal sequence are challenging cognitive skills that probably need to be well developed in their own right before they can be implemented as a strategic means to a memory goal (Flavell, 1985; Smirnov & Zinchenko, 1969). In a recent study, Baker-Ward and her collaborators (Baker-Ward, Ornstein, & Holden, 1984) demonstrated that when preschoolers are presented with familiar toys and instructed to remember as many of them as possible, children as young as 3 years of age show some evidence of intentional memory behavior. They named, visually inspected, and manipulated the toys more and played with them less than a control group not instructed to remember them. Although labeling the objects showed no relationship to the children's memory performance until 6 years of age, the precursors of rehearsal as a strategic device could be seen in the children's behaviors years earlier. Baker-Ward's study supports the idea that a memory strategy has to be well established before it can serve as an effective memory aid. Even when young children are capable of rehearsing, until the strategy becomes less effortful and more automatic, they have trouble applying it successfully in a memory problem.

Organization. Rehearsal is not the most effective memory strategy available to a resourceful information processor. **Organization** goes beyond mere repetition and mimicry by grouping and relating to-be-remembered items with one another, causing recall to improve dramatically.

Like rehearsal, the faint beginnings of organization can be seen in the behavior of young preschool children when they are asked to recall small sets of familiar items. Goldberg, Perlmutter, and Myers (1974) gave 2-year-olds two-item lists of objects to remember. When the objects were semantically related (e.g., a cookie and a lollipop —both food items), the children remembered more of them and recalled them faster than when they were unrelated (e.g., M&Ms and a lion). Nevertheless, except when assisted to do so by obvious associations among adjacent items or by hints and instructions from adults, young children will not rearrange pictures or objects into organized groups, whereas older children will do so spontaneously and deliberately (Moely et al., 1969; Neimark, Slotnick, & Ulrich, 1971). A great many studies using subjects from kindergarten through grade 9 have reported age-related increases in both organization of presented items and subsequent recall performance (e.g., Cole, Frankel, & Sharp, 1971; Wachs & Gruen, 1971; Kobasigawa & Middleton, 1972).

When experimenters train children to apply organizational strategies by instructing them to sort items into groups of things "that go together or are alike," subjects as young as 4 or 5 show enhanced category clustering as well as improved recall (Moely et al., 1969). But like the training studies on rehearsal, gains from instructing children to organize do not transfer to new memory problems, nor are they maintained on later trials of the same memory task after adults stop giving young children directions to categorize (Liberty & Ornstein, 1973; Williams & Goulet, 1975). These results suggest an early production deficiency for organization similar to the one we described earlier for rehearsal.

Also like rehearsal, the quality of children's organizational strategies changes with age. Young children are less parsimonious organizers than older children and adults in that they divide their lists into a greater number of categories and leave many isolates (Frankel & Rollins, 1982; 1985). In addition, young children's categorization schemes are far less stable than those of older individuals, and considerable resorting takes place from one trial to the next (Liberty & Ornstein, 1973; Moely, 1977). The shifting, piecemeal quality of children's first organizational efforts may be partly due to the fact that during the early elementary school years, most children are not consciously aware that they are organizing at all! Whereas adults have little difficulty indicating why they group certain items together, children often cannot name their sorting categories or say why they organized them as they did (Bjorklund & Zeman, 1983; Liberty & Ornstein, 1973).

Why are children initially not aware of how and why they categorize? When investigators have looked at exactly what children do when putting information together in a memory task, they repeatedly find that below age 9 or 10, grouping is largely restricted to items that are *high in associative strength* — in other words, that easily cue one another because they commonly occur together in everyday experience. For example, look at the following set of items:

| hat | carrot | head | rabbit |
| feet | monkey | banana | shoes |

When memorizing them, children below fourth grade spontaneously organize the words into associative pairs, such as "hat-head," "feet-shoes," and "monkey-banana." In contrast, older children and adults employ nonassociative categorical relations. In the example given above, they group items together using the categorical criteria of body parts, clothing, animals, and food. The less mature method of organizing by associative relations is probably not very deliberate and effortful. In fact, a number of investigators believe that associative pairing takes place fairly automatically, without much awareness on the part of the child (Bjorklund & Jacobs, 1985; Frankel & Rollins, 1982; 1985; Lange, 1978). In a recent study, Bjorklund and de Marchena (1984) found a gradual developmental shift between first and seventh grade from memory organization based on associative criteria to memory organization based on categorical relations (see Figure 7.10). They believe that the younger child's organizational memory is really not strategic, since it rests on the automatic activation of associative relations. However, grouping by associativity may play an important role in facilitating the development of categorical organization. Once children engage in an automatic grouping process, they may notice it, think about its significance, and start to consciously apply more cognitively mature forms of relating items together (Bjorklund & Jacobs, 1985).

Finally, since young children are primarily associative organizers, whether or not they do organize depends on favorable task circumstances. As long as they are given highly familiar and strongly associated words to memorize, preadolescents will cluster items together in recall (Steinmetz & Battig, 1969; Wachs & Gruen, 1971). When presented with items that have less obvious characteristics in common, they show little if any organization (Bjorklund & Hock, 1982; Ornstein, Hale, & Morgan, 1977;

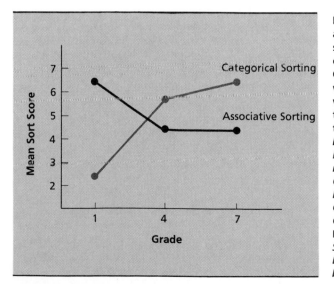

Figure 7.10. Age changes in associative and categorical sorting in the Bjorklund and de Marchena (1984) study. Children were given a set of words on cards, told they would need to remember them, and then asked to sort them into groups. *(From D. F. Bjorklund & M. R. de Marchena, 1984, "Developmental Shifts in the Basis of Organization Memory: The Role of Associative Versus Categorical Relatedness in Children's Free Recall,"* Child Development, 55, 956. ©The Society for Research in Child Development, Inc. Adapted by permission.)

Moely, 1977). As children get older and understand more about categorical relations, they gradually apply such knowledge more broadly, and they are better able to engage in organizational strategies under less favorable task conditions.

Elaboration. **Elaboration** involves creating a relationship, or shared meaning, between two or more pieces of information that do not bear any natural categorical relationship to one another. It is commonly studied in *paired-associate learning tasks,* in which the subject is asked to learn pairs of stimulus-response items (e.g., fish-pipe) so that when the stimulus is presented (fish), the response (pipe) is easily recalled. If, in trying to learn this pair, you generated a mental image of a fish smoking a pipe, or you recited a sentence to yourself expressing this relationship (e.g., "The fish puffed the pipe"), you were engaging in elaboration. A substantial body of research reveals that elaboration is one of the most effective methods of cementing information in memory (Pressley, 1982).

Compared to other strategies, elaboration is a late-developing memory skill that typically appears after the age of 11 and gradually increases into young adulthood (Pressley, 1982; Rohwer & Litrownik, 1983; Pressley & Levin, 1977a). When individuals finally do use it, elaboration is so effective in producing high memory performance that it tends to replace other memory strategies (Pressley & Levin, 1977a).

The very reasons that explain why elaboration is so successful also provide insight into why it is so late to arrive on the scene as a spontaneous strategy. When individuals use mental imagery to elaborate, they must process deeply, going well beyond the information given in a paired-associate task. Recall that the levels of processing model suggests that the more deeply we process material by weaving meaningful connections with other previously stored information, the more likely it is that the new material will be remembered. But deep elaborative processing is a late-developing skill because it makes substantial information processing demands on the individual. For example, when you use mental imagery to elaborate, you must first take the items to be remembered, translate them into pictures, and then generate an imaginal interaction between them. Children develop skill at such internal imaginal manipulations only very gradually over the course of middle childhood (Dean, 1976). Their storehouse of knowledge about how different items may be related to one another in an elaborative representation undoubtedly expands over this time period as well (Pressley, 1982).

Investigators used to think that younger children depended on concrete mental imagery as an elaborative device, while older children and adults relied on purely verbal elaboration, of the type that occurs when two unrelated words are connected together in a sentence. Recent evidence shows that this once well accepted assumption is not correct. In fact, there appears to be little development of purely verbal elaborative skills over the course of childhood. Even preschoolers can be taught the relatively simple technique of inserting a verb or preposition between two words as a way to improve their memory of the items. In contrast, the success of instructing individuals in the use of mental imagery increases with age (Pressley, 1982). Levin, McCabe, and Bender (1975) showed that providing children with simple instructions to engage in elaborative mental imagery in order to remember pairs of toys failed to improve the memory performance of children younger than 5 or 6 years of age. However, if preschool children are required to manipulate the toys to show the experimenter the content of their mental images, they do show enhanced learning (Bender & Levin, 1976). In addition, children below the age of 7 or 8 only profit from instruction in elaborative mental imagery if the to-be-learned items are concrete objects or pictures of objects. By the middle of the elementary school years, they can use the strategy successfully with purely verbal materials (Pressley, 1982), and the effectiveness of instruction gradually increases until 11 years of age (Levin & Pressley, 1978; Pressley & Levin, 1977b), around the time that children begin to generate the strategy spontaneously.

Even during the high school and college years, individual differences exist in the extent to which people rely on elaboration in memory tasks. Although virtually all adolescents and young adults use rehearsal and organization, there are still some who never think of using elaboration in learning tasks in which they have to associate discrete pieces of information with one another (Rohwer & Bean, 1973; Pressley, 1982). Why elaboration is a less universally applied strategy than other memory techniques remains a topic for future research.

Environmental Contexts and Memory Strategies

In the many laboratory studies cited above, memory is the one and only goal of the subject's activity. But in most everyday tasks, individuals are not just engaged in the business of committing information to memory for its own sake. Rather, they engage in a variety of meaningful daily activities that produce excellent memory as a natural by-product of the activity itself (Paris & Lindauer, 1982).

An interesting finding from cross-cultural research is that very much like young children, people in non-Western cultures without formal schooling do not spontaneously generate or benefit very easily from instruction in the use of memory strategies. Instead, they rely on external, culturally specific memory aids, such as poems, songs, knotted ropes, and carved sticks, when they need to remember information to successfully engage in an activity. When psychologists test people in non-Western cultures, they consistently find that memory difficulties appear on tasks in which the material is presented as isolated units, devoid of obvious structure and removed from external cues of the kind found in everyday life that assist in the recall of needed information (Cole & Scribner, 1977; Paris & Lindauer, 1982). In an intriguing study, Istomina (1975) showed that some of the performance difficulties of young children on laboratory memory tasks reside in learning how to remember information for its own sake when its usefulness is unclear. Three- to 7-year-old children were required to remember a list of five words under two different conditions. In one, they played a game of grocery store and had to remember the items so they could buy them. In the other, they were simply told to learn the list. Children recalled nearly twice as many items in the grocery store game as they did in the list-learning condition.

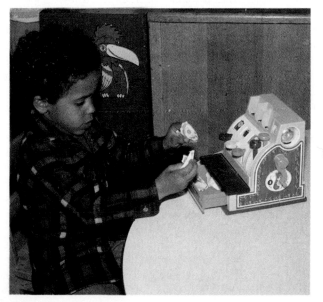

By learning about money within the familiar context of play with a cash register, this child remembers the value of each bill more easily than if he were simply told to learn a list. (Nancy Sheehan)

A repeated finding of cross-cultural investigations is that educated subjects remember more information than uneducated subjects when tasks require the use of memory strategies. This suggests that the kind of experience that promotes strategic memorizing is formal schooling. Deliberate memorization is a much more common activity in school than out of school, and school tasks provide children with a great deal of practice and motivation for using strategies (Cole & Scribner, 1977; Paris & Lindauer, 1982). Looked at in this way, the development of memory strategies is not just a matter of the emergence of a more competent and facile information processing system. It is also a product of environmental demands and cultural conditions.

In summary, use of memory strategies during early childhood is characterized by both production and control deficiencies. Preschoolers do not spontaneously generate strategies to improve their memory, nor do they show lasting benefits from training. By the time they enter school, children start to acquire greater competence in rehearsal and organization. Skills of elaboration develop later, emerging after age 11 and increasing into young adulthood. Finally, besides improvement in the functioning of the information processing system, environment and culture influence the use of memory strategies.

LONG-TERM MEMORY

Retrieval of Information

So far, we have discussed storage mechanisms that put things into memory. Once information enters the long-term store, it must be retrieved in order to be used again. Retrieval refers to recovering information from memory or remembering what has been stored. Information processing theorists study three different types of retrieval: recognition, recall, and reconstruction.

Recognition. **Recognition** involves noticing that a stimulus is identical or similar to something previously experienced. It is the simplest form of retrieval, since the material to be remembered is fully present during testing to serve as its own retrieval cue. Recognition memory is present in early infancy, as shown by the habituation studies that we discussed in Chapter 4. In fact, as early as the second year of life recognition memory for stimuli to which children have been exposed for very brief periods of time lasts much longer than most people would expect. Using the habituation-dishabituation paradigm, Daehler and Bukatko (1977) showed toddlers and preschool children long sequences of pictures. Each picture was presented once alone during the memorization phase of the study, and a second time paired with a novel picture, during testing. Even when as many as 50 pictures intervened between the two presentations, 19-month-olds consistently dishabituated, or looked longer at the novel picture, indicating that they recognized the familiar picture as one that they had seen before.

By the end of the preschool years, children's recognition memory is very accurate (Perlmutter, 1984). Brown and Campione (1972) found that one week after viewing a series of 80 pictures, 4-year-olds discriminated the old pictures from new ones with 90-percent accuracy. Because recognition memory appears so early in development and young children are able to recognize large numbers of stimuli successfully, it is regarded as a rather automatic process that is less dependent on systematic search of the memory store than other types of retrieval (Perlmutter & Lange, 1978).

Even though young children's recognition memory approximates that of adults on many tasks, it does improve with age. Research shows that the ability of older children and adults to apply strategies during storage increases the number of stimuli later recognized, particularly when the stimulus events are complex and not very familiar (Hoffman & Dick, 1976; Mandler & Robinson, 1978; Nelson & Kosslyn, 1976). In addition, growth in the general storehouse of knowledge held in long-term memory undoubtedly helps to support improvement in recognition memory, for with age there are simply fewer stimuli around that children have had no prior experience with (Perlmutter, 1984).

Recall. In contrast to recognition, **recall** is a form of *productive memory* in that it involves the ability to spontaneously remember something that is not present. In recognition, the original stimulus is available, but in recall there may be only a few cues as to what it is, or perhaps none at all besides the general context in which the material was originally learned. Therefore, recall always demands generation by the memory system of a mental representation of the absent stimulus, although how much must be generated differs from one recall task to another, depending on the degree of stimulus support, or availability of external retrieval cues at time of testing (Perlmutter, 1984).

The beginnings of recall appear before 1 year of age as long as there is considerable external support for what is being remembered. Ashmead and Perlmutter (1980) had parents keep diary accounts of their babies' memories. For infants as young as 7 months of age, many examples of memory for people, places, and objects not perceptually present at the time of recall appeared in the records. The following diary entry of a 7-month-old's recall of his father is an example:

> My husband called from work and I let him talk to Rob. (Rob) looked puzzled for a while and then he turned and looked at the door. Rob thought of the only time he hears his dad's voice when he knows Dad isn't home is when his dad just got home. He heard his dad's voice and based on past experiences, he reasoned that his dad must be home, so he looked at the door. (P. 4)

In another diary study, 21- to 27-month-old children were able to remember experiences that had happened several months previously, in some cases from a time prior to when they had learned to talk, although all the memories were strongly cued in some way. For example, one child remembered a friend whom he had not seen in several months when passing the friend's house (Nelson & Ross, 1980).

By the time children are 3 or 4 and researchers can study their memory abilities in the laboratory, the most obvious feature of their performance is their much poorer recall as opposed to recognition memory (Perlmutter, 1984). Of course, recognition is much easier than recall for adults as well, but in comparison to adults, children's recall performance is quite deficient, and there is far greater improvement in recall than recognition with age (Hasher & Zacks, 1979; Perlmutter & Lange, 1978; Perlmutter, 1984). In fact, the ability to recall lists of information accurately over extended periods of time continues to improve through adolescence (Brainerd, Kingma, & Howe, 1985).

We have already mentioned one major reason that younger children's recall is poorer than that of older children and adults in earlier sections of this chapter. Younger and older children differ in the extent to which they meaningfully organize knowledge to aid remembrance of specific information. When information is strategically organized and structured at encoding so that it is deeply processed and connected with other material in long-term memory, individuals can rely on a wide variety of internal retrieval cues to stimulate its recall. During the elementary school years, semantic organization of the knowledge base increases as children develop increasingly consistent and stable criteria for defining category memberships and begin to link categories together into hierarchically structured networks of information (Ford & Keating, 1981; Nelson, 1984; Perlmutter, 1984). In some studies, the degree to which children rely on semantic organization for recall of information has been examined by looking at the extent to which their production of recalled items is clustered into categories. Clustering is related to better recall performance, and greater spontaneous clustering of information occurs with increasing age (Perlmutter, 1984).

In summary, over the course of infancy, memory retrieval evolves from simple recognition of previously experienced stimuli to recall in the presence of salient external retrieval cues over longer periods of time. Later development involves greater reliance on internal retrieval cues as stored information becomes better organized and integrated with other material in memory. As a result, the older child engages in more deliberate efforts at retrieval, as opposed to fairly unintentional, automatic recall that is passively instigated by an external retrieval cue.

Reconstruction. Read the following passage about George, an escaped convict trying to break out of prison. Then close the book and try to recall it by telling the story to a friend or writing it down:

> George was alone. He knew they would soon be here. They were not far behind him when he left the village, hungry and cold. He dare not stop for food or shelter for fear of falling into the hands of his pursuers. There were many of them; they were strong and he was weak. George could hear the noise as the uniformed band beat its way through the trees not far behind him. The sense of their presence was everywhere. His spine tingled with fear. Eagerly he awaited the darkness. In darkness he would find safety. (Brown et al., 1977, p. 1456)

When you have retold the story, compare your rendition with the original version above. Is it a perfectly faithful reproduction?

In studies of adult memory carried out in the early part of this century, Bartlett (1932) showed that when people are given complex, meaningful material to remember instead of isolated bits and pieces of information, an extraordinarily high proportion of inaccuracies, distortions, and additions occur that are not just the result of memory failure. Instead, they are the outcome of a radical transformation of the stimulus material. Bartlett advocated a *constructivist* view of human memory, suggesting that much of the meaningful information to which we are exposed in our daily lives, such as prose passages and spoken language, is not copied verbatim into the system at storage and then faithfully reproduced at retrieval. Instead, we construct interpretations of such inputs, and "information undergoes blending, condensation, omission, invention, and similar constructive transformations" (p. 35). Basic to the constructivist position is the view that new information is selected, interpreted, and embellished based on its correspondence with the individual's existing knowledge base. As a result, exact reproductions of meaningful stimulus events are rare. In fact, once the material is transformed, people may not be able to distinguish what they have internally constructed from what was initially presented (Paris & Lindauer, 1977; Flavell, 1985). Recall from Chapter 6 that Piaget's theory is also a constructivist position. He believed that knowledge could not be imposed ready-made on the organism from without; instead, it is constructed by the mind through the mental functions of adaptation and organization. Does the constructivist view of human memory remind you of these Piagetian concepts? It is, in fact, very congruent with Piaget's basic ideas (Piaget & Inhelder, 1973).

Constructive memory processing can take place during any phase of stimulus flow through the information processing system. It can occur during storage, for the strategies of organization and elaboration are clearly within the province of constructive memory, since they emphasize generated relationships among stimuli. However, we already know that young children rarely produce and employ these encoding strategies efficiently. Constructive processing can also involve **reconstruction** of information while it is in the system and generation of new relationships at retrieval. Do children reconstruct stored information in these ways? The answer clearly is yes.

Children's reconstructive processing has largely been studied by asking them to recall prose material. Like adults, when children are asked to retell a story, they engage in condensations, integrations, reorganizations, and additions of information. Research shows that by 6 or 7 years of age, children tend to recall the important features of a story and forget the unimportant ones (Christie & Schumacher, 1975; Mandler & Johnson, 1977), and they amalgamate information expressed in different sentences into more tightly knit, efficient units. For example, consider the following sentences, "On the first day of school, Bob was introduced to his new teacher. The principal who introduced him was very nice." When children as young as 6 years of age were asked to remember this material, they often produced something like this: "On the first day of school, the principal introduced Bob to his new teacher" (Barclay & Reid, 1974). In addition to paring down extensive textual material to its meaningful essentials, elementary school children, like adults, reorder the sequence of events in a story so that it is more logically consistent (Bischofshausen, 1985), and they frequently recall information that fits with the meaning of a passage but was not really presented. For example, when Brown and her colleagues (1977) told third, fifth, and seventh graders the story of George, the escaped convict, presented at the beginning of this section, the following sorts of statements were generated as part of their recollections:

> All the prison guards were chasing him.
> He climbed over the prison walls.
> He was running so the police would be so far away that their dogs would not catch his trail. (P. 1459)

In reordering and embellishing their recall in meaningful ways, children provide themselves with a multitude of potentially helpful retrieval cues that they can use in trying to remember the information. Thus, from the early elementary school years and on, the nature of children's recollection of meaningful materials is similar to that of adults in its emphasis on semantic reconstruction of information.

Between 4 and 12 years of age reconstruction goes even further as the ability to make inferences about actions and actors within story material gradually improves (Paris & Lindauer, 1977). Preschoolers can draw inferences when story statements concern the physical causes of events. For example, given the sentence, "As Jennifer was walking to the store, she *turned a somersault* and lost her dollar," 4-year-olds are able to infer how Jennifer lost her money. But it is not until the early to mid-elementary school years that children can make inferences from information about psychological causes, as in the following sentence: "As Jennifer was walking to the store, she *became very excited* and lost her dollar." Young children's prior understanding and experience with physical causation is much greater than it is with psychological causation, a difference that affects their ability to comprehend and infer relationships (Thompson & Myers, 1985). Because research shows a strong link between a child's ability to understand implied relationships within a story and long-term retention of its main ideas, generation of inferences may be an especially important strategy for remembering semantic information (Paris, 1975).

In summary, children, like adults, often recall stored information in reconstructed forms. Reconstructive processing, including the ability to make inferences, improves across the elementary school years, enabling children to better understand and remember information. Developmental psychologists regard changes in children's reconstructive memory as largely the result of growth in the knowledge structures they have available to interpret incoming information (Paris & Lindauer, 1977; Kail & Hagen, 1982). In the next section, we consider how the size and structure of the long-term knowledge base changes with age, as well as additional evidence for the enormous effect its breadth and organization have on what children learn and remember.

The Knowledge Base

Knowledge as an Explanation for Age Differences in Memory Performance. In several earlier sections of this chapter, we suggested that the child's rapidly developing storehouse of knowledge may be crucial for memory development and for the deployment of increasingly successful memory strategies. The extent to which expansion of the knowledge base during the childhood years serves as an adequate and complete explanation for age differences in memory performance is a topic of great interest to developmental psychologists. Many now believe that cognitive development may be largely a matter of acquisition of **domain-specific knowledge** — knowledge of specific content areas that subsequently renders new, related information more familiar and meaningful and therefore easier to store and retrieve (Chi, 1978; Flavell, 1985; Mandler, 1983; Siegler, 1983a). Becoming more knowledgeable in a particular area may also improve strategy use, for experts in specific domains of knowledge probably can deploy highly efficient, content-adapted strategies for storing and retrieving information. Chi (1982) demonstrated the importance of the knowledge base for strategic memory processing in a study that showed that the facility with which a 5-year-old could use an alphabetical strategy for retrieving children's names was heavily dependent on her familiarity with the to-be-remembered material. When asked to retrieve the names of pupils in her own classroom — domain-specific knowledge that she knew very well — the child learned and applied the alphabetical strategy quickly. When required to use it to retrieve a set of names of people she did not know, she had great difficulty doing so.

If children's growing knowledge of task-related stimuli serves as a viable explanation for age-related increments in memory performance, then in content domains where some children happen to be more knowledgeable than most adults, such child experts should also have superior memories. In an intriguing study, this prediction was, in fact, borne out. Chi (1978) solicited six third- through eighth-grade children from a local chess tournament and compared their recall for legitimate chessboard arrangements with the memory performance of adult subjects who could play chess to some degree, but who were not especially knowledgeable. As shown in Figure 7.11A, children's reproductions on the first trial were far more accurate than those of

Figure 7.11. Performance of skilled child chess players and adults on two tasks — memory for chessboard arrangements and standard digit span — in the Chi (1983) study. (A) Child chess experts recalled more items on the first trial of the chess task, whereas adults recalled more on the digit span task. (B) Child chess experts required fewer trials to perfect recall on the chess task, whereas adults required fewer on the digit span task. *(Adapted from M. T. H. Chi, 1978.)*

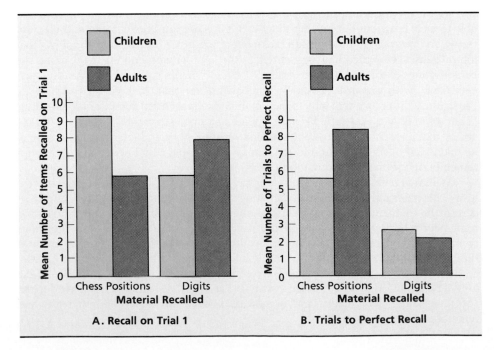

adults. Even when their initial response was not perfect, the young chess players required fewer repeated recall trials to get the chess configurations completely right (see Figure 7.11B). Chi's striking results cannot be attributed to the selection of an unusual sample of especially bright children with superior memories, for on a standard memory span task in which the subjects were asked to recall a list of numerical digits, the adults did better.

In Chi's study of chess-playing children, memory skill differences were largely attributed to differences in *quantity* of knowledge in a particular domain. But the differences may also have been due to the *structure* of knowledge, or the way that experts versus novices relate and connect the concepts in a particular content area with one another. We have already discussed how important the ability to organize and interrelate discrete pieces of information is for memory performance. In another study by Chi and Koeske (1983), the domain-specific knowledge of a 4½-year-old dinosaur enthusiast was studied. Remarkably, his dinosaur knowledge conformed to a hierarchically organized pattern, much like that found among adults who are skilled in a particular knowledge domain. This finding suggests that the basic organization of long-term memory is similar throughout development. Age-related changes are probably ones of greater interrelatedness as knowledge increases in quantity and becomes more familiar, rather than fundamental revisions in format (Mandler, 1983).

Although the knowledge base clearly plays a central role in memory development, whether or not it is the only factor involved is still a matter of controversy. Some recent research shows that beyond the size and structure of the knowledge base, children differ in the degree to which they spontaneously utilize their available storehouse of information to understand and learn new material. Bransford and his colleagues (1981) discovered differences between academically successful and less successful fifth graders in the extent to which they would access their current knowledge to clarify the significance of new information. In one task, the children were given written passages describing two different kinds of robots, one (the extendible robot) used to wash outside windows on two-story houses and the other (the nonextendible robot) used to wash windows on high-rise apartment buildings. A brief description of the functions of each robot was given in the opening paragraph of the passage, followed by several additional paragraphs describing the properties of the robots. For example, the extendible robot was made of heavy steel and had spiked feet that stuck in the ground, while the nonextendible robot was light, had suction-cup feet, and was equipped with a parachute in case it should fall. The children had to memorize each robot's characteristics. The academically successful pupils used the information about the functions of the robots to understand the meaning of each of the robot's features, and their recall was exceptionally good. In contrast, even though the same functional knowledge was available to the less successful students, they failed to make use of it in interpreting the significance of the robot characteristics. As a result they remembered much less.[1]

Bransford believes that failure to approach memory tasks by asking oneself how previously stored information can clarify the meaning and significance of new material may, in the long run, seriously interfere with the development of an adequate knowledge base, for it restricts the individual's opportunity to learn new information. Looked at in this way, inadequacies in the quantity and structure of the knowledge base are not only causes of memory problems, but consequences as well. As Brown et al. (1983) point out, children "vary not only in what they know but also in what they do with what they know. Knowledge is necessary but not sufficient for performance,

---

[1] Did you make use of your previously acquired knowledge to process the information in this section more deeply? Notice that what the more successful students did in the Bransford et al. (1981) study was to engage in *reconstructive processing* of information. They drew *inferences* about relationships between robot functions and characteristics and then were able to rely on them as retrieval cues when recalling the robot properties.

for it is the efficiency with which a learner uses whatever is available that defines intelligence" (p. 100).

Young Children's Scripts: Basic Building Blocks of Structured Knowledge. Think back to Chi and Koeske's (1983) investigation of the 4-year-old dinosaur expert we mentioned earlier. The study provided evidence that young children's semantic knowledge is not fragmented and disorganized. Instead, children seem to form the rudiments of a structured long-term knowledge base at a very early age. How do children begin to build a coherent knowledge system as early as the preschool years, and in what ways does it change with age?

Our vast, intricately organized general knowledge system, which, for purposes of clarity, we now refer to as **semantic memory,** must somehow grow out of the young child's **episodic memory,** or memory for a great many personally experienced events (Tulving, 1972; Posner & Warren, 1972; Nelson & Brown, 1978). How semantic memory emerges from a foundation of specific real-world experiences is considered by some developmental psychologists as the quintessential question of memory development (Nelson & Brown, 1978).

Nelson (1986) and her colleagues have explored the nature of young children's episodic memory representations. Like adults, children as young as 3 remember familiar daily experiences in terms of **scripts.** Scripts are organized representations of event sequences that provide a general description of what occurs and when it occurs in a given situation (Schank & Abelson, 1977). An experience coded in script form provides the child with a basic organizing device for interpreting everyday experiences, such as going to nursery school or eating lunch. Scripts that are held in long-term memory can be used to predict what will happen in the future on similar occasions. An example of a script structure, based on common acts mentioned by children when asked to tell about lunchtime at their day care center, is given in Figure 7.12.

For young preschool children, scripts begin as a very general structure of main acts. For example, when asked to tell what happens when you go to a restaurant, a 3-year-old might say, "You go in, get the food, eat and then pay." Even though children's first scripts contain few acts, they are almost always reported in a temporally and causally correct sequence. With increasing age as well as repetitions of a particular kind of experience, children's scripts become more elaborate and complex, as in the following restaurant rendition: "You go in. You can sit in the booths or at a table. Then you tell the waitress what you want. You eat. If you want dessert, you can have some. Then you pay and go home" (Fivush, 1984; McCarthy & Nelson, 1981; Nelson & Gruendel, 1981).

Nelson believes that scripts serve as a basic means through which children organize and interpret their world. For example, young children rely on scripts when listening to and telling stories. They recall more events from stories based on familiar than unfamiliar event sequences (Hudson & Nelson, 1983), and they also use script structures for the stories they make up and act out in play. Listen carefully to preschool children at play, and you will hear scripts reflected in their dialogues when they pretend to put the baby to bed, go on a trip, or play school (Nelson & Gruendel, 1981).

Nelson regards scripts as the developmental link in the progression from early episodic memory to a mature, semantically organized, long-term memory store (Nelson & Brown, 1978; Nelson & Gruendel, 1981). Objects that share the same function in a script structure provide the basis for the child's first semantic relationships. Lucariello and Nelson (1985) discovered that a list of script-related items (e.g., peanut butter, bologna, cheese [foods often eaten at lunchtime]) was recalled in clustered form and remembered more easily by 3- and 4-year-old children than a typical categorical list (toast, cheese, ice cream [foods]). It appears that relationships among items are first understood in terms of familiar events that children take part in within

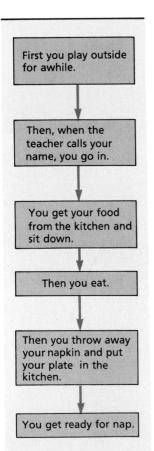

Figure 7.12. "Lunchtime at the day care center" script. This script is typical of ones generated by children of 5 or 6 years of age. Younger children give scripts that are less detailed and that contain fewer main acts.

Through repeated experience of daily events, such as brushing teeth before bedtime, young children build mental scripts that help them organize, interpret, and predict their world. (Randy Matusow/Monkmeyer Press Photo Service)

an organized script framework. Once children develop an array of script sequences, objects sharing the same function but occurring in different scripts (eating toast for breakfast, peanut butter for lunch) may be joined together under a single, more typical semantic category (food).

A final word about scripts and the development of long-term memory deserves mention. To the extent that any one occasion is like others, it is fused into the same script representation, and any specific instance of a scripted experience becomes difficult to recall. For example, unless it was out of the ordinary, you would probably have difficulty remembering what you had for dinner two days ago. The same is true for young children (Fivush, 1984). Nelson and Ross (1980) believe that the early merging of specific memories with the more general knowledge system may help to explain infantile amnesia, the fact that practically none of us can retrieve any specific autobiographical events that happened to us before 3 years of age. To find out more about the various ways that developmental psychologists account for this fascinating phenomenon, refer to Box 7.3.

In summary, age differences in memory processing are at least partly due to changes in the size and structure of children's underlying knowledge base. However, the extent to which children spontaneously use their current knowledge to remember information is also important. How our vast, intricate long-term storehouse of information evolves from memories of everyday experience is one of the most fascinating yet puzzling questions about memory development. Children's tendency to remember daily events in scripted format serves as one possible basis for this change.

Box 7.3
Infantile Amnesia

Groucho: Chicolini, when were you born?

Chico: I don't remember. I was just a little baby at the time.*

One of the most striking features of our efforts to recollect past experiences is an inability to remember any specific autobiographical events from the first few years of our lives. When adults are asked to describe early memories, the average age at first reported event is about 3½ years (Dudycha & Dudycha, 1941). There is no single, well-substantiated answer to the question of why we cannot recall our earliest experiences. A variety of explanations exist, each of which makes its own unique contribution to our understanding (White & Pillemer, 1979).

Freud (1953) first called attention to this phenomenon and named it **infantile amnesia.** Our early memories, he believed, are so emotionally charged with themes of infantile sexuality that they are unacceptable to our socialized, conscious selves. Therefore, we build a heavy wall of repression that prevents their easy recall. Because the few early recollections that most of us have are of rather ordinary, insignificant events, Freud (1963) explained that what we recall is a relatively safe memory fragment or a substitute for an emotionally laden experience that is not fully available.

*From the Marx Brothers' 1933 movie, *Duck Soup* (cited by Nadel & Zola-Morgan, 1984).

One goal of psychoanalysis is to help people retrieve and come to terms with these repressed memories. However, Freud's interpretation runs into difficulty as a satisfactory explanation of infantile amnesia, for psychoanalytic patients are unable to recall their early childhood years even when their analysis is complete (White & Pillemer, 1979).

As an alternative, Schachtel (1947) and Neisser (1967) suggest that infantile amnesia results from changes in children's categories of thought as they grow older. For recall of early experiences to be successful, the categories we possess now must be similar to those we used to store events in memory long ago. Otherwise, the stored fragments of experience will be uninterpretable, and recall will be unsuccessful. Adults, according to these authors, can no longer think as young children do, largely because of the change from preverbal to verbal modes of representing experience during early childhood.

Physiological explanations that place the roots of infantile amnesia in the child's growing nervous system also exist. For example, Nadel and Zola-Morgan (1984) believe that maturation of a structure called the *hippocampal formation,* situated in the temporal lobe of the brain, is responsible. Research suggests that the time frame of infantile amnesia matches the postnatal maturation of the hippocampus. In addition, humans and animals whose hippocampal formations are damaged retain the ability to learn perceptual-motor skills, but they cannot remember the spatial and temporal context of their experiences. Nadel and Zola-Morgan believe that infants and young children fail to retain the time and place of events they experience until the hippocampal system matures. As a result, early events are not remembered because they cannot be retrieved in any environmentally specific way.

Finally, a number of information processing explanations of infantile amnesia have been developed. One suggests that the experiences of infants and young children are stored before they are mature enough to engage in active, deliberate information processing. Yet only information that we process consciously and strategically at storage is easily accessible through purposeful retrieval efforts (White & Pillemer, 1979). Another information processing interpretation is offered by Nelson and Ross's (1980) research on young children's scripts. They suggest that most things children experience in early life are eventually repeated and do not remain novel. As young children construct common scripts for these similar events, individual instances quickly lose their identity and become difficult to recall. Nelson and Ross also believe that only after children have established general expectations about familiar events through well-established script sequences will unique autobiographical memories stand out as distinguishable from them. This general base of scripted knowledge probably takes the first few years of life to build up.

METACOGNITION

In previous sections of this chapter, we have made many references to the fact that children's cognitive processing abilities seem to become more conscious, reflective, and deliberate with age. These trends indicate that in addition to children's expanding knowledge of the world around them, another form of knowledge that we have not yet considered may have an important bearing on how efficiently and effectively they are able to remember and solve problems. **Metacognition** refers to awareness and understanding of one's own cognitive processes. The prefix "meta-," meaning "beyond or higher," is applied to the term because the central meaning of metacognition is "thinking about thought." It is cognition that takes as its object any aspect of the mind and its activities. Cognitive psychologists believe that to work most effectively, the information processing system must be aware of itself. It needs, for example, to be able to arrive at such realizations as "I had better write that phone number down or I'll forget it," "This paragraph is complicated; I had better read it again to understand the author's point," and "I had better try to group these items together in some way if I am going to remember them" (Paris & Lindauer, 1982).

Metacognitive knowledge can be as wide-ranging as the functioning of the information processing system itself. Below we discuss three aspects of metacognitive knowledge: knowledge of the self as a cognitive processor, knowledge of task variables, and knowledge of strategies. Once children develop these understandings, they must be able to put them into action while solving a task. They do this through *self-regulation* — constantly monitoring their progress toward a goal, checking outcomes, and redirecting efforts that prove unsuccessful. In the last part of this section, we take up the development of this on-line, continuous, and conscious monitoring of cognitive activity.

Metacognitive Knowledge

Knowledge of the Self as a Cognitive Processor. What do children know about themselves as cognitive processors and remembering beings, and how early does an appreciation of the existence and functioning of their own mental worlds appear?

Recent research shows that the first awareness of the separateness of mental events from external events appears remarkably early, around the middle of the third year of life. Such words as "think," "remember," and "pretend" are among the first verbs that young children add to their vocabulary (Limber, 1973), and after 2½ years of age they use them appropriately to refer to internal states, as when they say, "It's not real, I was just pretending," or "I thought the socks were in the drawer, 'cept they weren't" (Wellman, 1985, p. 176). Although at one time it was thought that preschool children could not distinguish between internal mental, symbolic acts and external, physical behaviors (Piaget, 1926/1930), new evidence shows that this is not true. Johnson and Wellman (1982) presented 4- through 9-year-olds with a trick condition in which the discrepancy between their own mental state and an external act was made very salient. Each child was shown an object hidden in one of two boxes and then was asked to pick the box in which it was located. Children picked correctly, but the experimenter had secretly moved the object from the box in which it had been hidden to the other box instead. The behavioral act of not finding the object did not lead even the youngest children to say they had forgotten where the object was. Instead, they insisted that they knew and remembered.

Although preschool children have some understanding of mentality, at first it is rudimentary and incomplete. Not until the very end of the preschool years do they grasp the difference among distinct mental acts. Johnson and Wellman (1980) found that 4-year-olds did not comprehend the difference between remembering, knowing, and guessing. The children claimed to know and remember in situations where it was obvious that they happened to guess right, and they sometimes said they were guessing when their responses were clearly based on knowing and remembering. Around age 5½, children develop a differentiated and conventionally accepted understanding of these mental processes (Miscione, Marvin, et al., 1978). During early elementary school, they can provide elaborate definitions of them (Kreutzer, Leonard, & Flavell, 1975).

If very young children have some appreciation of the independent existence of an internal cognitive system, how early are they aware that it is a limited capacity processing device? Research shows that even preschoolers understand that they occasionally have trouble paying attention and that noise, lack of interest, and thinking about other things can hinder their attentiveness to a task (Miller & Zalenski, 1982). Elementary school children are more aware of the impact of psychological factors on attention. They recognize that optimal conditions for attending involve being interested in the task, concentrating on it, wanting to do it, and not being tempted by anything else around them (Miller & Bigi, 1979). By 5 or 6 years of age, most children also realize that their memory is limited—that briefly presented information is likely to be lost, that having to retain information for a long period of time makes memory uncertain, and that at times they do forget (Kreutzer, Leonard, & Flavell, 1975; Wellman, 1978).

Despite some consciousness of a limited capacity processing device, young children still tend to overestimate their own performance. In one study, children were presented with groups of 10 pictures at a time and asked how many they thought they could remember. Nursery school and kindergarten children thought they could remember them all, and their estimates continued to be unrealistic even after they performed the memory task and were given feedback that their recall was far from perfect. During the early elementary school years, predicted and actual memory span come closer together (Flavell, Friedrichs, & Hoyt, 1970). However, when memory span prediction takes place in a task context that is meaningful to young children, such as a game or shopping activity, realistic estimates of memory performance are obtained at younger ages (Schneider, 1985).

By school entry, children show a limited appreciation of individual differences in cognitive abilities in that they recognize that adults are better than children at attending and remembering (Miller & Bigi, 1979; Wellman, 1977). However, children's appreciation of their own cognitive performance in relation to the capabilities of their peers takes more time to develop. As we shall see in Chapter 11 when we discuss the development of self-concept, it does not emerge until second grade.

Knowledge of Task Variables. To perform in an optimal fashion, a learner must be able to evaluate the nature of the task before attempting a solution. Preschool and early elementary school children understand some things about what makes a task easy or hard. For example, the majority of them know that increasing the number of items makes memory performance more difficult (Wellman, 1977; Kreutzer, Leonard, & Flavell, 1975). Kindergartners are also aware that more study time gives them a better chance to learn and recall information and that certain attributes of items, such as their perceptual salience (e.g., being brightly colored) and familiarity, can enhance performance (Kreutzer, Leonard, & Flavell, 1975). They also understand that it is far easier to be asked to recognize items than to have to recall them (Speer & Flavell, 1979).

Older elementary school children have a more differentiated understanding of task variables. During the middle elementary school years, they become conscious of the facilitating role of inter-item relationships in a memory problem. For example, they recognize that a list of semantically related items is easier to remember than a list of unrelated items (Moynahan, 1973; Tenney, 1975). In addition, they have a more sophisticated appreciation of how certain task variables affect the retrievability of material. For example, they know that their memory for a list will suffer if, in between learning and recall, they must study another set of items that is similar to the original list, and they also realize that having to recall prose material word for word is more difficult than being asked for a paraphrase (Kreutzer, Leonard, & Flavell, 1975).

Knowledge of Strategies. Middle childhood is also the time that children become conscious of effective strategies for processing information. By first grade, children recognize a systematic, planful visual search strategy as the most effective way to discover which stimulus in an array of similar stimuli differs from the others, although they do not always deploy it (Miller & Bigi, 1979). By 8 or 9 years of age, they are aware of the need to adapt attentional strategies to momentary task demands, for they realize that in studying material for later recall, it is helpful to devote most effort to the items that they know least well (Kreutzer, Leonard, & Flavell, 1975). In addition, by third grade, children have developed a sophisticated awareness of memory strategies. Kindergartners and first graders have some of this knowledge. For example, they are aware that enlisting the aid of outside memory sources, such as writing yourself a note or asking someone to remind you, is helpful. But when given a hypothetical memory task, older children can think of many more strategic things to do. Witness the following response of an 8-year-old to the question of what she would do to remember a phone number:

> Say the number is 663-8854. Then what I'd do is — say that my number is 663, so I won't have to remember that, really. And then I would think now I've got to remember 88. Now I'm 8 years old, so I can remember, say, my age two times. Then I say how old my brother is, and how old he was last year. And that's how I'd usually remember that phone number. [Is that how you would most often remember a phone number?] Well, usually I write it down. (Kreutzer, Leonard, & Flavell, 1975, p. 11)

Once children are consciously aware of the benefits of strategies, they combine this knowledge with other metacognitive information about person and task variables to form an integrated understanding of cognition, or what Wellman (1985) calls a "naive theory of mind." Even preschool children are sometimes aware of the simultaneous influence of two variables — for example, that both the number of items you must learn and the effort you expend to do so operate jointly to influence memory performance (Wellman, Collins, & Glieberman, 1981). However, older children are far more likely to take account of such interactions (Hale & Kail, 1984; Wellman, 1978). A comprehensive understanding of how a variety of factors, such as the age and motivational level of the learner, the nature and difficulty of the task, and effective deployment of strategies, work together is not achieved until well into the elementary school years (Flavell, 1985; Wellman, 1985).

Self-Regulation

Despite growth of metacognitive knowledge over the childhood years, most studies report that it is only weakly related to task performance (e.g., Moynahan, 1973; Flavell, 1976; Byrd & Gholson, 1985). This disappointing association is most likely due to the fact that a great number of factors can intercede between children's knowledge of what to do and the way they actually behave when confronted with a problem. Children might know about a strategy, but not be good at using it, simply choose to use a different one, think the task is easy enough to do without the strategy, or just not bother to implement it (Flavell & Wellman, 1977; Siegler, 1983a). Still another reason that metacognitive knowledge is only remotely connected to task performance is that younger children have been found to be relatively poor at **self-regulation.** They have difficulty using what they know about cognition to continuously monitor their progress toward a goal, and they often continue with a particular approach even when it is obviously ineffective (Paris & Lindauer, 1982; Brown et al, 1983).

In one study, DeLoache, Sugarman, and Brown (1981) observed the self-regulatory activity of young preschoolers trying to put together a set of nesting cups. When a pair of cups did not fit together, 2-year-olds either applied brute force or took the entire set apart and started over again. Three-year-olds were somewhat better at self-correction on the task. For example, they used their awareness of the serial relationship among the cups when they ran into trouble, reversing two nonfitting cups so the smaller one fit inside the larger one. They only reverted to the brute force technique as a last resort, when they had tried a number of unsuccessful approaches.

Even older children do not seem to interpret their momentary cognitive states while performing a complex task with a great deal of accuracy. When reading or listening to spoken language, sensitivity to the sudden feeling that we do not understand part of a passage is called **comprehension monitoring.** Markman (1979b) examined comprehension monitoring in third-, fifth-, and sixth-grade children by having them listen to short essays containing inconsistent information, as in the following passage:

> To make (Baked Alaska) they put ice cream in a very hot oven. The ice cream in Baked Alaska melts when it gets that hot. Then they take the ice cream out of the oven and serve it right away. When they make Baked Alaska the ice cream stays firm and it does not melt. (P 646)

Children of all grades were poor at noticing such inconsistencies, and similar results have been found in other studies of both spoken and written prose (Flavell et al., 1981; Harris et al., 1981). Sixth graders will reduce their reading speed and look back through the material to a greater extent than third graders when a text is not clear (Capelli & Markman, 1980; Zabrucky & Ratner, 1986), and even younger children will show puzzled facial expressions, although they have trouble verbalizing what is wrong (Flavell et al., 1981). It has been suggested that one impediment to young children's self-regulation is that they have difficulty interpreting their own feelings of uneasiness and discomfort when they encounter ambiguities and contradictions that interfere with successful task performance (Brown et al., 1983; Flavell, 1981a). Poor readers of all ages are especially deficient in self-regulation. They seldom look forward and backward to check their own understanding as they read (Baker & Brown, 1984).

Current evidence suggests that self-regulation is a late-developing skill. In fact, Piaget (1978) believed that it did not appear in sophisticated form until adolescence. In line with this conclusion, there is some evidence that by the adolescent years, metacognitive knowledge and task performance become better related to one another (Waters, 1982).

Still, it is possible to facilitate the development of younger children's self-regulatory behavior. Parents and teachers can help children by promoting conscious awareness of task demands, personal planning, and self-correction (Collins & Stevens, 1982). As adults ask children questions and help them regulate their behavior in circumstances where they are likely to encounter difficulties, then children can internalize these procedures and make them part of their own effective self-regulatory skills.

Think about these practical suggestions for fostering self-regulation. Do they resemble Vygotsky's (1934/1962) ideas about the self-guiding function of private speech, which we discussed in Chapter 6? The ideas are much the same, for Vygotsky emphasized that the self-regulatory role of private speech has its origins in social interactions with others. In fact, Vygotsky's theory has been a source of inspiration for recent research on the effects of *metacognitive training* on children's task performance (Reeve & Brown, 1985). A number of training studies show that providing children with instructions to use self-guiding verbalizations while they perform a task has a substantial effect on how well they do (Meichenbaum & Asarnow, 1979). In addition, training that informs children of the reasons that a strategy is useful enhances the extent to which children will apply it spontaneously in new situations (Kennedy & Miller, 1976; Paris & Jacobs, 1984). When adults tell children *why* and not just *what* to do, they provide a rationale for future action. Then children learn not just how to get a particular task done, but also what to do when faced with new problems. When adults use such approaches to teach children, as Brown and her colleagues (1983) suggest, they help children "learn how to learn."

In summary, metacognition, or conscious awareness of the self as a cognitive processor, improves from the preschool through the school years, gradually encompassing a wider variety of person, task, and strategic aspects of the cognitive system. Eventually the child integrates these with one another into a personal theory of the self as a thinking being, or a "naive theory of mind." However, metacognitive understanding shows a disappointingly weak relationship with children's task performance during the middle childhood years. One reason is that children's ability to apply their metacognitive knowledge in a self-regulatory fashion is not well developed until adolescence. However, younger children can be encouraged and trained to improve their self-regulatory skills.

APPLICATIONS OF THE INFORMATION PROCESSING APPROACH TO COMPLEX TASKS: SCIENTIFIC PROBLEM SOLVING

Research from the information processing perspective that we have discussed so far focuses on the functioning of separate parts of the system. Few efforts have been made to construct general, integrative theories that capture the development of children's thinking and problem solving as a whole. An exception is Siegler's (1981; 1983a; 1983b) **rule-assessment approach**, which offers a precise and effective description of the development of childhood thinking that competes quite well with Piaget's stages. Siegler restudies the responses of children to a variety of Piagetian problem-solving tasks within an information processing perspective. He concludes that cognitive development involves the acquisition of increasingly sophisticated and broadly applicable rules for solving problems. Based on previous studies of children's responses to particular problems, Siegler generates rules that children and adults may be using to solve the task. Then he formulates a set of variations of the problem that yield distinct patterns of answers for individuals using each rule. So far, Siegler has

Siegler's research shows that when solving problems, older children encode and coordinate more pieces of information than their younger counterparts. (Freda Leinwand)

applied the rule-assessment approach to a wide range of scientific problem-solving tasks. His goal is to examine how development proceeds in each specific task domain and from there to look for similarities across different tasks to arrive at general conclusions about the development of the cognitive system.

In the most well known of Siegler's investigations, children from 3 to 17 years of age were presented with a balance scale with four pegs on each side of a fulcrum, much like one of Piaget's formal operational tasks (Siegler, 1976; 1978). Weights were placed on a single peg on each side of the scale. On some trials, the total weight on each side was equal, and on others it was unequal. In addition, sometimes the distances of the weights from the fulcrum were the same, and sometimes they differed. Each time the child was asked to indicate whether the scale would balance or not. Siegler predicted that children would use four different developmentally ordered rules to solve the problem:

Rule I. Subjects using this rule take into account only the number of weights on each side of the fulcrum, ignoring distance. If the number of weights is equal, they predict that the scale will balance. If it is not equal, they predict that the scale will not balance.

Rule II. Subjects following this rule also take into account only weight, except under one circumstance—when the weights on both sides are equal. Under equal-weight conditions, the subjects predict that the scale will balance if the two distances are equal. If they are not equal, they predict that the scale will not balance.

Rule III. Subjects consider both weight and distance. If one dimension is equal and the other is not, they base their decision on the unequal dimension. However, if both dimensions are unequal, they cannot take account of the situation and merely guess.

Rule IV. Subjects consider both weight and distance by computing the torques on each side. They realize that multiplying the number of weights by the distance they are from the fulcrum on one side and seeing if the result is equal to the weight $\times$ distance product obtained on the other side will tell them if the scale will balance.

As shown in Figure 7.13, use of each rule predicts a particular pattern of response across problems on the balance scale. Siegler (1976) found that the great majority of children between 5 and 17 responded in accord with one of the rules. Five-year-olds conformed to Rule I, 9-year-olds usually used Rule II or III, and 13- and 17-year-olds most often used Rule III. Practically no children at any age used Rule IV. Finally, a systematic, rule-governed approach to the problem seemed to emerge between the ages of 3 and 5, for the great majority of 3-year-olds performed randomly, using no rule at all, but by age 4, half of the children had acquired an understanding of Rule I (Siegler, 1978). Applying the rule-assessment approach to other tasks, Siegler again found that preschool children frequently showed no evidence of consistent rule-using and that older children conformed to a parsimonious set of rules much like those described above.

Further research by Siegler showed that feedback to children about whether they were correct or not on each trial led many of them to move toward use of more advanced balance scale rules. However, children differed in the extent to which they profited from such experience. For example, Rule I 8-year-olds who witnessed violations of their current approach generally advanced to Rule II or III. In contrast, many 5-year-olds did not change at all. Siegler observed that the younger Rule I users failed to notice the distance of the weights from the fulcrum; they never encoded this aspect of the problem. When trained to encode distance, they quickly advanced in their rule-governed solutions (Siegler, 1976). Inadequate encoding also explained the complete absence of rule use in many preschoolers, who failed to notice the dimension of weight. When 3- and 4-year-olds were trained to take account of weight, they used Rule I quite effectively. Similarly, 13- and 17-year-olds grasped Rule IV when given feedback on their incorrect responses along with aids designed to facilitate discovery of the torque principle (Siegler, 1978).

Siegler (1983b) concludes that children profit most from new information that pinpoints specific inadequacies in what they already know. His observation that poor encoding is a major obstacle to the development of more sophisticated problem-solving procedures is another information processing finding that has important implications for education. If teachers want children to develop enhanced understanding, they must make sure that their pupils take in all relevant dimensions of a situation.

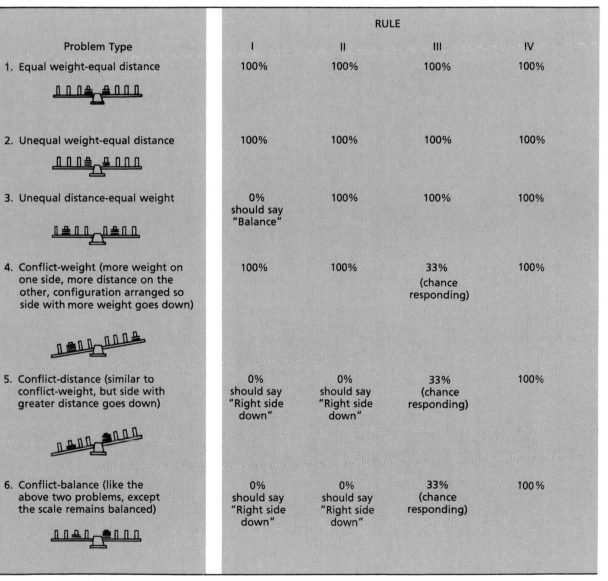

Problem Type	RULE			
	I	II	III	IV
1. Equal weight-equal distance	100%	100%	100%	100%
2. Unequal weight-equal distance	100%	100%	100%	100%
3. Unequal distance-equal weight	0% should say "Balance"	100%	100%	100%
4. Conflict-weight (more weight on one side, more distance on the other, configuration arranged so side with more weight goes down)	100%	100%	33% (chance responding)	100%
5. Conflict-distance (similar to conflict-weight, but side with greater distance goes down)	0% should say "Right side down"	0% should say "Right side down"	33% (chance responding)	100%
6. Conflict-balance (like the above two problems, except the scale remains balanced)	0% should say "Right side down"	0% should say "Right side down"	33% (chance responding)	100%

Figure 7.13. Percentage of correct responses expected on Siegler's (1978) balance scale problems for children using different rules. For each problem type, children are asked to indicate whether they think the scale will balance or whether the right or left side will go down. *(From "The Origins of Scientific Reasoning" by R. S. Siegler. In R. S. Siegler [Ed.], Children's Thinking: What Develops? [pp. 104–149]. Hillsdale, NJ: Erlbaum. Copyright 1978 by Lawrence Erlbaum Associates. Adapted by permission.)*

When children lack detailed knowledge, they rely on what Siegler calls *fall-back rules* — approaches in which they focus on a single obvious dimension of a situation, such as the Rule I focus on weight in the balance scale task described above.[2] Siegler recommends that teachers carefully assess children's initial rule-oriented understanding and develop instructional experiences in relation to those rules. Only when teaching efforts are systematically tuned to the child's current knowledge, he says, can they be maximally effective.

Can all of children's thinking and problem solving be captured by Siegler's rule-assessment approach? A number of investigators think not. For example, some critics suggest that it may only be applicable to well-structured tasks (Strauss & Levin, 1981). Siegler (1981) himself acknowledges that numerous tasks with varying characteristics will need to be examined to build a comprehensive theory of children's problem solving. Nevertheless, at the present time his rule-assessment technique offers a promising way of getting at the basic nature of the cognitive system within a single framework, and it has also generated precise and useful suggestions for education.

EVALUATION OF THE INFORMATION PROCESSING APPROACH TO COGNITIVE DEVELOPMENT

The major strength of the information processing approach, already noted at the beginning of this chapter, is its explicitness and precision in breaking down cognitive performance into a set of sequentially operating processes. Information processing has been successful in providing a detailed specification of how younger versus older and more versus less skilled individuals perceive, attend, memorize, and solve problems. Its findings emphasize the commonalities between adult and childhood thinking and continually underscore the fact that few general statements can be made about how people process information without specifying the nature of their task environments. An additional contribution of the information processing approach has been in the study of how children process information in educationally important domains, such as reading, mathematics, and science. Information processing researchers have already been successful in identifying factors responsible for more versus less effective performance on school-related tasks and coming up with successful ways to help children learn (Glaser, 1982).

Nevertheless, the information processing perspective has a variety of serious limitations that prevent it from serving as a completely adequate account of cognitive development. The first, ironically, stems from its central strength: by breaking cognition down into its component parts, information processing has had difficulty integrating all of the elements into a broad, comprehensive developmental theory. Although information processing has outlined basic developmental changes in perception, attention, memory, and higher cognitive processes such as problem solving, at present we know little about how all these facets of cognition are put together over the course of childhood. Because information processing has not yet been successful in reducing the wide array of changes in children's thinking to manageable proportions, there are still many developmental psychologists who resist abandoning Piaget's theory in favor of it (Carey, 1985).

[2] Notice how similar Siegler's notion of fall-back rules is to the Piagetian preoperational characteristic of centration described in Chapter 6. However, in contrast to Piaget, Siegler does not consider young children's tendency to focus on a single aspect of a problem to the neglect of other important aspects to be an inherent property of their mental organization. Instead, he regards it as a temporary means of resolving a problem that both children and adults resort to when they have limited knowledge about a task.

Another difficulty is that the information processing approach has, to date, not provided an explicit account of how developmental change takes place (Siegler, 1983a; Kuhn, 1988; Flavell, 1985). Information processing theorists have complained that Piagetian mechanisms of change — assimilation, accommodation, and organization — are vague and imprecise (e.g., Klahr & Wallace, 1976), but they have yet to replace them with more detailed and effective explanations of how change occurs. Although many rely, in one form or another, on gradual increases in domain-specific knowledge to explain development, it is now well established that in a variety of situations, even a great deal of additional knowledge as well as practice in applying it will not elevate the young child's performance to the level of the older, more skilled learner. That such limitations on development do exist has meant that information processing psychologists have not been able to dismiss completely the Piagetian emphasis on years of maturation and generalized experience in a rich and varied external world as important contributors to cognitive change (Case, 1978).

In addition, the computer metaphor, although bringing exactitude and precision to research on the internal workings of the human mind, has its own inherent limitations. Information processing theorists uniformly reject the behaviorist assumption of a passive, purposeless organism shaped by environmental contingencies and think of the human being as an active, strategic processor of information. But their reliance on the computer as an analogy for mental functioning has been attacked as another sterile conception of human cognition. Task performances that can be simulated on computers, while complex in their own right, do not mirror the richness of many real-life learning situations. For example, they tell us little about some facets of cognition that are not linear, logical, and unidirectional in nature, such as daydreaming and creative imagination. In addition, computers cannot feel, and they do not have self-generated goals and intentions. While they can interact with other machines through phone lines and modems, computers do not make friends, develop affectional ties to one another, take each other's perspectives, or adopt morals and social values. It is perhaps because of the narrowness of the computer metaphor that information processing has not told us much about the links between cognition and other areas of development, such as emotion, motivation, and social functioning. Currently there is considerable interest on the part of developmental psychologists in finding out whether information processing can enhance our appreciation of how children think about their social world. We will see a few examples of this new emphasis in later chapters of this book. However, it is still the case that extensions and elaborations of Piaget's theory prevail when it comes to research on children's social cognition and moral thought.

Finally, information processing research has emphasized the verbal symbolic arena of human mental functioning. Less is known about nonverbal thought, such as children's representations of actions and spatial relations, than has been gleaned from extensions of Piaget's theory. The verbal symbolic emphasis of information processing models has also meant that not much effort has been devoted to explaining how the preverbal infant is transformed into a symbol-manipulating preschooler. Once again, Piaget has told us more about this important transitional period. Information processing research has yet to do an effective job of covering and linking together the entire continuum of child development.

Despite its deficiencies, the information processing approach holds promise for the future. It has already contributed invaluably to our appreciation of the wide array of cognitive changes that take place during childhood, and it continues to generate a wealth of important research findings. Siegler (1983a) predicts that it will surmount a number of its shortcomings. He forecasts increased attention to identifying mechanisms of development, new research on the early symbolic child, and a continuation of the current trend toward studying educationally relevant task domains in the years to come.

CHAPTER SUMMARY

1. Information processing rose to the forefront of cognitive development as the result of dissatisfaction with both Piagetian and behaviorist perspectives. The approach views the mind as a complex, symbol-manipulating system, much like a digital computer. The computer metaphor provides a means of analyzing thought into separate internal processes that can be studied individually to yield a detailed understanding of what children and adults do when faced with a task or problem.

2. Major models of the information processing system include Atkinson and Shiffrin's store model, which assumes that information travels through a sequence of three finite-capacity stores. Control processes, or strategies, operate on material in each store so that it can be retained and used efficiently. Research on the serial position effect supports Atkinson and Shiffrin's distinction between short- and long-term memory. However, variable findings on the capacities of the stores have led some investigators to turn toward a levels of processing model. It assumes that retention of information is a function of the depth to which an incoming stimulus is analyzed. Superficially processed information is quickly forgotten, but information linked with other knowledge is retained for a longer period of time. Instead of fixed-capacity stores, levels of processing theorists attribute the limited capacity of the system to the extent to which individuals can distribute their attention across different activities. With increasing age, cognitive operations become better learned and more automatic, and attentional resources are freed for other concurrent activities. Other information processing models focus less on discrete strategies and more on whole programs of processing. This larger view is just beginning to appear in research on children.

3. The major perspective on the processing of sensory information is differentiation theory, which views development as the detection of increasingly fine-grained distinctions among objects and patterns with age. Differentiation theory helps explain the way in which children discriminate written symbols from one another as they learn to read. Enrichment theory, a competing approach to sensory processing, emphasizes the application of cognitive schemes to the interpretation of stimulus events.

4. Attentional processes determine the sources of information that will be considered in any task or problem. With age, children's allocation of attention becomes more controlled and sustained as well as planful and systematic. Also, older children are better able to adapt attentional resources to task demands and increments in their own learning.

5. Strategies commonly used by adults to keep information in short-term memory and facilitate its transfer to the long-term store are rarely employed by preschool children. Although young children can be trained to use strategies, without continued adult prompting, they quickly abandon them. During the elementary school years, children use re-

hearsal and organization spontaneously and with greater effectiveness. Elaboration is a late-developing memory skill that typically does not appear until after age 11. Like young children, people in non-Western cultures without formal schooling do not use memory strategies spontaneously. Classroom learning experiences seem to play a role in facilitating the emergence of deliberate memorization.

6. Information in permanent, long-term memory must be retrieved in order to be used again. Recognition is the simplest form of retrieval. By the preschool years, children's recognition memory is excellent, although it continues to improve with age. In contrast, their recall is poor; during the preschool years children depend on salient external retrieval cues for remembering absent stimuli. Recall improves as children encode information in a more organized fashion. Unlike lists of items, complex, meaningful material generally undergoes reconstruction when it is remembered. When 6- or 7-year-old children are asked to recall prose material, like adults, they engage in condensations, integrations, and additions of information. During elementary school, children's ability to draw inferences from prose material gradually improves. Developmental psychologists attribute changes in children's reconstructive memory to growth in the knowledge base available to interpret incoming information.

7. A growing number of investigators believe that cognitive development may be largely a matter of the acquisition of domain-specific knowledge that renders new information more familiar and easier to store and retrieve. Although children who are more knowledgeable than adults in particular content areas have superior memories, whether knowledge is the only factor involved in memory development is a matter of controversy. Some evidence indicates that children differ not only in how much they know, but also in how effectively they use their knowledge to clarify the meaning of new information.

8. Early in development, children represent their everyday experiences in terms of scripts, general descriptions of what occurs and when it will occur in a given situation. Script structures become more complex and better specified with age. They serve as an early, basic form of memory organization and may be the link between early episodic memory and a mature, semantically organized long-term memory store.

9. Metacognitive knowledge is believed to have an important bearing on how efficiently and effectively children can remember and solve problems. Knowledge of the self as a cognitive processor, knowledge of task variables, and knowledge of strategies improve during middle childhood. However, metacognitive knowledge is only weakly related to performance, possibly because children are relatively poor at using what they know to regulate their task-related behavior. Current evidence suggests that self-regulation does not appear in mature form until adolescence.

10. Siegler's rule-assessment approach is unique among information processing research on children in that it aims to characterize the development of thinking and problem solving as a whole. Examining children's patterns of performance on scientific problem-solving tasks, Siegler concludes that cognitive development involves the acquisition of increasingly sophisticated and broadly applicable rules for solving problems. Siegler finds that poor encoding is a major obstacle to better problem-solving procedures. He believes that effective instructional experiences must be based on children's current rule-oriented understandings.

11. Major strengths of the information processing approach include its explicitness and precision, its emphasis on important commonalities between adult and childhood thinking, and its contribution of successful techniques to help children learn. As yet, information processing research has not led to a broad, integrative theory of cognitive development, and it has not offered clear explanations of how developmental change takes place. Furthermore, information processing has told us little about aspects of thinking that are not linear and logical in nature, nor has it shed light on how cognition is related to other facets of development. Despite these shortcomings, information processing continues to contribute in many important ways to our understanding of children's cognitive development.

IMPORTANT TERMS AND CONCEPTS

black box model
reversal and nonreversal learning
mediational theory
overjustification hypothesis
store model
control processes or strategies
sensory store
short-term memory store
long-term memory store
serial position effect
levels of processing model
M-space

differentiation theory
enrichment theory
incidental learning
attention deficit-hyperactivity
    disorder
rehearsal
production deficiency
control deficiency
organization
elaboration
recognition
recall

reconstruction
domain-specific knowledge
semantic memory
episodic memory
scripts
infantile amnesia
metacognition
self-regulation
comprehension monitoring
rule-assessment approach

The Crabbers, by Ian Nathan.
Felix Rosenstiel's Widow & Son Ltd.

CHAPTER 8

Intelligence: A Psychometric Perspective

The psychometric or measurement approach to children's intellectual growth serves as the basis for the wide variety of mental tests currently available for the assessment of children. As we will see shortly, in recent years the content of some mental tests has been influenced by the Piagetian and information processing perspectives that we discussed in Chapters 6 and 7. However, when compared to these other two views, the psychometric perspective is far more "product-oriented" than "process-oriented" in its approach to intellectual development. In other words, the psychometric perspective focuses on outcomes and results—*how many* and *what kinds* of questions children can answer correctly at different ages. It places less emphasis on *how* children arrive at solutions to problems at various points in development. Psychometricians pose such questions as: What factors or dimensions make up intelligence, and how do these factors change with age? How can intellectual development be measured quantitatively so that scores are useful for predicting school achievement, career attainment, and other consequences of intellectual success? How can the intelligence of different children be meaningfully compared, and what background characteristics explain these differences?

We begin our consideration of the psychometric approach by reviewing historical and current definitions of intelligence. After discussing how IQ scores are computed and distributed in the general population and describing some commonly used intelligence tests, we turn to research on the stability of the IQ score and how effectively it predicts scholastic performance and later life success and satisfaction. Racial/ethnic and social class differences in intelligence are at the heart of the nature-nurture debate waged among psychologists over the course of this century. We continue our discussion by considering current evidence on genetic and environmental determinants of IQ, as well as the controversial issue of whether intelligence tests are biased against

313

ethnic minority children. Finally, we conclude by moving "beyond IQ" to consider the development of creativity. Although creativity is among the most highly valued of human attributes in all literate societies, it is one mental ability that is not represented on current intelligence tests for children.

DEFINITIONS OF INTELLIGENCE

Take a moment to jot down a list of behaviors that you regard as typical of people who are highly intelligent. Did you come up with just one or two attributes or a great many? In a recent study, Sternberg and his co-workers (Sternberg et al., 1981; Sternberg, 1982) asked nearly 500 laypersons to complete a similar exercise. He found that ordinary people have very definite notions of what intelligence is, and their ideas show a surprisingly close correspondence to the views of experts. Psychologists and laypersons alike typically regard intelligence as a complex construct made up of practical problem solving, verbal ability, and social competence. These findings suggest that people do not consider a single dimension as adequate for describing intelligence. Instead, their definitions incorporate a variety of attributes.

The problem of defining children's intelligence is even more complicated, because as they grow and develop, behaviors judged to reflect intelligent behavior change as well. In a study similar to the Sternberg work described above, Siegler and Richards (1980) asked students in an introductory psychology course to list five traits they thought characterized intelligent 6-month-olds, 2-year-olds, 10-year-olds, and adults. As shown in Table 8.1, common descriptors of intelligent behavior differed from one developmental period to another, in much the same fashion as Piaget suggested intelligence changes over the course of childhood. For example, with age, problem solving and reasoning became more important as intelligent characteristics, and sensorimotor responsiveness became less so. Furthermore, beyond infancy, respondents stressed verbal and symbolic knowledge as the major basis of intelligence, an emphasis that fits with both the Piagetian and information processing views. The investigators also asked the students to estimate the correlations among the traits they mentioned for each age. The students' responses revealed that they thought there would be some close connections between different mental abilities, but they

Table 8.1. Five Traits Most Frequently Mentioned by College Students as Characterizing Intelligence at Different Ages

6-MONTH-OLDS	2-YEAR-OLDS	10-YEAR-OLDS	ADULTS
1. Recognition of people and objects	1. Verbal ability	1. Verbal ability	1. Reasoning
2. Motor coordination	2. Learning ability	2,3,4. Learning ability; problem solving; reasoning (all three tied)	2. Verbal ability
3. Alertness	3. Awareness of people and environment		3. Problem solving
4. Awareness of environment	4. Motor coordination		4. Learning ability
5. Verbalization	5. Curiosity	5. Creativity	5. Creativity

Source: R. S. Siegler & D. D. Richards, 1980. College Students' Prototypes of Children's Intelligence. Paper presented at the annual meeting of the American Psychological Association, New York. Copyright 1980 by the American Psychological Association. Adapted by permission of the author.

predicted considerable distinctiveness as well. As we review important historical and current conceptions of mental ability in the sections below, you will see that the evolution of scientific theories reveals this same tension between a view of intelligence as a single, overarching characteristic as opposed to a collection of only loosely related cognitive skills.

Early Conceptions of Intelligence

Foundations of the Intelligence Testing Movement. From the end of the nineteenth century to the middle of the twentieth century, the mental testing movement evolved from crude beginnings to an advanced state of development. The rise of mental testing was stimulated by the intellectual, social, and educational climate of this time period. During the latter part of the nineteenth century, Darwin's theory of evolution helped draw the attention of behavioral scientists to individual differences (which were at that time largely presumed to be hereditary) in people's ability to adapt to the demands of a newly industrialized society. The initiation of universal public education in Europe and the United States by the early 1900s opened the schoolhouse doors to children who previously would not have been admitted to an educational system that was restricted to society's privileged classes. As a result, new methods were needed to identify children who could not profit from regular classroom instruction. Moreover, the emergence of the mental testing movement coincided with a major war that brought with it the enormous practical problem of selecting and training millions of men for military combat. By the beginning of World War I, mental testing had progressed far enough that psychologists were able to apply the new methodology to this mass selection effort (Carroll, 1982).

Sir Francis Galton and James McKeen Cattell. The British psychologist and statistician Sir Francis Galton (1883) and the American psychologist James McKeen Cattell (1890) can be credited with the invention of the very first mental tests. But like others before the turn of the century, they adhered to a crude conception of intelligence, believing that it could be revealed by simple tests of sensory acuity and speed of reaction. Intelligence test items, such as reaction time to sound and time for naming colors, were chosen to reflect the ability of the nervous system to respond sensitively and quickly. However, these measures were soon shown to have little practical

By the early 1900s, universal public education had become prevalent in Europe and the United States. Intelligence tests responded to a new need for ways to identify children who could not profit from regular classroom instruction. (Photograph by Jacob A. Riis, Jacob A. Riis Collection, Museum of the City of New York)

utility. They were poor indicators of individual differences in mental functioning, and they bore no relationship to academic achievement (Wissler, 1901).

Alfred Binet. In the early 1900s, the French psychologist Alfred Binet and his colleague Theodore Simon discovered the first effective way to measure intelligence. Binet's successful approach was motivated by the challenging task of recommending to the French Minister of Public Instruction a method for identifying Paris schoolchildren who could not benefit from regular classroom experiences and needed special instruction. Binet concluded that instead of measures of sensory acuity and reaction time, test items resembling the mental activities of everyday life were needed. Believing that intelligence involved sophisticated mental powers of reasoning, good judgment, memory, and abstraction, he devised a test of "general mental ability" that included a diverse array of complex verbal and nonverbal reasoning tasks. Binet's test was also the first *developmental* approach to test construction. The criterion for including an item on the test was that it had to show a consistent increase in performance with age.

The Binet test proved to be so successful in predicting school performance that it became the basis for new intelligence tests developed in other countries. In 1916, it was adapted for use with American schoolchildren by Lewis Terman at Stanford University. Since then, its American version has been known as the Stanford-Binet Intelligence Scale. The Stanford-Binet has undergone several revisions over the course of this century, but the content of the current test can still be traced back to Binet's original scale.

Alfred Binet (1857–1911) devised the first effective measure of intelligence. His test of "general mental ability" was the first to successfully predict children's school performance. (Culver Pictures)

From Individual to Group Testing. Binet's instrument was designed to be individually administered to one child at a time, but psychologists soon realized that many of the items that appeared on it could be adapted for more efficient, group testing. One of the first widespread applications of group testing was implemented during World War I. A team of prominent American psychologists devised the Army Alpha Examination, which was given to more than a million army recruits to aid in their selection and rejection. Early trials revealed a surprisingly high rate of illiteracy in the recruit population. As a result, the new group testing approach was attended to by educators, who felt that group tests might help teachers assess the learning capacities of their pupils. A flood of group intelligence tests appeared that imitated the format of the army examination, bringing the concept of intelligence into widespread usage (Carroll, 1982).

Currently, a wide variety of group intelligence tests are available for use in schools. These mass testing instruments permit the simultaneous examination of large numbers of children and require little training of teacher-examiners (Anastasi, 1982). However, most intelligence tests that enter into important educational decisions, such as the placement of children into special educational programs, are individually administered and demand considerable training and experience to give well. In contrast to group-administered tests, individual tests permit an in-depth diagnosis by a skilled examiner who not only considers the child's scores, but also makes clinical observations of the child's functioning during the test, such as attentiveness to and interest in the tasks and whether the child adequately understood the test instructions. The examiner also looks for indicators of certain internal states, such as anxiety or wariness of the tester, that might lead the results to underestimate the child's ability. This information is combined with additional data on the cultural and educational background of the child in interpreting the test scores (Kaufman, 1979).

Because group tests do not permit the gathering of such clinical evidence, they involve greater risk of error than individual tests. Consequently, their practical usefulness is restricted to instructional planning for large groups of children and *screening,* or the identification of children who require more extensive evaluation with individually administered tests. In recent years, heightened sensitivity to the limitations of group tests has led their designers to no longer refer to them as tests of "intelligence" or "mental ability," but instead to call them by less assuming names, such as "academic aptitude," "scholastic aptitude," "school ability," or "cognitive abilities" (Lennon, 1985).

Toward Clearer Definitions: The Early Factor Analysts. The efforts of Binet and others during the early period of the mental testing movement were oriented toward a wholistic appraisal of intelligence. They used a single score to measure individual differences in overall ability (Guilford, 1985). However, as shown in Figure 8.1, a wide variety of tasks appear on typical intelligence tests. In view of the diversity of mental performances subsumed under the construct "intelligence," psychologists seeking clearer definitions of intelligence had to face the important issue of whether it really was an all-inclusive entity that could be represented by a single score, or whether it was a collection of many different abilities.

To resolve the dilemma, researchers began to carefully study the performances of individuals on successful intelligence tests. The statistical technique of **factor analysis** was used early on as a tool for examining relationships among mental test items in order to identify the various components of intelligence. Factor analysis is a complicated correlational procedure whereby scores on many separate test items are combined together into just a few factors, which substitute for the separate scores. Then the psychologist gives each of the factors a name, based on the common characteristics of items that are closely correlated with the factor. For example, if vocabulary, verbal comprehension, and verbal analogies items all correlate highly with the same factor, the factor might be labeled "verbal ability." Using this technique, many efforts were made to identify the underlying mental abilities that account for successful performance on intelligence tests.

Charles Spearman's "General Factor." An early influential factor analyst who worked to establish a clearer definition of intelligence was British psychologist Charles Spearman (1927). Spearman found that all of the test items he examined correlated to a greater or lesser extent with one another. He therefore proposed that they had in common an underlying **general factor,** or what he termed **"g."** In addition, since the test items were not perfectly correlated, Spearman suggested that each also measured a **specific factor,** called **"s,"** which was unique to the task. Spearman's identification of "g" and "s" led his theory of mental abilities to be called the *two-factor theory of intelligence.*

Spearman was especially interested in the psychological nature of "g," or whatever it is that tends to produce positive correlations among all mental test scores. He concluded that "g" represented some kind of abstract reasoning power, for intelligence test problems that require individuals to extract relationships and apply general principles seemed to be the strongest correlates of "g," and they also offered the best prediction of intellectual performance in other situations.

Later on in his research, Spearman discovered something that contradicted his earlier two-factor view. He found that some subsets of test items correlated more highly with one another than they did with other items. This finding led him to add to his theory a set of **group factors** that were of moderate degrees of generality, in addition to "g" and "s." With additional empirical research, Spearman identified four such group factors: verbal, visual, and numerical abilities, and another factor that was social in nature, in that it involved awareness of the mental states of other people. Out of these findings emerged a new, better articulated view of intelligence as a set of hierarchically structured abilities. Still, from Spearman's point of view, "g" was central and supreme, at the top of the hierarchy of mental abilities. The existence of a general factor underlying a wide variety of separate mental abilities is currently accepted by many (but not all) psychometric experts, and "g" ranks as Spearman's

Item Type	TYPICAL VERBAL ITEMS
Vocabulary	Tell me what "carpet" means.
General Information	How many ounces make a pound? What day of the week comes right after Thursday?
Verbal Comprehension	Why are policemen needed?
Verbal Analogies	A rock is hard; a pillow is _____ .
Logical Reasoning	Five girls are sitting side by side on a bench. Jane is in the middle and Betty sits next to her on the right. Alice is beside Betty, and Dale is beside Ellen, who sits next to Jane. Who are sitting on the ends?
Number Series	Which number comes next in the series? **4 8 6 12 10** ____

TYPICAL NONVERBAL ITEMS

Picture Oddities	Which picture does not belong with the others?

Spatial Visualization	Which of the boxes on the right can be made from the pattern shown on the left?

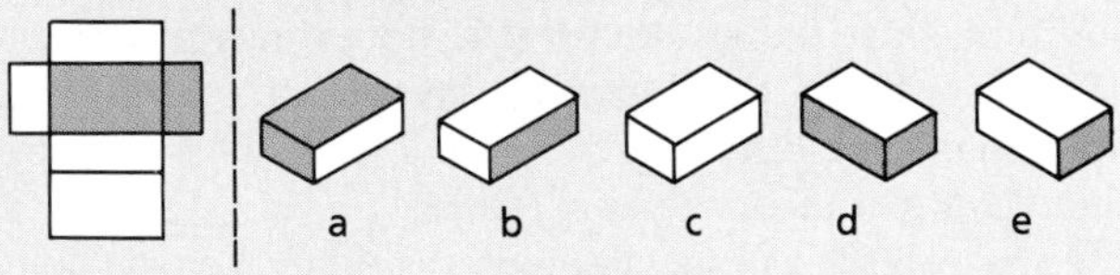

Figure 8.1. Sample intelligence test items appropriate for children of different ages. The items are similar, but not identical, to ones that appear on common individually and group-administered tests. In contrast to verbal items, nonverbal items do not require reading or direct use of language. Performance items are also nonverbal, but they require the individual to draw or construct something rather than merely give a correct answer. As a result, they appear only on individually administered intelligence tests. *(Logical reasoning, picture oddities, spatial visualization, and figure matrices examples are adapted with permission of The Free Press, a Division of Macmillan, Inc. from* Bias in Mental Testing *by Arthur R. Jensen. Pp. 150, 154, 157, 160. Copyright © 1980 by Arthur R. Jensen.)*

longest-lasting contribution to scientific efforts directed at unraveling the nature of intelligence.

Louis Thurstone's "Primary Mental Abilities." Louis Thurstone, an American contemporary of Spearman, did not originally view intelligence as unitary. Instead, he saw it as a multidimensional construct. Thurstone gave 50 intelligence tests to a large number of college students, analyses of which yielded seven clear factors. He concluded that intelligence was composed of seven distinct **primary mental abilities:** verbal meaning, perceptual speed, reasoning, number, rote memory, word fluency, and a spatial or visualization factor. As an outgrowth of this theory, Thurstone developed the Primary Mental Abilities Test (Thurstone, 1938), a group-administered instrument that consisted of separate subtests, each designed to measure one of the factors. A version was eventually developed for schoolchildren (Thurstone & Thurstone, 1953). With further research, Thurstone found that his primary mental abilities correlated moderately with one another. Consequently, he eventually acknowledged

Figure Matrices   Which pattern fills the blank space?

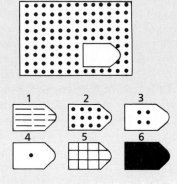

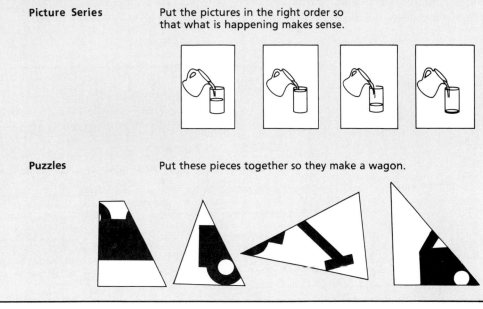

TYPICAL PERFORMANCE ITEMS

Picture Series   Put the pictures in the right order so
that what is happening makes sense.

Puzzles   Put these pieces together so they make a wagon.

the existence of "g" as well as second-order group factors fewer in number than the seven primary factors.

Spearman's and Thurstone's respective findings are generally taken to represent two different schools of thought about mental abilities, the first stressing one general ability tapped by all tests, the other emphasizing that there are numerous independent mental abilities. In actuality, each view is supported by research and accounts for part of the story. Still, Thurstone's work emphasized a different view from the one that dominated the early period of the mental testing movement. His research underlined the notion that intelligence tests were mixtures of very diverse mental tasks, and a single, composite score could conceal important information about a person's pattern of abilities. Thurstone increased psychologists' and educators' receptiveness to the idea that individuals could have a variety of intellectual strengths and weaknesses. As a result, children who scored low on measures of general intelligence were not doomed to failure in all intellectual activities. Beneath their low scores might lie special intellectual talents (Carroll, 1982).

The Modern Factor Analysts

J. P. Guilford's "Structure-of-Intellect" Model. Modern mental ability theorists follow in the tradition of the early factor analysts. One of the most prominent of them is J. P. Guilford (1967, 1985), who proposes a complex, three-dimensional **structure-of-intellect model** (see Figure 8.2). In the model, mental activity is classified along three dimensions: (1) its mental operation; (2) its contents; and (3) the product resulting from the mental operation. For example, a common memory span task in which a child is asked to remember a list of numbers would be classified as memory (operation), symbolic (content), and units (product). A test that asks a subject to decide which of a set of words belong to the same class (e.g., jacket, socks, tie, pencil) involves evaluation (operation), semantic (content), and classes (product). The structure-of-intellect model generates a total of 150 possible separate ability factors, and Guilford claims empirical support for at least 98 of them (Guilford & Hoepfner, 1971).

Unusual features of Guilford's model include a "behavioral" content category, which is responsive to the conjectures of early theorists, like Spearman, that a separate "social intelligence" may exist, involving sensitivity to the mental states of others. In addition, Guilford added tests of creative thinking to his factor analytic studies, realizing that a person who exhibited signs of creativity may be especially intelligent and that items of this type were conspicuously absent from standard intelligence tests. Guilford (1950) suggested that one of the mental operations that is

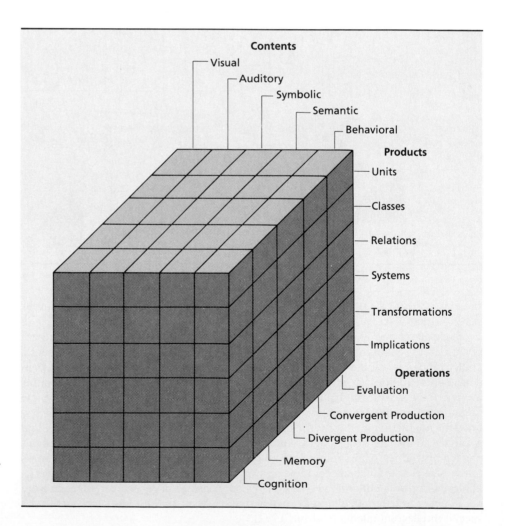

Figure 8.2. Guilford's structure-of-intellect model. *(From J. P. Guilford, 1985, "The Structure-of-Intellect Model." In B. B. Wolman [Ed.],* Handbook of Intelligence. *Copyright © 1985 by John Wiley & Sons, Inc. Reprinted by permission of John Wiley & Sons, Inc.)*

centrally involved in creative thinking is *divergent production,* which involves fluency in production of ideas and a ready ability to think of a wide variety of alternatives to meet a particular need (e.g., "Think of as many meanings for the word 'bolt' as you can). It can be contrasted with the noncreative type of thinking involved in *convergent production,* in which one is asked to converge on or arrive at a single best answer (e.g., "Bolt" most nearly means [a] to paint [b] to sing [c] to run [d] to hang). Guilford also conjectured that creative thinking is flexible thinking. It involves a ready ability to switch categories of thought, an aspect represented in Guilford's model by the product category *transformations.* As we shall see when we consider creativity in greater detail at the end of this chapter, test materials commonly used to assess it are responsive to Guilford's ideas.

Although Guilford's structure-of-intellect model is the most comprehensive model of mental abilities available, many psychologists have questioned his extensive proliferation of mental factors beyond the seven originally identified by Thurstone. Studies providing support for the structure-of-intellect model have been criticized on methodological grounds (Horn & Knapp, 1974). Investigators have also raised such issues as: "Do the factors correspond to the nature of human mental life?" "To what extent are each of Guilford's mental abilities important in school, everyday life, and other activities?" (Carroll, 1982). As yet, these questions have not been fully answered by research.

Raymond Cattell's "Fluid Versus Crystallized Intelligence." A different, more parsimonious approach to defining mental abilities is reflected in the work of Raymond B. Cattell (1963; 1971), who distinguishes between **crystallized and fluid intelligence.** Using Spearman's terminology, R. B. Cattell refers to these two types of intelligence as broad "group factors" that exist in addition to "g."

Crystallized intelligence is heavily dependent on culturally loaded, fact-oriented learning. Tasks highly correlated with this factor include vocabulary, general information, and arithmetic problems. In contrast, **fluid intelligence** demands little in the way of specific informational content. It involves the ability to see complex relationships and solve problems, as is the case in the number series, spatial visualization, and figure matrix examples displayed in Figure 8.1. These tasks are good examples of items that correlate highly with Cattell's fluid ability factor.

When samples of children are similar in cultural and educational background, there is usually a high correlation between crystallized and fluid intelligence, often so high that the two types of mental abilities cannot be distinguished from one another using factor analysis. In such instances, the strong relationship is probably the result of the fact that children high in fluid intelligence tend to acquire specific information more efficiently and extensively. However, when children have had very different cultural and educational backgrounds, crystallized and fluid intelligence are easier to distinguish, and children with the same fluid capacity may show very different performances on tests that are heavily loaded with crystallized items. Thus, R. B. Cattell's theory of crystallized and fluid intelligence has important implications for the issue of cultural bias in intelligence testing. Efforts to devise culture-fair tests that will not discriminate against individuals from disadvantaged backgrounds usually involve de-emphasizing crystallized abilities and placing greater emphasis on fluid abilities.

Crystallized and fluid intelligence follow different patterns of development over the life span (Cattell, 1971; Horn, 1967; Horn & Cattell, 1967). As shown in Figure 8.3, fluid intelligence shows a steady and rapid increase through childhood and adolescence, reaching a maximum in the late teens and early 20s after which it gradually declines. In contrast, crystallized scores reveal a more gradual and continuous increase from infancy until about 60 or 70 years of age. However, we must be cautious in interpreting these cross-sectional trends, for the exact causes of them are not made clear by the findings. For example, it is possible that the post-adolescent

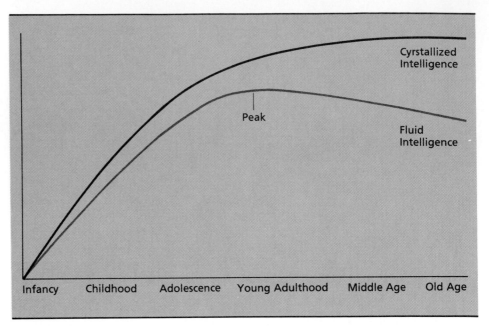

Figure 8.3. Developmental changes in crystallized and fluid intelligence over the life span. The graph depicts cross-sectional averages taken from several studies, each involving several hundred people. *(Published by permission of Transaction, Inc., from "Intelligence: Why It Grows, Why It Declines," by J. L. Horn, Trans-Action, 5, [1], 1967. Copyright © 1967 by Transaction, Inc.)*

decline in fluid intelligence results from physiological changes during adulthood. Alternatively, because the curves in Figure 8.3 are only age averages, perhaps the trend is accounted for by only a few individuals whose scores drop sharply with age. Recent longitudinal evidence supports a decline in mental abilities during adulthood, but the drop is negligible until after the age of 60, and substantial individual differences related to health and lifestyles exist in the extent to which people conform to the pattern (Schaie & Hertzog, 1983).

Recent Developments: Combining Cognitive and Psychometric Approaches

Although the factor analytic approach has been the major methodological route to defining mental abilities, a number of investigators believe that its value will remain limited unless it is combined with other theoretical approaches to the study of human cognition. Psychometric researchers have been criticized for devoting too much attention to the identification of factors and too little effort to explaining them in terms of the dynamics of their mental processes. As Carroll (1982) points out, factors by themselves are of little usefulness unless psychologists can explain why performances on tasks that are correlated with the factor happen to be linked together. Like any correlational research strategy, factor analysis does not provide investigators with the reasons behind the linkages among different mental performances.

The latest developments in theorizing about mental abilities have arisen from attempts to combine the psychometric perspective with the information processing approach discussed in Chapter 7. Researchers involved in this effort think that performance on mental tests can be understood in terms of a number of basic, underlying information processing components: sensory apprehension, attention, memory strategies, symbolic comparison and transformation, metacognitive processes, as well as others. These investigators believe that individual differences in such processing components are at the heart of varying performances on intelligence test items (Carroll, 1976; 1981; Sternberg, 1980; 1985a; 1985b). To study these relationships, some psychologists correlate subjects' scores on mental test factors with their performance on laboratory tasks designed to reveal the speed and effectiveness of different information processing skills (e.g., Carroll & Maxwell, 1979; Keating

& Bobbitt, 1978; Sternberg, 1977). The findings of such studies have been provocative, and more effort is currently being devoted to extending them. The hope is that information processing can fill in the details about mental abilities left open by psychometric approaches because of the inherent limitations of the factor analytic technique (Sternberg, 1981; 1985b).

Finally, cognitive theories have direct implications for the expansion of testing procedures. For example, it has been suggested that traditional intelligence tests could be supplemented by items that reflect important information processing skills. Such tasks might be particularly effective in isolating specific cognitive processes in which improvement is needed in order to augment general intellectual performance (Sternberg, 1981). Psychometricians have already begun to realize the usefulness of cognitive theory for mental testing. The authors of one of the newest intelligence tests for children, the Kaufman Assessment Battery, relied heavily on information processing for the design of their mental tasks (Kaufman & Kaufman, 1983a). Piaget's theory has also left its mark on intelligence testing, as several Piagetian-based instruments have been developed over the last several decades. We will describe these tests, as well as some important ones that represent the traditional psychometric approach, shortly. But first let's consider how the IQ score is computed, and what IQ differences among individuals actually mean.

THE COMPUTATION AND DISTRIBUTION OF IQ SCORES

Once an intelligence test is given, the examiner computes a raw score on the basis of the child's answers. Then the raw score is converted to an **IQ (intelligence quotient)** that provides a ready means by which the child's performance can be compared to the scores of other individuals.

The Traditional IQ Score

In the original Stanford-Binet scale, IQs were obtained by converting the raw score on the test to a **mental age (MA).** The mental age equivalent of a particular raw score is determined by finding the chronological age at which children, on the average, obtain that score. For example, if the mean raw score of 8-year-olds on an intelligence test is 40, then a raw score of 40 is equivalent to a mental age of 8. A child's IQ, considered to be an index of brightness or rate of mental development, is then computed by entering the mental age into the following formula:

$$IQ = (MA/CA) \times 100$$

Using this method, children with IQs of 100 are considered to be of average mental ability, for they do just as well as would be expected for their chronological age. Those with IQs higher than 100 are above average, for they obtain raw scores comparable to those of older children Those with IQs lower than 100 are below average for a similar reason.

Although the mental age approach provides a convenient way of comparing the test scores of different children, it has come under criticism and is rarely used today. Mental growth is known to be far more rapid at younger ages than older ages. In other words, the difference in intellectual functioning between a 2- and 3-year-old is much greater than the difference between a 10- and 11-year-old, but an IQ computation based on mental age does not take this into account. In addition, the mental age equivalent leads people who are not familiar with the basis of the score to draw the erroneous conclusion that an 8-year-old child with a mental age of 12 is like a 12-year-old in all respects. Yet the assumption that such a child could keep pace with children 4 years her senior in academic learning and social situations is unreasonable

(Sattler, 1988). It is best not to make this inference and, instead, to merely regard the 8-year-old as a very intellectually superior child in comparison to her own age group.

The Modern IQ Score

The modern method of arriving at an IQ avoids the problems inherent in the mental age approach by making a direct comparison of a child's raw score to the scores of a representative sample of children of the same chronological age. This approach is often referred to as a **deviation IQ,** because it is based on a statistical determination of the extent to which a child's performance deviates from the mean of his or her particular age group. When an intelligence test is standardized, it is given to a large number of individuals, and the performances of children at each age level form a frequency distribution that closely approximates the *normal curve* shown in Figure 8.4. Two important features of the normal curve are its *mean,* or the average of the test scores, and its *standard deviation,* which gives a measure of the average variability, or "spread-outness" of the scores from the mean.

Knowing the mean and standard deviation of the raw scores, we can determine the exact percentage of the population that will fall above or below a certain score. Figure 8.4 shows the percentage of individuals falling into each area of the normal curve when the distribution is marked off in standard deviation units. Most intelligence tests recalibrate their raw scores so that the mean is set at 100 and the standard deviation at 15. Then when we talk about an IQ of a particular magnitude, we know precisely what it means. For example, a child who obtains an IQ of 100 performs better than 50 percent of the population of same-age children. A child with an IQ of 85 does better than only 15.9 percent of her agemates, while a child with an IQ of 130 outperforms 97.7 percent of them. Look at Figure 8.4 again and notice how most of the scores cluster near the mean. The great majority of the population (95.5 percent) falls between an IQ of 70 and 130, and only a few people achieve very high or very low scores.

REPRESENTATIVE INTELLIGENCE TESTS FOR CHILDREN

Given the diversity of scientific models of intelligence, it is not surprising that a multitude of tests have been developed to represent them. Among the variety of instruments currently available, the Stanford-Binet and Wechsler scales are the ones most often used for diagnosis of children with learning problems, identification of highly intelligent children, and decisions regarding special educational placement.

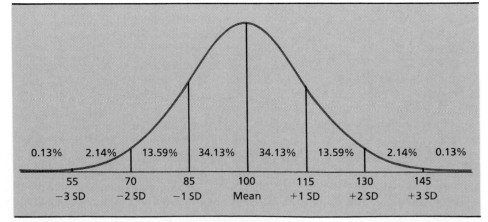

Figure 8.4. The normal curve, with the baseline scaled in both IQ and standard deviation (SD) units. Areas under the curve are given in percentages. By summing the percentages to the left of an individual's IQ, we can obtain a percentile rank, which refers to the proportion of people of the same age that the individual scored better than on the test.

The Stanford-Binet Intelligence Scale

For over half a century, the *Stanford-Binet* has been the most popular individual intelligence test for children. Translated and adopted throughout the world, it has frequently served as the yardstick against which the worth of new intelligence tests has been measured (Jensen, 1980). Like earlier editions, the 1986 revision is suitable for testing individuals from 2 through 18 years of age.

In contrast to older versions, the new Stanford-Binet measures both overall intellectual performance as well as multiple factors. It is based on a hierarchial model of intelligence that incorporates the theories of Spearman, R. B. Cattell, and Horn, whose extensions of Cattell's work have shown that short-term memory is an additional factor that is independent of crystallized and fluid intelligence (Horn, 1985; Stankov, Horn, & Roy, 1980). As shown in Figure 8.5, the three-level model uses a wide variety of item types to assess each area of mental ability. Separate scores obtained for each of the 15 subtests that make up the entire scale permit a more detailed analysis of each child's performance (Thorndike, Hagen, & Sattler, 1986). Another feature of the new Stanford-Binet is a standardization sample more representative of the American population than was used in earlier editions. Also, the new test materials are designed to be sensitive to minority and handicapped youngsters and to reduce sex bias. Pictures of children from different racial/ethnic groups, a child in a wheelchair, and "unisex" figures that can be interpreted as either male or female are included (see Figure 8.6).

Nevertheless, the new Stanford-Binet has been criticized on several grounds. Some of the subtests are not strongly correlated with the factors they are supposed to represent, raising questions about the meaningfulness of the separate mental ability scores and concerns about whether the test actually reflects the model of mental ability adopted by the test designers. In addition, the test takes an especially long time to administer — up to 2 hours for some children (Sattler, 1988).

The Wechsler Intelligence Scales

The *Wechsler Intelligence Scale for Children (WISC)*, first published in 1949, revised in 1974, and now known as the *WISC-R*, and the *Wechsler Preschool and Primary Scale of Intelligence (WPPSI)*, published in 1967, are the only individual tests of mental ability that have successfully competed with the Stanford-Binet in popularity. The

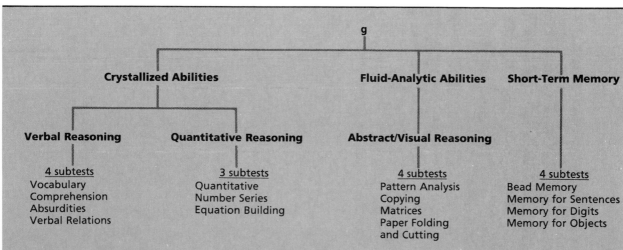

Figure 8.5. Mental abilities appraised by the 1986 revision of the Stanford-Binet Intelligence Scale. *(Adapted from R. L. Thorndike, E. P. Hagen, & J. M. Sattler, 1986.)*

Wechsler tests offered differentiated scoring long before it was incorporated into the Stanford-Binet, and consequently, over the past two decades they have become the preferred mental assessment tools of clinical and school psychologists (Jensen, 1980; Wade et al., 1978). The WISC-R is appropriate for children from 6 through 16 years of age, and the WPPSI is intended for children 4 through 6½ years of age (Wechsler, 1967; 1974). The WPPSI is currently undergoing revision; the new version will span a wider age range, from 3 through 7¼ years.

Figure 8.7 shows the factor structure of the WISC-R; the one for the WPPSI is similar. Both Wechsler tests consist of verbal and performance subtests that combine to yield separate Verbal and Performance Scale IQs. Together, all the subtests provide an overall measure of intelligence, called the Full Scale IQ. Although the Verbal IQ is a better predictor of academic performance (Hale, 1978; Wikoff, 1979), the Performance IQ provided one of the first means through which non-English-speaking children and children with speech and language disorders could demonstrate their intellectual strengths.

In addition, the Wechsler tests have broadly representative standardization samples. Developed in the 1960s and early 1970s when psychologists and educators were becoming increasingly sensitive to the needs of the ethnically different child, the tests were the first to be standardized on samples adequately representing the total population of the United States, including racial minorities (Zimmerman & Woo-Sam, 1978). The Wechsler standardization procedures have served as models for many later intelligence tests.

Other Intelligence Tests

The Kaufman Assessment Battery for Children. The *Kaufman Assessment Battery for Children (K-ABC)* is the first major assessment instrument to be theoretically grounded in cognitive psychology. Published in 1983, the K-ABC measures the intelligence of children from 2½ through 12 years of age on the basis of two general classes of information processing skills: simultaneous processing and sequential processing. It provides a unique array of subtests as well as a separate score to represent each (see Figure 8.8).

Sequential processing refers to the capacity of the human information processing system to solve problems in a step-wise fashion. Tasks that sample this ability emphasize solutions that are dependent on temporal or serial relationships among stimulus elements. In contrast, *simultaneous processing* involves the ability of the information processing system to grasp the overall configuration among several

Figure 8.6. "Unisex" child in the new Stanford-Binet, designed to reduce sex bias in the test. *(From R. L. Thorndike, E. P. Hagen, & J. M. Sattler, 1986,* The Stanford-Binet Intelligence Scale *[4th ed.], Chicago: Riverside Publishing. Reprinted by permission.)*

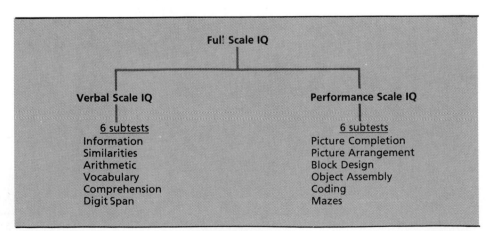

Full Scale IQ

Verbal Scale IQ

Performance Scale IQ

6 subtests
Information
Similarities
Arithmetic
Vocabulary
Comprehension
Digit Span

6 subtests
Picture Completion
Picture Arrangement
Block Design
Object Assembly
Coding
Mazes

Figure 8.7. Mental abilities appraised by the Wechsler Intelligence Scale for Children-Revised (WISC-R).

Modern intelligence tests are standardized on samples that represent the racial/ethnic and socioeconomic diversity of the American child population. (Rhoda Sidney/ Monkmeyer Press Photo Service)

related elements and meaningfully integrate a variety of stimuli at the same time. The two processing components combine to yield an overall intelligence or information processing measure, called the Mental Processing Composite.

In the construction of both mental processing scales, a concerted effort was made to reduce cultural bias through the provision of items with content familiar to all children. As a result, the K-ABC mental processing scales are, for the most part, nonverbal in nature and heavily laden with items reflecting R. B. Cattell's concept of fluid intelligence. Crystallized items involving the acquisition of culturally based knowledge and skills are not regarded as unimportant, but they are assessed by a separate intellectual dimension — the Achievement Scale. It includes subtests traditionally associated with verbal intelligence as well as measures of school-related skills.

Like the Wechsler tests, the K-ABC's standardization sample is highly representative. Diverse ethnic, racial, and socioeconomic groups as well as gifted, emotionally disturbed, and learning disabled children are all included in the same proportions as they occur in the American population. National norms are further supplemented by

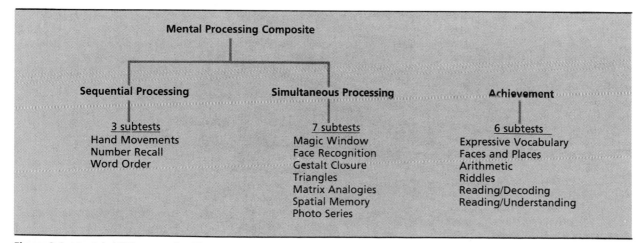

Mental Processing Composite		
Sequential Processing	**Simultaneous Processing**	**Achievement**
3 subtests	7 subtests	6 subtests
Hand Movements	Magic Window	Expressive Vocabulary
Number Recall	Face Recognition	Faces and Places
Word Order	Gestalt Closure	Arithmetic
	Triangles	Riddles
	Matrix Analogies	Reading/Decoding
	Spatial Memory	Reading/Understanding
	Photo Series	

Figure 8.8. Mental abilities appraised by the Kaufman Assessment Battery for Children (K-ABC). *(From A. S. Kaufman & N. L. Kaufman, 1983,* Kaufman Assessment Battery for Children: Interpretive Manual. *Circle Pines, MN: American Guidance Service. Adapted by permission.)*

separate norms for blacks and whites and, within these two racial groups, norms for different income levels. These separate sociocultural norms permit each child's performance to be compared to the scores of a representative sample of children who have experienced comparable opportunities for learning (Kaufman & Kaufman, 1983a).

Extra efforts to respond to the special needs of minority children are also apparent in K-ABC's unusually flexible administration and scoring procedures. Deviating from virtually all other tests, the K-ABC permits the examiner to "teach the task" to any child who fails one of the first three items in any subtest. The tester may use alternate wording, gestures, and physical prompts and may even communicate in a language other than English (Kaufman & Kaufman, 1983a; 1983b). Also, credit is given when children provide correct verbal responses in a foreign language. These special features make the K-ABC stand apart as one of the fairest measures of intelligence currently available for children from ethnic minority and low-income backgrounds.

Like the new Stanford-Binet, the K-ABC is not without its critics. For example, Goetz and Hall (1984) and Sternberg (1984) claim that there is little support in the information processing literature for the simultaneous/sequential processing dichotomy on which the test is based. The battery has also been criticized for overemphasizing short-term memory and rote learning (Sternberg, 1984). Nevertheless, the test represents a new wave of enthusiasm among psychometricians for measuring intelligence on the basis of contemporary cognitive theory, and it is likely to inspire the construction of new instruments that draw on information processing models.

Piagetian-Based Tests. During the 1960s and early 1970s, psychometricians became interested in whether the tasks Piaget devised to reflect children's stage-wise progress could be used to assess individual differences in intellectual performance. Among the first Piagetian-based mental scales was Goldschmid and Bentler's (1968a) *Concept Assessment Kit — Conservation,* a standardized test that measures elementary school children's performance on 12 different conservation problems. Research on the Goldschmid and Bentler test shows that children who are ahead of their agemates in solving Piagetian conservation tasks also do well on traditional measures of intelligence. Scores on it also correlate positively with school grades (Goldschmid & Bentler, 1968b).

Nevertheless, Piagetian-based tests designed to assess operational thinking in childhood have not caught hold strongly, largely because they have not worked better than existing intelligence tests for practical purposes. In addition, most general intelligence tests sample a much wider range of mental abilities than Piagetian tasks, which, in middle childhood, are limited primarily to reasoning ability (Elkind, 1971).

Piagetian theory has had a greater impact in the area of infant assessment. Two tests based on Piaget's sensorimotor period have been developed (Escalona & Corman, 1969; Užgiris & Hunt, 1975). The most recent of them, Užgiris and Hunt's *Infant Psychological Development Scale,* is designed to measure intellectual development between 2 weeks and 2 years of age. The test contains eight subscales, each of which assesses the development of an important sensorimotor capacity, such as object permanence and vocal and gestural imitation. A study by Wachs (1975) revealed that among the Užgiris-Hunt subscales, repeated assessments of object permanence at 3-month intervals between 12 and 24 months of age all predicted performance on the Stanford-Binet at 31 months of age. As will become apparent in the section below, Piagetian-based infant scales are somewhat more successful than traditional infant intelligence tests in predicting later mental ability measures, perhaps because they focus more directly on infant problem solving and conceptual understanding than most early assessment devices (Lewis & Sullivan, 1985).

Infant Intelligence Tests. Psychometrically based instruments for infants consist largely of perceptual and motor performances, such as lifting the head, following a moving object with the eyes, and building a tower of cubes. Since babies are often less than cooperative subjects, infant scores tend to be more unreliable than those obtained on older children, and some tests depend heavily on information supplied by parents in order to compensate for the unpredictability of these very young test-takers. Also, because of skepticism about whether the behaviors on infant scales reflect the same construct of intelligence measured by tests for children and adults, most scores on infant tests are conservatively labeled **developmental quotients (DQ)** rather than IQs. However, the DQ is computed in the same way as an IQ, with a score of 100 indicating average performance.

The roots of tests for babies can be traced to the work of Arnold Gesell, one of the founders of the normative tradition in child development. Virtually all infant tests have either borrowed or adapted items from *The Gesell Developmental Schedules,* first introduced in 1925 and designed to measure the developmental progress of babies from 3 to 24 months of age (Honzik, 1983; Lewis & Sullivan, 1985). Besides the Gesell test, another instrument developed in the 1930s by Nancy Bayley, *The Bayley Scales of Infant Development,* became widely used. Both currently exist in revised forms (Bayley, 1969; Knobloch, Stevens, & Malone, 1980).

The Bayley infant test was the first to be designed for the purpose of predicting future intellectual competence. But despite careful efforts to establish its reliability and standardize it on a representative sample, the Bayley test is a poor predictor of intelligence during the childhood years, at least for samples of normal babies (Bayley, 1970; Lewis & McGurk, 1972; McCall, Hogarty, & Hurlburt, 1972). The consistency of this finding has led investigators to conclude that the perceptual and motor behaviors tapped in infancy are qualitatively different from the verbal, conceptual, and problem-solving skills assessed at later ages. The differences between the behavioral domains sampled by infant and childhood tests appear to preclude prediction from one to the other.

Some investigators have speculated that infant tests miss early information processing behaviors that might be expected to predict later cognitive functioning, such as attentiveness to the environment, as assessed by the habituation-dishabituation paradigm. Recent research indicates that infant attention predicts intelligence during the preschool years more effectively than traditional infant instruments (Fagan & McGrath, 1981; Lewis & Brooks-Gunn, 1981). Finding ways to include such cognitive processing measures in new infant tests holds considerable promise for improving the predictability of early assessment devices (Lewis & Fox, 1983)

Infant tests do show somewhat better long-term predictive validity for at-risk, very low scoring babies (Honzik, 1983; Knobloch & Pasamanick, 1967; Siegal, 1981; Werner & Smith, 1982). In view of this finding, many investigators believe that the major usefulness of infant testing is for screening purposes—identifying babies for further diagnosis and possible intervention whose initial low scores may mean that they have a high probability of experiencing delayed or abnormal development in the future (Lewis & Sullivan, 1985). The original Gesell Schedules were used extensively in this way by pediatricians, and they inspired the development of another widely used pediatric screening device for infants and preschool children: *The Denver Developmental Screening Test (DDST)* (Frankenberg & Dodds, 1967; Frankenberg et al., 1975). Like the Gesell, the DDST provides scores in four behavioral domains: personal-social, fine motor-adaptive, language, and gross motor. Unlike other tests, it does not produce a DQ or IQ. Instead, considering the number of items on which a child shows extreme developmental delays, the test classifies the child as normal, questionable, or abnormal. Follow-up research shows that the abnormal category on the DDST accurately identifies over 85 percent of infants and preschoolers who continue to be developmentally delayed into the middle childhood years, the majority of whom experience serious learning problems after they enter school (Frankenberg et al., 1975).

In summary, current widely used intelligence tests for children are based on hierarchical models of intelligence in which both general ability as well as numerous separate abilities are measured. In addition, each major test has incorporated features into its design that respond to the special needs of ethnic minority children. In general, infant mental test scores do not predict later mental functioning. However, infant tests are useful for identifying babies whose extremely low scores suggest they may be experiencing serious developmental difficulties.

WHAT AND HOW WELL DO INTELLIGENCE TESTS PREDICT?

We have already seen that in the great majority of cases, infant tests are poor predictors of later cognitive functioning, but what about the more frequently administered childhood intelligence tests? Most school districts conduct testing programs in which IQ scores are used to help characterize the learning needs of large groups of pupils as well as to make decisions regarding the educational placement of individual children. Psychologists and educators who rely on test scores in these ways assume they are good predictors of future intellectual and scholastic performance. Let's see how well the IQ fares as a predictive measure based on research evidence.

The Stability of IQ Scores

Stability refers to how effectively IQ scores serve as predictors of themselves from one developmental period to another. Do children who obtain a particular IQ at age 3 or 4 perform about the same during the elementary school years, and again when tested during high school? Scores on intelligence tests have traditionally been assumed to represent a fairly constant attribute that changes minimally with time. Whether or not this assumption is true is of crucial practical importance, for we would have little faith in educational placement decisions based on IQ if the scores shifted dramatically from one year to the next. To investigate the stability of IQs, psychologists must follow children longitudinally, retesting them at regular intervals. Such studies are expensive and time-consuming to conduct. Therefore, investigators have relied on already-existing data from major longitudinal investigations, especially the Berkeley and Fels studies, to which you were introduced in Chapter 2.

Correlational Stability. One way of examining the stability of the IQ is to correlate scores obtained from repeated testings on the same group of children. This information tells us whether children who score low or high in comparison to their agemates at one point in time continue to do so at later ages. Examination of the Berkeley longitudinal data reveals lower correlations when the first of two IQ testings is obtained at an early age. For example, the correlation between IQs taken at 2 and 5 years of age is only .32. It rises to .70 between 5 and 8, and to .85 between 9 and 12 (Honzik, Macfarlane, & Allen, 1948). Preschool IQs do not predict school-age scores as well as later measures, but after age 6 there is good stability, with many of the correlations remaining in the .70s and .80s. Relationships between two testings obtained during the adolescent years are as high as the .80s and .90s (Bayley, 1949; Honzik, Macfarlane, & Allen, 1948; Sontag, Baker, & Nelson, 1958). Also, across the entire period of development, scores at adjacent ages always correlate much better than scores at ages that are distant from one another. For example, a 4-year IQ correlates with a 5-year score at .72, but the prediction drops by age 6 to .62, and by age 18, it has declined to .42 (Honzik, Macfarlane, & Allen, 1948).

Looking at the correlational evidence as a whole, two generalizations about the stability of mental test performance can be made: (1) The older the child at time of first testing, the better the prediction of current IQ status; and (2) the closer in time two testings are, the stronger the relationship between the scores. These summary statements indicate that stability of mental test performance is strongly dependent on when the scores are taken. Before the age of 5 or 6, IQ should be regarded as largely an indicator of present ability and not as a dependable, enduring measure.

You might reasonably be wondering why early childhood scores do not predict as well as later assessments. One frequently cited reason is similar to the one we discussed earlier with regard to infant tests. Differences in the nature of intelligence test items may play an important role. Concrete, basic intellectual knowledge tends to be tested at younger ages and abstract, problem-solving ability later on, and it is possible that skill at the former is not necessarily predictive of skill at the latter (Siegler & Richards, 1982). Another explanation is that during early periods of rapid growth, one child may spurt ahead of another and reach a plateau, while a second child, moving along slowly and steadily from behind, may gain on and gradually overtake the first. Because children frequently change places with one another in a distribution during periods of rapid change, all measures of developmental status, including height and weight, are less stable and predictable at these times, and IQ seems to be no exception.

The Stability of Absolute Scores. So far, the stability evidence we have presented centers on the strength of correlations, which tell us the degree to which children maintain their relative IQ standing among agemates over time. It is also possible to view stability in absolute terms. We can compare each child to him- or herself by examining the profile of IQ scores obtained on a series of repeated testings. Recall from Chapter 2 that we presented examples of individual IQ growth trends from the Fels and Berkeley studies. The evidence revealed that the majority of children experienced substantial IQ fluctuations. To refresh your memory with just one example, the Berkeley findings indicated that 85 percent of the children studied showed changes of 10 or more points, and a third of the sample changes of 20 or more points, between 6 and 18 years of age (Honzik, Macfarlane, & Allen, 1948). Individual IQ variations of children in the Fels sample were even more dramatic (Sontag, Baker, & Nelson, 1958).[1]

The Berkeley and Fels profiles of IQ change tended to be orderly. Steadily increasing or decreasing performances rather than random, unpredictable fluctuations occurred. Also, large shifts were often associated with important alterations in the child's life experiences. For example, dramatic declines were linked to such events as loss of a parent, removal to a foster home, and serious illness, whereas increases occurred during time of greater happiness, expansion of interests, and improved emotional stability (Honzik, Macfarlane, & Allen, 1948). In the Fels study, IQ gains and losses were also associated with children's personality characteristics and parental child-rearing practices. IQ gainers were more independent and scholastically competitive, and their parents' special interest in their intellectual accomplishments was reflected in greater pressure to succeed in school along with moderate, rational disciplinary practices. Children who showed declines had parents who made little effort to stimulate them and who showed extremes in discipline — either very severe or very lax punishment techniques (McCall, Appelbaum, & Hogarty, 1973; Sontag, Baker, & Nelson, 1958).

Longitudinal studies generally report overall IQ gains for their samples as a whole (although a handful of subjects always show decreases). However, when low-income children and children of disadvantaged minority groups are selected for special study, a large number of them show progressive declines during childhood and adolescence. This decrement has been attributed to the cumulative effects of an underprivileged background on IQ, an explanation referred to as the **cumulative deficit hypothesis.** The cumulative deficit hypothesis suggests that due to the compounding effects of

---

[1] Return to Chapter 2, pages 55–58, to review this evidence in greater detail, and to Figure 2.2 on page 57 to examine some sample IQ profiles of individual children.

depressed rearing conditions, early intellectual deficiencies lead to more deficiencies, and they become progressively more difficult to counteract as children get older. This idea was at the heart of the rationale for the early intervention movement initiated in the mid-1960s, which was a massive attempt to offset such declines.

Although cross-sectional studies conducted since the early part of this century have lent support to the cumulative deficit hypothesis, they have methodological difficulties. Older and younger age groups could have been exposed to different life experiences and therefore may not have been comparable (Jensen, 1974). Well-designed longitudinal studies are scarce, but one recent British investigation found evidence in favor of the cumulative deficit. Inner-city disadvantaged British children declined steadily on a wide variety of intellectual measures between 7 and 15 years of age, whereas more advantaged controls showed no such trend (Cox, 1983a; 1983b).

Nevertheless, longitudinal studies such as this one do not tell us for sure that depressed environments are the cause of the IQ decline. A competing hypothesis is that genetically determined differences in children's intellectual growth curves exist and are responsible for the progressive drops among the disadvantaged. However, in a study of American black children, Jensen (1977) reported evidence that contradicts a genetic explanation. He compared the IQ scores of younger and older children in the same families, reasoning that if a true cumulative deficit exists, older siblings should obtain lower test scores than their younger brothers and sisters. Jensen found just such an effect for black children growing up under severely depressed environmental circumstances in the rural South. Among a sample of less disadvantaged, California-reared black children, no such sibling effect appeared.

To briefly summarize what we have said about the stability of IQ, a surprising number of children show substantial shifts in the absolute value of their scores over the course of childhood and adolescence. Upward shifts are typical of children from advantaged backgrounds, while downward shifts occur often among low-income and ethnic minority children. Nevertheless, IQs obtained after school entry are good indicators of a child's intellectual status in comparison to agemates. And once IQ becomes reasonably stable in a correlational sense, it predicts a variety of outcome measures, as we shall see in the sections that follow.

IQ as a Predictor of Scholastic Success

Thousands of studies have examined the relationship between intelligence and scholastic performance, and they are remarkably consistent in revealing that intelligence tests have accomplished the goal of predicting academic achievement. IQ scores show a moderate to high relationship with achievement test performance during elementary and high school. The correlations generally range from about .40 to .70, with typical figures hovering around .50 (Jensen, 1980; Siegler & Richards, 1982). Children with higher IQs also get better grades, and they stay in school longer. As early as age 7, IQ scores are moderately correlated with adult educational attainment (McCall, 1977).

Why does IQ predict scholastic success so well? Psychologists differ in how they answer this question. Some believe that the relationship between IQ and achievement results from the fact that tests of intelligence and achievement both sample from the same pool of culturally specific information. From this point of view, an intelligence test is at least partly an achievement test, and relevant past experiences determine whether children do well or poorly on both types of measures (Zigler & Seitz, 1982). Support for this position comes from research that shows that past achievement test scores (which represent acquired knowledge to a greater extent than do intelligence tests) do a slightly better job of predicting future achievement than does IQ (Crano, Kenny, & Campbell, 1972). In addition, when IQ is partitioned into separate abilities, verbal scores (which are heavily dependent on acquired knowledge or Cattell's crystallized intelligence) show the strongest relationships with academic performance (Siegler & Richards, 1982). In fact, when test designers make a conscious and systematic effort to separate crystallized and fluid abilities from one another, fluid intelligence does a much poorer job of predicting achievement than its crystallized counterpart (Kaufman, Kamphaus, & Kaufman, 1985).

Other psychologists believe that the IQ-achievement relationship does not just come about because both measure children's opportunity to acquire the same body of culturally relevant information. Instead, they believe that IQ predicts achievement because both measures depend on cognitive processes that underlie Spearman's "g"—the ability to form mental relationships and to reason abstractly. That IQ correlates best with achievement scores in the more highly academic and abstract school subjects, such as English, mathematics, and science, has been taken to support this interpretation (Jensen, 1980).

Exactly why IQ predicts achievement as well as it does remains a matter of controversy, but as you can probably imagine, psychologists who believe that environmental factors account for most of the IQ variation among individuals prefer the former explanation, whereas those who believe that genetic influences play a crucial role prefer the latter. But whether one or the other (or both) of the above interpretations is correct, it is important to note that IQ is definitely not the only correlate of achievement, for the correlation between the two variables is not perfect. Even when IQ and achievement are correlated at their best, intelligence only accounts for about half of the individual differences that exist among children in academic performance.[2] The other half must be determined by a different set of influences, such as some combination of motivational and personality characteristics that lead some children to try hard and want to do well in school. Whatever these other factors, they are at least as important as IQ in explaining individual differences among children in scholastic success (Zigler & Seitz, 1982).

IQ as a Predictor of Vocational Success

Psychologists and educators would be less preoccupied with the origins and measurement of IQ if it only predicted academic outcomes while individuals remained in school and was unrelated to longer-term measures of life success. However, research indicates that childhood IQ predicts adult occupational status just about as well as it

---

[2] When two variables, such as IQ and achievement, are correlated, psychologists determine the proportion of variation in one that can be explained by the other by squaring the correlation. The highest correlations obtained between IQ and achievement are around .70. This figure, when squared, equals .49. The result indicates that only about half of the variation, or differences among individuals, in achievement can be accounted for by IQ.

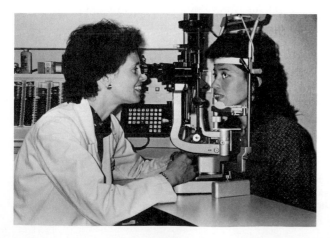

By second grade, children's IQ scores are moderately predictive of adult occupational success. (Gloria Karlson)

correlates with school achievement. By second grade, pupils with the highest IQs are the ones most likely to enter the most prestigious occupations, such as physician, scientist, accountant, lawyer, and engineer (McCall, 1977). Longitudinal follow-ups of Terman's famous sample of children with IQs above 135 provide additional support for the relationship between childhood mental test performance and vocational success. By middle age, more than 86 percent of the men in the sample had entered high-status professional and business occupations, a higher proportion than would have been expected for a random sample of individuals having similar home backgrounds, or even among college graduates of the same era. Terman's subjects also had incomes that exceeded the earnings of individuals in the general population who had attained a comparable level of occupational status (Terman & Oden, 1959).[3] Recent evidence reveals that IQ is not just effective in predicting occupational prestige and income. It also correlates well with measures of job training success and how well people perform at work across the entire range of occupations, from very low to very high status vocational endeavors (Hunter & Hunter, 1984).

But like the IQ–school achievement connection, relationships between mental test scores and occupational attainments are not perfect, and other variables must figure importantly into the picture. For example, among Terman's gifted sample, not all were equally professionally successful, and those who fared best differed from other members of the sample in that they appeared to have "a special drive to succeed, a need to achieve, that had been with them from grammar school onward" (Goleman, 1980, p. 31). In addition, it is difficult if not impossible to determine what causes the positive associations that exist among IQ, education, occupational status, and income, for correlations themselves do not provide satisfactory explanations. It is possible that factors related to family background cause the complex of correlations, rather than IQ being at the heart of them. However, home background cannot be the whole story, for the occupational status and income of brothers raised in the same family often differ substantially from one another (Jencks, 1972), and differences among family members in vocational achievements are also related to their IQ scores (Waller, 1971). But once again, the picture is not simple, for IQ cannot account for all such within-family variation in occupational success.

IQ as a Predictor of Social and Emotional Adjustment

Even if it could be proved with certainty that IQ is the most important cause of individual differences in occupation and income, there are other indicators of life success, such as social and emotional adjustment, that extend beyond the confines of the schoolroom and workplace, and we might reasonably ask whether IQ is so pervasively influential that it also predicts these characteristics. A number of studies show that during the elementary school years, pupils with higher IQs tend to be better accepted socially by their classmates (Hartup, 1983), but again, the origins of this relationship are obscure, and it could have come about for all manner of reasons. For example, peers may simply tend to admire those classmates who are highly regarded by teachers and especially successful in school. Differences among children in social skills are just as likely to originate from factors having to do with socioeconomic status, child-rearing practices, health, physical appearance, and personality (all of which are correlated with IQ) as they are from mental ability.

Another way of exploring the relationship between IQ and psychological adjustment is to look at the intellectual performance of children who are clearly poorly

---

[3] Born in the early part of this century during an era quite different from our own, nearly half of the women in Terman's study became housewives. However, of those who did work, there were examples of outstanding vocational accomplishments. Among them were scientists (one of whom contributed importantly to the development of the polio vaccine), several novelists and journalists, and a number of highly successful businesswomen (Terman & Oden, 1959).

adjusted, such as highly aggressive youngsters who engage in norm-violating and delinquent acts. IQ and delinquency are negatively related, with most delinquents falling in the lower half of the IQ distribution (Hirschi & Hindelang, 1977). However, like other correlational findings discussed above, there is no evidence that IQ has a direct impact on delinquency. Furthermore, there must be other contributing factors, for there are many more delinquent males than females, but no differences in general intelligence exist between the sexes. Like the variable of vocational attainment considered earlier, delinquency is correlated with socioeconomic status, and conditions related to low income and poverty may explain its relationship to IQ. Some investigators believe that the probability of delinquency is increased by negative school experiences in combination with an underprivileged family background. They suggest that children from nonsupportive families who fail repeatedly in the classroom are likely to react to the pain of these events by turning to antisocial behavior (Berman, 1978; Hirschi & Hindelang, 1977), an explanation that is supported by the finding that as soon as delinquent youngsters leave school, their antisocial behaviors decline (Phillips & Kelly, 1979). However, for some children, the association between IQ and aggressive, acting-out behavior is apparent as early as 3 or 4 years of age (Richman, Stevenson, & Graham, 1982). For these children, the relationship cannot be mediated by school failure, for it is present before school entry. In such cases, it is likely that personality or familial background variables simultaneously predispose children to both intellectual deficits and antisocial conduct (Rutter & Garmezy, 1983). Thus, there are several plausible explanations for the IQ–antisocial behavior relationship in which IQ itself does not play a direct causal role.

Finally, it is important to note that a good number of other childhood adjustment disorders, such as excessive anxiety, fearfulness, withdrawal, and depression, are unrelated to IQ scores (Graham, 1979).

In summary, IQ is an effective predictor of a wide variety of measures of personal success and life satisfaction. However, the causal factors involved in each of the obtained relationships are not clearly established by the available research. Home background and personality characteristics appear to be at least as effective as IQ in predicting individual differences in educational, occupational, and personal success.

RACIAL/ETHNIC AND SOCIOECONOMIC DIFFERENCES IN IQ

The academic and vocational outcomes of which IQ is predictive are unevenly distributed among racial, ethnic, and socioeconomic groups in the United States (Cleary et al., 1975). In searching for the roots of these disparities, social scientists have turned to studies of IQ differences among major sectors of the American population. The results of these investigations are responsible for kindling the IQ nature-nurture debate. If children of various racial/ethnic and socioeconomic classifications differ in IQ, then there must either be genetic differences between rich and poor and black and white children, or children from impoverished sectors of the population must have fewer environmental opportunities to acquire those skills required for successful test performance.

The IQ nature-nurture controversy reached epic proportions during the decade of the 1970s, following publication of a 1969 *Harvard Educational Review* article by psychologist Arthur Jensen entitled, "How much can we boost IQ and scholastic achievement?" Jensen's answer to this question was *not much,* because, he argued, racial and socioeconomic differences in IQ scores are largely traceable to genetic origins.

Jensen's work was followed by an outpouring of responses and research studies, some in favor and some opposed to his position. In addition, there were ethical challenges from scientists deeply concerned that his conclusions would be used inappropriately to fuel existing social prejudices. This concern was intensified by the fact that Jensen's findings were highly tenuous and debatable. The controversy has since died down. Most scientists have come to the reasoned conclusion that individual differences in IQ scores are genetically as well as environmentally determined, and, as we explained in Chapter 3, the two sets of influences are often impossible to disentangle. But before we consider evidence on the genetic versus environmental roots of intelligence, let's take a look at the nature and extent of racial, ethnic, and socioeconomic differences in IQ, since they have been at the heart of this controversy.

Differences in General Intelligence

It is a well-substantiated finding that American black children score, on the average, about 15 points below white children on measures of general intelligence (Brody, 1985; Cleary et al., 1975; Loehlin, Lindzey, & Spuhler, 1975; Jensen, 1980). Socioeconomic differences in IQ also exist, but they are generally smaller in magnitude than black-white differences. In one large-scale study, low-income children scored about 9 points below their middle-income counterparts (Jensen & Figueroa, 1975). Since a disproportionate number of black families are low income, it is reasonable to ask whether socioeconomic differences in IQ fully account for the obtained racial discrepancy. They explain some of it, but not all of it. When members of both racial groups are matched on the basis of socioeconomic status, the black-white IQ gap is reduced by only a third (Jencks, 1972).

The socioeconomic and racial differences described above are group averages, and there is substantial IQ variation within each race and socioeconomic level. For example, as shown in Figure 8.9, the distributions of intelligence test scores for blacks and whites overlap a great deal; 15 to 20 percent of blacks actually score above the white mean, and the same percentage of whites score below the black mean. Therefore, regardless of how high one chooses to draw a line on the intellectual dimension, there will always be blacks who score above it, only there will be proportionately fewer of them than whites (Cleary et al., 1975). In fact, racial and socioeconomic differences account for only about one fourth of the total variation that exists in IQ (Jensen, 1980). Still, racial and socioeconomic differences are sufficiently large and of serious enough consequence that they cannot be ignored.

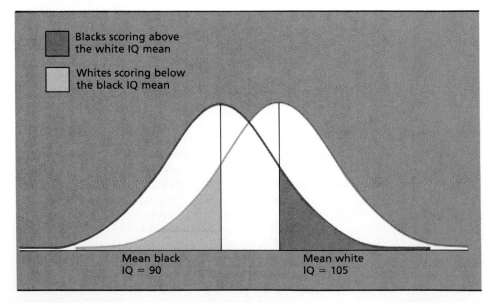

Figure 8.9. Comparison of the distributions of IQ scores for black and white children. The means represent approximate values obtained in studies of children reared by their biological parents.

Differences in Specific Mental Abilities

337

CHAPTER 8
INTELLIGENCE:
A PSYCHOMETRIC
PERSPECTIVE

Although many studies have compared racial and social class groups in terms of general intelligence, more detailed comparisons of particular mental abilities are less frequent. In one well-known theory about racial and social class variations in different mental abilities, called the **Level I–Level II theory,** Jensen (1969; 1973; 1980) argued that subgroup disparities are greater for some intellectual abilities than others.

The Level I–Level II theory distinguishes between two kinds of mental abilities. Mental test items that reflect Level I emphasize rote memory, or the ability to register, store, and engage in short-term recognition and verbatim recall of information. The digit span items on many intelligence tests are a good example of Level I ability. In contrast, Level II involves complex cognitive processing and problem solving. Items highly correlated with Spearman's "g" reflect Level II abilities, such as vocabulary and verbal comprehension, spatial visualization, and figure matrices. Jensen and his collaborators have presented evidence to suggest that black-white IQ differences, and to a lesser extent socioeconomic differences, are largely accounted for by Level II abilities and that population subgroups differ very little in Level I capacity (Jensen, 1985; Jensen & Figueroa, 1975; Reynolds & Jensen, 1983). In addition, Jensen suggested that among Level II abilities, black children do worst on the least culturally loaded, fluid ability, problem-solving type items and best on the most culturally loaded, crystallized items, such as vocabulary and general information. Therefore, Jensen argued, black-white IQ differences cannot be accounted for by any cultural biases inherent in the tests. The conclusion drawn, that blacks obtain lower IQ scores than whites because they are least well endowed with higher-order, conceptual forms of intelligence, is one aspect of Jensen's research that intensified public outcries about the racist connotations of his work.

Jensen's Level I–Level II theory has not been substantiated by the work of others. For example, Stankov, Horn, and Roy (1980) found that children's short-term memory performance (Level I) as well as fluid and crystallized ability scores (Level II) all declined in a similar fashion from high to middle to low socioeconomic classifications. These findings leave open the possibility that a wide variety of factors, among them cultural bias in the tests, might be operating across all mental ability scores. In another study of a large representative sample of black and white adolescents, Scarr and Barker (1981) reported results in direct opposition to Jensen's. The largest mental ability differences between black and white children occurred on the most culturally loaded tests (vocabulary) and the smallest differences on tests of memory and conceptual understanding, although black children did worse than white children on all measures.

In one of the most comprehensive investigations of social class and racial/ethnic variations in specific mental abilities, Lesser and his co-workers (Lesser, Fifer, & Clark, 1965; Stodolsky & Lesser, 1967) tested a large sample of lower- and middle-class 6- and 7-year-old children belonging to four different ethnic minority groups: Chinese, Jewish, black, and Puerto Rican. Each child was given measures of four different mental abilities. As shown in Figure 8.10, both social class and ethnicity made a difference in children's overall performance. Within each ethnic classification, middle-class children consistently outperformed lower-class children. In addition, Chinese and Jewish children did generally better than blacks and Puerto Ricans. But the most striking finding was that each ethnic group showed a distinct pattern of mental ability performance that remained unaltered across social class. For example, black children of both social classes achieved their best performances on verbal and reasoning items and did least well on number tasks. In contrast, Puerto Rican children did best on reasoning, number, and spatial tasks and poorest on the verbal items.

Lesser's findings suggest that Jensen's Level I–Level II theory is an oversimplification of the complex mental ability profiles associated with racial/ethnic identities.

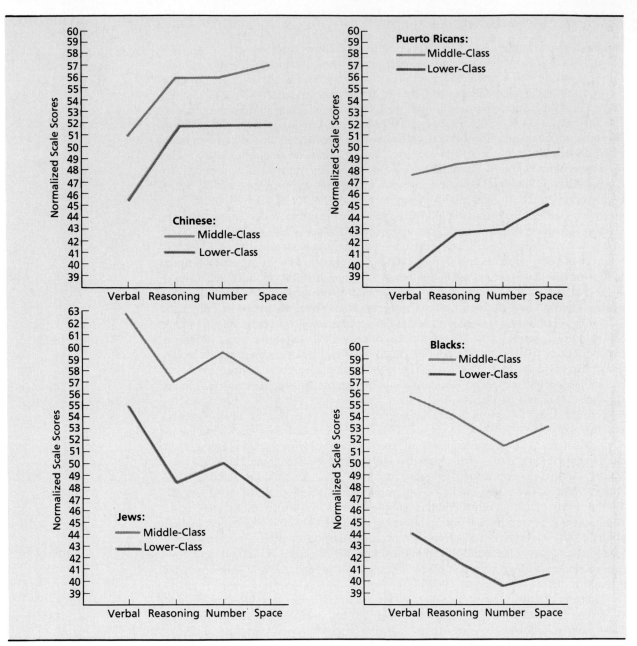

Figure 8.10. Patterns of mental abilities obtained by Lesser and his co-workers among middle-class and lower-class children from four different ethnic groups. *(From S. Stodolsky & G. Lesser, "Learning Patterns in the Disadvantaged,"* Harvard Educational Review, *1967, 37, 546–593. Copyright © 1967 by the President and Fellows of Harvard College. All rights reserved.)*

More than two ability factors distinguished the different ethnic groups. What explains these complex patterns? Genetic variation among ethnic groups may play some role, although Lesser and his colleagues believe that ethnic differences in stimulation and encouragement of specific intellectual functions are responsible. The exact causes of the ethnically related patterns remain conjectural, but what is known is that the patterns are subtle, intricate, and unlikely to be accounted for in simple ways.

In summary, although racial and socioeconomic differences in overall intelligence are well documented, research on specific mental abilities reveals complex patterns of strengths and weaknesses that pose a serious challenge to Jensen's Level I–Level II theory. Now that we have a clear picture of the IQ variations that figure importantly into the nature-nurture debate, we turn to a closer examination of the evidence regarding genetic and environmental influences that affect the IQ score.

EXPLAINING INDIVIDUAL DIFFERENCES IN IQ

Genetic Influences

Heritability of Intelligence. Because intelligence is a polygenic trait (influenced by a complex array of genes), knowledge of the specific hereditary pathways that affect intellectual variation among normal individuals is a long way off, and many scientists believe that they will never be precisely understood. Therefore, research on the role that genetic factors play in the development of intelligence is limited to indirect methods of study. In Chapter 3, we introduced the most popular of these methods, the **heritability estimate,** which calculates the extent to which individual differences in IQ scores can be traced to genetic origins. You may recall from Chapter 3 that heritability estimates are obtained from *kinship studies.* The IQs of pairs of individuals of different degrees of genetic relationship to one another are correlated. Then, by means of a complicated statistical procedure, the correlations are compared to arrive at an index of heritability, ranging from 0 to 1, which reflects the proportion of individual variation in IQ that is attributable to genetic factors. Let's begin our consideration of genetic influences on IQ by examining the correlational evidence from which heritability estimates are derived.

Averaging the results of over a hundred of the most carefully conducted studies, Bouchard and McGue (1981) summarized worldwide findings on IQ correlations between kinship pairs. The correlations, shown in Table 8.2, are consistent with a polygenic model of inheritance of IQ, because they show that the greater the propor-

Table 8.2. Bouchard and McGue's (1981) Worldwide Summary of IQ Correlations Between Kinship Pairs

KINSHIP PAIR	AVERAGE WEIGHTED CORRELATION	TOTAL NUMBER OF KINSHIP PAIRS INCLUDED	NUMBER OF STUDIES
Identical twins reared together	.86	4,672	34
Identical twins reared apart	.72	65	3
Fraternal twins reared together	.60	5,546	41
Siblings reared together	.47	26,473	69
Siblings reared apart	.24	203	2
Biological parent — offspring living together	.42	8,433	32
Biological parent — offspring living apart	.22[a]	814	4
Nonbiological siblings (adopted — natural pairings)	.29	345	5
Nonbiological siblings (adopted — adopted pairings)	.34	369	6
Adoptive parent — offspring	.19	1,397	6

[a] This correlation is lower than the values obtained in two recent American cross-fostering studies (Horn, 1983; Scarr & Weinberg, 1983), which reported correlations of .31 and .43 respectively.

Source: T. J. Bouchard & M. McGue, 1981. "Familial Studies of Intelligence: A Review," *Science, 212,* 1056. Copyright 1981 by the AAAS.

tion of genes two relatives have in common, the higher the correlation between their IQs. In fact, two of the correlations reveal that heredity is, without question, a partial determinant of general intelligence. The correlation for identical twins reared apart (.72) is considerably higher than for fraternal twins reared together in the same household (.60). In a recent longitudinal study of identical and fraternal twins that examined how relationships between their IQs changed from infancy into the adolescent years, the correlations for identicals became stronger and those for fraternals became weaker with age (see Figure 8.11) (Wilson, 1983). Do these developmental trends remind you of the *niche-picking* concept that we discussed in Chapter 3? Common rearing experiences seem to maximize the similarity between fraternal twins during childhood, but as they move toward adolescence and are gradually released from the influence of their immediate family environment, each fraternal twin pursues a course of development, or finds a niche, that is in accord with his or her unique genotype, and their IQ scores begin to diverge. In contrast, the genetic likeness of identical twins leads them to seek out niches that are very similar to one another in adolescence. Consequently, their IQ similarity is even greater than it was during the childhood years.

Although twin comparisons verify the importance of genetic factors, careful inspection of all of the correlations given in Table 8.2, taking into account the magnitude of the differences between them and clear effect of common rearing experiences, provides support for only a moderate role for heredity in the determination of intelligence. For example, the average correlation between identical twins reared apart is far from the perfect value that would be expected if IQ differences were solely determined by the genes (although its high magnitude is also difficult to explain on the basis of any strict environmental hypothesis). In addition, the correlation between identical twins reared apart is considerably less than when they are reared together, a difference that points to the importance of family environment. Other comparisons that stress the role of the environment include: the stronger correlation for fraternal twins as opposed to ordinary siblings reared together (generally attributed to more similar rearing conditions experienced by twins); the stronger correlation for siblings reared together than apart; and the stronger correlation for biological parents and offspring living together than apart. Finally, adoptive parents' and their adoptive

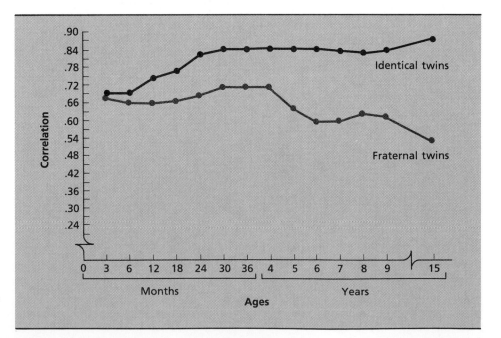

Figure 8.11. Age changes in IQ correlations for identical and fraternal twins in the Louisville Twin Study. *(R. Wilson, 1983, "The Louisville Twin Study: Developmental Synchronies in Behavior,"* Child Development, 54, *311.* © The Society for Research in Child Development, Inc. Reprinted by permission.)

offspring, as well as unrelated siblings, show low positive IQ correlations, again providing support for the impact of common rearing conditions.

Heritability estimates are generally computed using comparisons of the correlations of identical and fraternal twins. The values arrived at in recent investigations, which employ improved statistical methodology over previous research, range from .30 to .70. Scarr and Kidd (1983) suggest that the true value is probably somewhere around .50, which means that half of the variation in IQ can be attributed to differences among people in genetic makeup. This is a much more modest estimate than reported in earlier studies, such as the value of .80 arrived at by Jensen as part of his controversial 1969 article on racial and social class differences in intelligence. In addition, as we indicated in Chapter 3, it is still possible that the moderate heritabilities reported above may be inaccurate, for twins reared together experience very similar overall environments, and even in the few instances where they are reared apart, they are often placed in foster and adoptive homes that are advantaged and alike in many ways. When the range of environments to which twin pairs are exposed is restricted, heritabilities underestimate environmental influences and overestimate genetic influences. This problem also raises questions about the generalizability of heritability estimates. Due to placement in similar and superior homes, the rearing environments of separated twins are unlikely to be representative of the broad range of environmental variation experienced by children growing up in an average community.

Despite inherent limitations of the heritability estimate, Jensen (1969; 1973) relied heavily on it to support the argument that racial and socioeconomic differences in general intelligence have a strong genetic basis. This line of reasoning is widely regarded as inappropriate, for heritability estimates computed *within* a population (largely on white twin samples) provide no direct evidence about what is responsible for *between*-group racial/ethnic and socioeconomic differences in IQ. In a well-known example, Lewontin (1976) showed that generalizing within-group heritabilities to explain between-group differences is like comparing different seeds in different soil. Suppose we take a handful of "white" corn seeds and pot them all with the same special nutrient designed to encourage plant growth. Then we take a handful of "black" seeds and grow them under quite different conditions, with half as much nutrient. We chart plant growth and find that although the plants in each group vary in height, the "white" seeds, on the average, grow taller than the "black" ones. Within each group we can attribute individual differences in plant height to genetic factors (since growth environments were much the same), but it would be wrong to account for the between-group difference in this way. Instead, it must be largely environmentally determined, since the nutrient given the "black" seeds was far less plentiful.

Furthermore, high heritabilities have been *assumed* by Jensen to imply that the malleability of the IQ score is very limited. In actuality, the correlational findings on which heritability estimates are based offer no precise information on the extent to which heredity restricts future opportunities for environment to influence the IQ score. In comparison to twin correlations, **cross-fostering studies,** in which children are reared in environments very different from their family of origin, provide much more useful information. Correlations of the same set of children with their biological as well as adoptive family members can be studied for insight into the relative importance of heredity and environment. In addition, changes in the absolute value of the IQ score as the result of being reared in an advantaged family setting can also be examined.

Cross-Fostering Research. Several classic adoption studies were carried out during the 1930s and 1940s, and then the adoption design lay dormant for nearly three decades, until the nature-nurture debate during the 1970s sparked renewed interest in it. The most well known of these early studies was conducted by Skodak and Skeels

(1949). They gave repeated IQ testings during childhood and adolescence to a sample of 100 children placed in adoptive homes prior to 6 months of age. Although the children's biological parents were largely from low socioeconomic backgrounds, the adoptive families were well above average in economic security and educational status. Due to advantaged rearing experiences, the absolute value of the adopted children's IQ scores remained above the population mean throughout middle childhood and into the adolescent years, a finding that proves that the IQ is, in fact, highly malleable! Nevertheless, the children's IQs still showed considerable correlation with the scores of their biological mothers. Also, children of biological parents with higher intellectual ability profited more from adoptive placement than those of biological parents with lower intellectual ability. These latter two findings provide support for the role of heredity in determining IQ.

Selective placement in adoption procedures is a problem that plagues most cross-fostering studies, and it appeared to be operating in the Skodak and Skeels investigation. When selective placement occurs, both biological and adoptive parents bear similarities in IQ and other salient characteristics. As a result, hereditary and environmental influences cannot be disentangled from each other completely. However, the findings of Skodak and Skeels have been replicated in a recent cross-fostering investigation in which the effects of selective placement were judged to be minimal. The Texas Adoption Project (Horn, Loehlin, & Willerman, 1979; Willerman, 1979; Horn, 1983) resulted from the discovery of a large private adoption agency that had administered IQ tests routinely to hundreds of unwed mothers while they resided in its residential facility. Two extreme groups of biological mothers — those with IQ scores below 95 and those with IQ scores above 120 — were chosen for special study. As shown in Figure 8.12, when tested during middle childhood, children of the low-IQ mothers scored above average in IQ, but they did not do nearly as well as the children of the brighter natural mothers who were raised in comparable adoptive families. In addition, adopted children's IQs correlated more strongly with the scores of their biological mothers than with their adoptive mothers who had reared them from birth. Thus, cross-fostering research shows that *both* family environment *and* heredity contribute significantly to individual differences in IQ.

Given that lower-IQ natural mothers are usually from less advantaged family backgrounds, the fact that their adopted offspring repeatedly score above average in IQ suggests that social class differences in intelligence have a substantial environmental component. However, concluding that social class differences in IQ are entirely

Figure 8.12. IQs of adopted children as a function of biological mothers' IQ in the Texas Adoption Project. A 4-point difference between the two groups in the IQs of the adoptive mothers occurred, suggesting a mild selective placement effect. However, it was not great enough to account for the substantial difference in children's IQs as a function of biological mothers' scores. *(Adapted from L. Willerman, 1979.)*

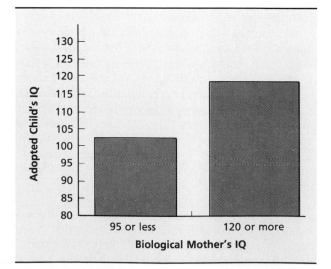

accounted for by differences in family environments is probably too extreme (Bouchard & Segal, 1985). Children of low-IQ biological mothers adopted into upper-middle-class families (although they attain above-average IQs) generally score somewhat lower than their adoptive parents' natural children, with whom they share equally privileged rearing conditions. In addition, cross-fostering studies repeatedly reveal stronger correlations between the IQ scores of biological as opposed to adoptive relatives (Horn, 1983; Plomin & DeFries, 1983; Scarr & Weinberg, 1983). On the basis of such evidence, a number of investigators have concluded that the social class–IQ connection is partly genetic in origin (Bouchard & Segal, 1985; Scarr & Weinberg, 1978).

The findings of the cross-fostering studies we have reviewed so far are based on white samples and tell us nothing about the origins of the black-white IQ gap. In an unusual investigation of black children adopted into white middle-class families, Scarr and Weinberg (1976; 1983) found that the poorer test performance of American black children is socioculturally determined and cannot be explained by racially linked, inferior genes. See Box 8.1 for a description of this important study.

FOCUS ON THEORY, RESEARCH, AND APPLICATIONS

Box 8.1
The Transracial Adoption Study

Theory. The Transracial Adoption Study, carried out by Sandra Scarr and Richard Weinberg (1976; 1983), was aimed at finding out how well black children adopted by upper-middle-class white families and reared "in the culture of the tests and schools" would do on IQ and achievement tests. If Jensen's claim that black children are limited in intellectual potential is correct, then the IQs of black adoptees should fall considerably below those of other children reared in the same advantaged white homes. However, if black children have the hereditary prerequisites to benefit from advantaged rearing conditions, then adopted black children should show an overall rise in test performance, and their scores should resemble their white adopted counterparts.

Research. The families of over a hundred adopted black children participated in the study. Approximately two thirds of the children were adopted during the first year of life, and one third after 12 months of age. The white adoptive parents scored in the high-average to superior range on intelligence tests, were well above average in occupational status and income, and exceeded the educational

attainment of the biological parents by 4 to 5 years.

Scarr and Weinberg's findings paralleled the dramatic results of cross-fostering investigations involving white adoptees. During childhood and adolescence, the black children showed an average IQ score of 106, well above the general population mean, and their school achievement was similarly elevated. The IQ scores of those who had been adopted within the first 12 months of life were even higher. Averaging 110, they were 20 points above scores of comparable children reared in the black community. The investigators concluded that genetic factors do not play a major role in black children's typically depressed intellectual performance.

Like correlational findings of other cross-fostering investigations, those obtained in the Transracial Adoption Study provide support for both genetic and environmental determinants of IQ. The scores of adoptive siblings were moderately correlated with one another (.25), again providing support for the importance of family environment, but this correlation was not as strong as the one obtained for biological siblings reared together (.42), indicating that genetic factors also play a significant role. Similarly, the IQs of the adopted children were related to the scores of their adoptive parents (.29), but not nearly as strongly

as they correlated with the educational level of their biological mothers (.43). Thus, the high scores obtained by the black children show that black adoptees, like their white adopted counterparts, are responsive to rearing environments that provide stimulation relevant to the skills and knowledge sampled by IQ tests. At the same time, the correlational results indicate that *both* genetic and environmental factors are responsible for individual differences among adopted children, regardless of their racial origins.

Applications. Results of the Transracial Adoption Study negate a genetic explanation of the black-white IQ gap and suggest that the typically poor mental test performance of black children is due to the fact that tests and schools share a common culture to which black children are not fully exposed. Scarr and Weinberg (1976) are careful to point out that their study is not an endorsement for widespread adoption of black children into white homes. Instead, they call for more research aimed at identifying specific ways that family environments can promote intellectual skills, as well as societal efforts aimed at changing the circumstances associated with poverty and minority status that exert a detrimental effect on children's psychological development.

Research on Racial Ancestry. Another way of investigating whether racial groups are genetically different in intelligence is to compare individuals of relatively pure versus mixed racial ancestry. If it were true that racial differences do contribute to the difference in IQ between blacks and whites, then blacks with higher degrees of African ancestry should perform more poorly than those with some white ancestry (Jensen, 1973). A study conducted by Scarr and her co-workers of several hundred socially classified black children revealed no support at all for this hypothesis. Children with more African ancestry (determined by careful analyses of blood group phenotypes) scored just as high on a battery of intelligence tests as did children with less African ancestry (Scarr et al., 1977). Thus, the findings of both adoption and racial ancestry research are in agreement that the genes contributing to blackness do not act to lower IQ scores.

In summary, heritability estimates support a moderate role for genetic factors in the determination of intelligence. However, heritabilities cannot be generalized to explain racial and social class differences in IQ, and they do not tell us whether further environmental interventions can raise test scores. In contrast, cross-fostering studies demonstrate that the absolute value of the IQ is highly malleable, even though the contribution of heredity is clearly evident in stronger IQ correlations between biological than adoptive relatives.

Environmental Influences

Although genetic factors play an undeniable part in the IQ variation in the general population, at present there are no ethically acceptable routes to controlling such influences. It is much more fruitful for people interested in bettering the lives of children to concentrate on things they can do something about — the environmental factors that explain the sizable remaining variation in IQ once genetic influences are accounted for. While predictive of children's IQ scores, global indices of the environment, such as parental occupation, income, and education, do not tell us much about the numerous specific aspects of experience — details of the child's sociocultural background, home environment, and schooling — that contribute to the overall relationships. Once such precise information is known, psychologists and educators will have more powerful tools at their disposal for planning effective interventions. During the last two decades, researchers have made substantial progress in identifying these important environmental factors.

Sociocultural Background and Bias in the Tests. Both professionals and laypersons have raised the question of whether taking the intellectual behaviors of the majority as the standard against which the performance of all children is assessed yields a biased picture of minority children's abilities. The issue of test bias has produced a voluminous and controversial research literature. Psychologists are not of one mind, either about how to define test bias or whether it exists.

Some investigators (e.g., Ebel, 1975; Jensen, 1980; Oakland & Parmelee, 1985) believe that test bias should be viewed strictly in terms of objective assessments of an intelligence test's validity. From this perspective, if a test yields the same factor structure of abilities among minority children as it does among majority children, and if it also predicts scholastic performance equivalently for different subgroups of children, it is not biased. Using these criteria, intelligence tests have stood up very well (Kaplan, 1985; Oakland & Parmelee, 1985; Reschly, 1978; Reynolds & Nigl, 1981). However, some known exceptions exist (Mercer, 1979a; Oakland, 1978), and the validity of every test needs to be established for children of different backgrounds. Otherwise, it is possible for a test to have very different meanings for different kinds of children (Kaplan, 1985).

Once a test behaves in the same way for different subgroups with regard to these validity issues, those who subscribe to a strict definition of test bias regard the instruments as equally fair for all children. They claim that intelligence tests were intended to represent important aspects of success in the common culture. As long as they do so, any additional bias (if it exists) is not in the tests so much as it is in the attitudes, values, and child-rearing practices of particular subgroups that do not adequately prepare their children to succeed in the prevailing culture. These psychologists believe that minority interests are not well served by blaming the tests for disadvantaged children's poorer scores (Ebel, 1975; Oakland & Parmelee, 1985).

Other psychologists adhere to a much broader definition of test bias. In addition to issues of uniform factor structure and prediction of academic performance, they regard a test as biased if it samples culturally specific knowledge and skills that not all subgroups have had equal opportunity to become acquainted with (Mercer, 1975; Zigler & Seitz, 1982). From this point of view, when certain subgroups have not been adequately exposed to information sampled by the test or have learned a set of survival skills that is maladaptive in testing situations, then scores are biased because they reflect differential learning opportunities, not true differences in ability. These psychologists point to familiarity of item content, language differences, and motivational variables as factors that cause poor and ethnic minority children to score lower than their actual abilities permit. Let's examine each of these important factors in turn.

Familiarity of Item Content. Many researchers have argued that intelligence test scores are affected by knowledge of specific information that is acquired as part of white, middle-class upbringing. Lacking access to such knowledge, many minority children, these investigators believe, have less chance of doing well on standardized tests.

Unfortunately, efforts to change standardized tests either by basing verbal items on more familiar content or by eliminating the test's dependence on culturally based, crystallized knowledge altogether have not changed the scores of ethnic minority children very much (Jensen, 1980; Kaplan, 1985). For example, *Raven's Progressive Matrices* is one of the best researched and most extensively used culture-fair tests of fluid intelligence. To see a typical item, look back at the figure matrix task shown in Figure 8.1. Despite the Raven's lack of dependence on specific verbal information and its simple instructions, research shows that minority children continue to perform more poorly on it, and on other tests like it, than white middle-class children (Jensen, 1980).

It is still possible that high scores on fluid tests like Raven's Matrices are dependent on less obvious learning opportunities than the ones involved in verbal tests. In one recent study, Dirks (1982) discovered that children's performance on the Block Design subtest of the WISC-R (also a measure of fluid intelligence) was related to the extent to which they had played an expensive commercial game that, like the subtest, required them to arrange cubes to duplicate a geometric pattern as quickly as possible. When children inexperienced at playing the game were given a brief exposure to it, their Block Design scores rose dramatically. Opportunities to interact with games and objects may be especially important for the development of some nonverbal intellectual skills, and some minority children may be especially deficient in such experiences. In fact, it has been suggested that because black children are raised in more "people-oriented" than "object-oriented" homes, they experience fewer opportunities to manipulate objects and discover their properties and relationships (Hale, 1982).

Language Differences. IQ scores are biased indicators of true ability when non-English-speaking and bilingual children are not given tests in their native or dominant

Opportunities to manipulate objects and discover their properties and relationships contribute to the development of nonverbal intellectual skills. (Linda Hirsch)

language. Such children frequently obtain higher scores on nonverbal and performance than on verbal scales when tests are administered in English, but under these circumstances it would be entirely incorrect to conclude that this profile indicates a real deficiency in verbal ability (Jensen, 1980; Oakland & Parmelee, 1985).

Many black children from low-income backgrounds speak a dialect that is different from standard English, and like bilingual children, they are often assumed to be at a disadvantage when intelligence tests are administered in standard English. However, when tests have been translated into black dialect, black children's scores have not changed (Quay, 1972; 1974). This same finding does not necessarily generalize to all dialect-speaking children. One recent study reported that children who spoke a Hawaiian-English dialect did better on a verbal comprehension test when it was administered in their dialect instead of in standard English (Speidel & Tharp, 1985).

Another prevalent claim is that intelligence tests, and the classroom learning experiences that resemble them, are not relevant to the early language customs of many minority children. For example, some investigators believe that black subculture gives rise to unique language skills that are ignored in the usual educational and mental assessment process. Well-known psychometric experts dismiss black children's unique verbal experiences as an appropriate basis for assuming that intelligence tests are biased against them (e.g., Ebel, 1975; Jensen, 1980; Sattler, 1988). However, a number of anthropologists who have spent many hours observing black children at home and in school have concluded that tests and school learning activities do emphasize language characteristics to which black children are inadequately exposed. For example, Michaels (1980) observed sharing time in an urban first-grade classroom composed of half black and half white pupils and noted that the two groups of children had very different oral presentation styles. The white middle-class children used a tightly organized, *topic-centered style* that focused on a single topic or series of related topics. In contrast, low-income black children used a *topic-chaining style* that flowed easily from one topic to another and that usually dealt with aspects of personal relationships. The white teacher had trouble following and responding to the black children's narratives, which appeared to her to be poorly focused, rambling responses.

How do such different verbal approaches to the same classroom learning experience on the part of black and white children develop? In a study described in Box 8.2, anthropologist Shirley Brice-Heath suggests some provocative answers to this ques-

Box 8.2
Questioning at Home and School: Early Language Environments of Black and White Children

Theory. Anthropologist Shirley Brice-Heath (1982) studied the language customs of Trackton, a small black community in a southeastern American city, and compared them to white teachers' communications with their own children at home and their pupils at school. She predicted that such information would help explain why many ethnic minority children approach school learning situations differently from other youngsters. Brice-Heath also hypothesized that sharing her language observations with white teachers of the Trackton children could spur the development of more effective teaching strategies that take into account the unique language experiences of black youngsters.

Research. Children of Trackton attended integrated public schools where they were taught by white teachers. Trackton parents were disturbed by their children's extreme dislike of school and discomfort communicating in the classroom. The teachers commented that many of the children seemed unable to answer even simple questions. Some teachers thought the difficulty might lie in differences between black dialect used in Trackton and standard English used at school. Others believed that the

communication breakdown was more basic, although they could not pin down exactly what the problem was.

Brice-Heath compared uses of language in Trackton with language customs in the white community. She concentrated on question asking, for questions are a particularly important classroom communication tool. Watching the white teachers communicate with their own young children, Brice-Heath discovered that they constantly communicated in questions. Over 50 percent of their utterances were interrogatives, most of which were used to train children in knowledge about the world, as in "What color is it?" "Where's the puppy?" "What's this story about?" Moreover, Brice-Heath found that the teachers' classroom discourse also consisted largely of questions, and the types of questions used by teachers at home were the same ones used in school.

In comparison to white children, Brice-Heath found that black pupils from Trackton were asked questions at home far less frequently. As a rule, Trackton adults postponed asking questions until their children were seen as competent conversationalists and reliable sources of information. When black children got older, the questions asked were of a very different sort than white teachers posed to their children. Instead of knowledge-training questions, black parents asked analogy questions (e.g., "What's that like?") or story-starter questions (e.g., "Didja hear Miss Sally this morning?") that called for elaborate responses about

whole events for which there was no single "right answer."

Once Brice-Heath got teachers to incorporate these kinds of questions into classroom activities, Trackton children changed from passive, reticent members of the classroom to eager, lively participants. Using photos of the community, teachers started by asking such questions as, "Tell me what you did when you were there?" "What's that like?" Then they taped children's responses, added specific questions identifying attributes and objects to the tapes, and placed them in learning centers where children could listen to themselves give responses appropriate in their own community alongside classroom discourse strategies. Gradually the children were helped to prepare new questions and answers for the tapes. As the result of these experiences, they soon caught on to classroom verbal customs and began to realize that school-type questions need not threaten their ways of talking at home.

Applications. Brice-Heath's study illustrates a unique approach to helping ethnic minority children become more successful in school. When teachers understand the cultural experiences that give rise to the distinct verbal customs of black children, they can incorporate those customs into classroom activities, thereby building effective bridges between black children's natural learning styles and the styles of learning necessary for school success.

---

tion. Brice-Heath and others (Hale, 1982; Havighurst, 1976; Yando, Seitz, & Zigler, 1979) who take the position that minority children's backgrounds do not prepare them to be successful in the test-taking and academic world, advocate a *difference* rather than *deficit* approach as the basis for understanding and helping the minority child. They stress the need for instructional experiences that recognize the minority child's cognitive strengths and that build bridges between their natural learning styles and the expectations of classroom learning and testing situations.

Motivational Variables. Intelligence tests are known to be greatly influenced by a variety of motivational variables. Zigler and Seitz (1982) point out that when faced with an unfamiliar adult, children from poverty backgrounds often reply "I don't know" to the simplest of questions, including "What's your name?" The response does not stem from lack of cognitive competence. Instead, it reflects wariness of the examiner and the test situation. Consequently, the fearful child behaves in ways that are aimed at minimizing interaction and terminating the unpleasant situation as soon as possible. Besides suspicion and discomfort in the presence of strangers, many ethnic minority children do not define test situations in achievement terms. They are more motivated to look for signs of attention and approval and less motivated to be correct for the sake of correctness alone. Often they will settle for lower levels of achievement success than their abilities would allow (Zigler & Butterfield, 1968).

A number of studies show that substantial IQ gains result when testing conditions are modified so disadvantaged children have an opportunity to become familiar with the examiner, are provided with generous amounts of praise and encouragement, and are given easier test items immediately after incorrect responses to minimize the emotional consequences of failure (Ali & Costello, 1971; Zigler, Abelson, & Seitz, 1973; Zigler & Butterfield, 1968). In the most impressive of these investigations, preschool children from poverty backgrounds scored 10 IQ points higher after either being given a 10-minute play period with the examiner prior to testing or being individually tested a second time by the same examiner who tested them on the first occasion. In contrast, gains of advantaged children under the same optimal testing conditions amounted to only about 3 IQ points (Zigler, Abelson, & Seitz, 1973).

Although familiarization with the examiner and modification of testing procedures minimize the effects of motivational difficulties pertaining to features of the testing situation, Zigler and his colleagues (Zigler et al., 1982) believe that many disadvantaged children suffer from more deep-seated self-defeating attitudes and motives. Far more extensive intervention is necessary to treat these problems. Zigler suggests that IQ gains that result from attending preschool early intervention programs are, for the most part, not true cognitive gains. Instead, they are the result of the effectiveness of such programs in helping disadvantaged children develop motivational attributes that permit them to fully utilize their intellectual capabilities. Recently, Zigler and his co-workers (1982) found that preschool children attending a year-long Head Start program showed IQ gains, but comparable children who did not attend experienced IQ declines accompanied by increased wariness of strange adults. These findings suggest that poor motives and attitudes underlie disadvantaged children's low test scores and lesser readiness to profit from classroom learning experiences at school entry. As such children experience repeated academic failure, a self-defeating motivational style marked by withdrawal, disengagement, and reduced effort becomes more firmly entrenched in their personality dispositions and increasingly difficult to modify.

Overcoming Test Bias. Evidence that many disadvantaged and racial/ethnic minority children score lower on IQ tests than their true abilities permit has led to a national controversy about whether biased testing procedures lead to overlabeling of minority children as retarded and their disproportionate assignment to special public school classes that provide an inferior education. Sociologist Jane Mercer has been a leading proponent of this position. Studies by Mercer conducted during the early 1970s in Riverside, California, revealed that of a total 812 persons defined as mentally retarded by community agencies, the schools were the principal labelers, contributing 429, or more than half of the diagnoses. Poor children as well as blacks and Hispanics were overrepresented, especially among the public school nominees. When Mercer interviewed mothers of "mentally retarded" schoolchildren, she found that in the eyes of family and friends, many were considered quite normal. Mercer concluded that such children were really "six-hour retardates": situationally retarded at school due to the application of a culturally biased, middle-class assessment framework (Mercer, 1972; 1975). Results of more extensive surveys than those conducted by Mercer indicate that the overrepresentation of minority students in special classes for the retarded and their underrepresentation in programs for the academically gifted is a pervasive national problem (Reschly, 1979).

As a remedy for culturally biased testing procedures believed to be responsible for disproportionate placement, Mercer suggested that adaptive behavior inventories, designed to assess children's ability to cope with the everyday demands of the environment, be used as a supplement to IQ scores in the identification of children for special educational placement. Her findings indicate that adding a test of adaptive behavior to IQ makes little difference in the assessment of retardation as far as white middle-class children are concerned. However, it has a substantial effect for minority children, for Mercer reported that 91 percent of blacks and 60 percent of Hispanics with IQs below 70 did well on the behavioral assessment. Because of the dangers of unfairly penalizing ethnic minority children, Mercer (1972; 1975) advocates that very stringent criteria be used to define children as retarded, recommending that only those who fall in the lowest 3 percent on both intelligence and adaptive behavior scales be so labeled.

Also, Mercer has been a strong advocate of assessment approaches that deliberately take cultural differences into account. To that end, she developed the *System of Multicultural Pluralistic Assessment (SOMPA)*, which is based on the assumption that a culturally fair testing system must adjust for the minority child's different life experiences (Mercer, 1979b; Mercer & Lewis, 1978). The SOMPA adds extra points to the child's IQ score to compensate for an underprivileged sociocultural background. Its purpose according to Mercer is, once again, to help prevent minority children from being overidentified as mentally retarded.

Critics of Mercer's approach believe that the effects of labeling children in special educational placements are of little psychological consequence. They maintain that low-IQ children, regardless of what they are called, need extra help in school, and Mercer's system may prevent them from getting it and leave many frustrated pupils in learning situations where they cannot keep up. Because the socioculturally adjusted scores on the SOMPA are poor predictors of school success, critics also claim that the approach is less valid than sticking to traditional IQs (Goodman, 1979; Oakland, 1979; Sattler, 1988; Reschly, 1981). Others take more of a "wait-and-see" attitude toward the SOMPA and believe that time will tell if minority children not placed in special classes who otherwise would have been are benefiting educationally (Kaplan, 1985).

A less radical approach to reducing test bias than the SOMPA is exemplified by the K-ABC. Recall that designers of the K-ABC took special steps to correct a number of important contributing factors to culturally biased test scores, including eliminating items with biased content and permitting flexible administration procedures. These efforts cut the typical IQ discrepancy between black and white children in half and nearly equalized the performance of Hispanics and white youngsters (Kaufman, Kamphaus, & Kaufman, 1985). These findings are encouraging, for the K-ABC has managed to reduce commonly obtained racial/ethnic differences in IQ while accumulating a substantial record of reliability and validity (Kaplan, 1985).

Should the problems of test bias and the potential for misusing IQ scores be resolved by banning the tests altogether? Even psychologists who believe that intelligence tests suffer from serious biases regard this alternative as unacceptable, for it totally relinquishes important decisions about children to subjective impressions, an approach that could increase the discriminatory placement of minority children. As Reschly (1981) points out, IQ tests reduce the degree of overrepresentation in special classes that would exist from teacher referral alone, and when wisely used and interpreted, they yield information not available through other means. Rather than banning the tests entirely, it is much more fruitful to continue to refine current mental testing practices and build safeguards into decision-making processes involving IQ scores.

In summary, the criteria for defining test bias differ among psychologists. Those who adopt strict, objective definitions find little evidence of bias against low-income and ethnic minority children. In contrast, proponents of culture-fair assessment procedures argue that unfamiliar item content, different language customs, and motivational factors lead IQ tests to underestimate disadvantaged children's true abilities. Test bias and misuse of IQ scores have been held responsible for the overidentification of minority children as mentally retarded in the public schools. Assessments of adaptive behavior and testing procedures that take cultural differences into account have been recommended as remedies for these problems.

Home Environment and IQ. Despite the overwhelming attention accorded them, racial/ethnic and social class differences are not the only important IQ variations with environmental explanations. As we indicated earlier in this chapter, individual children of the *same* ethnic and socioeconomic backgrounds also differ in IQ. Below we consider some important home environmental factors believed to contribute to these differences.

Variations in home environments that affect children's IQ scores are of two general types. The first type, **between-family influences,** are the ones most often studied and include factors related to the overall "intellectual climate" of the home. They are called between-family influences because they permeate the general atmosphere of the home and therefore can be expected to affect all children within a family to the same extent. The availability of stimulating toys and books, parental encouragement for achievement, and modeling by parents of intellectual activities and accomplishments are good examples. The second type, **within-family influences,** have only recently begun to capture the attention of developmental psychologists. They are factors that make siblings *different* from one another. Examples include differential treatment of children by parents, birth order and spacing of siblings, as well as serendipitous events like moving to a new neighborhood that affect one sibling more than another. Let's see what research reveals about each of these two important classes of environmental influences.

Between-Family Influences. A large body of research carried out over the last 40 years has consistently shown that children's concurrent as well as later IQ scores can be predicted from assessments of their home environments taken as early as the first 2 years of life. Longitudinal investigations, such as the Berkeley and Fels studies, were among the first to illuminate aspects of parental behavior and home atmosphere that were potent predictors of children's IQ scores. Stimulation provided by the physical setting, parental encouragement of intellectual achievement, and the emotional climate created by parental interactions loomed as especially important in these first studies. As indicated in our previous discussion of the stability of mental test performance, early assessments of these dimensions not only correlated with IQ scores (Honzik, 1967; Moore, 1968) but also predicted profiles of IQ change over the course of childhood.

Because of the promising nature of these early findings, Caldwell and her collaborators developed a broadly applicable technique that permits precise measurement of subtle aspects of the young child's home environment. Currently, the *Home Observation for Measurement of the Environment (HOME)* is the most widely used technique for investigating the relationship of between-family environmental characteristics to children's intellectual performance. It gathers information through direct observation as well as parental interview. Two versions of HOME exist: one for assessment during infancy (Elardo, Bradley, & Caldwell, 1975) and the other for the preschool years (Bradley & Caldwell, 1979). The subscales measured by each are shown in Table 8.3.

Research with HOME provides overwhelming confirmation of the findings of earlier research—that quality of stimulation provided in the early years of life is linked to cognitive development. All HOME subscales are correlated with children's intellectual performance, but elements of the home environment that loom as especially important change with age. Organization of the physical and temporal environ-

Table 8.3. Home Observation for Measurement of the Environment (HOME) Subscales

INFANCY VERSION	PRESCHOOL VERSION
1. Emotional and verbal responsivity of the mother	1. Stimulation through toys, games, and reading material
2. Avoidance of restriction and punishment	2. Language stimulation
3. Organization of the physical and temporal environment	3. Physical environment: Safe, clean, and conducive to development
4. Provision of appropriate play materials	4. Pride, affection, and warmth
5. Maternal involvement with the child	5. Stimulation of academic behavior
6. Opportunities for variety in daily stimulation.	6. Modeling and encouragement of social maturity
	7. Variety of stimulation
	8. Avoidance of physical punishment

Sources: Bradley & Caldwell, 1979; Elardo, Bradley, & Caldwell, 1975.

ment and opportunities for variety in daily stimulation seem most strongly related to infant mental development. After children enter the preschool years, maternal involvement with the child (which includes actively encouraging achievement), emotional and verbal responsivity of the mother, and the provision of appropriate play materials become more powerful predictors, and their relationship to intelligence remains substantial throughout early childhood (Elardo, Bradley, & Caldwell, 1975; Bradley & Caldwell, 1976a; Elardo, Bradley, & Caldwell, 1977). Research with HOME also adds to our understanding of environmental factors related to IQ gains and declines over the early childhood years. Mothers who encourage and challenge their infants to develop new skills and provide them with stimulating play materials have children who show large mental test increases (of 21 or more points) from 1 to 3 years of age. Children who show early declines of a comparable magnitude have parents who do a particularly poor job of organizing the home environment (Bradley & Caldwell, 1976b).

Studies examining home environments within different social class and ethnic groups have reported findings similar to the ones described above (Bee et al., 1982; Bradley & Caldwell, 1981; 1982; Engel, Nechin, & Arkin, 1975; McGowan & Johnson, 1984). No matter how economically and ethnically homogeneous the sample, certain aspects of maternal behavior — provision of appropriate play materials, encouragement of achievement and independence, warmth and affection, and verbal stimulation and responsiveness — repeatedly predict infant and childhood mental test scores.

But caution should be exercised with regard to these correlational findings, for they tell us nothing definite about causation. In all the investigations reviewed so far, children were reared by their biological parents, with whom they share not only a common environment but also common genes. As long as heredity and environment are merged in this way, it is possible for family environment–IQ relationships to be explained genetically. Parents who have genes for high IQ may simply provide particular kinds of experiences for their children as well as give birth to offspring with higher IQs. Some investigators interpret the home environment–IQ linkage in this way (e.g., Longstreth et al., 1981), but evidence from adoption studies suggests that this conclusion is not warranted. For example, Plomin and DeFries (1983) showed that later prediction of IQ from early HOME measures is as powerful among adopted children as it is among children reared by their biological parents. This finding indicates that HOME–IQ correlations *are* environmentally mediated. Furthermore, research directed at finding out the extent to which early HOME assessments contribute to children's mental test performance *beyond* the effect of maternal IQ indicates that HOME variables do make an independent contribution (Plomin & DeFries, 1983; Wilson, 1983; Yeates et al., 1983).

Still, it is important to keep in mind that the relationship of home environment to the development of intelligence is undoubtedly very complex. We have already seen that different home variables exert their strongest influence at different periods of development. Also, as our discussion of genetic-environmental correlation in Chapter 3 indicated, different children *evoke* different environmental inputs from their families, and the way they do so changes over the childhood years. Putting all these possibilities together, we see that the early home environment–IQ connection is the outcome of an intricate set of interdependencies. Bradley, Caldwell, and Elardo (1979) suggest that the relationship between home environment and mental performance may reach a steady state at some point, with neither being the primary cause, and the point in development at which the steady state is reached may depend on the particular kind of environmental influence and mental ability involved.

Finally, to add to the complexity of the home environment–IQ picture, it is worth noting that virtually all research on between-family influences focuses on the infancy and preschool periods. Information is still needed on how home experiences during later childhood impinge on intellectual development. Despite the wider range of settings to which school-age children are exposed, they continue to spend considerable time in the family. Also, it is now known that experiences in salient extra-familial settings, such as day care centers and schools, have a significant impact on cognitive development. We take up what has been discovered about them in later chapters.

Within-Family Influences. Rowe and Plomin (1981) argue that within-family environmental influences on intelligence, those that make siblings different from one another, are at least as important as between-family influences. The most obvious examples of within-family influences are family configurational variables, such as birth order and spacing of children. In an effort to sort out their effects, Zajonc and Markus proposed a complex theory called the **confluence model** (Zajonc & Markus, 1975; Zajonc, Markus, & Markus, 1979). It regards children's mental growth as a function of the quality of the intellectual environment experienced within the family, which is affected by contributions of all family members. With each new child born into the family, environmental quality is diluted, for infants are cognitively immature beings who consume the attentions of the most mature family members but contribute little to its overall level. However, as children get older and mature intellectually, environmental quality rises. Based on these assumptions, the confluence model leads to a number of specific predictions about the effects of family configurational factors on intelligence. Children's scores should be higher in smaller families with wider spacing among siblings. In addition, IQ should decline with birth order, except when wide spacing cancels the negative effect of being born into a large family.

Do the complex predictions of confluence theory hold up under research scrutiny? An extensive study that analyzed data from military files on almost all males born in Holland at the end of World War II revealed supportive findings (Zajonc, 1976; Zajonc & Markus, 1975). As shown in Figure 8.13, both family size and birth order had the expected depressing effects on IQ (Belmont & Marolla, 1973). However, exceptions to confluence theory predictions also appeared. The performance of only children, who are from the smallest family size, is lower then expected. Also, the last child of each family size shows a greater drop in intelligence than occurs for other birth order positions. Zajonc and Markus explain these deviations from the overall pattern by suggesting that only and last-born children are alike in that neither has the opportunity to serve as an intellectual resource to younger siblings. Experiences in teaching younger brothers and sisters, they believe, offer a special intellectual advantage to the older sibling who serves as the teacher.

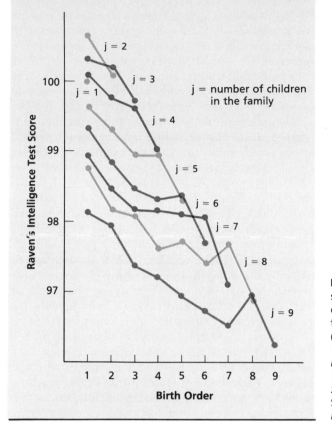

Figure 8.13. Intelligence test scores plotted as a function of family size and birth order from Belmont and Marolla's (1973) Dutch sample of 19-year-old males. *(From L. Belmont & F. A. Marolla, 1973, "Birth Order, Family Size, and Intelligence,"* Science, 182, *1097. Copyright 1973 by the AAAS.)*

The confluence model has recently been the subject of heated controversy. While some studies have confirmed its predictions (Berbaum & Moreland, 1985), others have not (Brackbill & Nichols, 1982; Galbraith, 1982). Some researchers suggest that rather than trying to test the model in its entirety, a more fruitful approach would be to study each family configurational variable separately with the aim of discovering the precise processes responsible for its effects (Rodgers, 1984; McCall, 1985). In a

According to confluence theory, the birth of a new baby dilutes the intellectual quality of the family environment and is associated with a decline in children's IQ scores. (Myrleen Ferguson/ PhotoEdit)

recent reanalysis of the Fels longitudinal data, McCall (1984) reported that the IQs of children who experienced the birth of a younger sibling dropped 10 points during the following 2 years in comparison to singleton children and 6 points in comparison to last-born children in families of comparable size. The decline was temporary; the older siblings gradually compensated for it, and the differences were no longer apparent by 17 years of age. In two other studies, the birth of a new baby was associated with less positive and playful communication as well as more negative interaction on the part of mothers with their older children (Dunn & Kendrick, 1980; Stewart et al., 1987). Taken together, these results are consistent with an important tenet of confluence theory — that the birth of a new child reduces the intellectual atmosphere of the home and temporarily slows the mental development of older children — but more than that, the findings help to illuminate just how this effect is set in motion.

Another important assumption of confluence theory has to do with the value of being in a position to teach younger siblings, an effect experienced by all children in a family except only and youngest children. Many studies indicate that children and adolescents do benefit intellectually from tutoring other children in school (e.g., Bargh & Schul, 1980; Devin-Sheehan, Feldman, & Allen, 1976; Goldschmid & Goldschmid, 1976), but to date only one study has explored the phenomenon in connection with sibling relationships. Smith (1984) found that among a large sample of 6th- through 12th-grade students, the relationship between responsibility for younger siblings and school grades was actually far more complex than predicted by confluence theory. Among white students, a moderate amount of sibling responsibility was related to higher grades, but either very little or a great deal of responsibility predicted lower grades. In contrast, among black students sibling responsibility was consistently related to lower grades. These findings indicate that sibling teaching opportunities may have quite different meanings for children of different ethnic origins. They also suggest that burdening any child with too much responsibility for younger brothers and sisters may drain time and energy away from schoolwork and other pursuits that are far more important for intellectual growth than opportunities to teach younger children.

On the whole, confluence theory has received only mixed support. Even its proponents admit that family size, spacing, and birth order do not account for very much of the variation in intelligence test scores (Berbaum, 1985; Zajonc, Markus, & Markus, 1979). Perhaps you already noticed in examining Figure 8.13 that differences among first- and later-born children growing up in different family sizes are only a matter of a few IQ points. Does this mean that within-family environmental influences are really not very important in the development of children's intelligence? The evidence is not all in on this issue. As McCall (1983) points out, some potentially very powerful within-family factors are isolated, one-time events. Unlike spacing and birth order, they are not continuously present and are therefore quite difficult to capture and study. A particularly inspiring English teacher, a summer vacation spent with an attentive and caring grandparent, or a period of especially intense rivalry with a sibling are examples of such experiences. The most important within-family environmental influences may be of this kind, but understanding their impact requires far more intensive longitudinal study of children within the same family than has been accomplished to date.

In summary, a stimulating physical environment along with parental warmth, verbal stimulation, and encouragement for achievement are between-family influences that are consistently related to mental test performance during the early childhood years. Effects of within-family factors, such as birth order and spacing, also show relationships with IQ, but they are not very powerful. Other within-family influences are probably more important than these family configurational variables, but they remain to be studied.

EARLY INTERVENTION AND INTELLECTUAL DEVELOPMENT

A wide variety of early intervention programs for children of poverty were launched in the 1960s, during a decade of great optimism about the malleability of young children's intelligence. The programs were based on the assumption that the learning problems of low-income children were best treated early, before formal schooling began, as well as the hope that early enrichment would offset the declines of IQ and school achievement common among children from disadvantaged backgrounds.

Intervention programs continue to exist in large numbers today. The most widespread is Project Head Start, which began in 1965. A typical Head Start program provides children with a year of preschool education prior to school entry, along with nutritional and medical services. In addition, parent involvement is a central part of the Head Start philosophy. Parents serve on policy councils as decision-makers in program planning. They also work directly with children in classrooms, attend special programs on parenting and child development, and receive services directed at their own socioemotional and vocational needs. Although Head Start has had a shaky history with its federal funding several times in jeopardy, it now stands solidly on its feet. Its 2,000 centers located around the country reach approximately 400,000 children annually (Brown, 1985; Zigler & Berman, 1983).

Fifteen years of research establishing the long-term benefits of early intervention has played a major role in the survival of Head Start. But the first widely publicized evaluation of the program yielded adverse findings and seriously threatened its existence. Conducted by the Westinghouse Learning Corporation in cooperation with Ohio University (and now known as the Westinghouse Report), the initial study indicated that a year of Head Start had only marginal effects on children's intelligence and school achievement (Cicerelli, Evans, & Schiller, 1969). The study was immediately criticized by many researchers, for it was seriously flawed. Carried out retrospectively, a year or more after children in the sample had already completed Head Start, the evaluation suffered from inadequate matching of Head Start and control children and poor sampling of the variety of Head Start interventions available at the time (Smith & Bissell, 1970). Still, many people were convinced by the Westinghouse Report, and its findings became an important part of Jensen's (1969) argument that the low IQs of poor children were largely genetically determined and could not be raised very much.

Fortunately, new evaluations were completed during the 1970s and 1980s in which powerful longitudinal designs replaced the questionable retrospective approach of the Westinghouse Report. The most important of these was coordinated by the Consortium for Longitudinal Studies, a group of 12 investigators who pooled long-term follow-up data from a variety of preschool intervention programs. This massive evaluation effort showed that attending programs providing from 1 to 3 years of cognitive enrichment increased IQ and school achievement among low-income children through the early elementary school years (although the scores declined thereafter). More importantly, it revealed that real-life indicators of school adjustment that did not involve the measurement of IQ emerged in the primary grades and lasted through the high school years. Intervention significantly reduced the number of children assigned to special education classes and retained in grade. Also, there were motivational and attitudinal benefits. Children who attended the programs were more likely than controls to give achievement-related reasons for being proud of themselves, and their mothers had higher vocational aspirations for them (Lazar & Darlington, 1982). A separate report on the long-term outcomes of one of the Consortium programs revealed benefits that lasted into adulthood. Besides improving the ability of students to meet basic school requirements, this program was associated with a reduction in delinquency and teenage pregnancy and an increase in the likelihood of employment (Berrueta-Clement et al., 1984). These findings had a tremendous impact on the nation's funding and preservation of early intervention, for scientific evidence clearly supported its value.

Other smaller-scale longitudinal studies of intervention programs are consistent with the Consortium results. Almost all show an eventual **washout effect** for intelligence and achievement test scores. In other words, when test performance is the major focus of evaluation, gains do not last for more than a few years beyond termination of the intervention. This is not surprising, for preschool educational experiences gradually become less relevant to test and classroom learning content as children mature. For intervention to be most effective, it must be continuous. Dovetailed programs, each appropriate for a particular period of development and extending all the way from infancy into the adolescent years, would undoubtedly produce more permanent cognitive gains than a short-term preschool intervention (Zigler & Berman, 1983). In fact, many intervention programs *are* starting earlier and lasting longer. Head Start has spawned a successful downward extension, the Parent Child Centers for infants and their families (Andrews et al., 1982), and an upward extension, Project Follow Through, which provides classroom enrichment and other support services during the early elementary school years (Becker & Gersten, 1982).

The fact that short-term preschool programs of only a year or two in length result in impressive changes in children's ability to meet basic school requirements, without permanently changing the IQ score itself, has been one of the most important revelations of intervention research (Becker & Gersten, 1982; Lazar & Darlington, 1982; Seitz, Rosenbaum, & Apfel, 1985; Sprigle & Schaefer, 1985). Are these lasting outcomes mediated by IQ gains during the period immediately following the program, even though the scores themselves do not last? Or, are they largely the result of changes in the attitudes and behaviors of program parents, who are more satisfied with their children's schoolwork and develop higher expectations for their performance?

As yet, the precise mechanisms through which these long-term outcomes are achieved are not known, but researchers are working to find out. Many experts believe that the addition of a few extra IQ points does not bring lasting advantages to children of poverty, and programs that have as their singular goal the raising of test scores are regarded as far too narrowly focused (Seitz, Rosenbaum, & Apfel, 1985; Zigler & Berman, 1983; Zigler, 1985). Comparisons of the effectiveness of different intervention programs reveal that the most successful ones always work closely with parents (Bronfenbrenner, 1975; Gray & Wandersman, 1980). Actively involving parents builds bridges between center and home, thereby making it more likely that program effects will be sustained.

Recently, social scientists have experimented with interventions that direct their primary effort toward working with parents, and evaluations reveal striking long-term gains comparable to programs that emphasize cognitive stimulation of children. One such program provided impoverished mothers with social, psychological, and medical services as well as day care when it was needed during the first 2½ years of their children's lives. The benefits were still evident 10 years after the program ended. In comparison to controls, program mothers were more likely to be employed and to be better educated, and their enhanced sense of self-esteem and control over their own lives seemed to transfer to their offspring. Though their children showed no lasting cognitive gains, they did show enhanced school adjustment, for they were described by their teachers as likable, socially well adjusted pupils. Their school attendance was good, and boys in particular had a lessened need for special educational services. In contrast, control children were often truant and had serious learning and behavior problems. The investigators concluded that the link between early intervention and positive outcomes for children probably could be found in a nurturant, supportive parent-child relationship, which carries benefits for children into later years (Seitz, Rosenbaum, & Apfel, 1985).

Perhaps future research will show that the most effective interventions are those that provide *both* long-term family support *and* cognitive enrichment, leading to improved adjustment as well as higher IQs. Early intervention is an evolving concept, and social scientists continue to experiment with it and to build on its demonstrated achievements (Zigler, 1985). Unfortunately, due to the complex forces associated with poverty that act to limit human intellectual potential, it is unlikely that intervention experiments will ever produce gains for disadvantaged youngsters that equal the life chances of children born into economically privileged homes (Ramey, 1982).

BEYOND IQ: THE DEVELOPMENT OF CREATIVITY

As indicated at the beginning of this chapter, the concept of intelligence, to experts and laypersons alike, means much more than just traditional academic behaviors that predict success in school. One type of ability not sampled by major intelligence tests is creativity. Some evidence indicates that low-income children demonstrate special capabilities in this area that, besides academic intelligence, deserve to be fostered educationally (Kogan, 1983; Yando, Seitz, & Zigler, 1979).

In adults, creativity is generally regarded as the demonstration of unusual accomplishment at some intrinsically meaningful activity, such as writing, music, painting, science, or mathematics (Wallach, 1985). Of course, children are not yet experienced and mature enough to make such outstanding contributions, so in childhood, creativity has taken on a more restricted definition that has its origins in Guilford's distinction between convergent and divergent production. **Convergent thinking,** with its emphasis on arriving at a single correct answer to a problem, is the kind of cognition called for by tasks on traditional intelligence tests, whereas **divergent thinking** refers to the generation of multiple possibilities. Tests that measure divergent thinking ask children to describe as many problems as possible that are suggested by particular happenings, to name as many uses for common objects as they can (e.g., a newspaper), or to think of as many instances of a particular class of objects (e.g., "all the round things") as possible (Wallach & Kogan, 1965). Responses can be scored for their ideational fluency, or the number of different ideas generated, as well as their originality or unusualness. For example, saying that a newspaper can be used as "handgrips for a bicycle" would be a more unusual response than indicating that it can be used "to clean things."

The above-mentioned tasks are verbal tests of creativity, but figural or drawing measures also exist (Torrance, 1966). For example, Figure 8.14 shows the responses of a highly creative 8-year-old child on a figural measure requiring her to come up with as many drawings based on a circular motif as she could think of.

The ability of children to display creativity on divergent thinking tasks has little to do with whether they are capable of earning high scores on conventional intelligence tests. Among the general population of children, IQ and divergent thinking show only a low positive correlation with one another, and at high levels of intelligence, the relationship is virtually nil. Thus, children who are both highly intelligent and highly creative are the exception rather than the rule, and most creative children do not have high IQs. These findings hold true over a wide span of ages, extending from nursery school through the college years (Kogan, 1983; Torrance, 1976). The absence of a close association between intelligence and creativity has even been documented in adulthood for a great variety of professions, including art (Barron, 1963), writing (Barron, 1983), architecture, science (MacKinnon, 1968), and mathematics (Helson & Crutchfield, 1970; MacKinnon & Hall, 1973). These findings underline the importance of sampling a wider range of mental abilities than those encompassed by traditional IQ tests when identifying children who have special intellectual talents (Torrance, 1976).

Heritability research involving comparisons of identical and fraternal twins reveals that genetic influences on divergent thinking are extremely weak (Pezzullo,

Figure 8.14. Responses of a highly creative child to one of Torrance's (1966) figural measures of creativity. This 8-year-old was asked to make as many objects or pictures as she could from the circles on the page. The titles she gave her drawings, from left to right, are as follows: "dracula," "one-eyed monster," "pumpkin," "hula-hoop," "poster," "wheel chair," "earth," "moon," "planet," "movie camera," "sad face," "picture," "stop light," "beach ball," "the letter O," "car," "glasses." *Copyright © 1980 by Scholastic Testing Service, Inc. Reprinted by permission of Scholastic Testing Service, Inc. From The Torrance Tests of Creative Thinking by E. P. Torrance.)*

Thorsen, & Madaus, 1972). Thus, there may be an especially wide margin in which creative thinking can be enhanced by experience. Research on family environments shows that parents of creative children value nonconformity, emphasize intellectual curiosity and freedom of exploration, and are highly accepting of their children's individual characteristics (Getzels & Jackson, 1962). In view of this background of early support, it is not surprising that studies of personality characteristics of creative children and adults reveal them to be broad in their interests, attracted by complexity, and unconcerned about complying with conventional social norms (Barron & Harrington, 1981; Wallach, 1985).

Complementing the home background findings, cross-sectional evidence on the development of creativity during the school years suggests that the fact- and memory-oriented emphasis in many school classrooms may inhibit divergent thinking. Moran and several co-workers (1983) found that kindergartners gave a higher proportion of original responses to creativity tasks than did individuals from second grade through the adult years. Moran suggested that the answer-centered approach of traditional school curricula may make children and adolescents more cautious about expressing unusual ideas than preschoolers, who spend time in less formal settings. Consistent with this interpretation, open classrooms, which provide greater freedom and choice in learning activities, have a facilitating effect on divergent thinking when compared to traditional classrooms, at least for the young elementary school child (Thomas & Berk, 1981).

A major concern of researchers interested in creativity has been how to foster venturesome and original thinking in childhood. A variety of successful techniques for stimulating divergent thinking have been identified, including modeling of a fluent, freely flowing style of responding (Belcher, 1975) and direct instruction in question-asking techniques (Cliatt, Shaw, & Sherwood, 1980; Franklin & Richards, 1977). Question-asking training provides children with experiences in *problem finding* (as opposed to problem solving), a cognitive ability judged to be so important to creative productivity in all fields of endeavor that Arlin (1975) views it as the zenith of human cognitive capacity and as a qualitatively distinct kind of cognition that lies beyond Piaget's formal operational stage. A strong link between play and divergent thinking has also been established. Because of its imaginative, experimental quality, make-believe play is especially facilitating. Whether young children engage in it spontaneously or it is induced by an experimenter, make-believe play is consistently related to enhanced performance on divergent-thinking tasks (Dansky, 1980; Dansky & Silverman, 1975; Pepler & Ross, 1981).

Despite the availability of successful methods for augmenting divergent thinking, not all experts in the field of creativity think that these efforts are worthwhile. Wallach (1985) believes that to justify interventions aimed at improving divergent test scores, they must clearly be shown to predict real-life creative accomplishments. Yet evidence is inconsistent on this issue, and at best, divergent thinking seems to be an imperfect predictor of real-world creativity (Kogan, 1983). Partly because of this finding, the attentions of many investigators interested in giftedness have turned away from the general abilities of intelligence and creativity toward the assessment of specialized talents, for there is very clear evidence that outstanding performances in domain-specific areas, such as mathematics, science, music, art, and athletics, have their roots in specialized skills that are evident in childhood (Wallach, 1985). Retrospective accounts by highly accomplished adult pianists, research mathematicians, and Olympic swimmers of their childhood years point to the importance of long-term, systematic instruction in their field of achievement beginning at an early age, appren-

Specialized talents, like playing the violin, are rooted in native ability, but they also depend on long-term systematic instruction, beginning at an early age. (Nancy Sheehan)

ticeship under eminent and inspiring teachers, and deeply committed parents who assist with their instruction (Bloom, 1982; Bloom & Sosniak, 1981). Sheer natural talent plays an undeniable role in the accomplishments of these outstanding people, but intense, field-specific education over a period of a decade or longer is a crucial part of their development. These findings suggest that the most effective way to foster creativity is to provide children with systematic training aimed at thorough mastery of a particular domain of knowledge, helping the talented student to reach the limits of a particular field as quickly as possible, and then move beyond.

At present, there are no longitudinal studies of creative children—either those who excel at divergent thinking or those who display exceptional domain-specific talents—that trace the long-term trajectory of their accomplishments and the factors that support their special abilities. Psychologists agree that longitudinal information is essential, both for improving ways of identifying creative children and designing educational programs aimed at helping them realize their unique potential (Kogan, 1983; Sternberg & Davidson, 1985; Wallach, 1985). How best to maximize the creative resources of the coming generation—the future poet and scientist as well as the everyday citizen—is a challenging task for future research.

CHAPTER SUMMARY

1. Influenced by the social, intellectual, and educational climate of the times, attempts to measure intelligence began in the latter part of the 1800s, and by the early 1900s, the French psychologist Alfred Binet had developed the first successful intelligence test for children. An individually administered test, the Binet was adapted for use in the United States in 1916, and soon it inspired the construction of a multitude of more efficient group-administered instruments for both children and adults.

2. Factor analysis surfaced as the central means for arriving at clearer definitions of what intelligence tests measure. Spearman and Thurstone's factor analytic studies led to two schools of thought about the nature of intelligence, the first emphasizing one general ability ("g"), the second stressing that intelligence is a collection of distinct, relatively independent mental capacities. Modern factor analysts follow in the tradition of these early theorists. Guilford's structure-of-intellect model defines a total of 150 separate factors, whereas R. B. Cattell's fluid versus crystallized dichotomy represents a much more parsimonious approach to identifying mental capacities.

3. The procedure for computing an IQ score evolved from the early mental age approach to the modern deviation IQ. Current widely used intelligence tests for children are the Stanford-Binet Intelligence Scale, the Wechsler scales, and the Kaufman Assessment Battery for Children, all of which provide a differentiated profile of IQ scores. Piagetian-based tests for children also exist, but they have not caught hold strongly. Infant tests are useful for identifying babies likely to experience delayed or abnormal development, but they have little predictive value for most children.

4. IQs obtained after school entry are fairly stable indicators of children's later intellectual status in comparison to agemates, although a large number of children show substan-

tial changes in the absolute value of their scores during childhood and adolescence. While middle-class children generally show longitudinal gains, low-income and ethnic minority children show progressive declines that result from the compounding effects of depressed rearing conditions.

5. IQ is an effective predictor of scholastic success, educational attainment, occupational status, job performance, income, and social and emotional adjustment. However, the underlying causes of these correlational findings are not established. Home background and personality characteristics appear to be as effective as IQ in explaining them.

6. Low-income and black children score lower on IQ tests than do white middle-class children, a finding that is responsible for kindling the IQ nature-nurture controversy, which reached epic proportions during the 1970s following publication of Arthur Jensen's work. Jensen proposed a Level I–Level II theory that attributes the poorer scores of low-income and black children to genetic deficiencies in complex cognitive processing. However, the theory is not supported by research.

7. Heritability estimates arrived at by comparing identical and fraternal twins support a moderate role for genetic influences in determining IQ. However, cross-fostering investigations offer a wider range of information. They provide clear evidence that IQ is highly malleable, for advantaged rearing conditions raise the absolute value of adopted children's IQ scores substantially. At the same time, heredity is also important, for the IQs of adopted children correlate more strongly with the scores of their biological than adoptive relatives. Research on black children reared in white middle-class homes shows that the black-white IQ gap is socioculturally determined and cannot be explained by racially linked genes. Evidence on racial ancestry and IQ supports this conclusion.

8. Psychologists disagree on how to define test bias and whether it exists. Some believe that if tests have equivalent factor structures and predict scholastic performance to the same degree for different subgroups of children, they are not biased. Others think that tests are biased if some groups of children have less opportunity to learn the knowledge and skills required for successful performance. Research shows that lack of familiarity with item content, different language customs, and motivational factors lead minority children to achieve lower scores than their true abilities permit. Cultural bias in the tests is believed by Mercer, as well as others, to be responsible for the overlabeling of minority children as mentally retarded in the public schools and their disproportionate assignment to special education classes.

9. Children of the same racial/ethnic and social class backgrounds also differ in IQ. Besides heredity, both between- and within-family environmental influences account for this variation. A variety of aspects of home stimulation show substantial relationships with IQ scores during the childhood years. The confluence model is a complex theory of family configurational effects that attempts to clarify the effect of several within-family variables, such as birth order and spacing, on children's intelligence. So far, it has received only limited research support.

10. Longitudinal studies of low-income children who have experienced early intervention repeatedly show that IQ and achievement score gains wash out with time. However, lasting benefits occur in students' school adjustment and ability to meet basic educational requirements. The precise mechanisms responsible for these favorable outcomes are not known, but recent research suggests that they are probably mediated by positive changes in parent-child relationships that result from parent involvement in early intervention programs.

11. One type of ability not represented on intelligence tests is creativity. Intelligence and creativity are weakly related in the general child population. Children who score high in divergent thinking come from homes that value nonconformity and intellectual curiosity. Some evidence suggests that the fact-oriented emphasis of traditional school classrooms may act to dampen divergent thinking, while open classrooms may foster it. Successful techniques for stimulating divergent thinking have been developed. However, since divergent thinking is an imperfect predictor of real-life creativity, some psychologists question the value of efforts to augment it. They regard specialized talent as a better index of creativity and advocate the identification and systematic training of highly talented children beginning at an early age.

IMPORTANT TERMS AND CONCEPTS

factor analysis
general factor ("g")
specific factor ("s")
group factors
primary mental abilities
structure-of-intellect model
crystallized intelligence
fluid intelligence

intelligence quotient (IQ)
mental age (MA)
deviation IQ
developmental quotient (DQ)
cumulative deficit hypothesis
Level I–Level II theory
heritability estimate
cross-fostering study

between-family environmental
   influences
within-family environmental
   influences
confluence model
washout effect
convergent thinking
divergent thinking

Reading, by Theodore E. Butler.
Private Collection, California; photograph courtesy of Daniel B. Grossman Gallery, New York.

CHAPTER 9
Language Development

"**B**ah-bah!" waves 1-year-old Mark, snugly strapped into his infant seat as his mother backs the car out of the driveway at grandmother's house. As she pulls on to the freeway and heads for home, Mark begins to call demandingly, "Bel! Bel!" He tugs at his seat belt, looking alternately at it and his mother seated beside him.

"The seat belt, Mark?" his mother responds. "Let's keep it on." "Look!" she says. "Here's something," handing him a cracker.

"Caa-caa. Caa-caa," says Mark, who begins to eat contentedly.

"Can you shut the front door?" Susan's father shouts from upstairs to his 3-year-old daughter.

"There. Dad, I shutted it," calls Susan up the stairs after closing the door.

Four-year-old Connie reaches for a piece of toast as she looks over the choices of jam and jelly jars at the breakfast table. "Mamma, there's no more honey, is there?" she says.

"That's right, we ran out," her mother acknowledges. "We need to buy some more."

"You go get it because I don't want to," Connie states emphatically.

"All right," Connie's mother agrees. "I can get some later while you're at nursery school."

Language—the most complex and fascinating of human abilities—develops with extraordinary rapidity over the early childhood years. The impressive accomplishments of young language learners are so diverse and sophisticated that they seem nearly miraculous. At age 1, Mark can use single words to name familiar objects and communicate his desires. Three-year-old Susan already shows a subtle understanding of the conventions of human communication. Even though her father's message is phrased as a question, she knows that he really intends it to be a directive and willingly complies by closing the front door. In her report of the accomplished act, she uses grammatical rules to combine words into meaningful statements. In fact, Susan's incorrect construction, "shutted," attests to her active, rule-oriented approach to linguistic production, for she generalizes the "verb + ed" past tense construction to an irregular verb, a common error among children her age. With a larger vocabulary, 4-year-old Connie produces longer utterances and shows that she is in command of a number of sophisticated grammatical forms, including the tag question and use of conjunctions. Following generally accepted conversational rules, Connie takes turns in a short discussion with her mother. Research aimed at determining how young children achieve so much in such a short time has mushroomed over the last two decades. The cumulative literature on language development is vast — larger than the literature on any other aspect of child development (Flavell, 1985).

A common practice of psycholinguists is to divide human language skill into four components: phonology, semantics, grammar, and pragmatics. **Phonology** concerns how we understand and produce the speech sounds of language. If you have ever visited a foreign country where you had little or no facility with the language, you probably wondered how anyone could segment the rapid, unbroken flow of speech sounds emitted by native speakers into organized strings of words. In addition, native listeners probably had trouble understanding you because of your unfamiliar word sounds and intonation patterns. Yet in English, you easily comprehend and produce complicated sound patterns. How you acquired this facility is the story of phonological development.

Semantics refers to word meaning, or the way that underlying concepts are expressed in words and word combinations. Over the preschool years, children acquire a vast number of new words. As we shall see shortly, intensive study of young children's vocabulary growth lends insight into how they go about the Herculean task of mapping thousands of words onto previously unlabeled concepts and eventually make these connections according to the conventions of their language community.

Once mastery of vocabulary is on its way, young children begin to combine words and modify them in meaningful ways. Knowledge of **grammar** includes two main facets: *syntax,* the rules by which words are arranged into comprehensible sentences; and *morphology,* the application of grammatical markers that denote number, tense, case, person, gender, active versus passive voice, as well as other meanings in various languages (the -s and -ed endings serve as examples of these markers in English).

Finally, **pragmatics** refers to the communicative side of language. It deals with how to engage in linguistic discourse with others — how to take turns, maintain topic relevance, and communicate clearly, as well as how to use gestures, tone of voice, and the context in which a verbal message occurs to accurately gauge a speaker's intended meaning. Pragmatics also includes *sociolinguistic knowledge,* for society often dictates how language should be spoken. To be successful communicators, children must eventually acquire certain socially accepted interaction rituals, such as verbal greetings and leave-takings and they must learn to adjust their speech acts to mark important social relationships between speaker and listener, such as differentials in age and status.

In this chapter, we begin with a short history of the field of language development, including the fiery theoretical debate of the 1950s between behaviorist B. F. Skinner and linguist Noam Chomsky that inspired the burst of research since that time. Next we take up several current issues in the study of child language, and we discuss infant preparatory skills that set the stage for the child's first words around the beginning of the second year of life. The central portion of our discussion is organized around the four main areas of language skill. For each area, we describe *what* changes and then

To be successful communicators, children must learn socially accepted interaction rituals, such as verbal greetings and leave-takings. (Linda Hirsch)

treat the more controversial question of *how* young children acquire so much in so little time. As we proceed, you will see that the four areas of language facility are really mutually interdependent; children learn bits and pieces of each at the same time.

A SHORT HISTORY

During the early and middle parts of the twentieth century, research on language acquisition was primarily descriptive — aimed at establishing norms of development. The first studies identified basic milestones that characterized children growing up around the globe: all babbled by the middle of the first year, said their first words between 8 and 18 months of age, combined words at the end of the second and beginning of the third year, and were in command of a great many grammatical constructions by 4 to 5 years of age. The regularity of these achievements regardless of the language children spoke suggested a maturational process much like rolling over, crawling, and beginning to walk. Given a reasonably stimulating linguistic context in which to grow, it appeared that children could not help but acquire language. Yet, at the same time, language also seemed to be learned, for without exposure to a spoken language, children who, for example, were congenitally deaf or seriously neglected did not acquire verbal language (McNeill, 1970). This seeming contradiction set the stage for a nature-nurture debate as virulent as any that has been waged in the field of psychology. By the end of the 1950s, two major figures had taken opposite sides in the controversy.

Nature versus Nurture and the Skinner-Chomsky Debate

In his book *Verbal Behavior,* published in 1957, B. F. Skinner took the radical behaviorist stance that language, like any other behavior, was learned as adults applied the principles of reinforcement to the utterances of infants and young children. Beginning with the child's spontaneous babbling, parental contingencies shaped the child's utterances through successive approximations until they became more like adult speech.

Although adherents to a behaviorist account of language acquisition still exist (e.g., Moerk, 1983; Whitehurst & Valdez-Menchaca, 1988), they are few in number. Think, for a moment, about the process of language development proposed by Skinner. Shaping babbled syllables into words and words into sentences so that, by kindergarten age, children readily produce complex grammatical forms and have a usable vocabulary of over 14,000 words is a physically impossible task, even for the most conscientious of parents. We now know that no parent engages in such intensive language tutoring. For this reason, as well as others, the behaviorist view of language as impressed on a passive child who responds to the reinforcements of intrusive adult tutors is no longer widely accepted.

Linguist Noam Chomsky's book, *Syntactic Structures,* published during the same year as Skinner's volume, along with Chomsky's (1959) critical review of Skinner's theory, first convinced the scientific community that even small children assume much of the responsibility for their own language learning. In addition to the problems noted above, Chomsky mentioned a variety of other difficulties with Skinner's theory, including the fact that many things children say, like Susan's use of the word "shutted" in the conversational vignette at the beginning of this chapter, could not have been directly taught. Such utterances are self-generated, novel productions governed by a working knowledge of grammatical rules.

Chomsky's alternative was a staunchly nativist theory. He pointed out that other animal species have communication systems, but none come close to the complexity and flexibility found in human language. Chomsky viewed our extraordinary language facility as a uniquely human attribute dependent on innate mechanisms. Focusing on children's grammatical achievements, he reasoned that the structure of language is too complex to be directly taught to or independently discovered by the cognitively immature preschool child. Chomsky theorized that children are born with a **language acquisition device (LAD),** an innate grammatical representation that underlies all human languages. It enables children, immediately upon acquiring a sufficient vocabulary, to combine words into novel but grammatically consistent utterances and to understand the meaning of the language they hear. It is the existence of the LAD, according to Chomsky, that permits children to develop language so early and so swiftly.

Linguist Noam Chomsky believes that an innate language acquisition device (LAD) enables children to combine words into grammatically consistent utterances and understand the speech of other people at an early age. (Massachusetts Institute of Technology)

Chomsky proposed a theory of *transformational grammar* to explain how a single LAD can account for children's acquisition of grammatically diverse language systems around the world. The theory is extremely complex — in fact, Chomsky and others are still trying to clarify it — so we will give only its basic flavor here. Chomsky (1957) distinguished between the *surface structure* of a sentence, or what people actually say, and its *deep structure,* or basic underlying meaning. Upon hearing spoken sentences, we translate grammatically diverse surface structures into their common underlying meanings using *transformational rules* contained in the LAD. For example, the following two sentences have grammatically different surface structures: "Jim gave Mary a present," and "The present was given by Jim to Mary." Because we can apply a transformational rule that takes us from the two different surface sentences to the same underlying deep structure, we know immediately that the two sentences mean the same thing. The above example applies to language comprehension, but language production simply works the opposite way. It starts with the deep structure and applies transformational rules to produce grammatically correct surface sentences. According to Chomsky, language development is a matter of gaining facility in applying these rules during early childhood. Children are not taught to use them; instead, their ability to do so matures spontaneously with mere exposure to a language environment.

Chomsky's position, like Skinner's, has been criticized. Although some language development specialists continue to find value in it (e.g., Flavell, 1985; Gleitman & Wanner, 1988), others regard it as an inadequate account of how language acquisition takes place (Whitehurst, 1982; Maratsos, 1983). Critics point out that it is not clear exactly what transformational rules are acquired by children. Currently, at least four competing transformational grammars exist, each devised by different linguists (Fodor, 1977), and Chomsky himself has changed important details of his original theory (Chomsky, 1965). Since transformational rules have not been clearly described, Chomsky's approach has provided little that is definite and specific about how language development proceeds.

Also, investigators have questioned the "psychological existence" of deep grammatical structures. There is good evidence that the first word combinations of very young children are not based on a consistent application of formal grammatical categories, such as the subject of a sentence and the object of the main verb. Instead, as we shall see in greater detail later on, at first children use words belonging to the same grammatical class in variable and unpredictable ways that do not fit with an innate knowledge of grammar (Braine, 1976; Maratsos & Chalkley, 1980).

Finally, children's language acquisition is no longer viewed as being accomplished as quickly as nativist theory assumes. Although extraordinary strides are made during the preschool years, children's progress in mastering many sentence constructions is steady and gradual, showing little evidence of sudden, innately determined insights (Brown, 1973; Knapp, 1979). In fact, complete mastery of some common grammatical forms (such as the passive voice) is not achieved until well into middle childhood (Horgan, 1978), and many grammatical subtleties continue to be learned into the adult years (Menyuk, 1977).

Despite their deficiencies, the theories of Skinner and Chomsky have contributed to our understanding of language development. Although language acquisition cannot be reduced to the mechanisms of reinforcement and modeling, we will encounter many examples in this chapter that show that once children grasp a new linguistic form, its refinement is facilitated by adult feedback and example. Moreover, behaviorist principles continue to be of practical value to speech and language therapists in their efforts to help children with language delays and disabilities overcome their problems (Lovaas, 1967; Whitehurst et al., in press). Chomsky's theory, especially, has left a lasting legacy, for it is now widely accepted that children are active, rule-oriented, hypothesis-testing beings who acquire much of their language at their own initiative. Moreover, Chomsky's work has sparked fruitful new lines of research. For example, his strong belief that a grammatically complex, flexible language system is a uniquely human capacity has served as the impetus for a number of attempts to teach primates systems of linguistic communication. The outcomes of these efforts are summarized in Box 9.1.

The Interactionist Perspective

New theories of language acquisition have been developed that emphasize linkages and interactions between inner predispositions and environmental inputs, replacing the dichotomy that grew out of the Skinner-Chomsky debate. Although several interactionist models exist, all stress the social context of language learning. An active child, well endowed for learning language, observes and engages in social exchanges with others. From this experience the child builds a linguistic system that relates the form and content of language to its social meaning. Both native endowment and a rich communicative environment assist the child in discovering the functions and regularities of language (Bloom & Lahey, 1978; McLean & Snyder-McLean, 1978).

Although all interactionists regard the child as an active, communicative being from birth, there is little agreement about the precise nature of children's innate abilities. Some investigators believe that children make sense of their complex language environments by applying powerful analytic capacities of a general cognitive kind, rather than ones that are uniquely fitted for linguistic analysis. As we chart the course of language growth, we will describe some of these new views, but it is important to note that none are completely verified yet, and Chomsky's basic idea may still prove to be close to the truth (Flavell, 1985). In fact, observations of a group

Box 9.1
Can Apes Learn Language?

Is the ability to acquire a language system that is grammatically complex as well as flexibly productive, in that speakers can recombine forms they already know to create novel utterances, a uniquely human attribute? The linguistic achievements of a number of great apes who have been given long-term, intensive language instruction indicate that this capacity does seem to be unique to the human species.

An early study of a chimpanzee raised in a home and treated much like a human child demonstrated that chimps do not have the physiological capacity to articulate human speech. After six years of patient instruction, the ape in question, Viki, was only able to say four words (''mama,'' ''papa,'' ''cup,'' and ''up''), and pronunciation was extremely difficult (Hayes, 1951). Viki's limited accomplishments left open the question of whether chimps, the animal on earth that is genetically most similar to human beings, could acquire a language system that is not

dependent on vocal speech. To find out, several efforts were made to teach chimps simplified artificial languages, such as the manipulation of plastic tokens of different colors and shapes (Premack, 1976) and the use of a computer console that produces visual symbols (Rumbaugh, 1977). But the most famous attempts to get chimps to use linguistic communication have involved teaching them a natural human language — American Sign Language (ASL), a nonverbal system used by the deaf that is as extensive in its vocabulary and as elaborate in its grammar as any spoken language. The best-known of these efforts include the training of Washoe at the University of Nevada (Gardner & Gardner, 1969; 1980) and Nim Chimsky at Columbia University (Terrace, 1979; Terrace et al., 1980). A gorilla named Koko has also been trained at Stanford University (Patterson, 1980).

Although trainers of Washoe and Koko claimed that the sign combinations of their primate subjects were grammatically consistent and productive (Gardner & Gardner, 1980; Patterson, 1980), subsequent careful

Nim Chimsky tries to follow along as a trainer teaches him his name in American Sign Language. (Susan Kuklin/Photo Researchers)

analyses of their sign strings indicated that ape language abilities were far more limited than originally believed. When Terrace and his colleagues (1980) examined tapes of Washoe's and Koko's signing behavior, they discovered that most of their longer and seemingly grammatical utterances resulted from a great deal of drilling and prompting by their teachers. Many

of congenitally deaf children who received no language input but nevertheless developed their own systematically structured sign language are currently among the strongest evidence that something like Chomsky's innate deep structure may exist. See Box 9.2 for a description of this research.

IMPORTANT ISSUES IN LANGUAGE DEVELOPMENT

In this section, we consider three basic issues about the course of language growth. The first two — whether there is a critical period during which human beings are especially receptive to acquire language, and whether language development proceeds according to a sequence that is universal for all children — are offshoots of the nature-nurture debate. If the human organism is equipped with something like an LAD that leads it to be especially prepared to learn language easily and rapidly, then we would anticipate childhood to be the time of greatest receptivity to language learning. We would also expect development to proceed in a uniform fashion for all children. The third issue we address is how to assess children's language progress: through their language production, that is, what they are able to *say,* or through their comprehension, what they are able to *understand* but might not yet be able to produce in their own speech.

were merely imitations of the trainer's prior sign productions.

To investigate the issue of ape language capabilities more conclusively, Terrace embarked on the training of Nim Chimsky, raising him in a home environment from early infancy and exposing him to trainers who consistently communicated in ASL. Much like Washoe and Koko, Nim built an impressively large vocabulary of over 100 signs during several years of training. Not only did he use signs to name desired objects ("cat," "banana," "book") and familiar actions ("give," "eat," "tickle"), but he also used them appropriately to refer to emotional states, such as "angry" and "sorry." In addition, Nim's two-sign combinations, which first appeared around 16 months, were quite similar to the early two-word utterances of 1- and 2-year-old human children (e.g., "groom me," "hug Nim," "Nim book").

However, for sign strings longer than two combinations, Nim's productions bore little resemblance to human grammar. Instead of adding new information when combining 3, 4, 5, or more signs, Nim repeated information he had signed in shorter strings. For example, typical 3- and 4-word utterances were: "Eat Nim eat," and "Play me Nim play." One of Nim's longest utterances, a 16-sign combination, went like this: "Give orange me give eat orange me eat orange give me eat orange give me you" (Terrace et al., 1980). Analyses of videotapes also revealed that Nim was a poor conversationalist. He had difficulty taking turns and often interrupted his trainer. In contrast, young children rarely interrupt others during the early phases of language learning, and by the preschool years they have a good sense of their conversational responsibilities.

Apes do possess some language ability, including a symbolic capacity much like that of the very early language-learning child. However, getting them to use even basic language skills is an arduous process requiring extensive training and reinforcement. To date, there is no convincing evidence that they can master complex grammatical as well as conversational rules. Nevertheless, it would be premature to conclude that apes' lack of a humanlike grammatical system proves the nativist argument that a specialized LAD exists in human beings. We do not know exactly what accounts for the linguistic differences between apes and humans — a specialized language capacity, certain cognitive abilities, or social and motivational factors (Slobin, 1979).

Finally, it is important to note that not all species of apes have been studied as extensively as the common chimp, the subject of the research described above. Recent work by Savage-Rumbaugh (1987) with pygmy chimps, who are far more adept at observational learning than common chimps, reveals more rapid vocabulary development and better language comprehension than ever before attained by subhuman primates. Savage-Rumbaugh used a new instructional approach, teaching these chimps to comprehend a wide range of linguistic expressions before they were required to produce them. Her research suggests that combining the right method of teaching with an especially bright animal produces improved language competencies.

Is There a Critical Period for Language Development?

Lenneberg (1967) first proposed that language acquisition must occur during a critical period of development that parallels the age span during which lateralization (or localization) of language functions takes place in the left hemisphere of the brain. Lenneberg believed that brain lateralization was complete around the age of puberty; exposure to a linguistic environment, he thought, had to occur before this time or language acquisition would not be possible. You may recall from Chapter 5 that localization of language in the left hemisphere begins far earlier than Lenneberg speculated — during the first few years of life. This new evidence does not refute the existence of a critical period for language learning, although if the period is tied to lateralization, it may end earlier and be much shorter than Lenneberg believed. In fact, that normal children around the world acquire language rapidly during the preschool years fits with Lenneberg's hypothesis that the period of cortical lateralization sets developmental boundaries for language acquisition. It is also possible that a critical period (if it exists) may not be defined by lateralization, but may, instead, be related to some other biological factor (Reich, 1986). In any case, to verify the critical period notion, we need to show that when language learning is delayed beyond a certain time, it is far more difficult for children to acquire it, or it cannot be acquired at all. Two kinds of research shed light on this issue. The first are studies of severely abused and neglected children who were not exposed to language in early childhood. The second are investigations of second language learning aimed at finding out whether an additional language can be acquired more easily during childhood than later on.

History contains some accounts of *feral children,* children thought to have been abandoned in the wild at an early age, but who nevertheless survived and were eventually returned to human society. Among the 60 recorded cases, a great many never learned any language, but 11 of them, ranging in age between 4 and 18 at the time of discovery, acquired some, although their linguistic competence remained very immature (Reich, 1986). Since precise information about the early experiences of these children is not available, the records of feral children merely provide evidence that is consistent with the existence of an early critical period for learning language.

More definitive information comes from cases of severely abused children who experienced minimal human contact during their early childhood years. The most

FOCUS ON CONTEMPORARY ISSUES

Box 9.2
Language Development in Deaf Children Without a Language Model

Some exposure to language is necessary for children to acquire the language of their social community. But what happens when children are not exposed to a conventional language system in early childhood at all? If such children devise a communication system much like that of youngsters reared in normal spoken language environments, this would serve as powerful evidence for the nativist argument that human beings are prepared for language learning in a specialized way.

Susan Goldin-Meadow and her collaborators (Goldin-Meadow, 1979; Goldin-Meadow & Mylander, 1983; Goldin-Meadow & Morford, 1985) studied the early gestural language development of ten congenitally deaf children between 1 and 4 years of age. Their parents had decided against exposing them to a conventional sign language, and, instead, sent them to a school that emphasized an oral approach. Despite intensive efforts to train them in sound production, the children had made little progress in acquiring English. Thus, at the time of Goldin-Meadow's observations, none of the children had made use of conventional oral input, and none had been exposed to a sign system at home or at school.

Carefully analyzing videotapes of the deaf children's manual communications with their mothers in informal play sessions, Goldin-Meadow compared their gestures to the earliest stages of language acquisition in hearing children. She found that deaf children spontaneously produced two basic types of wordlike gestures: (1) *pointing gestures,* which, like the words "this" and "there," served to single out objects, people, and places in the environment; and (2) *characterizing gestures,* which were signs related to particular objects, actions, or attributes by physical similarity. For example, a twisting motion was used to represent the act of opening a container, and two fists moving up and down in the air represented the beating of a drum.

When the developmental course of sign production was examined, it was remarkably similar to the early stages of language development in hearing children. At first, single gestures were used in ways quite similar to the hearing child's use of single spoken words—largely to refer to familiar objects and actions. At about the same time as hearing children produce two-word utterances, Goldin-Meadow's young deaf subjects used two-gesture sign combinations. Furthermore, all the deaf subjects elaborated their self-generated signing systems into complex gesture sentences between 2 and 3 years of age, only slightly later than hearing children produce verbal utterances that

are three words or longer. When the deaf children's complex signing was compared to the speech of same-age hearing children, they were found to produce fewer and somewhat shorter utterances. But despite these differences in quantity, their manual utterances emerged in the same sequence and bore a structural resemblance to the verbal productions of children exposed to a normal language environment.

The fact that the deaf children developed a structured communication system in the absence of any obvious tutoring or modeling is among the most convincing pieces of evidence to date for the nativist argument that human beings enter the world with a strong, built-in bias to communicate in language-like ways. Still, it is important to note that there are critics of Goldin-Meadow's conclusions (e.g., Bohannon & Warren-Leubecker, 1986; Whitehurst, 1982). The signing competencies of the deaf subjects may have been the product of some important but as yet unidentified aspects of interactive exchanges with their parents, for it is known that children deprived of such communicative experiences do not acquire normal language. For example, in a different investigation—this time of a hearing child born to deaf parents who was exposed to spoken language only through television—the child failed to acquire normal speech (Bonvillian, Nelson, & Charrow, 1976).

recent and thoroughly studied of such children is Genie, a child isolated at 20 months of age[1] in the back room of her parents' house and harnessed to a potty chair. She was not discovered until 13½ years of age (Curtiss, 1977). Genie's early environment was linguistically (as well as emotionally) impoverished. No one was permitted to talk to her, and she was severely beaten when she made any noise herself. When found, she did not vocalize at all; even her crying was silent. Over several years of training with warm, dedicated caregivers who taught her language and social skills, Genie's language developed, but not nearly at the rate or to the same extent as normal children. Although she eventually developed a large vocabulary and good comprehension of everyday conversation, her grammatical abilities were much narrower, and she never acquired some syntactic forms, such as the use of pronouns. Genie's speech also showed poor pitch control, and she was not able to use intonation to express some meanings. Although she was eager to join in conversations, she was slow to respond. Asked something, Genie might not answer right away, but would return 5 or 10 minutes later to deliver the requested information (Curtiss, 1977).

Genie's case is consistent with the operation of a "weak" critical period, or the sensitive phase notion we introduced in Chapter 4. Genie *was* able to acquire a first language, but she did not do so as easily, naturally, and competently as preschool children do. Neurolinguistic assessments revealed that Genie used the right hemisphere of her brain to process linguistic information. Curtiss (1977) believes that by the time she was found, the developmental period had passed during which specialized language areas in the left hemisphere could easily accomplish the task of language learning. Nonlanguage areas, particularly in the right hemisphere, were forced to take over functioning, but they could do so only to a limited extent. Consistent with this idea, Genie's accomplishments resembled the attainments of other right-hemispheric language cases and, to some degree, nonhuman primates, who when given language training also have difficulty with grammar. Thus Genie's development fits with the conjecture that language learning is optimal when it occurs during the period of brain lateralization, although we cannot tell how early and limited that period might be.

What about acquiring a second language? Is this task harder during adolescence and adulthood, after a critical or sensitive phase for language learning has passed? Surprisingly, research suggests otherwise. In one of the most comprehensive studies of second language learning, Snow and Hoefnagel-Höhle (1978) spent one year tracking the acquisition of Dutch by English-speakers ranging in age from 3 years to adulthood. All were picking up the language at school or work, with little or no formal instruction. Except for pronunciation (where attainment at year's end was similar for all ages), virtually all acquisition differences favored the older subjects, with 12- to 15-year-olds learning the fastest and preschoolers the slowest. It seems that increasing age actually predicts faster acquisition of a second language, at least up to a point well beyond the time frame during which the brain has been regarded as especially receptive to language learning. These results are contrary to the expectations of a critical period hypothesis. Snow and Hoefnagel-Höhle believe that motivational and social factors, rather than biological readiness, influence second language learning. People of a wide range of ages acquire a foreign language quickly if it is needed to get along in daily life. Older children, who have developed better learning strategies, progress more quickly than younger ones.

In summary, evidence on children deprived of early exposure to language supports the existence of a period of special biological receptivity for first language acquisition. Once a first language has been learned, second language learning does not proceed in a way that is consistent with the critical period hypothesis.

---

[1] Pediatric records of Genie's early infancy suggest that she was an alert, responsive baby. Her early motor development was normal, and her mother reported that she said her first words just before her confinement, after which all language disappeared. Thus, mental retardation is regarded as an unlikely alternative explanation for the course of her later development.

Universals versus Individual Differences in Language Development

Due to Chomsky's influence, the majority of work on language acquisition between the 1950s and early 1970s involved a search for *universals,* or similarities in the way children master their first language. A variety of commonalities were identified that we will discuss in greater detail later on. They were assumed to reflect the maturational unfolding of a genetically determined linguistic competence, and variations among children were not seen as particularly interesting or important (Goldfield & Snow, 1985; Wells, 1986).

As Chomsky's theory began to be questioned, research on language universals waned. Investigators realized that universals could as easily be attributed to experiences common to all children as they could to an innate LAD. The genetic versus environmental causes of universal language milestones were difficult, if not impossible, to sort out (Hardy-Brown, 1983), yet researchers wanted to move beyond mere description of language development toward an understanding of factors responsible for its acquisition.

Individual differences in *rate* of language development had long been recognized (McCarthy, 1954), but by the 1970s, studies reported differences not only in rate, but also in *route* or form of language development. Children seemed to learn language in variable rather than perfectly uniform ways. Researchers began to recognize that studying differences as well as similarities was crucially important if the origins of language were to be fully understood.

Nelson (1973) was one of the first to identify important individual differences in route of language development, and her findings have been documented and extended in subsequent research (Bloom, Lightbown, & Hood, 1975; Bretherton et al., 1982). Following a sample of 1- to 2½-year-olds as they acquired their first 50 words, Nelson noticed that the children differed in the words and phrases they produced. The majority fit a **referential style** of language learning. Their early vocabularies consisted of a large number of nouns (familiar object names, such as "ball" and "car"), and fewer verbs, proper names, and adjectives. A smaller number of children had an **expressive style.** Compared to referential children, they used a large number of pronouns and social formulas, such as "stop it," "I want it," "what d'you want," and relatively fewer nouns, verbs, and adjectives. Children uttered these social phrases without pause in the form of compressed wholes, much like single words. Nelson suggested that the two types of children had developed different early notions about the uses of language. Referential children had the idea that language largely served the purpose of talking about things, while expressive children seemed to think it was for talking about the self and other people, as well as for expressing feelings, needs, and social forms. Thus, children's first notions of what language was all about were reflected in the unique makeup of their early vocabularies.[2]

Children's early styles soon became linked to other aspects of language development. Expressive children used more pronouns in their early sentences, whereas referential children showed clearer articulation, and their vocabularies grew faster. The referential advantage in vocabulary size is not surprising. Languages provide the child who talks mostly about things with many object labels, but far fewer social phrases are available for the expressively oriented child. Vocabulary differences diminished as children broadened their first primitive notions about the functions of language (Nelson, 1973; 1975), but some referential versus expressive variations persisted well into the preschool years. For example, Horgan (1980; 1981) reported that referential children later tended to elaborate noun phrases with descriptive

---

[2] Nelson notes that there are some children who employ both styles from the very beginning, suggesting that the referential-expressive distinction is a continuum rather than two completely separate language learning strategies. Also, nouns were the most frequent words in the vocabularies of all of the children, although some children used more nouns than others.

information (e.g., "*The great big mean dog* ran home"). Expressive children elaborated verb phrases (e.g., "He *might have been going* home"). Thus, early stylistic variations evolved into new individual differences as children matured.

Psycholinguists are currently devoting more attention to individual differences in language development, because the genetic and environmental factors underlying them may be easier to specify than is the case for language universals. Recent research suggests that a rapidly developing, referential-style child may be one with an especially active interest in exploring objects, whose home life provides a rich variety of play materials that stimulate object labeling, and whose parents eagerly respond with words for things to their child's first attempts to talk. In contrast, an expressive-style child may have a more socially oriented personality and may experience a linguistic environment in which speech is frequently used to mediate social relationships (Nelson, 1973; Lieven, 1978; Wells, 1986). These findings suggest that, like other aspects of development, important factors affecting language acquisition are bidirectional and reciprocal, involving an interdependency between children's inherent attributes and their physical and social environments.

The Comprehension versus Production Distinction

A final important issue is the distinction between **comprehension** (the language children understand) and **production** (the language they use). Most research on early language development is based on what children say rather than what they comprehend. But inferences about development based only on production may give a distorted picture, for young children understand many words long before they produce them (Goldin-Meadow, Seligman, & Gelman, 1976).

The distinction we made in Chapter 7 between recognition and recall will help you understand why language comprehension proceeds ahead of production. Comprehension merely requires recognition of a word, along with a memory search for the concept it designates, whereas production demands active retrieval of words, plus an evaluation of whether they appropriately express one's intended meaning (Clark, 1983; Kuczaj, 1986). Because production is cognitively more difficult, failure to produce a word is not good evidence that children do not understand it. In fact, children just beginning to learn language can follow many simple instructions, such as "Bring me the book" or "Put the toy on the shelf," long before they are able to produce the words themselves. Children with more reserved, cautious personalities may show especially large comprehension-production discrepancies during the early phases of language growth. In comparison to their more outgoing agemates, these youngsters begin to talk later and often show sudden spurts in language production (Nelson, 1973). Thus, relying only on production to make judgments about language functioning leads to underestimates of linguistic knowledge that are greater for some children than for others. In assessing children's language competence, it is important to look at not just one, but both of these processes.

Now that we have covered these basic, prefacing issues, let's chart the course of language development itself.

PRELINGUISTIC PREPARATION

The prelinguistic infant enters the world with a variety of neonatal behaviors that serve as powerful cues for parents to communicate with their tiny newcomer. From the very beginning, babies are prepared to develop language. In the sections below, we discuss some important inborn capabilities and infant developmental attainments that pave the way for the dawn of linguistic communication.

Receptivity to Speech Sounds

Human infants, as indicated in Chapter 4, are pretuned to respond to human speech sounds. Recall that the infant is especially sensitive to the pitch range of the human voice, that human speech is more rewarding to infants than other sounds, and that infants have an astonishing ability to detect differences between language sounds that exceeds the capacity of adults. Because this last-mentioned skill may help children crack the phonological code of their language, let's consider it in greater detail.

As adults, we hear speech sounds in terms of sound categories, or **phonemes.** That is, when we listen to speech, we attend to certain features that permit us to divide it into small but distinct units, such as the difference between the initial consonants in "pa" and "ba." Phonemes are not the same across all languages. For example, "ra" and "la" are distinct sounds to English speakers, but Japanese individuals are unable to distinguish between them (Miyawaki et al., 1975). Conversely, English speakers do not make some distinctions that are important in other languages (Sachs, 1985).

When individuals are asked to discriminate artificially generated sounds that belong to the same phonemic category in their native language, but are actually slightly different acoustically, they have considerable difficulty doing so. This tendency to perceive as identical a range of sounds that belong to the same phonemic class is called **categorical speech perception.** Research shows that categorical speech perception is not only characteristic of adults, but also of 1-month-old infants. Furthermore, as indicated earlier, young infants around the world can discriminate phoneme categories that adults confuse because the particular contrast involved is not used in the language the adults speak (Aslin, Pisoni, & Jusczyk, 1983).

Do these findings indicate that infants are born with a speech decoder, an innate device for verbal language perception that permits them to analyze the sound stream of any language to which they are exposed? A decade or two ago, psychologists thought this was the case, but new research has led this view to be questioned. Recent evidence reveals that babies have a built-in tendency to look for well-defined boundaries in *both* speech and nonspeech sounds, but the nature of the speech stream is such that it is more easily separable into perceptual categories than other sound stimuli (Aslin, Pisoni, & Jusczyk, 1983).

Eventually, infants focus more intently on the sounds of their own language. By 8 to 10 months of age, English-learning babies start to lose the ability to discriminate sounds not used in English (Werker & Tees, 1984). Jusczyk (1985) believes this shift is not just the result of infants' increased exposure to a particular language environment. That it occurs around the time that infants start to talk suggests that it may be related to their increased desire to communicate. As children attend selectively to speech sounds that lead to changes of meaning in their own language, certain phonemic discriminations atrophy because they are not used. Like adult speakers, toddlers trying to understand verbal communication quickly learn to ignore or deemphasize sounds that are not relevant to the phonological constraints of their native tongue (Aslin, Pisoni, & Jusczyk, 1983).

Babbling

Sometime between 3 and 6 months of age, infants start to babble, and they continue to do so even after they produce their first words, between 1 and 1½ years of age. The onset and early course of babbling seems to be controlled maturationally, for babies from all linguistic environments begin babbling at around the same age and produce a similar repertoire of early sounds. Even deaf babies and infants of deaf parents who cannot respond to their babies' sounds make some typical babbling sounds (Lenneberg, Rebelsky, & Nichols, 1965; Stoel-Gammon & Otomo, 1986). However, the continuation of babbling is dependent on the ability to hear speech sounds of the self and others. Babbling containing the sounds of mature spoken languages appears in hearing babies around 7 months of age; in hearing-impaired infants, it rarely occurs before the second year of life, and observations of one totally deaf child revealed a complete absence of speechlike babbles (Oller & Eilers, 1988). Nevertheless, among hearing infants a maturational component continues to be evident in the *form* of babbling throughout the first year, for adults cannot change the babbling sounds infants make through reinforcement and modeling, although they can, to some extent, influence the overall *amount* of babbling (Dodd, 1972; Todd & Palmer, 1968). In addition, the phonetic development of babbling follows a universal pattern. Infants initially produce a limited number of vowel and consonant sounds that expands to include a much broader range by 12 months of age, and the addition of a wide variety of stress and intonation patterns makes the 1-year-old's babbling stream seem much like conversational speech without intelligible words. This gradual expansion of babbled sounds is believed to result from maturation of the vocal structures and of the brain areas responsible for articulation (de Villiers & de Villiers, 1978; Sachs, 1985).

At one time, it was thought that the child's first words emerged directly out of babbling—that infants babbled all possible sounds and adults simply reinforced those most similar to their own language (Winitz, 1969). Think about what we have said about the development of babbling so far, and you will see that this explanation cannot possibly be correct. Not only is adult feedback ineffective in changing babbling sounds, but babbling *expands* with development; it does not contract to become more like the language the child will learn, and only its intonation patterns, not its sounds, resemble those of the child's language community (Boysson-Bardies, deSagart, & Durand, 1984; Thevenin et al., 1985).

That infants do not stop babbling when they first begin to talk suggests that babbling plays some role in the development of speech production, although investigators are not entirely certain what it is. In a recent study, Elbers and Ton (1985) recorded the speech of a young toddler and discovered a continuous interplay between the child's babbling and early words. New words influenced the sound characteristics of babbling, and babbling, in turn, seemed to pave the way for the production of additional new words. As we shall see later on, one factor, among others, that contributes to early word choice is the presence of sound patterns in the child's speech repertoire that can be adapted to fit a new word. Babbling may enable speech sounds to develop in a preparatory way that then facilitates their integration into the child's first words.

The Emergence of Communicative Competence

Research suggests biological preparedness for some aspects of conversational behavior. For example, newborn infants quickly integrate their attentional behavior into preverbal communicative patterns. They can initiate interactions by making eye contact and terminate them by averting their gaze. By 4 months of age (when their tracking is sufficiently mature), infants follow their mother's line of regard. Thus, the attention of mother and infant becomes jointly directed at an early age, and mothers often verbally comment on what their infants are observing (Bruner, 1974). Researchers used to believe that innate readiness for communication also resided in the neonate's capacity to move in synchrony to the sound patterns of human speech (Condon & Sander, 1974). However, recent studies have failed to replicate this phenomenon (Dowd & Tronick, 1986; Pack, 1983).

By about three months of age, the beginnings of conversational turn-taking can be observed. **Pseudodialogues,** which mimic the form but do not yet serve the function of verbal exchange, appear between caregivers and infants. The baby vocalizes, the adult vocalizes in return, then waits for a response, and vocalizes again (Bateson, 1975). In western cultures, these vocal exchanges are a frequent occurrence between mother-infant pairs (Lewis & Freedle, 1972). To participate, infants must be capable of remaining quietly alert for longer periods of time and must have begun to coo and babble. But beyond this basic infant readiness, indications are that the mother is initially responsible for sustaining the interaction sequence. She does this by responding to the temporal flow of her baby's behavior — replying, fitting into, and supporting the infant's signals. In this way, the baby's responses become integrated into a dialogue-like sequence before infants have any real awareness that conversational expectations exist (Schaffer, 1979).

Bruner (1977) believes that early social games help infants grasp the conversational routine and pair its turn-taking form with its information exchange function. Between 6 and 12 months of age, conventional infant games, such as peekaboo and pat-a-cake, increase in frequency and variety. The games contain complementary roles that are almost always reversible. At first, the parent elaborates the game, and the amused infant is a passive spectator. Gradually, the baby learns to anticipate game events, and around age 1, infant and parent alternate the roles of agent and experiencer (Ratner & Bruner, 1978). Simple, predictable game structures are an ideal setting for infants to connect parents' spoken utterances to the ongoing action of the games. In fact, between 13 and 16 months of age, children begin to linguistically mark their own participation (Camaioni & Laicardi, 1985).

At the end of the first year, the baby starts to intentionally use nonverbal signals to direct and control the behavior of other people. Bates and her colleagues found that infants use two preverbal forms of basic speech acts. The first is the **protodeclarative,** in which the baby makes an assertion about an object by touching it, holding it up, or pointing to it while looking at others to make sure they see it. The second is the **protoimperative,** in which the infant gets another person to do something by pointing, reaching, and often calling and making sounds at the same time. These preverbal speech acts coincide with Piaget's sensorimotor substage 5, in which the child learns that it is possible to bring about changes through various means, one of these being to use another person to achieve a goal rather than to carry it out directly oneself (Bates, 1979; Bates, Camaioni, & Volterra, 1975). However, preverbal intentional communication is also encouraged by the caregiver's responses to infant signals, which help babies make the connection that their cries, smiles, vocalizations, and gestures produce predictable results. In time, babies send out these signals deliberately because

According to Bruner, early social games like pat-a-cake help infants grasp the turn-taking form of conversation along with its information exchange function. (Erika Stone)

they have learned, as the result of maternal responsiveness, to anticipate their future effects on others (Bruner, 1977).

Early in the second year of life, turn-taking and children's preverbal intentional communication are brought together, especially in situations where children's messages initially fail to communicate clearly. When 8- to 12-month-olds use adults to achieve their goals and fail in their first attempt, they do not engage in communicative repairs and frequently revert to less mature behaviors, such as whining and crying. Older infants negotiate their failed messages. Sometimes such exchanges last for a number of turns before infants achieve their goal, as in the following example of a 14-month-old's repeated attempts to get his mother to give him a sponge on the kitchen counter:

Jordan: (Vocalizes repeatedly until his mother turns around.)

Mother: (Turns around to look at him.)

Jordan: (Points to one of the objects on the counter.)

Mother: Do you want this? (Holds up milk container.)

Jordan: (Shakes head "no.") (Vocalizes, continues to point.)

Mother: Do you want this? (Holds up jelly jar.)

Jordan: (Shakes head "no.") (Continues to point.) (2 more offer-rejection pairs.)

Mother: This? (Picks up sponge.)

Jordan: (Leans back in high chair, puts arms down, tension leaves body.)

Mother: (Hands Jordan sponge.) (Golinkoff, 1983, pp. 58–59)

Soon words are uttered along with the same reaching and pointing gestures that made up the infants' preverbal communicative acts. Then the gestures start to diminish, eventually becoming a redundant adjunct to vocal language (Goldin-Meadow & Morford, 1985).

In summary, during the first two years of life, young children develop a rich interactional framework in which to embed linguistic messages. This foundation rests on a combination of biological predispositions, cognitive-developmental achievements, and a responsive social environment. Throughout our discussion, we have stressed that the changes that occur are heavily dependent on caregivers involving infants in dialogue-like contexts. However, caution should be exercised in judging how essential these interactive experiences are. Recent cross-cultural evidence reveals that there are societies, such as the people of Western Samoa and the Kaluli of Papua, New Guinea, who rarely treat their infants as communicative partners and never play social games with them, yet their children become speakers of their native language within the normal time frame of development (Ochs, 1982; Schieffelin & Ochs, 1983). Perhaps deliberate parental molding of the infant's expressive behaviors into reciprocal exchanges is not essential, but when it occurs, it facilitates communicative development. Additional cross-cultural comparisons are needed to determine how crucial maternal-infant reciprocal interaction really is for the development of communicative competence (Shatz, 1983).

The Beginnings of Conceptual Understanding

In Chapter 6 as well as in the discussion above, we indicated that certain cognitive acquisitions provide a foundation for language development. A flexible ability to coordinate sensorimotor means with ends is related to infants' realization that language is a tool for influencing others, and development of the symbolic function in Piaget's sensorimotor substage 6 underlies the 2-year-old's ability to use words and sentences to refer to objects and events that are not immediately present. Children must also acquire a foundation of prelinguistic conceptual understandings onto which they can map their first words, for as we shall soon see, children's early vocabulary reflects the cognitive knowledge they have amassed about objects and situations during infancy. Thus language builds on prior cognitive advances, but as we showed in Chapter 6, the relationship between language and thought quickly becomes reciprocal. Children require a cognitive base for learning the labels of their language, but learning new words and verbal expressions also facilitates cognitive development by making meanings salient and explicit, freeing thought from its ties to the here and now, and increasing the efficiency and flexibility of human thinking.

Now that we have seen how children are prepared to become competent, linguistic beings during the first two years of life, let's turn to a consideration of the various facets of language development—phonological, semantic, grammatical, and pragmatic—during the much lengthier, linguistic period of childhood.

PHONOLOGICAL DEVELOPMENT

Think about the sounds you might hear if you listened in on a 1- or 2-year-old child trying out her first handful of words. You probably conjured up an assortment of rather interesting pronunciations, such as "nana" for banana, "oap" for soap, "weddy" for ready, as well as some puzzling productions that the child uses like words, but that have no resemblance to adult forms. For "translations" of these latter items, you have to ask the child's parent. Acquiring accurate pronunciation skills is a complicated process that depends on children's increasing control over the articulatory apparatus, improved ability to attend to complex phonological sequences, and growing capacity to monitor and revise their own faulty productions so that they match adult speech. Between 1 and 4 years of age, children make considerable progress at this task (Ingram, 1986).

Experts in phonology currently view children mastering the pronunciation of their language as young problem solvers. In trying to figure out how to talk like people around them, they adopt a variety of temporary strategies for producing sounds in order to bring adult words within their current range of physical and cognitive capabilities (Ingram, 1986; Menn, 1985; Menyuk, Menn, & Silber, 1986). Let's look at the characteristics of this progression.

The Early Phase: First Words, Sound Play, and Jargon Stretches

During the transition from babbling to speech, children engage in trial-and-error efforts to pronounce their first words, some of which are produced fairly accurately, while others are only loosely approximated. Children's first productions are limited by the small number of sounds they can voluntarily control. In the first few months of phonological development, they apply a single phonetic form to a variety of words, a feature of their speech that often makes them difficult to understand. In one case described by Ingram (1986), "bat" was substituted by a child for as many as 12 different words, including "bad," "bark," "bent," and "bite."

During this period, first words often become the subject of **sound play** episodes as children practice and expand their new-found phonological capacities (Garvey, 1977). Your author's older son, upon acquiring the word "book" at 14 months, was fond of producing vocal variations on it, which sounded something like this: "book-a-book-a-dook-a-dook-a-book-a-nook-a-book-aaaa." Also, children of this period frequently produce **jargon stretches,** which are babbled sequences with real words embedded in them that are uttered with eye contact and communicative intent (Menyuk, Menn, & Silber, 1986). Young language learners seem to recognize that words are embedded by adults in extended sound streams, and they emulate this form with the limited vocabulary and phonological resources that they have.

Early semantic and phonological development are interdependent, for the first words children choose to say are partly influenced by what they can successfully pronounce. For example, Menn's (1976) subject Jacob understood many words beginning with "b," "k," and "d" at the time he began to speak, but he only attempted to say those beginning with "d." Some children are quite conservative in this respect and only try to say words within their current phonological repertoire. Others are more daring and will try to say just about anything, but most fall somewhere in between these two extremes and are simply more likely to produce words with familiar sounds (Schwartz & Leonard, 1982).

The Appearance of Phonological Strategies

Soon children apply systematic strategies to simplify words so they fit with their phonological capabilities. The strategies mark an intermediate phase of development in which children's pronunciation of many words is partly right and partly wrong, but their errors are fairly consistent. Although children vary greatly in the rules they adopt, a few typical ones are shown in Table 9.1. Phonological strategies often lead children to pronounce different words identically — for example, both "wing" and "ring" as "wing." But such errors do not result from an inability to perceive sound differences between the words. Children can point to a correct picture when presented with each of the adult pronunciations, even though they cannot yet say both words correctly (Barton, 1980). Here again, comprehension is clearly ahead of production.

Children's pronunciation undergoes marked improvement over the preschool years. Maturation of the vocal apparatus and the child's own active problem-solving efforts are largely responsible for this change, for children's phonological errors are quite resistant to adult correction. However, parents and others provide effective models from which children do learn. When speaking to young children, adults and older children tend to limit their communications to simple sentences with exagger-

Table 9.1. Common Phonological Strategies Used by Young Children to Simplify the Task of Pronouncing Adult Words

STRATEGY	EXAMPLES
Repeating the initial consonant-vowel in a multisyllable word	"TV" becomes "didi," "cookie" becomes "gege"
Deletion of unstressed syllables in a multisyllable word	"banana" becomes "nana," "granola" becomes "nola," "giraffe" becomes "raffe"
Replacing fricatives (hissing sounds) with stop consonant sounds	"sea" becomes "tea," "say" becomes "tay," "sing" becomes "ting"
Replacing consonant sounds produced in the rear and palate area of the vocal tract with ones produced in the frontal area	"shoe" becomes "zue," "shop" becomes "zop," "goose" becomes "doose"
Replacing liquid sounds ("l" or "r") with glides ("j" or "w")	"lap" becomes "jap," "ready" becomes "weddy"
Reducing consonant-vowel-consonant words to a consonant-vowel form by deleting the final consonant	"bib" becomes "bi," "bike" becomes "bai," "more" becomes "muh"
Replacing an ending consonant syllable with a vowel	"apple" becomes "appo," "bottom" becomes "bada"
Reducing a consonant cluster to a single consonant	"clown" becomes "cown", "play" becomes "pay," "train" becomes "tain"

Source: Ingram, 1986.

ated intonation and very clear pronunciation, a form of speech called **motherese** (Newport, Gleitman, & Gleitman, 1977). Parents do not seem to use motherese in a deliberate attempt to teach language, as many of the same speech characteristics are used by native speakers when communicating with foreigners. Motherese probably arises unconsciously out of parental efforts to keep children's attention and assure that they understand (Brown, 1977). Motherese may not be essential for language development, but it is probably facilitating. Its high articulatory precision offers a linguistic context that undoubtedly eases the young child's task of making phonological sense out of a complex speech stream.

Later Phonological Development

Although phonological development is largely complete by the time the child goes to school, a few acquisitions involving accent patterns are not mastered until later childhood and adolescence. Using appropriate stress patterns to signal differences in meaning between such words as "greenhouse" and "green house" develops gradually from first to sixth grade (Atkinson-King, 1973). Changes in syllabic stress after words take on endings, such as -ity ("humid," "humidity") and -al ("method," "methodical") are not mastered until adolescence. These late developments may have something to do with the semantic complexity of the words to which they apply. Even among young children, phonology is more systematic when applied to semantically less complex words (Camarata & Leonard, 1986). As indicated in Chapter 7, the human information processing capacity is limited, and working on both the form and meaning of a new word at the same time may overload the system, leading form to be sacrificed temporarily until the word's meaning is better understood.

In summary, phonological development begins with young children's trial-and-error efforts to pronounce their first words, followed by an intermediate period in which systematic strategies are used to pronounce difficult words. Although the sound features of motherese facilitate early phonological development, the child is an active problem-solver in mastering the phonology of language. Phonological development is mostly complete by school entry, except for a few complex accent patterns.

SEMANTIC DEVELOPMENT

The Early Phase

Maternal reports indicate that on the average, children utter their first word between 11 and 12 months, with a range of about 8 to 18 months for normal children (Whitehurst, 1982). By age 6, children have a vocabulary of around 14,000 words (Templin, 1957). To accomplish this monumental task, children add about 9 words to their vocabulary each day (Clark, 1983).

Learning words is largely a matter of identifying which concept within one's current cognitive repertoire each label picks out in a particular language community. In view of the sensorimotor foundations that precede language learning, it is not surprising that children's first words generally refer to manipulable, movable objects and to events that have salient properties of change. As Nelson (1973) points out, in their first 50 vocabulary words, children rarely include names for things that just *sit there* (e.g., table, stove, vase). Instead, important people ("dada," "mama"), animals ("cat," "bird"), vehicles ("car," "truck"), toys ("ball," "book"), food ("cookie") body parts ("eye"), articles of clothing the child acts on ("socks"), household implements ("spoon"), greetings ("hi," "bye-bye"), familiar actions ("up," "no," "more"), game routines ("peekaboo"), and modifiers that are the outcome of some action ("dirty," "broken") are typical early words (Clark, 1983).

Children's first words often refer to perceptually salient, animated objects, like this family pet. (Suzanne Szasz/Photo Researchers)

Research demonstrates the remarkable ease with which children connect a new word with an underlying concept after just one brief encounter with it, a process called **fast mapping.** It helps account for how young children build up a large vocabulary with extraordinary speed (Carey, 1978). Dollaghan (1985) presented 2- to 5-year-olds with a novel nonsense word, "koob," and its referent, an oddly shaped plastic ring, in a game in which the object was labeled only once. Even 2-year-olds were able to infer the connection between the novel word and its referent after a single encounter.

Representations for words heard only once do not fade quickly. When children are tested several days after hearing a new label, they are as likely to use it and recognize its referent as children who heard the label very recently (Dickinson, 1984). Thus, fast mapping provides powerful cognitive support for vocabulary growth. However, once children fast map a word, their acquisition is not yet complete. During a second, extended phase of word learning, children refine their initial representation of the word's meaning based on subsequent encounters with the word.

Careful examination of the kinds of words children acquire and how they use them provides psycholinguists with important information about the course of semantic development. Clark (1983) divides children's early words into three different categories: words for objects, words for actions, and words for states (modifiers of objects and actions)

Object Words. Although, as indicated earlier, there are individual differences in the first words children choose to learn, virtually all early language learners have far more object than action words in their beginning vocabularies (Gentner, 1982; Greenfield & Smith, 1976; Nelson, 1973; Goldin-Meadow, Seligman, & Gelman, 1976). Object labels comprise 60 to 70 percent of children's first 50 to 100 words, while action terms make up only 10 to 30 percent (Gentner, 1982). If actions are an especially important means through which infants find out about their world, why this early predominance of object over action words? Investigators have explained the finding in two different ways.

The first explanation is that concepts referred to by nouns are particularly accessible to young children because they are perceptually bounded, highly cohesive, and easily identifiable. By the time children start to talk, all they need to do is to match objects with their appropriate linguistic referents[3] (Gentner, 1982). In contrast, verbs are conceptually more complex in that they require an understanding of the connections between objects and actions (Huttenlocher & Lui, 1979).

A second explanation involves the characteristics of adult speech to young children. Although motherese does not contain a greater number of object than action words (Nelson, 1973; Schnur & Shatz, 1984), the way nouns are used by mothers may lead them to be learned more easily by children (Bridges, 1985). For example, in one study of mothers' speech to 14-month-olds, the most heavily stressed words were nouns (names of toys). Also, nouns, more often than verbs, occur as single-word utterances or at the ends of sentences (at least in English), and there is evidence that children find it easiest to pay attention to and learn the ending parts of adult verbalizations (Kuczaj, 1979; Slobin, 1973).

Whether characteristics of the linguistic environment can completely account for the object word emphasis in children's early vocabularies is best settled by cross-cultural evidence, and recent research argues against it. Higher proportions of nouns are found in the vocabularies of children learning a wide variety of languages. However, in some of these languages, word order is such that verbs rather than nouns generally occur in final sentence positions, but verbs are still not acquired by children in greater frequency (Gentner, 1982). Moreover, in cultures where adults show little interest in teaching children the names of objects, they still have many more object than action words in their initial vocabularies (Gentner, 1982). Thus the disproportionate number of nouns in children's early speech largely reflects the dependence of language on cognitive development, a theme, as we shall see below, that continues to assert itself as vocabulary growth proceeds. However, as we have stressed repeatedly, there are important individual differences in vocabulary as well as other aspects of language development in which parental input does play an important role.

Action Words. When children first begin to talk about actions, they do not necessarily do so in ways that conform to adult usage. For example, in their early word productions, children use verbs ("open"), nouns ("door"), and prepositions ("out") to refer to actions. As their vocabulary and utterance length expand, children use many more words to refer to actions that, for adults, are verbs (Clark, 1983). By age 3, they clearly distinguish between words for objects and actions. When presented with a nonsense word embedded in the following sentence, "Do you know what it means *to sib*?" children consistently point to a picture of an action, whereas when asked, "Do you know what *a sib* is?" they point to an object (Brown, 1957).

Researchers have studied how very young children use action words to talk about cause and effect. Between 1 and 2 years of age, they focus only on the results of actions, saying "broken" for a toy that is broken or "stuck" for a finger stuck in a small hole (Clark, 1983). As early as age 2, they use expressions containing actions plus an indication of the effect they lead to, such as "eat allgone" or "push out." Words and word combinations that express causal relations (i.e., the notion that particular actions lead to predictable results) emerge early in children acquiring very different languages (Ammon & Slobin, 1979). In addition, appropriate usage of such causal connectives as "if," "because," and "so" follows shortly thereafter, appearing as soon as children can produce longer utterances, around 3 and 4 years of age (e.g., "If you drink paint, you'll get sick") (McCabe et al., 1983; French & Nelson, 1985). Early correct usage of these causal terms when children talk about familiar events is one finding, like many others described in Chapter 6, that has led recent investigators to conclude that preschool children's thought is far more orderly and logical than was once believed to be the case.

---

[3] You may wish to turn back to Chapter 4 to review how, during the first year of life, infants acquire the concept of the object as a perceptually independent, bounded whole. It is interesting that young children take a word uttered by an adult while pointing at an object as a name for that object as a whole, and not, as would certainly be logically possible, as a name for just some part of it (Macnamara, 1972).

State Words. Consistent with the sensorimotor underpinnings of early language, children's first state words refer to transient conditions of objects that are the outcome of some action, such as "dirty," "wet," and "hot." Between 2 and 2½ years of age, children's range of modifiers expands to include labels for salient perceptual attributes, such as their size and color ("big," "red"), as well as possession ("my toy," "Mommy purse"). Modifiers that refer to the functions of objects (e.g., "dump truck," "pickup truck") follow soon after (Nelson, 1976).

In instances in which modifiers are related to one another in meaning, the least conceptually complex and most broadly applicable terms are acquired first. For example, a stable order exists in the acquisition of dimensional adjectives: big-small first; followed by tall-short, high-low, and long-short; and finally wide-narrow and deep-shallow. The same applies to temporal terms, which serve as modifiers of actions. Children first master "now" versus "then," followed by "today" versus "yesterday" and "tomorrow" (Clark, 1972, 1983).

Children's state words designating the location and orientation of objects provide additional examples of how the development of conceptual knowledge influences vocabulary acquisition. In one study, children were given an imitation task in which they were asked to do as an experimenter did in placing an object in, on, and under a container or support. Those below the age of 2 could mimic placing objects in and on, but not under, and their ability to follow verbal instructions containing these prepositions (e.g., "Put the x *in [on, under]* the y") showed an order of acquisition that paralleled their nonlinguistic imitations: "in" was mastered first, followed by "on" and then "under," with all three achieved around 2½ years of age (Clark, 1973a). Children's understanding of words describing the orientation of objects—top, bottom, front, and back—reveals a similar pattern of development. "Top" and "bottom" are understood first, around 2½ or 3 years, followed by "front" and "back" between 4 and 5 (Clark, 1980).

Children's acquisition of new words takes place in an order that conforms to their mastery of underlying concepts. With respect to state words designating an object's location, "in" is acquired first, followed by "on" and then "under." (Nancy Sheehan)

State words perform a vital conceptual service for children. By permitting distinctions among objects and actions, children can use them to name new concepts that cannot be designated with just a single label. Thus state terms contribute significantly to the flexible, productive nature of human language. In addition, children's understanding and use of them reveal much about their underlying conceptual development (Nelson, 1976).

Mismatches, Underextensions, and Overextensions. During early vocabulary acquisition, children make three types of errors of word use. In fast mapping a new word into their initial vocabularies, children may **mismatch** the new label with an underlying concept, applying it to an inappropriate set of events. For example, your author's younger son, at age 2, was offered a "new" Pooh bear to replace a tattered "old" one that had become a highly treasured toy. He rejected the new bear vehemently and a day later produced the words "new" and "old" for the first time. After refusing a cookie he was offered, he pointed to a box of a different kind and said, "Want *old* cookie, not *new* cookie." Using "old" to mean "something I want" and "new" to mean "something I don't want," he began with the wrong hypothesis about adult conventions for the words.

Two additional types of early vocabulary errors are **underextension,** which involves applying a term to a smaller collection of events than is acceptable in conventional usage (e.g., only using the word "doll" to denote a particular doll), and **overextension,** applying it to a wider collection of events than is appropriate (e.g., using the word "car" to refer to trucks, trains, and bikes). Underextension is hard to detect, for children use the word in question appropriately, but simply extend it to a very limited range of instances. It is possible that underextension, in the form of picking up a new word in a very specific context, constitutes the first stage of acquisition of a great many words (Clark, 1983).

Overextensions are the most frequently observed word errors between 1 and 2½ years of age (Clark, 1978). Because they occur often in production, psycholinguists have exploited them for information about how children gradually develop adult word meanings. Overextensions reveal a surprisingly early sensitivity to categorical relations in toddlers and young preschoolers. Children do not overextend words randomly. Instead, they apply them to a class of similar referents, such as calling several animals "doggie" or using the word "open" to mean opening a door, peeling fruit, and undoing shoelaces (Clark, 1983). As children enlarge their vocabularies, they make finer distinctions, and overextended words become more constricted in their application (Rescorla, 1980). Following the development of these words reveals how young children strive at a very early age to clarify how words differ in meaning from one another (Clark, 1983).

Nevertheless, the study of overextensions underestimates what children really know about word meanings, for they overextend many words in production that they do not overextend in comprehension. That is, they may refer to trucks, trains, and bikes as "cars," but they can pick out these objects correctly when given their names in a comprehension task (Clark, 1978; Nelson et al., 1978; Rescorla, 1980). Overextension may be a special communicative technique that young children use as long as their vocabularies and memories are very limited. In other words, they may overextend deliberately because they have no suitable word or because they cannot remember the right word. From this perspective, overextension is a strategy children use to stretch their limited language resources to the utmost (Clark, 1978).

Coining New Words. Another means that young children use to stretch their limited vocabularies is coining new words, which occurs as early as age 2. Coined words, like overextensions, fill in for words children have not yet acquired or cannot retrieve, or they label concepts for which there is no word. Children's word coinages follow the principles of word formation in their language. The earliest strategies operate on whole words, as in the technique of compounding—"break-machine" for a machine that breaks things and "plant-man" for a gardener. Also, children invent new action words by converting a noun into a verb, as in one child's use of "needle it" to refer to mending something. In a similar way, they change verbs to nouns, such as "a chop" to refer to an axe. Later, children discover more specialized word coinage techniques, as in the addition of the ending -er to identify a doer of a particular action—"pounder" (for a hammer) and "crayoner" (for a child using crayons instead of paints). Children relinquish coined words as soon as they acquire conventional labels for their intended meanings (Clark & Hecht, 1982), but their inventiveness in constructing them is an additional linguistic feature that attests to their remarkable, rule-governed approach to language learning at an early age.

Later Vocabulary Development

Vocabulary continues to increase during middle childhood and adolescence, more than doubling in size from school entry until adulthood, for a mature linguistic repertoire consists of more than 30,000 words. During the school years, children use words more precisely and conventionally, and their semantic knowledge becomes better organized and hierarchically arranged. As indicated in Chapter 7, this occurs earlier in some domains of knowledge than others, especially those that are very familiar to the child.

Older children continue to fast map words into their vocabulary, but in connecting verbal labels with underlying concepts, 11- and 12-year-olds profit far more than 6- and 7-year-olds from being given explicit definitions (Dickinson, 1984). Similarly, the ability to use language to explain the meanings of words improves with age. During the early school years, children's word definitions are highly concrete, consisting primarily of descriptions of a referent's function or appearance (e.g., knife: "when you're cutting carrots"; bicycle: "it's got wheels, a chain, and handlebars"). Later on, children give more abstract responses involving synonyms, explanations, and descriptions of categorical relationships (e.g., knife: "Something you could cut with. A saw is like a knife. It could also be a weapon."). This advance reflects the older child's ability to deal with word meanings on an entirely verbal plane (Litowitz, 1977), as well as movement from word meanings based largely on personal experience to ones that reflect more general, socially shared information (Wehren, DeLisi, & Arnold, 1981).

Finally, during the school years, children display an improved ability to interpret words on multiple levels. They begin to appreciate the meaning of metaphors, such as "spilling the beans," "sharp as a tack," and "left high and dry." As with other aspects of language, at first children comprehend the meanings of these figures of speech, and only later on can they produce definitions of them (Winner, Rosenstiel, & Gardner, 1976).

Older children's appreciation of metaphor and their ability to deal with word meanings on an entirely linguistic plane reflect growth in *metalinguistic awareness,* or conscious ability to reflect on language as a system. Conscious awareness of language improves not only in the semantic area, but in other domains of language as well. We will comment more fully on it in a later section of this chapter.

New Ideas About How Semantic Development Takes Place

Adults are known to correct the inaccuracies of children's word usage, and research indicates that adult feedback helps the process of semantic development along. Ninio and Bruner (1978) observed dialogues between a mother and her young child during joint picture book reading. The child's incorrect labels for pictures were corrected, and appropriate word usage was usually followed by positive feedback from the mother. In a recent study, three types of adult feedback for incorrect labeling were compared: (1) correction (e.g., "That's not a car. It's a truck."); (2) correction plus an explanation that points out features of the referent ("That's a truck. See, it has a place to put things in."); and (3) acceptance of an incorrect label ("Yes, that's a car."). Correction with explanation was most effective in helping 1- to 1½-year-old children move toward adultlike word meanings, followed by simple correction, which was more effective than acceptance (Chapman, Leonard, & Mervis, 1986).

Still, there is no way that an adult, in naming instances of categories and providing children with feedback, can indicate exactly what a word picks out. For example, if an adult points to a dog and calls it a "doggie," it is not automatically clear whether the word refers to four-legged animals, the dog's shaggy ears, the shape of its wagging tail, or its barking sound. A major role in vocabulary development must be played by the child's own active cognitive processing. Children have to look for consistencies in adult usage of words, try words out based on initial hypotheses about their meaning, and then make adjustments based on additional adult usage and feedback from others (Clark, 1983). Finding out exactly how children go about deriving word meanings has been a challenging task for psycholinguists. Major theoretical accounts have been adopted and discarded over the years (e.g., Clark, 1973b).

Recently, Clark (1983) proposed a new explanation to account for semantic development, **lexical contrast theory.** It assumes that two fundamental principles govern the acquisition of word meaning. The first is *conventionality,* children's natural desire to acquire words and word meanings that are accepted by their linguistic community. Children attend to conventionality from a very early age, for they ask for names of unfamiliar objects, and they drop coined words as well as refine over- and underextensions as soon as new labels and meanings are added to their semantic repertoire. The second principle is *contrast,* which explains how new word meanings are acquired. Children assume the meaning of each word they hear is unique, so when they hear a new label, they immediately try to figure out what it refers to by contrasting it with words they already know. At the same time, each new word provides a comparative basis for revising the understanding of old ones. Recent research indicates that the principle of contrast is a vocabulary acquisition strategy used by children as young as 2 years of age (Taylor & Gelman, 1988). Besides accounting for the gradual refinement of word meanings as children enlarge their vocabularies, a major advantage of lexical contrast theory is that it regards children's strong desire to communicate as a central force in vocabulary development.

In summary, semantic development proceeds with extraordinary rapidity as preschoolers fast map thousands of words into their vocabularies. The course of vocabulary growth reflects children's cognitive development. At first object words predominate, while action and state words are less frequent. Errors of mismatch, underextension, and overextension occur often in children's use of new words but gradually disappear as preschoolers enlarge and refine their vocabularies. An increasingly flexible, abstract understanding of word meanings emerges in middle childhood and adolescence. Adult feedback assists with the monumental task of vocabulary building, but a major role is played by the child's active cognitive processing. Lexical contrast theory, which emphasizes acquisition principles of conventionality and contrast, is a new account of how semantic development takes place.

GRAMMATICAL DEVELOPMENT

Grammar requires more than just a single word to be evident in children's speech. Therefore, grammatical progress is charted using an index called **mean length of utterance (MLU).** Utterance length is measured in terms of number of **morphemes,** the smallest meaningful unit of adult speech. MLU is strongly related to the number of words in an utterance, but not perfectly so. For example, a young child's utterance, "see boat," is 2 morphemes long, whereas "see boats" contains 3 morphemes, due to the additional element, -s. MLU is determined by averaging the lengths of a large sample of utterances emitted by a child. During the first few years, the acquisition of grammatical features correlates with children's MLU, so grammatical development is often divided into phases based on this index.

A major controversy in the area of grammatical development concerns how early children develop an appreciation of adult grammatical categories, such as subject-verb-object. Evidence for a very early grasp of formal grammatical distinctions would provide Chomsky's nativist theory with continued support, whereas findings indicating that children's appreciation of grammar is not present in their early word combinations open the possibility that other factors, such as powerful cognitive processing abilities, may account for the acquisition of grammar. We consider evidence relevant to this issue as we chart the course of grammatical development below.

The One-Word Phase: Is an Appreciation of Grammar Already Present?

Between 1 and 2 years, many utterances children produce are single words, yet by combining them with gestures and intonation, they can express meanings that seem sentence-like in nature. One interpretation of single-word utterances is that children already have a full sentence in mind; they simply are not yet able to display this inherent grammatical knowledge because their vocabulary and ability to remember and produce longer word strings are limited. Investigators who believe that children's one-word utterances stand for complete thoughts term them **holophrases** (meaning one-word sentences), but whether this view is correct or not has been the subject of considerable debate. A number of investigators reject the notion (e.g., Bloom, 1973; Dore, 1985), preferring to postpone judgments about the child's grammatical knowledge until the MLU has expanded and grammar can be studied directly.

First Word Combinations: The Two-Word Utterance Phase

Sometime between 1½ and 2½ years of age, children combine two words together, such as "Mommy shoe," "go car," and "more cookie." Children's two-word utterances have been called **telegraphic speech.** Like a telegram, they omit smaller and less important words, such as articles ("the," "a"), auxiliary verbs ("can," "am," "will"), and prepositions ("on," "at," "in"). Also, as yet there are no grammatical morphemes added to the words, such as -s and -ed endings (Brown, 1973). Despite the restricted form of the two-word utterance, young children the world over use it to express a very similar and impressive variety of meanings, the most common of which are summarized in Table 9.2.

But do children in the two-word utterance phase use a consistent word order, the kind of evidence that would suggest an inherent grasp of grammatical categories? Investigators used to think so, but current evidence argues against it, for there is no uniform word order tendency during this phase (Maratsos, 1983; Maratsos & Chalkley, 1980). For example, children are just as likely to say "cookie give" as "give cookie" (which conforms to English grammar).

Children's two-word speech contains some word-bound formulas, such as "want + X" or "more + X." These are productive in nature, as children insert a variety of words in the X position. When a number of these formulas appear at once, they give the appearance that the child has captured a grammatical rule, but such formulas are actually very limited in their initial application. For example, Jonathan, a child studied by Braine (1976), produced several actor-action combinations at about the same time, such as "Mommy sit," "Daddy sleep," and "Daddy work." However, they did not represent a general understanding of subject-verb grammatical relations,

Table 9.2 Common Semantic Relationships Expressed by Children During the Two-Word Utterance Phase

MEANING	EXAMPLE
Agent and action	"Tommy hit"
Action and object	"Give cookie"
Agent and object	"Mommy truck" (meaning Mommy push the truck)
Action and location	"Put table" (meaning put X on the table)
Entity and location	"Daddy outside"
Possessor and possession	"My truck"
Entity and attribution	"Big ball"
Demonstrative and entity	"That doggie"
Notice and noticed object	"Hi mommy" "Hi truck"
Recurrence	"More milk"
Nonexistence and nonexistent or disappeared object	"No shirt" "No more milk"

Source: Brown, 1973.

for Jonathan only used them when an agent was moving from one place to another, such as his father going to bed or leaving for work. He had really constructed a very specific rule for expressing a particular semantic relationship, which was something like this: "mover of self + movement." Furthermore, many of the creative combinations children produce during the two-word period to not conform to adult grammatical restrictions. For example, based on a "more + X" rule, Andrew, another child studied by Braine (1976), said "more hot" and "more read," but these combinations are not acceptable in English grammar.

The evidence cited above indicates that learning how to express a small set of semantic relations is the major task of the two-word phase. It is now widely agreed that the unification of words into grammatical classes is a later achievement. As further evidence for this conclusion, de Villiers and de Villiers (1973a) asked children just beginning to make two-word combinations to act out sentences with toys in which both agents and objects were animate, such as "Make the *boy* kiss the *girl*." The children's responses were random; they were as likely to have the girl kiss the boy as the boy kiss the girl. Similarly, their spontaneously produced agent-action and action-object formulas tend to be limited to "*animate agent* + action" and "action + *inanimate object*" forms (see Table 9.2 for examples) (Bloom, Lightbown, & Hood, 1975; Brown, 1973). However, the piece-by-piece learning of word-based rules that goes on during the two-word phase may provide the foundation for the emergence of formal grammatical structure. Pieces that are similar to one another may eventually be drawn together, a general tendency that characterizes much of cognitive development (Maratsos, 1983).

From Two-Word Utterances to Complex Speech

Between 2 and 3 years of age, as the MLU moves from 2 toward 3, simple sentences appear. In English, one of their salient characteristics is a relatively fixed word order: subject-verb-object. Historically, the subject-verb-object sequence was thought to be close to Chomsky's deep structure and to represent a natural order of thoughts. However, as cross-linguistic research accumulated, it became clear that the order is not basic. It is not characteristic of children learning a wide variety of languages—Finnish, Samoan, Hungarian, Turkish, German, Italian, and Serbo-Croatian, to name just a few—in which different orderings of subject, verb, and object are typical. Children in these linguistic communities adopt the word orders reflected in the adult speech to which they are exposed, and they do not find their native tongue more difficult to learn than children born into English-speaking communities do (Maratsos, 1983).

The Acquisition of Grammatical Morphemes. During this period, children acquire grammatical morphemes, and expressions with small additions over the two-word phase, such as "he *is* eating" and "John's dog," become frequent. However, these acquisitions are not the result of sudden, rule-guided grammatical insights. They are mastered very gradually, and children do not use them consistently for months or even years after they first appear (Maratsos, 1983).

A striking finding is that morphemes are acquired in a highly regular order by English-speaking children between 1½ and 3½ years of age, a pattern first observed by Brown (1973) in an intensive longitudinal study of the early language development of three children and later replicated cross-sectionally on large samples (de Villiers & de Villiers, 1973b; Kuczaj, 1977a). The sequence of acquisition is displayed in Table 9.3.

Table 9.3. Order of Acquisition of English Grammatical Morphemes

MORPHEME	EXAMPLE
1. Verb present progressive ending (-ing)	"He singing."
2. Preposition "on"	"On horsie."
3. Preposition "in"	"In wagon."
4. Noun plural "-s"	"Cats."
5. Verb irregular past tense	"He ran." "It broke."
6. Noun possessive	"Daddy's hat."
7. Verb uncontractible "be" form used with adjective, preposition, or noun phrase	"Are kitties sleepy?"
8. Articles "a" and "the"	"A cookie." "The bunny."
9. Verb regular past tense ending (-ed)	"He kicked it."
10. Verb present tense, third person singular regular ending (-s)	"He likes it."
11. Verb present tense, third person singular irregular ending (-s)	"She has (from have) a cookie." "He does (from do) eat cookies."
12. Auxiliary verb uncontractible "be" forms	"Are you eating?"
13. Verb contractible "be" forms used with adjective, preposition, or noun phrase	"He's inside." "They're sleepy."
14. Auxiliary verb contractible "be" forms	"He's coming." "Doggie's eating."

Source: Brown, 1973.

There are different explanations about why this regular order occurs. One has to do with the frequency of adult use of the various morphemes, which bears some relationship to their order of acquisition (Moerk, 1980). However, all of the forms listed in Table 9.3 are highly frequent in adult speech, and adult usage is definitely not the only important factor. A second explanation has to do with the *structural complexity* of each of the grammatical forms. For example, adding the endings -ing or -s is structurally less complex than using the various forms of the verb "to be." In these, the child has to figure out the different forms that express tense, and also has to make the verb form agree with the noun person and number (e.g., "I *am* coming" versus "They *are* coming"). Besides structural complexity, *semantic complexity,* the number and difficulty of the meanings encoded in the acquisition, can also affect morphological development. For example, noun pluralization by adding -s involves just one semantic distinction, the difference between one versus more than one. In contrast, distinguishing among the various forms of the verb "to be" involves many more, including an understanding of number, person, and time of occurrence. Analyzing the structural and semantic complexity of the morphemes shown in Table 9.3, Brown (1973) concluded that both factors predicted their order of acquisition fairly well.

Structural and semantic complexity are hard to tease apart, for generally speaking, the more complex the grammatical construction, the more complicated the meaning it expresses. However, cross-linguistic research provides support for the independent contribution of both factors. Because of differences in the structural complexity of the expression, the time of emergence of constructions having similar meanings may vary considerably for children learning different languages. For example, Johnston and Slobin (1979) found that acquisition of the morphology used to express location (in English, this would be prepositions such as "in" and "on") occurred earlier for children learning English, Italian, and Turkish than Serbo-Croatian, in which locational expression is structurally more complex. At the same time, semantic complexity is partly responsible for morphological development, for across languages, there is considerable similarity in the order of acquisition of morphemes with the same meaning (Slobin, 1982).

Slobin (1982) uses the analogy of a waiting room to show how semantic and structural complexity work together to affect grammatical development. If we think of each linguistic form shown in Table 9.3 as having its own waiting room, children first gain entry to the room with a cognitive appreciation of the expression's underlying meaning as the key. Once in the room, they must figure out how the meaning in question is encoded in the grammatical structure of their language. This task takes varying amounts of time and effort, depending on the complexity of the linguistic features involved, but finally the child leaves the particular waiting room with the completed structure in hand. As Slobin explains, "The important point of the waiting-room metaphor is its two doors: the cognitive entry door and the linguistic exit. . . . we cannot hope to understand language acquisition without understanding the path between these two doors." (p. 169)

Overregularization. Look again at Table 9.3, and you will see that grammatical morphemes with irregular forms are acquired before those with regular forms. For example, children use such past tense irregular verbs as "broke" and "ran" before they acquire the regular -ed form. But once children get a regular morphological rule, they **overregularize,** or extend it inappropriately to irregular instances. For example, such expressions as "breaked," "runned," "goed," "feets," and "mouses" are frequent occurrences in the speech of 3-year-olds. The phenomenon of overregularization is extremely important in what it reveals about grammatical development. Since children do not hear mature speakers of English say "breaked" or "feets," the mistakes show that they develop productive grammatical rules at an early age. Additional evidence for the productive use of morphological rules comes from a famous study by Berko (1958) in which children were shown pictures of unusual objects and actions that were given nonsense syllable names, such as "wug" for a birdlike creature and "rick" for a swinging motion (see Figure 9.1). The nonsense labels were embedded in sentences that Berko asked children to complete in order to find out if they could add the appropriate elements. Preschoolers were able to supply correct morphemes to many novel nouns and verbs (e.g., they completed the sentences shown in Figure 9.1 with the expressions "wugs" and "ricked"). The findings support the conclusion that children construct *mental rules* for the application of grammatical morphemes. They do not learn them in a rote fashion by imitating adult usage.

An interesting question concerns why children use a number of correct irregular forms before they begin to overregularize. Whitehurst (1982) points out that irregular forms in all languages are applied to important, frequently used words. In English, words like "broke" and "ran" are few in number when considering the language system as a whole, but young children hear them very often. As a result, they may initially learn these instances by rote memory, but as soon as they grasp a morphological rule, they apply it broadly, and irregular words are overregularized for a time. Application of morphological rules does not drive out irregular forms completely. Kuczaj (1977b) showed that there is alternation in the young child's speech between overregularized and irregular versions of words for many months and sometimes years, until the child has managed the difficult task of sorting out the exceptions from the regular instances.

The Emergence of Formal Grammatical Understandings. Around the time the MLU reaches 3 and children are about 2½ years of age, they first show an appreciation of the formal grammatical categories of their language. In a recent study, Valian (1986) analyzed a large number of utterances of 2-year-old children to see if words that are members of particular grammatical categories obeyed the regularities characteristic of adult English usage. If so, Valian suggested, then children's knowledge of these categories could be inferred. For example, we would know that young children have formed the grammatical category of "adjective" (even though they do not

THIS IS A WUG.

NOW THERE IS ANOTHER ONE.
THERE ARE TWO OF THEM.
THERE ARE TWO _____ .

THIS IS A MAN WHO KNOWS HOW TO RICK. HE IS RICKING. HE DID THE SAME THING YESTERDAY. WHAT DID HE DO YESTERDAY? YESTERDAY HE _____ .

Figure 9.1. Two examples from Berko's (1958) "wug test." *From J. Berko, 1958, "The Child's Learning of English Morphology,"* Word, *14, pp. 154–155. Reprinted by permission.*

consciously label it as such) if they consistently place words adults classify as adjectives before nouns and after articles ("a *big* dog"), understand that adjectives can be sequenced ("a *big bad* dog") or repeated ("a *big big* dog"), and realize that they can appear as predicates ("The dog is *big*.") Valian found that by the middle of the third year, the distributional properties of children's speech were highly consistent, suggesting that they had implicit knowledge of the formal grammatical categories of adjective, article, noun, noun phrase, preposition, and prepositional phrase.

Psycholinguists have different ideas about exactly how young children achieve this amazing structural organization of language at such an early age. Some think that the *semantic* properties of grammatical classes play a prominent role in early category formation. For example, children may begin by grouping together words with "object qualities" as nouns and words with "action qualities" as verbs and then merge these basic semantic classes with observations they make about how particular words are used in sentence contexts (Bates & MacWhinney, 1982). Others believe that grammatical categories are largely shaped by observations children make about the *structural* properties of linguistic usage. That is, children notice which words appear in the same positions in sentences, take the same morphological endings, and are similarly combined with other words and gradually group them together (Maratsos & Chalkley, 1980). It is probably some complex combination of both semantic and structural properties that leads children to this accomplishment (Maratsos, 1983). Psycholinguists still have much to learn about exactly how children construct their first grammatical classifications.

The Development of Complex Grammatical Forms. The appearance of forms of the auxiliary verb "to be" opens the door to a variety of new expressions around 3 to 3½ years of age. In English, auxiliary verbs play central roles in a great many sentence structures that are complex variations on the early-appearing subject-verb-object form. Two important examples are negations and questions.

The development of negation reflects a complex interaction of grammatical, semantic, and parental input factors that combine to produce some interesting developmental patterns. Research on children's first use of negatives contains examples in which they initially place "no" or "not" in front of an utterance, such as "no want green beans," as well as integrate negatives into sentences, such as, "That not Mommy." Investigators who have studied these negative forms report that children use different rules to form different kinds of negatives. Three semantic types of negation exist, and they appear in children's speech in the following order: (1) *nonexistence,* in which the child remarks on the absence of something, such as "no cookie" or "allgone crackers"; (2) *rejection,* in which the child expresses opposition to something, such as "no take bath"; and (3) *denial,* in which the child denies the truthfulness of something, such as, "That not my kitty" (Bloom, 1970; Clancy, 1985). Young children tend to use the rule "no + utterance" to express nonexistence and rejection, but they use an internal form of negation to express denial. de Villiers and de Villiers (1979) suggest that the different forms are derived from parental speech patterns. For example, when parents express rejection, they often use constructions in which "no" appears at the beginning of the sentence, such as, "No, you can't have another cookie." Around 3 to 3½ years of age, children add auxiliary verbs to their utterances and become sensitive to the way they are combined with negatives by adult speakers. Consequently, appropriate grammatical constructions for all types of negation appear, such as, "There aren't any more cookies" (nonexistence), "I don't want a bath" (rejection), and "That isn't my kitty" (denial).

Like negatives, question forms also emerge over the early to middle preschool years. English-speaking children are able to rely on rising intonation to convert an utterance into a *yes-no question* (e.g., "Mommy baking cookies?"), and as a result, they produce them at an earlier age than children learning languages in which the construction of yes-no questions is more complex (Bowerman, 1973). Other kinds of questions, the so-called *wh- questions* that begin with "what," "where," "who," "when," "why," and "how," require that children invert the subject and auxiliary verb and place the wh- word at the beginning of the sentence. One of the best-known phenomena in English grammatical development is the initial noninversion of these sentences by children between 2 and 3 years of age. They can be heard using such expressions as, "What you doing?" and "Where Daddy going?" A little later, they include the auxiliary without inverting (e.g., "What you are doing?"), and finally they can incorporate all the rules for producing a correctly formed wh- question.

The acquisition of wh- questions follows an order that conforms to both semantic and structural complexity. "What," "where," and "who" questions, which ask about concrete objects, places, and people, appear first in children's speech. "When," "how," and "why" refer to more difficult concepts — time, manner, and causality — and they appear later on. The latter questions are also structurally more complex, for answers to them generally require whole sentences rather than just a single word (Tyack & Ingram, 1977).

Between 3 and 6 years of age, and as the MLU advances from 3 to 4 and beyond, children acquire increasingly complex grammatical forms. Conjunctions appear connecting whole sentences (e.g., "Mom picked me up, and we went to the park") and verb phrases ("I got up and ate breakfast"). Conjunctions with "and" appear first, followed by ones expressing a variety of other relations between clauses (e.g., "because," "although," "if") (Bloom et al., 1980). In the late preschool years, children also begin to produce embedded sentences (e.g., "I think *he will come*"), tag questions ("He isn't coming, *is he?*"), indirect object-direct object constructions ("The boy showed his friend the present"), and passive sentence forms ("The dog was patted by the girl") (Whitehurst, 1982). In addition, by school entry, children have acquired some of the subtleties involved in the use of pronouns. For example, they understand that "he" and "Bill" can co-refer in, "After he ate, Bill went to the movies," but not in "He said Bill should eat dinner now" (Solan, 1983). Thus, as the preschool years draw to a close, children have mastered an impressive variety of grammatical constructions. Still, grammatical development is by no means complete, and there is still a long period of development beyond early childhood.

Later Grammatical Development

The passive voice is an example of a grammatical construction that is not completely mastered until well into middle childhood. Studying passive sentences that 2- to 13-year-old children used to describe pictures, Horgan (1978) found that children of all ages produced more *truncated passives* (e.g., "It got broken"; "They got lost") than *full passives* ("The glass was broken by Mary"), although the production of full passives increased steadily from the preschool through the early adolescent years. Before children begin to produce very many passives, they show evidence of understanding them, but they comprehend some types more easily than others. Preschool and early school-age children understand passives based on action verbs, such as "hit" or "kiss," better than those based on experiential verbs, such as "like" or "know." The latter are not well understood until the mid-elementary school years (Sudhalter & Braine, 1985). Also, when children are asked to act out passive sentences, *irreversible passives,* in which only one noun in the sentence could plausibly serve as the subject ("The cup is washed by the girl"), are understood before *reversible passives,* in which *both* nouns could conceivably be the subject (e.g., "The boy is pushed by the girl") (Bever, 1970). Thus, mastery of the passive form in its full range of possibilities is a long development that is not complete before the end of middle childhood.

Another grammatical achievement that develops during the school years is the understanding of infinitive phrases, such as the difference between "John is eager to please" (in which "John" is the agent of "please") and "John is easy to please" (in which "John" is the object of "please"). Carol Chomsky (1969) tested children's understanding of this construction by presenting them with a blindfolded doll and asking them to respond to the question, "Is the doll *easy or hard to see?*" The results indicated that 5-year-old children always equated the grammatical subject ("doll" in this instance) with the agent role. That is, they respond "hard to see," as if they understood the question to mean something like, "Is the doll able to see?" Between 5 and 10, children gradually separate subject from agent in these kinds of sentences (Karmiloff-Smith, 1979).

The above examples reflect the broad scope of grammatical development. Like semantic development, later grammatical acquisitions are facilitated by the older child's cognitive maturity and metalinguistic awareness. School-age children can deal with less explicitly stated relationships and are more attentive to subtle linguistic cues in interpreting the meaning of utterances. These developments play major roles in helping them understand the most intricate grammatical constructions (Wallach, 1984).

New Ideas About How Grammatical Development Takes Place

As Chomsky's theory failed to find consistent support, a number of investigators turned toward a view of grammar as one product of general cognitive development, children's tendency to search the environment for consistencies and patterns of all sorts (Bever, 1982; Maratsos, 1983; Whitehurst, 1982). Other theorists, while also focusing on cognitive processing mechanisms, have not rejected the possibility that they are specially tuned for language learning. For example, Slobin (1973; 1985) proposes that children do not start out with an innate knowledge of grammatical rules (as Chomsky believed), but they do have a special **language-making capacity (LMC)** — a set of cognitive procedures for analyzing linguistic input that supports the discovery of grammatical regularities. On the basis of cross-linguistic studies, Slobin has begun to specify the processing procedures that all children may be using to master the grammar of their language. His theory still requires a great deal of research to be verified. Whether the LMC actually exists, is innately specified at birth, and is specially tuned to analyze linguistic features of the environment remain controversial issues (Bowerman, 1985).

In addition to children's inherent capacities, investigators have been interested in what aspects of linguistic input may make the task of grammatical mastery easier. In a well-known study, Brown and Hanlon (1970) found that parents of preschoolers give feedback not on the basis of grammaticality, but in response to the "truth value" of children's utterances. For example, the statement, "Her curling my hair," was met with an approving response because the child's mother was, in fact, curling her hair, whereas "There's the animal farmhouse" led a parent to respond that the building was really a lighthouse and not a farmhouse. These findings, as well as others (Hirsh-Pasek, Treiman, & Schneiderman, 1984; Penner, 1987), indicate that preschool children receive little direct guidance in formulating their grammar and must figure out its intricacies largely on their own. However, adults do model the necessary examples from which children draw the patterns, and the way they do so seems to ease the child's task.

We have already indicated that motherese provides children with input in the form of short, simple syntactic structures that are clearly pronounced. In addition, it is slower in tempo than speech to adults and contains distinct pauses between major grammatical units, such as noun and verb phrases (Sorenson, Cooper, & Paccia, 1978). Adults also adjust their utterance length so it is just ahead of the child's MLU, thereby fine-tuning it to children's changing developmental needs (Gleitman, Newport, & Gleitman, 1984).

Furthermore, mothers frequently engage in **expansions** of children's utterances. For example, a parent hearing a child say "go car" may say, "Yes, we're going to the car now." Parental responses that incorporate and expand children's verbalizations are helpful. In one study, preschool children progressing most rapidly in language development had mothers who made especially frequent use of expansions (Cross, 1978). In another, an experimenter manipulated children's exposure to them. Those receiving expansions showed a greater increase in sentence complexity over time than control children who heard completely new sentences (Nelson, Carskaddon, & Bonvillian, 1973). Recently, Penner (1987) discovered that parents tend to use expansions in response to grammatically incorrect utterances, while they use topic extensions (in which they continue the topic of interaction) in response to grammatically correct ones. These contingencies are far less obvious than direct approval or disapproval, but they can be regarded as a kind of feedback to children about grammaticality. Topic extensions offer children indirect information that their utterances are understood, whereas expansions suggest ways to alter grammatically incorrect forms.

In summary, research shows that children are active, rule-oriented learners who acquire basic grammatical categories of their language during the early preschool years and master a wide variety of complex grammatical constructions by school entry. A number of interacting factors account for grammatical development. These include basic cognitive processing strategies for analyzing linguistic input, the difficulty of the meanings expressed by the structures to be learned, the complexity of the structures themselves, and the extent to which examples of them are available in the environment and are communicated clearly to the child. Psycholinguists still have much to figure out about each of these contributing variables and how they work together. The acquisition of grammar continues to be one of the most awesome achievements of childhood.

PRAGMATIC DEVELOPMENT

During development, children must learn to use language in ways that permit them to send and receive messages successfully in social contexts. To do so, they must employ nonlinguistic channels of communication to supplement linguistic ones, be able to send messages that are clear and precise, and adhere to social conventions that govern how speakers and listeners should relate to one another. In the following sections, we address this pragmatic or communicative side of language development.

Becoming an Effective Conversationalist

As we indicated in our discussion of prelinguistic communication, by the end of the first two years, children already appreciate conversational turn-taking and are able to provide content-relevant verbalizations in response to parental speech. During the preschool years, children's conversational abilities develop further.

At age 2, children's ability to participate in a sustained verbal exchange is still limited, for they rarely continue a conversation beyond two turns. One reason is that although 2-year-old children *respond* in a relevant fashion to prior utterances, they rarely use conventional techniques that help sustain interaction, such as **turnabouts,** in which the conversationalist not only comments on what has just been said, but also adds some other kind of request to get the partner to respond again. Children's production of turnabouts increases over the preschool years (Kaye & Charney, 1980; Goelman, 1986). Its restricted use by very young preschoolers may be due to their very limited MLU, for as yet they cannot use very many words in each turn. During early childhood, children not only engage in more sustained discourse, but maintain a single topic of conversation over a greater number of turns (Byrne & Hayden, 1980;

Martlew, 1980; McDonald & Pien, 1982). Between 5 and 9 years, children learn to use more advanced conversational strategies, such as **shading,** in which a change of conversational topic is initiated gradually by modifying its focus, rather than through an abrupt topical change, which is typical of younger children (Brinton & Fujiki, 1984; Wanska & Bedrosian, 1985).

Although the child's participatory role increases, adults continue to assume much responsibility for maintaining conversational structure and cohesiveness when interacting with preschool children (Wanska & Bedrosian, 1985). In doing so, adults demonstrate effective conversational strategies. In fact, opportunities for conversational give-and-take with adults may provide an especially facilitating context for all aspects of early language development. Conversational extension and topic maintenance between adults and children are positively related to general measures of preschool language growth (Byrne & Hayden, 1980). Furthermore, research reported in Box 9.3 suggests that the slower rate of language development among twins as opposed to singletons may be explained by twins' reduced opportunity to engage in conversational participation with their parents.

If children are to carry on effective discourse, they must also be sensitive to the **illocutionary intent** of utterances — that is, what a speaker *means to say,* regardless of whether the linguistic form of the utterance is perfectly consistent with it. For example, the question, "Would you like to make cookies?" can be a request for information, an offer to provide an activity, or a directive to do something, depending on the context in which it is said. The ability to take context into account in interpreting the meaning of language emerges early in the preschool years and undergoes continued refinement into middle childhood. By age 3, the way children respond in everyday discourse indicates that they comprehend a variety of utterances as requests for action even when they are not directly expressed that way, such as "I need a pencil" or "Why don't you tickle me?" (Garvey, 1974). In addition, preschoolers are able to make requests of others using a variety of linguistic forms (Dore, 1974; Read & Cherry, 1978).

Conveying meaning through language seems to depend as much on illocutionary elements as it does on phonological, semantic, and grammatical factors, and children are sensitive to this fact at a surprisingly early age. Perhaps they appreciate the multiple interpretations of verbal messages so early because they are exposed to a wide variety of parental form-intention pairings during the first few years of life. Shatz (1979) reported that mothers of 1- and 2-year-olds use many linguistic forms to express a single intention, and they express a variety of intentions with the same form.

During the school years, children's illocutionary knowledge undergoes further development. Third graders are able to grasp illocutionary intents that are expressed in very unconventional ways just as well as adults. For example, in the context of having forgotten to do his chore of taking the garbage out, an 8-year-old understands very clearly that his mother's declarative statement, "The garbage is beginning to smell," really means, "Take the garbage out!" Comprehending form-intention pairings like this one requires children to make subtle inferences between context and utterance that are beyond the preschool child's cognitive capabilities (Ackerman, 1978).

Learning to Communicate Clearly

Effective communication also involves the ability to phrase a message one sends as clearly as possible, as well as the ability to recognize when a message one receives is not clear so that one can ask for more information. Both of these abilities — the *speaker's skill* at sending informative messages and the *listener's skill* at detecting when a message is not informative enough — are called **referential communication skills.**

Box 9.3
Language Learning Environments
of Twins and Singletons

Theory. Twins learn language at a slower rate than singletons during the early years of life (Savic, 1980). The difference could be due to twins' less advantaged prenatal conditions, for twins must share space and nutrition in utero, and they are generally born several weeks preterm. For these reasons twins may experience a slower course of early intellectual development. But twins' language-learning environments could also account for their slower linguistic growth. Twins' conversational experiences with their mothers are almost always *triadic* rather than *dyadic*. That is, they almost always take place in the presence of a same-age sibling. Michael Tomasello, Sara Mannle, and Ann Kruger (1986) hypothesized that the presence of the second child reduces the effectiveness of the mother's conversational style, resulting in detrimental consequences for twins' language growth.

Research. Six pairs of toddler-age twins were matched with singleton children on socioeconomic status and age. Along with their mothers, they were videotaped at home, with each singleton dyad and twin triad interacting with toys and the mothers told to do what they normally do when playing and conversing with their children. The videotapes were coded for the amount and quality of mother-child conversations, and for the size of children's vocabularies as a general indicator of their language growth.

The findings indicated that the twins were substantially behind singletons in vocabulary development at 21 months of age. As shown in Figure 9.2, singletons produced nearly 4 times the total number of words and 5 times as many different words as twins during the videotaping session. As expected, the triadic interactive situation had a substantial effect on the quantity and quality of mother-child conversations. Overall, twin mothers did not spend less time interacting with their children than did mothers of singletons, but each twin got less than half the quantity of direct input that was accorded to singletons. Also, the utterances used by mothers of twins were shorter in length and contained a higher proportion of directives and a lower proportion of comments and questions designed to extend the interaction. Furthermore, the quantity of maternal utterances and use of conversation-extending devices were positively related (and directives negatively related) to children's vocabulary development.

Applications. The presence of a twin may dramatically alter parent-child conversations in a way that affects language development, and parents of twins should make an effort to interact separately with each of their children. Arranging special times for one-to-one conversation may also be important for laterborn siblings. In a study similar to the one described above, the presence of a closely spaced older sibling led mothers to offer the younger child less responsive verbal stimulation. Some evidence suggests that laterborns are slower than firstborns in early language development (Jones & Adamson, 1987).

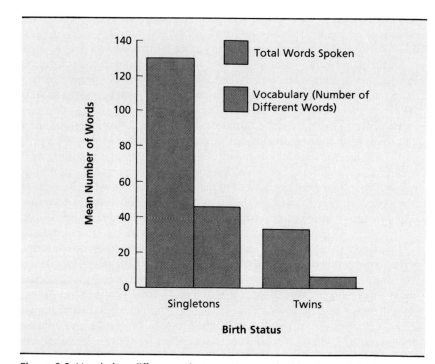

Figure 9.2. Vocabulary differences between 21-month-old twins and singletons in the Tomasello, Mannle, and Kruger (1986) study. The means indicate the total number of words spoken as well as the number of *different* words spoken (an estimate of vocabulary size) in a 15-minute recording session. *(Adapted from Tomasello, Mannle, and Kruger, 1986.)*

The ability to phrase messages clearly begins to develop during the preschool years, although it is not well developed until middle childhood. Not until age 3 do children revise their own utterances in response to requests for more information (Gallagher, 1981). But when preschoolers do clarify their messages, they rely heavily on gestures (such as pointing), and they are unlikely to give full verbal accounts of exactly what they mean (Pechmann & Deutsch, 1982; Van Hekken, Vergeer, & Harris, 1980).

Factors responsible for the production of clear verbal messages are both cognitive and linguistic in nature. Cognitively, skilled speakers must be able to determine the attributes of a referent that discriminate it from other possible alternatives, and linguistically, they must be in command of the vocabulary and grammatical skills that permit them to designate those attributes in a verbal message. Even when preschool children have acquired these abilities, they do not necessarily make use of them. For example, Deutsch and Pechmann (1982) displayed several eight-object arrays to 3- to 10-year-old children as well as adults. In each array, several of the objects were similar in size, shape, and color, and subjects were asked to indicate which object they liked best as a birthday present for an imaginary friend. Most of the 3-year-olds gave ambiguous descriptions, a tendency that declined steadily with age.

An interesting finding is that when children's messages *are* inadequate and there is a breakdown in communication, preschool and kindergarten children tend to blame their listeners rather than themselves. Young children may have reason to do so, for many parents patiently try to figure out the meaning of children's utterances and rarely tell them explicitly why their messages are not understood. When parents do give feedback about the inadequacy of children's messages, they are likely to say something like, "Which one?" instead of providing more informative feedback, such as, "There are four balls, and I don't know whether you mean a large or a small one or a red or a green one." Providing such explicit feedback in laboratory experiments has been found to increase the clarity of 5- and 6-year-olds' subsequent messages as well as to reduce their listener-blaming tendencies (Robinson, 1981).

Children's capacity to evaluate the communicative adequacy of messages they receive also improves from the preschool years into middle childhood. Around age 3, children start to ask for clarification from others when a message is ambiguous (Revelle, Karabenick, & Wellman, 1981). Asking for more information is a sophisticated accomplishment, for it requires children to monitor the situation for the kind of information they need, match this against the content of linguistic inputs, and translate any lack of agreement into an appropriate request for clarification. Still, young children only gradually become aware of the inadequacies of different kinds of uninformative messages. Recognition that a message provides an ambiguous description of a concrete object emerges earlier than recognition that a message is inconsistent with something a speaker said earlier in a conversation. Detection of this last kind of difficulty involves greater cognitive processing demands. Instead of just comparing the content of a message to stimuli available in the environment, the listener must retrieve previous discourse from memory and then match it against the spoken message (Sonnenschein, 1986a). Noticing inconsistencies in spoken language requires the comprehension monitoring skills we discussed in Chapter 7. It is a late-developing achievement that undergoes gradual improvement over the course of middle childhood and adolescence.

Children with learning problems often show deficits in referential communication skills. They communicate information less accurately, have more difficulty rephrasing their messages when asked to do so, and are less likely to ask for more information when a message they receive is unclear (Feagans & Short, 1986). Referential communication skills can be trained with techniques that stress the importance of messages that indicate their referents unambiguously. However, at least among preschool children, training speaker skills will not generalize to listener skills, and training listener skills will not generalize to speaker skills. Early in development, children seem to lack knowledge of the commonalities between these two highly related tasks (Sonnenschein & Whitehurst, 1983). How they eventually come to discover the relations between them and what experiences help them do so are, as yet, unanswered questions.

The Development of Sociolinguistic Understanding

Besides expressing meanings, verbal messages have sociolinguistic implications. That is, they carry information having to do with the social relationships between people, such as status differentials and familiarity, and they also vary according to the communicative demands of particular situations. Psycholinguists refer to speech variations that adapt to changes in social expectations as **speech registers.** As adults, we move through a variety of settings and play many different roles in the course of a given day — parent, employee, supervisor, friend, and casual acquaintance, to name just a few. To be socially acceptable, we have to master several different registers. Over the course of development, children must learn how to adjust their linguistic performance in accordance with social demands, for whether or not they do so may determine if a listener is willing to receive their message at all.

Children are sensitive to the age, sex, and social status of their communicative partners at an early age. In one study, 4- to 7-year-old children were asked to act out

At an early age, children adjust their speech in accord with the age, sex, and social status of their communicative partners. (Erika Stone)

different roles with hand puppets. Even the youngest children understood stereotypic linguistic features of different social positions. They used more imperatives when playing socially dominant and "male" roles, such as teacher, doctor, and father, and more politeness routines and indirect requests when playing less dominant and "feminine" roles, such as pupil, patient, and mother (Anderson, 1984). Older children have acquired an even more subtle appreciation of register adjustments that mark social status. Between 5 and 8 years of age, they increase the degree of deference expressed in requests they make of adults when the adult is preoccupied with another task and could be expected to be disturbed by the interruption (Ervin-Tripp, O'Connor, & Rosenberg, 1984). Speech adjustments based on familiarity with a listener also appear during the preschool and early elementary school years. Children give fuller explanations in messages directed to an unfamiliar listener than someone with whom they share common experiences, such as a friend or a familiar adult (Menig-Peterson, 1975; Sonnenschein, 1986b).

Sociolinguistic understanding appears early and seems to parallel children's mastery of language itself. Children probably learn a great deal about speech registers through direct observation, but parents also make a concerted effort to teach some social forms that make children acceptable speakers in their society. From age 2 on, children get intensive instruction in politeness routines. When they fail to say "please," "thank you," or "hi" and "good-bye" in contexts that call for them, parents generally demand an appropriate response. This is true not only in our culture, but in others as well (Schieffelin & Ochs, 1983), for a child can get by in the world without perfectly correct grammar, pronunciation, and an extensive vocabulary, but failing to use socially acceptable linguistic forms can lead to ostracism and rejection. Anything that has such drastic social consequences cannot be unimportant, and parents' insistent tutoring in social niceties suggests that they are well aware of this fact (Grief & Gleason, 1980).

In summary, during early and middle childhood, children acquire pragmatic skills that enable them to participate as competent conversationalists in sustained discourse with others. During the same period, the ability to detect the illocutionary intent of others and referential communication also improve. Finally, children's sociolinguistic understanding, or sensitivity to social expectations conveyed through language, appears early and undergoes further refinement during the school years.

THE EMERGENCE OF METALINGUISTIC AWARENESS

We have already indicated in several sections of this chapter that **metalinguistic awareness** — the ability to think about and reflect on language itself — is involved in a variety of later language achievements. Psychologists and educators have been interested in when metalinguistic awareness emerges and the role that it plays in a number of language-related accomplishments, especially learning to read.

Laboratory studies show that a diverse array of metalinguistic skills appears during the preschool years. For example, some 3-year-olds and many 4-year-olds are aware that word labels are arbitrary and not actually a part of the objects they denote. When asked if an object could be called by a different name in a new language, they respond affirmatively. In addition, 4-year-olds demonstrate some phonological awareness, for they are able to pick out words that rhyme from those that do not. They can also make some conscious syntactic judgments — for example, that a puppet who says "nose your touch" or "dog the pat" is saying his sentences "the wrong way around." Furthermore, these beginning metalinguistic accomplishments are strongly correlated with vocabulary and grammatical development during the preschool years (Smith & Tager-Flusberg, 1982).

Still, many metalinguistic abilities do not emerge until middle childhood. Around age 7 children can divide meaningful phrases into their constituent words (Hakes, Evans, & Tunmer, 1980; Tunmer, Bowey, & Grieve, 1983), and at about 8 they can segment spoken words into phonemes (Tunmer & Nesdale, 1982). Whereas preschoolers cannot make judgments about the grammatical correctness of a sentence if its meaning does not suit them, between ages 5 and 8 the ability to separate meaning from linguistic structure and to recognize grammatically correct sentences shows marked improvement (Bialystok, 1986; Hakes, Evans, & Tunmer, 1980; Scholl & Ryan, 1980). These findings indicate that during the elementary school years, children are much better at reflecting on the properties of language than they were when they were rapidly acquiring basic language skills. Some investigators believe that refinement of metalinguistic skills may be a function of the improved metacognitive control over the information processing system that also occurs during middle childhood (see Chapter 7). However, much more research is needed to determine the links between metacognitive and metalinguistic development (Tunmer & Bowey, 1984).

Many studies report that kindergartner's scores on a variety of metalinguistic measures are good predictors of their reading achievement in first grade (Ehri, 1979). That metalinguistic abilities are intimately involved in successful reading makes perfect sense, for in order to map printed text onto oral language effectively, children must have some conscious knowledge of the structural features of spoken language. However, investigators differ with regard to how they think metalinguistic abilities and reading are related. Some believe that the process of learning to read itself is responsible for increasing children's conscious awareness of the properties of language (Donaldson, 1978), while others think that a certain amount of metalinguistic knowledge is necessary before a child can learn to read (Calfee, Chapman, & Venezky, 1972). It is possible that each of these views is partially correct and that metalinguistic development and reading mutually support one another. Although some level of metalinguistic knowledge may be critical for reading success, researchers do not yet know which metalinguistic skills are essential and exactly what levels of awareness are required. However, once more is known, special training in metalinguistic skills may prove to be an especially effective means for facilitating reading progress (Tunmer & Bowey, 1984).

BILINGUALISM: LEARNING TWO LANGUAGES AT A TIME

For most of this chapter, our discussion has focused on children's learning of their first language, but a common occurrence throughout the world is that children are exposed to two languages, and sometimes more than two, during their childhood years. Current estimates indicate that 4.5 million American school-age children speak a native language other than English at home (Hakuta, 1986).

Until recently, a commonly held belief among Americans was that learning more than one language in early childhood undermined proficiency in either language, led to intellectual deficits, and promoted a sense of personal rootlessness because the bilingual child was believed to identify only weakly with mainstream American culture. The long American tradition of negative attitudes toward childhood bilingualism has been fueled by racial and ethnic prejudices, for bilingualism in the United States is strongly associated with low-income and minority status. In addition, during the early part of this century, the view was bolstered by the findings of seriously flawed research (Diaz, 1983). Today, more carefully conducted investigations show that there are no negative consequences from an early bilingual experience. To the contrary, bilingualism has intellectually enriching consequences.

Children may become bilingual in two ways: through *simultaneous acquisition* of both languages, or through *sequential acquisition* in which second language learning follows proficient mastery of the first. Case studies of young children reveal no serious linguistic retardation in either language as the result of simultaneous acquisition. For a short period during the second year of life, children exposed to two languages do appear to develop more slowly, but this is because they shift between the two vocabularies, often apply the grammar of one language to the vocabulary of the other, and sometimes mix the two phonological systems. Between 2 and 3, children become aware that they are dealing with two separate languages, and from then on they develop as independent systems. By age 4, children show normal native ability in the language of their community, and good to native ability in the second language, depending on the extent to which they have been exposed to it. When two languages are learned sequentially (one before and one after age 3), it generally takes about a year to achieve a level of fluency that is roughly comparable to native-speaking agemates (Reich, 1986).

Contrary to a commonly held belief in the United States, bilingualism in childhood has intellectually enriching consequences. (Bill Anderson/Monkmeyer Press Photo Service)

A landmark study conducted by Peal and Lambert (1962) showed for the first time that bilingualism had a positive influence on cognitive development. Comparing 10-year-old Canadian children who were equally fluent in both English and French to monolingual controls, the investigators found that the bilinguals performed better on a variety of verbal and nonverbal intellectual measures. Although Peal and Lambert's research suffered from methodological difficulties in that their two groups were not perfectly matched on important characteristics (e.g., grade in school), better designed studies have replicated and extended their findings. When compared to monolinguals, balanced bilingual children show advantages on tests of analytic reasoning, concept formation, and metalinguistic awareness (Ben-Zeev, 1977; Bialystok, 1986; Cummins, 1978; Ianco-Worrall, 1972). Diaz (1985) recently examined the relationship between degree of proficiency in a second language (English) and cognitive development among kindergarten and first-grade Spanish-speaking children. Even after children's socioeconomic status and native language proficiency were controlled, a strong positive relationship between second language fluency and a variety of intellectual measures remained.

The cognitive advantages of bilingualism provide strong justification for the expansion of bilingual education programs to serve the 3.5 million children with limited English proficiency in America's public schools (Hakuta, 1986). Bilingual education programs are committed to maintaining children's first language while fostering mastery of English. By providing instruction in the native language and gradually introducing English as children become ready for it, bilingual programs communicate to American minority groups that their languages and cultures are respected. In addition, by avoiding abrupt submersion of the child in an English-speaking environment, the programs prevent the cognitive and educational risks of *semilingualism* — inadequate proficiency in both languages for a period of several years. Disadvantaged non-English-speaking children are at special risk for semilingualism when schools provide only English instruction, for facility in their native language gradually recedes if it is not exercised and fostered.

The last two decades have brought a gradual increase in federal support for bilingual education. Public school programs have expanded, with most serving children during the early elementary school years. However, it is still the case that few bilingual children receive much in the way of maintenance of their native language in America's schools, and over half still receive no instruction in their first language at all (O'Malley, 1982). Bilingualism is part of the ethnic minority child's right to be fully educated, but beyond this, it provides one of the best examples of how language, once learned, becomes an important tool of the intellect and fosters cognitive growth. As Hakuta (1986) suggests, the goals of schooling could justifiably be broadened to include the development of *all* students as functional bilinguals, with the aim of promoting the linguistic, cognitive, and cultural enrichment of the entire American populace.

CHAPTER SUMMARY

1. Increased interest in language development was sparked by the Chomsky-Skinner debate of the 1950s. Both Skinner's environmentalist theory and Chomsky's nativist theory have since been criticized, and an interactionist perspective now dominates the field. Current theorists regard children as active, hypothesis-testing beings who, supported by a rich linguistic social environment, acquire the complexities of language largely at their own initiative.

2. Three basic issues regarding language development

concern whether a critical period exists for language learning, whether language acquisition follows a strict universal sequence, and whether linguistic progress should be assessed using language comprehension or production. Evidence on children deprived of early language exposure is consistent with a "weak" critical period for first language learning, but second language learning does not conform to the critical period hypothesis. Although there are universal features of language development, striking individual variations in rate and route exist. Language comprehension is generally ahead of production, and an accurate appraisal of language development requires that both processes be assessed.

3. Infants are specially prepared for language development. Neonates are capable of categorical speech perception. Initially they discriminate phonemic categories that adults confuse with one another, but by the end of the first year, they focus more intently on the speech sounds of their own language. Between 3 and 6 months, babies begin to babble, and the range of sounds they produce expands during the first year. In Western cultures, adults encourage conversational turn-taking by responding to infants' vocalizations and initiating social games with them. By the end of the first year babies express preverbal intentions, and soon words accompany these early gestures. During infancy, children also acquire a prelinguistic conceptual foundation onto which they map their first words.

4. Phonological development involves understanding and producing the sound patterns of one's native language. During the transition from babbling to speech, children engage in trial-and-error efforts to pronounce their first words. Slightly later, they use systematic phonological strategies that bring adult utterances within the limits of their physical and cognitive capabilities. Pronunciation undergoes marked improvement over the preschool years. Maturation of the vocal apparatus coupled with children's active problem-solving efforts are largely responsible for this change, but the features of motherese appear to ease the child's task. Although phonological development is mostly complete by school entry, a few stress and accent patterns are mastered during middle childhood and adolescence.

5. Semantic development involves identifying which underlying concept each verbal label picks out in one's language community. To build an extensive vocabulary rapidly, children engage in fast mapping, a cognitive process that permits them to connect an underlying concept with a word after only a brief encounter. The order of children's word acquisitions reveals how cognitive development influences vocabulary growth. Labels for objects are most common, while action and state words are less frequent in early vocabularies. When first learning new words, children make errors involving mismatches, underextensions, and overextensions. Overextensions, as well as word coinages, are communicative devices that help children stretch their limited vocabularies to the utmost. During the school years, children are better able to grasp new word meanings from verbal definitions, and they show an appreciation of metaphor. Adults correct children's inaccuracies in word usage, but they cannot teach them exactly what referent every word picks out. A major role in vocabulary development must be played by the child's own active cognitive processing. Lexical contrast theory is a new approach to explaining semantic development in which children rely on principles of conventionality and contrast to build their vocabularies.

6. Grammatical development is generally divided into phases based on mean length of utterance (MLU). During the one-word phase, children use single words to express meanings that seem sentence-like in nature, but there is no definite evidence that their one-word utterances are really holophrases. During the two-word phase, children combine words to express many meanings, but they do not follow adultlike grammatical rules. As MLU moves from 2 to 3, simple sentences reflecting the word order conventions of children's linguistic community appear. Children also acquire grammatical morphemes in a consistent order that reflects their structural and semantic complexity. Soon children overregularize, or extend morphological rules inappropriately to irregular instances. About the time the MLU reaches 3, children achieve an implicit appreciation of some formal grammatical categories of their language, and complex grammatical constructions, such as negations and questions, appear. Mastery of additional constructions such as conjunctions, tag questions, and subtle uses of pronouns, occurs between 3 and 6 years of age. The passive voice and infinitive phrases are examples of grammatical forms that continue to develop during middle childhood. Current theorists believe that powerful cognitive processing mechanisms help young children discover the regularities of grammar, but debate continues about whether or not they are specially tuned to analyze linguistic information. Although parents do not deliberately correct children's grammatical errors, the simple syntactic structure of motherese and adult expansions of children's utterances facilitate grammatical development.

7. Pragmatic development involves the communicative side of language. During the preschool years, children become more effective conversationalists, participating in sustained discourse and maintaining a single topic of conversation over a greater number of turns. In addition, the ability to appreciate illocutionary intent (what a speaker means to say, even though the linguistic form of the utterance is not consistent with it) emerges early in the preschool period and undergoes continued refinement into middle childhood. Referential communication skills, involving the ability to send unambiguous messages and to recognize when a message one receives is unclear, also develop over the preschool and elementary school years. Sociolinguistic understanding is reflected in children's adjustment of speech acts to differentials in age, sex, and social status as early as the preschool years.

8. Metalinguistic awareness, the ability to step back and consciously reflect on language as a system, is intimately related to language development as well as language-related accomplishments, such as learning to read. Preschoolers show metalinguistic skills, but many do not emerge until middle childhood.

9. Although the United States has a sizable bilingual population, Americans have traditionally held negative attitudes toward the learning of multiple languages in childhood. Recent research shows that bilingual children are cognitively advantaged when compared to their monolingual counterparts. During the last two decades, federal support for bilingual education programs in America's public schools has increased, but far too few non-English-speaking ethnic minority children are served by them.

IMPORTANT TERMS AND CONCEPTS

phonology
semantics
grammar
pragmatics
language acquisition device (LAD)
referential style
expressive style
comprehension
production
phonemes
categorical speech perception
pseudodialogues

protodeclarative
protoimperative
sound play
jargon stretches
motherese
fast mapping
mismatch
underextension
overextension
lexical contrast theory
mean length of utterance (MLU)
morpheme

holophrases
telegraphic speech
overregularization
language-making capacity (LMC)
expansions
turnabouts
shading
illocutionary intent
referential communication
speech registers
metalinguistic awareness

PART IV

Personality and Social Development

In Disgrace, by Charles Burton Barber.
© Camden Graphics Ltd., 1986.

CHAPTER 10
Emotional Development

In this chapter we consider the child's emotions, a topic that has captured the fascinated attention of investigators from virtually every major theoretical persuasion in developmental psychology. Although the affective side of growth and development lay in the shadow of cognition for several decades, today new excitement surrounds the topic, for accumulating evidence reveals that emotions play a central role in all aspects of human behavior.

Our discussion brings together three lines of research that have to do with various aspects of children's emotions. First, we chart the general course of emotional development. In doing so, we underscore the importance of emotions in cognition, social behavior, and physical health, and we describe major developmental changes in children's ability to express as well as recognize and interpret emotional signals. Second, our attention turns to the topic of individual differences in temperament and personality. We examine both biological and environmental origins of these differences, as well as their long-term consequences for development. Finally, we address the development of attachment to the caregiver, the child's first affectional tie that emerges over the course of infancy. This formative social relationship is forged from a complex interaction between the baby's emotional signals and the caregiver's responsiveness to infant cues. The feelings of affection and security that emanate from this bond serve as a vital source of support for many aspects of psychological growth. As we consider these diverse topics, you will see that a unifying theme that weaves its way though virtually all current research is that feelings play an important, adaptive role in behavior and serve as regulating forces for all of human development.

THE COURSE OF EMOTIONAL DEVELOPMENT

Between the 1940s and 1970s, developmental psychologists rarely stopped to consider the possibility that emotions might occupy a central role in the social and intellectual life of the child. The 1970 *Handbook of Child Psychology,* which summarized the status of the field, did not even include a chapter on emotional development. This was in stark contrast to the four previous handbooks, which, in responding to the importance that both behaviorist and psychoanalytic theories had accorded emotions in prior decades, had each included a chapter (Campos et al., 1983). Today, the field of child development is experiencing a rebirth of interest in emotional development. The most recent *Handbook of Child Psychology,* published in 1983, compensates for the 1970 omission by devoting over 100 pages to the topic. This return was sparked, in part, by the perfection of new methods that permit psychologists to assess human emotional reactions more accurately and at an earlier age than was previously thought possible.

Methods of Measuring Emotional Reactions

A variety of procedures for classifying the patterning of facial expressions as indicators of underlying emotions were developed in the 1970s (Ekman & Oster, 1979), and they are the most common methods used to study emotional development today. The refinement of these techniques was inspired by cross-cultural evidence indicating that the facial behaviors people associate with basic emotions are universal. For example, Ekman and his colleagues (Ekman & Friesen, 1972; Ekman, Sorenson, & Friesen, 1969) reported that subjects from the United States, Japan, a variety of South American countries, and even preliterate societies discriminated happiness, sadness, disgust, and anger from still photographs in the same way. The consistency of these findings suggested that a number of facial emotional patterns were under biological control, had important adaptive value, and might even be discernible in early infancy.

Recently, the vocal channel has also been used to study children's emotions. Although the techniques are not as well developed as those for facial patterns, different emotions can be identified consistently in vocal expressions (e.g., Scherer, 1982). This is even true early in life, for as we indicated in Chapter 4, newborn infants already express some vocal affects through a set of differentiated cries that are clearly recognizable to their caregivers (Wolff, 1969).

Expressions of emotion involving postural movements have received less attention, although they offer promise as measures of children's affects. In one study, Lewis and Michalson (1982) reported that mothers of 1-year-olds often use bodily responses to infer and label their children's emotions. For example, throwing objects, kicking, and stomping are taken as evidence of anger; moving away and refusing to look as fear; and skipping and strutting as happiness.

Finally, physiological measures indexing autonomic nervous system reactivity, such as galvanic skin response, heart rate, blood pressure, and respiration rate, have been used to measure emotional arousal for decades. However, by themselves physiological measures are limited indices of emotion. As yet there has been little success in linking them with discrete emotional states, although they serve as good measures of the intensity of emotional reactions (Lacey & Lacey, 1970; Lewis & Michalson, 1983).

The Functions of Emotions

In the following sections, we look at developmental psychologists' new view of emotions as vital determinants of a wide variety of psychological and physiological processes, including cognition and learning, social behavior, and physical health.

Current methods of assessing children's emotional reactions rely on facial, vocal, and postural channels of communication. (Erika Stone)

Emotions as Regulators of Cognitive Processing. A substantial body of evidence indicates that emotions have a profound influence on learning and cognitive processing. Campos and his collaborators (1983) point out that emotional behavior can lead to learning that is crucial for survival. For example, the newly mobile infant does not have to receive a shock from an electric outlet or fall down a steep staircase to learn to avoid these dangerous situations. Instead, the caregiver's emotional reactions are sufficient to get the baby to acquire these self-protective behaviors.

Emotions of the learner affect the storage and retrieval of information in memory. Research by Bower (1981) reveals that we remember things better when we are in the same emotional state in which we originally learned them. Using hypnotic suggestion, Bower induced a variety of emotional states in adults and found improved memory for word lists, childhood experiences, and personal events recorded in a daily diary when moods during learning and recall were congruent. In addition, emotions had a powerful effect on such cognitive processes as free association, imaginative fantasies, and judgments of others. For example, angry subjects generated angry free associations, reported hostile fantasies, and tended to find fault with other people.

Intensity of emotional arousal also affects performance on cognitive tasks, with the relationship generally following an inverted U-shaped function (see Figure 10.1). The effect of anxiety on school performance conforms to this pattern, with large and small amounts of anxiety leading to poorer outcomes than a moderate amount of anxiety, which can be facilitating (Sarason, 1980). This same inverted U has been found for a very different feeling state — happiness — among children as young as 16 months of age. After a group of toddlers played joyfully with puppets, they were given problems to solve in which they had to rotate a bar to bring a toy within reach. The greater the intensity of happiness expressed in the puppet play situation, the better the infants' subsequent problem solving, up to an intermediate point, after which performance declined. However, when a negative emotional state was induced by separating toddlers from their mothers prior to the problem-solving task, the U-shaped function did not hold. Instead, the more toddler distress upon separation, the poorer their performance on the tasks (Campos et al., 1983). Thus, recent evidence suggests that the well-known inverted U-shaped function between emotional intensity and cognitive performance may hold only for certain ages, emotional states, and situational conditions.

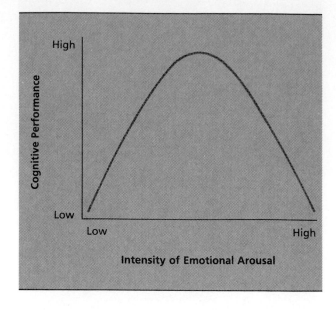

High

Cognitive Performance

Low

Low   High

Intensity of Emotional Arousal

Figure 10.1. Relationship of intensity of emotional arousal to cognitive performance.

Of course, any effort to determine which factor is more important in development — emotion or cognition — is a futile enterprise. We shall repeatedly encounter evidence in this chapter that demonstrates the reciprocal, interwoven relationship between the two. Nevertheless, the research cited above provides clear justification for placing more emphasis on the importance of emotions in learning and cognition than has been typical in the past.

Emotions as Regulators of Social Behavior. Besides their role in cognitive processing, emotions help organize behavior in social contexts. Children's emotional expressions, such as smiling, crying, and attentive interest, affect the behavior of caregivers in powerful ways, and beginning at an early age the emotional reactions of others also regulate children's emotional responses. For example, Tronick and his collaborators (1978) instructed mothers to assume either a still-faced, unreactive pose or a depressed emotional state. Babies as young as 3 months looked away from their mothers' faces and engaged in intense crying and protest behavior. Toward the end of the first year, infants deliberately seek emotional information from others and use it to appraise events about which they are uncertain, a phenomenon called *social referencing,* to which we return later in this chapter. The phenomenon is a clear demonstration of how infants rely on the emotions of others as crucial evaluative resources (Campos & Stenberg, 1981). Finally, another way emotions regulate social behavior is through *empathy,* the perception and vicarious experience of emotions expressed by others. Because empathy is of crucial significance in fostering prosocial and altruistic behavior, we also discuss its development in a subsequent section.

Emotions as Contributors to Physical Health. A growing body of evidence indicates that emotions affect physical health. When experienced for extended periods of time, negative emotions, such as depression, anxiety, and anger, are thought to affect the body's immunological system by lowering resistance to infection. Negative emotions also affect physical health when they are associated with prolonged changes in autonomic nervous system functioning.[1] In support of the connection between emo-

---

[1] You may wish to return to Chapter 3, page 102, to refresh your memory about some of the specific mechanisms through which emotional stress can influence physical health.

tional well-being and physical health, a longitudinal study of 100 Harvard graduates revealed that of those considered to be poorly adjusted during college, nearly half had become seriously ill or died by their early 50s, whereas among those in the best mental health, only 2 had become ill or died (Valliant, 1977). Evidence for a relationship between emotional well-being and physical health as early as infancy was reported by psychoanalyst René Spitz in the 1940s. Studying institutionalized infants, Spitz found that babies separated from their mothers during the first year of life not only became weepy, withdrawn, and depressed, but also lost weight and showed extreme susceptibility to infection, despite the fact that they received adequate physical care (Spitz, 1946).

Recent research indicates that certain emotional states that form the basis of enduring personality dispositions may contribute to the development of cardiovascular disease and cancer. The most widely publicized of these dispositions, the type A personality, has been linked to heart disease. As indicated in Box 10.1, developmental psychologists are currently studying the childhood origins of this disposition in an effort to prevent its later-life consequences as early as possible.

FOCUS ON THEORY, RESEARCH, AND APPLICATIONS

Box 10.1
Type A Behavior in Children

Theory. In the late 1950s, Friedman and Rosenman (1959) first presented evidence that linked the **type A personality** to increased risk of heart disease in adulthood. When confronted with competition-eliciting circumstances, type A adults exhibit excessive time consciousness, impatience, restlessness, anger, and competitiveness. The physiological correlates of these responses include elevated blood cholesterol levels (Glass et al., 1980) as well as heightened blood pressure during challenging tasks (Dembroski et al., 1979), factors that increase the chances of arteriosclerosis (hardening of the arteries). Statistics indicate that the incidence of heart disease is about twice as high in type A as opposed to type B individuals. Recently, researchers have begun to explore whether the type A behavior pattern and its cardiovascular correlates are already evident during the childhood years.

Research. Investigators generally distinguish type A from type B children by asking teachers to rate pupils in their classrooms on a variety of behaviors associated with the type A

personality (e.g., "This child is competitive"; "When this child has to wait for others, he [or she] becomes impatient"). Then children are subjected to a set of tasks designed to elicit type A responding. In one investigation, Matthews and Angulo (1980) found that type A second through sixth graders aggressed against a Bobo doll sooner and with less experimenter encouragement, won a car race against a female adult by a greater margin of victory, and emitted more impatient behaviors (sighed, squirmed, and clicked their tongues) during a frustrating drawing task than their type B counterparts. In another study involving younger children, type A and B 2- to 5-year-olds were paired with one another in competitive games. The A's were more often the winners. Furthermore, when observed in their classrooms, they showed more frequent interruptions of their peers, more facial signs of annoyance, and greater gross motor activity than B's (Vega-Lahr & Field, 1986). These findings suggest that the seeds of the type A personality may surface as early as the preschool years.

So far, at least two investigations have reported that type A children show elevated physiological responsiveness in competitive situations. Lundberg (1983) discovered that type A preschool children display a greater

rise in blood pressure than type Bs when confronted with the challenge of running as fast as possible up and down a day care center corridor. Studying 11- and 12-year-olds, Lawler and her colleagues (1981) reported a rise not only in blood pressure, but also in heart rate and galvanic skin response for type As under challenging task conditions.

Applications. The above findings provide convincing evidence that type A behavioral and physiological characteristics are already present in children. As yet it is not known if type A responses in childhood are predictive of heart disease in the same way they are in adulthood, although it is conceivable that they might be, for some evidence reveals that coronary artery pathology can begin as early as the first or second decade of life (Friedman, 1969).

Research on type A children is still in its early stages, and psychologists have much to discover about the constitutional and environmental foundations of the type A personality. Once more is known about factors that contribute to the emergence of stable type A behaviors, early intervention programs can be designed to prevent this important cause of heart disease in the fourth and fifth decades of life.

Theories of Emotional Development

In the sections below, we review three important theoretical approaches to emotional development — behaviorist, cognitive-developmental, and the new organizational approach. While organizational theories have gained in popularity because of their comprehensive explanatory power, each of these perspectives has made important contributions to our understanding of emotional development.

Behaviorist Theory. The early behaviorist, John Watson (1913), accorded emotional reactions a prominent role in explaining behavior. Watson proposed three innate emotions that he claimed to have observed in neonates: fear, elicited by loud noises or loss of support; rage, elicited by restriction of bodily movements; and love, evoked by tactile stimulation. As we indicated in Chapter 1, one of Watson's major empirical contributions was his finding that emotional responses to new stimuli can be learned through classical conditioning. By associating the appearance of a furry white rat with a loud, fear-eliciting sound, Watson produced a fear reaction (intense crying) to the rat as well as to other white furry objects in a 9-month-old baby (Watson & Raynor, 1920). Watson concluded that all emotional reactions came to be associated with novel stimuli in just this way. In the 1950s and 1960s, a second behaviorist paradigm, operant conditioning, became the focus of attention. Several researchers showed that infant smiling, vocalizing, and crying could be manipulated through the careful application of reinforcers and punishments (Brackbill, 1958; Etzel & Gewirtz, 1967; Rheingold, Gewirtz, & Ross, 1959).

Although some emotional reactions are acquired according to conditioning principles, the behaviorist approach to emotional development is a limited one. It cannot explain why some emotional responses emerge spontaneously, without any prior association with unpleasant experiences. For example, around 8 months of age, normal, family-reared babies often show fear of strangers. The fear occurs despite the fact that infants previously reacted positively to strangers and the strangers continue to smile and initiate playful interaction with the baby. Another difficulty with the behaviorist perspective is that it regards only overt expressions of emotion, not underlying affective states, as important. For example, a behaviorist would assume that a fearful, unhappy child who has given up sending signals to others about her anxious internal state is no longer emotionally troubled. Yet this conclusion runs the risk of leaving feelings untended that, in some instances, may have long-term consequences for the child's psychological adjustment.

Cognitive-developmental Discrepancy Theory. Instead of viewing emotions as central forces in development, cognitive-developmental theorists explain them in cognitive terms. The first to take this position was Donald Hebb (1946, 1949), who outlined a **discrepancy theory** of emotional development, which explained how distress reactions came to be elicited by novel stimuli. According to discrepancy theory, when the child encounters a new stimulus, it is compared to a mental representation, or scheme, of a familiar object. The child's emotional response to the stimulus is determined by the degree of similarity between the novel stimulus and the child's internal scheme. Little discrepancy produces very little distress, but as the magnitude of the discrepancy increases, the child's distress reaction intensifies. When the discrepancy is very great, the stimulus can no longer be assimilated. At this point, the child's distress reaction falls off until there is no reaction at all. As shown in Figure 10.2, Hebb's theory predicts an inverted U-shaped relationship between cognitive discrepancy and emotional distress.

Hebb's theory was later modified by Kagan (1971, 1974; Kagan, Kearsley, & Zelazo, 1978) and McCall (McCall & McGhee, 1977), who argued that it could account for a wide variety of emotional phenomena. For example, the positive emotions of interest and smiling were believed to be produced by a moderate degree of

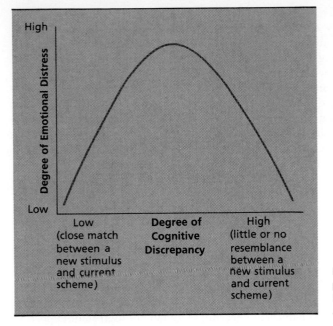

Figure 10.2. Hebb's proposed relationship between cognitive discrepancy and emotional distress.

discrepancy between a current scheme and new event. Fear of strangers was thought to occur just after the child formed a coherent scheme for the mother, but the discrepancy between the maternal scheme and unfamiliar people was still fairly large.

Cognitive discrepancy is especially effective in explaining children's interest in many objects and stimuli in the environment. McCall, Kennedy, and Applebaum (1977) reviewed the results of many studies in which infants were exposed to a wide variety of visual stimulus arrays (e.g., checkerboards, random shapes, arrows, and three-dimensional objects) that varied systematically in their divergence from a standard. In each case, infants looked longest at members of a stimulus set that were moderately discrepant from the standard with which they had been familiarized. For example, 10-week-old babies who were first shown a picture of an arrow in one orientation (e.g., ↕) looked longest at new arrows that were moderately discrepant (↗) as opposed to widely discrepant (↔) in orientation from the initial stimulus. Applied to everyday life, discrepancy theory explains why young children play happily with new toys while ignoring familiar old ones, and why parents and teachers often find it useful to rotate toys in and out of children's play space every few weeks as a means of fostering absorbed interest in objects. Discrepancy theory is also consistent with a phenomenon that we addressed in Chapter 4: overwhelming children with too much stimulation in the form of an overabundance of patterns, objects, or activities can be disturbing and lead them to withdraw from their surroundings.

Although discrepancy theory works well in explaining children's exploration of the inanimate environment, it does poorly when it comes to providing a full account of children's emotional reactions. In the case of fear of strangers, one major difficulty is that babies have well-established memories of their mothers long before fear of strangers emerges late in the first year. Yet discrepancy theory implies that as soon as the maternal scheme is present, distress reactions to discrepant stimuli should appear. Furthermore, in one intriguing investigation of infants' emotional reactions to *different* strangers — a normal-sized adult, an adult midget, and a 5-year-old child — infant reactions did not conform to discrepancy theory predictions. The babies responded with fear to the full-sized adult, friendliness to the unfamiliar child, and uncertainty to the midget. If the infants had used a maternal scheme as the reference point for making cognitive comparisons, the strange child and small adult, not the normal-sized adult, should have elicited the greatest negative affect (Brooks & Lewis, 1976). Discrepancy theory also has difficulty accounting for situational influences that modify the quality of emotional reactions. For example, when infants are held in their mother's arms, smiling at strangers predominates and crying is rare, but when separated from the mother and especially when picked up, infants often cry in response to a stranger (Bronson, 1972).

A final difficulty with discrepancy theory is that it cannot explain why very familiar experiences do not consistently elicit boredom, withdrawal, or a lack of emotional response. For example, the approach of the mother (who is a very familiar person indeed) repeatedly elicits smiling and pleasure from infants, and preschool children are known for their tireless requests to have the same story read to them over and over again. There is no question that infants and children display positive affect to some events with which they are thoroughly familiar.

Lewis and Michalson (1983) clarify the role that discrepancy plays in emotional reactions by suggesting that its chief consequence is not to produce a particular affective response, but instead to arouse and alert the organism. Specific emotional reactions occur only after a discrepancy is noticed, and they depend on situational context as well as the momentary goals of the individual. For example, a mother putting on a mask is a discrepant event that will capture the attention of a baby, but whether the infant responds by laughing or crying depends on the situation and the baby's needs at the time. If the baby is hungry and seated in her high chair expecting to eat, she may cry because she cannot comprehend how her masked mother is related to the context of eating. However, if the mask is donned in the context of play, it may produce laughter and great delight. In that situation, the baby easily grasps its game-like quality.

New Organizational Theories. New theories, gathered together under the **organizational approach to emotional development,** have emerged as a result of the rediscovery of the importance of emotions. Although a number of different organizational theories exist (e.g., Campos et al., 1983; Emde, 1980; Sroufe, 1979), all share an emphasis on emotions as central forces in virtually all aspects of human behavior.

Organizational theorists recognize the adaptive role of emotions in fostering exploration of the environment, retreat from threatening situations, and bonding human beings together. In addition, the organizational approach is unique in viewing emotions as important in the development of self-awareness, a topic we will take up in detail in Chapter 11. For example, the sense of interest and excitement associated with acting on novel objects provides infants with their first opportunities to gain a notion of the *self* as *agent,* capable of affecting events in their surrounding world.[2] Once a rudimentary sense of self has developed by the second year of life, complex emotions, such as shame, guilt, envy, and pride, that are related to one's sense of self, begin to appear (Campos et al., 1983; Izard, 1978; Lewis & Brooks, 1978; Sroufe, 1979). Thus, emotions facilitate the emergence of self-awareness, and when the beginnings of a stable self-image exist, the door is opened for the experience of new, increasingly complex emotional states.

Most organizational theorists also see emotion and cognition as intimately interdependent. Lewis, Sullivan, and Michalson (1984) liken the continuous, dynamic interplay between emotion and cognition to a musical fugue[3] in which these two major themes of experience are inseparably interwoven into a single stream of behavior. In one study, they reported evidence for the existence of reciprocal emotion-cog-

---

[2] You may wish to return to Chapter 6 to review Piaget's description of how infants' sensorimotor exploratory activity eventually leads to a decline in egocentrism and a growing appreciation of the self as an object in a world of objects.

[3] A fugue is a musical composition in which several statements of a theme are interwoven in such a way that they seem to appear, disappear, and reappear as they weave in and out and respond to one another.

nition relationships as early as the first 6 months of life. Babies were presented with an apparatus in which pulling a lever resulted in a pleasant audiovisual event (a color slide of a happy baby and a recording of a children's song). Tracking facial reactions and vocalizations as infants learned the task, the researchers found interest high upon first exposure to the situation, increases in vigilance and wariness as initial arm pulls produced the first recurrences of the rewarding stimulus, and a rise in interest, surprise, and happiness as a higher rate of arm-pulling revealed that the babies had figured out the connection between action and outcome. Finally, indications of sadness emerged at the end of the task (see Figure 10.3)

All organizational theorists agree that examination of discrete emotions, and not just the intensity of globally positive and negative states, is necessary to understand the emotion-cognition relationship. In the study above, emotional reactions served both as consequences of prior learning and the foundation for each new learning phase. For example, infants' negative emotion of sadness at the end of the task may have been set off by the peak of enjoyment that followed their discovery of what made the audiovisual stimulus recur. Among adults, a negative emotion can be precipitated by a preceding positive one (Solomon & Corbitt, 1974), and "post-task blues" (provided they are not too intense) may help individuals reorient toward new tasks. For the infants described above, sadness may have served this very function, acting as "the first note in the next sequence of the cognitive emotional fugue" (Lewis, Sullivan, & Michalson, 1984, p. 283).

Finally, organizational theorists emphasize that emotional development includes increasing control over the expression of affect, as well as developmental changes in the conditions under which affect is expressed (Campos et al., 1983). At first, babies modulate emotional arousal by looking away or engaging in mouthing and sucking when its intensity gets too high. As motor development proceeds, infants can approach or withdraw from an emotion-arousing stimulus in response to their affective state. Later on, the emergence of representation and language provides an additional means for controlling emotional experience. When an 18-month-old is told by her mother, "I'll be back soon. You play with the dolly," the infant may look longingly at

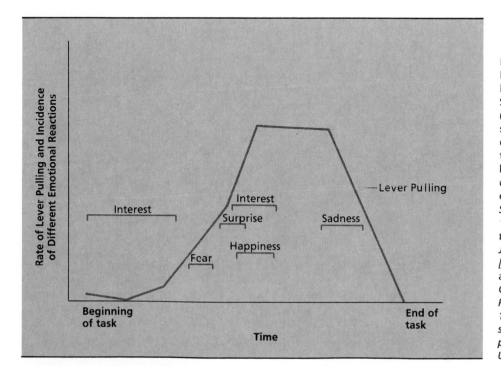

Figure 10.3. Relationship between emotions and learning in the Lewis, Sullivan, and Michalson (1984) study. The figure shows the peaks in various discrete emotional reactions that occurred as infants learned to pull a lever to produce a pleasant audiovisual event. *(From M. Lewis, M. W. Sullivan, & L. Michalson, 1984, "The Cognitive-Emotional Fugue." In C. E. Izard, J. Kagan, & R. B. Zajonc [Eds.], Emotions, Cognition, and Behavior. New York: Cambridge University Press. Pp. 280–281. © Copyright 1984 by Cambridge University Press. Reprinted with the permission of Cambridge University Press.)*

the door and then turn to the doll and repeat, "Mama go, play dolly." In this instance, linguistic representation helps control emotions, because it reminds the child that her mother will return after an intervening period of play (Sroufe, 1979). With age, emotions also become socialized. Cultures specify *emotional display rules* — the circumstances under which it is acceptable to express emotions — and investigators have begun to study how children learn these rules so that, by late childhood, few emotions are expressed as openly and freely as they were during the early years of life.

In summary, organizational theorists believe that emotions are major adaptive forces in human behavior, are inseparably intertwined with cognition, and undergo important developmental changes in the circumstances in which they are expressed. Yet organizational theorists also differ from one another. As we shall see below, one major difference of opinion concerns how early discrete emotional states are present in the young infant.

Development of the Expression of Discrete Emotions

Some organizational theorists believe that a set of differentiated, basic emotions exists at birth. Others believe that the neonates' emotional capacities are more limited and that qualitatively distinct emotions gradually emerge from early global arousal states. We consider current evidence on this controversy, along with research on the development of some basic emotions, in the sections that follow.

To What Extent Are Newborns Capable of Discrete Emotional Expressions? In Chapter 4, we indicated that newborn infants respond with distinct facial reactions to sweet versus sour and bitter substances (Steiner, 1979) and display a set of differentiated cries (Wolff, 1969). These findings offer support for the existence of discrete emotional states in the neonate. Even theorists who believe that a full set of basic emotions is not present in early infancy acknowledge that a few, such as interest, distress, and disgust, are already observable in the newborn baby (e.g., Sroufe, 1979).

Campos and his colleagues (1983) take the position that all of the **basic emotions,** including happiness, interest, surprise, fear, anger, sadness, and disgust, are probably present in the early weeks of life, and interviews with mothers about their infants' emotional expressions support this view. In two such investigations, the majority of mothers with infants under 3 months of age reported that their babies showed surprise, anger, and fear, in addition to the reactions of interest, happiness, and distress that have been observed in laboratory studies (Johnson et al., 1982; Klinnert et al., 1984). The mothers based their judgments on infant facial, vocal, and gestural cues. For example, when asked how they knew their babies were surprised, they described components of the classic "surprise expression," such as wide open eyes and mouth opened in an "O" shape, along with a bodily startle response. These reports indicate that there may be a remarkably diverse core of emotions present in early infancy (Emde, 1983).

The Development of Some Basic Emotions. Among the basic emotions, happiness, anger, sadness, and fear have received the most research attention. We take up their early course of development below.

Happiness. The literature on children's emotions is replete with studies of smiling and laughter. As one of the infant's first emotional and social behaviors, the smile "serves many masters" (Kagan, 1971), playing an important role in the child's total development. Smiling simultaneously serves as a mechanism for release of tension and expression of emotional pleasure in cognitive mastery. The smile also elicits positive emotions in adults, binding them to the infant and young child and thereby serving social and survival functions. The functions of smiling are complementary and interrelated. We shall see how this is the case as we trace the development of smiling, and its more intense and joyful counterpart, laughter, below.

The first smiles, which can be observed soon after birth, are called **endogenous smiles** because they occur in the absence of external stimulation, most commonly during REM sleep (Emde, Gaensbauer, & Harmon, 1976). Already, the relationship between smiling and tension release is present, for electrical recordings of brain activity indicate that the endogenous smile is associated with spontaneous neural discharge in the brain stem and limbic system[4] (Sroufe & Waters, 1976).

Exogenous smiles, those elicited by external stimulation, appear during the first and second weeks of life. Initially, they are most easily elicited by low level tactile and auditory stimulation while the infant is asleep or drowsy. By the third week, the infant begins to smile in response to mild stimulation in the waking state, with light touches, blowing on the skin, gentle jogging, and a soft, high-pitched voice being the most effective stimuli (Emde & Koenig, 1969; Wolff, 1963). By the fourth week, the mother's voice is especially effective, even causing the baby to interrupt a feeding in order to smile. Around the fifth week, infants also begin to smile at visual stimuli, but the stimulus must be active and dynamic — a nodding head, or a moving object that jumps suddenly across the baby's field of vision (Wolff, 1963). In the second month, the human face becomes a potent stimulus of smiling as long as it remains in motion, leading the smiling response at this time to be called the **social smile** (Wolff, 1963; Shirley, 1933). Presentation of stationary faces or other static visual stimuli does not consistently yield smiling until about the eighth or tenth week. By this time, the initial soft turning up of the corners of the mouth that occurred during the neonatal period has become a broad, active grin that is often accompanied by pleasurable cooing (Sroufe & Waters, 1976).

Perhaps you can already see that changes in infant smiling parallel the development of the baby's perceptual capacities — in particular, sensitivity to moving stimuli and complex visual patterns, including the human face — that we discussed in Chapter 4. Investigators agree that one important elicitor of smiling is active processing of stimulus information, which goes on during physiological excitation — relaxation cycles in the waking state. The smile occurs at the point at which the infant assimilates or masters the stimulus event, after which arousal begins to decrease.

Some psychologists think that the earliest waking-state exogenous smiles differ very little from those that occur during REM sleep. They believe that smiling is not really mediated by *active* cognitive processing of information until around 3 months of age (Emde, Gaensbauer, & Harmon, 1976; Sroufe, 1979; Sroufe & Waters, 1976). About this time, laboratory studies show that rate of smiling gradually habituates, or declines in response to repeatedly presented visual stimuli (Shultz & Zigler, 1970; Zelazo, 1972; Zelazo & Komer, 1971). These results suggest an active effort on the part of babies of several months of age to assimilate the content of stimulation, followed by a pleasurable emotional response that falls off as mastery is attained. However, there is dispute about whether the smiles of younger infants are purely passive, reflexive reactions. Oster (1978) found that in babies as young as 3 weeks, brow-knitting (associated with concentration and puzzlement in adults) preceded exogenous smiles. She believes that the knitted brow reflects an active attempt on the part of even very young babies to "make sense of" or assimilate complex patterns of stimulation.

Laughter is a more intense expression of positive affect than smiling, requiring a steeper build-up and more rapid release of tension. It generally does not appear until 12 to 16 weeks of age (Sroufe & Wunsch, 1972), although it has occasionally been seen as early as 5 to 9 weeks (Wolff, 1963). As with smiling, infants' first laughs are to

---

[4] The limbic system is a portion of the forebrain involved in the regulation of emotional behavior and learning.

Infants' first smiles and laughs occur in response to tactile and auditory stimulation. (Myrleen Ferguson/PhotoEdit)

physical and auditory stimulation, but the stimulus must be dynamic and intrusive, as when the mother says playfully, "I'm gonna get you" and kisses the baby's tummy. From 4 to 6 months of age, laughter occurs in response to less vigorous tactile and vocal stimulation, and in the second half of the first year, babies laugh at more subtle visual stimuli — a soundless game of peekaboo or the caregiver's approach with a covered face. By 12 months of age, infants laugh at situations providing obvious elements of discrepancy, such as the mother walking like a penguin or sucking on the baby's bottle. Around this time, infants also start to laugh in anticipation of events, such as the mother beginning to kiss the baby's tummy. As with early smiling, events that produce laughter go hand in hand with the baby's cognitive achievements.[5] However, laughter reflects faster assimilation of stimuli than smiling. Laughter generally builds from neutral reactions and smiles, during which the infant forms an initial representation of the novel stimulus. When the stimulus event occurs again, the prior mental representation hastens the infant's processing, and a laugh follows (Sroufe & Wunsch, 1972).

In addition to their role in cognitive mastery, expressions of happiness take on a vital social function, eliciting the approach and positive engagement of others. By 3 months of age, the smile has become a major component in the infant's greeting behavior, is performed differentially to familiar figures, and is seen more frequently when infants are with people than when they are alone (Vine, 1973). The baby's smile motivates the caregiver to be affectionate as well as more stimulating, for it signals well-being and encourages the caregiver to repeat cognitively interesting events. Thus, the social and cognitive consequences of the baby's expressions of happiness support one another. In addition, changes in the stimuli babies smile at offer a window through which we can observe cognitive growth.

Anger and sadness. During the first two months of life, infants express anger in response to physical restraint, such as having their arms forcibly held (Stenberg, 1982), and to painful stimuli. In a longitudinal study of babies' facial expressions following routine inoculations from 2 to 18 months, the all-out emergency reaction of pain declined and was replaced by an increase in anger, with the largest rise occurring

---

[5] Infants' developing grasp of object permanence underlies their amusement at peekaboo, and their ability to anticipate events is the reason they laugh as soon as their mothers initiate the tummy-kissing game. Turn back to the discussion of Piaget's sensorimotor stage in Chapter 6 if you need to refresh your memory about these important cognitive achievements.

between 7 and 19 months (see Figure 10.4) (Izard, Hembree, & Huebner, 1987). By the end of the first year, anger is sometimes observed in response to brief separations from the mother (Hyson & Izard, 1983; Shiller, Izard, & Hembree, 1986) as well as other blocked goals, such as the removal of a teething biscuit from the baby's mouth. The intensity of the anger response is affected by situational conditions. Anger rises with the repetition of a frustrating event and when a familiar individual from whom the infant expects comforting behavior is the agent of frustration (Stenberg, Campos, & Emde, 1983).

The sharp rise in anger after 7 months of age may be due to improvements in infants' cognitive capacity to appraise the agent of a painful stimulus or a blocked goal. In addition, maturation of inhibitory mechanisms in the brain may enable infants to cut short a reflexive pain response and substitute an angry emotional reaction. The rise in angry reactions at the end of the first year can also be viewed as adaptive. Improved motor capacities permit older babies to use the energy mobilized by anger either to defend themselves or to overcome obstacles (Izard, Hembree, & Huebner, 1987). At the same time, the expression of anger is a potent social signal that motivates adults to comfort a suffering infant and, in the case of separation, may discourage them from leaving again soon (Bowlby, 1973).

Expressions of sadness also occur in response to painful stimuli and brief separations, but they are far less frequent than anger (Izard, Hembree, & Huebner, 1987; Shiller, Izard, & Hembree, 1986). However, infants who are separated from their mothers for extended periods of time and who do not receive care from a sensitive parental substitute show a dramatic increase in sadness that corresponds to a severe depressive reaction (Gaensbauer, 1980; Spitz, 1945). We will discuss the significance of this response later when we take up the topic of infant-mother attachment.

Fear. Fear reactions occur infrequently during the first 7 months of life, but like anger they rise dramatically between 7 and 9 months of age. For example, infants of this age display fear of heights, and they sometimes hesitate before reaching for novel

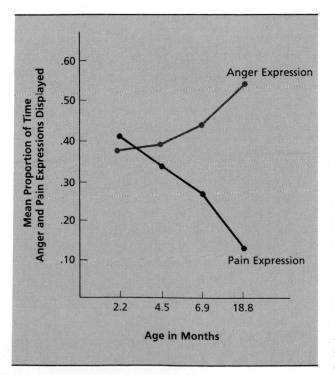

Figure 10.4. Proportion of time following a routine inoculation that infants of different ages showed pain and anger facial expressions in the Izard, Hembree, and Huebner (1987) study. *(From C. E. Izard, E. A. Hembree, & R. R. Huebner, 1987, "Infants' Emotion Expressions to Acute Pain,"* Developmental Psychology, 23, *105–113.* © Copyright 1987 by the American Psychological Association. Reprinted by permission of the author.)*

objects that they grasped immediately at an earlier age (Schaffer, Greenwood, & Parry, 1971). At this time, expressions of fear in response to strange adults are frequently observed; this reaction is commonly called **stranger distress** (Gaensbauer, Emde, & Campos, 1976). At the same time that increased fearfulness emerges, a diverse array of additional developmental changes is also taking place: new sensorimotor acquisitions, a rise in protest reactions when the baby is separated from the familiar caregiver, and the emergence of self-produced locomotion. Fear of strangers is best understood in relation to these cognitive, social, and exploratory capacities. But before we see how it fits in, let's discuss the characteristics of this new wariness of unfamiliar people.

Stranger distress typically occurs when an unfamiliar adult approaches, greets, and then picks up the infant (Schaffer, 1966; Emde, Gaensbauer, & Harmon, 1976), but it is strongly influenced by situational factors. Babies, may behave in a friendly fashion toward strangers if the threat posed by the unknown person is reduced by a period of infant-controlled acquaintance before the stranger comes near. For example, if infants are allowed to move about the environment freely while the stranger sits still, babies frequently display positive and curious behavior toward unknown adults, including smiling, visual exploration, and spontaneous approach, although they rarely make physical contact (Bretherton & Ainsworth, 1974; Harmon, Morgan, & Klein, 1977; Horner, 1980). The adult's style of interaction also makes a difference. If the stranger presents an attractive toy, begins to play a familiar game, or approaches the infant slowly as opposed to quickly and abruptly, the baby's fear can be reduced. Close proximity of the mother also serves to allay a fearful reaction (Rheingold & Eckerman, 1973; Ross, & Goldman, 1977; Trause, 1977).

Between 7 and 9 months of age, many infants display stranger distress at the approach of an unfamiliar adult. (Mimi Forsyth/ Monkmeyer Press Photo Service)

The fact that stranger distress is influenced by situational context helps us understand the significance of greater fearfulness around 8 months of age. Like other affective responses, fear has an adaptive function that is especially relevant at the end of the first year. It holds in check the baby's compelling exploratory urge to venture away from the caregiver, which comes with the onset of crawling and walking (Ainsworth, 1973; Bowlby, 1969). The rise in fear responses highlights the caregiver's role as a **secure base** from which exploration of the environment can be made and as a "haven of safety" when distress occurs. As part of this adaptive system, encounters with unfamiliar individuals activate two conflicting tendencies in the baby: approach (signified by interest and friendly affiliation) versus avoidance (signified by wariness and fear). The infant's resulting behavior is a careful balance between the two (Clarke-Stewart, 1978). But what tips this balance in one direction or the other has to do with new cognitive capacities, for the older infant has a more advanced ability to appraise unfamiliar experiences.

As we mentioned earlier, infants do not show the same degree of wariness to all unfamiliar people. They rarely respond with fear to small children, although why this is the case is not completely clear. Lewis and Brooks's (1978) explanation is that once the infant develops a rudimentary concept of the self as separate from the surrounding world, the self begins to be used as a basis of comparison in encounters with unfamiliar people, and the cognitive determination that small children are more like the self than adults leads the infant to be less afraid. The unique stimulus value of small children may also play a role, especially their animated and friendly behavior.

Eventually, children's fear of strangers wanes as their developing cognitive capacities permit them to differentiate more effectively between threatening and non-threatening encounters. In addition, a broader array of strategies for coping with fear, including improved locomotion and the capacity to represent the whereabouts and return of the mother, leads to more effective control over the fearful affect around two years of age (Sroufe, 1977). Thus, infant reactions to strangers can only be understood in relation to a complex set of factors, including the context of the encounter with the stranger, the adaptiveness of the fear response, and the baby's emerging cognitive competencies.

The Socialization of Emotional Expression. Society dictates how and under what circumstances particular affects should be expressed. Children's acquisition of conventionally accepted **emotional display rules** is crucial for successful social interaction with others. For example, an individual who openly expresses dislike for an unattractive birthday present or who laughs in response to the injury of another runs the risk of serious negative social consequences, ranging from disapproval to outright scorn and rejection. In addition, membership in society creates the need for certain **complex emotions,** such as shame, guilt, envy, and pride. These feelings result from evaluation of the self by other people (shame and guilt) or comparison of the self to others (envy and pride), and they underscore important societal standards. In the following two sections, we consider these important facets of the socialization of emotional expression.

Acquiring Emotional Display Rules. As early as the first few months of life, infants are exposed to socialization experiences aimed at suppressing emotional expression, particularly negative affect. Malatesta and her colleagues (Malatesta & Haviland, 1982; Malatesta et al., 1986) filmed mothers playing with their 2- to 7-month-old babies. The mothers showed an overall decline in acknowledgment of infant emotional expressions as the babies increased in age. Although sometimes they imitated their babies' emotional reactions, they were selective in the way that they did so. Imitations were restricted to the positive emotions of interest, happiness, and surprise; mothers rarely duplicated negative emotional displays.

Although caregiver shaping of emotional behavior begins early, it is not until well into elementary school that children become adept at regulating their own emotional reactions. In a study in which 6- to 12-year-old children were interviewed about their likes and dislikes and then asked to deliberately act differently than they felt, the 10- to 12-year-olds were better at inhibiting negative emotional expressions than younger children. Interestingly, children of all ages showed high "leakage" of their true feelings when asked to control a positive emotional state. There are fewer rules against displaying positive as opposed to negative affect, and children may have difficulty masking positive feelings because they have had little experience in doing so (Shennum & Bugental, 1982).

During middle childhood, children do not just achieve better use of display rules, they develop a conscious awareness and understanding of them. Saarni (1979) presented 6-, 8-, and 10-year-olds with hypothetical scenarios involving a child in a stressful situation with an onlooker present. For example, in one, the child boasted about his skating ability and afterwards fell down. The subjects were asked to choose from an array of facial expressions the one that ended the scene and to explain why the choice was appropriate. The 10-year-olds exceeded the 6- and 8-year-olds in the number of display rules they used and the complexity of reasoning they gave as the basis for picking the final facial expression. In addition, many more older children justified the use of display rules by referring to social norms (e.g., "It's impolite to show you feel that way"). In contrast, younger children justified them as a way to avoid scolding and ridicule from others or maintain self-esteem (e.g., "He'd be pretty stupid to show he's hurt after he's been bragging how good he is"). Saarni (1982) believes that children initially learn to conform to display rules as a way to avoid punishment and gain the approval of others. Eventually they see that the rule is consistently applied over time, and they come to understand it as a generally accepted standard for expressive behavior.

Successful use of display rules and conscious understanding of them develop in tandem and are facilitated by socialization experiences and cognitive development. Relevant cognitive influences are consciousness of the distinction between inner emotional experience and expressive behavior and advanced perspective-taking abilities that enable the older child to view the self from the perspective of others (Saarni, 1982; Shennum & Bugental, 1982). Better muscle coordination also contributes to older children's improved ability to regulate facial, vocal, and gestural expressions so that they conform to display rules.

The Emergence of Complex Emotions. Only at the end of infancy do complex emotions, such as shame, guilt, envy, and pride, emerge. An important feature of these emotions is that they involve either injury to or enhancement of the person's sense of self. Shame involves injury to important aspects of the self-concept, guilt involves injury to one's moral standards, envy is a negative appraisal of the self's ability to secure desired goods and experiences, and pride involves delight in the self's achievements. These complex emotions have much in common with basic emotions, including their capacity to influence the individual's cognition and social behavior and the fact that they are adaptive. For example, guilt plays an important role in self-responsibility and morality, and shame, pride, and envy motivate the achievement of socially valued skills and goals.[6]

But complex emotions are also different from basic emotions, in that they require specific socialization experiences to develop (Campos et al, 1983; Erikson, 1950; Harter, Wright, & Bresnick, 1987). For example, children must first have experiences in which the parent is ashamed or proud of the child to feel shame or pride themselves. In addition, children must be taught what situations appropriately elicit com-

---

[6] It is important to note that any of these emotions can be maladaptive if they are either too intense or last for too long a time (Campos et al., 1983)

plex emotions in their own culture. In American society, children are taught to feel pride over individual achievement, and they engage in smiling and general excitement after winning a game or getting good grades. Among the Zuni Indians, children learn that the goals of the individual must be subordinated to the group. Shame and embarrassment—lowering the eyes and hanging the head—occur in response to purely personal success (Benedict, 1934).

According to Sroufe (1979), children show evidence of experiencing shame by 18 months and guilt and pride by 3 years of age. Envy has also been observed in preschool children (Freud & Dann, 1951). However, even though behavioral manifestations of these emotions are present early, the circumstances under which children experience them change markedly over the elementary school years. For example, when provided with vignettes designed to evoke pride (e.g., a child accomplishing a gymnastic feat) and shame (e.g., a child taking money from a jar that belongs to her parents) and asked how they would feel, early elementary age children only reported the appropriate emotion if an adult was there to observe the act. In contrast, older children reported experiencing the emotion in the absence of observation by others, and they provided much better definitions of shame and pride than their younger counterparts (Harter, Wright, & Bresnick, 1987). In another study, which asked 6- to 11-year-old children to tell about experiences that made them feel guilty, the youngest subjects reported feeling guilty for any act that could be described as wrongdoing, even if it was accidental. Older children reported guilt for clearly intentional wrongdoing, such as ignoring one's responsibilities, cheating, or lying (Graham, Doubleday, & Guarino, 1984). Taken together, these investigations show that complex emotions are *outcome-related* for the youngest children. Experiencing them is dependent on others' reactions and obvious consequences of one's behavior. Eventually, complex affects are experienced in the absence of parental surveillance and are integrated with a conscious awareness of the self as a causal agent.

In summary, although a set of basic emotions may be present in the newborn infant, the development of emotional expression is a gradual process that continues throughout early and middle childhood. Changes in the expression of happiness, anger, and fear during the first year reflect the infant's growing cognitive capacities and serve social as well as survival functions. From an early age, children are exposed to socialization experiences aimed at suppressing the free expression of emotion. However, it is not until well into the elementary school years that children are adept at conforming to emotional display rules, an achievement that goes hand in hand with cognitive development. Finally, socialization experiences and cognitive development also support the appearance and refinement of complex emotions during the preschool and elementary school years.

Recognizing and Responding to the Emotions of Others

In addition to emotional expression, children's recognition and responsiveness to the emotional signals of others are important. In the sections below, we consider how children's sensitivity to the affective behavior of other people changes with age.

Emotional Recognition in Infancy. The ability to respond to the facial expressions of others is evident early in the first year of life. Habituation studies of infant perception show that babies can discriminate some aspects of facial configurations during the first six months (see Chapter 4), and we noted earlier that infants as young as 3 months of age become upset when confronted with the depressed, immobile faces of their mothers.

However, investigators are not sure whether young infants' differential responding to facial expressions actually reflects sensitivity to emotional cues, or whether they are responding to featural details of the human face that have no true emotional significance (Nelson, 1987). Consequently, child development specialists have not been able to pinpoint exactly when infants first begin to meaningfully interpret emotional information conveyed by others. What little research there is indicates that infants recognize and respond to a number of discrete emotions by 5 to 7 months of age, an ability that improves over the second half of the first year (Buhler, 1930; Kreutzer & Charlesworth, 1973; Walker-Andrews, 1986). By 8 or 9 months, babies actively seek out information about other people's feelings, and social referencing begins at this time.

Social Referencing. **Social referencing** involves relying on another person's emotional reaction to form one's own appraisal of an uncertain situation. Two major cognitive prerequisites acquired by the end of the first year enable infants to engage in social referencing. First, as indicated in the section above, infants can recognize the affective messages of others. Second, they start to evaluate encounters with events and objects in the environment, for they pause longer to study a new object or person than they did at a younger age.

Research shows that the mother's emotional expression (e.g., happiness, fear, or anger) influences whether the baby will show distress in reaction to a stranger (Boccia & Campos, 1983), be willing to approach an unfamiliar toy (Svejda & Campos, 1982), or cross an uncertain drop-off on the visual cliff (Sorce et al., 1981). In fact, the mother's provision of affective cues during moments of uncertainty may be a major reason that she serves as a secure base for exploration. In one study, 2-year-olds were observed under three conditions: when the mother was visible in a play room and facing the child; when the mother was visible but had her back turned; and when she was seated behind a partition. The children showed a strong desire to be within "eyeshot" of their mothers. In the latter two conditions, they positioned themselves within the mother's visual field for nearly half the play period and were willing to abandon exploration of an attractive set of toys in order to do so (Carr, Dabbs, & Carr, 1975). Staying within the caregiver's visual field is one means of retaining access to her facial and gestural cues. The importance of the caregiver as a source of emotional information in uncertain situations is also evident in the tendency of infants to look toward her after falls or other painful events. Many parents are aware that, depending on their own emotional reaction, the baby's tears can be prevented or encouraged in these situations.

The infant's capacity to make use of others' emotional cues improves with age. Younger babies can only engage in *direct* social referencing. That is, they make use of affective information that is transmitted directly to them. By the middle of the second year, infants engage in *indirect* social referencing in that they pick up emotional cues by watching the behavior of other people with whom they are not directly engaged. For example, a 15-month-old will become less wary of a stranger as the result of just observing the stranger conversing pleasantly with her mother (Feiring, Lewis, & Starr, 1984). A 10-month-old must be directly smiled at and talked to in a soothing tone of voice to profit from the caregiver's emotional cues (Feinman & Lewis, 1983). Although there is little research on social referencing during the early preschool years, sensitivity to other people's emotional evaluations undoubtedly becomes more finely tuned as cognitive and language development proceed. Also, while infants look to their mothers as the favored source for social referencing, an expanding social world leads older children to include other significant individuals, such as fathers, siblings, teachers, and peers, as influential sources of affective appraisal (Feinman, 1982).

Social referencing is a vital information-processing strategy when infants and children are faced with new situations in which they do not know how to respond. Social referencing is also an important mediator of socialization. Through it children learn how mature members of society react emotionally to a great many everyday events.

Further Changes in Emotional Recognition During Childhood. Children emerge from infancy with a sophisticated ability to discriminate and respond appropriately to the positive and negative affective cues of others. Additional advances in the ability to recognize and understand other people's emotions take place over the childhood years.

During the preschool period, children acquire a vocabulary of emotional terms and underlying concepts that facilitates their recognition of emotional stimuli. However, when very young children use a word to describe a feeling, they often do not mean exactly what an adult means by the term. When preschoolers are asked to match words with photos of different facial expressions, their performance is far less accurate than that of adults. For example, for the word "mad," 3-year-olds are just as likely to select a picture illustrating an expression of disgust or fear as one of an angry expression. Preschoolers' mislabeling of emotional expressions is not random. Particular emotions have characteristics in common, and children initially confuse related affects. In other words, young children initially *overextend* emotion-laden terms, just as they do many other additions to their vocabulary during the preschool years (see Chapter 9). By age 5 children's use of many emotional terms is adultlike in nature (Bullock & Russell, 1984).

Inferences about how people feel can be made on the basis of a variety of situational as well as expressive cues. Research reveals an age-related increase in children's ability to take multiple sources of information into account in interpreting emotional reactions. In a study by Gnepp (1983), children were provided with conflicting cues about a person's feelings. One cue was situational and the other was conveyed through a facial expression. For example, children were shown a picture of a happy-faced child with a broken bicycle. When asked how the child in the picture felt, preschoolers tended to rely on the facial cue alone. By sixth grade, children showed no preference for one cue over the other, suggesting that older children consider neither type of information sufficient by itself for making inferences about another's feelings. Older children are also better at taking past experiences into account in explaining why a person reacts in an atypical way to a particular situation. Children are not very adept at this skill until the end of middle childhood and beyond, and it is probably dependent on repeated exposure to occasions in which people do not respond with an expected emotional reaction. By trying to make sense of these occurrences, children may slowly learn that prior experiences are relevant to how people interpret current events and that not all people respond emotionally in the same way (Gnepp & Gould, 1985).

Finally, by 8 or 9 years of age, children recognize that a person can experience more than one emotion at a time — in other words, that they can have "mixed feelings." They are also aware that people can change their feelings by using self-initiated strategies (e.g., "When sad, try to think of something to make yourself happy"). This advanced appreciation of affective states is a function of cognitive developmental achievements of the middle childhood years, but the child's opportunities for modeling and reinforcement of emotional sensitivity are also important (Carroll & Steward, 1984).

The Development of Empathy. In **empathy,** recognition and expression of emotion are intimately interwoven, for both awareness of the feeling states of others and a vicarious affective response to those feelings are required for empathic behavior. Current theorists agree that empathy involves a complex interaction of cognition and affect. The cognitive ability to distinguish among different emotions, perspective-taking capacity to comprehend another person's emotional experience, and feelings aroused within the self all combine to produce a mature empathic response (Hoffman, 1984).

Hoffman (1984) believes that empathic responding is possible at any age, but a growing ability to discern the feelings of others and imagine oneself in another's place leads the empathic experience to change over the course of childhood. Consistent with Hoffman's idea, empathy seems to have roots early in development, for as mentioned in Chapter 4, newborn babies will cry in response to the cry of another baby. The behavior is only a primitive precursor of mature empathic behavior, because babies cannot yet put themselves in another individual's place and imagine what the other person is feeling. But it suggests that human beings come into the world predisposed to experience the emotional states of others.

Like the complex emotions we discussed earlier, empathy requires a cognitive appreciation of the self as separate and distinct from other people. As children become aware of this distinction during the second year of life, for the first time they recognize when another individual, and not the self, is the victim of a distressing experience (Thompson, 1987). This is illustrated by the fact that toddlers no longer cry vigorously and seek comfort for themselves in reaction to another child's tears. Instead, they start to give to others what they themselves would find most comforting. For example, Hoffman (1984) describes a 13-month-old child who responded with a distressed look to an adult who appeared sad and then gave the adult her favorite doll. The child's facial affect indicated that she was responding empathically, and her attempt to soothe the adult is an early manifestation of the important role that empathy plays in fostering altruistic behavior.

Preschool children recognize and respond empathically to the emotions of others in simple situations. For example, they laugh in response to another child's joy and offer comfort and reassurance when another child is sad or hurt (Strayer, 1980). However, an increase in empathic responding occurs over the elementary school years (Bryant, 1982a; Feshbach & Feshbach, 1969; Marcus, Telleen, & Roke, 1979). Older children's understanding of a wider range of emotions, as well as their ability to take multiple cues into account in accurately discerning what another person feels, contributes to advances in empathic ability. In addition, elementary school children are better able to imagine themselves in another person's place. Experimental instructions to do so increase the intensity of emotional reactions in older children and adults (Stotland, 1969; Thompson & Hoffman, 1980), but have little effect on preschoolers (Cantor & Wilson, 1984). Hoffman (1984) suggests that advances in perspective-taking over late childhood and early adolescence permit an empathic re-

An increase in empathic responding occurs over the elementary school years, due to the older child's improved ability to accurately detect the emotions of others and imagine the self in another's place. (Susan Johns/Photo Researchers)

sponse not just to other people's immediate distress, but also to their general life condition. He regards the ability to empathize with the plight of the poor, oppressed, and sick as the most mature form of empathic distress, because it demands an advanced form of perspective-taking in which the child understands that people lead continuous affective lives beyond the immediate situation.

The development of empathy is molded by cognitive development in general and perspective-taking in particular, but it is also affected by early experience. Parents who are nurturant and encouraging and who show a sensitive, empathic concern for their youngsters have children who are more likely to react in a concerned way to the distress of others (Radke-Yarrow & Zahn-Waxler, 1984). In a recent study, Main and George (1985) observed a group of severely physically abused toddlers to see how they responded to naturally occurring incidents of other children's distress in a day care center. Unlike their nonabused counterparts, not one showed any evidence of empathy. Instead, they responded to agemates' distress with fear, anger, and physical attacks. These findings reveal that by the second year of life the reactions of abused children already resemble the behavior of their parents, for both respond with anger and aversion to others' distress. Harsh, punitive parenting seems to be related to interruptions in the normal course of empathic development at a very early age.

In summary, the ability to recognize and meaningfully interpret emotional reactions improves markedly during infancy, and by the end of the first year, babies engage in social referencing in which they actively seek affective information from others. During the preschool and elementary school years, children's emotional recognition skills continue to expand. By age 5, their use of many emotional words is adultlike, and toward the end of elementary school, they take multiple sources of information into account in discerning the feelings of others. Finally, due to cognitive development and social experience, the ability to respond empathically undergoes gradual improvement from early infancy into the adolescent years.

TEMPERAMENT AND DEVELOPMENT

While virtually all individuals manifest joy, anger, sadness, fear, interest, and increased or diminished activity levels in certain situations, as we get to know people well, the way their emotional responsiveness is unique and different from others becomes increasingly apparent. We take note of these individual differences when we describe one person as particularly cheerful and "upbeat" in personality, another as especially cautious and hesitant when faced with uncertain situations, a third as prone to angry outbursts and slow to calm down after provocation, and a fourth as having a calm and quiet disposition. The term **temperament** encompasses this potpourri of stable individual differences among people in quality and intensity of emotional reaction (Goldsmith, 1987). Developmental psychologists have become increasingly interested in the causes and consequences of temperamental differences among infants and children, for the child's style of emotional responding is believed to form the cornerstone of the adult personality.

Research on temperament was inspired by findings of the classic Berkeley and Fels longitudinal studies, which, as we indicated in Chapter 2, were the first to identify continuities in personality development from infancy into the adult years (Kagan & Moss, 1962; Schaefer & Bayley, 1963). Interest in temperament was also sparked by the practical concerns of child guidance professionals who worked with problem children. They quickly realized that a one-sided emphasis on the environment as responsible for children's adjustment difficulties could not account for what they saw. Sometimes children with psychological difficulties experienced family environments that differed very little from the environments of those who did not develop problems, and a few children appeared to be relatively free of adjustment difficulties, even after experiencing family disorganization and poor parental care.

These observations served as the impetus for the New York Longitudinal Study, initiated in 1956 by Alexander Thomas and Stella Chess, who followed 141 children over a period that now extends into adulthood in order to chart the impact of temperament on the course of development. Their findings indicated that temperamental characteristics were major factors in predisposing children to vulnerability or buffering them from stress. When negative factors piled up in childhood, especially difficult temperament combined with insensitive caregiving and severe parental conflict, a high likelihood of poor psychological adjustment occurred. However, temperamental characteristics were not fixed and immutable, for some children were not constant, and environmental circumstances seemed to modify their reactions and behavior.

The findings of the New York Longitudinal Study inspired a growing body of research on temperament and development, including new studies of the stability of temperament, its biological roots, its relationship to social and cognitive functioning, and its interaction with child-rearing practices. But before we review what is known about these issues, let's look at some current models of temperament and at how temperament is measured.

Models of Temperament

A variety of classification systems of temperament currently exist, with Thomas and Chess's (1977) dimensions serving as the first systematic model from which all others have been derived. Analyzing detailed descriptions of infants' and children's behavior obtained from parental interviews, Thomas and Chess identified nine dimensions of temperament, which are summarized in Table 10.1. When these dimensions were used to rate the behavior of children in their longitudinal sample, certain characteristics seemed to cluster together, yielding 3 temperamentally different types of children:

The easy child (40 percent of the sample). This child quickly establishes regular routines in infancy, is generally cheerful, and adapts easily to new experiences.

The difficult child (10 percent of the sample). This child is irregular in daily routines, slow to accept new experiences, and tends to react negatively and cry a great deal.

The slow-to-warm-up child (15 percent of the sample). This child is inactive, somewhat negative, and exhibits mild, low-key reactions to environmental stimuli.

Note that a large minority of children in the New York Longitudinal sample (35 percent) did not fit any one of these patterns. Instead, they showed diverse mixtures of temperamental traits that did not add up to a clear characterization.

The difficult temperament type has been of special interest to child psychologists, for it places children at greater risk for adjustment problems than any other set of temperamental characteristics. In the New York Longitudinal Study, 70 percent of infants classed as difficult developed behavior problems by school age, whereas only 18 percent of the easy infants did (Thomas, Chess, & Birch, 1968). Despite these findings, the temperamentally difficult pattern has been criticized by some investigators, who suggest that it is too global and that there may be more than one kind of difficult child (Campos et al., 1983). In addition, critics have noted that what is difficult to some parents may not be difficult to others, especially when temperament is viewed in cross-cultural context. Nevertheless, for a great many American parents, a young child who reacts with fussing and turmoil when faced with new foods, new people and new places and whose hunger, sleep, and elimination patterns are irregu-

Table 10.1. Two Models of Temperament

THOMAS AND CHESS		ROTHBART	
DIMENSION	DESCRIPTION	DIMENSION	DESCRIPTION
Activity level	Proportion of active periods to inactive ones	Activity level	Level of gross motor activity
Rhythmicity	Regularity of functions, such as hunger, excretion, sleep, and wakefulness	Smiling and laughter	Frequency of expression of happiness and pleasure
Distractibility	Degree to which extraneous stimuli alter behavior	Undisturbed persistence	Duration of orienting and interest
Approach/withdrawal	Response to a new object or person, in terms of whether the child accepts the new experience or withdraws from it	Fear	Wariness and distress in response to intense or novel stimuli
Adaptability	Ease with which the child adapts to changes in the environment	Soothability	Reduction of fussing, crying, or distress when soothing techniques are used by the caregiver or child
Attention span and persistence	Amount of time devoted to an activity, and the effect of distraction on the activity	Distress to limitations	Fussing, crying, and showing distress when desires are frustrated
Intensity of reaction	Intensity or energy level of response		
Threshold of responsiveness	Intensity of stimulation required to evoke a response		
Quality of mood	Amount of friendly, pleasant, joyful behavior as contrasted with unpleasant, unfriendly behavior		

Sources: A. Thomas, S. Chess, & H. G. Birch, 1970, "The Origins of Personality," *Scientific American, 223*(2), 102–109.
© August 1970 by Scientific American, Inc. All rights reserved. M. K. Rothbart, 1981, "Measurement of Temperament in Infancy," *Child Development, 52,* 569–578. © The Society for Research in Child Development, Inc. Reprinted by permission.

lar is harder to raise than others, a finding that has been confirmed in many investigations (Thomas, Chess, & Korn, 1982). It is interesting to note that the development of slow-to-warm-up children has received far less attention than that of difficult children, probably because these youngsters usually do not present difficulties in the early years. Their problems emerge later, after they enter school and peer group settings in which they are expected to respond actively and quickly. Chess and Thomas (1984) reported that 50 percent of these children began to show adjustment difficulties during the school years.

A second model of temperament, devised by Rothbart (1981), is also shown in Table 10.1. Rothbart's typology was stimulated by Thomas and Chess's model, but it has fewer dimensions because it combines those of Thomas and Chess that overlap with one another (e.g., "distractibility" and "attention span" are merged into "undisturbed persistence"). It also includes some temperamental characteristics, such as soothability and distress to limitations, that are not represented by Thomas and Chess. Other models of temperament also exist (e.g., Buss & Plomin, 1984), but the dimensions displayed in Table 10.1 provide a fairly comprehensive representation of those most often studied.

Measuring Temperament

Temperament is usually assessed in one of three ways: through interviews or questionnaires given to parents; through behavior ratings by pediatricians, nurses, teachers, or other individuals familiar with the child; or through direct observation either in the home or the laboratory. The most common method is to rely on parental reports, for parents have a depth of knowledge about the child that cannot be matched by any other source of information. A widely used assessment tool is the *Carey Infant Temperament Questionnaire* (Carey & McDevitt, 1978), which asks parents to indicate their degree of agreement with 70 statements about their baby's specific behaviors, such as, "The infant lies quietly in the bath" (an item that assesses activity level). The questionnaire also asks parents to describe in their own words their impressions of the baby's temperament. Parental perceptions, even though they include subjective elements, are regarded as useful for understanding the way parents view and respond to the baby's behavior (Hubert et al., 1982; Sirignano & Lachman, 1985).

Most measures, whether parental report or observational, can only assess temperament across a very narrow age range, because the way a particular temperamental trait is expressed may change considerably with development (Lerner et al., 1982). For example, a child who is high in fearfulness and withdrawal may vehemently reject his first spoonfuls of cereal at 3 months of age, cry vigorously in response to unfamiliar people at 8 months, refuse to sleep in a strange bed at 1 year, avoid new children on the playground as a preschooler, and hide behind his mother when first entering kindergarten.

The Stability of Temperament

We have already mentioned the Fels, Berkeley, and New York longitudinal studies, all of which provide evidence for the long-term stability of some temperamental characteristics. Their findings are supported by other investigations, which report moderate stability for sociability, shyness, activity level, and irritability over the period of infancy (Kagan, Reznick, & Snidman, 1987; Korner et al., 1981; Matheny et al., 1981; Matheny, Riese, & Wilson, 1985; Riese, 1987) and into the childhood years (Buss & Plomin, 1984). Research also offers some support for the stability of temperament across situations. For example, infants who tend to smile and laugh, have high activity levels, or show distress when frustrated in one situation also tend to do so in others (Rothbart, 1981).

Evidence for the stability of temperamental characteristics is crucially important, for without it, temperament cannot be regarded as an enduring disposition of the individual. Nevertheless, the findings as a whole indicate that the stability of temperament is not high. The characteristics of many children change considerably over time, suggesting that temperament is a malleable aspect of the individual that can be modified substantially by child-rearing experiences. Furthermore, no study has shown that children maintain early temperamental characteristics in the absence of environmental supports. Instead, environmental factors contribute to stability, for as we discussed in Chapter 3, children's behavioral tendencies shape experience by evoking, controlling, and modifying the environmental events to which they are exposed.

Biological Foundations of Temperament and Personality

Heritability. The very term "temperament" implies a biological foundation for individual differences in personality. Some theorists believe that a valid measure of temperament not only must be stable and predictive of adult personality, but also must be heritable (Buss & Plomin, 1975; Plomin & Rowe, 1979).

Table 10.2. Twin Correlations for Temperament, Personality, and Intelligence

	INFANT TEMPERAMENT[a]	PERSONALITY MEASURED IN CHILDHOOD AND ADULTHOOD[b]	INTELLIGENCE[c]
Identical twins reared together	.46	.52	.86
Fraternal twins reared together	.30	.25	.60

Note: Correlations presented are averages across a variety of temperamental and personality characteristics.

[a] From Goldsmith and Gottesman (1981).
[b] From Nichols (1978). Correlations reported are averages over published studies.
[c] From Bouchard & McGue (1981). Correlations reported are averages over published studies.

In recent years, many kinship studies have compared individuals of differing degrees of genetic relationship to one another to determine the extent to which temperament and personality are heritable. As with the heritability of intelligence, the most common approach has been to compare identical and fraternal twins. The findings of these studies are remarkably consistent in demonstrating that across a wide range of temperamental traits (activity level, sociability, distress to limitations, intensity of emotional reaction, attention span, and persistence) as well as childhood and adult personality measures (introversion, extroversion, anxiety, and impulsivity), identical twins are more similar than fraternals at just about any age they are assessed (Campos et al., 1983; Nichols, 1978; Scarr & Kidd, 1983).

The degree of resemblance between twins is fairly similar across different temperamental and personality dimensions (Scarr & Kidd, 1983). Representative average correlations are given in Table 10.2, and it can easily be seen that they are much lower than those obtained for intelligence. When heritability estimates (reflecting the proportion of variation among individuals in temperament and personality that can be attributed to genetic factors) are computed from twin studies, they are only moderate, around 40 to 50 (Matheny, 1980; Scarr & Kidd, 1983).

However, as we indicated in earlier chapters, the twin method of arriving at heritabilities is suspect, for it probably leads to an overestimation of the variation attributable to heredity. Cross-fostering studies, in which the characteristics of children reared in adoptive families are compared to both their biological relatives (with whom they share genes) and adoptive relatives (with whom they share a common rearing environment) provide a more powerful approach to the study of genetic influences on behavior[7] (Scarr & Kidd, 1983). The few such studies available for personality report correlations that are strikingly low for both biological and adoptive pairs. For example, Scarr and her collaborators (1981) gave a battery of personality tests to almost 200 adolescents who had been adopted in infancy, as well as to their adoptive relatives. A sample of adolescents reared by their biological parents was also tested. The correlations obtained are reported in Table 10.3. Comparisons between adoptive parent-child correlations and biological parent-child correlations produced heritabilities that were only around .20 (Scarr et al., 1981). This finding suggests a very modest role for genetic factors in the development of personality.

An intriguing finding of adoption studies is the light they shed on the role that environment plays in the development of personality. Look at Table 10.3 again, and you will see that a notable finding is the almost total lack of correlation between biological or adoptive children who are reared together in the same family. How can

---

[7] Return to Chapter 8, pages 341–343, to review the reasons that cross-fostering investigations are generally regarded as more useful and valid than twin comparisons.

Table 10.3. Kinship Correlations for Personality from Scarr et al.'s (1981) Cross-Fostering Study

	KINSHIP CORRELATION
Biological parent-child	.20
Adoptive parent-child	.06
Biological siblings	.20
Unrelated siblings	.07

Note: Correlations presented are averages across a variety of personality characteristics.
Source: Scarr et al., 1981.

this be explained, when their resemblance, as we showed in Chapter 8, is considerably higher for intelligence? Recall from Chapter 8 that there are two broad classes of environmental influences: *between-family* influences, factors that make one home environment different from another and affect all children in a family to the same extent; and *within-family* influences, those that act to make children growing up in the same household different from each other.[8] The fact that siblings reared in the same household show no consistent resemblance in personality suggests that between-family influences, such as socioeconomic status and overall climate of the home, are not very influential in explaining individual differences in personality traits. This conclusion is also supported by the finding that rearing identical twins apart in separate families (instead of together) does not affect their resemblance in personality (Bouchard, 1984; Rowe, 1987).

These results have led behavioral geneticists to conclude that the environmental factors most salient in personality development are within-family influences that accentuate genetically based differences among siblings and bring out each child's uniqueness (Rowe & Plomin, 1981). In other words, when it comes to children's personalities, parents may look for and act in such a way as to emphasize differences. This is reflected in the comments of many parents after the birth of a second child: "She's nothing like the first one," "He's so much calmer," "She's a lot more active," or "He's more sociable." Schachter and Stone (1985) found that parents' descriptions of their offspring as temperamentally easy or difficult are governed by a sharp contrast effect. To the extent that one child is perceived as easy, another is regarded as difficult. Children, in turn, evoke reactions from caregivers that are consistent with both parental views and with their actual temperamental dispositions. Furthermore, as they get older, they may actively seek ways in which they can be different from their siblings (Schachter et al., 1976). This is especially true when children are of the same sex or come from large families. Under these conditions, the child's need to "stand out" as someone special is particularly great (Huston, 1983). However, it is important to note that not all developmental psychologists agree with behavioral geneticists that within-family influences are supreme in personality development. In Chapter 14, we will see that investigators who have assessed between-family environmental influences directly (such as parents' overall child-rearing styles) report that they *do* affect personality development. As Hoffman (1985) points out, we must think of personality as resulting from many different inputs. For some qualities, child-specific experiences may be important; for others, the general family environment may be important; and perhaps for most, both within- and between-family factors are involved.

[8] If you need to review our earlier discussion of between- and within-family environmental influences, return to Chapter 8, pages 350–354.

Beginning at birth, Chinese-American infants are calmer than Causasian-American babies. This finding suggests the existence of biologically based racial/ethnic differences in early temperament. (Alan Oddie/PhotoEdit)

Finally, consistent racial/ethnic differences have emerged for some infant temperamental characteristics that may be indicative of group differences in the biological substrate of personality. For example, Chinese-American neonates are calmer, more easily soothed when upset, and better at self-quieting than Caucasian-American neonates (Freedman, 1974; 1976). Chinese-American infants also show greater inhibition and vigilance when faced with novel and uncertain situations (Kagan, Kearsley, & Zelazo, 1978; Kagan, 1984). But determining how these temperamental variations interact with the environment to produce ethnic group differences in personality and behavior later on in development remains a task for future research.

Heredity and the Development of Psychopathology. Genetic influences on psychopathological conditions are usually determined through **concordance rates** — the percentage of instances in which both members of a twin pair show a disorder when it is present in one pair member. Using this index, psychologists have found evidence for the operation of heredity in a wide variety of disorders. Among the severe disturbances for which genetic factors have been implicated is *schizophrenia,* a disorder characterized by serious difficulty in distinguishing fantasy from reality, frequent delusions and hallucinations, and irrational and inappropriate behaviors. Although concordances for schizophrenia vary somewhat from one study to another, they are consistently higher for identical (35 to 68 percent) than for fraternal twins (9 to 26 percent) (O'Rourke et al., 1982). *Depression,* an affective disorder involving frequent and extended periods of sadness and hopelessness, also appears to have a genetic basis. Once again, concordance rates are much higher for identical than fraternal twins (69 versus 13 percent). Moreover, the incidence of both of these conditions is greater among biological than adoptive relatives (Cadoret, 1976; Kessler, 1980; Mendlewicz & Rainer, 1974).

Though heredity is undeniably important, environmental factors also play a role in whether children of seriously disturbed parents manifest the same disorder. For example, offspring of schizophrenics are more prone to psychopathology in general, but the specific form it takes varies a great deal, and the chances that a child of a schizophrenic parent will also become schizophrenic are only 7 to 19 percent (O'Rourke et al., 1982). Rutter (1979) showed that temperamentally unattractive and abrasive children are especially likely to develop psychopathological conditions. However, whether or not they do so depends on the number and intensity of environmental stressors to which they are exposed, including parental quarrelsomeness and disharmony (a particularly important precipitating factor), low socioeconomic status, and living in a large family with crowded home conditions. Children exposed to environmental stressors who have sources of support outside the family, in the form of caring adults or satisfying peer relationships, may escape the worst of these effects. Thus, environmental factors are significant in determining whether and in what form severe emotional disturbance in children with a genetic predisposition occurs.

Interestingly, the consequences of being reared by a schizophrenic parent appear to be less severe than those that follow from having a chronically depressed mother. While schizophrenic mothers may be erratic and unpredictable in their behavior, they are more emotionally available to their children than are depressed mothers. The extreme sadness of depressed parents leads them to become detached from their youngsters, a circumstance that interferes considerably with sensitive and responsive caregiving. Maternal depression is a strong predictor of disturbances in infant-mother attachment and is associated with a high incidence of early behavior problems (Gaensbauer et al., 1984; Zahn-Waxler et al., 1984; Radke-Yarrow et al., 1985). Also, the young child's keen sensitivity to the negative emotional signals conveyed by a depressed mother may be an important reason, in addition to genetic predisposition, that the incidence of depressive symptoms in the offspring of depressed mothers is quite high (Cytryn et al., 1985).

In summary, research on the nature-nurture issue in the realm of temperament and personality indicates that the role of heredity cannot be ignored. At the same time, the findings demonstrate that individual differences in both normal personality and abnormal behavior can only be explained by a model that stresses complex transactions and interdependencies between genetic and environmental factors.

Temperament as a Predictor of Individual Differences in Children's Behavior

Earlier in this chapter we saw how emotions serve as powerful regulators of cognitive and social behavior. Since temperament involves a person's characteristic style of emotional responding, it should be an effective predictor of individual differences in those behaviors that emotions are thought to organize (Campos et al., 1983). A rapidly accumulating body of research reveals that this is, indeed, the case.

Temperament and Cognitive Performance. Temperamental dispositions play an important role in cognitive performance, with interest and persistence showing strong relationships with learning and cognitive functioning almost as soon as they can be reliably measured. For example, 2- to 3-month-old infants rated high in persistence show faster operant conditioning rates than their less persistent counterparts (Dunst & Linderfelt, 1985). Persistence also correlates with concurrent infant mental test scores between 6 and 24 months of age (Matheny, Dolan, & Wilson, 1974) as well as later IQ at age 4 (Goldsmith & Gottesman, 1981). During the school years, persistence, in the form of teacher-perceived task orientation, continues to predict IQ, grades in school, and teacher estimates of children's academic ability. In contrast, distractibility, avoidance of new situations, and lack of adaptability are related to poor school performance (Keogh, 1985).

Temperamental characteristics grouped under the rubric of **cognitive style** — an individual's general manner of perceiving and reacting to cognitive problems — have a particular bearing on intellectual performance. One cognitive style dimension that has been investigated extensively is **reflection-impulsivity.** It refers to the degree to which a child will pause to reflect about a solution to a problem when a number of possible answers are available and there is uncertainty as to which one is correct. The instrument most often used to measure it is Kagan's *Matching Familiar Figures Test* (Kagan, 1965). It presents children with a series of items in which they must select from an array of complex stimuli the one that exactly matches a standard (see sample item in Figure 10.5). Reflective children search the alternatives carefully, taking a long time to respond, and they generally perform more accurately. In contrast, impulsives dash headlong toward an answer, and they tend to make more errors. Although all children show a developmental trend toward greater reflectivity over the elementary school years, reflection-impulsivity is, nevertheless, a stable characteristic that predicts performance on a wide variety of cognitive tasks (Messer, 1976).

Most children who are impulsive on the Matching Familiar Figures Test are not "hyperactive" in a general behavioral sense, although children diagnosed as hyperactive do score toward the impulsive extreme on Kagan's measure (Campbell, 1973). For the majority of children, measures of reflection-impulsivity only predict behavior when they are working on cognitive tasks in which a solution is not immediately

Figure 10.5. Sample item from the *Matching Familiar Figures Test.* The child is asked to point to the picture in the array that matches the standard at the top. Impulsive children dash quickly toward an answer, frequently making mistakes, while reflective children take more time and are more accurate. *(From J. Kagan, 1965,* Matching Familiar Figures Test. *Cambridge, Mass.: Harvard University. Reprinted by permission.)*

apparent (Kagan & Messer, 1975). Emotional factors underlying the fast-inaccurate responding of impulsives are anxious self-doubt and intense fear of making mistakes (Block, Block, & Harrington, 1974; Yap & Peters, 1985), feelings that seem to be translated into an urge to escape the task quickly by responding as fast as possible. In view of this, it is not surprising that impulsive children achieve less well in school and show particular deficits in reading skills when compared to their reflective counterparts (Barrett, 1977; Messer, 1976).

The foundations of impulsive children's poorer cognitive performance may also be rooted in the information-processing strategies they use to solve problems. Impulsive children focus more on the stimulus as a whole, doing better on tasks that require global analysis, whereas reflective children pay more attention to fine details (Zelnicker et al., 1972), a strategy that leads them to search stimuli more exhaustively and places them at an advantage in academic situations. However, one underlying difference between a detailed versus global information-processing strategy is degree of persistence and effort, and we have already seen how this temperamental characteristic predicts cognitive performance from the earliest ages (Kogan, 1983).

Techniques used to teach elementary school children to be more reflective include training in the use of more efficient stimulus-scanning strategies (Egeland, 1974), insistence by an adult that the child take more time to respond (Zelnicker, Cochavi, & Yered, 1974), and teaching the child to use verbal self-instruction as a means of self-control (Meichenbaum & Goodman, 1971). These procedures lead the high error rates of impulsive children to be modified successfully on a short-term basis. However, there is no evidence that the effects are long-lasting, and impulsive children cannot be trained to the performance level of their more reflective counterparts.

Although reflective children perform better on cognitive tasks, some investigators believe that extremes at either end of the impulsivity-reflectivity dimension may be maladaptive. Children who delay responding for a very long time may also feel self-doubt and uncertainty in learning situations. In agreement with this interpretation, Kagan (as reported by Asher, 1987) found that temperamentally fearful, inhibited children score at both extremes on the Matching Familiar Figures Test. In view of these findings, interventions could fruitfully be implemented with both kinds of youngsters, although to date they have focused only on children who fall at the impulsive extreme.

Temperament and Social Interaction. Individual differences in temperament are associated with important variations in social interaction. Several studies report that temperament predicts social behavior in preschool classrooms. For example, highly active preschoolers are very sociable with their peers, but they also become involved in more conflict than their inactive counterparts. Emotionally sensitive preschoolers with a low threshold of reaction tend to interact physically by hitting, touching, and taking things away from agemates. Shy, withdrawn children do more watching of their classmates and engage in behaviors that discourage social interaction, such as pushing other children away and speaking to them less often (Billman & McDevitt, 1980; Hinde, Stevenson-Hinde, & Tamplin, 1985). Temperament even influences children's prosocial behavior, for shy preschoolers are less likely to help an unfamiliar adult who, for example, spills a box of gold stars (Stanhope, Bell, & Parker-Cohen, 1987).

In some cases, the social behavior seems to be a direct outcome of the temperamental characteristic in question, as is the case with shy children. In other cases, it results from the response of other people to the child's temperamental trait. For example, highly assertive and active children evoke more negative communications from others and therefore become embroiled in more arguments and disagreements. This is nicely illustrated by research on sibling relationships, for sibling conflict increases when one member of a sibling pair is emotionally intense or highly active

(Brody, Stoneman, & Burke, 1987). Early high activity level and emotional reactivity also predict aggression in adolescence, but the connection seems to result from the inclination of many mothers to be permissive of antisocial behavior in children with these characteristics (Olweus, 1980b). Thus, individual differences in temperament lead to differences in the reactions of others toward children, which, in turn, regulate their social development.

Temperament and Child-rearing: The "Goodness-of-Fit" Model

The evidence reviewed so far shows that only a bidirectional relationship between temperamental and environmental factors can explain healthy or maladaptive development for a particular individual. The nature of this relationship determines whether the child's initial behavioral tendencies will be maintained, modified, or changed over time, and this outcome, in turn, affects the nature of future organism-environment interactions. Thomas and Chess (1977; Chess & Thomas, 1984) propose a **"goodness-of-fit" model** as a useful summary of how temperamental style and environmental influences act in concert to determine the course of later development. The model states that when the organism's style of behaving and environmental influences are in harmony or achieve "good fit" with one another, then optimum development results. When there is dissonance or a "poor fit" between temperamental dispositions and environmental demands, then the outcome is maladaptive functioning and distorted development.

The goodness-of-fit model helps explain why children with difficult temperaments are at risk for later psychological disturbance. Such children, at least in American middle-class society, frequently experience child-rearing environments that fit poorly with their behavioral styles. Many studies indicate that babies identified as having a difficult temperament experience less responsive caregiving and stimulating contact with their mothers in infancy (Crockenberg, 1986). By the second year of life, mothers of difficult children are likely to use more intrusive and punitive discipline. In response, temperamentally difficult children react with recalcitrance and disobedience, and then their mothers often behave inconsistently, rewarding the child's noncompliant behavior by giving in to it, although they initially resisted (Lee & Bates, 1985). The difficult child's temperament combined with the mother's intrusive and inconsistent child-rearing techniques form a "poor fit" that serves to maintain and even increase the child's irritable, reactive, conflict-ridden style.

In the goodness-of-fit model, individual differences in temperament tend to evoke certain caregiving behaviors, but caregiving also depends on characteristics of caregivers and the social and cultural context in which they live. In some ethnic groups, difficult temperament does not necessarily evoke demanding and inconsistent parental reactions. For example, difficult children from working-class Puerto Rican families are not more likely to show behavioral maladjustment than their temperamentally easier counterparts, presumably because they are exposed to more accepting child-rearing attitudes and practices (Gannon & Korn, 1983).

Even in cultures in which difficult temperament and maladjustment are related, the outcome is not inevitable. Change is possible when dissonant organism-environment connections are replaced with child-rearing practices that are more consonant with the child's dispositions. Thomas and Chess (1977; Chess & Thomas, 1984) advocate interventions that encourage parents to be warm and accepting, but at the same time to make firm, reasonable, and consistent demands for mastering new experiences and situations.

A good fit between the child's temperamental style and child-rearing practices is best accomplished at an early age, before unfavorable temperament-environment relationships heighten difficult behavior and are hard to change. Carey (1982) finds the goodness-of-fit model useful for pediatricians as a basis for counseling parents during the baby's first year about suitable child-rearing practices, given a particular temperamental style. Also, goodness-of-fit is especially important in the development of infant-mother attachment. Attachment depends on the quality of social interaction between caregiver and infant, and the emotional responsiveness of both infant and mother contribute to it. In the final portion of this chapter, we turn to the development of this crucial and formative socioemotional relationship.

THE DEVELOPMENT OF ATTACHMENT

Attachment is the strong affectional tie we feel for special people in our lives that leads us to feel pleasure when we interact with them and to be comforted by their nearness during times of stress. Its first manifestation is in the baby's tendency to send positive emotional signals and seek physical closeness to the primary caregiver (generally the mother) in preference to other individuals — behaviors that are clearly evident by the middle to end of the first year of life.

Freud first suggested that the infant's emotional tie to the mother serves as the prototype for all later social relations and continues to exert its influence throughout the life span. Today, research on the development of children deprived of establishing an early attachment bond indicates that Freud's conjecture about the importance of attachment was correct. However, attachment has also been the focal point of intense debate for decades. Behaviorist and psychoanalytic theories were early views that vied with one another to explain how attachment developed and the reasons for its significance. The deficiencies of each of these perspectives eventually led to the emergence of a new view of infant-mother attachment, ethological theory, which is most popular today.

Early Views

Behaviorist Theory. In the history of research on attachment, the concept of *dependency* preceded the term attachment and was linked to behaviorist or social learning theory. A number of behaviorists adopted a **drive reduction model** that accorded central importance to the role of feeding in the infant-mother relationship. The baby's dependency behaviors — seeking closeness by clinging, following the mother about, and crying and calling in her absence — were viewed as a secondary or learned drive, acquired as a result of the mother's repeated association with satisfaction of infant hunger. However, the drive reduction model was soon overturned by both animal and human evidence. A famous study of rhesus monkeys by Harlow and Zimmerman (1959) played a major role in its demise. Baby monkeys separated from their mothers at birth and reared with terry cloth and wire mesh surrogates preferred to cling to the terry cloth substitute, even though the wire mesh "mother" held the bottle and infants had to climb on it to be fed. "Contact comfort," not feeding, was shown to be a central component of dependency behavior, a finding that was completely at odds with the drive reduction model.

Observations of human infants soon showed that they became attached to a variety of people who did not feed them, even other babies their own age. Freud and Dann (1951) followed the development of six German-Jewish orphaned babies whose parents had been killed in the gas chambers during World War II and who remained together throughout infancy and early childhood. The children developed a passionate attachment to one another, preferring each other's company, becoming upset when separated for even short moments, and actively rejecting the positive overtures of adults. In another study of 60 Scottish family-reared infants, Schaffer and Emerson (1964) reported that although the babies showed a special preference for their mothers, they frequently directed attachment behaviors toward other familiar people

Harlow found that baby monkeys preferred to cling to a terry cloth "mother" instead of a wire mesh "mother" that held a bottle. This result contradicts the drive reduction explanation of infant dependency as rooted in maternal feeding. (Harlow Primate Laboratory, University of Wisconsin)

who did not participate in routine care activities, such as fathers, grandparents, and siblings. Finally, perhaps you have observed that many toddlers develop strong emotional ties to soft cuddly objects, such as blankets and teddy bears (see Box 10.2). Obviously such objects have never played an active role in infant feeding!

Another variant of behaviorist theory is an **operant conditioning model** of infant social responsiveness (Gewirtz, 1969). According to this view, infants exhibit behaviors of looking, smiling, and seeking proximity to their mothers because their mothers reciprocate with contingent smiles, vocalizations, pats, and hugs, thereby reinforcing the infant's social engagement. The greater the number of infant behaviors that have been consistently reinforced by and have therefore come under the stimulus control of a particular person, the stronger the attachment relationship is said to be. A mechanism like this undoubtedly plays a role in the development of pleasurable and satisfying social exchanges between mother and baby, but by itself it cannot serve as a satisfactory explanation for the attachment bond. One reason is that attachment behaviors emerge even under conditions of serious infant maltreatment. Harlow and his collaborators reported that socially deprived mother monkeys (who had themselves been isolated in infancy) behaved violently toward their babies, but the infants continued to seek physical contact (Seay, Alexander, & Harlow, 1964). Similar attempts to approach nonreinforcing, abusive mothers have been observed in human children.

A major deficiency of drive reduction and operant conditioning explanations is that neither can explain why an attachment relationship, once formed, persists over long periods of time in which attachment figures are absent and do not satisfy primary drives or provide contingent reinforcement for social behavior. Think about your own feelings of attachment for a loved one whom you have not seen (and been reinforced by) in many months. Behaviorist theory would predict that the attachment relationship should be extinguished, yet clearly it is not. Because behaviorism ignores the child's growing capacity to form a stable, internal representation of the attachment figure that continues to exist despite extended absences of the person, it cannot account for the remarkable persistence of human attachments over time and space (Ainsworth, 1969).

Psychoanalytic Theory. Like the drive reduction model, **psychoanalytic theory** emphasizes that the infant becomes attached to the mother through dependency on her for satisfying hunger and sucking needs, for the oral zone of the body is regarded as the locus of instinctual gratification during the first year of life. Also like behaviorism, the psychoanalytic perspective views the infant as initially passive in the establishment of this bond. When the mother consistently satisfies the baby's urgent pangs of hunger and her feeding practices are accompanied by sensitive, loving care, the baby gains a sense of trust, or confident expectation, that his needs will be satisfied (Erikson, 1950). This feeling of trust and security provides an emotional shelter that frees the baby from total preoccupation with biological tensions and, instead, enables the infant to turn his attention outward toward the environment. This process supports the development of the baby's *ego*, or self-system, and eventually the infant develops a sense of self that is separate from the mother and the surrounding world. At

---

FOCUS ON THEORY, RESEARCH, AND APPLICATIONS

Box 10.2
Blankets and Teddies: Young Children's Attachment to Soft Objects

Theory. The importance of special objects to small children, such as blankets, teddy bears, and other cuddly toys, has long been recognized by parents. Such attachments are highly frequent, occurring in more than 50 percent of children in Western cultures (e.g., Passman & Halonen, 1979). Children especially appreciate the presence of their favorite soft object when exposed to unfamiliar situations, when going to sleep, or when tired or ill. In fact, almost half the children who form such attachments during the first or second year still display them in middle childhood (Sherman et al., 1981).

One interpretation of the significance of attachments to soft objects is that they help children manage the stress and anxiety of maternal separation and serve as substitutes for special people when they are not available (Winnicott, 1953). Richard Passman and Paul Weisberg (1975) decided to test this conjecture by investigating whether blanket-attached children would use their special object as a secure base of exploration in the

same way that they depend on their mothers when exposed to unfamiliar environments.

Research. Two- and 3-year-old children were assigned to one of four conditions in which they were accompanied by their mother, a familiar blanket, a favorite hard toy, or no object to a strange playroom. Half the children were blanket-attached and half were not. As shown in Figure 10.6, children attached to a blanket who had it with them played longer without becoming distressed than nonattached children who were provided with a blanket, and also longer than children in the toy-present and no-object conditions. Also, the extent of their play and exploration was comparable to blanket-attached children who had their mother (but not their object of attachment) with them. These findings indicate that distress can be alleviated and play promoted by favorite objects that offer young children clinging and contact comfort. However, blankets are not always as comforting as mothers. In another study, Passman (1976) showed that when a strange playroom is made more fear-arousing by dimming the lights and piping strange clicking noises through a loud-speaker, "security blankets" become

ineffective, and only the mother's presence is successful in promoting exploration and alleviating distress.

Passman and Weisberg's research provides insight into the functions of attachment objects, but it does not tell us why some children become attached to them and others do not. The phenomenon is more frequent among higher socioeconomic groups in many countries (Gaddini & Gaddini, 1970), but absent in non-Western societies in which caregivers are continuously available to infants (Hong & Townes, 1976). These findings suggest that parental accessibility, the provision of soft toys, and adult encouragement may have something to do with these attachments. In addition, temperamental characteristics may be involved. One study found that college students who reported having an attachment object in early childhood tended to be high in restlessness and excitability; they may have experienced more difficulty calming down when highly aroused than their nonattached counterparts (Cohen & Clark, 1984). Finally, there is no evidence that object-attached children develop differently from other children or that they experience unsatisfactory parental affectional ties (Mahalski, Silva, & Spears, 1985).

the same time, a more mature form of attachment emerges in which a permanent, positive internal representation of the mother is maintained, independent of the baby's momentary need state. By the last half of the first year, the baby has developed an affectional tie to the mother that is not as need-dominated as before. Now if the mother leaves, she is not forgotten, and babies begin to show considerable distress at her departure and in her absence.

In general, psychoanalytic theory offers a richer perspective on attachment than behaviorism. It emphasizes that the quality of mother-infant interaction has a profound effect on later social and personality development, and it also views the attachment bond as providing the necessary emotional security for exploration of the environment and cognitive mastery. Nevertheless, in viewing attachment as originating in the mother's relief of the baby's hunger, the psychoanalytic position suffers from some of the same problems as behaviorist theory. In addition, because the newborn baby is incorrectly regarded as totally passive, psychoanalysts place too much emphasis on faulty maternal behavior as the cause of developmental problems and too little on what the infant brings to the relationship in the way of temperamental dispositions and readiness to respond.

Applications. Objects of attachment are normal and effective sources of security during a developmental period in which children start to increase their physical and psychological separateness from parents. Such objects help children recapture the soft, tactile comfort of physical closeness to the mother and provide emotional support when children are tired, frustrated, or exposed to strange, fear-arousing situations. No harm results from allowing a child who so chooses to become dependent on a cuddly comforter.

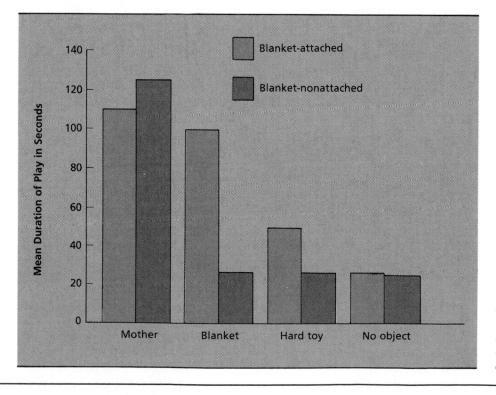

Figure 10.6. Effects of presence of mother versus different familiar objects on duration of play in an unfamiliar room in the Passman and Weisberg (1975) study. The blanket was as effective a source of emotional support as the mother among blanket-attached children. *(Adapted from Passman & Weisberg, 1975.)*

Bowlby's Ethological Theory

Today, **ethological theory** is the most widely accepted view of the attachment relationship. The influence of ethology on attachment theory was initially inspired by Lorenz's studies of *imprinting,* the early following behavior of the offspring of certain species of birds that appears during a restricted time period of development and, once established, is difficult to modify. Lorenz's view of imprinting as an adaptive behavior that helps insure survival influenced John Bowlby (1969), originally a psychoanalyst, to formulate an approach to human attachment in which the infant's emotional tie to the mother is viewed in adaptive, evolutionary terms. In developing the theory, Bowlby updated the psychoanalytic perspective by emphasizing that the infant is biologically prepared to be an active contributor to the attachment relationship from the very beginning. At the same time, he retained a number of psychoanalytic contributions, such as the importance of attachment in providing emotional support for exploration of the environment and the vital role of cognitive development in the emergence of a mature attachment relationship.

The central feature of Bowlby's theory is that the human infant, like other animal species, is endowed with a set of built-in behaviors that elicit parental care and, as a result, increase the baby's chances of survival. This repertoire of attachment-related behaviors — sucking, clinging, crying, smiling, gazing at the mother's face, and eventually following her when the infant can move about independently — brings the baby into close proximity to the mother and thereby provides protection from danger. Contact with the mother also ensures that the infant will be fed, but Bowlby was careful to point out that hunger satisfaction is not the basis for attachment. Instead, the attachment bond itself has strong biological roots, and it can only be understood within an evolutionary framework in which survival of the species is of paramount importance.

Although Bowlby's theory was stimulated by evidence on imprinting, it is important to note that imprinting cannot adequately account for the development of human attachment. In contrast to the imprinted bird whose time for learning is short and for whom the variability of what is to be learned is very narrow, human infants have a long period of immaturity and an extraordinary capacity for learning. As a result, the infant's relationship to the mother is not fixed, but changes considerably over the course of infancy. According to ethological theory, it evolves from a set of instinctive behaviors that summon the mother to the neonate's side into a true attachment relationship, which is highly selective in having the mother as the preferred target of physical closeness and social interaction. Then it moves toward increased independence from the caregiver, a process that is supported by a history of warm, responsive caregiving as well as by cognitive development during the second and third years of life. Bowlby divides this developmental progression into four phases, which are summarized below.

The Developmental Course of Attachment

1. **The preattachment phase** (birth – 6 weeks). During this first phase, the behavior of the infant is largely a matter of genetically determined reflexive responses with survival value. By grasping, smiling, crying, and tracking with the eyes, infants orient toward and signal other human beings. They are also biased toward responding to stimuli that come from other people, for they are soothed and comforted by being picked up, stroked, and talked to softly. Infant signals are especially important in promoting physical contact during this period. In their study of Scottish family-reared babies, Schaffer and Emerson (1964) found that being put down from the arms of an adult was the situation that most often evoked protest from very young babies (see Figure 10.7).

Rudimentary sensory recognition of the mother appears during this phase. As we

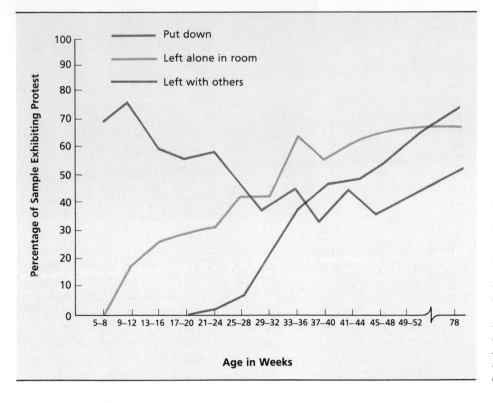

Figure 10.7. Age changes in infant protest in response to being put down, left alone in a room, and left with people other than the mother in the Schaffer and Emerson (1964) study. *(From H. R. Schaffer, P. E. Emerson, 1964,* The Development of Social Attachments in Infancy. *Monographs of the Society for Research in Child Development, 29 (3, Serial No. 94), 35–36. © The Society for Research in Child Development, Inc. Adapted by permission.)*

noted in Chapter 4, even neonates prefer their own mother's smell and voice to that of another adult, although as yet they show no specific attachment to her. However, the process of beginning to distinguish mother from stranger is facilitated by maternal emotional cues. Young infants only recognize their mother's voice when it carries emotional information. When the mother deliberately speaks in a monotone, they fail to make the discrimination (Mehler et al., 1978; Fernald, 1984).

2. **The "attachment-in-the-making" phase** (6 weeks – 6 to 8 months). Infants in this second phase orient toward and respond in more marked preference to the mother than they did before. For example, the baby will smile and vocalize more freely to the mother, quiet more quickly when she picks him up, and keep track of her whereabouts more consistently than that of a stranger. However, a specific attachment has not yet developed, since infants of this period will not protest when separated from the mother, despite the fact that they are able to distinguish her perceptually from an unfamiliar individual. During this period, it is not separation from the mother per se, but rather separation from other human beings that causes babies to be especially anxious and upset. As shown in Figure 10.7, responding with distress to being left alone in a room begins during this phase and rises steadily over the course of the first year.

3. **The phase of "clearcut" attachment** (6 to 8 months – 18 months to 2 years). Now attachment to the mother is clearly evident. Babies of this period show **separation anxiety** in that they become very upset when the mother leaves. As Schaffer and Emerson (1964) report, until about 7 months of age, departure of the mother is the least likely situation to arouse protest. After this age reactions to it rise dramatically until at 18 months more infants become upset in this situation than in any other (see Figure 10.7). With their new-found powers of crawling and walking, babies of this period also act more deliberately to maintain the mother's presence by approaching,

During the phase of "clearcut" attachment, babies display a clear preference for the familiar caregiver, who serves as a secure base for exploration and a haven of safety to which to return. (Erika Stone)

following, and climbing on her in preference to others, and using her as a secure base from which to explore the environment and a haven of safety to which to return.

It is no accident that the period of "clearcut" attachment is concurrent with the emergence of Piagetian object permanence. Infants cannot have a discriminating attachment to the mother and engage in efforts to find her when she is not in view without a cognitive appreciation of her as a permanent object, separate from the self and others. In fact, babies who have not yet mastered object permanence usually do not protest when separated from their mothers (Lester et al., 1974). The importance of cognitive development in the emergence of a discriminating attachment is also supported by the finding that high scores on infant mental tests predict earlier appearance of this phase (Schaffer & Emerson, 1964; Reed & Leiderman, 1983).

4. **Formation of a reciprocal relationship** (18 months to 2 years and on). Rapid growth in language and mental representation at the end of the second year enables children to better appreciate factors that influence the mother's coming and going and to predict her return. As a result, separation anxiety declines over the third year. In addition, children start to engage in active efforts to alter the mother's goals, using request and persuasion, rather than merely adjusting their own behaviors to suit hers (by clinging and crawling after the mother). Understanding and attempting to modify the mother's goals requires considerable cognitive competence, including a beginning ability to see things from another person's perspective. Children start to develop these capacities during the early preschool years, but they can be facilitated or hampered by the extent to which parents clarify their goals for children. Weinraub and Lewis (1977) found that mothers who "slipped out" without giving the child advance warning at the time of departure had 2-year-olds who were most likely to cry during the period of separation. In contrast, mothers who explained that they were leaving, would return soon, and also gave the child an explicit instruction about what to do in the interim (e.g., "Build me a house with Tinkertoys while I'm gone") had youngsters who accepted the mother's departure far more easily. Explanations that fit the child's cognitive level of understanding work best. Short descriptions of where the mother is going and when she will return are most effective, whereas lengthy, repetitive explanations delivered long in advance of the departure actually heighten the young child's separation protest (Adams & Passman, 1981).

Bowlby's four phases show that a positive, enduring affectional tie to the caregiver emerges from the experiences of the first two years of life. Once established, the attachment bond bridges time and distance, and children no longer need to engage in proximity-seeking behaviors as insistently as they did before. Bowlby's model is bidirectional, for secure attachment depends on the baby's equipment for evoking responsive caregiving as well as on a history of sensitive maternal responsiveness. Therefore, according to ethological theory, deviations in the development of attachment can result from problems on the infant's side, when the behavioral system responsible for infant signaling is not intact, or problems on the environmental side, when responsive caregiving is either infrequent or entirely absent. Also, each side — the infant's as well as the mother's — can influence and modify the adequacy of the other.

Now that we have traced the developmental course of attachment, let's turn to a consideration of individual differences in the quality of this formative emotional bond.

Measuring the Security of Attachment: Ainsworth's Strange Situation

The **Strange Situation** is the most widely used technique for assessing the quality of attachment to the caregiver between 1 and 2 years of age. In designing it, Mary Ainsworth and her colleagues (Ainsworth & Wittig, 1969; Ainsworth et al., 1978) reasoned that if the development of attachment has gone along as it should, the baby should show feelings of security in the presence of the mother and use her as a secure base from which to explore a strange environment. In addition, the quality of the baby's attachment ought to be most evident when fear and distress are activated, first by introducing a stranger into the situation, and then by the departure of the mother as well as the unfamiliar person so that the infant is left alone. Therefore, as summarized in Table 10.4, the Strange Situation takes the baby through 8 short episodes that

Table 10.4. Episodes in Ainsworth's Strange Situation

EPISODE	PERSONS PRESENT	DURATION	EVENTS AND PROCEDURES	ATTACHMENT BEHAVIORS ACTIVATED
1	Mother and baby	30 seconds	Experimenter introduces mother and baby to room and then leaves.	
2	Mother and baby	3 minutes	Mother is seated while baby plays with toys for exploration.	Mother as a "secure base"
3	Mother, baby, and stranger	3 minutes	Stranger enters, is seated, and talks to mother.	Reaction to unfamiliar adult Mother as a "haven of safety"
4	Stranger and baby	3 minutes or less[a]	Mother leaves room. Stranger responds to baby's initiations and offers comfort if baby is upset.	Separation anxiety
5	Mother and baby	3 minutes or more[b]	Mother returns, greets baby, and if necessary offers comfort.	Reaction to reunion
6	Baby alone	3 minutes or less[a]	Mother leaves room.	Separation anxiety
7	Stranger and baby	3 minutes or less[a]	Stranger enters room and offers comfort.	Ability to be soothed by stranger
8	Mother and baby	3 minutes	Mother returns, greets baby, if necessary offers comfort, and tries to reinterest baby in toys.	Reaction to reunion

[a] Episode is cut short if the baby becomes very distressed.
[b] Episode is extended if more time is needed for the baby to become reinvolved in play.

Source: From M. D. S. Ainsworth, M. Blehar, E. Waters, & S. Wall, 1978. *Patterns of Attachment.* Hillsdale, N.J.: Lawrence Erlbaum Associates, p. 37. Adapted by permission.

simulate brief separations and reunions commonly experienced by infants in our culture.

Observing the responses of infants to these episodes, Ainsworth identified three different behavior patterns that describe individual differences in the quality of attachment. Two of them — avoidant and ambivalent — are insecure patterns, while the third designates secure attachment. Each is summarized below.

Avoidantly attached. These babies are usually not distressed during separation, but when they are, it seems to be due to being left alone rather than to the mother's absence, for they react to the stranger in much the same way as the mother. During reunion, these infants typically avoid the mother, or they mingle proximity-seeking with avoidance. When picked up, they often fail to cling, although they do not resist physical contact. About 20 to 25 percent of American middle-class infants show this pattern.

Ambivalently attached. Before separation, these infants seek proximity to the mother, but after she returns, they combine contact-seeking with conspicuously angry, resistive behavior. Sometimes they even hit or push the mother away, and they continue to cry for a period of time after reunion. This pattern is found in approximately 15 percent of American middle-class infants.

Securely attached. These infants may or may not cry on separation, but if they do, it is due to the mother's absence, for they show a marked preference for the mother over the stranger. When the mother returns, they actively seek contact with her and reduce their crying immediately. About 65 percent of American middle-class babies show this pattern.

The Strange Situation has proved to be a powerful tool for assessing attachment, since infant behavior in it shows a clear relationship to comparable behavior in everyday life (Ainsworth, Bell, & Stayton, 1971). In addition, behavior in the Strange Situation is responsive to changes in family circumstances. As long as caregiving conditions are stable, attachment classification is fairly stable (Waters, 1978). When family conditions change, attachment classification also tends to change. For example, one study showed that an increase in stressful life events predicted movement from secure to insecure attachment in low-income families (Vaughn et al., 1979).

However, new cross-cultural evidence reveals that Strange Situation behavior may need to be interpreted differently for children of different cultural origins. For example, German babies show a higher incidence of avoidant attachment than American infants, but German parents deliberately encourage their babies to be nonclinging and independent, and the baby's response is probably an intended outcome of parental training (Grossman et al., 1985). An unusually high proportion of Japanese babies show an ambivalently attached pattern, but infants in Japan are rarely separated from their mothers and left in the care of strange people. Consequently, the Strange Situation may create far greater stress in Japanese babies than it does among babies in countries where brief mother-infant separations are common (Miyake et al., 1985). Despite these cultural variations, it is still the case that the secure attachment pattern is the most frequent Strange Situation response in all societies that have been studied to date (van IJzendoorn & Kroonenberg, 1988).

Factors that Affect the Development of Attachment

Maternal Deprivation and Institutionalization. Research has consistently shown that early experience that prevents the formation of a secure attachment relationship to one or a very few caregivers leads to seriously impaired development. In a series of landmark studies, Spitz (1945, 1946) observed the development of institutionalized babies abruptly separated at weaning from their mothers (who had made the decision to give them up) sometime between the third month and end of the first year of life.

The infants were placed on a general ward in unstimulating individual cubicles where they shared a nurse with at least 7 other babies. From the time of separation, babies showed extreme susceptibility to infection as well as marked delays in development, with practically none speaking, walking, or eating alone by 2 years of age.

Besides severely delayed development, many infants who experienced prolonged maternal separation during the second half of the first year showed a severe depressive disorder that Spitz (1946) called **anaclitic depression.** In contrast to the happy, outgoing behavior they exhibited before separation, these babies showed extreme weepiness and withdrawal, lying in their cots with averted faces and refusing to take part in their surroundings. This behavior persisted for 2 to 3 months, during which time the infants lost weight and suffered from insomnia. If the mother was not restored or an adequate caregiving relationship supplied, the depression deepened rapidly.

Spitz noticed that not all institutionalized infants became depressed. The reaction was most severe in babies whose mothers were rated as having a "good" relationship with the infant. In those with a "bad" relationship, depression rarely occurred, for children who have not developed an affectional tie cannot miss it when the caregiver is withdrawn. Depression also did not occur when an effective caregiver replaced the mother, so it was not solely the result of maternal departure. Spitz concluded that anaclitic depression was caused by the combined effects of separation from a warm, familiar caregiver and placement in an environment that did not provide an adequate mother substitute.

In agreement with Spitz's observations, subsequent studies of institutionalized infants indicate that lasting developmental disruptions are not the result of separation from the natural parent per se, but instead occur when babies are prevented from forming an emotional bond with one or a few adults. Although Bowlby argued that the human infant has a built-in bias to become attached to a single caregiver, we now know that infants can cope quite well with several caregivers at once or with the replacement of one caregiver by another as long as each provides sensitive, responsive care. However, they suffer when exposed to a rapid turnover of adults in their world (Rutter, 1979).

Longitudinal studies of institutionalized infants have consistently found that when large numbers of staff care for children and close personal relationships are discouraged, language development and socioemotional adjustment remain impaired (Goldfarb, 1943; Pringle & Bossio, 1958; Tizard & Rees, 1975; Tizard & Hodges, 1978). In the most recent of these investigations, Tizard studied children reared in an institution that offered a good caregiver-child ratio and a rich selection of books and toys. However, staff turnover was so rapid that the average child experienced a total of 50 caregivers by the age of 4½! Although the stimulating physical conditions offset many of the cognitive deficits previously found in institutionalized samples, socioemotional difficulties persisted into childhood, with children showing an insatiable desire for attention, indiscriminate friendliness toward strange adults, difficulties with peer relationships, and inability to concentrate in comparison to home-reared counterparts.

Many children in Tizard's sample became "late adoptees" who were placed in home environments after the age of 4. Since most developed deep relationships with their adoptive parents, Tizard's study indicates that a first attachment bond can be developed as late as 4 to 6 years. However, throughout middle childhood these late-adopted children continued to show the same social and attentional problems as those who remained in the institution, a finding which suggests that fully normal development depends on establishing attachment bonds in infancy. The evidence is consistent with a possible sensitive period for optimal attachment in the early years of life (Rutter, 1979).

The research reviewed above should not be taken as a blanket indictment of institutional upbringing. Neither Bowlby nor Spitz claimed that all institutions are

Research on Israeli kibbutz youngsters shows that when institutional rearing is responsive to children's needs, it does not lead to disturbances in personality development. (Louis Goldman/Photo Researchers)

harmful or that all children separated from their mothers suffer permanent damage. The *conditions* of institutional rearing are of central importance. For example, in special agricultural settlements in Israel called *kibbutzim,* children are deliberately reared in institutional environments that are responsive to their needs in order to free both parents for full participation in the work life of the community. Between 6 and 12 weeks of age kibbutz babies enter a children's house where they spend most of their day and sleep at night (although for several hours each evening they visit with their parents). Communally reared kibbutz children show no evidence of increased psychopathology when compared to family-reared Israeli children (Beit-Hallahmi & Rabin, 1977).

Quality of Caregiving. Ethological theory predicts that even when infants are reared in families, those who experience caregiving that is not sensitive to their signals and needs will develop anxious, insecure attachments. Although virtually everyone agrees that good parenting is a matter of warmth, affection, and sensitive responsiveness to infant cues, there is controversy over how crucial these factors are for the emergence of a satisfactory attachment relationship (Campos et al., 1983; Sroufe, 1985). Some investigators believe that the nuances of early caregiving — prompt, reliable responding to infant distress and expressions of pleasure in interacting with the baby — have a limited impact on attachment security, and what the infant brings to the caregiving circumstance in the way of temperamental dispositions is of central importance (e.g., Kagan, 1982). However, research over the past two decades on the antecedents of attachment behavior has moved this controversy toward a clearer resolution. As we shall see in this section and the one that follows, just as Bowlby's original theoretical formulation assumes, *both* maternal and infant contributions are important, for the quality of infant-mother attachment is the result of a *relationship* between the two that builds over the first year of life (Belsky & Rovine, 1987; Thompson, 1986).

Extremely inadequate maternal care, including child abuse and neglect, is a powerful predictor of insecure attachment. In the case of neglect, when the infant's needs for attention, food, cleanliness, and safety are not attended to, babies show an increase in angry, ambivalent attachment behavior, whereas when they experience physical abuse, there is a marked increase in avoidant attachment (Egeland & Sroufe, 1981; George & Main, 1979; Schneider-Rosen et al., 1985).

Caregiving need not consist of extreme abuse and neglect to affect the attachment relationship. Ainsworth and her collaborators (1978) reviewed the findings of a number of studies in which direct observations as well as ratings of maternal behavior in the home during the first year were related to Strange Situation classification at 1 year of age. Securely attached infants had mothers who, during the first 3 months, responded promptly to infant crying, handled their babies tenderly and carefully, and paced their behavior to fit the tempo of the baby's behavior. In contrast, insecurely attached infants had mothers who disliked physical contact, handled them ineptly, and tended to behave in a "routine" manner when face to face with the infant. These differences in maternal sensitivity persisted over the first year. Between 9 and 12 months of age, mothers of securely attached babies were more affectionate, more accepting rather than rejecting of infant social initiatives, and more cooperative as opposed to interfering with the infant's ongoing behavior. Ainsworth's conclusion — that securely attached infants have mothers who are more sensitive and psychologically available — is supported by many recent studies involving highly diverse samples, including low-income and middle-income mother-infant pairs (Bates, Maslin, & Frankel, 1985; Belsky, Rovine, & Taylor, 1984; Egeland & Farber, 1984; Kiser et al., 1986).

As we have already indicated in this and in previous chapters, quality of caregiving can only be fully understood in relation to the larger social and environmental context in which mother and infant are situated. In this regard, a number of factors have been identified that exert an important influence on maternal precursors of attachment security. In families where there is stress, instability, and resulting disorganization in infant care, the incidence of insecure attachment is especially high (Sroufe, 1985). However, the availability of social supports, especially a good marital relationship and the father's assistance in caregiving, ameliorates stress and is related to greater attachment security (Goldberg, 1982; Durrett, Otaki, & Richards, 1984).

Although it has long been known that intergenerational continuity plays a role in child maltreatment, with many abusive parents having been neglected and battered as children themselves (Bowlby, 1980; Rutter, 1979), even less extreme variations in caregiver behavior may be predictable from the parent's own early care. Several studies have found a relationship between maternal reports of their own childhood experiences and the security of infant attachment (Main, Kaplan, & Cassidy, 1985; Morris, 1981; Ricks, 1985). In these investigations, parents describing their own mothers as warm, competent caregivers were those most likely to have securely attached babies of their own. However, parents who remembered unsatisfactory attachment-related experiences, but who looked back on them in a forgiving, understanding way, also had securely attached infants. These findings indicate that not all parents experiencing an unhappy and disturbed upbringing become insensitive or abusive parents themselves. The intergenerational cycle is strengthened by poverty, family disorganization, bearing of children during the teenage years, and lack of available social supports to buffer the debilitating consequences of high life stress (Rutter, 1979).

Infant Characteristics. As early as the neonatal period, infant characteristics affect the security of the attachment bond. Recall from Chapter 4 that prematurity, birth complications, and neonatal illness make caregiving more taxing for new parents, and there is good evidence that many children who are later abused begin life as difficult newborns (Sameroff & Chandler, 1975). But as long as parents have the personal resources to care for a baby with special needs and the infant is not very ill, an at-risk newborn is likely to fare quite well in the development of attachment (Rode et al., 1981). Nevertheless, some infants are likely to challenge the resources of just about any parent. For example, a substantial number of preterm babies born with severe respiratory distress syndrome[9] later develop ambivalent attachment relationships, probably because the illness demands such extraordinary attention and creates sufficient parental anxiety to interfere with optimal caregiving (Meisels et al., 1984).

Although normal infants do not strain parental resources to the same degree as sick babies, their temperamental characteristics contribute importantly to the quality of the attachment bond. The clearest linkage established to date is between neonatal irritability and subsequent ambivalent attachment (Crockenberg, 1981; Miyake et al., 1985; Sagi et al., 1985; Waters, Vaughn, & Egeland, 1980). Other research reports a relationship between neonatal orienting, or expression of "interest," and secure attachment classification, with the connection maintained for as long a period as 18 months (Grossmann et al., 1985). In contrast to these neonatal indicators, efforts to link parental reports of infant temperament to attachment security have not shown consistent relationships, and they continue to require further study (Lamb et al., 1984).

As we indicated earlier, the precise role that temperament plays in the unfolding of the infant-caregiver relationship has been a matter of dispute, with some investigators suggesting that it may fully account for individual differences observed in the Strange Situation. They believe, for example, that babies who are prone to irritability, fearfulness, and anxiety may simply react to strange environments and transient separations from the mother with undue alarm, regardless of the parent's sensitivity to the baby. However, most experts reject this view as far too simplistic (Campos et al., 1983; Crockenberg, 1986; Sroufe, 1985; Thompson, 1986). Evidence arguing against it is that quality of attachment to mother, father, and substitute caregiver are often different from one another (Lamb et al., 1984; Oppenheim, Sagi, & Lamb, 1988; Sagi et al., 1985). If infant characteristics were the only important influences, we would expect attachment to be constant across all attachment figures.

A more likely explanation is that temperamental variations influence security of attachment by affecting subtle nuances of the caregiver-infant relationship. Crockenberg's (1981) findings provide a good example of the bidirectional relationship that exists between temperament and attachment. In her study, neonatal irritability did not predict insecure attachment for all infants, but only for those whose mothers reported few available social supports in the form of help from husbands, extended family, and friends. Such supports increased mothers' capacity to be sensitive to an irritable baby. Miyake and his collaborators (1985) also found that infant temperament and maternal behavior are interwoven. Mothers of Japanese irritable infants who behaved intrusively by frequently interrupting their baby's behavior were especially likely to have ambivalently attached infants.

One reason that many temperamental characteristics have not shown a straightforward relationship with secure attachment may be that temperament largely exerts its effect on attachment through "goodness-of-fit." From this perspective, *many* temperamental characteristics may be associated with secure attachment as long as the caregiver is able to harmoniously adjust her behavioral style to accommodate the infant. In fact, as Sroufe (1985) suggests, the reason that maternal sensitivity is an especially effective predictor of attachment security is that the very concept of sensitive caregiving implies a mother who is able to adjust her behavior to suit the unique characteristics of her infant.

Nevertheless, when babies arrive with behavioral styles that make them very difficult to adjust to, or gradually build those characteristics as the result of highly

---

[9] Otherwise known as hyaline membrane disease, this condition occurs in about 25,000 newborn infants each year, most of whom are premature. The lungs of the baby are underdeveloped, causing collapse of the air sacs and formation of an abnormal fibrous membrane that leads to extremely difficult breathing and, in some cases, death by suffocation. Modern medical treatment keeps many such babies alive long enough for their lungs to become sufficiently developed, and most who recover from the illness suffer no permanent physical consequences.

insensitive early care, then even the ministrations of a very responsive mother or substitute caregiver may meet with less than optimal success. Thompson (1986) believes that some very difficult babies may continue to be uncertain about their caregiver's accessibility, despite conscientious efforts of parents to be as sensitive and responsive to them as possible. In this way, variations in temperament may, at times, shape an infant's *appraisal* of caregiver sensitivity in ways that do not accurately reflect actual quality of care. Thompson's intriguing idea has not yet been investigated, but it provides an excellent illustration of the intricacies likely to emerge as researchers continue to unravel the complex transactions between infant characteristics and maternal caregiving that are central to attachment security.

Multiple Attachments: The Father's Special Role

We have already seen that most infants develop a number of attachment relationships that include fathers, grandparents, siblings, substitute caregivers, and sometimes peers. Although Bowlby (1969) made room for such subsidiary attachments in his theory, he believed that infants were biologically predisposed to direct their attachment behaviors toward a single preferred figure, especially when they were distressed. Observations of family-reared babies between 8 and 16 months of age lend some support to Bowlby's assumption. When an anxious, unhappy baby is permitted to choose between the mother and father as a source of comfort and security, the infant generally shows a preference for the mother (Cohen & Campos, 1974; Lamb, 1976). However, when babies are not distressed, they will approach, touch, ask to be held by, vocalize to, and smile equally at both parents (Kotelchuk, 1976; Ross et al., 1975), and sometimes they show a preference for their fathers (Clarke-Stewart, 1978). Even under conditions of distress, attachment behaviors directed toward the mother and father become more similar over time, until by 18 months of age, there is little difference between the two (Schaffer & Emerson, 1964). Furthermore, when babies are left with their fathers, they show identical proximity-seeking behaviors and are just as easily comforted, and fathers are preferred by infants over unfamiliar adults (Lamb, 1976).

Research indicates that fathers are salient figures in the lives of babies, beginning to build relationships with them as early as the first few days after birth. Interviews with fathers of newborn infants reveal that most are elated by the birth of their baby and experience a feeling state that Greenberg and Morris (1974) call **engrossment,** a term that captures the sense of absorption and interest that fathers display toward their newborn child. Regardless of their social class or whether they participate with their wives in childbirth classes, fathers touch, look at, vocalize to, and kiss their newborn babies just as much as mothers. When they hold the infant, they sometimes exceed mothers in stimulation and affection (Parke & Tinsley, 1981). Also, when feeding the baby, fathers are just as sensitive as mothers to infant cues (Parke & Sawin, 1980).

As infancy progresses, the circumstances under which mothers and fathers build attachment relationships diverge, and each parent relates to the infant in different ways. In most families, mothers devote a high proportion of the time they are engaged with the baby to caregiving functions, such as changing, bathing, and feeding, whereas a greater percentage of time spent with fathers is taken up in stimulating and playful interactions (Kotelchuk, 1976). In addition, the play initiations of mothers and fathers tend to be different. Mothers offer toys and verbal stimulation, and initiate more conventional games like pat-a-cake and peekaboo, while fathers engage in unconventional, highly physical, bouncing and lifting games, especially with boys (Yogman, 1981). In view of these differences, it is not surprising that babies tend to look to their mothers when in distress, and to their fathers for playful interaction (Lamb, 1976; Clarke-Stewart, 1980).

Elated by the birth of his baby, this father displays the absorbed interest in his newborn known as engrossment. (Erika Stone)

Even in the eyes of parents, the view of "mother as caregiver" and "father as playmate" is widely held (Parke & Tinsley, 1981). However, this picture is changing in some families as a result of the revised work status of women. Working mothers engage in more playful stimulation of their babies than nonworking mothers, and their husbands engage in less social play (Pedersen et al., 1980). Perhaps mothers who spend the day away from their infants return in the evening with a heightened desire to interact with them, thereby reducing the father's opportunity for playful engagement. In families where fathers and mothers reverse responsibilities so that the father is the primary caregiver and the mother assumes a secondary role, fathers retain their highly arousing play style and at the same time increase their attentiveness to the baby's physical well-being (Hwang, 1986). Such highly involved fathers tend to be less stereotypical in their sex-role orientations and hold beliefs that the father's role in child development is especially important. In addition, their wives are highly encouraging and supportive of them in their revised paternal role (Palkovitz, 1984).

Research on fathers as attachment figures helps us appreciate the complex, multidimensional nature of the infant's socioemotional world. Both mothers and fathers are affectively salient figures to infants and are equally capable of behaving sensitively and responsively. In most families, mothers spend much more time with babies than do fathers, but the great majority of fathers spend enough time to promote the development of deep affectional ties. No evidence exists to support the commonly held assumption that women are biologically constituted to be more effective caregivers than are men.

Quality of Attachment and Later Development

Both psychoanalytic and ethological theories predict that the inner feelings of security and affection that emanate from a healthy attachment relationship provide the foundation for virtually all aspects of later psychological functioning, including exploration and mastery of the inanimate environment and cooperative, sociable interactions with others. Some research findings indicate that assessments of attachment security between 12 and 18 months of age are predictive of a number of aspects of cognitive and socioemotional development during the preschool years.

Short-term longitudinal research reveals that youngsters who have developed secure relationships with their mothers show more sophisticated make-believe play and greater flexibility and persistence on problem-solving tasks by 2 years of age. Also, in comparison to their insecurely attached counterparts, they approach cognitive activities with more enthusiasm and positive affect, and on very difficult tasks they are less easily frustrated and are able to make constructive use of adult assistance without becoming overly demanding and dependent on it (Matas, Arend, & Sroufe, 1978).

In the socioemotional sphere, a recent study reported that 4-year-olds who had been securely attached infants were rated by their preschool teachers as high in self-esteem, socially competent, cooperative, autonomous, popular, and empathic. In contrast, their avoidantly attached peers were viewed as isolated, disconnected, and elusive, while those who were ambivalently attached were seen as disruptive, difficult, and tantrumy. Teachers also reported that both types of insecurely attached children were immaturely dependent. For ambivalently attached preschoolers, dependency appeared as chronic, low-level attention-seeking behavior. These children hovered around teachers during free play and waited for them to provide help during activities the children could carry out by themselves. Avoidantly attached children's dependency was more subtle. They withdrew when injured or disappointed and only sought adult contact when their level of stress was very low, a behavior pattern that is strikingly reminiscent of their earlier reactions in the Strange Situation (Sroufe, 1983; Sroufe, Fox, & Pancake, 1983). Furthermore, insecurely attached babies tend to experience difficulties in interacting with agemates when they become preschoolers. Avoidantly attached preschoolers receive few positive responses from peers, whereas ambivalently attached children attract an elevated number of aggressive and resistive reactions (Jacobson & Wille, 1986).

These correlational findings have been taken by some as evidence that an early secure attachment relationship causes increased autonomy and competence during the preschool years (e.g., Sroufe, 1983). However, there is as yet no definite evidence for a causal connection, for some of the associations described above have not been easy to replicate, and alternative interpretations are also possible. Lamb and his colleagues (1985) believe that later differences in children's adjustment may not result from the early attachment relationship per se, but rather from continuity in the quality of the child's care throughout the early childhood years. From this perspective, current patterns of parent-child interaction, not just the formative attachment bond, could contribute to the differences in behavior described above. In support of this view, among samples of children who have experienced major changes in family and caregiving circumstances, correlations between early attachment security and later functioning are generally not found (Sroufe, 1978; Erickson, Sroufe, & Egeland, 1985). Clearly, more research is needed to determine whether an early secure attachment relationship is critical for a variety of aspects of later behavior among family-reared youngsters.

Attachment and Societal Change: Day Care and the Working Mother

With the tremendous rise in the number of women entering the labor force during the last several decades, routine substitute care has become common for infants and very young children. By 1986, 54 percent of American mothers with children under 3 were employed. The proportion of working mothers with babies 1 year of age and younger has increased faster than that of any other age sector — from 31 percent in 1975 to over 50 percent in 1986 (U.S. Department of Labor, 1986). In response to this trend, child development specialists as well as concerned lay people have raised questions about the impact of day care and repeated daily separations of infant from mother on the attachment bond. Both psychoanalytic and ethological theories imply that arrangements depriving infants of fairly continuous access to their mothers should threaten the child's emotional security.

Some studies indicate that maternal employment during the first year of life is a "risk" factor for a somewhat higher incidence of infants with insecure attachments to their mothers (Barglow, Vaughn, & Molitor, 1987; Schwartz, 1983) and, for boys, to their fathers as well (Belsky & Rovine, 1988; Chase-Lansdale & Owen, 1987). However, other studies show no such effects (Owen et al., 1984; Easterbrooks & Goldberg, 1985; Hock, 1980). As yet, we do not know how a host of moderating variables — timing of the mother's return to work, parental attitudes toward maternal employment, and infant characteristics, to name just a few — affect the attachment relationship. But there is clear evidence that the quality of substitute care does make a difference.

Many investigations carried out during the 1970s reported that day care and home-reared children did not differ in their response to separation from and reunion with their mothers (e.g., Brookhart & Hock, 1976; Doyle, 1975; Kagan, Kearsley, & Zelazo, 1978). In the few studies in which differences were found, they appeared to be the result of a temporary distress reaction to initial placement in day care that waned as the infant became accustomed to substitute caregivers (Belsky, 1984). However, virtually all of this early research was conducted in high quality, university-based centers with generous caregiver/infant ratios and exceptionally well-trained staffs. More recent research provides information on the effects of day care for children who are not fortunate enough to be enrolled in such programs. One study showed that infants from low-income families who were exposed to insensitive, barren, and unstable substitute care were at risk for developing avoidant attachments to their mothers, especially if day care began before the first birthday (Vaughn, Gove, & Egeland, 1980). Even a highly positive maternal relationship does not buffer the child against such care. For example, infants evaluated as securely attached at 18 months who had experienced poor quality day care since the first year of life displayed less competent and more maladaptive behavior on a problem-solving task at age 2 than their home-reared counterparts (Vaughn, Dean, & Waters, 1983). Furthermore, the consequences of purely custodial care may return to affect aspects of mother-child interaction that help to sustain warm, affectional ties. Peterson and Peterson (1986) found that 3- to 5-year-old children enrolled in low quality day care were less compliant and cooperative and carried on less sustained verbal dialogues with their mothers than those who either attended good day care or were reared at home.

Unfortunately, infants exposed to the poorest and most unstable day care are often those who experience the greatest family disorganization. Highly stressed parents generally have little time and energy to monitor the quality of their youngsters' substitute care. This is true not only for low-income children (Vaughn, Gove, & Egeland, 1980), but also in more economically advantaged families. Middle-class parents who place their toddlers in low-quality day care tend to lead complex and stressful lives that interfere with involvement in their children's daily activities (Howes & Olenick, 1986). As a result, many infants experiencing unsatisfactory day care arrangements are at special risk for developmental difficulties. They receive a double dose of vulnerability, both at home and in the substitute care setting.

These findings underline the importance of insuring that all infants receive substitute care that safeguards their emotional needs while their mothers are at work. What are the components of such high quality care? According to Belsky (1984), day care that is supportive of early development consists of an environment that harmoniously integrates the four levels of Bronfenbrenner's ecological model, discussed in Chapter 1, in the following ways:

At the level of the *microsystem* — stable care in which frequent changes are not made in children's placement or in the staff within a placement; a generous caregiver/child ratio;[10] and caregivers who engage in sensitive, one-to-one interaction and provide age-appropriate learning experiences.

At the level of the *mesosystem* — frequent communication between parents and caregivers, so that each is cognizant of the infant's life at home and in the substitute care environment.

At the level of the *exosystem* — supervisory agencies that license and oversee the day care environment to assure high quality care, and employers that permit parents to arrange work schedules that are compatible with good early caregiving experiences.

At the level of the *macrosystem* — a national social policy that embodies respect for the complex, sophisticated, and vital role of the substitute caregiver and that places a high value on quality day care to meet the formative developmental needs of young children while their parents are at work.

In Chapter 14, we will return to the topics of maternal employment and day care and consider their consequences for development during the preschool, school-age, and adolescent years.

CHAPTER SUMMARY

1. The field of child development is experiencing a rebirth of interest in emotions, a revival sparked by evidence documenting their central role in virtually all aspects of human behavior. Behaviorist theory, cognitive-developmental discrepancy theory, and the new organizational approach have each enhanced our understanding of emotional development. However, the behaviorist and cognitive developmental views cannot account for many emotional phenomena, and the organizational perspective has broadest explanatory power. It regards emotions as adaptive forces in human behavior, as interdependent with cognition, and as facilitating exploration, self-awareness, and social interaction.

2. A diverse set of basic emotions may already be present in the neonate, although substantial changes in the way they are expressed occur with age. Smiling and laughter serve vital social functions, and their development reflects as well as supports the emergence of infant perceptual and cognitive capacities. Anger and fear reactions increase substantially after 7 months of age and can be understood in terms of infants' improved ability to cognitively appraise environmental events. These emotional reactions also have adaptive significance. Older babies can use the energy mobilized by anger to defend themselves or overcome obstacles, and fear holds in check the baby's compelling exploratory urge to venture away from the caregiver.

3. In early infancy, mothers start to socialize children's emotional reactions according to culturally accepted display rules. However, children do not become adept at regulating

---

[10] Kagan, Kearsley, and Zelazo (1978) reported a caregiver/child ratio of 1 to 3 for infants and 1 to 5 for toddlers in a model day care center of very high quality. The standards of most American states are not this stringent.

their emotional behavior until the elementary school years, about the same time as they achieve conscious awareness and understanding of these rules. Increased self-awareness at the end of infancy and over the preschool years, along with socialization experiences, leads to the emergence of complex emotions, such as shame, guilt, envy, and pride. The circumstances under which these emotions are experienced change markedly with age.

4. The ability to recognize and interpret emotional expressions improves during the first year of life. By 8 months of age, infants engage in social referencing, actively seeking emotional information from others in uncertain situations. Over the preschool years, children acquire a vocabulary of emotional terms and concepts that facilitates the processing of emotional information. During middle childhood, they become better at taking multiple cues into account in appraising the feelings of others. The capacity to respond empathically also undergoes development from infancy into childhood, due to advances in perspective-taking, comprehension of others' emotions, and exposure to sensitive, empathic parenting.

5. Temperamental characteristics are important predisposing factors in the development of adjustment problems; temperamentally difficult children are especially prone to behavior problems. A number of temperamental characteristics show moderate stability over the period of infancy and into childhood, and temperament and personality are modestly heritable. Concordance rates reveal that hereditary transmission is also involved in the development of severe psychopathological disorders like schizophrenia and depression. Despite the importance of genetic predispositions, complex transactions and interdependencies between heredity and environment are necessary to explain individual differences in normal and abnormal personality functioning. Behavioral geneticists regard within-family environmental factors as especially influential in the development of personality, but other research indicates that between-family factors are also important.

6. Temperament affects both cognitive performance and social behavior. Persistence is related to cognitive functioning at an early age, and reflection-impulsivity also predicts intellectual performance. Many temperamental characteristics are associated with variations in children's social behavior. In most instances the outcomes result from bidirectional influences in which temperament affects the reactions of others to the child, and these, in turn, modify the child's social behavior. The goodness-of-fit model summarizes the varied ways in which temperamental style and child-rearing practices combine to yield positive or negative developmental outcomes.

7. Infant–caregiver attachment has been the focal point of intense theoretical debate for decades, with behaviorist and psychoanalytic theories vying with one another to explain the development of this formative affectional tie. Currently, the most well accepted perspective is Bowlby's ethological theory, which views attachment in adaptive, evolutionary terms. Attachment begins with a set of instinctive behaviors and evolves into a true attachment relationship around 8 months of age. At about this time, the mother becomes the preferred target of physical closeness and social interaction and serves as a secure base for exploration. The emergence of a positive inner image of the caregiver permits the child to move in the direction of increased independence from the attachment figure over the preschool years. The entire process is supported by infant behaviors that evoke caregiving, cognitive development, and a history of sensitive, responsive care. Ainsworth's Strange Situation is the preferred procedure for assessing the quality of the attachment bond. The baby's reactions to a series of brief separations from and reunions with the mother yield assessments of infant attachment as either avoidant, ambivalent, or secure.

8. Studies of institutionalized infants reveal that babies deprived of developing affectional ties with one or a few adults show socioemotional deficits that extend into the childhood years. However, family rearing by itself does not assure a healthy attachment relationship, for children who experience early caregiving that is not sensitive and responsive tend to develop anxious, insecure attachments. Infant characteristics, in terms of temperament and neonatal readiness to respond, affect the quality of attachment through their impact on the caregiver–infant relationship. Besides attachments to mothers, infants develop strong emotional ties to their fathers that build through stimulating, playful interaction. Some studies report that attachment quality predicts cognitive and social functioning into the preschool years, but a causal association has not yet been established.

9. Maternal employment may be a ''risk'' factor for insecure attachment, but not all studies report this association, and it is undoubtedly affected by a host of moderating variables. High quality day care does not interfere with the establishment of affectional ties. However, when substitute care is insensitive and unstable and working parents lead stressful lives, infants are at serious risk for developing insecure attachments.

IMPORTANT TERMS AND CONCEPTS

type A personality	endogenous smile	emotional display rules
discrepancy theory	exogenous smile	complex emotions
organizational approach to emotional development	social smile	social referencing
basic emotions	stranger distress	empathy
	secure base	temperament

easy child
difficult child
slow-to-warm-up child
concordance rates
cognitive style
reflection-impulsivity
goodness-of-fit model
attachment

drive reduction model
operant conditioning model
psychoanalytic theory
ethological theory
preattachment phase
"attachment-in-the-making" phase
phase of "clearcut" attachment
separation anxiety

formation of a reciprocal relationship
Strange Situation
avoidantly attached
ambivalently attached
securely attached
anaclitic depression
engrossment

Tanis, by Daniel Garber.
From the Warner Collection of Gulf States Paper Corporation, Tuscaloosa, AL.

CHAPTER 11

The Self and Social Understanding

This chapter addresses the development of **social cognition,** or how children come to understand their multifaceted social world. Like cognitive development, which we considered in Chapters 6 and 7, the changes to which we now turn are concerned with matters of perceiving, thinking and interpreting experience, but the experience of interest is no longer the child's physical, inanimate surroundings. Instead, social cognition has a unique content: the behavior and inner characteristics of the self and other people. Social-cognitive psychologists want to know how children and adults conceptualize themselves and others as psychological beings and how they understand relationships between people. Although historically social and cognitive development were studied separately, in the last two decades efforts have been made to put them together. Today, developmental psychologists recognize that children are active social thinkers who bring cognitive skills to social interactions and take meaning from these interactions according to their current cognitive capacities (Youniss, 1975).

In this chapter, you will see that many of the same developmental trends that we identified for nonsocial thinking apply to social cognition as well. This is understandable, for after all, it is the same being who is thinking and reasoning in both domains. Furthermore, people as "objects" of thought have characteristics in common with physical objects. Both are separate, permanent entities that exist in space and participate in events that take place over time (Flavell, 1985). As a result, all of the basic mental capacities that serve nonsocial cognition emerge in the social domain as well.

Like nonsocial cognition, the development of social cognition proceeds from *concrete to abstract*. Children first understand the immediately observable aspects of their social world, such as people's physical appearance and overt behavior. Only

461

later do they grasp less obvious, covert psychological processes, such as perceptions, intentions, motivations, abilities, attitudes, and beliefs. Also like nonsocial cognition, social thinking becomes *better organized and integrated* with age, as children gather their observations of people's separate behaviors into coherent, socially relevant concepts, such as personalities and identities. Over time, children also revise their conceptions of the causes of behavior, moving from *simple, one-sided explanations to complex interacting relationships* that take into account both person and situational variables.

Finally, social cognition, like nonsocial cognition, *moves toward a metacognitive level of understanding*. As children get older, they not only think about social reality, but also *think about the social thoughts* of themselves and others. As we indicated in Chapter 6, adolescents are often preoccupied with their own and others' socially relevant thoughts, and they ruminate about what they believe others think of them for hours. In addition, as development proceeds, children become more adept at the metacognitive activity of *self-regulation* in the social arena. They begin to oversee and appraise their social activities on a moment-by-moment basis, taking appropriate corrective action when they need to go differently (Flavell, 1981b).

While nonsocial and social cognition have many features in common, they also differ. The world of physical objects is far more predictable than the realm of social experience. Movements of things can be fully understood from knowledge of the physical forces that act on them, but people are not just objects that can be acted on; they move and act themselves. As a result, people's behavior is not the simple result of others' actions toward them; it is also mediated by inner psychological states not directly observable to others. This makes people more complex than physical objects, since their behavior is determined by an interplay of observable and unobservable forces.

Given this complexity, we might expect the development of social cognition to always lag behind nonsocial thinking, yet surprisingly, it does not (Hoffman, 1981). In this chapter, we will return to a theme that appears repeatedly in many parts of this book: children demonstrate some sophisticated cognitive understandings at early ages, even though many others require an extensive time period of development to achieve.

The rather surprising rapidity of social-cognitive development is facilitated by special features of social experience that help children make early sense out of its complexity. First, the fact that people are animated beings as well as objects of deep emotional investment leads them to be particularly attractive objects of contemplation, for children as well as adults. Second, the interactive context in which social cognition takes place is an ideal setting for promoting *disequilibrium* and resulting cognitive change. Social interaction continually presents children with discrepancies between the behaviors they expect and the behaviors that occur, motivating *accommodation,* or reassessments of their thoughts about social concerns. Finally, children and the people with whom they interact are all human beings, with the same basic nervous system and a shared background of similar experiences. As a result, assessing another's behavior from the self's point of view leads to correct inferences in many instances and helps make people's behavior more predictable and understandable (Flavell, 1985; Hoffman, 1981; Shantz, 1983). In situations where one's own perspective leads to incorrect predictions, human beings are equipped with a unique capacity — *perspective-taking* — that permits them to imagine what another's thoughts and feelings may be. Perspective-taking is so important for a variety of psychological developments that we have already made frequent reference to it in earlier parts of this book. We will devote considerable attention to its development and social significance in this chapter.

Our discussion begins with a brief review of historical influences that led to the rising prominence of social cognition in the field of child development, along with typical methods of investigation. Then we turn to an overview of what is known about the following three facets of social-cognitive development: the child's conception of self, of other people, and of relationships between people.

Before we begin, perhaps you have already noticed, based on the brief introduction given above, that we considered some social-cognitive topics in previous chapters. Good examples are children's referential communication skills (Chapter 9) and recognizing and understanding others' emotions (Chapter 10). Children's developing sense of morality — how people *ought to* behave toward each other as opposed to how they *do* behave — is another important social-cognitive topic, but research on the development of moral reasoning is so extensive that it merits a chapter of its own. We will consider it in Chapter 12.

HISTORICAL INFLUENCES AND RESEARCH METHODS

A major influence on studies of social-cognitive development has been the work of Piaget. Although Piaget's best-known contribution was his broad theory of cognitive development, a smaller portion of his work dealt with children's social reasoning and behavior. Recall from Chapter 6 that Piaget believed that *egocentrism* — an inability to differentiate between the self's perspective and that of others — was the overriding feature responsible for the immaturity of young children's thought, in both social and nonsocial domains. Although preschoolers are not as egocentric as Piaget believed, their ability to take the perspective of others improves substantially over childhood and adolescence. Piaget's ideas about egocentrism, even though they proved to be incorrect, inspired new theories of children's perspective-taking skill and understanding of social relationships, such as friendship and authority, in which perspective-taking plays a prominent role (Cooney & Selman, 1978; Damon, 1977; Selman, 1980; Youniss & Volpe, 1978). In keeping with the Piagetian tradition, each of these theories includes a series of *stages* that children traverse as they move from the least to the most mature forms of social understanding.

As we indicated in Chapter 1, Piaget also left his mark on methods for investigating children's social cognition, with variations of his flexible, open-ended *clinical interview* serving as the most popular research technique. Recall from Chapter 2 that the clinical interview's great strength is that it permits children to display what they know in terms most likely to resemble their thoughts about social experiences in everyday life. The method also has limitations, however. It may underestimate the capacities of children who have difficulty putting thoughts into words, or who are not yet old enough to do so (Berndt & Heller, 1985). Consequently, other methods are sometimes used to substitute for or supplement it. These include direct observations of children's social interactions, from which inferences are drawn about their social-cognitive skills, and structured questionnaires and rating scales, which reduce the verbal demands made of the child (Barenboim, 1985).

Another influential theoretical perspective comes from *attribution theory* in academic social psychology (e.g., Heider, 1958; Kelley, 1973; Weiner, 1974, 1987). **Attributions** are our common, everyday speculations about the causes of behavior — the answers we provide to the question, "Why did he (or I) do that?" to make behavior meaningful and understandable. Adults group the causes of their own and others' behavior into two general categories: *external, environmental causes* and *internal, psychological causes*. Then they subdivide the category of psychological causes into *ability* (what a person is *able* to do) and *effort* (what a person is *trying* to do). When explaining behavior, they apply the cause most closely associated with people's actions. For example, if a behavior occurs for a great many people, but only in a single situation (e.g., the whole class gets an A on Ms. Apple's French test), it is seen as caused by the situation (an easy test). However, if an individual exhibits a behavior in many situations (e.g., Johnny always gets A's on French tests), it is seen as caused by some aspect of the person (ability, effort, or both). As this last example suggests, attribution theory is most often applied to children's understanding of their successes and failures in achievement situations. Developmental psychologists have been interested in when and how children's achievement-related attributions emerge and how they affect behavior in learning situations (Dweck & Elliott, 1983). Like other social-cognitive topics, research on children's attributions has depended heavily on open-ended interviews, although structured research techniques have occasionally been used.

Finally, Erikson's psychoanalytic theory has influenced research on the development of the self, particularly adolescent identity formation. Typical social-cognitive research methods have been applied to empirically test and extend Erikson's ideas.

CONCEPTUALIZING THE SELF

Infancy: The Emergence of Self-recognition

Infancy is a rich, formative period for the development of social understanding. As we showed in Chapter 10, by the middle to end of the first year, infants demonstrate a complex set of social cognitions, including the capacity to recognize and respond appropriately to others' emotions and the ability to identify familiar people. This period also brings landmark achievements in nonsocial cognition, as the work of Piaget and his followers has revealed (see Chapter 6). The fact that both objects and people achieve an independent, stable existence in infancy implies that knowledge of the self as a separate, permanent entity emerges at about this time. As we shall see shortly, acting on objects and interacting with people do not just inform infants about the physical and social environment; they also pave the way toward self-recognition, which is well-established by the end of the second year of life.

Researchers rely on clever laboratory observations in which they expose babies to images of themselves in mirrors, on videotapes, and in still photos to illuminate the

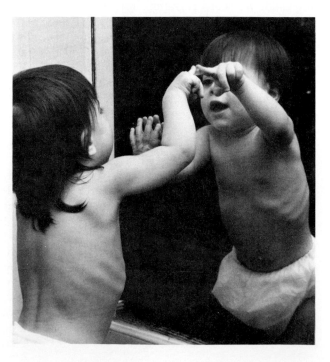

The perfect correspondence between one's own movements and the movements of the image in the mirror is a cue that enables children to recognize themselves at a very young age. (Erika Stone)

infant's developing sense of self. As early as the first few months, infants enjoy observing their own behavior in a mirror, for they watch intently, smile, and return friendly social behaviors to the image. At what age do they realize that the charming baby gazing and grinning back at them is really the self?

To find out, Lewis and Brooks-Gunn (1979) brought infants between 9 and 24 months of age into a laboratory, where each was placed in front of a large mirror. Then, under pretext of wiping the baby's nose, each mother was asked to rub red dye on her infant's face, and the researchers watched to see how the babies responded to their transformed images. Younger infants smiled, vocalized, and touched the mirror as if the red marks had little to do with any aspect of the self, but by 15 months of age, "mark-directed" behavior began to appear, and it rose steadily until at age 2 the majority of infants touched and rubbed their strange-looking little red noses. As age increased, so did the probability that infants would entertain themselves by acting silly or coy in front of the mirror, responses that also reflect the beginnings of self-recognition.

Mirrors offer two kinds of cues that can be used to recognize the self: *contingency cues*, which provide a perfect correspondence between one's own bodily movements and the movements of the image in the mirror, and *featural cues,* which have to do with the unique visual appearance of the self. Research using videotapes of infant behavior permits the separation and exploration of each of these cues and, consequently, provides important insights into how the baby's first awareness of self develops.

When Lewis and Brooks-Gunn (1979) showed infants a "live" video playback of their ongoing behavior, babies as young as 9 to 12 months of age engaged in "contingent play" with the image, initiating a kind of peekaboo game in which they moved their heads, bodies, or hands out of the camera's view and back again, a pattern of behavior that rose steadily throughout the second year of life. When videotaped sequences of noncontingent behavior were shown, even young infants would "test" the image by trying to play contingently, but when it did not respond, they immediately stopped trying.

Between 15 and 18 months, infants begin to respond to specific perceptual features of the self in videotaped sequences. At this age, they react differently to a film of a strange infant than they do to a film of themselves. They smile, move toward, and attend more closely to the unfamiliar baby, but they imitate and try contingent play in response to themselves. By the end of infancy, recognition of the self's perceptual features is well established, for 2-year-olds look and smile more at a still photo of themselves than at one of a same age peer, and almost all of them use their own name or a personal pronoun to label a picture of themselves (Lewis & Brooks-Gunn, 1979).

The research reviewed above indicates that contingency information provides babies with their first cues regarding the self's existence. Featural information only becomes salient later on, at the end of the second year of life. As young infants act on the environment, different contingencies between behavior and aspects of the external world probably help them sort out self and social and nonsocial facets of experience. For example, batting a mobile and seeing it swing in a pattern and rhythm different from the infant's own actions informs the baby about the nature of the physical world, whereas smiling and vocalizing at a caregiver who reciprocally smiles and vocalizes back help specify the nature of the social world (Bahrick & Watson, 1985). But all types of contingency cues are necessary for understanding each facet of experience, for it is the contrast among them that enables infants to build a clear and active image of the self as distinct from external reality (Lewis, Brooks-Gunn, & Jaskir, 1985).

Once awareness of the self's existence is well established, it quickly becomes an integral part of children's social and cognitive lives. As we saw in Chapter 10, the development of complex emotional responses and empathy cannot occur until a sense of self emerges. The capacity to form plans and recognize the consequences of one's own actions also requires an active, independently existing self. In addition, self-recognition is the first step toward developing a differentiated psychological self-concept, which is a major social cognitive achievement of the childhood years.

From Childhood to Adolescence: The Development of Self-concept

From the preschool period through adolescence, children work on constructing a **self-concept,** or "personal theory" of what the self is like as an experiencing, functioning individual. Like any theory, the self-concept is subject to continual change as it is exposed to new information and as the child becomes a more sophisticated thinker about the self and the social world (Epstein, 1973; Harter, 1983).

The Categorical Self. As soon as representational thought and language appear at the end of infancy, children start to construct a **categorical self.** They use a number of concrete descriptors that refer to salient dimensions on which people differ, such as sex ("boy" or "girl," "lady" or "man") and age (e.g., "baby," "boy," or "man"). Young children apply such terms appropriately, indicating that they categorize the self and the social world on the basis of these dimensions almost as early as they can talk (Lewis & Brooks-Gunn, 1979). However, as we indicated in Chapter 6, several characteristics of the self that are permanent and unchangeable, such as the child's sex and humanness, have not yet attained *constancy* for the preschool child. For example, while the 2- to 4-year-old may say today that she is a girl and a person, she is also likely to indicate that by dressing up, wearing a mask, or playing with her brother's cars and trucks that she can change genders or species in the future (Carey, 1985; DeVries, 1969; Emmerich, 1982; Guardo & Bohan, 1971; Kohlberg, 1966).

These unstable self-descriptions are thought to be due to the preschool child's cognitive limitations, but growth of the young child's body and feedback from the social environment may also contribute to them. After all, many aspects of the child's physical self *do* change, including height, weight, strength, and hair length. In addition, adults often emphasize change when they make such comments as "My, how big and tall you're getting to be!" or "You're getting smarter all the time; you know your ABCs!" Young children may make the mistake of generalizing these prominent dimensions of change to stable self-attributes, only gradually accomplishing the task of sorting out constant from changing characteristics around the late preschool and early school years (Harter, 1983).

During elementary school, constancy of the categorical self is established. However, many 6-year-olds still cite their unchanging name as the basis for self-sameness and think that they would not be the same person if their name were taken away from them. By age 8, children recognize that names are arbitrary and have nothing to do with the continuity of self (Guardo & Bohan, 1971).

The Inner Self. During the preschool years, children first become aware of an **inner self** made up of private thoughts and imaginings accessible only to themselves and not to others. Piaget (1926/1930) first discovered that preschoolers regard dreams as tangible phenomena, like a kaleidoscope of passing pictures outside the self. Only at around 7 to 8 do they understand dreams as subjective experiences that are generated "inside their heads." But because most dreams are visual phenomena that resemble the world the child sees, their subjective nature may be understood later than conscious, everyday thoughts.

Recently, Flavell, Shipstead, and Croft (1980) studied 3- and 4-year-olds' awareness of an inner, private self by asking them such questions as, "Where is the part of you that knows your name and thinks about things?" Of the children interviewed, 64 percent localized the thinking part of themselves inside their heads (or very close by) and indicated that other people cannot see these activities or the part of the self that does them. Moreover, research we reviewed in Chapter 7 indicating that preschoolers use such words as "think," "remember," and "pretend" to distinguish between internal mental states and external reality suggests remarkably early awareness of an inner self.[1]

The Psychological Self. Perhaps you have already deduced from our discussion so far that prior to the middle childhood years, children's self-concepts are largely based on highly concrete, observable characteristics, such as names, physical appearance, possessions, and typical behaviors. Keller, Ford, and Meacham (1978) asked 3- to 5-year-olds to tell about themselves. The most frequently mentioned responses were actions that children typically engaged in (e.g., "I go to school." "I can wash my hair by myself." "I help mommy."). These findings indicate, in agreement with Piaget (1937/1954) and other theorists (Cooley, 1902; Erikson, 1950), that acting on the environment and finding out *what one can do* is an especially important early basis for self-definition.

During the elementary school years, children's descriptions of themselves change from a catalogue of observable, external characteristics to an emphasis on internal psychological dispositions, with a major shift occurring around 8 to 11 years. The following self-descriptions written by children of different ages reflect this movement away from concrete, surface aspects of the self toward more abstract, internal traits and abilities:

A boy age 7. I am 7 and I have hazel brown hair and my hobby is stamp collecting. I am good at football and I am quite good at sums and my favourite game is football and I love school and I like reading books and my favourite car is an Austin. (Livesley & Bromley, 1973, p. 237)

A girl age 11½. My name is A. I'm a human being. I'm a girl. I'm a truthful person. I'm not pretty. I do so-so in my studies. I'm a very good cellist. I'm a very good pianist. I'm a little bit tall for my age. I like several boys. I like several girls. I'm old-fashioned. I play tennis. I am a *very* good swimmer. I try to be helpful. I'm always ready to be friends with anybody. Mostly I'm good, but I lose my temper. I'm not well-liked by some girls and boys. I don't know if I'm liked by boys or not. (Montemayor & Eisen, 1977, pp. 317–318)

A girl almost age 13. I have a fairly quick temper and it doesn't take much to rouse me. I can be a little bit sympathetic to the people I like, but to the poor people I dislike my temper can be shown quite easily. I'm not thoroughly honest, I can tell a white lie here and there when it's nessersary, but I am trying my hardest to redeem myself, as after experience I've found it's not worth it. If I cannot get my way with various people I walk away and most likley never talk to that person again. I take an interest in other people and I like to hear about their problems as more than likley they can help mesolve my own. My friends are used to me now and I don't realy worry them. I worry a bit after I have just yelled somebody out and more than likely I am the first to appologise. (Livesley & Bromley, 1973, p. 239 [original spellings retained])

If you look carefully at these descriptions, you will see that the number of stable psychological characteristics mentioned about the self increases with age. In addition, when trait descriptions first appear, they focus on overall qualities of character (e.g., "smart," "honest," "helpful," "friendly," "truthful") and emotional characteristics ("happy," "cheerful," "able to control my temper") as the child forms general ideas about the self. A developmental shift occurs during early adolescence, from these global evaluative terms to the use of qualifiers ("I have a *fairly* quick temper." "I'm *not thoroughly* honest."), along with indicators of how psychological characteristics are manifested in different situations. This trend reflects the adolescent's in-

---

[1] Turn back to Chapter 7, page 301, to review these findings.

creasing understanding that the behavior of the self is best understood as a complex interaction of psychological characteristics and situational influences (Barenboim, 1977; Livesley & Bromley, 1973). In addition, during adolescence, a greater emphasis on interpersonal virtues, such as being sociable, considerate, and cooperative, appears in self-descriptions, a change that reflects greater concern with being liked and viewed in a positive light by others (Rosenberg, 1979).

What factors are responsible for these changes in the self-concept? Cognitive development determines the changing *structural organization* of the self, from an array of concrete, isolated behavioral attributes during the preschool years to the consolidation of typical behaviors into stable psychological attributes during late childhood and adolescence (Harter, 1983; Paget & Kritt, 1986). But the *content* of the developing self is largely gleaned from interaction with others, although, as we mentioned earlier, feedback from acting directly on the environment also plays an important role (Shavelson, Hubner, & Stanton, 1976; Shavelson & Bolus, 1982).

Early in this century, sociologist C. H. Cooley (1902) proposed that the role of other people in the child's emerging self-definition is like a social mirror, for what eventually becomes the self is the synthesis of what we imagine significant others think of us. Cooley called this reflected or social self *the looking-glass self*. Several decades later, George Herbert Mead (1934) elaborated on Cooley's idea with his concept of the **generalized other,** which suggested that a coherent, psychological self truly emerges when the child is able to assume the attitude that others take toward the self. Mead theorized that in stepping outside the self, assuming this role of a generalized other, and then looking back at the self, "we appear as social objects, as selves" to ourselves (p. 270).

Cooley's and Mead's ideas indicate that perspective-taking skills emerging during middle childhood and adolescence — in particular, the ability to imagine what other people are thinking — play a crucial role in the development of a psychological self. These skills permit the child to construct a "generalized other," consisting of descriptions of how the self appears to others as well as evaluative statements about how others judge that appearance. The shift during adolescence, noted earlier, toward interpersonal virtues as part of the self-concept is a clear indication of the operation of the "generalized other." Such traits reveal that adolescents place increasing emphasis on psychological attributes that have to do with their attractiveness as people and personalities in the eyes of others. In addition, the existence of the generalized other has been repeatedly supported by research (Rosenberg, 1979). In one recent study adolescents in grades 6 to 12 were asked to describe the impressions that parents and peers formed of them. An increase with age was found in their tendency to think that others perceive them as individuals with stable psychological dispositions and personalities, rather than solely in terms of surface characteristics (Herzberger et al., 1981).

The work of Cooley and Mead suggests that the contents of people's self-concepts differ from one another because sources of the generalized other vary from person to person. Parents and teachers send different messages to different children, and as a result, children come to value and incorporate a particular constellation of psychological qualities into their sense of self. In addition, the significant others that children look to as sources of the self-concept — the ones whose opinions they care about and value — increase in number and then eventually come to be selected more deliberately with age. Consequently, the older child's self-concept depends not only on the attitudes of others toward the child, but also on the child's attitude toward others with whom he or she comes in contact. Between 8 and 15 years of age, peer evaluations become more important sources of self-definition. A related change is that, during adolescence, the self-concept starts to become increasingly vested in those who are deliberately chosen — the individual's closest friends (Rosenberg, 1979).

However, parental influences do not, as commonly believed, decline during this period. In a survey of over 3,000 adolescents, Douvan and Adelson (1966) found that

*During adolescence, peer
evaluations become more
important as sources of
self-definition. (Erika Stone)*

of all people, 14- to 16-year-olds admired their parents most and, in general, felt they had honest and trusting relationships with them. In a British study, adolescent alienation from parents was also uncommon. An increase in petty disputes about clothes, hair, and going out did occur, but few teenagers reported being overly critical and rejecting of their parents, and most continued to share parental values (Rutter et al., 1976).

Self-esteem: The Evaluative Side of Self-concept

In the discussion above, we focused on the general structure and content of the self-concept and how it changes with age. An additional component of self-concept is **self-esteem,** the judgments we make about the worth of ourselves (Coopersmith, 1967; Rosenberg, 1979; Harter, 1983). According to Rosenberg (1979), "a person with high self-esteem is fundamentally satisfied with the type of person he is, yet he may acknowledge his faults while hoping to overcome them." (p. 31). Thus, high self-esteem implies a realistic appraisal of the self's characteristics and competencies, coupled with an attitude of self-acceptance, self-respect, and self-worth.

Self-esteem is such a conspicuous part of people's reflections about themselves that many investigators who study it make no distinction between self-esteem and the broader idea of self-concept. In fact, the great majority of studies of self-concept are really studies of self-esteem. The interest of psychologists in this evaluative side of the self has been so great that it has generated a virtual mountain of research.

One Self-esteem or Many? Although the first studies of self-esteem emphasized a single global self-evaluation, new evidence indicates that as early as the preschool period children make distinctions about how they feel about various aspects of the self. Today, researchers believe that in addition to general self-esteem, it is important to assess a number of separate self-evaluations, such as perceptions of cognitive and academic competence, feelings of acceptance by parents and peers, and evaluations of one's physical abilities and appearance. In fact, recent research suggests that children develop an array of separate self-esteems first, only later combining and integrating them into an overall impression. Thus, the course of self-esteem development appears to be one of *differentiation* of a number of separate self-evaluations, followed by their eventual *integration* into an overall sense of self-worth, producing a hierarchically organized system of self-appraisal. Harter (1981; 1983) believes that prior to middle childhood, a general self-esteem cannot exist, since children have not yet constructed a coherent psychological picture of themselves. They only evaluate specific behaviors as good or bad.

Researchers have investigated the multidimensional nature of self-esteem in the same way that they have tried to answer the question of whether there is only one intelligence or many: by applying the technique of *factor analysis*[2] to children's ratings of themselves on a great many characteristics. Results reveal that during the preschool and early elementary school years, children already distinguish between two separate self-esteems: social acceptance and competence (being "good" at doing things). However, the 4- to 7-year-old does not yet discriminate among competence in different activity domains. Perceiving the self as good at one activity (e.g., schoolwork) is fused with perceptions of competence at others (e.g., sports and games) (Harter, 1983). By 7 to 8 years of age, children differentiate among a variety of self-esteems, with independent dimensions of cognitive or academic competence, physical prowess, and social self-worth appearing in many studies. Shavelson's hierarchical model, shown in Figure 11.1, depicts how self-esteem is organized by the mid-elementary school years (Marsh et al., 1984; Shavelson, Hubner, & Stanton, 1976; Shavelson & Bolus, 1982). By this time, in addition to a set of independent self-evaluations, children have also begun to build an overall view of how they feel about themselves (Harter, 1982). As children move toward adolescence, the hierarchical structure of self-esteem is reflected even more clearly in factor-analytic studies (Marsh et al., 1984; Mullener & Laird, 1971), and it appears among socioeconomically and ethnically diverse samples of children (Cauce, 1987).

Developmental Changes in the Level of Self-esteem. Once the child formulates a sense of self-esteem, does it remain stable over childhood or does it fluctuate a great deal? The results of cross-sectional studies suggest that self-esteem drops over the early elementary school years (Eshel & Klein, 1981; Marsh et al., 1984; Nicholls, 1979; Ruble et al., 1980; Stipek, 1981). This decline can be explained by the fact that young children's self-judgments are at first inordinately high and show a poor match with the opinions of others and with objective performance. In one study, Stipek (1981) had children in kindergarten through third grade rate their own and each of their classmate's "smartness" at school. Pupils in all grades could provide assessments of classmates' abilities that correlated with teacher perceptions. However, the self-ratings of kindergartners and first graders were overly favorable and showed no relationship with teacher or peer judgments. Not until second grade did pupil self-ratings reflect the opinions of those around them. Similarly, Ruble and her colleagues reported that second graders were able to make use of social comparison information (their own score along with the scores of several peers) in judging how well they themselves did on a task, but younger pupils were not (Ruble et al., 1980). As children become better able to incorporate information from the environment regarding their performance, self-esteem adjusts to a more realistic level and gradually becomes more

---

[2] You may find it helpful to reread the description of factor analysis on page 317 of Chapter 8.

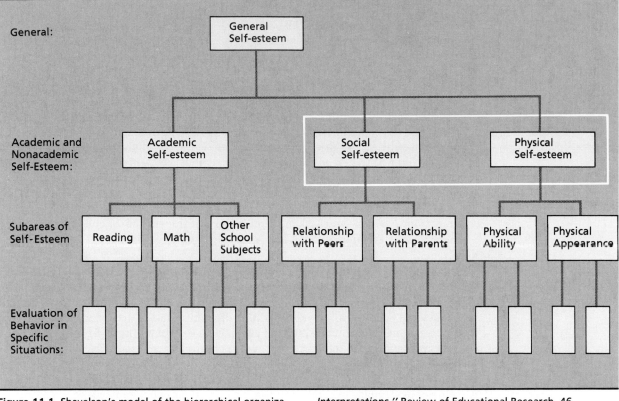

Figure 11.1. Shavelson's model of the hierarchical organization of self-esteem. *(From R. J. Shavelson, J. J. Hubner, & J. C. Stanton, 1976, "Self-concept: Validation of Construct Interpretations,"* Review of Educational Research, 46, *407–441. Adapted by permission.)*

strongly correlated with teacher ratings, test scores, and direct observations of the child's behavior.

Both longitudinal and cross-sectional findings indicate that from fourth grade on and continuing throughout the adolescent years, self-esteem, based on global assessments as well as the separate areas of social and physical self-worth, is on the rise for most individuals (Nottelmann, 1987; O'Malley & Bachman, 1983; Savin-Williams & Demo, 1984; Wallace, Cunningham, & Del Monte, 1984). One exception to this trend is a temporary decline in self-esteem associated with the period surrounding the transition from elementary to junior high school (Rosenberg, 1979; Simmons et al., 1979). Entry into a new school, accompanied by new expectations on the part of teachers and peers, may lead adolescents to have difficulty making realistic judgments about their behavior and performance for a period of time.

Aside from this exception, the fact that self-esteem shows a steady increase from late childhood on is one reason that researchers now question the long-held assumption that the transition to adolescence is a time of serious emotional turmoil. To the contrary, improved self-evaluations suggest that for a great many young people, becoming an adolescent is relatively free from disturbance and, on the whole, fosters feelings of pride and self-confidence. (Nottelmann, 1987; Offer, Ostrov, & Howard, 1981). Most adolescents feel good about growing up, look forward to greater freedom and independence, and reap personal benefits from new responsibilities and expectations, not just in terms of what they learn, but also in terms of a growing sense of competence, self-worth, and self-respect.

The Antecedents of Self-esteem

From middle childhood on, strong relationships exist between children's self-evaluations and their everyday behavior and performance. For example, academic self-esteem predicts children's school achievement and their curiosity and motivation to engage in challenging tasks (Harter, 1981; Marsh et al., 1984; Marsh, Smith, & Barnes, 1985), and children with high social self-esteem are consistently rated as better liked by their peers (Harter, 1982). Large sex differences in self-esteem, with physical abilities favoring boys and reading favoring girls (Marsh, Relich, & Smith, 1983; Marsh et al., 1984), parallel clear behavioral differences between the sexes. Boys generally outperform girls in athletic power and skill during middle childhood (see Chapter 5), whereas girls do better in school, particularly in the verbal areas (Maccoby & Jacklin, 1974). The fact that self-esteem is so powerfully related to important individual differences in behavior is the major reason that psychologists have been interested in studying its origins. If ways can be found to improve children's sense of self-worth, then many important dimensions of children's development may be enhanced as well.

Child-rearing Practices. Investigators interested in the antecedents of self-esteem have focused on the importance of a nurturant home environment that provides children with firm but reasonable expectations for behavior. Warm, positive parental behavior is believed to provide children with confirmation that they are accepted as competent and worthwhile human beings. Firm expectations, backed up with rational explanations, are thought to encourage children to make sensible choices, evaluate their own behavior against reasonable standards, and feel confident about the decisions they make. In contrast, repeated use of parental coercion communicates a sense of inadequacy to children. It suggests that their behavior needs to be controlled by others and that they are ineffective in managing it themselves.

Although research relating child-rearing practices to self-esteem is limited (Wylie, 1979), the evidence that does exist is consistent with the predictions noted above (Coopersmith, 1967; Openshaw, Thomas, & Rollins, 1984). However, we must be cautious in interpreting these relationships, for they are merely correlational. Although parental acceptance is probably an important prerequisite for a positive sense of self-worth, we cannot separate the extent to which child-rearing styles are causes of or reactions to children's characteristics and behavior (Wylie, 1979).

Research that has been far more successful at isolating the antecedents of self-esteem involves attribution theory, which focuses on how children interpret the multiple environmental cues that provide them with information about themselves. Unlike the correlational findings reported above, attribution research has been able to identify powerful adult communication styles that cause changes in children's sense of self-worth. In the next section, we look at how one set of influential attributions develops — children's explanations for their successes and failures in academic learning situations.

Making Attributions: Speculating about the Causes of Success and Failure. In Chapter 8, we showed that although intelligence predicts school achievement, it is imperfectly correlated with it. Differences among children in **achievement motivation** — the tendency to display initiative and persistence when faced with challenging tasks — are an important reason that some less intelligent children do better in school than their brighter counterparts and that children who are equally endowed intellectually often respond quite differently in achievement situations (Dweck & Elliott, 1983). Because achievement motivation spurs us on to acquire new knowledge and skills, to master the unknown, and to increase the self's competence, it is highly valued in all human societies (Fyans et al., 1983) and worthy of encouragement at an early age.

Middle childhood is an especially important period for consolidation of the "achieving self." Recall from Chapter 1 that psychoanalyst Erik Erikson (1950) viewed the development of *industry,* or the capacity for productive involvement in activities that have meaning in one's own culture, as the major developmental task of this period. Erikson saw the development of industry as crucial, because it provides children with important skills and achievement strivings that form the foundation for later vocational direction, which is a major concern of the soon-to-follow adolescent and young adulthood years. Today, developmental psychologists regard children's attributions — their beliefs about the causes of their own successes and failures — as the major reason that some children are competent learners who are oriented toward mastery in the face of obstacles to success, while others treat failure as insurmountable and readily give up when task goals are not immediately achieved.

The Development of Achievement-related Attributions. As we have seen in previous chapters, children begin to engage in competence-increasing activities almost as soon as they enter the world. In Chapter 10, we showed that infants derive great pleasure from physical and mental activity. When mastery is attained as a consequence of babies' own actions (e.g., pulling a string to make a mobile turn), the satisfaction experienced reinforces their behavior, motivating them to engage in similar activities in the future. Infants do not yet cognitively evaluate the outcomes of their actions against internally or externally imposed standards, nor do they take the results of their actions as an indication of the worth or goodness of the self. Instead, they are naturally driven toward mastery of activities that foster their own development. More complex, later-developing motives, such as achievement motivation, are believed to have roots in this early drive (White, 1959).

By age 3, children are capable of cognitively reacting to their performance by making attributions about their successes and failures. The development of these attributions is important, for they affect children's *expectancies of success,* and these expectancies, in turn, influence the extent to which children will be motivated to persist when confronted with similar tasks in the future.

Children age 6 and below view their own ability as extremely high, often underestimate task difficulty, and as a result hold very high expectancies of success. Even in the face of repeated failure, 5-year-olds, in comparison to older grade school children, will keep trying for a longer period of time (Rholes et al., 1980). When asked to react to a situation in which one person does worse on a task than another, young children indicate that the lower-scoring person can still succeed if he keeps on trying, and they believe that a smart person is one who expends more effort (Nicholls, 1978). In short, preschoolers and early elementary school children are "learning optimists" (Dweck & Elliott, 1983). They develop naive explanations for their successes and failures that support a continuation of the mastery-oriented behavior they freely displayed as infants. As evidence for this optimism, when kindergartners and first graders are asked to indicate how well they think they are doing in school, most rank themselves at the top of the class (Nicholls, 1979; Stipek, 1981).

Of course, part of the reason that young children arrive at these positive attributional conclusions is that they are not yet capable of the complex reasoning that older grade-school children use to explain their successes and failures. Young children do not notice and separate relevant variables from one another in the sphere of physical cognition (see Chapters 6 and 7); neither do they do so in the realm of social cognition. Several studies report that preschool and early elementary school children fail to isolate and coordinate effort and ability in making achievement-related attributions (Kun, 1977; Nicholls, 1978). Instead, they view all good things as going together: a person who tries hard is also a smart person who is going to succeed (Kun, 1977).

During middle childhood, children can separate the attributional variables of ability and effort, and they take a wider array of information into account in explaining why they succeed and fail. Elementary school children who are high in academic self-esteem develop **mastery-oriented attributions** that are adaptive in sustaining achievement motivation on the more intellectually demanding tasks of the school years. These children attribute their successes to high ability, and since they understand ability to be a characteristic of the self that they can depend on in the future to help them succeed, their causal attribution engenders high expectancies of success. When failure occurs, mastery-oriented children attribute it to factors about the self or the environment that can be changed and controlled, such as insufficient effort or an especially difficult task. Consequently, regardless of whether they succeed or fail, their attributions result in a willingness to approach challenging tasks with vigor, and they retain the enthusiasm for learning that characterized them during their earlier years (Nicholls, 1976).

Learned Helplessness. Unfortunately, some elementary school children use their new-found capacities for social reasoning to arrive at far less flattering explanations for task outcomes. Dweck and her collaborators (Dweck & Elliott, 1983; Dweck et al., 1978) refer to a phenomenon called **learned helplessness** that characterizes children who believe that failure is insurmountable. The achievement strivings of such children are seriously disrupted when they encounter obstacles to success or receive negative feedback from parents and teachers. Under these circumstances, their performance quickly deteriorates, and they show decreased persistence and signs of giving up.

Learned-helpless children construct a very different pattern of attributions than their mastery-oriented counterparts. They explain their failures (and not their successes) as due to ability, and since they have come to regard ability as a fixed characteristic of the self that is difficult to change, they have little confidence in themselves, develop low expectancies of success, and when failure hits, they regard themselves as hopelessly inadequate in the face of it (Diener & Dweck, 1978; 1980). Because learned helplessness engenders disrupted performance along with feelings of anxious lack of control, it acts to sustain itself, providing children with repeated confirmation of their failure-related explanations. Learned-helpless children soon select less challenging tasks in order to protect themselves from the debilitating psychological consequences of failure, and over the long term they choose less challenging courses and even less demanding careers (Parsons, 1983). Thus, learned helplessness prevents children from pursuing tasks that they are actually capable of mastering because their attributions lead to low expectancies of success.

What accounts for the very different attributions of learned-helpless and mastery-oriented children? Children pick up some information about how capable they are from their actual performance and how well it compares to that of their peers. But the kind of feedback they receive from adults also plays a significant role. In a recent study, Parsons, Adler, and Kaczala (1982) reported that among children of equivalent performance in mathematics, those with low expectancies of success had parents who believed that they were less able and had to work harder to succeed, and the children shared these beliefs. In another, Dweck and her colleagues (1978) experimentally manipulated the feedback fourth- and fifth-grade children received after they failed at a task. Those receiving negative evaluations implicating their ability were far more likely to attribute their poor performance to lack of ability than children receiving feedback suggesting insufficient effort was involved. Dweck's research shows that the evaluative messages adults send to children are a strong determinant of how they interpret failure experiences. According to the chain of events depicted in Figure 11.2, once such attributions are formed, they affect children's self-evaluations and future expectancies of success, which in turn moderate their achievement motivation and performance in learning situations.

At this point, it is important to note that girls are far more likely than boys to exhibit the helpless pattern of attributions and low expectancies of success described above (Crandall, 1969; Dweck, Goetz, & Strauss, 1980; Stipek & Hoffman, 1980).

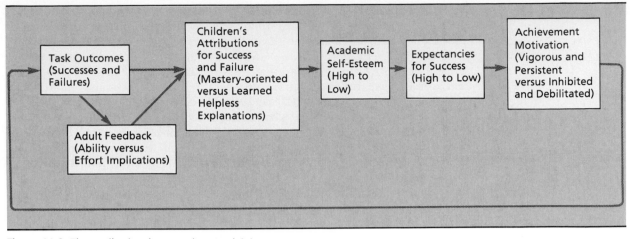

Figure 11.2. The attributional approach to explaining children's achievement motivation.

Girls more often blame their ability for poor performance, and they are also more likely to show decreased persistence and impaired performance following failure (Dweck & Gilliard, 1975; Dweck & Reppucci, 1973; Nicholls, 1975; Phillips, 1981; Weisz & McGuire, 1980). Girls also tend to receive evaluative feedback from adults (both teachers and parents) that credits their effort when they succeed, but denigrates their ability when they fail, whereas the reverse is true for boys (Dweck et al., 1978; Parsons, Adler, and Kaczala, 1982). Although the greater learned helplessness of girls is not related to poorer achievement in the grade-school years, the low sense of self-esteem and expectancies for success engendered by it may pave the way for future diminished achievement and an increased likelihood of falling short of realizing their intellectual potential during adolescence and adulthood (Dweck & Licht, 1980; Parsons, 1983).

Attribution Retraining. At one time achievement motivation was viewed as a relatively fixed, enduring characteristic of the personality that developed early in life because some children (especially boys) were encouraged by parents to be more independent and self-reliant than others (McClelland et al., 1953; Rosen & D'Andrade, 1959). Today, this is no longer the prevalent view. The attributional account suggests that achievement motivation can be changed by modifying self-deprecating attributions. However, effective remolding of attributions may need to take place prior to adolescence, before individuals form a stable, coherent conception of the self's characteristics, some of which may be resistant to change (Harari & Covington, 1981).

Attribution retraining involves methods that try to get children who have been identified as low achievers or who exhibit learned helplessness to view failure as surmountable if additional effort is exerted. Most often, children are asked to work on tasks that are hard enough so that some failure experiences are bound to occur, and then they are provided with repeated feedback from an adult that helps them revise their failure-related attributions, such as "You can do it if you try harder" (e.g., Dweck, 1975). In addition to reinterpreting failures, many programs encourage children to ascribe their successes to both ability and effort as opposed to chance factors like good luck, by giving them additional feedback after they succeed, such as, "You're really good at this" or "You really tried hard on that one" (Chapin & Dyck, 1976; Fowler & Peterson, 1981; Medway & Venino, 1982; Schunk, 1983). Other helpful techniques are exposure to models who demonstrate self-effort statements (e.g., "I tried hard and found out I could do it.") and persistence in the face of obstacles to task success (Cecil & Medway, 1986; Schunk, 1981; Schunk, Hanson, & Cox, 1987). These easy-to-implement procedures are remarkably effective at enhancing children's judgments of their own performance capabilities, increasing task persistence, and improving ultimate task success. In addition, the greater task persistence that accrues from attribution retraining generalizes to new tasks and endures over long periods of time (Chapin & Dyck, 1976; Rhodes, 1977).

According to Dweck (1986), when children replace learned helpless with mastery-oriented attributions, their motivational style changes from a *fixed* to an *incremental* view of their ability. Even if ability is low to begin with, it can be improved by trying hard. Attribution retraining is a simple, practical tool for helping teachers and parents replace destructive feedback practices (criticisms for errors, negative comparisons with peers, and unreasonably high expectations) with communication patterns that foster the fullest possible development of children's intellectual potential.

Adolescence: Constructing an Identity

The following self-searching statement was written by a 17-year-old girl asked to compose a short essay to answer the question, "Who am I?" As you read it, consider how it differs from the sample self-descriptions of younger children given on page 467:

> I am a human being. I am a girl. I am an individual. I don't know who I am. I am a Pisces. I am a moody person. I am an indecisive person. I am an ambitious person. I am a very curious person. I am not an individual. I am a loner. I am an American (God help me). I am a Democrat. I am a liberal person. I am a radical. I am a conservative. I am a pseudoliberal. I am an atheist. I am not a classifiable person (i.e., I don't want to be). (Montemayor & Eisen, 1977, p. 318)

This response exemplifies the direction of self-development during adolescence: toward a sense of **identity,** a coherent conception of the self consisting of an integrated set of goals, values, and beliefs to which the individual is solidly committed. The young person who wrote this statement is still formulating her identity, for we see her reviewing, reflecting, and vacillating about a large number of ideological beliefs. As she gradually builds a well-developed self-structure, various elements will be added and discarded, until she patterns the disparate parts into a consistent, organized self-system worthy of giving direction and meaning to her life (Erikson, 1950; Marcia, 1980; Waterman, 1984).

Erikson's (1950; 1968) theory, summarized in Chapter 1, has provided the major inspiration for virtually all current research on identity development. According to Erikson, establishing an identity involves a search for *continuity* of the self's attributes over time. Adolescents must sort through the attributes that defined the self during childhood and mold them into a mature self-conception that provides a sense of sameness and consistency as they move toward adulthood. Another important component of identity formation involves *unity*. Adolescents must construct a unified self that integrates the new roles they will assume — occupational, sexual, and ideological (e.g., religious, political, and moral) — into an organized configuration. Thus, attaining an identity is a matter of synthesizing childhood self-definitions into more mature commitments having to do with getting a job, establishing new relationships, and becoming a citizen.

Is Adolescence Inevitably a Period of Storm and Stress? In a complex society that confronts the adolescent with many possible directions and choices, each young person who successfully formulates an identity experiences an **identity crisis** — a temporary period of heightened self-consciousness and self-focusing as the individual experiments with a variety of alternatives before settling on a set of goals and values. Erikson believes that adolescent commitments arrived at without a period of inner "soul searching" are not true identity formations, for a secure identity results from personally sifting through many choices and assuming the formidable responsibility of choosing goals and values that fit with the self's strengths and weaknesses. As part of this process, adolescents must not only affirm a set of commitments, but also relinquish some fantasized, glamorous possibilities of what they once thought they would become as unrealistic, impractical, and unattainable.

A few adolescents experience identity crises that are traumatic and totally preoccupying, but Erikson recognized that for most, identity formation proceeds in a very gradual, uneventful way. The many daily decisions that an adolescent makes — "whom to date, whether or not to break up, having intercourse, taking drugs, going to college or working, which college, what major, studying or playing, being politically active" — and the bases on which these decisions are made, eventually are integrated into a unified self-structure (Marcia, 1980, p. 161). As we indicated earlier, for most young people adolescence is not a period of intense emotional upheaval that brings with it an increased risk of serious adjustment difficulties, although it has often been thought of in this way. In fact, as part of the Isle of Wight Study, an intensive investigation of the distribution of childhood and adolescent psychological disorders among a population of 100,000 residing on an island off the coast of England, Rutter and his colleagues (1976) reported that the rate of serious psychological disturbances increased only slightly from middle childhood to adolescence (from 5.7 percent at age 10 to 7.7 percent at age 15). Among the mild rise in psychological problems during the teenage years, depression and suicide are common occurrences (see Box 11.1). But it is important to keep in mind that an identity crisis is a normal and necessary experience during adolescence, not a cataclysmic and seriously disruptive event that predisposes young people to high rates of psychopathology.

Paths to Identity Formation. Because Erikson's account of identity was originally intended for clinical purposes, its initial impact rested on its usefulness in the psychoanalytic interpretation of case histories. As a result, some of his ideas appeared vague to developmental psychologists (Waterman, 1982). Recently, Erikson's theory has been tested and extended using social-cognitive research methods that clarify the course of identity development and the various means that adolescents use to arrive at a coherent, integrated sense of self.

Marcia (1966; 1980) used a semistructured interviewing technique to evaluate the extent to which young people are in a period of crisis or have made commitments to occupational choices and religious and political values. He found evidence for four identity statuses that indicate the degree of progress individuals have made toward formulating a mature personal identity. Marcia's four identity statuses are an outgrowth of Erikson's theory, but they also add to it by making the various paths toward identity formation explicit, measurable, and testable:

1. **Identity achievement.** These individuals have already experienced a period of crisis and decision making and now manifest a secure sense of commitment to an occupation or ideology.
2. **Moratorium.** The word "moratorium" refers to a temporary delay or holding pattern. These individuals have suspended definite commitments while they go through an identity crisis, searching for an appropriate occupation and ideology in which to make a positive self-investment.
3. **Identity foreclosure.** Like identity-achieved individuals, foreclosed young people have committed themselves to occupational and ideological positions. However, they have dodged the task of attaining a mature identity, for their commitments are not self-chosen, but merely the choices of authority figures, usually parents. Foreclosed adolescents have avoided a period of crisis and, instead, have

Box 11.1
Adolescent Suicide: Annihilation of the Self

Over the last 30 years, the suicide rate has tripled among adolescents and young adults, currently ranking as the third most common form of death (following accidents and homicides) among this age sector of the population. More than 5000 die from suicide each year (Pfeffer, 1986).

Marked sex differences in suicidal behavior exist, with the number of boys who kill themselves exceeding girls by four or five to one. Girls more often make unsuccessful suicide attempts and use methods with a likelihood of resuscitation, such as a sleeping pill overdose. In contrast, boys select more active and instantaneously lethal methods, such as firearms or hanging (Holden, 1986; Shaffer, 1974). These differences may be partly the result of societal sex-role expectations, for there is less tolerance for feelings of helplessness and failed efforts in males than in females (Smith, 1981).

Many studies point to a common set of internal and external factors that predispose young people to suicidal actions. Suicidal adolescents often show signs of severe depression during the period preceding the suicidal act, with many verbalizing the wish to die, losing interest in school or hobbies, and manifesting a pervasive sense of gloom and hopelessness (Triolo et al., 1984; Shafii et al., 1985). These depressive symptoms appear in two different types of suicidal youngsters.

In one group are adolescents of superior intelligence who lead a solitary, withdrawn existence, hold themselves to inordinately high standards of performance, and are very self-critical. A second, larger group is characterized by antisocial tendencies. These adolescents engage in bullying, fighting, and stealing, and many have a history of school truancy and drug and alcohol abuse. These behavior patterns indicate that many suicidal young people do not just turn aggression inward; they are also hostile and destructive in their actions toward others (Holden, 1986; Shaffer, 1974; Shaffer & Fisher, 1981).

Family turmoil, parental emotional problems, and marital breakups are prevalent in the backgrounds of suicidal adolescents. However, since these factors, as well as the behavior constellations noted above, can be found in young people who do not commit suicide, psychologists believe that other precipitating events are also involved. Common circumstances just before a suicide include the breakup of an important peer relationship or learning that parents will be informed about the adolescent's antisocial behavior. Such experiences trigger shame and humiliation in a young person whose sense of self is already extremely precarious. Also, exposure to the suicidal behavior of relatives and friends seems to be important, for from one-third to two-thirds of suicide victims have known someone who has attempted or completed suicide (Holden, 1986; Shaffer, 1974; Shafii et al., 1985).

Why is suicide extremely rare before age 12 but on the rise thereafter? Investigators believe that the adolescent's improved ability to engage in planning and foresight and greater awareness of the self as seen by others play significant roles. Many who succeed in their suicidal intent plan it out purposefully and secretively; few adolescent suicides are sudden and impulsive. In addition, cognitive advances may cause depression to be experienced differently during adolescence than it was at earlier ages. Depressed teenagers are believed to be extremely self-preoccupied and self-focused, a circumstance that may lead them to the exaggerated conclusion that no one could possibly understand them or could ever experience the intense psychological pain they feel. Thus, cognitive maturity is an added factor that may contribute to the hopelessness, isolation, and despair of an already vulnerable adolescent (Pfeffer, 1986; Shaffer & Fisher, 1981).

Prevention and treatment of suicide is a multidimensional activity. Young people who show warning signs, such as suicidal threats and comments, a sense of hopelessness and gloom, and declining interest in activities, need professional help and the sympathetic understanding of adults who take their despair seriously. Family and peer survivors of suicide victims also need help, to assist them in emotionally integrating the event and as a means for preventing additional suicides in the future (Smith, 1980).

---

reached a premature commitment to a ready-made identity that others have formulated for them.

4. **Identity diffusion.** These individuals differ from the above three identity statuses in that they do not have firm occupational or ideological commitments and are not actively trying to reach them. Diffused adolescents are characterized by a lack of direction. They may have never experienced an identity crisis, or they may have had a period of crisis that they were unable to resolve.

In the process of forming an identity, adolescents often shift from one status to another until an identity is finally achieved. In a cross-sectional study of college-bound males between the ages of 12 and 24, Meilman (1979) found that young adolescents often start out as identity diffused or foreclosed, but gradually shift toward the moratorium and identity-achieved statuses between 18 and 21 years of

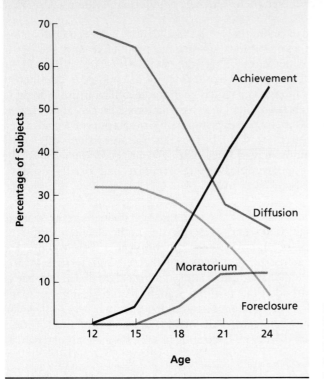

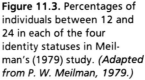

Figure 11.3. Percentages of individuals between 12 and 24 in each of the four identity statuses in Meilman's (1979) study. *(Adapted from P. W. Meilman, 1979.)*

age (see Figure 11.3), a trend that has been documented for both males and females in a more representative sample of both college- and non-college-oriented adolescents (Archer, 1982). Late adolescence seems to be an especially important time for identity achievement, and longitudinal research on college youth confirms this, for many undergraduates show shifts from a moratorium to an identity-achieved status between their freshman and senior years (Adams & Fitch, 1982; Waterman & Waterman, 1971; Waterman, Geary, & Waterman, 1974). The diversity of experiences provided by college environments undoubtedly triggers considerable self-searching and suggests various resolutions for identity concerns. However, young people who go to work following high school are not handicapped in formulating a sense of identity. They are not more foreclosed or diffused; in fact, they are less so. They simply move toward identity achievement sooner than their college-bound counterparts (Munro & Adams, 1977).

As you have probably surmised, identity achievement and moratorium are regarded as healthy and adaptive avenues to identity formation, whereas foreclosure and diffusion are considered maladaptive. In general, research supports this idea, for individuals who are either identity-achieved or experiencing a moratorium tend to "do better and feel better about themselves" than their less well-developed counterparts (Marcia, 1980, p. 181). They have a higher sense of self-esteem, report greater similarity between their ideal self (what they had hoped to become) and their real self, are more advanced in moral reasoning, and are more likely to assume personal responsibility for their decisions and the direction of their lives (Marcia, 1980; Waterman & Goldman, 1976). In addition, identity-achieved individuals, more than the other three statuses, have moved beyond the preoccupation with an *imaginary audience*[3] that characterizes adolescents upon entry into the formal operational stage. They are less self-focused and preoccupied with how others regard them and more

[3] Return to Chapter 6, pages 253–254, to review the concept of the *imaginary audience*.

self-assured and outer-directed than their same-age counterparts (Adams, Abraham, & Markstrom, 1987).

What factors are involved in facilitating adolescent identity achievement? Waterman (1982) speculates that opportunities to observe productive and successful models and exposure to a wide range of identity alternatives are important. In addition, parenting styles that are involved but democratic as opposed to dominating (likely to yield foreclosure) or uninvolved (likely to promote diffusion) are thought to play a role. Although research bears out these associations between child-rearing practices and identity statuses, once again, it is impossible to sort out cause and effect. A profitable direction for future research will be to isolate the antecedents of identity development, so that interventions aimed at facilitating identity consolidation can be initiated, thereby maximizing opportunities for adolescents to lead socially responsible as well as personally satisfying adult lives.

In summary, in the sections above we have seen that vast changes in the sense of self occur from infancy through adolescence. The first step in the development of the self is self-recognition, which is attained by the second year of life. To this, the preschooler adds concrete categorical descriptors of the self and awareness of a private, inner self. In middle childhood, internal psychological attributes appear in children's self-descriptions. In addition, a differentiated, hierarchically organized self-esteem develops that is strongly influenced by feedback from others. Self-development culminates during the adolescent years with the formation of an identity, a coherent, integrated conception of the self consisting of self-chosen goals and values.

CONCEPTUALIZING OTHER PEOPLE

Children's developing cognitions about other people — their descriptions of others as personalities and the inferences they make about their behavior and internal thoughts — constitute the largest area of social-cognitive research. As we examine how children's understanding of others develops, you will see that it has much in common with their developing conceptions of themselves. Thoughts about other people become more abstract and psychologically based, and increasingly differentiated, well-organized, and integrated with age.

Person Perception: Understanding Others as Personalities

Person perception deals with how we conceptualize the personalities of people with whom we are familiar. To study its development, investigators use methods much like those used to illuminate how children think about themselves: asking them to give free descriptions of people they know, such as "Can you tell me what kind of person ———— is?"

Like their self-descriptions, children younger than age 8 describe others in terms of concrete, observable characteristics, such as appearance, possessions, and routine activities. Around third grade, children discover consistencies in the overt behavior of people they know. As a result, they begin to describe them in terms of motives, beliefs, abilities, interests, and attitudes (Barenboim, 1977; Livesley & Bromley, 1973; Peevers & Secord, 1973). However, the sophistication of children's descriptions of others as unique, differentiated personalities builds slowly and gradually. The first mention of inner attributes is closely tied to others' behavior and consists only of *implied* dispositions, such as "He is always fighting with people" or "He steals and he lies" (Peevers & Secord, 1973). Later, children mention psychological characteristics directly, but they are global and stereotyped descriptors, such as "good," "nice," or "acts smart," that reflect little in the way of differentiation of the other person's character. Eventually these broad, amorphous impressions evolve into sharper descriptions, and adjectives like "honest," "trustworthy," "generous," "polite," "likable," and "selfish," appear (Livesley & Bromley, 1973; Scarlett, Press, & Crockett, 1971). Moreover, elementary school children start to make comparisons among people at about the same time they begin to compare themselves to others. Their comparisons follow the concrete-to-abstract progression noted above, for in the early elementary school years they cast these comparisons in behavioral terms (e.g., "Billy runs a lot faster than Jason."). Only between 10 and 12, after they have had sufficient experience inferring psychological attributes from regularities in others' behavior, do they make psychological comparisons between people (e.g., "Paul's a lot more considerate than thick-headed Del.") (Barenboim, 1981, p. 133).

Throughout middle childhood children's character sketches remain poorly organized, with different descriptors strung together in a fairly random, unintegrated way. Between 14 and 16 years of age, person perception undergoes a major change in this regard, for adolescents begin to construct integrated descriptions of other people (Livesley & Bromley, 1973). To do so, they present rich descriptions of people they know that operate on several levels, simultaneously referring to external attributes, overt behavior, inner dispositions, and their complex interconnections. In addition, they recognize that their own experiences with a particular person, and therefore their constructed impressions of them, may differ from the opinions of other people (Barenboim, 1977; Livesley & Bromley, 1973).

The research discussed above shows that young people become capable amateur "personality theorists" by the midadolescent years, an accomplishment that is facilitated by improved abstract reasoning and perspective-taking abilities as well as a broader range of social experiences. Adolescents' capacity to synthesize unique combinations of behavior and inner characteristics into complex, integrated descriptions of others is useful and adaptive, for it permits them to understand as well as predict the actions of people they know far more effectively than they could at an earlier age.

Understanding Others' Intentions

Besides coming to know others as unique personalities, children, like adults, must observe and interpret the ongoing behavioral stream of other people to know how to react to it. Making behavior meaningful and responding to it appropriately often depend on being able to separate deliberate and intentional actions from those that are accidental and fortuitous. By two years of age, children already have intentionality on their minds, for they will use "gonna," "hafta," and "wanna" to announce actions that they are about to perform (Brown, 1973). In a number of studies, children have been shown filmed sequences of behavior and asked to describe what is happening. Even 4- and 5-year-olds spontaneously infer intentions, making such statements as, "He wants to know . . . ," "He's trying to . . . ," and "He needs . . . ," a tendency that increases over the school years (Flapan, 1968; Livesley & Bromley, 1973).

Children have the capacity to infer intentions at a very early age, but how good are they at distinguishing people's accidental from intentional acts? Parents' and teachers' anecdotal reports indicate that very young preschoolers clearly distinguish between their unintentional and intended behaviors when it is in their own best interests to do so. After being reproached by an adult for bumping into a playmate or spilling a glass of milk, they will defend themselves by exclaiming, "It was an accident!" or "I didn't do it on purpose!" (Shultz, 1980). Some evidence suggests that preschoolers separate the accidental from the intended at a somewhat earlier age for themselves than they do for others (Keasey, 1977). Adults help them make this distinction by providing relevant feedback — assigning blame for intentional behaviors and excusing or ascribing less blame for unintended ones. In addition, children

Even young children have the capacity to understand the difference between an intended and an unintended act. (Michal Heron)

are aided in making the discrimination by noticing how they themselves are thinking, feeling, and acting, for the cognitive experience of doing something one wants to do is very different from the experience of finding oneself doing something that one did not try to do (Shultz, 1980; Flavell, 1985). Once children appreciate this difference for themselves, they may generalize it to the behavior of others.

Children's ability to diagnose the intended and accidental behavior of others must follow quickly behind self-understanding, for some ingenious laboratory studies reveal that even 3-year-olds separate intended actions from unintentional behaviors such as mistakes and reflexes. Shultz, Wells, and Sarda (1980) had children repeat an easy-to-pronounce sentence ("She lives in a house") or a tongue twister ("She sells sea shells by the sea shore") in which they invariably made mistakes, after which an adult asked them, "Did you mean to say it that way?" Three-year-olds knew that an incorrectly repeated tongue twister was not intended to be spoken with errors, regardless of whether they did the speaking or watched another child make the mistake. In a second study, an experimenter elicited a knee-jerk reflex by tapping the child's knee and also had the child imitate a similar voluntary leg movement. Three- and 4-year-olds showed some tendency to distinguish these voluntary from involuntary movements in themselves and others, an ability that improved markedly by 5 years of age.

In the above instances, the researcher stated ahead of time exactly what the child's purposeful action was to be (e.g., repeating a sentence or moving one's leg like the experimenter). Recently, Shultz and Wells (1985) showed that children between the ages of 2½ and 12 rely heavily on a *matching rule* to separate intended from unintended behavior. If the self's or another person's prior stated intention matches the subsequent behavioral result, then the behavior must have been deliberate. but if it does not match, then the behavior was not intended. The matching rule always works for judging the self's behavior, but it cannot always be relied on to infer the intentions of others, because people often do not announce what they will do before they do it. Therefore, in many instances, children must notice environmental cues to figure out whether an actor's behavior was purposeful or not. Important cues are whether the result of an action leads to a positive or negative outcome (e.g., if you drop an empty milk carton in a garbage pail, the behavior was probably intended, but if you drop it on the floor it probably was not); whether or not the actor is monitoring his own actions (concentrating on what one is doing implies intentionality, whereas not paying attention suggests unintentionality); and whether an external cause can account for the person's behavior (e.g., stumbling over a box in the middle of a room is probably an accidental behavior). Smith (1978) showed 4- to 6-year old children films in which these cues were varied and found that 4-year-olds did not use them, but 5-year-olds clearly did. By the late preschool years children already have at their command a rich set of cognitive tools for separating others' behaviors into deliberate and unintended actions.

The range of intentional behaviors of which people are capable extends beyond the ones examined in the studies above, for we can intentionally simulate unintentional acts, like falling over an object or bumping into someone, and we can also deliberately refrain from acting, but pretend our lack of response was unintentional (e.g., "I forgot all about it!"). How children come to understand these subtle, deceptive forms of intentional behavior remains a topic for future research, but since they require that children imagine what another person is thinking, they probably depend on perspective-taking skills, a topic to which we turn in the next section.

Finally, as the result of their unique personalities and history of social experiences, children come to differ from one another in how they interpret other people's intentions. In research described in Box 11.2, Dodge and his collaborators found that

---

FOCUS ON THEORY, RESEARCH, AND APPLICATIONS

Box 11.2
Inferring Intentions: The Special Case of the Aggressive Child

Theory. The inferences that children make about the intentions of others are major determinants of how they respond in social situations. For example, if Bobby's knocking down the block tower is seen as deliberate and hostilely motivated, his classmates are likely to retaliate with verbal or physical aggression. But if destroying the tower is seen as prosocially motivated (carried out in the process of helping to clean up the room) or purely accidental, his peers are likely to refrain from seeking revenge.

Since children often respond with aggression when they regard the behavior of others as hostile and threatening, Kenneth Dodge hypothesized that highly aggressive and socially rejected children may behave as they do because they perceive hostile intentions in social situations where, in fact, they do not exist. To find out if such children suffer from serious social-cognitive deficits in their ability to use behavioral cues to interpret others' intentions, Dodge examined aggressive-rejected and nonaggressive boys' interpretations of peer behavior in which cues about the peer's intentions were systematically varied.

Research. Aggressive and nonaggressive boys in grades 2, 4, and 6 were told that they could win a prize for putting together a puzzle and that another (fictitious) boy was working on a similar puzzle in an adjoining room. When each subject was partly finished, the experimenter borrowed his puzzle, ostensibly to show it to the other boy. Moments later, the subject heard his puzzle crashing apart, along with one of three taped messages providing different cues about the peer's intentions: a *hostile condition,* in which the other boy says he does not want the subject to win a prize; a *prosocial condition,* in which the boy says he will help the subject get more done, but as he puts another piece in, he accidently knocks the puzzle over; and an *ambiguous condition,* in which the puzzle can be heard breaking apart, but the intentions of the boy are not made clear. Then the experimenter returned with the subject's destroyed puzzle as well as the other child's partly finished one. The subject was told to look over the puzzles while the adult was out of the room, and the researchers filmed his response. Although both groups of subjects responded to the hostile condition with retaliatory aggression (messing up the other boy's puzzle) and to the prosocial condition with restraint and helping behavior, in the ambiguous condition aggressive and non-aggressive boys differed sharply, with the aggressive boys reacting much more hostilely. The results indicated that in circumstances where the intentions of a peer are unclear, the social inferences of aggressive boys are distorted in the direction of hostile intentions, and they react accordingly (Dodge, 1980).

Another study showed that when aggressive boys feel personally threatened (for example, when they are led to expect an imminent conflict with a peer), their processing of intentional cues deteriorates even further. Under these conditions, they interpret both ambiguous and accidental intentional cues as hostile (Dodge & Somberg, 1987).

Dodge's research reveals that aggressive-rejected children have difficulty appraising intentions accurately. Primed to interpret the actions of others in a hostile fashion, they react with aggressive behavior that leads peers to respond in kind, creating an escalating spiral of peer-directed aggressive interaction. By the end of the elementary school years, normal peers have become biased in the way they view the intentions of highly aggressive boys, perceiving malice in instances where their intent is benign, due to the aggressive child's long history of belligerent behavior (Dodge & Frame, 1983).

Applications. Dodge's work suggests that social-cognitive interventions aimed at teaching aggressive boys to accurately interpret the intentional cues of others may help reduce their aggressive behavior. Once aggressive children's appraisal of others begins to change, peers need to be taught to view them differently, so that the past reputation of aggressive children does not continue to provoke antagonistic reactions that serve to perpetuate their overly hostile view of the world.

highly aggressive children exhibit striking biases in inferring the intentions of peers. Children's ability to observe and reason about the human behavioral stream is also of great applied significance. It is especially important in children's eyewitness testimony in court proceedings, a topic that we address in Box 11.3.

Understanding Another's Viewpoint: The Development of Perspective-taking Skills

In this and other chapters, we have repeatedly emphasized that children's capacity for **perspective-taking** — their ability to imagine what other people may be thinking and feeling[4] — is important for a wide variety of social-cognitive achievements, including referential communication skills (Chapter 9), empathic responding (Chapter 10), self-concept and self-esteem, conceptualizing other people as unique personalities, and making meaningful sense out of their ongoing stream of behavior. Selman's theory of the development of perspective-taking, which follows in the Piagetian tradition, is well grounded in empirical research. The perspective-taking advances he identified have proved to be critical factors in children's understanding of social relationships and the development of mature social behavior.

Selman's Stages of Perspective-taking. Selman (1980; Selman & Byrne, 1974) has developed a four-stage model that describes major changes in children's understanding of others' cognitive perspectives in relation to their own. Selman's stages, like Piaget's, are assumed to mark qualitatively distinct ways of thinking, to develop in an invariant sequence, and to apply universally to all children. The stages were originally formulated from age-related changes in children's responses to social dilemmas like this one:

> Holly is an 8-year-old girl who likes to climb trees. She is the best tree climber in the neighborhood. One day while climbing down from a tall tree she falls off the bottom branch but does not hurt herself. Her father sees her fall. He is upset and asks her to promise not to climb the trees any more. Holly promises.
>
> Later that day, Holly and her friends meet Sean. Sean's kitten is caught up in a tree and cannot get down. Something has to be done right away or the kitten may fall. Holly is the only one who climbs trees well enough to reach the kitten and get it down, but she remembers her promise to her father. (Selman & Byrne, 1974, p. 805)

Questions are then asked that focus on the characters' perspectives, such as, "Does Sean know why Holly cannot decide whether or not to climb the tree? What will Holly's father think? Will he understand why if she climbs the tree?"

Selman's four stages are as follows:

Level 0: Undifferentiated and egocentric perspective-taking (about 3–6 years). At this stage, the existence of the self's and others' inner thoughts and feelings is recognized, but the two are frequently confused. Children seldom acknowledge that another person can respond to and interpret the same situation differently from themselves.

Typical response to the "Holly" dilemma: The child predicts that Holly will save the kitten because she does not want it to get hurt and believes that Holly's father will feel just as she does about her climbing the tree: "Happy, he likes kittens" (Selman, 1976, p. 303).

Level 1: Differentiated and subjective perspective-taking (about 5–9 years). Children of this stage clearly understand that cognitive interpretations of

---

[4] Sometimes an alternative term — *role-taking* — is used to refer to this phenomenon in the research literature.

Box 11.3
Children's Eyewitness Testimony in Court Proceedings

Increasingly, children are being called upon to testify in court cases involving child abuse and neglect, child custody, adoption, and other civil and criminal cases. Having to provide such testimony can be difficult and traumatic. Not only are children confronted with a strange and unfamiliar situation—at the very least an interview in the judge's chambers and at most an open courtroom with an audience of judge, jury, and spectators and the possibility of unsympathetic cross-examination—but they may be asked to give testimony against a parent or other relative toward whom they have strong feelings of loyalty. For these reasons, when children's eyewitness accounts are not absolutely necessary, it is best to protect them from having to testify. Nevertheless, sometimes their testimony is essential. For example, in allegations of child abuse, the child is not only the victim, but often the only witness to the crime (Whitcomb, Shapiro, & Stellwagen, 1985).

Once a child's testimony is deemed important, judgments must be made concerning whether the child is mature enough to provide reliable and accurate information. Although some states have legal rules that exclude very young children from testifying, in others the court makes a judgment about each child's competence (Ross, Miller, & Moran, 1987). Nevertheless, it is rare for children under 5 to be asked to testify, while those 6 and older often are, and children between 10 and 14 are generally assumed to be sufficiently mature to appear in court (Saywitz, 1987). These guidelines make good sense in view of what we know about the development of children's social-cognitive capacities. Compared to preschoolers, school-age children are better able to recall and give detailed descriptions of past experiences, make accurate inferences about others' motives and intentions, and base their judgments on many different pieces of information instead of just a single event. Also, older children are more resistant to misleading and suggestive questions of the sort asked by attorneys when they probe for more information or, in cross-examination, try to influence the content of the child's responses (Goodman, Aman, & Hirschman, 1987).

Still, each child's competence to testify should be reviewed on an individual basis. When children are under stress, as is the case after a traumatic experience or separation from abusive, neglectful, or divorcing parents, they may experience distortions in social-cognitive processes. Misperceptions, misidentifications, overgeneralizations, and other errors in thinking can occur, seriously diminishing the child's accuracy as a witness (Peters, 1987). Evaluations by child guidance specialists may be helpful, in which the veracity of the child's account as well as the child's ability to withstand the stress of court testimony is assessed, particularly in cases where children are asked to testify against a parent. As part of the evaluation, children can be asked to give their account in several different interviews. If they have not been unfairly coached by an interested party, the wording should vary but the story should remain the same (Terr, 1980).

Children judged competent as witnesses need to be prepared so that they understand the courtroom process and know what to expect. At present, little research exists on how to go about preparing a child witness (Melton & Thompson, 1987a). One suggestion is to use role playing, in which children practice giving testimony to adults who act as judge and lawyers (Bernstein et al., 1982). As part of this process, children can be encouraged to admit not knowing an answer rather than guessing or going along with what an adult appears to expect of them (Cole & Loftus, 1987). If the child is likely to experience emotional trauma or later retribution (e.g., in a family dispute) as a result of appearing in court, then mechanisms exist for permitting expert witnesses to provide testimony that reports on the child's psychological condition and that contains important elements of the child's story (Terr, 1980).

---

social situations by the self and others may be the same or different, and they recognize that different perspectives may result because different people have access to different information. However, a Level 1 child is not yet capable of coordinating perspectives. He cannot put himself in the place of another person to judge that person's actions or reflect upon himself, and he also cannot appreciate that his own view of the other person is influenced by what he imagines the other's view of himself to be.

Typical response to the "Holly" dilemma: When asked how Holly's father will react when he finds out that she climbed the tree, the child responds, "If he didn't know anything about the kitten, he would be angry. But if Holly shows him the kitten, he might change his mind." The child clearly recognizes that depending on the information Holly's father has available for interpreting the situation, he may or may not be angry and his perspective may or may not be the same as Holly's.

Level 2: Self-reflective or reciprocal perspective-taking (about 7–12 years). Level 2 children are capable of engaging *reciprocal perspective-taking*. They can see their own thoughts, feelings, and behavior from another person's perspective and recognize that others can do the same. Therefore, Level 2 children are better able to anticipate others' reactions to their behavior than are children at earlier stages. However, they cannot move outside a two-person situation and view it from a third-party perspective.

Typical response to the "Holly" dilemma: When asked what punishment Holly might regard as fair if she climbs the tree, the child responds, "None. [Holly] knows that her father will understand why she climbed the tree, so she knows that he won't want to punish her at all" (Selman, 1976, p. 305). This response indicates that Holly's point of view is influenced by her assumption that her father will be able to "step in her shoes" and understand her motive for saving the kitten.

Level 3: Third-party or mutual perspective-taking (about 10–15 years). This individual can step outside a two-person situation and imagine how the self and others are viewed from a third-party "generalized other" position. The third party can be a typical member of a group or class of people (e.g., other children or parents) or simply a disinterested spectator. Assuming a third-party position enables the Level 3 individual to engage in *mutual perspective-taking,* which involves looking at the relationship between two perspectives simultaneously. Mutual perspective-taking is *recursive,* in that the person's viewpoint can take itself as an object of thought. For example, the individual can imagine that "Holly thinks that her father thinks that she thinks . . . ."

Typical response to the "Holly" dilemma: A Level 3 individual may respond to the question of whether Holly should be punished by her father as follows: "No, because Holly thought it was important to save the kitten, but she also knows that her father told her not to climb the tree and that he didn't know about the kitten, so she'd only think that she shouldn't be punished if she could get her father to understand why she thought it was important to climb the tree." This response steps outside the immediate situation to view both Holly's and her father's perspectives simultaneously. In addition, it has a recursive quality, in that Holly's viewpoint takes itself as an object of thought.

Level 4: In-depth and societal perspective-taking (about 14 years–adult). This stage is marked by an appreciation that mutual coordination of perspectives can take place on multiple or progressively deeper levels of understanding, including the levels of superficial information, shared interests, common expectations, or at a deeper level of unverbalized feelings and values. However, each of these levels is understood as influenced by one of a number of possible societal perspectives, such as "the American viewpoint," "the democratic viewpoint," or "the Judeo-Christian perspective." Thus a distinguishing feature of this stage is the capacity to view mutual perspective-taking as shaped by one or more systems of larger societal values.

Typical response to the "Holly" dilemma: At this level, the individual can make reference to larger societal values for whether Holly should save the kitten, how her father should view her action, and whether he should punish her. For example, a Level 4 adolescent may suggest that the value of humane treatment of animals justifies Holly's retrieval of the kitten and that her father's appreciation of this value will lead him not to punish her.

Research Confirming Selman's Developmental Sequence. As shown in Table 11.1, responses of cross-sectional samples between 4 years of age and adulthood to Selman's dilemmas indicate that maturity of perspective-taking rises steadily with

Table 11.1 Percentage of Subjects Reaching Each of Selman's Perspective-taking Levels Between 4 Years of Age and Adulthood

LEVEL	AGE 4	AGE 6	AGE 8	AGE 10	AGE 13	AGE 16	ADULT
0	80	10	0	0	0	0	0
1	20	90	40	20	7	0	0
2	0	0	50	60	50	21	0
3	0	0	10	20	36	58	0
4	—	—	—	—	7	21	100

Source: From R. L Selman & D. F. Byrne, 1974, "A Structural-Developmental Analysis of Levels of Role Taking in Middle Childhood," *Child Development, 45,* 803–806. © The Society for Research in Child Development, Inc. Additional data from D. F. Byrne, 1973, "The Development of Role Taking in Adolescence, unpublished doctoral dissertation, Harvard University.

age. In addition, longitudinal research reveals gradual movement toward successively higher stages over a period of 2 to 5 years, with no subjects skipping stages (Selman, 1980) and practically none regressing to a previous stage (Gurucharri & Selman, 1982). These findings provide strong support for Selman's assumption that perspective-taking skills develop in an age-related, invariant sequence.

In addition, advances in perspective-taking are related to the development of nonsocial-cognitive capacities. Maturity of perspective-taking is moderately correlated with general intelligence (Rubin, 1973; 1978) and is also associated with Piagetian cognitive performance. Individuals who fail Piaget's concrete operational tasks tend to be at Selman's Level 0, those who pass concrete but not formal operational tasks tend to be at Levels 1 and 2, and those who are increasingly formal operational tend to be at Levels 3 and 4 (Krebs & Gillmore, 1982; Keating & Clark, 1980). These findings offer additional support for Selman's developmental sequence as a stage-wise progression. Research also indicates that attainment of each Piagetian cognitive stage tends to occur somewhat earlier than its related perspective-taking level (Krebs & Gillmore, 1982; Walker, 1980). Because Piagetian milestones are reached first and are not a perfect guarantee of parallel perspective-taking competence, they are regarded as *necessary but not sufficient conditions* for the attainment of Selman's perspective-taking stages. Investigators believe that additional (as yet unidentified) social-cognitive competencies are also required. As Shantz (1983) points out, we still do not know much about the precise cognitive processes that underlie and facilitate perspective-taking competence.

Besides children's interview responses to social dilemmas, "games and the delights of deception" offer ideal opportunities to study perspective-taking skills (Selman, 1980, p. 49). Many studies have been conducted using game-like tasks, and age-related findings are consistent with Selman's overall sequence of development. For example, Mossler, Marvin, and Greenberg (1976) played a simple "privileged information game" with 2- to 6-year-old children, who were shown videotaped stories while their mothers were out of the room. Once the mother returned, the videotape was shown again, but this time with the sound turned off. Then the child was asked questions about the mother's knowledge of the story that could only be derived from the audio portion. Much like the change between Selman's Level 0 and Level 1, a steady age-related increase in preschoolers' ability to take the mother's perspective occurred, with none of the 2-year-olds and all of the 6-year-olds realizing that their mothers did not have the audio-conveyed information.

A large number of game-like tasks have focused on the development of **recursive thought,** the reflective, self-embedded cognitive endeavor that involves thinking about what another person is thinking. Selman's theory suggests that the ability to think recursively undergoes rapid improvement during the early to mid-adolescent years, a trend that has been confirmed in numerous studies. For example, Miller, Kessel, and Flavell (1970) asked first- through sixth-grade children to verbally describe cartoon drawings depicting one- and two-loop recursive thinking (see Figure 11.4). As expected, one-loop recursions were achieved before two-loop recursions, but at sixth grade, only 50 percent of the children displayed simple recursive thought, and two-loop recursions were rare. By midadolescence, young people have mastered the complexities of recursive understanding (Flavell et al., 1968).

The recursive thought that grows out of advances in perspective-taking has been of particular interest to developmental psychologists, for it is one feature of human social interaction that makes it truly reciprocal and interactive (Shultz, 1980). In everyday conversations, people depend on recursive thinking to clear up misunderstandings, as when they say, "I thought you would think I was just kidding when I said that." Recursive thought is also involved in our attempts to disguise our real feelings and cognitions (e.g., "He'll think I'm jealous if I tell him I don't like his new car, so I'll pretend I do"), and it may be an important reason that older elementary school children and adolescents are far better than younger children in conforming to the emotional display rules we discussed in Chapter 10. Finally, recursive reflection is an integral part of the intense self-focusing and preoccupation with an imaginary audience that is typical at adolescence. As Miller, Kessel, and Flavell (1970) point out, "Often to their pain, adolescents are much more gifted at this sort of wondering than first graders are" (p. 623).

Perspective-taking and Social Behavior. Children's developing ability to understand the perspectives of others provides an important cognitive basis for effective interpersonal functioning. As early as the preschool years, children's budding recognition that others may have momentary needs different from the self underlies their altruistic attempts to share, help, and comfort others. Eisenberg-Berg and Neal (1979) waited in a nursery school until 4- and 5-year-old children engaged in spontaneous altruistic behavior and then immediately asked them, "Why did you do that?" Nearly a quarter of the answers referred to the needs of others (e.g., "He's hungry." "He can't

Figure 11.4. Cartoon drawings depicting recursive thinking in the Miller, Kessel, and Flavell (1970) study. *(From P. H. Miller, F. S. Kessel, & J. H. Flavell, 1970, "Thinking about People Thinking about People Thinking about . . . : A Study of Social Cognitive Development,"* Child Development, *41, 613–623. ©The Society for Research in Child Development, Inc. Reprinted by permission.)*

One-loop recursion
"The boy is thinking that he is thinking about himself."

Two-loop recursion
"The boy is thinking that the girl is thinking of the father thinking of the mother."

carry it by himself."), and stereotypical and approval-oriented reasons for behaving prosocially (e.g., "It's nice to help." "My teacher wants us to.") were rare.

In studies using laboratory tasks and games, the perspective-taking skills of both preschool and elementary school children have also shown positive relationships with effective interpersonal behavior, including altruism (Barnett, King, & Howard, 1979; Buckley, Siegel, & Ness, 1979; Cutrona & Feshbach, 1979; Eisenberg-Berg & Hand, 1979; Rothenberg, 1970) and *social problem-solving,* or the ability to think of effective ways of handling difficult social situations (Marsh, Serafica, & Barenboim, 1981). Also, good perspective-takers tend to be sociable (LeMare & Rubin, 1987) and especially well-liked by their peers (Deutsch, 1974; Rubin & Maioni, 1975). Nevertheless, some contradictory relationships between perspective-taking and interpersonal functioning have emerged (Iannotti, 1985; Kurdek, 1978; Waxler, Yarrow, & Smith, 1977), which suggest that the relationship of perspective-taking to social behavior is, in reality, quite complex and moderated by other factors.

A careful examination of the research reveals that a wide array of tasks and social situations have been used to relate perspective-taking to social behavior, only some of which produce positive results. In those that do, the recipients of the child's helpfulness, generosity, comfort, and cooperation tend to be hypothetical peers or peers actually known to the subject child rather than strange adults. Perhaps at first children are better at taking the perspective of another person with whom they share common experiences, and only later do they become adept at putting themselves in the place of people whose backgrounds differ from their own (Chandler & Helm, 1984).

In addition, perspective-taking tasks that are good predictors of positive interpersonal behavior require the child to comprehend another person's feeling state (Iannotti, 1985). Appreciating the affective states of others increases the chances that children will empathize, a response that makes the others' needs and feelings even more salient and improves the likelihood that children will act on their awareness. In contrast, other perspective-taking tasks—tasks that require the child to imagine what an opponent is thinking in a competitive game or describe how different characters view a scene in a story—often show no relationship to prosocial behavior or, on occasion, even evoke responses that are incompatible with it. In one study, elementary school children who did well on these kinds of tasks were actually rated by their teachers as *more* disruptive in the classroom (Kurdek, 1978). These results indicate that, depending on the contexts in which perspective-taking and social behavior are assessed, skilled perspective-takers may be as concerned with defending and supporting their own viewpoints as they are with helping other people. In fact, a few mildly antisocial behaviors, such as knowing how to needle your sister to triumphantly "get her goat," sometimes make use of masterful perspective-taking skills.

Even the ability to appreciate other people's feelings does not uniformly lead to altruistic behavior, partly because additional factors, such as temperament and personality along with the context in which social behavior takes place, affect the extent to which children act on their social cognitions. Barrett and Yarrow (1977) found that among 5- to 8-year-old children who scored high in affective perspective-taking, assertiveness was the crucial factor in determining whether they spontaneously helped their peers. In another study, shy, withdrawn preschoolers less often lent a helping hand to a strange adult in need than their more gregarious counterparts (Stanhope, Bell, & Parker-Cohen, 1987). Thus, although perspective-taking is evident in a great many prosocial acts, being skilled at it does not guarantee altruistic responding, for social behavior is multiply determined—by social-cognitive functioning, personality characteristics, and situational conditions.

Nevertheless, among youngsters who display extremes of antisocial behavior, substantial developmental delays in perspective-taking have been found. Chronic delinquents have a very limited capacity to imagine the thoughts and feelings of others (Chandler, 1973; Jurkovic & Prentice, 1977), a social-cognitive deficit that may be responsible for the fact that they mistreat and manipulate others for their own ends without experiencing guilt and remorse. In one investigation, delinquents between the ages of 11 and 15 achieved perspective-taking scores that were so immature that they resembled the performance of children only half their age. Even when intellectual differences between delinquents and nondelinquents were controlled, they continued to differ sharply in the ability to recognize that others can have feelings and viewpoints that contrast with their own (Chandler, 1973). Because severe deficits in perspective-taking may help sustain antisocial activity in aggressive and delinquent youth, psychologists have experimented with techniques that induce perspective-taking as a way to lessen antisocial behavior and facilitate prosocial responding.

Training Perspective-taking Skills. Training experiences that encourage children and adolescents to step outside their own egocentric vantage point and assume either real-world or fantasy-type roles can improve perspective-taking. Chandler (1973) had delinquent boys make up, act out, and videotape brief skits about persons their own age. At the end of a 10-session training period, delinquent boys showed significant improvement in perspective-taking when compared to a control group participating in a film-making activity that did not offer role-taking practice. Furthermore, improved perspective-taking was associated with a substantial reduction in delinquent behavior over a subsequent 18-month period. In Chapter 6, we showed that sociodramatic play involving role enactment leads to advances in perspective-taking competence among preschoolers. The same seems to be true for older children and adolescents who are very poor perspective-takers. That perspective-taking and everyday social functioning undergo simultaneous improvement after relatively short-term interventions provides additional support for the central role of this social-cognitive skill in effective human interaction.

In summary, a number of important changes in children's cognitions about other people occur over childhood and adolescence. During middle childhood, person

Research shows that children who display extremes of antisocial behavior have a limited capacity to imagine the thoughts and feelings of others. (Hugh Rogers/ Monkmeyer Press Photo Service)

perception shifts from a focus on concrete characteristics to increasingly abstract, psychological dimensions. The ability to infer others' intentions from their ongoing stream of behavior emerges during the preschool years. Children's understanding of others' viewpoints undergoes vast changes from the preschool through adolescent years, from a rudimentary awareness that others have thoughts and feelings different from the self to advanced societal and recursive perspective-taking capacities.

CONCEPTUALIZING RELATIONS BETWEEN PEOPLE

As children develop, they apply their capacity to appreciate the inner psychological worlds of themselves and others to an understanding of relationships between people. A relatively new research focus in social cognition has to do with how children reason about dyadic relations, including friendship, authority, and conflict, and how their increasingly sophisticated insights affect their social behavior.

Understanding Friendship

Stages of Friendship Relations. To an adult, friendship is not a one-sided relationship. It is not enough to just like or be attracted to another person, for you can like someone without being a friend to that person, and your liking may not be reciprocated. Instead, friendship is a mutually satisfying psychological relationship involving companionship, sharing, understanding of thoughts and feelings, and caring for and comforting one another in times of need. In addition, a friendship is a relationship that endures over time and transcends occasional conflicts.

Children's ideas about friendship do not start out this way. Several investigators have conducted interviews with preschool through adolescent youngsters, generally by asking them to name a best friend, explain why that child is a friend, and indicate what they expect of a close friend. Another technique has been to present children with story dilemmas about friendship that tap such issues as motives for friendship formation, characteristics of friendships, ways in which good friends resolve conflicts, and how and why friendships break up. From children's responses, a number of theories regarding children's conceptions of friendship have emerged (Damon, 1977; Selman, 1980, 1981; Youniss, 1975; Youniss & Volpe, 1978). All emphasize that the understanding of friendship evolves from a concrete, behavioral relationship involving sharing material goods and pleasurable activity to a more abstract conception of a relationship of mutual consideration and psychological satisfaction. Damon (1977) has synthesized the developmental progressions of other investigators into a three-stage sequence of children's appreciation of friendship.

Level 1: Friendship as a handy playmate[5] (about 5–7 years). During this stage, friendship is concrete and activity-based. Friends are regarded as associates with whom one frequently plays, and friendship is affirmed by giving or sharing material goods. As yet there is no sense of liking or disliking the personality traits of the other person, for (as we saw earlier) young children have little appreciation of the stable psychological characteristics of self and other. Because friendship is merely pleasurable play association and material exchange, young children regard it as easily begun—for example, simply by meeting in the neighborhood and saying, "Hi." However, it does not yet have a long-term enduring quality, for Level 1 children suggest that a friendship is easily terminated by refusing to share, hitting, or not being available to meet and play. The following response from a 5-year-old boy to the question, "What makes a good friend?" sums up the Level 1 child's view of friendship: "Boys play with boys, trucks play with trucks, dogs play with dogs." When the

---

[5] Titles for each of the stages have been provided by this author to assist you in remembering them.

Children's understanding of friendship evolves from a relationship based on sharing pleasurable activities to a more abstract relationship involving mutual consideration and psychological satisfaction. (Myrleen Ferguson/ PhotoEdit)

interviewer probed, "Why does that make them good friends?" the child answered, "Because they do the same things" (Selman, 1980, p. 136).

Level 2: Friendship as mutual trust and assistance (about 8–10 years). During middle childhood, friendship evolves into a consensual relationship in which both parties respond to each other's needs and desires. Since friendship is now a matter of mutual consent, getting it started is not as simple as it was at an earlier age. Older children regard it important to *offer* to get together or *invite* another child to play, an action that assumes willing participation by both individuals. As in the previous stage, friendship can be affirmed by gift-giving and other material offers, but it goes beyond these concrete exchanges to include help-giving and other acts of kindness that signify that each person can be counted on to support and not harm or take advantage of the other. Thus, mutual trust becomes a central defining element of friendship, and older elementary school children regard violations of trust, such as not helping when the other needs help, breaking promises, or gossiping behind the other's back, as serious breaches of friendship expectations. At younger ages friendships simply resume after squabbles over activities and material possessions dissipate, but at this level, friendship violations require some acknowledgment that trust has been broken, in the form of apologies and explanations, to reinstate the former relationship. Finally, Level 2 respondents recognize that friendship involves psychological and not just concrete elements, and they like or dislike others on the basis of their inferred dispositions and qualities. The following response of an 8-year-old child to queries about her best friend illustrates some of the qualities of a Level 2 friendship:

> Who is your best friend? *Shelly.* Why is Shelly your best friend? *Because she helps when I'm getting beaten up, she cheers me when I'm sad, and she shares.* Do you share with Shelly? *Yes. I share so she'll share. . . .* How come you like Shelly better than anyone else? *She's done the most for me. She never disagrees, she never eats in front of me, she never walks away when I'm crying, and she helps me on my schoolwork.* (Damon, 1977, p. 159–160)

Level 3: Friendship as intimacy and mutual understanding (11–15 years and older). By early adolescence, conceptions of friendship take on greater depth. Friends are now regarded as persons who understand and accept one another as individuals and who share their innermost thoughts and feelings. Because friendship has this depth dimension to it, individuals regard it as a stable relationship that is established and affirmed over a long period of time by "getting to know someone," and a good friendship rests on impressions of one another that promote feelings of compatibility and closeness. Since each party in a friendship knows the other well, friendships are regarded as important in alleviating psychological problems, such as loneliness, sadness, and fear. Also, since true mutual understanding implies forgiveness, only serious disaffection and breaches of the relationship can lead Level 3 friendships to dissolve. One Level 3 early adolescent characterized his best friendship as follows:

> *Well, you need someone you can tell anything to, all kinds of things that you don't want spread around. That's why you're someone's friend.* Is that why Jimmy is your friend? Because he can keep a secret? *Yes, and we like the same kinds of things. We speak the same language. My mother says we're two peas in a pod. . . .* Do you ever get mad at Jimmy? *Not really.* What if he did something that got you really mad? *He'd still be my best friend. I'd tell him what he did wrong and maybe he'd understand. I could be wrong too, it depends.* (Damon, 1977, p. 163)

Many studies report findings that are in remarkable agreement with this developmental progression. For example, Bigelow (1977; Bigelow & LaGaipa, 1975) analyzed first through eighth graders' essays about expectations of a best friend and found three clusters of friendship expectations, each emerging at successive ages and showing close agreement with the stages described above (see Table 11.2). Also, virtually every study shows that while more psychological conceptions of friendship emerge with age, earlier concepts, such as engaging in common activities, are not relinquished. Instead, they are reconceptualized and integrated into successively higher levels. As additional support for a stage-wise progression of friendship concepts, Selman (1981) found that friendship stages are related to advances in perspective-taking. We would certainly expect this to be the case, for the adolescent who comments that intimacy and mutual disclosure are important dimensions of friendship must be able to appreciate that people can understand one another's thoughts and feelings. Finally, reference to the intimacy and faithfulness of friends tends to be more common among girls than boys (Bigelow, 1977; Bigelow & LaGaipa, 1975; Hunter & Youniss, 1982), a finding that is probably explained by societal sex-role standards that permit girls to be more open and expressive of their inner feelings.

Are Children's Developing Conceptions of Friendship Related to Features of Their Real Friendships? If social understanding plays a vital role in everyday social behavior, then children's changing ideas about friendship should be related to a number of age-related changes in the qualities of their real friendships.

Table 11.2. Children's Changing Expectations of Their Friends from First Through Eighth Grade

GRADES 1–3 SITUATIONAL EXPECTATIONS	GRADES 4–5 NORMATIVE EXPECTATIONS	GRADES 6–8 INTERNAL PSYCHOLOGICAL EXPECTATIONS
Propinquity (physical nearness)	Character admiration	Acceptance
Common activities		Loyalty and commitment
Evaluation		Genuineness
		Common interests
		Intimacy potential

Source: Bigelow, 1977.

First, we would expect friendships to show greater stability as mutual trust and loyalty become more important in what one expects of a friend. In general, research bears out this prediction. In a study in which mutual friendship choices of first, fourth, and eighth graders were assessed in both the fall and spring of the school year, friendships did become more stable from first to fourth grade, although the number of stable friendships showed no change from fourth to eighth grade. However, the researchers discovered that the eighth graders permitted a larger number of friendships to dissolve than younger children and were reluctant to add new people to their friendship repertoire. As adolescents place a higher premium on friendships with psychological depth and intimacy, they seem to restrict their friendships to people with whom they feel comfortable sharing their innermost thoughts. An eighth grader expressed this idea when he explained why one of his friendships ended, saying, "[name of friend] is trying to single out his friends now. At the beginning of the year, he was friends with almost everybody because he wanted to be friends over [during] the school year with a lot of kids. Now he's singling out best friends" (Berndt & Hoyle, 1985, p. 1013).

Although changes in friendship stability do occur, it is important to note that children's friendships are actually remarkably stable at all ages. Even during the preschool years, two-thirds of children who identify one another as friends do so again 4 to 6 months later (Gershman & Hayes, 1983). However, lasting friendships at younger ages are more a function of the constancy of social environments—the preschool and neighborhood—than of social-cognitive processes. In one study, preschoolers only maintained friendships across a summer vacation period if parents made special arrangements for mutual home visits and periods of interaction (Schaivo & Solomon, 1981).

In addition to stability, more mature conceptions of friendship should lead older children to behave with more mutual responsiveness, sympathetic understanding, and altruism toward friends. Actually, positive social exchanges and mutuality occur more among friends than nonfriends at all ages (Hartup, 1983). Masters and Furman (1981) observed 4- and 5-year-olds at play and found that children gave twice as much positive reinforcement, in the form of greetings, smiles, praise, and compliance, to friends than to nonfriends, and they also received more from them. In addition, when friends participate in joint activities, they are more interactive and emotionally expressive, talking, laughing, and looking at each other to a greater extent than in nonfriendship interactions. Also, the conversational strategies of friends are more mutually directed (e.g., "Let's do it this way") as opposed to being aimed at the other person as an individual (e.g., "Put your piece over there") (Newcomb, Brady, & Hartup, 1979). In several studies in which friends and nonfriends worked on challenging tasks together, the greater social responsivity and harmonious interaction of friends led to more extensive exploration of materials and improved problem-solving performance (Nelson & Aboud, 1985; Newcomb, Brady, & Hartup, 1979; Schwartz, 1972). Apparently, sensitivity, spontaneity, and intimacy characterize friendship relations very early, although verbalizing that these qualities are essential to a good friendship does not occur until later ages.

Altruism among friends does increase over middle childhood. When pairs of friends worked on a task that allowed them to help and share with each other, fourth graders helped more than first graders did (Berndt, 1981). Generosity and helpfulness toward friends undergoes additional increments from middle childhood into adolescence (Berndt, 1985). In fact, one study showed that fifth- and sixth-grade children who had close friendships, as opposed to ones who did not, performed better on an affective perspective-taking task, and when observed at school they behaved more altruistically toward others in general (McGuire & Weisz, 1982). Many altruistic behaviors may emerge first in the context of friendship, and then generalize to other people.

Elementary school children do not just behave more prosocially with their friends;

when paired with one another in competitive games they compete with each other to a greater extent than nonfriends (Berndt, 1983), and they also openly express disagreement on topics about which they hold differing opinions (Nelson & Aboud, 1985). As early as middle childhood, friends seem to be secure enough in their mutual approval of one another to risk being direct and open about their different points of view. As a result, friendship probably provides an important context in which children learn to tolerate argument, criticism, and disagreement.

The value that adolescents accord to feeling especially "in sync" with their close associates would lead us to expect friends to resemble one another more in interests, attitudes, and values at older ages. Research reveals that the attributes on which friends are most alike throughout childhood and adolescence are age and sex (Duck, 1975; Kandel, 1978a).[6] Friends also tend to be of the same racial/ethnic background, even in integrated schools where opportunities to form cross-race friendships are available (Singleton & Asher, 1979). These findings indicate that an inclination to make friends with children who are like the self in observable characteristics exists from an early age. However, the association of these characteristics with friendship choice is, to some extent, the result of age-graded contexts in which peers gather together (e.g., school) as well as adult influence and social pressures. By middle childhood perceived similarity in interests affects friendship associations (Davitz, 1955), and during adolescence, stable friendship pairs, as opposed to those that dissolve, are more alike in educational aspirations, political values, as well as in their tendency to use drugs and engage in minor delinquent acts. Friendships may also have a socializing influence on attitudes and values, for adolescents who choose to continue their friendship become even more similar in these psychological characteristics over time (Kandel, 1978b).

Do adolescent friends, because of the greater intimacy of their relationship, "know" each other better as individuals than their younger grade-school counterparts? It appears that they do. In a study in which fourth and eighth graders were asked about their best friend's personality, preferences, and typical behavioral and emotional reactions, accuracy of knowledge (determined by comparing the child's responses with the friend's self-reports) increased with age. No age changes occurred in knowledge of external characteristics, such as birth date and phone number (Diaz & Berndt, 1982).

In summary, as children get older, greater stability, prosocial responding, psychological similarity, and intimate personal knowledge characterize their friendship relations. These developmental trends fit with children's changing understanding of the nature of friendship. Because friendships are based on emotional sensitivity and social reciprocity between individuals who meet on an equal footing, they provide children with invaluable contexts in which they can learn to resolve social conflicts, form new attachments, and get to know another person as a unique individual. In fact, friendships may be as vital for development as early family attachments. Several decades ago, noted psychiatrist Harry Stack Sullivan (1953) wrote about the significance of friendship:

> . . . if you will look very closely at one of your children when he finally finds a chum — somewhere between eight-and-one-half and ten — you will discover something very different in the relationship — namely, that your child begins to develop a real sensitivity to what matters to another person. And this is not in the sense of "what should I do to get what I want," but instead "what should I do to contribute to the happiness or to support the prestige and feeling of worthwhileness of my chum." So far

[6] Although opposite-sex peer associations increase during early adolescence, stable friendships continue to be limited to members of the same sex throughout the adolescent years. In a survey of 1,879 high school students between the ages of 13 and 18, a total of 91 percent reported best-friend choices that were restricted to members of the same sex (Kandel, 1978a).

as I have been able to discover, nothing remotely like this appears before. . . . The developmental epoch of preadolescence is marked by the coming of integrating tendencies which, when they are completely developed, we call love. . . . " (pp. 245–246)

Research on the development of children's friendship relations bears out Sullivan's vision.

Understanding Authority

In contrast to the world of friendships where children meet on an equal footing, in the adult-child world one person has controlling power and can impose things on another. Relationships with authority figures are a pervasive part of children's daily experiences, and they are of crucial importance. Out of them emerge many competencies that are extended and elaborated in the world of peers.

Due to their physical immaturity and limited knowledge and experience, young children are subordinates who are expected to obey the dictates of parents and teachers, and sometimes this deference is demanded by more socially powerful peers as well. However, at an early age children construct cognitive rationales for their obedience and arrive at explanations for the legitimacy of authority figures—that is, which personal qualities justify that a powerful person be recognized and respected as such.

Compared to research on friendships, comparatively little attention has been devoted to children's understanding of authority. Damon (1977) has investigated it, again by asking children to respond to dilemmas having to do either with parental authority (a mother who will not let a child go on a picnic because he did not clean up his room) or peer authority (children on an athletic team who must choose a captain). Children between 4 and 9 were asked to answer such questions as whether the mother was fair and had a right to tell the child what to do, and how to choose a team captain and what the captain could tell others to do. Their responses suggested three sequential stages of reasoning:

Level 0: Egocentric authority perspective[7] (about 5 years and younger). Early in this stage, children generally fail to differentiate between what they want and what an authority expects of them. For example, they say they obey authority figures because they "want to" or "like to," or in the case of a peer leader, because "he's like me." Later on, authority is viewed as separate from the self, but it is regarded as having no other purpose than constraining the self's desires. In addition, very young children legitimize authority by referring to physical characteristics, such as large size (e.g., being a "big, grown-up person") or dress (e.g., a team captain "wears a different colored shirt").

Level 1: Authority as physical and social power (about 6–9 years). At this intermediate level, obedience to authority is rationalized on the basis of reciprocal exchange; an authority should be obeyed because the superior person has helped and cared for the child in the past and will do so in the future (e.g., a child should clean up her room on request because "if you were sick and asked your mother for a glass of water she would do it for you"). Children of this stage legitimize authority by pointing to social as well as physical attributes that enable authority figures to enforce demands (e.g., being "the boss of the house") and slightly later, to special talents and abilities (e.g., being able to "do lots of things you can't do," or for a team captain, being "the best hitter").

Level 2: Authority as capable leadership (about 9 years and older). Older chil-

---

[7] Titles for each of the stages are provided by this author. Examples of children's responses are adapted from Damon, 1977, pages 185–199.

As children grow older, they no longer view authority figures as omnipotent in all situations. Instead, they respond to a parent's demand for help when it seems legitimate and in the best interests of all. (Robert Brenner/PhotoEdit)

dren no longer view authority as a matter of domination by strong individuals over weaker, less knowledgeable people. Instead, they see authority as a consensual relationship, adopted temporarily for the welfare of all. Authority is legitimized by characteristics that make a person more capable of leading and commanding (e.g., a mother should be obeyed because "she knows more about things that matter in bringing kids up"). In addition, at this stage authority figures are not omnipotent and legitimized in all situations, but only in those for which they possess relevant characteristics (e.g., just because mothers know more about kids, "that doesn't mean they could be president").

Children's responses to authority dilemmas are related to reasoning about the same issues in real life situations. Damon (1977) organized same-age children between 4 and 10 years of age into four-member basketball teams and asked them how they would select a leader and how they would decide whether or not to obey that person. Children's maturity of authority reasoning was negatively related to an egocentric tendency to want to choose themselves as team captain. Also, children at the lower two stages thought a captain should give everyone on the team an equal opportunity to shoot baskets, regardless of what that strategy might mean for the performance of the team as a whole. In contrast, Level 2 children made self-interest secondary to the collective interest of the team. They accorded their captain the authority to lead the team in a manner that would make winning most likely, including devising a strategy that permitted the best shooter to shoot more often than the others.

As yet, developmental psychologists do not know how children's conceptions of authority figures affect developmental changes in their obedience to adults. Perhaps older children's more rational view of authority determines at least some of the circumstances under which they are willing to comply. As parents and teachers are well aware, with increasing age children are much more likely to ask "why they have to," and they are less prone to take things on faith from adults.

Finally, young children's unilateral and unquestioning view of authority is believed by prominent theorists of moral development to be a major limiting factor in their moral reasoning. Therefore, we will return to the significance of children's understanding of authority relations when we discuss the emergence of morality in Chapter 12.

Understanding Social Conflict: Social Problem Solving

Children, even when they are best friends, come into conflict with one another. Recall from Chapter 6 that social conflict was accorded an important role in development by Piaget, who believed that peer interactions involving arguments and disagreements helped children overcome their egocentrism. According to Piaget, social conflict prods children to scrutinize their own viewpoints and the merits of their own reasoning. This, in turn, facilitates their cognitive development as well as their ability to engage in effective, mutually satisfying social discourse (Piaget, 1923/1926).

As Shantz (1987) points out, adults often equate children's conflicts with aggression and socially disruptive behavior. Although conflicts occasionally resolve into aggression, intensely hostile reactions among children are rare, while arguments, disagreements, refusals, denials, and opposition are far more typical. Furthermore, conflicts are not very frequent when compared to children's harmonious interactions (Hay, 1984). When they do occur, most are brief in duration and settled by children themselves (Bakeman & Brownlee, 1982; O'Keefe & Benoit, 1982).

But despite their infrequency and brevity, peer conflicts are not unimportant. Watch children work out their disputes over possession and use of play objects ("That's mine!" "I had it first!"), entry into and control over the social environment ("I'm on your team, Jerry." "No you're not!"), and disagreements over ideas, facts, and beliefs ("I'm taller than he is." "No you aren't."). You will see that they take these matters quite seriously. Recent research reveals that social conflicts offer children invaluable learning opportunities in **social problem solving.** In their efforts to resolve conflict effectively—in ways that are socially acceptable but at the same time achieve results that are beneficial to the self—children must bring together a variety of social-cognitive skills. These include encoding and interpreting social information pertaining to a social goal, generating alternative strategies for reaching the goal, and evaluating the effectiveness of these strategies as a prelude to selecting one and translating it into a behavioral response. Dodge (1986) regards social problem solving as a special, interpersonal form of the more general problem-solving process. He organizes the steps of social problem solving into the temporal sequence depicted in Figure 11.5.

With age, children become more proficient social problem solvers in both hypothetical and real-life situations. But at all ages, substantial individual differences exist, and social problem solving is currently regarded as one of the most important dimensions of social competence (Rubin & Krasnor, 1985; Shantz, 1983).

The Development of Social Problem Solving. Spivack and Shure (1974) initiated the large body of research that now exists on social problem solving. They focused on the strategy generation part of the process by asking young children to generate as many possible ways as they could for dealing with hypothetical conflicts, such as wanting to play with a toy someone else has. Spivack and Shure's work, along with

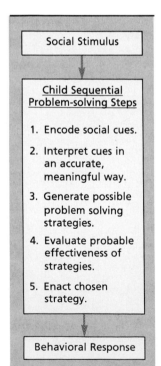

Figure 11.5. A social problem-solving flow chart. *(Adapted from Dodge, 1986.)*

more recent findings, indicates that the ability to flexibly generate a variety of solutions to hypothetical social conflicts increases over the preschool and early school years. Also, children's repertoire of problem-solving strategies is moderately related to friendly, sociable peer interaction and teacher ratings of social adjustment (Rubin & Krasnor, 1985; Spivack & Shure, 1974).

Besides quantity of strategies, the quality of strategies generated by children changes with age. During elementary school, younger children, as well as children with especially poor peer relations, describe strategies that impulsively meet their own needs, such as grabbing, physically pushing away another child, or ordering another to do what one wants. Older children and those with good peer relations assert the self's needs in ways that take into account the needs of others, such as friendly persuasion and compromise (Renshaw & Asher, 1983; Rubin & Daniels-Beirness, 1983; Selman et al., 1983; Selman & Demorest, 1984).

Recently, investigators have expanded their study of social problem solving in an effort to find out at what other points, besides strategy generation, things may go awry for children who have difficulty getting along with peers. In one recent study, Dodge and his collaborators (1986) assessed grade-school children's social-cognitive skillfulness at each of the five problem-solving steps depicted in Figure 11.5. A videotape presented children with a dramatized problem involving how best to gain entry into a play group. In the first scene, two children were seated at a table playing a board game, and the investigators assessed each subject's ability to *encode and correctly interpret social cues* about the video characters' willingness to let the subject join the game. Then subjects were asked to *generate strategies* for joining the game, and their responses were coded into one of five categories: competent (polite requests to play and other friendly comments); aggressive (threats, physical violence, or barging in without permission); self-centered (statements about the self, such as "Hey, I know how to play that"); passive (shy, hovering responses, such as waiting or "hanging around"); and authority intervention ("The teacher said I could play"). Next, children viewed five more scenes in which a child tried to enter the game using each of the strategy types noted above, and the subject was asked to engage in *strategy evaluation* by indicating whether or not the particular technique would succeed. Finally, children engaged in *strategy enactment* by demonstrating a way of asking to join the game. In a separate session, Dodge examined children's actual social competence in the laboratory by having them try to gain entry into a real peer group activity. Results showed that all of the five social problem-solving skills predicted children's performance, and in a second investigation, the predictability of the social-cognitive measures generalized to children's group entry effectiveness on their school playground.

Perhaps you have already noticed, based on the flow chart depicted in Figure 11.5, that Dodge takes an *information processing* approach to the study of social problem solving. Information processing research in the social-cognitive arena is aimed at finding out precisely how a child thinks in the process of social negotiations and how a particular set of processing steps results in a social response. Once this is known, specific processing deficiencies at the heart of the social incompetencies of particular children can be assessed, and individualized treatment programs can be implemented.

Social information processing has only just begun to infiltrate research on social development. Nevertheless, research like that of Dodge and his coworkers is an indication that the study of social-cognitive development may follow in the footsteps of its nonsocial-cognitive partner. In our efforts to explain and predict children's social behavior, social information processing may very well be an important new wave of the future.

Training Social Problem Solving. Like perspective-taking, social problem solving can be trained. A well-known intervention program for preschool and kindergarten children has been developed by Spivack and Shure (1974; Shure, 1981). During daily sessions over a number of months, children participate in games involving puppet dramatizations of social problems and discussions of effective and ineffective means to resolve conflicts. In addition, teachers intervene as problems arise to point out consequences and suggest alternatives. After applying the training program in low-income inner city classrooms with children at risk for later social adjustment problems, Spivack and Shure found that trained pupils, as opposed to untrained controls, improved in both social reasoning skills and teacher-rated social adjustment, and these gains were still evident a year after completion of training. Spivack and Shure's findings have been replicated (Ridley & Vaughn, 1982; Feis & Simons, 1985), and comparable interventions have proved effective with older elementary school children (Stiefvater, Kurdek, & Allik, 1986). As yet, investigators do not know exactly which training ingredients are most effective in social problem-solving interventions, and current programs are not individually tailored to fit the social-cognitive deficits of particular children (Urbain & Kendall, 1980). However, it is in precisely these ways that the information processing approach to social problem solving promises to make a unique contribution.

On a final note, social-cognitive techniques are not the only means for helping children with deficiencies in social competence. We consider other approaches, including reinforcement, modeling, and direct teaching of social skills, in Chapter 15.

CHAPTER SUMMARY

1. The development of social cognition deals with how children's understanding of themselves, other people, and relationships between people change with age. A major influence on current theory and research is the work of Piaget, whose concept of egocentrism inspired new stage theories of children's social understanding. Piaget's clinical interviewing procedure is the most frequently used social-cognitive research method, although more structured questioning techniques and direct observations of social interaction are also employed. Attribution theory has influenced research on children's conceptions of themselves as academic achievers, and Erikson's psychoanalytic theory has been important in the study of adolescent identity development.

2. Research reveals that infants have completed the task of self-recognition by the end of the second year of life. In the early preschool years, children develop a categorical self based on salient characteristics such as sex and age, but they do not accurately separate constant from changing features of the self until the late preschool and early elementary school years. By 3 to 4 years of age, children are already aware of a private, inner self not accessible to others.

3. During middle childhood, children's self-concepts change from a catalogue of observable characteristics to an emphasis on internal psychological dispositions, a transformation that is facilitated by general cognitive development as well as perspective-taking skills. In adolescence, the self-concept becomes even more differentiated and subtle. Adolescents place a heavier emphasis on interpersonal virtues in their self-descriptions, a change that reflects their increasing concern with being liked and viewed in a positive light by others.

4. Self-esteem differentiates into a number of separate self-evaluations by 7 to 8 years of age, including academic, social, and physical self-worth. During the middle elementary school years, children also build a global sense of self-esteem. Level of self-esteem declines over the early grade-school years as children become increasingly sensitive to social comparison information and others' opinions of themselves. From late childhood into adolescence, self-esteem is on the rise, an indication that new responsibilities and greater independence foster feelings of pride, self-confidence, and self-respect.

5. A warm, approving parenting style along with firm but reasonable expectations is positively related to self-esteem, although the extent to which child-rearing practices cause changes in self-esteem is not clarified by correlational findings. Studies of children's attributions for their successes and failures in learning situations have identified adult communication styles that cause changes in self-esteem. During middle childhood, some children attribute their successes to high ability and their failures to insufficient effort. As a result, they approach learning tasks with enthusiasm and high expectancies of success. In contrast, learned helpless children attribute their failures to low ability, and when faced with obstacles to task success, they show decreased persistence and signs of giving up. Children who consistently receive negative evaluations about their ability develop the learned helpless pattern. Attribution retaining programs have succeeded in improving the self-evaluations and task performance of low-achieving and learned helpless youngsters.

6. Developing an identity is a major task of the adolescent years. In complex societies, an identity crisis and period of moratorium is a necessary step before identity is achieved. For

most young people, adolescence is not a period of storm and stress that engenders serious emotional turmoil and risk of maladjustment. Adolescents who respond to pressures from authority figures (identity foreclosed) or who fail to move toward occupational and ideological commitments (identity diffused) show less mature psychological functioning than their moratorium and identity-achieved counterparts.

7. Like their self-concepts, children's perceptions of others become more psychologically based, differentiated, and organized with age. By the end of the preschool years, children can distinguish between intentional and unintentional acts. Some children with social adjustment difficulties, such as highly aggressive youngsters, show deficits in the ability to accurately interpret intentions from behavioral cues.

8. The ability to appreciate the perspectives of others undergoes substantial development during childhood and adolescence. Selman's five-stage theory shows that perspective-taking gradually takes on reciprocal, third-party, and societal dimensions. Children's ability to understand the viewpoints of others is an important basis for effective interpersonal functioning. Youngsters who show extreme forms of antisocial behavior are seriously delayed in the development of perspective-taking. These deficits can be reduced through training programs that encourage them to step outside their egocentric vantage points.

9. Conceptions of interpersonal relationships change dramatically with age. Ideas about friendship evolve from a concrete relation based on sharing material goods and pleasurable activities to a more abstract conception based on mutual consideration, intimacy, and psychological satisfaction. In line with this trend, children's real friendships show increases in prosocial responding, psychological similarity, and intimate personal knowledge with age. During middle childhood, children's view of authority changes from a physically omnipotent individual to a consensually chosen leader who is legitimized by special talents and skills.

10. In their efforts to resolve conflicts effectively, children must bring together a variety of social-cognitive skills in complex interaction. With increasing age, children generate a wider variety of strategies for solving social problems and are better able to take into account the needs and perspectives of others. Besides strategy generation, other components of social problem solving, including encoding and interpretation of social cues and strategy evaluation and enactment, predict children's social competence. The information processing approach to social problem solving may soon make it possible to design interventions tailored to fit the social-cognitive deficits of particular children.

IMPORTANT TERMS AND CONCEPTS

social cognition
attributions
self-concept
categorical self
inner self
generalized other
self-esteem
achievement motivation

mastery-oriented attributions
learned helplessness
attribution retraining
identity
identity crisis
identity achievement
moratorium
identity foreclosure

identity diffusion
person perception
perspective-taking
stages of perspective-taking skill
recursive thought
stages of friendship relations
stages of authority relations
social problem solving

Daughters of Edward Darley Boit, by John Singer Sargent.
Museum of Fine Arts, Boston.

CHAPTER 12

The Development of Morality and Self-control

Moral development — how human beings come to resolve discrepancies between their self-centered, egoistic needs and obligations to act in favor of the needs of others — has been of intense interest to developmental psychologists since the early part of this century. Today, the empirical literature on the topic is so vast that in sheer numbers of research studies it exceeds all other topics in the field of social development (Flavell, 1985). The understanding of human morality and the related practical matter of how to motivate children to behave morally are not just twentieth-century research concerns. They are age-old preoccupations, for it has long been recognized that behavior aimed at benefiting others is essential to the survival of the individual and the continued existence of human groups. Infants and children cannot live and grow unless they are cared for by morally responsible, giving adults, and all societies have procedures for settling conflicts that protect the general welfare of the citizenry (Radke-Yarrow, Zahn-Waxler, & Chapman, 1983; Rest, 1986).

The determinants of human morality exist on multiple levels. Although morality is protected by an overarching cooperative social organization, it also has roots in each major facet of the human psyche. First, as we indicated in Chapter 10, morality has a vital *emotional component,* for powerful affective reactions cause us to empathize when we witness another's distress or feel guilty when we are the cause of it. Second, morality has an important *cognitive component.* As we showed in Chapter 11, human beings actively think about their social experiences, and children's developing social understanding permits them to make increasingly sophisticated moral judgments about actions they believe to be right or wrong. Third, morality has a *behavioral component,* for experiencing morally relevant feelings and cognitions only increases the probability, but does not guarantee, that people will actually follow through and behave in accord with them.

Traditionally, these different facets of morality have been investigated separately: psychoanalytic psychologists have focused on emotions, cognitive-developmental psychologists on moral thought, and behaviorists on moral behavior. But even though major theorists have emphasized very different aspects of morality, there is one point on which there is fairly common agreement. At first, the child's morality is *externally imposed and controlled* by direct instruction, supervision, and the rewards and punishments of authority figures. Eventually children *internalize* moral rules and principles, taking over the responsibility for regulating their own moral conduct. **Internalization**—the shift from externally controlled responses to behavior governed by internal standards and principles—permits children to behave in a moral fashion in the absence of adult monitoring and vigilance. The concept of internalization underscores a quality that most people accept as indispensable to moral functioning. Truly moral individuals do not just comply with the momentary social influences of others. Instead, they have adopted relatively permanent, general standards of conduct that govern their behavior with many people, across many settings, and over a wide variety of occasions.

In this chapter, we begin our consideration of moral development with a brief overview of the philosophical foundations of major theories. Then we discuss biological, psychoanalytic, behaviorist, and cognitive-developmental perspectives on moral development, highlighting the strengths and shortcomings of each view. We conclude this chapter with a consideration of the child's capacity for *self-control,* the ability to inhibit the expression of spontaneous impulses. The development of an inner resolve to keep the self from doing anything it feels like doing—from painting on the walls and playing with matches in the young preschooler to ignoring one's chores, insulting an agemate, or breaking a promise in the older child—is a major determinant of the extent to which inner moral commitments actually become translated into moral action.

THEORIES OF MORALITY

For centuries preceding modern scientific study of the child, philosophers mused about what morality is and how it develops. Many of their views anticipated present-day perspectives and found their way into modern theories. Recall from Chapter 1 that the sixteenth-century Protestant doctrine of original sin held that only through severe disciplinary practices could children learn to subordinate their innate, self-centered depravity to behavior that served the public good. This philosophical position resembles Freud's idea of a harsh, punitive conscience as the inner force assuring moral behavior. Jean Jacques Rousseau's (1762/1955) natural philosophy of childhood, with its vision of the child as innately good and naturally motivated by sympathy, compassion, and caring for others, is similar to the modern-day biological perspective on the origins of morality. The philosophy of John Locke (1690/1892), with its image of the child as a "blank slate"—born neither good nor bad but molded into a moral being by wise, consistent adult tutoring—finds its modern parallel in behaviorist theories emphasizing modeling and reinforcement of moral action.[1] Finally, the German philosopher Immanuel Kant (1785/1952) regarded human beings as motivated by *both* selfish and benevolent passions and concluded that only reason could resolve the conflicting tendencies between the two. To Kant, the essence of morality was acting according to rational principles of justice, fairness, and respect for other persons. Kant's philosophy foreshadows the modern cognitive-developmental ap-

---

[1] You may wish to return to Chapter 1, pages 8–10, to review these basic philosophical preludes to modern developmental theories in greater detail.

proach to moral development, as exemplified by Piaget's theory and its more recent extension by Lawrence Kohlberg.

The diverse philosophical and theoretical orientations mentioned above can be organized into three fundamental positions on the origins of morality: (1) morality as rooted in human nature, or the biological perspective; (2) morality as the adoption of externally imposed societal norms, which includes both the Freudian and behaviorist perspectives; and (3) morality as rational understanding of social justice, or the cognitive-developmental perspective. As we shall see below, no single theory provides a complete account of the foundations of morality and the essence of moral development (Rest, 1983). Rather, by highlighting different facets, each adds to our appreciation of the complex, interacting factors that contribute to the emergence of moral functioning in children and adolescents.

MORALITY AS ROOTED IN HUMAN NATURE: THE BIOLOGICAL PERSPECTIVE

During the 1960s and 1970s, biological theories of human social behavior became prominent, spurred by a controversial new discipline called **sociobiology.** Sociobiology advanced the idea that morally relevant human behaviors, including cooperation, helping, and other prosocial responses, were rooted in the genetic heritage of the species (Wilson, 1975). This view was supported by observations of ethologists, who reported cases of animals helping other members of their species, often at considerable risk to their own survival. For example, some small birds, including robins, thrushes, and titmice, emit a warning call that lets others know of an approaching predator, even though the sound itself may betray the caller's presence. Certain types of insects, such as bees, ants, and termites, show extremes of self-sacrificial behavior. Large numbers of them will viciously sting or bite an animal that threatens the hive, a defensive response that often results in death to the attackers. Among primates, chimpanzees can be seen sharing meat after a cooperative hunt and practicing adoption when a baby loses its mother. Based on such animal evidence, sociobiologists reasoned that evolution must have made similar provisions for prosocial behavior in humans, perhaps in the form of genetically prewired emotions such as empathy that serve to motivate altruistic behavior (Trivers, 1971).

It is likely that human prosocial behavior does have biological roots, although the evidence for this hypothesis is sparse. As we pointed out in earlier chapters, human neonates show a rudimentary empathic response, for they will cry when they hear the cry of another baby, and by the second year of life empathy is already an important motivator of behavior aimed at alleviating another person's pain and unhappiness. But like most other human behaviors, morally relevant actions are only partially accounted for by their biological foundations. As we showed in Chapter 10, the development of empathy requires strong environmental supports to be realized. Recall that it hinges on experiences with adults who respond in a sensitive, caring way to the child, and its mature expression depends on cognitive development, especially advances in perspective-taking skill. Furthermore, although affective motivation is one basis for moral action, it is not a complete explanation, for there are instances in which blindly following one's empathic feelings is not necessarily moral. For example, most of us would question the morality of a parent who decides not to take a sick child to the doctor because she empathizes with the youngster's fear and anxiety (Rest, 1983). Still, the biological perspective on morality is a useful one, for it reminds us of the adaptive significance of moral action and suggests some intriguing ideas about its evolutionary foundations.

MORALITY AS THE ADOPTION OF SOCIETAL NORMS: THE PSYCHOANALYTIC AND BEHAVIORIST PERSPECTIVES

Although psychoanalytic and behaviorist theories emphasize vastly different mechanisms of development, both approaches regard moral development as the adoption of standards for behavior that conform to societal prescriptions for good conduct, or norms.

The Psychoanalytic Perspective

According to Freud, the seat of morality rests in a portion of the personality called the **superego,** which is the end product of the young boy's Oedipal conflict during the phallic, or early childhood, stage of development (a comparable Electra conflict exists for girls). In the Oedipal conflict, the young boy desires to have his mother all to himself and feels hostile and rivalrous toward his father. These feelings soon lead to intense anxiety, since the boy fears he will lose his parents' love and be punished for his unacceptable desires. To master the anxiety, avoid punishment, and maintain the continued affection of parents, the child forms a superego by **identifying** with the same-sex parent, emulating that parent's characteristics, and in the process internalizing parental standards and prohibitions that reflect society's norms. In addition, the child turns inward the hostility previously aimed at the same-sex parent, which results in the self-punitive affect of guilt. These events lead to the formation of the superego, which is made up of two basic components: an *ego ideal,* or set of ideal standards (derived from parental identification) against which the worth of the self is measured; and a *conscience,* or judging and punishing agency that leads the child to experience guilt each time the standards of the ego ideal are violated. According to Freud's theory, children are motivated to act in accord with societal prescriptions in order to avoid guilt. Freud regarded the process of moral development as largely complete by 5 or 6 years of age, with some additional solidification of the superego during the period of middle childhood (Freud, 1925/1961b; Freud, 1933).

Is Psychoanalytic Theory of Morality Supported by Current Research?

Although Freud's theory of conscience development is still widely accepted by psychoanalytic writers, most developmental psychologists disagree with it on a number of grounds. For example, few current researchers accept Freud's view of guilt as a hostile impulse toward the parent that is redirected toward the self. Instead, they regard guilt as a complex emotion arising from experiences in which a person intentionally engages in a morally unacceptable behavior. From this perspective, young children cannot experience guilt in mature form without first having attained certain cognitive prerequisites. These include awareness of themselves as autonomous beings who make choices about their own actions and the capacity to distinguish between intentional and unintentional acts (Hoffman, 1988; Campos et al., 1983). If you return to our discussion of complex emotions in Chapter 10 and our consideration of children's self-development and understanding of intentions in Chapter 11, you will see that the cognitive capacities that support the guilt response emerge during the preschool years and undergo continued refinement into middle childhood. Although this is the same period that Freud assigned to conscience formation, the basis of the guilt response is now regarded as decidedly different from what Freud described in his Oedipal theory.

Although Freud was not very explicit about the child-rearing practices he thought would promote strong conscience formation, the dynamics of the Oedipal conflict suggest that practices promoting fear of punishment and loss of parental love should motivate children to behave morally. However, research does not support this conclusion (Hoffman, 1977). The findings of a large number of studies indicate that parents who rely on either love-withdrawal techniques of discipline (e.g., ignoring, refusing to speak or listen to, or explicitly stating a dislike for the child) or power assertion (e.g., threats, commands, or physical force) have children who are *less likely* to feel guilty about acting harmfully toward others than children of parents who rely on a form of discipline called **induction.** Induction is a strategy that points out the effect a child's behavior has on others, either directly, by using such statements as, "If you keep pushing him, he'll fall down and cry," or indirectly, by saying something like, "Don't yell at him. He was only trying to help" (Hoffman, 1988, p. 524). Induction may also include suggestions for making amends, such as apologies or ways of compensating for the wrongs done to others. Inductive discipline is somewhat more effective with school-age than preschool children, probably because older children are better able to comprehend the parental reasoning involved (Brody & Shaffer, 1982). However, some research indicates that induction can be useful with children as young as 2 years of age. Zahn-Waxler, Radke-Yarrow, and King (1979) found that mothers who delivered explanations about the unhappiness their young preschoolers caused in others had children who were more likely to engage in reparations after a transgression. Such children were also more altruistic, in that they spontaneously gave hugs, toys, and verbal sympathy to others in distress.

Virtually all parents resort to coercive discipline at one time or another. An occasional power assertion administered by parents who normally use induction may actually facilitate conscience development, because it lets children know that the parent feels strongly about an issue and may get the child to stop doing something long enough to pay attention to the parent's inductive communication. But extreme reliance on either power assertion or love withdrawal does not promote conscience development. Why does induction work so much better? According to Hoffman (1988), induction communicates to children the harmful consequences of their actions, a prohibition against harming others, and the reasons that particular actions are right or wrong in such a way that children can cognitively organize and store the information in memory as a moral norm. Then, in future situations in which the child is tempted to act in a harmful manner, cues from the situation activate the norm along with unpleasant feelings of guilt for having harmed another person. Hoffman believes that disciplinary techniques that rely too heavily on power assertion or love withdrawal may produce such high levels of fear and anxiety in children that they interfere with effective processing of the moral norm. As a result, although these methods may suppress unacceptable behavior temporarily, they are ineffective in motivating moral internalization.

Although there is little empirical support for psychoanalytic mechanisms of conscience development, Freud was still correct in regarding guilt as an important motivator of moral action. Hoffman (1975b; 1976; Hoffman & Saltzstein, 1967) gave 10- to 12-year-olds stories in which a child like themselves committed a transgression, such as cheating or harming another person. Then subjects completed the stories by telling what the protagonist thought and felt and "what happened afterward." Almost all the children made reference to guilt reactions, followed by efforts to make amends on the part of the story character, which served to reduce the guilt. When reparation was precluded by the story conditions (i.e., it was too late for anything to be done), children described prolonged guilt. In addition, story characters were often portrayed as resolving to become less selfish and more considerate in the future. This last finding suggests that guilt may contribute to moral behavior in older children by triggering a process of self-examination and an increased resolve to behave in accordance with moral norms and values. Thus, guilt may eventually become part of a generalized motive to behave morally that goes beyond avoiding transgressions and providing immediate restitution to a victim (Hoffman, 1980).

Despite the effectiveness of guilt as a moral motive, it is not the only force that propels us to act morally, and Freud's theory suffers from one-sidedness in regarding it as such. Furthermore, a wealth of evidence that we will review later on in this chapter indicates that, contrary to what Freud believed, moral development is not an abrupt event that is virtually complete by 5 or 6 years of age. Instead it is a far more gradual process, beginning in early childhood and extending into the adulthood years.[2]

On a final note, Freud's theory places a heavy burden on parents as crucial agents of socialization who assure through their disciplinary practices that children develop an internalized conscience. The research findings summarized above lend considerable support to the idea that parents occupy center stage when it comes to conscience development. However, we have emphasized repeatedly in earlier chapters that parent-child interaction is a two-way street with both parties influencing each other. In line with this idea, research shows that children's personality characteristics affect the discipline they receive from adults. For example, highly attentive, socially responsive children are more likely to evoke inductions than their less socially responsive counterparts, who engender more power-assertive techniques (Keller & Bell, 1979). Research also indicates that the precise nature of children's moral transgressions influences parental methods of discipline. Inductions occur most often when children hurt other people, whereas power assertions are especially frequent when children belligerently damage physical property, display explosive, ill-tempered behavior, or refuse to share (Grusec & Kuczynski, 1980; Zahn-Waxler & Chapman, 1982). Finally, the degree to which a child complies with an initial parental demand affects the parent's subsequent disciplinary response. When children are recalcitrant and noncompliant, their behavior is stressful for parents, and under these conditions parents often escalate their punitiveness (Mulhern & Passman, 1981; Parke, 1977). Thus, moral socialization within the family, like other aspects of development, is best understood as a bidirectional, transactional process between parent and child.

In summary, Freud's theory falls short as an adequate account of moral development. Although he was correct that guilt is an important motivator of moral action, developmental psychologists no longer accept Freud's view of guilt as hostility redirected toward the self. Furthermore, in contrast to predictions drawn from Freudian theory, disciplinary practices that engender fear of punishment and loss of parental love are not effective in promoting moral internalization. Instead, induction is far more successful. Whereas Freud regarded socialization during the preschool years as crucial for conscience development, moral development is actually a far more gradual process in which both parental practices and child characteristics play an influential role.

The Behaviorist Perspective

Unlike psychoanalytic theory, behaviorist approaches to moral development do not consider moral functioning to be a special form of human activity that follows a unique course of development. Rather, moral behavior is seen as acquired just like

---

[2] Contemporary descendants of Freudian theory, while accepting the punitive, restrictive dimension of the superego, place greater emphasis on its positive, constructive side. For example, Erikson (1950) describes the psychological outcome of the Oedipal period as a *sense of initiative,* which provides the foundation for a realistic sense of ambition and purpose in life. Children develop initiative by identifying with heroic and idealized representatives of their society, whose roles they act out in play. Unlike Freud, Erikson (1968) views conscience development as extending from early childhood into adulthood. Recall from Chapter 11 that an important component of identity development is the adolescent's search for an ideology, or a set of ethical values, to have faith in. These values are selected during late adolescence as identity is achieved, and they undergo further refinement during the adulthood years.

any other set of responses: through the learning mechanisms of reinforcement and modeling.

Reinforcement. According to the traditional operant conditioning view, behavior in conformity with societal norms increases because adults follow it up with positive reinforcement in the form of approval, affection, and other rewards, whereas behavior that violates normative standards is punished by reproof, loss of privileges, and other outcomes that make it less likely to occur in the future. Most behaviorists regard positive reinforcement as a far more effective means than punishment for promoting socially desirable behavior. However, one social learning theory modification of the operant conditioning paradigm views punishment as a prime motivator of moral action and comes very close to Freud's idea of a harsh, guilt-ridden conscience. In fact, the inspiration for this account came from the efforts of some social learning theorists to translate psychoanalytic ideas into learning theory terms. The theory states that due to a history of punishment for deviant acts, painful anxiety becomes associated with unacceptable behavior. Since anxiety is reexperienced each time the child starts to deviate again, it is best avoided by not engaging in the act (Aronfreed, 1968; Mowrer, 1960). However, this explanation suffers from the same difficulties we mentioned earlier in connection with Freud's theory. Punitive parental tactics that provoke high levels of anxiety are less effective in motivating resistance to transgression than rational, inductive techniques. Box 12.1 will tell you more about why punishment works so poorly as a method for inducing conscience development and self-control, when its use is justified, and how adults can apply it so that its adverse consequences are reduced to a minimum.

Other social learning theorists point out that it is probably unlikely that very many prosocial behaviors are initially acquired according to the principle of operant conditioning. For a behavior to be reinforced, it must first occur spontaneously, and many morally relevant behaviors, like sharing, helping, or comforting a distressed playmate, do not occur often enough by chance for reinforcement to account for their rapid acquisition in early childhood. Consequently, these social learning theorists assume that children learn to behave morally largely through observation and imitation of models who demonstrate socially acceptable behavior (Bandura & Walters, 1963; Bandura, 1977). But once children acquire a prosocial response, reinforcement in the form of praise and the presence and vigilance of adults who remind children of the rules for appropriate behavior are factors that increase its frequency (Gelfand et al., 1975; Zarbatany, Hartmann, & Gelfand, 1985). However, we might question whether prosocial behaviors maintained in this way are truly "moral." As we noted in the introduction to this chapter, becoming increasingly independent of the pressures of the immediate situation and governed by internalized standards is generally regarded as an essential part of moral development. However, traditional behaviorists differ from most other theorists in that they do not look upon morality in this fashion.

Modeling. Laboratory evidence indicates that exposure to models who behave in a helpful or generous fashion is very effective in encouraging children to act more prosocially themselves (Bryan & London, 1970; Canale, 1977; Elliott & Vasta, 1970; Gray & Pirot, 1984). Furthermore, an altruistic behavioral example will continue to affect children's behavior from several hours to several weeks after the original exposure to the model (Midlarsky & Bryan, 1972; Yarrow, Scott, & Waxler, 1973). Recent studies indicate that altruistic models exert their most powerful effects on children below the age of 7 or 8. Older children who have a history of consistent exposure to caring, giving adults tend to behave altruistically in situations where generosity and helping are appropriate regardless of whether a nearby adult's behavior is charitable or selfish (Lipscomb et al., 1982; 1985). By middle childhood, altruism is based on cognitive mediators, or *internalized normative prescriptions* abstracted from repeated experiences in which children have seen others help and give, heard them state the importance of doing so, and been encouraged to behave in a similar fashion themselves (Mussen & Eisenberg-Berg, 1977). In fact, by 7 to 9 years of age, children can spontaneously verbalize the norm of helping people in need (Bryan & Walbek, 1970). As a result, they are more apt to follow this internalized prescription whether behavior consistent with the norm is modeled for them or not. In contrast, younger children are still formulating the norm and finding out under what conditions to apply it. Thus they look to adult models for information about where, when, and what kinds of altruistic behaviors are appropriate (Peterson, 1982).

Research shows that characteristics of models affect children's willingness to imitate their behavior. Warmth and affection are consistently associated with children's prosocial inclinations. In an experiment by Yarrow, Scott, and Waxler (1973), an altruistic caregiver interacted with two groups of preschoolers. In one condition,

---

FOCUS ON THEORY, RESEARCH, AND APPLICATIONS

Box 12.1
Punishment and the Socialization of Moral Behavior

Punishment is a form of discipline that presents children with noxious stimulation aimed at inhibiting undesirable behavior. All parents rely on it sometimes, and the use of sharp verbal reprimands and physical force to restrain or move a child from one place to another is warranted when children engage in behaviors that need to be stopped immediately because they can result in serious harm to the child or others. But punishments involving unpleasant pokes, taps, and spankings or verbal rebukes that denigrate the child's worth as a person are never justified. Such tactics are inhumane and ineffective, and they promote a series of unfortunate side effects that may accelerate parental punitiveness as well as children's undesirable behavior. Research highlights several important reasons for avoiding these types of punishments:

1. Punishment only promotes temporary suppression of a response, not long-term internalization of a prohibition. Frequently punished children inhibit an undesirable behavior while the punishing agent is present, but they revert back to engaging in the act as soon as the adult leaves the scene and they can "get away with it." In fact, children of highly punitive parents are known to be especially aggressive and hard to control in settings

outside the home situation (Eron et al., 1974).

2. Punishments involving physical or verbal injury provide children with examples of adult-instigated aggression that they can model and incorporate into their own behavioral repertoires. Naturalistic studies have repeatedly shown that parental punitiveness is associated with high levels of aggression in children (Parke & Slaby, 1983), and experimental evidence confirms that children adopt the punitive tactics used by adults in their own interactions with peers (Gelfand et al., 1974). The aggressive behaviors displayed by physically abused children are especially extreme. At home and in school, they verbally threaten and physically assault both peers and adults far more often than their nonabused counterparts (George & Main, 1979; Reid, Taplin, & Lorber, 1981).

3. Frequently punished children soon learn to protect themselves by avoiding punitive agents (Redd, Morris, & Martin, 1975). When children refrain from approaching and interacting with those responsible for their upbringing, adults have fewer opportunities to teach desirable behaviors, and their power as socializing agents is severely reduced.

4. As punishment "works" to temporarily suppress children's unacceptable behavior, it offers immediate relief to punitive agents, and they are reinforced for applying the punitive techniques. Consequently, a

punitive adult is likely to punish with greater frequency over time, a course of action that may spiral into serious child abuse (Parke & Collmer, 1975).

For obvious ethical reasons, investigators cannot study highly punitive methods of discipline in the laboratory. Instead, they are limited to the use of loud buzzers or verbal reprimands that do not cover the full range of noxious consequences to which children are exposed in natural environments. Nevertheless, experimentation with these techniques has identified ways in which sharp warnings and admonitions can be combined with other disciplinary tactics to increase children's behavioral inhibition. Factors that affect children's responsiveness to punishment include its timing, intensity, and consistency. Characteristics of punitive agents and whether or not a verbal explanation accompanies the punishment are also important.

Timing. Punishment delivered early, soon after the child initiates a prohibited act, is most effective (Walters, Parke, & Cane, 1965; Cheyne & Walters, 1969). Laboratory findings suggest that delaying punishment for several hours after a transgression occurs markedly reduces its inhibition of undesirable behavior (Parke, 1977).

Intensity. A highly intense reprimand, as opposed to a mild one, is more effective in producing response inhibition during the period just after the caregiver behaved warmly and nurturantly while she demonstrated a wide variety of prosocial behaviors. In the other condition, the caregiver was equally altruistic, but her mood was cold and aloof. Children in the first group were far more likely to behave like the model. Warmth of emulated figures continues to be related to prosocial behavior during middle childhood (Hoffman, 1975a) and into adolescence. In a study of college civil rights activists, Rosenhan (1970) found that the most committed students had a warm and congenial relationship with at least one parent, and their parents were also highly dedicated prosocial activists who were especially effective in passing their altruistic values on to their children. Warmth and nurturance may facilitate prosocial behavior by making children more receptive to the model, and as a result, more attentive to the model's behavior. In addition, warm, affectionate responding is itself a model of altruism, and part of what children may be imitating is this aspect of the model's behavior itself.

punishment is delivered. However, severe punishment also poses risks, for the high levels of fear and anxiety engendered by it may interfere with adaptive cognitive processing and moral internalization.

Consistency. Punishment that is erratic and intermittent is related to especially high rates of aggression and disobedience in children. When parents react to the same violation with laxity on some occasions and punitiveness on others, children's inhibition of prohibited behavior is markedly reduced (Parke & Deur, 1972).

Characteristics of Punitive Agents. Punishment administered by an adult who has a warm relationship with the child produces more immediate behavioral inhibition (Parke & Walters, 1967). Children of involved and caring parents probably find the disruption of parental affection that accompanies punishment to be especially unpleasant. As a result, they are motivated to regain the positive attentions of their parents as quickly as possible.

Verbal Rationales. The most successful way to improve the effectiveness of punishment is to accompany it with a verbal rationale that gives children reasons for not engaging in a deviant act (Harter, 1983). Such reasoning can take the form of inductions that tell children how their behavior affects others,

instructions about how to behave in a particular situation, or explanations of adult motives for punishing the child. The addition of a cognitive rationale does more than increase immediate behavioral inhibition. Resistance to transgression lasts over time because children internalize the adult's reasoning and call on it in future situations to induce self-control. Reasoning also eliminates the relevance of most variables that moderate the effectiveness of punishment. For example, the addition of reasoning increases the success of late-timed punishment administered hours after a deviant act (Walters & Andres, 1967). Moreover, when punishment is coupled with a cognitive rationale, the punishing agent's effectiveness is no longer dependent on nurturance, and low intensity punishment is just as effective as high intensity punishment in promoting immediate behavioral inhibition (Parke, 1969). However, for reasoning to be effective, its complexity must match the child's level of cognitive development. A rationale cannot facilitate response inhibition if children do not comprehend it. Concrete explanations that focus on the physical consequences of an action (e.g., "That vase might break," "You might get hurt") work best with preschoolers. With increasing age, explanations that focus on feelings (e.g., "I'll feel very sad if you do that"), intentions (e.g., "It's wrong for you to want that toy"), and basic rights (e.g., "That belongs to

someone else") become more effective (Pressley, 1979).

On a final note, several alternatives to physical and verbal punishment exist that permit adults to discipline children effectively and, at the same time, avoid the undesirable side effects of punishment. One is a procedure called *time out,* in which children are removed from the immediate setting and the opportunities it offers for positive reinforcement until they are ready to behave acceptably. For most children, time out requires only a few minutes to change behavior, and it also offers a "cooling off" period for parents who may be highly angered by a child's unacceptable actions. Another commonly used technique is withdrawal of privileges, such as loss of allowance or deprivation of a special experience like going to the movies. Removing privileges may generate some anger and resentment in children, but at least parents are not engaging in punitive behaviors that could easily escalate into abuse and violence. Finally, parental practices that do not wait for children to misbehave, but that encourage and reward children for good conduct, are, in the long run, the most effective forms of discipline. When adults help children acquire acceptable behaviors that they can use to replace prohibited actions, the need to use punishment in the socialization of children is greatly reduced (Parke, 1977).

Other influential characteristics of models are power and competence, dimensions that are believed to be especially important in the father's impact on children's moral development. Research shows that the types of disciplinary strategies used by fathers have far less influence on children's moral behavior than those used by mothers (Brody & Shaffer, 1982), perhaps because in most families the mother is the primary caregiver and therefore the child's chief disciplinarian (Mulhern & Passman, 1981). Instead, the father's impact on children's morality seems to derive primarily from his portrayal of an instrumentally competent role model.[3] Social learning theorists believe that powerful individuals serve as effective models because children want to be like them in order to acquire their power, mastery, and other resources. Acting like the model is rewarding to children because it signifies that they, too, may be able to attain the model's desirable goal states (Bandura, 1977).

An additional characteristic of models that affects children's tendency to emulate their behavior is whether they "practice what they preach"—that is, demonstrate consistency between what they say and what they actually do. One study found that grade-school children were more likely to place money they had won in a game in a jar for the needy if a model who played the game first made a charitable statement (e.g., "It's a good thing to give, especially when you know it will make others happy") and also behaved charitably than if the model's statement and behavior contradicted one another (Midlarsky & Bryan, 1972). When adults say one thing and do another, in choosing between their words and actions children generally opt for the most lenient standard of adult-demonstrated behavior (Mischel & Liebert, 1966).

The evidence reviewed above indicates that children pick up many positive, prosocial behaviors by observing parents and other adults. Social learning theorists have also been interested in finding out whether modeling facilitates children's self-control and restraint—the *inhibition* of behaviors that violate social prohibitions. The evidence is not as clear on this issue. Laboratory studies reveal that the effects of watching a model who shows lapses in self-control far exceed the effects of watching a model who resists temptation (Fry, 1975; Rosenkoetter, 1973; Stein, 1967). These findings suggest that models can easily encourage deviant behavior, but they are far less effective in helping children overcome their self-centered, egoistic impulses. However, several studies indicate that under certain conditions, models *can* foster children's resistance to temptation (Bussey & Perry, 1977; Grusec et al., 1979). Grusec and her colleagues (1979) had a person first try to lure a model and then 5- to 8-year-old subjects away from a boring task to play with toys that the experimenter had forbidden them to touch. A model who verbalized that she was resisting temptation and clearly stated her reason for doing so (e.g., "I can't come play with the toys because I'm here to sort cards, and I always try to do what's right"), was more effective in promoting children's resistance to temptation than a model who merely demonstrated resistance. Grusec's findings indicate that the behavior of a self-controlled model is more likely to rub off on children when the model makes her own efforts at behavioral inhibition obvious by verbalizing them. In addition, the verbalization provides children with a cognitive rationale that they can internalize and rely on at a later time to facilitate resistance to temptation.

In summary, adult modeling of prosocial behavior is highly successful in encouraging children to behave helpfully and generously toward others, especially at younger ages. Several characteristics of prosocial models increase children's willingness to imitate their behavior, including warmth, power, competence, and consistency between words and deeds. Laboratory research indicates that resistance to temptation is less likely to be imitated by children than a model's lapses in self-control. However, imitation of self-controlled behavior is enhanced when adult models make the nature of their behavior explicit by describing and explaining it to children.

---

[3] It is important to keep in mind that the parental differences described here may not operate in nontraditional families where mothers provide models of competent, mastery-oriented behavior and fathers participate in household and child care responsibilities.

Consistency across Situations in Moral Behavior

513

CHAPTER 12
THE DEVELOPMENT
OF MORALITY
AND SELF-CONTROL

Once children are old enough to have internalized normative standards, we would expect them to show a reasonable degree of consistency in moral conduct from one occasion to another. To what extent do children develop *traits of character,* such as honesty, generosity, and helpfulness (or their opposites—deceitfulness, selfishness, and inconsiderateness) that predict how they will behave across a wide variety of situations?

Six decades ago, in a study that examined consistency of moral conduct among 11,000 children between the ages of 8 and 16 who were tempted to steal, lie, or cheat in a variety of contexts, Hartshorne and May (1928) found that children's moral behavior varied substantially from one situation to another. Knowing that a child behaved honestly or dishonestly on one occasion was not a good clue as to whether the child would behave that way on another. Instead, expediency seemed to account for children's behavior. When circumstances made it safe and easy to cheat and when other children approved of the cheating, a child was likely to do so. Hartshorne and May concluded that morality was entirely specific to the situation; there was no such thing as a moral character guaranteeing that a person would behave honorably under all or even most conditions.

However, more recent research indicates that Hartshorne and May's conclusion was too extreme. Burton (1963; 1976) reanalyzed their data, eliminating assessments of dishonesty that were unreliable and applying more sophisticated data analysis techniques. He found that children do have a moderate tendency to behave in a morally consistent fashion across situations. Furthermore, children's behavioral consistency becomes fairly strong when assessments of their conduct are taken in situations that are similar to one another. For example, the extent to which a child will cheat on an examination is much the same across different classroom contexts, but cheating on tests at school will not necessarily predict cheating in a ball game on the playground or while playing Monopoly at home. Burton's results indicate that moral behavior is neither completely situation-specific nor entirely stable and predictable. Instead, its consistency lies somewhere between these two extremes, a conclusion that has also been confirmed by other investigations (Nelson, Grinder, & Mutterer, 1969; Rushton, 1980).

A moderate level of individual consistency in moral conduct does not rule out the possibility that situational factors affect moral behavior to some degree, and a long history of research on children's classroom cheating behavior indicates that situational variables do play a contributing role. For example, the level of honesty of peer associates affects children's tendency to cheat. Cheaters generally sit close to one

Children learn to behave generously toward others from exposure to warm, caring adults who display altruistic behavior themselves. (Mimi Forsyth/ Monkmeyer Press Photo Service)

another in the classroom, and students who happen to sit near or next to a cheater are more likely to cheat themselves (Sherrill et al., 1970). Siblings and close friends also resemble one another in cheating behavior, and in college, fraternity and sorority group membership is associated with a rise in self-reported cheating (Harp & Taietz, 1966).

Furthermore, situational factors that increase children's anxieties about not doing well in school will augment their tendency to cheat. A comparative study of high school students in the United States, Canada, and Scotland found that in all three societies, students perceived the major cause of classroom cheating to be fear of failure (Schab, 1971). When teachers give pupils information about the superior performance of classmates in comparison to themselves, place a high premium on doing well on a particular task, or give children assignments that are beyond their ability to accomplish successfully, cheating behavior rises accordingly (Pearlin, Yarrow, & Scarr, 1967; Taylor & Lewit, 1966; Vitro, 1969). Although strong parental pressure to succeed predicts better academic performance, it is also related to cheating. This is especially true in low-income families where the disparity between educational goals and financial resources is very great and parents may try to overcome the gap by making achievement demands that are extreme (Pearlin, Yarrow, & Scarr, 1967).

In summary, situational determinants of honesty and dishonesty provide evidence of variability in moral behavior, but there is also a counterbalancing picture of consistency. Situational temptations do not affect all children to the same degree; a morally well-socialized child is less likely to succumb to a ready opportunity to copy from a neighbor, use crib notes in class, or change a test score. Effective child-rearing and disciplinary practices do contribute to the development of internal dispositions to behave morally that are generalizable across contexts. At the same time, evidence on the role of situational factors suggests that honest conduct can be enhanced by arranging environments in such a way as to minimize children's temptation to cheat. One way of doing so would be to reduce extreme parental and school pressures placed on children for competitive success (Burton, 1976).

Critique of the "Morality as Social Conformity" Perspective

Learning to behave in conformity with societal norms is, without question, an important dimension of moral development. Nevertheless, a major criticism of psychoanalytic and behaviorist theories, which treat morality as entirely a matter of social conformity, is that sometimes normative prescriptions conflict with important ethical principles and social goals. Under these conditions, deliberate violation of norms is not immoral; it is justifiable and often very courageous. Cases of famous nonconformists, whose actions dramatized the inadequacy of societal norms at great personal sacrifice, illustrate the difficulty of equating morality with social conformity. Few of us would place Susan B. Anthony, Mahatma Ghandi, or Martin Luther King in the same moral class as Al Capone or Jack the Ripper, although all have in common the fact that they were nonconformists who were seriously at odds with prevailing societal standards (Rest, 1983).

Furthermore, many normative matters are not primarily moral matters. Instead, they involve arbitrary **social conventions,** such as dress styles, table manners, and customs of social interaction. At a fairly early age children understand that social conventions differ from moral acts, and the distinctions they make do not seem to result from direct teaching, modeling, or reinforcement. For example, Nucci (1981) asked individuals between 7 and 19 years of age what would be more wrong — engaging in behaviors like calling a teacher by her first name or eating lunch with one's fingers (breaking with social convention) or committing such acts as lying, stealing, or hitting another person (violating moral rules). Subjects of all ages consistently indicated that moral violations were more serious, giving as reasons that they

Susan B. Anthony's (1820 – 1906) leadership in the campaign for women's suffrage illustrates how behavior at odds with prevailing societal norms is sometimes highly moral and courageous. (North Wind Picture Archives)

result in harm to others, deprive people of what is rightfully theirs, or simply should not be committed. In contrast, violations of social conventions were regarded as merely unmannerly, disruptive, or unpleasantly messy. Furthermore, when asked if it would be all right to steal in another country that has no rule against stealing, children as young as 6 indicated that it would still be wrong to steal, but when asked if it would be okay to play games by different rules in other countries, children thought this would be quite permissible (Turiel, 1983).

Even preschoolers seem to appreciate the distinction between moral and social conventional matters. When observed in nursery school they frequently respond to moral transgressions of their peers by verbalizing their own injury or loss, reacting emotionally, telling another child to stop, or retaliating. In contrast, they seldom respond to their classmates' social conventional transgressions, leaving these for teachers to handle. In addition, when asked, preschoolers answer that moral transgressions are wrong regardless of the presence or absence of school rules pertaining to them, but they think violating social conventions is only wrong if a school rule prohibits the behavior (Nucci & Turiel, 1978).

Based on these findings, Turiel (1983) has proposed that social conventions and morality constitute distinct domains of behavior and social understanding that undergo separate lines of development. At an early age, Turiel believes, moral violations come to be understood as wrong because of the consequences these actions have for others (e.g., doing harm and violating rights). In contrast, social conventions are understood as arbitrary and relative, to be adhered to simply as a matter of assuring social orderliness. It is interesting that preschoolers have already begun to make this distinction, despite the fact that adults model conformity to social conventions and are at least as insistent that children act in accord with them as they are about their obedience to moral norms (Grief & Gleason, 1980). However, although adults may react equally often to both kinds of transgressions, the *way* they respond differs between the two. Parents and teachers more often provide rationales and comment on the feelings of others in response to moral transgressions, whereas they refer to institutional rules and the disorderliness likely to ensue in the case of social conventional infractions. Furthermore, children experience moral transgressions differently from social conventional violations. In moral situations, they are sometimes victims whose rights have been violated, and if they are perpetrators of the violation, they receive the distinct forms of feedback from adults and children described above. Turiel and his coworkers believe that it is not through modeling and reinforcement, but rather through *actively thinking about* their different experiences in social conventional and moral domains that children come to differentiate between the two.

Although Turiel makes a strong case for the distinctiveness of moral and social conventional domains, he believes that situations do arise in which the two overlap. Sometimes violations of social conventions *are* moral matters. For example, getting assigned work done on time, greeting a coworker in the morning, or sending a thank you note after receiving a gift are arbitrary practices arrived at by social consensus. However, violating any one of them can cause harm to other people (in the examples given above, by placing additional work burdens on others or hurting another person's feelings). Turiel believes the ability to coordinate and integrate the social conventional and moral implications of behavior is an important feature of mature moral understanding. Preliminary evidence indicates that by the adolescent and college years, individuals seem to appreciate the overlapping nature of these two domains, whereas at younger ages each is understood in a separate, uncoordinated way (Turiel, 1983).

Turiel's research, as well as the work of others, shows that children strive to *make sense* out of social rules. They make moral judgments, deciding what is right or wrong on the basis of underlying concepts they have about justice and fairness. As Rest (1983) indicates, "Children do not just learn lists of prescriptions and prohibitions; they also come to understand the nature and function of social arrangements," including promises, bargains, divisions of labor, and fair principles and procedures for settling conflicts and organizing social relationships (p. 616). The cognitive-developmental position on morality is unique in its view of the child as a thinking moral being who wonders about right and wrong and actively searches for moral truth. We will see later on that Piaget's and Kohlberg's theories, which comprise the major cognitive-developmental research tradition in moral development, do not make the same distinction between moral and social conventional matters adhered to by Turiel. However, all of these theorists are in full agreement that children *reason* about the rightness and wrongness of social acts and that changes in their reasoning are at the heart of moral development.

MORALITY AS SOCIAL UNDERSTANDING: THE COGNITIVE-DEVELOPMENTAL PERSPECTIVE

Cognitive-developmental theorists study how moral reasoning changes with age. They believe that increasing cognitive maturity and social experience gradually lead children to gain a better understanding of cooperative social arrangements that regulate moral responsibilities. Children's understanding of social arrangements evolves from a simple, concrete grasp of obligations between people to a more abstract, comprehensive appreciation of society-wide institutions and law-making systems. As the understanding of society and social structures changes, children's moral ideals — their conceptions of what ought to be done when the needs and desires of people are in conflict with one another — also undergo revision, toward increasingly just, fair, and balanced solutions to moral problems (Rest, 1983).

Before we summarize the theories of Piaget and Kohlberg and the large body of research they have inspired, it is important to stress once more that a cognitive-developmental explanation cannot be considered a complete account of morality, any more than the other perspectives we have already discussed. This is because thinking about what is moral does not guarantee that people will actually behave in accord with their cognitions. Plenty of examples exist to demonstrate that children and adults often compromise their ideals of fairness, permitting self-interest to prevail even when they believe it is wrong to do so. Decades ago in their classic investigation of moral conduct, Hartshorne and May found a low relationship between children's moral reasoning and their actual behavior in a wide variety of situations (Hartshorne, May, & Shuttleworth, 1930).

Nevertheless, an integral part of the cognitive-developmental approach is that moral understanding does affect moral motivation. Therefore, cognition should bear some relationship, although an imperfect one, to moral action. Cognitive-developmental theorists believe that as children come to understand the purpose and function of cooperative social arrangements, they develop increased respect for the arrangements themselves and for the people who work to uphold and protect them. As a result, children gradually realize that behaving in line with the way one thinks is an important part of creating and maintaining a just social world (Rest, 1983). Based on this idea, the cognitive-developmental approach predicts a very specific relationship between moral thought and behavior: the two should come closer together as individuals advance toward higher levels of moral understanding. An important reason that the research of Hartshorne and May, cited above, found very little association between moral reasoning and conduct may have been that their subjects were insufficiently advanced in moral development to have integrated thought with action. As we shall see later on, recent evidence indicates that among older children, adolescents, and adults, there is moderate consistency between moral reasoning and moral behavior. Thus, moral thinking is not independent of and irrelevant to moral action. Instead, it is one important factor, among a great many factors, that helps explain why people behave as they do.

Piaget's Theory of Moral Development

517

CHAPTER 12
THE DEVELOPMENT
OF MORALITY
AND SELF-CONTROL

Piaget's book, *The Moral Judgment of the Child* (1932/1965), published over half a century ago, served as the original inspiration for the cognitive-developmental perspective on morality and continues to be highly influential in contemporary research. Although Piaget agreed with other theorists of his time that the younger child's morality was largely a matter of uncritical acceptance of adult prescriptions, he was the first to argue that all morality is not "imposed by the group upon the individual and by the adult upon the child" (p. 341). Instead, as children's understanding of social arrangements changes, their morality also undergoes revision, from a rigid view of moral rules as sacred, unalterable dictates of authority figures to an appreciation of them as flexible instruments of human purposes that are subject to change in response to human needs.

Piaget's Stages of Moral Understanding. To study children's ideas about morality, Piaget relied on his open-ended clinical interviewing procedure, questioning scores of Swiss children between 5 and 13 years of age about their understanding of rules in the game of marbles. In addition, he gave children pairs of stories in which characters' intentions to engage in right or wrong action and the outcomes resulting from their behavior were varied. In the best-known of these stories, children were asked to judge which of the following two boys, well-intentioned John who causes much damage or ill-intentioned Henry who does little damage, is naughtier and why:

> Story A: A little boy who is called John is in his room. He is called to dinner. He goes into the dining room. But behind the door there was a chair, and on the chair there was a tray with fifteen cups on it. John couldn't have known that there was all this behind the door. He goes in, the door knocks against the tray, bang go the fifteen cups, and they all get broken!

> Story B: Once there was a little boy whose name was Henry. One day when his mother was out he tried to get some jam out of the cupboard. He climbed up on to a chair and stretched out his arm. But the jam was too high up and he couldn't reach it and have any. But while he was trying to get it he knocked over a cup. The cup fell down and broke. (Piaget, 1932/1965, p. 122)

Based on children's responses, Piaget identified two broad stages of moral development, as follows:

1. **The stage of heteronomous morality,[4] or moral realism** (about 5–10 years). During the early preschool years and prior to the beginning of this stage, children show little understanding of social rules. When they play rule-oriented games like marbles, they do so for the sheer pleasure of exploring and manipulating the materials and are generally unconcerned about winning, losing, or systematically coordinating their actions with those of other players. Around 5 or 6 years of age, as children enter the period of heteronomous morality, they start to show great concern and respect for rules. However, they view rules as fixed, external regularities that are created and handed down by adult authorities. For example, young children state that the rules of the game of marbles cannot be changed, explaining that "God didn't teach (the new rules)," "you couldn't play any other way," or "it would be cheating. . . . A fair rule is one that is in the game" (pp. 58, 59, 63). Many of Piaget's younger subjects claimed that rules originate with God or their fathers, or that the rules have existed in their current form since the beginning of time.

Piaget believed that the heteronomous child's view of rules as sacred and unchangeable results from two factors that limit the young child's moral understanding: (1) the coercive constraint of adult authority, which promotes an unquestioning

---

[4] Heteronomous means under the authority of another.

To study children's moral judgment, Piaget interviewed schoolchildren about their understanding of rules in the game of marbles. He reported that young children view rules as fixed, external regularities handed down by authorities. At older ages, they regard rules as flexible instruments of human purposes that can be changed to suit the will of the majority. (Sybil Shelton/ Monkmeyer Press Photo Service)

attitude toward rules and the adults who enforce them; and (2) cognitive immaturity, particularly the young child's egocentrism. Egocentrism causes children's moral understanding to be characterized by **realism,** an inability to separate subjective and objective aspects of experience. In other words, because young children make the egocentric assumption that everyone else's thoughts are identical to their own, they externalize rules and treat them as permanent fixtures in reality, like gravity and other physical laws, instead of viewing them as subjective, internal principles that can be modified at will.

Together, egocentrism and realism lead to other deficiencies in children's moral judgments. For example, the heteronomous child bases an action's wrongness on *objective consequences,* not on people's subjective intent to do harm. In the stories about John and Henry given above, John is regarded as the naughtier of the two boys because he broke the greatest number of cups, despite the fact that he did not do so on purpose. Also, since young children do not distinguish between violating a social rule and violating a physical law, they believe in **immanent justice,** that wrongdoing inevitably leads to punishment. Inescapable punishment for bad acts is regarded as the way in which the physical world maintains moral order, and it may do so through a variety of unfortunate experiences and accidents, such as making children fall off their bikes, break treasured toys, or have bad dreams during the night. Finally, the heteronomous child believes in *absolutism of moral perspectives,* the idea that there is only one correct moral viewpoint in a situation and that everyone involved automatically adheres to it. Given a story in which the classmates of a lazy schoolboy are forbidden by their teacher to help him with his homework, but one child helps the lazy pupil anyway, heteronomous children believe that all participants in the situation — the teacher, the lazy boy, the helping child, and the other classmates — think the same way about the rightness or wrongness of the helping child's disobedience. There cannot be different perspectives (Lerner, 1937).

2. The stage of autonomous morality, or the morality of cooperation (about 10 years and older). Due to cognitive development, gradual release from adult vigilance and constraint, and interaction with peers, children eventually shift from heteronomous to autonomous moral functioning. Piaget regarded social experiences with peers as particularly important in this transition. Peer experiences promote a decline in egocentrism (see Chapter 6). As a result, children recognize that different people may have different perspectives about moral action, and the subjective intentions of people, not the objective consequences of their actions, serve as the basis for judging behavior.

In addition, as children participate as co-equals in social exchanges with peers, they learn to settle conflicts in mutually beneficial ways. Gradually they become aware of **reciprocity** as the organizing principle of cooperative social relations. By reciprocity, Piaget meant a rational ideal of fairness, a concern for the welfare of others in the same way that each person is concerned about the welfare of the self, or, phrased in a very familiar form: "Do unto others as you would have them do unto you." Piaget believed that an appreciation of reciprocity was at the heart of the transition from heteronomous to autonomous moral functioning. For example, autonomous children no longer view rules as fixed and immutable. They see them as flexible, socially agreed upon principles of cooperation that can be changed to suit the will of the majority. Therefore, not all rules enunciated by adults need to be upheld. At times, there may be good reason to break a rule, and unquestioning obedience to authority is no longer regarded as a sound basis for moral action. Furthermore, an understanding of reciprocity leads to a new perspective on punishment. Bad acts are no longer seen as inevitably punished. Instead, the autonomous child believes that punishment should be reciprocity-based, or rationally related to the offense. That is, the severity of punishment should fit the seriousness of the transgression as well as the intentions of the transgressor. Also, where possible punishment should be a logical consequence of the offender's crime, requiring him to make active restitution or allowing him to suffer the natural consequences of his action (e.g., a cheater whom no one will play with; a liar whom no one will believe anymore, even when he tells the truth). Finally, punishment should be meted out in an evenhanded, nonarbitrary fashion to all participants in a situation, guaranteeing "equal justice for all."

Critique of Piaget's Theory. Follow-up research on Piaget's theory has upheld his general vision of moral development. In a large number of studies, some conducted in different cultures, the diverse moral attributes that distinguish heteronomous from autonomous morality show the expected differences between younger and older subjects, even though the timing of the changes varies substantially from one sample to another (Lickona, 1976). Furthermore, as indicated in Box 12.2, research documents Piaget's conclusion that very young children do not comprehend the moral concept of reciprocity and that their appreciation of this vital principle of cooperative social relations improves during middle childhood. Piaget did not test his belief that moral reasoning is facilitated by release from the coercive constraint of adult authority, intellectual growth, and peer interaction, but there is evidence to support the relevance of all of these factors. A well-documented relationship exists between parental power assertion and immaturity of moral judgment (Hoffman, 1976; Hoffman & Saltzstein, 1967). In addition, IQ, cognitive perspective-taking skill, and performance on Piagetian logical tasks are all positively related to measures of moral judgment maturity (Lickona, 1976; Kurdek, 1980). As we will see later on, extensions of Piaget's work by Kohlberg and his followers have led to a more refined analysis of the connection between cognitive development and moral reasoning, and they also provide support for the role of peer associations in stimulating the growth of moral understanding.

Nevertheless, certain aspects of Piaget's theory have been the subject of considerable criticism. Recall that earlier in this chapter, we summarized work by Turiel and his coworkers indicating that as early as the preschool years, children do not regard all rules with equal reverence and respect. They make cognitive distinctions between social conventional and moral rules and regard the former as far less permanent and immutable than the latter.

Box 12.2
The Development of Children's Understanding of Moral Reciprocity

Theory. Piaget (1932/1965) proposed that an understanding of moral reciprocity—the importance of "treat[ing] others as [one] would wish to be treated" (p. 196)—underlies the shift from a morality of obedience to authority to a morality of social cooperation. Although he suggested that children's appreciation of reciprocity improves between 6 and 12 years of age, he did little to chart its course of development.

Reciprocity can be understood in two different ways. The first is on a concrete plane—as a matter of equal exchanges between people. A person who understands reciprocity in this way believes that justice is promoted when the favors or unkindnesses of other people are returned in a similar fashion, a notion that is summed up by the Biblical quotation, "An eye for an eye and a tooth for a tooth." Reciprocity can also be appreciated on a more abstract, idealistic plane, in the sense expressed by Piaget above. In "The Golden Rule" account of reciprocity, kind behavior is warranted regardless of how another person behaves, and hostile retaliation is not justified. Instead, morality is based on treating others as one would want to be treated by them. Consider this more advanced notion of reciprocity and what you learned about the development of children's perspective-taking abilities in Chapter 11. Thinking about how you would want to be treated if you and another person had to exchange places requires Selman's complex, *mutual perspective-taking* skill. Therefore, we would not expect children to have an advanced appreciation of reciprocity until the early adolescent years. Although no single study has investigated children's

understanding of reciprocity over an extended age period, by piecing together the results of several investigations, we can get some sense of its progression of development.

Research. During the preschool years, children do not understand reciprocity, even in its concrete form. Berndt (1979b) showed 3- to 5-year-olds a series of cartoons. Some portrayed concrete reciprocal exchanges (returning a favor or an aggressive retaliation), and others depicted nonreciprocal behavior in which a character engaged in spontaneous helping or unprovoked aggression. After each cartoon, children were asked whether the actor was good or bad and then told to rank the actor from a little bit good (bad) to very, very good (bad). Preschool children simply gave more positive evaluations for prosocial than for aggressive behavior. They did not differentiate between episodes portraying reciprocal versus nonreciprocal actions.

By five years of age, children regard concrete reciprocity as an important basis for moral judgment (Baldwin & Baldwin, 1970; Berndt, 1977; Peterson, Hartmann, & Gelfand, 1977), and they shift toward an ideal notion of reciprocity by the late childhood and early adolescent years. Baldwin and Baldwin (1970) gave children pairs of stories designed to assess judgments of kind behavior. One pair required children to indicate which of two behaviors was kinder: returning a favor for a past favor received or doing a favor irrespective of the generosity of a person's past behavior. The majority of kindergartners judged a concrete exchange of favors to be kinder. However, the proportion of children judging a situation in which a person performed a favor without basing it on prior benefits received as the greater kindness increased steadily over middle

As children's understanding of moral reciprocity becomes more abstract, they are more likely to perform a favor without expecting to receive one in return. (Alan Oddie/PhotoEdit)

childhood and early adolescence, a trend that has been confirmed by other research (Peterson, Hartmann, & Gelfand, 1977).

Applications. The findings summarized above indicate that children's understanding of reciprocity becomes more abstract and idealistic over the elementary school years. However, it is not yet clear what factors underlie this change. Because ideal reciprocity requires advanced perspective-taking skill, cognitive development must play a major role. But certain kinds of experiences may also be necessary. Offering children opportunities to witness other people behaving helpfully and generously without the expectation of favors returned; encouraging children, at least on occasion, to give without receiving; and providing them with rationales that justify the value of ideal reciprocity may facilitate its acquisition. Clearly more work needs to be done on how this important basis for mature moral judgment develops.

Furthermore, it is now known that Piaget's story vignettes underestimated young children's moral understanding. Look again at the stories about John and Henry on page 517. Because they confound character intentions with objective consequences (e.g., bad intentions are always coupled with minor consequences and good intentions with serious consequences, but alternative combinations are not included), the stories yield a biased picture of the extent to which young children can consider people's intentions in making moral judgments. In Chapter 11, we showed that preschoolers are quite sensitive to social cues regarding people's intentions. When Piagetian stories are modified, young children's remarkable ability to consider intentions in judging behavior *is* reflected in their moral reasoning. For example, Grueneich (1982) presented kindergarten and third- and sixth-grade children with stories containing all possible combinations of intentions and consequences. He found a developmental progression from reliance on a single cue (either intentions or consequences) by younger children to increasing integration of both kinds of information in making judgments about the wrongness of an action during the elementary school years. Do these findings remind you of young children's tendency to rely on single as opposed to multidimensional rules in dealing with conservation and other cognitive problems? The ability of preschool and early elementary school children to judge ill-intentioned characters as naughtier than well-intentioned ones is especially apparent when story presentations help them notice and remember each character's intentions — either by holding consequences constant and varying only intentions, giving character intentions last in the story sequence, or making story events very salient by acting them out on film (Chandler, Greenspan, & Barenboim, 1973; Grueneich, 1982; Nelson-Le Gall, 1985). Many researchers now believe that Piaget's younger subjects responded to his interviews immaturely because of biases in the wording of his stories that accentuated the prominence of consequences while minimizing character intentions.

A final criticism of Piaget's theory is that the characteristics of his stages do not correlate very highly with one another, as one would expect if each stage represented a general, unifying organization of moral judgment (Harris, 1970). As Lickona (1976) puts it, "The child's moral thought, as it unfolds in Piagetian interviews, is not all of a piece but more of a patchwork of diverse parts" (p. 240). The various features of heteronomous and autonomous morality are best viewed as separate dimensions of morality, not as manifestations of closely knit stages.

Moral development is now regarded as a more extended process than Piaget believed, for Kohlberg's theory, to which we now turn, identifies three stages beyond Piaget's autonomous morality. Over the past two decades, Piaget's ground-breaking work has been supplanted by Kohlberg's more comprehensive six-stage sequence, but it is clear that Kohlberg's theory is a direct continuation of the research that Piaget began: the search for universal stages of moral development, and the study of how children's conceptions of morality are intimately tied to the course of cognitive growth (Lickona, 1976).

Kohlberg's Extension of Piaget's Theory

Kohlberg based his stage sequence on responses to hypothetical situations quite different from Piaget's stories. Whereas Piaget asked children to judge the naughtiness of a character who had already decided on a moral course of action, Kohlberg gave his subjects hypothetical **moral dilemmas** in which competing courses of action were possible and asked them to indicate what an actor should do and why. Because he had subjects both decide on and justify a course of action, he was able to obtain a clearer idea of the reasoning on which subjects' moral decisions were based.

Methods of Assessment. Before we summarize Kohlberg's theory, let's look at the dilemmas he used to assess moral understanding, his extensive interviewing procedure, as well as another "objective" approach to assessing moral judgment that is faster and more efficient than the clinical interviewing technique.

The Clinical Interview. Like Piaget, Kohlberg regarded the clinical interview as the preferred method for studying children's moral development. Each moral dilemma that serves as the basis for an interview involves a genuine crisis situation that pits one moral value against another. The best-known of these dilemmas, the "Heinz dilemma," asks individuals to choose between the value of upholding the law (not stealing) and the value of human life (saving a dying person). It goes like this.

In Europe a woman was near death from a very special kind of cancer. There was one drug that the doctors thought might save her. It was a form of radium that a druggist in the same town had recently discovered. The drug was expensive to make, but the druggist was charging ten times what the drug cost him to make. He paid $200 for the radium and charged $2,000 for a small dose of the drug. The sick woman's husband, Heinz, went to everyone he knew to borrow the money, but he could only get together about $1,000, which is half of what it cost. He told the druggist that his wife was dying, and asked him to sell it cheaper or let him pay later. But the druggist said, "No, I discovered the drug and I'm going to make money from it." So Heinz got desperate and broke into the man's store to steal the drug for his wife. Should Heinz have done that? Why? (Colby et al., 1983, p. 77)

Kohlberg emphasized that it does not matter which moral value — in the above instance, upholding the law or saving a life — the subject favors in choosing a course of action. In other words, the moral *content* of the response is not important. Instead it is the *structure* of the answer — how the individual reasons about a course of action — that is critical for determining its level of moral maturity. For example, if a person responds, "Heinz shouldn't steal the drug because it would be against the law," Kohlberg would want to know how the subject thinks about the law — in terms of simple fear of punishment or as a system that is worthy of respect in its own right. Similarly, if the subject indicates, "Heinz should steal the drug to save his wife's life," it is necessary to find out why her life is so important — because Heinz feels gratitude toward her for doing things for him, because it is a husband's duty to protect his wife, or because life is among the highest of human values. As we shall see shortly, each of these justifications implies a qualitatively distinct organization of moral thought and a different stage of moral development (Kohlberg, 1969; 1976).

To bring out the structure of the subject's moral reasoning, Kohlberg's interviewing procedure is lengthy and free-ranging. After a dilemma is presented, a series of follow-up questions elicits the individual's views on such issues as obedience to laws and authority figures and understanding of higher moral values like respect for human life. In the case of the Heinz dilemma, the interviewer would ask, "If Heinz does not love his wife, should he still steal the drug for her?" "Is it important for people to do everything they can to save another's life?" "It is against the law for Heinz to steal. Does that make it morally wrong?" and "Why or why not?" (Colby et al., p. 77). After the answers are obtained, they are subjected to an elaborate scoring procedure that assures strict separation of the content of the response from its structure before classifying it at a particular stage of development.

Lawrence Kohlberg's (1927–1987) stage sequence of moral development extends Piaget's theory by providing a more complete description of qualitative changes in moral reasoning from childhood into adulthood. (Harvard University)

An Objective Instrument: The Defining Issues Test. Once the characteristics of Kohlberg's stages were well known, some investigators worked on developing less time-consuming methods for assessing moral maturity. Rest's **Defining Issues Test (DIT)** is the most widely used objective measure. It asks individuals to read a series of dilemmas, among them the familiar Heinz problem, and then rate the importance of each of a series of "moral issue" statements for deciding on a course of action. Each statement captures the crux of moral reasoning associated with a particular stage, and by scoring the ratings, the investigator can identify a subject's stage of reasoning as well as the relative importance that the subject attaches to "principled morality," or Kohlberg's highest two stages. Several DIT issue statements associated with the Heinz dilemma are given in Table 12.1. Which ones seem most important to you in making a decision about what Heinz should do? (Look at the fine print at the bottom of the table to find the stage of reasoning represented in each statement.)

DIT scores correlate moderately well with Kohlberg's clinical interview assess-

Table 12.1. "Heinz Dilemma" Issue Statements from the Defining Issues Test (DIT)

WHICH ISSUES ARE MOST IMPORTANT IN MAKING A DECISION ABOUT WHAT HEINZ SHOULD DO?[a]

1. Whether a community's laws are going to be upheld.

2. Is Heinz willing to risk getting shot as a burglar or going to jail for the chance that stealing the drug might help?

3. Isn't it only natural for a loving husband to care so much for his wife that he'd steal?

4. What values are going to be the basis for governing how people act toward each other?

5. Whether the law in this case is getting in the way of the most basic claim of any member of society.

[a] 1. Stage 4. 2. Stage 2. 3. Stage 3. 4. Stage 6. 5. Stage 5.

Source: J. R. Rest, 1979b, *Revised Manual for the Defining Issues Test.* Minneapolis: Moral Research Projects. (Reprinted by permission.)

ments (Rest, 1979a). However, subjects generally appear more advanced in moral development on the DIT. This finding is not surprising, in view of the fact that Kohlberg's method asks subjects to *produce* a rationale for a course of action, whereas the DIT only requires that they *recognize* and indicate their preferences for stage-linked reasoning. Recall from Chapter 7 that recognition is a far less demanding cognitive process than active production of a response.

Nevertheless, both DIT and clinical interviewing scores produce similar longitudinal developmental trends, correlate similarly with other cognitive measures, and show similar changes in response to interventions designed to facilitate moral reasoning (Rest, 1983). Because of its efficiency of administration and impressive reliability and validity, the DIT has been used more often than any other single measure in moral reasoning research, including Kohlberg's method. Since its development in the early 1970s, over 500 studies employing the DIT have been conducted (Rest, 1986).

Kohlberg's Stages of Moral Understanding. Kohlberg intended his stage sequence to describe very closely and accurately the qualitative changes in moral thinking that take place from childhood into adulthood. Consequently, he made strong statements about the properties of his six stages. First, the stages were assumed to form an *invariant* sequence, or fixed series of steps that people traverse sequentially, without skipping any stages. Second, each new stage was regarded as a more *equilibrated* way of making and justifying moral judgments. In other words, each successive step integrates and builds upon the reasoning of the previous stage, resulting in a more broadly applicable and logically consistent notion of justice than its predecessor. Finally, each stage was believed to form a tightly *organized,* structural whole — that is, a qualitatively distinct pattern of moral reasoning that a person applies across a wide range of moral situations. Note that these are strict stage characteristics in the Piagetian sense of the word.[5]

Furthermore, Kohlberg regarded change in moral reasoning as motivated by the same basic factors that Piaget thought were important for cognitive growth: (1) *cognitive disequilibrium,* or actively noticing inadequacies in one's current moral reasoning and revising it accordingly; and (2) *advances in perspective-taking.* As you read the descriptions of Kohlberg's stages below, look for qualitative changes in the nature of thought and in perspective-taking that each of the stages assumes.

Kohlberg organized his six stages into three general levels of moral progress. To illustrate Kohlberg's belief that the structure of moral reasoning changes indepen-

[5] You may wish to review the various concepts that Kohlberg borrowed from Piaget to formulate the characteristics of his moral stages. They can be found on pages 224–225 of Chapter 6.

dently of its content, we present two examples of typical thinking at each stage: one a "pro-stealing" and the other an "anti-stealing" response to the Heinz dilemma. Kohlberg's developmental progression is as follows:

I. **The preconventional level.** At this level, morality is still externally governed. Preconventional children justify actions as right or wrong on the basis of whether they lead to pleasurable or punitive consequences. Behaviors that result in punishment are regarded as bad, and those that result in rewards or concrete exchanges of favors are thought of as good.

Kohlberg's preconventional level is much like Piaget's heteronomous morality of adult constraint. However, unlike Piaget, Kohlberg did not regard children as motivated to conform to adult dictates out of awe and reverence for their authority. Instead, Kohlberg agreed with Damon's (1977) findings on the young child's conception of authority figures, which we discussed in Chapter 11. Preconventional children conform because of the physical power of those who state the rules. They are very much aware that adults have the size and strength to enforce their dictates.

The preconventional level is subdivided into the following two stages:

Stage 1: The punishment and obedience orientation. Children of this stage find it difficult to consider two points of view in a moral dilemma. Unaware that people's interests and perspectives may differ, they ignore the motives and intentions of others in judging the goodness or badness of an action. Instead, they unquestioningly accept an authority's perspective as their own and focus on avoidance of punishment and deference to superior powers as reasons for behaving morally. The following responses to the Heinz dilemma reflect the Stage 1 child's orientation toward obedience and fear of punishment:

> *Pro-stealing:* "If you let your wife die, you will get in trouble. You'll be blamed for not spending the money to help her and there'll be an investigation of you and the druggist for your wife's death." (Kohlberg, 1969, p. 381).

> *Anti-stealing:* "You shouldn't steal the drug because you'll be caught and sent to jail if you do. If you do get away, your conscience would bother you thinking how the police would catch up with you any minute." (Kohlberg, 1969, p. 381).

Stage 2: The naive hedonistic orientation. Awareness that people can have different points of view in a moral dilemma appears at this stage, but this understanding is initially very concrete. Right action is regarded as what satisfies one's own needs in a very physical, pragmatic way, and others are also viewed as acting out of self-interest. If some sacrifice for another person is to be made, Stage 2 individuals base it on a need for the services of that person, a desire for something the other person has, or the expectation that the other person will do the same for them sometime in the future. Stage 2 individuals grasp the idea of concrete reciprocity, for their idea of fairness is equal exchange of favors—"you do this for me and I'll do that for you." Their hedonistic, self-gratifying morality is reflected in the following two interview responses:

> *Pro-stealing:* "The druggist can do what he wants and Heinz can do what he wants to do. It's up to each individual to do what he wants with what he has. But if Heinz decides to risk jail to save his wife, it's his life he's risking; he can do what he wants with it. And the same goes for the druggist; it's up to him to decide what he wants to do." (Rest, 1979a, p. 26)[6]

> *Anti-stealing:* "[Heinz] is running more risk than it's worth unless he's so crazy about her he can't live without her. Neither of them will enjoy life if she's an invalid." (Rest, 1979a, p. 27)

---

[6] All quotations from Rest, 1979a, reprinted by permission of University of Minnesota Press.

II. **The conventional level.** At this level, the individual continues to regard conformity to social norms as the basis for morality, but upholding them is no longer motivated by the immediate consequences of one's actions. Instead, active maintenance of the social order is regarded as important in its own right. The conventional individual believes strongly in supporting and preserving the laws and rules of the current social system.

Stage 3: The "good boy—good girl" orientation, or the morality of interpersonal concordance. Belief in the importance of adhering to social prescriptions for their own sake makes its first appearance in relationships with people one knows well. The Stage 3 individual is oriented toward maintaining the continued affection and approval of relatives and friends by being a "good person"—trustworthy, loyal, respectful, helpful, and nice. Newly acquired capacities for mutual perspective-taking and the understanding of ideal reciprocity support this revised conception of morality. The Stage 3 individual can anticipate what another person is thinking and feeling and knows that the other person can simultaneously do the same, as the following responses to the Heinz dilemma indicate:

Pro-stealing: "No one will think you're bad if you steal the drug, but your family will think you're an inhuman husband if you don't. If you let your wife die, you'll never be able to look anyone in the face again." (Kohlberg, 1969, p. 381)

Anti-stealing: "It isn't just the druggist who will think you're a criminal, everyone else will too. After you steal it, you'll feel bad thinking how you've brought dishonor on your family and yourself; you won't be able to face anyone again." (Kohlberg, 1969, p. 381)

Stage 4: The social-order-maintaining orientation. At this stage the individual is able to step outside a two-person, mutual relationship and take into account a third perspective of societal laws in deciding on a course of action. As a result, morality is no longer restricted to those with whom one has personal ties. Instead, rules must be uniformly applied and enforced in an evenhanded fashion for everyone, and each member of society has a personal duty to uphold them. When asked, the Stage 4 individual responds that laws cannot be disobeyed under any circumstances, because they are indispensable for assuring societal order and preventing the social system from breaking down. The following are typical Stage 4 answers to the Heinz dilemma:

Pro-stealing: "He should steal it. Heinz has a duty to protect his wife's life; it's a vow he took in marriage. But it's wrong to steal, so he would have to take the drug with the idea of paying the druggist for it and accepting the penalty for having stolen later on."

Anti-stealing: "It's a natural thing for Heinz to want to save his wife, but it's still always wrong to steal. You have to follow the rules regardless of how you feel or regardless of the special circumstances. Even if his wife is dying, it's still his duty as a citizen to obey the law. No one else is allowed to steal, why should he be? If everyone starts breaking the law in a jam, there'd be no civilization, just crime and violence." (Rest, 1979a, p. 30)

III. **The Postconventional or Principled Level.** Postconventional individuals move beyond unquestioning adherence to the moral dictates of their own society. They make an effort to define morality in terms of abstract principles and values that are valid and applicable in all situations and all societies.

Stage 5: The social contract, legalistic orientation. At Stage 5, individuals become aware that any single rule system is only one of many possible rule systems, and they are able to envision alternatives to their own social order. Consequently, they no longer regard rules as established givens, but as flexible instruments for furthering human values. At this stage, there is an emphasis on fair, rational procedures for interpreting and changing the law when there is an ethically valid reason to do so.

When laws are consistent with individual rights and with the interests of the majority, one's obligation to abide by them stems from a *social contract orientation* — free and willing participation in the system because it brings about more good for the self and others than if no such arrangement existed. A rational consideration of rules and laws and adherence to the social contract as the reason for observing them appears in the following two statements:

> *Pro-stealing:* "Although there is a law against stealing, the law wasn't meant to act in such a way as to violate a person's right to life. Taking the drug does violate the law, but Heinz is justified in stealing in this instance. If Heinz is prosecuted for stealing, the law needs to be reinterpreted to take into account situations in which it goes against people's natural right to keep on living."

> *Anti-stealing;* "Heinz has to respect the general will of society as it is set down in the law. The law represents the basis of how people have agreed to live with each other. By continuing to live in that society, he has agreed to respect and maintain its laws. The law states that stealing is a violation." (Rest, 1973, p. 96)

Stage 6: The universal ethical principle orientation. At this highest stage, right action is defined by self-chosen ethical principles that are comprehensive, rational, and universally applicable. These principles transcend legal formulations; there is recognition at Stage 6 that some moral obligations and values are valid for all humanity, regardless of law and social agreement. Typical principles referred to at Stage 6 are equal consideration of the claims of all human beings and respect for the worth and dignity of each person as an individual. These values are abstract and ethical, not concrete moral rules like the Ten Commandments, and they are justified by an appeal to one's inner, private conscience. According to Kohlberg, a very abstract form of perspective-taking underlies moral reasoning at this stage. Stage 6 individuals make moral decisions by simultaneously considering the perspectives of all parties in a moral dilemma and then choosing an action that they could endorse if they did not know ahead of time which role (e.g., Heinz, his wife, or the druggist) they would play. The following responses reflect Stage 6 moral reasoning:

> *Pro-stealing:* "If Heinz does not do everything he can to save his wife, then he is putting some value higher than the value of life. It doesn't make sense to put respect for property above respect for life itself. Men could live together without private property at all. Respect for human life and personality is absolute and accordingly men have a mutual duty to save one another from dying." (Rest, 1979a, p. 37)

> *Anti-stealing:* "If you stole the drug, you wouldn't be blamed by other people but you'd condemn yourself because you wouldn't have lived up to your own conscience and standards of honesty." (Kohlberg, 1969, p. 382)

Research Aimed at Verifying Kohlberg's Stage Theory

Since its original construction, a large body of research has been directed at verifying Kohlberg's stage-wise progression. If Kohlberg's theory is correct, movement through his stages should be related to age, cognitive growth, and improvements in perspective-taking capacity. In addition, developmental changes in moral reasoning should be consistent with strict Piagetian stage characteristics. We consider the evidence on these issues in the following sections.

Age-related Changes and an Invariant Developmental Sequence. A wealth of evidence reveals that maturity of moral reasoning is strongly related to age. Thoma (as reported by Rest, 1986) combined data from many cross-sectional studies, arriving at a sample size of approximately 6,000 subjects, and found that age correlated with moral maturity at .72. Similarly powerful relationships have been identified in other large-scale cross-sectional investigations (Gibbs & Widaman, 1982; Rest, Davison, & Robbins, 1978).

Longitudinal studies provide the most convincing evidence for Kohlberg's developmental sequence. The most extensive of these is a 20-year continuation of Kohlberg's initial study of adolescent boys in which 58 of the 84 original subjects were retested at regular 3- to 4-year intervals. Like cross-sectional findings, the correlation between age and moral maturity was strong, at .78. In addition, the results supported Kohlberg's assumption that the stages form an invariant developmental sequence. With few exceptions, subjects proceeded through the stages in the prescribed order, without skipping a stage or regressing to an earlier level once a stage had been attained (Colby et al., 1983). Results of other longitudinal studies also confirm the invariance of the stages (Rest, 1986; Nisan & Kohlberg, 1982; Snarey, Reimer, & Kohlberg, 1985).

Age trends in moral reasoning provide information about when, on the average, individuals move from one moral stage to another and how long it takes them to achieve each major transformation in moral thought. Figure 12.1 shows the extent to which subjects between 10 and 36 years of age used each stage of moral reasoning in the 20-year longitudinal study conducted by Kohlberg and his collaborators. The age trends reveal that the development of moral reasoning is extremely gradual. Stages 1 and 2 decrease from age 10 on, Stage 3 increases until about 16 to 18 and then decreases, and Stage 4 rises steadily from early adolescence into adulthood when it becomes the typical response; very few subjects move beyond it to Stage 5 (Colby et al., 1985). Other longitudinal and cross-sectional findings confirm this very gradual development of moral thought (Gibbs & Widaman, 1982; Nisan & Kohlberg, 1982; Snarey, Reimer, & Kohlberg, 1985). In fact, principled morality is such a rarity in most samples studied that there is no clear evidence to date that Kohlberg's Stage 6 actually follows Stage 5. The distinctiveness of the highest stage of moral development is still a matter of speculation.

Do Kohlberg's Stages Form Tightly Knit, Structural Wholes? If each of Kohlberg's moral stages forms an organized, structural whole, then individuals ought to apply the same level of moral reasoning consistently across many tasks and situations. Research shows that when Kohlberg's interviewing procedure is used, most subjects do display fairly uniform reasoning from one moral dilemma to another

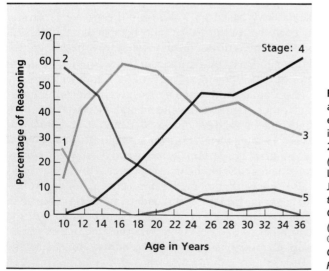

Figure 12.1. Mean percentage of moral reasoning at each stage for each age level in the Colby et al. (1983) 20-year longitudinal study. *(From A. Colby et al., 1983,* A Longitudinal Study of Moral Judgment, *Monographs of the Society for Research in Child Development, 48, (1–2, Serial No. 200), 46.* ©*The Society for Research in Child Development, Inc. Reprinted by permission.)*

(Colby et al., 1983; Snarey, Reimer, & Kohlberg, 1985). However, Kohlberg's scoring procedure tends to minimize variability in subjects' responses. When alternative scoring approaches are used, people show greater diversity in the types of reasoning they produce (Rest, 1983).

Furthermore, when the procedures used to elicit moral thinking are systematically varied, moral reasoning changes as well. We have already mentioned that using an objective assessment procedure like the DIT will produce more advanced moral judgments than Kohlberg's interviewing procedure. Changing the story elements in the dilemmas has a profound effect as well. In one study, Sobesky (1983) gave high school and college students the Heinz dilemma, presenting the original version in addition to several new ones. In one version, the consequences Heinz would experience for stealing were high; the story indicated that he would ''be caught for sure and sent to prison.'' In another they were low; Heinz could ''take the drug and the druggist [would] never miss it'' (p. 578). When consequences were severe, students were less certain that stealing the drug would be appropriate, and they gave fewer principled answers and more preconventional responses. Sobesky suggests that highlighting the possibility of punishment for Heinz increased subjects' concern with self-interest, a major preconventional basis of morality. Other investigations have found that when subjects are given moral dilemmas set in practical, familiar contexts, their reasoning changes, sometimes in an upward and sometimes in a downward developmental direction (Gilligan & Belenky, 1980; Leming, 1978).

Earlier in this chapter we indicated that situational factors reduce the consistency of children's moral behavior, and the findings summarized above indicate that they produce variability in moral judgments as well. Because varying testing materials and procedures affects maturity of moral reasoning, Kohlberg's stages do not look like the tightly knit, structural wholes he originally envisioned. Subjects do not seem to be completely ''in'' one stage or another. Instead, they manifest a number of different moral structures that depend on the type of task. Rest (1979a) suggests that Kohlberg's sequence be viewed in terms of a much looser, more flexible stage conception, in much the same way that Flavell regards Piaget's stages of cognitive development, as we indicated in Chapter 6. While retaining the idea of qualitatively distinct organizations of moral thought, Rest believes that developmental changes do not proceed one step at a time, but instead consist of shifting distributions of moral responses in which less mature reasoning gradually declines as more mature thinking becomes increasingly prominent. From this perspective, developmental periods vary in the *range of possible types of reasoning* that are evident, not in a single stage response.

Cognitive Prerequisites for Moral Reasoning. Like Piagetian moral judgment scores, assessments of moral maturity based on Kohlberg's theory are positively correlated with IQ, Piagetian cognitive performance, and perspective-taking skill (Rest, 1979a). However, these correlations do not tell us in what way these cognitive variables are related to moral thought. Do cognitive and moral development undergo separate but fairly similar lines of development, or is moral development actually dependent on the acquisition of certain cognitive and perspective-taking structures?

Kohlberg (1969; 1976) and other cognitive-developmental theorists (Damon, 1977; Selman, 1977) have argued that moral development depends on cognitive and perspective-taking skills in a very specific way. As shown in Table 12.2, each moral stage is assumed to require the attainment of certain cognitive and perspective-taking stages, based on Piaget's and Selman's developmental sequences. However, cognitive-developmental theorists also believe that moral development cannot be entirely reduced to these other facets of cognitive growth. Moral understanding is assumed to involve some additional cognitive reorganizations that are entirely unique to the moral domain. Consequently, Kohlberg and others have hypothesized that cognitive and perspective-taking stages are *necessary but not sufficient conditions* for each of the moral stages.

Recall from Chapter 11 that the necessary but not sufficient condition applies to the relationship between Piaget's cognitive and Selman's perspective-taking stages, for Piagetian competencies are generally achieved before their respective perspective-taking counterparts. If Kohlberg is correct that the necessary but not sufficient assumption also applies to moral development, then moral maturity should either keep pace with or lag behind the attainment of corresponding cognitive and perspective-taking stages, but never be ahead of them. To what extent does research bear out this prediction?

Although no single study has examined the entire continuum of stage relationships shown in Table 12.2, several have focused on portions of it, and their findings are remarkably consistent with Kohlberg's predictions. Krebs and Gillmore (1982) studied the cognitive prerequisites for Kohlberg's first two stages and found a pattern of stage relationships consistent with the necessary but not sufficient hypothesis. However, their results suggest that Kohlberg overestimated the cognitive prerequisites of preconventional morality shown in Table 12.2. Only preoperational thinking and Level 0 perspective-taking were required for moral Stage 1, and only Level 1 perspective-taking (in addition to concrete operations) was required for moral Stage 2.

Other studies provide evidence that beginning formal operations and mutual perspective-taking skill (Selman's Level 3) are necessary but not sufficient conditions for moral Stage 3. In a study of 64 fourth through seventh graders, Walker (1980) found that all children who demonstrated Stage 3 moral reasoning scored at either a higher or the equivalent stage of cognitive development and perspective-taking skill, and only one subject who lacked the necessary cognitive prerequisites showed evidence of Stage 3 morality. Furthermore, Walker as well as other investigators report that interventions designed to stimulate moral reasoning are more effective when subjects are at advanced stages of cognitive development than when they are not. Also, moral development cannot be stimulated beyond the stage for which an individual possesses the appropriate cognitive prerequisites (Arbuthnot et al., 1983; Walker & Richards, 1979).

Table 12.2. Hypothesized Parallel Stages in Cognitive, Perspective-taking, and Moral Development

PIAGET'S COGNITIVE STAGE	SELMAN'S PERSPECTIVE-TAKING STAGE	KOHLBERG'S MORAL STAGE
Preoperational	0 Undifferentiated and egocentric perspective-taking	0 Premoral
Transitional preoperational and concrete operational	1 Differentiated and subjective perspective-taking	1 Punishment and obedience orientation
Concrete operational	2 Self-reflective or reciprocal perspective-taking	2 Naive hedonistic orientation
Early formal operational	3 Third party or mutual perspective-taking	3 "Good boy–good girl" orientation
Consolidated formal operational	4 In-depth and societal perspective-taking	4 Social-order-maintaining perspective
		5 Social contract, legalistic orientation
		6 Universal ethical principle orientation

Source: Selman, 1976.

The research summarized above indicates that both nonsocial-cognitive and perspective-taking achievements are crucial building blocks for moral reasoning, but they are not enough by themselves. What other cognitive factors besides the achievement of Piaget's and Selman's stages might promote moral maturity? Earlier we mentioned Kohlberg's belief that experiences that induce cognitive disequilibrium are vital for moral change. That is, exposing people to conflicting information just ahead of their present moral level challenges them to revise their reasoning in the direction of more advanced moral thinking. A number of theorists believe that cognitive conflict is the most fundamental ingredient of change in moral understanding (Berkowitz, 1985; Haan, Aerts, & Cooper, 1985; Kohlberg, 1984; Turiel, 1977), and it may be the critical factor that bridges the gap between children's cognitive and perspective-taking attainments and their moral stage. As we shall see in the discussion that follows, the development of moral structures is related to many environmental factors, including peer interaction, child-rearing practices, formal education, and cultural variations. When environmental influences facilitate moral reasoning, it is conceivable that one important means by which they do so is through inducing cognitive disequilibrium — providing children and adolescents with just those cognitive challenges deemed essential for moral growth.

Antecedents of Change in Moral Reasoning

Experiences that foster the development of moral reasoning have been investigated through a wealth of correlational studies. The weakness of this research literature is one we have discussed a great many times before: correlational investigations cannot guarantee that an important experiential cause of moral reasoning has been isolated. Fortunately, in a few instances correlational studies have been supplemented with experiments that manipulate the environmental variable in question, providing more convincing evidence of the role of certain experiential factors.

Membership in social organizations is positively related to children's maturity of moral reasoning. (Michal Heron)

Peer Interaction. Recall that Piaget believed that interaction with peers is a major means of facilitating moral understanding. Such peer experiences, he claimed, encourage children to take the perspective of others, and they may also induce cognitive disequilibrium by exposing children to reasoning of agemates more advanced than themselves.

Results of studies relating peer experiences to progress through Kohlberg's moral stages fit very well with Piaget's idea. Maturity of moral reasoning is correlated with peer popularity, participation in social organizations, and service in leadership roles (Enright & Sutterfield, 1980; Harris, Mussen, & Rutherford, 1976; Keasey, 1971). Research conducted in Africa underlines the importance of exposure to differing peer value systems for stimulating moral thought. Kenyan and Nigerian students attending culturally heterogeneous high schools and colleges were advanced in moral judgment in comparison to those enrolled in homogeneous settings (Edwards, 1978; Maqsud, 1977). Culturally diverse educational environments may confront students with opposing viewpoints that are especially challenging. In fact, the African college students attributed the greatest change in their personal values to encountering ethnic and racial diversity at school (Edwards, 1981).

Peer experiences have provided the framework for a number of interventions aimed at improving moral understanding. A major feature of most of them is peer discussion and role-playing of moral problems. A study by Blatt and Kohlberg (1975) is one of the most impressive in terms of its findings. After participating in teacher-led classroom discussions of moral dilemmas for one semester, many sixth and tenth graders moved partially or totally to the next stage, a change that was not found in subjects who had no opportunity for moral discussion. The gains were maintained in follow-up testing a year later. Other peer discussion interventions have also produced upward changes in moral reasoning, although in most instances the stage gains are slight (Arbuthnot, 1975; Berkowitz, Gibbs, & Broughton, 1980; Colby et al., 1977; Crockenberg & Nicolayev, 1979).

A major shortcoming of the studies noted above is that we cannot tell exactly what aspects of peer discussion serve as catalysts for moral change. Yet it is precisely this kind of information that psychologists and educators need in order to design more effective moral education programs. Recently, researchers have begun to tackle this question by conducting fine-grained analyses of ongoing peer dialogues, comparing the features of those that produce greater stage change with those that lead to little or no change. Berkowitz and Gibbs (1983) found that college students who gained in moral maturity as the result of a discussion experience spent a great deal of time penetrating each other's reasoning by confronting, critiquing, and attempting to clarify one another's statements. Nongainers spent less discussion time this way. Instead, they made independent assertions, gave personal anecdotes, or expressed confusion about the task. In another study, Haan, Aerts, and Cooper (1985) had small friendship groups of university students participate in weekly interaction sessions. Some groups discussed hypothetical moral dilemmas, while others played games that were designed to stir up actual moral problems among friends (e.g., a game called "Ghetto" in which citizens confront a corrupt staff person who represents "the system"). In the games, students engaged in more emotionally intense expressions of disagreement, while during discussions, the interchanges tended to be emotionally controlled, intellectual responses to conflict. Games facilitated the development of moral reasoning far more effectively than discussions. Taken together, the findings of these investigations indicate that interactions in which peers merely express reasoning in disagreement with one another are less effective in stimulating moral development than cognitively penetrating, emotionally involved exchanges in which participants experience one another's moral indignation.

Child-rearing Practices. Family influences favorable to the development of moral understanding are those that reflect rational, democratic processes. Adolescent youngsters who are at the conventional as opposed to preconventional level of moral reasoning have parents who are more advanced in moral judgment themselves and who encourage their youngsters to contribute actively to family discussions (Holstein, 1972; Parikh, 1980). Such parents also rely on disciplinary methods that facilitate modeling and internalization of parental beliefs and practices, including low levels of power assertion and high levels of warmth, involvement, and inductive control techniques (Saltzstein, 1976). Edwards (1981) sums up the kind of parent who facilitates children's moral understanding as one who is verbal, rational, and affectionate and who promotes a cooperative style of family life. However, as noted earlier, children themselves make active contributions to parental practices. When viewed in the family context, upward movement through the moral stages, like other aspects of morality, is undoubtedly the result of a dynamic interchange between parent and child.

Formal Education. Since children and adolescents at higher levels of education are inevitably older, we cannot separate the impact of schooling on moral judgment from other age-related variables in youthful samples. However, studies of adults provide an opportunity to disentangle the effects of age and education. Among adult samples, older subjects need not have completed more formal education than younger subjects. The results of many such investigations indicate that formal schooling is one of the most powerful predictors of moral change. For example, Dortzbach (1975) examined the relationship of age and education to moral judgment scores on the DIT among individuals age 25 to 74. As shown in Figure 12.2, mature reasoning increased dramatically with education, whereas it declined slightly when the subjects were grouped by age. Even the decline among older adults could be accounted for by education, for most subjects in the 65- to 74-year-old age group had attained only a grade-school education, while the younger adults in the sample tended to be college educated.

Additional research shows that adults do not show much advance in moral reasoning beyond that accounted for by their level of education. Rest and Thoma (1985) conducted a six-year longitudinal study of subjects who did not differ from each other in moral reasoning at the time they graduated from high school. Those who went to college continued to show gains in moral judgment maturity, whereas those who did not leveled off in development. In general, moral reasoning seems to advance regularly as long as a person remains in school, but when formal education is discontinued, it tends to stabilize (Rest, 1979a).

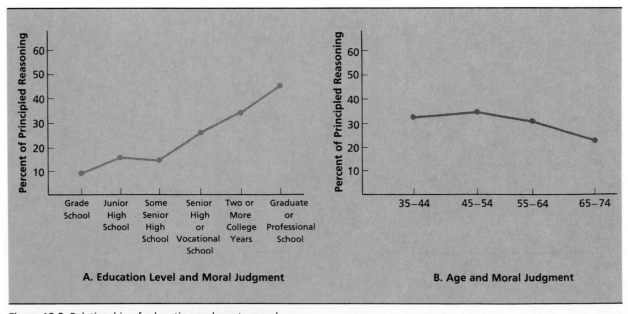

Figure 12.2. Relationship of education and age to moral judgment in the Dortzbach (1975) study. *(Adapted from J. R. Dortzbach, 1975.)*

Why is formal education such an important contributor to the development of moral understanding? Its impact could be the result of many factors, including extracurricular participation, academic learning, and other elements of the school milieu. As yet, the precise mechanisms of school influence have not been identified, and further research is needed to clarify them.

Culture. Cross-cultural research on Kohlberg's stages indicates that the rate and end point of moral development vary substantially from one society to another. A great many studies indicate that individuals in technologically advanced societies move through the stages more rapidly and advance to higher levels than do individuals in less industrialized and more rural environments. Stages 4 and above are not reached by members of isolated peasant and tribal communities, whereas they are achieved by high school- and college-educated adolescents and adults in a variety of Western and non-Western samples (Edwards, 1981).

Why these cultural differences exist remains a matter of some speculation and debate. It is possible that Kohlberg's dilemmas are inappropriate for eliciting moral reasoning in some cultures and, in these instances, underestimate moral understanding. A second explanation addresses the role of societal institutions in stimulating moral development. Kohlberg (1969) argued that greater societal complexity in terms of governmental institutions and legal systems is necessary for a culture to foster the highest stages. In traditional peasant and tribal communities, participation in village life, with its emphasis on interpersonal expectations as the primary basis for cooperation, fosters reasoning as high as Stage 3. More advanced reasoning is not needed to carry out the activities of the social group. The existence of formalized systems of government and law as well as opportunities to participate in them are believed to be necessary for Stage 4 and above. In support of this interpretation, Snarey, Reimer, and Kohlberg (1985) found that the moral stage scores of Israeli kibbutz-reared adolescents and young adults, who receive participatory training in the cooperative institutions of their society from an early age, were unusually high. When compared to Americans, kibbutz-reared young people were advanced at all ages between 13 and 26, and a greater proportion of them eventually reached Stage 5. In fact, by third grade, children growing up on a kibbutz already verbalize more concerns about societal laws and norms when discussing moral conflicts than do Israeli city-reared or American children (Fuchs et al., 1986).

The fact that reasoning at the highest three stages is absent in traditional village societies is a serious limitation in further efforts to verify Kohlberg's stage sequence. Since the higher stages are not manifested among these peoples at all, we cannot tell if advanced reasoning would emerge if they were exposed to more complex societal conditions or not. Questions also remain about whether the highest stages represent a culturally specific, rather than universal, form of moral reasoning that only emerges in Western European societies that emphasize individual rights, democracy, and appeal to an inner, private conscience. One way to find out would be to study the development of moral reasoning in societies that are just as complex as Western industrialized nations, but guided by very different political and economic ideologies, such as China or the Soviet Union (Edwards, 1981).

Taken together, the findings on antecedents of moral reasoning suggest a powerful role for environmental contexts in the development of moral understanding. Higher stages are not realized unless appropriate environmental supports exist on multiple levels, including family, peers, schooling, and institutions of the wider society.

Are There Sex Differences in Moral Reasoning?

One of the most controversial questions about Kohlberg's theory concerns whether it fails to tap important aspects of moral thought that are uniquely feminine. Carol Gilligan (1977; 1982) is the most prominent figure among those who have argued that

Kohlberg's theory is sex-biased. Gilligan noticed that the findings of a handful of early studies indicated that the moral reasoning of females lagged behind that of males. Girls appeared to advance to Stage 3 and then remain there, while boys moved beyond, reaching Stages 4 and 5 by late adolescence and adulthood (e.g., Haan et al., 1968; Holstein, 1976). If these findings are accurate, they support a widely held stereotype that men develop an abstract, rational commitment to moral ideals, whereas women embed their morality in a less mature, concrete concern for interpersonal approval and maintenance of harmonious relationships.

Gilligan accepts the idea that female morality is embedded in human relationships, but she believes that a feminine commitment to an "ethic of care" is not a mark of moral inferiority. Instead, she argues that Kohlberg's stages are limited to a description of how individuals arrive at *abstract justice reasoning* and do not adequately incorporate other valid bases of morality, such as a *concern for others*. Gilligan has proposed an alternative sequence of development in which a "morality of care" moves from an egoistic, self-centered emphasis to a concrete commitment to people with whom one has close affectional ties (a Stage-3-like conception), and finally to an abstract understanding of care as a universal obligation (a principle of postconventional judgment).

As yet there is little empirical support for Gilligan's assumption that a distinct "morality of care" exists. Her own explorations of children's and adult's responses to interview questions designed to elicit caring as well as justice reasoning were informal and anecdotal, and the generalizations drawn from them remain uncertain. Furthermore, systematic efforts to test Gilligan's ideas raise doubts about their validity. Walker and de Vries (1985) examined the results of 80 studies that, taken together, included responses from over 10,000 subjects to Kohlberg's interviews. In the vast majority of these investigations, no sex differences were found. In another comprehensive review, this time of 56 samples involving a total of 6,000 subjects who responded to the DIT, females scored *higher* than males at every age and level of education examined, although the size of the discrepancy was very small (Thoma, 1986). In both of these summary analyses, the investigators concluded that there was little evidence to support Gilligan's claim that females score lower than males on justice-oriented measures of moral development.

However, it is still possible that important sex differences in moral understanding would emerge if researchers focused on subjects' reasoning about issues of interpersonal commitment and care. Responding to Gilligan's suggestion that subjects' responses to everyday moral problems might better evoke this kind of reasoning than Kohlberg's moral dilemmas, Walker, de Vries, and Trevethan (1987) asked first-, fourth-, seventh-, and tenth-grade youngsters as well as adults to recall a personal moral conflict that they had actually experienced. In addition, the subjects responded to standard hypothetical dilemmas. In both problem situations, the researchers looked at how each subject oriented to the moral problem — that is, whether they defined it as a matter of personal relationship concerns or impersonal rights and fairness concerns. Contrary to Gilligan's claim that females orient toward interpersonal concerns more often than males, for the majority of subjects, both caring and justice orientations emerged in everyday as well as hypothetical dilemma responses, and this was especially true for individuals who scored at the highest stages of Kohlberg's scheme. Furthermore, when females did raise interpersonal issues, they were not down-scored by Kohlberg's assessment system. No sex differences were found in stage of moral reasoning with respect to either personally generated or hypothetical moral problems.

These findings suggest that although Kohlberg emphasized fairness and justice as opposed to interpersonal commitment and care as the highest of moral ideals, his theory and methods may, in actuality, encompass both sets of values. For example, the Stage 6 person's appeal to universal moral principles, such as the dignity and worth of each individual, may combine abstract notions of justice with a deep, abiding concern for other human beings. Although current evidence indicates that justice and caring are not sex-specific moralities, Gilligan's work has had the effect of broadening cognitive-developmental conceptions of the highly moral person. As Brabeck (1983) indicates,

> [Gilligan's] major contribution rests in a redefinition of what constitutes an adequate description of the moral ideal. When Gilligan's and Kohlberg's theories are taken together, the moral person is seen as one whose moral choices reflect reasoned and deliberate judgments that ensure justice be accorded each person while maintaining a passionate concern for the well-being and care of each individual. Justice and care are then joined . . . and the need for autonomy and for interconnection are united in an enlarged and more adequate conception of morality. (p. 289)

Moral Reasoning and Behavior

In line with the cognitive-developmental assumption that moral reasoning is an important aspect of moral motivation, many studies indicate that progress through the moral stages does predict moral behavior. Blasi (1980) reviewed 75 investigations relating moral reasoning to behavior; 76 percent of them found clear relationships. The wide variety of morally relevant responses measured in these studies indicates that the link between moral thought and action is broad and pervasive. Maturity of moral reasoning is related to altruistic behavior, including helping, sharing, and defending victims of injustice (e.g., Harris, Mussen & Rutherford, 1976; Staub, 1974). It also predicts honesty, as measured by cheating behavior at school and resistance to temptation in laboratory tasks that require children to not touch forbidden toys or to return money that does not belong to them (e.g., Harris, Mussen, & Rutherford, 1976; Nelson, Grinder, & Biaggio, 1969).

Moral understanding is also related to student protest behavior in colleges and universities. In a well-known study, Haan, Smith, and Block (1968) interviewed a large sample of university students during a period of frequent campus demonstrations over free speech and other human rights issues in the 1960s. In general, postconventional students were more involved in political-social matters and were more likely to protest than the conventionally moral. Some preconventional students were also politically active. However, their reasons for participation reflected reactive and rebellious motivations. In contrast, postconventional students appeared to be acting on higher moral principles, for they described a deep personal commitment to civil liberties and the rights and roles of students as citizens in a university community. Other studies also report that advanced moral reasoning is related to the value stances people take on controversial public issues. For example, Kohlberg's principled morality is associated with a firm belief in the right of free speech, due process, and opposition to capital punishment (Rest, 1986; de Vries & Walker, 1986). Commitment to such values may be an important intermediate link between postconventional moral structures and political behavior.

Despite a clear connection between moral reasoning and a broad range of behaviors, it is important to note that the strength of these associations is, in all instances, only moderate. Kohlberg acknowledged that the relationship between moral reasoning and behavior would be imperfect. He showed in the Heinz dilemma, for example, that two people may reason at the same stage, but one person will choose to steal the drug and the other will not. As we indicated earlier, the relationship of moral understanding to behavior is mediated by a great many factors, including emotional reactions such as empathy and guilt and social background and experiences that affect moral choices and decision making. As yet little is known about how these variables interact with moral reasoning to affect behavioral outcomes. Once investigators learn how all aspects of moral motivation work together as parts of a complex, functioning whole, prediction of moral behavior will undoubtedly improve (Blasi, 1983).

In 1988, students protested the appointment of a nondeaf president at Gallaudet University, a campus with an all-deaf student body. Participants in campus demonstrations are often morally mature individuals with deep commitments to civil liberties. (Paul Conklin/ Monkmeyer Press Photo Service)

Overall Evaluation of Kohlberg's Theory

Our review of Kohlberg's work and the research stimulated by it indicates that considerable evidence exists to support his theory. To briefly summarize, although moral reasoning seems to fit a looser, more flexible stage conception than Kohlberg originally envisioned, the stages conform to an orderly, invariant developmental sequence. From late childhood into adulthood, morality gradually evolves from concrete, externally governed reasoning toward increasingly abstract, comprehensive, and ethically adequate justifications for moral choices and actions. Each moral stage builds upon cognitive and perspective-taking capacities, and a broad range of experiences also affects development, including moral discussions with peers and family members, formal education, and citizenship activities in the wider political and economic arena of society. Although recent research indicates that Kohlberg's theory is not sex-biased, as yet there is not enough cross-cultural evidence to be certain that the stage sequence is universally applicable to all people, regardless of nationality. In addition, the scarcity of Stage 6 reasoning has prevented investigators from determining whether it is, in fact, the culminating moral stage.

Other unresolved questions about Kohlberg's theory remain. Kohlberg's insistence that moral structure and content are separate — that how one reasons is independent of the specific moral choices one reasons about — has been troubling to many developmental psychologists. Emergence of the higher moral stages would hardly be of much consequence unless it could be argued that they produce commitments to certain moral contents that differ from those of the lower stages. In fact, the findings discussed above on the relationship of moral reasoning to behavior suggest that the higher stages *are* associated with specific moral contents, including values and behaviors embodying a commitment to civil liberties, consideration for others, and basic human rights. Because Kohlberg pushes the independence of moral structure and content to an extreme, his theory may seem to suggest that advanced reasoning can be used to justify any moral content. Yet this is clearly not what Kohlberg intended, for he rejected the idea that human morality was an arbitrary, relative matter. Current followers of Kohlberg now recognize the need to specify how each advance in quality of moral structures also implies improvements in moral content, or particular kinds of moral choice (Locke, 1983).

A related controversy over Kohlberg's theory has to do with his ideas regarding moral education. Look back at the kinds of experiences Kohlberg regarded as important for facilitating moral growth. They do not focus on direct teaching of moral prescriptions and rules. Instead, they emphasize cognitive challenges that are likely to induce disequilibrium and consequent revision of moral structures. In fact, for many years Kohlberg opposed approaches to moral education that taught children prescriptions for good behavior, regarding them as a form of indoctrination that inhibited cognitive development and prevented children from building their own rational moral structures. However, others differed with Kohlberg, arguing that direct teaching of moral content was not only necessary, but compatible with his theory. For example, Hamm (1977) suggested that teaching children particular rules and behaviors that constitute specific instances of higher moral principles provides them with concrete examples that can later be organized and incorporated into more abstract, broadly applicable moral ideals. When adults encourage children not to cause pain to others, to be honest, to keep promises and abide by contracts, and not to lie or cheat, they actually support the cause of justice, rather than interfere with it. Kohlberg (1978; 1980) later revised his conception of moral education to include direct teaching of moral attitudes and behavior, acknowledging that it could facilitate solid attainment of the conventional level. However, he continued to regard other experiences —in particular, social interaction that encourages young people to question the validity of societal rules and laws—as essential for the attainment of postconventional moral thought.

Finally, Kohlberg's stages focus on broad transformations in moral understanding that take place between late childhood and adulthood. Since most of the research on his theory concentrates on children age 10 and older, it tells us little about changes in moral reasoning that take place during early and middle childhood. Moreover, Kohlberg's moral dilemmas are remote from the experiences of young children and may not be clearly understood by them. Consequently, the dilemmas are inappropriate for gathering information about moral understanding during the preschool and early elementary school years. Recent research in which young children have been provided with moral problems related to their everyday experience indicates that Kohlberg's Stage 1, much like Piaget's stage of heteronomous morality, underestimates the moral reasoning of the younger child. We turn to a consideration of this evidence in the sections that follow.

THE MORAL REASONING OF YOUNG CHILDREN

Two bodies of research have used moral dilemmas specifically designed for children age 12 and below: (1) studies of children's **distributive justice,** or how they think rewards should be allocated among group members, and (2) investigations of children's responses to *prosocial moral dilemmas* in which they must choose between satisfying their own needs and those of others. Besides being relevant to children's real-life experiences, the moral problems used in these studies differ from Kohlberg's in that the importance of laws, punishment, and formal obligations is deemphasized, and there are few obvious rules on which to base a course of action. When dilemmas are formulated in this way, young children reveal some surprisingly sophisticated moral judgments.

Young Children's Understanding of Distributive Justice

In everyday life, children are frequently the recipients of adults' and peers' distributive decisions, and they dispense rewards to others as well. How much weekly allowance is to be given to siblings of different ages, who has to sit where in the family car on an extended vacation, and in what way an eight-slice pizza is to be shared by six hungry playmates are all questions of distributive justice.

Damon (1977) gave children between 4 and 9 years of age a distributive justice interview in which they were asked to react to dilemmas like this one:

> All of these boys and girls are in the same class together. One day their teacher lets them spend the whole afternoon making paintings and crayon drawings. The teacher thought that these pictures were so good that the class could sell them at the fair. They sold the pictures to their parents, and together the class made a whole lot of money. Now all the children gathered the next day and tried to decide how to split up the money. What do you think they should do with it? Why? (p. 66)

Based on children's responses, Damon identified a six-level sequence of distributive justice reasoning. As shown in Table 12.3, preschool children's ideas about how rewards should be allocated start out as egocentric; fairness is equated with self-interest. By middle childhood, children consider a variety of claims to rewards, including work accomplished and special needs of participants. Eight-year-olds also believe that the distribution of rewards should serve some higher social goal, such as helping the group do better next time or promoting positive feelings among group members.

Damon's progression of distributive justice reasoning is supported by both cross-sectional and longitudinal evidence (Blotner & Bearison, 1984; Damon, 1977; Enright, Franklin, & Manheim, 1980; Enright et al., 1980). Furthermore, like Piaget's

Table 12.3. Damon's Levels of Children's Distributive Justice Reasoning

LEVEL	APPROXIMATE AGE	DESCRIPTION
O-A	4	Fair allocation of rewards is confused with the child's momentary desires. Children of this level believe that they themselves should get more simply because they want more.
O-B	4–5	Children cite an objective attribute as a fair basis for distribution, but it is arbitrary and irrelevant to the situation. A child should get more for being the oldest, a fast runner, or having the most friends.
1-A	5	There is recognition that each participant has a stake in the rewards, but children of this level think the only way competing claims can be resolved is by strictly equal distribution. Special considerations like merit or need are not taken into account.
1-B	6–7	Fair distribution is equated with deservingness and concrete reciprocity. There is recognition that some people may have a greater claim to rewards for having worked harder.
2-A	8	Children recognize a variety of conflicting claims to justice, including equal treatment, merit, and need. Each claim is weighed, and parties with special needs, such as a younger child who cannot produce as much or a child who does not get any allowance, are given consideration.
2-B	8 and older	As in 2-A, all claims are considered. In addition, a fair distribution of rewards is seen as one that furthers the social goals of the group—for example, by encouraging future productivity or promoting friendship and group solidarity.

Source: Damon, 1977.

and Kohlberg's developmental sequences, distributive justice concepts are related to Piagetian cognitive capacities and children's perspective-taking skill. For example, Damon's Level 1-B (refer to Table 12.3) is associated with the attainment of Piagetian concrete operations and clear awareness by the child that others can have thoughts and feelings different from the self (Enright, Franklin, & Manheim, 1980; McNamee & Peterson, 1986).

A mature understanding of distributive justice also predicts everyday social behavior. Enright and Sutterfield (1980) found that first graders who used high level reasoning were better social problem solvers (see Chapter 11) and were rated as more popular and fair-minded by classmates than their less mature counterparts. Children who reason at advanced levels are also less selfish in situations in which they actually have an opportunity to allocate rewards to peer group members (Damon, 1977; McNamee & Peterson, 1986), and they are also more likely to share or help another child when there is no adult pressure to do so (Blotner & Bearison, 1984).

Research on children's ideas of distributive justice suggests that complex, internalized concepts of fairness emerge at a much earlier age than Kohlberg's punishment-oriented Stage 1 would have us believe.[7] In fact, fear of punishment and deference to authority do not even appear as themes in children's distributive justice rationales. Because Damon's dilemmas minimize the relevance of these factors to moral choice, they permit some unusually elaborate and mature moral reasoning on the part of children to rise to the surface.

Young Children's Prosocial and Altruistic Reasoning

Earlier, when we considered Gilligan's challenge to Kohlberg's theory, we showed that Kohlberg's stages and moral dilemmas do tap a caring and interpersonal orientation, in addition to a morality of fairness and justice. Nevertheless, prosocial choices in Kohlberg's dilemmas are always pitted against legal prohibitions or an authority's dictates (Eisenberg, 1982; Eisenberg, Lennon, & Pasternack, 1986). For example, in the Heinz dilemma, to help his wife, Heinz has no choice but to break the law and steal. In most everyday situations in which children must decide whether or not to do something for another person, the primary cost is not disobeying a law or an authority figure. Instead, the cost is a personal one of not satisfying one's own wants or needs. Eisenberg has constructed a set of prosocial moral dilemmas that, like Damon's distributive justice problems, deemphasize external prohibitions and make the primary sacrifice involved in aiding another person a matter of giving up one's own desires. Here is a typical prosocial dilemma that Eisenberg gives to younger children:

> One day a girl named Mary was going to a friend's birthday party. On her way she saw a girl who had fallen down and hurt her leg. The girl asked Mary to go to her house and get her parents so the parents could come and take her to the doctor. But if Mary did run and get the child's parents, she would be late for the birthday party and miss the ice cream, cake, and all the games. What should Mary do? Why? (Eisenberg, 1982, p. 231)

Interviewing children from preschool through twelfth grade, Eisenberg found that their responses to prosocial moral problems fell into five age-related levels, which are summarized in Table 12.4. Both cross-sectional and longitudinal evidence support this developmental pattern (Eisenberg, Lennon, & Roth, 1983; Eisenberg et al., 1987; Eisenberg-Berg, 1979; Eisenberg-Berg & Roth, 1980).

Perhaps you have already noticed that Eisenberg's developmental sequence bears considerable similarity to Kohlberg's stages. Her hedonistic, pragmatic orientation is

[7] Note that the very same conclusion is supported by Turiel and Nucci's research on children's moral versus social conventional understanding described earlier in this chapter. By the early elementary school years, children are aware that a distinguishing feature of moral transgressions is that they violate another person's right to be treated fairly and humanely.

Table 12.4. Eisenberg's Levels of Prosocial Moral Reasoning

LEVEL	APPROXIMATE AGE	DESCRIPTION
1. Hedonistic, pragmatic orientation	Preschool, early elementary school	Right behavior satisfies one's own needs. Reasons for helping or not helping another refer to gains for the self, e.g., "I wouldn't help because I might be hungry."
2. "Needs of others" orientation	Preschool, elementary school	Concern for the physical, material, and psychological needs of others is expressed in simple terms, without clear evidence of perspective-taking or empathic feeling, e.g., "He needs it."
3. Stereotyped, approval-focused orientation	Elementary school and high school	Stereotyped images of good and bad persons and concern for approval justify behavior, e.g., "He'd like him more if he helped."
4. Empathic orientation	Older elementary school and high school	Reasoning reflects an emphasis on perspective-taking and empathic feeling for the other person. e.g., "I'd feel bad if I didn't help because he'd be in pain."
5. Internalized values orientation	Small minority of high school students, no elementary school pupils	Justifications for moral choice are based on internalized values, norms, desire to maintain contractual obligations, and belief in the dignity, rights, and equality of all individuals, e.g., "I would feel bad if I didn't help because I'd know that I didn't live up to my values."

Source: Eisenberg, 1982.

like Kohlberg's Stage 2, her "needs of others" and approval-focused orientations are like Kohlberg's Stage 3, and her internalized values orientation includes forms of reasoning that match Kohlberg's Stages 4 through 6. But several features of Eisenberg's research differ from Kohlberg's. First, like the distributive justice findings noted above, authority- and punishment-oriented reasoning is completely absent from the prosocial dilemma responses of children of all ages. Second, children's prosocial understanding is clearly accelerated when compared to the timing of Kohlberg's stages. For example, Kohlberg reported that approval-focused (Stage 3) reasoning was rare until midadolescence, but when children are given Eisenberg's prosocial dilemmas, it occurs often during the elementary school years. Finally, Eisenberg's dilemmas bring out a new form of moral reasoning that she calls "empathic." By the late elementary school years, children realize that empathy is an important motivator of behaviors aimed at benefiting others. The appearance of empathic reasoning also indicates that children's prosocial understanding has become truly altruistic, for empathic justifications include a clear willingness to share and help others without expecting concrete rewards or social approval in return.[8]

In a recent study, Eisenberg and her colleagues found that 9- and 10-year-old children who empathized easily with others advanced to higher levels of prosocial reasoning during the period of early adolescence than their less empathic counterparts (Eisenberg et al., 1987). Eisenberg believes that the ability to react empathically may encourage the development of advanced prosocial reasoning as well as strengthen its realization in everyday behavior. In line with this idea, research shows that children who score at the higher stages of prosocial reasoning do behave in a

---

[8] Return for a moment to Box 12.2 and note that around this time children begin to understand the notion of ideal reciprocity, which also supports a truly altruistic orientation toward helping others in need.

more prosocial and altruistic fashion than those who show less advanced prosocial judgments (Eisenberg-Berg, 1979; Eisenberg-Berg & Hand, 1979). Eisenberg is one investigator who has made an important start at putting the cognitive, affective, and behavioral components of morality together.

Viewed together with Kohlberg's theory, Damon's and Eisenberg's research on young children's moral reasoning indicates that moral understanding is a rich and multifaceted phenomenon. Its dimensions and complexity are not exhaustively described by any single theory or set of moral dilemmas. Children's responses to a wide range of moral problems, including dilemmas that focus on societal justice, fair distribution of material goods, and prosocial behavior, are needed for an accurate picture of early moral-cognitive capacities, as well as a comprehensive description of the development of moral thought.

THE DEVELOPMENT OF SELF-CONTROL

The study of moral reasoning tells us what people think they would do and why when faced with a moral problem, but we have already indicated that people's good intentions often fall short. Whether children and adults actually follow through on what they believe is partly due to characteristics we call iron will, firm resolve, strong character, or more simply: **self-control.** Self-control in the moral arena involves inhibiting behaviors that conflict with a moral course of action. Sometimes it is referred to as resistance to transgression or resistance to temptation. You are already familiar with these terms, for we referred to them in the first part of this chapter. Recall that children's self-control is enhanced by explanations and inductive discipline, as well as by models who demonstrate and explicitly verbalize self-controlled behavior. Thus we have already seen that the practices of socialization agents play an important role in the development of self-control. However, children cannot be affected by these practices until they have developed the ability to internalize parental prohibitions and resist temptation. When and how does the child's own capacity for self-control develop?

The Beginnings of Self-control: Late Infancy and Early Childhood

Developmental psychologists who have studied the emergence of self-control all agree that a fundamental level of cognitive development has to be attained before children can internalize caregiver expectations and control their own behavior. The beginnings of self-control are supported by a number of cognitive achievements that come together during the second year of life and that we discussed in earlier chapters. Children cannot deliberately resist temptation until they are aware of the self as a separate, autonomous being and understand that their actions have consequences that are controllable by the self (Chapters 6 and 11). Self-control also requires representational and memory capacities (Chapters 6 and 7) that enable children to internalize caregiver directives and apply them to their own behavior (Kopp, 1982). As these abilities mature and consolidate, the first glimmerings of self control appear in the form of **compliance.** Between 12 and 18 months of age, children show clear awareness of caregiver wishes and expectations and can voluntarily obey adult commands and requests. Compliance is a landmark achievement on the way to self-controlled behavior in the absence of adult prompting and monitoring (Kopp, 1982; Vygotsky, 1934/1962; Luria, 1961).

Parents are generally delighted at their young toddler's new-found ability to comply, for it signals that the child is ready to begin learning the rules of social life. In addition, adults can moderate the child's behavior more easily and from a greater distance than was possible at an earlier age. Toddlers now respond to simple verbal directives, such as "Give the toy to Billy," "Put the candy back," and "Don't touch." But control of the child's actions during the second year is still tied to the here and now of caregiver commands, and adults must repeatedly call the child's attention to expectations for acceptable behavior. According to the Russian theorist Vygotsky (1934/1962), children cannot control their own behavior until they are able to incorporate adult directives into their own speech and use it to instruct the self. You may remember from Chapter 6 that this self-directed form of language is often referred to as *private speech.*[9]

The first investigations of very young children's ability to use private speech to control their own actions were conducted by one of Vygotsky's followers, Alexander Luria (1961). Luria was interested in how early in development children could *initiate* physical acts in response to self-instructions, as well as *inhibit* or stop engaging in a behavior when they told themselves to do so. The ability to voluntarily inhibit action is especially important for morally relevant self-control, for without it, young children clearly cannot resist temptation. In Luria's research, 1½- to 5-year-olds were given a bulb-squeezing task in which each child was requested to say "press" and squeeze a rubber bulb, following which the child was told to say "don't press" and release the bulb. Children below the age of 3 could respond to their own verbal instructions to initiate behavior, but curiously, they could not use a verbal command to inhibit an ongoing action. Upon giving themselves the directive "don't press," they actually squeezed the bulb even harder! Based on this finding, Luria concluded that before 3 years of age, children cannot use self-directed speech to control their own behavior. According to Luria, the 2-year-old simply reacts to the energizing, motor quality of the speech rather than to its meaningful content. Therefore, regardless of whether they tell themselves to press or not press the bulb, they continue to engage in bulb-squeezing behavior.

Luria's formative research has since been followed up, and recent investigations indicate that his conclusion regarding the 2-year-old's lack of self-control was not entirely correct (Pressley, 1979). The bulb-squeezing task is a type of motor inhibition problem that requires children to stop a behavior that is already in progress, and in line with Luria's findings, new research indicates that 2-year-olds do find this kind of problem to be quite difficult. For example, when asked to stop playing with a very attractive toy, they inhibit their own behavior far less effectively than do 3- and 4-year-olds (Masters & Binger, 1976). However, the 2-year-old *can* make use of language to inhibit behavior in situations that call for **delay of gratification.** In a delay-of-gratification task, children must hold in check an impulse to respond that has not yet been initiated. Many everyday problems in self-control are of this kind — waiting to eat a piece of candy until after dinner, refraining from going outside until an adult is ready to go too, or not turning on the TV set until homework and household chores are finished, to name just a few.

In a study aimed at investigating 2-year-olds' capacity to delay gratification, Vaughn, Kopp, and Krakow (1984) gave 18-, 24-, and 30-month-old children a series of three tasks. In the first task, the child was instructed not to touch an interesting toy telephone that was within arm's reach. In the second, raisins were hidden under cups, and the child was told to wait until the experimenter said it was all right to pick up a cup and eat a raisin. In the third task, the child was told not to open an attractively wrapped gift until the experimenter had finished her work. As shown in Figure 12.3, on all three problems, the ability to delay gratification increased dramatically from 18 months to 2½ years of age. Furthermore, by age 2½, clear individual differences in the ability to exercise self-control were evident, and the single best predictor of them was language development.

[9] You may wish to return to Chapter 6, pages 256–258, to review Vygotsky's ideas about the function and development of private speech.

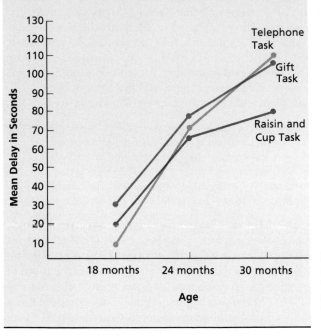

Figure 12.3. Age changes in delay of gratification in the Vaughn, Kopp, and Krakow (1984) study. *(Adapted from Vaughn, Kopp, and Krakow, 1984.)*

These findings reveal that self-control undergoes an important period of development and consolidation around 2 to 2½ years of age, considerably earlier than Luria's bulb-pressing research indicated. However, Vaughn, Kopp, and Krakow's results are clearly supportive of Luria and Vygotsky's view that speech and language are intimately tied to children's ability to control their own behavior. In fact, the investigators informally noted that 2-year-olds used a number of verbal techniques to help themselves wait, including singing and talking out loud to themselves.

In summary, research on very young children indicates that self-control has its origins in cognitive and representational development during the second year of life. Control over behavior initially takes the form of toddler compliance to caregiver requests. By 2 years of age, children start to shift from dependence on external sources of control to internal sources. Self-directed verbalizations begin to be used for the purpose of inhibiting behavior, and true self-control appears.

The Development of Self-control during the Late Preschool and Middle Childhood Years

The capacity for self-control is in place by the third year of life, but it is not completely developed. Improved cognitive abilities permit older children to use a variety of effective *self-instructional strategies* for resisting temptation. As a result, delay of gratification undergoes steady improvement during the preschool and elementary school years (Mischel & Metzner, 1962; Weisz, 1978).

Strategies for Self-control. Mischel has studied exactly what older children think and say to themselves that enables them to resist temptation more effectively than their younger counterparts. His research was initially inspired by Freud's suggestion that delay of gratification is facilitated when children create a mental image of a desired object or activity and think about the gratification it will bring (Freud, 1925/1961a). Freud believed that thoughts about the object substitute for real satisfaction, reduce the feeling of need, and help the child to delay. However, an early study by Mischel and Ebbesen (1970) suggested that Freud's theory was incorrect. Preschool children were given a delay-of-gratification problem in which they could choose between a highly desirable food reward that they would have to wait to eat and a less desirable food reward that they could eat any time during the waiting period. Informal observations of the most self-controlled preschoolers indicated that rather than focusing their attention on the reward, they did just the opposite. They used any technique they could think of to *distract* themselves from the desired object. For example,

> Some children covered their eyes with their hands, rested their heads on their arms, and found other similar techniques for averting their eyes from the reward objects. Many seemed to try to reduce the frustration of delay of reward by generating their own diversions: they talked to themselves, sang, invented games with their hands and feet, and even tried to fall asleep while waiting — as one child successfully did. (p. 335)

In everyday situations, preschoolers find it extremely difficult to keep their minds off tempting activities and objects for very long (Mischel, 1974). Mischel and his colleagues discovered that when children's thoughts do turn to an enticing but prohibited object, instructions that get them to engage in *cognitive transformations* of the mental stimulus are highly effective in promoting delay of gratification. In one study, Mischel and Baker (1975) had some preschoolers think about marshmallows imaginatively as "white and puffy clouds" and others focus on their realistic, "sweet and chewy" properties. In the realistic condition, children had much more difficulty waiting to eat the reward. These results show that not all mental images containing the desired object interfere with response inhibition. Instead, the nature of the cognitive representation is the critical feature that influences a child's capacity to delay. When diverting attention from rewards is difficult, thinking about them in stimulus-transforming, imaginative ways that deemphasize their arousing qualities improves children's self-control.

In each of the studies described above, an experimenter taught preschool children to use delay-enhancing strategies. How good are preschoolers at thinking up successful self-instructional techniques on their own? Research shows that they are not nearly as capable as their elementary school counterparts. Toner and Smith (1977) compared the performance of preschool and early elementary school children in a "waiting game" in which pieces of candy were put on a table in front of the child one at a time. In this task, the longer the child resisted the temptation to eat the candy, the more candy the child received. Some children in this study were given a task-oriented verbalization in which they periodically had to say out loud, "It's good if I wait." Others were told to use a counting verbalization that diverted their attention from the rewards, while a third group received no instructions. Older children who had not been instructed to say anything did just as well as those who had been given strategies by the experimenter, whereas without experimenter instructions the preschoolers did poorly. These findings suggest that by first and second grade, children are good at thinking up and applying their own strategies for resisting temptation. Of course, even very young preschoolers can generate some effective self-control strategies (as the examples given earlier indicate), but the ability to do so improves markedly over the early elementary school years.

Perhaps you have already noticed that the results described above parallel findings on children's strategy use in the memory development literature. In Chapter 7, we showed that preschoolers' performance on memory tasks improves when they are trained to apply strategies that help them recall, but below the age of 5 or 6 children rarely produce strategies independently. The ability to spontaneously generate cognitive strategies seems to be a major reason that delay of gratification, as well as performance on a wide variety of cognitive tasks discussed in earlier chapters, shows steady gains with age.

Knowledge of Strategies. Recently, Mischel investigated children's knowledge of the self-control process itself. Recall from Chapter 7 that conscious awareness of which mental strategies are likely to be successful is an important aspect of *metacognitive understanding*. Metacognition plays a role in how effectively children deploy strategies, as well as whether it occurs to them to use certain strategies at all.

Mischel and Mischel (1983) interviewed 3- to 11-year-old subjects to find out how much they knew about situational conditions and self-instructions likely to facilitate self-control. First children were asked whether exposing or shielding rewards from view would best help them wait during a delay period. Then they were asked to suppose that the rewards were left in full view and to describe what they could say to help themselves wait. Finally, children were asked to choose from pairs of self-instructional phrases the one that would best help them delay. Results showed that not until 5 or 6 years of age did children realize that covering the rewards would create a more effective environment for self-control. Around this time they also recognized that self-instructions that focus on the task of waiting (e.g., "I am waiting for the two marshmallows") rather than on the rewards (e.g., "The marshmallows taste yummy and chewy") would increase delay. Although most of the preschoolers had great difficulty describing strategies they would use, some were aware that directing their attention elsewhere would be helpful, for they gave such suggestions as "Close two eyes" and "Talk to the wall." As children moved through the elementary school grades, they came up with an increasingly broad array of delay tactics, and older children also described why certain techniques worked by referring to their arousal-reducing properties. Finally, not until the late elementary school years did children mention strategies involving cognitive transformations of rewards and their own arousal states. For example, one creative 11-year-old recommended saying, ". . . the marshmallows are filled with an evil spell." Another indicated he would tell himself, "I hate marshmallows I can't stand them. But when the grown-up gets back, I'll tell myself 'I love marshmallows' and eat it" (p. 609). Perhaps the reason that awareness of strategies involving transforming ideation appears so late in development is that it requires the abstract, hypothetical reasoning processes of formal operational thought.

Metacognitive understanding undoubtedly plays an important role in children's steadily improving ability to generate effective self-control strategies. Preschoolers do poorly when it comes to thinking up very many techniques for resisting temptation, and in comparison to older youngsters, they do not have a clear understanding of which self-control techniques work best and why. Do the findings of Mischel and his coworkers enhance your understanding of why disciplinary practices that include inductions and verbal explanations (discussed earlier in this chapter) are so effective in promoting behavioral inhibition in children? Such practices fit with the child's natural inclination to use self-guiding and self-inhibiting instructions to control their own behavior. They also provide children with examples of successful strategies for resisting temptation, and they offer rationales that promote metacognitive awareness of which strategies work best and why.

From Self-control to Responsibility. There is one final factor that contributes to the older child's improved capacity for self-control. During middle childhood and adolescence, self-control starts to become an important part of the young person's self-concept. In one study, children between 6 and 12 were asked to explain why they did chores that they did not like to do, such as cleaning their rooms, going to bed on time, and doing what their parents asked without talking back or arguing. Younger respondents focused on pleasing authority figures, whereas older children mentioned the achievement of goals they had set for themselves (Chandler, 1981). In another study, nearly a thousand students between 8 and 19 years of age were asked to describe themselves as persons. In telling what they liked best about themselves, older subjects were more likely to mention matters of self-control, such as "The way I apply myself," "I don't lose my temper easily," and "My attitude—if I don't like something, I won't get nasty about it." Also, nearly a third of the adolescents mentioned a concern about some self-control problem, such as "Sometimes I get mad at my sister over nothing" or "It's hard for me to force myself to do homework or whatever I'm supposed to do." In contrast, only 15 percent of the elementary school pupils mentioned such issues (Rosenberg, 1979, pp. 210, 213). As young people make the transition from childhood to adolescence, self-control starts to become an internalized value of considerable importance—a matter of *personal commitment and responsibility.*

Recall from Chapter 11 that children construct their self-concepts—in this case, a picture of oneself as more or less in command of one's own actions—largely on the basis of feedback they get from others. In a study of how adults' statements affect children's self-control, Toner, Moore, and Emmons (1980) exposed kindergarten through second-grade girls to a delay-of-gratification task. Before it began, half the children were given a task-relevant personal label. The experimenter commented in the course of a short conversation, "I hear you are very patient because you can wait for nice things when you can't get them right away." The other half received a task-irrelevant label—"I hear that you have some very nice friends at school." The results indicated that adult feedback to children about their capacity to wait was an extremely effective motivator of self-control. Children labeled as patient were able to delay gratification far longer than those who were told they had nice friends.

These findings indicate that besides suggesting effective self-instructional strategies, adults can facilitate children's resistance to temptation by bolstering their images of themselves as patient, self-disciplined personalities. Once self-control becomes a valued dimension of the child's self-concept, it is sustained not just by children's understanding that it is the sensible thing to do, but also by a firm inner resolve that it is what they want and ought to do.

CHAPTER SUMMARY

1. Moral development is concerned with how individuals come to resolve discrepancies between their self-centered, egoistic needs and obligations to act in favor of the needs of others. Four theoretical perspectives, each with roots in Western philosophical tradition, provide different accounts of moral development. Despite their different emphases, most theories agree that the general direction of moral development is toward internalization. At first the child's morality is externally imposed and controlled by adults. Eventually children develop internalized moral rules and principles, taking over the responsibility for regulating their own moral conduct.

2. The biological perspective on moral development assumes that the motivation to behave morally is grounded in the genetic heritage of the species. Human prosocial behavior may have genetic roots, but the biological perspective is a limited one, for there is much evidence to suggest that human morality requires strong environmental supports to be realized.

3. Although psychoanalytic and behaviorist theories propose different mechanisms of development, both regard morality as the adoption of societal prescriptions for good conduct, or norms. According to Freud, human morality resides in a portion of the personality called the superego, which results

from resolution of the Oedipal and Electra conflicts during early childhood. Fear of punishment and loss of parental love lead children to internalize adult rules and prohibitions and to redirect hostile impulses toward the self, in the form of guilt. Although guilt is an important motivator of moral action, Freud's interpretation of how guilt reactions develop is no longer widely accepted. Furthermore, in contrast to predictions drawn from Freudian theory, power assertion and love withdrawal do not foster an internalized conscience. Inductive discipline is far more effective. Moral development is also much more gradual than Freud assumed, extending beyond the preschool years into adolescence and adulthood.

4. Behaviorists regard morality as learned in the same way as all other behaviors: according to the principles of reinforcement and modeling. Positive reinforcement is a far more effective means than punishment for promoting socially desirable behavior. When punishment is severe and frequently applied, it leads to a series of unfortunate side effects, including imitation by children of adult aggressive behavior, avoidance of punitive agents, and increased risk of child abuse. In addition, punishment does not foster moral internalization. Modeling is a successful means for promoting prosocial behavior. Children are especially likely to imitate models who are warm and affectionate, powerful and competent, and who

demonstrate consistency between what they say and what they do. In comparison to positive, prosocial behaviors, impulse control is not as easily encouraged by modeling. Although children easily pick up on adult lapses in self-control, they are only likely to copy a model who resists temptation if the model makes her efforts at behavioral inhibition explicit by verbalizing and explaining them to the child.

5. Even after children internalize moral prescriptions, consistency in moral conduct from one occasion to another is only moderate. Situational conditions affect children's tendency to behave honestly or dishonestly. For example, the general level of honesty of children's peer associates and adult achievement pressures affect children's tendency to cheat on assignments and examinations in school.

6. In contrast to psychoanalytic and behaviorist theories, the cognitive-developmental perspective does not regard morality as a matter of conforming to societal norms. Instead, cognitive-developmental theorists believe that children actively think and reason about moral issues. Due to cognitive maturity and broadening social experience, children's conceptions of justice and fairness become more abstract and morally adequate with age. Piaget's work served as the original inspiration for the cognitive-developmental perspective. He identified two broad stages of moral development: (1) the stage of heteronomous morality, in which moral rules are regarded as unalterable dictates of authority figures; and (2) the stage of autonomous morality, in which rules are viewed as flexible instruments of human purposes established through cooperative social agreement. Research has confirmed Piaget's general vision of moral development, although it has failed to support a number of specific aspects of his theory. Kohlberg's six-stage sequence, which follows in the tradition of Piaget, has supplanted his two-stage theory.

7. According to Kohlberg, between middle childhood and adulthood, moral reasoning advances through three levels, each of which contains two separate stages: (1) the preconventional level, in which morality is externally governed by rewards, punishments, and the power of authority figures; (2) the conventional level, in which conformity to laws and rules is viewed as necessary to preserve the current social system; and (3) the postconventional level, in which individuals develop abstract, universally applicable moral principles and values. Research indicates that Kohlberg's stages are strongly related to age and form an invariant developmental sequence. However, moral development requires a less tightly organized stage conception than Kohlberg originally envisioned. Maturity of moral reasoning is moderately related to a wide variety of moral behaviors.

8. Research suggests that Piaget's cognitive and Selman's perspective-taking stages are necessary but not sufficient conditions for the attainment of Kohlberg's stages of moral thought. Experiences related to the development of moral understanding include peer interaction; warm, rational, and democratic child-rearing practices; and higher education. A certain level of societal complexity may be necessary for a culture to promote the higher moral stages, since individuals living in isolated peasant and tribal communities do not advance beyond Stage 3. It is also possible that Kohlberg's dilemmas are culture-bound and underestimate the moral reasoning of some peoples.

9. Research does not support the claim that Kohlberg's theory is sex-biased. However, his insistence that moral structures are independent of moral content has been challenged. Moreover, Kohlberg's theory, like Piaget's, underestimates the young child's moral understanding. Research on distributive justice and prosocial moral reasoning reveals that elementary school children are capable of some surprisingly sophisticated moral judgments.

10. The development of self-control is supported by cognitive and representational capacities that emerge during the second year of life. Self-control makes its initial appearance in the form of compliance. By age two children can use self-directed speech to delay gratification. During the preschool period, children profit from adult-provided self-control strategies, but cannot generate very many of them independently. Over the elementary school years, children produce an increasingly broad array of strategies themselves, and they become consciously aware of which ones work best and why. Finally, during late childhood and early adolescence, self-control becomes a vital component of the self-concept — a matter of personal commitment and responsibility.

IMPORTANT TERMS AND CONCEPTS

internalization
sociobiology
superego
identification
induction
social conventions
heteronomous morality

realism
immanent justice
autonomous morality
reciprocity
moral dilemma
Defining Issues Test (DIT)
preconventional morality

conventional morality
postconventional morality
distributive justice
self-control
compliance
delay of gratification

Calm Morning, by Frank Benson.
Museum of Fine Arts, Boston. Gift of Charles A. Coolidge and Family.

CHAPTER 13

The Development of Sex Differences and Sex Roles

Four-year-old Jenny arrives at her preschool classroom and enters the housekeeping corner, where she dons a frilly long dress and grown-up-looking high heels. Karen, while setting the table, produces whimpering sound effects for the swaddled baby doll in the crib. Jenny lifts the baby and gently whispers, "You need milk and a new diaper." She picks up a bottle, sits down in the rocker, and pretends to feed the doll. In a few moments, Jenny says to Karen, "I think the baby's sick. Ask Rachel if she'll be the nurse." Karen goes off to find Rachel, who is coloring at the art table.

In the same classroom, Nathan hurriedly hangs up his jacket and calls to Tommy, "Wanna play traffic?" Both boys dash energetically toward the cars and trucks in the block corner. Soon David joins them. "I'll be policeman first!" says Nathan, who pulls a chair into the block area and stands on it. "Green light, go!" shouts the young police officer. With this signal, Tommy and David scurry on all fours around the chair as fast as possible, each pushing a large wooden truck. "Red light," exclaims Nathan, and the trucks screech to a halt.

"My truck beat yours," says Tommy to David.

"Only 'cause I need gas," retorts David, who pulls off to the side and pretends to fill the tank.

"Let's build a runway for the trucks," suggests Nathan. The three construction engineers begin to gather large blocks and boards for the task.

The activity preferences and play behaviors of these preschoolers indicate that at a tender age, they have already begun to adopt the sex-typed standards of their cultural community. Jenny and Karen gravitate to play with dresses, dolls, and household props, act out a stereotypically feminine scene of nurturance and caregiving, and summon Rachel to assume the occupational role of nurse, not doctor. The play of Nathan, Tommy, and David, with its traffic scene turned racecourse, is active, competitive, and thematically masculine. Already, all of these four-year-olds interact more often with children of their own than of the opposite sex. In addition, the boys seldom enter the housekeeping area, and the girls rarely choose to build with large blocks or use the cars and trucks.

What causes play preferences and social orientations to become so rigidly sex-typed at an early age, and how do children's sex-typed knowledge and behavior change over time? Do societal expectations limit the way children *think about themselves* as masculine and feminine beings, with implications for the development of their self-concepts, personal attributes, and behavior? Finally, to what extent do widely held beliefs about the characteristics of males and females reflect reality? Is it the case that the average man is fairly aggressive, assertive, competitive, and good at spatial and mathematical skills, while the average woman is passive, conforming, nurturant, socially responsive, and better at verbal skills? How large are the differences that exist between the sexes, and what are their origins in childhood socialization and the biology of the organism? These are the central questions asked by researchers who study the development of sex typing, and we consider evidence that responds to them in this chapter.

The acquisition of sex-typed characteristics has been of central concern to child development specialists for decades, and interest in the topic has continued to grow in recent years. The wealth of accumulated studies is vast; there are comparisons of the sexes on virtually every form of behavior imaginable (Deaux, 1985). The research is also highly controversial. Like investigations into children's intelligence, the study of sex typing has become embroiled in the nature-nurture debate and taken on a political flavor because of its implications for gender equality.

Perhaps more than any other area of child development, the study of sex typing has responded to the winds of societal change. Largely as a consequence of social and political progress in the area of women's rights, during the past two decades there have been major shifts in how sex differences are regarded. Until the early seventies, psychologists, educators, and parents considered the adoption of sex-typed behavior as a desirable goal of socialization and as crucial for optimal psychological adjustment. Today, psychologists recognize that some extremely sex-typed behaviors are actually threats to mental health. Unrelenting aggressiveness and competitiveness on the part of men and dependency, conformity, and passivity on the part of women are maladaptive behavior patterns for any person. This realization has led modern research to be guided by the new assumption that the adoption of some sex-typed behaviors may not be good, because it limits developmental possibilities for individuals of both sexes (Huston, 1983; Ruble, 1988).

Like other aspects of child development, theoretical revision marks the study of sex differences and sex roles. Psychoanalytic theory at one time offered a prominent and persuasive account of how children, like Jenny and Nathan described earlier, acquired masculine and feminine characteristics. According to Freud, sex-typed attitudes and behavior were adopted in the same way as other societal norms (see Chapter 12). Both resulted from identification with the same-sex parent during the late preschool years (Freud, 1925/1961b). However, recent evidence shows that same-sex parental identification is only one of many socializing influences on sex typing. Interactions with peers, teachers, and opposite-sex parents also make a difference, as do examples of sex-appropriate behavior provided by the broader social environment. Furthermore, psychologists now know that the age range during which sex-typed learning takes place begins earlier and extends beyond the time frame Freud assigned to it, continuing into the middle childhood, adolescent, and even adulthood years (Huston, 1983). Finally, Freudian theory and subsequent extensions of it (e.g., Erikson, 1950) view sex typing as a natural and normal outcome of biological differences between males and females. Although debate continues about the truth of this assumption, firm adherence to it by psychoanalytic theorists has not been helpful in the quest to discover how people might become free of the constraints of gender-based definitions of appropriate behavior. Consequently, child psychologists have, for the most part, abandoned the psychoanalytic framework and turned toward other theoretical perspectives.

Social learning theory, with its emphasis on the learning mechanisms of modeling and reinforcement, and cognitive-developmental theory, with its focus on children as active thinkers about their social world, are the major contemporary approaches for understanding the development of sex typing. Neither has proved entirely adequate by itself. We will see later on that a new, integrative perspective called *gender schema theory* combines elements of both of these theories to explain the acquisition of sex-typed knowledge and behavior.

Along with new research and new theories has come a proliferation of new terms. *Sex* and *gender* are labels that have distinct meanings to some investigators (e.g., Deaux, 1985) but are used interchangeably by others (Huston, 1983; Ruble, 1988). We will adopt the second convention in this chapter.[1] Other important terms are sex stereotypes, sex roles, and sex-role identity. Sex stereotypes and sex roles are the public face of gender in society, and they support and influence one another. **Sex stereotypes** refer to widely held beliefs about the characteristics associated with one sex as opposed to another (Ruble & Ruble, 1982). **Sex roles** are the reflection of these stereotypes in behaviors regarded as culturally appropriate for males and females (Rosen & Rekers, 1980). In the first portion of this chapter, we consider the content of current stereotypes and sex-role expectations and how children's knowledge and understanding of them change with age. The term **sex-role identity** has a private connotation. It refers to the individual's perception of the self as relatively masculine or feminine in characteristics, capabilities, and behaviors. In the second part of this chapter, we consider how children's images of themselves as masculine or feminine beings develop, and we also discuss the relationship of sex-role identity to sex-typed behavior. Finally, in the last part of this chapter we turn to the question of how different males and females really are in intellectual abilities and personality attributes, and the biological versus environmental roots of these differences.

SEX STEREOTYPES AND SEX ROLES

Beliefs about sex differences have appeared in religious, philosophical, and literary writings for centuries, and they have been closely linked to the roles of the sexes in society. For example, in ancient times, Aristotle wrote:

> Woman is more compassionate than man and has a greater propensity to tears. She is, also, more envious, more querulous, more slanderous, and more contentious. Farther still, the female is more dispirited, more despondent, more impudent and more given to falsehood than the male. . . . But the male . . . is more disposed to give assistance in danger, and is more courageous than the female. (Cited in Miles, 1935, p. 700)

Although the latter part of the twentieth century has brought a new level of awareness about the wide range of role possibilities for each sex, strong beliefs about differences between males and females continue to exist. Systematic research on sex stereotyping did not begin until the latter part of the 1960s. Using a variety of techniques, including open-ended responses, checklists, and rating scales, investigators asked people what characteristics they believed to be typical of men and women.

[1] The term *sex* is often taken to imply biologically-based differences between males and females, whereas *gender* invokes explanations based on social influences. However, differences may be due to both biological and environmental factors. In this chapter, use of the terms sex and gender does not imply specific assumptions about the determinants of differences being discussed.

Despite the diversity of methods employed and samples studied, considerable consensus emerged in adults' beliefs about sex-related attributes (Ruble & Ruble, 1982).

For example, in 1968 Rosenkrantz and his colleagues asked college students to rate the extent to which they thought a large number of characteristics were typical of males and females. Masculine-rated traits reflected competence, rationality, and self-assertion — personality characteristics termed **instrumental** in the psychological literature. Feminine-associated traits were warm, caring, and emotional — characteristics labeled as **expressive** in nature. During the 1970s and early 1980s, a period of intense political activism with respect to women's rights, these stereotypes remained essentially the same (Broverman et al., 1972; Ruble, 1983; Spence, Helmreich, & Stapp, 1975). A list of attributes that college students of the 1980s regarded as associated with males and females is provided in Table 13.1. It bears a strong resemblance to the findings Rosenkrantz obtained a decade and a half earlier. Furthermore, in a recent cross-cultural study that included respondents from 30 nations, Williams and Best (1982) reported that the instrumental-expressive dichotomy continues to be a widely held sex-stereotypic viewpoint around the world.

In addition to the personal attributes listed in Table 13.1, other components of sex stereotypes have been identified, including physical characteristics (e.g., tall, strong, and sturdy for men; soft, dainty, and graceful for women) and occupations (e.g., truck driver, insurance agent, and chemist for men; telephone operator, elementary school teacher, and nurse's aide for women) (Deaux & Lewis, 1984). The variety of attributes that are sex-stereotypic, their constancy over time, and their generality across samples suggest that sex stereotypes are salient, deeply ingrained patterns of thinking. In the following sections, we consider when children become aware of sex stereotypes, and the implications of stereotyping for the development of sex-role behavior.

Table 13.1. Some Characteristics Regarded as Stereotypically Masculine and Feminine by College Students in the 1980s

MASCULINE CHARACTERISTICS	FEMININE CHARACTERISTICS
Independent	Emotional
Aggressive	Home-oriented
Skilled in business	Kind
Mechanical aptitude	Cries easily
Outspoken	Creative
Acts as a leader	Considerate
Self-confident	Devotes self to others
Takes a stand	Needs approval
Ambitious	Gentle
Not easily influenced	Aware of others' feelings
Dominant	Excitable in a major crisis
Active	Expresses tender feelings
Makes decisions easily	Enjoys art and music
Doesn't give up easily	Tactful
Stands up under pressure	Feelings hurt
Likes math and science	Neat
Competitive	Likes children
Adventurous	Understanding

Source: Ruble, 1983.

HOW EARLY DO CHILDREN DISPLAY SEX STEREOTYPED KNOWLEDGE?

Recall from our discussion of social cognition in Chapter 11 that as early as two years of age, children apply common gender-linked labels, such as mommy, daddy, lady, man, boy, and girl, to categorize other people, and they label their own gender correctly as well (Lewis & Brooks-Gunn, 1979; Weinraub et al., 1984). As soon as basic gender categories are established, children start to sort out what they mean in terms of activities and behaviors, and a wide variety of sex stereotypes in the prevailing culture are quickly mastered. Many toys, articles of clothing, tools, household objects, games, and occupations are associated by the young preschooler with one sex as opposed to the other (Blakemore, LaRue, & Olejnik, 1979; Edelbrock & Sugawara, 1978; Thompson, 1975; Nemerowicz, 1979; Weinraub et al., 1984). In one study, children as young as 2½ were shown a series of pictures. As each one was presented, the experimenter described it by making a statement about a sex-typed behavior (e.g., "I can hit you"), a physical characteristic (e.g., "I am strong"), an activity (e.g., "I like to play ball"), or a future role (e.g., "When I grow up, I'll fly an airplane"). Both boys and girls at this young age indicated that girls "like to play with dolls," "talk a lot," "never hit," say "I need some help," and later on as grown-ups will "clean the house" and "be a nurse." They also believed that boys "like to help father," say "I can hit you," and as future adults will "be boss" and "mow the grass" (Kuhn, Nash, & Brucken, 1978).

Even before children can verbalize their own gender and match up statements and objects with a male or female stimulus figure, their play behavior suggests that they have acquired some implicit knowledge about "sex-appropriate" activities. This is particularly evident in sex-typed game and toy choices, which are present by 1½ years of age (Fagot, Leinbach, & Hagan, 1986). The tendency of toddlers and young 2-year-olds to play with "same-sex" toys more than toys regarded as appropriate for the other gender has been found in home observations, laboratory settings, and in free play in a preschool setting (Fagot, 1978; Fein et al., 1975; O'Brien, 1980). Between 1 and 3 years of age, sex-typed toy and game choices become highly consistent for both sexes (O'Brien & Huston, 1985).

A notable feature of preschool children's sex stereotypes is that they are rigid and inflexible, much like other aspects of their thinking at this young age (see Chapter 6). Shown a picture of a Scottish bagpiper wearing a kilt, a 4-year-old is likely to state emphatically, "Men don't wear skirts!" At nursery school, children can be heard exclaiming to one another that girls don't drive fire engines and can't be police officers and boys don't take care of babies and can't be the teacher. While such statements are definitely influenced by the surrounding environment of sex-typed activities and roles, they are also a function of preschoolers' limited cognitive capacities. As we will see in greater detail when we discuss the development of sex-role identity, concrete, observable characteristics—play activities, toy choices, occupational roles, hair styles, and clothing—are the defining features of gender to the child of 4 or 5 and below. Change the most obvious characteristics of how males or females look and what they do, and to the preschooler, the person's sex miraculously changes as well.

CHANGES IN SEX STEREOTYPING DURING MIDDLE CHILDHOOD AND ADOLESCENCE

During middle childhood and adolescence, awareness of sex stereotypes increases, particularly in the less obvious areas of personality attributes and achievement. At the same time, the understanding of gender-related characteristics becomes more flexible. Older children recognize that behaviors and activities are *associated,* not *defining* features of biological sex (Ullian, 1976). Consequently, some notions about "sex-appropriate" characteristics actually become less stereotypic by the late childhood years, particularly with respect to activities and occupations.

Sex Stereotyping of Personality Attributes

In Chapter 11, we showed that before age 8, children's descriptions of themselves and others consist of concrete lists of particular activities, interests, and behaviors. Only in middle childhood do they engage in abstractions from behavior and think about people in terms of inner psychological characteristics. This same developmental trend appears in research on children's awareness of sex stereotypes.

An instrument called the Sex Stereotype Questionnaire is frequently used to collect information on elementary school children's stereotyping of personality dispositions. Children are given masculine adjectives (e.g., tough, aggressive, rational, dominant) and feminine adjectives (gentle, appreciative, excitable, affectionate) and asked to assign them to either a male or female stimulus figure. Best and her colleagues (1977) administered this measure to 5-year-olds, 8-year-olds, 11-year-olds, and college students. As shown in Figure 13.1, the kindergartners responded at better than chance, but the tendency to stereotype increased markedly over the elementary school years and into adolescence. Best also reported that masculine-stereotyped traits were learned at an earlier age than feminine ones by children of both sexes. Perhaps male stereotypes are acquired sooner because boys are permitted far less freedom than girls to engage in "cross-sex" activities. Boys' earlier and more complete conformity to sex-stereotypic behaviors may lead children to abstract the inner dispositions typically associated with the male role at an earlier age (Williams, Bennett, & Best, 1975).

Several cautions should be kept in mind about the developmental trends described above. Virtually all the work on children's knowledge of personality stereotypes has used forced-choice techniques in which children have had to assign a characteristic to either one gender or the other. Only a handful of investigations have

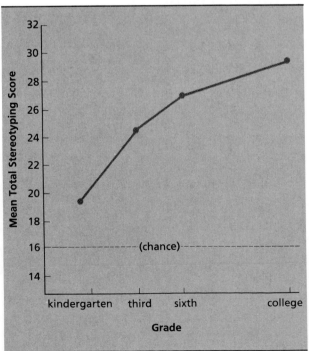

Figure 13.1. Age changes in sex stereotyping of personality attributes in the Best et al. (1977) study. *(From D. L. Best et al., 1977, "Development of Sex-trait Stereotypes among Young Children in the United States, England, and Ireland,"* Child Development, *48, 1357–1384. © The Society for Research in Child Development, Inc. Reprinted by permission.)*

asked subjects whether a personality attribute might be appropriate for *both* genders. The results of these studies suggest that the forced-choice technique leads to an overestimation of children's stereotyping of personality attributes (Marantz & Mansfield, 1977; Kelly & Smail, 1986). Furthermore, awareness of sex-stereotyped characteristics is not the same as endorsement of them. There is some limited evidence that although older elementary school children recognize many personality attributes as associated with one gender rather than the other, they do not necessarily approve of these distinctions (Kelly & Smail, 1986).

Sex Stereotyping of Achievement Areas

Not long after children enter elementary school, they figure out which academic subjects and skill areas are considered masculine and which are feminine. Stein and Smithells (1969; Stein, 1971) asked second, sixth, and twelfth graders whether they thought activities in six achievement areas were more for boys or more for girls. As shown in Figure 13.2, children of all ages thought that reading, artistic (art and music), and social skills were feminine and athletics, mechanical skills, and mathematics were masculine. While sex stereotyping of achievement areas is present in the early grades, it also increases with age, especially in areas that are considered more appropriate for the opposite sex. For example, in Stein and Smithells's research, boys' ratings of reading and girls' ratings of athletics and mathematics changed the most. These findings suggest that children start out by assuming that many achievement areas are quite appropriate for their own gender. What they seem to learn over the school years is which ones to exclude.

Other important but subtle forms of achievement stereotyping also emerge during middle childhood. Recall our discussion of achievement-related attributions in Chapter 11. We reviewed evidence indicating that attributing failure to ability (a relatively permanent deficiency that cannot be easily altered) as opposed to effort (a modifiable attribute that is under the control of the individual) has an undermining effect on achievement motivation.[2] Research indicates that elementary school children explain the failures of females, particularly in "cross-sex" activities, as due to ability. In

[2] Turn back to Chapter 11, pages 472–476, if you need to review the research on the development of children's achievement-related attributions.

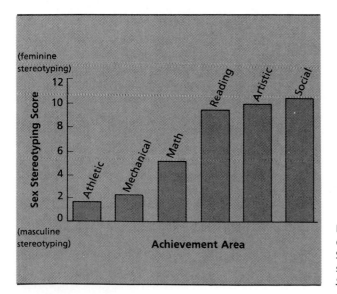

Figure 13.2. Sex stereotyping of achievement areas in the Stein and Smithells (1969) study. *(Adapted from Stein & Smithells, 1969.)*

contrast, they interpret comparable male failures as a matter of insufficient effort or learning opportunities. For example, Nemerowicz (1979) asked elementary school children why men and women do not engage in activities stereotyped for the other sex. The children often responded that women do not perform masculine activities like carpentry, truck driving, or playing baseball because they lack physical strength or ability. They thought men performed more poorly at cooking and domestic activities because they have not learned the necessary skills.

Similar results showing that children devalue the achievements of females, particularly in masculine-stereotyped areas, have emerged in laboratory studies. Etaugh and Rose (1975) presented seventh, ninth, and eleventh graders with short articles that had appeared in magazines for teenagers. Some were on feminine subjects like child care and grocery shopping, some on masculine subjects such as car racing and space exploration, and others were sex-neutral. A fictitious author's name followed each of the articles, and they were described as entries in a writing contest. The subjects were asked to judge the merits of the writing and the ability of the author. The work of male authors was judged better than female authors, especially when the article was on a masculine topic. This pattern of results occurred at all age levels and among both male and female participants, and it duplicates the findings of similar studies conducted with adults (Mischel, 1974).

Furthermore, by the mid-elementary school years, children have acquired a more general stereotype of achievement as a "masculine" norm. Hawkins and Pingree (1978) told third through twelfth graders stories about a woman (Anne) and a man (John) who either succeeded or failed in medical school and had them rate how nice each was under both conditions. For male and female subjects of all ages, Anne was somewhat less nice than John when they both succeeded, but John was much less nice than Anne when they both failed. Although children are biased in favor of males who succeed, they seem to evaluate a male who fails at an important achievement activity especially negatively.

Sex Stereotyping of Activities and Occupations

In studies of children's stereotyping of activities and occupations, researchers have gone beyond asking children whether a particular endeavor is appropriate for males or females. They have also asked whether members of each sex *can* or *should* engage in the activity. Results repeatedly indicate that although awareness of stereotypes increases with age, a more flexible and varied appreciation of what males and females can and should do emerges as well (Cummings & Taebel, 1980; Garrett, Ein, & Tremaine, 1977; Meyer, 1980). In one study, children's flexible appreciation of activity and occupational stereotypes paralleled the development of their understanding of social conventions, a topic that we discussed in Chapter 12. In other words, children's grasp of the idea that sex-stereotyped activities are arbitrary, socially defined matters went hand in hand with their appreciation that social conventions (e.g., eating with a knife and fork as opposed to one's hands) are not fixed, immutable laws, but relative practices arrived at by group consensus (Carter & Patterson, 1982). These findings suggest that sex-stereotyped activities and social conventions are part of the same domain of social-cognitive understanding. Both become more flexible as children's understanding of the social origins of certain rules improves during middle childhood. In agreement with this interpretation, between 6 and 18 years of age, children's answers to the question, "Why do you think boys and girls are different/do different things?" focus less on biological explanations (e.g., "Boys have different things in their innards than girls") and more on societal roles and different socialization experiences (e.g., "We do different things because it is the way we have been brought up") (Smith & Russell, 1984; Ullian, 1976).

In summary, during the preschool years children develop well-defined stereotypes about concrete aspects of sex roles, including activities, playthings, and occupations. More abstract dimensions of sex stereotypes, including personality and achievement attributes, emerge in middle childhood and undergo further refinement during adolescence. At the same time, a more flexible view of sex-stereotyped activities and occupations develops. As children grasp the arbitrary nature of social rules, they also come to understand that people can engage in "cross-sex" activities, and that what is stereotyped in one culture need not be so in another.

GROUP DIFFERENCES IN SEX STEREOTYPING

Besides the developmental trends noted above, group differences exist in children's sex-stereotyped thinking. The strongest and most consistent of these is between boys and girls. In many investigations, boys have been found to hold more stereotyped views. In toddlerhood, boys play more often with toys stereotyped for their own gender, a difference that persists throughout the preschool years (O'Brien & Huston, 1985; O'Brien, Huston, & Risley, 1983). By middle childhood and adolescence, boys make more stereotyped judgments on all of the dimensions discussed above, including personality attributes, achievement areas, occupations, and activities (e.g., Archer, 1984; Cummings & Taebel, 1980; Fennema & Sherman, 1977; Kleinke & Nicholson, 1979; Raymond & Benbow, 1986). In addition, boys are less flexible in their view of occupational stereotypes than girls, and they show a greater tendency to devalue feminine achievement performance and attribute gender differences to biological rather than social causes (Etaugh & Rose, 1975; Nemerowicz, 1979; Smith & Russell, 1984).

Studies that have included American minority children in their samples report that black children hold less stereotyped views of women than white children (Kleinke & Nicholson, 1979; Bardwell, Cochran, & Walker, 1986). This finding may be linked to differences in black and white family lifestyles. For example, more black than white women with children under 18 are employed (U.S. Department of Labor, 1986). This means that black children are more likely to have mothers whose lives reflect less traditional sex roles. Although lower social class groups are generally more rigidly stereotyped than members of the middle class during adolescence and adulthood (e.g., Bayer, 1975; Canter & Ageton, 1984; Tomeh, 1979), research on children has failed to provide clear confirmation of this same difference. In several studies, no socioeconomic differences were found in children's stereotyping of activities, achievement areas, and occupations (Cummings & Taebel, 1980; Nemerowicz, 1979; Stein, 1971). In one study, low-income kindergarten children actually appeared less stereotyped than their middle-class agemates (Bardwell, Cochran, & Walker, 1986).

Cross-cultural investigations of children's stereotyping of personality attributes have also been conducted. Like the findings on adults described earlier, the instrumental-expressive dichotomy has held up in a variety of countries (Best et al., 1977; Williams et al., as cited by Huston, 1983). But as yet, a great many national groups, especially non-Western cultures, have not been studied. Therefore, the extent of cross-cultural variation in children's sex-stereotyped beliefs is not fully known.

The fact that gender and racial group differences in stereotyping do exist indicates that growth in social-cognitive understanding is not sufficient to explain the development of stereotyped attitudes. Socialization experiences must also contribute. But before we consider these influences, let's look at whether sex-stereotyped attitudes actually affect children's sex-role adoption. If we were to find that stereotyping only influences children's patterns of thinking and not their actual behavior, there would be little reason to be concerned that stereotypes limit the development of each child's full potential.

DOES SEX STEREOTYPING AFFECT SEX-ROLE ADOPTION?

Correlational evidence, especially in the area of sex stereotypes about achievement, indicates that children's knowledge of stereotypes is related to their sex-typed behavior. An impressive number of studies report that children and adolescents show greater motivation and mastery when they regard an achievement area as consistent with their own sex role, and less motivation and mastery when they view it as an opposite-sex endeavor (Dwyer, 1974; Kelly & Smail, 1986; Paulsen & Johnson, 1983; Sherman & Fennema, 1977; Sherman, 1980; Stein, 1971). Strong evidence for this relationship has even been obtained in quite young children. In a longitudinal study that followed children from 4 to 6 years of age, sex stereotypes about intellectual achievement predicted children's expectancy of success at each time of measurement. In addition, stereotyped thinking at age 4 was related to changes in children's expectancies over the following year (Crandall, 1978).

More definite evidence of the power of stereotypes to affect sex-typed interests and behavior comes from experimental research in which investigators take gender-neutral tasks and artificially label them as appropriate for one sex or the other. In one such study, 6- to 8-year-olds played a game in which they had to toss as many marbles as possible into a clown's body within a short time limit. In one condition, the game was labeled as an activity for girls, in another for boys, and in a third it was not given a gender-associated label. Children of both sexes judged the game as more attractive and also performed better when it was labeled as sex-appropriate or not labeled at all than when they were told it was an opposite-sex activity (Montemayor, 1974).

Experimental findings in combination with correlational evidence provide strong support for the influence of sex stereotypes on children's attraction to tasks, effortful behavior, and performance. The impact of stereotypes on behavior is likely to be even more potent as children take their knowledge of stereotypes and integrate it into their sex-role identities — self-perceptions about what they can and should do at play, in school, and as future participants in society. But the emergence of sex-role identity is a topic that we treat at a later point in this chapter. For now, let's consider various influences that may serve to promote children's sex-stereotyped view of the world.

BIOLOGICAL AND ENVIRONMENTAL INFLUENCES ON SEX STEREOTYPING AND SEX-ROLE ADOPTION

Virtually all psychologists agree that the content of sex stereotypes is conveyed to children by socialization agents as well as through information available about sex-role expectations in the broader social environment. Social learning theorists emphasize direct teaching, modeling, and reinforcement of stereotypical knowledge and behavior as the major mechanisms by which sex-role standards are transmitted to children. We shall see shortly that a great deal of research supports their view. Nevertheless, some individuals argue that biological variations lead each sex to be uniquely suited to fill particular roles and that the great majority of societies merely promote sex-role differentiation that is grounded in the biological makeup of the organism. What evidence, if any, exists to support the idea that biological differences between males and females are congruent with sex stereotypes and serve to constrain sex-role development?

Are Sex Stereotypes and Traditional Sex Roles Grounded in Biological Differences Between the Sexes?

While practically no modern psychologist would argue that "biology is destiny" — that women are constitutionally ordained to stay home and care for children and men to serve as economic providers, warriors, and protectors — serious questions about the influence of biological factors on sex-role development remain (Ruble, 1988). Cross-cultural similarities in stereotypes and sex-role behavior are sometimes taken as evidence for biological influences on sex-role differentiation. Earlier in this chapter we indicated that the instrumental-expressive dichotomy is represented in the sex stereotyping of a great many national groups. Although this evidence appears to support the argument that the socialization practices of most cultures simply adapt to biological differences between the sexes, it must be interpreted with caution. A careful examination of the anthropological literature reveals that although most societies encourage instrumental traits in boys and expressive traits in girls, the distinctions made are not always strong. Substantial cultural diversity exists in the *magnitude* of the sex difference, even when the *direction* of the difference is the same from one society to another (Hendrix & Johnson, 1985). Furthermore, reversals of traditional sex roles are not absent from the cross-cultural literature, as Margaret Mead's (1935/1963) well-known study of three tribal societies in New Guinea revealed over half a century ago. Among the Arapesh, both men and women were trained to manifest "feminine" characteristics of cooperativeness, unaggressiveness, and responsiveness to the needs of others. Among the Mundugumore, both sexes were ruthless and aggressive and showed little evidence of parental caring and nurturance. Among the Tchambuli, a reversal of sex-stereotyped characteristics appeared. Women were trained to be dominant, impersonal, and assertive, while men were given less economic responsibility and were emotionally dependent and docile. Mead concluded that personality characteristics traditionally regarded as masculine and feminine could not be explained in biological terms, since cultural variations among these New Guinean tribespeople were so pronounced.

Mead's cross-cultural comparisons indicate that sex-role behavior is enormously malleable, but it can still be argued that cultural deviations from sex-stereotypic patterns of behavior are more the exception than the rule. Biological pressures may still be operating, manifesting themselves in behavior as long as cultural pressures against them are not extreme. Because cross-cultural research is inconclusive, in recent years scientists have turned to a direct examination of biological mechanisms that might be involved in moderating the sex-role development of boys and girls.

It is well known that genetic makeup and associated hormones have a direct effect on anatomical development of the sexes. Between the ninth and twelfth weeks of prenatal life, the presence of androgen hormones causes differentiation of the male genitalia in the fetus. In the absence of androgens, physical characteristics of the fetus are feminized (Moore, 1983). Again during puberty, an upsurge of sex hormones in varying balances regulates maturation of male and female primary and secondary sexual characteristics (see Chapter 5). In addition, sex hormones are known to affect central nervous system differentiation and neural activity in many animal species, and they probably do so in humans as well (McEwen, 1981). Can sex hormones, which so pervasively affect the development of bodily structures, be said to carry over to the development of sex-role behavior as well?

Animal research, in which hormone levels can be experimentally manipulated and studied for their effects on behavior, suggests that exposure to sex hormones during certain critical periods, such as the prenatal phase and puberty, does affect behavioral development. For example, prenatally administered androgens increase the incidence of rough-and-tumble play in both male and female nonhuman mammals. Androgens also induce male-typical sexual behavior, lessened maternal behavior, higher activity levels, and greater aggression in a wide variety of animal species

(Bardin & Catterall, 1981; Parsons, 1982; Quadagno, Briscoe, & Quadagno, 1977).

Ethical considerations preclude manipulating hormone levels in human subjects to find out if they have a generalized influence on sex-role behavior. Instead, human research is limited to circumstances in which hormone levels vary inadvertently or are modified for medical reasons. A classic series of investigations by Money and Ehrhardt involved such cases (Money & Ehrhardt, 1972; Ehrhardt & Baker, 1974; Ehrhardt, Epstein, & Money, 1968). They studied children afflicted with **adrenogenital syndrome (AGS),** a disorder in which prenatal exposure to unusually high levels of androgens or androgen-like hormones occurred. In some of the AGS subjects, a genetic defect caused the unborn child's adrenal system to malfunction. In others, the mother had been given a synthetic hormone during pregnancy to prevent miscarriage that had androgenizing consequences for the fetus. All of the girls were born with masculinized external genitalia. Most underwent surgical correction in infancy or childhood; a few experienced it in later life. In addition, those with genetic AGS were placed on continuous drug therapy to correct the hormonal imbalance.

Assessing gender-related behaviors by interviewing subjects and family members, the investigators found that AGS girls exhibited masculinized sex-role behavior. They preferred boys over girls as playmates; liked cars, trucks, and blocks better than dolls; showed little interest in fantasizing about traditional feminine roles such as bride and mother; and were less concerned about matters of appearance, such as clothing, jewelry, and hairstyle, than normal controls. In addition, both boys and girls with AGS showed heightened physical activity levels, as manifested by greater participation in active sports and outdoor games.

Money and Ehrhardt concluded from this evidence that prenatal androgen exposure is a biological factor that contributes significantly to the development of masculine sex-role behavior. However, their studies have been criticized for not ruling out the possibility that subtle environmental pressures were responsible for the differences found. For example, genital abnormalities, which in some cases were not corrected until well beyond infancy, may have caused family members to perceive afflicted girls as boyish and unfeminine and to treat them accordingly (Huston, 1983; Quadagno, Briscoe, & Quadagno, 1977). In addition, genetic AGS girls required prolonged medical contact to treat their condition. In the course of clinic visits they were given information about their disorder, and it is very likely that they were informed that menarche would be delayed and that as adults they might have difficulty conceiving a child. These girls may have shown little interest in fantasizing about the maternal role because they had reason to be unsure of their futures as women and mothers, not because of prenatal androgen exposure. In fact, a careful examination of Money and Ehrhardt's (1972) data indicates that girls with nongenetic AGS, who after surgical intervention required no further medical treatment, did not show the same degree of disinterest in fantasizing about marriage and motherhood as did the more severely affected genetic AGS subjects.

Studies of individuals exposed to abnormal levels of prenatal hormones, but without the consequence of genital abnormalities, eliminate some of the problems that plague the Money and Ehrhardt research. Although the majority of these investigations report no behavioral effects (Hines, 1982), a few lend support to Money and Ehrhardt's conclusions. For example, one study of children whose mothers took progesterone during pregnancy (which has androgen-like consequences) reported increases for both males and females in self-reported hostility and preference for aggressive solutions to problems on a questionnaire (Reinisch, 1981). Another reported a rise in activity level and participation in active sports (Ehrhardt, 1975), and a third found increases in stereotypically masculine personality characteristics such as independence, individualism, self-sufficiency, and self-assurance (Reinisch & Karow, 1977).

Taken together, research on hormonal variations suggests that biological differences between the sexes may affect the emergence of a variety of aspects of sex-role functioning. However, since none of the behavioral differences described above were very large, biological predispositions appear to be modest influences at best. In addition, it is important to keep in mind that even biological factors are subject to environmental modification. For example, in animals, environmental stress and social dominance have been found to increase the level of androgen production (Macrides, Bartke, & Dalterio, 1975; Rose, Holaday, & Bernstein, 1976).

Finally, some additional human research in which children were reared as members of the opposite sex because they had abnormal or ambiguous genitalia suggests that in the majority of cases, sex-role orientation is consistent with sex of rearing, irrespective of genetic sex (Baker, 1980). The most widely cited example of this strong "sex-of-rearing effect" is a longitudinal case study of a pair of identical twins described in Box 13.1. However, as you read about this study, you will see that it, too, is subject to varying interpretations and has provoked considerable controversy.

The only reasonable conclusion that can be drawn from the available evidence is one that we have arrived at many times before in earlier chapters of this book. As with other domains of development, there is no simple and easy answer to the question of why sex-role variations exist. Both hereditary and environmental factors appear to be important in the emergence of sex-role differentiation, but their independent contributions have proved difficult to disentangle in virtually all human studies. A challenging problem for future research will be to specify the exact nature of the relationships between biology and experience that underlie various aspects of sex-role development. In the final portion of this chapter, we will see that scientists have already begun to tackle this difficult task.

Environmental Influences on Children's Sex Stereotyping and Sex-Role Adoption

A large body of evidence indicates that even if biological predispositions are involved in human sex-role differentiation, environmental factors provide powerful support for children's early acquisition of sex-typed attitudes and behavior. As we will see in the sections that follow, adults view boys and girls differently, and they treat them differently. In addition, the social environments to which children are exposed on a daily basis provide them with plenty of opportunity to observe people behaving in ways that are consistent with widely held stereotypes. Finally, as soon as young children enter the world of the peer group, their playmates teach and reinforce conformity to sex-role standards of the larger cultural community.

Perceptions and Expectations of Adults. Sex-stereotyped perceptions of children exist in the "eye of the adult beholder," even when cues that could evoke them are absent from children's behavior. In several studies, researchers have asked adults to observe the behavior of children artificially labeled as boys or girls. When all else is held constant, people "see" qualities that fit with a child's artificially assigned sex. For example, in one study, college students viewed a crying baby as angrier if they thought it was a boy and more fearful if they thought it was a girl. In addition, the students rated the baby as slightly more active under the "boy" than the "girl" condition (Condry & Condry, 1976).

Studies of real parents reveal an even stronger tendency for children to be regarded in a sex-stereotypic fashion. Rubin, Provenzano, and Luria (1974) interviewed parents within the first 24 hours after the birth of their first child. Although their male and female newborns did not differ in weight, length, or Apgar scores, the parents clearly perceived them differently. Sons were rated as firmer, larger-featured, better-coordinated, more alert, stronger, and hardier, and daughters were regarded as softer, finer-featured, more awkward, more inattentive, weaker, and more delicate.

During childhood and adolescence parents continue to have different perceptions

Box 13.1
Can Sex-Role Socialization
Overcome Biology? A
Longitudinal Case Study of a Pair
of Identical Twins

During the 1970s, a study by John Money and Anke Ehrhardt (1972; Money & Tucker, 1975) of the development of a pair of identical twins captured the attention of scientists and the general public. It suggested that the path of sex-role development remained wide open during the first few years of life and that biological predispositions could be overcome by child-rearing conditions. The twins were born as normal males, but at 7 months one experienced a surgical mishap during circumcision. On the basis of medical advice, the parents made the decision to rear the child as a girl at 17 months of age. Surgical reconstruction as a female began soon after, and the medical team made plans to regulate growth and feminization at puberty with estrogen therapy. During childhood, the parents and their daughter visited the medical clinic annually for psychological support and guidance. Reports by the mother and observations of the child during these sessions provided insight into the girl's development in comparison to that of her twin brother.

The mother began to reorient the rearing of her new daughter by making a concerted effort to dress her in a feminine fashion. Within a year, the girl showed a clear preference for dresses over slacks and took pride in her long hair. At age 5, she asked for dolls, a doll house, and a doll carriage for Christmas; her twin brother asked for cars, gas pumps, and tools. The twins also expressed different future goals; the son wanted to be a fireman or

police officer, the daughter a doctor or a teacher. But despite her feminine characteristics, the girl was also reported to have a variety of tom-boyish traits, such as abundant physical energy and dominative behavior toward peers, which persisted even in the face of repeated efforts by her mother to discourage them.

On the basis of this as well as other cases involving children with ambiguous or traumatized genitalia, Money and Ehrhardt (1972) concluded that gender reassignment is easily accomplished in the first 3 to 4 years of life, during which time socialization practices can successfully mask biological propensities. After this sensitive phase, they regarded gender reassignment as difficult if not impossible to achieve.

However, as Money and Ehrhardt's subjects moved closer to maturity, some investigators began to take issue with their conclusions. In a follow-up of the twin girl at age 13, Diamond (1982) described her as "beset with problems" (p. 183). Despite estrogen therapy, she looked somewhat masculine, seemed ambivalent about her gender status, aspired to be a mechanic, and expressed the belief that boys have a better life. In addition, she was regarded as an unhappy adolescent and had difficulty making friends. Diamond believes that the girl's status at adolescence indicates that biology is the primary organizing force in sex-role functioning and sets limits on the degree of gender variation that any person can display.

Other research suggests, in agreement with Diamond's conclusion, that sex-role orientation consistent with biological sex and prenatal hormone exposure will prevail at adolescence, especially if genetically programmed pubertal events are al-

lowed to run their course. Imperato-McGinley and her colleagues (1979) studied a group of 38 genetic males from three rural villages in the Dominican Republic who, due to the inheritance of a recessive trait, were born with feminine-appearing external genitalia. Eighteen of them were raised as girls, yet during adolescence when masculinization of their bodies occurred, nearly all successfully switched to the male sex role. Without feminine hormone therapy at puberty, the effect of androgens predominated in these individuals, overriding their prior rearing history. Imperato-McGinley concluded, in contrast to Money and Ehrhardt, that successful gender reassignment can take place well beyond the early childhood years — during adolescence and even adulthood — as long as it is consistent with the individual's biological makeup.

But Imperato-McGinley's findings have also been challenged! The genital appearance of her Dominican subjects was not that of a completely normal female, and the culture allowed common river bathing and did little to assure physical privacy. As a result, their unusual genitals were probably known to others, and their rearing may not have been as singularly feminine as Imperato-McGinley assumed (Rubin, Reinisch, & Haskett, 1981). These individuals may have been confused and ambivalent about their gender identity for many years before most of them settled into a masculine orientation.

In answer to the question, "Can sex-role socialization overcome biology?" Money and Ehrhardt respond affirmatively, Diamond and Imperato-McGinley negatively. This issue, as well as the question of whether there is an early sensitive period for gender reassignment, remains unresolved.

and expectations of their sons and daughters. They persist in interpreting the behaviors of boys and girls in stereotypical ways (Fagot, 1981), want their preschoolers to play with "sex-appropriate" toys (Schau et al., 1980), and voice beliefs that boys and girls should be raised differently. For example, when asked about their child-rearing values, parents describe achievement, competitiveness, and the control of emotional expression as important for boys, and warmth, "ladylike" behavior, and close supervision of activities as important for girls (Block, 1983). Despite increased attention given to women's rights, parental expectations for boys and girls have changed very little during the last several decades (Emihovich, Gaier, & Cronin, 1984; Brooks-Gunn, 1986). Furthermore, in several studies, men's stereotyped perceptions and expectations of children were found to be more extreme than those of women (Fagot, 1981; Rubin, Provenzano, & Luria, 1974).

Differential Treatment by Parents. Do adults actually treat children in accord with their stereotypical beliefs? Using the same basic procedure described earlier in which a child's gender is artificially assigned — only this time, the adult is asked to interact with the baby in a laboratory playroom — investigators have found that differential treatment *does* emanate from adults' stereotypical views of boys and girls. Adults play in a masculine way with a baby they think is a boy and in a feminine way with one they think is a girl. For example, the toys offered are influenced by the infant's gender label (Frisch, 1977; Sidorowicz & Lunney, 1980), and adults encourage girl babies to engage in more "nurturance play" with dolls and puppets than boys (Frisch, 1977).

Similar findings appear when parents' interaction with their own children is studied. Parents more often encourage gross motor activity in boy than girl babies (Smith & Lloyd, 1978), and they are more likely to respond contingently to the smiles, babbles, and reaches of infant sons than daughters (Parke & Sawin, 1976; Yarrow, 1975). By the second year of life, parents react favorably to sex-stereotypic and negatively to "cross-sex" play and behavior. In one study, parents and their young

Observations of parents interacting with their own children indicate that toys offered are strongly influenced by the baby's sex. (Linda Hirsch)

toddlers were observed as they went about their daily activities at home. Mothers and fathers differentially reinforced boys and girls in a sex-stereotypic fashion for a great many behaviors, including block play, doll play, large motor activities of running and jumping, assisting with household tasks, and seeking help and physical closeness (Fagot, 1978).

During the preschool and elementary school years, parental treatment of sons and daughters undergoes further differentiation as children's behavioral skills expand and issues of achievement, independence, and exploration of environments beyond the home become increasingly salient (Block, 1978). Observations of parents interacting with their youngsters in teaching situations show that higher levels of independent task performance are demanded from boys than from girls. For example, parents are more likely to respond quickly to girls' requests for help on cognitive tasks, while they more often ignore or actively refuse to respond to similar requests from boys (Rothbart & Rothbart, 1976). When parents do provide help in achievement situations to children of both sexes, they do so in very different ways. They behave in a more task-oriented, mastery-emphasizing fashion with sons, setting higher standards and pointing out important cognitive elements of the task. In contrast, parents often use a teaching situation with a girl to cement a positive but dependent interpersonal relationship. For example, they will digress from a task-oriented agenda to joke and play with a daughter more often than they will with a son (Block, Block, & Harrington, 1975). In addition, parents frequently interrupt the conversational initiatives of daughters and talk simultaneously with them, subtly delivering the message that what a girl has to say is of little consequence. They tend to let sons finish their statements before responding (Grief, 1979).

In middle childhood, boys are allowed to range farther from home without adult supervision than are girls. In a study of over 700 English children whose mothers were interviewed about supervision of children's whereabouts and activities, girls were more often picked up after school or required to go home directly and less often permitted to be at home in the absence of an adult. In addition, girls more often brought friends into the house instead of playing in the neighborhood (Newson & Newson, 1976). While girls are generally assigned chores, such as food preparation, cleaning, and babysitting, that keep them close to home, boys are often given responsibilities that take them into the surrounding world, such as yard work and running errands (Saegert & Hart, 1976; Whiting & Edwards, 1974).

Earlier we noted that fathers more than mothers view children in sex-stereotypic ways. Similarly, in most aspects of parental behavior in which differential treatment of boys and girls occurs, fathers are the ones who differentiate the most. For example, fathers engage in far more active, physically stimulating play with boy as opposed to girl babies than do mothers (Parke & Suomi, 1980; Yogman, 1981). By 15 months of age fathers vocalize twice as much to their sons as to their daughters, and fathers are twice as interactive with their sons as mothers are (Lamb, 1977). In childhood, there is greater sex differentiation in encouragement for cognitive performance by fathers than mothers. In addition, when physical punishment is meted out by a parent, boys are targets of it more often than girls, and fathers generally deliver it (Jacklin & Maccoby, 1983). The greater pressure exerted by fathers to get children to conform to sex-role expectations is dramatically illustrated by the findings of a study reported in Box 13.2 in which parental reactions to children's "sex-appropriate" as well as "inappropriate" play in a laboratory were observed.

Parents also seem to feel an especially strong commitment to assure the sex-role socialization of the child of their own gender. While mothers go on shopping excursions and bake cookies with their daughters, fathers play catch, help coach the Saturday morning soccer game, and take fishing trips with their sons. The special significance of the same-sex parent-child relationship in sex-role socialization may be partly responsible for the finding that among children of divorced parents, boys in father-absent and girls in mother-absent homes are less sex-stereotyped in their activity and play preferences (Santrock, Warshak, & Elliott, 1982; Stevenson & Black, 1988). Furthermore, this same-sex child bias is another aspect of sex-role socialization that is more pronounced for fathers than it is for mothers. When asked in an interview if certain parts of a child's rearing belonged to one parent or the other, parents of boys indicated that fathers have a special responsibility to serve as role models and play companions to their sons (Fagot, 1974).

What are the developmental implications of parents' differential treatment of boys and girls? Block (1983) suggests that important sex differences in cognitive abilities may accrue from the fact that boys' toys (e.g., blocks, chemistry sets, and model airplanes) encourage manipulation, inventive possibilities, and feedback from the physical world, whereas girls' toys (e.g., dolls, dress-up clothing, and tea sets) emphasize imitation and offer fewer opportunities for discovery and innovation. In addition, parental help-giving and communicative patterns are likely to convey subtle messages to girls that they are less competent and that their achievement efforts are less important than those of boys. Finally, parents' more intense surveillance of their daughter's whereabouts may lead girls to miss important opportunities for developing feelings of independence, self-reliance, and confidence about venturing beyond the family milieu into the wider world.

FOCUS ON THEORY, RESEARCH, AND APPLICATIONS

Box 13.2
The Special Place of Fathers in Sex-Role Socialization

Theory. Recent theorists of sex-role socialization suggest that fathers serve as the primary tutors of sex-typed behavior during the childhood years (e.g., Johnson, 1981). Mothers, because of their expressive orientation, are thought to treat children of both sexes nurturantly and supportively. In contrast, fathers are believed to differentiate at an early age, assuming the special responsibility of pushing sons in the direction of an instrumental role. To test these assumptions, Judith Langlois and Chris Downs (1980) watched closely to see how mothers and fathers reacted when their 3- to 5-year-old sons and daughters played with "sex-appropriate" as well as "sex-inappropriate" toys.

Research. Preschool children came to a laboratory, some with their mothers and others with their fathers. Each child and parent participated in two short play sessions. In one, children were asked by the experimenter to play with a set of highly masculine toys as boys would. In a second, they were given a set of highly feminine toys and asked to play with

them as girls would. After each child had begun to play, the mother or father was permitted to enter the room, and play behavior as well as parental reactions to it were recorded.

The results revealed that mothers were generally warm, expressive, and

Fathers exert more pressure than mothers to get children to conform to sex-role expectations, especially with their sons. (Janice Fullman/The Picture Cube)

nurturant to children of both sexes, regardless of which type of toys they happened to be playing with. In contrast, fathers' reactions varied sharply between the two play sessions. When children engaged in "sex-appropriate" play, the fathers were rewarding—smiling, praising, talking pleasantly, and joining in the child's play. When "sex-inappropriate" play occurred, the fathers reacted punitively by taking toys away, shaking their heads "no," frowning in disgust, or directing other negative verbal communications to the child. These differential reactions were especially pronounced among fathers who participated in play sessions with their sons.

Applications. Langlois and Downs's research suggests that fathers' role in the socialization of traditionally sex-typed behaviors is important, more so than that of mothers (however, evidence reviewed elsewhere in this chapter indicates that the role of mothers cannot be discounted). In an era of transition away from sex-stereotypic values and behavior, modification of paternal treatment of sons and daughters may be especially crucial for opening up a wider array of role possibilities for boys and girls.

Differential Treatment by Teachers. Parents are not the only agents of socialization who encourage sex-stereotypic behaviors in children. Teachers do so as well, but to some extent they do so in different ways than parents. Schools are often thought of as feminine-oriented environments in which quiet, passive obedience is rewarded and assertiveness is discouraged. This "feminine bias" is believed to promote discomfort for boys in elementary school classrooms. However, it may be equally or even more harmful for girls, who willingly comply with typical classroom demands for passivity and conformity, with possible long-term negative consequences for their sense of independence and self-esteem (Huston, 1983). In support of the feminine bias of school environments, the findings of many studies indicate that preschool and elementary school teachers positively reinforce children of both sexes for "feminine" rather than "masculine" instructional and play activities (Brophy & Good, 1974; Etaugh, Collins, & Gerson, 1975; Fagot, 1985a; Fagot & Patterson, 1969; Oettingen, 1985; Robinson & Canaday, 1978). Surprisingly, experienced male teachers do so as strenuously as female teachers (Fagot, 1985a; Robinson & Canaday, 1978).

At the same time, teachers act in ways that serve to maintain or even increase the sex-typed patterns of behavior that have already been fostered in the home. For example, when introducing new materials into the preschool, teachers call on boys rather than girls to demonstrate how to use a masculine-stereotyped item, thereby contributing to sex-typed activity preferences (Serbin, Connor, & Iler, 1979). Teachers also differentially reinforce social behaviors in male and female pupils. Fagot and her colleagues (1985) observed the interaction of teachers with very young children who were participants in toddler play groups. The teachers reacted to the children's social initiatives in terms of sex stereotypes. They attended to boys' assertive behaviors (e.g., pushing another child, grabbing a toy, crying or whining for attention) by talking to them, giving them a new toy, or physically moving them. Comparable behaviors were ignored in girls. In contrast, girls' less intense social initiatives, such as gestures, gentle touches, and talking, were responded to more often than the same behaviors of boys. Although the children in this study did not differ in their use of communicative acts at the start of the play groups, when they were observed nine months later, there were clear sex differences in behavior. The boys were more assertive, and the girls talked to teachers more.

During the preschool and elementary school years, teachers discourage aggressive acts and other forms of misbehavior in children of both sexes, but they do so more loudly, emphatically, and frequently for boys (Etaugh & Harlow, 1975; Serbin et al., 1973). Teachers' greater scolding and disapproval of boys seems to result from their expectation that boys will misbehave more often than girls, a belief based partly on real behavioral differences that have emerged during the early childhood years and partly on stereotypical beliefs about the sexes (Huston, 1983).

A series of natural experiments conducted by Serbin and her colleagues in preschool classrooms reveals that changing teacher reinforcement contingencies and cues about the sex-appropriateness of play activities can quickly modify the way that boys and girls respond at school. For example, when teachers introduce new play materials nonstereotypically, as appropriate for children of both sexes, or reinforce pupils when they show independence and persistence and ignore attention-seeking and dependency, children's behavior changes accordingly (Serbin, Connor, & Iler, 1979; Serbin, Connor, & Citron, 1978). Also, when teachers move out of "feminine" activity areas, such as fine motor skills and arts and crafts (where they tend to spend most of their time) and locate themselves in male-preferred contexts such as the block and transportation toy centers, children follow their lead (Serbin, Connor, & Citron, 1981). However, girls are more responsive to teacher-delivered contingencies than boys, even when male teachers provide the feedback. Furthermore, changes in children's behavior as a result of teacher interventions are transient and short-lived, for as soon as the usual reinforcement patterns are permitted to reassert themselves in the classroom, children's activity choices and behavior rapidly return to their former levels. Traditional sex-role behaviors of young children, once acquired, are extremely tenacious and difficult to modify in any lasting fashion, especially among boys.

Observational Learning. In addition to direct pressures from adults, a wide variety of models of sex-stereotypic behavior are readily available in children's everyday social environments. As Huston (1983) points out,

> Although American society has changed to some degree, most adults continue to manifest sex-stereotyped patterns of household responsibility, occupational activity, recreational interests, and achievement. The average child sees women cooking, cleaning, and sewing; working in "female" jobs such as clerical, secretarial, sales, teaching, nursing; choosing to dance, sew, or play bridge for recreation; and achieving in artistic or literary areas more often than in science and engineering. That same child sees men mowing the lawn, washing the car, or doing household repairs; working in "male" occupations . . . choosing team sports, fishing, and nights with "the boys" for recreation; and achieving in math, science, and technical areas more often than in poetry or art. In school, the teachers of young children are women; the teachers of older students and the administrators with power are usually men. Peers and siblings pursue sex-stereotyped activities, games, and interests more often than they engage in cross-sex activity. Hence, although there are some individual differences, most children are exposed continually in their own environments to models of sex-stereotyped activities, interests, and roles. (pp. 420–421)

Not only do many real people with whom the child comes in contact conform to traditional sex-role expectations, but media portrayal, as we shall see in Chapter 15, is highly sex-stereotypic as well. Little overall change in the way that males and

Teachers can reduce sex-stereotyped behavior in the classroom by moving out of "feminine" activity areas and spending more time in male-preferred contexts. (Linda Hirsch)

females are represented in television programs has taken place in recent years (Huston, 1983). Moreover, content analyses of children's storybooks and textbooks reveal that they commonly portray males and females in traditional roles. In the majority of books, boys and men far outnumber girls and women as main characters, and males take center stage in most of the exciting and adventurous plot activities. Females, when they do appear as important characters, are generally engaged in such "feminine" pursuits as housekeeping and caring for children. Although more sex-equitable reading materials for children have become available in recent years, school texts have been particularly slow to change (Scott & Schau, 1985).

Modeling not only encourages conformity to sex stereotypes, but promotes nonstereotypic behavior as well. Children who see their parents behaving in a nonstereotypic fashion on a day-to-day basis — mothers who work and fathers who take over household and child care responsibilities — are less sex-stereotyped in their views of men and women (Carlson, 1984; Selkow, 1984; Weinraub et al., 1984). Furthermore, girls who have career-oriented mothers show a number of changes in sex-role behavior. They more often engage in typically masculine pursuits such as physically active play, and they report higher educational aspirations as well as more nontraditional career choices (Hoffman, 1984; Tauber, 1979). We will take up the relationship of maternal employment to child development in greater detail in Chapter 14.

Peer Influences. Once children's sex-typed play preferences start to emerge, peers do a great deal to maintain them. Observations of preschool children in both laboratory settings and natural environments reveal that by age 3, children positively reinforce one another for sex-typed play by praising, approving, imitating, or joining in the activity of an agemate who exhibits the "gender-appropriate" response (Fagot & Patterson, 1969; Langlois & Downs, 1980). This encouragement comes primarily from peers of the same sex, although preschool boys do send messages of approval to girls for sticking to stereotypically feminine activities (Lamb & Roopnarine, 1979). Similarly, when preschoolers engage in "sex-inappropriate" play — for example, when boys play with dolls or girls with the woodworking tools — they receive criticism and social ostracism from their peers. Social rejection is greater for boys than girls who frequently cross gender lines. Their male peers ignore them even when they enter masculine activities (Fagot, 1977a). Due to these reinforcement contingencies, preschoolers quickly learn to inhibit "cross-sex" play as soon as a peer arrives on the scene (Serbin et al., 1979).

Same-sex peers reinforce one another for "sex-appropriate" play, and in reciprocal fashion, similar play interests bring like-sex children together, creating a mutually supportive system that serves to perpetuate and strengthen sex-typed behaviors. **Sex cleavage** in social interaction — the tendency of boys to play with boys and girls to play with girls — is one of the most conspicuous characteristics of children's peer associations, and it surfaces surprisingly early in development. More frequent interaction with same-sex peers is already evident at age 2 when children are just beginning to play socially with one another (Jacklin & Maccoby, 1978; La Freniere, Strayer, & Gauthier, 1984). While sex cleavage is sustained by, as well as contributes to, stereotypical play choices, adults also promote it. Beginning in toddlerhood, mothers more often seek out same-sex than opposite-sex playmates for their children (Lewis et al., 1975). In addition, teachers frequently organize groups of children by gender — asking the girls to line up for snack time, library period, or outdoor play first, followed by the boys, or vice versa.

Sex cleavage is found in a wide variety of cultures and also characterizes the peer interaction of nonhuman juvenile primates (Rosenblum, Coe, & Bromley, 1975; Sackett, 1970). Consequently, the pattern is regarded by some investigators as a biologically determined, natural, and normal aspect of children's development. However, same-sex interaction can easily be modified environmentally. This can be done on a short-term basis by having teachers comment approvingly when mixed-sex pairs

Children's preference for peer companions of the same sex appears early in development and increases over the course of middle childhood. (Richard Hutchings)

or groups of children play together (Serbin, Tonick, & Sternglanz, 1977). Mixed-sex interaction is sustained on a long-term basis in nontraditional classrooms where transmission of nonstereotyped values to children is an important part of the school curriculum (Berk & Lewis, 1977; Bianchi & Bakeman, 1978; Lockheed, 1986).[3] Mixed-sex play can also be promoted by changing the design of preschool environments. In one study, a wall of shelves separating the housekeeping and block areas was removed so that these two sex-typed play contexts were joined. In response to the change, boys and girls interacted much more often with one another (Kinsman & Berk, 1979). Encouraging cooperative mixed-sex play appears to be a vital means for broadening the developmental possibilities of children of both genders. It reduces sex-stereotyped activity choices and increases children's exposure to behavioral styles generally deemed "appropriate" for the opposite sex (Lloyd & Smith, 1985).

In the absence of interventions deliberately aimed at modifying same-sex peer interaction, such interaction increases over the course of middle childhood, reaching a peak in early adolescence, at which time it begins to decline as interest in members of the opposite sex accompanies the physical changes of puberty (Hartup, 1983). During the elementary school years, sex cleavage continues to be related to sex-typed variations in the play behaviors of boys and girls. Around the neighborhood, boys congregate in larger groups than girls. Roughhousing, vigorous bike riding, animated snowball fights, and ball games are typical pastimes of these young male gatherings. Girls more often play in pairs, and the friendships they develop are more exclusive and intimate than those of boys. In addition, the outdoor activities of female play-mates in the middle childhood years — hopscotch, cartwheels, jump rope, and cheer-leading practice — are considerably more tranquil than those of their male counter-parts.

[3] You may wish to turn back to Chapter 2, Box 2.2, to reread the summary of Bianchi and Bakeman's (1978) study of same- and mixed-sex play in a traditional and open school.

Sibling Influences. Growing up with siblings of the same or opposite gender also affects sex typing. However, sibling influences are more complex than peer influences, because their impact is moderated by other family configurational variables, such as birth order and family size.

If sibling effects operated just like peer influences, we might expect a family of same-sex siblings to encourage stereotyped interests and behavior among one another and a family of mixed-sex siblings to do just the opposite. Some evidence exists to support this prediction. In a classic study that examined sibling influences on sex typing, Brim (1958) analyzed teacher ratings of several hundred 5- and 6-year-old children on a great many masculine and feminine attributes. Children with same-sex siblings were viewed as having more "sex-appropriate" traits than those with opposite-sex siblings. The effect was especially pronounced for the younger members of sibling pairs. Similar results emerged in a recent naturalistic study of the play behaviors of 4- to 9-year-old sibling pairs in their homes. Play activities selected by same-sex siblings were highly sex-typed. However, among opposite-sex sibling pairs, play choices were determined by the gender of the older child. Girls with older brothers engaged in more "masculine" activities and boys with older sisters in more "feminine" activities. In fact, the effect was so strong that boys with older sisters actually played "house" and "dolls" as much as pairs of sisters did. In contrast, boys with older brothers never engaged in such pursuits (Stoneman, Brody, & MacKinnon, 1986).

But curiously, other research directly contradicts these findings. For example, Tauber (1979) videotaped 8- and 9-year-old children while each played with toys in a laboratory. In her study, play with "opposite-sex" toys was more common among children who came from families where all of the siblings were of the same gender. Similarly, several other studies report that individuals with same-sex siblings have less sex-typed interests and personality characteristics than those from mixed-gender families (Grotevant, 1978; Leventhal, 1970). How can such puzzling and conflicting results be explained?

Recall from Chapter 10 that an important *within-family* environmental influence on children's personality development is that siblings often strive to be different from one another in order to win recognition for their own uniqueness.[4] This effect is most pronounced when children are of the same sex and when they come from large families. A close look at the studies reported above reveals that those investigations that report a *modeling and reinforcement effect* (an increase in sex typing among same-sex siblings) were limited to children from small, two-child families. In contrast, those that report a *differentiation effect* included children from large families. In the latter studies, an older sibling of the same sex may have provided an effective sex-typed model, but the younger child may not have responded to it out of a need to be different or a reluctance to compete with an older sibling in an area where that child was already quite competent.

It is also possible that parents may relax pressures toward sex typing among offspring of the same sex. The results of one study are consistent with this idea. When asked to choose gifts for their younger children, mothers more often selected "opposite-sex" toys if the child's older sibling was of the same gender (Stoneman, Brody, & MacKinnon, 1986). Furthermore, in all-girl and all-boy families, children are more likely to be encouraged to take on "cross-sex" household responsibilities. In such families, girls may be asked to mow the lawn and take out the garbage, and boys to cook and wash the dishes, because no "gender-appropriate" child is available to do the job! Thus, families in which siblings are all of the same sex may provide some special opportunities for expansion of traditional sex roles.

In summary, beginning at a very early age adults treat boys and girls differently. Parents encourage infants and children to engage in sex-stereotypic play activities,

---

[4] You may wish to return to Chapter 10, pages 433–434, to refresh your memory about within-family environmental influences on personality development.

and they promote independence, assertiveness, and cognitive mastery among boys and nurturant, dependent behavior among girls. Fathers make these sex-typed distinctions to a greater degree than do mothers, and fathers also show a special concern for the instrumentally oriented socialization of their sons. Traditional sex-role learning receives further support from teachers and playmates as children enter the world of the school and peer group. Sibling influences on sex typing are less straightforward than other environmental influences. Sibling effects may vary considerably, depending on how several family configurational variables combine with one another, including gender mixture, birth order, and family size.

SEX-ROLE IDENTITY

So far, we have considered biological predispositions and a wide array of environmental pressures as important factors in children's acquisition of sex-role preferences and behaviors. An additional variable that eventually comes to moderate children's sex typed patterns of responding is *sex-role identity*, which we defined at the beginning of this chapter as a person's perception of the self as relatively masculine or feminine in characteristics. In the sections that follow, we consider how children's sex-role identity develops. In addition, we look at the implications of individual differences in the content of children's self-perceptions for their general psychological adjustment and behavior.

Masculinity, Femininity, and Androgyny

The first studies of sex-role identity assumed that all normally developing, well-adjusted individuals viewed themselves as either masculine or feminine in attributes —whichever happened to be congruent with their biological gender. By the 1970s, it became apparent that this assumption was incorrect. First, not all traditionally sex-typed individuals turned out to be pictures of psychological health. In 1970, Broverman and her colleagues asked psychologists experienced in treating people for adjustment problems to rate a series of stereotypically masculine and feminine attributes in terms of how well they represented the characteristics of a "mature, healthy, socially competent" individual. The masculine items were regarded as far healthier than the feminine ones. Furthermore, an accumulating body of evidence indicated that most people regarded masculine instrumental attributes as more desirable than feminine ones (e.g., Rosenkrantz et al., 1968). Taken together, these findings suggested that a masculine-oriented male was advantaged in psychological adjustment over a feminine-oriented female, probably because masculine attributes are essential for positions of power and prestige in society.

Moreover, additional research revealed that many men and women did not view themselves in a traditionally sex-typed fashion. In 1974, Sandra Bem presented evidence that around 30 to 40 percent of people have an **androgynous** sex-role identity. When given a list of masculine and feminine attributes and asked to indicate how well each describes themselves, androgynous people score high on both sets of characteristics (Bem, 1974; 1977). Bem hypothesized that a person with a mixed or androgynous identity would be particularly advantaged in psychological adjustment. An androgynous orientation, she reasoned, should permit greater behavioral adaptability—masculine independence as well as feminine nurturance, depending on what the situation calls for—than a traditional sex-role orientation, which is narrower and more inhibiting in its behavioral possibilities.

The first studies to examine the behavioral correlates of androgyny indicated that androgynous people did show greater psychological well-being and behavioral flexibility than either traditionally sex-typed individuals or those who identified weakly with the attributes of both sex roles. For example, androgynous subjects comfortably displayed "cross-sex" behavior (Bem, 1975), and they scored higher in self-esteem

(Bem, 1977; Spence, Helmreich, & Stapp, 1975) and maturity of moral judgment than individuals with other sex-role identities (Block, 1973).

But as more research on androgyny accumulated, Bem's ideas were challenged. When a large number of studies reporting on a diverse array of adjustment measures were carefully examined, masculine-oriented individuals again appeared advantaged. Furthermore, the masculine component of androgyny was found to be largely responsible for the superior psychological health of androgynous females over those with traditional sex-role identities (Taylor & Hall, 1982; Whitley, 1983; 1985).

Nevertheless, the studies of androgyny clearly demonstrated that individuals vary considerably in the content of their sex-role orientations. Possessing masculine attributes does not preclude the adoption of feminine ones; being independent, forceful, and interested in baseball and science does not mean that one cannot also be affectionate, compassionate, and interested in cooking and poetry as well. Moreover, in a futuristic society in which feminine characteristics are socially rewarded to the same degree as masculine ones, androgynous individuals may very well excel in psychological health. Perhaps a blend of masculine and feminine attributes does represent the ideal personality, even though the feminine side is not valued as much as the masculine one in our present-day culture.

The Development of Sex-Role Identity

How do children develop sex-role identities that consist of varying mixtures of traditionally masculine and feminine characteristics? Both social learning and cognitive-developmental answers to this question exist. Social learning theory stresses that *behavior is primary.* Modeling and reinforcement of sex-typed responses cause children to learn society's rules for gender-related behavior, which are accepted as appropriate for the self. In contrast, cognitive-developmental theory emphasizes that *behavior is secondary to thought.* Children actively organize their experiences into gender-linked perceptions of themselves. Once formed, these self-perceptions serve as cognitive plans for action, and children strive to behave in ways that are consistent with their cognitive structures.

According to cognitive-developmental theory, the development of sex-role identity begins with **gender constancy,** an appreciation of the fact that one's own gender is a permanent dimension of the self that does not change with superficial variations in appearance or characteristics. Cognitive-developmental theorists assume that before children understand that their gender is permanent, they do not engage in sex-typed behavior, because no consistent cognitive structure is available to guide and sustain it. But once children attain gender constancy, they are believed to use this knowledge as the basis for forming a sex-role identity. From the vast array of alternatives available in the environment, they actively select preferences and values that fit with their own gender, and they start to pattern their behavior after same-sex models judged similar to the self.

Cognitive-developmental and social learning theory lead to different predictions about sex-role development. The cognitive-developmental viewpoint assumes that sex-typed behavior follows after gender constancy, while social learning theory states that the behavior is there first. Before we look at what research says about the accuracy of these two hypotheses, let's trace the emergence of gender constancy during the early childhood years.

The Emergence of Gender Constancy. Lawrence Kohlberg (1966) first proposed that between the ages of 2 and 7 children gradually acquire a cognitive appreciation of the constancy of their own gender by moving through three stages of development:

1. **Gender labeling** (about 2–3½ years). During this stage, the child learns such sex-linked verbal labels as man, boy, lady, and girl and applies them systematically to

the self and others. But below the age of 3½ children can only label their gender correctly. They do not understand its constancy. When asked such questions as "When you (a girl) grow up, could you ever be a daddy?" or "Could you be a boy if you wanted to?" children of this stage freely answer yes (Slaby & Frey, 1975). In addition, when shown a doll whose hairstyle and clothing are transformed before their eyes, young children believe that the doll's sex is no longer the same (Marcus & Overton, 1978). Even when the doll's clothing is transparent and children can see a girl's genitals beneath masculine clothing or a boy's genitals beneath feminine clothing, children of this stage still think the gender of the doll fits with its most obvious outward appearance (McConaghy, 1979). Genital differences, hidden beneath clothing and observed far less than other gender-linked attributes, are of little importance in the preschool child's definition of male and female.

2. **Gender stability** (about 3½ – 4½ years). During this intermediate stage, children have a partial understanding of the permanence of their own gender. They grasp the constancy of gender across time — its *temporal stability*. However, their knowledge of gender constancy is still incomplete and contradictory. Although they know that male and female babies eventually become boys and girls and men and women, they continue to assert, as they did at younger ages, that changing hairstyle, clothing, and "sex-appropriate" activities will lead a person to switch genders as well (Coker, 1984; Fagot, 1985b; Slaby & Frey, 1975).

3. **Gender consistency.** Sometime between 4 and 7 years of age, children become certain of the *situational consistency* of their sex (Marcus & Overton, 1978; Siegal & Robinson, 1987). They know that their gender will remain the same, even if on a particular occasion they decide to dress in an "opposite-sex" fashion or engage in "cross-sex" activities. At first, children demonstrate a preliminary understanding of gender consistency. They answer motivational questions correctly (e.g., "If you really wanted to be a [member of the opposite sex], could you be?"). However, they are still influenced by irrelevant perceptual variations in a person's clothing or hairstyle (Marcus & Overton, 1978). Around the same time that children begin to pass Piagetian conservation problems, they also grasp the unchangeability of their gender in the face of "opposite-sex" transformations in appearance and behavior (DeVries, 1974; Kohlberg, 1966; Marcus & Overton, 1978). As further evidence for the cognitive basis of this stage, 7-year-olds usually justify gender consistency with explanations that reflect concrete operational reasoning (e.g., "The clothes a person wears don't make a difference; if you're born a girl, you're still a girl"). Four-year-olds, even when they happen to give a correct answer to a gender consistency question, are seldom able to justify it (Emmerich, 1981).

Around 7 to 9 years of age, children are fully aware that their sex is solely determined by their genitals (McConaghy, 1979; Thompson & Bentler, 1971). From a myriad of gender-linked characteristics, they have isolated the constant physical features that define their sex, and knowledge of gender constancy is complete.

How Well Does Gender Constancy Predict Sex-Role Preferences and Behavior? Is cognitive-developmental theory correct that gender constancy is the single major determinant of sex-role behavior during the childhood years? From findings that we discussed earlier in this chapter, perhaps you have already concluded that the evidence for this assertion is weak. Long before the ages of 4 to 7, children show sex-typed activity choices and behaviors and are aware of a diverse array of societal sex stereotypes. In the case of modeling, even children at the lower two stages of development prefer to imitate the behavior of same-sex rather than opposite-sex adults. Furthermore, same-sex modeling appears to be determined by social learning, for boys exhibit it to a greater extent than girls, and we have already seen that boys receive more systematic reinforcement than girls for conforming to sex-stereotypic expectations (Bussey & Bandura, 1984).

Sex-typed behaviors appear so early in development that direct reinforcement and modeling must be of formative importance in the early preschool years. But even though gender constancy is not a prerequisite for sex typing, some of the cognitive acquisitions that precede and contribute to it may facilitate the child's tendency to respond to the world in sex-linked terms. In two recent investigations, Fagot and her colleagues (Fagot, 1985b; Fagot, Leinbach, & Hagan, 1986) found that children who had attained the stage of gender labeling differed in sex-role behaviors from those who had not. Those who used gender labels correctly played more often with sex-stereotypic toys and same-sex peers. In addition, girls who succeeded at a gender labeling task showed lower rates of aggression in their play with other children than girls who did not use gender labels consistently, whereas no such difference occurred for boys. Fagot's findings suggest that as soon as children become aware of the gender category to which they belong, they actively modify their behavior, bringing it into conformity with sex-typed expectations.

If a complete understanding of gender constancy is not necessary for the adoption of sex-typed behaviors, then just what role, if any, does it play in children's sex-role development? Researchers are continuing to explore this question. One speculation is that instead of increasing conformity to societal standards, gender constancy may free children to experiment with "opposite sex" choices during the period of middle childhood. Prior to attaining gender constancy, children may engage in behaviors that fit with their own sex because they believe that doing so is what makes them a boy or a girl. Once gender constancy is achieved, they understand that their gender will remain the same regardless of their sex-role preferences. As a result, nonstereotypic activity choices and behaviors become less threatening (Huston, 1983; Marcus & Overton, 1978). There is some research to support this idea. In the early elementary school years, children's understanding of gender constancy is positively related to the number of sex-stereotypic attributes they rate as appropriate for both sexes (Urberg, 1979). In addition, gender-constant youngsters understand that the adoption of sex-typed behaviors is ultimately a matter of individual choice, whereas non-gender-constant children tend to view it as a rigid necessity (Ullian, 1976).

The Development of Sex-Role Identity During Middle Childhood and Adolescence. Once children enter elementary school, researchers use questionnaires much like those given to adults to find out how their masculine, feminine, and androgynous self-perceptions change with age. A finding that appears repeatedly in such studies is that boys' and girls' sex-role identities follow different paths of development. From third to sixth grade, boys strengthen their identification with a same-sex, masculine role. They describe a greater number of stereotypically masculine attributes (e.g., active, adventurous, persevering, independent) as typical of themselves. In contrast, girls' identification with same-sex, feminine characteristics (e.g., kind, gentle, emotionally expressive) declines over the same age period, and they begin to adopt some "opposite-sex" traits. Girls' overall orientation still leans toward the feminine side, but they identify with a more diverse mixture of characteristics than boys, and they are clearly the more androgynous of the sexes (Hall & Halberstadt, 1980). In early adolescence, an upsurge in same-sex orientation occurs for both sexes. This diminishes by the college years, although it does so to a greater extent for females than it does for males (Leahy & Eiter, 1980).

Children's activity preferences and behaviors show similar developmental patterns. Girls, unlike boys, do not continue to increase in their preference for "sex-appropriate" interests and activities during middle childhood. Instead, they do some exploring of "masculine" pursuits—participating in organized sports, taking up science projects, and building forts in the backyard (Huston-Stein & Higgins-Trenk, 1978). Then a temporary return to same-sex interests emerges in early adolescence

During middle childhood, girls feel freer than boys to engage in "opposite-sex" pursuits. These preadolescent girls participate in a team sport typically reserved for boys and men. (Tony Freeman/PhotoEdit)

that becomes less pronounced in the late adolescent years (Leahy & Eiter, 1980; Stoddart & Turiel, 1985; Ullian, 1976).

These developmental trends can be accounted for by a mixture of social and cognitive forces. We have seen that society attaches greater prestige to masculine attributes and to the male role in general. Girls undoubtedly become aware of this as they grow older. As a result, they start to identify with masculine attributes and are attracted to some typically masculine activities. The heightened same-sex orientation during early adolescence may be a function of new perspective-taking competencies that emerge during the teenage years. Because adolescents are often preoccupied with what others think of them, they have a greater need to adhere to social conventions and to avoid being seen as different and deviant than they did at an earlier age. As they move toward establishing a mature personal identity (see Chapter 11), they become less concerned with others' evaluations of their behavior and more involved in finding meaningful attributes to incorporate into their self-definitions. As a result, highly stereotypic self-perceptions decline by late adolescence (Leahy & Eiter, 1980; Ullian, 1976).

Although sex-role identity follows the general path of development described above, individual differences exist at all ages, and they are moderately predictive of sex-typed behavior. A more masculine and less feminine identity is associated with better performance on spatial and mathematical tasks (Signorella & Jamison, 1986). In the personal-social domain, adolescent girls with feminine orientations are more popular with agemates, but masculine-oriented youngsters of both sexes are more assertive, less dependent, and have a higher sense of self-esteem (Hall & Halberstadt, 1980). At the present time, androgynous children, much like their adult counterparts, do not seem to be especially advantaged either intellectually or socially. Instead, it is a masculine sex-role orientation that is the key factor in predicting positive behavioral outcomes for children of both sexes.

Since these relationships are correlational in nature, the perennial "chicken-and-egg" question emerges as soon as we try to explain them. We do not know the extent to which masculine and feminine self-perceptions *arise* from particular activities and behaviors (as social learning theory assumes) or serve as *determinants* of behavior (as cognitive-developmental theory would predict). According to a new perspective on the origins and consequences of sex-role identity — gender schema theory — the answer is probably *both,* as we will see in the section that follows.

Gender Schema Theory: A New Approach to Sex-Role Identity. Gender schema theory is an integrative approach to the development of sex typing that contains both social learning and cognitive-developmental features. It also combines a number of separate elements of the sex-typing process—stereotyping, sex-role identity, and sex-role preferences and behavior—into a unified picture of how and why sex-typed orientations emerge and are often tenaciously maintained (Bem, 1981; 1983; Martin & Halverson, 1981).

Schema theory states that children learn from the environment stereotypical definitions of maleness and femaleness and incorporate them into masculine and feminine cognitive categories, or *gender schemas,* which they actively use to interpret their world. Once these basic schemas are formed, children select the contents associated with their own sex and construct a sex-role identity, or set of attributes appropriate for and characteristic of the self. As a result, children's self-perceptions become sex-typed, and they also function as gender schemas that children use to interpret incoming information from the environment and to moderate their own behavior.

Figure 13.3 shows exactly how this network of gender schemas works to organize and regulate sex-typed preferences and behavior. Let's take the example of a child who has been taught that "dolls are for girls" and who also knows that she is a girl. Our young child uses this schematic information to interpret the environment and make decisions about how to behave. Because her schemas lead her to conclude that "dolls are for me," she approaches the doll, explores it, and learns more about it. In contrast, on seeing a truck, she uses her gender schemas to conclude that "trucks are not for me" and responds by avoiding the "sex-inappropriate" toy (Martin & Halverson, 1981).[5]

Gender schema theory explains why stereotypes and sex-role orientations are self-perpetuating and difficult to modify, and exactly how they restrict behavioral alternatives. The reason is that schemas structure experience so that schema-

[5] Does this flowchart of how gender schemas work make you think of an information processing approach to children's cognition? In fact, gender schema theory is one of the few examples of the application of information processing to children's understanding of themselves and their social world. Recall that the topic of social problem solving, discussed in Chapter 11, is another.

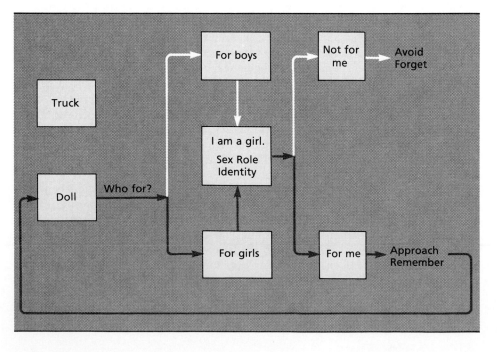

Figure 13.3. Model of how gender-relevant stimuli are encoded into sex-role identity and used to organize sex-role preferences and behavior. *(From C. L. Martin & C. F. Halverson, 1981, "A Schematic Processing Model of Sex-typing and Stereotyping in Children,"* Child Development, 52, *1119–1134.* © The Society for Research in Child Development, Inc. Adapted by permission.)

consistent information is attended to and approached, while schema-inconsistent information is ignored, misinterpreted, or actively rejected. In fact, investigators have found that when children see others behaving in gender-inconsistent ways, they either have difficulty remembering what they have seen, or they change the sex of the actor or distort the nature of the activity to make the two elements fit with one another. For example, when shown a picture of a boy cooking at a stove, many children recall the picture as a girl rather than a boy, and when shown a film that includes a male nurse, they remember him as a doctor instead of a nurse (Martin & Halverson, 1983; Cordua, McGraw, & Drabman, 1979; Signorella & Liben, 1984). Schema theory also helps us understand why the same-sex modeling effect, described earlier, evaporates when preschoolers are shown a same-sex model engaged in a "sex-inappropriate" activity. Under these conditions, the gender schema "Not for me!" prevails. In fact, children are far more willing to imitate a model of either sex engaged in an activity that fits with their own gender than a model who tries to teach them a "gender-inconsistent" response (Masters et al., 1979). The result of this schematic processing is that over time, children begin to increase their detailed knowledge of "things for me" that are consistent with their own gender schemas, and they learn much less about "opposite-sex" activities and behaviors.

Among children who have strong stereotypical beliefs and self-perceptions, gender-schematic thinking is especially extreme (Signorella & Liben, 1984). But gender-schematic thinking could not operate at all to restrict behavior and learning opportunities if society did not teach children an extensive network of gender-linked associations. Thus, schema theory tells us that children would not view themselves and others in such a gender-biased fashion if their social environments did not exaggerate distinctions between the sexes (Bem, 1983).

In summary, both social learning and cognitive-developmental perspectives help us understand how sex-role identity emerges and eventually comes to moderate sex-typed behavior. Some sex-typed responses appear so early in development that gender constancy cannot have preceded them, and modeling and reinforcement must govern their initial acquisition. Nevertheless, research confirms that gender constancy develops in a three-stage sequence over the preschool years, and once it is attained, it may be partly responsible for children's more flexible appreciation of sex stereotypes during middle childhood. Boys' and girls' sex-role identities follow different developmental paths during the elementary school years. Boys become more same-sex oriented, but girls become less so. An increase in same-sex identification occurs for both sexes during early adolescence. But at all periods of development, individual differences in sex-typed self-perceptions exist, and they are moderately predictive of sex-typed behavior. Finally, gender schema theory is a new, integrative approach that combines social learning with cognitive-developmental theory and puts the various pieces of sex-typed functioning together. Culturally transmitted stereotypes lead children to construct gender schemas, or cognitive interpretations of the environment and of themselves, that serve to limit learning opportunities and perpetuate sex-typed preferences and behaviors.

TO WHAT EXTENT DO BOYS AND GIRLS *REALLY* DIFFER IN COGNITIVE ABILITIES AND PERSONALITY ATTRIBUTES?

So far in this chapter, we have looked at the relationship of biological, environmental, and cognitive-developmental factors to children's acquisition of a wide variety of sex-stereotypic preferences and behaviors. At the same time, we have said little about the extent to which boys and girls are measurably different in cognitive and personality attributes on which we might expect them to differ, given the pervasive stereotypes available in our culture. Over the past three decades, there have been thousands of efforts to measure sex differences in these characteristics. At the heart of all of these studies is the age-old nature-nurture debate, couched in gender-related terms. Investigators have looked for stable differences between males and females and, from there, have searched for the biological and environmental roots of each specific variation.

In 1974, Eleanor Maccoby and Carol Jacklin published *The Psychology of Sex Differences,* a monumental review of the sex differences literature. Examining 1600 studies conducted between 1966 and 1973 and comparing the number that reported sex differences to the number that did not, they concluded that actual sex differences were far less prevalent than commonly believed. Convincing evidence, they indicated, could be found in only four areas: verbal ability (in favor of girls); and spatial ability, mathematical ability, and aggression (all in favor of boys).

Careful scrutiny of Maccoby and Jacklin's procedures quickly produced criticisms of their overall findings (Block, 1976). A major shortcoming was that many studies included in their review were based on such small and potentially biased samples that some sex differences may have gone undetected. Since 1974, many new literature reviews have been conducted. But instead of tabulating the results of individual studies, researchers now reanalyze the data of many investigations together, thereby avoiding the pitfall of giving too much weight to findings based on limited numbers of subjects. This approach has another advantage. It not only tells us whether a sex difference exists, but also provides an estimate of how large the difference is between males and females.

New findings, summarized in Table 13.2, indicate that Maccoby and Jacklin's synthesis of research *did* underestimate sex differences, particularly in the realm of personality. However, even though more sex differences have since been confirmed, many common assumptions about gender variations continue to be unfounded. For example, contrary to popular belief, girls are not more sociable, suggestible, kinder, and more giving and helpful to others. Also, boys are not "smarter." They do not excel at complex, analytical thinking, and girls are not better at rote, repetitive tasks.

Furthermore, a repeated conclusion of new research is that the disparities between boys and girls are quite small—surprisingly so, in view of pervasive societal stereotypes. Gender accounts for no more than 5 percent of individual differences among children in any characteristic, leaving most to be explained by other factors (Deaux, 1985).[6] Also, some sex differences have changed over time. For example, over the last several decades, sex differences have narrowed in all areas of intellectual abilities in which they have been identified, except for upper level mathematics, where boys' advantage has remained constant (Becker & Hedges, 1984; Feingold, 1988; Rosenthal & Rubin, 1982). This trend is a reminder that currently established sex differences are not settled for all time. The general picture of how boys and girls differ may not be the same in a decade or two as it is today.

Sex Differences in Cognitive Abilities

Sex differences in the intellectual domain continue to be consistent with the findings of Maccoby and Jacklin—favoring girls in verbal and boys in spatial and mathematical skills. There is considerable agreement that heredity is involved in the verbal and spatial disparities. In recent years, scientists have turned their attention toward

---

[6] Although this estimate is quite small and means that the distributions of boys' and girls' scores on every ability and personality characteristic overlap considerably, psychologists still regard a difference of this size as meaningful. For example, even if sex accounted for only 4 to 5 percent of individual differences, this would still amount to 60 percent of one group but only 40 percent of the other scoring above the mean on the attribute in question.

Table 13.2. Confirmed Differences Between Boys and Girls

1. **Physical and Motor Development:** Boys are slightly larger than girls at birth, but they lag behind girls in physiological and skeletal maturation throughout childhood. Sex differences in body size and strength are small during infancy and childhood. Boys surpass girls in size and muscle strength at adolescence (see Chapter 5).

2. **Verbal Abilities:** Sex differences in verbal skills favor girls and appear early in development. Differences in reading skill as well as other tested verbal abilities are evident in the early school years. A slight difference in some verbal skills persists through high school.

3. **Spatial Abilities:** Boys out-perform girls in spatial abilities by the mid-elementary school years, a difference that persists into adulthood. However, the sex difference is only evident on certain types of spatial tasks.

4. **Mathematical Abilities:** Beginning in adolescence, boys do better than girls on tests of mathematical reasoning. The difference is especially pronounced at the high end of the distribution; more boys than girls are exceptionally talented in math.

5. **School Achievement:** From kindergarten through third grade, girls outperform boys in all areas of school achievement. Beyond this age, sex differences are no longer evident, and by junior high and high school, boys start to show an advantage in some areas, such as mathematics.

6. **Achievement Motivation:** Sex differences in achievement motivation are linked to type of task. Boys perceive themselves as more competent and have higher expectancies of success in "masculine" achievement areas, such as mathematics, athletics, and mechanical skills. Girls have higher expectancies and set higher standards for themselves in "feminine" areas, such as English and art.

7. **Emotional Sensitivity:** As early as the preschool years, girls are more effective interpreters and senders of nonverbal emotional cues. They also score higher on self-report measures of empathy, although they do not appear more empathic in real-life situations.

8. **Fear, Timidity, and Anxiety:** Girls are more fearful, timid, and anxious than boys. These differences may be present as early as the first year of life. In school, girls are more anxious about failure and expend more energy trying to avoid failure than boys. In contrast, boys are more daring and greater risk-takers than girls. This difference is reflected in boys' higher accident rates at every age between 4 and 18.

9. **Compliance and Dependency:** Beginning in the early preschool years, girls are more compliant than boys in response to directives from either adults or peers. They also engage in more help-seeking from adults and score higher on measures of dependency. In contrast, boys are the more dominant and socially assertive of the two sexes.

10. **Activity Level:** Although some studies report no sex difference, those that do consistently find boys to be more active than girls.

11. **Aggression:** Boys are more aggressive than girls; reliable differences between the sexes appear as early as the preschool years.

12. **Developmental Difficulties:** Boys are overrepresented among children with many types of developmental problems, including speech and language disorders, reading disabilities, and behavior problems such as hyperactivity, hostile acting-out behavior, and social and emotional immaturity. More boys than girls are born with genetic defects, physical impairments, and mental retardation. Overall, boys are the more vulnerable of the two sexes.

Sources: Benbow & Stanley, 1980, 1983; Feingold, 1988; Hogrebe, Nist, & Newman, 1985; Hyde, 1981; 1984; Hall, 1978; Hall & Halberstadt, 1981; Linn & Petersen, 1985; Jacklin & Maccoby, 1983; Richardson, Koller, & Katz, 1986.

unraveling the specific biological mechanisms responsible for these differences, and we will see that a diverse array of speculative hypotheses exist. But no biological factor ever operates in a cultural or experiential vacuum. In the case of each type of mental ability, environment has been shown to play a crucial role, and sometimes experience is so powerful that it can totally eradicate the differences between boys and girls.

Verbal Abilities. In infancy, girls are already the more verbal of the two sexes. Between 6 and 12 months of age, girls are more responsive to their mothers' verbalizations and initiate more interactions (Gunnar & Donahue, 1980). By age 2, girls speak in longer sentences (Schachter et al., 1978), and at school entry, they learn to read earlier, achieve higher scores on standardized reading tests, and account for a lower percentage of children referred for remedial reading instruction (Dwyer, 1973). In middle childhood and adolescence, girls continue to outperform boys on a number of tested verbal skills. However, the disparity diminishes with age, and overall it is quite small (Feingold, 1988). Current estimates indicate that gender accounts for only one percent of the variation among elementary and high school students in verbal skills (Hyde, 1981; Hogrebe, Nist, & Newman, 1985).

The most frequently suggested biological explanation for this difference is girls' faster rate of physiological maturation. But a purely maturational account is not sufficient, because girls' maturational advantage should support superior development in all areas of cognitive skill, yet girls are not ahead of boys in spatial and numerical abilities. Consequently, the importance of maturation rate has been combined with speculations about sex differences in brain lateralization[7] that would lead to higher verbal than spatial scores for girls, and the opposite for boys. Since this hypothesis concerns spatial as well as verbal abilities, we discuss it in the next section. For now, it is important to note that it is the only current theory that poses a specific biological mechanism to account for girls' superior verbal performance.

While girls' more rapid language acquisition is difficult to explain in purely environmental terms (especially since boys are generally the recipients of more parental interaction), later-appearing sex differences in reading and other tested verbal skills might very well be accounted for by experience. Many studies suggest that conflict between the masculine sex role and the demands of the typical classroom environment place limits on boys' early reading competence. Earlier in this chapter we indicated that children think of reading as a ''feminine'' subject and that schools are ''feminine-biased'' settings in which boys' greater activity level and noncompliance lead them to experience more scolding from teachers than girls. Other studies show that girls' advantage in reading is reduced or eliminated in countries where reading and early school learning are regarded as well suited to the male sex role (e.g., Preston, 1962). Furthermore, certain kinds of experiences are successful in minimizing the verbal gender gap. In one study of first graders, a program of computer-assisted instruction was associated with equivalent reading performance for children of both sexes (Atkinson, 1968). The masculine appeal of the mechanical teaching devices may have been responsible for boys' improved performance.

Spatial Abilities. Spatial skills involve the ability to mentally manipulate nonverbal, pictorial information. The sex difference in spatial performance is larger than the verbal difference, but it is not very large, accounting for only 4 to 5 percent of individual differences among children (Hyde, 1981). But because gender variation in spatial skills has implications for math and science education and later entry into scientific careers, it has commanded far more attention from researchers than the verbal area.

The study of sex differences in spatial ability is complicated by the fact that a variety of spatial tasks exist, and sex differences appear on some but not all of them (see Figure 13.4). The gender gap is strongest for *mental rotation tasks* in which subjects must rotate a three-dimensional figure rapidly and accurately inside their heads. Sex differences also occur on *spatial perception tasks* in which people must determine spatial relationships based on the orientation of their own bodies. Interestingly, no systematic sex difference appears on *spatial visualization tasks* that involve very complex, multi-step manipulations of spatially presented material. Many mental strategies can be used to solve these problems. While males may solve them with spatial manipulations, perhaps females come up with other equally effective cognitive strategies and, for this reason, perform just as well (Linn & Petersen, 1985).

Until the 1980s, investigators thought that sex differences in spatial skills did not appear until the adolescent years, but recent evidence indicates that they are clearly evident in middle childhood and persist throughout the life span (Johnson & Meade, 1987; Linn & Petersen, 1985). The pattern is consistent enough to suggest the operation of a biological mediator, and three controversial hypotheses about the specific biological mechanisms involved exist.

---

[7] Recall from Chapter 5 that lateralization refers to specialization of functions between the hemispheres of the brain. For most individuals, verbal skills tend to localize in the left and spatial skills in the right hemisphere. You may wish to return to Chapter 5, pages 202–203, to review what is known about the development of brain lateralization in childhood.

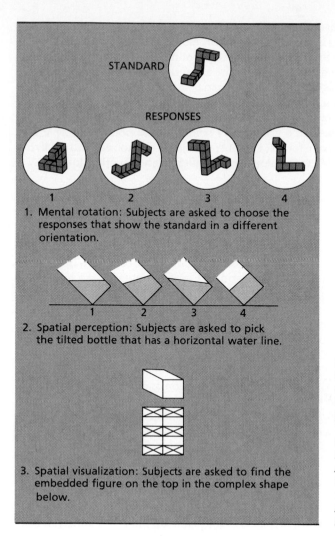

STANDARD

RESPONSES

1   2   3   4

1. Mental rotation: Subjects are asked to choose the responses that show the standard in a different orientation.

1   2   3   4

2. Spatial perception: Subjects are asked to pick the tilted bottle that has a horizontal water line.

3. Spatial visualization: Subjects are asked to find the embedded figure on the top in the complex shape below.

Figure 13.4. Types of spatial tasks on which the performance of males and females has been compared. *(From M. C. Linn & A. C. Petersen, 1985, ''Emergence and Characteristics of Sex Differences in Spatial Ability: A Meta-analysis.''* Child Development, 56, *1479–1498.* © *The Society for Research in Child Development, Inc. Reprinted by permission.)*

1. The Brain Lateralization/Maturation Rate Hypothesis. Although there have been several accounts of how maturation rate and brain lateralization may work together to explain sex differences in mental abilities, one of the most widely known is Waber's (1976). She suggested that girls' faster rate of physiological maturation leads to an earlier but less strongly lateralized brain than that of boys. Early hemispheric specialization in girls is thought to enhance verbal skills, which develop quickly during the first few years of life. In contrast, boys' slower maturation rate and stronger lateralization during adolescence are believed to provide maximum opportunity for later-emerging spatial functions to develop.

Recall from Chapter 3 that the cognitive strengths and weaknesses of children afflicted with certain sex-linked chromosomal disorders provide some support for Waber's hypothesis.[8] However, studies of genetically normal children have produced mixed findings. When the verbal and spatial scores of early- and late-maturing adolescent boys and girls are compared, some studies find the expected association between speed of maturation and cognitive abilities, while others do not (Newcombe & Dubas, 1987). An additional difficulty is that even when late maturers outperform early maturers on spatial tasks, they do not necessarily show evidence of stronger lateralization. The lateralization/maturation rate hypothesis is an intriguing idea, but it requires a great deal of additional research to be confirmed.

[8] Return to Chapter 3, pages 84–87, if you wish to review this evidence.

2. *The X-linked Recessive Gene Hypothesis.* This explanation suggests that a recessive gene for spatial abilities is carried on the X chromosome. Since girls have two Xs, they must inherit two recessive genes for the "spatial trait" to be manifest. In contrast, boys need only one, and as a result, they are advantaged. To test this hypothesis, investigators study relationships among the spatial scores of family members. For example, since boys get their X chromosome from their mothers, their spatial scores should be more strongly correlated with the scores of mothers than fathers. This prediction has been examined in a great many studies. Since both supportive and contradictory evidence has been found (Parsons, 1982), it is also too early to tell if this hypothesis provides a viable explanation for sex differences in spatial skills.

3. *The Androgen Hormone Hypothesis.* A third hypothesis is that exposure to androgen hormones prenatally or during puberty accounts for the male advantage in spatial abilities. Of all biological mechanisms, this one has received the least support. Studies of adrenogenital syndrome girls provide no evidence of an association between prenatal androgens and later cognitive functioning (Parsons, 1982). In addition, the fact that differences in spatial performance are present prior to adolescence suggests that a pubertal hormone explanation cannot fully explain sex differences in spatial skills. Furthermore, to the extent that pubertal hormones do play a role, their effects are not simple. Although high levels of pubertal androgens do predict better spatial scores in females (Broverman, Klaiber, & Vogel, 1980), the reverse has actually been reported for males (Petersen, 1979). A number of investigators believe that hormonal influences, if they exist, may exert their effects by interacting with other biological mechanisms, such as brain lateralization and maturation rate, but a great deal of work needs to be done to sort out these complex relationships.

Very little attention has been devoted to the environmental bases of sex differences in spatial ability, but a few studies suggest that experience can widen or reduce the gender gap. Boys' early play activities may contribute to their spatial advantage, for children of both sexes who play with highly manipulative, "masculine" toys do better on spatial problems (Fagot & Littman, 1976). In addition, girls' more limited awareness of certain scientific principles may sometimes prevent them from demonstrating their true spatial competencies. In a recent study of college students, Liben and Golbeck (1984) found that when females were given information about a relevant physical rule prior to solving the spatial perception problem shown in Figure 13.4, their performance equaled that of males. Another study reported that sex differences in spatial performance disappeared when males and females who had completed the same number of high school math and science courses were compared (Fennema & Sherman, 1977). Finally, on spatial rotation tasks for which sex differences are largest, males and females differ only in speed, not accuracy! Perhaps females' greater cautiousness and anxiety about failing in achievement situations contributes to their slower performance, although use of less efficient cognitive strategies may also play a role (Linn & Petersen, 1985).

Mathematical Skills. The male advantage in mathematics is clearly evident by age 15 (Meece et al., 1982), but among highly intellectually gifted youngsters it is present earlier — by age 13. Although the magnitude of the difference is not large, it is greater at the upper end of the ability distribution. In a series of studies, Benbow and Stanley (1980; 1983) examined the mathematical performance of thousands of high-achieving seventh- and eighth-grade youngsters who were invited to take the Scholastic Aptitude Test (SAT) long before they were required to do so for college admission. Year after year, the boys out-scored the girls on the mathematics subtest. Twice as many boys as girls had scores above 500; 13 times as many scored over 700. Sex differences in mathematics achievement do not occur on all kinds of test items. Boys and girls perform equally well on tests of basic math knowledge, and girls sometimes do better in computational skills. The difference occurs on tests of mathematical reasoning, primarily in solving word problems (Parsons, 1982).

Some researchers believe that the gender gap in mathematical performance is biologically based and rooted in boys' superior spatial skills. If this is the case, then children's spatial and mathematical scores should be positively correlated, but the literature as a whole shows inconsistent patterns of relationships, and in some studies verbal skills are as effective as spatial skills in predicting math achievement (Parsons, 1982; Linn & Petersen, 1985). Some investigators believe that the link between spatial and mathematical skills occurs only at fairly advanced levels of mathematical reasoning. There is some support for this idea (Fennema & Sherman, 1977), but it requires additional study.

Even if we could be sure that spatial and mathematical scores were consistently related, we would not be able to tell from the correlation if boys' spatial advantage actually caused them to be ahead in mathematics achievement. In fact, mathematical performance is also related to a variety of other important variables, including number of math courses taken in high school (boys take more than girls) and the extent to which math is regarded as a "sex-appropriate" subject (both boys and girls think of math as a "male domain") (Dwyer, 1974; Fennema & Sherman, 1977; Sherman & Fennema, 1977; Paulsen & Johnson, 1983; Sherman, 1980). Furthermore, girls' inclination to attribute their academic failures to insufficient ability (rather than effort) is known to undermine self-confidence and promote debilitating anxiety in achievement situations. Girls display this self-defeating style of attributional reasoning particularly strongly in mathematics (Stipek, 1984). The fact that they do so in elementary school, long before consistent sex differences in mathematical performance are evident, suggests that girls' self-derogating attributions may be partly responsible for the fact that many stop taking math courses as soon as they are not mandatory and, ultimately, achieve less well than boys by the high school years. In Chapter 11, we showed that children develop their attributional biases largely from the evaluative messages they get from others. There is evidence that teachers as well as parents expect girls to do less well in math and subtly communicate this message to children (Meece et al., 1982; Parsons, Adler, & Kaczala, 1982). Taken together, these findings indicate that lack of confidence in oneself as a learner is just as plausible an account of girls' inferior math performance as any biologically based difference between the sexes.

Sex Differences in Personality Attributes

In the sections that follow, we consider the origins of several important sex differences in personality attributes: emotional sensitivity, compliance and dependency, and aggression.

Emotional Sensitivity. Females are stereotyped as the more emotionally sensitive of the two sexes, and recent reviews of many studies indicate that, in fact, they are more emotionally responsive and expressive than males. The difference, although small, appears quite early. In studies in which subjects are asked to make judgments of others' emotional states using nonverbal cues communicated through facial expression, bodily posture, or tone of voice, girls perform better than boys at every age from the preschool years into adulthood (Hall, 1978). Girls are also more effective nonverbal senders of their feelings than boys, although the difference is restricted to facial and bodily expressiveness and does not apply to the vocal channel (Hall & Halberstadt, 1981).

It would be reasonable to expect these sex differences to carry over to empathic responding, but to date the evidence is mixed. On self-report measures of empathic arousal, girls consistently score higher than boys. However, in the few studies in

Research indicates that girls communicate feelings through facial and bodily gestures more effectively than do boys. (Nancy Sheehan)

which children have been observed for behavioral indicators that they are actually experiencing the distress of a nearby person, boys and girls show no difference (Eisenberg & Lennon, 1983).

As with other attributes, both biological and environmental explanations for sex differences in emotional sensitivity exist. One speculation is that females are genetically prewired to be especially sensitive to nonverbal cues so that later on as mothers they will be able to detect and respond quickly to the distress signals of their offspring. Against this interpretation is a growing body of evidence that girls are not "naturally" more nurturant than boys. Prior to age 5 boys and girls spend equal amounts of time talking to and playing with a baby during interaction sessions arranged in either laboratory or natural environments (Berman, 1986; Berman & Goodman, 1984; Fogel et al., 1987). After that age, boys' willingness to interact with infants declines, although they continue to respond with just as much care and affection to other targets of nurturance, such as pets and elderly relatives (Melson & Fogel, 1988). Moreover, sex differences in emotional responsiveness do not occur in adulthood when parents interact with their own babies. In Chapter 10 we showed that fathers respond very affectionately to their infants, and they are just as competent caregivers as mothers. In Chapter 4, we noted that men respond to the cries of babies in much the same way as women.

A more likely explanation for sex differences in emotional sensitivity is that children learn very quickly what is expected for their gender. Earlier in this chapter, we showed that in infancy and early childhood parents encourage girls to be warm and expressive and boys to be emotionally distant and controlled. Moreover, the fact that the sex difference in ability to interpret others' emotional reactions widens with age is consistent with an environmentally based explanation (Blanck et al., 1981).

Compliance and Dependency. Beginning in the preschool years, girls are the more passive and compliant of the two sexes in the face of both adult and peer requests and demands (Block, 1976; Jacklin & Maccoby, 1978). In addition, girls more often seek help and information from adults and score higher in dependency on personality inventories (Block, 1976). No evidence exists that a specific biological mechanism underlies these sex differences. Instead, there is widespread agreement that they are learned, and some intriguing new research suggests how this learning comes about.

According to Carpenter (1983), the reason boys and girls differ in compliance and dependency has much to do with the activity environments in which they spend their time. From an early age, girls are encouraged to remain in close proximity to adults both at home and in preschool. Because they spend so much time near adults, they soon learn to prefer highly structured activities in which guidelines for appropriate performance are explicitly provided. In contrast, boys gravitate to low-structure activities in which adults are either minimally involved or entirely absent. The result of this process is that boys and girls end up practicing very different social behaviors. Compliance, requests for adult attention, and bids for help appear more often in adult-structured activities, whereas assertiveness, leadership, and creative use of materials occur more often in unstructured activities (Carpenter & Huston-Stein, 1980). Since optimal development involves the ability to lead and assert as well as the capacity to comply and fit into structures imposed by others, Carpenter recommends that parents and teachers deliberately encourage children of both sexes to participate in a balanced array of structurally different activities. In a recent study, she showed that the compliant and assertive tendencies of preschool children of both sexes could easily be modified by assigning them to classroom activities that differ in degree of adult structure (Carpenter, Huston, & Holt, 1986).

Aggression. Sex differences in aggression have attracted more attention from researchers than any other gender variation. The findings are the same in study after study: beginning in the preschool years, boys engage in more physical and verbal aggression, and by adolescence they are five times more likely than girls to be involved in antisocial behavior and violent crime (Johnson, 1979). Although the sex difference appears very reliably, it is small in childhood, accounting for only 5 percent of individual variability (Hyde, 1984), and aggressive behavior is by no means absent among girls. In fact, some psychologists believe that current research may underestimate girls' aggressiveness. Most studies have focused on highly visible aggressive acts, such as physical assaults and verbal insults. By late childhood, girls may develop some less obvious forms of aggression, such as tattling, malicious gossip, and social exclusion, that may be just as hostile and harmful to a victim as boys' overt, aggressive outbursts (Brodzinsky, Messer, & Tew, 1979). These more subtle forms of interpersonal hostility are difficult for researchers to observe and study, but more needs to be known about them if we are to fully understand the nature and extent of sex differences in aggressive behavior.

Sex Similarities and Differences in the Development of Aggression. The seeds of aggressive outbursts are already apparent by the end of the first year of life. In Chapter 10, we showed that angry emotional reactions in response to frustration and blocked goals increase after 7 months of age. As infants develop the cognitive capacity to isolate sources of frustration and the motor skills to lash out at them, two basic forms of aggression appear. The first is **instrumental aggression,** in which the child tries to gain access to an object, privilege, or space and, in doing so, pushes, shouts at, or otherwise attacks another individual who is in the way. In this type of aggression, there is little or no hostile intent toward the victim. Instead, the child is merely trying to reach a desired goal. A second form is **hostile aggression.** It is person-oriented and

As early as the preschool years, physically aggressive interchanges occur more often in boy-boy interactions than in boy-girl and girl-girl pairs. (Gloria Karlson)

meant to hurt, as when the child hits or insults a playmate with no other aim in mind but to injure the other individual.

In children of both sexes, the form of aggression as well as the avenue through which it is expressed (physical or verbal) change with age. In a classic study of the development of early aggressive behavior, Goodenough (1931) asked mothers of preschoolers to keep records of their children's angry outbursts. Physical aggression increased until the third year of life, after which it declined and began to be replaced by verbally mediated aggression. The change parallels children's rapid gain in language competence during the preschool years, but it is also the result of negative reactions on the part of adults and peers to instances of physical aggression (Parke & Slaby, 1983). In another study, Hartup (1974) recorded the aggressive displays of 4- to 7-year-old children at school and reported a decline over this age period in instrumental aggression and a gradual increase in hostile, person-oriented outbursts. An interesting finding was that tattling, criticism, and ridicule frequently provoked hostile reactions in 6- and 7-year-olds, but seldom did so in 4- and 5-year-olds. The rise in hostile aggression occurs during the same period in which children become better able to assess the intentions and motives of other people (see Chapter 11). As a result, when the behavior of another child is deliberately hostile, older children are more likely to "read" it as such and respond with an aggressive retaliation.

Although there are similarities, differences between boys and girls in the development of aggression also exist. By 18 months of age the frequency of temper tantrums and strong frustration reactions begins to decline in girls but is maintained in boys (Goodenough, 1931). During the preschool and elementary school years, boys display more overt peer aggression of all kinds (Barrett, 1979; Maccoby & Jacklin, 1980), and cross-cultural observations in many nations reveal a similar picture (Omark, Omark, & Edelman, 1975; Whiting & Whiting, 1975). In addition, analyses of the circumstances in which peer and sibling aggressive encounters occur show that physically aggressive interchanges are especially frequent in boy-boy interactions and less so in boy-girl or girl-girl pairs (Barrett, 1979; Maccoby & Jacklin, 1980; Strauss, Gelles, & Steinmetz, 1980). Boys are also far more likely than girls to respond with retaliatory aggression when they are physically attacked (Darvill & Cheyne, 1981).

From middle childhood on, aggression is a very stable individual characteristic, especially among males (Kagan & Moss, 1962; Huesmann et al., 1984; Olweus, 1979). In a longitudinal investigation of more than 400 subjects that spanned 22 years, very aggressive 8-year-olds became 30-year-olds who were more likely to score high in aggressive inclinations on a personality inventory, use severe punishment with their children, and be convicted of serious criminal offenses (see Figure 13.5). In this study, the researchers also tracked the aggressive tendencies of the subjects' family members. Strong intergenerational continuity emerged, especially when comparisons of relatives were made as they reached the same age. For example, subjects' aggression at age 8 was highly predictive of their children's aggression two decades later when they were about 8 years old (Huesmann et al., 1984). Finally, by the mid-elementary school years aggressive behavior shows considerable consistency across situations. Children who display it in one setting are more likely to display it in others. Once again, this is particularly true for boys (Olweus, 1980a; Deluty, 1985).

Recently, investigators have made considerable progress in unraveling the complex, intricate ways in which biological and environmental factors work together to promote and sustain aggressive behavior. We turn to a consideration of what they have discovered in the following two sections.

Biological Influences. Since the sex difference in aggression is apparent early in life, generalizes across cultures, and is found in many animal species, almost all researchers agree that biological mechanisms must be involved. As we mentioned earlier in this chapter, androgen hormones are related to aggressive behavior in animals, and they are also believed to play a role in human beings. But think back for a moment to our discussion of sex-role development among adrenogenital syndrome children. These youngsters were exposed to abnormally high levels of prenatal androgens, but there was little evidence of increased aggression among them (although they consistently showed higher activity levels). This finding suggests that in humans, no more than a *predisposition* for aggression results from androgen exposure. Investigators currently believe that androgen hormones affect intervening response tendencies that, when combined with learning and environmental influences, lead to a higher likelihood of aggressive outcomes.

One speculation is that prenatal androgens promote higher levels of physical activity, which may or may not be translated into aggression, depending on child-rearing conditions (Parsons, 1982). For example, a very active youngster who partici-

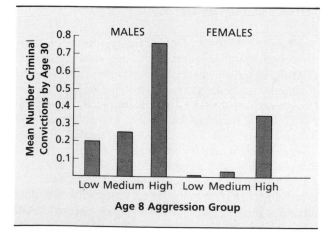

Figure 13.5. Relationship of childhood aggression to criminal behavior in adulthood in the Huesmann et al. (1984) study. *(From L. R. Huesmann, L. D. Eron, M. M. Lefkowitz, & L. O. Walder, 1984, "Stability of Aggression over Time and Generations,"* Developmental Psychology, 20, *1120–1134. Copyright 1984 by the American Psychological Association. Reprinted by permission of the author.)*

pates in aggressive-conducive activities as an outlet for his energies, such as water fights, boxing matches, and tackle football, is more likely to display aggressive behavior than a comparable child who is encouraged to participate in vigorous but nonaggressive pursuits, such as running track, playing baseball, or working out in the gym. Some recent findings lend support to this idea. In a longitudinal study of third and fourth graders, Bullock and Merrill (1980) had children indicate their own activity preferences as well as nominate the most aggressive youngsters in their class in the fall of the school year and one year later. Girls showed little attraction to aggressive-conducive activities, and their activity choices had no predictive value as far as aggressive behavior was concerned. But for boys who were neither high nor low in aggression at the beginning of the study, activity preferences had a strong impact on behavior. Those who found aggressive-conducive pursuits attractive were regarded by their peers as much higher in aggressive attributes the following year.

Another biological hypothesis is that prenatal hormone levels influence the basic organization of the nervous system in ways that affect children's later emotional reactions and mood states. According to this theory, hormone levels induce more frequent displays of certain feelings, such as anger, generalized excitement, or anxiety, and these have an increased likelihood of culminating in aggression in the presence of certain environmental conditions. In support of this idea, one study found that early hormone levels (measured at birth from umbilical cord blood samples) were positively related to excited as opposed to calm emotional states during the first two years of life for boys, although no relationships appeared for girls (Marcus et al., 1985).

Besides the prenatal period, adolescence is a second phase during which hormone levels have important implications for aggressive responding. Adolescent boys who are high in androgens experience more sad and anxious emotional reactions, and they also display more aggressive behavioral attributes, such as hostile retaliations to threatening provocations, low frustration tolerance, and delinquent and rebellious behavior (Nottelmann et al., 1987; Olweus et al., 1980; Susman et al., 1987). In one recent study, higher estrogen and androgen levels were associated with an increase in expressions of anger on the part of adolescent girls when interacting with their parents in a laboratory discussion session (Inoff-Germain et al., 1988).

These results are intriguing, but they require replication and extension, for there is still much that remains to be learned about hormonal processes and aggressive behavior. However, from the little evidence that already exists it is apparent that there are multiple pathways between hormones and aggression, that each involves a complex series of steps, and that each may vary with the sex and age of the child. It is also clear that whether hormonally induced intervening responses, such as activity level or emotional state, are eventually channeled into aggressive outbursts or other forms of behavior is heavily dependent on child-rearing conditions. Next we turn to the environmental side of children's aggressive behavior.

Environmental Influences: The Family as Training Ground for Aggressive Behavior. A wealth of research exists on environmental provocations of aggressive behavior. Parental child-rearing practices; strife, anger, and discord in the family; and television violence have been the most commonly studied sources. In this section, we focus on familial factors, reserving our consideration of television influences for Chapter 15.

Many studies reveal that the same child-rearing dimensions that undermine the development of moral internalization and self-control (see Chapter 12) are also correlated with aggressive behavior. Parental love withdrawal and rejection, power-assertive and physically punitive discipline, and inconsistent punishment are associated with higher levels of aggression from the preschool through adolescent years in children of both sexes (Parke & Slaby, 1983). When parents repeatedly discipline children with anger and hostility, they provide examples of aggressive behavior, fail to teach youngsters acceptable behavioral alternatives, and frustrate children's needs for nurturance so that they are likely to lash out toward others in return. Unfortunately, a variety of ineffective and destructive child-rearing practices are often found together in the same family, compounding their harmful consequences for some children. After questioning parents of 13- to 16-year-old boys, Olweus (1980b) reported that mothers who had highly aggressive sons recalled not only being negative, rejecting, and indifferent to their youngsters at an early age, but also using power-assertive discipline.

The use of coercive tactics within the family is likely to spread from one member to another and become part of a self-perpetuating cycle that elicits and maintains aggression among all family members. Making detailed home observations of typical sequences of interaction that occur in aggressive families, Patterson (1981; 1982) discovered how this happens. As indicated in Figure 13.6, the pattern begins with dominative and forceful disciplinary practices, which are made more likely by parental personality characteristics, stressful life experiences, or a temperamentally difficult child (see Chapter 10). Once the parent acts coercively, the child responds in kind by whining, yelling, and refusing, until the parent eventually finds the child's behavior too much to take and "gives in." This pattern is likely to repeat itself in the future, since at the end of the interchange both parent and child experience immediate relief and reinforcement for stopping the negative, unpleasant behavior of the other. The next time the child misbehaves, the parent is likely to react even more coercively and the child more recalcitrantly until one member of the pair again experiences the

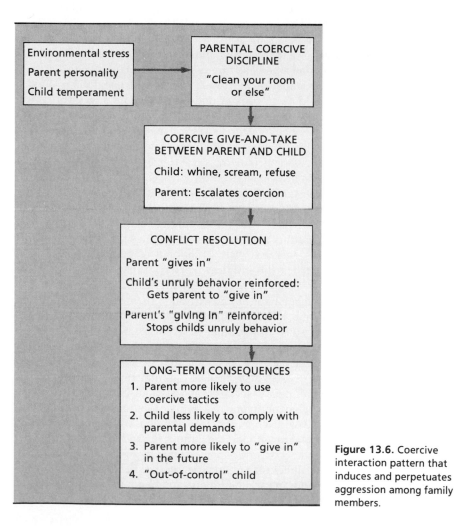

Figure 13.6. Coercive interaction pattern that induces and perpetuates aggression among family members.

behavior of the other as unbearable and "begs off." Coercive tactics soon generalize to other family members, creating a conflict-ridden family atmosphere in which communication and successful problem solving are seriously disrupted and children become "out of control," unmanageable youngsters.

Aggressive children who are products of these family processes soon learn to approach the world from a hostile and violent perspective. Because they expect others to behave coercively, they begin to "see" malicious intent in the actions of other people even when it does not exist. As a result, they engage in a large number of unprovoked aggressive attacks, which stimulate additional hostile reactions among family members and peers, contributing further to the spiraling aggressive cycle. You may recall our discussion of Dodge's work, presented in Chapter 11, which showed that highly aggressive youngsters are especially prone to misinterpret the innocent behaviors of others as hostilely motivated.

For a variety of reasons, boys are more likely than girls to become embroiled in family interaction patterns that serve as a training ground for aggressive behavior. Parents more often use physical punishment with boys, which encourages them to adopt the same tactics in their own interactions with others. In contrast, inductive discipline, which promotes self-control and empathy for a victim (see Chapter 12), is used more often with girls (Block, 1978). In addition, while many parents intervene when they observe an aggressive act committed by a child of either sex, some evidence suggests that parents are less likely to interpret fighting as aggressive when it occurs among boys (Condry & Ross, 1985). The stereotype embodied in the familiar adage, "Boys will be boys," may lead many adults to overlook male hostility except when it is extreme, thereby setting up conditions in which it is encouraged, or at least tolerated, to a greater extent than among girls.

Furthermore, there is evidence that arguing and bickering between husband and wife, while stimulating aggression among all family members, may do so to a greater extent among boys. In a recent experiment, Cummings, Iannotti, and Zahn-Waxler (1985) exposed 2-year-old children to backgrounds of warm and angry verbal exchanges between adults while they played with familiar peers. Friendly adult interaction had the effect of slightly dampening peer aggression in children of both sexes. In contrast, angry interaction led to changes in the way children behaved that were different for boys and girls. Girls showed distress reactions (e.g., tensely freezing in place, covering or hiding their faces), while boys engaged in more interpersonal aggression, a response that was especially pronounced after they were exposed to the argumentative adults on a second occasion. In line with our earlier discussion of emotional mediators of aggressive behavior, these findings suggest that boys may be "primed" to react to familial hostility and discord with feelings that are easily translated into aggressive impulses, whereas girls' emotional reactions, while no less intense, are more likely to lead to fearful, withdrawn behavior that is less of a problem to others.

Besides teaching aggressive behavior directly through their communication and disciplinary practices in the home, parents influence children's aggression indirectly, as "managers" of their youngsters' environments (Parke & Slaby, 1983). When parents provide young children with aggressive toys, such as pistols and rifles, they encourage play that is thematically aggressive and likely to lead to peer hostility and conflict (Turner & Goldsmith, 1976). Also, lack of parental supervision over children's whereabouts, selection of peer associates, and style of interaction with age-mates is related to aggressive behavior. In one recent investigation, absence of parental monitoring was associated with court-reported delinquency, peer quarreling, talking back to teachers, and breaking school rules among junior high and high school pupils (Patterson, Stouthamer-Loeber, & Loeber, as cited by Parke & Slaby, 1983). Again, these factors are more likely to heighten aggressive behavior among boys. Provision of aggressive playthings in early childhood and freedom to come and go as one pleases during adolescence are more typical of parental practices with sons than with daughters.

Helping Children and Families to Control Aggression. We have seen that encouragement and maintenance of aggression within the family are the result of bidirectional influences in which the hostility exchanged between family members becomes part of a self-maintaining system. Help for aggressive children and their parents must break this chain and equip each party with effective techniques for preventing the destructive cycle from reasserting itself. Over the past several decades, a variety of approaches for treating childhood aggression have been proposed and studied. Among them are the catharsis approach; coaching, modeling, and reinforcing alternative parent and child behaviors; training empathy and perspective-taking skills; and changing the physical environment to minimize aggression.

The Cathartic Approach. Catharsis is the oldest treatment technique and was originally inspired by psychoanalytic theory, which assumed that aggressive urges build up in the organism and, unless drained off, inevitably result in hostile outbursts. Cathartic treatment is aimed at discharging pent-up anger and frustration before it reaches dangerously high levels. This is done by offering children "safe" opportunities to behave aggressively, such as a session with a punching bag, a Bobo doll, or a violent video game. Another approach is to provide children with passive exposure to the aggression of others. Violent television programs, comic books, and stories are assumed to reduce hostility as children identify with aggressive characters and experience their behavior vicariously.

On the basis of what we have said about modeling in this and other chapters, are you skeptical of the effectiveness of cathartic treatment? If so, you are correct. It has received very little research support. In fact, there is considerable evidence that aggression can be stimulated by such experiences (e.g., Mallick & McCandless, 1966; Parke et al., 1977). Catharsis is a widely held popular belief that many people use to rationalize an appetite for violent media fare, but it is an ineffective and even counterproductive method for controlling aggressive behavior.

Coaching, Modeling, and Reinforcing Alternative Parent and Child Behaviors. A far more successful approach to treating childhood aggression is to interrupt the destructive family processes that contribute to it. Techniques based on social learning theory have been developed that teach both parents and children new ways of interacting with one another.

On the parent's side, modeling and coaching in child management skills have been effectively applied by Patterson (1976). A therapist carefully observes the parent's inept disciplinary practices, describes and demonstrates alternative means of handling the child, and has the parent practice and apply them. Parents learn not to give in to a hostile, acting-out child and not to escalate their coercive efforts to control misbehavior. In addition, they are taught to pair commands with reasons and to replace verbal insults and spankings with more effective punishments, such as time out and withdrawal of privileges (see Chapter 12). Patterson's (1981) research shows that ineffective parenting skills contribute significantly to parents' anger, anxiety, and doubt about their own competence, further limiting their ability to control their children. Although parents of aggressive youngsters often need help with marital conflicts and other problems, one way to help them make their own lives less stressful is to teach them to manage their children more successfully.

On the child's side, aggressive youngsters benefit from programs in which they are taught alternative techniques for resolving conflict, such as cooperation and sharing, that are incompatible with aggressive behavior. Sessions in which these nonaggressive alternatives are explained, modeled, and role-played and children have opportunities to see that they result in rewarding social outcomes reduce aggression and increase positive social behavior (Chittenden, 1942; Zahavi & Asher, 1978). Once aggressive children demonstrate more acceptable interaction patterns, their parents need to be reminded to give them attention and approval for their prosocial behavior. The coercive cycles of parents and aggressive children are often so pervasive that these youngsters even get punished when they do behave appropriately (Patterson, 1982).

Empathy and Perspective-taking Training. Aggression is inhibited by empathic reactions to another person's pain and suffering. However, highly aggressive boys respond with more, not less, aggression after observing a victim's distress (Hartmann, 1969), and they show little sign of pain or remorse after injuring another individual (Perry & Bussey, 1977). Because aggressive children often come from homes in which they have had little opportunity to witness family members behaving in a sensitive, caring way to one another, they miss early experiences that are vital for nurturing empathic reactions (see Chapter 10). In such children, empathy may have to be deliberately taught. One study found that training sessions in which children were encouraged to identify others' feelings and express their own reduced hostile interactions among peers and increased prosocial behaviors of cooperation, helping, and generosity (Feshbach & Feshbach, 1982). Empathy training necessarily involves practice in perceiving situations from the perspective of others. In Chapter 11, we showed that the delinquent acts of highly aggressive boys could be substantially reduced by an intervention program that improved perspective-taking skills through dramatic role playing. Perhaps the reason this program worked so well was that it promoted empathic responding, which then served as a deterrent to antisocial behavior.

Modifying the Physical Environment. A final technique for reducing aggression is to change aspects of the physical environment that are known to encourage it. Toys that stimulate aggressive play can be removed by parents and teachers. In preschools and day care centers, steps can be taken to reduce crowding so that knocks, jostles, and bumps among children do not resolve into aggressive retaliations. The physical resources available also make a difference. When there are few toys and many youngsters in a play setting, children congregate in larger groups, and both crowded conditions and competition over scarce materials result in more aggression (Smith & Connolly, 1980). Sometimes adults cannot do much to modify the physical environment. If this is the case, it is especially important that they remain nearby and ready to intervene in any hostile interactions among the youngsters in their charge.

In the sections above, we have seen that boys and girls differ in a variety of intellectual and personality characteristics. Biological factors operate in several of them, but biology only makes it slightly easier for one sex as opposed to the other to acquire certain attributes. Both boys and girls can learn all of them, and socialization experiences determine whether sex differences among children are minimized or maximized. Finally, given the myriad of ways in which it is possible for human beings to vary, our overall conclusion must be that males and females are really much more alike in developmental potential than they are different from one another.

RAISING NON-SEX-STEREOTYPED CHILDREN

A comparison of the different roles and achievements of men and women in our society with the actual sex differences discussed above leads to the conclusion that the developmental horizons of many children are seriously limited by pervasive gender stereotyping in our culture. Although psychologists now recognize the importance of raising children who feel free to express their human qualities without fear of violating gender-related expectations, no easy recipe exists for accomplishing this difficult task. It undoubtedly needs to be tackled on many fronts — in the home, at school, and at the level of the wider society.

Throughout this chapter we have mentioned ways to minimize sex stereotyping and sex-role adoption in childhood. These include behaviors of parents and teachers that respond to children as individuals rather than in terms of stereotyped expectations, and environmental modifications that reduce sex-stereotyped play and bring about more mixed-sex peer activity. But even children who are fortunate enough to grow up in family, school, and peer settings that minimize stereotyping will eventually encounter it in the media and in their observations of what men and women typically do in the surrounding community. Until societal values change, children need early experiences with astute caregivers who repeatedly counteract their readiness to absorb our culture's extensive network of gender-linked associations.

Bem (1983; 1984) suggests that parents make a concerted effort to delay the young child's absorption of sex-stereotyped messages from the surrounding culture as long as possible. Parents can begin by eliminating sex stereotyping from their own behavior and from the alternatives they provide for their children. For example, mothers and fathers can take turns making dinner, bathing children, and driving the family car, and they can ensure that all children have trucks and dolls to play with and both pink and blue clothing. In addition, adults can deliberately shield young children from media presentations indicating that the sexes differ in what they can and should do.

At the same time, parents can teach young children that anatomy and reproduction are the only characteristics that determine a person's gender. In this chapter, we have seen that children, at least in our society, typically do not learn to view sex in terms of genital characteristics until quite late, and they mistakenly assume that many cultural correlates of maleness and femaleness are defining features of gender. By

By engaging in non-sex-stereotyped activities themselves, parents can limit young children's acquisition of sex-typed preferences and behavior. (Robert Brenner/ PhotoEdit)

encouraging preschoolers to construct their earliest gender-linked associations based on biology, parents can capitalize in a favorable way on their tendency to interpret rules and categories rigidly and inflexibly. If children grasp at an early age that sex is narrowly defined in terms of anatomy and reproduction, then they should be less likely to view it in terms of arbitrary social conventions that must be strictly obeyed (Bem, 1984).

Once children are exposed to the vast array of sex-stereotypic associations that prevail in our culture, parents and other adults can take steps to prevent these stereotypes from being absorbed into the child's gender schemas. For example, arrangements can be made for children to see males and females pursuing nontraditional activities and careers. In addition, older children can be informed directly about the historical roots and current consequences of gender inequalities in our society — why, for example, there has never been a female president; why few fathers stay home with their children; and why stereotypical views of men and women adhered to by the mass media and by many people in the larger community are so pervasive and hard to change (Bem, 1984). As such efforts help the next generation build conceptions of themselves and their social world that are not governed by the male-female dichotomy, they contribute to the transformation of societal values, and they bring us closer to a time when individuals will be released from the constraints of conformity to traditional sex roles.

CHAPTER SUMMARY

1. Sex stereotypes are deeply ingrained, widely held beliefs about the characteristics of males and females that children begin to learn in the early preschool years. By middle childhood, children are aware of a broad array of stereotypes, including those associated with personality attributes, achievement areas, activities, and occupations. Although preschoolers' understanding of gender-related characteristics is rigid and inflexible, elementary school children recognize that some stereotypes are socially defined and can vary from one culture to another. Boys hold more stereotypes than girls, and they are also more likely to attribute sex differences to biological than social causes. Both correlational and experimental evidence indicates that sex stereotyping is an important determinant of sex-role adoption.

2. Cross-cultural similarity in sex stereotyping has been taken as evidence for biological influences on sex-role development. Although most cultures adhere to the instrumental-expressive sex-role dichotomy, some cultural diversity exists, including instances of traditional sex-role reversal, as Margaret Mead's study of New Guinean tribal societies illustrates. Research on adrenogenital syndrome (AGS) children suggests that prenatal hormone levels may influence general sex-role adoption, but the impact of biological factors is modest at best, and a variety of socialization influences provide powerful support for sex-stereotyped attitudes and behavior. Parents hold sex-typed perceptions and expectations of their children, and they reinforce their sons and daughters for a great many "sex-appropriate" activities and behaviors. Fathers differentiate more than mothers, although each parent is more influential in the sex-role development of the same-sex child. Teachers and peers also reinforce sex-typed behaviors and activity

choices. In addition, children have ample opportunity to pick up traditional sex roles from people they observe in their everyday environments and from the content of television, storybooks, and textbooks. Sibling influences on sex-role development depend on the way a variety of family configurational factors, such as family size and birth order, combine with one another.

3. Sex-role identity, one's perception of the self as relatively masculine or feminine in characteristics, changes over the childhood and adolescent years. According to cognitive-developmental theory, sex-role identity begins with gender constancy, a cognitive appreciation of the permanence of one's own gender, which is attained at about the same time as Piagetian conservation. In contrast to cognitive-developmental predictions, sex-typed behavior is acquired much earlier than gender constancy and is not dependent on it. Instead, the attainment of gender constancy seems to free children to experiment with "opposite-sex" choices during middle childhood. During the elementary school years, boys strengthen their identification with the same-sex masculine role, while girls become more androgynous. Same-sex identification increases in early adolescence for both sexes and declines thereafter. Psychologists at one time thought that androgynous individuals would show better psychological adjustment than traditionally oriented individuals. However, masculine-oriented children and adults are consistently advantaged, probably because of the greater societal value attached to the male sex role.

4. Gender schema theory combines features of social learning and cognitive-developmental theory to explain the

acquisition of sex-stereotyped knowledge and behavior. Children learn from the environment basic definitions of sex-appropriate behavior that form networks of gender-related schemas. These schemas are then used by children to process new experiences. Schema-consistent information is attended to and explored, while schema-conflicting information is ignored, rejected, or distorted to fit the schema. As a result, children learn much more about "same-sex" than "opposite-sex" activities and behavior.

5. A variety of sex differences in cognitive abilities and personality attributes have been identified. Girls excel in verbal skills and are more emotionally sensitive, compliant, and dependent, while boys are advantaged in spatial and mathematical abilities and are more aggressive than girls. In all instances the variations are small, and overall there are many more ways in which boys and girls are alike than different from one another. Hereditary factors may underlie sex differences in verbal and spatial abilities, and investigators have searched for the specific biological mechanisms responsible for them. At the same time, it is clear that environment plays an important role in each sex difference in mental ability. Girls' advantage in emotional sensitivity is probably the result of parental reinforcement for warmth and expressiveness, and their greater compliance and dependency can be accounted for by their frequent engagement in adult-structured activities.

6. Aggression first appears in children of both sexes during late infancy. Changes in the avenue through which aggression is expressed (from physical to verbal) and the form of aggression (from instrumental to hostile) take place during early childhood. Boys show more aggression of all kinds than girls. Aggressive behavior is also more stable over time and situationally consistent among boys. Prenatal and pubertal androgen levels appear to contribute to this sex difference, but they exert their effects indirectly, perhaps through intervening response tendencies that, when combined with certain environmental factors, lead to a higher likelihood of aggressive reactions. Parental disciplinary practices and anger and discord in the home promote self-perpetuating cycles of aggressive behavior between parents and children, and boys are more likely to become embroiled in coercive family processes than girls. Among treatments designed to reduce aggression, the cathartic technique has been shown to be ineffective. Interventions based on social learning theory that teach parents and children new ways of interacting with one another are far more successful. Aggression can also be reduced through empathy and perspective-taking training as well as modifications of the physical environment.

IMPORTANT TERMS AND CONCEPTS

sex stereotypes
sex roles
sex-role identity
instrumental traits

expressive traits
adrenogenital syndrome (AGS)
sex cleavage
androgyny

gender constancy
gender schema theory
instrumental aggression
hostile aggression

PART V

Contexts for Development

The Boating Party, by Mary Cassatt.
National Gallery of Art, Washington; Chester Dale Collection.

CHAPTER 14
The Family

In this chapter, we consider the child's first and formative context for development — the family. Other social settings also have important consequences for development, but the impact of the family is, without a doubt, the most profound. In Chapter 10, we showed that the family is the source of unique ties to others, for within it, children experience their first relationships of abiding commitment and love. The affectional bonds formed with parents and siblings generally endure over the life span, and they serve as prototypes for social relationships in the wider world of neighborhood and school. Within the family, children also experience their first social conflicts. As we saw in Chapters 11 and 12, disciplinary encounters with parents and arguments between siblings give children valuable lessons in compliance and cooperation, as well as early opportunities to learn how to influence the behavior of others. Finally, in several previous chapters we showed that the parent-child relationship is an essential context for the development of intellectual skills, language competence, and social and moral values. Thus the family provides the foundation for an impressively diverse array of characteristics that makes each of us human.

Research on the family has a long history in the social sciences. However, for many years it was primarily studied by sociologists and anthropologists. They paid less attention to its impact on child development than to describing its *structure* — the roles and relationships of its members — and *functions* — the purposes it serves in the everyday lives of people in comparison to other institutions of society (Hareven, 1984). When psychologists first turned to the study of family-related issues, they did so in a very restricted way. From the 1940s to the 1970s, most research was limited to the mother-child dyad and emphasized one-way effects of parental treatment on children's behavior. You are already aware from many earlier sections of this book that today, child development specialists are intensely interested in reciprocal, bidirectional influences between parents and children. In addition, they want to know

599

how parent-child interaction is affected by other family members, as well as by forces outside the family context.

Child development researchers now conceive of the family as a complex system of multiple, interacting relationships. To understand it, they have moved beyond their original focus on the mother-child dyad to the study of fathers, siblings, and extended family members. In addition, they have joined forces with those in other disciplines. New trends include an interest in looking at the family from an *ethological* perspective, in terms of its evolutionary origins and adaptive value. The family is currently studied from an *ecological* standpoint as well. Investigators now believe that the consequences of the family for children's development can only be understood when it is viewed in terms of its connections with other social institutions and as embedded in a larger context of cultural customs, attitudes, and values.

We begin our discussion of the family by examining the reasons that this formative social unit came into being and has survived over thousands of years as the primary context for human development. Then we describe the current view of the family as a *social system* of complex, interacting relationships with multiple sources of influence on the child. Next we take a close look at the family as the core socializing agency of society. Parental efforts to train children in the rules and tasks of the larger social group differ widely among families, social classes, and ethnic groups. We consider how to conceptualize this diverse array of parental child-rearing behaviors, and we examine their consequences for children's development.

In the last portion of this chapter, we take up the significance of a variety of changes in the American family for children's psychological development. The current trend toward fewer children per family unit means that more youngsters grow up with only one sibling, or none at all, than they did in decades past. The modern family is also more mobile, moving from one community to another with greater frequency than it did during the first half of this century. After 1960 the divorce rate rose dramatically, leading many children to spend a substantial portion of their childhood in single-parent homes. Many divorced parents eventually remarry, and their children must adjust to living arrangements that include an increasingly complex array of family figures and relationships. Over the last several decades, mothers have entered the labor force in rising numbers, and children spend much time in alternative care arrangements during their early years.

Finally, the modern family unit appears especially vulnerable to a breakdown in protective, emotionally supportive relationships of parent with child. Child abuse and neglect are prevalent in the United States, ranking as one of our most serious national problems. We consider why some parents mistreat their children, and why destructive family relationships are common in American society. We conclude this chapter with a discussion of the vital importance of developing broad national policies that support the American family in its child-rearing role.

EVOLUTIONARY ORIGINS

The structure of the human family as it exists in its most common form — a lifelong commitment between a man and woman who feed, shelter, and nurture their children until they reach maturity — had its origins tens of thousands of years ago among our hunting-and-gathering ancestors. A group living arrangement specially adapted for human survival, the family is unique to our species. Nonhuman primates also live in social groups and give birth to offspring who are protected by adult members of their species. But apes and monkeys do not organize themselves into family units where food is shared and both parents invest in the rearing of offspring. Instead, their young cling to and are nursed by the mother until they are able to move about themselves. After that time, they travel with the larger group and are protected from predators, but they must forage to feed themselves (Lancaster & Whitten, 1980).

Anthropologists believe that *bipedalism*—the ability of humans to walk upright on two legs—was an important evolutionary development that led to the formation of the family unit. Bipedalism permitted division of labor among adults. Once arms were freed to carry things, our evolutionary ancestors could cooperate and share, especially in providing food for the young. Men traveled to hunt for game and brought it back to women and children, and women gathered fruit and berries that provided a temporary food supply when game was scarce. The human family pattern in which a specific male assumed special responsibility for a single female and their joint off-spring soon appeared because it enhanced survival. It assured a relatively even balance of male hunters and female gatherers within a social group, thereby providing the maximum possible protection against starvation in times when game was scarce. Also, it led to the emergence of the "husband-father" role, which has no true counter-part among nonhuman primates. Furthermore, the economic and social obligations of parents to each other and to their children were so important to the survival of early humans that they could not be entrusted to rational thinking alone. The capacity for strong emotional bonds evolved to assure long-term commitment among family members (Lancaster & Whitten, 1980; Lovejoy, 1981; Mitchell & Shively, 1984).

Ninety-nine percent of the cumulative history of our species was spent in the hunting-and-gathering stage. Although a hunting-and-gathering economy no longer sustains the family ties of the vast majority of living humans, the special demands of this lifestyle appear to have left a lasting imprint on modern familial behavior (Lancaster & Whitten, 1980).

FUNCTIONS OF THE FAMILY

The family unit of our evolutionary ancestors not only promoted the survival of its own members, but also performed vital services for the larger society of which it was a part. Winch (1971) describes five functions that must be performed for society as a whole to survive:

1. *Reproduction:* replacements for dying members of society must be provided.
2. *Economic services:* goods and services must be produced and distributed for the support of members of society.
3. *Societal order:* procedures must exist for reducing conflict and maintaining orderly relationships among members of society.
4. *Socialization:* the young must be trained to become competent, participating members of society.
5. *Emotional support:* there must be procedures for binding individuals together, harmonizing their goals with those of other members of society, dealing with emotional crises, and fostering in each individual a sense of commitment, direction, and purpose.

In the early history of our species, families probably served all or most of these functions. But as the environments in which human beings lived became increasingly complex, the demands placed on the family became too much for it to sustain alone. As a result, other institutions took over or shared in certain functions that originally belonged to the family unit, and families became linked to larger social structures of society and culture (Lerner, Spanier, & Belsky, 1982). For example, political and law-making institutions assumed responsibility for insuring societal order, and schools built on the family's socialization function by educating children to partici-pate in an increasingly complex social world. Religious institutions supplemented the socialization and emotional support functions by providing educational services and offering family members a set of common beliefs that enhanced their sense of pur-posefulness and shared goals. Finally, although in preindustrial society the family was the basic unit of economic activity, today this is no longer true (Hareven, 1984).

In preindustrial society, the family was the basic unit of economic activity, and parents and children worked together to produce goods and services for society. Today, children are liabilities rather than contributors to the family's economic well-being. (University of Reading, Museum of English Rural Life)

While members of some families still carry out economic tasks together (as in the case with family-run farms and businesses), in modern mass societies economic productivity has, for the most part, been taken over by institutions that make up the world of work (Winch, 1971). In fact, today the economic role of the family is largely limited to consumption of goods and services, not to production. As a result, whereas children used to be important contributors to the economic well-being of the family, today they are ''economic liabilities.'' In fact, the cost of raising an American child born in the late 1980s from birth through four years of college is about $80,000 to $117,000.[1] The money required to give children the care and educational opportunities necessary to prepare them for the roles they will assume as adults is one factor, among others, that has contributed to the declining birth rate in modern industrialized nations (Espenshade, 1980).

While important functions have been taken over by or are now shared with other institutions, three of the functions mentioned above — reproduction, socialization, and emotional support — remain primarily the province of the family. Interestingly, these three functions are the ones that are especially related to children, for they include the tasks of giving birth to, rearing, and nurturing the young. Researchers interested in finding out how modern families go about serving these functions take a **social systems approach** to understanding the family, viewing it as a complex set of mutually influencing relationships affected by the larger social context of which it is a part.

THE FAMILY AS A SOCIAL SYSTEM

The social systems perspective on the family grew out of the efforts of family researchers and therapists to describe and explain the complex patterns of social behavior they observed among family members (Kantor & Lehr, 1975). As we review its fundamental features here, you will see that it has much in common with Bronfen-

---

[1] These figures are based on a 1980 estimate, corrected for subsequent inflation (U.S. Department of Labor, 1988). The estimate includes basic expenses related to food, housing, clothing, medical care, and education.

brenner's (1979) ecological model, which we discussed in Chapter 1.[2] According to the social systems view, the family is not a unidirectional social mold in which the child is shaped by parental (largely maternal) treatment. Instead, it consists of a complex interplay of interdependent parts that, together, form a network of reciprocal causal effects. Thus, basic to the social systems perspective is that children and parents influence each other. Furthermore, the reciprocal, bidirectional quality of familial interaction is affected by the quality of other relationships in the family setting, or what we referred to in Chapter 1 as the effect of *third parties*. For example, research has shown that mothers and fathers feel more competent as parents, praise and stimulate their children more, and nag and scold them less when their marital relationship is warm and supportive (Belsky, 1984b; Bandura & Walters, 1959; Sears, Maccoby, & Levin, 1957). In contrast, high marital hostility is linked to frequent use of coercion and punishment, techniques that often lead children to respond noncompliantly and aggressively in return. Take a moment to think about other examples of third-party influences within the family — for example, the impact of sibling relationships on parent-child communication, and vice versa. Have you conjured up an image of family interaction that looks much like a web of intricately crossed fibers in which pulling any single thread bends and shapes the others nearby?

To make matters even more complicated, the social systems approach views the complex interplay of forces within the family as dynamic, progressive, and ever-changing (Kantor & Lehr, 1975). Individuals continue to grow and change throughout the life span. As a result, the interactive nature of the family is not static; it shifts across time. For example, as children develop, so does parental participation in child rearing, and changes in parents' behavior toward their physically, cognitively, and socially more competent children pave the way for new competencies and further changes in family relationships. In fact, no other social unit is required to accommodate to such vast developmental changes in its members as is the family.

Finally, the social systems approach, as we indicated earlier, views relationships among mothers, fathers, and children as situated in larger social contexts. In other words, continuous, complex interchange does not just take place within the system; it also occurs across the boundary between the inner, family environment and the outer, external world (Kantor & Lehr, 1975). Connections to the community — both in terms of *formal organizations,* such as the school, work place, day care center, church, or synagogue, as well as *informal social networks* of relatives, friends, and neighbors — are regarded as significant for family well-being, and a wealth of research supports this view (Bronfenbrenner, Moen, & Garbarino, 1984). For example, higher rates of psychopathology — particularly disturbances that appear early in development, last a long time, and are typically accompanied by severe parental discord — are more prevalent in urban than rural communities (Rutter, 1981). Although population density and poverty contribute to this finding, they are not the only factors responsible. Psychological disturbance is greatest in metropolitan areas characterized by fragmented communication networks — high population mobility, weak community leadership, lack of organized leisure time activities, and few telephones and visits among friends and neighbors (Hughes et al., 1960). In addition, child abuse and neglect are greatest in urban neighborhoods where unemployment is high (Steinberg, Catalano, & Dooley, 1981) and residents report dissatisfaction with the community, describing it as a socially isolated place where few individuals take an interest in one another's welfare (Garbarino & Sherman, 1980). In contrast, when family ties to the community are strong — as reflected in regular church attendance and participation in informal networks of friends and relatives — family stress and child psychopathology are reduced (Werner & Smith, 1982). Furthermore, the results of several studies suggest that links established between family and community enhance children's

---

[2] You may wish to return to Chapter 1, pages 22–23, to review Bronfenbrenner's ecological model at this time.

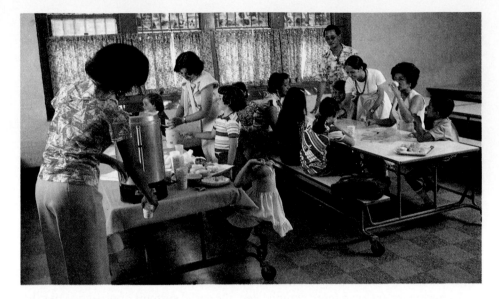

The social systems approach views formal and informal ties to the community as essential for optimal family functioning. (Michal Heron)

development. In one study, support from relatives and membership in social and religious organizations predicted the extent to which mothers of high-risk newborn babies provided their children with a stimulating home environment during the preschool years (Pascoe et al., 1981). In another study, parents who were more involved in school activities and organizations had children who showed superior school achievement (Stevenson & Baker, 1987).

Why do social ties to the community serve as an effective buffer against family stress and facilitate child development? Social systems theorists think this is true for a number of reasons. First, social supports provide parents with interpersonal acceptance. A neighbor or relative who listens sympathetically and tries to allay a parent's doubts and concerns enhances the parent's self-confidence and self-esteem. The parent, in turn, is likely to behave more patiently and sensitively toward her children. Second, social networks provide parents with opportunities to exchange valuable information, goods, and services. A friend who offers useful advice about where a parent might go to find a new job, better living arrangements, or a good doctor, or who looks after children while the parent attends to other pressing needs, helps make the multiple roles of spouse, economic provider, and caregiver easier to fulfill. As a result, benefits return to the parent-child relationship. Third, informal social networks as well as links with formal community organizations provide parents with child-rearing controls and role models. By giving advice, friends and relatives may encourage or discourage particular patterns of parent-child interaction, and during mutual visits, they may provide parents with observable examples of what they should be doing with their children. Finally, as children participate in the informal social networks of their parents, other adults can influence their development directly by providing warmth, encouragement, and exposure to a wider array of competent adult models (Cochran & Brassard, 1979; Mitchell & Trickett, 1980).

In summary, the social systems approach views family functioning as the product of a complex set of interacting, bidirectional relationships that constantly evolve and readjust as family members change over time. The quality of these relationships and the extent to which they enhance or undermine children's development are, in part, dependent on links established between family and formal and informal social supports in the larger community. No investigator could possibly study all facets of family functioning encompassed by the social systems perspective at the same time. However, as we address each piece of the larger family puzzle in the course of this chapter, it is important to keep in mind the many interlocking parts that simultaneously contribute to children's development.

605

CHAPTER 14
THE FAMILY

SOCIALIZATION WITHIN THE FAMILY

Socialization — the process by which members of society shape the behaviors of immature individuals so that they grow into competent, contributing participants — has been of greatest interest to child development specialists who study the family. A large number of investigations have addressed the question of how children's developing social, emotional, and cognitive competencies are influenced by the quality of their interactions with parents. In previous chapters, we discussed numerous ways in which parents can foster children's development — by being sensitively responsive to infants' momentary behaviors and needs (Chapter 10); by serving as models and reinforcers of children's socially acceptable behavior (Chapter 12); by relying on reasoning, explanation, and inductive disciplinary techniques to promote moral internalization and self-control (Chapter 12); and by communicating causal attributions that implicate children's effort rather than ability when they fail, thereby encouraging a mastery-oriented rather than learned-helpless approach to challenging tasks (Chapter 11).

Socialization pressures begin in earnest during the second year of life when children are first able to comply with parental demands (Maccoby & Martin, 1983). Effective caregivers pace their expectation in accord with children's ability to control their own actions. For example, parents who are in tune with their child's development do not impose a range of "don'ts" on a small infant. Instead, they put away breakable objects, place barriers across steep staircases, and remove babies physically when they start to behave in ways that are dangerous or bothersome to others. As soon as parents place greater emphasis on socialization toward the end of the infancy period, they vary considerably in how they go about the task. Researchers have been interested in describing the overall quality of parent-child interaction that distinguishes parents who are especially effective from those who are less effective at socializing the child.

Dimensions of Child Rearing

In a series of influential studies, Diana Baumrind gathered information on child-rearing practices by making naturalistic home observations and structured laboratory observations of parent-child interaction in families with preschool children. Two broad dimensions of parenting behavior emerged from the data (Baumrind, 1967; 1971; Baumrind & Black, 1967). The first is **control** or demandingness. Some parents establish high standards for what they expect of their children and insist that their youngsters meet those standards. Other parents demand very little and rarely redirect or inhibit their children's behavior. The second dimension is **responsiveness** or child-centeredness. Some parents are highly accepting of and responsive to their children; they frequently engage in open discussion and verbal give-and-take. Others are aloof, rejecting, and unresponsive to their youngster's social initiatives.

When looked at together, these two parenting dimensions sum up basic differences in how parents go about the task of socialization. As shown in Table 14.1, the various combinations of control and responsiveness yield four types of parents. Baumrind's research focused on three of them: the authoritative, the authoritarian, and the permissive parent. The fourth type — the indifferent parent — has been studied by other investigators. Each parenting pattern predicts important aspects of child development. Overall, research indicates that authoritative parents have socially active, responsible, and cognitively competent children, whereas parents who rely on

Table 14.1. A Two-dimensional Classification of Parenting Styles

	RESPONSIVE, CHILD-CENTERED	UNRESPONSIVE, PARENT-CENTERED
CONTROLLING, DEMANDING	Authoritative parent	Authoritarian parent
LOW IN CONTROL, UNDEMANDING	Permissive parent	Uninvolved parent

Source: Adapted from E. E. Maccoby & J. A. Martin, 1983, "Socialization in the Context of the Family: Parent-Child Interaction," in P.H. Mussen, (ed.), *Handbook of Child Psychology* (Vol. 4, pp. 1–101). New York: Wiley. Copyright 1983 by John Wiley & Sons. Reprinted by permission.

the other three styles have youngsters who develop less optimally in a number of ways. We take a close look at each of these parenting styles in the sections that follow.

The Authoritative Parent. In Baumrind's (1967) first study, preschool children were separated into categories based on ratings by psychologists who observed them over several months in the nursery school. As shown in Figure 14.1, one group, the mature preschoolers, differed sharply from the others in that their parents used a set of child-rearing tactics that were clearly **authoritative** in style. Parents of these youngsters were controlling and demanding. They had high expectations for mature behavior and firmly enforced them by using commands and consequences for disobedience when necessary. At the same time, they were warm and nurturant, listened patiently and sensitively to their youngster's point of view, and encouraged children's input into family decision making. These authoritative parents used a rational, democratic approach to child rearing in which the rights of both parents and children were recognized and respected. Psychologists observing their youngsters rated them as buoyant, zestful, and content in mood; self-reliant in their mastery of new tasks; and self-controlled in their ability to show sustained effort and inhibit behaviors that would be disruptive to others. Subsequent studies by Baumrind replicated these findings (Baumrind & Black, 1967) and also revealed that independent, achievement-oriented behavior among girls and friendly, cooperative social behavior among boys showed especially strong associations with authoritative parenting (Baumrind, 1971). Furthermore, follow-up research by other investigators indicated that the authoritative style continues to predict a variety of dimensions of competence during middle childhood and adolescence, including high self-esteem (Coopersmith, 1967; Loeb, Horst, & Horton, 1980), internalized moral standards (Hoffman, 1970), and superior academic performance in high school (Dornbusch et al., 1987).

The Authoritarian Parent. **Authoritarian** parents are also demanding and controlling, but they place such a high value on conformity and obedience that they are unresponsive — even outright rejecting — when children assert opposing opinions and beliefs. Consequently, little communicative give-and-take occurs between these parents and their youngsters. Rather, children are expected to accept their parent's word for what is right in an unquestioning manner. If they do not, authoritarian parents resort to punitive, forceful measures to curb the child's will. The authoritarian style is clearly biased in favor of parents' needs, with little room accorded to the child's independent self-expression. In Baumrind's (1967) early research, preschoolers whose parents fit this pattern were withdrawn and unhappy (see Figure 14.1). They appeared anxious and insecure when interacting with their peers and showed a tendency to react hostilely when frustrated. In subsequent research, the

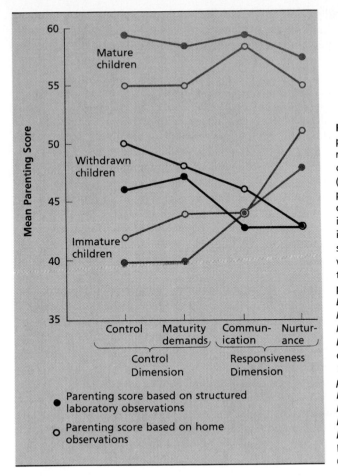

Figure 14.1. Relationship of parental control and responsiveness to children's competence in the Baumrind (1967) study. Assessments of parenting were based on observations of parent-child interaction in the home and in a structured laboratory situation in which parents were given an opportunity to teach and play with their preschool child. *(From D. Baumrind, "Child Care Practices Anteceding Three Patterns of Preschool Behavior," Genetic Psychology Monographs, 75, p. 73, 1967. Reprinted with permission of the Helen Dwight Reid Educational Foundation. Published by Heldref Publications, 4000 Albermarle Street N.W., Washington, DC 20016 © 1967.)*

preschool daughters of authoritarian parents were especially dependent and lacking in exploration and achievement motivation. In addition, some boys who were products of authoritarian child rearing showed high rates of anger and defiance, a pattern of response that was not found in girls (Baumrind, 1971). Furthermore, you may remember from Chapter 12 that authoritarian, power-assertive discipline is negatively related to internalization of moral prohibitions (Hoffman, 1970), and it is also associated with low self-esteem (Coopersmith, 1967).

The Permissive Parent. **Permissive** parents are nurturant, communicative, and accepting, but they avoid asserting their authority or imposing controls of any kind. They are overly tolerant and permit children to make virtually all of their own decisions. Children of permissive parents eat meals and go to bed when they feel like it, watch as much television as they want, do not have to learn good manners or be responsible for household chores, and are allowed to interrupt and annoy others without parental intervention. While some permissive parents consciously believe that a lax style of child rearing is good for children, many others lack confidence in their ability to influence their youngster's behavior and are disorganized and ineffective in running their households. Baumrind (1967) found it difficult to identify many parents who were extremely permissive among her research participants, but some leaned in that direction. As indicated in Figure 14.1, their children were highly immature youngsters. They had difficulty controlling their impulses, were overly dependent and demanding of adults, and showed less sustained involvement in classroom activities than children of parents who exerted more control. In addition, they were disobedient and explosive when asked to do something that conflicted with their current desires. Later findings indicated that the association of permissive parenting with passive, dependent, nonachieving behavior held for boys, but not for girls (Baumrind, 1971).

The Uninvolved Parent. When undemanding parenting is combined with indifferent or rejecting behavior, it falls within the **uninvolved** cell of the diagram in Table 14.1. Uninvolved parents display little commitment to their role as caregivers and socialization agents beyond the minimun effort required to maintain the child as a member of the household. Often these parents are overwhelmed by many daily pressures and stresses in their lives, and they have little time and energy left to spare for children. As a result, they cope with the requirements of parenting by keeping the child at a distance and are strongly oriented toward avoiding inconvenience. They may respond to the child's immediate demands for food and easily accessible objects, but any efforts that have to do with long-term goals, such as establishing and enforcing rules about homework or setting standards for acceptable social behavior, amount to little more than fleeting, feeble attempts to get the child to conform (Maccoby & Martin, 1983).

At its extreme, uninvolved parenting ranks as a form of child maltreatment called neglect. Especially when it begins early, it leads to disruptions in a great many aspects of development. Research reveals that detached, emotionally uninvolved, depressed mothers who are disinterested in their babies have children who by two years of age show deficits in virtually all aspects of psychological functioning, including substantial intellectual declines, attachment difficulties, lack of participation in play and feeding situations, and a rise in angry, noncompliant, as well as dependent behavior (Egeland & Sroufe, 1981).

Even when parental disinterest and detachment are less pronounced, child development is far from optimal. In a longitudinal investigation of the relationship between early parent-child interaction and children's behavior, Martin (1981) reported that uninvolved as opposed to responsive mothers had preschoolers who were noncompliant, demanding, and interfering in behavior. Required to wait while the mother filled out a questionnaire, they tugged and pulled at her clothing, grabbed her pencil, and sometimes kicked and hit her. Other studies have examined the correlates of an uninvolved, parent-centered approach at older ages. In longitudinal research carried out in Finland, Pulkkinen (1982) found that parents who rarely had conversations with their adolescents, took little interest in their life at school, and were seldom aware of their whereabouts and activities had youngsters who were low in frustration tolerance and emotional control, lacked long-term goals, and more often had records of delinquent acts than adolescents of involved parents. These differences persisted when the sample was followed up at 20 years of age. Other longitudinal findings support an association between a distant, indifferent, and unconcerned parenting style and impulsive, undercontrolled behavior throughout the childhood and adolescent years (Block, 1971).

As children get older, effective parents adjust their level of involvement to fit the child's changing capacity for independent, autonomous functioning. While too little parental involvement is associated with serious developmental difficulties, too much involvement can be overbearing and intrusive. A gradual lessening of parental monitoring and vigilance as children get older supports their movement toward mature, responsible behavior, as long as it continues to be built on high parental commitment and a warm, openly communicative relationship (Maccoby & Martin, 1983).

What Makes Authoritative Child Rearing So Effective?

The repeated association of authoritative parenting with socioemotional and intellectual maturity led Baumrind to conclude that the authoritative style plays a causal role in the superior development of children who are exposed to it. But like other correlational findings discussed throughout this book, these results are open to different interpretations. Recently, Lewis (1981) suggested that authoritative child rearing is largely a reaction to children's personality dispositions, rather than the cause of them. According to Lewis, parents of well-socialized children use firm, demanding tactics because their youngsters happen to have cooperative, obedient dispositions, not because firm control is an essential ingredient of effective parenting. Baumrind (1983) has countered Lewis's challenge by pointing out that many children of authoritative parents do not submit willingly to adult authority. Disciplinary conflict occurred often in the authoritative homes she studied, but parents handled it firmly, patiently, and rationally. They neither gave in to children's unreasonable demands, nor did they respond in a harsh, arbitrary fashion. Baumrind emphasizes that it is not the exercise of firm control per se, but rather the rational and reasonable use of firm control, that has positive consequences for children's development.

Nevertheless, children's characteristics undoubtedly contribute to the ease with which parents are able to implement an authoritative pattern. We saw in earlier chapters that temperamentally difficult youngsters are more likely than other children to receive highly coercive discipline, and when children react recalcitrantly and disobediently, some parents respond inconsistently by giving in to the child's unruly behavior, thereby rewarding it and increasing the chances that it will occur again. Children of parents who go back and forth between authoritarian and passive, indifferent child-rearing styles have especially impulsive, aggressive, and irresponsible youngsters who do very poorly in school (Dornbusch et al., 1987; Olweus, 1980b; Patterson, 1982). As Maccoby and Martin (1983) point out, the direction of influence between parenting practices and children's characteristics goes both ways. Impulsive and difficult children make it harder for parents to remain firm as well as democratically involved, but parenting practices may serve to either sustain or reduce children's difficult behavior.

Why do authoritative practices support such a wide array of positive developmental outcomes and help to bring the demanding, unruly behavior of poorly socialized children under control? There are a number of reasons. First, as we saw in Chapter 12, control exercised in a way that appears fair and reasonable to the child, not impetuous and arbitrary, is far more likely to be complied with and internalized. Second, nurturant, nonpermissive parents who are secure in the standards they hold for their youngsters provide children with models of caring concern for others as well as confident, assertive behavior (Kuczynski, Zahn-Waxler, & Radke-Yarrow, 1987). In addition, such parents are likely to be more effective reinforcing agents, praising the child for behaviors that meet their expectations as well as making more successful use of disapproval, which works best when applied by a nurturant parent who is able to withstand counterpressures from the child. Finally, parents who rely on authoritative techniques make demands that are sensitive and responsive to their children's developing capacities. By adjusting expectations so they fit with children's ability to take responsibility for their own behavior, these parents communicate to children a sense that they are competent beings who can do things successfully for themselves. As a result, high self-esteem and mature, autonomous functioning are fostered (Kuczynski et al., 1987).

Cultural, Social Class, and Ethnic Variations in Child Rearing

The same dimensions of parenting that underlie the child-rearing styles discussed above apply to a wide range of cultures around the world. Rohner and Rohner (1981) rated descriptions of parent behavior from anthropological records collected in 186 societies and found that children everywhere seem to experience differing degrees of control and nurturant involvement from parents and other major caregivers. Although cross-cultural variability does exist, the most common pattern of child rearing in the cultures studied by the Rohners was a style that is warm and controlling but neither very lax nor restrictive, much like Baumrind's authoritative pattern. As the investigators put it, ". . . the majority of [cultures] . . . have discovered for themselves over the centuries a 'truth' that has only recently emerged from empirical research in the western world—healthy psychosocial development of children is promoted most effectively by love with at least moderate parental control" (p. 257).

In American society as well as other Western nations, consistent social class differences in child-rearing patterns have been identified (Duvall, 1946; Gecas, 1979; Hoffman, 1984; Kohn, 1977). When asked about qualities they would like to encourage in their children, parents who work in semiskilled and skilled manual occupations (e.g., machinists, truck drivers, and custodians) place a high value on external characteristics, such as obedience, neatness, and cleanliness. In contrast, white-collar and professional parents more often emphasize internal psychological characteristics, such as curiosity, happiness, and self-control. These differences in child-rearing values are reflected in social class differences in parenting behaviors. Middle-class parents use more explanations, verbal praise, and inductive disciplinary techniques. In contrast, commands, such as "You'll do that because I told you to," as well as criticism and physical punishment, occur more often in low-income and working-class households (Kohn, 1977; Laosa, 1981). These coercive practices are verbally restricted, and they do not encourage children to compare and evaluate alternative courses of action. As a result, they contribute to the cognitively less enriching home environments experienced by many low-income children (Bernstein, 1964; Hess & Shipman, 1965).

Social class variations in child-rearing practices can be understood in terms of a number of differences in life conditions that exist between low-income and middle-income families. Low-income parents often feel a sense of powerlessness in their relationships with institutions beyond the family, a circumstance that has consequences for the way they rear their children. For example, several theorists suggest that because lower-class parents are continually subjected to the rules and authority of others in the workplace, their parent-child interaction duplicates their own experiences, only with them in the authority roles. Working-class occupations generally require the worker to follow the explicit rules of a supervisor, whereas middle-class occupations allow more room for self-direction and place greater emphasis on the manipulation of ideas and symbols. The values and behaviors required for success in the world of work are thought to affect parents' ideas about characteristics important to train in their children, who are expected to enter similar work roles in the future. Social class differences in educational attainment may play a role in these child-rearing variations as well. Middle-class parents' concern with nurturing their children's internal psychological characteristics is probably facilitated by years of higher education, during which they have learned to think about abstract, subjective ideas. Furthermore, the greater economic security of middle-class parents frees them from the burden of having to worry about making ends meet on a daily basis. As a result, they can devote more energy and attention to thinking about and encouraging the inner characteristics of themselves and their children (Hoffman, 1984; Kohn, 1977; 1979).

The constant stresses that impinge on many low-income families constitute an additional factor that contributes to social class differences in child-rearing patterns. Families of poverty experience an extraordinarily high frequency of daily crises and hassles—bills to pay, arguments with one's spouse, the car breaking down, termination of welfare and unemployment payments, something stolen from the house, a family member arrested, school reports of child misbehavior or truancy, to name just a few (Brown, Bhrolchain, & Harris, 1976; Tonge, James, & Hillam, 1975). When daily crises arise, parental irritability and coercive interactions within the household increase as well (Patterson, 1982).

Nevertheless, within a single social class there is considerable variation in factors that affect child rearing. The family structure, customs, and practices of some ethnic groups have been found to buffer the stress and disorganization that result from living in poverty. A case in point is the American black family, which has been studied extensively in recent years in an effort to find out how its members have managed to survive generations of severe economic deprivation and racism. A far greater proportion of American black than white families live below the poverty level (31 versus 9 percent), and a greater percentage experience the stresses associated with marital breakup and widowhood as well as out-of-wedlock and teenage pregnancy (Reid, 1982; Wilson, 1986).

The black cultural tradition of **extended family households,** in which one or several grandparents, uncles, aunts, siblings, or cousins live together with the parent-child **nuclear family unit,** is a vital feature of the black family that has enabled its members to survive and, in some instances, surmount highly adverse social conditions. The salience of the black extended family can be traced to the African heritage of most black Americans. In many African societies, a newly married couple does not move away from kin and start a new household. Instead, individuals marry into a large extended family that assists its members with essential family functions. The tradition of a broad network of highly committed kinship ties was transferred to the United States during the period of slavery. Since then, it has served as a protective mechanism against the destructive impact of poverty and racial prejudice (Foster, 1983) Today, more black than white adults have relatives other than their own children living in the same household. Black parents also see more kin during the week and perceive them as more salient figures in their lives — respecting the advice of relatives and caring deeply about what they think is important (Hays & Mindel, 1973; Wilson, 1986).

Research has consistently shown that the black extended family structure helps to reduce the stress of poverty and single parenthood by providing emotional support and reciprocal sharing of income and essential resources. In addition, extended family members often act as effective surrogate parents in the rearing of children (Wilson, 1986). The presence of grandmothers in the households of many black teenagers and their infants protects babies from the negative influence of an overwhelmed and inexperienced young mother. In one study, black grandmothers exhibited more responsive and less punitive interaction with the babies of their teenage daughters than the teenage mothers did themselves, and they also transmitted to the young mothers basic information about how infants develop (Stevens, 1984). Furthermore, black adolescent mothers who live in extended families tend to become productive, contributing members of the household. They are more likely to complete high school and get a job and less likely to receive welfare than mothers living on their own (Furstenberg & Crawford, 1978). During the middle childhood years, black extended family living arrangements are associated with positive outcomes for children. The presence of multiple adults leads to more give-and-take in adult-child interaction (Wilson & Tolson, 1985), along with better school achievement and improved psychological adjustment (Kellam, Ensminger, & Turner, 1977).

Active and involved extended families also characterize other American poverty minorities (Harrison, Serafica, & McAdoo, 1984). The study of such families increases our appreciation of the ability of the family unit to mobilize its cultural traditions to support its members under conditions of high life stress.

THE CHANGING AMERICAN FAMILY

Over the last several decades, rapid changes in family life have pervaded all sectors of the American populace, challenging the once widely held assumption of stability in the American family. Shrinking family size due to a declining birth rate; increasing family mobility; a rise in marital dissolution and single-parent households; and increasing participation in the labor market by mothers with children of all ages have reshaped modern family functioning. Today, the traditional family form in which the father earns a livelihood while the mother stays home and assumes primary responsibility for household tasks and the rearing of two or more children characterizes a small minority of family units. In 1955, 60 percent of families fit this traditional pattern; in the mid-1980s, only 7 percent conformed to it (Hodgkinson, 1985). In the sections that follow, we take up these changes in the American family, placing special emphasis on how each affects the roles and relationships of family members and, ultimately, children's development. Consistent with the social systems approach, we will see that what transpires within the family as a consequence of these changes is heavily influenced by the larger community and societal context in which family members are situated.

From Large to Small Families

Birth rate statistics indicate that although the size of the American family declined from the early to the middle part of this century, childbearing increased dramatically from 1945 to 1957, a period known as the post-World War II baby boom. During that time, many couples were making up for births they had postponed during wartime, and the average family size was greater than three children. However, birth rates dropped steadily thereafter. Today there are many more one- and two-child families than in earlier decades, as well as more couples opting to have no children at all. This trend is likely to continue. When women between 18 and 39 years of age were asked in 1986 to indicate how many children they expected to have, their projections averaged 2.1 children, in comparison to 3.1 in 1960 (U.S. Bureau of the Census, 1987a). Fertility rates are expected to drop even further by the early part of the twenty-first century, to a record low of 1.5 births per woman of childbearing age (Westoff, 1978).

Declining family size among all sectors of the population is the result of a number of broad social changes in the United States. Improved contraceptive effectiveness as well as the 1972 Supreme Court decision legalizing abortion make the current period one of greater choice with respect to whether or not to have children. In addition, increased entry into the labor market and career advancement among women over the past few decades have meant that many have chosen to divide their energies between work and family. A smaller family size is certainly more compatible with this dual commitment to career and child rearing. Furthermore, more couples are now delaying the birth of their first child until they are well established professionally and secure economically. This trend has repercussions for family size, for the woman who postpones childbirth is also likely to have fewer children than if she had begun her family at an earlier age (David & Baldwin, 1979; Hofferth, 1984). Finally, greater marital instability is another reason that families are smaller, for more couples today get divorced before their childbearing plans are complete (Falbo, 1984).

Family size has consequences for parent-child interaction as well as children's opportunities to grow up with siblings. In the sections that follow, we consider the implications of the smaller American family for child development by looking at its impact on relationships among nuclear family members.

Family Size and Parent-Child Interaction. In general, the trend toward a smaller family size has favorable consequences for parent-child interaction and, in turn, for many aspects of children's development. The results of many studies show that parental attitudes and treatment of children change systematically as more youngsters are added to the household. More children mean less time that husband and wife have to devote to one another as well as to each youngster's activities, school work, and other concerns. As a result, parents of large families tend to feel less satisfied with their marital relationships and parenting roles (Hurley & Palonen, 1967; Rutter & Madge, 1976). Furthermore, disciplinary practices become more authoritarian and punitive as family size increases and parents try to keep large numbers of youngsters "in line." Crowding and lack of a special place each child can call his own promote additional tension in a household with many children, with further repercussions for parent-child relationships (Blau, 1981). Investigators believe that together, these factors are responsible for the fact that children growing up in larger families have somewhat lower intelligence test scores, poorer school achievement, and lower self-esteem. Forms of child maladjustment also vary with family size. A smaller number of children provides some parents with ample opportunity to pressure their youngsters too much, leading anxiety to be somewhat more common among children from small families. In contrast, antisocial behavior and delinquency appear more often among children and adolescents who have many siblings (Wagner, Schubert, & Schubert, 1985).

However, an important qualification regarding the above findings is in order, for family size is strongly correlated with socioeconomic status, with larger families less well off economically than smaller ones. In fact, the birth of additional children contributes to the family size – socioeconomic relationship, given the cost mentioned earlier in this chapter of rearing a child to maturity. As a result, the impact of family size on parent-child interaction and child development is never completely separate from the family's standard of living. Rutter and Madge (1976) believe that the negative impact of increased family size on children's intellectual and socioemotional functioning is largely due to insufficient financial and material resources, which result in less adequate housing, poorer nutrition, greater parental stress, and consequent deterioration in the quality of the parent-child relationship. Consistent with this interpretation is evidence that unfavorable developmental outcomes associated with growing up in a large family are substantially reduced in economically well-off households with many children (Page & Grandon, 1979; Kennett & Cropley, 1970).

Growing Up with Siblings. Despite the shrinking family size, the two-child family is still very common in the United States, accounting for 42 percent of families who have children. Most American children still grow up with at least one sibling. In a survey in which married individuals were asked to explain why they desired more than one child, the most frequently mentioned reason was sibling companionship, cited by nearly half of the respondents (Bulatao & Arnold, 1977). The consequences of growing up with brothers and sisters have received relatively little research attention until recently, given the historical focus of investigators on the mother-child dyad. However, new research indicates that siblings exert important influences on development, both directly through the relationships siblings establish with one another, and indirectly, through the effects that the presence of an additional child has on the attitudes and behaviors of parents. In previous chapters, we looked at some developmental consequences of having brothers and sisters, including birth order effects on intelligence (Chapter 8), the impact of siblings on personality development (Chapter 10), and sibling effects on sex typing (Chapter 13). In this chapter, we focus more directly on the quality of the sibling relationship itself and its implications for childhood socialization and development.

Among adults, sibling associations generally conjure up images of rivalry and competition — thoughts of brothers and sisters competing with one another for a fair share of parental attention, approval, and material resources. The common assumption that jealousy and rivalry are key elements in sibling interactions originated with psychoanalytic theory, which stressed that sibling relationships are mediated by each youngster's desire to monopolize the attention and love of the parent (Levy, 1937). While some siblings are highly conflictual and rivalrous, we now know that this dimension of sibling interaction is only one element in a complex array of feelings and social exchanges that take place among youngsters growing up in the same family.

In a longitudinal study of the early development of sibling relationships, Dunn and Kendrick (1982) conducted parent interviews and made home observations of 40 preschoolers from a point late in their mother's second pregnancy through the infancy of the younger child. A drop in maternal involvement with the firstborn child occurred immediately after the birth of the infant. As a result, jealousy was an element in the older child's feelings toward the new arrival. Many preschoolers responded by becoming demanding and clingy and engaging in instances of "deliberate naughtiness" while the mother was preoccupied with caring for the baby. But resentment about being displaced by the new infant was only one of a wide range of emotions displayed by the older child. Positive social approaches and expressions of affection and concern for the baby also occurred. By the time the infant was 8 months old, the two siblings had become salient social partners for each other. A high frequency of interactions occurred, with the preschoolers comforting, sharing toys with, imitating, and expressing friendliness toward the baby, in addition to showing signs of anger and ambivalence. By 14 months of age, imitations by the baby of the firstborn child became frequent. Older children were already serving as influential models and agents of socialization for their younger brothers and sisters.

Substantial individual differences in the quality of relationships established by firstborn preschoolers with their siblings appear in the first few weeks after the second child's birth and remain remarkably stable over the early childhood years. As we indicated in Chapter 10, children's temperamental characteristics have some bearing on how positive or conflictual sibling interactions will be. But sibling relationships are also affected by the mother's manner of responding to her youngsters. Dunn and Kendrick found that when mothers were positive and playful in their style of interaction, feelings of rivalry emerged in older children, who were slightly less friendly toward the babies than older siblings with less playful mothers. In contrast, among firstborns who had experienced tense maternal relationships or whose mothers were especially tired and depressed after the second birth, a warm and caring relationship with the sibling often developed that relieved the stressful impact of the parent's behavior and contributed to the preschooler's emotional well-being. Moreover, mothers who frequently discussed the baby's feelings and intentions had preschoolers who were more likely to comment on the baby as a person with special wants and needs. Such children displayed more than twice as much friendly and considerate behavior toward their younger brothers and sisters as those who did not hear the mother discuss the baby in this way.

During middle childhood, when children begin to participate in sports, music, and school activities that highlight their special talents, parental comparisons of each child's abilities and accomplishments occur more frequently. When these evaluations are communicated to children, they accentuate sibling rivalry. The child who gets less parental attention, more disapproval, and the "short end of the stick" in terms of rewards and material resources is likely to express resentment and ill will toward a sibling who receives preferential treatment (Bryant & Crockenberg, 1980; Pfouts, 1976). Social comparisons are probably an important source of conflict for all siblings during the middle childhood years, and the common tendency of many siblings to strive to be different from one another in activities, talents, and interests (see Chapter 10) may be a major way children try to minimize this aspect of sibling rivalry. But despite some increased potential for sibling conflict during the elementary school years, many preadolescent youngsters also rely on siblings as important sources of social support. Siblings provide companionship, assistance with everyday tasks, and comfort during times of emotional stress, and they generally continue to do so throughout adolescence and adulthood (Bryant, 1982b). Warm, enduring bonds among brothers and sisters occur especially often in large families. More offspring dilute the attention each child receives from parents, a circumstance that appears to intensify children's rapport with one another (Bossard & Boll, 1956).

The research summarized above suggests that sibling associations offer a rich interactional context in which children learn and practice a wide range of social skills, including affectionate caring, conflict resolution, and control of competitive and hostile feelings. Child development specialists actually know very little about how experiences with siblings influence social relationships outside the family. In general, laterborn children are more popular with agemates than firstborn children (Miller &

Although rivalry is one dimension of sibling relationships, positive interactions are also prevalent. Siblings often provide one another with companionship and assistance with everyday tasks. (Tony Freeman/ PhotoEdit)

Maruyama, 1976; Sells & Roff, 1964). Perhaps as the result of learning to get along with larger, more powerful brothers and sisters, younger siblings become especially adept at negotiating, accommodating, and accepting less favorable outcomes, and they transfer these skills to their peer associations. However, much more research is needed to establish causal connections between children's sibling relationships and their social competence in the wider world of neighborhood and school.

The Only Child. Without opportunities to experience the closeness and conflicts inherent in sibling relationships, are children born into one-child families disadvantaged as far as social and emotional development goes? Many Americans think so. Parents of only children frequently report that relatives pressure them to have a second, believing that an only child is destined to become a spoiled, self-centered, dependent, socially inadequate adult (Falbo, 1984). This popular stereotype has been reinforced by the pessimistic pronouncements of many child development specialists, which can be traced at least as far back as 1907, when the eminent American psychologist G. Stanley Hall remarked, "Being an only child is a disease in itself" (Fenton, 1928, p. 547).

A great deal of research now indicates that the stereotypical view that siblings are indispensable for normal social development is incorrect. In fact, during the preschool years, there is some evidence that only youngsters are advanced in sociability. Snow, Jacklin, and Maccoby (1981) observed 2-year-old children with an unfamiliar peer in a laboratory playroom. Only children, when compared to youngsters from two-child families, showed more social behavior of all kinds, including positive as well as assertive-aggressive interactions, while second-borns showed the least. Later in development, only children as well as firstborns are more willing to lean on others in times of stress than laterborns (Hoyt & Raven, 1973; Schachter, 1959). Perhaps they do so because their parents were able to respond especially promptly to their signs of discomfort when they were infants and young children, a circumstance that may have led them to develop a high expectation that other people will be comforting when they are anxious and worried. By college age, only children do report a smaller circle of friends and membership in fewer organizations than individuals with siblings. But they do not appear to suffer socially or emotionally because of this, for they have just as many close friends as non-only borns and do not describe themselves as lonelier. Furthermore, as adults they report a level of life satisfaction and general happiness that is equal to that of other people (Blake, 1981; Falbo, 1978).

On the average, only children do better in school and attain higher educational levels than children with siblings (Claudy, 1984; Falbo & Polit, 1986). This difference is also thought to result from special parent-child relationships experienced by only youngsters. Research indicates that onlies as well as firstborns receive greater pressure for mature behavior than do laterborn children (Clausen, 1966; Kammeyer, 1967). In addition, the achievement of only children may be enhanced by the fact that they have only adult models in the home, a circumstance that may accelerate their acquisition of adultlike behavior. Only children also experience a higher overall level of parent-child interaction (Lewis & Kreitzberg, 1979), and their relationships with parents are more positive and affectionate than those of non-only youngsters (Falbo & Polit, 1986). We have already seen that the combination of high parental standards and warm, nurturant involvement — namely, authoritative parenting — is especially conducive to competent, mastery-oriented behavior.

In summary, no evidence exists to document the widely held belief that there are negative developmental consequences from being raised as an only child in the United States. Instead, both advantages and disadvantages are associated with family constellations that have just one or more than one youngster. In a survey in which only children and their parents were questioned about what they liked and disliked about living in a single-child family, the overwhelming majority of respondents depicted their lifestyle in positive terms (Hawke & Knox, 1978). However, they did mention a set of pros and cons, which are summarized in Table 14.2. Prospective parents might consider this list when deciding on how many children would best fit with their personal and family life plans, rather than basing their decision on the erroneous assumption that only children are destined to grow up as selfish, lonely, and maladjusted.

On a final note, we indicated earlier that the trend toward smaller families in general, and one-child families in particular, is associated with a tendency for many more women to postpone childbirth until their education is complete and their careers are well under way. Turn to Box 14.1 for some interesting research on how

Table 14.2. Advantages and Disadvantages of Living in a One-child Family

ADVANTAGES		DISADVANTAGES	
MENTIONED BY CHILDREN	MENTIONED BY PARENTS	MENTIONED BY CHILDREN	MENTIONED BY PARENTS
Avoiding sibling rivalry	Having time to pursue one's own interests and career	Not getting to experience the closeness of a sibling relationship	Walking a "tightrope" between healthy attention and overindulgence
Having more privacy	Less financial pressure	Feeling too much pressure from parents to succeed	Having only one chance to "make good" as a parent
Enjoying greater affluence	Not having to worry about "playing favorites" among children	Having no one to help care for parents when they get old	Being left childless in case of the child's death
Closer parent-child relationship			

Source: Hawke & Knox 1978.

Box 14.1
Bearing Children Past 30:
Consequences for Caregiving
Attitudes and Behavior

Theory. Although the overall birth rate declined during the 1970s, first births for women in their early 30s more than doubled, and they have continued to rise through the 1980s (Ventura, 1982; U.S. Bureau of the Census, 1987a). In years past, delayed child rearing depended on marriage opportunities and fertility. Today, it is largely the result of career commitments and finances.

Waiting to have a baby until a later period in the life course is likely to affect a mother's attitudes and behavior as a parent and, in turn, her children's development. Popular wisdom has it that giving birth during the twenties is optimal, not only because the risk of having a baby with genetic abnormalities is reduced (see Chapter 3), but also because younger parents are better equipped with energy levels needed to keep up with active children. Alternatively, since older mothers are economically better off and have had more experience in nonparenting roles, they may be better

able to invest in parenting. As a result, they may perform child care tasks more effectively. Arlene Ragozin and her colleagues (1982) examined the child care attitudes and behaviors of 17- to 38-year-old mothers of preterm and full-term newborns to find out how they compared in child-rearing enthusiasm and competence.

Research. One month after discharge from the hospital, over a hundred mothers were asked about their perceptions of and satisfactions with parenting, and their interactions with their infants were observed in a laboratory playroom. After background variables such as family income and maternal education were controlled, age continued to predict both parenting attitudes and behavior. The more stable life circumstances and emotional maturity of older mothers seemed to help them cope with the stress of caring for a preterm baby. These mothers reported greater pleasure in the maternal role, more involvement in child care responsibilities, and less social time away from their babies than their younger counterparts. Among mothers with full-term babies, maternal age showed strong relationships with several

aspects of mother-infant interaction. However, as shown in Figure 14.2, the nature of these associations depended on number of prior births. For those having their first child, the older the mother, the more she vocalized and was sensitively responsive to her baby's cues. These positive maternal age – behavior associations declined in strength until they became negative for mothers who had more than two children. Ragozin and her colleagues suggested that older mothers with several children, having already experienced parenthood a number of times, were less interested in the new baby and eager to turn to extrafamilial roles, while those giving birth to their first child were especially committed to the parenting experience.

Applications. Ragozin's research challenges the popular assumption of less optimal parenting, at least during early infancy, on the part of older mothers. While little is known about the consequences of parents' age for their relationships with older children and adolescents, the findings reported above suggest that positive developmental outcomes may accrue for first-born and at-risk babies from delaying parenthood until a later age.

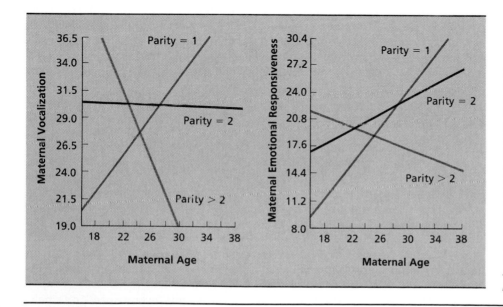

Figure 14.2. Relationship of mothers' age and parity (number of births) to their vocalization and emotional responsiveness to full-term babies in the Ragozin et al. (1982) study. *(Adapted from A. S. Ragozin, R. B. Basham, K. A. Crnic, M. T. Greenberg, & N. M. Robinson (1982), "Effects of Maternal Age on Parenting Role,"* Developmental Psychology, 18, *627–634. Copyright 1982 by the American Psychological Association. Adapted by permission of the author.)*

these more "mature" mothers, in comparison to their younger counterparts, feel about parenthood and interact with their newborn babies.

Family Mobility

Mobility rates of American families rose dramatically after World War II and have continued to increase gradually since 1960. Currently, one fifth of America's population moves each year (U.S. Bureau of the Census, 1987a). Relocating invariably leads to disruptions in families' formal and informal ties to neighborhood and community. However, why and where a family moves has much to do with how easily it can build supportive links to its new social surroundings and, ultimately, how well children fare after resettling in a new locale.

Better educated, economically advantaged parents usually move willingly, in response to opportunities for vocational advancement or better housing. Although they make more long-distance moves to places where they have no preexisting contacts than low-income families, they generally adjust quite well. Middle-class families have sufficient resources to preserve old community ties through phone calls and travel until they have had a chance to develop new supportive relationships (Fischer, 1977). In addition, affluent, well-educated parents who frequently relocate pick up social skills that facilitate their rapid integration into new communities. Such parents are in an especially good position to help their youngsters adjust to unfamiliar schools, neighborhoods, and peer groups. Research shows that their children do as well academically as their less mobile counterparts and are not harmed socially or emotionally (Fischer, 1977; Long, 1975).

But low-income and impoverished members of the population usually move for different reasons than well-off families. They are generally forced to relocate, as the result of unemployment, urban renewal, or eviction (Fischer, 1977). For families like these, even a short-distance move to a new neighborhood is an added stressor that can seriously disrupt supportive relationships with relatives and friends. Children subjected to frequent moves who come from families experiencing economic instability make especially poor progress in school (Long, 1975). One study indicated that these youngsters also display adjustment problems in the form of increased dependency and aggressiveness during the adolescent years (Pulkkinen, 1982).

In summary, the developmental consequences of America's highly mobile lifestyle have much to do with parental choice and availability of resources. When families move voluntarily and can choose destinations where they are likely to find compatible social relationships, relocating has no long-term psychological ill effects. In contrast, when they are forced to relocate, must take up residence in unreceptive destinations, and are poor, moving is likely to disrupt family functioning and increase the chances that an already vulnerable child will experience behavior and learning problems.

The Rising Rate of Divorce

Parental separation and divorce have become extremely common in the lives of American children. The incidence of marital breakup in the United States is the highest in the world, nearly doubling that of the second-ranked country, Sweden (Bronfenbrenner, 1986). Between 1960 and 1980, the American divorce rate tripled, and then stabilized. Currently, over one million children experience the separation or divorce of their parents each year, and recent census figures indicate that a total of 13 million children under 18 years of age (23 percent of all of America's youngsters) live in single-parent households. While the great majority (89 percent) live with their mothers, the number residing in father-headed households increased slightly between 1980 and 1985, from 9 to 11 percent (U.S. Bureau of the Census, 1987a).

The average period of time that children whose parents divorce spend in a single-parent home is 6 years, amounting to one-third of their total childhood years (Hetherington, 1979). But for many children, divorce leads to new family relationships. Approximately two thirds of divorced parents marry a second time (Glick & Lin, 1987), merging parent, stepparent, and children into a new family structure called the **reconstituted family.** Half of these children eventually experience a third major change in their family lives — the dissolution of their parent's second marriage (Bumpass, 1984).

These figures reveal that divorce is not a single event in the lives of parents and children. Instead, it is a transition that leads to a series of new family arrangements that are often accompanied by shifts in residence, financial resources, and familial roles and responsibilities. Since the 1960s, many studies have reported that the stress of marital breakup is associated with negative social, emotional, and cognitive consequences for children's development. But the research has also revealed considerable individual variability in how children respond. Some youngsters adjust with comparative ease, while others suffer prolonged psychological difficulties. Recently, investigators have begun to understand these different outcomes in terms of a complex array of variables that affect how well the family unit is able to adapt to stress and sustain a pattern of interaction that is supportive of children's development. Factors that make a difference in children's adjustment include adult psychological functioning; child characteristics such as temperament, sex, and age; and the availability of social supports in the surrounding community.

Effects of Divorce on Children's Development. In the sections that follow, we consider what is known about how well children take the major life changes associated with parental divorce. Our knowledge is enhanced by several longitudinal studies that have tracked children's development over extended periods of time, as well as a large number of short-term investigations.

Immediate Reactions. The period surrounding divorce is almost always accompanied by an escalation of family conflict as parents separate and try to settle disputes over personal belongings, finances, and child custody. Once one parent moves out, a cluster of additional, highly stressful events generally ensues that further threatens the adaptive functioning of the custodial parent and children. Mother-headed households typically experience a dramatic drop in income. Often the family must relocate for economic reasons, generally to poorer quality housing and neighborhoods, a circumstance that reduces supportive ties to neighbors and friends. Many single mothers who previously did not work must find immediate employment. Those with little occupational training and experience end up in low-paying jobs with incomes that barely cover family necessities. As a result, young children are likely to experience inadequate child care while the mother is at work and an overburdened, distracted, and unavailable caregiver when she is at home. Research indicates that the life circumstances of many newly divorced mothers often promote a highly disorganized family situation that Wallerstein and Kelly (1980) termed "minimal parenting." Predictable household events and routines — scheduled mealtimes and bedtimes, regular completion of household chores, and joint parent-child recreational activities — usually disintegrate. Disciplining of children vacillates between detachment and highly authoritarian, restrictive practices as mothers try to recapture control of youngsters who are distressed, confused, and angry about their less secure home lives (Hetherington, Cox, & Cox, 1982). Divorced fathers generally spend more time with their youngsters immediately after divorce, but for many children this contact diminishes over time. Infrequent paternal visitation often brings with it highly indulgent and permissive parenting that conflicts with the mother's style of discipline and increases her difficulties in managing the youngster on a day-to-day basis (Furstenberg, Spanier, & Rothschild, 1982; Hetherington, Cox, & Cox, 1982; Furstenberg & Nord, 1985; Weitzman, 1985).

In view of these changes in family relationships and living conditions, it is not surprising that many studies report that children experience painful emotional reactions and a rise in behavior problems during the period surrounding parental divorce. Common initial responses of preschool through adolescent-age youngsters are anger, fear, depression, divided parental loyalty, and guilt (Hetherington, 1979; Wallerstein & Kelly, 1980). However, the intensity of these feelings and the manner in which they are translated into behavior vary considerably from child to child and are partly dependent on the youngster's sex. Preschool and elementary school boys show more severe behavioral disorganization than girls, typically reacting to parental battles and inconsistent discipline with noncompliance, demandingness, and hostile behavior (Guidubaldi & Perry, 1985; Hetherington, Cox, & Cox, 1982; Wallerstein & Kelly, 1980). Recall from Chapter 13 that boys are more assertive and noncompliant than girls to begin with. They seem to engage in these behavior patterns even more strongly when they encounter high parental conflict and unpredictable disciplinary tactics. Boys also receive less nurturance and are viewed more negatively by custodial mothers, teachers, and peers in the period immediately surrounding divorce, perhaps because their behavior is especially difficult to manage. In addition, some mothers may react more negatively to their sons because the male child serves as a reminder of the divorcee's ex-husband. These unsympathetic reactions increase the stress and frustration that boys experience and further magnify their undercontrolled behavior. Girls are also intensely affected by parental separation, but they usually show more internalized reactions, such as crying, self-criticism, and withdrawal, which are easier for parents to deal with in a patient, sympathetic manner (Emery, 1982). Moreover, the demanding, attention-getting behavior that girls do display when exposed to divorcing parents' inconsistent discipline is less intense than that of their male counterparts (Hetherington, Cox, & Cox, 1982). While children of both sexes show declines in school achievement during the aftermath of divorce, once again, school difficulties are far more prevalent among boys (Guidubaldi & Cleminshaw, 1985; Guidubaldi & Perry, 1985; Wallerstein & Kelly, 1980).

Besides children's sex, developmental maturity influences their response to divorce. The more limited cognitive competencies of preschool and early elementary school children make it difficult for them to accurately appraise the reasons behind their parents' separation. These youngsters often blame themselves, imagine that they must have done something wrong to cause the departure of one parent from the household, and take the marital rupture as a sign that they could be abandoned by both of their parents. Consequently, younger children are often profoundly upset, revert to more immature behaviors, and display intense separation anxiety (Wallerstein & Kelly, 1975). In contrast, older children and adolescents are better able to understand their parents' divorce in terms of irreconcilable differences of opinion, incompatible personalities, and lack of caring for one another (Neal, 1983). Older youngsters' ability to appropriately assign responsibility may moderate some of the pain that they feel. Nevertheless, many adolescents display intense behavioral reactions, although the way they respond is qualitatively different from the reactions of younger children. Some enter into a variety of undesirable peer activities that provide an escape from their unpleasant home lives, and truancy, running away from home, smoking, school discipline problems, and delinquent behavior become increasingly common (Dornbusch et al., 1985). Girls in particular show a rise in sexual activity that often coincides with the discovery of parental sexual infidelities. However, not all adolescents react in this fashion. For some — especially oldest children in the family — divorce can be a catalyst for more mature behavior. These youngsters may respond by taking on greater responsibility for household tasks, care and protection of younger siblings, and emotional support of a depressed, anxious mother. Nevertheless, some investigators speculate that too much responsibility may lead some older youngsters to feel overburdened and resentful, eventually causing them to withdraw from the family into some of the more destructive behavior patterns described above (Wallerstein & Kelly, 1980).

Long-term Outcomes. If the immediate crisis of parental separation is not compounded by continuing family hardships, both parents and children show markedly improved adjustment by two years after the divorce. But when poor parent-child relationships continue for an extended period, long-term negative outcomes accrue, especially for children whose characteristics limit their resilience when they are confronted with stressful life conditions.

Children with histories of maladjustment preceding parental divorce are especially likely to show lasting emotional difficulties (Hetherington, 1979). In addition, boys remain more vulnerable in the long run than girls. Many show continued problems with school performance as well as heightened dependency, poor self-control, and increases in aggressive behavior (Hetherington, Cox, & Cox, 1982; 1985; Guidubaldi & Perry, 1985). Research suggests that contact with fathers is particularly important in how well boys eventually adjust, for regular paternal visitation and a good father-son relationship are associated with improved long-term outcomes (Hetherington, Cox, & Cox, 1982; Wallerstein & Kelly, 1980). Moreover, the limited evidence available on paternal custody suggests that sons who live with their fathers show special benefits in terms of socioemotional adjustment, including less demanding and more mature behavior than that of their mother-custody counterparts (Santrock & Warshak, 1979). Fathers appear to be able to evoke more compliance and cooperation from their male children than mothers, perhaps because of the way they interact with and discipline boys. One study reported that divorced fathers ignore their sons' disruptive behavior less and offer praise for following directions more than do mothers (Hetherington, Cox, & Cox, 1982). The father's image of greater power and authority may be an added reason that he is able to engender more obedience in sons (Hetherington, 1979). In addition, sons whose fathers maintain frequent contact have more opportunities to identify with and adopt their father's self-controlled behavior.

Girls experience far fewer lasting problems than boys, particularly when they reside in mother-headed households. Their singular long-term difficulty is the appearance of precocious sexual activity at adolescence and a continuation of short-lived sexual relationships into early adulthood, an outcome that characterizes even those girls who experienced their parents' separation as long ago as the preschool and middle childhood years and who showed good adjustment prior to the time that they became teenagers (Hetherington, 1972; Kalter et al., 1985; Wallerstein, 1985). These findings indicate that a good father-daughter relationship is important for the girl's adolescent heterosexual adjustment, even though it seems to be less crucial for her overall social and emotional well-being during early and middle childhood than a supportive maternal relationship (Santrock & Warshak, 1979; Wallerstein & Kelly, 1980).

The research described above underlines the importance of positive relationships with both parents for optimal child development, with the same-sex parent appearing as especially important for many aspects of psychological adjustment during early and middle childhood. In fact, the ability of divorcing couples to put aside their conflicts and support one another in their respective parenting roles is the single most important factor in assuring that a single-parent family will serve as an effective context for the development of competent, stable, and happy children (Hetherington, 1979; Wallerstein & Kelly, 1980). Where parental cooperation is not possible, the assistance of extended family members and friends can lead to improved child adjustment (Colletta, 1979). In addition, school environments make a difference. Hetherington, Cox, and Cox (1982) found that during the two years following divorce, the social and cognitive development of preschoolers was enhanced if they attended schools in which teachers provided them with consistent structure, used warm but firm disciplinary techniques, and made reasonable demands for mature behavior. Note that these are the same characteristics of authoritative parenting associated with competent social and intellectual development among children raised in intact families. Young children clearly benefit from a safe, predictable, and nurturant classroom environment when comparable experiences are not available at home.

Changing Societal Attitudes Toward Divorce. Several decades ago, the prevalent view of divorce in American society was that children were doomed to maladjustment if they were raised in a single-parent household. Professionals and lay persons alike believed that unhappily married couples should avoid separation at almost any cost, and many remained together for the sake of their children. Today, divorce carries little of the social stigma that it did a generation or two ago, and child rearing has become an activity governed less by constraint and obligation and more by voluntary choice (Furstenberg & Nord, 1985). As a result, children figure less importantly into parents' decision to dissolve a marriage than they did in decades past. Some people wonder whether these changes in attitudes are for the better, or if most youngsters would be better off if their parents returned to the practice of tolerating a conflict-ridden, unfulfilling relationship to safeguard their children's development.

A longitudinal study carried out by Hetherington, Cox, and Cox (1982) sheds light on this question. They followed the development of two groups of preschool children. In one, children resided in divorced families; in the other they lived in intact households. In each group, some families had high and others had low levels of family discord. In the first year following divorce, children in divorced families were functioning less well than those in either high- or low-conflict nondivorced homes. But by two years following the divorce, this pattern had changed. Children from stressed, intact families were more poorly adjusted than youngsters who had weathered the stormy transition to a single-parent family and were living in low-conflict households.

These findings suggest that in the long run, it is probably not a good idea for parents to remain in a strife-ridden marriage for the sake of children if they can work toward a harmonious single-parent arrangement. Nevertheless, when we look at the research as a whole, it is abundantly clear that children suffer deeply from experiencing their parents' divorce — more so than many researchers expected when they set out to study the problem. An overwhelming majority of children from divorced families are much less content with the quality of their family relationships than children who live in intact homes, and they report that they do not get all the affection and attention that they need. They would much rather be together with both of their parents than in their current living arrangements. Although an involved noncustodial parent can ease the strain that children feel, shared parenting among formerly married couples takes place in only a minority of cases. Many children of divorce indicate that they no longer feel close to both their mother and father, miss the nonresidential parent deeply, and are grateful for the small amount of contact that they have (Furstenberg & Nord, 1985). Finally, although school performance and psychological adjustment ratings improve over time for many children, deep-seated inner feelings remain. Conducting interviews with adolescents and young adults who had experienced their parents' marital breakup ten years earlier, Wallerstein (1984; 1985) found that those old enough to recall the circumstances surrounding the divorce retained vivid, emotionally painful memories of their own suffering at the time. Even among those who remembered little, the dissolution of their parents' marriage remained a salient aspect of their lives and often evoked tears and sadness as they spoke of it. Most of these young people had resolved to avoid the unhappiness associated with divorce in their own adulthood, and as a group they were strongly committed to the traditional ideal of a lasting marriage for the sake of their own as yet unborn children.

So the question of whether divorce is best for children if their parents' marriage is unhappy really has no simple, satisfactory answer. We must conclude, overall, that the dissolution of a strife-ridden marital relationship has significant costs, as well as benefits, for the youngsters who experience it.

The Reconstituted Family. For many children whose parents divorce, life in a single-parent household is a temporary condition. Their parents marry again before they become young adults. Remarriage often leads to improvements in the life circumstances of single-parent families — a better standard of living, another adult to share the household tasks and responsibilities, and an end to the loneliness and isolation that many divorced parents experience. As a result, it is often associated with greater life satisfaction for the remarried adult (Hetherington, Cox, & Cox, 1982). But remarriage also creates a new and complex set of relationships for all family members, as stepparents, stepchildren, stepsiblings, stepgrandparents, and others begin to play roles in family life. For some children, this expanded network of family ties is a gratifying turn of events that compensates for the loss in parental attention associated with divorce. But for most youngsters, it presents difficult adjustments. Stepparents and children must define a relationship in the absence of clear guidelines like those that exist for biological parents and their offspring. Many stepparents wonder how and whether to discipline their spouse's youngster, and when they do, they often use different practices than the child was used to in the "old" family. Having to switch to a new set of rules and expectations is stressful for many youngsters (Lutz, 1983). Moreover, some children view the entry of steprelatives into the household as an intrusion into their relationship with the custodial parent (Cherlin, 1981). Remarriage also leads to changes in children's opportunities to interact with the noncustodial parent. For example, remarried noncustodial fathers visit their children far less often, especially if they are daughters (Hetherington, Cox, & Cox, 1982; Furstenberg, Spanier, & Rothschild, 1982).

The limited evidence available on children's adaptation to reconstituted family arrangements indicates that many go through a trying period of adjustment, but how well they fare varies with the sex of parent and child. Children accommodate best to mother-stepfather families, the most frequent form of reconstituted arrangement (since mothers generally retain custody of the child). When custodial mothers remarry, boys in particular acclimate quickly, welcoming a relationship with a stepfather who establishes a responsive, authoritative relationship with the child and offers relief from the inconsistent discipline and coercive cycles of interaction that tend to build between divorced mothers and their sons (Wallerstein & Kelly, 1980). One study indicated that less than two years after remarriage, boys in mother-stepfather households were functioning almost as well as those living in nondivorced families (Hetherington, Cox, & Cox, 1985). In contrast, girls adapt less favorably to a mother-stepfather arrangement. They display an increase in behavior problems for a period of time, perhaps because of disruption in the close ties many established with their mothers while living in a single-parent family (Hetherington, Cox, & Cox, 1985; Clingempeel & Segal, 1986; Peterson & Zill, 1986; Santrock, Warshak, & Elliott, 1982).

Although only a few studies have focused on father-stepmother remarriages, the evidence consistently reveals more confusion and problematic interaction in these homes (Ihinger-Tallman & Pasley, 1987). This outcome may be due to the fact that stepmother families generally start out with more problems. When biological fathers obtain custody of their children, the arrangement is often not a matter of choice, but of necessity. The biological mother can no longer handle the difficult, unruly child (usually a boy), and the father and his new wife are faced with a youngster who has experienced an especially troubled mother-child relationship (Grief, 1985; Risman, 1986). In other cases, the father assumes custody because of a close relationship with the child, but his remarriage jeopardizes this bond. Although one study reported that girls adjust better than boys to the stepmother-father arrangement (Santrock, Warshak, & Elliott, 1982), several others have come to contrary conclusions — that girls have an especially difficult time getting along with their stepmothers (Clingempeel, Brand, & Ievoli, 1984; Clingempeel, Ievoli, & Brand, 1985; Ferri, 1984; Hobart & Brown, 1988). Paternal custody of girls is a rare arrangement that may occur in instances of a very warm father-daughter relationship, which (as indicated above) is threatened by the entry of a stepmother. Other evidence suggests that noncustodial mothers (unlike their paternal counterparts) maintain regular contact with their children, but frequent visits by the nonresident mother are associated with less positive stepmother-stepdaughter interaction. Perhaps girls are especially likely to become embroiled in loyalty conflicts between their two mother figures, a circumstance that promotes an ambivalent and strained relationship with the stepmother. However, the longer girls live in father-stepmother households, the more positive stepmother-daughter relationships become. Over time, the relative child-rearing roles of biological mothers and stepmothers seem to be effectively negotiated, and girls eventually benefit from the support of a second mother figure (Clingempeel & Segal, 1986).

These findings indicate that children in stepmother families, and daughters in particular, have the most difficult time adjusting to parental remarriage. However, the quality of the stepparent-child relationship is probably much more important than the precise makeup of the reconstituted family in moderating the consequences of remarriage for children (Clingempeel & Segal, 1986; Hetherington & Camara, 1984). To date, research has only scratched the surface with regard to how children feel about and interact with their remarried parents and new steprelatives. Furthermore, most of the evidence summarized above is based on preadolescent and early adolescent youngsters, who may find it harder to adjust to their parents' remarriage than their younger counterparts (Hobart, 1987; Kaplan & Pokorny, 1971; Wallerstein & Kelly, 1980). Older children are more perceptive about the implications of remarriage for their own life circumstances. As a result, they may initially challenge some aspects of the reconstituted family that younger children simply accept, thereby creating more relationship issues with their steprelatives. Finally, it is important to note that the impact of reconstituted families, as well as repeated divorce in instances of failed remarriage, on the long-term trajectory of development is still unknown.

Helping Children and Families Cope with Divorce and Remarriage. The stressful events that surround divorce and remarriage leave many parents and children in need of supportive services during these times of family transition. A wide variety of resource and intervention programs have been initiated by local community agencies as well as single-parent and stepparent associations. The largest of these organizations is Parents Without Partners, with a national membership of 180,000. It provides informative publications, telephone referrals, and programs through local chapters that are designed to alleviate the problems of single parents in relation to the upbringing of their children (Koek & Martin, 1988). The aim of most of these efforts is prevention—working with parents and children before serious maladjustment develops. Some offer informal self-help sessions in which small groups of single parents or stepparents meet together on a regular basis to share experiences, discuss problems, and provide one another with social support. Formal psychological services also exist, consisting of individual, family, or group counseling in which health professionals teach parents communication and child discipline skills and offer specific information about what to expect after entry into a single-parent or reconstituted family arrangement. Support groups are also available for children, often sponsored by schools, churches, synagogues, and mental health agencies, in which youngsters can share fears and concerns and learn anger control and other coping skills (Emery, Hetherington, & DiLalla, 1984). The limited evidence available on the effectiveness of such interventions suggests that they can reduce stress and promote improved communication among family members (e.g., Stohlberg, Cullen, and Garrison, 1982).

Another recently developed service is **divorce mediation.** It consists of a series of meetings between the divorcing parents and a trained professional who tries to facilitate agreement on disputed issues, such as child custody and property settlement. Its purpose is to permit divorcing parties to remain involved in important decisions, rather than turning them over to the court entirely, and to avoid extended courtroom battles that lead to an escalation of conflict within the family. In some states, divorce mediation is voluntary, while in others it is mandatory and must be attempted before a case is heard by a judge (Emery, Hetherington, & DiLalla, 1984). Research indicates that divorce mediation increases out-of-court settlements and feelings of well-being among divorcing adults (Bahr, 1981). Little is known about its consequences for children's adjustment, although by reducing parental conflict, divorce mediation may ease the stress that children experience once their parents decide to divorce.

Joint Custody. Child custody arrangements condoned by the American legal system are far more flexible today than they were several decades ago. In addition to the traditional **sole custody** arrangement in which one parent assumes responsibility for the education and welfare of the child, **joint custody,** which grants both parents an equal right to be involved in important decisions about the child's upbringing, is now possible in most states. Joint custody may promote increased contact on the part of each parent with the child and reduce the stress of perpetual caregiving that often comes with single parenthood. In addition, it eliminates a "winner" and "loser" resolution to child custody disputes, a circumstance that sometimes diminishes the "loser's" willingness to spend time with the children. All of these factors may lead joint custody to be beneficial for children's adjustment (Emery, Hetherington, & DiLalla, 1984).

Nevertheless, joint custody is a controversial practice, and not all psychologists and legal professionals advocate it. *Joint legal custody* is not synonymous with *joint physical custody*—a shared parenting arrangement in which both mother and father participate equally in the care and upbringing of the child (Ihinger-Tallman & Pasley, 1987). In fact, practically speaking, joint legal custody translates into a multitude of different child living arrangements. In some instances, children reside primarily with one parent and see the other on a fixed visitation schedule, much like the typical sole custody arrangement. In other cases, parents do share in the physical custody of their children, who must alternate between parental homes, sometimes on a daily and other times on a weekly, monthly, or even yearly basis. Some of these transitions require a shift not just in residence, but also in school and peer group. As a result, they introduce a new kind of instability into children's lives that is especially difficult for some youngsters to handle. The success of joint physical custody requires a reasonably cooperative relationship between divorcing parents. When parental interaction following separation continues to be argumentative and destructive, shared custody prolongs children's immersion in a conflict-ridden family atmosphere (Steinman, 1981).

Unfortunately, there is not much research on the advantages and disadvantages of joint custody. The available evidence suggests that like other child-rearing arrangements, its consequences are mediated by a variety of factors. These include the quality of the divorcing parents' relationship, child characteristics, and the proximity of the two parents' homes to one another. In addition, attitudes of extended family members and friends toward the shared custody arrangement, as well as support from formal organizations (e.g., schools that permit flexible busing arrangements so that children can alternate easily between parents' homes) are important. Some investigators speculate that joint custody may ease children's adjustment to parental remarriage, since living arrangements and interaction patterns with at least one parent remain unchanged (Clingempeel & Reppucci, 1982). However, the moderating effect of joint custody on children's adaptation to reconstituted family environments has not been studied.

Maternal Employment and Day Care

For many years, divorce has been associated with a high rate of maternal employment, due to the financial strains experienced by women who are responsible for maintaining their own families. However, over the last several decades, women of all sectors of the population—not just those who are single and poor—have gone to work in increasing numbers. The most dramatic change in labor force participation has occurred among mothers in two-parent families. The percentage of employed married women with children under 18 years of age has more than doubled since 1960, from about 30 to over 67 percent. The greatest rise has been among mothers of infants, but impressive increases have also occurred for those with preschoolers, elementary school children, and adolescents. In fact, maternal employment is no longer the exception; it is the modal pattern. Today, single and married mothers are in the labor market in nearly equal proportions (U.S. Department of Labor, 1987), and when children in both types of families are considered together, at any given age more than 50 percent of their mothers work (U.S. Department of Labor, 1986).

In Chapter 10, we discussed the impact of maternal employment and day care on the development of infant-mother attachment and concluded that for babies, the consequences depend on the quality of substitute care as well as the nature of the continuing parent-child relationship. Research on the relationship of maternal employment to development during the childhood and adolescent years comes to much the same conclusion. Moreover, a growing body of evidence indicates that a host of additional moderating variables — the sex of the child, the social class of the family, the mother's satisfaction with her work, the support she receives from her husband, and her daily work schedule — have a bearing on whether children show benefits or decrements from growing up in a working-mother family. We consider the implications of maternal employment, and the related topic of day care, for children's socioemotional adjustment and intellectual performance in the following two sections.

Effects of Maternal Employment on Child Development. Much like societal attitudes toward divorce, the popular view of the working mother has changed in recent years. Prior to the 1960s, most people frowned on employed mothers, and many were under pressure to demonstrate to family and friends that their employment was not having adverse consequences for children (Bronfenbrenner & Crouter, 1982; Hoffman, 1984). Today, this public censure is much diminished. During a period in which the cost of living has soared, maternal employment has come to be regarded as an economic necessity. In addition, families are now smaller, marriages less stable, and life expectancies longer, and modern technology has reduced the time needed for housework and food preparation. As a result, the traditional expectation that a woman must derive virtually all of her personal satisfactions from home, hearth, and children is no longer widely accepted (Hoffman, 1977). Women's desire for accomplishment and fulfillment has expanded, and work is recognized as a major way in which these needs can be met. Consistent with this new positive perspective, research indicates that maternal employment can bring many benefits to women, and also to their preschool- through adolescent-age youngsters.

In both low-income and middle-income families, employed mothers report a higher sense of competence and self-worth, feel less lonely, and express less ambivalence and regret about their children's growing independence than their nonemployed counterparts (Gold & Andres, 1978a; 1978b; 1978c; Walshok, 1978). Overall, the children of working mothers also show indications of better social and emotional adjustment — a higher sense of self-esteem and better family and peer relations (Cherry & Eaton, 1977; Gold & Andres, 1978a; 1978b; Gold, Andres, & Glorieux, 1979). A mother who has a gratifying life of her own outside the family tends to interact more effectively with her youngsters when she is at home. In addition, when compared to full-time mothers, working mothers seem willing to grant their children greater independence when they are ready for it — a likely reason that many children of employed women display such competent social behavior (Hoffman, 1984). But there are other factors that probably contribute to these positive child outcomes as well. Maternal employment often leads to a conscious decision on the part of mothers to compensate for their absence by scheduling special, uninterrupted times to devote to their children (Hoffman, 1984). In addition, to have the household function smoothly, employed mothers often find it necessary to lay down consistent rules for their children's behavior. As a result, there is greater consistency between child-rearing theory and practice in the homes of working than nonworking mothers. Furthermore, during middle childhood and adolescence, children of working mothers are more often given regular household responsibilities (Hoffman, 1974; 1977), and as long as these assignments are reasonable, they are positively associated with children's self-esteem and intellectual performance (Medrich, 1981; Smokler, 1975). Finally, both sons and daughters of working women are less sex-stereotyped in their beliefs and attitudes. They have more flexible ideas regarding appropriate roles and activities for males and females, regard women as more competent and effective, and view men as warmer than do children whose mothers are not employed (Gold & Andres, 1978c; Gold, Andres, & Glorieux, 1979; Vogel et al., 1970).

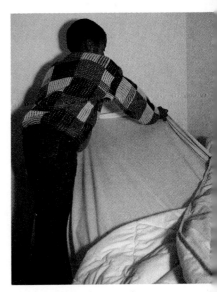

Nevertheless, some qualifications regarding these encouraging findings are in order. First, much like the findings on divorce, the outcomes associated with maternal employment are more favorable for daughters than for sons. Girls of working mothers more often have higher educational aspirations and voice plans to work in adulthood (Hoffman, 1974), and at the college level, they are more likely to choose nontraditional careers, such as law, medicine, and physics (Tangri, 1972). In contrast, the relaxation of traditional sex stereotypes is less pronounced for boys in low-income families (Gold & Andres, 1978a). In fact, several studies suggest that lower-class boys whose mothers work experience strain in the father-son relationship and are less admiring of their fathers (Gold & Andres, 1978a; Hoffman, 1974; 1980). Perhaps a lingering belief exists in many lower-class families that when a mother works, the father has failed in his traditional provider role.

Another negative outcome for boys has appeared repeatedly in the research literature. This time, the sons affected are those of middle-class working mothers. They score lower in intelligence and academic achievement than boys whose mothers do not work (Gold & Andres, 1978b; Moore, 1975; Rees & Palmer, 1970). Investigators do not know exactly why this finding occurs. One hypothesis is that the difference is not really a true difference in ability. Instead, it results from greater compliance on the part of continuously mothered boys to intense achievement pressures from their mothers. Consistent with this interpretation, some evidence indicates that middle-class nonworking mothers overinvest in their youngsters, becoming excessively involved in their academic achievement in comparison to mothers who are employed (Birnbaum, 1975). In addition, one study reported that sons of middle-class nonemployed mothers are more dependent, conforming, and inhibited in personality than those whose mothers work (Moore, 1975).

An alternative explanation regards the lower test scores of boys with employed mothers as an indication of real developmental problems. According to Hoffman (1980), full-time employment may result in less effective socialization of sons because their more active behavior requires greater parental monitoring and intervention than is necessary for girls. Research exists to support this interpretation as well. In one study, highly educated full-time employed mothers, in comparison to their part-time employed and nonworking counterparts, described their 3-year-old sons in especially negative terms (Bronfenbrenner, Alvarez, & Henderson, 1984). When the content of the mothers' statements was examined, those who worked full-time frequently mentioned their sons' activity level as especially bothersome, and they also remarked that their boys seemed demanding and noncompliant (Alvarez, 1985). These findings are consistent with Hoffman's belief that maternal employment, when it introduces heavy demands into the mother's daily schedule, can lead to inadequate socialization of sons during the early years.

It is interesting that a comparable pattern of intellectual deficits for sons of employed mothers in lower-class families does not exist, even though (as we mentioned earlier) these boys experience difficulties in relating to their fathers. In fact, some research even suggests that intellectual benefits accrue for low-income children whose mothers work (Cherry & Eaton, 1977). One possible explanation is that the additional income reduces stress and leads to improved daily living conditions in lower-class households—circumstances that compensate for any negative consequences boys in these families might ordinarily experience.

Beyond the sex and social class differences noted above, several other factors make a difference in how children adjust to maternal employment. As we mentioned earlier, a mother's feelings of life satisfaction are important, and many mothers do derive a special sense of challenge, stimulation, and achievement from their work. Nevertheless, women continue to have less prestigious jobs than men, and they also earn less money than men in comparable occupations. Because these factors affect their financial status and morale, they are likely to affect how mothers feel and behave when they arrive home at the end of the working day (Mortimer & Sorensen, 1984). Furthermore, issues surrounding work time and scheduling are often highly problematic for mothers who work full-time or are in very demanding careers. Several studies show that part-time maternal employment has benefits for children across the entire age range, probably because it provides a flexible enough time schedule for mothers to meet the needs of youngsters with a wide range of characteristics (Alvarez, 1985; Douvan, 1963; Kappel & Lambert, 1972). Finally, when a mother works, her husband's support is especially crucial. If he does not assist with family responsibilities, she experiences a double load, at home and at work, a circumstance that leads to fatigue, distress, and reduced time and energy to interact with children in an optimal fashion. Recent evidence indicates that working mothers continue to shoulder most of the burden of household and child care tasks, although their husbands participate to a greater extent than those of nonworking mothers (Baruch & Barnett, 1986; Hoffman, 1984). Employed mothers' psychological well-being is known to increase when husbands provide at least some child care assistance (Kessler & McRae, 1981; 1982).

Research on maternal employment suggests a variety of ways that work settings can support parents in their child-rearing roles and, at the same time, increase their effectiveness as employees. More opportunities for part-time employment, permission to bring suitable work home during normal working hours, and liberal paternity and maternity leaves (including time off for childhood illness) would help many parents juggle the multiple demands of jobs, household maintenance, and child rearing more successfully. Moreover, the availability of high quality substitute child care is a vital component of parents' peace of mind during the working day (Kamerman, 1980a), and, as we shall see shortly, it has major implications for children's development.

Effects of Day Care on Child Development. Although research on the consequences of day care for children's development has increased over the past several decades, our knowledge continues to be limited because of the wide variety of child care arrangements utilized by working mothers in the United States. A recent national survey indicated that the majority of children of all ages are placed in home-based care (see Table 14.3). Home care is an especially common arrangement for infants and school-age children; a greater proportion of 3- and 4-year-olds attend day care centers. These trends are due to the fact that most center facilities specialize in preschool care; very few accommodate infants or offer before- and after-school services. As a result, most working mothers with non-preschool-age youngsters must seek other options. In fact, a close look at the figures in Table 14.3 reveals an alarming statistic: 20 percent of school-age children whose mothers work receive no supervised care at all (U.S. Bureau of the Census, 1987b).

Since organized child care facilities are easiest for researchers to study, most investigations have focused on center-based care for preschoolers. In recent years more research has reported on children's experiences in *family day care homes,* a form of care in which a neighborhood woman looks after a small group of youngsters in her

Table 14.3. Who's Minding America's Children?

629

CHAPTER 14
THE FAMILY

PERCENTAGE OF CHILDREN WITH EMPLOYED MOTHERS
IN DIFFERENT TYPES OF CHILD CARE ARRANGEMENTS

AGE OF CHILD	HOME-BASED CARE (*See breakdown below*)	ORGANIZED CHILD CARE FACILITIES (DAY CARE CENTERS)	PARENT CARES FOR CHILD WHILE ON THE JOB	CHILD "SELF-CARE"
2 years and under	75.5	16.3	8.2	—
3–4 years	58.0	33.9	8.1	—
5–14 years	66.6	7.6	5.8	20.0

PERCENTAGE OF CHILDREN IN DIFFERENT TYPES OF HOME-BASED CARE

AGE OF CHILD	CARE IN CHILD'S OWN HOME		CARE IN ANOTHER HOME	
	BY RELATIVE	BY NONRELATIVE	BY RELATIVE	BY NONRELATIVE
2 years and under	27.5	6.5	15.8	25.7
3–4 years	22.1	5.0	13.2	17.7
5–14 years	37.8	3.8	12.1	12.8

Note: Many children experience more than one type of child care arrangement in the course of a single day. The figures for children 4 years of age and younger refer to settings in which children spend *most* time while their mothers are at work. Since the majority of children between 5 and 14 are in school during their mother's employment hours, these figures reflect the child care arrangements in which children spend most time during out-of-school hours.
Source: U.S. Bureau of the Census, 1987b.

In family day care homes where group size is small and caregivers are knowledgeable about child development, children experience more stimulating and responsive adult-child interaction. (Sarah Putnam/The Picture Cube)

own household. However, there are still very few of these studies. Moreover, at present we know practically nothing about how the millions of children watched by relatives or baby-sitters in their own or someone else's home fare in response to these types of care. And only in the last few years have researchers started to look into the consequences of releasing large numbers of children to "self-care" during after-school hours (see Box 14.2).

The very first investigations of day care, carried out in the 1960s and 1970s, compared preschool children enrolled in high quality, university-sponsored centers with children of the same social class who were being reared at home. Although the environments sampled were limited to high quality model programs, the research responded to the concerns of many people that the development of preschool children would suffer from long hours spent in group care arrangements. The findings were reassuring and encouraging. With respect to intellectual development, test scores of middle-class day care children did not differ from those of their home-reared coun-

FOCUS ON CONTEMPORARY ISSUES

Box 14.2
Latchkey Children

Latchkey children are youngsters who regularly care for themselves after school with no adult supervision. Over the last two decades their numbers have risen dramatically, along with maternal employment. One recent estimate indicates that just over one million children between 5 and 14 years of age regularly care for themselves when not in school (U.S. Bureau of the Census, 1987b). Other projections are considerably higher, some as great as 5 to 7 million children (Simons & Bohen, 1982; U.S. Department of Labor, 1982). While many latchkey children return home to an empty house, others "hang out" with peers in the neighborhood or in nearby shopping malls in the late afternoon and evening hours.

Widespread public concern exists about the dangers to which latchkey children are exposed, as well as the possibility that in the absence of adult supervision, many will engage in undesirable, antisocial behavior. However, research yields contradictory findings. Some investigators have found that latchkey children have problems that adult-supervised children do not, including low self-esteem, poor academic achievement, inadequate social skills, and greater anxiety and fearfulness. In contrast, other researchers report no detrimental conse-

quences as the result of after-school "self-care" (Robinson, Rowland, & Coleman, 1986). But much of the research has failed to take account of the type of latchkey arrangement as a critical factor in the child's psychological well-being. In a recent study, Laurence Steinberg (1986; 1988) showed that the way latchkey youngsters spend their time and whether or not parents supervise them "in absentia" make a difference in one important aspect of their adjustment: susceptibility to peer antisocial activity.

Steinberg asked a large number of fifth- through eighth-grade children residing in a small Midwestern city to answer a series of questions about how they spent their afternoon time, what their parents' child-rearing practices were like, and whether or not they would join in the activities of a best friend who had decided to engage in antisocial behavior, such as vandalism and stealing. The findings showed that the more removed the children's after-school care was from an adult-related environment, the more susceptible they were to peer pressure. Youngsters who frequently "hung out" with agemates described themselves as willing to follow along in a peer's antisocial activities more often than those who spent time at friends' homes after school. Both of these groups were, in turn, more susceptible to peer influence than children who returned to their own homes once the school day was over. Moreover,

whether or not parents knew their children's whereabouts had a substantial impact on their ability to be persuaded by peers. Latchkey children who were "monitored from a distance" by telephone calls or given regular after-school chores differed very little from those who experienced direct adult supervision. In contrast, youngsters left entirely to their own devices were particularly susceptible to peer influence. Finally, authoritative child rearing greatly increased latchkey children's resistance to undesirable peer pressures. The greater social responsibility and internalized moral standards encouraged by warm but firm parental control appeared to serve as a powerful buffer against peer antisocial tendencies.

Steinberg's research suggests that when parents can find no alternative to after-school self-care, distal supervision of their youngster's activities along with authoritative child-rearing practices reduces the chances that latchkey children will become problems to themselves, their peers, and the community. Parents are wise to try to arrange appropriate after-school supervision of children while they finish the working day. And communities need to provide more after-school care alternatives, to prevent the many American school-age youngsters whose mothers are employed from being exposed to the risks of unsupervised after-school hours.

terparts. And in some studies of low-income children, enriched day care experiences actually predicted better intellectual performance. For these youngsters, good day care seemed to provide an effective form of early intervention, offsetting the negative impact of growing up in an impoverished family environment. Several studies also indicated that group care could lead to social benefits for children. When compared to home-reared youngsters, children attending high quality day care programs were advantaged in sociability, although a rise in negative as well as positive peer interactions appeared (Belsky & Steinberg, 1978).

Once research had established that day care need not be harmful and could be beneficial for children's development, investigators turned to the study of child care programs available in ordinary communities. These new studies improved on the first wave of day care research by comparing children's experiences and development in day care environments differing widely on dimensions of quality. Their aim was to identify specific conditions of care that support healthy psychological development, as well as those that were likely to undermine it. Once the precise ingredients of good care were known, parents could be encouraged to rely on them in choosing a child care setting. And legislators could use the information in devising day care licensing standards that safeguard the development of our nation's children.

The *National Day Care Study,* which included over 60 day care centers serving low-income children in three large cities, and the *National Day Care Home Study,* involving several hundred family day care homes serving a diverse urban population, are the largest comparative investigations of day care that have been conducted to date (Divine-Hawkins, 1981; Ruopp et al., 1979). The goal of both studies was to determine the impact on children of such dimensions of quality as group size (number of children accommodated in a single classroom or well-defined physical space), caregiver/child ratio, and staff educational preparation. In each study, systematic observations of caregiver and child behavior were collected. The center study also included standardized tests of intellectual and language development administered in the fall and spring of the year.

The findings were remarkably consistent. In both center and home environments, group size and the related variable of adult/child ratio influenced caregivers' style of interaction. As number of children decreased (to around 2 to 4 in day care homes, and to about 14 preschoolers accompanied by at least 2 caregivers in day care centers), management of children became easier. Under these conditions, caregivers spent less time commanding and correcting and more time in positive, stimulating verbal interaction. Furthermore, training in early childhood education, child development, or a related field showed widespread relationships with caregiver behavior. Caregivers knowledgeable about children's development were more verbally stimulating as well as responsive to children's needs, helping and comforting them more often than their untrained counterparts. Finally, in the center study, both smaller group size and caregiver training predicted large gains in intelligence and language test scores over a year's time.

Other comparative studies have replicated as well as extended these findings. In one series of investigations, day care centers serving low-income children were studied on the island of Bermuda, where approximately 85 percent of children enter substitute care by the age of 2. Adult stimulating verbal interaction along with a global rating of center quality (based on a wide variety of characteristics, from physical facilities to program activities) predicted a broad array of positive child outcomes, including cognitive, language, and social skills (McCartney, 1984; McCartney et al., 1985; Phillips, McCartney, & Scarr, 1987). Other research indicates that these dimensions of quality predict enhanced social and intellectual development among middle-class children as well (Clarke-Stewart & Gruber, 1984; Howes, 1988; Vandell & Powers, 1983).

In summary, investigators still have much to learn about the wide variety of child care arrangements experienced by America's children. But even though our knowledge is limited, research has established that not all day care has identical implications for development. High quality settings in which group size is small, caregiver-child ratios are low, staff training is high, and adults communicate in stimulating, responsive, and affectionate ways contribute positively to many aspects of children's psychological functioning. At the same time, poor quality care interferes with children's optimal development.

Do the findings on day care remind you of our discussion of parenting styles earlier in this chapter? Much like authoritative parents, caregivers who are involved with children, responsive to their needs, and neither too lax nor restrictive in their demands are those who promote cognitive and social competence among the youngsters in their charge. In programs where adults are knowledgeable about child development and their resources are not overextended by too many children and insufficient play materials and space, "authoritative caregiving" is likely to occur. As a result, child development is fostered. This seems to be as true in day care as it is in the family environment (Belsky, 1984a).

THE VULNERABLE FAMILY: CHILD MALTREATMENT

Families, as we indicated in the first part of this chapter, contribute in essential ways to the maintenance of society by serving as contexts in which children are loved, protected, and encouraged to develop into competent, productive adults. Throughout our discussion of the changing American family, we highlighted conditions under which family functioning is strained and parent-child relationships are likely to be less than optimal. When these circumstances become extreme, the family can be transformed from a supportive child-rearing context into a dangerous environment for children.

Incidence and Definitions

Child maltreatment is as old as the history of humankind. However, only in the latter half of the twentieth century has there been widespread public and professional acceptance that the problem exists, research aimed at understanding its psychological and social roots, and programs directed at helping maltreated children and their families (Oates, 1982). Perhaps the recent upsurge in professional and public concern is due to the fact that child maltreatment is especially common in large, industrialized nations like the United States (Gelles & Cornell, 1983). Although estimates of how often it occurs vary considerably from study to study, all of them are high, and most are underestimates, since the majority of cases go unreported (Starr, 1979). In one effort to estimate the actual incidence of child abuse, Gelles (1978) telephoned a representative sample of American households and asked about violence among family members. About 3.5 percent of parents admitted that at least once during the previous year they had acted so violently toward their child that they could have caused physical injury. Extrapolated to the total American child population, this figure suggests that each year, between 1.4 and 1.9 million youngsters experience physical mistreatment. Yet Gelles's estimate is undoubtedly very conservative, for it relied on parents' willingness to admit to severely punitive behavior and only included families with children between 3 and 7 years of age. When reported instances of child abuse are considered, the largest number involve 1- to 3-year-old youngsters (Johnson & Showers, 1985; U.S. Department of Health and Human Services, 1981).

Child maltreatment assumes a wide variety of forms, only one of which emphasizes physical aggression. The following varieties of maltreatment are generally included in legal statutes and professional definitions:

1. *Physical abuse:* assaults on children that produce pain, cuts, welts, bruises, burns, broken bones, and other injuries

2. *Sexual abuse:* sexual molestation, intercourse, and exploitation of children
3. *Physical neglect:* living conditions in which children receive insufficient food, clothing, shelter, medical attention, or supervision
4. *Emotional neglect:* failure of caregivers to meet children's needs for nurturance and emotional support
5. *Psychological abuse:* actions that damage children's emotional, social, or intellectual functioning

Although mental health and legal professionals agree that these five forms exist, they do not agree on the range of adult behaviors that actually constitute mistreatment. Definitions vary in the *frequency* and *intensity* of behaviors regarded as abusive and the emphasis they place on *intentionality*—whether or not the harm is deliberately inflicted by an adult (Gelles & Cornell, 1983). Consensus on a definition of child maltreatment is important, for if we cannot define it, we are hampered in studying its origins and consequences for children's development and in designing effective intervention programs (Starr, 1979). The greatest definitional problems arise in the case of subtle, interpretable behaviors. For example, some investigators regard psychological abuse, in which children are rejected, scapegoated, ridiculed, humiliated, or terrorized by adults, as the most prevalent and potentially destructive form (Garbarino, Guttman, & Seeley, 1986; Hart & Brassard, 1987). But definitions of psychological abuse are especially complex and serious in their consequences for children and families. If they are too narrow and include only the most severe instances of mental cruelty, they allow many harmful actions toward children to continue unchecked and untreated. If they are too lenient, they can result in arbitrary, disruptive legal intrusions into family life (Melton & Davidson, 1987; Melton & Thompson, 1987b).

The Origins of Child Maltreatment

When child maltreatment first became a topic of research in the early 1960s (Kempe et al., 1962), most child development specialists viewed it as rooted in adult psychopathology. The first studies showed that adults who abused or neglected their offspring usually had one or more of the following characteristics: a history of abuse or neglect during their own childhoods; unrealistic expectations that children satisfy their own unmet psychological needs; and poor control of aggressive impulses (Spinetta & Rigler, 1972). These early findings suggested that only particular "kinds of people" mistreated children. However, it soon became apparent that many adults who had been abused as children did not repeat the cycle with their own offspring and that even "normal" parents were capable of abusive behavior (Gil, 1970–1973). A more comprehensive explanation than a "disturbed adult personality" was needed to explain the widespread occurrence of child abuse and neglect in our society. Psychologists turned for help to the social systems approach to family functioning, which views child maltreatment as multiply determined—not just by forces within the individual, but also by characteristics of the family, community, and culture of which parent and child are a part (Belsky, 1980; Garbarino, 1977).

At the level of the individual, besides parental characteristics, attributes of children increase the chances that child maltreatment will occur. A premature or very sick baby or a child with a difficult temperament, a hyperactive behavioral style, or other developmental difficulties has an increased likelihood of becoming the target of abusive treatment. Boys, who are more active and display a greater number of developmental deviations than girls, also experience higher rates of abuse.[3] Moreover, a passive, lethargic youngster can also engender mistreatment, especially in the form of neglect, simply by not demanding care and attention from parents (Belsky,

[3] An exception is sexual abuse, which is committed against girls more often than boys. Approximately 14 percent of reported child maltreatment cases involve sexual offenses. In the majority of instances, the perpetrators are parents or close parental associates (Kempe & Kempe, 1984; U.S. Department of Health and Human Services, 1981).

1980; Parke & Collmer, 1975). Once both the parent's and child's role in maltreatment are appreciated, our understanding of it moves beyond the level of the individual to a problem that is embedded in a family relationship.

In many instances, child abuse begins with small interactive discrepancies that are magnified and multiplied over time until maladaptive parent-child interaction becomes acute (Garbarino, 1977). Research shows that asynchronous interactions between abusive mothers and their infants sometimes appear as early as the first few weeks of life (Kennell, Voos, & Klaus, 1976). By the preschool years, abusive and neglectful families are characterized by low levels of parent-child interaction. When parent communication does occur, it tends to be negative and coercive (Burgess & Conger, 1978; Patterson, 1976; Trickett & Kuczynski, 1986). Maltreated children, in turn, display especially high rates of misbehavior, aggressing against peers and caregivers and reacting with defiance to parental intervention (George & Main, 1979; Howes & Eldredge, 1985; Trickett & Kuczynski, 1986). Maladaptive parenting and child recalcitrance feed on one another and escalate, until maltreatment becomes a chronic family pattern. Children who consistently experience any form of abuse or neglect quickly develop very serious adjustment and learning problems (Egeland & Sroufe, 1981; Kempe & Kempe, 1984; Lamphear, 1985; Brassard, Germain, & Hart, 1987). These outcomes contribute to the continuation of their mistreatment, as well as to the intergenerational maintenance of child abuse and neglect.

Nevertheless, most parents have sufficient self-control not to respond to their children's misbehavior with abuse, and not all children with developmental difficulties are mistreated. Other factors must combine with these conditions to precipitate an extreme parental response. Research shows that unmanageable parental stress is almost invariably associated with child maltreatment. Unemployment, marital conflict, large, closely spaced families, overcrowded living conditions, and extreme household disorganization are common in abusive homes — factors that increase the chances that tolerable levels of parental stress will be passed. Furthermore, abusive parents generally have few effective ways of coping with life's adversities. Many studies show that the overwhelming majority are isolated from formal and informal social supports in their communities (Belsky, 1980; Garbarino, 1977). The causes of this social isolation are multiple. Due to their own life histories, many abusive and neglectful parents have learned to mistrust and avoid other people and have failed to develop the skills necessary for establishing positive interpersonal relationships. At the same time, these parents are often rejected by extended family and neighbors because they are seen as deviant and unlikely to reciprocate when assistance is offered (Polansky et al., 1985). In addition, maltreating parents are more likely to live in neighborhoods that provide little in the way of supportive links between family and community (Garbarino & Sherman, 1980). Consequently, during particularly stressful times, they lack "lifelines" to other people and often have no one to turn to for help.

One final factor — the broad ideology and customs of our culture — profoundly affects the chances that child maltreatment will occur when parents feel stressed and overburdened. In societies where force and violence are viewed as appropriate techniques for solving problems, including those that arise in the rearing of children, the stage is set for child abuse. These conditions exist in the United States (Garbarino, 1977; Hart & Brassard, 1987; Belsky, 1980). Although all 50 states as well as the federal government have enacted child abuse legislation, there is still strong societal support for the use of physical force in American caregiver-child relations. During the past two decades, the United States Supreme Court has twice upheld the legal right of school officials to use corporal punishment to discipline children. One survey of educators, police officers, and clerics indicated that two thirds condone physical discipline in the form of spanking, and more than 10 percent believe that hitting children with belts, straps, and brushes is justifiable (Viano, 1974). High crime rates permeate American cities, and television sets beam graphic displays of violence into family living rooms. In view of the widespread acceptance of violent behavior in American culture, it is not surprising that most American parents employ physical punishment at one time or another to discipline their children. In countries where corporal punishment is not condoned, such as China and Sweden, child abuse is rare (Belsky, 1980).

Preventing Child Maltreatment

Because child maltreatment is embedded in families, communities, and society as a whole, efforts to prevent it must be directed at each of these levels. Techniques that have been suggested include interventions that teach high-risk parents effective caregiving and disciplinary practices; efforts to make child development knowledge and experience with children a regular part of the high school curriculum; and broad social programs that have as their goal full employment and improved economic conditions for low-income families (Belsky, 1978; Rosenberg & Reppucci, 1985; Zigler, 1978). We have already seen in earlier parts of this chapter that providing social supports to families is extraordinarily effective in minimizing parental stress. Consequently, it is not surprising that it sharply reduces the incidence of child maltreatment as well (Garbarino, 1977). Parents Anonymous, a national organization consisting of 10,000 members that has as its main goal the rehabilitation of child-abusing parents, does so largely through providing social supports to abuse-prone families. Each of its 1,500 local chapters offers self-help group meetings, daily phone calls, and regular home visits to relieve social isolation and encourage the use of effective parenting techniques (Koek & Martin, 1988). Crisis intervention services also exist in many communities. Nurseries provide temporary child care when parents feel they are about to lose control, and telephone hotlines offer immediate help to parents under stress and refer them to appropriate community agencies when long-term assistance is warranted. Other preventive approaches include media campaigns, such as public service announcements in newspapers, magazines, and on television and radio, which are designed to educate lay people about child maltreatment and

Public service announcements help prevent child abuse by educating people about the problem and informing them of how and where to seek help.

12 alternatives to lashing out at your kid.

You don't have to lift a hand to hurt your child. Words hit as hard as a fist. The next time everyday pressures build up to such a pitch that you feel like lashing out...stop! And try any of these simple alternatives.

1. Put your hands over your mouth. Count to 10. Or better yet, 20.
2. Stop in your tracks. Press your lips together and breathe deeply.
3. Phone a friend.
4. Phone the weather.
5. Say the alphabet out loud.
6. If someone can watch the children, go outside and take a leisurely walk.
7. Take a hot bath or splash cold water on your face.
8. Pick up a pencil and write down your thoughts.
9. Close your eyes and imagine you're hearing what your child hears.
10. Turn on the radio or TV.
11. Hug a pillow.
12. Write for prevention information: National Committee for Prevention of Child Abuse, Box 2866, Chicago, IL 60690.

Take time out. Don't take it out on your kid.

CHILD ABUSE CAMPAIGN
MAGAZINE AD NO. CA-2207-87—4⅝" X 5" [110 SCREEN]

CM-1-87

Words hit as hard as a fist.

"You're pathetic. You can't do anything right!"
"You disgust me. Just shut up!"
"Hey stupid! Don't you know how to listen."
"Get outta here! I'm sick of looking at your face."
"You're more trouble than you're worth."

"Why don't you go and find some other place to live!"
"I wish you were never born!"
Children believe what their parents tell them. Next time, stop and listen to what you're saying. You might not believe your ears.
Take time out. Don't take it out on your kid.

Write: National Committee for Prevention of Child Abuse, Box 2866E, Chicago, IL 60690

CHILD ABUSE CAMPAIGN
MAGAZINE AD NO. CA-2209-87—4⅝" X 5" [110 SCREEN]

CM-1-87

inform them of where and how to seek help (Rosenberg & Reppucci, 1985). In addition to these efforts, substantial changes in the overall attitudes, practices, and priorities of our culture are needed. Many psychologists believe that child maltreatment cannot be eradicated as long as parents must rear their children in a society where violence is rampant and corporal punishment continues to be regarded as an acceptable child-rearing alternative (Belsky, 1980; Garbarino, Guttman, & Seeley, 1986; Gil, 1987; Hyman, 1987; Melton & Thompson, 1987b).

Although more cases reach the courtroom today than in decades past, child maltreatment remains a crime that is very difficult to prove. Most of the time, the only witnesses are child victims themselves or other loyal family members. Even in court cases where the evidence is strong, judges are hesitant to impose the ultimate preventive to further mistreatment — permanent removal of the child from the family. There are several reasons for this reluctant posture. First, in our society, state intervention into family life is viewed as a last resort, to be imposed only when there is near certainty that a child will be denied basic care and protection by parents. Second, despite destructive family relationships, maltreated children and their parents are usually attached to one another, and most of the time, neither desires separation. Finally, the tendency of the American legal system to regard children as parental property, rather than as human beings in their own right, also serves to impede court-ordered protection (Hart & Brassard, 1987). Yet despite intensive intervention and therapy, some adults persist in their abusive acts. Approximately 1,000 abused children end up as fatalities each year (U.S. Department of Health and Human Services, 1981). In cases where parental rehabilitation is unlikely, society's obligation to assure safe and healthy rearing environments for children should be paramount, even if this requires the drastic steps of separating parent from child and legally terminating parental rights.

Child maltreatment is a distressing and horrifying topic. When we consider how often it occurs in a society such as our own that claims to place a high value on the dignity and worth of the individual, it is all the more shocking. Nevertheless, there is reason to be optimistic, for enormous strides have been made in understanding and preventing child maltreatment over the last several decades. Although we still have a long way to go, the situation for abused and neglected children is far better now than it has been at any time in history (Kempe & Kempe, 1984).

STRATEGIES FOR SUPPORTING THE AMERICAN FAMILY

In the course of this chapter, we have seen that the modern American family faces many serious problems, and we have also shown that parents and children function best when supportive links are established between the family and the broader social context in which it is embedded. In Chapter 1, when we discussed the macrosystem level of Bronfenbrenner's (1979) ecological model, we indicated that for children to develop optimally, society as a whole must give top priority to encouraging favorable child-rearing environments. Many child development experts believe that governmental policies that promote positive, nurturant family contexts are the most effective way to improve the lives of America's children (Goffin, 1983).

However, the United States lags far behind many other countries in developing policies that support children and families. For example, America is the only industrialized country in the world that has no statutory regulations guaranteeing women a paid leave for childbirth and the early care of their young infants. Often, employed mothers must use their own sick leave time, or take leave without pay, during the weeks preceding and following the birth of a new baby. In contrast, European countries typically offer 6 to 12 months paid maternity or paternity leave, and they also permit parents to stay home when a child is ill during the first few years of life (Kamerman, 1980b).

To be sure, there are government-sponsored programs that do help parents and children in the United States. The large majority are aimed at the neediest sectors of the population. For example, income assistance, medical care, supplementary food programs, job training, and day care subsidies are available for low-income families. But these programs have been enacted piecemeal, over a long period of time, with little attention given to their interrelatedness. Moreover, they are largely crisis-oriented, aimed at handling the most severe of America's family difficulties, rather than at preventing problems before they happen. In addition, funding for most of these efforts — insufficient to begin with — has waxed and waned and been seriously threatened at various times (Hayes, 1982; Takanishi, DeLeon, & Pallak, 1983). As Zigler and Finn-Stevenson (1988) point out, "it is difficult to identify any overarching and consistent goals for the support of children and families in America" (p. 620).

What accounts for America's slow progress in providing for children and families on a national scale? Like any country, American responsiveness to child and family concerns is guided by complex social, political, and economic factors. In the United States, many people believe that parents should assume total responsibility for rearing their children — an ideology that reflects the historical emphasis our society has placed on individualism, self-sufficiency, and the privacy of family life. The prevalence of these values has led government to be unwilling to become heavily involved in family matters (Goffin, 1988). In addition, unlike the aged, who have made greater strides in obtaining services in support of their needs, children are a "forgotten constituency" because they cannot vote. They must depend on the good will of adults to become an important governmental priority (Takanishi, DeLeon, & Pallak, 1983).

A revised set of values guides the efforts of those trying to expand and strengthen America's role in meeting the needs of children and families. These child advocates — child development specialists, legislators, and committed citizens — also think that children's needs are best met by their families. At the same time, they believe that society should provide a full array of coordinated services to strengthen the family's capacity to rear children successfully, and that in doing so, government can be supportive of family life, without being intrusive (Bronfenbrenner & Weiss, 1983; Edelman, 1981; Keniston, 1977). We have seen in the course of this chapter that parents are not always directly responsible for what becomes of their children. Many problems faced by families are beyond their individual control and are due to the external conditions under which they live. Our nation has been slow to accept this alternative point of view, for any pervasive national outlook is hard to change. However, there is reason to be optimistic, for efforts are being made to improve the attention given to children's needs on America's legislative agenda. One example is a recent movement to strengthen the government's role in funding day care and regulating its quality. Scientific and professional organizations with an interest in children's welfare have been working together to stimulate legislation that would lead to better day care for all children, and more affordable care for low- and moderate-income families (Weintraub & Furman, 1987)

Progress on the problems experienced by America's families can be made on many fronts, and each effort to do so helps build a national climate that is supportive of family well-being. For example, business and industry have begun to realize that worker productivity is augmented by a satisfying family life (Fernandez, 1986). A few firms now offer parental leave benefits as well as conveniently located day care services, at a cost their employees can afford.

Many child and family researchers are working hard to provide the kind of knowledge needed to design and implement better family services. Researchers' growing interest in contributing to sound family policies is not yet widely accepted by those in charge of governmental planning. The findings of research are not always consistent enough to point to clear solutions. And even when results are conclusive, they are often not powerful enough to overcome the clash of opinions and special interests that is an inherent part of the American lawmaking process. But researchers are becoming increasingly skilled at communicating to legislators what they know about optimal child development (Lindblom, 1986). In addition, child development specialists are doing a better job of disseminating information to the general public about family needs, so that society as a whole grasps the immediacy of family problems in the United States and, in turn, presses for change (Zigler & Finn-Stevenson, 1988).

Finally, despite the limited resources currently available, many professionals who work directly with children — teachers, caregivers, psychologists, pediatricians, and social workers — can continue to build active relationships with families that motivate parents to fulfill their child-rearing responsibilities to the best of their ability. Even when national priorities improve, the work of these individuals will remain indispensable to the creation of social contexts that permit children and families to reach their full potential.

CHAPTER SUMMARY

1. The origins of the human family can be traced to our hunting and gathering ancestors, for whom it was essential for survival. In addition to safeguarding its own members, the family performs essential functions for society by giving birth to, nurturing, and socializing the young. Currently, investigators view the family as a social system — a complex network of mutually influencing relationships affected by the larger community and societal context of which it is a part.

2. Two broad dimensions — control and responsiveness — describe individual differences in how parents go about socializing the child. When combined with one another, these dimensions yield four parenting types: authoritative, authoritarian, permissive, and uninvolved. Authoritative parents, who are both controlling and responsive, are especially effective agents of socialization. Their rational, democratic style promotes socially active, responsible, and cognitively competent child behavior. Authoritarian parents, who are high in control but low in responsiveness, tend to have anxious, withdrawn, dependent children who react hostilely when frustrated. Permissive parents are warm and responsive, but lacking in control; their youngsters are often dependent and demanding and display poor impulse control. Finally, uninvolved parents are low in both responsiveness and control. Their indifferent, rejecting behavior is associated with deficits in all aspects of psychological functioning.

3. Authoritative parenting has emerged as the most common form of child rearing in many cultures around the world. Nevertheless, systematic social class differences in parenting behavior exist in modern industrialized nations. Low-income, working-class families are more authoritarian and punitive than their middle-class counterparts. In contrast, middle-class parents emphasize the development of children's internal psychological characteristics, and they more often use explanations, verbal praise, and inductive disciplinary techniques. These differences can be understood in terms of the life conditions of lower- and middle-class parents, including variations in work roles, education, and degree of stress impinging on the

family. The cultural traditions of some low-income minorities, such as the black extended family, provide a buffer against the stresses of living in poverty.

4. Over the last several decades, substantial changes in American family life have occurred. The current trend toward smaller families has had consequences for parent-child interaction, as well as children's opportunities to grow up with siblings. In households with large numbers of children, parents tend to be more authoritarian and punitive, and children score somewhat lower in intelligence, school achievement, and self-esteem. However, these unfavorable outcomes are reduced in economically well-off households with many youngsters. Sibling relationships offer children practice in a wide range of social skills, but they are not essential for normal social and emotional development. Only children have just as many close friends and are not lonelier than other youngsters. Furthermore, they are more likely to experience authoritative parenting, and they do somewhat better in school and attain higher educational levels than children with siblings.

5. The American family is far more mobile today than it was during the first half of this century. The consequences for children of moving to a new neighborhood or community have much to do with why and where a family moves. When parents relocate willingly, in response to better housing or job opportunities, as is the case for most economically advantaged families, children are not harmed academically, socially, or emotionally. In contrast, when impoverished families are forced to relocate, moving is an added stressor that predicts poorer academic progress and adjustment problems.

6. Divorce has become extremely common in the lives of American children. Although most children experience painful emotional reactions in the period surrounding divorce, there are substantial individual differences in the way they respond. Boys show more severe behavioral disorganization than girls, reacting to parental conflict and inconsistent disci-

pline with noncompliant, hostile behavior and a marked increase in school difficulties. Preschool and early-school-age children have difficulty understanding their parents' estrangement and are often more deeply affected than their older counterparts. By two years after the divorce, most children show improved adjustment. Nevertheless, boys in mother-custody homes remain vulnerable to lasting academic and socioemotional problems, although a continuing positive father-son relationship alleviates these difficulties. The single consistent long-term outcome for girls is precocious heterosexual activity at adolescence. Children in divorced families are better adjusted in the long run than those who reside in strife-ridden, intact homes. However, the research as a whole indicates that children suffer deeply from their parents' divorce and, even many years later, continue to wish that they could have grown up in a happy, intact home.

7. Many divorced parents remarry, and their children must adjust to a complex array of new family figures and relationships. Like the period immediately surrounding divorce, most children experience the transition into a reconstituted household as difficult and stressful. How well they fare in the long run varies with the sex of parent and child. Boys do especially well in mother-stepfather families. Children in father-stepmother families, and girls in particular, display the greatest adjustment difficulties.

8. Over the last several decades, women have entered the labor force in rising numbers. A variety of positive child outcomes are associated with maternal employment, including a higher sense of self-esteem, better family and peer relations, and less sex-stereotyped attitudes. Girls of working mothers have higher educational and occupational aspirations. However, sons do not fare as well as daughters. Lower-class boys experience strain in the father-son relationship, and middle-class boys score lower in intelligence and academic achieve-

ment. Some studies indicate that children of all ages adjust best under conditions of part-time maternal employment. A flexible work schedule and assistance by fathers with household responsibilities help mothers balance the multiple demands of work and child rearing.

9. American children experience a diverse array of child care arrangements while their mothers are at work. Although most children are placed in home-based care, organized child care facilities are most frequently studied. Research comparing child care settings on dimensions of quality indicates that when group size is small, caregiver/child ratios are generous, staff training is high, and adults communicate in stimulating, responsive ways, many aspects of child development are fostered.

10. Child maltreatment is especially common in the United States and other modern industrialized nations. Recent research shows that it is multiply determined—by characteristics of individuals, families, communities, and the larger culture of which parent and child are a part. Certain child attributes, such as prematurity and other developmental difficulties, as well as unmanageable parental stress and isolation from supportive ties to the community, increase the chances that maltreatment will occur. Child abuse is fostered in societies, like the United States, where force and violence are sanctioned as appropriate means for solving problems.

11. The United States lags behind many countries in the development of national policies that support children and families. The American tradition of individualism, self-sufficiency, and family privacy has led government to be reluctant to become involved in family matters, except when problems become extreme. Although this outlook is pervasive and hard to change, efforts are being made on many fronts to build a national climate that fosters family well-being.

IMPORTANT TERMS AND CONCEPTS

social systems approach
socialization
control
responsiveness
authoritative parenting

authoritarian parenting
permissive parenting
uninvolved parenting
extended family household
nuclear family unit

reconstituted family
divorce mediation
sole custody
joint custody
latchkey children

The Country School, by Winslow Homer.
The Saint Louis Art Museum.

CHAPTER 15

Peers, Media, and Schooling

$\mathbf{B}$eginning at an early age, socialization in the family is supplemented by experiences in the wider world of peers, media, and school. In this final chapter, we take up the significance of these three major extrafamilial contexts for development.

We begin by considering children's peer relations. In all human societies, children receive extensive, informal exposure to other children during their daily lives. In no culture are they reared entirely by adults. From our discussion of social cognition in Chapter 11, you already know that one special type of peer relationship, friendship, changes substantially over the course of childhood and contributes uniquely to socioemotional and cognitive development. In this chapter, we take a broader look at how peer sociability changes with age. Then we turn to the topic of *peer acceptance*. Perhaps you remember from your own childhood years that some of your classmates were especially well liked and sought after as play companions, while others were actively rejected by peers. We consider the origins of peer acceptance in children's personal characteristics and social behaviors, along with its significance for the long-term psychological adjustment of the individual. Next we discuss children's *peer groups*—self-generated informal associations that become increasingly common during middle childhood and adolescence. We trace how peer groups form, factors that affect their functioning, and the role they play in the development of the child. We conclude our discussion of peer influences by taking a detailed look at the processes through which children serve as socialization agents for one another—peer reinforcement and modeling during childhood and conformity to the peer group during the adolescent years.

Children are profoundly affected by major technological advances in our culture. In this chapter, we concentrate on two highly prevalent and influential innovations of this century: television and computers. We review what is known about the effects of these captivating electronic devices on children's intellectual and social development and discuss how best to assure that both serve as constructive forces in the lives of children, helping them to acquire new cognitive skills as well as prosocial values and behaviors.

Finally, our discussion turns to the school, an institution established by society to assist the family in its mission of transmitting culturally valued knowledge and skills to the next generation. We consider how schools accomplish their socializing goal. We begin with physical setting — the implications of such factors as physical layout and school size for children's academic and social learning. Next we take up the basic philosophical orientation of the classroom, focusing on the implications of traditional versus open schooling for classroom experiences and academic outcomes. Then we turn to the teacher's role as mediator of classroom learning. We place special emphasis on *teacher expectations* for pupil performance — how these expectations form, their effects on teacher-pupil interaction, and their motivational and achievement consequences. Problems faced by schools in accommodating pupils with special needs — the child with learning difficulties as well as the intellectually gifted youngster — are considered next. Our chapter concludes with a discussion of the success of schools in contributing to two major societal goals — improving the life chances of America's racial/ethnic minorities and equipping America's young people to keep pace with their increasingly well-educated counterparts in other industrialized nations around the world.

PEER RELATIONS

Research on children's peer relations began early in this century, stimulated by the interest of sociologists and social psychologists in effects of group processes on individual behavior. A lull occurred around World War II, a period in which child development specialists were intensely preoccupied with the study of parent-child relations. The past two decades have brought renewed interest in peer associations, stimulated by more effective techniques of observing child-child interaction and provocative speculations about the vital place of peers in socioemotional and cognitive development.

Much like the study of the family, contemporary research on peers has been heavily influenced by the field of *ethology*. In the 1960s, ethologists moved beyond the classic motherless monkey studies to investigate the consequences of early peer deprivation. Maternally reared rhesus monkeys with no peer contact displayed a broad array of behavioral disturbances, including immature play, excessive aggression and fearfulness, and less effective cooperation among group members at maturity (Harlow, 1969). However, additional primate studies revealed that optimal development depended on *both* parental and peer rearing. Maternally deprived peer-raised monkeys also showed behavior problems, including heightened dominant and submissive (as opposed to friendly) interaction and deficient sexual behavior (Goy & Goldfoot, 1974). The complementary socialization roles of parents and peers suggested by these findings have become a major current emphasis in human peer research. Moreover, social behaviors observed among a wide variety of mammalian species, such as dominance hierarchies and rough-and-tumble play, have led researchers to search for similar qualities in children's peer associations, and to study their evolutionary significance and adaptive function.

Also like research into family relations, an *ecological* perspective has become increasingly common in studies of peers. We will see later on that the peer network is an organized, structured system that functions in concert with other social systems, such as the family and school. Also, child-child interactions are molded in part by situational influences, such as the number, age range, and familiarity of peer participants and the type of play materials available, to name only a few. We will return to the role of environmental contexts in children's peer associations many times in the course of our discussion.

Before we begin, a word of caution about the limitations of contemporary research on peers is appropriate. Strictly speaking, the term *peer* means "equal in rank or standing." Most research bears the mark of this definition, as it focuses on children who are close in age. But this one-sided emphasis on agemate interaction is not just an outgrowth of the meaning of the word. Children are most accessible to researchers in age-graded settings, such as schools, clubs, and summer camps. Yet in the neighborhood, where children's social activities are harder to track, more than half of their contacts are with children who differ by a year or more from their own age (Barker & Wright, 1955; Ellis, Rogoff, & Cromer, 1981). Moreover, in cultures where children are not segregated by age for schooling and recreation, cross-age interaction is even more common (Weisner & Gallimore, 1977; Whiting & Whiting, 1975). We will point out what is known about the importance of mixed-age peer associations as our discussion proceeds. But it is important to note that the heavy research focus on same-age relationships limits what we currently know about the breadth and significance of children's peer experiences (Hartup, 1983).

The Development of Peer Sociability

Child-child interaction appears early in cultures where children experience regular contact with peers during the first year of life. Mothers' anecdotal reports indicate that about 60 percent of American 6- to 12-month-olds see other babies at least once a week (Vandell & Mueller, 1980). Observations of these infant playmates reveal that peer interaction begins with isolated, nonreciprocated social contacts. Gradually these evolve into the complex, coordinated interaction sequences that are typical of the childhood and adolescent years. The development of peer sociability parallels the acquisition of important cognitive and linguistic capacities that we discussed in earlier chapters. Changes in each domain occur in tandem and undoubtedly support one another.

Infant Beginnings. How skilled a peer social partner is the infant during the first two years of life? Early claims that babies fail to interact socially with one another

The beginnings of peer sociability emerge in infancy, in the form of looks, touches, and gestures that increase in frequency over the second half of the first year. (Nancy Sheehan)

(e.g., Parten, 1932) have recently been challenged. Investigators mark the occurrence of a true social act when an infant looks at another person's face while engaging in an attention-getting behavior. When pairs of babies are brought together in a laboratory, looking accompanied by touching occurs at 3 to 4 months, and peer-directed smiles and babbles are evident by 6 months (Vandell & Mueller, 1980). These social acts increase in frequency during the second half of the first year, and occasional reciprocal exchanges also occur in which babies smile, laugh, gesture, or otherwise duplicate each other's behavior (Eckerman & Whatley, 1977; Vandell, Wilson, & Buchanan, 1980). Between 1 and 2 years, the quantity and complexity of infant social behavior develops further. Isolated social initiations recede and coordinated interaction occurs more often. Also, toddlers combine more behaviors into a single social act—for example, they look, vocalize, gesture, and smile at the same time (Bronson, 1981; Mueller & Brenner, 1977). In addition, the emotionally expressive component of peer sociability becomes more evident. Both positive and negative affect increase in frequency during the second year (Mueller & Rich, 1976), although a positive emotional tone predominates (Rubenstein & Howes, 1976). By age 2, when both the mother and a peer are present, attempts to engage the peer in play occur more often than initiations to the mother (Eckerman, Whatley, & Kutz, 1975).

Nevertheless, it is important not to exaggerate the baby's social capacities. Even in highly focused playroom situations where infants have little else to capture their attention besides one another, social contacts between babies are infrequent, and sustained interaction is extremely rare. You may recall from Chapter 9 that the ability of infants and young preschoolers to actively participate in reciprocal turn-taking with adults is also limited. Therefore, it is not surprising that the same skill is tenuous and fleeting in their earliest encounters with peers, who are far less optimal social partners than most adults. True mutuality in peer interaction hinges on a more sophisticated understanding of the rules of human communication, and on the capacity to apply them, than is available to the preverbal infant (Bronson, 1981; Brownell, 1986).

But rudimentary peer sociability is present during infancy, and researchers have been interested in how it grows out of the baby's earliest experiences. One hypothesis is that infants' animated play with objects captures the attention of other babies, who soon want to join in their activities (Mueller & Lucas, 1975). This idea may have some validity, but it cannot serve as a complete explanation. Social development does not proceed from an initial focus on toys to a focus on peers during the first two years of life. In fact, babies as young as 6 months of age are much more responsive to each other when toys are absent than when they are present in a laboratory playroom (Eckerman & Whatley, 1977; Vandell, Wilson, & Buchanan, 1980). A second idea is that early peer social skills are supported by the infant's growing attachment to the caregiver. By the end of the first year, the attachment bond creates a secure base that frees the baby to venture away from the adult and approach other children (see Chapter 10). Also, from interacting with sensitive, responsive adults, babies may learn how to send and interpret emotional signals in their first peer associations (Bronson, 1981; Parke et al., in press; Jacobson et al., 1986). In support of this explanation, research indicates that the looks, touches, smiles, and vocalizations that characterize infant-infant responsiveness resemble salient qualities of mother-infant interaction (Eckerman, Whatley, & Kutz, 1975; Vandell, 1980; Vandell & Wilson, 1987). Furthermore, babies who experience a sensitive, warm parental relationship engage in more extended social exchanges with other infants (Howes & Stewart, 1987; Vandell & Wilson, 1987), and they display more socially competent behavior during the preschool years (Sroufe, 1983).

The Preschool Years. During the preschool period, the frequency and quality of child-child interaction changes substantially. Both positive and negative social behaviors become more prevalent (Lougee, Grueneich, & Hartup, 1977; Charlesworth

& Hartup, 1967), although as during infancy, friendly social acts are more common (Hay, 1984; Walters, Pearce, & Dahms, 1957). In addition, preschoolers gradually abandon immature social behaviors in favor of more mature and effective ones. For example, when observed in nursery school, 2-year-olds often stand and watch their peers, retreat from conflict, cry, and orient toward the teacher. In contrast, 4- and 5-year-olds come closer together in play, and they talk, smile, and trade play materials (Jones, 1972; Smith & Connolly, 1972). Older preschoolers also engage in longer verbal exchanges, and they convey their social intent more clearly than they did at younger ages by establishing eye contact when speaking and listening and using such attention-getting devices as touching, calling a play partner by name, or saying "Hey!" (Mueller, 1972).

These findings suggest that a major change in peer sociability — from one-way social initiatives to reciprocal, coordinated interaction — takes place between 2 and 5 years of age. In a classic study of preschool social behavior, Parten (1932) observed nursery school children at play and concluded that social development proceeds in a three-step sequence. It begins with nonsocial activity — unoccupied, onlooker behavior and solitary play — and then shifts to a limited degree of social participation called **parallel play,** in which the child plays near other children with similar materials, but does not interact with them. Toward the middle of the preschool years, truly social, **cooperative play,** in which children converse, borrow and share toys, and act out complementary roles, predominates as the other play forms decline.

However, recent efforts to replicate Parten's findings (see Table 15.1) reveal that the development of preschool social behavior does not conform to this straightforward developmental progression. Although nonsocial activity does decrease with age, it is still the most frequent form of behavior among preschoolers, and among kindergartners it continues to consume as much as a third of children's free-play time. Moreover, solitary and parallel play remain fairly stable from 3 to 6 years of age, and together, these categories account for as much of the young child's play activity as highly social, cooperative interaction. Social development during the preschool years is not simply a matter of eliminating nonsocial and partially social activity from the young child's behavioral repertoire.

We now know that it is the *type,* rather than the amount, of solitary and parallel play that undergoes important developmental changes during the early years. In a detailed study of preschool children's play behavior, Rubin, Watson, and Jambor (1982) looked at the cognitive maturity of nonsocial, parallel, and cooperative play among 4- and 5-year-old children by applying Smilansky's (1968) cognitive play

Table 15.1. Changes in Occurrence of Parten's Social Play Types from Preschool to Kindergarten Age

	PRESCHOOL 3–4 YEARS	KINDERGARTEN 5–6 YEARS
Total nonsocial activity	41%	34%
Uninvolved and onlooker behavior	19%	14%
Solitary play	22%	20%
Parallel play	22%	23%
Cooperative play	37%	43%

Sources: Preschool figures are averages of those reported by Barnes (1971); Rubin, Maioni, & Hornung (1976); Rubin, Watson, and Jambor (1978); and Smith (1978). Kindergarten figures are averages of those reported by Barnes (1971) and Rubin, Watson, and Jambor (1978).

categories, shown in Table 15.2. Within each of Parten's social play types, 5-year-olds engaged in more cognitively mature behavior than 4-year-olds. At the same time, cooperative make-believe play—a form we called *sociodramatic* in Chapter 6[1]—became increasingly prevalent with age.

Parents and teachers often voice concerns about children who frequently play in a solitary fashion and engage in low rates of interaction with peers. In line with the findings described above, current evidence indicates that only certain kinds of nonsocial activity—aimless wandering and functional play involving immature, repetitive motor actions—are predictive of lags in cognitive development and early difficulties in relating to peers. Most nonsocial play of preschoolers is not of this kind. Instead, it is positive and constructive, and preschool teachers encourage it when they set out art materials, puzzles, and construction toys for children to choose during free play. Contrary to popular belief, children who spend much of their play time in these activities are not maladjusted. Instead, they are bright, socially competent youngsters who enjoy and do especially well at complex problem-solving tasks (Rubin, 1982).

In the preschool years, contact with agemates provides children with opportunities to learn and practice a wide variety of social skills. But young children, who are limited in mobility and independence, are largely dependent on parents to help them establish rewarding peer associations. Parents influence children's peer relationships in many ways. One is through the neighborhood they choose to live in. Neighborhoods differ substantially in the extent to which they permit easy contact and play among young children. Berg and Medrich (1980) examined the impact of different residential areas in Oakland, California, on peer interaction. Monterrey, an affluent hilly subdivision in which secluded homes on large lots were set back from busy roads that lacked sidewalks, constricted children's opportunities to move about freely and congregate with peers. In contrast, the flat, densely populated inner city neighborhood of Yuba offered ready access to a rich and varied neighborhood social life. Children played often in large, mixed-age groups, made use of the streets for sponta-

---

[1] In Chapter 6, we discussed the emergence of sociodramatic play during the preschool years along with its significance for children's social and cognitive development. You may wish to return to Box 6.1, page 236 to review these findings.

Table 15.2. Smilansky's (1968) Developmental Sequence of Cognitive Play

PLAY TYPE	DEFINITION	EXAMPLES	AGES AT WHICH ESPECIALLY COMMON
Functional play	Simple, repetitive muscle movements with or without objects	Running around a room, rolling a car back and forth, kneading clay with no intent to construct with it	1–2
Constructive play	Creating or constructing something	Making a house out of toy blocks, drawing a picture, putting together a puzzle	3–6
Make-believe play	Acting out everyday and imaginary roles in play	Playing house, school, or police officer. Acting out fairy tale or television characters	3–7
Play and games with rules	Understanding and conforming to rules in play activities	Playing board games, cards, hopscotch, baseball	6–11

Sources: Smilansky (1968); Rubin, Fein, & Vandenberg (1983).

neous games, built secret hidaways in empty lots, and traveled together to make small purchases in nearby shops.

Parents also act as social planners and "booking agents" for young children, scheduling visits between playmates and enrolling them in preschool and other organized activities where contact with agemates is provided. Older children arrange more peer experiences for themselves, but preschoolers must rely on their parents' efforts, especially if the neighborhood prevents them from gathering spontaneously. Parents also influence their children's social behavior by offering advice and guidance about how to interact with playmates. Finally, adult social relationships provide children with influential examples of how to act toward peers, and as we saw in earlier chapters, young children quickly integrate parental styles of interaction into their own social behavior (Rubin & Sloman, 1984).

Neighborhood play life and parental support, guidance, and modeling of social skills continue to be influential beyond the preschool years. Throughout childhood, the social worlds of family and peers are linked in fundamental ways.

Children's opportunities to interact with peers are influenced by the physical and social characteristics of their neighborhood. Neighborhoods with flat terrain and a rich variety of child residents permit youngsters to move about freely and gather together in mixed-age play groups. (Nancy Sheehan)

Middle Childhood and Adolescence. With the beginning of formal schooling, children's contact with a diversity of peers increases substantially. The school's emphasis on intellectual tasks soon makes it apparent that agemates vary in achievement-related characteristics, and children also learn that peers differ in many other ways, including ethnicity, religion, interests, and personality. Greater breadth of peer contact contributes to heightened awareness by elementary school children that others have viewpoints that differ from their own (see Chapter 11). Peer interaction, in turn, profits from children's improved perspective-taking capacity. Children's communication skills with agemates undergo marked improvement during middle childhood. For example, eye contact in peer conversations increases between 4 and 9 years of age (Levine & Sutton-Smith, 1973), and children become better at accurately interpreting the intentions of others and taking them into account in peer dialogues.

Children's ability to moderate their own social behavior in accord with multiple sources of information — for example, the rules of a game and the momentary reactions of a playmate — improves over the elementary school years. Hartup, Brady, and Newcomb (1983) had first and third graders play a board game with a fictitious peer partner seated in another room. Half the children were given competitive rules in which the player progressing farthest around the board would get a prize. The other half were given cooperative rules in which rewards would be dispensed on the basis of the players' combined progress. Within each of these conditions, half of the fictitious partners behaved competitively and half cooperatively, irrespective of the rules of the game. When rules and partner behavior were inconsistent, first graders adjusted what they did to match the behavior of the partner and ignored the rules. By third grade, children took both sources of information into account, responding with a mixture of cooperation and competition when rules and playmate behavior were inconsistent.

In middle childhood, peer interaction also becomes increasingly governed by social norms that promote courteous, prosocial behavior. Recall from Chapter 12 that sharing, helping, and other forms of altruism are more common in middle childhood than during the preschool years. In the study described above, by fifth grade, when game rules and partner behavior were in conflict, children showed a bias toward cooperation. Also, older children differ from their younger counterparts in the way they go about helping others. Kindergartners move right in and give assistance, regardless of whether it is desired or not. Older children offer to help and wait for a peer to accept it before they behave altruistically (Melburg, McCabe, & Kobasigawa, 1980, cited by Hartup, 1983). During adolescence, agemates work more cooperatively in groups — staying on task, interacting more, interrupting each other less, asking for opinions, and acknowledging one anothers' contributions (Smith, 1960; Smith, 1973).

In line with children's increasing adherence to prosocial expectations, the overall incidence of quarreling and aggressive interchanges decreases over the late preschool and middle childhood years, although, as we indicated in Chapter 13, the form of aggression makes a difference. Verbal insults continue into adolescence, while physical attacks decline, although both occur more often among boys than among girls.

Another form of peer interaction becomes more common in the late preschool and middle childhood years. Watch children at play in a public park or school yard, and you will see them wrestle, roll, jump, hit, and run after one another while smiling and laughing. This friendly chasing and play-fighting is called **rough-and-tumble play.** Research indicates that it is a good-natured, sociable activity that is quite distinct from aggressive fighting. Children initiate it with peers whom they like especially well, and they continue interacting after a rough-and-tumble episode, rather than separating (as they do at the end of an aggressive encounter). The resemblance of rough-and-tumble play to the juvenile social behavior of a wide variety of mammalian species raises questions about its adaptive significance. By 11 years of age, children choose rough-and-tumble partners who are not only likable, but similar in strength to themselves. In our evolutionary past, this form of interaction may have been important for the development of dominance and fighting skill (Humphreys & Smith, 1987). Rough and tumble play occurs more often among boys, but girls also engage in it. However, girls' rough-and-tumble behaviors largely consist of running and chasing, while boys engage in more playful wrestling and hitting (Jones, 1972; Smith & Connolly, 1972; Humphreys & Smith, 1987).

Over the course of middle childhood, children interact increasingly often with

During the late preschool and middle childhood years, children engage in friendly chasing and play-fighting known as rough-and-tumble play. (Paul Conklin/ Monkmeyer Press Photo Service)

peers, until at adolescence, more time is spent in peer associations than with any other agent of socialization (Medrich et al., 1982). Why do children choose to spend so much time with agemates? Common interests, novel play activities, comparable social skills, and opportunities to interact with others on a relatively equal footing make peer relationships especially satisfying. As childhood draws to a close, the average young person emerges from these frequent and intense social encounters with a great many sensitive and sophisticated social behaviors (Hartup, 1983).

Situational Influences on Peer Interaction

At all ages, peer interaction is highly subject to situational influences. In the following sections we consider a number of important ones: the play materials available, and the group size, age mixture, and familiarity of peer participants.

Play Materials. The quantity and kind of play materials available have an important bearing on the nature of peer interaction. Play with small objects — especially when there are too few to go around — is the most common setting for fights and quarrels among young children (DeStefano & Mueller, 1982; Maudry & Nekula, 1939; McGrew, 1969). In preschool classrooms, certain play contexts, such as the art and reading areas, promote solitary and parallel play, while others, such as the housekeeping and block areas, stimulate cooperative social behavior (Rubin, 1977). Active play spaces, such as school playgrounds or indoor slides and jungle gyms, also encourage high levels of coordinated interaction as well as rough-and-tumble play (Humphreys & Smith, 1984; Vandenberg, as cited by Hartup, 1983).

Providing children with toys that have highly specific functions (e.g., trucks, dolls, stove) as opposed to materials with ambiguous functions (e.g., pipe cleaners, cardboard cylinders, paper bags) also influences peer sociability. In one study, small groups of preschoolers came together for two play sessions — one with specific and the other with ambiguous play objects. Children used the specific toys to enact realistic roles, such as mother, doctor, and baby. In contrast, the ambiguous materials encouraged fantastic role play, such as pirate and creature from outer space. Fantastic roles, in turn, led to more social interaction, especially planning statements, such as, "I'll be the pirate and you be the prisoner" or "Watch out! Now I'm going to jump ship!" Since fantastic role play is not governed by familiar, everyday scripts, children devote more time to planning each episode and explaining what they are doing to play companions (McLoyd, Warren, & Thomas, 1984).

Group Size. A smaller group size encourages more intense and cooperative social behavior at all ages. Interacting in twosomes seems to be especially conducive to the development of early social skills. Tracking the development of peer sociability among toddlers over a 6-month period, Vandell and Mueller (1977) reported that the number and complexity of exchanges increased under conditions of dyadic (but not group) interaction. Similarly, in family day care homes with only 2 or 3 youngsters, children are more likely to talk and play among themselves (Howes & Rubenstein, 1985). When day care homes have more than 5 children, preschoolers perform poorly on perspective-taking tasks, and their behavior is less socially competent (Clarke-Stewart & Gruber, 1984). This same trend carries over into the middle childhood years. In elementary school classrooms, small discussion and study groups of about five members promote more involved and cooperative peer interaction than larger group sizes (Hare, 1953; Hertz-Lazarowitz, Sharan, & Steinberg, 1980).

Age Mix of Child Participants. The theories of Piaget and Vygotsky, which we reviewed in Chapter 6, suggest that children derive different benefits from interacting with same- as opposed to different-age peers. Piaget (1932/1965) emphasized the importance of experiences with children of equivalent status who challenge the young child's egocentric viewpoint, thereby fostering cognitive, social, and moral growth. In contrast, Vygotsky (1930–1935/1978) believed that children derive unique advantages from interacting with older, more capable peers, who encourage more mature behavior in their younger counterparts.

Research reveals that children accommodate quite differently to the presence of same- and different-age youngsters. In several studies, preschool and early elementary school children were brought together in laboratories to play or work on problem-solving tasks. Mixed-age conditions evoked more social interaction from younger children, along with special accommodations by older youngsters, who reduced their rate of social communication and assumed more responsibility for task performance than they did with same-age partners (Lougee, Grueneich, & Hartup, 1977; Graziano et al., 1976; Brody, Graziano, & Musser, 1983). Moreover, children freely imitate behaviors of same-age and older youngsters, but they rarely imitate a younger child (Brody & Stoneman, 1981; Thelen & Kirkland, 1976). Similarly, observations of child-child interaction in classrooms that combine preschool and early school-age children reveal that younger children cross age boundaries more often than older children, who are more likely to initiate to same-age partners. However, for children of both age levels, same-age interaction is more positive, more verbal, and more likely to evoke cooperative play (Day & Hunt, 1975; Lederberg et al., 1986; Roopnarine & Johnson, 1984). Children in mixed-age settings seem to gravitate to same-age companions because play interests are more compatible and social engagement is more reinforcing. Younger children also turn toward older classmates because of their superior knowledge and power, and because their play appears especially stimulating and exciting.

By the beginning of elementary school, children are consciously aware of the different social functions of older, younger, and same-age peers. When asked, they indicate that they prefer to establish friendships with agemates; to seek help, comfort, and instruction from older children; and to give help and sympathy to younger ones (French, 1984). Although more needs to be learned about the unique developmental consequences of same- and mixed-age relationships, research suggests that children profit cognitively and socially from both types of associations. As we indicated in Chapters 11 and 12, from interacting with coequals, children learn to cooperate and resolve conflicts, and they develop important moral notions of justice and reciprocity. Moreover, younger children do acquire new competencies from older companions, and when more mature children teach their less mature counterparts, they practice nurturance, guidance, and other prosocial behaviors (Whiting & Whiting, 1975; Hartup, 1983).

Finally, age is not the only child characteristic that affects peer sociability. Recall from Chapter 13 that children often choose companions of the same sex and that same- and mixed-sex peer associates differ substantially in the activities they pursue and their style of interaction. Later on, when we take up the topic of school desegregation, we will see that children also prefer companions of their own racial/ethnic group. However, research indicates that peer relations do not change in quality when children of different racial/ethnic origins choose to interact with each other (Finkelstein & Haskins, 1983; Lederberg et al., 1986).

Familiarity of Peer Associates. "Familiarity breeds sociability" in the case of peer companions. As children get to know one another better, they interact more frequently, intensely, and competently. Gestures, imitation, and reciprocal exchanges among infants; maturity of play among preschoolers; and verbal interaction and group problem solving among elementary school children are all enhanced when peers are acquaintances rather than strangers (Becker, 1977; Brody, Graziano, & Musser, 1983; Doyle, Connolly, & Rivest, 1980; Harper & Huie, 1985; Young & Lewis, 1979). Peer familiarity may augment sociability for at least two reasons. First, much like adults, when children get to know each other better, their social behaviors probably achieve a "better fit" with one another as smooth, comfortable interaction replaces the stilted, awkward exchanges of strangers. Second, among infants and young children, well-known peers (much like familiar caregivers) serve as a secure base for exploration, thereby promoting vigorous, competent behavior toward social as well as inanimate surroundings (Ipsa, 1981). In line with this idea, one recent study indicated that children who enter kindergarten classes with a large number of peers whom they knew in nursery school the previous year like school better and show fewer anxious symptoms than children who have few familiar companions (Ladd & Price, 1987).

In summary, situational factors have a major bearing on the quantity and quality of peer sociability. Liberally equipped play environments; nonspecific toys; small group sizes; and same-age, familiar companions are among the factors that promote positive, highly verbal, cooperative child-child interaction. Cross-age contact provides older children with opportunities to practice important prosocial skills, and it permits younger children to benefit from the expertise of their older companions. Research on situational factors suggests ways to design programs and play spaces to promote a wide range of positive social behaviors.

Peer Acceptance and Popularity

Although the quantity and complexity of social behavior increase with age for virtually all children, not all youngsters are equally liked and sought after as peer companions. Popularity refers to likability — how well a child is regarded by others as a worthy social partner. Investigators generally measure it with **sociometric techniques.** These are self-report measures that ask peers in the same classroom to evaluate one another's likability. A variety of sociometric methods have been developed to assess peer opinion. Children may be asked to nominate several peers in their class whom they especially like or dislike; to indicate for all possible pairs of classmates which one they prefer to play with; or to rate each peer on a scale from "like very much" to "like very little" (Asher & Hymel, 1981). Pupils as young as 4 years old can answer sociometric questions reliably (Hymel, 1983).

Until very recently, researchers made global distinctions between popular and unpopular children, failing to recognize that among children classed as unpopular, those actively disliked and those simply not chosen were very different kinds of youngsters. Currently, sociometric methods are used to distinguish among four types of social acceptance: (1) **popular children,** who receive many positive votes; (2) **rejected children,** who are actively disliked; (3) **controversial children,** who receive a large number of positive and negative choices; and (4) **neglected children,** who are seldom chosen, either positively or negatively. Together, these four kinds of children comprise about two thirds of the pupils in a typical elementary school classroom. The remaining one third are *average* in peer acceptance; they do not receive extreme scores on sociometric measures (Coie, Dodge, & Coppotelli, 1982; Gottman, 1977).

Assessments of peer acceptance remain reasonably stable over childhood and adolescence. At any given year from preschool on, those children who are liked most and liked least tend to retain their status the following year (Bukowski & Newcomb, 1984; Ladd & Price, 1987; Roff, Sells, & Golden, 1972; Rubin & Daniels-Bierness, 1983). Although the stability of sociometric choices declines as the interval between assessments lengthens, even over a 5-year period, there is moderate consistency in peer opinion, with the rejected status remaining the most stable over time (Coie & Dodge, 1983). Moreover, by first grade, children have formed a fairly accurate notion of how well liked each of their classmates is, and by third grade they can accurately appraise their own peer reputation (Krantz & Burton, 1986). Popularity is a salient social attribute in the minds of children by the early school years.

Peer acceptance has been of special interest to child development specialists

Children who are rejected by peers feel unhappy and alienated, and they have a high probability of experiencing later-life adjustment problems. (Elizabeth Ely/PhotoEdit)

because it is a powerful variable in forecasting current as well as later psychological well-being. Rejected children, especially, are unhappy, alienated, poorly achieving youngsters who have a low sense of self-esteem. Both parents and teachers view them as having a wide range of socioemotional difficulties (Achenbach & Edelbrock, 1981; Green et al., 1981; French & Waas, 1985). A recent comprehensive review of research on the relationship of peer acceptance to later-life problems reveals similar findings. Peer rejection in middle childhood is associated with dropping out of school, delinquency, and criminality, and to a lesser extent, with serious psychological difficulties in adolescence and young adulthood (Parker & Asher, 1987). In contrast, neglected children, at one time assumed to be at risk for adjustment problems, are indistinguishable from youngsters of average social status in mental health assessments. Although peer acceptance predicts a wide variety of later life problems and certainly may contribute to them, it is important to keep in mind that the evidence described above is correlational, and peer relations may not be a major causal factor. Peer acceptance may be linked to psychological adjustment through other prior influences, such as children's personality characteristics, parental child-rearing practices, or some combination of the two. As yet, investigators have not sorted out the precise connections between peer acceptance and the wide variety of other factors that are also associated with later life adjustment.

Correlates and Causes of Acceptance in the Peer Situation. To better understand how peer acceptance emerges in the context of child-child relations, researchers have correlated a wide variety of child characteristics and social behaviors with sociometric scores. Many of these investigations have led to provocative speculations about what leads some children to be liked and others to be rejected by their classmates, but most cannot tell us for sure what engenders these different reactions. However, in several recent studies, investigators have successfully made use of the longitudinal research design to isolate causal connections between children's social behaviors and peer acceptance. In each case, initially unacquainted children were brought together for repeated sessions in a laboratory, and behaviors that eventually turned them on or off to one another were tracked over time. We will discuss the findings of these groundbreaking investigations shortly. But first, let's look at the significance of some nonbehavioral characteristics for children's popularity — their names and physical appearance.

Names. Do offbeat names like Bertha and Horatio reduce a child's chances of being accepted by peers, and common ones like Karen and Michael enhance it? McDavid and Harari (1966) asked 10- to 12-year-olds to rate the attractiveness of a large number of first names and then provide sociometric ratings of children in their classrooms. A positive relationship emerged between children's name preferences and the likability of children who bore the names. It is unlikely that children's attitudes toward classmates simply generalize to their names, because the name preferences of peers who do not know each other also predict popularity. McDavid and Harari believe that children and adults are prone to judge others by their labels. Popular, socially desirable names are associated with positive personal qualities, while rare and unusual ones produce negative personal images. However, it is possible that the connection between names and peer likability is more complex than this interpretation suggests. Perhaps parents who give their children offbeat names are nonconformists who place little value on peer popularity and raise their children in ways that limit acquisition of social skills needed for peer acceptance. At present, information that would permit us to choose between these different explanations is not available.

Physical Appearance. In Chapter 5, we indicated that physical attractiveness has an important bearing on peer acceptance. Recall that children who deviate from society's ideal standards of physical beauty are less well accepted by peers. As early as age 4, children have different social expectations of attractive and unattractive age-mates. When asked to guess the characteristics of unfamiliar peers from their photographs, preschool and elementary school pupils attribute friendliness, smartness, and niceness to good-looking peers, and aggressiveness and other negative social behaviors to physically unattractive youngsters (Adams & Crane, 1980; Langlois & Stephan, 1977). Attractiveness also predicts popularity and behavior ratings among children who know each other well, although these relationships are stronger among girls than boys (Langlois & Styczynski, 1979).

Do children derive their opinions about attractive and unattractive youngsters from the way these children behave or from stereotypes associated with physical appearance? In one study, good-looking children did behave differently from their less handsome counterparts. Langlois and Downs (1979) paired same-age and same-sex 3- and 5-year-olds with one another to form three types of dyads: two attractive children; two unattractive children; and one attractive and one unattractive child. Then the social behaviors of each pair were observed in a laboratory playroom. No behavioral differences based on attractiveness were found among the 3-year-olds, but 5-year-old unattractive children more often aggressed against their partners than attractive youngsters did. These findings indicate that unattractive children actually display some of the negative behaviors attributed to them by their peers. But the fact that behavioral differences did not appear until the end of the preschool years leaves open the possibility that unattractive youngsters responded the way they did because of others' prior reactions to their physical appearance.

Parents and teachers hold the same "beauty is best" bias exhibited by peers in their behavioral expectations of children (Adams, 1978). In one study, the stronger the bias held by a mother against unattractive children, the more likely her child was to prefer the handsomer of two agemates as a play partner (Adams & Crane, 1980). When combined with the research summarized above, these results suggest that the physical attractiveness–peer popularity connection is multiply determined. Parents may react differently to their own children based on physical appearance, and along with the media, they teach children a variety of stereotypes about physical beauty. Over time, the reactions of adults and peers may promote different behaviors in attractive and unattractive youngsters. These, in turn, sustain the social preferences of agemates with whom the child comes in contact.

Interpersonal Behavior. Although physical appearance influences popularity ratings, its importance pales in comparison to a child's social behavior (Dodge, 1983; Reaves & Roberts, 1983). Popular, rejected, controversial, and neglected youngsters interact with agemates in distinct ways that serve to evoke as well as sustain peer opinion.

Popularity is consistently associated with cooperative, friendly social behavior

(Coie, Dodge, & Coppotelli, 1982; Hartup, Glazer, & Charlesworth, 1967; Ladd & Price, 1987). Moreover, well-liked youngsters are especially effective social problem solvers who communicate with peers in a mature and sensitive fashion. When they do not understand another child's reaction, they are likely to ask for an explanation (Gottman, Gonso, & Rasmussen, 1975; Rubin, 1972). If they disagree with a play partner in a game, they go beyond voicing their displeasure; they suggest what the other child could do instead (Putallaz & Gottman, 1981). In addition, popular children gain entry into ongoing play groups by adapting their behavior to the flow of peer activity, offering relevant comments about the game instead of hovering around the outskirts of the group (as neglected children often do) or barging in and disrupting the activity (an approach that is typical of rejected youngsters) (Dodge et al., 1983; Putallaz, 1983). In view of these findings, it is not surprising that popular children are judged by classmates as especially willing and helpful companions who possess leadership qualities (Carlson, Lahey, & Neeper, 1984).

Rejected social status is associated with a wide range of negative social behaviors — high rates of conflict, aggression, hyperactive-distractible behavior, and immature forms of social and cognitive play (Carlson, Lahey, & Neeper, 1984; Coie, Dodge, & Coppotelli, 1982; Dodge, Coie, & Brakke, 1982; Ladd & Price, 1987; Rubin & Daniels-Bierness, 1983; Shantz, 1986). Peer-rejected children also show deficits in a number of social-cognitive skills that we discussed in Chapter 11. For example, they are more likely than other children to misinterpret innocent acts of peers as hostile (Dodge, Murphy, & Buchsbaum, 1984), and they generate few prosocial solutions to hypothetical social problems (Rubin & Daniels-Bierness, 1983). These social-cognitive deficits contribute to rejected children's inept and hostile style of relating to agemates. Moreover, the fact that rejected youngsters experience many conflictual and aggressive exchanges with peers serves to limit their social-cognitive development. Because they seldom engage in extended conversational exchanges in which they are confronted with an agemate's point of view, they have few opportunities to improve their perspective-taking capacities and learn to accurately read another's intentions.

Controversial children display a blend of positive and negative social behaviors that is consistent with the mixed peer opinion they engender. Like rejected youngsters, they are active and disruptive, yet they also engage in high rates of positive, prosocial acts. As a result, they are salient individuals to their classmates and, much like popular children, are regarded as leaders (Milich & Landau, 1984; Coie, Dodge, & Coppotelli, 1982). As yet, controversial children are an understudied group. We do not know whether their antisocial tendencies lead to adjustment problems later on, or whether their positive social skills reduce the chances that they will experience long-term developmental difficulties.

Neglected children fall at the opposite extreme of controversial children, engaging in low rates of peer interaction of all kinds. These youngsters often choose to play alone; classmates regard them as shy children who seldom call attention to themselves (Carlson, Lahey, & Neeper, 1984; Dodge, Coie, & Brakke, 1982; Gottman, 1977). However, these findings should not be taken to mean that neglected children are less socially skilled than their average counterparts. Instead, these are the youngsters discussed earlier in this chapter who have a repertoire of effective social behaviors but are simply content to pursue their solitary interests. Despite their low rates of social interaction, they do not report feeling especially lonely (Asher & Wheeler, 1985). However, it is still possible that some neglected children—those who are extremely withdrawn and lack the ability to form peer relationships of any kind — are at risk for psychological problems. But these constitute no more than a very small fraction of the neglected category (Asher, 1983). Moreover, recent research suggests that very withdrawn children who deliberately avoid peers and display inappropriate behavior in their presence eventually become rejected, rather than neglected, at older ages (Hymel & Rubin, 1985; Rubin, LeMare, & Lollis, in press).

The findings summarized above are based on correlational studies of already acquainted agemates. As mentioned earlier, they do not tell us for sure if social behavior is actually responsible for variations in peer acceptance. Recently, by making creative use of the longitudinal research design, several investigators have established that behavioral styles *do* play a causal role in peer opinion. Dodge (1983) brought groups of unacquainted second-grade boys together for a series of play sessions in a laboratory and looked at how their interaction patterns predicted sociometric assessments at the end of the study. Much like the constellations of findings reported above, boys who came to be popular engaged in friendly conversation and cooperative play; those who became rejected engaged in high frequencies of antisocial acts; while those who developed a controversial status displayed both prosocial and antisocial behaviors. Neglected boys showed some inappropriate social responses, but they were noticeably low in aggressive behavior. In another similar study, Coie & Kupersmidt (1983) reported much the same findings, except for the fact that many youngsters neglected by familiar classmates showed highly competent social behavior when brought together with unfamiliar agemates in a laboratory. Under these conditions, they broke away from their usual pattern of playing by themselves and became more sociable. The fact that neglected children can behave in a positive, socially outgoing manner when they enter new situations may be one reason that as a group, they do not experience psychological adjustment problems.

Although social behavior is a major cause of peer acceptance, once a child's peer reputation is established, it contributes to the maintenance of particular interaction patterns. Research indicates that popular youngsters come to be viewed as "friendly" and "nice" by their classmates, while rejected youngsters are seen as "malicious" and "hostile." In line with their respective reputations, well-accepted children end up being excused by peers for their undesirable behaviors, while rejected youngsters are quickly blamed (Hymel, 1986). Because popular children rarely experience peer ostracism when they do behave antisocially, they have an easy time remaining popular, for children who are seldom shunned and tormented by peers are less likely to behave negatively in the future (Dodge, 1983; Coie & Kupersmidt, 1983).

In summary, popular children interact positively and rejected children antisocially, while controversial children display a mixture of both types of behavior. Although neglected youngsters engage in low rates of peer interaction, most are socially competent, well-adjusted children who enjoy solitary endeavors. Maladaptive behavior patterns, social-cognitive deficits, and negative peer reputations of rejected children feed on one another and are carried over from year to year. Therefore, interventions with such children are best begun early, before their antisocial tendencies and social skill deficits become so well practiced that they are difficult, if not impossible, to change.

Helping Unpopular Children. A variety of intervention programs aimed at helping unpopular children achieve more satisfactory peer relations have been developed. Most employ behaviorist and social learning theory principles to teach positive social skills, such as how to initiate peer interaction, cooperate in play, and respond to another child with friendly emotion and approval. Three basic types of interventions have been tried: (1) reinforcement for peer contact and positive interaction; (2) modeling of appropriate social behaviors; and (3) direct teaching, or coaching, in how to interact effectively with other children. Reinforcement programs are effective in increasing rates of very simple social behaviors. However, since they require children to spontaneously exhibit a desirable response before adult approval can be administered, they do not work well with extremely aggressive, disruptive, or socially withdrawn youngsters. Moreover, the effects of reinforcement are rarely maintained once adult contingencies are withdrawn (O'Connor, 1972), and reinforcement programs are not well suited to teaching complex or completely new social skills. Modeling programs in which children are shown films of youngsters engaging in complex social behaviors have met with greater success, with some interventions producing gains in positive social acts that persist up to several weeks after the treatment (O'Connor, 1969; O'Connor, 1972). Finally, a number of coaching programs that provide verbal lessons in the principles of effective peer interaction, practice in enacting them, and feedback to children on how well they have performed have produced impressive gains in social skill and peer acceptance that last from several weeks to a year after the treatment (Bierman, 1986; Ladd, 1981; Oden & Asher, 1977). Coaching programs may work well for at least two reasons. First, several methods — direct teaching, modeling, and reinforcement — are integrated into the training procedures. Second, because verbal coaching involves explanations that encourage children to think about the consequences of their actions, it probably promotes greater understanding, internalization, and generalization of effective social skills.

Despite the success of some interventions, others have shown mixed or negative outcomes, and a great deal remains to be learned about how to help children who are not accepted by their peers. In most studies, rejected and neglected pupils have been combined into a global category of unpopular children and then subjected to the same treatment. Yet we have already seen that the majority of neglected children are socially competent and not in need of intervention (Asher, Markell, & Hymel, 1981). Few programs have targeted rejected children, who are most in need of help. In one that did, intensive academic tutoring proved to be more effective in increasing social acceptance than coaching in social skills (Coie & Krehbiel, 1984). Although the precise reasons for this finding are not clear, it does suggest that satisfactory school achievement may be a vital indirect link to successful social relations in the classroom.

Finally, because rejected children display high levels of aggressive and disruptive behavior, some psychologists believe that to produce lasting changes in peer acceptance, techniques designed to reduce these antisocial acts must be combined with coaching in social skills and academic remediation (Krehbiel & Milich, 1986). In one recent study, including verbal prohibitions against antisocial behaviors and negative consequences for engaging in them in a coaching program led to better social acceptance among rejected elementary school boys than a program that focused only on teaching positive social skills (Bierman, Miller, & Stabb, 1987). Other investigators recommend combining social-cognitive interventions (such as training in perspective-taking) with direct instruction in social skills (Ladd & Mize, 1983), but the impact of such comprehensively designed programs on rejected children's social status remains to be studied.

Peer Groups

In the sections above, our major focus has been on developmental changes and individual differences in dyadic peer interaction. Beginning in the preschool years, collectives of three to a dozen or more children assemble on a regular basis in the neighborhood or school yard. Younger children, when gathered together in this fashion, "behave simply as a number of independent persons, each mainly concerned with his own immediate ends." By middle childhood, an important change occurs. Aggregates of older youngsters give the impression of greater interdependence — "more developed and reciprocal social relationships, with a settled organization" (Isaacs, 1933, p. 213). When peer participants feel a strong desire to belong to a social unit, generate shared rules or norms of conduct beyond those maintained by society at large, and develop a hierarchical social structure of roles and relationships that govern their interaction with one another, a **peer group** is formed (Hartup, 1983).

In Chapter 11, we showed that close, one-to-one friendship ties in middle childhood and adolescence contribute uniquely to the development of trust and sensitivity to other people. During the same period, experiences in multimember social groups also provide a unique context for social learning. The group teaches children how to engage in cooperative activity aimed at collective rather than individual goals. In addition, through group membership, children experience social structures first-hand, practice the skills associated with leadership and followership, master control of hostile impulses toward fellow members, and learn to mobilize aggression in the service of group loyalty by directing it toward "outsiders" (Fine, 1980).

A classic study by Sherif and his colleagues (1961) called the *Robbers Cave experiment* illustrates how peer groups form, their essential features, and the functions they serve in the social life of the child.

Peer Group Formation. Fifth-grade boys selected on the basis of being well-adjusted in school and in peer group relations were brought to a summer campground known as Robbers Cave, divided into two clusters of 11 members each, and removed to separate campsites. Friendships developed as the boys in each collective mingled freely with one another, but a strong, cohesive group structure did not emerge until the camp staff arranged circumstances that required cooperation and interdependent activity. Backpacking excursions into the woods as well as opportunities to improve a swimming area and clean up a rough field for athletics led the campers to create a division of labor, and several individuals with superior skills soon took on greater status — one boy for his cooking, another for his athletic prowess, and a third for his entertaining personality and ability to "horse around." Over time, shifting patterns of leaders and followers from one activity to the next began to stabilize. One boy in each group ranked highest, followed by several other prestigious associates. A few members sifted toward the bottom of the emerging structure, while still others were intermediate in respect and influence. As the group structure coalesced, the boys at each campsite also developed distinct notions of appropriate behavior and ways of doing things. For example, one group generated a "norm of toughness" adhered to so strongly that members suppressed any signs of hurt after an injury and refused treatment for cuts and scratches. In the other group, a very different "norm of good behavior" emerged. In contrast to the swearing and rowdy behavior of the "tough" group, these boys used "clean" language and were polite and considerate toward one another. At each campsite, group members coined nicknames for one another, and special jargon, jokes, and ways of performing tasks developed. Wayward campers who failed to do things "right" or did not contribute to the goals of the group found themselves reprimanded, ridiculed, and even given "the silent treatment." Soon behavior in conformity with group norms took place smoothly, with little need for corrective measures. Eventually the groups took names for themselves — the Rattlers and the Eagles. Boys in each displayed considerable pride in their collective accomplishments and a strong group identity.

The next phase of Sherif's study showed that group norms and social structures evolve further, based on the group's relationship with "outsiders." The camp counselors arranged for the Rattlers and Eagles to "discover" one another, and a tournament of competitive activities was initiated in which only one group could be the winner. Although the games began in an atmosphere of cordiality and good sportsmanship, these conditions quickly deteriorated. The consequences of losing for the solidarity of each group were striking. Members became angry and vindictive, blaming each other for defeat, and disintegration of established group structures ensued. The leader of the Eagles was deposed when he proved reluctant to confront the hostilities of the out-group. Among the Rattlers, a large bully whose aggressiveness had been squelched during the early period of group formation emerged as a hero during periods of team competition. Revised group structures and new normative behaviors based on intergroup rivalry started to develop. Members devoted themselves to hurling animosities and retaliating against the out-group after defeat. Name calling, physical scuffles, stealing and burning of team flags, and destructive cabin raids ensued, with each successful attack increasing intragroup harmony and solidarity. Over time, both the Rattlers and Eagles showed a strong tendency to stereotype each other as nasty and sneaky, reactions that further magnified the social distance between the groups.

In the final phase of Sherif's study, the camp staff faced the challenging task of how to bring two groups with extremely negative images of one another into harmonious interaction. Pleasurable joint recreational activities, such as a trip to the movies and Fourth of July fireworks, were tried, but these were disasters. Far from reducing conflict, they served as opportunities for each group to renew its berating of the other. But once the staff arranged activities with *superordinate goals* that each group desired but neither could achieve without the cooperation of the other, intergroup hostility began to subside. In one instance, the camp water supply "broke down," and in another, a truck preparing to get food for the hungry campers "stalled" — circumstances that required interdependent action among all the boys to solve a common problem. After a series of these experiences, members of each group started to feel friendlier toward each other. Negative stereotyping of the out-group diminished, and new friendship choices emerged that cut across group lines.

The Robbers Cave study shows that peer groups form when individuals perceive that others share common goals. Norms and role structures gradually emerge in the service of shared motivations, and as goals change, these basic determinants of group cohesion are modified as well. Group functioning is affected by situational factors external to the group. Although differences in ethnicity and skin color are known to promote prejudice and negative stereotyping, Sherif's study reveals that hatred by an in-group of an out-group can be generated without them. Competition for scarce but highly desired resources is sufficient to produce deep-seated intergroup animosities. Activities with superordinate goals that one group cannot reach without the help of the other gradually reduce intergroup hostilities and foster positive feelings and attitudes.

In the sections that follow, we take a closer look at two processes shown in Sherif's study to be essential for peer group cohesion: the emergence of group norms and group social structures.

Group Norms. Group norms are responsible for the existence of "peer cultures" — unique systems of knowledge, beliefs, and behavioral customs that bind group members together, creating a sense of joint commitment and solidarity. In earlier chapters, we showed that societal norms, such as sex-role stereotypes and moral standards, begin to affect child-child interaction as early as the preschool years. But these norms are derived from adults. Self-generated norms in the peer group, such as a specialized language, unique codes of dress, musical preferences, and a place to "hang out" during leisure hours — are not evident until late childhood and adolescence. Once they do appear, different peer groups generate quite distinct normative prescriptions. Hartup (1983) describes the array of peer group norms that emerged in one Minnesota high school in the mid-1970s:

> *Sporties* . . . are adolescents of both sexes who engage in sports, who attend sports activities, and who drink beer. *Workers* are students who have jobs, who are motivated to accumulate money, who own cars, and whose social lives revolve mostly around the automobile. *Crispies* are students who use drugs on other than a one-time basis, who are the best football players, and who do not work very hard at school. *Musicians* are students who spend much time in the music room, who attend or assist with performance activities of one type or another, and who drink alcoholic beverages. *Debaters* are those who read a lot, get good grades, participate in clubs focused on intellectual activities and who drink Pepsi-Cola at their parties. (p. 146)

What governs the assortment of peers into separate groups with unique normative standards? Recent longitudinal studies in which adolescent values and peer associates have been tracked over time show that selection of group companions and the norms generated by them are a blend of family and peer group influences (Britt & Campbell,

1977; Downs, 1985; Chassin et al., 1986). In other words, when young people join a group, they select associates likely to create norms compatible with their current values. Then the new norms generated modify members' original beliefs and behaviors. A study by Chassin and her coworkers (1986) illustrates this process. Nearly 4,000 sixth through eleventh graders were surveyed about their own smoking behavior and that of their parents and peers. The same questions were asked again one year later. Adolescents who took up smoking on a regular basis during the year of the study, when compared to their nonsmoking counterparts, were more likely to have both parents and peer associates who smoked. You may recall from our discussion of identity development in Chapter 11 that contrary to popular belief, adolescence is not a period in which a radical break with parental values occurs. Chassin's findings support this conclusion; many norms generated by the peer group are an extension of those acquired at home.

Nevertheless, the onset of peer group ties during preadolescence coincides with a period in which some of the "nicest children begin to behave in the most awful way" (Redl, 1966, p. 395). As we saw in the Robbers Cave experiment, the peer group is a context in which hostility directed toward outsiders can occur. Prank-playing, such as egging a house, making a funny phone call, or ringing a door bell and running away, is usually performed with agemates, who provide temporary social support for breaking the normative traditions of society. Interviewing a sample of 48 middle-class 12-year-old boys, Fine (1980) reported that 70 percent had participated in such activities at one time or another. At school, peer groups may become status-conscious with respect to other rival groups with whom they jockey for power, influence, and visibility. These conditions intensify the exclusive, condescending behavior of some cliques toward outsiders. Clique members are renowned for engaging in negative gossip about nonmembers, making catty remarks about their "weird" dress and behavior that intensify the clique's tightly knit organization and sense of collective identity (Savin-Williams, 1980b).

Pranks and petty antagonisms are mild forms of antisocial behavior when compared to the delinquent acts perpetrated by a small number of juvenile gangs. Do children and adolescents learn behaviors and attitudes conducive to delinquency within the peer group? At present, investigators continue to debate the question of whether most delinquents are highly social individuals with strong bonds to agemates who share their antisocial norms, or whether they are social misfits who fail to establish effective peer relations. Currently, evidence in favor of both these positions exists. The home lives of most delinquent youths are characterized by stress, disorganization, and poverty, leading them to be poorly equipped to succeed in the mainstream world of peers and school. Gradually, these youngsters come to view conventional routes to achievement and self-esteem as unreachable, and these goals are replaced by their very opposite — aggressive, antisocial, and destructive behavior — through which the adolescent gains acceptance in the eyes of like-minded peers. Relations within delinquent gangs can be strong. Moreover, the gang may function as a surrogate family in which the alienated youth experiences a sense of loyalty and belonging not achieved in other settings (Campbell, 1980).

For most youngsters, peer cultures do not constitute a strongly antisocial force. Instead, they promote important dimensions of personal development during the adolescent years. The unique normative structure of the peer group fosters security, belongingness, and opportunities to experiment with new commitments in a supportive social context. In fact, the intensification of peer group loyalties during early adolescence can be viewed as one means by which young people establish a temporary, interim sense of identity as they separate from the family and begin to build a personally meaningful identity of their own (Erikson, 1950).

Group Social Structures. In all groups, members differ in power or status, an arrangement that facilitates division of responsibility and smooth coordination of behavior among group participants. Some children become leaders who direct the group's activities; others end up as followers who cooperate with leader-set objectives. Group norms and group social structures are interdependent. Leaders are usually the major norm-setters, and high-status children's ideas are often sufficient to alter the group's opinion (Fine, 1980). On what basis do status hierarchies emerge in children's groups?

Research by ethologists demonstrates that group social structures are sometimes based on dominance, or toughness and assertiveness. A **dominance hierarchy** is a stable ordering of individuals that predicts who will win under conditions of conflict between group members. Dominance hierarchies exist in the social organization of many animal species, and research indicates that they are a basic feature of human group cohesion as well. Observations of exchanges between children in which physical attacks, threats, and struggles over objects occur reveal a consistent lineup of winners and losers as early as the preschool years. This hierarchy becomes increasingly stable during middle childhood and adolescence (Strayer & Strayer, 1976), especially among boys (Savin-Williams, 1979). Although dominance relations are visible to observers of peer interaction, nursery school children are not aware of them. When asked, they cannot agree on who is toughest or strongest in their classroom (Sluckin & Smith, 1977; Strayer, Chapeskie & Strayer, 1978). Agreement among agemates on which group members are dominant and which are submissive is first evident in kindergarten and increases over the early elementary school years (Edelman & Omark, 1973).

Dominance hierarchies among humans, like those among other primates, serve the adaptive function of limiting aggression between group members. Once dominance relations are clearly established, intragroup hostility rarely occurs. When it does, it is very restrained, often taking the form of verbal insults delivered in a playful manner that can be accepted with equanimity by the target (Fine, 1980; Savin-Williams, 1980a). Active hostility toward insiders promotes group disintegration, and by adolescence children take heed of its destructive consequences. The gradual substitution of friendly insults for more direct aggression between group members may be functional in helping youngsters learn how to appropriately express and control their aggressive impulses.

Think back to the findings of the Robbers Cave study once more, and you will see that group structures are not always a matter of the largest and strongest children rising to the top. When the goals of the group involve the conquest of "outsiders," then a group organization based on dominance is likely to emerge, as it did when the Rattlers and Eagles confronted one another in competitive games. Under other conditions, many personal qualities become relevant. During adolescence, group structures are less dependent on physical size and prowess and more dependent on characteristics that support a group's current normative activities, such as being good at arts and crafts, knowing what to do on a camp-out, possessing athletic skill, being especially bright, or behaving in a friendly and sociable manner (Savin-Williams, 1980a). Effective group leaders are not always tough and coercive. Rather, individuals who possess a combination of attributes that best facilitate the group's current objectives are likely to rise to the top of the status hierarchy. Since groups vary in their normative orientations, social power often accrues to different children in different social situations (Hartup, 1983).

Peer Relations and the Socialization of the Child

We have seen that peer interaction contributes importantly to the acquisition of a wide variety of skills that help children adapt successfully to their social world. In the sections below, we consider the precise mechanisms by which peers socialize one another. Peers use some of the same techniques that parents do to influence each other's behavior. Reinforcement, modeling, and direct pressures to conform to peer expectations[2] are among the mechanisms that have been studied.

Peer Reinforcement and Modeling. Children's social responses to one another operate as reinforcers, modifying the extent to which they display certain behaviors in peer social contexts. Peer reinforcement increases over the course of childhood, and children often employ this socialization mechanism to positive ends. Preschoolers value the positive, prosocial behaviors of their peer associates. Children who engage in attentive, approving, and affectionate social acts are likely to be the recipients of similar behaviors in return (Charlesworth & Hartup, 1967; Leiter, 1977).

However, children are just as receptive to peer reinforcement for aggressive, antisocial responses as they are for prosocial behavior. A well-known study by Patterson, Littman, and Bricker (1967) shows how peer reactions to aggressive initiations modify the future occurrence of aggressive behavior among preschoolers. The investigators recorded instances in which a child insulted, hit, kicked, or grabbed a toy from a classmate, the reaction of the target child, and the subsequent behavior of the attacker. When the target cried, did nothing, or withdrew, the initiator was more likely to perform the same aggressive act in the future. In other words, these responses served as positive reinforcers for aggressive behavior. In contrast, successful retaliations by the target — for example, hitting back or hanging on to the desired toy — served as punishments. Under these conditions, the aggressor either moved on to a new victim or tried a new form of assertive behavior. If you study these contingencies carefully, you will see that they quickly lead to conditions in which the least aggressive children in a classroom are victimized the most. But after many instances of being the target of others' aggression, even a very passive child is likely to strike back at one time or another, a response that is reinforced when the attacker retreats. A striking finding of this study was a steady increase in aggressive behavior on the part of initially nonaggressive youngsters who successfully counterattacked after being victimized. Peer feedback is an important means through which children's aggression is enhanced as well as controlled, and even mild-mannered children can learn to behave aggressively if they are frequently the targets of hostile attacks.

Besides dispensing social reinforcement, peers provide each other with models of a wide variety of social behaviors. Peer imitation is a common occurrence from infancy through the preschool years, but by middle childhood, imitation of both peer and adult models declines (Grusec & Abramovitch, 1982). As we indicated in Chapter 12, once children grasp and internalize the rules of social life, there is less need to rely on observations of others for information about how to behave. Although peers will copy each other's negative behaviors, children who have been guided by adults toward socially acceptable standards of conduct are able to resist these influences, and they provide effective models of prosocial behavior for other youngsters (Hartup & Coates, 1967; Toner, Parke, & Yussen, 1978). However, like adult models (see Chapter 12), not all peer exemplars are equally effective in influencing the behavior of other children. An especially important attribute is knowledgeability and competence. As we mentioned earlier in our discussion of mixed-age interaction, children much prefer to imitate the behavior of an older or same-age peer than that of a younger child. Perceived similarity in background and interests, as well as friendly relations between peer models and child observers, also enhances children's willingness to emulate their agemates (Hartup & Coates, 1967; Rosekrans, 1967).

The powerful effects of peer reinforcement and modeling have led psychologists to experiment with peers as behavior change agents in remediating a wide variety of problematic behaviors in children. Socially adept children can be trained to model

[2] You may recall from our discussion of sex role development in Chapter 13 that peer reinforcement and modeling in early childhood and conformity in early adolescence are important mechanisms through which children acquire sex-typed orientations and behaviors. Turn back to page 568 and pages 574–575 to review this evidence.

and reinforce socially competent acts in less skilled youngsters, and both trainers and targets show gains in social maturity as a result (Strain, 1977). Even younger children can sometimes be used as effective "therapists" for children who lack the necessary social skills for relating to peers. In a study in which highly withdrawn preschoolers participated in a series of short play sessions with a younger but socially competent child, the withdrawn children showed dramatic increases in positive peer interaction in their regular classrooms that exceeded the gains of those who played with same-age therapists (Furman, Rahe, & Hartup, 1979). The younger play partners may have freely reinforced the social initiations and leadership behaviors of these withdrawn subjects, something that seldom occurred in their play with agemates. Peers can also serve as effective tutors for less knowledgeable youngsters at school, teaching, modeling, and reinforcing academic skills. Carefully planned peer tutoring programs in which tutors are trained and supervised by adult teachers have been found to promote self-esteem and academic progress in both tutor and tutee (Bargh & Schul, 1980; Devin-Sheehan, Feldman, & Allen, 1976).

Although other societies have long recognized the utility of peer assistance in teaching academic and social skills, peers remain an untapped potential in the United States (Damon, 1984). In most American classrooms, teachers seldom make use of peers to foster educational goals. In contrast, in cultures such as the Soviet Union and the Israeli kibbutz, the capacity of peers to socialize one another is harnessed by adults to teach the dominant values of society. Communally reared kibbutz children report receiving more discipline as well as help with problems and school work from peers than they do from parents (Avgar, Bronfenbrenner, & Henderson, 1977). In Russian elementary schools, peers are trained to reinforce one another for academic excellence and for meeting appropriate standards of grooming and social behavior. Pupils who meet these expectations are given praise and high marks by the peer collective, while those who perform poorly may be criticized or even publicly shamed (Bronfenbrenner, 1970). The American value of individualism prevents adults from transforming the autonomous, informal peer network into a formal agent of socialization in the United States. Nevertheless, these cross-cultural findings demonstrate that American schools could make far better use of peers than they currently do to promote a wide variety of socially valued behaviors. They also show that broad cultural ideologies have a major impact on how peers in different societies socialize one another.

Peer Conformity. The adolescent period is noted for a special mechanism of peer socialization — *conformity,* or acting in concert with the pressures of a particular social group. We have already seen in our discussion of group norms that parental influences are not relinquished during the teenage years. Nevertheless, it is widely believed that adolescence is a period in which young people slavishly "follow the crowd." Many parents are concerned that when conflicts between parental and peer values do arise, young people will turn toward their peers.

In actuality, peer conformity is a complex process that fluctuates with the adolescent's age, need for social approval, and the situation (Hartup, 1983). Several studies report a rise in peer conformity between 11 and 14 years of age, especially in the area of peer-sponsored misconduct, that diminishes during the late adolescent years (Berndt, 1979; Bixenstine, DeCorte, & Bixenstine, 1976; Devereux, 1970). You may recall from our discussion of self-esteem in Chapter 11 that early adolescence is a period during which young people are especially concerned about what their age-mates think of them. However, when compared to other spheres of influence, peer pressures toward antisocial behavior are not strong. In a recent study, Brown, Lohr, and McClenahan (1986) asked nearly 400 junior and senior high school students how much pressure they felt from peers to engage in various behaviors. In addition, they were questioned about their adoption of peer values — how important they thought it was to engage in the behaviors and the frequency with which they actually performed them. As shown in Figure 15.1, adolescents perceived greatest pressure to conform to

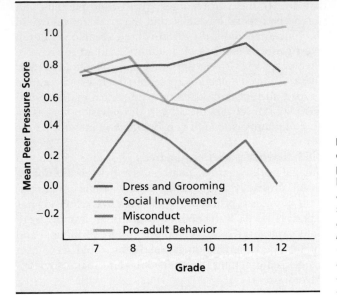

Figure 15.1. Grade differences in perceived peer pressure for four areas of behavior in the Brown, Lohr, and McClenahan (1986) study. *(From B. B. Brown, M. J. Lohr, and E. L. McClenahan, 1986, "Early Adolescents' Perceptions of Peer Pressure,"* Journal of Early Adolescence, 6, *147. Reprinted by permission.)*

the most visible aspects of the peer culture — dressing and grooming like everyone else and engaging in peer-condoned social activities (having a boyfriend or girlfriend and going to parties, school functions, or the local teenage hangout). Furthermore, they reported that peer pressure to engage in pro-adult behavior (achieving good grades, getting along with parents) was also strong. Although peer pressures toward misconduct (drinking alcohol, smoking cigarettes, and having sex) rose in early adolescence, compared to all other areas they were low, and a substantial number of respondents indicated that peers actively discouraged these activities. Moreover, peer pressures were only moderately related to adolescent values and behavior. These young people did not blindly follow the dictates of their peers.

In instances in which parental and peer pressures are in opposition to one another, adolescents do not always lean toward peers as a means of rebelling against the family. Instead, parents and peers are likely to differ in their spheres of greatest influence. Parents usually exceed peers in the areas of educational aspirations and job expectations (Kandel & Lesser, 1972), whereas peers exceed parents in matters of grooming, preferred music, and choice of friends. With respect to less desirable behaviors — smoking, alcohol use, delinquency, and early sexual activity — we have already seen that what an adolescent does is a joint product of peer and parental influences. Moreover, personal characteristics make a difference. Adolescents who view themselves as competent, worthwhile individuals are less likely to feel a need to fall in line with their peers (Landsbaum & Willis, 1971). Finally, you may recall from Chapter 14 that an effective deterrent to participation in peer antisocial behavior is authoritative child-rearing, a warm but demanding parent-child relationship that fosters high self-esteem and social and moral maturity.

MEDIA

Television

Television is pervasive in American society, and in many other countries of the Western world. Ninety-eight percent of American homes have at least one television set, over 50 percent have two or more, and a TV set is switched on in a typical household for a total of 7.1 hours per day. Television's popularity is nearly universal, but for some, the set conjures up images of passive, vegetating individuals mesmerized by a "plug-in drug" that diverts them from other worthwhile pursuits and teaches antisocial lessons, stereotyped social attitudes, and materialistic values. In fact, there is good reason to be concerned about the effects of television on children and youth. In an unusual investigation, residents of a small Canadian town were studied just before and then two years after TV reception became available in their community. Grade school children showed a decline in reading fluency and creative thinking, a rise in sex-stereotyped attitudes, and increases in verbal and physical aggression during spontaneous play. Moreover, the advent of television was associated with a marked drop in community participation by adolescents and adults (Williams, 1986).

Disturbing findings like these have surfaced in hundreds of studies conducted over the last four decades. But the negative consequences of television are not an inherent part of the medium itself. Instead, they result from the way it is used in our society (Greenfield, 1984). As our discussion proceeds, you will see that television has as much potential for good as it does for ill. If the content of TV programming were substantially changed and adults capitalized on it to enhance children's interest and participation in their physical and social surroundings, television could serve as a powerful, cost-effective means of strengthening the intellectual and social development of millions of American youngsters.

How Much Television Do Children View? The amount of time American children spend in front of TV is extraordinary. The average child between 2 and 18 years of age watches over 3 hours a day, clocking in a total of 25 hours in a single week (Nielsen Television Services, 1985). Considering the time the set is on during weekends, school holidays, and summer vacations, children spend more time watching television than they do in any other waking activity, including going to school, interacting with family members, and getting together with peers. Even babies are surprisingly committed viewers. In one study in which the activities of a small sample of toddlers were tracked at home, the average time spent attending to the set was 1.1 hours per day, a very long time in the life of an 18-month-old (Nelson, 1973). Parents admit that they sometimes use TV as a babysitter for young children (Hollenbeck & Slaby, 1979). And most older youngsters who initiate their own viewing are permitted to watch with few adult restrictions on time or content (Rossiter & Robertson, 1975).

Individual differences exist in television viewing; some children gravitate to the set much more than others. As shown in Figure 15.2, age makes a difference. Viewing time rises steadily over the preschool years, shows a slight dip around the time of school entry, then increases steadily into early adolescence, at which point it levels off and declines slightly. During the teenage years, boys exceed girls by about 1½ hours per week (Nielsen Television Services, 1985). But at all ages, children who have lower IQs, who come from low-income family backgrounds, and who are members of America's poverty minorities tend to watch the most (Liebert & Sprafkin, 1988). Excessive TV viewing is often associated with other problems, such as family and peer difficulties (Liebert, 1986) and less trusting perceptions of other people (Singer, Singer, & Rapaczynski, 1984).

The Development of "Television Literacy." The young child, confronted with the television medium for the first time, faces a formidable problem in making sense of its complexity. The television stimulus presents a rapid stream of people, objects, places, words, and sounds. Only gradually do children learn to interpret this flow of perceptual events in a coherent, undistorted fashion.

Television, or film, has its own specialized symbolic code of conveying information. Investigators liken the task of cracking this code to that of learning to read and therefore refer to it as **television literacy** (Anderson & Smith, 1984; Greenfield, 1984). The symbolic learning required to understand television is not as great as that demanded by reading, but it is still considerable. Television literacy has two basic

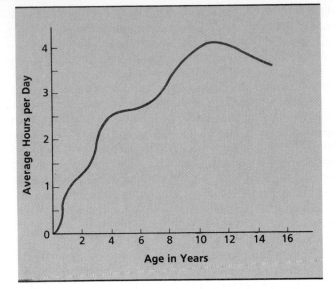

Figure 15.2. Estimated average hours of television viewing by age, based on research conducted over the past 20 years. (*Reprinted with permission from R. M. Liebert and J. Sprafkin,* The Early Window: Effects of Television on Children and Youth *(3rd ed.), 1988, Pergamon Books Ltd. P. 5.*)

parts. The first involves making sense of the *form* of the message. Children must master the meaning of a wide variety of visual and auditory effects, such as camera zooms, panoramic views, scene switches, fade-outs, split screens, instant replays, and sound effects. Second, children must process the *content* of the message, deriving an accurate story line by integrating scenes, character behavior, and dialogue into a meaningful whole. These two parts are really interdependent, because television form provides essential cues for interpreting a program's meaning. For example, young children will come to the wrong conclusion about television content if they do not understand that a scene switch from the exterior of a house to a family dinner means that the family is in that house, or that an instant replay is a repeated rendition of a single event, not two identical events occurring in succession.

Throughout the preschool and early elementary school years, children are captivated by television's most salient perceptual features, such as quickly paced character movement, special effects not seen in the real world, loud music, sound effects, nonhuman speech, and children's voices. At other times, they look away, play with toys, or talk to others in the same room (Rice, Huston, & Wright, 1982; Wright et al., 1984). While involved in other activities, preschoolers quickly learn to follow the TV sound track. They turn back to the set when they hear cartoon character and puppet voices and certain words such as "Big Bird" and "cookie," features that signal that the content is likely to be child-oriented and related to their own experience (Alwitt et al., 1980).

These findings indicate that young children are selective and strategic processors of televised information, but how much do they really understand when they watch a television show? Not a great deal, according to current research. Before age 8, children have difficulty integrating separate scenes into a continuous story line. Instead, they treat each scene as an isolated incident (Collins et al., 1978). Because they do so, children have difficulty relating a TV character's behavior to its prior motives and eventual consequences (Collins, 1973; Collins, Berndt, & Hess, 1974). Other TV forms are confusing as well, such as fades that signal the passage of time (Anderson & Smith, 1984) and instant replays, which preschoolers take as repeated events (Rice, Huston, & Wright, 1986). In addition, young children have difficulty distinguishing between true-to-life and fantasized televised material. They assume the medium reflects their world unless extraordinary violations of physical reality occur, such as Superman shooting across the sky (Kelly, 1981). Moreover, 5- to 7-year-olds, who have little knowledge of the mechanics of television, think TV puppets and cartoon figures are alive and real rather than make-believe characters (Quarfoth, 1979).

Cognitive development, growth in the child's general storehouse of information, and specific experience with the TV medium itself are responsible for gradual improvement in television literacy during middle childhood and adolescence (Greenfield, 1984; Salomon, 1979). Understanding of cinematic forms and memory for information important to plot comprehension improve dramatically from grade school into high school, and older children also go beyond concrete televised data to make inferences about implicit content (Collins, 1983; Newcomb & Collins, 1979). For example, a fifth to eighth grader recognizes that a character who seems like a "good guy" at first but who unexpectedly behaves callously and aggressively toward others is really a double-dealing "bad guy" in the end. In this kind of episode, younger children have a harder time reconciling their initial positive expectations with the character's eventual bad behavior, and they end up evaluating the character and his actions much more positively (Collins, 1983).

The research summarized above indicates that preschool and early school-age children misunderstand a great deal of televised material. Piecemeal assimilation, realistic appraisal, and inability to evaluate televised content are factors that increase young children's willingness to indiscriminately mimic what they see on the screen. For example, televised violence that seems real and justified is more likely to be imitated than violence that a child can associate with negative consequences to the aggressor (Hearold, 1986). But special steps can be taken to improve children's television literacy. One way is through special programming adjusted to children's cognitive capacities. For example, when the rapid pace of televised material is reduced, young children recall its content far more accurately (Wright et al., 1984), and when the events displayed are familiar, preschoolers grasp the implications of many more cinematic forms (Anderson & Smith, 1984). But children spend long hours watching adult-oriented entertainment that is not suited for young viewers. In these instances, parents can place limits on children's TV consumption, and when children do watch, parents can help them understand what they see. When adults make comments about how scenes in a show fit together, children comprehend the meaning of a program much better than they otherwise would (Watkins et al., 1980). Also, when adult coviewers express disapproval of on-screen behavior, raise questions about the realism of a portrayal, and encourage children to talk about televised events that are troubling to them, they teach children to evaluate TV content rather than absorb it uncritically (Collins, 1983). Through efforts like these, it is possible to counteract the adverse effects of television viewing on children's development that we take up in the following sections.

Television and Social Learning. Since the 1950s, scientists and public citizens have been concerned about the kinds of social attitudes and interaction patterns that TV cultivates in child and adolescent viewers. The largest number of studies focus on the implications of high levels of TV violence for the development of antisocial conduct, but research exists on television's power to teach undesirable sex-role and racial/ethnic attitudes as well. In addition, a growing body of evidence illustrates television's as yet untapped potential to contribute positively to children's social development.

Aggression. Most American television—in fact, 82 percent of all programs broadcast—contain at least some violence, with particularly high levels appearing in material specifically designed for children. Cartoons contain more acts of aggression that any other type of programming—21 violent acts per hour, a rate over 4 times greater than prime-time adult-oriented and family programming (Gerbner et al., 1986).

Many reviewers of a now massive research literature have concluded that TV violence can and does increase aggressive behavior in children and adolescents (Dorr & Kovaric, 1980; Friedrich-Cofer & Huston, 1986; Hearald, 1986; Liebert & Sprafkin, 1988; Parke & Slaby, 1983). A few studies have not produced consistent findings, and there are critics who believe a causal association is not yet proven (Freedman, 1984). But most experts think that the cumulative weight of the evidence argues in favor of a causal relationship. The case is strengthened by the fact that similar results emerge in studies employing a wide variety of research designs, methodological procedures, and subjects. In addition, the relationship between TV violence and aggression remains the same even after many factors that might otherwise account for it are controlled, such as social class, IQ, school achievement, and parental child-rearing practices (Friedrich-Cofer & Huston, 1986; Parke & Slaby, 1983).

In Chapter 2, we provided examples of important correlational and experimental findings that support a short-term link between televised violence and antisocial conduct.[3] Longitudinal studies, lasting from 1 to as many as 22 years, suggest that the effects are long-lasting and that TV violence is one factor (among others) that contributes to the development of a hostile, undercontrolled personality disposition. In the most extensive longitudinal study conducted to date, boys who watched a great many violent programs at age 8 were more likely to be rated by peers as highly aggressive at age 19 (Lefkowitz et al., 1972). A second followup at age 30 revealed a continuing association between early violent TV viewing and adult aggressiveness, measured this time in terms of serious criminal activity (see Figure 15.3) (Huesmann, 1986b).

In our discussion of the development of aggression in Chapter 13, we indicated that childhood aggressiveness also predicts adult criminal behavior. In fact, highly aggressive children (who are generally boys) show a greater appetite for violent TV, and they are more profoundly affected by it as well (Greenberg, 1975; Huesmann, 1986a; Parke et al., 1977; Friedrich & Stein, 1973; Huesmann, Lagerspetz, & Eron, 1984; Singer & Singer, 1981). Several researchers believe that television violence and aggressive behavior feed on one another in a bidirectional, reciprocal fashion. Violent TV instructs children in aggressive modes of solving problems, and greater knowledge of and familiarity with hostile interpersonal tactics promotes attraction to media violence, leading to a spiraling pattern of cumulative learning that, if left unchecked, results in enduring patterns of antisocial responding by early adulthood (Huesmann, 1986b; Friedrich-Cofer & Huston, 1986).

Television violence does not just augment children's aggression; it also "hardens" them so they are more likely to tolerate aggressive behavior in others. Drabman and Thomas (1976) had fifth graders view either an aggressive detective show or a nonaggressive excerpt from an exciting baseball game. Afterwards, each subject was left "in charge" of two younger children (who were allegedly playing in an adjacent

[3] Return to Chapter 2, pages 52–55 to review this research.

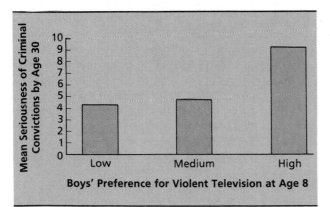

Figure 15.3. Relationship between boys' violent television viewing at age 8 and seriousness of criminal convictions at age 30 in the Huesmann (1986b) study *(From R. L. Huesmann, 1986, "Psychological Processes Promoting the Relation between Exposure to Media Violence and Aggressive Behavior by the Viewer,"* Journal of Social Issues, 42, *129. Reprinted by permission.)*

room and could be watched through a video monitor) and told to notify the experimenter if anything went wrong. A prepared film showed the younger children becoming increasingly hostile toward one another and destructive toward physical property. Subjects who had seen the aggressive film took much longer to seek help; many were willing to tolerate all but the most violent acts among their charges.

Other research indicates that heavy viewers of violent TV, in comparison to light viewers, overestimate violence and danger in society (Gerbner et al., 1979; Singer, Singer, & Rapaczynski, 1984). These findings suggest that violent television modifies children's attitudes toward social reality so they increasingly match the world reflected on TV. Children who watch a great deal begin to think of their social world as a mean and scary place in which aggressive acts are a widespread and appropriate means for dealing with other people.

Sex-Role and Racial/Ethnic Stereotypes. Television conveys sex-role and racial/ethnic stereotypes that are common in American society. Women are underrepresented as characters, and when they do appear, their marital and child-rearing roles are emphasized. If they work, they generally perform "feminine" jobs, such as nurse, teacher, or secretary, while professional and law enforcement roles are given to men. The personalities of TV characters also conform to a sex-stereotyped pattern. Women are deferent, passive, and emotional, while men are active, dominant, and rational (Barcus, 1983; Macklin & Kolbe, 1984). Even formal features of television reflect sex-stereotypic views. In an analysis of TV toy commercials, Welch and her colleagues (1979) found that those aimed at boys had more variability of scenes, rapid cuts, loud music, and sound effects, conveying a masculine image of "fast, sharp, and loud." Those directed at girls had camera fades and background music, communicating a feminine message of "gradual, soft, and fuzzy." By first grade, children recognize these subtle features as indications that an ad is aimed at one sex rather than the other (Huston et al., 1984).

In the early days of television, blacks rarely appeared on TV, and when they did, they were portrayed in subservient roles. The civil rights movement of the 1960s led to an increase in black television figures, and their social and occupational status rose as well (Clark, 1972; Roberts, 1970). But although blacks appear more often on TV than they once did, they are largely segregated from whites in programs for both children and adults (Barcus, 1983). Other racial/ethnic minorities continue to be underrepresented on television, and when they do appear, they are usually depicted negatively, as villians or victims of violence (Gerbner et al., 1986).

Are children's sex-role and racial attitudes affected by these stereotyped portrayals? Much like the reciprocal relationship between TV violence and aggressive behavior, a bidirectional association between TV viewing and sex stereotyping may exist. Research indicates that highly sex-typed adolescents may be especially attracted to TV and select programs with sex-stereotypic characters because they approve of their behavior (Friedrich-Cofer et al., 1978; Morgan, 1982). At the same time, longitudinal findings reveal that television viewing is associated with increments in sex-stereotyped beliefs over time (Kimball, 1986). In one study, this was especially true for middle-class adolescent girls, who are less sex-typed to begin with (and therefore have more room to change) than their male and lower-class female counterparts (Morgan, 1982).

In comparison to research on sex stereotyping, investigations into television's impact on children's racial attitudes are scarce. In one study, black and white children were shown cartoons that either portrayed blacks in a positive light (as competent, hardworking, and trustworthy) or a negative light (as inept, destructive, lazy, and powerless). The racial attitudes of black children became more favorable regardless of which films they saw. Apparently, the mere presence of black TV characters was enough to make their attitudes more positive. Among white children, attitudes conformed to the content of the film, with those shown a negative portrayal changing more than any other group in the study (Graves, 1975). An impressive outcome of this investigation was that substantial changes in children's racial attitudes occurred after only a single viewing session.

Consumerism. Television commercials directed at children "work" by increasing product sales. In the aisles of grocery and toy stores, young children can be seen asking for advertised products, and adult refusals often result in arguments between parents and children (Atkin, 1978). Although children can distinguish a TV program from a commercial as early as 3 years of age (Levin, Petros, & Petrella, 1982), below age 8 they seldom understand the selling purpose of the ad (Blatt, Spencer, & Ward, 1972; Gaines & Esserman, 1981; Ward, Reale, & Levinson, 1972). When asked, "What are commercials for?" one typical 5-year-old replied, "So people know how to buy things. So if somebody washes their clothes, they'll know what to use" (Blatt, Spencer, & Ward, 1972, p. 457). This child thought TV ads were simply well-intentioned efforts by film makers to be helpful and informative to viewers. Around age 8 or 9, most children understand that commercials are intended to persuade, and by age 11, they realize that advertisers will resort to clever techniques to achieve their objectives. During this period, they also become increasingly skeptical of the truthfulness of commercial messages (Ward, Wackman, & Wartella, 1977).

Despite increased awareness of the advertising agenda, even older children find many commercials alluring and convincing. In one study of 8- to 14-year-old boys, celebrity endorsement of a racing toy made the product more attractive, and inclusion of live race track footage led to exaggerated estimates of the toy's positive features as well as decreased awareness that the ad was staged (Ross et al., 1984). Commercials for heavily sugared food products comprise about 80 percent of advertising aimed at children (Barcus, 1978), and heavy viewers come to prefer these foods and believe they are highly nutritious (Atkin, Reeves, & Gibson, 1979; Gorn & Goldberg, 1982). Moreover, pronutrition messages are not very effective in counteracting the effects of such ads. Children absorb the pronutrition content, but their actual choice of snack foods does not change (Jeffrey, McLellarn, & Fox, 1982; Peterson et al., 1984). Apparently, long-term exposure to commercials for sugared products is not easily reversed by short-term interventions. The ease with which television advertising can manipulate the beliefs and preferences of children, especially young children who do not grasp the selling intent of the ads, has raised questions about the extent to which child-directed commercials constitute fair and ethical practice by the broadcasting industry (Singer & Singer, 1983).

Prosocial Behavior. Many programs on television include acts of altruism, cooperation, and sympathetic understanding of others (Liebert & Poulos, 1975). A recent large-scale review of research on prosocial television leaves little doubt that it can have socially desirable consequences for children, increasing their willingness to share, help, and cooperate with others (Hearold, 1986). But research also reveals some important qualifications with regard to television's prosocial impact. First, virtually all of the demonstrated effects are short-term and limited to circumstances quite similar to those shown on the program. Longitudinal studies that examine the effects of exposure to prosocial TV over extended periods of time have not been conducted (Liebert & Sprafkin, 1988). Second, television programs often mix prosocial intentions and behavior with antisocial acts. Recall from our earlier discussion of television literacy that young children process TV material piecemeal; they have difficulty integrating televised information about motives, behavior, and consequences. When prosocial and antisocial content are combined, preschool and elementary school children usually attend to the hero's aggressions and miss the prosocial message, and their antisocial behavior rises accordingly (Collins, Berndt, & Hess, 1974; Liss, Reinhardt, & Fredriksen, 1983). These findings indicate that prosocial TV only has positive consequences when it is unencumbered by violent content. Finally, parents who discipline their children authoritatively, with warmth and reasoning rather than commands and physical force, have children who watch more prosocial programs (Abelman, 1985). Thus, children from families that already promote social and moral maturity probably benefit most from prosocial television fare.

Television, Academic Learning, and Imagination. Since the early days of television, educators have been captivated by the potential of TV to support and supplement the school's curriculum, especially for low-income youngsters who enter kindergarten academically behind their middle-class peers. *"Sesame Street,"* the most well-known and popular of children's educational programs, was created for public television with this goal in mind. Today, it is seen by almost half of America's 2- to 5-year-olds on a regular basis, and it is broadcast in more than 40 countries around the world (Liebert & Sprafkin, 1988). Combining the expertise of child development and media specialists, the designers of "Sesame Street" capitalized on the attention-grabbing power of fast-paced action, lively sound effects and music, and humorous puppet characters to foster basic academic skills, including letter and number recognition, counting, vocabulary, and conceptual understanding.

How well does "Sesame Street" work as an academic tutor? During the first year of the program, researchers conducted an evaluation of its effectiveness on a socio-economically diverse sample of about 950 preschoolers. To make sure that some children watched more than others, a publicity campaign was launched in which investigators described the program to parents, distributed written material about it, and made weekly home visits to encourage program viewing. After approximately 6 months, children were divided into four groups on the basis of how much they viewed, and gains on tests designed to measure the learning goals of the program were compared. As shown in Figure 15.4, children did acquire academic skills from "Sesame Street," and the more they watched, the more they learned (Ball & Bogatz, 1970). Moreover, a second, similarly designed study that included only urban disadvantaged preschoolers replicated these findings. It also showed that when regular

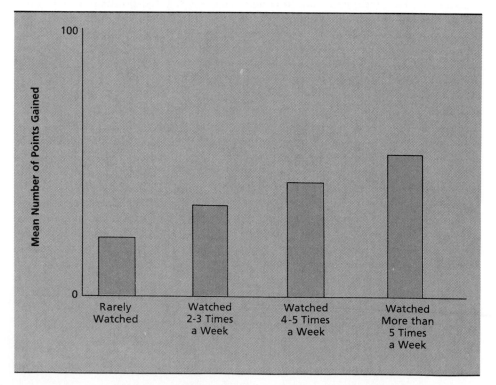

Figure 15.4. Relationship between amount of "Sesame Street" viewing and preschoolers' gains on tests of basic academic knowledge in the Ball and Bogatz (1970) evaluation. (*From Ball and Bogatz, 1970.*)

"Sesame Street" viewers from low-income families entered first grade, they were rated by teachers as better prepared for school than their light-viewing counterparts (Bogatz & Ball, 1972).

These results indicate that educational television can assist children in acquiring important school readiness skills. But it is only fair to note that the early "Sesame Street" evaluations, as well as the program format itself, have been the subject of considerable controversy. Cook and his collaborators (1975) noted that parents of viewers in the early studies were encouraged by the investigators to get their children to watch; when test scores of those who viewed without such encouragement were examined, learning gains were far less impressive, and they were largely accounted for by middle-class children, who watched the program more often. Perhaps the encouraged parents interacted with their children in special ways that facilitated their acquisition of "Sesame Street" content. That adult teaching and reinforcement may be necessary for significant academic gains from educational television is supported by research on *"The Electric Company,"* an educational program aired from 1970 to 1985 that was aimed at teaching elementary school children basic reading skills. Findings showed that children who watched at school with teacher support gained in reading skills; those who watched at home benefited very little (Ball & Bogatz, 1973; Corder-Bolz, 1980).

Moreover, the rapid-paced, densely packed information format of "Sesame Street," as well as other children's programming, has not earned high marks in the area of imagination and creativity. Longitudinal research reveals that less TV viewing at 3 and 4 years of age is associated with more elaborate make-believe play in the older preschooler and higher creativity scores in the elementary school child (Singer & Singer, 1981; Singer & Singer, 1983). In experimental studies in which TV treatments have facilitated young children's imaginative play, gains only occurred for slow-paced, nonviolent material providing high continuity of story line, not for programs that offer rapid-paced, disconnected bits of information (Huston-Stein et al., 1981; Tower et al., 1979). Furthermore, children do not gain as much from television as they do from spending the same amount of time with a live adult who encourages them to pretend (Singer & Singer, 1976). Some experts argue that because television presents more complete data to the senses than other media, such as radio or the printed page, in heavy doses it promotes reduced mental effort and shallow information processing, circumstances that undermine children's thoughtfulness and constructive learning. In addition, too much television subtracts from the time children devote to other activities, such as reading, playing, and conversing, that require more sustained concentration and active thinking skills (Peterson, Peterson, & Carroll, 1986). However, television can have positive intellectual consequences as long as children's viewing is not excessive, when it is accompanied by sensitive parental guidance, and when programs are specially designed to take into account children's cognitive-developmental needs.

In summary, in the sections above we have seen that children's television literacy improves only gradually over the course of childhood. The attention of the preschooler and young elementary school child is grabbed by perceptually salient features of the TV medium, but before age 8 children have difficulty processing fast-paced, adult-oriented TV content in an interconnected, undistorted fashion. Heavy TV viewing leads to a rise in aggressive behavior and sex-stereotyped beliefs, and television can modify children's attitudes toward racial/ethnic minorities in a single viewing session. Although the right kind of program content can foster children's prosocial behavior, the television medium seldom capitalizes on its positive potential. Research on TV's impact on academic skills and imaginative thought processes indicates that children learn best from television when they have ample time to think about the material, when its pace and novelty are not too great, and when an adult serves as an intermediary between the set and the young child.

Evidence that television is a major socializer of undesirable attitudes and behavior has led to efforts to restrict its content by major professional organizations and by citizens' groups, such as Action for Children's Television, a 20,000-member organization aimed at encouraging quality programming for children. However, the First Amendment right to freedom of speech has made the federal government reluctant to place limits on the content of television broadcasting, and the heavy doses of violence and commercialism beamed at the American public have not declined in recent years (Liebert & Sprafkin, 1988). Social scientists are currently involved in advising the broadcasting industry in hopes of achieving better self-regulation and more child-appropriate TV content. But until children's television does improve, creating a discriminating audience by educating parents about the dangers of excessive TV viewing and providing children with instruction in critical viewing skills (e.g., Dorr, Graves, & Phelps, 1980; Singer, Zuckerman, & Singer, 1980) may be the most effective approach to reducing the harmful impact of television on children's social development.

Computers

Invention of the microcomputer chip in the 1970s sharply reduced the cost and cumbersomeness of computer circuitry and made it possible for the general public to have ready access to computer technology. Today, microcomputers are a familiar fixture in most schools and in many homes, bringing a wide range of new entertainment and learning tools within easy reach of preschool through adolescent youngsters. Children are fascinated by this new technology. They generally prefer it to television, perhaps because computers combine the visual and auditory dynamism of TV with an active, participatory role for the child. As one child commented, "It's fun because you get to control it. TV controls itself" (Greenfield, 1984, p. 128). What is the impact of this new interactive medium on the human mind and the world we live in? Many researchers believe that a good way to answer this question is to study how microcomputers affect children—their impact on intellectual development, everyday activities, and social behavior.

Research on computers and child development has proliferated rapidly in the last few years. Most studies have been carried out in classrooms, where computers are used as learning aids and children's reactions to them can easily be observed. Findings

In classrooms, computers provide learning environments that are stimulating as well as socially interactive. Small groups often gather around the machine, and children take turns as well as help each other figure out next steps. (Paul Conklin/Monkmeyer Press Photo Service)

reveal that computers can have rich educational and social benefits. Children as young as 3 years of age like computer activities and are able to type in simple commands on a standard keyboard. At the same time, they do not find the computer so captivating that it diverts them from other worthwhile play activities (Campbell & Schwartz, 1986). Moreover, preschool and elementary school pupils generally use computers socially. Small groups often gather around the machine, and children take turns as well as help each other figure out next steps (Kull, 1986; Hawkins et al., 1982). Thus the common fear that computers channel children into solitary, mechanistic pursuits is unfounded, although exactly what children learn from computers depends on how teachers use them in the classroom.

Three major uses of computer technology in schools are computer-assisted instruction, word processing, and programming. In *computer-assisted instruction,* children acquire new knowledge and practice academic skills with the help of learning software. The unique properties of many instructional programs make them effective and absorbing ways to learn. For example, pupils can begin at points that fit with their current level of mastery; programs are often written to intervene when children's responses indicate that special help is needed; and multiple communication modes of text, graphics, animation, voice, and music enhance children's attention and interest. While some programs provide drill and practice on basic academic skills, others involve gamelike activities that encourage more indirect and experiential learning. For example, in one, children operate a lemonade stand and learn about economic principles of cost, profit, supply, and demand in a familiar context. Many studies report significant gains in achievement when computer-assisted instruction is integrated into the curriculum, with elementary school students benefiting most from this highly responsive teaching medium (Kulik, 1986).

In *word processing,* the computer does not instruct; instead, it serves as a tool for writing and editing text material. Children are able to use word-processing programs as soon as they have acquired minimal reading and writing skills. When word processing becomes part of the language arts curriculum, it enables children to write freely and to experiment with letters and words, without being encumbered by the fine motor task of handwriting. As a result, children write material that is longer and of higher quality, since they are less worried about making mistakes and find it easy to revise and polish their work (Levin, Boruta, & Vasconellos, 1983).

Finally, *programming* offers children the highest degree of control over the computer, since they must tell it just what to do. Specially designed computer languages are available to introduce children to programming skills. Research shows that when teachers encourage and mediate children's efforts, computer programming increases kindergartners' problem-solving performance (Degelman et al., 1986), and it helps 9- to 11-year-olds learn formal operational concepts in mathematics once thought beyond their level of understanding (Pea & Kurland, 1984). In addition, because children must detect errors in their programs to get them to work, computer programming helps them reflect on their own thought processes, and several studies report gains in the metacognitive skill of comprehension monitoring[4] as the result of programming experience (Clements, 1986; Miller & Emihovich, 1986). Increases in general *computer literacy* also accrue from learning to program. Children know more about the uses of computers and how they function (Pea & Kurland, 1984), and as a result they are better prepared to participate in a society in which computers are becoming increasingly important in daily life.

Although computers provide children with many learning advantages, they raise serious concerns as well. Computers appear more often in the homes and schools of economically well-off children, a circumstance that could widen the intellectual performance gap that already exists between lower- and middle-class youngsters (see

---

[4] Recall from Chapter 7 that comprehension monitoring refers to continuous assessment of the degree to which information in a text passage one is reading or listening to can be understood.

Chapter 8). Moreover, by the end of elementary school, boys spend much more time with computers than do girls. Consequently, certain gender differences in cognitive abilities may also be exaggerated by computer usage (see Box 15.1). Finally, video games take up a large proportion of the out-of-school recreational use of computers by children and adolescents, especially boys. Many parents are seriously concerned about the allure of these fast-paced electronic amusements, fearing that their youngsters will become overly involved as well as more aggressive because of the games' highly violent themes. However, as yet little research exists on this aspect of children's computer-related activities.

SCHOOLING

Unlike the informal world of peer relations, school is a formal institution deliberately established to supplement the family's function of transmitting to children the knowledge and skills required to become productive members of society. Children spend many long hours in school — 6 hours a day, 5 days a week, 36 weeks of the year — totaling, altogether, about 15,000 hours by graduation from high school. Do schools make a difference in the lives of children? This question was explored in the 1960s and 1970s by investigators who pitted family and school variables against one another as predictors of intellectual and occupational attainment (Coleman et al., 1966; Jencks, 1972). They reached the startling conclusion that quality of schooling is relatively unimportant and that the attitudes, abilities, and family support systems children bring with them to the classroom are primarily responsible for their academic and vocational success. But these studies focused on only a very narrow range of school variables and pupil outcomes, such as expenditures per child, teacher/pupil ratio, and achievement test scores. They did not look at what happens inside schools or at the broader implications of schooling for social as well as academic development. Research examining characteristics of schools as complex social systems — their physical environments, educational philosophies, teacher-pupil interaction patterns, and the relationship of these features to the larger societal context in which schools are

FOCUS ON CONTEMPORARY ISSUES

Box 15.1
Sex Differences and Computers

Psychologists and educators have been especially concerned about the impact of microcomputer technology on equality of access to computer literacy for children of both sexes. Observations in classrooms indicate that boys and girls do not differ in their attraction to computer activities during the preschool years (Campbell & Schwartz, 1986). But girls' involvement decreases while boys' increases with age. Parents with sons are twice as likely as those with daughters to install a microcomputer in the home, and by late childhood, participation in special computer programming courses and

summer camps shows large sex differences in favor of boys, especially at the more advanced and costly levels of activity (Hess & Miura, 1985). In addition, by emphasizing themes of war and violence and male sex-typed sports such as baseball, basketball, and football, much computer game software is unappealing to girls, and it may even have the unfortunate consequence of turning them off to computers in general (Lepper, 1985).

Girls' decreasing attraction to computers is not a matter of any deficiency in basic skills required for computer literacy. When girls do enroll in computer courses, they perform as well as or better than males (Linn, 1985), and the cognitive benefits of learning to program are similar for

both sexes (Lockheed, 1985). But girls' reduced interest in computers may have the effect of compounding already existing sex differences in spatial and mathematical performance (see Chapter 13). This is especially unfortunate since computers could do just the opposite. Non-sex-biased computer environments are needed in which software programs appeal to girls as well as boys and in which all children are encouraged to explore the new medium. Early exposure to and mastery of the microcomputer may be especially important for girls, as a means of reducing male domination of the new technology and assuring that females realize their developmental potential in mathematical and scientific fields.

embedded—indicates that schooling exerts powerful influences on many aspects of individual development (Minuchin & Shapiro, 1983).

The Physical Environment

Although the physical plants of all schools bear similarities—each has classrooms, hallways, a lunchroom, and a play yard—they are also decidedly different. Schools vary in how many children are enrolled, how much space is available for work and play, and how classrooms are furnished and arranged. Crowding and room arrangements make an important difference in the quality of children's life at school.

In a series of careful studies, Smith and Connolly (1980) examined the effects of classroom crowding by systematically varying group size, amount of space, and the quantity of material resources in preschools. Extreme social density—less than 15 square feet per child (the size of a 3 x 5 throw rug)—led to a rise in aggressive behavior. Moreover, when greater social density was not accompanied by more plentiful materials, aggression was further magnified. Although crowded classroom conditions promote conflict and disruptiveness, teachers can reduce these negative outcomes through effective management of children's behavior. In one study of a Dutch nursery school that was very crowded by American standards, pupils did not react aggressively; instead, many positive and friendly interactions occurred. The teachers at this school reduced children's opportunities to fight over toys and space by assigning them to particular play areas. The program sacrificed free choice of activities for an arrangement that permitted large numbers of children to coexist amicably in a small classroom space (Fagot, 1977). Although research on classroom crowding focuses on preschool children, similar effects may occur at the elementary school level as well.

Is there an optimal class size that fosters smooth classroom functioning and effective pupil learning? In classes that contain no more than 15 or 20 pupils, elementary school children show improved academic achievement, but above this threshold, class size has little consequence for learning outcomes (Educational Research Service, 1980). Also, teachers in classrooms with fewer children spend less time disciplining and more time providing their pupils with individualized attention, factors that may be responsible for the achievement gains noted above. Moreover, when class size is small, both teachers and pupils report greater satisfaction with their life at school (Smith & Glass, 1979).

Room arrangements are another feature of the physical setting that affects children's school experiences. A teacher's decision to seat pupils in one configuration as opposed to another is often a function of his or her educational philosophy. The familiar row-and-column seating plan is generally associated with a traditional approach to classroom learning, while desks arranged in circles or clusters reflect a more open orientation (we will take up the significance of these two educational philosophies shortly). Therefore, it is difficult to study the impact of room arrangements separately from the teacher's instructional program, but a few researchers have been successful at isolating the effects of physical setting alone. In the row-and-column seating plan, pupil location is a strong determinant of classroom participation, with pupils located "front and center" interacting with teachers the most (see Figure 15.5) (Adams, 1969). Although children who are gregarious and talkative tend to choose central desks and those who are shy and reticent avoid them, the seating effect is not just a function of pupil personality. When very sociable youngsters sit away from the center, they consistently show a drop in participation (Koneya, 1976).

Do these findings imply that teachers should locate noninteractive pupils "front and center," where they will be forced to participate in class discussion? It is possible that doing so may result in considerable psychological discomfort for shy youngsters, thereby undermining their learning rather than enhancing it. A better approach might be to rearrange the seating configuration as a whole so that participation of all pupils is encouraged. In an experiment in which three seating plans—row-and-column,

Figure 15.5. Area associated with highest pupil participation rates in Adams's (1969) study of row-and-column classroom seating arrangements. (*Adapted from Adams (1969).*)

large circle, and small clusters of adjoining desks — were compared, the circular configuration was most effective in facilitating children's participation and attentiveness during class discussion. The cluster arrangement ranked second, while the row-and-column configuration produced more pupil withdrawal and off-task behavior than either of the other conditions (Rosenfield, Lambert, & Black, 1985).

By the time students reach junior high and high school, they no longer spend most of their time in a single, self-contained classroom. Instead, older students come in contact with a wider range of teachers and peers than they did at earlier ages, and they are offered many activity choices outside of academic classes. As a result, the relevant physical context becomes the school as a whole. One feature of the general school environment that shows consistent relationships with high school students' behavior is student body size. You may recall from our discussion of ecological psychology in Chapter 1 that a greater proportion of students in small than large high schools are actively involved in the extracurricular life of their schools. Schools of 500 students or less promote personalized conditions because there are fewer people around to assure that clubs, sports events, and social activities will continue to function. As a result, a greater percentage of students are pressed into participation and hold positions of responsibility and leadership. In contrast, there are plenty of people available to fill activity slots in large schools, and only a small elite can be genuinely active (Barker & Gump, 1964). In view of these findings, it is not surprising that students in small schools report a greater sense of personal responsibility, competence, and challenge from their extracurricular experiences. This is even true for "marginal" students — those with academic difficulties, low IQs, and impoverished backgrounds — who, under other conditions, display little commitment to school life (Willems, 1967). Some evidence indicates that the incidence of truancy and delinquency is lower in small schools (McPartland & McDill, 1977; Reynolds et al., 1980). Perhaps this occurs because involvement in extracurricular activities prevents the otherwise alienated youngster from retreating to the fringes of the environment and becoming involved in socially deviant peer groups (Garbarino, 1980). Small schools are not associated with better academic achievement, but the experience they offer in productive social roles is an equally important gain, increasing students' feelings of satisfaction and promoting a sense of social obligation that may one day transfer to community participation in adult life.

In summary, a variety of physical qualities of the school environment have a substantial impact on pupil behavior. Crowding in the classroom leads to increases in aggression among young children, while small class size is associated with better academic achievement and feelings of satisfaction on the part of classroom inhabitants. Circular and clustered seating arrangements are more conducive to pupil participation and attentiveness than the traditional row-and column configuration. Among older students, size of the student body affects participation in extracurricular life at school; small schools promote greater involvement and a reduced incidence of deviant social behavior. The physical plan of the classroom is often related to teachers' educational philosophy and curricular goals; it is this dimension of schooling to which we turn in the following section.

The Educational Philosophy: Traditional versus Open Classrooms

Each teacher brings an educational ideology to the classroom that plays a major role in determining the structure and organization of children's school experiences. Two global philosophical orientations have been studied in American education: traditional and open. They differ in what children are taught, how they are believed to learn, the extent to which decision making is vested in teacher or child, and how pupil progress is evaluated.

Traditional classrooms stress socialization of the child toward culturally approved behavior and levels of achievement; the goal of education is to convey already established knowledge and standards of conduct. Children are relatively passive in the learning process; they absorb information presented by the teacher, who serves as the sole authority for knowledge, rules, and decision making. A traditional classroom is easily recognized by the fact that the teacher is the center of attention and does most of the talking; children spend much time seated at their desks — listening, responding when called on, and completing teacher-assigned tasks. Pupil progress is determined by how well children keep pace with a common set of expectations for all pupils in their grade; children are compared to one another and to age-related, normative standards of performance.

In **open classrooms,** acquisition of culturally valued knowledge is deemed important, but not to the exclusion of other goals. Greater emphasis is placed on nurturing social and emotional development, in addition to children's academic progress. The open philosophy regards children as active agents in their own development. Consequently, the teacher assumes a flexible authority role, sharing decision making with children in accord with their developing capacity to formulate classroom rules and select appropriate learning activities. Evaluation is based on children's progress in relation to their own prior development, and only secondarily to classmates' performance and normative standards. A glance inside the door of an open classroom reveals richly equipped learning centers, small groups of pupils conversing and collaborating on learning tasks, and a teacher who moves about from one area to another, guiding, supporting, and instructing in response to children's individual needs (Minuchin & Shapiro, 1983).

Perhaps you have already surmised that traditional education is the most preva-

In open classrooms, teachers assume a flexible authority role. Pupils take more responsibility for their own learning, and teachers move about the classroom, guiding and instructing in response to children's individual needs. (Erika Stone)

lent approach in the United States today; open classrooms are far less common. But at various times during the course of this century, there have been bursts of interest in open education that have receded only to blossom again a decade or two later. These swings in the popularity of educational ideologies are related to changes in society at large, and they also reflect the dominant views of educational philosophers and child development theorists during particular time periods. In the early part of this century, philosopher John Dewey (1916/1966; 1938/1963) conceived of the ideal classroom as a microcosm of democracy in which children are active participants and learning encompasses moral as well as intellectual goals. In addition, Freud's theory became known during this period; his concern with the child's emotional well-being contributed to an embrace of open education during the 1930s. However, many teachers misapplied Dewey's and Freud's ideas, allowing planlessness and permissiveness to take root in their classrooms. Soon school officials became disenchanted with the open approach and reverted back to a traditional orientation (Cremin, 1961; Silberman, 1970). Enthusiasm for open education returned in the 1960s, sparked by disillusionment with the ability of traditional classrooms to meet the needs of America's poverty and ethnic minority children. During this decade, American educators were also introduced to the ideas of Piaget; his view of the child as an active, intrinsically motivated learner was highly consistent with the open philosophy. The 1970s brought declining achievement test scores and grave doubts about whether American schools were placing sufficient emphasis on academic preparation of the nation's children. A swing back to a traditional orientation occurred that is still evident today.

The aims of open education include the development of active, autonomous learners who feel positively about themselves, are tolerant and respectful of individual differences, and respond to learning with pleasure and enthusiasm. The combined results of many studies suggest that open environments are successful in achieving these goals. Open classroom pupils are more independent; they express less need for social approval and explicit direction than traditionally instructed youngsters. Although most studies report no differences in self-esteem, when differences do appear, they favor children in open classrooms. Moreover, traditional and open pupils are decidedly different in attitudes and social behavior. In both laboratory and classroom observations, children exposed to open education cooperate more effectively when working on common tasks. In addition, sociometric measures reveal fewer extremes of peer popularity and rejection in open classrooms. In these environments, pupils with a wide range of characteristics are liked, and children more often select peer associates who differ from themselves in sex and race. Finally, children in open environments like school better than those in traditional classrooms, and their attitudes toward school become increasingly positive as they spend more time in the setting (Hedges, Giaconia, & Gage, 1981; Horwitz, 1979; Peterson, 1979; Walberg, 1986).

Although open education is associated with social and attitudinal advantages, it does not lead to better academic achievement. Most investigations show no difference on this score; when they do show differences, open pupils actually perform slightly below their traditional counterparts. One careful synthesis of research revealed that open programs placing greatest emphasis on child-directed learning and individualized assessment of pupil progress were especially effective in promoting self-esteem and positive attitudes toward school, but they sacrificed achievement gains to some degree. Perhaps children in these settings did less well on conventional achievement tests because their classroom experiences seldom presented them with testlike situations (Giaconia & Hedges, 1982). An additional complicating factor in assessing the learning outcomes of traditional and open education is that some children may perform better under one approach than the other. However, as yet, research is not conclusive about which pupils fare best in which type of classroom. Some findings suggest that it is best to place children in classrooms that are consistent with their personality dispositions—for example, anxious and conforming pupils in highly structured, traditional environments and autonomous, self-directed learners in open settings (Grimes & Allinsmith, 1961; Peterson, 1977). But other results indicate just the opposite—that children fare best when placed in school environments emphasizing a mode of learning that they might otherwise avoid (Solomon & Kendall, 1979).

Currently, we do not know if long-term consequences for development accrue from open as opposed to traditional education. Furthermore, the dichotomous traditional-open distinction described above appears to oversimplify the real world of classroom philosophical differences. In several studies, some classrooms could not be classified as either traditional or open; instead, they fell somewhere in between (Aitken, Bennett, & Hesketh, 1981; Minuchin et al., 1969; Thomas & Berk, 1981). In the future, more precise distinctions among educational philosophies may be needed to improve our understanding of how classroom environments affect children's development. Perhaps a balanced mixture of traditional and open education will turn out to be the optimal kind of learning environment, because it can accommodate the needs of many types of children. Finally, even teachers with very similar ideologies differ substantially in how they interact with their pupils on a day-to-day basis (Carew & Lightfoot, 1979). In the sections that follow, we consider the implications of this finer level of classroom experience for children's learning and development.

Teacher-Pupil Interaction

The classroom is a complex social system in which a myriad of interactions between teachers and children take place on a daily basis. Teachers play a central role in this highly social environment, engaging in as many as one thousand interpersonal exchanges with pupils each day (Jackson, 1968). While most teacher talk centers on communicating academic content and some on managing the complex flow of classroom events (Jackson & Lahaderne, 1968), a substantial portion is evaluative in nature. Children get feedback from teachers about whether their ideas and answers are right or wrong and whether their behavior fits with what is expected of them in the student role. A large body of research exists on teacher-pupil interaction, the bulk of which deals with its significance for the most salient goal of schooling—academic achievement.

Classroom time devoted to academic instruction and pupil involvement in academic work show consistent positive associations with achievement (Brophy & Good, 1986; Minuchin & Shapiro, 1983). But for children to learn effectively in an environment as busy, crowded, and potentially distracting as an elementary school classroom, teachers must arrange conditions that make work possible. Teacher behaviors that show the strongest relationships with pupil achievement involve classroom management skills (Brophy & Evertson, 1976; Good & Power, 1976; Gage, 1978). Effective classroom managers establish learning environments in which activities flow easily from one to the next. Little time is devoted to transitions between lessons, and there are few disruptions and discipline problems. Teachers who create these conditions plan carefully ahead of time, so they do not need to devote much effort to organizing and giving directions midstream, while the classroom day is in motion. In addition, successful classroom managers possess a special quality called *withitness,* a term coined by Kounin (1970) to describe a teacher's ability to monitor what is happening in all parts of the room, regardless of what he or she is doing at the moment. Teachers who are "withit" interrupt disruptive behavior in its early stages, nipping it in the bud before it accelerates and spreads to other pupils in the class. Moreover, they deal with problems calmly and patiently. Explosive teachers who react angrily to misconduct cause tension and anxiety in their pupils, which interferes with learning and magnifies rather than controls disruptive behavior. Teachers who manage the complexities of classroom life effectively have few discipline problems, smooth-running daily programs, and more time available for teaching. As a result, their pupils spend more time learning, which is reflected in higher achievement test scores.

In addition to management skills, the quality of teachers' instructional messages affects children's task involvement and consequent learning. Disappointingly, much research shows that American elementary schools place greater emphasis on rote repetitive drill of factual information than on cognitively challenging tasks, such as applying concepts and skills and analyzing and synthesizing ideas and information. However, individual differences among teachers do exist, and both cognitively simple and complex instruction occur in all classrooms to some degree. In a recent study, Stodolsky (1988) conducted extensive observations in a large number of fifth-grade classes and found that teachers' instructional style varied across the school day in accord with the subject matter being taught. Math lessons were heavily laden with lower-level intellectual activity — memorization of number facts and computational routines. In contrast, the mental processes encouraged by social studies lessons were more diverse and included both fact acquisition and higher-level processes. Stodolsky discovered that within each subject, students were far more attentive when given complex tasks than simple, factual exercises, and overall, their level of engagement was greater in social studies than in math. Although some factual learning in school is necessary, many investigators believe that American teachers place far too much emphasis on it (e.g., Dossey et al., 1988; Goodlad, 1984; McKnight et al., 1987; Sirotnik, 1983). Introducing more cognitively complex activities into the school curriculum (as long as they have a good fit with pupil capabilities) is likely to increase children's involvement in classroom activities and their academic achievement as well.

So far, we have emphasized one-way effects of teacher communication on pupil behavior and performance, but as you already know from many earlier discussions in this book, social relationships are bidirectional and reciprocal, with each participant influencing the behavior of the other. Teacher communication is not equivalent for all children; over time, some receive more attention, praise, and criticism than others. Interviewing a large number of elementary school teachers, Silberman (1969; 1971) and Brophy and Good (1974) identified four types of pupils. Each is associated with distinct teacher attitudes, child characteristics, and patterns of teacher-pupil interaction. The first type — pupils to whom teachers are strongly *attached* — are high

Pupils who evoke teacher concern are low-achieving youngsters who often ask for help with academic work and are well-behaved in the classroom. Teachers respond to their needs by providing extra attention and support. (Rick Friedman/The Picture Cube)

achieving, well-behaved youngsters who make few demands on the teacher's time. These children are more often asked to share ideas with the class, receive more public praise, and when they do misbehave are less often harshly reprimanded than their classmates. The second type of pupil evokes *concern;* teachers view these children as especially in need of help and support. Concern pupils are low-achieving youngsters who make extensive but appropriate demands of teachers, often asking for help with academic work and behaving in a dependent, compliant fashion. In line with their behavior, these children receive an extra dose of adult attention; teachers monitor their performance more, encourage them after an incorrect response, and react positively to their frequent requests for assistance. A third type of pupil engenders teacher *indifference.* These children keep pace with what is expected of them academically, but they respond with passivity and withdrawal in the classroom, avoiding contact with teachers and seldom contributing to class discussion. Teachers respond by seldom interacting with indifferent pupils; when they do, their communication tends to be brief and bland in emotional tone. Finally, a fourth type of pupil evokes teacher *rejection* and dislike. These children, like the concern group, are low-achieving youngsters, but at the same time, they are active and disruptive. Teacher-rejected pupils receive high levels of criticism for their classroom work and behavior, and they are rarely called on during class discussion. Moreover, in contrast to concern pupils (who are allowed to approach teachers freely), when teacher-rejected youngsters seek special help or permission, their requests are generally denied.[5]

These findings reinforce the conclusions of other investigators that teachers prefer children who are high-achieving, well-motivated, and conforming, and especially dislike those who are active, independent, and disruptive (e.g., Feshbach, 1969). Unfortunately, once established, teacher attitudes are in danger of becoming more extreme and stereotyped than is warranted by children's behavior. If teachers rigidly and inflexibly treat pupils in ways that fit with their impressions, they may engage in discriminatory practices that have long-term consequences for children's motivation and academic progress. Child development specialists have been especially interested in whether teachers harbor unfair biases about the intellectual capabilities of

---

[5] Both concern and teacher-rejected children tend to be boys, who consistently achieve less well in elementary school than girls. But teacher-rejected boys combine low achievement with behavior that violates teacher preferences for compliance and dependency. In Chapter 13, we indicated that schools tend to be "feminine-biased" places in which boys are targets of far more scolding and disapproval than girls, because of their independent, active, and assertive behavior. Teacher-rejected boys appear to be especially heavy recipients of these unfavorable communications, because they meet neither the academic nor the conduct expectations of the school.

some pupils, based on their classroom behavior, racial/ethnic background, or social class. We take up this issue in the sections that follow.

Teacher Expectations of Children's Academic Performance. The idea that teacher expectations for pupils' academic performance may become realities, causing some children to do better and others to do worse than they otherwise would, is known as the educational **self-fulfilling prophecy.** In the early 1960s, psychologist Robert Rosenthal found that maze performance of rats could be modified by experimenter beliefs about an animal's "brightness" or "dullness" (Rosenthal & Fode, 1963). Rosenthal reasoned that if rats learn more effectively when expected to, the same might be true for children whose teachers believe in their ability to learn. With Lenore Jacobson, Rosenthal conducted a famous experiment in which he tested this hypothesis.[6] First, children in an elementary school were administered an IQ test, and teachers were given erroneous information that the test results could identify pupils expected to "bloom," or show an intellectual growth spurt, during the ensuing months. Each teacher was provided with a list of "bloomers" in her classroom (who were actually randomly chosen by the researchers). Then the IQ test was readministered at the end of the school year. Results showed that first and second graders for whom teachers expected gains actually showed them. However, self-fulfilling prophecy effects did not emerge in the third through sixth grades (Rosenthal & Jacobson, 1968).

Rosenthal and Jacobson's research was soon criticized on methodological grounds, and numerous attempts to replicate it failed to produce the same findings. Scores of new studies conducted over the past two decades suggest that educational self-fulfilling prophecies do exist, but they are complex and multidimensional; they do not operate in a simple fashion. The most informative investigations do not provide teachers with false feedback about the capabilities of their students. Many teachers, especially those who are self-confident and experienced, will reject experimenter-provided expectancy information if it disagrees with their firsthand observations (Carter et al., 1987).

The research that has done most to advance our understanding of how self-fulfilling prophecies operate in classrooms focuses on teachers' *naturally formed* expectations for children, the quality of their interaction with individual pupils (through which expectations are communicated), and children's consequent learning. The combined results of many studies reveal that for the great majority of teachers, self-fulfilling prophecies are minimal. Although teachers do interact differently with high-achieving and low-achieving pupils, in most cases their behavior is a reality-based response to pupil characteristics and does not cause children to do well or poorly in school. But in a few instances, teachers *have* been found to harbor unfair pupil expectations; unfortunately, they are usually biased in a negative rather than a positive direction, leading to more unfavorable classroom experiences and learning outcomes than would otherwise occur (Brophy, 1983).

Research suggests that these self-fulfilling prophecies interact in complex ways with teacher and pupil characteristics. In other words, certain teachers are more likely to promote these effects, and some pupils are especially susceptible targets. For example, teachers who regard low-achieving pupils as limited by ability rather than effort or opportunity to learn are likely to provide them with little encouragement for mastering new and difficult tasks. In addition, some research suggests that teachers who have a strong fear of losing control of their class more often initiate negative self-fulfilling prophecies. They do so by avoiding public communication with low-achieving pupils (who are often behavior problems and threats to teacher control) and

---

[6] Although most research on self-fulfilling prophecies focuses on the teacher-pupil relationship, the phenomenon can occur in other social contexts, such as parent-child and peer associations, as well. Try to think of other findings we have discussed, in this and earlier chapters, that can be viewed as self-fulfilling prophecies.

giving them feedback that is abrupt, inconsistent, and not contingent on the quality of their work. When this happens, pupils attribute their classroom performance to external forces beyond their control. This lowers their expectancies for success, their motivation to achieve, and, ultimately, academic achievement itself (Cooper, 1979). Note that this explanation of how teachers' self-fulfilling prophecies are realized is drawn from *attribution theory* of achievement motivation, which we considered in Chapter 11. Moreover, it suggests that certain children are especially likely to experience negative self-fulfilling prophecies — namely, low achievers who are serious behavior problems in the classroom. There is good evidence to support this view. Recall from our earlier discussion that teacher-rejected children (who display this combination of characteristics) are seldom called on publicly, often have their requests refused, and receive especially high levels of criticism from teachers. Brophy (1983) believes that quiet, noninteractive youngsters, to whom many teachers react with indifference, may also be candidates for negative self-fulfilling prophecies. Because these children approach teachers infrequently, they provide little evidence about what they are actually like as learners, a circumstance that makes it easier for teachers who hold inappropriate expectations to sustain them.

Finally, in many classrooms and schools, children are *ability grouped* or *tracked* into classes in which children of similar achievement levels are taught together, a practice designed to ease the teacher's task of having to accommodate a wide range of academic needs in the same learning environment. Some investigators believe that differential teacher treatment of these intact groups and classes may be an especially powerful mediator of self-fulfilling prophecies (Brophy, 1983; Corno & Snow, 1986). Although some teachers flexibly switch children from one ability group to another (Barr & Dreeben, 1983), in most cases, there is little movement of children between groups once they are assigned (Brophy & Good, 1974; Persell, 1977). Moreover, high and low groups are instructed differently. Low-group pupils receive more drill on basic facts and skills, are exposed to a slower learning pace, and spend less time engaged in academic pursuits than high-group youngsters (Borko, Shavelson, & Stern, 1981; Brookover et al., 1979; Evertson, 1982). Over time, children in low groups display a drop in self-esteem and achievement motivation, are socially stigmatized as "not smart," and limit their friendship choices to those within their own group. In view of these findings, it is not surprising that ability grouping is associated with a widening of the school performance gap between high and low achievers (Calfee & Brown, 1979; Good & Stipek, 1983; Rosenholtz & Wilson, 1980).

Teacher Reactions to Children's Racial/Ethnic and Social Class Backgrounds. The American school has often been characterized as a white, middle-class institution in which social attitudes of the larger society prevail (Minuchin & Shapiro, 1983). There is good evidence that teachers often respond in stereotyped ways to children from poor and minority backgrounds, making them especially susceptible to negative self-fulfilling prophecies. In most (but not all) studies examining differential treatment of black and white pupils, black pupils received less favorable communication from teachers (Aaron & Powell, 1982; Byers & Byers, 1972; Hillman & Davenport, 1978; Irvine, 1986). One study reported that as early as the preschool years, teachers provide less verbal stimulation when they teach classes of low-income than middle-income children (Quay & Jarrett, 1986).

In Chapter 8, we indicated that ethnic minority children often have unique customs of social interaction that are not well understood at school. Teachers who are unaware of this fact may interpret the minority child's behavior as an indication of uncooperativeness or disruptiveness when, in fact, it is not. For this reason, it is vitally important that teachers understand the communication practices that culturally different children bring to school. Then they can adjust classroom expectations to take into account the child's prior experiences, and negative self-fulfilling prophecies with serious consequences for the minority child's future academic performance can be avoided.

Teaching Children with Special Needs

Effective teachers flexibly adjust their curriculum to meet the needs of the majority of schoolchildren, accommodating pupils with a wide range of aptitudes for learning. But making such adjustments becomes increasingly difficult at the very low and high ends of the ability distribution. How do schools serve youngsters with very special learning needs?

Mainstreaming Children with Learning Difficulties. In 1975, Congress passed *Public Law (PL) 94-142, the Education for All Handicapped Children Act.* It required that schools grant handicapped children an *appropriate* public education and place them in the *least restrictive environment* needed to meet their educational needs. The intent of the legislation was to better prepare handicapped children to participate in a nonhandicapped world by providing educational experiences as similar as possible to those of nonhandicapped pupils.

PL 94-142 requires school districts to offer an array of alternative placements to meet the varied needs of handicapped pupils. Among the options, ranging from most to least restrictive, are special schools; self-contained classrooms in regular school buildings; and integration into classrooms serving nonhandicapped children for part or all of the school day. **Mainstreaming** is a term that refers to this last alternative. PL 94-142 recognizes that regular classroom placement is not appropriate for all handicapped children and does not require it. But since passage of the law, the "least restrictive environment" concept has been translated into a nationwide reduction in self-contained classes and an increase in mainstreaming for pupils with mild handicapping conditions (MacMillan, Keogh, & Jones, 1986). Research has focused on the academic and social consequences of regular classroom instruction for mildly retarded and learning disabled children, since they are the most likely candidates for mainstreaming.[7]

Does mainstreaming accomplish the dual goal of providing more appropriate academic experiences for mildly handicapped children as well as integrated participation in the nonhandicapped social world? At present, the weight of the evidence is not positive on either of these points. Achievement differences between mainstreamed pupils and those instructed in self-contained classrooms have not been dramatic (MacMillan, Keogh, & Jones, 1986). Furthermore, a large number of studies indicate that mildly retarded children are consistently rejected by their nonhandicapped schoolmates (Hartup, 1983; MacMillan & Morrison, 1984). Overwhelmed by the social competence of normal agemates, many mainstreamed retarded children exhibit high levels of avoidant and withdrawn behavior. When asked, they report considerable dissatisfaction and anxiety about their peer experiences as well as intense feelings of loneliness (Taylor, Asher, & Williams, 1987).

Do these findings indicate that mainstreaming is not a good way to meet the educational needs of mildly handicapped children? This conclusion is not warranted, since most research does not consider variations in quality among mainstreaming programs. Educators agree that successful mainstreaming requires a carefully individualized instructional program that takes into account each pupil's strengths and weaknesses and that minimizes comparisons between handicapped children and their higher achieving peers. In a handful of well-designed studies in which mainstreamed youngsters were placed in classrooms with these characteristics, they showed gains in self-esteem and achievement over their nonmainstreamed counterparts (Madden & Slavin, 1983; Wang & Baker, 1985–1986). Furthermore, as we saw earlier in this chapter, children seek out peer companions who, in comparison to themselves, are either equivalent or more advanced in social maturity. Therefore,

---

[7] Mildly retarded children are those whose IQ scores fall between 55 and 70 (Grossman, 1983). Learning disabled children have specific learning difficulties in verbal or mathematical areas that are not attributable to general intellectual impairment, physical handicaps, or socioemotional causes.

without special encouragement, interaction between handicapped and nonhandi-capped pupils is unlikely to occur. Bender (1986–1987) recommends that socal skills training be implemented to help handicapped children develop an effective set of peer interaction skills prior to being mainstreamed. Once children enter the regular classroom, cooperative learning projects in which a handicapped child and several nonhandicapped peers work together on the same task have been found to promote friendly interaction and improved social acceptance of mainstreamed pupils (Ballard et al., 1977; Johnson, Johnson, & Maruyama, 1984; Slavin, Madden, & Leavey, 1984). Finally, teachers can prepare children for the arrival of a handicapped youngster and encourage them to welcome and assist the new pupil. Under these conditions, main-streaming may lead to valuable gains in emotional sensitivity, perspective-taking, and altruistic behavior among nonhandicapped peers. Once better ways are devised to achieve mainstreaming, it may very well break down social barriers and foster early integration of persons with disabilities into the mainstream of American life.

Teaching the Gifted. Since the early part of this century, the term *gifted* has been used to designate individuals with superior mental abilities. Terman's longitudinal study of high-IQ children, to which you were introduced in Chapter 1, initiated a widespread identification of giftedness with superior intelligence test performance. However, you may recall from Chapter 8 that intelligence tests do not sample the entire range of human mental skills. Only within the last two decades have concep-tions of giftedness not based on IQ gained acceptance in public schools (Getzels & Dillon, 1973). Today, definitions of giftedness encompass high general intelligence, creativity, and talent in a specific field of endeavor. In Chapter 8, we discussed the development of highly intelligent, creative, and talented youngsters. Here we focus on how schools meet the challenge of nurturing their exceptional abilities.

Enrichment activities provided in regular classrooms and pull-out programs in which bright youngsters are gathered together for special instruction have been common ways of serving gifted children for decades. But these approaches are limited in effectiveness, because the same enrichment experience is generally provided to all pupils, without consideration for each child's unique talents and skills. Current trends in gifted education place greater emphasis on experiences that build on each child's special abilities. These include mentorship programs in which a highly skilled adult tutors the gifted youngster in a relevant field and accelerated learning programs in which gifted pupils are provided with fast-paced instruction in a particular subject or permitted to advance to a higher grade (Torrance, 1986).

Acceleration is among the most controversial practices in gifted education be-cause of concerns that intellectually precocious children may suffer socially if placed with older pupils. Yet when applied selectively to mature and able students, it is highly successful. Longitudinal case studies of accelerated students indicate that they continue to be socially well-adjusted and demonstrate exceptional academic attain-ments (Stanley, 1976; 1978).

Another controversial practice involves identifying gifted children during the preschool years and providing very early educational programming. However, gifted preschool programs pose the danger of premature academic training during a period in which children need relaxed opportunities to explore their surroundings through play. As a result, early gifted education has raised some of the same objections as the current movement to extend the age range for public schooling downward to include 4-year-olds (see Box 15.2). Furthermore, assessment of giftedness is difficult during the preschool years. IQ is not yet very stable, and young children are insufficiently mature to display many talents that will become apparent at older ages. As an alternative to early gifted education, Johnson (1983) recommends child-responsive preschool environments that serve the educational needs of all children, including gifted children who can be identified early as well as those whose exceptional talents are not yet apparent.

Box 15.2
Extending Schooling Downward:
Should Four-Year-Olds Go To
School?

Recently, many child development specialists have reacted with alarm to the growing movement to extend compulsory education downward to include 4-year-olds (e.g., Zigler, 1987; Zimiles, 1985). The trend is motivated by a widespread belief that early academic training will enhance the ultimate scholarly attainments of the nation's youth, as well as an urgent need for day care programs to serve the rising numbers of preschool children whose mothers are employed (see Chapter 14). In addition, enthusiasm for early schooling has been fueled by the success of many early intervention programs in improving the motivation and academic performance of disadvantaged youngsters (see Chapter 8).

Research indicates that there is little to be gained by exposing 4-year-olds to universal public education, and for many it may be harmful. A large body of evidence demonstrates that middle-class children exposed to preschool education are not advantaged in achievement during the school years (Clarke, 1984). Moreover, as we indicated in Chapter 8, the success of early intervention for disadvantaged youngsters is not tied to academic training. Instead, programs that work best provide assistance to the family as a whole, under the assumption that the basic needs of both parents and children must be met before schooling can have a positive impact on development. Furthermore, premature schooling in which 4-year-olds are required to sit quietly for long hours while being drilled on reading, writing, and numerical skills does not fit with their developmental needs. These demands are likely to frustrate even the most patient preschoolers and cause them to react negatively to the school situation. Early academic training also takes time away from experiences known to foster young children's socioemotional and cognitive development, including play, peer interaction, and rich, stimulating conversations between adult and child. Finally, the compulsory dimension of many proposed early schooling plans has angered parents who do not wish to enroll their 4-year-olds and set them in opposition to teachers and principals before their children enter school — a poor beginning to the positive home-school relationship that is vital for children's educational success (Zigler, 1987).

Many educators and child development specialists believe that early childhood programs rooted in an understanding of how young children develop could profitably be housed in school buildings, a circumstance that would foster a smooth transition between preschool and elementary school when the time comes for children to begin their formal education. Such programs could also provide conveniently located, high-quality day care for families that need it and ensure integration of children with diverse social and racial/ethnic backgrounds at an early age. As Zigler (1987) notes, in the right kind of environment, "four-year-olds do have a place in school, but it is not at a school desk" (p. 259).

The School and American Society

Society often turns to its schools for solutions to pressing social problems. In the sections below, we review the accomplishments of American education in two areas relevant to concerns of the larger society. First, we discuss how well schools have fared in promoting increased contact among children of diverse racial/ethnic backgrounds and in bringing us closer to the goal of equal educational opportunity for all American children. Second, we evaluate the overall quality of American education. We consider the extent to which it produces a well-educated populace, and how well it measures up to the educational preparation of young citizens in other technologically advanced nations around the world.

Desegregation. In 1954, an historic Supreme Court decision, *Brown* versus *Board of Education of Topeka,* affirmed the injustice of separate educational facilities for racially different children growing up in an egalitarian society. The law gradually resulted in the desegregation of many American schools, but not without substantial community polarization in many areas of the country. Racial prejudice, fierce defense of the neighborhood school, and strong objections to mandatory busing led many white parents to oppose the practice, if not the principle, of school desegregation. Even in school districts where desegregation took place with relative calm, merging white and black children into the same school building did not guarantee equitable educational services. In many instances, blacks were resegregated inside the building. Rigid ability grouping practices and prejudicial teacher attitudes led to the continuation of inferior instruction for black pupils, and little positive contact took place that permitted black and white children to get to know each other as individuals.

In view of these conditions, it is not surprising that by 1975, a large literature on the impact of school desegregation revealed little in the way of gains in self-esteem and school achievement for black youngsters (St. John, 1975). But an additional decade of research in which investigators looked closely at classroom social arrangements and instructional methods produced findings much like those on mainstreaming discussed earlier in this chapter. School desegregation results in clear benefits for children when active efforts are made to change educational practices in racially mixed classrooms.

Many studies reveal that cooperative learning experiences in which small, racially mixed groups of children help one another work toward common academic goals are highly successful in producing cross-race peer acceptance, and they lead to gains in black children's self-esteem and school achievement as well (Johnson, Johnson, & Maruyama, 1984). In addition, multiethnic curricula and projects focusing on racial issues are beneficial (Genova & Walberg, 1984). When teachers help pupils understand the customs of different ethnic groups and directly inform them of the destructive impact of racial discrimination, children can internalize this information and call upon it in their future peer associations. Teachers' educational philosophies are also important. In classrooms where competitive success is deemphasized, peer status hierarchies in which whites fall at the top and blacks at the bottom are less likely to develop. Under these conditions, white children's resistance to interracial contact is reduced, and they identify a greater number of black classmates as best friends. In addition, small class size promotes cross-race sociability. In large classes, students usually have a sufficient number of same-race peers from whom to choose their companions, and they do not need to cross racial barriers to establish satisfying peer relationships (Hallinan & Teixeira, 1987).

Unfortunately, the constructive potential of mixed-race classrooms for providing minority children with a better education and helping racially different children understand one another has only been realized in a few American schools. But enough research has accumulated to show that educational practices under the school's control are crucial determinants of the success of school desegregation. When carefully implemented, mixed-race learning environments can foster harmonious intergroup relations and bring us closer to the realization of equality of educational opportunity for all American children.

How Well Are Schools Educating America's Children? *A Nation at Risk* was the 1983 conclusion of the National Commission on Excellence of Education, a group of

The success of desegregated schools depends on teachers' active efforts to arrange classroom activities that promote cross-race peer acceptance. Cooperative learning experiences and projects in which pupils learn about the customs of different ethnic groups are helpful. (Frank Siteman/The Picture Cube)

scholars, educators, and citizens appointed by the federal government to examine the quality of American education and report back to the nation. American schools, they found, were plagued by a "rising tide of mediocrity that threatens our very future as a Nation and as a people" (p. 5). Among the indicators of a seriously deficient educational system were steadily plummeting Scholastic Aptitude Test (SAT) scores of high school students between 1963 and 1980; severe deficiencies in basic academic skills among America's poverty minorities; and a population of gifted youngsters who, as a group, were not achieving up to their potential. Similar trends were documented in a recent Nation's Report Card, which summarized the academic competence of America's youth.

The Nation's Report Card: Academic Skills of Young Americans. In response to a mandate from Congress for continuous monitoring of the performance of young Americans in various learning areas, several national assessments of the reading, writing, and mathematical achievement of American schoolchildren were conducted from the early 1970s into the mid-1980s. Large representative samples of 9-, 13-, and 17-year-olds were tested every 4 to 5 years during this time period, and achievement trends carefully examined. Although the findings pointed to some hopeful signs, they revealed a worrisome overall picture.

On the positive side, the Nation's Report Card showed that the majority of American children master basic literacy skills by 9 years of age. In addition, gains in reading and mathematical performance occurred during the late 1970s and 1980s, partially offsetting an earlier decline. However, this recovery was largely confined to low-level academic skills. The average performance of 17-year-olds in the mid-1980s did not reach a level in reading permitting them to understand and explain moderately complicated information. In math, it did not move beyond an intermediate level of skill required to read simple graphs and solve basic algebraic equations (Dossey et al., 1988; National Assessment of Educational Progress, 1985). Moreover, although achievement gaps between poverty minorities and their white counterparts diminished over the period of the national assessments, large differences still remained, and black and Hispanic children continued to be seriously at risk for poor academic performance. Finally, the findings on writing ability were least encouraging. Only 41 percent of 9-year-olds could write a description of a series of simple pictures, and only 65 percent of 17-year-olds could prepare a clear paragraph for a job application. Tasks requiring students to write a well-reasoned paper on a particular subject were very difficult at all ages (Applebee, Langer, & Mullis, 1986).

Authors of the Nation's Report Card concluded that too many young people emerge from American high schools ill-equipped for college study or entry into the many technical vocations prevalent in modern, industrialized nations. Supplementary information collected by the investigators suggested several probable causes of the disappointing findings. Consistent with results discussed in several earlier chapters, a stimulating home environment predicted better academic performance. But quality of schooling also played a major role, for the researchers found that classroom instructional emphases were clearly associated with student achievement. For example, amount of homework assigned was positively correlated with performance. By 1986, teachers were giving more homework than in previous years, but as many as 30 percent of high school students still reported less than one hour per night, and 6 percent had none. In mathematics, the cognitive level of most classroom teaching matched the mediocre level of pupil performance. As Stodolsky (1988) found and we reported earlier in this chapter, math instruction that moved beyond basic fact and rule memorization was extremely rare. Moreover, children's enjoyment of math and belief in its usefulness waned as they progressed through school. Most regarded the subject as consisting mainly of rule memorization, expected to have little use for it in their future lives, and elected not to take the most advanced courses in high school (Dossey et al., 1988).

Cross-national Research on School Achievement. The trends described above would be less disheartening if the achievement of American children, despite its deficiencies, were still on a par with that of young people in other industrialized nations. But cross-national research on school achievement reveals that this is not the case. In every cross-cultural study conducted to date, Asian youngsters have been among the top performers, especially in mathematics and science, while Americans have scored no better than at the mean, and often at the bottom of the pack (Husén, 1967; Comber & Keeves, 1973; McKnight et al., 1987; Stevenson, Lee, & Stigler, 1986).

These differences are apparent early in development. In a recent study comparing the achievement of elementary school children in Japan, Taiwan, and the United States, large cross-cultural differences in mathematics were evident as early as kindergarten and became progressively greater with increasing grade. Furthermore, achievement differences were not limited to math. Less extreme disparities emerged in reading, where Chinese children scored highest, Japanese children lowest, and American children in between (Stevenson, Lee, & Stigler, 1986). Cross-national comparisons conducted with older youngsters reveal a similar picture. For example, a recent comprehensive survey of the mathematics achievement of eighth- and twelfth-grade students in countries around the world showed American junior high pupils to be at about the international average in computational skills, but well below it in higher-order problem solving. Among students about to complete high school, the most talented American performers — those enrolled in the most advanced high school math courses — scored substantially below the average of all participating countries. When all college-bound high school seniors were considered, America ranked among the poorest-performing nations in the study (see Table 15.3) (McKnight et al., 1987).

Table 15.3. Mathematics Achievement of College-bound Graduating High School Students in Fifteen Nations

COUNTRY (IN RANK ORDER OF PERFORMANCE)	MEAN PERCENT CORRECT ON ACHIEVEMENT TESTS[a]
Hong Kong	74%
Japan	70%
Finland	61%
England and Wales	60%
Sweden	58%
New Zealand	55%
Belgium (Flemish)	52%
Canada (Ontario)	51%
Belgium (French)	48%
Israel	46%
Scotland	43%
United States	40%
Canada (British Columbia)	38%
Thailand	35%
Hungary	32%

Source: McKnight et al. (1987).

[a] The percentage given is an average of each nation's performance on the following six achievement tests: sets and relations, number systems, algebra, geometry, elementary functions and calculus, and probability and statistics.

A comparison of home and school influences in top-scoring Asian countries and the United States adds to our appreciation of why America has become an underachieving nation. Asian pupils are not "smarter" when they begin school; they do not score higher than American children on intelligence tests (Stevenson et al., 1985), and Asian parents do not hurry their youngsters into academic work during the preschool years (Leetsma et al., 1987; Song & Ginsburg, 1987). Instead, stronger parental pressures to perform well after school entry and a more intensive process of education appear to underlie their extraordinary performance. For example, Japanese and Taiwanese parents and teachers believe that all children have the potential to master a challenging academic curriculum if they work hard enough; in contrast, many more of their American counterparts regard native ability as the key to academic success (Stevenson, Lee, & Stigler, 1986; McKnight et al., 1987). Asian parents report spending a great deal of time helping their children with homework; American parents spend very little and, at least during elementary school, do not regard homework as an especially important activity. In the United States, the school year is considerably shorter than in Japan or Taiwan, and much less class time is devoted to academic instruction (Stevenson et al., 1986). Moreover, instructional time is used differently in the United States than in higher-achieving nations. For example, a comparison of American and Japanese mathematics curricula revealed more superficial treatment of topics and much more time devoted to repetition of material taught the previous year in the United States. Finally, Japanese teachers do not make early educational decisions about pupils on the basis of their school performance. There are no separate ability groups or tracks in Japanese grade schools; instead, all pupils receive the same high-quality education. Later on, Japanese students take nationwide competitive examinations to determine which high school and university they will enter. Because of these exams, even young children are encouraged to study hard in order to have the best possible preparation (McKnight et al., 1987; Stigler, Lee, & Stevenson, 1987; Leetsma et al., 1987).

Our discussion ends on a note of concern mixed with hopefulness about the quality of America's schools. Education defines the ability of a society to compete in a complex world economy, make new discoveries, transmit a common cultural identity to each new generation, and enjoy an enriched quality of life. Success in improving American education is crucial for the optimal development of children and the future of the nation as a whole. America's educational system has risen to challenges before; today it provides basic education to a greater proportion of its citizenry than any other country in the world. Already, every state has responded to the current educational crisis with some needed reforms. In many areas of the country, school curricula are being strengthened, high school graduation requirements raised, and teacher certification standards upgraded. These are encouraging signs that reflect the firm desire of many educators and concerned citizens to rebuild an educational system capable of nurturing American children toward a prosperous and civilized adulthood in a rapidly changing world.

CHAPTER SUMMARY

1. Peer sociability begins in infancy with isolated touches, smiles, and vocalizations that increase in frequency and combine with one another during the second year of life. During the preschool years, coordinated peer exchanges become more prevalent, and both nonsocial and social play become more cognitively mature. In middle childhood and adolescence, children's interactions become more sensitively tuned to the viewpoints of peer partners and increasingly governed by societal norms that promote courteous, prosocial behavior. At all ages, child-child interaction is heavily influenced by situational factors. The quantity and quality of play materials available affect the extent to which young children quarrel and fight, engage in cooperative play and verbal conversation, or spend time in solitary pursuits. Smaller group sizes, same-age peers, and familiar companions encourage more intense and cooperative peer exchanges. Mixed-age peer experiences provide older children with practice in helping, comforting, and instructing others, and younger children ben-

efit from the superior knowledge and skill of their older companions.

2. Children differ from one another in peer acceptance or popularity—the extent to which agemates regard them as likable social partners. Sociometric techniques are used to distinguish four types of children on the basis of peer acceptance: (1) popular children, who are liked by many agemates; (2) rejected children, who are actively disliked; (3) controversial children, who are both liked and disliked; and (4) neglected children, who are seldom chosen, either positively or negatively. Although well-liked children are often good-looking youngsters with names judged attractive in our culture, the most powerful predictor of peer acceptance is social behavior. Popular children are socially skilled youngsters who interact in a mature and sensitive fashion with agemates. In contrast, rejected children engage in negative, antisocial acts and are seriously at risk for lasting adjustment problems. Controversial children display a blend of positive and negative peer behaviors, while neglected youngsters have a repertoire of effective social skills, but prefer to play alone rather than interact with agemates. Among the variety of interventions developed to help rejected children achieve better peer acceptance, coaching in social skills and intensive tutoring to remediate academic problems have proved most effective.

3. Beginning in middle childhood, children spontaneously organize themselves into peer groups, cohesive social units that collectively generate unique norms and hierarchical social structures. Peer groups form when members perceive that they share common goals. Although intergroup rivalry increases the solidarity of group participants, it also promotes negative stereotyping and hostility toward the out-group. When rivalrous groups work toward common goals, intergroup conflict gradually diminishes. Selection of peer group companions and generation of group norms result from a blend of family and peer influences. Group social structures are sometimes based on dominance hierarchies. During adolescence, dominance becomes less important, and group structures are more dependent on special talents and skills that further group members' common objectives.

4. Peers serve as socialization agents for one another by reinforcing and modeling a wide variety of social behaviors. In some cultures, such as the Soviet Union and the Israeli kibbutz, the power of peers to shape each other's behavior is harnessed by adults to transmit the dominant values of society. Adolescence is noted for a special mechanism of peer socialization—conformity to peer group pressures. Although peer pressures are salient social forces during adolescence, peers seldom demand total conformity, and most peer pressures are not in conflict with important adult values.

5. Children spend more time watching television than they devote to any other waking activity. Viewing time increases with age, and the heaviest child viewers tend to have lower IQs, come from low-income families, and experience family and peer difficulties. Only gradually do children acquire television literacy, the ability to process the form and content of TV messages in an accurate fashion. High levels of violence appear in American TV programs. Violent TV viewing has been linked to both short- and long-term increments in aggressive behavior, and it hardens children to the aggressive acts of others. In addition, much televised material conveys sex-role and racial/ethnic stereotypes that children readily incorporate into their own belief systems, and TV commercials successfully manipulate toy and food preferences, especially among young children who do not comprehend the selling purpose of the ads. At the same time, appropriately designed TV programs can foster positive developmental outcomes, including prosocial attitudes and behavior and basic academic skills.

6. The diffusion of microcomputers into American homes and schools has brought a wide range of new entertainment and learning tools within easy reach of children. Computers can have rich educational and social benefits for children. In classrooms, children use them collaboratively and cooperatively. Gains in academic performance result from computer-assisted instruction and word-processing programs. Specialized programming languages teach children about how computers function and promote advanced cognitive skills. Nevertheless, concerns that computers may widen already existing intellectual gaps between social class groups and boys and girls have been raised. In addition, the violent content of video games may foster aggressive behavior, although little research exists on this aspect of the computer medium.

7. Children spend many long hours in school, and the quality of their experiences affects many aspects of development. The physical characteristics of the school setting exert their greatest impact on social behavior. Crowded classrooms promote increases in aggression, while small class size is associated with more individual attention from teachers and better academic achievement. In the traditional row-and-column seating arrangement, pupil participation depends on location; children placed "front and center" interact with teachers the most. In contrast, circular and clustered seating plans induce a more even distribution of teacher-pupil interaction, as well as greater attentiveness to class discussion. Small high schools provide students with an enhanced extracurricular experience; in large high schools, active involvement is restricted to an elite few.

8. Two broad educational philosophies have been studied in American schools: traditional and open. Research indicates that open classrooms achieve their goal of developing active, autonomous learners who feel positively about themselves, are tolerant of individual differences, and respond to learning with enthusiasm and pleasure. However, children in open classrooms are not advantaged in academic achievement, and the long-term benefits of open schooling have not yet been studied.

9. Patterns of teacher-pupil interaction affect children's engagement in classroom activities and their academic progress. Teachers who are effective classroom managers have pupils who are attentive and achieve especially well. Instruc-

tion that focuses on rote repetitive drill as opposed to cognitively challenging activities reduces children's interest and involvement. Teachers do not interact with all pupils in the same way. In most instances, their behaviors are reasonable reactions to the characteristics of different children. However, sometimes negative self-fulfilling prophecies occur in which teachers behave in a biased fashion and cause children to display poorer school progress than would otherwise occur. Disruptive, poorly achieving youngsters; children who are members of racial/ethnic minority groups; and pupils assigned to low ability tracks are especially susceptible to negative teacher expectation effects.

10. Children who fall at the extremes of the ability distribution require special services to meet their learning needs. The legal mandate that handicapped children be placed in "least restrictive environments" has led to widespread mainstreaming of mildly retarded and learning-disabled children into regular classrooms. Without deliberate efforts on the part of teachers to promote positive peer relations, retarded children are consistently rejected by their nonhandicapped classmates. Most research on mainstreaming reveals little in the way of academic benefits, but in a few studies in which mainstreaming was accompanied by individualized educational programming, handicapped youngsters experienced gains in self-esteem and achievement. Gifted children are best served by educational programs that build on their special strengths. Academic acceleration is a controversial practice in gifted education, but when carefully implemented, it is highly successful.

11. In many schools, the constructive potential of desegregated classrooms for fostering positive intergroup relations and providing minority children with a better education has not been realized. Successful mixed-race learning environments depend on educational practices that promote positive interaction among racially different children. Cooperative learning experiences, multiethnic curricula, teaching practices that minimize comparisons among pupils, and small class sizes help break down social barriers between black and white youngsters.

12. National assessments of the academic performance of American pupils, along with cross-national comparisons of the achievement of young people in industrialized countries, reveal the United States to be a seriously underachieving nation. Family influences are partly responsible for this trend, but quality of American schooling has also contributed to it. Recent concern about the academic preparation of American youth has stimulated educational reforms in every state in the nation.

IMPORTANT TERMS AND CONCEPTS

parallel play
cooperative play
rough-and-tumble play
sociometric techniques
popular children

rejected children
controversial children
neglected children
peer group
dominance hierarchy

television literacy
traditional classroom
open classroom
self-fulfilling prophecy
mainstreaming

Glossary

Accommodation. A form of Piagetian cognitive adaptation in which schemes are revised and adjusted to take into account newly apprehended properties of the environment.

Achievement Motivation. The tendency to display initiative and persistence when faced with challenging tasks.

Action-Consequence Learning. The active efforts of infants to explore and control events around them and to repeat those behaviors that lead to interesting effects. Distinguished from the behaviorist view that the infant passively responds to environmental contingencies.

Active Genetic-Environmental Correlation. A type of genetic-environmental correlation in which children play an active role in selecting environments that are compatible with their own genetic predispositions. Distinguished from passive or evocative correlations.

Adaptation. A central principle of Piagetian cognitive theory that suggests that mental structures achieve a better fit with external reality through the complementary processes of assimilation and accommodation.

Adrenocorticotropic Hormone (ACTH). A hormone released by the pituitary gland that stimulates the adrenal cortex to produce corticoids and androgens.

Adrenogenital Syndrome (AGS). A congenital disorder caused by prenatal androgen exposure. AGS-affected girls are born with masculinized external genitalia.

Allele. Each of the two forms of a gene located at identical places on the autosomes.

Ambivalent Attachment. A pattern of insecure attachment characterizing infants who mix contact-seeking with angry resistive behavior when reunited with the mother after a brief separation.

Amniocentesis. A medical test for chromosomal abnormalities in which a sample of amniotic fluid is extracted through a needle inserted into the maternal abdominal wall. Cannot be performed prior to 15 or 16 weeks' gestation.

Amnion. The thin, inner fetal membrane that forms a protective sac around the embryo and contains fluid in which the embryo is suspended.

Anaclitic Depression. An infant depressive reaction that occurs when there is no adequate mother substitute to replace a familiar caregiver from whom the infant is permanently separated and to whom the infant had previously formed an affectional tie.

Androgens. A group of hormones produced by the adrenal cortex and testes, high levels of which are evident at puberty. Androgens play an important role in the adolescent growth spurt, appearance of body hair, and development of male sexual characteristics.

Androgyny. A type of sex-role identity characterized by both masculine and feminine characteristics.

Animistic Thinking. Young children's belief that inanimate objects have thoughts, wishes, feelings and other lifelike qualities. Believed by Piaget to result from preoperational egocentrism.

Anorexia Nervosa. A severe emotional and physical disorder prevalent among adolescent females involving self-induced starvation.

Anoxia. A harmful condition in which insufficient oxygen reaches the brain of the infant during labor and delivery; can cause brain damage.

Apgar Scale. A rating scale used by physicians to assess the newborn infant's physical condition immediately after birth.

Aphasia. Difficulty in either comprehending or producing speech caused by brain damage in areas of the cerebral cortex that control verbal functions.

Assimilation. A form of Piagetian cognitive adaptation in which the external world is interpreted in terms of currently available schemes.

Attachment. The strong affectional tie that humans feel toward special people in their lives. Its first behavioral manifestation is the infant's tendency to send positive emotional signals and seek physical closeness to the primary caregiver.

Attention Deficit–Hyperactivity Disorder. A childhood disorder involving inattentiveness, impulsive responding, and hyperactivity. Often leads to social problems, academic failure, and low self-esteem.

Attribution Retraining. Modifying the self-deprecating beliefs of low-achieving and/or learned helpless children through feedback that encourages them to view failure as surmountable if additional effort is exerted.

Attributions. Common, everyday speculations about the causes of one's own and others' behavior.

Authoritarian Parenting. A parenting style that is high in control and demandingness, but low in responsiveness to children's rights or needs. Conformity and obedience are valued over open communication between parent and child, and punitive, coercive discipline is used to curb the child's will.

Authoritative Parenting. A parenting style that is controlling and demanding, but also warm and responsive. A rational, democratic approach in which both parents' and children's rights are recognized and respected.

Autonomous Morality. The highest Piagetian stage of moral development in which rules are viewed as flexible instruments of human purposes established through cooperative social agreement. Usually characteristic of children 10 years and older.

Autosomes. The 22 homologous pairs of chromosomes. Distinguished from the nonhomologous 23rd pair, called sex chromosomes.

Autostimulation Theory. The theory that REM sleep provides spontaneous stimulation necessary for central nervous system development in the immature organism.

Avoidant Attachment. The pattern of insecure attachment characterizing infants who are not distressed by separation from the mother and who upon reunion avoid the mother or mingle proximity-seeking with avoidance.

Axon. A long fiber extending from the cell body of a neuron that sends impulses to other neurons.

Basic Emotions. The set of discrete emotions believed by some investigators to be present during the early weeks of life. Includes happiness, interest, surprise, fear, anger, sadness, and disgust.

Behavior Modification. A set of practical procedures derived from behaviorism and social learning theory, including reinforcement, modeling, and the manipulation of situational cues, that are used to replace children's undesirable behaviors with socially acceptable responses.

Behavior Setting. A unit of the environment that is spatially bounded and that has a set of typical behaviors, such as a classroom where teachers instruct and children learn or a park playground where children climb, swing, and run. Employed within the field of ecological psychology to study the impact of the environment on children's behavior.

Behaviorist Theory. A theoretical approach that regards directly observable events—stimuli and responses—as the important focus of psychological study. This position views the child as a passive entity shaped from without and development as a quantitative increase in learned responses.

Between-Family Environmental Influences. Factors related to the general climate of the home that affect all children within a family to the same extent.

Biased Sampling. Failure to select subjects who are representative of the population of interest; threatens the validity of a study.

Binocular Cues. Cues for depth that rely on each eye receiving a slightly different view of the visual field.

Black Box Model. The traditional behaviorist view that only the environmental stimuli impinging on the organism and the overt responses that emerge are proper objects of psychological study. Investigation of inner mental processes is rejected.

Blastocyst. The zygote four days after fertilization, after numerous cell divisions have yielded a hollow cluster of 60 to 70 cells.

Canalization. The tendency for growth to return to a genetically predetermined path in spite of environmental influences that may temporarily deflect it.

Catch-Up Growth. Physical growth that returns to its genetically predetermined growth path after being deflected off course by environmental factors.

Categorical Self. Early classification of the self according to observable, concrete characteristics on which people differ, such as sex and age.

Categorical Speech Perception. The tendency to perceive a range of sounds that belong to the same phonemic class as identical to one another.

Centration. Young children's tendency to focus attention on one detail of a situation at a time, to the neglect of other important features. A quality of Piagetian preoperational thought.

Cephalocaudal Trend. A head-to-foot sequence of growth that applies to certain aspects of physical and motor development.

Cerebral Cortex. The deeply infolded gray matter making up the surface layer of the brain that houses the "higher brain centers" and accounts for the highly developed intelligence of the human species.

Child Development. The field of study devoted to understanding all facets of human growth and change from conception into adolescence.

Chorion. The outer membrane that encases the embryo and subsequently develops into the fetal portion of the placenta.

Chorionic Villi Biopsy. A relatively new prenatal diagnostic method that permits analysis of fetal tissue for chromosomal abnormalities. Can be used as early as 6 to 8 weeks' gestation.

Chromosomes. Rodlike structures within the cell nucleus that store and transmit genetic information.

Chunking. Grouping pieces of information into meaningful units or chunks, thereby expanding the capacity of short-term memory.

Circular Reaction. A Piagetian sensorimotor learning mechanism in which the infant repeats a chance behavior that leads to an interesting or satisfying result, until eventually the response becomes consolidated into a new scheme.

Class Inclusion. A Piagetian concrete operational task that requires the child to systematically organize objects into hierarchies of classes and subclasses.

Classical Conditioning. A learning paradigm that involves a new association between a neutral stimulus (CS) and a stimulus (UCS) that reliably elicits a reflexive response (UCR). After repeated pairings of the CS and UCS, the CS presented by itself produces the reflexive response (now called the CR), and learning has occurred.

Clinical Interview. A research method that employs flexible, open-ended questions to probe for the subject's point of view.

Clinical Method. A method that collects information on the unique functioning of the individual child by synthesizing interview material, psychological test results, and observations of the child's behavior.

Codominance. The pattern of autosomal inheritance in which both alleles in a heterozygous combination are expressed phenotypically.

Cognitive Maps. Mental representations of environmental space.

Cognitive Style. An individual's general manner of perceiving and reacting to the environment.

Cohort Effects. See cultural-historical change.

Complex Emotions. Emotions involving either injury to or enhancement of the sense of self. Examples are shame, guilt, envy, and pride.

Compliance. Voluntary obedience to adult commands and requests. In young children, a beginning form of self-control.

Comprehension Monitoring. Continuous assessment of the degree to which one understands a passage being read or listened to.

Concordance Rate. The percentage of instances in which both members of a twin pair show a disorder when it is present in one member.

Concrete Operational Stage. The third Piagetian stage of cognitive development in which reasoning becomes more logical, systematic, and rational in its application to concrete objects but abstract thinking is still lacking. Characteristic of children between about 7 and 11 years of age.

Conditioned Response (CR). In classical conditioning, an originally unconditioned, reflexive response that is produced by a conditioned stimulus (CS).

Conditioned Stimulus (CS). In classical conditioning, an originally neutral stimulus that, through repeated pairings with an unconditioned stimulus (UCS), evokes a new response (CR).

Confluence Model. The view that children's mental growth is a function of family size, birth order, and spacing between children — variables that affect the quality of the intellectual environment in the home.

Consanguinity. The extent to which a couple is genetically related through descent from a common ancestor in the last few generations. Used in genetic counseling to help predict the odds that parents may bear an abnormal child.

Conservation. The Piagetian term for knowledge that certain physical attributes of objects, like their mass and weight, do not vary when the object changes shape.

Continuum of Caretaking Casualty. The range of risk factors associated with caretaking environments in which children develop.

Continuum of Reproductive Casualty. The range in severity of biological insults to the organism during the prenatal and perinatal phases of development.

Control Deficiency. In information processing, the inability to skillfully implement a strategy.

Control Processes. In information processing, mental strategies, such as attention, rehearsal, and organization, that individuals use to increase the capacity of the cognitive system.

Conventional Morality. Kohlberg's intermediate level of moral development in which the desire to conform to social norms and preserve the social order underlie moral judgments.

Convergent Thinking. Seeking a single correct answer to a problem or task. The opposite of divergent, or creative, thinking.

Corpus Callosum. The large bundle of myelinated neural fibers that connects the two hemispheres of the brain and transmits information from one side to the other.

Corpus Luteum. A ruptured ovarian follicle that secretes hormones that ready the uterine lining for implantation of the ovum.

Correlation Coefficient. A numerical estimate of the relationship between two variables that indicates the strength as well as the direction of the relationship.

Correlational Design. A type of research design that indicates whether two or more variables are related to one another. In contrast to experimental designs, a correlational design cannot determine cause and effect, since there is no manipulation of an independent variable.

Corticoids. A type of hormone released by the adrenal cortex that regulates the body's protein-carbohydrate balance.

Critical Period. A period of development in which harmful environmental influences can result in permanent damage to a bodily structure or behavior that is developing rapidly.

Cross-Fostering Study. An investigation of the development of children reared in environments that differ from their family of origin.

Cross-Sectional Design. A developmental research design in which subjects of different ages are observed at a single point in time.

Cross-Validation Study. A type of study in which the investigator tries to replicate results in new situations and with different samples of children. Used to establish external validity.

Crossing Over. Exchange of segments between a pair of homologous chromosomes during meiosis so that genes from one chromosome are replaced by genes from another. Increases genetic variability among offspring.

Crystallized Intelligence. A form of intelligence that is culturally loaded and fact-oriented. Distinguished from fluid intelligence.

Cultural-Historical Change. Shifts in cultural conditions that may compromise the validity of longitudinal and cross-sectional studies. Also called cohort effects.

Cumulative Deficit Hypothesis. The view that attributes the progressive decline in IQ scores to the compounding effect of depressed environmental conditions.

Debriefing. Providing a full account and justification of research activities to subjects who participated in a study in which deception was used. Raises special ethical concerns in research with children.

Decoding. In information processing, interpreting the meaning of information by comparing and combining it with other previously stored information.

Deferred Imitation. The ability to replicate the behaviors of models no longer present in the immediate perceptual field.

Defining Issues Test (DIT). A widely used objective instrument for assessing moral maturity in which subjects rate the importance of statements that represent different stages of moral reasoning.

Delay of Gratification. A form of self-control that involves the capacity to wait before acting on an impulse.

Dendrite. A branchlike extension of a neuron that receives impulses from other neurons.

Deoxyribonucleic Acid (DNA). Long, double-stranded molecules that make up chromosomes, segments of which are genes containing the blueprint for the individual's characteristics and capacities.

Dependent Variable. In an experiment, behaviors that an investigator expects to be influenced by an independent or manipulated variable.

Depression. An affective disorder involving frequent and extended periods of sadness, hopelessness, irritability, and confusion.

Deprivation Dwarfism. A growth disorder characterized by short stature and weight that is proportionate to height. Believed to be caused by the negative impact of emotional deprivation on growth hormone production.

Developmental Psychology. The study of all changes that human beings experience throughout the life span.

Developmental Quotient (DQ). An index of infant intelligence, based primarily on perceptual and motor performances. Computed in the same manner as an IQ.

Deviation IQ. An IQ score based on the extent to which a child's performance deviates from the mean of his or her particular age group.

Differentiation Theory. The view that developmental changes in sensory processing reflect improvements in the ability to detect increasingly finely grained and subtle differences among objects and patterns.

Difficult Child. A child whose temperament is such that he or she is irregular in daily routines, is slow to accept new experiences, and tends to react negatively and cry a great deal.

Discrepancy Theory. The view that a child's emotional response to a novel stimulus is determined by the degree of similarity between the stimulus and an internal representation of a familiar object to which the new stimulus is compared.

Dishabituation. Recovery of a habituated response after stimulation changes.

Distance Curve. A growth curve that records the height and weight of an individual child, or the average height and weight of a group of children, for each age level. Shows the degree of progress toward mature size.

Distributive Justice. A concept of fairness concerning the allocation of rewards among group members.

Divergent Thinking. Fluency in generating ideas and a ready ability to think of a wide variety of alternatives to meet a particular need. Associated with creativity.

Divorce Mediation. A series of meetings between divorcing parents and a trained professional who tries to facilitate agreement on disputed issues, such as child custody and property settlement. Aimed at reducing family conflict during the period surrounding divorce.

Domain-Specific Knowledge. Knowledge in a specific content area that makes new information in that area more familiar and meaningful, thereby facilitating its storage in and retrieval from memory.

Dominant-Recessive Mode of Inheritance. A common pattern of autosomal inheritance in which, under heterozygous conditions, the influence of only the dominant allele becomes phenotypically apparent.

Down Syndrome. A disorder caused by abnormalities in the twenty-first pair of chromosomes. Associated with physical defects, slow motor development, and mental retardation.

Dyzygotic Twins. See fraternal twins.

Easy Child. A child whose temperament is such that he or she quickly establishes regular routines in infancy, is generally cheerful, and adapts easily to new experiences.

Ecological Psychology. A perspective that views natural environments as major sources of influence on behavior and that advocates naturalistic observation as a method of study.

Ego. In Freud's theory, the part of personality that moderates and redirects the id's impulses so that they are satisfied in accordance with reality.

Egocentric Speech. The name given by Piaget to children's verbal utterances that are not directly addressed to others or not expressed in ways that can easily be understood by others.

Egocentrism. A Piagetian term for the inability to distinguish one's own cognitive perspective from the perspectives of others.

Elaboration. A memory strategy in which a relationship, or shared meaning, is created between two or more pieces of information that do not bear any natural categorical relationship to one another.

Embryo. The prenatal organism from implantation to 8 weeks' gestation, during which time the groundwork for all bodily structures and systems is established.

Embryonic Disk. The inner cell mass projecting into the blastocyst cavity, from which will develop the future individual.

Emotional Display Rules. Cultural rules specifying the circumstances under which it is acceptable to express emotions.

Empathy. The perception and vicarious experience of others' emotions. Plays an important role in motivating prosocial and altruistic behavior.

Encoding. In information processing, entering information from the environment into the mental system and storing it in symbolic, representational form.

Endogenous Smiles. The earliest neonatal smiles that occur in the absence of external stimulation, most commonly during REM sleep.

Engrossment. The father's experience of elation and positive emotional involvement following the birth of his child.

Enrichment Theory. The view that sensory processing involves using internal mental schemes to interpret incoming stimulus information. As schemes are refined with development, perceptual intake is elaborated and enriched.

Epiphyses. Centers of bone ossification.

Episodic Memory. Memory for specific, personally experienced events, people, and objects.

Epistemology. A subdiscipline within the field of philosophy concerned with the study of knowledge and various forms of knowing.

Equilibration. A Piagetian concept referring to continuous movement between states of cognitive equilibrium and disequilibrium. Describes how assimilation and accommodation work together to produce cognitive change.

Erythroblastosis. A condition stemming from Rh blood incompatibility in which fetal and maternal bloodstreams mix, causing the mother's antibodies to destroy fetal red blood cells and reduce fetal oxygen supply.

Estrogens. Hormones produced by the ovaries that influence maturation of the breasts, uterus, and vagina at adolescence and, during the menstrual cycle, help ready the uterus for implantation in the event of fertilization of an ovum.

Ethological Theory of Attachment. A theory of attachment formulated by Bowlby that views the infant's emotional tie to the mother in adaptive, evolutionary terms. Regards the infant as an active, biologically prepared contributor to the attachment relationship.

Ethology. An approach concerned with understanding the adaptive or survival value of behavior and its evolutionary origins.

Event Sampling. A method of naturalistic observation in which an observer records every occurrence of a particular event or behavior during a specified time period.

Evocative Genetic-Environmental Correlation. A type of genetic-environmental correlation in which the child's genotype influences the responses the child receives from others. Distinguished from passive or active correlations.

Exogenous Smiles. Smiles elicited by external stimulation that first appear during the first to second week of life.

Exosystem. In Bronfenbrenner's ecological model of human development, settings that do not actually contain children, but that affect children's experiences in their immediate settings. Examples are the parents' workplace and the health and welfare services in the community.

Expansions. Parental responses that incorporate and elaborate on children's speech in ways that facilitate young children's language acquisition.

Experimental Design. A type of research design in which an independent variable is manipulated to determine its effect on a dependent variable, while other factors are controlled. Unlike a correlational design, experimental designs enable researchers to determine cause-and-effect relationships between variables.

Expressive Style. A style of early language learning characterizing children who use language to express feelings, needs, and social forms. Initial vocabularies emphasize pronouns and social formulas.

Expressive Traits. Feminine sex-typed personality characteristics that reflect warmth, caring, and emotion. Distinguished from instrumental traits.

Extended Family Household. A household in which parents and children plus other nonnuclear family members, such as grandparents, uncles, aunts, and cousins, live together.

External Validity. The accuracy with which research results can be generalized to other populations and situational contexts.

Extinction. Elimination of a response as the result of repeated nonreinforcement.

Factor Analysis. A statistical procedure that combines scores from many separate test items into just a few factors, which substitute for the separate scores.

Failure to Thrive. Growth retardation accompanied by psychological apathy during infancy for which there are no apparent organic or nutritional causes. Believed to be a consequence of inadequate maternal attention and affection.

Fast Mapping. The process by which children map a new word onto an underlying concept after just one encounter with the word. Accounts for the speed with which children build their early vocabularies.

Fetal Alcohol Syndrome. A cluster of abnormalities appearing in the offspring of mothers who ingest large quantities of alcohol during pregnancy; includes facial abnormalities, defects of the skeleton and internal organs, small body stature, and mental retardation.

Fetal Monitoring. A medical procedure in which fetal heart rate is tracked electronically during labor using devices affixed externally to the maternal abdomen or internally to the fetal scalp.

Fetoscopy. A method of prenatal diagnosis that permits visual inspection of the fetus to detect limb and facial malformations. Also permits sampling of fetal blood to detect certain genetic disorders.

Fetus. The prenatal organism from the beginning of the third month until the end of pregnancy, during which time organ systems are elaborated and refined and dramatic growth in body size takes place.

Field Experiment. An experiment in which investigators assign subjects to different treatments in the natural environment as opposed to an artificial laboratory setting.

Fluid Intelligence. A form of intelligence involving the ability to see complex relationships and solve problems that demands little specific informational content. Distinguished from crystallized intelligence.

Follicle Stimulating Hormone (FSH). A pituitary hormone that causes the gonads to release hormones affecting growth and sexual changes during adolescence. In females, FSH initiates the production of estrogens and is involved in regulating the menstrual cycle. In males, FSH causes the testes to produce sperm.

Fontanels. A group of six soft spots of fibrous tissue that separate the bones of the cranial vault at birth.

Formal Operational Stage. The fourth Piagetian stage of cognitive development during which the individual acquires the capacity for abstract, scientific thinking. Begins around 11 years of age.

Fragile X Syndrome. A sex chromosome abnormality in which an abnormal gap or break in a certain place on the X chromosome is present. Associated with mild facial deformities and mental retardation.

Fraternal Twins. Pairs of siblings resulting from two separately released and fertilized ova and who are not genetically identical; also called dizygotic twins. Distinguished from identical, or monozygotic, twins.

Gametes. Human sperm and ova, formed through meiosis, that contain half as many chromosomes as a body cell.

Gender Constancy. The understanding that one's own gender is permanent despite superficial variations in appearance or characteristics.

Gender Schema Theory. A theory that integrates aspects of social learning and cognitive-developmental theory to explain how sex-stereotyped knowledge and behavior are acquired.

Gene. A segment of a DNA molecule that contains hereditary instructions for the individual's characteristics and capacities.

General Factor ("g"). In Spearman's theory of intelligence, a single, common factor representing abstract reasoning power that underlies a wide variety of separate mental abilities.

Generalized Other. A synthesis of what we imagine significant others think of us; determines self-concept.

Genetic Counseling. Counseling that helps couples who want to have a child assess the likelihood of giving birth to a baby with a genetic disorder.

Genotype. The genetic makeup of the individual, which, in combination with environmental factors, determines physical and behavioral characteristics (phenotype).

Glial Cells. Brain cells whose function is myelinization and regulation of neuronal metabolism.

Goodness-of-Fit Model. Thomas and Chess's theory of how temperament and environmental pressures act together to determine the course of development. Optimal development is most likely when environmental demands are in harmony, or achieve a "good fit," with temperament.

Grammar. An area of language skill concerned with syntax, the rules by which words are arranged into comprehensible sentences, and morphology, the application of grammatical markers that denote number, tense, case, person, gender, and other meanings.

Group Factors. Mental ability factors of moderate degrees of generality, such as verbal, visual, and numerical ability.

Growth Hormone (GH). A pituitary hormone that affects growth of almost all body tissues except the central nervous system and possibly the adrenal glands and gonads.

Habituation. Gradual reduction in the strength of a response as the result of repetitive stimulation.

Hemophilia. An X-linked recessive disorder involving deficiencies in blood coagulation factors that cause blood to fail to clot normally.

Heritability Estimate. An index of the extent to which variation among individuals in complex behaviors can be attributed to genetic factors. Derived from kinship studies.

Heteronomous Morality. The initial Piagetian stage of moral development in which rules are regarded as fixed, externally imposed absolutes. Characteristic of children between about 5 and 10 years of age.

Heterozygous. Having two different alleles at a corresponding site on a pair of chromosomes. Often results in the dominant allele becoming phenotypically apparent, but co-dominance is also possible. Differs from homozygous inheritance.

Holophrases. The name given young children's one-word utterances by investigators who believe they function like sentences and stand for complete thoughts.

Home Observation for Measurement of the Environment (HOME). A technique employing direct observation of mother-child interaction in the home plus parental interviews to assess the relationship of between-family environmental influences to intelligence in infancy and early childhood.

Homologous. Having two chromosomes that correspond to one another in size, shape, and genetic function.

Homozygous. Having two identical alleles at a corresponding site on a pair of chromosomes, resulting in phenotypic appearance of the inherited trait. Differs from heterozygous inheritance.

Horizontal Décalage. A Piagetian term referring to the sequential mastery of concepts in different content areas within a single stage of development. For example, during the concrete operational stage, conservation of number is acquired prior to conservation of length, mass, and liquid.

Hormones. Chemical substances secreted into the bloodstream by specialized cells in one part of the body that pass to and influence cells in other parts of the body.

Hostile Aggression. Aggressive behavior purposely intended to harm another individual. Distinguished from instrumental aggression.

Hypothalamus. A structure located at the base of the brain that initiates and regulates pituitary gland secretions.

Hypothesis. A testable prediction about behavior drawn from a theory.

Hypothetico-Deductive Reasoning. A Piagetian formal operational problem-solving strategy. The adolescent begins with a general theory of all possible factors that could affect an outcome in a problem and deduces specific hypotheses, which are systematically tested.

Id. According to Freud, the portion of personality present at birth that is the source of basic biological needs and desires.

Identical Twins. Pairs of siblings who develop from a single fertilized egg and have identical genetic makeup; also called monozygotic twins. Distinguished from dizygotic or fraternal twins.

Identification. In Freudian theory, a process that leads to conscience formation in which the child emulates the same-sex parent and internalizes the parent's rules and prohibitions.

Identity. A coherent conception of the self composed of an integrated set of goals, values, and beliefs that develops during adolescence.

Identity Constancy. The knowledge that some qualitative characteristics of individuals, such as sex and species, are permanent despite superficial changes in appearance.

Identity Crisis. A normal, temporary period of inner struggle that precedes successful formulation of an identity during adolescence.

Identity Diffusion. An identity status characterizing adolescents who lack firm occupational or ideological commitments and are not actively engaged in seeking them.

Identity Foreclosure. A path toward identity formation involving premature commitment to occupational and ideological choices selected by authority figures, usually parents. Avoids the period of crisis necessary for mature identity achievement.

Illocutionary Intent. What a speaker means to say, regardless of whether that meaning is perfectly consistent with the linguistic form actually uttered.

Imaginary Audience. A kind of Piagetian formal operational egocentrism in which the adolescent believes that others are as concerned with and critical of the adolescent's behavior as adolescents are themselves.

Imitation. Learning in which the individual observes and then replicates the behavior of others.

Immanent Justice. The belief that wrongdoing inevitably leads to punishment. Characterizes children in Piaget's heteronomous stage of moral development.

Imprinting. The early following behavior of certain baby birds that assures that the young will stay close to the mother and be fed and protected from predators. Appears during a restricted early time period of development.

Incidental Learning. Learning of irrelevant aspects of a task. With age, attention to irrelevant stimuli is replaced by increased attentional control.

Independent Variable. An event in an experiment that the investigator manipulates and expects to cause changes in a dependent variable.

Induction. A disciplinary technique in which the effect of the child's own behavior on others is communicated to the child.

Infantile Amnesia. The inability to remember specific autobiographical events that happened during the first few years of life.

Information Processing. A general theoretical approach to the study of cognition that views the human mind as a complex, symbol-manipulating system through which information flows, operating much like a digital computer. Focuses on the operation of distinct, sequential mental processes and emphasizes the commonalities between child and adult thinking.

Informed Consent. An ethical procedure that entails explaining the nature of the research to prospective subjects to ensure that they have the freedom to make choices regarding their own participation. When subjects are children, parental permission must be obtained. Children's consent should be sought as soon as they are capable of making reasoned judgments about participation.

Inner Self. Aspects of the self, such as inner thoughts and imaginings, that are accessible only to the self and not to others.

Institutional Review Board. A panel of individuals established in research-oriented institutions and organizations to independently evaluate the ethical advisability of proposed research studies.

Instrumental Aggression. Aggressive acts aimed at gaining access to an object, privilege, or space and in which there is no direct intent to harm another person. Distinguished from hostile aggression.

Instrumental Traits. Masculine sex-typed personality characteristics that reflect competence, rationality, and self-assertion. Distinguished from expressive traits.

Intelligence Quotient (IQ). An index of mental development permitting an individual's performance on an intelligence test to be compared to the scores of other individuals.

Intentional Behavior. In Piaget's sensorimotor stage, a new action sequence deliberately aimed at attaining a goal. Also called goal-directed behavior.

Intermodal Coordination. Perceiving information offered to more than one sensory modality at a time as an integrated unit.

Internal Validity. The accuracy of a study's cause-and-effect conclusions. Present when there are no competing, uncontrolled factors internal to the design that serve as plausible alternative explanations of the results.

Internalization. The developmental shift from behavior that is externally controlled to behavior that is controlled by internal standards and principles.

Invariant. Unchanging or constant; applied to stages of development that emerge in a maturationally determined, fixed sequence that is universal for all children.

Invariant Features. According to differentiation theory of sensory processing, any stable, discriminable aspect of a stimulus that distinguishes it from its background or from other stimulus objects in the environment.

Jargon Stretches. Sequences of infant babbling that contain real words and are spoken with communicative intent and eye contact.

Joint Custody. A child custody arrangement following divorce in which the court grants both parents equal power over and participation in child rearing. Distinguished from sole custody.

Kinetic Cues. Depth cues resulting from changes in an object's retinal image size. Created by movements of the head or body or by movement of objects in the environment.

Kinship Study. Research comparing individuals of differing degrees of genetic relationship to one another. Used to infer the influence of heredity on behavior when knowledge of specific gene pathways is unavailable.

Klinefelter's Syndrome (XXY). A sex chromosome disorder in males due to the presence of an extra X chromosome. Associated with depressed verbal intelligence, tallness, incomplete development of secondary sex characteristics, and sterility.

Kwashiorkor. A dietary disease caused by extreme protein deficiency that commonly appears between 1 and 3 years of age. Leads to wasted condition of the body, skin rash, and swelling of the face, limbs, and abdomen.

Language Acquisition Device (LAD). According to Chomsky, an innate grammatical representation underlying all human languages that enables children to combine words into novel but grammatically consistent utterances and to understand the meaning of the language they hear.

Language-Making Capacity (LMC). A hypothetical set of innate cognitive procedures possessed by children for analyzing linguistic input that supports the discovery of grammatical rules.

Lanugo. White, downy hair covering the fetus, nearly all of which is shed prior to birth, that helps keep vernix on the skin.

Lateralization. Specialization of functions between the two hemispheres of the brain. For example, verbal processing is typically localized in the left hemisphere and spatial processing in the right hemisphere.

Learned Helplessness. The attributional pattern in which failures are ascribed to lack of ability. Contributes to low expectancies of success, decreased persistence when faced with challenging tasks, and impaired performance following failure.

Leboyer "Gentle Birth." A childbirth technique that focuses on easing the trauma of birth for the infant through a warm delivery room, reduced sound and light, and a bath and gentle massage.

Level I–Level II Theory. Jensen's controversial theory that racial and social class variations in intelligence are due to genetic differences in complex cognitive processing (Level II) abilities rather than basic rote memory (Level I) skills. The theory has not been substantiated by the work of other investigators.

Levels-of-Processing Model. An information processing model that suggests that retention of information is a function of the depth to which an incoming stimulus is analyzed. Allocation of attention determines the individual's information processing capacity.

Lexical Contrast Theory. A theory of semantic development that describes how children acquire a new word by contrasting it with those they already know and attending to the word's conventional usage in their linguistic community.

Long-Term Memory Store. In Atkinson and Shiffrin's store model, that part of the information processing system in which information is retained and filed permanently. The capacity of long-term memory is assumed to be limitless.

Longitudinal Design. A developmental research design in which repeated observations of a group of subjects are made at different ages.

Longitudinal-Sequential Design. A research design with both longitudinal and cross-sectional components in which several different samples born in different years are repeatedly tested over the same time span.

Luteinizing Hormone (LH). A pituitary hormone that, in females, causes the ovaries to release ova and produce progesterone. In males, LH stimulates testicular production of androgens.

M-Space. Mental space; in Case's information-processing version of Piaget's theory, the maximum number of schemes an individual can apply simultaneously. M-space increases in each successive Piagetian stage.

Macrosystem. In Bronfenbrenner's ecological model of human development, the overarching ideology, values, laws, regulations, rules, and customs of a culture that influence experiences and interactions at lower levels of the model.

Marasmus. A dietary disease resulting from general starvation that appears in the first year of life and leads to severe weight loss, muscular atrophy, and reduction in subcutaneous fat.

Mastery-Oriented Attributions. The attribution of success to high ability, and of failure to insufficient effort. Associated with high academic self-esteem and a willingness to undertake challenging tasks.

Matching. A research procedure in which subjects with comparable characteristics are matched and then assigned in equal numbers to different treatment groups.

Maturation. A naturally unfolding, genetically predetermined pattern of growth.

Mean. The average score in a distribution of scores.

Mean Length of Utterance (MLU). An index of grammatical development based on the average number of morphemes per utterance. Derived from a large sample of utterances made by a child.

Mechanistic Model. The view of the child as a passive recipient of environmental inputs. Represented by behaviorist and social learning theories.

Mediational Theory. Modern behaviorist position that recognizes the limitations of a black box model and acknowledges the need to study covert mental processes.

Meiosis. The process of cell division through which gametes are formed and in which the number of chromosomes in each cell is reduced by half.

Menarche. The first menstrual period.

Mental Age (MA). A measure of a child's performance on an intelligence test in terms of the chronological age at which children, on the average, obtain that score.

Mesosystem. In Bronfenbrenner's ecological model of human development, the interconnections among children's immediate contexts.

Metacognition. Awareness and understanding of one's own cognitive processes; thinking about thought.

Metacognitive Training. Training children to use self-guiding verbalizations to improve their task performance.

Metalinguistic Awareness. The ability to think about language as a system.

Microsystem. In Bronfenbrenner's ecological model of human development, the activities, roles, and relationships in the child's immediate surroundings.

Mismatch. A form of early vocabulary error in which the child applies a new label to an inappropriate set of events.

Mitosis. The process of cell duplication in which each new cell receives an exact copy of the original chromosomes and, therefore, the identical genetic material.

Modeling. Learning acquired through mere exposure to the behavior of others; also known as observational learning.

Modifier Gene. A gene that modifies the phenotypic expression of another gene by either enhancing or diluting its effects.

Monozygotic Twins. See identical twins.

Moral Dilemma. A hypothetical conflict situation in which the subject is asked to choose and justify a moral course of action. Used to assess the development of moral reasoning.

Moratorium. In identity formation, a temporary suspension of commitments while the adolescent searches for an occupational and ideological direction in which to make a positive self-investment.

Morpheme. The smallest meaningful unit of adult speech.

Motherese. The altered language adopted by adults when speaking to young children; includes simple sentences, exaggerated intonation, and very clear pronunciation.

Mutation. A sudden but permanent change in genetic material occurring spontaneously or in response to hazardous environmental substances.

Myelinization. The process whereby axons in the developing brain become coated with the insulating fatty sheath necessary for efficient conduction of nerve impulses.

Natural Experiment. A research design in which investigators study the effects of naturally occurring treatments.

Naturalistic Observation. A research method in which the investigator goes into the natural environment to observe behaviors of interest.

Neonatal Behavioral Assessment Scale (NBAS). An instrument developed by Brazelton for assessing the overall behavioral status of newborn infants, including neonatal reflexes, environmental responsiveness, state changes, and soothability.

Neurons. Cells in the central nervous system that transmit neural impulses.

Niche-Picking. Active genetic-environmental correlation; the tendency of individuals to actively choose environments that are compatible with their genotypes.

Noble Savage. Rousseau's view of the child as naturally endowed with a sense of right and wrong and with an innate plan for orderly, healthy growth.

Non-Rapid Eye Movement Sleep (NREM Sleep). A sleep state in which heart rate, respiration, and brain wave activity are slow and regular and body movements are essentially absent. Also called regular sleep.

Nonreversal Learning. A type of discrimination learning in which subjects who have learned to respond to an aspect of one stimulus dimension (e.g., large size) must switch to an aspect of another stimulus dimension (e.g., black color).

Normal Curve. A bell-shaped frequency distribution that denotes the variability of certain characteristics in a population. Most individuals cluster near the mean, while only a few people achieve very high or very low scores.

Normative Study. An approach to the study of development in which quantitative measurements of behavior are taken and age-related averages are computed to chart the course of development.

Nuclear Family Unit. The portion of the family that consists of parents and their children. Excludes extended family members.

Obesity. A nutritional disorder involving intake of excess nutrients that results in a greater than 20 percent increment over average body weight. Associated with heart disease, hypertension, and diabetes as well as psychological and social consequences.

Object Permanence. The knowledge that objects in the environment have a permanent existence independent of one's interaction with them. According to Piaget, a developmental achievement of the sensorimotor period.

Observational Learning. See modeling.

Oedipal Conflict. A series of events of Freud's phallic stage that result in the emergence of the superego, or conscience. The boy feels a sexual desire for his mother, but represses this urge out of fear of punishment. To gain his parents' approval, the boy identifies with his father's characteristics and social values. In a similar Electra complex, girls form a conscience by identifying with their mothers.

Operant Conditioning. A form of learning in which a spontaneously emitted behavior is followed by an outcome that either increases the probability that a response will occur again (reinforcement) or decreases it (punishment).

Operations. A Piagetian term for internalized mental actions that are logical. According to Piaget, operations are not present during the sensorimotor or preoperational stages of development.

Organismic Model. The view that children are active contributors to their own development. Represented by maturational, psychoanalytic, and cognitive developmental theories.

Organization. In Piaget's theory, a cognitive function involving constant internal rearrangement of schemes so that they form organized, integrated totalities. In information processing, a memory strategy that recodes new information into a more tightly knit, efficient form, increasing the probability that it will be transferred from short-term to long-term memory.

Organizational Approach to Emotional Development. An approach that emphasizes the central function of emotions in human behavior, the interdependency of emotion and cognition, and the adaptive role emotions play in fostering exploration, retreat from threatening situations, and attachment.

Ossification. The process by which cartilage hardens into bone.

Overextension. A form of early vocabulary error that involves applying a word to a wider collection of events than is appropriate.

Overjustification Hypothesis. The hypothesis that children's interest in a task that was intrinsically satisfying to begin with will decrease when the child is extrinsically rewarded for the task.

Overregularization. In language development, the inappropriate extension of a regular morphological rule to irregular instances. For example, saying "mouses" instead of "mice."

Paired-Associate Learning Task. A laboratory task used in memory studies in which subjects learn pairs of stimulus-reponse items (e.g., fish-pipe) so that when the stimulus is presented (fish), the response is recalled (pipe).

Parity. The number of children to whom a mother has given birth.

Passive Genetic-Environmental Correlation. A type of genetic-environmental correlation in which the rearing environments provided by parents are congruent with their own genotypes and therefore happen to fit well with their children's.

Pedigree. A pictorial representation of the occurrence of genetic disorders in a family's history that is prepared by a genetic counselor.

Permissive Parenting. A parenting style that is responsive and nurturant, but low in control and demandingness. Permissive parents are overly tolerant and rarely restrict their child's behavior.

Person Perception. The way individuals conceptualize the personalities of people they know in their everyday lives.

Perspective-Taking. The capacity to understand what another person is thinking and feeling.

Phenotype. An individual's physical and behavioral characteristics, which are determined by both genetic makeup (genotype) and environmental influences.

Phenylketonuria (PKU). A disease resulting from inheritance of a recessive gene pair that adversely affects protein metabolism and central nervous system development, leading to severe mental retardation. Treated through dietary intervention.

Phoneme. The smallest unit of speech sound that can be distinguished acoustically.

Phonology. The area of language skill concerned with understanding and producing speech sounds.

Pictorial Cues. Monocular depth cues, including linear perspective, texture gradients, shading, and interposition of objects.

Pincer Grasp. The well-coordinated grasp involving thumb and forefinger opposition that emerges at the end of the first year.

Pituitary Gland. A major endocrine gland located at the base of the brain near the hypothalamus that releases hormones affecting physical maturation.

Placenta. The organ that separates the fetal and maternal bloodstreams but permits exchange of nutrients and waste products.

Play. Pleasurable, spontaneous, self-expressive activity carried out for its own sake. Play involving simple, sensorimotor repetition appears during infancy; constructive and make-believe forms emerge during the preschool years; and games with rules develop during middle childhood.

Pleiotropism. In genetic terminology, the determination of more than one characteristic by a single gene.

Polygenic Inheritance. Genetic inheritance in which multiple genes determine a particular characteristic. Associated with traits like height, weight, intelligence, and personality.

Postconventional Morality. Kohlberg's highest level of moral development in which moral understanding is based on abstract, universal principles of justice.

Practice Effects. Alteration of subjects' natural responses as a consequence of repeated testing. A factor that threatens the validity of longitudinal studies.

Pragmatics. The communicative side of language skill concerned with how to engage in effective and appropriate discourse with others.

Preconventional Morality. Kohlberg's first level of moral development in which moral understanding is based on rewards, punishments, and the power of authority figures.

Preformationism. Medieval view of the child as a miniature, preformed adult.

Prenatal Diagnosis. Methods that permit detection of some fetal problems prior to birth.

Preoperational Stage. In the second Piagetian stage of cognitive development, children engage in internal representation of sensorimotor action patterns. However, their reasoning is prelogical and intuitive rather than rational. Characteristic of children between about 2 and 7 years of age.

Prereaching. The uncoordinated, primitive reaching movements of neonates.

Preterm. Premature infants who are born several weeks or more before the end of a full gestational period. The birthweight of preterm infants is low but may be appropriate for actual gestational age.

Primacy Effect. In memory tasks, better recall of items at the beginning of a list than in the middle.

Primary Mental Abilities. Thurstone's set of seven distinct mental ability factors (verbal meaning, perceptual speed, reasoning, number, rote memory, word fluency, spatial), which led him to conclude that intelligence is a multidimensional construct.

Private Speech. Children's verbal utterances that serve a self-communicative and self-guiding function. According to Vygotsky, especially evident when children are engaged in difficult tasks.

Production Deficiency. In information processing, the failure to spontaneously use an already available strategy.

Progesterone. A hormone produced by the ovaries that helps prepare the uterus in the event of fertilization of an ovum.

Propositional Reasoning. Thought that evaluates the logic of verbal assertions without making reference to concrete, real-world circumstances. Characteristic of Piaget's formal operational stage.

Protodeclarative. A preverbal communicative act through which infants make an assertion about an object by touching it, holding it up, and pointing to it.

Protoimperative. A preverbal communicative act in which infants point, reach, and make sounds to get another person to do something.

Proximodistal Trend. A principle of growth in which certain maturationally determined aspects of development proceed in direction from the center of the body outward.

Pseudodialogues. Sequences of infant and maternal vocalizations that mimic the form but do not yet serve the function of information exchange; provide a context for infants to learn conversational turn-taking.

Psychoanalytic Theory. The body of psychosexual and psychosocial theories of personality development, including those of Freud and Erikson, that emphasize the role of biological instincts and unconscious motivations in determining behavior and the formative importance of early experience in development.

Punishment. Any outcome following an organism's spontaneously emitted behavior that decreases the probability that the behavior will be repeated.

Random Assignment. A research procedure in which subjects are assigned to different treatment groups in such a way that any subject has an equal chance of being assigned to any group; examples include drawing numbers out of a hat or flipping a coin.

Range of Reaction. Each genotype's unique response to a range of environmental conditions.

Rapid Eye Movement Sleep (REM Sleep). An active sleep state associated with the presence of rapid eye movements, brain wave activity similar to that of the waking state, and heart rate, blood pressure, and respiration that are uneven and slightly accelerated. Also called irregular sleep.

Realism. According to Piaget, the young child's inability to separate subjective and objective aspects of experience.

Recall. The form of productive memory involving the ability to remember a stimulus that is not present.

Recency Effect. In memory tasks, better recall of items at the end of a list than items in the middle.

Reciprocity. The moral principle of fair exchange and cooperation; emerges in concrete form during middle childhood and in abstract form by the late childhood and early adolescent years.

Recoding. In information processing, internal revision of the symbolic structure of information when its form proves inadequate for further processing.

Recognition. Memory that involves noticing that a stimulus is identical or similar to one previously experienced.

Reconstituted Family. A family structure resulting from the remarriage of a divorced parent; includes parent, stepparent, and children of previous marriages.

Reconstruction. A constructive memory process in which previously stored information is reinterpreted and embellished based on its correspondence with the individual's existing knowledge base. Upon retrieval, the information is a radically transformed version of the originally encoded stimulus.

Recursive Thought. The reflective, self-embedded cognitive activity that involves thinking about what another person is thinking. Grows out of advances in perspective-taking skill.

Referential Communication Skills. The ability to produce clear verbal messages and to recognize when the meaning of others' verbal messages is not clear.

Referential Style. A style of early language learning characterizing children who use language to name and call attention to things. First words are mostly nouns.

Reflection-Impulsivity. A cognitive style dimension involving the extent to which a child will pause to consider a solution to a problem when a number of possible answers are available and there is uncertainty about which is correct.

Rehearsal. The strategy of repeating information that is to be remembered; increases the probability that information will be transferred from short-term to long-term memory.

Reinforcer. An outcome or reward following an organism's spontaneously emitted behavior that serves to maintain or increase the probability that the behavior will occur again.

Reliability. The extent to which a research method, when applied again within a short period of time, yields the same results.

Replication. Repetition of an investigation that leads to results similar to those of a prior study.

Retrieval. In information processing, recovering information from long-term memory.

Reversal Learning. A type of discrimination learning in which subjects who have learned to respond to one aspect of a stimulus dimension (e.g., large size) must switch to another aspect of the same dimension (e.g., small size).

Reversibility. A Piagetian characteristic of logical operations; involves the ability to mentally go through a series of reasonings or transformations in a problem and then reverse direction to return to the starting point.

Risks Versus Benefits Ratio. A comparison of the costs of research to the individual participant against its value for advancing knowledge and bettering children's conditions of life; used in assessing the ethics of research.

Rule-Assessment Approach. Siegler's information processing view that changes in children's thinking stem from the acquisition of more broadly applicable rules for solving problems.

Saccades. Sudden, swift eye movements that bring objects from the periphery to the center of the field of vision. Used to explore the visual field.

Scheme. A Piagetian term for a cognitive structure that changes with development.

Schizophrenia. A disorder characterized by serious difficulty in distinguishing fantasy from reality, frequent delusions and hallucinations, and irrational and inappropriate behaviors.

Script. An organized representation of a sequence of events that provides a general description of what occurs and when it occurs in a familiar situation. A basic means through which children organize and interpret their world.

Secular Trend. A progressive pattern of change over successive generations in the average age at which physical or behavioral milestones are achieved.

Secure Attachment. A pattern of attachment characterizing infants who are distressed upon separation from the mother but who, when reunited with her, actively seek contact and are easily comforted by her presence.

Secure Base. A mother's adaptive function as a base from which the infant confidently explores the environment and as a haven of safety when distress occurs.

Self-Concept. A personal theory of what the self is like as an experiencing, functioning individual.

Self-Control. The capacity to inhibit behavioral responses that conflict with a moral course of action; resistance to temptation.

Self-Esteem. The evaluative side of self-concept that includes judgments about the extent to which the self is good, capable, significant, and praiseworthy.

Self-Regulation. Continuous, conscious monitoring and evaluation of one's progress toward a goal, including checking outcomes and redirecting unsuccessful efforts.

Semantic Memory. The organized store of general information in long-term memory.

Semantics. The area of language skill concerned with the understanding of word meaning.

Sensitive Phase. A particular time period during which an organism is biologically prepared to acquire certain new behaviors, provided it is supported by the presence of an appropriately stimulating environment. Weaker form of the critical period concept.

Sensorimotor Stage. The first Piagetian stage of cognitive development, during which cognitive structures consist of perceptual and motor adjustments to the environment and internalized thinking is largely absent. Object permanence and intentional, goal-directed behavior are major stage achievements. Characteristic of infants from birth to about 2 years of age.

Sensory Store. In Atkinson and Shiffrin's store model of the information-processing system, the initial way station in which auditory and visual stimulation is held briefly before it decays or is transferred to short-term memory.

Separation Anxiety. An infant distress reaction to the departure of the primary caregiver. Typically appears during the latter half of the first year and declines during the third year.

Sequential Processing. The capacity of the information processing system to solve problems in a stepwise fashion.

Serial Position Effect. In memory tasks involving lists of items, the tendency to remember those located at the beginning and end of the list better than those in the middle.

Sex Chromosomes. The twenty-third pair of chromosomes, which determine the sex of the future individual; in females called XX and in males called XY.

Sex Cleavage. The tendency for children to socially interact and play with same-sex peers.

Sex-Role Identity. An individual's perception of the self as relatively masculine or feminine in characteristics, abilities, and behavior.

Sex Roles. Sex-stereotyped sets of behaviors deemed culturally appropriate for males and females in particular situations.

Sex Stereotypes. Widely held beliefs about the characteristics associated with one sex as opposed to the other.

Shading. A conversational strategy in which a change of topic is initiated gradually by modifying the focus of the conversation, rather than through an abrupt change of topic.

Shape Constancy. The ability to perceive the shape of an object as stable, despite changes in the shape projected on the retina.

Short-Term Memory Store. The central processing portion of Atkinson and Shiffrin's store model of the information-processing system, where information from the environment is consciously operated upon and combined with additional information from long-term memory.

Sickle-Cell Anemia. A genetic blood disorder resulting from the inheritance of a recessive gene pair, which results in the production of blood cells that contain defective, oxygen-deficient hemoglobin molecules.

Simultaneous Processing. The capacity of the information processing system to grasp the overall configuration among several related elements and meaningfully integrate a variety of stimuli at the same time.

Size Constancy. The ability to perceive the size of an object as constant, despite changes in its retinal image size.

Skeletal Age. An estimate of progress toward physical maturity based on skeletal maturation.

Slow-to-Warm-Up Child. A child whose temperament is such that he or she is inactive, is somewhat negative, and exhibits mild, low-key reactions to environmental stimuli.

Small for Dates. An infant whose birth weight is lower than that expected for his or her gestational age. A small-for-dates infant may be full term or preterm.

Smooth Pursuit Eye Movements. Visual fixation on a moving target that permits an object's motion to be tracked.

Social Cognition. Thinking and reasoning about the self, other people, and social relationships.

Social Conventions. Normative matters that are not primarily moral, such as dress styles, table manners, and customs of social interaction.

Social Learning Theory. The theoretical approach to psychology that emphasizes the role of modeling, reinforcement, and, more recently, intervening cognitive variables as determinants of human behavior.

Social Problem Solving. A process utilizing a combination of social-cognitive skills and strategies through which social conflicts are resolved in ways that are mutually acceptable to the self and others.

Social Referencing. Relying on another person's emotional reaction to form one's own appraisal of an uncertain situation.

Social Smile. A smile that occurs in response to the human face; first appears during the second month of life.

Social Systems Approach. The view of the family, peer group, school, or any other social aggregate as a complex set of mutually influential relationships affected by the larger social context in which it is embedded.

Socialization. The process by which members of society shape the behaviors of immature individuals so they develop into competent, contributing participants.

Sociobiology. The theory that complex human social behaviors have a genetic basis and have evolved because of their survival value.

Sole Custody. A child custody arrangement following divorce in which the court grants one parent primary responsibility for the care and upbringing of the child. Distinguished from joint custody.

Sound Play. Playful repetition of early words through which infants and young children expand their phonological capacities.

Specific Factor ("s"). In Spearman's theory of intelligence, factors corresponding to mental abilities that are unique to particular tasks.

Specimen Record. A running narrative account of a single child's stream of behavior and its immediate environmental context; used in naturalistic observation.

Speech Registers. Speech variations that are adapted to changes in social expectations.

Spermarche. The first spontaneous ejaculation of seminal fluid.

Stage. A qualitatively distinct organization of behavior and thought at a particular period of growth.

Standard Deviation. A measure of the average variability or "spread-outness" of scores from the mean of a distribution.

Store Model. The information processing model that views information as moving sequentially through three finite-capacity stores: the sensory register, the short-term memory store, and the long-term memory store. Deployment of control processes or strategies increases the efficiency and capacity of each part of the system.

Strange Situation. A structured laboratory procedure devised by Ainsworth to study the quality of infant-mother attachment between 1 and 2 years of age.

Stranger Distress. The infant's expression of fear in response to unfamiliar adults. Generally emerges during the second half of the first year and wanes by the beginning of the third year.

Structure-of-Intellect Model. Guilford's 150-factor, three-dimensional model of intelligence that classifies mental activity according to mental operations, contents, and products.

Structured Observation. An observational method in which the investigator sets up a cue for the behavior of interest and observes it in the laboratory.

Subject Attrition. Selective loss of subjects in the course of an investigation, which poses a threat to the validity of a study.

Subject Reactivity. Revisions in a subject's natural responses that stem from the subject's awareness of the experimental procedures employed.

Sudden Infant Death Syndrome (SIDS). Death of a seemingly healthy baby who stops breathing, usually during the night, without apparent cause. Responsible for more deaths of infants between 10 days and 1 year of age than any other factor.

Synapse. The gap between the axon of one neuron and the dendrites of another across which chemical transmission of neural messages takes place.

Tabula Rasa. Locke's conception of the child as a blank slate whose character is shaped by experience.

Telegraphic Speech. Children's early word combinations, which emphasize high-content words and omit smaller and less important words, such as auxiliary verbs, prepositions, and articles.

Temperament. Stable individual differences in quality and intensity of emotional responding. Thought to provide the biological foundation for individual differences in personality.

Teratogen. Any environmental agent that causes damage during the prenatal period.

Testosterone. A type of androgen secreted from the testes that influences male skeletal growth and appearance of secondary sex characteristics.

Theory. An orderly, integrated set of statements that explains and predicts behavior.

Thyroid Stimulating Hormone (TSH). A pituitary hormone that stimulates the release of thyroxin, produced by the thyroid gland, into the bloodstream.

Thyroxin. A hormone produced by the thyroid gland that plays an important role in growth of the fetal brain, skeletal growth, and sexual maturation.

Time Sampling. A method of naturalistic observation in which the investigator records whether or not certain behaviors occur during a sample of short time intervals.

Transductive Reasoning. Reasoning in which two events that occur close in time and space are linked together as if one caused the other. Characteristic of Piaget's preoperational stage.

Transitivity. A Piagetian logical operation involving mental seriation of a set of objects according to some quantitative characteristic.

Triple X Syndrome (XXX). A sex chromosome abnormality in which an extra X chromosome is present in the female, leading to tallness, low verbal intelligence, and delayed speech and language development.

Turnabout. A conversational strategy that sustains verbal interaction. The speaker not only comments on what has just been said, but also adds some other kind of request to get the partner to respond again.

Turner Syndrome (XO). A sex chromosome abnormality in which a second X chromosome or a part of it is missing. Affected individuals are phenotypic females. In most cases, ovaries do not develop prenatally and secondary sexual characteristics and menstruation do not appear at puberty. Associated with intellectual deficits in spatial perception and orientation.

Type A Personality. A personality disposition characterized by excessive competitiveness, impatience, anger, and irritation. Linked to increased risk of heart disease.

Ulnar Grasp. The clumsy grasp of the young infant, in which the fingers close against the palm.

Ultrasound. A method of prenatal diagnosis used to estimate gestational age and detect gross structural abnormalities. High-frequency sound waves are beamed at the uterus to reflect the size and shape of the fetus.

Umbilical Cord. A prenatal structure that delivers nutrients to and removes waste products from the fetus.

Unconditioned Response (UCR). In classical conditioning, a reflexive response that is reliably elicited by an unconditioned stimulus (UCS).

Unconditioned Stimulus (UCS). In classical conditioning, a stimulus that reliably elicits a reflexive response (UCR).

Underextension. An early vocabulary error in which a word is applied to a smaller collection of events than is acceptable in conventional usage.

Uninvolved Parenting. A parenting style that is low in control as well as responsiveness. Uninvolved parents display minimal commitment to the caregiver role and are indifferent or rejecting in their behavior toward children.

Validity. The extent to which measures taken in a research study accurately reflect what the investigator intended to measure.

Velocity Curve. A growth curve that shows the absolute amount of growth at each yearly interval. Clarifies the timing of growth spurts.

Vernix. A white, cheeselike substance covering the fetus during the second trimester. Prevents chapping and hardening of skin from constant immersion in the amniotic fluid.

Visual Acuity. Fineness of visual discrimination.

Visual Cliff. An experimental apparatus used to study depth perception in infants. Consists of a glass-covered table designed to create the perception of a shallow and a deep side.

Wash-Out Effect. The tendency for intellectual gains resulting from early intervention to last for only a few years following program termination.

Within-Family Environmental Influences. Factors that serve to make children in the same family different from one another, such as differential treatment of siblings by parents.

X-Linked Inheritance. A hereditary pattern in which a phenotypic characteristic is caused by a recessive gene on the X chromosome. Males are more likely to be affected than females, since male sex chromosomes are not homologous and there are no complementary alleles on the Y to suppress the effects of those on the X.

XYY Syndrome. A sex chromosome abnormality involving an extra Y chromosome in males. The belief that it leads to increases in aggressive and antisocial behavior has been refuted. Associated with tallness, large teeth, and in some cases severe acne.

Yolk Sac. The sac attached to the embryo that produces blood cells until the liver, spleen, and bone marrow are mature enough to take over this process during the second month of gestation.

Zone of Proximal Development. Vygotsky's term for the range of tasks that are too difficult for the child to accomplish alone, but that can be mastered with the verbal guidance and assistance of adults or other more skilled children.

Zygote. The prenatal organism during the two-week period of development between fertilization and implantation.

References

AARON, R., & POWELL, G. (1982). Feedback practices as a function of teacher and pupil race during reading groups instruction. *Journal of Negro Education, 51,* 50–59.

ABELMAN, R. (1985). Styles of parental disciplinary practices as a mediator of children's learning from prosocial television portrayals. *Child Study Journal, 15,* 131–145.

ABRAHAM, S., COLLINS, G., & NORDSIECK, M. (1971). Relationship of childhood weight status to morbidity in adults. *HSMHA Health Reports, 86,* 273–284.

ABRAMOV, I., GORDON, J., HENDRICKSON, A., HAINLINE, L., DOBSON, V., & LaBOSSIERE, E. (1982). The retina of the newborn infant. *Science, 217,* 265–267.

ABRAVANEL, E., & SIGAFOOS, A. D. (1984). Exploring the presence of imitation during early infancy. *Child Development, 55,* 381–392.

ACHENBACH, T. M. (1978). *Research in developmental psychology: Concepts, strategies, methods.* New York: The Free Press.

ACHENBACH, T. M., & EDELBROCK, C. S. (1981). Behavioral problems and competencies reported by parents of normal and disturbed children aged 4 through 16. *Monographs of the Society for Research in Child Development, 46* (1, Serial No. 188).

ACHENBACH, T. M., & WEISZ, J. R. (1975). A longitudinal study of developmental synchrony between conceptual identity, seriation, and transitivity of color, number, and length. *Child Development, 46,* 840–848.

ACKERMAN, B. P. (1978). Children's understanding of speech acts in unconventional frames. *Child Development, 49,* 311–318.

ACREDOLO, C., ADAMS, A., & SCHMID, J. (1984). On the understanding of the relationships between speed, duration, and distance. *Child Development, 55,* 2151–2159.

ACREDOLO, L. P., & HAKE, J. L. (1982). Infant perception. In B. B. Wolman (Ed.), *Handbook of developmental psychology* (pp. 244–283). Englewood Cliffs, NJ: Prentice-Hall.

ADAMS, G. R. (1978). Racial membership and physical attractiveness effects on preschool teachers' expectations. *Child Study Journal, 8,* 29–41.

ADAMS, G. R., ABRAHAM, K. G., & MARKSTROM, C. A. (1987). The relations among identity development, self-consciousness, and self-focusing during middle- and late-adolescence. *Developmental Psychology, 23,* 292–297.

ADAMS, G. R., & CRANE, P. (1980). An assessment of parents' and teachers' expectations of preschool children's social preference for attractive or unattractive children and adults. *Child Development, 51,* 224–231.

ADAMS, G. R., & FITCH, S. A. (1982). Ego stage and identity status development: A cross-sequential analysis. *Journal of Personality and Social Psychology, 43,* 574–583.

ADAMS, R. E., & PASSMAN, R. H. (1981). The effects of preparing two-year-olds for brief separations from their mothers. *Child Development, 52,* 1068–1070.

ADAMS, R. J., MAURER, D., & DAVIS, M. (1986). Newborns' discrimination of chromatic from achromatic stimuli. *Journal of Experimental Child Psychology, 41,* 267–281.

ADAMS, R. S. (1969). Location as a feature of instructional interaction. *Merrill-Palmer Quarterly, 15,* 309–321.

ADLER, L. L. (1982). Cross-cultural research and theory. In B. B. Wolman (Ed.), *Handbook of developmental psychology* (pp. 76–90). Englewood Cliffs, NJ: Prentice-Hall.

AINSWORTH, M. D. S. (1969). Object relations, dependency, and attachment: A theoretical review of the infant-mother relationship. *Child Development, 40,* 969–1025.

AINSWORTH, M. D. S. (1973). The development of infant-mother attachment. In B. Caldwell & H. Ricciuti (Eds.), *Review of child development research* (Vol. 3, pp. 1–94). Chicago: University of Chicago Press.

AINSWORTH, M. D. S., BELL, S. M. V., & STAYTON, D. J. (1971). Individual differences in strange situation behavior of one-year-olds. In H. Schaffer (Ed.), *The origins of human social relations* (pp. 17–52). London: Academic Press.

AINSWORTH, M. D. S., BLEHAR, M. C., WATERS, E., & WALL, S. (1978). *Patterns of attachment.* Hillsdale, N.J.: Erlbaum.

AINSWORTH, M. D. S., & WITTIG, B. (1969). Attachment and exploratory behavior of one-year-olds in a strange situation. In B. Foss (Ed.), *Determinants of infant behavior* (Vol. 4, pp. 111–136). New York: Wiley.

AITKEN, M., BENNETT, S. N., & HESKETH, J. (1981). Teaching styles and pupil progress: A reanalysis. *British Journal of Educational Psychology, 51,* 187–196.

ALI, F., & COSTELLO, J. (1971). Modification of the Peabody Picture Vocabulary Test. *Developmental Psychology, 5,* 86–91.

ALS, H., LESTER, B. M., TRONICK, E., & BRAZELTON, T. B. (1980). Toward a research instrument for the assessment of preterm infants' behavior (APIB). In H. E. Fitzgerald, B. M. Lester, & M. W. Yogman (Eds.), *Theory and research in behavioral pediatrics* (Vol. 1, pp. 35–63). New York: Plenum.

ALTEMEIER, W. A., O'CONNOR, S. M., SHERROD, K. B., & VIETZE, P. M. (1984). Prospective study of antecedents for nonorganic failure to thrive. *Journal of Pediatrics, 106,* 360–365.

ALVAREZ, W. F. (1985). The meaning of maternal employment for mothers and their perceptions of their three-year-old children. *Child Development, 56,* 350–360.

ALWITT, L. F., ANDERSON, D. R., LORCH, E. P., & LEVIN, S. R. (1980). Preschool children's visual attention to attributes of television. *Human Communication Research, 7,* 52–67.

American Psychiatric Association. (1987). *Diagnostic and statistical manual of mental disorders* (3rd ed., rev.). Washington, DC: Author.

American Psychological Association, Division on Developmental Psychology. (1968). Ethical standards for research with children. *Newsletter,* 1–3.

AMES, L. B., GILLESPIE, C., HAINES, J., & ILG, F. L. (1978). *The Gesell Institute's child from one to six.* New York: Harper & Row.

AMIEL-TISON, C. (1985). Pediatric contribution to the present knowledge on the neurobehavioral status of infants at birth. In J. Mehler & R. Fox (Eds.), *Neonate cognition: Beyond the blooming buzzing confusion* (pp. 365–380). Hillsdale, NJ: Erlbaum.

AMMON, M. S., & SLOBIN, D. I. (1979). A cross-linguistic study of the processing of causative sentences. *Cognition, 7,* 3–17.

ANASTASI, A. (1958). Heredity, environment and the question how? *Psychological Review, 65,* 197–208.

ANASTASI, A. (1982). *Psychological testing* (5th ed.). New York: Macmillan.

ANDERS, T. F. (1978). Home-recorded sleep in 2- and 9-month-old infants. *Journal of the American Academy of Child Psychiatry, 17,* 421–432.

ANDERS, T. F., & CHALEMIAN, R. J. (1974). The effect of circumcision on sleep-wake states in human neonates. *Psychosomatic Medicine, 36,* 174–179.

ANDERS, T. F., & ROFFWARG, H. P. (1973). The effects of selective interruption and deprivation of sleep in the human newborn. *Developmental Psychobiology, 6,* 77–89.

ANDERSON, D. R., & SMITH, R. (1984). Young children's TV viewing: The problem of cognitive continuity. In F. J. Morrison, C. Lord, & D. P. Keating (Eds.), *Applied developmental psychology* (Vol. 1, pp. 115–163). Orlando, FL: Academic Press.

ANDERSON, E. S. (1984). The acquisition of sociolinguistic knowledge: Some evidence from children's verbal role play. *Western Journal of Speech Communication, 48,* 125–144.

ANDERSON, N. H., & CUNEO, D. O. (1978). The height + width rule in children's judgments of quantity. *Journal of Experimental Psychology: General, 107,* 335–378.

ANDERSON-HUNTINGTON, R. B., & ROSENBLITH, J. F. (1976). Central nervous system damage as a possible component of unexpected deaths in infancy. *Developmental Medicine and Child Neurology, 18,* 480–492.

ANDREWS, S. R., BLUMENTHAL, J. B., JOHNSON, D. L., KAHN, A. J., FERGUSON, C. J., LASATER, T. M., MALONE, P. E., & WALLACE, D. B. (1982). The skills of mothering: A study of Parent Child Development Centers. *Monographs of the Society for Research in Child Development, 47* (6, Serial No. 198).

ANISFELD, M. (1979). Interpreting "imitative" responses in early infancy. *Science, 205,* 214–215.

ANOOSHIAN, L. J., HARTMAN, S. R., & SCHARF, J. S. (1982). Determinants of young children's search strategies in a large-scale environment. *Developmental Psychology, 18,* 608–616.

APGAR, V. (1953). A proposal for a new method of evaluation in the newborn infant. *Current Research in Anesthesia and Analgesia, 32,* 260–267.

APPLEBEE, A., LANGER, J., & MULLIS, I. V. S. (1986). *The Writing Report Card: Writing achievement in American schools.* Princeton, NJ: Educational Testing Service.

APPLETON, T., CLIFTON, R., & GOLDBERG, S. (1975). The development of behavioral competence in infancy. In F. D. Horowitz (Ed.), *Review of Child Development Research* (Vol. 4, pp. 101–186). Chicago: University of Chicago Press.

ARBUTHNOT, J. (1975). Modification of moral judgment through role playing. *Developmental Psychology, 11,* 319–324.

ARBUTHNOT, J., SPARLING, Y., FAUST, D., & KEE, W. (1983). Logical and moral development in preadolescent children. *Psychological Reports, 52,* 209–210.

ARCHER, C. J. (1984). Children's attitudes toward sex-role division in adult occupational roles. *Sex Roles, 10,* 1–10.

ARCHER, S. L. (1982). The lower age boundaries of identity development. *Child Development, 53,* 1551–1556.

ARIES, P. (1962). *Centuries of childhood.* New York: Random House.

ARLIN, P. K. (1975). Cognitive development in adulthood: A fifth stage? *Developmental Psychology, 11,* 602–606.

ARONFREED, J. (1968). *Conduct and conscience.* New York: Academic Press.

ARONSON, M., KYLLERMAN, M., SABEL, K. G., SANDIN, B., & OLEGARD, R. (1985). Children of alcoholic mothers. *Acta Paediatrica Scandinavia, 74,* 27–35.

ASHER, J. (1987, April). Born to be shy? *Psychology Today, 21*(4), 56–64.

ASHER, S. R. (1983). Social competence and peer status: Recent advances and future directions. *Child Development, 54,* 1427–1434.

ASHER, S. R., & HYMEL, S. (1981). Children's social competence in peer relations: Sociometric and behavioral assessment. In J. D. Wine & M. D. Smye (Eds.), *Social competence* (pp. 125–157). New York: Guilford Press.

ASHER, S. R., MARKELL, R. A., & HYMEL, S. (1981). Identifying children at risk in peer relations: A critique of the rate of interaction approach to assessment. *Child Development, 52,* 1239–1245.

ASHER, S. R., ODDEN, S. L., & GOTTMAN, J. M. (1976). Children's friendships in school settings. In L. G. Katz (Ed.), *Current topics in early childhood education* (Vol. 1, pp. 33–61). New York: Erlbaum.

ASHER, S. R., & RENSHAW, P. D. (1981). Children without friends: Social knowledge and social skills training. In S. R. Asher & J. Gottman (Eds.), *The development of children's friendships* (pp. 273–296). New York: Cambridge University Press.

ASHER, S. R., & WHEELER, V. A. (1985). Children's loneliness: A comparison of rejected and neglected peer status. *Journal of Consulting and Clinical Psychology, 53,* 500–505.

ASHMEAD, D. H., & PERLMUTTER, M. (1980). Infant memory in everyday life. In M. Perlmutter (Ed.), *New directions for child development* (No. 10, pp. 1–16). San Francisco: Jossey-Bass.

ASLIN, R. N. (1981). Development of smooth pursuit in human infants. In D. F. Fisher, R. A. Monty, & J. W. Senders (Eds.), *Eye movements: Cognition and visual perception* (pp. 31–51). Hillsdale, NJ: Erlbaum.

ASLIN, R. N. (1987). Visual and auditory development in infancy. In J. D. Osofsky (Ed.), *Handbook of Infant Development* (2nd ed., pp. 5–97). New York: Wiley.

ASLIN, R. N., PISONI, D. B., & JUSCZYK, P. W. (1983). Auditory development and speech perception in infancy. In M. M. Haith & J. J. Campos (Eds.), *Handbook of Child Psychology, Vol. 2. Infancy and developmental psychobiology* (4th ed., Vol. 2, pp. 573–687). New York: Wiley.

ATKIN, C. (1978). Observation of parent-child interaction in supermarket decision making. *Journal of Marketing, 42,* 41–45.

ATKIN, C., REEVES, B., & GIBSON, W. (1979). Effects of television food advertising on children. Paper presented at the meeting of the Association for Education in Journalism, Houston, TX.

ATKINSON, R. C. (1968). Computerized instruction and the learning process. *American Psychologist, 23,* 225–239.

ATKINSON, R. C., & SHIFFRIN, R. M. (1968). Human memory: A proposed system and its control processes. In K. W. Spence & J. T. Spence (Eds.), *Advances in the psychology of learning and motivation* (Vol. 2, pp. 90–195). New York: Academic Press.

ATKINSON-KING, K. (1973). Children's acquisition of phonological stress contrasts. *UCLA Working Papers in Phonetics, 25.*

AULT, R. L. (1983). *Children's cognitive development* (2nd ed.). New York: Oxford University Press.

AVGAR, A., BRONFENBRENNER, U., & HENDERSON, C. R., JR. (1977). Socialization practices of parents, teachers, and peers in Israel: Kibbutz, Moshav, and city. *Child Development, 48,* 1219–1227.

BAHR, S. J. (1981). An evaluation of court mediation for divorce cases with children. *Journal of Family Issues, 4,* 160–176.

BAHRICK, L. E. (1983). Infants' perception of substance and temporal synchrony in multimodal events. *Infant Behavior and Development, 6,* 429–451.

BAHRICK, L. E., WALKER, A. S., & NEISSER, U. (1981). Selective looking by infants. *Cognitive Psychology, 13,* 377–390.

BAHRICK, L. E., & WATSON, J. S. (1985). Detection of intermodal proprioceptive-visual contingency as a potential basis of self-perception in infancy. *Developmental Psychology, 21,* 963–973.

BAILLARGEON, R. (1987). Object permanence in 3½- and 4½-month-old infants. *Developmental Psychology, 23,* 655–664.

BAILLARGEON, R., SPELKE, E. S., & WASSERMAN, S. (1985). Object permanence in five-month-old infants. *Cognition, 20,* 191–208.

BAKEMAN, R., & BROWN, J. V. (1980). Early interaction: Consequences for social and mental development at three years. *Child Development, 51,* 437–447.

BAKEMAN, R., & BROWNLEE, J. R. (1982). Social rules governing object conflicts in toddlers and preschoolers. In K. H. Rubin & H. S. Ross (Eds.), *Peer relationships and social skills in childhood* (pp. 99–111). New York: Springer-Verlag.

BAKER, L., & BROWN, A. L. (1984). Metacognitive skills of reading. In D. Pearson (Ed.), *Handbook of reading research* (pp. 353–394). New York: Longman.

BAKER, S. W. (1980). Biological influences on human sex and gender. *Signs: Journal of Women in Culture and Society, 6,* 80–96.

BAKER-WARD, L., ORNSTEIN, P. A., & HOLDEN, D. J. (1984). The expression of memorization in early childhood. *Journal of Experimental Child Psychology, 37,* 555–575.

BALDWIN, C. P., & BALDWIN, A. L. (1970). Children's judgments of kindness. *Child Development, 41,* 29–47.

BALDWIN, W. (1983). Trends in adolescent contraception, pregnancy and sexual activity. In E. R. McAnarney (Ed.), *Premature adolescent pregnancy and parenthood* (pp. 3–19). New York: Grune & Stratton.

BALL, S., & BOGATZ, G. (1970). *The first year of Sesame Street: An evaluation.* Princeton, NJ: Educational Testing Service.

BALL, S., & BOGATZ, G. (1973). *Reading with television: An evaluation of the Electric Company.* Princeton, NJ: Educational Testing Service.

BALLARD, B. D., GIPSON, M. T., GUTTENBERG, W., & RAMSEY, K. (1980). Palatability of food as a factor influencing obese and normal-weight children's eating habits. *Behavior Research and Therapy, 18,* 598–600.

BALLARD, M., COREMAN, L., GOTTLIEB, J., & KAUFMAN, M. (1977). Improving the social status of mainstreamed retarded children. *Journal of Educational Psychology, 69,* 605–611.

BANCROFT, J., AXWORTHY, D., & RATCLIFFE, S. (1982). The personality and psycho-sexual development of boys with 47 XXY chromosome constitution. *Journal of Child Psychology and Psychiatry, 23,* 169–180.

BANDURA, A. (1967, March). Behavioral psychotherapy. *Scientific American, 216*(9), 78–86.

BANDURA, A. (1977). *Social learning theory.* Englewood Cliffs, NJ: Prentice-Hall.

BANDURA, A. (1986). *Social foundations of thought and action: A social-cognitive theory.* Englewood Cliffs, NJ: Prentice-Hall.

BANDURA, A., GRUSEC, J. E., & MENLOVE, F. L. (1967). Vicarious extinction of avoidance behavior. *Journal of Personality and Social Psychology, 5,* 16–23.

BANDURA, A., & WALTERS, R. H. (1959). *Adolescent aggression.* New York: Ronald.

BANDURA, A., & WALTERS, R. H. (1963). *Social learning and personality development.* New York: Holt, Rinehart & Winston.

BANDURA, A., ROSS, D., & ROSS, S. (1963). Imitation of film-mediated aggressive models. *Journal of Abnormal and Social Psychology, 66,* 3–11.

BANKS, M. S. (1980). The development of visual accommodation during early infancy. *Child Development, 51,* 646–666.

BANKS, M. S., & SALAPATEK, P. (1983). Infant visual perception. In M. M. Haith & J. J. Campos (Ed.), *Handbook of Child Psychology: Vol. 2. Infancy and Developmental Psychobiology* (pp. 436–571). New York: Wiley.

BARCLAY, J. R., & REID, M. (1974). Semantic integration in children's recall of discourse. *Developmental Psychology, 10,* 277–281.

BARCUS, F. E. (1978). *Food advertising on children's television: An analysis of appeals and nutritional content.* Newtonville, MA: Action for Children's Television.

BARCUS, F. E. (1983). *Images of life on children's television.* New York: Praeger.

BARDIN, C. W., & CATTERALL, J. F. (1981). Testosterone: A major determinant of extragenital sexual dimorphism. *Science, 211,* 1285–1293.

BARDWELL, J. R., COCHRAN, S. W., & WALKER, S. (1986). Relationship of parental education, race, and gender to sex role stereotyping in five-year-old kindergartners. *Sex Roles, 15,* 275–281.

BARENBOIM, C. (1977). Developmental changes in the interpersonal cognitive system from middle childhood to adolescence. *Child Development, 48,* 1467–1474.

BARENBOIM, C. (1981). The development of person perception in childhood and adolescence: From behavioral comparisons to psychological constructs to psychological comparisons. *Child Development, 52,* 129–144.

BARENBOIM, C. (1985). A response to Berndt and Heller. In S. R. Yussen (Ed.), *The growth of reflection in children* (pp. 61–67). Orlando, FL: Academic Press.

BARGH, J. A., & SCHUL, Y. (1980). On the cognitive benefits of peer teaching. *Journal of Educational Psychology, 72,* 593–604.

BARGLOW, P., VAUGHN, B. E., & MOLITOR, N. (1987). Effects of maternal absence due to employment on the quality of infant-mother attachment in a low-risk sample. *Child Development, 58,* 945–954.

BARKER, R. G., & GUMP, P. V. (1964). *Big school, small school.* Stanford, CA: Stanford University Press.

BARKER, R. G., & WRIGHT, H. F. (1955). *Midwest and its children.* New York: Harper & Row.

BARNES, A., COLTON, T., GUNDERSON, J., NOLLER, K., TILLEY, B., STRAMA, T., TOWNSEND, D., HATAB, P., & O'BRIEN, P. (1980). Fertility and outcome of pregnancy in women exposed in utero to diethylstilbestrol. *New England Journal of Medicine, 302,* 609–613.

BARNES, K. E. (1971). Preschool play norms: A replication. *Developmental Psychology, 5,* 99–103.

BARNET, A. B., WEISS, I. P., SOTILLO, M. V., & OHLRICH, E. S. (1978). Abnormal auditory evoked potential in early infancy malnutrition. *Science, 201,* 450–452.

BARNETT, M. A., KING, L. M., & HOWARD, J. A. (1979). Inducing affect about self or other: Effects on generosity in children. *Developmental Psychology, 15,* 164–167.

BARR, R., & DREEBEN, R. (1983). *How schools work.* Chicago: University of Chicago Press.

BARRERA, M. E., & MAURER, D. (1981a). Discrimination of strangers by the three-month-old. *Child Development, 52,* 559–563.

BARRERA, M. E., & MAURER, D. (1981b). Recognition of mother's photographed face by the three-month-old infant. *Child Development, 52,* 714–716.

BARRETT, D. E. (1977). Reflection-impulsivity as a predictor of children's academic achievement. *Child Development, 48,* 1443–1447.

BARRETT, D. E. (1979). A naturalistic study of sex differences in children's aggression. *Merrill-Palmer Quarterly, 25,* 193–203.

BARRETT, D. E., RADKE-YARROW, M., & KLEIN, R. E. (1982). Chronic malnutrition and child behavior: Effects of early caloric supplementation on social and emotional functioning at school age. *Developmental Psychology, 18,* 541–556.

BARRETT, D. E., & YARROW, M. R. (1977). Prosocial behavior, social inferential ability, and assertiveness in children. *Child Development, 48,* 475–481.

BARRON, F. (1963). *Creativity and psychological health.* Princeton, NJ: Van Nostrand.

BARRON, F. (1983). Creative writers. In R. S. Albert (Ed.), *Genius and eminence* (pp. 302–310). Oxford, Eng.: Pergamon Press.

BARRON, F., & HARRINGTON, D. M. (1981). Creativity, intelligence, and personality. In M. R. Rosenzweig & L. W. Porter (Eds.), *Annual Review of Psychology, 32,* 439–476.

BARTLETT, F. C. (1932). *Remembering.* Cambridge, Eng.: Cambridge University Press.

BARTON, D. P. (1980). Phonemic perception in children. In G. Yeni-Komshian, J. F. Kavanagh, & C. A. Ferguson (Eds.), *Child phonology. Vol. 2. Perception* (pp. 97–116). New York: Academic Press.

BARTOSHUK, A. K. (1962). Human neonatal cardiac acceleration to sound: Habituation and dishabituation. *Perceptual and Motor Skills, 15,* 15–27.

BARUCH, G. K., & BARNETT, R. C. (1986). Fathers' participation in family work and children's sex-role attitudes. *Child Development, 57,* 1210–1223.

BATES, E. (1979). *The emergence of symbols: Cognition and communication in infancy.* New York: Academic Press.

BATES, E., CAMAIONI, L., & VOLTERRA, V. (1975). The acquisition of performatives prior to speech. *Merrill-Palmer Quarterly, 21,* 205–226.

BATES, E., & MacWHINNEY, B. A. (1982). Functionalist approaches to grammar. In L. Gleitman & H. E. Wanner (Eds.), *Language acquisition: The state of the art* (pp. 173–218). Cambridge, Eng.: Cambridge University Press.

BATES, J. E., MASLIN, C. A., & FRANKEL, K. A. (1985). Attachment security, mother-child interaction, and temperament as predictors of behavior-problem ratings at age three years. In I. Bretherton & E. Waters (Eds.), Growing points of attachment theory and research. *Monographs of the Society for Research in Child Development, 50* (1–2, Serial No. 209).

BATESON, M. C. (1975). Mother-infant exchanges: The epigenesis of conversational interaction. In D. Aaronson & R. W. Rieber (Eds.), *Developmental psycholinguistics and communication disorders* (Vol. 263, pp. 101–113). New York: New York Academy of Sciences (Annals of the New York Academy of Sciences).

BAUMRIND, D. (1967). Child care practices anteceding three patterns of preschool behavior. *Genetic Psychology Monographs, 75,* 43–88.

BAUMRIND, D. (1971). Current patterns of parental authority. *Developmental Psychology Monograph, 4* (No. 1, Pt. 2).

BAUMRIND, D. (1983). Rejoinder to Lewis's reinterpretation of parental firm control effects: Are authoritative families really harmonious? *Psychological Bulletin, 94,* 132–142.

BAUMRIND, D., & BLACK, A. E. (1967). Socialization practices associated with dimensions of competence in preschool boys and girls. *Child Development, 38,* 291–327.

BAYER, A. E. (1975). Sexist students in American colleges: A descriptive note. *Journal of Marriage and the Family, 37,* 391–397.

BAYLEY, N. (1949). Consistency and variability in the growth of intelligence from birth to eighteen years. *Journal of Genetic Psychology, 75,* 165–196.

BAYLEY, N. (1969). *Bayley scales of infant development: Birth to two years.* New York: Psychological Corporation.

BAYLEY, N. (1970). The development of mental abilities. In P. Mussen (Ed.), *Carmichael's manual of child psychology* (3rd ed., Vol. 1, pp. 1163–1209). New York: Wiley.

BECKER, B. J., & HEDGES, L. V. (1984). Meta-analysis of cognitive gender differences: A comment on an analysis by Rosenthal and Rubin. *Journal of Educational Psychology, 76,* 583–587.

BECKER, J. M. T. (1977). A learning analysis of the development of peer-oriented behavior in nine-month-old infants. *Developmental Psychology, 13,* 481–491.

BECKER, W. C., & GERSTEN, R. (1982). A follow-up of Follow Through: The later effects of the Direct Instruction Model on children in the fifth and sixth grades. *American Educational Research Journal, 19,* 75–92.

BECKWITH, L., & COHEN, S. E. (1980). Interactions of preterm infants with their caregivers and test performance at age 2. In T. F. Field (Ed.), *High-risk infants and children* (pp. 155–178). New York: Academic Press.

BEE, H. L., BARNARD, K. E., EYRES, S. J., GRAY, C. A., HAMMOND, M. A., SPIETZ, A. L., SNYDER, C., & CLARK, B. (1982). Prediction of IQ and language skill from perinatal status, child performance, family characteristics, and mother-infant interaction. *Child Development, 53,* 1134–1156.

BEILIN, H. (1978). Inducing conservation through training. In G. Steiner (Ed.), *Psychology of the twentieth century* (Vol. 7, pp. 260–289). Munich: Kindler.

BEILIN, H. (1980). Piaget's theory: Refinement, revision, or rejection? In R. Kluwe & H. Spada (Eds.), *Developmental models of thinking* (pp. 245–261). New York: Academic Press.

BEISEL, W. R. (1977). Magnitude of the host nutritional responses to infection. *American Journal of Clinical Nutrition, 30,* 1236–1247.

BEIT-HALLAHMI, B., & RABIN, A. I. (1977). The kibbutz as a social experiment and as a child-rearing laboratory. *American Psychologist, 32,* 532–541.

BELCHER, T. L. (1975). Modeling original divergent responses: An initial investigation. *Journal of Educational Psychology, 67,* 351–358.

BELL, S. M., & AINSWORTH, M. D. S. (1972). Infant crying and maternal responsiveness. *Child Development, 43,* 1171–1190.

BELMONT, L., & MAROLLA, F. A. (1973). Birth order, family size, and intelligence. *Science, 182,* 1096–1101.

BELSKY, J. (1978). A theoretical analysis of child abuse remediation strategies. *Journal of Clinical Child Psychology, 7,* 113–117.

BELSKY, J. (1980). Child maltreatment: An ecological integration. *American Psychologist, 35,* 320–335.

BELSKY, J. (1984a). Two waves of day care research: Developmental effects and conditions of quality. In R. C. Ainslie (Ed.), *The child and the day care setting* (pp. 1–34). New York: Praeger.

BELSKY, J. (1984b). The determinants of parenting: A process model. *Child Development, 55,* 83–96.

BELSKY, J., GOODE, M., & MOST, R. (1980). Maternal stimulation and infant exploratory competence: Cross-sectional, correlational and experimental analyses. *Child Development, 51,* 1168–1178.

BELSKY, J., & MOST, R. K. (1981). From exploration to play: A cross-sectional study of infant free play behavior. *Developmental Psychology, 17,* 630–639.

BELSKY, J., & ROVINE, M. (1987). Temperament and attachment security in the Strange Situation: An empirical rapprochement. *Child Development, 58,* 787–795.

BELSKY, J., & ROVINE, M. (1988). Nonmaternal care in the first year of life and the security of infant-parent attachment. *Child Development, 59,* 157–167.

BELSKY, J., ROVINE, M., & TAYLOR, D. G. (1984). The Pennsylvania infant and family development project: III. The origins of individual differences in infant-mother attachment: Maternal and infant contributions. *Child Development, 55,* 718–728.

BELSKY, J., & STEINBERG, L. (1978). The effects of day care: A critical review. *Child Development, 49,* 929–949.

BEM, S. L. (1974). The measurement of psychological androgyny. *Journal of Consulting and Clinical Psychology, 42,* 155–162.

BEM, S. L. (1975). Sex role adaptability: One consequence of psychological androgyny. *Journal of Personality and Social Psychology, 31,* 634–643.

BEM, S. L. (1977). On the utility of alternative procedures for assessing psychological androgyny. *Journal of Consulting and Clinical Psychology, 45,* 196–205.

BEM, S. L. (1981). Gender schema theory: A cognitive account of sex typing. *Psychological Review, 88,* 354–364.

BEM, S. L. (1983). Gender schema theory and its implications for child development: Raising gender aschematic children in a gender-schematic society. *Signs: Journal of Women in Culture and Society, 8,* 598–616.

BEM, S. L. (1984). Androgyny and gender schema theory: A conceptual and empirical integration. In R. A. Dienstbier & T. B. Sonderegger (Eds.), *Nebraska Symposium on Motivation* (Vol. 34, pp. 179–226). Lincoln, NB: University of Nebraska Press.

BEMIS, K. (1978). Current approaches to the etiology and treatment of anorexia nervosa. *Psychological Bulletin, 85,* 593–617.

BENBOW, C. P., & STANLEY, J. C. (1980). Sex differences in mathematical ability: Fact or artifact? *Science, 210,* 1262–1264.

BENBOW, C. P., & STANLEY, J. C. (1983). Sex differences in mathematical reasoning: More facts. *Science, 222,* 1029–1031.

BENCH, J., COLLYER, Y., MENTZ, L., & WILSON, I. (1976). Studies in infant behavioural audiometry: I. Neonates. *Audiology, 15,* 85–105.

BENCH, J., & PARKER, A. (1971). Hyper-responsivity to sounds in the short-gestation baby. *Developmental Medicine and Child Neurology, 13,* 15–19.

BENDER, B. G., & LEVIN, J. R. (1976). Motor activity, anticipated motor activity, and young children's associative learning. *Child Development, 47,* 560–562.

BENDER, W. H. (1986–1987). Effective educational practices in the mainstream setting: Recommended model for evaluation of mainstream teacher classes. *Journal of Special Education, 20,* 475–487.

BENEDICT, R. (1934). Anthropology and the abnormal. *Journal of Genetic Psychology, 10,* 59–82.

BENNETT, E. L., DIAMOND, M. C., KRECH, D., & ROSENZWEIG, M. R. (1964). Chemical and anatomical plasticity of the brain. *Science, 146,* 610–619.

BEN-ZEEV, S. (1977). The influence of bilingualism on cognitive strategy and cognitive development. *Child Development, 48,* 1009–1018.

BERBAUM, M. L. (1985). Explanation and prediction: Criteria for assessing the confluence model. *Child Development, 56,* 781–784.

BERBAUM, M. L., & MORELAND, R. L. (1985). Intellectual development within transracial adoptive families: Retesting the confluence model. *Child Development, 56,* 207–216.

BERG, M., & MEDRICH, E. A. (1980). Children in four neighborhoods: The physical environment and its effects on play and play patterns. *Environment and Behavior, 12,* 320–348.

BERG, W. K., & BERG, K. M. (1979). Psychophysiological development in infancy: State, sensory function, and attention. In J. D. Osofsky (Ed.), *Handbook of Infant Development* (pp. 283–343). New York: Wiley.

BERK, L. E. (1984). Development of private speech among low-income Appalachian children. *Developmental Psychology, 20,* 271–286.

BERK, L. E. (1985a). Relationship of caregiver education to child-oriented attitudes, job satisfaction, and behaviors toward children. *Child Care Quarterly, 14,* 103–129.

BERK, L. E. (1985b, July). Why children talk to themselves. *Young Children, 40*(5), 46–52.

BERK, L. E. (1986a). Relationship of elementary school children's private speech to behavioral accompaniment to task, attention, and task performance. *Developmental Psychology, 22,* 671–680.

BERK, L. E. (1986b, May). Private speech: Learning out loud. *Psychology Today, 20*(5), 34–42.

BERK, L. E., & LEWIS, N. G. (1977). Sex role and social behavior in four school environments. *Elementary School Journal, 77,* 205–217.

BERKO, J. (1958). The child's learning of English morphology. *Word, 14,* 150–177.

BERKOWITZ, M. W. (1985). The role of discussion in moral education. In M. W. Berkowitz & F. Oser (Eds.), *Moral education: Theory and application* (pp. 197–218). Hillsdale, NJ: Erlbaum.

BERKOWITZ, M. W., & GIBBS, J. C. (1983). Measuring the developmental features of moral discussion. *Merrill-Palmer Quarterly, 29,* 399–410.

BERKOWITZ, M. W., GIBBS, J. C., & BROUGHTON, J. M. (1980). The relation of moral judgment stage disparity to developmental effects of peer dialogues. *Merrill-Palmer Quarterly, 26,* 341–357.

BERMAN, A. (1978). Delinquency as a learning disability. *Science News, 114,* 180–181.

BERMAN, P. W. (1986). Young children's responses to babies: Do they foreshadow differences between maternal and paternal styles? In A. Fogel & G. F. Melson (Eds.), *Origins of nurturance* (pp. 25–51). Hillsdale, NJ: Erlbaum.

BERMAN, P. W., & GOODMAN, V. (1984). Age and sex differences in children's responsiveness to babies: Effects of adults' caretaking requests and instructions. *Child Development, 55,* 1071–1077.

BERNDT, T. J. (1977). The effect of reciprocity on moral judgment and causal attribution. *Child Development, 48,* 1322–1330.

BERNDT, T. J. (1979a). Developmental changes in conformity to peers and parents. *Developmental Psychology, 15,* 608–616.

BERNDT, T. J. (1979b). Lack of acceptance of reciprocity norms in preschool children. *Developmental Psychology, 15,* 662–663.

BERNDT, T. J. (1981). The effects of friendship on prosocial intentions and behavior between friends. *Developmental Psychology, 17,* 408–416.

BERNDT, T. J. (1983). Social cognition, social behavior, and children's friendships. In E. T. Higgins, D. N. Ruble, & W. W. Hartup (Eds.), *Social cognition and social development: A sociocultural perspective* (pp. 158–189). Cambridge, Eng.: Cambridge University Press.

BERNDT, T. J. (1985). Prosocial behavior between friends in middle childhood and early adolescence. *Journal of Adolescence, 5,* 307–313.

BERNDT, T. J. & HELLER, K. A. (1985). Measuring children's personality attributions: Responses to open-ended questions versus trait ratings and predictions of future behavior. In S. R. Yussen (Ed.) *The growth of reflection in children* (pp. 37–60). Orlando, FL: Academic Press.

BERNDT, T. J., & HOYLE, S. G. (1985). Stability and change in childhood and adolescent friendships. *Developmental Psychology, 21,* 1007–1015.

BERNER, E. (1971). *Private speech and role-taking abilities in preschool children.* Unpublished doctoral dissertation, Harvard University.

BERNSTEIN, B. (1964). Elaborated and restricted codes: Their social origins and some consequences. In J. Gumperz & D. Hymes (Eds.), The ethnography of communication. *American Anthropologist Special Publication, 66,* 55–69.

BERNSTEIN, B. E., CLAMAN, L., HARRIS, J. C., & SAMSON, J. (1982). The child witness: A model for evaluation and trial preparation. *Child Welfare, 61,* 95–104.

BERRUETA-CLEMENT, J. R., SCHWEINHART, L. J., BARNETT, W. S., EPSTEIN, A. S., & WEIKART, D. P. (1984). Changed lives: The effects of the Perry Preschool Program on youths through age 19. *Monographs of the High/Soope Research Foundation, 8.*

BERTENTHAL, B. I., & CAMPOS, J. J. (1987). New directions in the study of early experience. *Child Development, 58,* 560–567.

BERTENTHAL, B. I., CAMPOS, J., & BARRETT, K. (1984). Self-produced locomotion: An organizer of emotional, cognitive, and social development in infancy. In R. Emde & R. Harmon (Eds.), *Continuities and discontinuities in development* (pp. 174–210). New York: Plenum.

BEST, D. L., WILLIAMS, J. E., CLOUD, J. M., DAVIS, S. W., ROBERTSON, L. S., EDWARDS, J. R., GILES, H., & FOWLES, J. (1977). Development of sex-trait stereotypes among young children in the United States, England, and Ireland. *Child Development, 48,* 1375–1384.

BEVER, T. G. (1970). The cognitive basis for linguistic structure. In J. R. Hayes (Ed.)., *Cognition and the development of language* (pp. 279–362). New York: Wiley.

BEVER, T. G. (1982). Some implications of the nonspecific bases of language. In E. Wanner & L. R. Gleitman (Eds.), *Language acquisi-*

tion: The state of the art (pp. 429–449). Cambridge, Eng.: Cambridge University Press.

BIALYSTOK, E. (1986). Factors in the growth of linguistic awareness. *Child Development, 57,* 498–510.

BIANCHI, B. D., & BAKEMAN, R. (1978). Sex-typed affiliation preferences observed in preschoolers: Traditional and open school differences. *Child Development, 49,* 910–912.

BIERMAN K. L. (1986). Process of change during social skills training with preadolescents and its relation to treatment outcome. *Child Development, 57,* 230–240.

BIERMAN, K. L., MILLER, C. L., & STABB, S. D. (1987). Improving the social behavior and peer acceptance of rejected boys: Effects of social skill training with instructions and prohibitions. *Journal of Consulting and Clinical Psychology, 55,* 194–200.

BIGELOW, B. J. (1977). Children's friendship expectations: A cognitive-developmental study. *Child Development, 48,* 246–253.

BIGELOW, B. J., & LaGAIPA, J. J. (1975). Children's written descriptions of friendship: A multidimensional analysis. *Developmental Psychology, 11,* 857–858.

BILLMAN, J., & McDEVITT, S. C. (1980). Convergence of parent and observer ratings of temperament with observations of peer interaction in nursery school. *Child Development, 51,* 395–400.

BINET, A., & SIMON, T. (1916). *The development of intelligence in children.* Baltimore: Williams & Wilkins.

BIRCH, L. L. (1981). Generalization of a modified food preference. *Child Development, 52,* 755–758.

BIRCH, L. L., ZIMMERMAN, S., & HIND, H. (1980). The influence of social-affective context on preschool children's food preferences. *Child Development, 51,* 856–861.

BIRNBAUM, J. A. (1975). Life patterns and self-esteem in gifted family oriented and career committed women. In M. S. Mednick, S. S. Tangri, & L. W. Hoffman (Eds.), *Women and achievement* (pp. 396–419). Washington, DC: Hemisphere.

BIRNS, B., & NOYES, D. (1984). Child nutrition: The role of theory in the world of politics. *International Journal of Mental Health, 12,* 22–42.

BISCHOFSHAUSEN, S. (1985). Developmental differences in schema dependency for temporally ordered story events. *Journal of Psycholinguistic Research, 14,* 543–556.

BIXENSTINE, V. E., DeCORTE, M. S., & BIXENSTINE, B. A. (1976). Conformity to peer-sponsored misconduct at four age levels. *Developmental Psychology, 12,* 226–236.

BJORK, E. L., & CUMMINGS, E. M. (1984). Infant search errors: Stage of concept development or stage of memory development. *Memory and Cognition, 12,* 1–19.

BJORKLUND, D. F., & DE MARCHENA, M. R. (1984). Developmental shifts in the basis of organization memory: The role of associative versus categorical relatedness in children's free recall. *Child Development, 55,* 952–962.

BJORKLUND, D. F., & HOCK, H. S. (1982). Age differences in the temporal locus of memory organization in children's recall. *Journal of Experimental Child Psychology, 32,* 347–362.

BJORKLUND, D. F., & JACOBS, J. W. III (1985). Associative and categorical processes in children's memory: The role of automaticity in the development of organization in free recall. *Journal of Experimental Child Psychology, 39,* 599–617.

BJORKLUND, D. F., & ZEMAN, B. R. (1983). The development of organizational strategies in children's recall of familiar information: Using social organization to recall the names of classmates. *International Journal of Behavioral Development, 6,* 341–353.

BLAKE, J. (1981). The only child in America: Prejudice versus performance. *Population and Development Review, 1,* 43–54.

BLAKEMORE, J. E. O., LaRUE, A. A., & OLEJNIK, A. B. (1979). Sex-appropriate toy preference and the ability to conceptualize toys as sex-role related. *Developmental Psychology, 15,* 339–340.

BLANCK, P. D., ROSENTHAL, R., SNODGRASS, S. E., DePAULO, B. M., & ZUCKERMAN, M. (1981). Sex differences in eavesdropping on nonverbal cues: Developmental changes. *Journal of Personality and Social Psychology, 41,* 391–396.

BLASI, A. (1980). Bridging moral cognition and moral action: A critical review of the literature. *Psychological Bulletin, 88,* 593–637.

BLASI, A. (1983). Moral cognition and moral action: A theoretical perspective. *Developmental Review, 3,* 178–210.

BLASS, E. M., GANCHROW, J. R., & STEINER, J. E. (1984). Classical conditioning in newborn humans 2–48 hours of age. *Infant Behavior and Development, 7,* 223–235.

BLATT, J., SPENCER, L., & WARD, S. (1972). A cognitive developmental study of children's reactions to television advertising. In E. A. Rubinstein, G. A. Comstock, & J. P. Murray (Eds.), *Television and social behavior* (Vol. 4, pp. 452–467). Washington, DC: U.S. Government Printing Office.

BLATT, M., & KOHLBERG, L. (1975). The effects of classroom moral discussion upon children's level of moral judgment. *Journal of Moral Education, 4,* 129–161.

BLAU, Z. S. (1981). *Black children/white children: Competence, socialization, and social structure.* New York: The Free Press.

BLOCK, J. (1971). *Lives through time.* Berkeley, CA: Bancroft Books.

BLOCK, J., BLOCK, J. H., & HARRINGTON, D. M. (1974). Some misgivings about the Matching Familiar Figures Test as a measure of reflection-impulsivity. *Developmental Psychology, 10,* 611–632.

BLOCK, J. H. (1973). Conceptions of sex role: Some cross-cultural and longitudinal perspectives. *American Psychologist, 28,* 512–526.

BLOCK, J. H. (1976). Issues, problems, and pitfalls in assessing sex differences: A critical review of "The Psychology of Sex Differences." *Merrill-Palmer Quarterly, 22,* 283–308.

BLOCK, J. H. (1978). Another look at sex differentiation in the socialization behavior of mothers and fathers. In J. Sherman & F. L. Denmark (Eds.), *Psychology of women: Future directions of research* (pp. 29–87). New York: Psychological Dimensions.

BLOCK, J. H. (1983). Differential premises arising from differential socialization of the sexes: Some conjectures. *Child Development, 54,* 1335–1354.

BLOCK, J. H., BLOCK, J., & HARRINGTON, D. (1975). Sex role typing and instrumental behavior: A developmental study. Paper presented at the meeting of the Society for Research in Child Development, Denver.

BLOOM, B. S. (1982). The role of gifts and markers in the development of talent. *Exceptional Children, 48,* 510–522.

BLOOM, B. S., & SOSNIAK, L. A. (1981). Talent development vs. schooling. *Educational Leadership, 39,* 86–94.

BLOOM, L. (1970). *Language development: Form and function in emerging grammars.* Cambridge, MA: MIT Press.

BLOOM, L. (1973). *One word at a time: The use of single word utterance before syntax.* The Hague: Mouton.

BLOOM, L., & LAHEY, M. (1978). *Language development and language disorders.* New York: Wiley.

BLOOM, L., LAHEY, M., LIFTEN, K., & FIESS, K. (1980). Complex sentences: Acquisition of syntactic connections and the semantic relations they encode. *Journal of Child Language, 7,* 235–256.

BLOOM, L., LIGHTBOWN, P., & HOOD, L. (1975). Structure and variation in child language. *Monographs of the Society for Research in Child Development, 40* (2, Serial No. 160).

BLOTNER, R., & BEARISON, D. J. (1984). Developmental consistencies in socio-moral knowledge: Justice reasoning and altruistic behavior. *Merrill-Palmer Quarterly, 30,* 349–367.

BLYTH, D. A., SIMMONS, R. G., BULCROFT, R., FELT, D., VAN CLEAVE, E. F., & BUSH, D. M. (1981). The effects of physical development on self-image and satisfaction with body-image for early adolescent males. In R. Simmons (Ed.), *Research in community mental health* (Vol. 2, pp. 43–73). Greenwich, CN: JAI Press.

BLYTH D. A., SIMMONS, R. G., & ZAKIN, D. F. (1985). Satisfaction with body image for early adolescent females. The impact of pubertal timing within different school environments. *Journal of Youth and Adolescence, 14,* 207–225.

BOCCIA, M., & CAMPOS, J. (1983). Maternal emotional signalling: Its effect on infants' reaction to strangers. Paper presented at the meeting of the Society for Research in Child Development, Detroit.

BOGATZ, G. A., & BALL, S. (1972). *The second year of Sesame Street: A continuing evaluation.* Princeton, NJ: Educational Testing Service.

BOGGIANO, A. K., & RUBLE, D. N. (1979). Perception of competence and the overjustification effect: A developmental study. *Journal of Personality and Social Psychology, 37,* 1462–1468.

BOHANNON, J. N., & WARREN-LEUBECKER, A. (1986). Theoretical approaches to language acquisition. In J. B. Gleason (1986). *The development of language* (pp. 173–226). Columbus, OH: Merrill.

BOISMIER, J. D. (1977). Visual stimulation and wake-sleep behavior in human neonates. *Developmental Psychobiology, 10,* 219–227.

BONVILLIAN, J., NELSON, K. E., & CHARROW, V. (1976). Language and language-related skills in deaf and hearing children. *Sign Language Studies, 12,* 211–250.

BORG, S., & LASKER, J. (1981). *When pregnancy fails.* Boston: Beacon Press.

BORKE, H. (1975). Piaget's mountains revisited: Changes in the egocentric landscape. *Developmental Psychology, 11,* 240–243.

BORKO, H., SHAVELSON, R., & STERN, P. (1981). Teachers' decisions in the planning of reading instruction. *Reading Research Quarterly, 16,* 449–466.

BORNSTEIN, M. H. (1975). Qualities of color vision in infancy. *Journal of Experimental Child Psychology, 19,* 401–419.

BOSSARD, J. H. S., & BOLL, E. S. (1956). *The large family system.* Philadelphia: University of Pennsylvania Press.

BOUCHARD, T. J., JR. (1981). *The Minnesota study of twins reared apart: Description and preliminary findings.* Paper presented at the meeting of the American Psychological Association.

BOUCHARD, T. J., JR. (1984). Twins reared together and apart: What they tell us about human diversity. In S.W. Fox (Ed.), *Individuality and determinism: Chemical and biological bases* (pp. 147–184). New York: Plenum.

BOUCHARD, T. J., JR., & McGUE, M. (1981). Familial studies of intelligence: A review. *Science, 212,* 1056.

BOUCHARD, T. J., JR., & SEGAL, N. L. (1985). Environment and IQ. In B. B. Wolman (Ed.), *Handbook of Intelligence* (pp. 391–464). New York: Wiley.

BOUKYDIS, C. F. Z., & BURGESS, R. L. (1982). Adult physiological response to infant cries: Effects of temperament of infant, parental status and gender. *Child Development, 53,* 1291–1298.

BOWER, G. (1981). Mood and memory. *American Psychologist, 36,* 128–148.

BOWER, T. G. R. (1964). Discrimination of depth in premotor infants. *Psychonomic Science, 1,* 368.

BOWER, T. G. R. (1971, October). The object world of the infant. *Scientific American, 225*(4), 30–38.

BOWER, T. G. R. (1972). Object perception in infants. *Perception, 1,* 15–30.

BOWER, T. G. R. (1974). *Development in infancy.* San Francisco: Freeman.

BOWER, T. G. R. (1982). *Development in infancy* (2nd ed.). San Francisco: Freeman.

BOWER, T. G. R., BROUGHTON, J. M., & MOORE, M. K. (1971). Infant responses to approaching objects: An indicator of response to distal variables. *Perception and Psychophysics, 9,* 193–196.

BOWERMAN, M. (1973). *Early syntactic development: A cross-linguistic study with special reference to Finnish.* Cambridge, Eng.: Cambridge University Press.

BOWERMAN, M. (1985). What shapes children's grammars? In D. I. Slobin (Ed.), *The crosslinguistic study of language acquisition, vol. 2. Theoretical issues* (pp. 1257–1319). Hillsdale, NJ: Erlbaum.

BOWLBY, J. (1969). *Attachment and loss: Vol. 1. Attachment.* New York: Basic Books.

BOWLBY, J. (1973). *Attachment and loss: Vol. 2. Separation, anxiety, and anger.* New York: Basic Books.

BOWLBY, J. (1980). *Attachment and loss: Vol. 3. Loss.* New York: Basic Books.

BOYSSON-BARDIES, B., deSAGART, L., & DURAND, C. (1984). Discernable differences in the babbling of infants according to target language. *Journal of Child Language, 11,* 1–15.

BRABECK, M. (1983). Moral judgment: Theory and research on differences between males and females. *Developmental Review, 3,* 274–291.

BRACHT, G. H., & GLASS, G. V. (1968). The external validity of experiments. *American Educational Research Journal, 5,* 437–474.

BRACKBILL, Y. (1958). Extinction of the smiling response in infants as a function of reinforcement schedule. *Child Development, 29,* 115–124.

BRACKBILL, Y. (1979). Obstetrical medication and infant behavior. In J. D. Osofsky (Ed.), *Handbook of infant development* (pp. 76–125). New York: Wiley.

BRACKBILL, Y., & NICHOLS, P. L. (1982). A test of the confluence model of intellectual development. *Developmental Psychology, 18,* 192–198.

BRADLEY, R. H., & CALDWELL, B. M. (1976a). The relation of infants' home environments to mental test performance at fifty-four months: A follow-up study. *Child Development, 47,* 1172–1174.

BRADLEY, R. H., & CALDWELL, B. M. (1976b). Early home environment and changes in mental test performance in children from 6 to 36 months. *Developmental Psychology, 12,* 93–97.

BRADLEY, R. H., & CALDWELL, B. M. (1979). Home Observation for Measurement of the Environment: A revision of the preschool scale. *American Journal of Mental Deficiency, 84,* 235–244.

BRADLEY, R. H., & CALDWELL, B. M. (1981). The HOME Inventory: A validation of the preschool scale for black children. *Child Development, 52,* 708–710.

BRADLEY, R. H., & CALDWELL, B. M. (1982). The consistency of the home environment and its relation to child development. *International Journal of Behavioral Development, 5,* 445–465.

BRADLEY, R. H., CALDWELL, B. M., & ELARDO, R. (1979). Home environment and cognitive development in the first 2 years: A cross-lagged panel analysis. *Developmental Psychology, 15,* 246–250.

BRADLEY, R. M. (1972). Development of the taste bud and gustatory papillae in human fetuses. In J. F. Bosma (Ed.), *The third symposium on oral sensation and perception: The mouth of the infant* (pp. 137–162). Springfield, IL: Thomas.

BRAINE, M. D. S. (1976). Children's first word combinations. *Monographs of the Society for Research in Child Development, 41* (1, Serial No. 164).

BRAINERD, C. J. (1970). The construction of the formal operations of implication-reasoning and proportionality in children and adolescents. *Dissertation Abstracts International, 31,* 6919B. (University Microfilms No. 71-11, 792).

BRAINERD, C. J. (1974). Inducing ordinal and cardinal representations of the first five natural numbers. *Journal of Experimental Child Psychology, 18,* 520–534.

BRAINERD, C. J. (1978). *Piaget's theory of intelligence.* Englewood Cliffs, NJ: Prentice-Hall.

BRAINERD, C. J., & ALLEN, T. W. (1971). Training and generalization of density conservation: Effects of feedback and consecutive similar stimuli. *Child Development, 42,* 693–704.

BRAINERD, C. J., & BRAINERD, S. H. (1972). Order of acquisition of number and liquid quantity conservation. *Child Development, 43,* 1401–1405.

BRAINERD, C. J., KINGMA, J., & HOWE, M. L. (1985). On the development of forgetting. *Child Development, 56,* 1103–1119.

BRANSFORD, J. D., STEIN, B. S., SHELTON, T. S., & OWINGS, R. A. (1981). Cognition and adaptation: The importance of learning to learn. In J. Harvey (Ed.), *Cognition, social behavior and the environment* (pp. 93–110). Hillsdale, NJ: Erlbaum.

BRASSARD, M. R., GERMAIN, R., & HART, S. N. (Eds.). (1987). *Psychological maltreatment of children and youth.* New York: Pergamon Press.

BRAZELTON, T. B. (1974). *Toddlers and parents.* New York: Delacorte Press.

BRAZELTON, T. B. (1983). *Infants and mothers.* New York: Delacorte Press.

BRAZELTON, T. B. (1984). *Neonatal behavioral assessment scale.* Philadelphia: Lippincott.

BRAZELTON, T. B., KOSLOWSKI, B., & TRONICK, E. (1976). Study of the neonatal behavior in Zambian and American neonates. *Journal of the American Academy of Child Psychiatry, 15,* 97–107.

BRAZELTON, T. B., ROBEY, J. S., & COLLIER, G. A. (1969). Infant development in the Zinacanteco Indians of southern Mexico. *Pediatrics, 44,* 274–290.

BRENNAN, W. M., AMES, E. W., & MOORE, R. W. (1966). Age differences in infants' attention to patterns of different complexities. *Science, 151,* 354–356.

BRENNER, D., & HINSDALE, G. (1978). Body build stereotypes and self-identification in three age groups of females. *Adolescence, 13,* 551–562.

BRENT, R. L. (1983). The effect of embryonic and fetal exposure to X-ray, microwaves, and ultrasound. *Clinical Obstetrics and Gynecology, 26,* 484–510.

BRETHERTON, I., & AINSWORTH, M. D. S. (1974). Responses of one-year-olds to a stranger in a strange situation. In M. Lewis & L. A. Rosenblum (Eds.), *The origins of fear* (pp. 131–164). New York: Wiley.

BRETHERTON, I., MCNEW, S., SNYDER, L, & BATES, E. (1982). Individual differences at 20 months: Analytic and holistic strategies in language acquisition. *Journal of Child Language, 10,* 293–320.

BRICE-HEATH, S. (1982). Questioning at home and at school: A comparative study. In G. Spindler (Ed.), *Doing the ethnography of schooling: Educational anthropology in action* (pp. 102–127). New York: Holt.

BRICKER, D., CARLSON, L., & SCHWARZ, R. (1981). A discussion of early intervention for infants with Down syndrome. *Pediatrics, 67,* 45–46.

BRIDGES, A. (1985). Actions and things: What adults talk about to 1-year-olds. In S. A. Kuczaj II & M. D. Barrett (Eds.), *The development of word meaning* (pp. 225–255). New York: Springer-Verlag.

BRIDGES, F. A., & CICCHETTI, D. (1982). Mothers' ratings of the temperament characteristics of Down syndrome infants. *Developmental Psychology, 18,* 238–244.

BRIM, O. G. (1958). Family structure and sex role learning by children: A further analysis of Helen Koch's data. *Sociometry, 21,* 1–16.

BRINTON, B., & FUJIKI, M. (1984). Development of topic manipulation skills in discourse. *Journal of Speech and Hearing Research, 27,* 350–358.

BRITT, D. W., & CAMPBELL, E. Q. (1977). Assessing the linkage of norms, environments, and deviance. *Social Forces, 56,* 532–550.

BRITTON, S. B., FITZHARDINGE, P. M., & ASHBY, S. (1981). Is intensive care justified for infants weighing less than 801 gm at birth? *Journal of Pediatrics, 99,* 937–943.

BRODY, G. H., GRAZIANO, W. G., & MUSSER, L. M. (1983). Familiarity and children's behavior in same-age and mixed-age peer groups. *Developmental Psychology. 19.* 568–576.

BRODY, G. H., & SHAFFER, D. R. (1982). Contributions of parents and peers to children's moral socialization. *Developmental Review, 2,* 31–75.

BRODY, G. H., & STONEMAN, Z. (1981). Selective imitation of same-age, older, and younger peer models. *Child Development, 52.* 717–720.

BRODY, G. H., STONEMAN, Z., & BURKE, M. (1987). Child temperaments, maternal differential behavior, and sibling relationships. *Developmental Psychology, 23,* 354–362.

BRODY, N. (1985). The validity of tests of intelligence. In B. B. Wolman (Ed.), *Handbook of intelligence* (pp. 353–389). New York: Wiley.

BRODZINSKY, D. M., MESSER, S. M., & TEW, J. D. (1979). Sex differences in children's expression and control of fantasy and overt aggression. *Child Development, 50,* 372–379.

BRODZINSKY, D. M., & RIGHTMYER, J. (1980). Individual differences in children's humour development. In P. F. McGee & A. J. Chapman (Eds.), *Children's humour* (pp. 181–212). Chichester, Eng.: Wiley.

BRONFENBRENNER, U. (1970). *Two worlds of childhood: U.S. and U.S.S.R.* New York: Russell Sage Foundation.

BRONFENBRENNER, U. (1972). Is 80% of intelligence genetically determined? In U. Bronfenbrenner (Ed.), *Influences on human development* (pp. 118–130). Hinsdale, IL: Dryden Press.

BRONFENBRENNER, U. (1975). Is early intervention effective? In M. Guttentag & E. L. Struening (Eds.), *Handbook of evaluation research* (Vol. 2, pp. 519–603). Beverly Hills, CA: Sage.

BRONFENBRENNER, U. (1977). Toward an experimental ecology of human development. *American Psychologist, 32,* 513–531.

BRONFENBRENNER, U. (1979). *The ecology of human development.* Cambridge, MA: Harvard University Press.

BRONFENBRENNER, U. (1986). Alienation and four worlds of childhood. *Phi Delta Kappan, 67,* 430–436.

BRONFENBRENNER, U., ALVAREZ, W. F., & HENDERSON, C. R., JR. (1984). Working and watching: Maternal employment status and parents' perceptions of their three-year-old children. *Child Development, 55,* 1362–1378.

BRONFENBRENNER, U., & CROUTER, A. C. (1982). Work and family through time and space. In S. B. Kamerman & C. D. Hayes (Eds.), *Families that work: Children in a changing world* (pp. 39–83). Washington, DC: National Academy Press.

BRONFENBRENNER, U., MOEN, P., & GARBARINO, J. (1984). Child, family, and community. In R. D. Parke (Ed.), *Review of child development research* (Vol. 7, pp. 283–328). Chicago: University of Chicago Press.

BRONFENBRENNER, U., & WEISS, H. (1983). Beyond policies without people: An ecological perspective on child and family policy. In E. Zigler, S. L. Kagan, & E. Klugman (Eds.), *Children, families, and government: Perspectives on American policy* (pp. 393–414). Cambridge, MA: Harvard University Press.

BRONSON, G. W. (1972). Infants' reactions to unfamiliar persons and novel objects. *Monographs of the Society for Research in Child Development, 37* (3, Serial No. 148).

BRONSON, W. C. (1981). *Toddlers' behaviors with agemates: Issues of interaction, cognition, and affect.* Norwood, NJ: Ablex.

BROOKHART, J., & HOCK, E. (1976). The effects of experimental context and experiential background on infants' behavior toward their mothers and a stranger. *Child Development, 47,* 333–340.

BROOKOVER, W., BEADY, C., FLOOD, P., SCHWEITZER, J., & WISENBAKER, J. (1979). *School social systems and student achievement: Schools can make a difference.* New York: Bergin.

BROOKS, J., & LEWIS, M. (1976). Infants' responses to strangers: Midget, adult, and child. *Child Development, 47,* 323–332.

BROOKS-GUNN, J. (1984). The psychological significance of different pubertal events to young girls. *Journal of Early Adolescence, 4,* 315–327.

BROOKS-GUNN, J. (1986). The relationship of maternal beliefs about sex typing to maternal and young children's behavior. *Sex Roles, 14,* 21–35.

BROOKS-GUNN, J., & RUBLE, D. N. (1980). Menarche: The interaction of physiology, cultural, and social factors. In A. J. Dan, E. A. Graham, & C. P. Beecher (Eds.), *The menstrual cycle: A synthesis of interdisciplinary research* (pp. 141–159). New York: Springer-Verlag.

BROOKS-GUNN, J., & RUBLE, D. N. (1983). The experience of menarche from a developmental perspective. In J. Brooks-Gunn & A. C. Petersen (Eds.), *Girls at puberty* (pp. 155–177). New York: Plenum.

BROOKS-GUNN, J., & WARREN, M. P. (1985). The effects of delayed menarche in different contexts: Dance and nondance students. *Journal of Youth and Adolescence, 14,* 285–300.

BROOKS-GUNN, J., WARREN, M. P., SAMELSON, M., & FOX, R. (1986). Physical similarity of and disclosure of menarcheal status to friends: Effects of grade and pubertal status. *Journal of Early Adolescence, 6,* 3–14.

BROPHY, J. E. (1983). Research on the self-fulfilling prophecy and teacher expectations. *Journal of Educational Psychology, 75,* 631–661.

BROPHY, J. E., & EVERTSON, C. (1976). *Learning from teaching: A developmental perspective.* Boston: Allyn & Bacon.

BROPHY, J. E., & GOOD, T. L. (1974). *Teacher-student relationships: Causes and consequences.* New York: Holt, Rinehart and Winston.

BROPHY, J. E., & GOOD, T. L. (1986). Teacher behavior and student achievement. In M. C. Wittrock (Ed.), *Handbook of research on teaching* (3rd ed., pp. 328–375). New York: MacMillan.

BROVERMAN, D. M., KLAIBER, E. L., & VOGEL, W. (1980). Gonadal hormones and cognitive functioning. In J. E. Parsons (Ed.), *The psychology of sex differences and sex roles* (pp. 57–80). Washington: Hemisphere Publishing.

BROVERMAN, I. K., BROVERMAN, D. M., CLARKSON, F. E., ROSENKRANTZ, P. S., & VOGEL, S. R. (1970). Sex-role stereotypes and clinical judgments of mental health. *Journal of Consulting and Clinical Psychology, 34,* 1–7.

BROVERMAN, I. K., VOGEL, S. R., BROVERMAN, D. M., CLARKSON, F. E., & ROSENKRANTZ, P. S. (1972). Sex-role stereotypes: A current appraisal. *Journal of Social Issues, 28,* 59–78.

BROWN, A. L., BRANSFORD, J. D., FERRARA, R. A., & CAMPIONE, J. C. (1983). Learning, remembering, and understanding. In J. H. Flavell & E. M. Markman (Eds.), *Handbook of child psychology: Vol 3. Cognitive development* (4th ed., pp. 77–166). New York: Wiley.

BROWN, A. L., & CAMPIONE, J. C. (1972). Recognition memory for perceptually similar pictures in preschool children. *Journal of Experimental Psychology, 95,* 55–62.

BROWN, A. L., & DeLOACHE, J. S. (1978). Skills, plans and self-regulation. In R. S. Siegler (Ed.), *Children's thinking: What develops?* (pp. 3–35). Hillsdale, NJ: Erlbaum.

BROWN, A. L., SMILEY, S. S., DAY, J. D., TOWNSEND, M., & LAWTON, S. Q. C. (1977). Intrusion of a thematic idea in children's recall of prose. *Child Development, 48,* 1454–1466.

BROWN, A. L., SMILEY, S. S., & LAWTON, S. Q. C. (1978). The effects of experience on the selection of suitable retrieval cues for studying texts. *Child Development, 49,* 829–835.

BROWN, B. (1985, July). Head Start: How research changed public policy. *Young Children, 40*(5), 9–13.

BROWN, B. B., LOHR, M. J., & McCLENAHAN, E. L. (1986). Early adolescents' perceptions of peer pressure. *Journal of Early Adolescence, 6,* 139–154.

BROWN, G. W., BHROLCHAIN, M., & HARRIS, T. O. (1976). Social class and psychiatric disturbance among women in an urban population. *Sociology, 9,* 225–254.

BROWN, J. L. (1964). States in newborn infants. *Merrill-Palmer Quarterly, 10,* 313–327.

BROWN, J. V., & BAKEMAN, R. (1980). Relationships of human mothers with their infants during the first year of life: Effects of prematurity. In R. W. Bell & W. P. Smotherman (Eds.), *Maternal influences and early behavior* (pp. 353–373). New York: SP Medical and Scientific Books.

BROWN, R. W. (1957). Linguistic determinism and the part of speech. *Journal of Abnormal and Social Psychology, 55,* 1–5.

BROWN, R. W. (1973). *A first language: The early stages.* Cambridge, MA: Harvard University Press.

BROWN, R. W. (1977). Introduction. In C. E. Snow & C. A. Ferguson (Eds.), *Talking to children* (pp. 1–27). New York: Cambridge University Press.

BROWN, R. W., & HANLON, C. (1970). Derivational complexity and order of acquisition in child speech. In J. R. Hayes (Ed.), *Cognition and the development of language* (pp. 11–53). New York: Wiley.

BROWN, W. T., FRIEDMAN, E., & JENKINS, E. C. (1982). Association of fragile X syndrome with autism. *Lancet, 1,* 100.

BROWNELL, C. A. (1986). Convergent developments: Cognitive-developmental correlates of growth in infant/toddler peer skills. *Child Development, 57,* 275–286.

BRUCH, H. (1970). Juvenile obesity: Its courses and outcome. In C. V. Rowlan (Ed.), *Anorexia and obesity* (pp. 231–254). Boston: Little, Brown.

BRUCH, H. (1978). *The golden cage: The enigma of anorexia nervosa.* Cambridge: Harvard University Press.

BRUNER, J. S. (1974). The ontogenesis of speech acts. *Journal of Child Language, 2,* 1–19.

BRUNER, J. S. (1977). Early social interaction and language acquisition. In H. R. Schaffer (Ed.), *Studies in mother-infant interaction* (pp. 271–289). London: Academic Press.

BRUNER, J. S., JOLLY, A., & SYLVA, K. (Eds.) (1976). *Play—Its role in development and evolution.* New York: Penguin.

BRYAN, J. H., & WALBEK, N. (1970). Preaching and practicing self-sacrifice: Children's actions and reactions. *Child Development, 41,* 329–353.

BRYAN, J. H., & LONDON, P. (1970). Altruistic behavior by children. *Psychological Bulletin, 73,* 200–211.

BRYANT, B. K. (1982a). An index of empathy for children and adolescents. *Child Development, 53,* 413–425.

BRYANT, B. K. (1982b). Sibling relationships in middle childhood. In M. E. Lamb & B. Sutton-Smith (Eds.), *Sibling relationships: Their nature and significance across the life span* (pp. 87–121). Hillsdale, NJ: Erlbaum.

BRYANT, B. K. (1985). The neighborhood walk: Sources of support in middle childhood. *Monographs of the Society for Research in Child Development, 50* (3, Serial No. 210).

BRYANT, B. K., & CROCKENBERG, S. B. (1980). Correlates and dimensions of prosocial behavior: A study of female siblings with their mothers. *Child Development, 51,* 529–544.

BRYANT, P. E., & TRABASSO, T. (1971). Transitive inferences and memory in young children. *Nature, 232,* 456–458.

BUCKLEY, N., SIEGEL, L. S., & NESS, S. (1979). Egocentrism, empathy, and altruistic behavior in young children. *Developmental Psychology, 15,* 329–330.

BUHLER, C. (1930). *The first year of life.* New York: John Day.

BUKOWSKI, W. M., & NEWCOMB, A. F. (1984). Stability and determinants of sociometric status and friendship choice: A longitudinal perspective. *Developmental Psychology, 20,* 941–952.

BULATAO, R. A., & ARNOLD, F. (1977). Relationships between the value and cost of children and fertility: Cross-cultural evidence. Paper presented at the General Conference of the International Union for the Scientific Study of Population, Mexico City.

BULLOCK, D., & MERRILL, L. (1980). The impact of personal preference on consistency through time: The case of childhood aggression. *Child Development, 51,* 808–814.

BULLOCK, M. (1985). Animism in childhood thinking: A new look at an old question. *Developmental Psychology, 21,* 217–225.

BULLOCK, M., & RUSSELL, J. A. (1984). Preschool children's interpretation of facial expressions of emotion. *International Journal of Behavioral Development, 7,* 193–214.

BUMPAS, L. L. (1984). Children and marital disruption: A replication and update. *Demography, 21,* 71–82.

BURGESS, R. L., & CONGER, R. D. (1978). Family interaction in abusive, neglectful, and normal families. *Child Development, 49,* 1163–1173.

BURKE, B. S., BEAL, V. A., KIRKWOOD, S. B., & STUART, H. C. (1943). The influence of nutrition during pregnancy upon the conditions of the infant at birth. *Journal of Nutrition, 26,* 569–583.

BURTON, R. V. (1963). Generality of honesty reconsidered. *Psychological Review, 70,* 481–499.

BURTON, R. V. (1976). Honesty and dishonesty. In T. Lickona (Ed.), *Moral development and behavior: Theory, research, and social issues* (pp. 173–197). New York: Holt, Rinehart and Winston.

BUSHNELL, E. W. (1985). The decline of visually guided reaching during infancy. *Infant Behavior and Development, 8,* 139–155.

BUSHNELL, I. W. R., GERRY, G., & BURT, K. (1983). The externality effect in neonates. *Infant Behavior and Development, 6,* 151–156.

BUSS, A. H., & PLOMIN, R. (1975). *A temperament theory of personality development.* New York: Wiley.

BUSS, A. H., & PLOMIN, R. (1984). *Temperament: Early developing personality traits.* Hillsdale, NJ: Erlbaum.

BUSSEY, K., & BANDURA, A. (1984). Influence of gender constancy and social power on sex-linked modeling. *Journal of Personality and Social Psychology, 47,* 1292–1302.

BUSSEY, K., & PERRY, D. G. (1977). The imitation of resistance to deviation: Conclusive evidence for an elusive effect. *Developmental Psychology, 13,* 438–445.

BUTLER, N. R., & GOLDSTEIN, H. (1973). Smoking in pregnancy and subsequent child development. *British Medical Journal, 4,* 573–575.

BYERS, P., & BYERS, H. (1972). Non-verbal communication in the education of children. In C. Cazden, V. John, & D. Hymes (Eds.), *Functions of language in the classroom* (pp. 3–31). New York: Teachers College Press.

BYRD, D. M., & GHOLSON, B. (1985). Reading, memory, and metacognition. *Journal of Educational Psychology, 77,* 428–436.

BYRNE, D. F. (1973). The development of role taking in adolescence. *Dissertation Abstracts International, 34,* 5647B. (University Microfilms No. 74-11, 314)

BYRNE, M. C., & HAYDEN, E. (1980). *Topic maintenance and topic establishment in mother-child dialogue.* Paper presented at the meeting of the American Speech and Hearing Association, Detroit, MI.

CADORET, R. (1976). The genetics of affective disorders. In R. G. Grennell & S. Gabay (Eds.), *Biological foundations of psychiatry* (Vol. 2, pp. 645–652). New York: Raven Press.

CALFEE, R. C., CHAPMAN, R., & VENEZKY, R. (1972). How a child needs to think to learn to read. In L. Gregg (Ed.), *Cognition in learning and memory* (pp. 139–182). New York: Halsted Press.

CALFEE, R., & BROWN, R. (1979). Grouping students for instruction. In D. L. Duke (Ed.), *Classroom management* (78th yearbook of the National Society for the Study of Education, pp. 144–182). Chicago: University of Chicago Press.

CAMAIONI, L., & LAICARDI, C. (1985). Early social games and the acquisition of language. *British Journal of Developmental Psychology, 3,* 31–39.

CAMARATA, S., & LEONARD, L. B. (1986). Young children pronounce object words more accurately than action words. *Journal of Child Language, 13,* 51–65.

CAMPBELL, A. C. (1980). Friendship as a factor in male and female delinquency. In H. C. Foot, A. J. Chapman, & J. R. Smith (Eds.), *Friendship and social relations in children* (pp. 365–389). Chichester, Eng.: Wiley.

CAMPBELL, D. T., & STANLEY, J. C. (1966). *Experimental and quasi-experimental designs for research.* Chicago: Rand McNally.

CAMPBELL, P. F., & SCHWARTZ, S. S. (1986). Microcomputers in the preschool: Children, parents, and teachers. In P. Campbell & G. Fein (Eds.), *Young children and microcomputers* (pp. 45–60). Englewood Cliffs, NJ: Prentice-Hall.

CAMPBELL, S. B. (1973). Cognitive styles in reflective, impulsive and hyperactive boys and their mothers. *Perceptual and Motor Skills, 36,* 747–752.

CAMPOS, J. J., CAPLOVITZ, K. B., LAMB, M. E., GOLDSMITH, H. H., STENBERG, C. (1983). Socioemotional development. In M. M. Haith & J. J. Campos (Eds.), *Handbook of child psychology: Vol. 2. Infancy and developmental psychobiology* (4th ed., pp. 783–915). New York: Wiley.

CAMPOS, J. J., LANGER, A., & KROWITZ, A. (1970). Cardiac responses on the visual cliff in prelocomotor human infants. *Science, 170,* 196–197.

CAMPOS, J. J., & STENBERG, C. (1981). Perception, appraisal, and emotion: The onset of social referencing. In M. E. Lamb & L. R. Sherrod (Eds.), *Infant social cognition: Empirical and theoretical considerations* (pp. 273–314). Hillsdale, NJ: Erlbaum.

CANALE, J. R. (1977). The effect of modeling and length of ownership on sharing behavior of children. *Social Behavior and Personality, 5,* 187–191.

CANTER, R. J., & AGETON, S. S. (1984). The epidemiology of adolescent sex-role attitudes. *Sex Roles, 11,* 657–676.

CANTOR, J., & WILSON, B. J. (1984). Modifying fear responses to mass media in preschool and elementary school children. *Journal of Broadcasting, 28,* 431–443.

CAPELLI, C. A., & MARKMAN, E. M. (1980). *Children's sensitivity to incomprehensible material in written texts.* Unpublished manuscript, Stanford University.

CARDOSO-MARTINS, C., & MERVIS, C. B. (1985). Maternal speech to prelinguistic children with Down syndrome. *American Journal of Mental Deficiency, 89,* 451–458.

CAREW, J. V., & LIGHTFOOT, S. L. (1979). *Beyond bias: Perspectives on classrooms.* Cambridge, MA: Harvard University Press.

CAREY, S. (1978). The child as a word learner. In M. Halle, J. Bresnan, & G. Miller (Eds.), *Linguistic theory and psychological reality* (pp. 264–293). Cambridge, MA: MIT Press.

CAREY, S. (1985). *Conceptual change in childhood.* Cambridge, MA: MIT Press.

CAREY, W. B. (1982). Clinical use of temperament data in pediatrics. In R. Porter & G. M. Collins (Eds.), *Temperamental differences in infants and young children, Ciba Foundation Symposium 89* (pp. 191–202). London: Pitman.

CAREY, W. B., & McDEVITT, S. C. (1978). Revision of the Infant Temperament Questionnaire. *Pediatrics, 61,* 735–739.

CARLSON, B. E. (1984). The father's contribution to child care: Effects on children's perceptions of parental roles. *American Journal of Orthopsychiatry, 54,* 123–136.

CARLSON, C. L., LAHEY, B. B., & NEEPER, R. (1984). Peer assessment of the social behavior of accepted, rejected, and neglected children. *Journal of Abnormal Child Psychology, 12,* 189–198.

CARON, R. F., CARON, A. J., & MYERS, R. S. (1982). Abstraction of invariant face expressions in infancy. *Child Development, 53,* 1008–1015.

CARPENTER, C. J. (1983). Activity structure and play: Implications for socialization. In M. Liss (Eds.), *Social and cognitive skills: Sex roles and children's play* (pp. 117–145). New York: Academic Press.

CARPENTER, C. J., HUSTON, A. C., & HOLT, W. (1986). Modification of preschool sex-typed behaviors by participation in adult-structured activities. *Sex Roles, 14,* 603–615.

CARPENTER, C. J., & HUSTON-STEIN, A. (1980). Activity structure and sex-typed behavior in preschool children. *Child Development, 51,* 862–872.

CARPENTER, N. J., LEICHTMAN, L. G., & SAY, B. (1982). Fragile X-linked mental retardation. *American Journal of Diseases of Children, 136,* 392–398.

CARR, S., DABBS, J., & CARR, T. (1975). Mother-infant attachment: The importance of the mother's visual field. *Child Development, 46,* 331–338.

CARROLL, J. B. (1976). Psychometric tests as cognitive tasks: A new "structure of intellect." In L. B. Resnick (Ed.), *The nature of intelligence* (pp. 27–56). Hillsdale, NJ: Erlbaum.

CARROLL, J. B. (1981). Ability and task difficulty in cognitive psychology. *Educational Researcher, 10,* 11–21.

CARROLL, J. B. (1982). The measurement of intelligence. In R. J. Sternberg (Ed.), *Handbook of human intelligence* (pp. 29–120). Cambridge, Eng.: Cambridge University Press.

CARROLL, J. B., & MAXWELL, S. E. (1979). Individual differences in cognitive abilities. *Annual Review of Psychology, 30,* 603–640.

CARROLL, J. J., & GIBSON, E. J. (1981). *Infants' differentiation of an aperture and an obstacle.* Paper presented at the meeting of the Society for Research in Child Development, Boston.

CARROLL, J. J., & STEWARD, M. S. (1984). The role of cognitive development in children's understanding of their own feelings. *Child Development, 55,* 1486–1492.

CARTER, D. B., & PATTERSON, C. J. (1982). Sex roles as social conventions: The development of children's conceptions of sex-role stereotypes. *Developmental Psychology, 18,* 812–824.

CARTER, K., SABERS, D., CUSHING, K., PINNEGAR, S., & BERLINER, D. C. (1987). Processing and using information about students: A study of expert, novice, and postulant teachers. *Teaching & Teacher Education, 3,* 147–157.

CASE, R. (1972). Validation of a neo-Piagetian capacity construct. *Journal of Experimental Child Psychology, 14,* 287–302.

CASE, R. (1977). Responsiveness to conservation training as a function of induced subjective uncertainty, M-space, and cognitive style. *Canadian Journal of Behavioural Science, 9,* 12–25.

CASE, R. (1978). Intellectual development from birth to adulthood: A neo-Piagetian approach. In R. S. Siegler (Ed.), *Children's thinking: What develops?* (pp. 37–71). Hillsdale, NJ: Erlbaum.

CASE, R. (1985). *Intellectual development: A systematic reinterpretation.* New York: Academic Press.

CASE, R., KURLAND, D. M., & GOLDBERG, J. (1982). Operational efficiency and growth of short-term memory span. *Journal of Experimental Child Psychology, 33,* 386–404.

CASEY, M. B. (1986). Individual differences in selective attention among prereaders: A key to mirror-image confusions. *Developmental Psychology, 22,* 58–66.

CATTELL, J. McK. (1890). Mental tests and measurements. *Mind, 15,* 373–381.

CATTELL, R. B. (1963). Theory of fluid and crystallized intelligence: A critical experiment. *Journal of Educational Psychology, 54,* 1–22.

CATTELL, R. B. (1971). *Abilities: Their structure, growth and action.* Boston: Houghton Mifflin.

CAUCE, A. M. (1987). School and peer competence in early adolescence: A test of domain-specific self-perceived competence. *Developmental Psychology, 23,* 287–291.

CAVALLI-SFORZA, L. L. (1977). *Elements of human genetics.* Menlo Park, CA: W. A. Benjamin.

CAVIOR, N., & LOMBARDI, D. A. (1973). Developmental aspects of judgment of physical attractiveness of children. *Developmental Psychology, 8,* 67–71.

CECI, S. J., & BRONFENBRENNER, U. (1985). "Don't forget to take the cupcakes out of the oven": Prospective memory, strategic time-monitoring, and context. *Child Development, 56,* 152–164.

CECIL, M. A., & MEDWAY, F. J. (1986). Attribution retraining with low-achieving and learned helpless children. *Techniques: A Journal for Remedial Education and Counseling, 2,* 173–181.

CERNOCH, J. M., & PORTER, R. H. (1985). Recognition of maternal axillary odors by infants. *Child Development, 56,* 1593–1598.

CHANDLER, C. L. (1981). The effects of parenting techniques on the development of motivational orientations in children. *Dissertation Abstracts International, 42,* 4594B. (University Microfilms No. 82-09,943)

CHANDLER, M. J. (1973). Egocentrism and antisocial behavior: The assessment and training of social perspective-taking skills. *Developmental Psychology, 9,* 326–332.

CHANDLER, M. J., GREENSPAN, S., & BARENBOIM, C. (1973). Judgments of intentionality in response to videotaped and verbally presented moral dilemmas: The medium is the message. *Child Development, 44,* 315–320.

CHANDLER, M. J., & HELM, D. (1984). Developmental changes in the contribution of shared experience to social role-taking competence. *International Journal of Behavioral Development, 7,* 145–156.

CHAPIN, M., & DYCK, D. G. (1976). Persistence in children's reading behavior as a function of n length and attribution retraining. *Journal of Abnormal Psychology, 85,* 511–515.

CHAPMAN, K. L., LEONARD, L. B., & MERVIS, C. B. (1986). The effect of feedback on young children's inappropriate word usage. *Journal of Child Language, 13,* 101–117.

CHARLESWORTH, R., & HARTUP, W. W. (1967). Positive social reinforcement in the nursery school peer group. *Child Development, 38,* 993–1002.

CHARNEY, E., GOODMAN, H. C., MCBRIDE, M., BARBRO, L., & PRATT, R. (1976). Childhood antecedents of adult obesity: Do chubby infants become obese adults? *New England Journal of Medicine, 295,* 6–9.

CHASE-LANSDALE, P. L., & OWEN, M. T. (1987). Maternal employment in a family context: Effects on infant-mother and infant-father attachments. *Child Development, 58,* 1505–1512.

CHASSIN, L., PRESSON, C. C., MONTELLO, D., SHERMAN, S. J., & MCGREW, J. (1986). Changes in peer and parent influence during adolescence: Longitudinal versus cross-sectional perspectives on smoking initiation. *Developmental Psychology, 22,* 327–334.

CHERLIN, A. J. (1981). *Marriage, divorce and remarriage.* Cambridge, MA: Harvard University Press.

CHERRY, R. R., & EATON, E. L. (1977). Physical and cognitive development in children of low-income mothers working in the child's early years. *Child Development, 48,* 158–166.

CHESS, S., & THOMAS, A. (1984). *Origins and evolution of behavior disorders.* New York: Brunner/Mazel.

CHEYNE, J. A., & WALTERS, R. H. (1969). Intensity of punishment, timing of punishment and cognitive structure as determinants of response inhibition. *Journal of Experimental Child Psychology, 7,* 231–244.

CHI, M. T. H. (1978). Knowledge structures and memory development. In R. S. Siegler (Ed.), *Children's thinking: What develops?* (pp. 73–96). Hillsdale, NJ: Erlbaum.

CHI, M. T. H. (1982). Knowledge development and memory performance. In M. Friedman, J. P. Das, & N. O'Connor (Eds.), *Intelligence and learning* (pp. 221–229). New York: Plenum.

CHI, M. T. H., & KOESKE, R. D. (1983). Network representation of a child's dinosaur knowledge. *Developmental Psychology, 19,* 29–39.

CHILDS, B. (1965). Genetic origin of some sex differences among human beings. *Pediatrics, 35,* 798–812.

CHITTENDEN, G. E. (1942). An experimental study in measuring and modifying assertive behavior in young children. *Monographs of the Society for Research in Child Development, 7* (1, Serial No. 31).

CHOMSKY, C. (1969). *The acquisition of syntax in children from five to ten.* Cambridge, MA: MIT Press.

CHOMSKY, N. (1957). *Syntactic structures.* The Hague: Mouton.

CHOMSKY, N. (1959). Review of B. F. Skinner's Verbal Behavior. *Language, 35,* 26–129.

CHOMSKY, N. (1965). *Aspects of the theory of syntax.* Cambridge: MIT Press.

CHRISTIE, D. J., & SCHUMACHER, G. M. (1975). Developmental trends in the abstraction and recall of relevant versus irrelevant thematic information from connected verbal materials. *Child Development, 46,* 598–602.

CICERELLI, V. G., EVANS, J. W., & SCHILLER, J. S. (1969). *The impact of Head Start: An evaluation of the effects of Head Start on children's cognitive and affective development* (Vols. 1–2). Athens, OH: Westinghouse Learning Corporation and Ohio University.

CLANCY, P. (1985). Acquisition of Japanese. In D. I. Slobin (Ed.), *The cross-linguistic study of language acquisition: Vol. 1. The data.* (pp. 323–524). Hillsdale, NJ: Erlbaum.

CLARK, C. C. (1972). Race, identification, and television violence. In G. A. Comstock, E. A. Rubinstein, & J. B. Murray (Eds.), *Television and social behavior* (Vol. 5, pp. 120–184). Washington, DC: U.S. Government Printing Office.

CLARK, E. V. (1972). On the child's acquisition of antonyms in two semantic fields. *Journal of Verbal Learning and Verbal Behavior, 11,* 750–758.

CLARK, E. V. (1973a). Nonlinguistic strategies and the acquisition of word meanings. *Cognition, 2,* 161–182.

CLARK, E. V. (1973b). What's in a word? On the child's acquisition of semantics in his first language. In T. E. Moore (Ed.), *Cognitive development and the acquisition of language* (pp. 65–110). New York: Academic Press.

CLARK, E. V. (1978). Strategies for communicating. *Child Development, 49,* 977–987.

CLARK, E. V. (1980). Here's the top: Nonlinguistic strategies in the acquisition of orientational terms. *Child Development, 51,* 329–338.

CLARK, E. V. (1983). Meanings and concepts. In J. H. Flavell & E. M. Markman (Eds.), *Handbook of child psychology: Vol. 3. Cognitive development* (pp. 787–840). New York: Wiley.

CLARK, E. V., & HECHT, B. F. (1982). Learning to coin agent and instrument nouns. *Cognition, 12,* 1–24.

CLARK, M., & HAGER, M. (May 12, 1986). A breakthrough against CF? *Newsweek, 57*(19), 69.

CLARKE, A. M. (1984). Early experience and cognitive development. In E. W. Gordon (Ed.), *Review of research in education II* (pp. 125–161). Washington, DC: American Educational Research Association.

CLARKE-STEWART, K. A. (1973). Interactions between mothers and their young children: Characteristics and consequences. *Monographs of the Society for Research in Child Development, 38* (6–7, Serial No. 153).

CLARKE-STEWART, K. A. (1978). Recasting the Lone Stranger. In J. Glick & K. A. Clarke-Stewart (Eds.), *The development of social understanding* (pp. 109–176). New York: Gardner Press.

CLARKE-STEWART, K. A. (1980). The father's contribution to children's cognitive and social development in early childhood. In F. A. Pedersen (Ed.), *The father-infant relationship: Observational studies in a family setting* (pp. 111–146). New York: Praeger.

CLARKE-STEWART, K. A., & GRUBER, C. (1984). Day care forms and features. In R. C. Ainslie (Ed.), *The child and the day care setting* (pp. 35–62). New York: Praeger.

CLAUDY, J. G. (1984). The only child as a young adult: Results from Project Talent. In T. Falbo (Ed.), *The single-child family* (pp. 211–252). New York: Guilford.

CLAUSEN, J. A. (1966). Family structure, socialization, and personality. In L. W. Hoffman & M. L. Hoffman (Eds.), *Review of child development research* (Vol. 2, pp. 1–53), New York: Russell Sage Foundation.

CLAUSEN, J. A. (1975). The social meaning of differential physical and sexual maturation. In S. E. Dragastin & G. H. Elder (Eds.), *Adolescence in the life cycle: Psychological change and the social context.* (pp. 25–47). New York: Halsted.

CLEARY, T. A., HUMPHREYS, L. G., KENDRICK, S. A., & WESMAN, A. (1975). Educational uses of tests with disadvantaged students. *American Psychologist, 30,* 15–41.

CLEMENTS, D. H. (1986). Effects of Logo and CAI environments on cognition and creativity. *Journal of Educational Psychology, 78,* 309–318.

CLIATT, M. J. P., SHAW, J. M., & SHERWOOD, J. M. (1980). Effects of training on the divergent-thinking abilities of kindergarten children. *Child Development, 51,* 1061–1064.

CLIFTON, R. K., MORRONGIELLO, B. A., KULIG, J. W., & DOWD, J. M. (1981). Developmental changes in auditory localization in infancy. In R. N. Aslin, J. R. Alberts, & M. R. Petersen (Eds.), *Development of perception: Psychobiological perspectives: Vol. 1. Audition, somatic perception and the chemical senses* (pp. 141–160). New York: Academic Press.

CLINGEMPEEL, W. G., BRAND, E., AND IEVOLI, R. (1984). Stepparent-stepchild relationships in stepmother and stepfather families: A multimethod study. *Family Relations, 33,* 465–473.

CLINGEMPEEL, W. G., IEVOLI, R., & BRAND, E. (1985). Structural complexity and the quality of stepfather-stepchild relationships. *Family Process, 23,* 547–560.

CLINGEMPEEL, W. G., & REPUCCI, N. D. (1982). Joint custody after divorce: Major issues and goals for research. *Psychological Bulletin, 91,* 102–127.

CLINGEMPEEL, W. G., & SEGAL, S. (1986). Stepparent-stepchild relationships and the psychological adjustment of children in stepmother and stepfather families. *Child Development, 57,* 474–484.

COCHRAN, N. M., & BRASSARD, J. A. (1979). Child development and personal social networks. *Child Development, 50,* 601–616.

COHEN, F. L. (1984). *Clinical genetics in nursing practice.* Philadelphia: Lippincott.

COHEN, K. N., & CLARK, J. A. (1984). Transitional object attachments in early childhood and personality characteristics in later life. *Journal of Personality and Social Psychology, 46,* 106–111.

COHEN, L. B. (1981). Examination of habituation as a measure of aberrant infant development. In S. L. Friedman & M. Sigman (Eds.), *Preterm birth and psychological development* (pp. 241–253). New York: Academic Press.

COHEN, L. B., DELOACHE, J. S., & STRAUSS, M. S. (1979). Infant visual perception. In J. D. Osofsky (Ed.), *Handbook of infant development* (pp. 393–438). New York: Wiley.

COHEN, L. J., & CAMPOS, J. J. (1974). Father, mother, and stranger as elicitors of attachment behaviors in infancy. *Developmental Psychology, 10,* 146–154.

COHEN, S., GLASS, D. C., & SINGER, J. E. (1973). Apartment noise, auditory discrimination and reading ability. *Journal of Experimental Social Psychology, 9,* 407–422.

COHEN, S. E., & PARMELEE, A. H. (1983). Prediction of five-year Stanford-Binet scores in preterm infants. *Child Development, 54,* 1242–1253.

COIE, J. D., & DODGE, K. A. (1983). Continuities and changes in children's social status: A five-year longitudinal study. *Merrill-Palmer Quarterly, 29,* 261–282.

COIE, J. D., DODGE, K. A., & COPPOTELLI, H. (1982). Dimensions and types of social status: A cross-age perspective. *Developmental Psychology, 18,* 557–570.

COIE, J. D., & KREHBIEL, G. (1984). Effects of academic tutoring on the social status of low-achieving, socially rejected children. *Child Development, 55,* 1465–1478.

COIE, J. D., & KUPERSMIDT, J. B. (1983). A behavioral analysis of emerging social status in boys' groups. *Child Development, 54,* 1400–1416.

COKER, D. R. (1984). The relationships among gender concepts and cognitive maturity in preschool children. *Sex Roles, 10,* 19–31.

COLBY, A. KOHLBERG, L., FENTON, E., SPEICHER-DUBIN, B., & LIEBERMAN, M. (1977). Secondary school moral discussion programmes led by social studies teachers. *Journal of Moral Education, 6,* 90–111.

COLBY, A., KOHLBERG, L., GIBBS, J., & LIEBERMAN, M. (1983). A longitudinal study of moral judgment. *Monographs of the Society for Research in Child Development, 48* (1–2, Serial No. 200).

COLE, C. B., & LOFTUS, E. F. (1987). The memory of children. In S. J. Ceci, M. P. Toglia, & D. F. Ross (Eds.), *Children's eyewitness memory* (pp. 178–208). New York: Springer-Verlag.

COLE, M., FRANKEL, F., & SHARP, D. (1971). Development of free recall learning in children. *Developmental Psychology, 4,* 109–123.

COLE, M., & SCRIBNER, S. (1977). Cross-cultural studies of memory and cognition. In R. V. Kail, Jr., & J. W. Hagen (Eds.), *Perspectives on the development of memory and cognition* (pp. 239–271). Hillsdale, NJ: Erlbaum.

COLEMAN, J. S., CAMPBELL, E. Q., HOBSON, C. J., MCPARTLAND, J., MOOD, A. M., WEINFELD, F. D., & YORK, R. L. (1966). *Equality of educational opportunity.* Washington, DC: U. S. Government Printing Office.

COLES, R. (1977). *Children of crisis: Vol. 4. Eskimos, Chicanos, Indians.* Boston: Little, Brown.

COLLARD, R. (1971). Exploratory and play behaviors of infants reared in an institution and in lower and middle class homes. *Child Development, 42,* 1003–1015.

COLLETTA, N. D. (1979). Support systems after divorce: Incidence and impact. *Journal of Marriage and the Family, 41,* 837–846.

COLLINS, A., & STEVENS, A. (1982). Goals and strategies of inquiry teachers. In R. Glaser (Ed.), *Advances in instructional psychology* (Vol. 2, pp. 65–119). Hillsdale, NJ: Erlbaum.

COLLINS, E. (1981). Maternal and fetal effects of acetominophen and salicylates in pregnancies. *Obstetrics and Gynecology, 58,* 57S-61S.

COLLINS, W. A. (1973). Effect of temporal separation between motivation, aggression, and consequences: A developmental study. *Developmental Psychology, 8,* 215–221.

COLLINS, W. A. (1983). Children's processing of television content: Implications for prevention of negative effects. *Prevention in Human Services, 2,* 53–66.

COLLINS, W. A., BERNDT, T. J., & HESS, V. L. (1974). Observational learning of motives and consequences for television aggression: A developmental study. *Child Development, 45,* 799–802.

COLLINS, W. A., WELLMAN, H., KENISTON, A. H., & WESTBY, S. D. (1978). Age-related aspects of comprehension and inference from a televised dramatic narrative. *Child Development, 49,* 389–399.

COMBER, L. C., & KEEVES, J. P. (1973). *Science education in nineteen countries.* New York: Wiley.

CONDON, W. S., & SANDER, L. W. (1974). Synchrony demonstrated between movements of the neonate and adult speech. *Child Development, 45,* 456–462.

CONDRY, J., & CONDRY, S. (1976). Sex differences: A study of the eye of the beholder. *Child Development, 47,* 812–819.

CONDRY, J. C., & ROSS, D. F. (1985). Sex and aggression: The influence of gender label on the perception of aggression in children. *Child Development, 56,* 225–233.

CONNERS, C. K., GOYETTE, C. H., SOUTHWICK, D. A., LEES, J. M., & ANDRULONIS, P. A. (1976). Food additives and hyperkinesis: A controlled double-blind experiment. *Pediatrics, 58,* 154–166.

CONSTANZO, P. R., & WOODY, E. Z. (1979). Externality as a function of obesity in children: Pervasive style or eating-specific attribute? *Journal of Personality and Social Psychology, 37,* 2286–2296.

COOK, T. D., APPLETON, H., CONNER, R. F., SHAFFER, A., TAMKIN, G., & WEBER, S. J. (1975). *"Sesame Street" revisited.* New York: Russell Sage Foundation.

COOKE, R. A. (1982). The ethics and regulation of research involving children. In B. B. Wolman (Ed.), *Handbook of Developmental Psychology* (pp. 149–172). Englewood Cliffs, NJ: Prentice-Hall.

COOLEY, C. H. (1902). *Human nature and the social order.* New York: Scribner.

COOMBS, L. C. (1977). Preferences for sex of children among U.S. couples. *Family Planning Perspectives, 9,* 259–265.

COONEY, E. W., & SELMAN, R. L. (1978). Children's use of social conceptions: Toward a dynamic model of social cognition. In W. Damon (Ed.), *New directions for child development* (No. 1, pp. 23–44). San Francisco: Jossey-Bass.

COONS, S., & GUILLEMINAULT, C. (1984). Development of consolidated sleep and wakeful periods in relation to the day/night cycle in infancy. *Developmental Medicine and Child Neurology, 26,* 169–176.

COOPER, H. M. (1979). Pygmalion grows up: A model for teacher expectation communication and performance. *Review of Educational Research, 49,* 389–410.

COOPERSMITH, S. (1967). *The antecedents of self-esteem.* San Francisco: W. H. Freeman.

CORAH, N. L., ANTHONY, E. J., PAINTER, P., STERN, J. A., & THURSTON, D. L. (1965). Effects of perinatal anoxia after seven years. *Psychological Monographs. 79* (3, Whole No. 596).

CORDER-BOLZ, C. R. (1980). Mediation: The role of significant others. *Journal of Communication, 30*(3), 106–118.

CORDUA, G. D., McGRAW, K. O., & DRABMAN, R. S. (1979). Doctor or nurse: Children's perceptions of sex typed occupations. *Child Development, 50,* 590–593.

CORMAN, H. H., & ESCALONA, S. K. (1969). Stages of sensorimotor development: A replication study. *Merrill-Palmer Quarterly, 15,* 351–360.

CORNELL, E. H., & BERGSTROM, L. I. (1983). Serial-position effects in infants' recognition memory. *Memory and Cognition, 11,* 494–499.

CORNELL, E. H., & GOTTFRIED, A. W. (1976). Intervention with premature human infants. *Child Development, 47,* 32–39.

CORNO, L., & SNOW, R. E. (1986). Adapting teaching to individual differences among learners. In M. C. Wittrock (Ed.), *Handbook of research on teaching* (3rd ed., pp. 605–629). New York: MacMillan.

COUTURIER, L. C., MANSFIELD, R. S., & GALLAGHER, J. M. (1981). Relationships between humor, formal operational ability, and creativity in eighth graders. *Journal of Genetic Psychology, 139,* 221–226.

COWART, B. J. (1981). Development of taste perception in humans: Sensitivity and preference throughout the life span. *Psychological Bulletin, 90,* 43–73.

COX, T. (1983a). Disadvantaged 11-year-olds. Book supplement to *Journal of Child Psychology and Psychiatry, No. 3.* Oxford, Eng.: Pergamon.

COX, T. (1983b). Cumulative deficit in culturally disadvantaged children. *British Journal of Educational Psychology, 53,* 317–376.

CRAIK, F. I. M. (1970). The fate of primary items in free recall. *Journal of Verbal Learning and Verbal Behavior, 9,* 143–148.

CRAIK, F. I. M., & LOCKHART, R. S. (1972). Levels of processing: A framework for memory research. *Journal of Verbal Learning and Verbal Behavior, 11,* 671–684.

CRAIK, F. I. M., & TULVING, E. (1975). Depth of processing and the retention of words in episodic memory. *Journal of Experimental Psychology: General, 104,* 268–294.

CRAIN, W. C. (1980). *Theories of development.* Englewood Cliffs, NJ: Prentice-Hall.

CRANDALL, V. C. (1969). Sex differences in expectancy of intellectual and academic reinforcement. In C. P. Smith (Ed.), *Achievement-related motives in children* (pp. 11–45). New York: Russell Sage.

CRANDALL, V. C. (1978). Expecting sex differences and sex differences in expectancies. Paper presented at the meeting of the American Psychological Association, Toronto.

CRANO, W. D., KENNY, D. A., & CAMPBELL, D. T. (1972). Does intelligence cause achievement? A cross-lagged panel analysis. *Journal of Educational Psychology, 63,* 258–275.

CRAWLEY, S. B., & SPIKER, D. (1983). Mother-child interactions involving two-year-olds with Down syndrome: A look at individual differences. *Child Development, 54,* 1312–1323.

CREMIN, L. A. (1961). *The transformation of the school.* New York: Knopf.

CROCKENBERG, S. B. (1981). Infant irritability, mother responsiveness, and social support influences on the security of mother-infant attachment. *Child Development, 52,* 857–865.

CROCKENBERG, S. B. (1986). Are temperamental differences in babies associated with predictable differences in care-giving? In J. V. Lerner & R. M. Lerner (Eds.), New directions for child development (No. 31, pp. 53–74). San Francisco: Jossey-Bass.

CROCKENBERG, S. B., & NICOLAYEV, J. (1979). Stage transition in moral reasoning as related to conflict experienced in naturalistic settings. *Merrill-Palmer Quarterly, 25,* 185–192.

CROOK, C. K. (1978). Taste perception in the newborn infant. *Infant Behavior and Development, 1,* 52–69.

CROOK, C. K., & LIPSITT, L. P. (1976). Neonatal nutritive sucking: Effects of taste stimulation upon sucking rhythm and heart rate. *Child Development, 47,* 518–522.

CROSS, T. G. (1978). Mothers' speech and its association with rate of linguistic development in young children. In N. Waterson & C. E. Snow (Eds.), *The development of communication* (pp. 199–216). New York: Wiley.

CUMMINGS, E. M., IANNOTTI, R. J., & ZAHN-WAXLER, C. (1985). Influence of conflict between adults on the emotions and aggression of young children. *Developmental Psychology, 21,* 495–507.

CUMMINGS, S., & TAEBEL, D. (1980). Sexual inequality and the reproduction of consciousness: An analysis of sex-role stereotyping among children. *Sex Roles, 6,* 631–644.

CUMMINS, J. (1978). Metalinguistic development of children in bilingual education programs: Data from Irish and Canadian Ukranian-English programs. In M. Paradis (Ed.), *The Fourth Locus Forum 1977* (pp. 127–138). Columbia, SC: Hornbeam.

CUNEO, D. O. (1980). A general strategy for quantity judgments: The height and width rule. *Child Development, 50,* 170–179.

CURTISS, S. (1977). *Genie: A psycholinguistic study of a modern-day "wild child."* New York: Academic Press.

CUSHNER, I. M. (1981). Maternal behavior and perinatal risks: Alcohol, smoking, and drugs. *Annual Review of Public Health, 2,* 201–218.

CUTRONA, C. E., & FESHBACH, S. (1979). Cognitive and behavioral correlates of children's differential use of social information. *Child Development, 50,* 1036–1042.

CYTRYN, L., McKNEW, D. H., ZAHN-WAXLER, C., & GERSHON, E. S. (1985). Developmental issues in risk research: The offspring of affectively ill parents. In M. Rutter, C. E. Izard, & P. B. Read (Eds.), *Depression in young people: Developmental and clinical perspectives* (pp. 163–188). New York: Guilford.

DAEHLER, M. W., & BUKATKO, D. (1977). Recognition memory for pictures in very young children: Evidence from attentional preferences using a continuous presentation procedure. *Child Development, 48,* 693–696.

DAMON, W. (1977). *The social world of the child.* San Francisco: Jossey-Bass.

DAMON, W. (1984). Peer education: The untapped potential. *Journal of Applied Developmental Psychology 5,* 331–343.

DANNER, F. W., & LONKEY, E. (1981). A cognitive-developmental approach to the effects of rewards on intrinsic motivation. *Child Development, 52,* 1043–1052.

DANSKY, J. L. (1980). Make-believe: A mediator of the relationship between play and associative fluency. *Child Development, 51,* 576–579.

DANSKY, J. L., & SILVERMAN, I. W. (1975). Play: A general facilitator of associative fluency. *Developmental Psychology, 11,* 104.

DARVILL, D., & CHEYNE, J. A. (1981). Sequential analysis of responses to aggression: Age and sex effects. Paper presented at the meeting of the Society for Research in Child Development, Boston.

DARWIN, C. (1936). *The descent of man.* New York: Modern Library. (Original work published 1871)

DARWIN, C. (1936). *The origin of species.* New York: Modern Library. (Original work published 1859)

DAVID, H. P., & BALDWIN, W. P. (1979). Childbearing and child development: Demographic and psychosocial trends. *American Psychologist, 34,* 866–871.

DAVIS, K. (1947). A final note on a case of extreme deprivation. *American Journal of Sociology, 45,* 554–565.

DAVITZ, J. F. (1955). Social perception and sociometric choice in children. *Journal of Abnormal and Social Psychology, 50,* 173–176.

DAY, B., & HUNT, G. H. (1975). Multiage classrooms: An analysis of verbal communication. *Elementary School Journal, 75,* 458–466.

DEAN, A. L. (1976). The structure of imagery. *Child Development, 47,* 949–958.

DEAUX, K. (1985). Sex and gender. In M. R. Rosenzweig & L. W. Porter (Eds.), *Annual review of psychology* (Vol. 36, pp. 49–81). Palo Alto, CA: Annual Reviews, Inc.

DEAUX, K., & LEWIS, L. L. (1984). Structure of gender stereotypes: Interrelationships among components and gender label. *Journal of Personality and Social Psychology, 46,* 991–1004.

DeCASPER, A. J., & FIFER, W. P. (1980). Of human bonding: Newborns prefer their mothers' voices. *Science, 208,* 1174–1176.

DEGELMAN, D., FREE, J. U., SCARLATO, M., BLACKBURN, J. M., & GOLDEN, T. (1986). Concept learning in preschool children: Effects of a short-term Logo experience. *Journal of Educational Computing Research, 2,* 199–205.

DeLISI, R., & STAUDT, J. (1980). Individual differences in college students' performance on formal operational tasks. *Journal of Applied Developmental Psychology, 1,* 201–208.

DeLOACHE, J. S., SUGARMAN, S., & BROWN, A. L. (1981). *Self-correction strategies in early cognitive development.* Paper presented at the meeting of the Society for Research in Child Development, Boston.

DeLONE, R. (1982). Early childhood development as a policy goal: An overview of choices. In L. A. Bond & J. M. Joffe (Eds.), *Facilitating infant and early childhood development* (pp. 485–502). Hanover, NH: University Press of New England.

DELUTY, R. H. (1985). Consistency of assertive, aggressive, and submissive behavior for children. *Journal of Personality and Social Psychology, 49,* 1054–1065.

DEMBROSKI, T. M., MacDOUGALL, J. M., HERD, J. A., & SHIELDS, J. L. (1979). Effect of level of challenge on pressor and heart rate responses in Type A and Type B subjects. *Journal of Applied Social Psychology, 9,* 209–228.

DENNIS, W. (1960). Causes of retardation among institutionalized children: Iran. *Journal of Genetic Psychology, 96,* 47–59.

DENNIS, W. (1973). *Children of the Creche.* New York: Appleton-Century-Crofts.

DENNIS, W., & DENNIS, M. G. (1940). The effect of cradling practices upon the onset of walking in Hopi children. *Journal of Genetic Psychology, 56,* 77–86.

DENNIS, W., & NAJARIAN, P. (1957). Infant development under environmental handicap. *Psychological Monographs, 71* (7, Whole No. 436).

DeSTEFANO, C. T., & MUELLER, E. (1982). Environmental determinants of peer social activity in 18-month-old males. *Infant Behavior and Development, 5,* 175–183.

DEUTSCH, F. (1974). Observational and sociometric measures of peer popularity and their relationship to egocentric communication in female preschoolers. *Developmental Psychology, 10,* 745–747.

DEUTSCH, F., & STEIN, A. H. (1972). The effects of personal responsibility and task interruption on the private speech of preschoolers. *Human Development, 15,* 310–324.

DEUTSCH, W., & PECHMANN, T. (1982). Social interaction and the development of definite descriptions. *Cognition, 11,* 159–184.

DEVEREUX, E. C. (1970). The role of the peer group experience in moral development. In J. P. Hill (Ed.), *Minnesota Symposium on Child Psychology* (Vol. 4, pp. 94–140). Minneapolis: University of Minnesota Press.

de VILLIERS, J. G., & de VILLIERS, P. A. (1973a). Development of the use of word order in comprehension. *Journal of Psycholinguistic Research, 2,* 331–341.

de VILLIERS, J. G., & de VILLIERS, P. A. (1973b). A cross-sectional study of the acquisition of grammatical morphemes in child speech. *Journal of Psycholinguistic Research, 2,* 267–278.

de VILLIERS, J. G., & de VILLIERS, P. A. (1978). *Language acquisition.* Cambridge, MA: Harvard University Press.

de VILLIERS, P. A., & de VILLIERS, J. G. (1979). Form and function in the development of sentence negation. *Papers and Reports on Child Language Development, 13,* 118–125.

DEVIN-SHEEHAN, L., FELDMAN, R. S., & ALLEN, V. L. (1976). Research on children tutoring children: A critical review. *Review of Educational Research, 46,* 355–385.

de VRIES, B., & WALKER, L. J. (1986). Moral reasoning and attitudes toward capital punishment. *Developmental Psychology, 22,* 509–513.

DeVRIES, R. (1969). Constancy of gender identity in the years three to six. *Monographs of the Society for Research in Child Development, 34* (3, Serial No. 127).

DeVRIES, R. (1974). Relationship among Piagetian, IQ, and achievement assessments. *Child Development, 45,* 746–756.

DEWEY, J. (1963). *Experience and education.* New York: MacMillan. (Originally published 1938)

DEWEY, J. (1966). *Democracy and education.* New York: Free Press. (Originally published 1916)

DIAMOND, M. (1982). Sexual identity, monozygotic twins reared in discordant sex roles and a BBC follow-up. *Archives of Sexual Behavior, 11,* 181–186.

DIAZ, R. M. (1983). Thought and two languages: The impact of bilingualism on cognitive development. *Review of Research in Education, 10,* 23–54.

DIAZ, R. M. (1985). Bilingual cognitive development: Addressing three gaps in current research. *Child Development, 56,* 1376–1388.

DIAZ, R. M., & BERNDT, T. J. (1982). Children's knowledge of a best friend: Fact or fancy. *Developmental Psychology, 18,* 787–794.

DICK-READ, G. (1959). *Childbirth without fear.* New York: Harper & Brothers.

DICKIE, J. (1973). Private speech: The effect of presence of others, task and interpersonal variables. *Dissertation Abstracts International, 34,* 1292B. (University Microfilms No. 73-20, 329)

DICKINSON, D. K. (1984). First impressions: Children's knowledge of words gained from a single exposure. *Applied Psycholinguistics, 5,* 359–373.

DIENER, C. I., & DWECK, C. S. (1978). An analysis of learned helplessness: Continuous changes in performance, strategy, and achievement cognitions following failure. *Journal of Personality and Social Psychology, 36,* 451–462.

DIENER, C. I., & DWECK, C. S. (1980). An analysis of learned helplessness: II. The processing of success. *Journal of Personality and Social Psychology, 39,* 940–952.

DIRKS, J. (1982). The effect of a commercial game on children's Block Design scores on the WISC-R test. *Intelligence, 6,* 109–123.

DIRKS, J., & GIBSON, E (1977). Infants' perception of similarity between live people and their photographs. *Child Development, 48,* 124–130.

DITTRICHOVA, J., BRICHACEK, V., PAUL, K., & TAUTERMANNOVA, M. (1982). The structure of infant behavior: An analysis of sleep and waking in the first months of life. In W. W. Hartup (Ed.), *Review of child development research* (Vol. 6, pp. 73–100). Chicago: University of Chicago Press.

DIVINE-HAWKINS, P. (1981). *Family day care in the United States: National day care home study final report, executive summary.* Washington, DC: U.S. Government Printing Office.

DiVITTO, B., & GOLDBERG, S. (1979). The effect of newborn medical status on early parent-infant interaction. In T. Field, A. Sostek, S. Goldberg, & H. H. Shuman (Eds.), *Infants born at risk: Behavior and development* (pp. 311–322). Jamaica, NY: Spectrum.

DIXON, R. A., & LERNER, R. M. (1984). A history of systems in developmental psychology. In M. Bornstein & M. Lamb (Eds.), *Developmental psychology: An advanced textbook* (pp. 1–35). Hillsdale, NJ: Lawrence Erlbaum.

DOBSON, J. C., KUSHIDA, E., WILLIAMSON, M., & FRIEDMAN, E. (1976). Intellectual performance of 36 phenylketonuria patients and their nonaffected siblings. *Pediatrics, 58,* 53–56.

DODD, B. J. (1972). Effects of social and vocal stimulation on infant babbling. *Developmental Psychology, 7,* 80–83.

DODGE, K. A. (1980). Social cognition and children's aggressive behavior. *Child Development, 51,* 162–170.

DODGE, K. A. (1983). Behavioral antecedents of peer social status. *Child Development, 54,* 1386–1399.

DODGE, K. A. (1986). A social information processing model of social competence in children. In M. Perlmutter (Ed.), *Minnesota Symposia on Child Psychology* (Vol. 18, pp. 77–125). Hillsdale, NJ: Erlbaum.

DODGE, K. A., COIE, J. D., & BRAKKE, N. P. (1982). Behavior patterns of socially rejected and neglected preadolescents: The roles of social approach and aggression. *Journal of Abnormal Child Psychology, 10,* 389–410.

DODGE, K. A., & FRAME, C. L. (1983). Social cognitive biases and deficits in aggressive boys. *Child Development, 53,* 620–635.

DODGE, K. A., MURPHY, R. R., & BUCHSBAUM, K. (1984). The assessment of intention-cue detection skills in children: Implications for developmental psychopathology. *Child Development, 55,* 163–173.

DODGE, K. A., PETTIT, G. S., McCLASKEY, C. L., & BROWN, M. M. (1986). Social competence in children. *Monographs of the Society for Research in Child Development, 51* (2, Serial No. 213).

DODGE, K. A., SCHLUNDT, D. C., SCHOCKEN, I., & DELUGACH, J. D. (1983). Social competence and children's sociometric status: The role of peer group entry strategies. *Merrill-Palmer Quarterly, 29,* 309–336.

DODGE, K. A., & SOMBERG, D. R. (1987). Hostile attributional biases among aggressive boys are exacerbated under conditions of threats to the self. *Child Development, 58,* 213–224.

DODWELL, P. C., MUIR, D., & DiFRANCO, D. (1976). Responses of infants to visually presented objects. *Science, 194,* 209–211.

DOLGIN, K. G., & BEHREND, D. A. (1984). Children's knowledge about animates and inanimates. *Child Development, 55,* 1646–1650.

DOLLAGHAN, C. (1985). Child meets word: "Fast mapping" in preschool children. *Journal of Speech and Hearing Research, 28,* 449–454.

DOLLARD, J., DOOB, L. W., MILLER, N. E., MOWRER, O. H., & SEARS, R. R. (1939). *Frustration and aggression.* New Haven, CN: Yale University Press.

DONALDSON, M. (1978). *Children's minds.* Glasgow, Scot.: Collins.

DORE, J. (1974). A pragmatic description of early language development. *Journal of Psycholinguistic Research, 4,* 423–430.

DORE, J. (1985). Holophrases revisited: Their logical development from dialog. In M. D. Barrett (Ed.), *Children's single-word speech* (pp. 23–58). Chichester, Eng.: Wiley.

DORNBUSCH, S. M., CARLSMITH, J. M., BUSHWALL, S. J., RITTER, P. L., LEIDERMAN, H., HASTORF, A. H., & GROSS, R. T. (1985). Single parents, extended households, and the control of adolescents. *Child Development, 56,* 326–341.

DORNBUSCH, S. M., RITTER, P. L., LEIDERMAN, P. H., ROBERTS, D. F., & FRALEIGH, M. J. (1987). The relation of parenting style to adolescent school performance. *Child Development, 58,* 1244–1257.

DORR, A., GRAVES, S. B., & PHELPS, E. (1980). Television literacy for young children. *Journal of Communication, 30*(3), 71–83.

DORR, A., & KOVARIC, P. (1980). Some of the people some of the time — But which people? Televised violence and its effects. In E. L. Palmer & A. Dorr (Eds.), *Children and the faces of television: Teaching, violence, selling* (pp. 183–199). New York: Academic Press.

DORTZBACH, J. R. (1975). Moral judgment and perceived locus of control: A cross-sectional developmental study of adults, aged 25–74. *Dissertation Abstracts International, 36,* 4662B. (University Microfilms No. 76-05, 160)

DOSSEY, J. A., MULLIS, I. V. S., LINDQUIST, M. M., & CHAMBERS D. L. (1988). *The Mathematics Report Card: Are we measuring up?* Princeton, NJ: Educational Testing Service.

DOUGLAS, V. I. (1980). Treatment and training approaches to hyperactivity: Establishing internal or external control? In C. K. Whalen & B. Henker (Eds.), *Hyperactive children: The social ecology of identification and treatment* (pp. 238–317). New York: Academic Press.

DOUGLAS, V. I., BARR, R. G., O'NEILL, M. E., & BRITTON, B. G. (1986). Short term effects of methylphenidate on the cognitive, learning and academic performance of children with attention deficit disorder in the laboratory and the classroom. *Journal of Child Psychology and Psychiatry, 27,* 191–211.

DOUGLAS, V. I., & PETERS, K. G. (1979). Toward a clearer definition of the attentional deficit of hyperactive children. In G. A. Hale & M. Lewis (Eds.), *Attention and cognitive development* (pp. 173–247). New York: Plenum.

DOUVAN, E. (1963). Employment and the adolescent. In F. I. Nye & L. W. Hoffman (Eds.), *The employed mother in America* (pp. 142–164). Chicago: Rand McNally.

DOUVAN, E., & ADELSON, J. (1966). *The adolescent experience.* New York: Wiley.

DOWD, J. M., & TRONICK, E. Z. (1986). Temporal coordination of arm movements in early infancy: Do infants move in synchrony with adult speech? *Child Development, 57,* 762–776.

DOWNS, W. R. (1985). Using panel data to examine sex differences in causal relationships among adolescent alcohol use, norms, and peer alcohol use. *Journal of Youth and Adolescence, 14,* 469–486.

DOYLE, A. (1975). Infant development in day care. *Developmental Psychology, 11,* 655–656.

DOYLE, A., CONNOLLY, J., & RIVEST, L. (1980). The effects of playmate familiarity on the social interactions of young children. *Child Development, 51,* 217–223.

DRABMAN, R. S., CORDUA, G. D., HAMMER, D., JARVIE, G. J., & HORTON, W. (1979). Developmental trends in eating rates of normal and overweight preschool children. *Child Development, 50,* 211–216.

DRABMAN, R. S., & THOMAS, M. H. (1976). Does watching violence on television cause apathy? *Pediatrics, 57,* 329–331.

DREYFUS-BRISAC, C. (1970). Ontogenesis of sleep in human prematures after 32 weeks of conceptional age. *Developmental Psychobiology, 3,* 91–121.

DUCK, S. W. (1975). Personality similarity and friendship choices by adolescents. *European Journal of Social Psychology, 5,* 351–365.

DUDYCHA, G. J., & DUDYCHA, M. M. (1941). Childhood memories: A review of the literature. *Psychological Bulletin, 36,* 34–50.

DUNN, J., & KENDRICK, C. (1980). The arrival of a sibling: Changes in patterns of interaction between mothers and first-born child. *Journal of Child Psychology and Psychiatry, 21,* 119–132.

DUNN, J., & KENDRICK, C. (1982). *Siblings: Love, envy and understanding.* Cambridge, MA: Harvard University Press.

DUNST, C. J., & LINDERFELT, B. (1985). Maternal ratings of temperament and operant learning in two- to three-month-old infants. *Child Development, 56,* 555–563.

DURRETT, M. E., OTAKI, M., & RICHARDS, P. (1984). Attachment and the mother's perception of support from the father. *International Journal of Behavioral Development, 7,* 167–176.

DUVALL, E. M. (1946). Conceptions of parenthood. *American Journal of Sociology, 57,* 193–203.

DWECK, C. S. (1975). The role of expectations and attributions in the alleviation of learned helplessness. *Journal of Personality and Social Psychology, 31,* 674–685.

DWECK, C. S. (1983). Achievement motivation. In P. H. Mussen (Ed.), *Handbook of child psychology: Vol. 4. Socialization, personality, and social development* (pp. 643–691). New York: Wiley.

DWECK, C. S. (1986). Motivational processes affecting learning. *American Psychologist, 41,* 1040–1048.

DWECK, C. S., DAVIDSON, W., NELSON, S., & ENNA, B. (1978). Sex differences in learned helplessness: II. The contingencies of evaluative feedback in the classroom and III. An experimental analysis. *Developmental Psychology, 14,* 268–276.

DWECK, C. S., & ELLIOTT, E. S. (1983). Achievement motivation. In E. M. Hetherington (Ed.), *Handbook of child psychology:* Vol. 4. *Socialization, personality, and social development* (4th ed., pp. 643–691). New York: Wiley.

DWECK, C. S., & GILLIARD, D. (1975). Expectancy statements as determinants of reactions to failure: Sex differences in persistence and expectancy change. *Journal of Personality and Social Psychology, 32,* 1077–1084.

DWECK, C. S., GOETZ, T. E., & STRAUSS, N. L. (1980). Sex differences in learned helplessness: IV. An experimental and naturalistic study of failure generalization and its mediators. *Journal of Personality and Social Psychology, 38,* 441–452.

DWECK, C. S., & LICHT, B. G. (1980). Learned helplessness and intellectual achievement. In J. Garber & M. E. P. Seligman (Eds.), *Human helplessness: theory and applications* (pp. 197–221). New York: Academic Press.

DWECK, C. S., & REPPUCCI, N. D. (1973). Learned helplessness and reinforcement responsibility in children. *Journal of Personality and Social Psychology, 25,* 109–116.

DWYER, C. A. (1973). Sex differences in reading: An evaluation and a critique of current theories. *Review of Educational Research, 43,* 455–467.

DWYER, C. A. (1974). Influence of children's sex role standards on reading and arithmetic achievement. *Journal of Educational Psychology, 66,* 811–816.

EASTERBROOKS, M. A., & GOLDBERG, W. A. (1985). Effects of early maternal employment on toddlers, mothers, and fathers. *Developmental Psychology, 21,* 774–783.

EBEL, R. L. (1975). Educational tests: Valid? Biased? Useful? *Phi Delta Kappan, 57,* 83–89.

ECKERMAN, C. O., & WHATLEY, J. L. (1977). Toys and social interaction between infant peers. *Child Development, 48,* 1645–1656.

ECKERMAN, C. O., WHATLEY, J. L., & KUTZ, S. L. (1975). Growth of social play with peers during the second year of life. *Developmental Psychology, 11,* 42–49.

EDELBROCK, C., & SUGAWARA, A. I. (1978). Acquisition of sex-typed preferences in preschool-aged children. *Developmental Psychology, 14,* 614–623.

EDELMAN, M. S., & OMARK, D. R. (1973). Dominance hierarchies in young children. *Social Science Information, 12,* 103–110.

EDELMAN, M. W. (1981). Who is for children? *American Psychologist, 36,* 109–116.

Educational Research Service (1980). *Class size: A critique of recent meta-analyses.* Arlington, VA: Educational Research Service.

EDWARDS, C. P. (1978). Social experiences and moral judgment in Kenyan young adults. *Journal of Genetic Psychology, 133,* 19–30.

EDWARDS, C. P. (1981). The comparative study of the development of moral judgment and reasoning. In R. L. Munroe, R. Munroe, & B. B. Whiting (Eds.), *Handbook of cross-cultural human development* (pp. 501–528). New York: Garland.

EGELAND, B. (1974). Training impulsive children in the use of more efficient scanning techniques. *Child Development, 45,* 165–171.

EGELAND, B., & FARBER, E. (1984). Infant-mother attachment: Factors related to its development and changes over time. *Child Development, 55,* 753–771.

EGELAND, B., & SROUFE, L. A. (1981). Attachment and early maltreatment. *Child Development, 52,* 44–52.

EGELAND, B., & SROUFE, L. A. (1981). Developmental sequelae of maltreatment in infancy. In R. Rizley & D. Cicchetti (Eds.), *New directions for child development* (No. 11, pp. 77–92). San Francisco: Jossey-Bass.

EHRHARDT, A. A. (1975). Prenatal hormone exposure and psychosexual differentiation. In E. J. Sachar (Ed.), *Topics in psychoendocrinology* (pp. 67–82). New York: Grune & Stratton.

EHRHARDT, A. A., & BAKER, S. W. (1974). Fetal androgens, human central nervous system differentiation, and behavior sex differences. In R. C. Friedman, R. M. Richart, & R. L. VandeWiele (Eds.), *Sex differences in behavior* (pp. 33–51). New York: Wiley.

EHRHARDT, A. A., EPSTEIN, R., & MONEY, J. (1968). Fetal androgens and female gender identity in the early treated adrenogenital syndrome. *Johns Hopkins Medical Journal, 122,* 160–167.

EHRI, L. C. (1979). Linguistic insight: Threshold of reading acquisition. In T. G. Waller & G. E. MacKinnon (Eds.), *Reading research: Advances in theory and practice* (Vol. 1, pp. 63–114). New York: Harcourt Brace Jovanovich.

EID, E. E. (1970). Follow up study of physical growth of children who had excessive weight gain in first six months of life. *British Medical Journal, 2,* 74–76.

EIMAS, P. D., SIQUELAND, E. R., JUSCZYK, P., & VIGORITO, J. (1971). Speech perception in infants. *Science, 171,* 303–306.

EIMAS, P. D., & TARTTER, V. C. (1979). The development of speech perception. In H. W. Reese & L. P. Lipsitt (Eds.), *Advances in child development and behavior* (Vol. 13, pp. 155–193). New York: Academic Press.

EISENBERG, N. (1982). The development of reasoning regarding prosocial behavior. In N. Eisenberg (Ed.), *The development of prosocial behavior* (pp. 219–249). New York: Academic Press.

EISENBERG, N., & LENNON, R. (1983). Sex differences in empathy and related capacities. *Psychological Bulletin, 94,* 100–131.

EISENBERG, N., LENNON, R., & PASTERNACK, J. F. (1986). Altruistic values and moral judgment. In N. Eisenberg (Ed.), *Altruistic emotion, cognition, and behavior* (pp. 115–159). Hillsdale, NJ: Erlbaum.

EISENBERG, N., LENNON, R., & ROTH, K. (1983). Prosocial development: A longitudinal study. *Developmental Psychology, 19,* 846–855.

EISENBERG, N., SHELL, R., PASTERNACK, J., LENNON, R., BELLER, R., & MATHY, R. M. (1987). Prosocial development in middle childhood: A longitudinal study. *Developmental Psychology, 23,* 712–718.

EISENBERG-BERG, N. (1979). Development of children's prosocial moral judgment. *Developmental Psychology, 15,* 128–137.

EISENBERG-BERG, N., & HAND, M. (1979). The relationship of preschoolers' reasoning about prosocial moral conflicts to prosocial behavior. *Child Development, 50,* 356–363.

EISENBERG-BERG, N., & NEAL, C. (1979). Children's moral reasoning about their own spontaneous prosocial behavior. *Developmental Psychology, 15,* 228–229.

EISENBERG-BERG, N., & ROTH, K. (1980). The development of children's prosocial moral judgment: A longitudinal follow-up. *Developmental Psychology, 16,* 375–376.

EKMAN, P., & FRIESEN, W. (1972). Constants across culture in the face and emotion. *Journal of Personality and Social Psychology, 17,* 124–129.

EKMAN, P., & OSTER, H. (1979). Facial expressions of emotion. *Annual Review of Psychology, 30,* 527–554.

EKMAN, P., SORENSON, E., & FRIESEN, W. (1969). Pancultural elements in the facial expression of emotion. *Science, 164,* 86–88.

ELARDO, R., BRADLEY, R., & CALDWELL, B. M. (1975). The relation of infants' home environments to mental test performance from six to thirty-six months: A longitudinal analysis. *Child Development, 46,* 71–76.

ELARDO, R., BRADLEY, R., & CALDWELL, B. M. (1977). A longitudinal study of the relation of infants' home environments to language development at age 3. *Child Development, 48,* 595–603.

ELBERS, L., & TON, J. (1985). Play pen monologues: The interplay of words and babbles in the first words period. *Journal of Child Language, 12,* 551–565.

ELDER, G. H. (1974). *Children of the Great Depression.* Chicago: University of Chicago Press.

ELDER, G. H., LIKER, J. K., & CROSS, C. E. (1984). Parent-child behavior in the Great Depression: Life course and intergenerational influences. In P. B. Baltes & O. G. Brim (Eds.), *Life-span development and behavior* (Vol. 6, pp. 109–158). New York: Academic Press.

ELDER, G. H., NGUYEN, T. V., & CASPI, A. (1985). Linking family hardship to children's lives. *Child Development, 56,* 361–375.

ELDER, J. L., & PEDERSON, D. R. (1978). Preschool children's use of objects in symbolic play. *Child Development, 49,* 500–504.

ELKIND, D. (1971). Two approaches to intelligence: Piagetian and psychometric. In D. R. Green, M. P. Ford, & G. B. Flamer (Eds.), *Measurement and Piaget* (pp. 12–28). New York: McGraw-Hill.

ELKIND, D. (1974). *A sympathetic understanding of the child.* Boston: Allyn & Bacon.

ELKIND, D. (1976). *Child development and education.* New York: Oxford.

ELKIND, D. (1981). *Children and adolescents: Interpretive essays on Jean Piaget* (3rd ed.). New York: Oxford.

ELLIOT, R., & VASTA, R. (1970). The modeling of sharing: Effects associated with vicarious reinforcement, symbolization, age, and generalization. *Journal of Experimental Child Psychology, 10,* 8–15.

ELLIS, S., ROGOFF, B., & CROMER, C. (1981). Age segregation in children's social interactions. *Developmental Psychology, 17,* 399–407.

ELLISON, P. T. (1982). Skeletal growth, fatness, and menarcheal age: A comparison of two hypotheses. *Human Biology, 54,* 269–281.

ELSTER, A. B., & PANZARINE, S. (1983). Adolescent fathers. In E. R. McAnarney (Ed.), *Premature adolescent pregnancy and parenthood* (pp. 231–252). New York: Grune & Stratton.

EMDE, R. N. (1980). Toward a psychoanalytic theory of affect. I. The organizational model and its propositions. In S. Greenspan & G. Pollock (Eds.), *The course of life: Psychoanalytic contributions toward understanding personality development* (pp. 85–112). Washington, DC: U.S. Government Printing Office.

EMDE, R. N. (1983). The prerepresentational self and its affective core. *The Psychoanalytic Study of the Child, 38,* 165–192.

EMDE, R. N., GAENSBAUER, T. J., & HARMON, R. J. (1976). Emotional expression in infancy: A biobehavioral study. *Psychological Issues* (Vol. 10, No. 37). New York: International Universities Press.

EMDE, R. N., & KOENIG, K. L. (1969). Neonatal smiling and rapid eye movement states. *American Academy of Child Psychiatry, 8,* 57–67.

EMERY, R. E. (1982). Marital turmoil: Interparental conflict and the children of discord and divorce. *Psychological Bulletin, 92,* 310–330.

EMERY, R. E., HETHERINGTON, E. M., & DiLALLA, L. F. (1984). Divorce, children, and social policy. In H. W. Stevenson & A. E. Siegel (Eds.), *Child development research and social policy* (Vol. 1, pp. 189–266). Chicago: University of Chicago Press.

EMIHOVICH, C. A., GAIER, E. L., & CRONIN, N. C. (1984). Sex-role expectations changes by fathers and their sons. *Sex Roles, 11,* 861–868.

EMMERICH, W. (1982). Non-monotonic developmental trends in social cognition: The case of gender constancy. In S. Strauss (Ed.), *U-shaped behavioral growth* (pp. 249–269). New York: Academic Press.

ENGEL, M., NECHIN, H., & ARKIN, A. M. (1975). Aspects of mothering: Correlates of the cognitive development of black male infants in the second year of life. In A. Davids (Ed.), *Child personality and psychopathology* (Vol. 2, pp. 17–60). New York: Wiley.

ENGEN, T., & LIPSITT, L. P. (1965). Decrement and recovery of responses to olfactory stimuli in the human neonate. *Journal of Comparative and Physiological Psychology, 59,* 312–316.

ENGEN, T., LIPSITT, L. P., & KAYE, H. (1963). Olfactory responses and adaptation in the human neonate. *Journal of Comparative and Physiological Psychology, 56,* 73–77.

ENGSNER, G., & WOLDEMARIAM, T. (1974). Motor nerve conduction velocity in marasmus and kwashiorkor. *Neuropadiatrie, 5,* 34–48.

ENNIS, R. H. (1971). Conditional logic and primary children. *Interchange, 2,* 126–132.

ENRIGHT, R. D., & SUTTERFIELD, S. J. (1980). An ecological validation of social cognitive development. *Child Development, 51,* 156–161.

ENRIGHT, R. D., ENRIGHT, W. F., MANHEIM, L. A., & HARRIS, B. E. (1980). Distributive justice development and social class. *Developmental Psychology, 16,* 555–563.

ENRIGHT, R. D., FRANKLIN, C. C., & MANHEIM, L. A. (1980). Children's distributive justice reasoning: A standardized and objective scale. *Developmental Psychology, 16,* 193–202.

EPSTEIN, H. T. (1974a). Phrenoblysis: Special brain and mind growth periods. I. Human brain and skull development. *Developmental Psychobiology, 7,* 207–216.

EPSTEIN, H. T. (1974b). Phrenoblysis: Special brain and mind growth periods. II. Human mental development. *Developmental Psychobiology, 7,* 217–224.

EPSTEIN, H. T. (1980). EEG developmental stages. *Developmental Psychobiology, 13,* 629–631.

EPSTEIN, L. H., & WING, R. R. (1983). Reanalysis of weight changes in behavior modification and nutrition education for childhood obesity. *Journal of Pediatric Psychology, 8,* 97–100.

EPSTEIN, L. H., WING, R. R., KOESKE, R., ANDRASIK, F., & OSSIP, D. J. (1981). Child and parent weight loss in family-based behavior modification programs. *Journal of Consulting and Clinical Psychology, 49,* 674–685.

EPSTEIN, S. (1973). The self-concept revisited or a theory of a theory. *American Psychologist, 28,* 405–416.

ERICKSON, M. F., SROUFE, L. A., & EGELAND, B. (1985). The relationship between quality of attachment and behavior problems in preschool in a high-risk sample. In I. Bretherton & E. Waters (Eds.), Growing points of attachment theory and research. *Monographs of the Society for Research in Child Development, 50* (1–2, Serial No. 209).

ERIKSON, E. H. (1950). *Childhood and society.* New York: Norton.

ERIKSON, E. H. (1968). *Identity: Youth and crisis.* New York: Norton.

ERON, L. D., WALDER, L. O., HUESMANN, L. R., & LEFKOWITZ, M. M. (1974). The convergence of laboratory and field studies of the development of aggression. In J. deWit & W. W. Hartup (Eds.), *Determinants and origins of aggressive behavior* (pp. 347–380). The Hague: Mouton.

ERVIN-TRIPP, S., O'CONNOR, S., & ROSENBERG, J. (1984). Language and power in the family. In M. Schulz & C. Kramerae (Eds.), *Language and power* (pp. 116–135). Belmont, CA: Sage Press.

ESCALONA, S. K., & CORMAN, H. (1969). *Albert Einstein scales of sensorimotor development.* New York: Albert Einstein College of Medicine, Yeshiva University.

ESHEL, Y., & KLEIN, Z. (1981). Development of academic self-concept of lower-class and middle-class primary school children. *Journal of Educational Psychology, 73,* 287–293.

ESPENSCHADE, A. (1971). Motor performance in adolescence. In M. C. Jones, N. Bayley, J. W. MacFarlane, & M. P. Honzik (Eds.), *The course of human development* (pp. 86–90). Waltham, MA: Xerox Publishing.

ESPENSHADE, T. J. (1980). Raising a child can now cost $85,000. *Intercom 8(9),* 10–12.

ETAUGH, C., COLLINS, G., & GERSON, A. (1975). Reinforcement of sex-typed behaviors of two-year-old children in a nursery school setting. *Developmental Psychology, 11,* 255.

ETAUGH, C., & HARLOW, H. (1975). Behaviors of male and female teachers as related to behaviors and attitudes of elementary school children. *Journal of Genetic Psychology, 127,* 163–170.

ETAUGH, C., & ROSE, S. (1975). Adolescents' sex bias in the evaluation of performance. *Developmental Psychology, 11,* 663–664.

ETZEL, B. C., & GEWIRTZ, J. L. (1967). Experimental modification of caretaker-maintained high rate operant crying in a 6- and a 20-week-old infant (Infans tyrannotearus): Extinction of crying with reinforcement of eye contact and smiling. *Journal of Experimental Child Psychology, 5,* 303–317.

EVANS, D., HANSEN, J. D. L., MOODIE, A. D., & SPUY, H. I. J. (1980). Intellectual development and nutrition. *The Journal of Pediatrics, 97,* 358–363.

EVANS, G. W., MARRERO, D. G., & BUTLER, P. A. (1981). Environmental learning and cognitive mapping. *Environment and Behavior, 13,* 83–104.

EVELETH, P. B., & TANNER, J. M. (1976). *Worldwide variation in human growth.* Cambridge, Eng.: Cambridge University Press.

EVERTSON, C. (1982). Differences in instructional activities in higher- and lower-achieving junior high English and math classes. *Elementary School Journal, 82,* 329–350.

FABRICUS, W. V., & WELLMAN, H. M. (1984). Memory development. *Journal of Children in Contemporary Society, 16,* 171–187.

FABRIKANT, J. I. (1983). Radiation and health. *Western Journal of Medicine, 138,* 387–390.

FAGAN, J. F. III. (1971). Infants' recognition memory for a series of visual stimuli. *Journal of Experimental Child Psychology, 11,* 244–250.

FAGAN, J. F. III. (1973). Infants' delayed recognition memory and forgetting. *Journal of Experimental Child Psychology, 16,* 424–450.

FAGAN, J. F. III. (1976). Infants' recognition of invariant features of faces. *Child Development, 47,* 627–638.

FAGAN, J. F. III. (1977). Infant recognition memory: Studies in forgetting. *Child Development, 45,* 351–356.

FAGAN, J. F. III. (1984). Infant memory. In M. Moscovitch (Ed.), *Infant memory* (pp. 1–27). New York: Plenum Press.

FAGAN, J. F. III, & McGRATH, S. K. (1981). Infant recognition memory and later intelligence. *Intelligence, 5,* 121–130.

FAGAN, J. F. III, & SINGER, L. T. (1979). The role of simple feature differences in infants' recognition of faces. *Infant Behavior and Development, 2,* 39–45.

FAGOT, B. I. (1974). Sex differences in toddlers' behavior and parental reaction. *Developmental Psychology, 10,* 554–558.

FAGOT, B. I. (1977a). Consequences of moderate cross-gender behavior in preschool children. *Child Development, 48,* 902–907.

FAGOT, B. I. (1977b). Variations in density: Effect on task and social behaviors of preschool children. *Developmental Psychology, 13,* 166–167.

FAGOT, B. I. (1978). The influence of sex of child on parental reactions to toddler children. *Child Development, 49,* 459–465.

FAGOT, B. I. (1981). Stereotypes versus behavioral judgments of sex differences in young children. *Sex Roles, 7,* 1093–1096.

FAGOT, B. I. (1985a). Beyond the reinforcement principle: Another step toward understanding sex role development. *Developmental Psychology, 21,* 1097–1104.

FAGOT, B. I. (1985b). Changes in thinking about early sex role development. *Developmental Review, 5,* 83–98.

FAGOT, B. I., HAGAN, R., LEINBACH, M. D., & KRONSBERG, S. (1985). Differential reactions to assertive and communicative acts of toddler boys and girls. *Child Development, 56,* 1499–1505.

FAGOT, B. I., LEINBACH, M. D., & HAGAN, R. (1986). Gender labeling and the adoption of sex-typed behaviors. *Developmental Psychology, 22,* 440–443.

Fagot, B. I., & Littman, I. (1976). Relation of pre-school sex-typing to intellectual performance in elementary school. *Psychological Reports, 39,* 699–704.

FAGOT, B. I., & PATTERSON, G. R. (1969). An in vivo analysis of reinforcing contingencies for sex-role behaviors in the preschool child. *Developmental Psychology, 1,* 563–568.

FALBO, T. (1978). Only children and interpersonal behavior: An experimental and survey study. *Journal of Applied Social Psychology, 8,* 244–253.

FALBO, T. (1984). Only children: A review. In T. Falbo (Ed.), *The single-child family* (pp. 1–24). New York: Guilford.

FALBO, T., & POLIT, D. (1986). A quantitative review of the only child literature: Research evidence and theory development. *Psychological Bulletin, 100,* 176–189.

FANNING, D. M. (1967). Families in flats. *British Medical Journal, 4,* 382–386.

FANTZ, R. L. (1961, May). The origin of form perception. *Scientific American, 204* (5), 66–72.

FANTZ, R. L. (1963). Pattern vision in newborn infants. *Science, 140,* 296–297.

FANTZ, R. L., FAGAN, J. III, & MIRANDA, S. (1975). Early visual selectivity. In L. Cohen & P. Salapatek (Eds.), *Infant perception: From sensation to cognition. Vol. 2. Basic visual processes* (pp. 249–341). New York: Academic Press.

FANTZ, R. L., ORDY, J. M., & UDELF, M. S. (1962). Maturation of pattern vision in infants during the first six months. *Journal of Comparative Physiological Psychology, 55,* 907–917.

FAUST, M. S. (1960). Developmental maturity as a determinant in prestige of adolescent girls. *Child Development, 31,* 173–186.

FAUST, M. S. (1977). Somatic development of adolescent girls. *Monographs of the Society for Research in Child Development, 42* (1, Serial No. 169).

FAUST, M. S. (1983). Alternative constructions of adolescent growth. In J. Brooks-Gunn & A. C. Petersen (Eds.), *Girls at puberty: Biological and psychosocial perspectives* (pp. 105–125). New York: Plenum.

FEAGANS, L., & SHORT, E. J. (1986). Referential communication and reading performance in learning disabled children over a 3-year period. *Developmental Psychology, 22,* 177–183.

FEIN, G., JOHNSON, D., KOSSON, N., STORK, L., & WASSERMAN, L. (1975). Sex stereotypes and preferences in the toy choices of 20-month-old boys and girls. *Developmental Psychology, 11,* 527–528.

FEIN, G. G. (1975). A transformational analysis of pretending. *Developmental Psychology, 11,* 291–296.

FEIN, G. G. (1979). Play and the acquisition of symbols. In L. Katz (Ed.), *Current topics in early childhood education* (pp. 195–225). Norwood, NJ: Ablex.

FEINGOLD, A. (1988). Cognitive gender differences are disappearing. *American Psychologist, 43,* 95–103.

FEINMAN, S. (1982). Social referencing in infancy. *Merrill-Palmer Quarterly, 28,* 445–470.

FEINMAN, S., & LEWIS, M. (1983). Social referencing at ten months: A second-order effect on infants' responses to strangers. *Child Development, 54,* 878–887.

FEIRING, C., LEWIS, M., & STARR, M. D. (1984). Indirect effects and infants' reaction to strangers. *Developmental Psychology, 20,* 485–491.

FEIS, C. L., & SIMONS, C. (1985). Training preschool children in interpersonal cognitive problem-solving skills: A replication. *Prevention in Human Services, 3,* 59–70.

FEITELSON, D., & ROSS, G. S. (1973). The neglected factor—play. *Human Development, 16,* 202–223.

FENNEMA, E., & SHERMAN, J. (1977). Sex-related differences in mathematics achievement, spatial visualization, and affective factors. *American Educational Research Journal, 14,* 51–71.

FENTON, N. (1928). The only child. *Journal of Genetic Psychology, 35,* 546–556.

FERGUSON, L. R. (1978). The competence and freedom of children to make choices regarding participation in research: A statement. *Journal of Social Issues, 34,* 114–121.

FERNALD, A. (1984). The perceptual and affective salience of mothers' speech to infants. In L. Feagans, C. Garvey, & R. Galinkoff (Eds.), *The origins of growth in communication* (pp. 5–29). Norwood, NJ: Ablex.

FERNANDEZ, J. (1986). *Child care and corporate productivity.* Lexington, MA: Heath.

FERRARI, F., GROSOLI, M. V., FONTANA, G., & CAVAZUTTI, G. B. (1983). Neurobehavioral comparison of low-risk preterm and fullterm infants at term conceptual age. *Developmental Medicine and Child Neurology, 25,* 450–458.

FERRI, E. (1984). *Stepchildren: A national study.* Windsor, Eng.: NFER-Nelson.

FESHBACH, N. D. (1969). Student teacher preferences for elementary school pupils varying in personality characteristics. *Journal of Educational Psychology, 60,* 126–132.

FESHBACH, N. D., & FESHBACH, S. (1969). The relationship between empathy and aggression in two age groups. *Developmental Psychology, 1,* 102–107.

FESHBACH, N. D., & FESHBACH, S. (1982). Empathy training and the regulation of aggression: Potentialities and limitations. *Academic Psychology Bulletin, 4,* 399–413.

FIELD, D. (1981). Can preschool children really learn to conserve? *Child Development, 52,* 326–334.

FIELD, J. (1977). Coordination of vision and prehension in young infants. *Child Development, 48,* 97–103.

FIELD, J., MUIR, D., PILON, R., SINCLAIR, M., & DODWELL, P. (1980). Infants' orientation to lateral sounds from birth to three months. *Child Development, 51,* 295–298.

FIELD, T. M., SCHANBERG, S. M., SCAFIDI, F., BAUER, C. R., VEGA-LAHR, N., GARCIA, R., NYSTROM, J., & KUHN, C. M. (1986). Effects of tactile/kinesthetic stimulation on preterm neonates. *Pediatrics, 77,* 654–658.

FIELD, T. M., WIDMAYER, S. M., STRINGER, S., & IGNATOFF, E. (1980). Teenage, lower-class, black mothers and their preterm infants: An intervention and developmental follow-up. *Child Development, 51,* 426–436.

FIELD, T. M., WOODSON, R., GREENBERG, R., & COHEN, D. (1982). Discrimination and imitation of facial expressions by neonates. *Science, 218,* 179–181.

FINE, G. A. (1980). The natural history of preadolescent male friendship groups. In H. C. Foot, A. J. Chapman, & J. R. Smith (Eds.), *Friendship and social relations in children* (pp. 293–320). Chichester, Eng.: Wiley.

FINKELSTEIN, N., & HASKINS, R. (1983). Kindergarten children prefer same-color peers. *Child Development, 54,* 502–508.

FINNEGAN, L. P. (1985). Smoking and its effect on pregnancy and the newborn. In S. Harel & N. J. Anastasiow (Eds.), *The at-risk infant* (pp. 127–136). Baltimore: Paul H. Brookes.

FISCHER, C. S. (1977). *Networks and places.* New York: Free Press.

FIVUSH, R. (1984). Learning about school: The development of kindergartners' school scripts. *Child Development, 55,* 1697–1709.

FLAPAN, D. (1968). *Children's understanding of social interaction.* New York: Teachers College Press.

FLAVELL, J. H. (1963). *The developmental psychology of Jean Piaget.* New York: Van Nostrand.

FLAVELL, J. H. (1976). Metacognitive aspects of problem solving. In L. B. Resnick (Ed.), *The nature of intelligence* (pp. 231–235). Hillsdale, NJ: Erlbaum.

FLAVELL, J. H. (1981a). Cognitive monitoring. In W. P. Dickson (Ed.), *Children's oral communication skills* (pp. 35–60). New York: Academic Press.

FLAVELL, J. H. (1981b). Monitoring social cognitive enterprises: Something else that may develop in the area of social cognition. In J. H. Flavell & L. Ross (Eds.), *Social cognitive development: Frontiers and possible futures* (pp. 272–287). New York: Cambridge University Press.

FLAVELL, J. H. (1982a). On cognitive development. *Child Development, 53,* 1–10.

FLAVELL, J. H. (1982b). Structures, stages and sequences in cognitive development. In W. A. Collins (Ed.), *Minnesota symposia on child psychology* (pp. 1–28). Hillsdale, NJ: Erlbaum.

FLAVELL, J. H. (1985). *Cognitive development* (2nd ed.). Englewood Cliffs, NJ: Prentice-Hall.

FLAVELL, J. H., BOTKIN, P. T., FRY, C. L., JR., WRIGHT, J. W., & JARVIS, P. E. (1968). *The development of role-taking and communication skills in children.* New York: Wiley.

FLAVELL, J. H., FRIEDRICHS, A. G., & HOYT, J. D. (1970). Developmental changes in memorization processes. *Cognitive Psychology, 1,* 324–340.

FLAVELL, J. H., GREEN, F. L., & FLAVELL, E. R. (1986). Development of knowledge about the appearance-reality distinction. *Monographs of the Society for Research in Child Development, 51* (1, Serial No. 212).

FLAVELL, J. H., SHIPSTEAD, S. G., & CROFT, K. (1980). What young children think you see when their eyes are closed. *Cognition, 8,* 369–387.

FLAVELL, J. H., SPEER, J. R., GREEN, F. L., & AUGUST, D. L. (1981). The development of comprehension monitoring and knowledge about communication. *Monographs for the Society for Research in Child Development, 46* (5, Serial No. 192).

FLAVELL, J. H., & WELLMAN, H. M. (1977). Metamemory. In R. V. Kail, Jr., & J. W. Hagen (Eds.), *Perspectives on the development of memory and cognition* (pp. 3–33). Hillsdale, NJ: Erlbaum.

FODOR, J. (1977). *Semantics: Theories of meaning in generative grammar.* New York: Thomas Y. Crowell.

FOGEL, A., MELSON, G. F., TODA, S., & MISTRY, T. (1987). Young children's responses to unfamiliar infants. *International Journal of Behavioral Development, 10,* 1071–1077.

FORD, M. E., & KEATING, D. P. (1981). Development and individual differences in long-term memory retrieval: Process and organization. *Child Development, 52,* 234–241.

FOREHAND, G., RAGOSTA, J., & ROCK, D. (1976). *Conditions and processes of effective school desegregation.* Princeton, NJ: Educational Testing Service.

FOSTER, H. J. (1983). African patterns in the Afro-American family. *Journal of Black Studies, 14,* 201–232.

FOWLER, J. W., & PETERSON, P. (1981). Increasing reading persistence and altering attributional style of learned helpless children. *Journal of Educational Psychology, 73,* 251–260.

FOX, R., ASLIN, R. N., SHEA, S. L., & DUMAIS, S. T. (1979). Stereopsis in human infants. *Science, 207,* 323–324.

FRAIBERG, S. (1977). *Insights from the blind.* New York: Basic Books.

FRANCIS-WILLIAMS, J., & DAVIES, P. A. (1974). Very low birth weight and later intelligence. *Developmental Medicine and Child Neurology, 16,* 709–728.

FRANK, L. K. (1943). Research in child psychology: History and prospect. In R. Barker, J. Kounin, & H. Wright (Eds.), *Child behavior and development* (pp. 1–15). New York: McGraw-Hill.

FRANKEL, E. (1979). *DNA: The ladder of life.* New York: McGraw-Hill.

FRANKEL, M. T., & ROLLINS, H. A. (1985). Associative and categorical hypotheses of organization in the free recall of adults and children. *Journal of Experimental Child Psychology, 40,* 304–318.

FRANKENBERG, W. K., & DODDS, J. B. (1967). The Denver Developmental Screening Test. *Journal of Pediatrics, 71,* 181–191.

FRANKENBERG, W. K., DODDS, J. B., FRANDAL, A. W., KAZUK, E., & COHRS, M. (1975). *Denver Developmental Screening Test: Reference manual.* Denver: University of Colorado Medical Center.

FRANKLIN, B. S., & RICHARDS, P. N. (1977). Effects on children's divergent thinking abilities of a period of direct teaching for divergent production. *British Journal of Educational Psychology, 47,* 66–70.

FREEDMAN, D. G. (1974). *Human infancy: An evolutionary perspective.* Hillsdale, NJ: Erlbaum.

FREEDMAN, D. G. (1976). Infancy, biology, and culture. In L. P. Lipsitt (Ed.), *Developmental psychobiology: The significance of infancy* (pp. 35–54). Hillsdale, NJ: Erlbaum.

FREEDMAN, D. G., & FREEDMAN, N. (1969). Behavioral differences between Chinese-American and European-American newborns. *Nature, 224,* 1227.

FREEDMAN, J. L. (1984). Effect of television violence on aggressiveness. *Psychological Bulletin, 96,* 227–246.

FRENCH, D. C. (1984). Children's knowledge of the social functions of younger, older, and same-age peers. *Child Development, 55,* 1429–1433.

FRENCH, D. C., & WAAS, G. A. (1985). Behavior problems of peer-neglected and peer-rejected elementary age children: Parent and teacher perspectives. *Child Development, 56,* 246–252.

FRENCH, L. A., & NELSON, K. (1985). *Young children's knowledge of relational terms: Some ifs, ors, and buts.* New York: Springer-Verlag.

FREUD, A., & DANN, S. (1951). An experiment in group upbringing. *Psychoanalytic Study of the Child, 6,* 127–168.

FREUD, S. (1933). *New introductory lectures on psychoanalysis.* New York: Norton.

FREUD, S. (1953). Three essays on the theory of sexuality. In J. Strachey (Ed.), *The standard edition of the complete psychological works of Sigmund Freud* (Vol. 7). London: Hogarth Press. (Original work published 1905)

FREUD, S. (1961a). Formulations regarding the two principles of mental functioning. In J. Strachey (Ed.), *Standard edition of the complete psychological works of Sigmund Freud* (Vol. 12, pp. 215–226). London: Hogarth Press. (Original work published 1925)

FREUD, S. (1961b). Some psychical consequences of the anatomical distinction between the sexes. In J. Strachey (Ed.), *Standard edition of the complete psychological works of Sigmund Freud* (Vol. 19, pp. 248–258). London: Hogarth Press. (Original work published 1925)

FREUD, S. (1963). Introductory lectures on psychoanalysis. In J. Strachey (Ed.), *The standard edition of the complete psychological works of Sigmund Freud* (Vols. 15–16). London: Hogarth Press. (Original works published 1916–1917)

FREUD, S. (1973). *An outline of psychoanalysis.* London: Hogarth. (Original work published 1938)

FREUD, S. (1974). *The ego and the id.* London: Hogarth. (Original work published 1923)

FREUDENBERG, R. P., DRISCOLL, J. W., & STERN, G. S. (1978). Reactions of adult humans to cries of normal and abnormal infants. *Infant Behavior and Development, 1,* 224–227.

FRIEDMAN, M. (1969). *Pathogenesis of coronary artery disease.* New York: McGraw-Hill.

FRIEDMAN, M., & ROSENMAN, R. H. (1959). Association of specific overt behavior patterns with blood and cardiovascular findings. *Journal of the American Medical Association, 169,* 1286–1296.

FRIEDRICH, L. K., & STEIN, A. H. (1973). Aggressive and prosocial television programs and the natural behavior of preschool children. *Monographs of the Society for Research in Child Development, 38* (4, Serial No. 151).

FRIEDRICH-COFER, L. K., & HUSTON, A. C. (1986). Television violence and aggression: The debate continues. *Psychological Bulletin, 100,* 364–371.

FRIEDRICH-COFER, L. K., TUCKER, C. J., NORRIS-BAKER, C., FARNSWORTH, J. B., FISHER, D. P., HANNINGTON, C. M., & HOXIE, K. (1978). Perceptions by adolescents of television heroines. Paper presented at the meeting of the Southwestern Psychological Association, New Orleans.

FRISCH, H. L. (1977). Sex stereotypes in adult-infant play. *Child Development, 48,* 1671–1675.

FRISCH, R. E. (1983). Fatness, puberty and fertility. In J. Brooks-Gunn & A. C. Petersen (Eds.), *Girls at puberty: Biological and psychosocial perspectives* (pp. 29–49). New York: Plenum.

FRISCH, R. E., GOTZ-WELBERGEN, A., MCARTHUR, J. W., ALBRIGHT, T., WITSCHI, J., BULLEN, B., BIRNHOLZ, J., REED, R. B., & HERMANN, H. (1981). Delayed menarche and amenorrhea of college athletes in relation to age of onset of training. *Journal of the American Medical Association, 246,* 1559–1563.

FRISCH, R. E., & MCARTHUR, J. (1974). Menstrual cycles: Fatness as a determinant of minimum weight for height necessary for their maintenance or onset. *Science, 185,* 949–951.

FRISCH, R. E., WYSHAK, G., & VINCENT, L. (1980). Delayed menarche and amenorrhea of ballet dancers. *New England Journal of Medicine, 303,* 17–19.

FRODI, A. M. (1985). When empathy fails: Aversive infant crying and child abuse. In B. M. Lester & C. F. Z. Boukydis (Eds.), *Infant crying: Theoretical and research perspectives* (pp. 263–277). New York: Plenum.

FRODI, A. M., LAMB, M. E., LEAVITT, L. A., BONOVAN, W. L., NEFF, C., & SHERRY, D. (1978). Fathers' and mothers' responses to the faces and cries of normal and premature infants. *Developmental Psychology, 14,* 490–498.

FRUEH, T., & MCGHEE, P. E. (1975). Traditional sex role development and amount of time spent watching television. *Developmental Psychology, 11,* 109.

FRY, P. S. (1975). The resistance of temptation: Inhibitory and disinhibitory effects of models in children from India and the United States. *Journal of Cross-Cultural Psychology, 6,* 189–202.

FUCHS, I., EISENBERG, N., HERTZ-LAZAROWITZ, R., & SHARABANY, R. (1986). Kibbutz, Israeli city, and American children's moral reasoning about prosocial moral conflicts. *Merrill-Palmer Quarterly, 32,* 37–50.

FURMAN, W., RAHE, D., & HARTUP, W. W. (1979). Social rehabilitation of low-interactive preschool children by peer intervention. *Child Development, 50,* 915–922.

FURSTENBERG, F. F., JR., & CRAWFORD, D. B. (1978). Family support: Helping teenagers to cope. *Family Planning Perspectives, 10,* 322–333.

FURSTENBERG, F. F., JR., & NORD, C. W. (1985). Parenting apart: Patterns of childrearing after marital disruption. *Journal of Marriage and the Family, 47,* 893–904.

FURSTENBERG, F. F., JR., SPANIER, G. B., & ROTHSCHILD, N. (1982). Patterns of parenting in the transition from divorce to remarriage. In P. W. Berman & E. R. Ramey (Eds.), *Women: A developmental perspective* (pp. 325–343). Bethesda, MD: NIH Publication No. 82-2298.

FUSON, K. C., SECADA, W. G., & HALL, J. W. (1983). Matching, counting, and conservation of numerical equivalence. *Child Development, 54,* 91–97.

FYANS, L. J., JR., SALILI, F., MAEHR, M. L., & DESAI, K. A. (1983). A cross-cultural exploration into the meaning of achievement. *Journal of Personality and Social Psychology, 44,* 1000–1013.

GADDINI, R., & GADDINI, E. (1970). Transitional objects and the process of individuation: A study in three different social groups. *Journal of the American Academy of Child Psychiatry, 9,* 347–365.

GADDIS, A., & BROOKS-GUNN, J. (1985). The male experience of pubertal change. *Journal of Youth and Adolescence, 14,* 61–69.

GAENSBAUER, T. J. (1980). Anaclitic depression in a three-and-one-half month-old child. *American Journal of Psychiatry, 137,* 841–842.

GAENSBAUER, T. J., EMDE, R. N., & CAMPOS, J. J. (1976). Stranger distress: A Confirmation of a developmental shift in a longitudinal sample. *Perceptual and Motor Skills, 12,* 99–106.

GAENSBAUER, T. J., HARMON, R. J., CYTRYN, L., & MCKNEW, D. H. (1984). Social and affective development in children with manic-depressive parents. *American Journal of Psychiatry, 141,* 223–229.

GAGAN, R. J. (1984). The families of children who fail to thrive: Preliminary investigations of parental deprivation among organic and non-organic cases. *Child Abuse and Neglect, 8,* 93–103.

GAGE, N. L. (1978). The yield of research on teaching. *Phi Delta Kappan, 59,* 229–235.

GAINES, L., & ESSERMAN, J. (1981). A quantitative study of young children's comprehension of television programs and commercials. In J. F. Esserman (Ed.), *Television advertising and children: Issues, research and findings* (pp. 96–105). New York: Child Research Service.

GALBRAITH, R. C. (1982). Sibling spacing and intellectual development: A closer look at the confluence model. *Developmental Psychology, 18,* 151–173.

GALLAGHER, T. M. (1981). Contingent query sequences within adult-child discourse. *Journal of Child Language, 8,* 51–62.

GALLER, J. R., RAMSEY, F., & SOLIMANO, G. (1985a). A follow-up study of the effects of early malnutrition on subsequent development. I. Physical growth and sexual maturation during adolescence. *Pediatric Research, 19,* 518–523.

GALLER, J. R., RAMSEY, F., & SOLIMANO, G. (1985b). A follow-up study of effects of early malnutrition on subsequent development. II. Fine motor skills in adolescence. *Pediatric Research, 19,* 524–527.

GALLER, J. R., RAMSEY, F., SOLIMANO, G., KUCHARSKI, L. T., & HARRISON, R. (1984). The influence of early malnutrition on subsequent behavioral development. IV. Soft neurological signs. *Pediatric Research, 18,* 826–832.

GALTON, F. (1883). *Inquiries into human faculty and its development.* London: Macmillan.

GANNON, S., & KORN, S. J. (1983). Temperament, cultural variation, and behavior disorder in preschool children. *Child Psychiatry and Human Development, 13,* 203–212.

GANON, E. C., & SWARTZ, K. B. (1980). Perception of internal elements of compound figures by one-month-old infants. *Journal of Experimental Child Psychology, 30,* 159–170.

GARBARINO, J. (1977). The human ecology of child maltreatment: A conceptual model for research. *Journal of Marriage and the Family, 39,* 721–736.

GARBARINO, J. (1980). Some thoughts on school size and its effects on adolescent development. *Journal of Youth and Adolescence, 9,* 19–31.

GARBARINO, J., GUTTMAN, E., & SEELEY, J. (1986). *The psychologically battered child: Strategies for identification, assessment and intervention.* San Francisco: Jossey-Bass.

GARBARINO, J., & SHERMAN, D. (1980). High-risk neighborhoods and high-risk families: The human ecology of child maltreatment. *Child Development, 51,* 188–198.

GARDNER, B. T., & GARDNER, R. A. (1980). Two comparative psychologists look at language acquisition. In K. E. Nelson (Ed.), *Children's language* (vol. 2, pp. 331–369). New York: Gardner Press.

GARDNER H. (1980). *Artful scribbles: The significance of children's drawings.* New York: Basic Books.

GARDNER, J. M., KARMEL, B. Z., & DOWD, J. M. (1985). Relationship of infant psychobiological development to infant intervention programs. In M. Frank (Ed.), *Infant intervention programs: Truths and untruths* (pp. 93–108). New York: Haworth.

GARDNER, L. I. (1972, July). Deprivation dwarfism. *Scientific American, 227*(1), 76–82.

GARDNER, R. A., & GARDNER, B. T. (1969). Teaching sign language to a chimpanzee. *Science, 165,* 664–672.

GARRETT, C. S., EIN, P. L., & TREMAINE, L. (1977). The development of gender stereotyping of adult occupations in elementary school children. *Child Development, 48,* 507–512.

GARRITY, L. I. (1975). An electromyographical study of subvocal speech and recall in preschool children. *Developmental Psychology, 11,* 274–281.

GARVEY, C. (1974). Requests and responses in children's speech. *Journal of Child Language, 2*, 41–60.

GARVEY, C. (1977). Play with language and speech. In S. Ervin-Tripp & C. Mitchell-Kernen (Eds.), *Child discourse* (pp. 27–47). New York: Academic Press.

GECAS, V. (1979). The influence of social class in socialization. In W. Burr, R. Hill, I. Reiss, & F. I. Nye (Eds.), *Contemporary theories about the family* (Vol. 1, pp. 365–404). New York: Free Press.

GELFAND, D. M., HARTMANN, D. P., CROMER, C. C., SMITH, C. L., & PAGE, B. C. (1975). The effects of instructional prompts and praise on children's donation rates. *Child Development, 46*, 980–983.

GELFAND, D. M., HARTMANN, D. P., LAMB, A. K., SMITH, C. L., MAHAN, M. A., & PAUL, S. C. (1974). The effects of adult models and described alternatives on children's choice of behavior management techniques. *Child Development, 45*, 585–593.

GELLES, R. J. (1978). Violence toward children in the United States. *American Journal of Orthopsychiatry, 48*, 580–592.

GELLES, R. J., & CORNELL, C. P. (1983). International perspectives on child abuse. *Child Abuse & Neglect, 7*, 375–386.

GELMAN, R. (1972). Logical capacity of very young children: Number invariance rules. *Child Development, 43*, 75–90.

GELMAN, R. (1979). Preschool thought. *American Psychologist, 34*, 900–905.

GELMAN, R., & BAILLARGEON, R. (1983). A review of some Piagetian concepts. In J. H. Flavell & E. M. Markman (Eds.), *Handbook of child psychology. Vol. 3: Cognitive development* (pp. 167–230). New York: Wiley.

GELMAN, R., BULLOCK, M., & MECK, E. (1980). Preschoolers' understanding of simple object transformations. *Child Development, 51*, 691–699.

GELMAN, R., & GALLISTEL, C. R. (1986). *The child's understanding of number*. Cambridge, MA: Harvard University Press.

GELMAN, R., & SHATZ, M. (1978). Appropriate speech adjustments: The operation of conversational constraints on talk to two-year-olds. In M. Lewis & L. A. Rosenblum (Eds.), *Interaction, conversation, and the development of language* (pp. 27–61). New York: Wiley.

GENOVA, W. J., & WALBERG, H. J. (1984). Enhancing integration in urban high schools. In D. E. Bartz & M. L. Maehr (Eds.), *Advances in motivation and achievement* (Vol. 1, pp. 243–283). Greenwich, CT: JAI Press.

GENTNER, D. (1982). Why nouns are learned before verbs: Linguistic relativity versus natural partitioning. In S. A. Kuczaj II (Ed.), *Language development: Vol. 2. Language, thought, and culture* (pp. 301–332). Hillsdale, NJ: Erlbaum.

GEORGE, C., & MAIN, M. (1979). Social interactions of young abused children: Approach, avoidance, and aggression. *Child Development, 50*, 306–318.

GERBNER, G., GROSS, L., SIGNORIELLI, N., & MORGAN, M. (1986). *Television's mean world: Violence Profile No. 14–15*. Philadelphia, PA: Annenberg School of Communications, University of Pennsylvania.

GERBNER, G., GROSS, L., SIGNORIELLI, N., MORGAN, M., & JACKSON-BEECK, M. (1979). The demonstration of power: Violence Profile No. 10. *Journal of Communication, 29*(3), 177–195.

GERSHMAN, E. S., & HAYES, D. S. (1983). Differential stability of reciprocal friendships and unilateral relationships among preschool children. *Merrill-Palmer Quarterly, 29*, 169–177.

GESELL, A. (1929). Maturation and infant behavior pattern. *Psychological Review, 36*, 307–319.

GESELL, A. (1933). Maturation and the patterning of behavior. In C. Murchison (Ed.), *A handbook of child psychology*. Worcester, MA: Clark University Press.

GESELL, A. (1972). *Infant development: The embryology of early human behavior*. Westport, CN: Greenwood Press. (Original work published 1952)

GESELL, A., & ILG, F. L. (1949). The child from five to ten. In A. Gesell & F. Ilg, *Child Development* (pp. 1–454). New York: Harper & Row. (Original work published 1946)

GESELL, A., & ILG, F. L. (1949). The infant and child in the culture of today. In A. Gesell & F. Ilg, *Child development* (pp. 1–393). New York: Harper & Row. (Original work published 1943)

GESELL A., & THOMPSON H. (1938). *The psychology of early growth*. New York: Macmillan.

GETZELS, J. W., & DILLON J. T. (1973). The nature of giftedness and the education of the gifted. In R. M. W. Travers (Ed.), *Second handbook of research on teaching* (pp. 689–731). Chicago: Rand McNally.

GETZELS, J. W., & JACKSON P. W. (1962). *Creativity and intelligence: Explorations with gifted students*. New York: Wiley.

GEWIRTZ, H. B., & GEWIRTZ, J. L. (1968). Caretaking settings, background and behavior differences in four Israeli child-rearing environments: Some preliminary trends. In B. M. Foss (Ed.), *Determinants of infant behavior* (Vol. 4, pp. 229–252). London: Methuen.

GEWIRTZ, J. L. (1969). Mechanisms of social learning: Some roles of stimulation and behavior in early human development. In D. A. Goslin (Ed.), *Handbook of socialization theory and research* (pp. 57–212). Skokie, IL: Rand McNally.

GEWIRTZ, J. L., & BOYD, E. F. (1977a). Does maternal responding imply reduced infant crying? A critique of the 1972 Bell and Ainsworth report. *Child Development, 48*, 1200–1207.

GEWIRTZ, J. L., & BOYD, E. F. (1977b). In reply to the rejoinder to our critique of the 1972 Bell and Ainsworth report. *Child Development, 48*, 1217–1218.

GIACONIA, R. M., & HEDGES, L. V. (1982). *Identifying features of open education*. Stanford, CA: Stanford University Press.

GIBBS, J. C., & WIDAMAN, K. F. (1982). *Social intelligence: Measuring the development of sociomoral reflection*. Englewood Cliffs, NJ: Prentice-Hall.

GIBSON, E., & RADER, N. (1979). Attention: The perceiver as performer. In G. Hale & M. Lewis (Eds.), *Attention and cognitive development* (pp. 1–21). New York: Plenum.

GIBSON, E. J. (1970). The development of perception as an adaptive process. *American Scientist, 58*, 98–107.

GIBSON, E. J., GIBSON, J. J., PICK, A. D., & OSSER, H. (1962). A developmental study of the discrimination of letter-like forms. *Journal of Comparative and Physiological Psychology, 55*, 897–906.

GIBSON, E. J., & LEVIN, H. (1975). *The psychology of reading*. Cambridge, MA: MIT Press.

GIBSON, E. J., SCHAPIRO, F., & YONAS, A. (1968). *Confusion matrices for graphic patterns obtained with a latency measure*. Final report, Cornell University and U.S. Office of Education Project No. 5-1213, Contract No. OE6-10-156.

GIBSON, E. J., & SPELKE, E. S. (1983). The development of perception. In J. H. Flavell & E. M. Markman (Eds.), *Handbook of child psychology: Vol 3. Cognitive development* (4th ed., pp. 1–76). New York: Wiley.

GIBSON, E. J., & WALK, R. D. (1960, April). The "visual cliff." *Scientific American, 202*(1), 64–71.

GIBSON, J. J. (1979). *The ecological approach to visual perception*. Boston: Houghton Mifflin.

GIBSON, K. (1977). Brain structure and intelligence. In S. Chevalier-Skolnikoff and F. Porter (Eds.), *Primate bio-social development* (pp. 113–157). New York: Garland Press.

GIL, D. G. (1970–1973). *Violence against children: Physical child abuse in the United States*. Cambridge, MA: Harvard University Press.

GIL, D. G. (1987). Maltreatment as a function of the structure of social systems. In M. R. Brassard, R. Germain, & S. N. Hart (Eds.), *Psychological maltreatment of children and youth* (pp. 159–170). New York: Pergamon Press.

GILBERT, E. H., & DEBLASSIE, R. R. (1984). Anorexia nervosa: Adolescent starvation by choice. *Adolescence, 76*, 839–846.

GILLIGAN, C. F. (1977). In a different voice: Women's conceptions of self and morality. *Harvard Educational Review, 47*, 481–517.

GILLIGAN, C. F. (1982). *In a different voice*. Cambridge, MA: Harvard University Press.

GILLIGAN, C. F., & BELENKY, M. F. (1980). A naturalistic study of abortion decisions. In R. L. Selman & R. Yando (Eds.), *New directions for child development* (No. 7, pp. 69–90). San Francisco: Jossey-Bass.

GINSBURG, H., & OPPER, S. (1979). *Piaget's theory of intellectual development (2nd ed.)*. Englewood Cliffs, NJ: Prentice-Hall.

GINSBURG, H. J., POLLMAN, V. A., & WAUSON, M. S. (1977). An ethological analysis of nonverbal inhibitors of aggressive behavior in male elementary school children. *Developmental Psychology, 13,* 417–418.

GLASER, R. (ED.) (1982). *Advances in instructional psychology* (Vol. 2). Hillsdale, NJ: Erlbaum.

GLASS, D. C., KRAKOFF, L. R., CONTRADA, R., HILTON, W. F., KEHOE, K., MANNUCCI, E. G., COLLINS, C., SNOW, B., & ELTING, E. (1980). Effect of harassment and competition upon cardiovascular and plasma catecholamine responses in Type A and Type B individuals. *Psychophysiology, 17,* 453–463.

GLEITMAN, L. R., NEWPORT, E. L., & GLEITMAN, H. (1984). The current status of the motherese hypothesis. *Journal of Child Language, 11,* 43–80.

GLEITMAN, L. R., & WANNER, E. (1988). Current issues in language learning. In M. H. Bornstein & M. E. Lamb (Eds.), *Developmental psychology: An advanced textbook* (2nd ed., pp. 297–356). Hillsdale, NJ: Erlbaum.

GLICK, J. (1975). Cognitive development in cross-cultural perspective. In F. D. Horowitz (Ed.), *Review of child development research* (Vol. 4, pp. 595–654). Chicago: University of Chicago Press.

GLICK, P. C., & LIN, S. (1987). Remarriage after divorce: Recent changes and demographic variations. *Sociological Perspectives, 30,* 162–179.

GNEPP, J. (1983). Children's social sensitivity: Inferring emotions from conflicting cues. *Developmental Psychology, 19,* 805–814.

GNEPP, J., & GOULD, M.E. (1985). The development of personalized inferences: Understanding other people's emotional reactions in light of their prior experiences. *Child Development, 56,* 1455–1464.

GOELMAN, H. (1986). The language environments of family day care. In S. Kilmer (Ed.), *Advances in early education and day care* (Vol. 4, pp. 153–179). Greenwich, CT: JAI Press.

GOETZ, E. T., & HALL, R. J. (1984). Evaluation of the Kaufman Assessment Battery for Children from an information processing perspective. *Journal of Special Education, 18,* 281–296.

GOFFIN, S. G. (1983). A framework for conceptualizing children's services. *American Journal of Orthopsychiatry, 53,* 282–290.

GOFFIN, S. G. (1988, March). Putting our advocacy efforts into a new context. *Young Children, 43*(3), 52–56.

GOLD, D., & ANDRES, D. (1978a). Developmental comparisons between 10-year-old children with employed and non-employed mothers. *Child Development, 49,* 75–84.

GOLD, D., & ANDRES, D. (1978b). Developmental comparisons between adolescent children with employed and nonemployed mothers. *Merrill-Palmer Quarterly, 24,* 243–254.

GOLD, D., & ANDRES, D. (1978c). Relations between maternal employment and development of nursery school children. *Canadian Journal of Behavioural Science, 10,* 116–129.

GOLD, D., ANDRES, D., & GLORIEUX, J. (1979). The development of Francophone nursery school children with employed and nonemployed mothers. *Canadian Journal of Behavioural Science, 11,* 169–173.

GOLD, M. (1985, April). The baby makers. *Science 85, 6*(5), 26–38.

GOLDBERG, S., BRACHFELD, S., & DIVITTO, B. (1980). Feeding, fussing, and play: Parent-infant interaction in the first year as a function of prematurity and perinatal medical problems. In T. M. Field (Ed.), *High-risk infants and children* (pp. 133–153). New York: Academic Press.

GOLDBERG, S., PERLMUTTER, M., & MYERS, N. (1974). Recall of related and unrelated lists by 2-year-olds. *Journal of Experimental Child Psychology, 18,* 1–8.

GOLDBERG, W. A. (1982). Marital quality and child-mother, child-father attachments. *Infant Behavior and Development, 5,* 96.

GOLDFARB, W. (1943). Effects of early institutional care on adolescent personality. *Journal of Experimental Education, 12,* 106–129.

GOLDFARB, W. (1945). Effects of psychological deprivation in infancy and subsequent stimulation. *American Journal of Psychiatry, 102,* 18–33.

GOLDFIELD, B. A., & SNOW, C. E. (1985). Individual differences in language acquisition. In J. B. Gleason (Ed.), *The development of language* (pp. 307–330). Columbus, OH: Merrill.

GOLDIN-MEADOW, S. (1979). Structure in a manual communication system developed without a conventional language model: Language without a helping hand. In H. Whitaker & H. A. Whitaker (Eds.), *Studies in neurolinguistics* (Vol. 4, pp. 125–209). New York: Academic Press.

GOLDIN-MEADOW, S., & MORFORD, M. (1985). Gesture in early language: Studies of deaf and hearing children. *Merrill-Palmer Quarterly, 31,* 145–176.

GOLDIN-MEADOW, S., & MYLANDER, C. (1983). Gestural communication in deaf children: Noneffect of parental input on language development. *Science, 221,* 372–374.

GOLDIN-MEADOW, S., SELIGMAN, M. E. P., & GELMAN, R. (1976). Language in the two-year-old. *Cognition, 4,* 189–202.

GOLDMAN, P. S., & RAKIC, P. T. (1979). Impact of the outside world upon the developing primate brain. *Bulletin of the Menninger Clinic, 43,* 20–28.

GOLDSCHMID, B., & GOLDSCHMID, M. L. (1976). Peer teaching in higher education: A review. *Higher Education, 5,* 9–33.

GOLDSCHMID, M. L., & BENTLER, P. M. (1968a). The dimensions and measurement of conservation. *Child Development, 39,* 787–802.

GOLDSCHMID, M. L., & BENTLER, P. M. (1968b). *Manual: Concept Assessment Kit—Conservation.* San Diego, CA: Educational and Industrial Testing Service.

GOLDSMITH, H. H. (1987). Roundtable: What is temperament? Four approaches. *Child Development, 58,* 505–529.

GOLDSMITH, H. H., & GOTTESMAN, I. I. (1981). Origins of variation in behavioral style: A longitudinal study of temperament in young twins. *Child Development, 52,* 91–103.

GOLEMAN, D. (1980, February). 1,528 little geniuses and how they grew. *Psychology Today, 13*(9), 28–53.

GOLINKOFF, R. M. (1983). The preverbal negotiation of failed messages: Insights into the transition period. In R. M. Golinkoff (Ed.), *The transition of prelinguistic to linguistic communication* (pp. 57–78). Hillsdale, NJ: Erlbaum.

GOLUMB, C. (1974). *Young children's sculpture and drawing: A study in representation development.* Cambridge, MA: Harvard University Press.

GOLUMB, C., & CORNELIUS, C. B. (1977). Symbolic play and its cognitive significance. *Developmental Psychology, 13,* 246–252.

GOOD, T. L., & POWER, C. N. (1976). Designing successful classroom environments for different types of students. *Journal of Curriculum Studies, 8,* 45–69.

GOOD, T. L., & STIPEK, D. J. (1983). Individual differences in the classroom: A psychological perspective. In G. D. Fenstermacher & J. I. Goodlad (Eds.), *Individual differences and the common curriculum* (82nd yearbook of the National Society for the Study of Education, Part 1, pp. 9–44). Chicago: University of Chicago Press.

GOODENOUGH, F. L. (1931). *Anger in young children.* Minneapolis: University of Minnesota Press.

GOODLAD, J. I. (1984). *A place called school.* New York: McGraw-Hill.

GOODMAN, G. S., AMAN, C., & HIRSCHMAN, J. (1987). Child sexual and physical abuse: Children's testimony. In S. J. Ceci, M. P. Toglia, & D. F. Ross (Eds.), *Children's eyewitness memory* (pp. 1–23). New York: Springer-Verlag.

GOODMAN, J. F. (1979). Is tissue the issue? A critique of SOMPA's models and tests. *School Psychology Digest, 8,* 47–62.

GORDON, D., COHEN, R. J., KELLY, D., AKSELROD, S., & SHANNON, D. C. (1984). Sudden infant death syndrome: Abnormalities in short term fluctuations in heart rate and respiratory activity. *Pediatric Research, 18,* 921–926.

GORDON, T., & FOSS, B. M. (1966). The role of stimulation in the delay of onset of crying in the newborn infant. *Quarterly Journal of Experimental Psychology, 18,* 79–81.

GORN, G. J., & GOLDBERG, M. E. (1982). Behavioral evidence of the effects of televised food messages on children. *Journal of Consumer Research, 9,* 200–205.

GOTTESMAN, I. I. (1963). Genetic aspects of intelligent behavior. In

N. R. Ellis (Ed.), *Handbook of mental deficiency* (pp. 253–296). New York: McGraw-Hill.

GOTTFRIED, A. E. (1985). Academic intrinsic motivation in elementary and junior high school students. *Journal of Educational Psychology, 77*, 631–645.

GOTTMAN, J. M. (1977). Toward a definition of social isolation in children. *Child Development, 48*, 513–517.

GOTTMAN, J. M., GONSO, J., & RASMUSSEN, B. (1975). Social interaction, social competence, and friendship in children. *Child Development, 46*, 709–718.

GOY, R. W., & GOLDFOOT, D. A. (1974). Experiential and hormonal factors influencing development of sexual behavior in the male rhesus monkey. In R. O. Schmitt & F. G. Worden (Eds.), *The neurosciences* (pp. 571–581). Cambridge, MA: MIT Press.

GRAHAM, F. K., ERNHART, C. B., THURSTON, D. L., & CRAFT, M. (1962). Development three years after perinatal anoxia and other potentially damaging newborn experiences. *Psychological Monographs, 76* (3, Whole No. 522).

GRAHAM, F. K., PENNOYER, M. M., CALDWELL, B. M., GREENMAN, M., & HARTMAN, A. F. (1957). Relationship between clinical status and behavior test performance in a newborn group with histories suggesting anoxia. *Journal of Pediatrics, 50*, 177–189.

GRAHAM, P. (1979). Epidemiological studies. In H. C. Quay & J. S. Werry (Eds.), *Psychopathological disorders of childhood* (pp. 185–246). New York: Wiley.

GRAHAM, S., DOUBLEDAY, C., & GUARINO, P. A. (1984). The development of relations between perceived controllability and the emotions of pity, anger, and guilt. *Child Development, 55*, 561–565.

GRANRUD, C. E., & YONAS, A. (1984). Infants' perception of pictorially specified interposition. *Journal of Experimental Child Psychology, 37*, 500–511.

GRANRUD, C. E., YONAS, A., & OPLAND, E. A. (1985). Infants' sensitivity to the depth cue of shading. *Perception and Psychophysics, 37*, 415–419.

GRAVES, S. N. (1975). How to encourage positive racial attitudes. Paper presented at the meeting of the Society for Research in Child Development, Denver, CO.

GRAY, R., & PIROT, M. (1984). The effects of prosocial modeling on young children's nurturing of a "sick" child. *Psychology and Human Development, 1*, 41–46.

GRAY, S. W., & WANDERSMAN, L. P. (1980). The methodology of home-based intervention studies: Problems and promising strategies. *Child Development, 51*, 993–1009.

GRAY, W. M. (1978). A comparison of Piagetian theory and criterion-referenced measurement. *Review of Educational Research, 48*, 223–250.

GRAY, W. M., & HUDSON, L. M. (1984). Formal operations and the imaginary audience. *Developmental Psychology, 20*, 619–627.

GRAZIANO, W. G., FRENCH, D., BROWNELL, C. A., & HARTUP, W. W. (1976). Peer interaction in same- and mixed-age triads in relation to chronological age and incentive condition. *Child Development, 47*, 707–714.

GREEN, J. A., GUSTAFSON, G. E., & WEST, M. J. (1980). Effects of infant development on mother-infant interactions. *Child Development, 51*, 199–207.

GREEN, J. A., JONES, L. E., & GUSTAFSON, G. E. (1987). Perception of cries by parents and nonparents: Relation to cry acoustics. *Developmental Psychology, 23*, 370–382.

GREEN, K. D., VOSK, R., FOREHAND, R., & BECK, S. J. (1981). An examination of the differences among sociometrically identified accepted, rejected, and neglected children. *Child Study Journal, 11*, 117–124.

GREENBERG, B. S. (1975). British children and televised violence. *Public Opinion Quarterly, 38*, 531–547.

GREENBERG, M., & MORRIS, N. (1974). Engrossment: The newborn's impact upon the father. *American Journal of Orthopsychiatry, 44*, 520–531.

GREENBOWE, T., HERRON, J. D., LUCAS, C., NURRENBERN, S., STAVER, J. R., & WARD, C. R. (1981). Teaching preadolescents to act as scientists: Replication and extension of an earlier study. *Journal of Educational Psychology, 73*, 705–711.

GREENFIELD, P. M. (1984). *Mind and media: The effects of television, video games, and computers.* Cambridge, MA: Harvard University Press.

GREENFIELD, P. M., & SMITH, J. H. (1976). *The structure of communication in early language development.* New York: Academic Press.

GREIF, E. B., & ULMAN, K. (1982). The psychological impact of menarche on early adolescent females: A review. *Child Development, 53*, 1413–1430.

GREIF, E. B. (1979). Sex differences in parent-child conversations: Who interrupts who? Paper presented at the meeting of the Society for Research in Child Development, Boston.

GREIF, E. B., & GLEASON, J. B. (1980). Hi, thanks, and goodbye: More routine information. *Language in Society, 9*, 159–166.

GRIEF, G. L. (1985). Single fathers rearing children. *Journal of Marriage and the Family, 47*, 185–191.

GRIMES, D., & GROSS, G. (1981). Pregnancy outcomes in black women aged 35 and older. *Obstetrics and Gynecology, 58*, 614–620.

GRIMES, S. W., & ALLINSMITH, W. (1961). Compulsivity, anxiety, and school achievement. *Merrill-Palmer Quarterly, 7*, 247–271.

GRINKER, J. A. (1981). Behavioral and metabolic factors in childhood obesity. In M. Lewis & L. A. Rosenblum (Ed.), *The uncommon child* (pp. 115–150). New York: Plenum.

GROBSTEIN, C., FLOWER, M., & MENDELOFF, J. (1983). External human fertilization: An evaluation of policy. *Science, 222*, 127–133.

GROSSMAN, H. J. (Ed.). (1983). *Classification in mental retardation.* Washington, DC: American Association on Mental Deficiency.

GROSSMANN, K., GROSSMANN, K. E., SPANGLER, G., SUESS, G., & UNZNER, L. (1985). Maternal sensitivity and newborns' orientation responses as related to quality of attachment in Northern Germany. In I. Bretherton & E. Waters (Eds.), Growing points of attachment theory and research. *Monographs of the Society for Research in Child Development, 50* (1–2, Serial No. 209).

GROTEVANT, H. D. (1978). Sibling constellations and sex-typing of interests in adolescence. *Child Development, 49*, 540–542.

GRUEN, G. E., & VORE, D. A. (1972). Development of conservation in normal and retarded children. *Developmental Psychology, 6*, 146–157.

GRUENEICH, R. (1982). Issues in the developmental study of how children use intention and consequence information to make moral evaluations. *Child Development, 53*, 29–43.

GRUSEC, J. E., & ABRAMOVITCH, R. (1982). Imitation of peers and adults in a natural setting: A functional analysis. *Child Development, 53*, 636–642.

GRUSEC, J. E., & KUCZYNSKI, L. (1980). Direction of effect in socialization: A comparison of the parent's versus the child's behavior as determinants of disciplinary techniques. *Developmental Psychology, 16*, 109–199.

GRUSEC, J. E., KUCZYNSKI, L., RUSHTON, J., & SIMUTIS, Z. (1979). Learning resistance to temptation through observation. *Developmental Psychology, 15*, 233–240.

GUARDO, C. J., & BOHAN, J. B. (1971). Development of a sense of self-identity in children. *Child Development, 42*, 1909–1921.

GUIDUBALDI, J., & CLEMINSHAW, H. K. (1985). Divorce, family health and child adjustment. *Family Relations, 34*, 35–41.

GUIDUBALDI, J., & PERRY, J. D. (1985). Divorce and mental health sequelae for children: A two-year follow-up of a nationwide sample. *Journal of the American Academy of Child Psychiatry, 24*, 531–537.

GUILFORD, J. P. (1950). Creativity. *American Psychologist, 4*, 444–454.

GUILFORD, J. P. (1967). *The nature of human intelligence.* New York: McGraw-Hill.

GUILFORD, J. P. (1985). The structure-of-intellect model. In B. B. Wolman (Ed.), *Handbook of intelligence* (pp. 225–266). New York: Wiley.

GUILFORD, J. P., & HOEPFNER, R. (1971). *The analysis of intelligence.* New York: McGraw-Hill.

GUILLEMINAULT, C., BOEDDIKER, M. O., & SCHWAB, D. (1982). Detection of risk factors for "near miss SIDS" events in full-term infants. *Neuropediatrics, 13*, 29–35.

GUMP, P. V. (1975). *Ecological psychology and children.* Chicago: University of Chicago Press.

GUNN, P., & BERRY, P. (1985). Down's syndrome temperament and maternal response to descriptions of child behavior. *Developmental Psychology, 21,* 842–847.

GUNNAR, M., & DONAHUE, M. (1980). Sex differences in social responsiveness between six months and twelve months. *Child Development, 51,* 262–265.

GURUCHARRI, C., & SELMAN, R. L. (1982). The development of interpersonal understanding during childhood, preadolescence, and adolescence: A longitudinal follow-up study. *Child Development, 53,* 924–927.

HAAF, R. A. (1974). Complexity and facial resemblance as determinants of response to face-like stimuli by 5- and 10-week-old infants. *Journal of Experimental Child Psychology, 18,* 480–487.

HAAKE, R. J., SOMERVILLE, S. C., & WELLMAN, H. M. (1980). Logical ability of young children in searching a large-scale environment. *Child Development, 51,* 1299–1302.

HAAN, N., AERTS, E., & COOPER, B. (1985). *On moral grounds: The search for practical morality.* New York: New York University Press.

HAAN, N., SMITH, M. B., & BLOCK, J. (1968). Moral reasoning of young adults: Political-social behavior, family background, and personality correlates. *Journal of Personality and Social Psychology, 10,* 183–201.

HAGEN, J. W., & HALE, G. A. (1973). The development of attention in children. In A. D. Pick (Ed.), *Minnesota Symposium on Child Psychology* (Vol. 7, pp. 117–140). Minneapolis: University of Minnesota Press.

HAGEN, J. W., HARGROVE, S., & ROSS, W. (1973). Prompting and rehearsal in short-term memory. *Child Development, 44,* 201–204.

HAGEN, J. W., JONGEWARD, R. H., & KAIL, R. V., JR., (1975). Cognitive perspectives on the development of memory. In H. W. Reese (Ed.), *Advances in child development and behavior* (Vol. 10, pp. 57–101). New York: Academic Press.

HAGEN, J. W., & STANOVICH, K. G. (1977). Memory: Strategies of acquisition. In R. V. Kail, Jr., & J. W. Hagen (Eds.), *Perspectives on the development of memory and cognition* (pp. 89–111). Hillsdale, NJ: Erlbaum.

HAGEN, J. W., & WILSON, K. P. (1982). Some selected thoughts on attention: A reply to Lane and Pearson. *Merrill-Palmer Quarterly, 28,* 529–532.

HAITH, M. M. (1980). *Rules that babies look by.* New York: Erlbaum.

HAKES, D. T., EVANS, J. S., & TUNMER, W. E. (1980). *The development of metalinguistic abilities in children.* Berlin: Springer-Verlag.

HAKUTA, K. (1986). *Mirror of language.* New York: Basic Books.

HALE, C. A., & KAIL, R. (1984). Rules for evaluating the difficulty of memory problems. *Bulletin of the Psychonomic Society, 22,* 33–36.

HALE, J. E. (1982). *Black children: Their roots, culture, and learning styles.* Provo, UT: Brigham Young University Press.

HALE, R. L. (1978). The WISC-R as a predictor of WRAT performance. *Psychology in the Schools, 15,* 172–175.

HALFORD, G. S., & BOYLE, F. M. (1985). Do young children understand conservation of number? *Child Development, 56,* 165–176.

HALL, G. S. (1904). *Adolescence.* (Vols. 1–2). New York: Appleton-Century-Crofts.

HALL, J. A. (1978). Gender effects in decoding nonverbal cues. *Psychological Bulletin, 85,* 845–857.

HALL, J. A., & HALBERSTADT, A. G. (1980). Masculinity and femininity in children: Development of the Children's Personal Attributes Questionnaire. *Developmental Psychology, 16,* 270–280.

HALL, J. A., & HALBERSTADT, A. G. (1981). Sex roles and nonverbal communication skills. *Sex Roles, 7,* 273–287.

HALL, J. G., SYBERT, V. P., WILLIAMSON, R. A., FISHER, N. L., & REED, S. D. (1982). Turner's syndrome. *West Journal of Medicine, 137,* 32–44.

HALLINAN, M. T., & TEIXEIRA, R. A. (1987). Opportunities and constraints: Black-white differences in the formation of interracial friendships. *Child Development, 58,* 1358–1371.

HALVERSON, H. M. (1931). An experimental study of prehension in infants by means of systematic cinema records. *Genetic Psychology Monographs, 10,* 107–286.

HAMBURG, B. A. (1985). Comments on the relationship of child development to modern child health care. *Historical Selections from the 50th Anniversary Meeting.* Topeka, KS: Society for Research in Child Development.

HAMM, C. M. (1977). The content of moral education, or in defense of the "bag of virtues." *School Review, 85,* 218–228.

HARARI, O., & COVINGTON, M. V. (1981). Reactions to achievement behavior from a teacher and student perspective: A developmental analysis. *American Educational Research Journal, 18,* 15–28.

HARDY-BROWN, K. (1983). Universals and individual differences: Disentangling two approaches to the study of language acquisition. *Developmental Psychology, 19,* 610–624.

HARE, A. P. (1953). Small group discussions with participatory and supervisory leadership. *Journal of Abnormal and Social Psychology, 48,* 273–275.

HAREVEN, T. K. (1984). Themes in the historical development of the family. In R. D. Parke (Ed.), *Review of child development research* (Vol. 7, pp. 137–178). Chicago: University of Chicago Press.

HARLOW, H. F. (1969). Age-mate or peer affectional system. In D. S. Lehrman, R. A. Hinde, & E. Shaw (Eds.), *Advances in the study of behavior* (Vol. 2, pp. 333–383). New York: Academic Press.

HARLOW, H. F., & ZIMMERMAN, R. (1959). Affectional responses in the infant monkey. *Science, 130,* 421–432.

HARMON, R. J., MORGAN, G. A., & KLEIN, R. P. (1977). Determinants of normal variation in infants' negative reactions to unfamiliar adults. *Journal of the American Academy of Child Psychiatry, 16,* 670–683.

HARP, J., & TAIETZ, P. (1966). Academic integrity and social structure: A study of cheating among college students. *Social Problems, 13,* 365–373.

HARPER, L. V., & HUIE, K. S. (1985). The effects of prior group experience, age, and familiarity on the quality and organization of preschoolers' social relationships. *Child Development, 56,* 704–717.

HARPER, P. S. (1981). *Practical genetic counseling.* Baltimore: University Park Press.

HARPER, R. M., LEAKE, B., HOFFMAN, H., WALTER, D. O., HOPPENBROUWERS, T., HODGMAN, J., & STERMAN, M. B. (1981). Periodicity of sleep is altered in infants with sudden infant death syndrome. *Science, 213,* 1030–1032.

HARRELL, R. F., WOODYARD, E., & GATES, A. I. (1955). *The effects of mothers' diets on the intelligence of offspring.* New York: Teachers College Press.

HARRIMAN, A. E., & LUKOSIUS, P. A. (1982). On why Wayne Dennis found Hopi Indians retarded in age at onset of walking. *Perceptual and Motor Skills, 55,* 79–86.

HARRIS, H. (1970). Development of moral attitudes in white and Negro boys. *Developmental Psychology, 2,* 376–383.

HARRIS, P. L. (1983). Infant cognition. In J. H. Flavell & E. M. Markman (Eds.), *Handbook of child psychology: Vol. 2. Infancy and developmental psychobiology* (4th ed., pp. 689–782). New York: Wiley.

HARRIS, P. L., KRUITHOF, A., TERWOGT, M. M., & VISSER, P. (1981). Children's detection and awareness of textual anomaly. *Journal of Experimental Child Psychology, 31,* 212–230.

HARRIS, S., MUSSEN, P. H., & RUTHERFORD, E. (1976). Some cognitive, behavioral, and personality correlates of maturity of moral judgment. *Journal of Genetic Psychology, 128,* 123–135.

HARRISON, A., SERAFICA, F., & McADOO, H. (1984). Ethnic families of color. In R. D. Parke (Ed.), *Review of child development research* (Vol. 7, pp. 329–371). Chicago: University of Chicago Press.

HART, S. N., & BRASSARD, M. R. (1987). A major threat to children's mental health: Psychological maltreatment. *American Psychologist, 42,* 160–165.

HART, R. A. (1979). *Children's experience of place.* New York: Irvington.

HARTER, S. (1981). A new self-report scale of intrinsic versus extrinsic orientation in the classroom: Motivational and informational components. *Developmental Psychology, 17,* 300–312.

HARTER, S. (1982). The perceived competence scale for children. *Child Development, 53,* 87–97.

HARTER, S. (1983). Developmental perspectives on the self-system. In E. M. Hetherington (Ed.), *Handbook of child psychology: Vol. 4.*

Socialization, personality, and social development (4th ed., pp. 275–385). New York: Wiley.

HARTER, S., WRIGHT, K., & BRESNICK, S. (1987). A developmental sequence of the emergence of self affects: The understanding of pride and shame. Paper presented at the meeting of the Society for Research in Child Development, Baltimore.

HARTMANN, D. P. (1969). Influence of symbolically modeled instrumental aggression and pain cues on aggressive behavior. *Journal of Personality and Social Psychology, 11,* 280–288.

HARTSHORNE, H., & MAY, M. A. (1928). *Studies in the nature of character: Vol. 1. Studies in deceit.* New York: Macmillan.

HARTSHORNE, H., MAY, M. A., & SHUTTLEWORTH, F. K. (1930). *Studies in the nature of character: Vol. 3. Studies in the organization of character.* New York: Macmillan.

HARTUP, W. W. (1974). Aggression in childhood: Developmental perspectives. *American Psychologist, 29,* 336–341.

HARTUP, W. W. (1983). Peer relations. In E. M. Hetherington (Ed.), *Handbook of child psychology: Vol. 4. Socialization, personality, and social development.* (4th ed., pp. 103–196). New York: Wiley.

HARTUP, W. W., & COATES, B. (1967). Imitation of a peer as a function of reinforcement from the peer group and rewardingness of the model. *Child Development, 38,* 1003–1016.

HARTUP, W. W., BRADY, J. E., & NEWCOMB, A. F. (1983). Social cognition and social interaction in childhood. In E. T. Higgins, D. N. Ruble, & W. W. Hartup (Eds.), *Social cognition and social development* (pp. 82–109). Cambridge, Eng.: Cambridge University Press.

HARTUP, W. W., GLAZER, J. A., & CHARLESWORTH, R. (1967). Peer reinforcement and sociometric status. *Child Development, 38,* 1017–1024.

HASHER, L., & ZACKS, R. T. (1979). Automatic and effortful processes in memory. *Journal of Experimental Psychology: General, 108,* 356–388.

HAVIGHURST, R. J. (1976). The relative importance of social class and ethnicity in human development. *Human Development, 19,* 56–64.

HAWKE, S., & KNOX, D. (1978). The one-child family: A new life-style. *The Family Coordinator, 27,* 215–219.

HAWKINS, J., SHEINGOLD, K., GEARHART, M., & BERGER, C. (1982). Microcomputers in schools: Impact on the social life of elementary school classrooms. *Journal of Applied Developmental Psychology, 3,* 361–373.

HAWKINS, R. P., & PINGREE, S. (1978). A developmental exploration of the fear of success phenomenon as cultural stereotype. *Sex Roles, 4,* 539–547.

HAY, D. F. (1984). Social conflict in early childhood. In G. Whitehurst (Ed.), *Annals of child development* (Vol. 4, pp. 1–44). Greenwich, CT: JAI Press.

HAYES, C. (1951). *The ape in our house.* New York: Harper & Row.

HAYES, C. D. (1982). *Making policies for children: A study of the federal process.* Washington, DC: National Academy Press.

HAYES, L. A., & WATSON, J. S. (1981). Neonatal imitation: Fact or artifact. *Developmental Psychology, 17,* 655–660.

HAYNES, C. F., CUTLER, C., GRAY, J., O'KEEFE, K., & KEMPE, R. S. (1983). Nonorganic failure to thrive: Implications of placement through analysis of videotaped interactions. *Child Abuse and Neglect, 7,* 321–328.

HAYNES, H., WHITE, B. L., & HELD, R. (1965). Visual accommodation in human infants. *Science, 148,* 528–530.

HAYS, W. C., & MINDEL, C. H. (1973). Extended kinship relations in black and white families. *Journal of Marriage and the Family, 25,* 51–57.

HEALD, F. P., & HOLLANDER, R. J. (1965). The relationship between obesity in adolescence and early growth. *Journal of Pediatrics, 67,* 35–38.

HEAROLD, S. (1986). A synthesis of 1043 effects of television on social behavior. In G. Comstock (Ed.), *Public communications and behavior* (Vol. 1, pp. 65–133). New York: Academic Press.

HEBB, D. O. (1946). On the nature of fear. *Psychological Review, 53,* 259–276.

HEBB, D. O. (1949). *The organization of behavior.* New York: Wiley.

HEDGES, L. V., GIACONIA, R. M., & GAGE, N. L. (1981). *Meta-analysis of the effects of open and traditional instruction.* Stanford, CA: Stanford University, Program on Teaching Effectiveness.

HEIDER, F. (1958). *The psychology of interpersonal relations.* New York: Wiley.

HEINONEN, O. P., SLONE, D., & SHAPIRO, S. (1977). *Birth defects and drugs in pregnancy.* Littleton, MA: PSG Publishing Company.

HELD, R., & HEIN, A. (1963). Movement-produced stimulation in the development of visually guided behavior. *Journal of Comparative and Physiological Psychology, 56,* 872–876.

HELSON, R., & CRUTCHFIELD, R. S. (1970). Mathematicians: The creative researcher and the average Ph.D. *Journal of Consulting and Clinical Psychology, 34,* 250–257.

HENDRIX, L., & JOHNSON, G. D. (1985). Instrumental and expressive socialization: A false dichotomy. *Sex Roles, 13,* 581–595.

HERBST, A. L. (1981). Diethylstilbestrol and other sex hormones during pregnancy. *Obstetrics and Gynecology, 58,* 35S–40S.

HERON, A., & KROEGER, E. (1981). Introduction to developmental psychology. In H. C. Triandis & A. Heron (Eds.), *Handbook of cross-cultural psychology: Vol. 4. Developmental psychology* (pp. 1–15). Boston: Allyn & Bacon.

HERRERA, M. G., MORA, J. O., CHRISTIANSEN, N., ORTIZ, N., CLEMENT, J., VUORI, L., WABER, D., DE PAREDES, B., & WAGNER, M. (1980). Effects of nutritional supplementation and early education on physical and cognitive development. In R. R. Turner & H. W. Reese (Eds.), *Lifespan Psychology: Intervention* (pp. 149–184). New York: Academic Press.

HERSHENSON, M. (1964). Visual discrimination in the human newborn. *Journal of Comparative and Physiological Psychology, 58,* 270–276.

HERTZ-LAZAROWITZ, R., SHARAN, S., & STEINBERG, R. (1980). Classroom learning style and cooperative behavior of elementary school children. *Journal of Educational Psychology, 72,* 99–106.

HERZBERGER, S. D., DIX, T., ERLEBACHER, A., & GINSBURG, M. (1981). A developmental study of social self-conceptions in adolescence: Impressions and misimpressions. *Merrill-Palmer Quarterly, 27,* 15–29.

HESS, R. D., & MIURA, I. T. (1985). Gender differences in enrollment in computer camps and classes. *Sex Roles, 13,* 193–203.

HESS, R. D., & SHIPMAN, V. C. (1965). Early experience and the socialization of cognitive modes in children. *Child Development, 34,* 869–886.

HETHERINGTON, E. M. (1972). Effects of father absence on personality development in adolescent daughters. *Developmental Psychology, 7,* 313–326.

HETHERINGTON, E. M. (1979). Divorce: A child's perspective. *American Psychologist, 34,* 851–858.

HETHERINGTON, E. M., & CAMARA, K. A. (1984). Families in transition: The processes of dissolution and reconsition. In R. D. Parke (Ed.), *Review of child development research* (Vol. 7, pp. 398–439). Chicago: University of Chicago Press.

HETHERINGTON, E. M., COX, M., & COX, R. (1979). Play and social interaction in children following divorce. *Journal of Social Issues, 35,* 26–49.

HETHERINGTON, E. M., COX, M., & COX, R. (1982). Effects of divorce on parents and children. In M. E. Lamb (Ed.), *Nontraditional families: Parenting and child development* (pp. 233–288). Hillsdale, NJ: Erlbaum.

HETHERINGTON, E. M., COX, M., & COX, R. (1985). Long-term effects of divorce and remarriage on the adjustment of children. *Journal of the American Academy of Child Psychiatry, 24,* 518–530.

HIER, D. B., & KAPLAN, J. (1980). Are sex differences in cerebral organization clinically significant? *The Behavioral and Brain Sciences, 3,* 215–263.

HIGGINS, A. T., & TURNURE, J. E. (1984). Distractibility and concentration of attention in children's development. *Child Development, 55,* 1799–1810.

HIGGINS, E. T., & PARSONS, J. E. (1983). Social cognition and the social life of the child: Stages as subcultures. In E. T. Higgins, D. N. Ruble, & W. W. Hartup (Eds.), *Social cognition and social development* (pp. 15–62). Cambridge, Eng.: Cambridge University Press.

HILL, R. M. (1973). Drugs ingested by pregnant women. *Clinical Pharmacology and Therapeutics, 14,* 654–659.

HILL, R. M., & STERN, L. (1979). Drugs in pregnancy: Effects on the fetus and newborn. *Drugs, 17,* 182–197.

HILLMAN, S. B., & DAVENPORT, G. G. (1978). Teacher-student interactions in desegregated schools. *Journal of Educational Psychology, 70,* 545–553.

HIMES, J. H., & MALINA, R. M. (1975). Age and secular factors in the stature of adult Zapotec males. *American Journal of Physical Anthropology, 43,* 367–370.

HINDE, R. A., STEVENSON-HINDE, J., & TAMPLIN, A. (1985). Characteristics of 3- to 4-year-olds assessed at home and their interactions in preschool. *Developmental Psychology, 21,* 130–140.

HINES, M. (1982). Prenatal gonadal hormones and sex differences in human behavior. *Psychological Bulletin, 92,* 56–80.

HIRSCHI, T., & HINDELANG, M. J. (1977). Intelligence and delinquency: A revisionist view. *American Sociological Review, 42,* 571–587.

HIRSH-PASEK, K., TREIMAN, R., & SCHNEIDERMAN, M. (1984). Brown and Hanlon revisited: Mothers' sensitivity to ungrammatical forms. *Journal of Child Language, 11,* 81–88.

HOBART, C. (1987). Parent-child relations in remarried families. *Journal of Family Issues, 8,* 259–277.

HOBART, C., & BROWN, D. (1988). Effects of prior marriage children on adjustment in remarriages: A Canadian study. *Journal of Comparative Family Studies, 19,* 381–396.

HOCK, E. (1980). Working and nonworking mothers and their infants: A comparative study of maternal caregiving characteristics and infants' social behavior. *Merrill-Palmer Quarterly, 46,* 79–101.

HODGKINSON, H. L. (1985). *All one system: Demographics of education, kindergarten through graduate school.* Washington, DC: Institute of Educational Leadership, Inc.

HOFFERTH, S. L. (1984). Long-term economic consequences for women of delayed childbearing and reduced family size. *Demography, 21,* 141–155.

HOFFMAN, C. D., & DICK, S. A. (1976). A developmental investigation of recognition memory. *Child Development, 47,* 794–799.

HOFFMAN, L. W. (1974). Effects of maternal employment on the child—A review of the research. *Developmental Psychology, 10,* 204–228.

HOFFMAN, L. W. (1977). Changes in family roles, socialization, and sex differences. *American Psychologist, 32,* 644–657.

HOFFMAN, L. W. (1980). The effects of maternal employment on the academic attitudes and performance of school-aged children. *School Psychology Review, 9,* 319–336.

HOFFMAN, L. W. (1984). Work, family and the socialization of the child. In R. D. Parke (Ed.), *Review of child development research* (Vol. 7, pp. 223–282). Chicago: University of Chicago Press.

HOFFMAN, L. W. (1985). The changing genetics/socialization balance. *Journal of Social Issues, 41,* 127–148.

HOFFMAN, M. L. (1970). Moral development. In P. H. Mussen (Ed.), *Carmichael's manual of child psychology* (3rd ed., Vol. 2, pp. 261–359). New York: Wiley.

HOFFMAN, M. L. (1975a). Sex differences in moral internalization. *Journal of Personality and Social Psychology, 32,* 720–729.

HOFFMAN, M. L. (1975b). Altruistic behavior and the parent-child relationship. *Journal of Personality and Social Psychology, 31,* 937–943.

HOFFMAN, M. L. (1976). Empathy, role taking, guilt, and development of altruistic motives. In T. Lickona (Ed.), *Moral development and behavior: Theory, research, and social issues* (pp. 124–143). New York: Holt, Rinehart & Winston.

HOFFMAN, M. L. (1977). Moral internalization: Current theory and research. In L. Berkowitz (Ed.), *Advances in experimental social psychology* (Vol. 10, pp. 85–133). New York: Academic Press.

HOFFMAN, M. L. (1980). Moral development in adolescence. In J. Adelson (Ed.), *Handbook of adolescent psychology* (pp. 295–343). New York: Wiley.

HOFFMAN, M. L. (1981). Perspectives on the difference between understanding people and understanding things: The role of affect. In J. H. Flavell & L. Ross (Eds.), *Social cognitive development: Frontiers and possible futures* (pp. 67–81). New York: Cambridge University Press.

HOFFMAN, M. L. (1984). Interaction of affect and cognition in empathy. In C. E. Izard, J. Kagan, & R. B. Zajonc (Eds.), *Emotions, cognition, and behavior* (pp. 103–131). Cambridge: Cambridge University Press.

HOFFMAN, M. L. (1988). Moral development. In M. H. Bornstein & M. E. Lamb (Eds.), *Developmental psychology: An advanced textbook* (2nd ed., pp. 497–548). Hillsdale, NJ: Erlbaum.

HOFFMAN, M. L., & SALTZSTEIN, H. D. (1967). Parent discipline and the child's moral development. *Journal of Personality and Social Psychology, 5,* 45–47.

HOFSTEN, C. VON. (1982). Eye-hand coordination in the newborn. *Developmental Psychology, 18,* 450–461.

HOFSTEN, C. VON. (1984). Developmental changes in the organization of prereaching movements. *Developmental Psychology, 20,* 378–388.

HOFTSEN, C. VON, & SPELKE, E. S. (1985). Object perception and object-directed reaching in infancy. *Journal of Experimental Psychology: General, 114,* 198–212.

HOGREBE, M. C., NIST, S. L., & NEWMAN, I. (1985). Are there gender differences in reading achievement? An investigation using the High School and Beyond data. *Journal of Educational Psychology, 77,* 716–724.

HOLDEN, C. (1986). Youth suicide: New research focuses on a growing social problem. *Science, 233,* 839–841.

HOLLENBECK, A. R., GEWIRTZ, J. L., & SEBRIS, S. L. (1984). Labor and delivery medication influences parent-infant interaction in the first post-partum month. *Infant Behavior and Development, 7,* 201–209.

HOLLENBECK, A. R., & SLABY, R. G. (1979). Infant visual and vocal responses to television. *Child Development, 50,* 41–45.

HOLSTEIN, C. B. (1972). The relation of children's moral judgment level to that of their parents and to communication patterns in the family. In R. Smart & M. Smart (Eds.), *Readings in child development and relationships* (pp. 484–494). New York: Macmillan.

HOLSTEIN, C. B. (1976). Irreversible, stepwise sequence in the development of moral judgment: A longitudinal study of males and females. *Child Development, 47,* 51–61.

HONG, K., & TOWNES, B. (1976). Infants' attachment to inanimate objects. *Journal of the Academy of Child Psychiatry, 15,* 49–61.

HONZIK, M. P. (1967). Environmental correlates of mental growth: Prediction from the family setting at 21 months. *Child Development, 38,* 337–364.

HONZIK, M. P. (1983). Measuring mental abilities in infancy: The value and limitations. In M. Lewis (Ed.), *Origins of intelligence* (2nd ed., pp. 67–105). New York: Plenum.

HONZIK, M. P., MACFARLANE, J. W., & ALLEN, L. (1948). The stability of mental test performance between two and eighteen years. *Journal of Experimental Education, 17,* 309–329.

HOOK, E. B. (1973). Behavioral implications of the human XYY genotype. *Science, 179,* 131–150.

HOOK, E. B. (1980). Genetic counseling dilemmas: Down syndrome, paternal age, and recurrence risk after remarriage. *American Journal of Medical Genetics, 5,* 145.

HOOK, E. B., & CHAMBERS, G. M. (1977). Estimated rates of Down syndrome in live births by one-year maternal age intervals for mothers aged 20–29 in a New York State study. Implications of the risk figures for genetic counseling and cost-benefit analysis of prenatal diagnosis programs. In D. Bergsma & R. B. Lowry (Eds.), *Numerical taxonomy of birth defects and polygenic disorders* (pp. 123–141). New York: Alan R. Liss for the National Foundation—March of Dimes, BD: OAS XII (3A).

HOOPER, F. H., & DEFRAIN, J. D. (1980). On delineating distinctly Piagetian contributions to education. *Genetic Psychology Monographs, 101,* 151–181.

HORGAN, D. (1978). The development of the full passive. *Journal of Child Language, 5,* 65–80.

HORGAN, D. (1980). Nouns: Love 'em or leave 'em. In V. Teller & S. White (Eds.), *Studies in child language and multilingualism* (Vol. 345, pp. 5–25). New York: New York Academy of Sciences (Annals of the New York Academy of Sciences).

HORGAN, D. (1981). Rate of language acquisition and noun emphasis. *Journal of Psycholinguistic Research, 10,* 629–640.

HORN, J. L. (1967). Intelligence: Why it grows, why it declines. *Trans-Action, 5*(1), 23–31.

HORN, J. L. (1985). Remodeling old models of intelligence. In B. B. Wolman (Ed.), *Handbook of intelligence* (pp. 267–300). New York: Wiley.

HORN, J. L., & CATTELL, R. B. (1967). Age differences in fluid and crystallized intelligence. *Acta Psychologica, 26*, 107–129.

HORN, J. L., & KNAPP, J. R. (1974). Thirty wrongs do not make a right: A reply to Guilford. *Psychological Bulletin, 81*, 502–504.

HORN, J. M. (1983). The Texas Adoption Project: Adopted children and their intellectual resemblance to biological and adoptive parents. *Child Development, 54*, 268–275.

HORN, J. M., LOEHLIN, J. C., & WILLERMAN, L. (1979). Intellectual resemblance among adoptive and biological relatives: The Texas Adoption Project. *Behavior Genetics, 9*, 177–201.

HORNER, T. M. (1980). Two methods of studying stranger reactivity in infants: A review. *Journal of Child Psychology and Psychiatry, 21*, 203–219.

HOROWITZ, F. D., & LINN, P. L. (1982). The neonatal behavioral assessment scale: Assessing the behavioral repertoire of the newborn infant. In M. Wolraich & D. Routh (Eds.), *Advances in developmental and behavioral pediatrics* (Vol. 3, pp. 233–255). New York: Plenum.

HORWITZ, R. A. (1979). Psychological effects of the open classroom. *Review of Educational Research, 49*, 71–86.

HOVERSTEN, G. H., & MONCUR, J. P. (1969). Stimuli and intensity factors in testing infants. *Journal of Speech and Hearing Research, 12*, 687–702.

HOWARD, J., PARMELEE, A. H., KOPP, C. B., & LITTMAN, B. (1976). A neurological comparison of pre-term and full-term infants at term gestational age. *Journal of Pediatrics, 88*, 995–1002.

HOWES, C. (1988). Relations between early child care and schooling. *Developmental Psychology, 24*, 53–57.

HOWES, C., & ELDREDGE, R. (1985). Responses of abused, neglected, and non-maltreated children to the behaviors of their peers. *Journal of Applied Developmental Psychology, 6*, 261–270.

HOWES, C., & OLENICK, M. (1986). Family and child care influences on toddler's compliance. *Child Development, 57*, 202–206.

HOWES, C., & RUBENSTEIN, J. (1985). Determinants of toddlers' experience in day care: Age of entry and quality of setting. *Child Care Quarterly, 14*, 140–151.

HOWES, C., & STEWART, P. (1987). Child's play with adults, toys, and peers: An examination of family and child-care influences. *Developmental Psychology, 23*, 423–430.

HOYT, M. P., & RAVEN, B. H. (1973). Birth order and the 1971 Los Angeles earthquake. *Journal of Personality and Social Psychology, 28*, 123–128.

HUBEL, D. H., & WIESEL, T. N. (1970). The period of susceptibility to the physiological effects of unilateral eye closure in kittens. *Journal of Physiology, 206*, 419–436.

HUBERT, N., WACHS, T. D., PETERS-MARTIN, P., & GANDOUR, M. (1982). The study of early temperament: Measurement and conceptual issues. *Child Development, 53*, 571–600.

HUDSON, J., & NELSON, K. (1983). Effects of script structure on children's story recall. *Developmental Psychology, 19*, 525–635.

HUESMANN, L. R. (1986a). Communalities in learning of aggression. In L. R. Huesmann & L. D. Eron (Eds.), *Television and the aggressive child: A cross-national comparison* (pp. 239–257). Hillsdale, NJ: Erlbaum.

HUESMANN, L. R. (1986b). Psychological processes promoting the relation between exposure to media violence and aggressive behavior by the viewer. *Journal of Social Issues, 42*, 125–139.

HUESMANN, L. R., ERON, L. D., LEFKOWITZ, M. M., & WALDER, L. O. (1984). Stability of aggression over time and generations. *Developmental Psychology, 20*, 1120–1134.

HUESMANN, L. R., LAGERSPETZ, K., & ERON, L. D. (1984). Intervening variables in the TV violence-aggression relation: Evidence from two countries. *Developmental Psychology, 20*, 746–775.

HUGHES, C. C., TREMBLAY, M. A., RAPOPORT, R. N., & LEIGHTON, A. H. (1960). *People of cove and woodlot.* New York: Basic.

HULME, C., THOMSON, N., MUIR, C., & LAWRENCE, A. (1984). Speech rate and the development of short-term memory span. *Journal of Experimental Child Psychology, 38*, 241–253.

HUMPHREY, T. (1978). Function of the nervous system during prenatal life. In U. Stave (Ed.), *Perinatal physiology* (pp. 651–683). New York: Plenum.

HUMPHREYS, A. P., & SMITH, P. K. (1984). Rough and tumble in preschool and playground. In P. K. Smith (Ed.), *Play in animals and humans* (pp. 241–266). Oxford, Eng.: Basil Blackwell.

HUMPHREYS, A. P., & SMITH, P. K. (1987). Rough and tumble, friendship, and dominance in schoolchildren: Evidence for continuity and change with age. *Child Development, 58*, 201–212.

HUNT, J. McV., MOHANDESSI, K., GHODESSI, M., & AKEYAMA, M. (1976). The psychological development of orphanage-reared infants: Interventions with outcomes (Tehran). *Genetic Psychology Monographs, 94*, 177–226.

HUNTER, F. T., & YOUNISS, J. (1982). Changes in functions of three relations during adolescence. *Developmental Psychology, 18*, 806–811.

HUNTER, J. E., & HUNTER, R. F. (1984). Validity and utility of alternative predictors of job performance. *Psychological Bulletin, 96*, 72–98.

HURLEY, J., & PALONEN, D. (1967). Marital satisfaction and child density among university student parents. *Journal of Marriage and the Family, 29*, 483–484.

HUSÉN, T. (1967). *International study of achievement in mathematics: A comparison of twelve countries.* New York: Wiley.

HUSTON, A. C. (1983). Sex-typing. In E. M. Hetherington (Ed.), *Handbook of child psychology: Vol. 4. Socialization, personality, and social development* (4th ed., pp. 387–467). New York: Wiley.

HUSTON, A. C., GREER, D., WRIGHT, J. C., WELCH, R., & ROSS, R. (1984). Children's comprehension of televised formal features with masculine and feminine connotations. *Developmental Psychology, 20*, 707–716.

HUSTON-STEIN, A., FOX, S., GREER, D., WATKINS, B. A., & WHITAKER, J. (1981). The effects of TV action and violence on children's social behavior. *The Journal of Genetic Psychology, 138*, 183–191.

HUSTON-STEIN, A., & HIGGINS-TRENK, A. (1978). Development of females from childhood through adulthood: Career and feminine role orientations. In P. B. Baltes (Ed.), *Life-span development and behavior* (Vol. 1, pp. 257–296). New York: Academic Press.

HUTTENLOCHER, J., & LUI, F. (1979). The semantic organization of some simple nouns and verbs. *Journal of Verbal Learning and Verbal Behavior, 18*, 141–162.

HUTTUNEN, M. O., & NISKANEN, P. (1978). Prenatal loss of father and psychiatric disorders. *Archives of General Psychiatry, 35*, 429–431.

HWANG, C. P. (1986). Behavior of Swedish primary and secondary caretaking fathers in relation to mother's presence. *Developmental Psychology, 22*, 749–751.

HYDE, J. S. (1981). How large are cognitive gender differences? *American Psychologist, 36*, 892–901.

HYDE, J. S. (1984). How large are gender differences in aggression? A developmental meta-analysis. *Developmental Psychology, 20*, 722–736.

HYMAN, I. A. (1987). Psychological correlates of corporal punishment. In M. R. Brassard, R. Germain, & S. N. Hart (Eds.), *Psychological maltreatment of children and youth* (pp. 59–68). New York: Pergamon Press.

HYMEL, S. (1983). Preschool children's peer relations: Issues in sociometric assessment. *Merrill-Palmer Quarterly, 19*, 237–260.

HYMEL, S. (1986). Interpretations of peer behavior: Affective bias in childhood and adolescence. *Child Development, 57*, 431–445.

HYMEL, S., & RUBIN, K. H. (1985). Children with peer relationship and social skills problems: Conceptual, methodological, and developmental issues. In G. J. Whitehurst (Ed.), *Annuals of child development* (Vol. 2, pp. 251–297). Greenwich, CT: JAI Press.

HYSON, M. C., & IZARD, C. E. (1983). Continuities and changes in emotion expressions during brief separations at 13 and 18 months. *Developmental Psychology, 21*, 1165–1170.

IANCO-WORRALL, A. (1972). Bilingualism and cognitive development. *Child Development, 43*, 1390–1400.

IANNOTTI, R. J. (1985). Naturalistic assessment of prosocial behavior in preschool children: The influence of empathy and perspective taking. *Developmental Psychology, 21*, 46–55.

IHINGER-TALLMAN, M., & PASLEY, K. (1987). *Remarriage.* Newbury Park, CA: Sage.

IMPERATO-MCGINLEY, J., PETERSEN, R. E., GAUTIER, T., & STURLA, E. (1979). Androgens and the evolution of male-gender identity among male pseudohermaphrodites with 5-reductase deficiency. *New England Journal of Medicine, 22*, 1233–1237.

INGRAM, D. (1986). Phonological development: Production. In P. Fletcher & M. Garman (Eds.), *Language acquisition* (2nd ed., pp. 223–239). Cambridge, Eng.: Cambridge University Press.

INHELDER, B. (1944). *Le diagnostic du raisonnement chez les debiles mentaux.* Neuchatel: Delachaux et Niestle.

INHELDER, B. (1960). Criteria of stages of mental development. In J. M. Tanner and B. Inhelder (Eds.), *Discussions on child development* (pp. 75–85). New York: International Universities Press.

INHELDER, B., & PIAGET, J. (1958). *The growth of logical thinking from childhood to adolescence: An essay on the construction of formal operational structures.* New York: Basic Books. (Original French edition 1955)

INHELDER, B., SINCLAIR, H., & BOVET, M. (1974). *Learning and the development of cognition.* Cambridge, MA: Harvard University Press.

INOFF-GERMAIN, G., ARNOLD, G. S., NOTTELMAN, E. D., SUSMAN, E. J., CUTLER, G. B., JR., & CROUSOS, G. P. (1988). Relations between hormone levels and observational measures of aggressive behavior of young adolescents in family interactions. *Developmental Psychology, 24*, 129–139.

IOSUB, S., FUCHS, M., BINGOL, N., & GROMISCH, D. S. (1981). Fetal alcohol syndrome revisited. *Pediatrics, 68*, 475–479.

IPSA, J. (1981). Peer support among Soviet day care toddlers. *International Journal of Behavioral Development, 4*, 255–269.

IRVINE, J. J. (1986). Teacher-student interactions: Effects of student race, sex, and grade level. *Journal of Educational Psychology, 78*, 14–21.

ISAACS, S. (1933). *Social development in young children: A study of beginnings.* London: Routledge.

ISTOMINA, Z. M. (1975). The development of voluntary memory in preschool-age children. *Soviet Psychology, 13*, 5–64.

IZARD, C. E. (1978). On the ontogenesis of emotions and emotion-cognition relationships in infancy. In M. Lewis & L. Rosenblum (Eds.), *The development of affect* (pp. 389–413). New York: Plenum.

IZARD, C. E., HEMBREE, E. A., & HUEBNER, R. R. (1987). Infants' emotion expressions to acute pain. *Developmental Psychology, 23*, 105–113.

JACKLIN, C. N., & MACCOBY, E. E. (1978). Social behavior at thirty-three months in same-sex and mixed-sex dyads. *Child Development, 49*, 557–569.

JACKLIN, C. N., & MACCOBY, E. E. (1983). Issues of gender differentiation in normal development. In M. D. Levine, W. B. Carey, A. C. Crocker, & R. T. Gross (Eds.), *Developmental-behavioral pediatrics* (pp. 175–184). Philadelphia: Saunders.

JACKSON, P. W. (1968). *Life in classrooms.* New York: Holt, Rinehart & Winston.

JACKSON, P. W., & LAHADERNE, H. M. (1968). Inequalities of teacher-pupil contacts. *Psychology in the Schools, 4*, 201–211.

JACOBSON, J. L., TIANEN, R. L., WILLE, D. E., & AYTCH, D. M. (1986). Infant-mother attachment and early peer relations: The assessment of behavior in an interactive context. In E. Mueller & C. Cooper (Eds.), *Process and outcome in peer relations* (pp. 57–78). New York: Academic Press.

JACOBSON, J. L., & WILLE, D. E. (1986). The influence of attachment pattern on developmental changes in peer interaction from the toddler to the preschool period. *Child Development, 57*, 338–347.

JACOBSON, M. (1975). Brain development in relation to language. In E. H. Lenneberg & E. Lenneberg (Eds.), *Foundations of language development* (Vol. 1, pp. 105–119). New York: Academic Press.

JARVIK, L. F., KLODIN, V., & MATSUYAMA, S. S. (1973). Human aggression and the extra Y chromosome: Fact or fantasy. *American Psychologist, 28*, 674–682.

JEANS, P. C., SMITH, M. B., & STEARNS, G. (1955). Incidence of prematurity in relation to maternal nutrition. *Journal of the American Dietetic Association, 31*, 576–581.

JEFFREY, D. P., MCLELLARN, R. W., & FOX, D. T. (1982). The development of children's eating habits: The role of television commercials. *Health Education Quarterly, 9*, 78–93.

JENCKS, C. (1972). *Inequality: A reassessment of the effect of family and schooling in America.* New York: Basic Books.

JENSEN, A. R. (1969). How much can we boost IQ and scholastic achievement? *Harvard Educational Review, 39*, 1–123.

JENSEN, A. R. (1973). *Educability and group differences.* New York: Harper and Row.

JENSEN, A. R. (1974). Cumulative deficit: A testable hypothesis. *Developmental Psychology, 10*, 996–1019.

JENSEN, A. R. (1977). Cumulative deficit in IQ of blacks in the rural South. *Developmental Psychology, 13*, 184–191.

JENSEN, A. R. (1980). *Bias in mental testing.* New York: Free Press.

JENSEN, A. R. (1985). The nature of the black-white difference on various psychometric tests: Spearman's hypothesis. *Behavioral and Brain Sciences, 8*, 193–263.

JENSEN, A. R., & FIGUEROA, R. A. (1975). Forward and backward digit-span interaction with race and IQ: Predictions from Jensen's theory. *Journal of Educational Psychology, 67*, 882–893.

JOHNSON, C. F., & SHOWERS, J. (1985). Injury variables in child abuse. *Child Abuse & Neglect, 9*, 207–215.

JOHNSON, C. N., & WELLMAN, H. M. (1980). Children's developing understanding of mental verbs: "Remember," "know," and "guess." *Child Development, 51*, 1095–1102.

JOHNSON, C. N., & WELLMAN, H. M. (1982). Children's developing conceptions of mind and brain. *Child Development, 53*, 222–234.

JOHNSON, D. W., JOHNSON, R. T., & MARUYAMA, G. (1984). Goal interdependence and interpersonal attraction in heterogeneous classrooms: A meta-analysis. In N. Miller & M. B. Brewer (Eds.), *Groups in contact: The psychology of desegregation* (pp. 187–212). New York: Academic Press.

JOHNSON, E. S., & MEADE, A. C. (1987). Developmental patterns of spatial ability: An early sex difference. *Child Development, 58*, 725–740.

JOHNSON, J. E., & HOOPER, F. H. (1982). Piagetian structuralism and learning: Two decades of educational application. *Contemporary Eductional Psychology, 7*, 217–237.

JOHNSON, L. D., DRISCOLL, S. G., HERTIG, A. T., COLE, P. T., & NICKERSON, R. J. (1979). Vaginal adenosis in stillborns and neonates exposed to diethylstilbestrol and steroidal estrogens and progestins. *Obstetrics and Gynecology, 53*, 671–679.

JOHNSON, L. G. (1983). Giftedness in preschool: A better time for development than identification. *Roeper Review, 5*(4), 13–15.

JOHNSON, M. M. (1981). Fathers, mothers, and sex typing. In E. M. Hetherington & R. D. Parke (Eds.), *Contemporary readings in child psychology* (2nd ed., pp. 391–403). New York: McGraw-Hill.

JOHNSON, R. E. (1979). *Juvenile delinquency and its origins.* New York: Cambridge University Press.

JOHNSON, W., EMDE, R. N., PANNABECKER, B., STENBERG, C., & DAVIS, M. (1982). Maternal perception of infant emotion from birth through 18 months. *Infant Behavior and Development, 5*, 313–322.

JOHNSTON, F. E. (1980). The causes of malnutrition. In L. S. Greene & F. E. Johnston (Eds.), *Social and biological predictors of nutritional status, physical growth, and neurological development* (pp. 1–6). New York: Academic Press.

JOHNSTON, J. R., & SLOBIN, D. I. (1979). The development of locative expressions in English, Italian, Serbo-Croatian, and Turkish. *Journal of Child Language, 16*, 531–547.

JONES, C. P., & ADAMSON, L. B. (1987). Language use in mother-child and mother-child-sibling interactions. *Child Development, 58*, 356–366.

JONES, E. F., FORREST, J. D., GOLDMAN, N., HENSHAW, S. K., LINCOLN, R., ROSOFF, J. I., WESTOFF, C. F., & WULF, D. (1985). Teenage pregnancy in developed countries: Determinants and policy implications. *Family Planning Perspectives, 17,* 53–63.

JONES, H. E. (1971). Psychological factors related to physical abilities in adolescent boys. In M. C. Jones, N. Bayley, J. W. MacFarlane, & M. P. Honzik (Eds.), *The course of human development* (pp. 279–280). Waltham, MA: Xerox Publishing.

JONES, K. L., SMITH, D. W., ULLELAND, C. N., & STREISSGUTH, A. P. (1973). Patterns of malformation in offspring of chronic alcoholic mothers. *Lancet, 1,* 1267–1271.

JONES, M. C. (1965). Psychological correlates of somatic development. *Child Development, 36,* 899–911.

JONES, M. C., & BAYLEY, N. (1950). Physical maturing among boys as related to behavior. *Journal of Educational Psychology, 41,* 129–148.

JONES, M. C., & MUSSEN, P. H. (1958). Self-conceptions, motivations, and interpersonal attitudes of early- and late-maturing girls. *Child Development, 29,* 491–501.

JONES, N. BLURTON (1972). Categories of child-child interaction. In N. Blurton Jones (Ed.), *Ethological studies of child behaviour* (pp. 97–127). Cambridge, Eng.: Cambridge Unversity Press.

JOOS, S. K., POLLITT, K. E., MUELLER, W. H., & ALBRIGHT, D. L. (1983). The Bacon Chow study: Maternal nutritional supplementation and infant behavioral development. *Child Development, 54,* 669–676.

JUDD, S. A., & MERVIS, C. B. (1979). Learning to solve class-inclusion problems: The roles of quantification and recognition of contradictions. *Child Development, 50,* 163–169.

JURKOVIC, G. J., & PRENTICE, N. M. (1977). Relation of moral and cognitive development to dimensions of juvenile delinquency. *Journal of Abnormal Psychology, 86,* 414–420.

JUSCZYK, P. W. (1985). On characterizing the development of speech perception. In J. Mehler & R. Fox (Eds.), *Neonate cognition: Beyond the blooming, buzzing confusion* (pp. 199–230). Hillsdale, NJ: Erlbaum.

KAGAN, J. (1964). American longitudinal research on psychological development. *Child Development, 35,* 1–32.

KAGAN, J. (1965). *Matching Familiar Figures Test.* Cambridge, MA: Harvard University.

KAGAN, J. (1971). *Change and continuity in infancy.* New York: Wiley.

KAGAN, J. (1974). Discrepancy, temperament and infant distress. In M. Lewis & L. Rosenblum (Eds.), *The origins of fear* (pp. 229–248). New York: Wiley.

KAGAN, J. (1976). Resilience and continuity in psychological development. In A. M. Clarke & A. D. B. Clarke (Eds.), *Early experience: Myth and evidence* (pp. 97–121). New York: Free Press.

KAGAN, J. (1982). *Psychological research on the human infant: An evaluative summary.* New York: W. T. Grant Foundation.

KAGAN, J. (1984). The idea of emotion in human development. In C. E. Izard, J. Kagan, & R. B. Zajonc (Eds.), *Emotions, cognition, and behavior* (pp. 38–72). Cambridge, Eng.: Cambridge University Press.

KAGAN, J., KEARSLEY, R. B., & ZELAZO, P. R. (1978). *Infancy: Its place in human development.* Cambridge, MA: Harvard University Press.

KAGAN, J., & KLEIN, R. E. (1973). Cross-cultural perspectives on early development. *American Psychologist, 28,* 947–961.

KAGAN, J., KLEIN, R. E., FINLEY, G. E., ROGOFF, B., & NOLAN, E. (1979). A cross-cultural study of cognitive development. *Monographs of the Society for Research in Child Development, 44*(5, Serial No. 180).

KAGAN, J., & MESSER, S. B. (1975). A reply to "Some misgivings about the Matching Familiar Figures Test as a measure of reflection-impulsivity." *Developmental Psychology, 11,* 244–248.

KAGAN, J., & MOSS, H. A. (1962). *Birth to maturity.* New York: Wiley.

KAGAN, J., REZNICK, J. S., & SNIDMAN, N. (1987). The physiology and psychology of behavioral inhibition in children. *Child Development, 58,* 1459–1473.

KAIL, R., & HAGEN, J. W. (1982). Memory in childhood. In B. B. Wolman (Ed.), *Handbook of developmental psychology.* (pp. 350–366). Englewood Cliffs, NJ: Prentice-Hall.

KAITZ, M., MESCHULACH-SARFATY, O., AUERBACH, J., & EIDELMAN, A. (1988). A reexamination of newborns' ability to imitate facial expressions. *Developmental Psychology, 24,* 3–7.

KALTER, N., RIEMER, B., BRICKMAN, A., & CHEN, J. W. (1985). Implications of parental divorce for female development. *Journal of the American Academy of Child Psychiatry, 24,* 538–544.

KAMERMAN, S. B. (1980a). *Parenting in an unresponsive society.* New York: Free Press.

KAMERMAN, S. B. (1980b). *Maternal and parental benefits and leaves: An international review* (Impact on Policies Series, Monograph No. 1). New York: Center for the Social Sciences, Columbia University.

KAMMEYER, K. (1967). Birth order as a research variable. *Social Forces, 46,* 71–80.

KANDEL, D. B. (1978a). Similarity in real-life adolescent friendship pairs. *Journal of Personality and Social Psychology, 36,* 306–312.

KANDEL, D. B. (1978b). Homophily, selection, and socialization in adolescent friendships. *American Journal of Sociology, 84,* 427–436.

KANDEL, D. B., & LESSER, G. S. (1972). *Youth in two worlds.* San Francisco: Jossey-Bass.

KANT, I. (1952). Fundamental principles of the metaphysics of morals. In C. W. Elliot (Ed.), *The Harvard classics: Vol 32. Literary and philosophical essays* (pp. 305–373). New York: P. F. Collier & Son Corporation. (Original work published 1785)

KANTOR, D., & LEHR, W. (1975). *Inside the family.* San Francisco: Jossey-Bass.

KAPLAN, B. J. (1972). Malnutrition and mental deficiency. *Psychological Bulletin, 78,* 321–334.

KAPLAN, H. B., & POKORNY, A. D. (1971). Self-derogation and childhood broken homes. *Journal of Marriage and the Family, 33,* 328–337.

KAPLAN, R. M. (1985). The controversy related to the use of psychological tests. In B. B. Wolman (Ed.), *Handbook of intelligence* (pp. 465–504). New York: Wiley.

KAPPEL, B. E., & LAMBERT, R. D. (1972). Self-worth among the children of working mothers. Unpublished manuscript, University of Waterloo, Ontario, Canada.

KARMILOFF-SMITH, A. (1979). Language development after five. In P. Fletcher & M. Garman (Eds.), *Language acquisition* (pp. 307–323). New York: Cambridge University Press.

KATO, S., & ISHIKO, T. (1966). Obstructed growth of children's bones due to excessive labor in remote corners of Japan. In K. Kato (Ed.), *Proceedings of International Congress of Sports Sciences.* Tokyo: Japanese Union of Sports Sciences.

KATZ, L. (1972, June). Condition with caution. *Young Children, 28*(5), 277–280.

KAUFMAN, A. S. (1979). *Intelligence testing with the WISC-R.* New York: Wiley.

KAUFMAN, A. S., & KAUFMAN, N. L. (1983a). *Kaufman Assessment Battery for Children: Interpretive Manual.* Circle Pines, MN: American Guidance Service.

KAUFMAN, A. S., & KAUFMAN, N. L. (1983b). *Kaufman Assessment Battery for Children: Administration and scoring manual.* Circle Pines, MN: American Guidance Service.

KAUFMAN, A. S., KAMPHAUS, R. W., & KAUFMAN, N. L. (1985). New directions in intelligence testing: The Kaufman Assessment Battery for Children (K-ABC). In B. B. Wolman (Ed.), *Handbook of intelligence* (pp. 663–698). New York: Wiley.

KAYE, K., & CHARNEY, R. (1980). How mothers maintain "dialogue" with two-year-olds. In D. Olson (Ed.), *The social foundations of language and thought* (pp. 211–230). New York: Norton.

KAYE, K., & MARCUS, J. (1981). Infant imitation: The sensory-motor agenda. *Developmental Psychology, 17,* 258–265.

KAYE, K., & WELLS, A. J. (1980). Mothers' jiggling and the burst-pause pattern in neonatal feeding. *Infant Behavior and Development, 3,* 29–46.

KEASEY, C. B. (1971). Social participation as a factor in the moral development of preadolescents. *Developmental Psychology, 5,* 216–220.

KEASEY, C. B. (1977). Young children's attribution of intentionality to themselves and others. *Child Development, 48,* 261–264.

KEATING, D. P. (1980). Adolescent thinking. In J. Adelson (Ed.), *Handbook of adolescent psychology* (pp. 211–246). New York: Wiley.

KEATING, D. P., & BOBBITT, B. L. (1978). Individual and developmental differences in cognitive-processing components of mental ability. *Child Development, 49,* 155–167.

KEATING, D. P., & CLARK, L. V. (1980). Development of physical and social reasoning in adolescence. *Developmental Psychology, 16,* 23–30.

KEENEY, T. J., CANIZZO, S. R., & FLAVELL, J. H. (1967). Spontaneous and induced verbal rehearsal in a recall task. *Child Development, 38,* 953–966.

KELLAM, S. G., ENSMINGER, M. A., & TURNER, J. T. (1977). Family structure and the mental health of children. *Archives of General Psychology, 34,* 1012–1022.

KELLER, A., FORD, L. H., & MEACHAM, J. A. (1978). Dimensions of self-concept in preschool children. *Developmental Psychology, 14,* 483–489.

KELLER, B., & BELL, R. Q. (1979). Child effects on adults' method of eliciting altruistic behavior. *Child Development, 50,* 1004–1010.

KELLEY, H. H. (1973). The processes of causal attribution, *American Psychologist, 28,* 107–128.

KELLMAN, P. J., & SPELKE, E. S. (1983). Perception of partly occluded objects in infancy. *Cognitive Psychology, 15,* 483–524.

KELLY, A., & SMAIL, B. (1986). Sex stereotypes and attitudes to science among eleven-year-old children. *British Journal of Educational Psychology, 56,* 158–168.

KELLY, H. (1981). Viewing children through television. In H. Kelly & H. Gardner (Eds.), *New directions for child development* (No. 13, pp. 59–71). San Francisco: Jossey-Bass.

KEMPE, C. H., SILVERMAN, B. F., STEELE, P. W., DROEGEMUELLER, P. W., & SILVER, H. K. (1962). The battered-child syndrome. *Journal of the American Medical Association, 181,* 17–24.

KEMPE, R. S., & KEMPE, C. H. (1984). *The common secret: Sexual abuse of children and adolescents.* New York: Freeman.

KENDLER, H. H., & KENDLER, T. S. (1962). Vertical and horizontal processes in problem-solving. *Psychological Review, 69,* 1–16.

KENDLER, H. H., & KENDLER, T. S. (1975). From discrimination learning to cognitive development: A neobehaviorist odyssey. In W. K. Estes (Ed.), *Handbook of learning and cognitive processes* (Vol. 1, pp. 191–247). Hillsdale, NJ: Erlbaum.

KENISTON, K. (1977). *All our children: The American family under pressure.* New York: Harcourt Brace Jovanovich.

KENNEDY, B. A., & MILLER, D. J. (1976). Persistent use of verbal rehearsal as a function of information about its value. *Child Development, 47,* 566–569.

KENNELL, J. H., VOOS, D. K., & KLAUS, M. H. (1976). Parent-infant bonding. In R. Helfer & C. H. Kempe (Eds.), *Child abuse and neglect: The family and the community* (pp. 25–54). Cambridge, MA: Ballinger.

KENNELL, J. H., VOOS, D. K., & KLAUS, M. H. (1979). Parent-infant bonding. In J. Osofsky (Ed.), *Handbook of infant development* (pp. 786–798). New York: Wiley.

KENNETT, K. F., & CROPLEY, A. J. (1970). Intelligence, family size and socioeconomic status. *Journal of Biosocial Science, 2,* 227–236.

KENNTNER, G. (1969). Absolute differences and changes of the average stature among the Chileans. *Biological Abstracts, 50,* 3248.

KEOGH, B. (1985). Temperament and schooling: Meaning of "Goodness of fit?" In J. V. Lerner & R. M. Lerner (Eds.), *New Directions for Child Development* (No. 31, pp. 89–108). San Francisco: Jossey-Bass.

KERWIN, M. L. E., & DAY, J. D. (1985). Peer influences on cognitive development. in J. B. Pryor & J. D. Day (Eds.), *The development of social cognition* (pp. 211–228). New York: Springer-Verlag.

KESSEN, W. (1967). Sucking and looking: Two organized congenital patterns of behavior in the human newborn. In H. W. Stevenson, E. H. Hess, & H. L. Rheingold (Eds.), *Early behavior: Comparative and developmental approaches* (pp. 147–179). New York: Wiley.

KESSEN, W. (1983). Preface to volume 1. In W. Kessen (Ed.), *Handbook of child psychology: Vol. 1. History, theory, and methods* (4th ed., pp. iix–x). New York: Wiley.

KESSEN, W., HAITH, M. M., & SALAPATEK, P. H. (1970). Human infancy: A bibliography and guide. In P. H. Mussen (Ed.), *Carmichael's manual of child psychology* (3rd ed., Vol. 1, pp. 287–445). New York: Wiley.

KESSLER, R. C., & MCRAE, J. A., JR. (1981). Trends in the relationship between sex and psychological distress: 1957–1976. *American Sociological Review, 46,* 443–452.

KESSLER, R. C., & MCRAE, J. A., JR. (1982). The effects of wives' employment on the mental health of married men and women. *American Sociological Review, 47,* 216–227.

KESSLER, S. (1980). The genetics of schizophrenia: A review. *Schizophrenia Bulletin, 6,* 404–416.

KIELMAN, A. A. (1977). Weight fluctuations after immunization in a rural preschool child community. *American Journal of Clinical Nutrition, 30,* 592–598.

KIMBALL, M. M. (1986). Television and sex-role attitudes. In T. M. Williams (Ed.), *The impact of television* (pp. 265–301). New York: Academic Press.

KINARD, E. M., & KLERMAN, L. V. (1983). Effects of early parenthood on the cognitive development of children. In E. R. McAnarney (Ed.), *Premature adolescent pregnancy and parenthood* (pp. 253–266). New York: Grune and Stratton.

KINSMAN, C. A., & BERK, L. E. (1979, November). Joining the block and housekeeping areas: Changes in play and social behavior. *Young Children, 35*(1), 66–75.

KISER, L. J., BATES, J. E., MASLIN, C. A., & BAYLES, K. (1986). Mother-infant play at six months as a predictor of attachment security at thirteen months. *Journal of the American Academy of Child Psychiatry, 25,* 68–75.

KISILEVSKY, B. S., & MUIR, D. W. (1984). Neonatal habituation and dishabituation to tactile stimulation during sleep. *Developmental Psychology, 20,* 367–373.

KLAHR, D., & WALLACE, J. G. (1976). *Cognitive development: An information processing view.* Hillsdale, NJ: Erlbaum.

KLATZKY, R. L. (1984). *Memory and awareness: An information processing perspective.* New York: Freeman.

KLEIMAN, A. (1974). *The use of private speech in young children and its relation to social speech.* Unpublished doctoral dissertation, University of Chicago.

KLEIN, A. R., & YOUNG, R. D. (1979). Hyperactive boys in their classroom: Assessment of teacher and peer perceptions, interactions, and classroom behaviors. *Journal of Abnormal Child Psychology, 7,* 425–442.

KLEINKE, C. L., & NICHOLSON, T. A. (1979). Black and white children's awareness of de facto race and sex differences. *Developmental Psychology, 15,* 84–86.

KLIGMAN, D., SMYRL, R., & EMDE, R. N. (1975). A "nonintrusive" longitudinal study of infant sleep. *Psychosomatic Medicine, 37,* 448–453.

KLINNERT, M., SORCE, J., EMDE, R. N., STENBERG, C., & GAENSBAUER, T. J. (1984). Continuities and change in early affective life: Maternal perceptions of surprise, fear, and anger. In R. N. Emde & R. J. Harmon (Eds.), *Continuities and discontinuities in development* (pp. 339–354). New York: Plenum.

KNAPP, D. (1979). Automatization in child language acquisition. *Dissertation Abstracts International, 40,* 5052B. (University Microfilms No. 80-06,891)

KNITTLE, J. L. (1972). Obesity in childhood: A problem of adipose tissue cellular development. *Pediatrics, 81,* 1048.

KNITTLE, J. L., GINSBERG-FELLNER, F., & BROWN, R. E. (1977). Adipose tissue development in man. *American Journal of Clinical Nutrition, 30,* 762–766.

KNITTLE, J. L., TIMMERS, K., GINSBERG-FELLNER, F., BROWN, R. E., & KATZ, D. P. (1979). The growth of adipose tissue in children and adolescents. *Journal of Clinical Investigation, 63,* 239–246.

KNOBLOCH, H., & PASAMANICK, B. (1967). Prediction from the assessment of neuromotor and intellectual status in infancy. In J. Zubin & G. A. Jervis (Ed.), *Psychopathology of mental development* (pp. 387–400). New York: Grune & Stratton.

KNOBLOCH, H., & PASAMANICK, B. (Eds.). (1974). *Gesell and Amatruda's developmental diagnosis.* Hagerstown, MD: Harper & Row.

KNOBLOCH, H., STEVENS, F., & MALONE, A. (1980). *A manual for developmental diagnosis.* New York: Harper & Row.

KOBASIGAWA, A., & MIDDLETON, D. B. (1972). Free recall of categorized items by children at three grade levels. *Child Development, 43,* 1067–1072.

KOBRE, K. R., & LIPSITT, L. P. (1972). A negative contrast effect in newborns. *Journal of Experimental Child Psychology, 14,* 81–91.

KODROFF, J. K., & ROBERGE, J. J. (1975). Developmental analysis of the conditional reasoning abilities of primary-grade children. *Developmental Psychology, 11,* 21–28.

KOEK, K. E., & MARTIN, S. B. (Eds.). (1988). *Encyclopedia of Associations* (2nd ed.). Detroit: Gale Research Company.

KOFF, E., RIERDAN, J., & SHEINGOLD, K. (1982). Memories of menarche: Age, preparation, and prior knowledge as determinants of initial menstrual experience. *Journal of Youth and Adolescence, 11,* 1–9.

KOGAN, N. (1983). Stylistic variation in childhood and adolescence. In J. H. Flavell & E. M. Markman (Eds.), *Handbook of child psychology: Vol. 3. Cognitive development* (pp. 630–706). New York: Wiley.

KOHLBERG, L. (1966). A cognitive-developmental analysis of children's sex-role concepts and attitudes. In E. E. Maccoby (Ed.), *The development of sex differences* (pp. 82–173). Stanford, CA: Stanford University Press.

KOHLBERG, L. (1969). Stage and sequence: The cognitive-developmental approach to socialization. In D. A. Goslin (Ed.), *Handbook of socialization theory and research* (pp. 347–480). Chicago: Rand McNally.

KOHLBERG, L. (1976). Moral stages and moralization: The cognitive-developmental approach (pp. 31–53). In T. Lickona (Ed.), *Moral development and behavior: Theory, research, and social issues* (pp. 31–43). New York: Holt, Rinehart & Winston.

KOHLBERG, L. (1978). Revisions in the theory and practice of moral development. In W. Damon (Ed.). *New directions for child development* (pp. 83–87). San Francisco, Jossey-Bass.

KOHLBERG, L. (1980). High school democracy and educating for a Just Society. In R. L. Mosher (Ed.), *Moral education* (pp. 20–57). New York: Praeger.

KOHLBERG, L. (1984). *Essays on moral development: Vol. 2. The psychology of moral development.* San Francisco: Harper & Row.

KOHLBERG, L., YAEGER, J., & HJERTHOLM, E. (1968). Private speech: Four studies and a review of theories. *Child Development, 39,* 691–736.

KOHN, M. L. (1977). *Class and conformity: A study in values* (2nd. ed.). Chicago: University of Chicago Press.

KOHN, M. L. (1979). The effects of social class on parental values and practices. In D. Reiss & H. A. Hoffman (Eds.), *The American family: Dying or developing* (pp. 45–68). New York: Plenum.

KOLATA, G. B. (1979). Scientists attack report that obstetrical medications endanger children. *Science, 204,* 391–392.

KOLATA, G. B. (1983a). Fetal surgery for neural defects? *Science, 221,* 441.

KOLATA, G. B. (1983b). First trimester prenatal diagnosis. *Science, 221,* 1031–1032.

KOLATA, G. B. (1984). Studying learning in the womb. *Science, 225,* 302–303.

KOLATA, G. B. (1986). Obese children: A growing problem. *Science, 232,* 20–21.

KOLUCHOVA, J. (1972). Severe deprivation in twins: A case study. *Journal of Child Psychology and Psychiatry, 13,* 107–114.

KONEYA, M. (1976). Location and interaction in row-and-column seating arrangements. *Environment and Behavior, 8,* 265–282.

KONNER, M. J. (1972). Aspects of the developmental ethology of a foraging people. In N. Blurton Jones (Ed.), *Ethological studies of child behaviour* (pp. 285–304). Cambridge, Eng.: Cambridge University Press.

KOOCHER, G. P. (1974). Talking with children about death. *American Journal of Orthopsychiatry, 44,* 404–411.

KOOPMAN, P. R., & AMES, E. W. (1968). Infants' preferences for facial arrangements: A failure to replicate. *Child Development, 39,* 481–487.

KOPP, C. B. (1982). Antecedents of self-regulation: A developmental perspective. *Developmental Psychology, 18,* 199–214.

KOPP, C. B. (1983). Risk factors in development. In M. M. Haith & J. J. Campos (Eds.), *Handbook of child psychology: Vol. 2. Infancy and developmental psychobiology* (pp. 1081–1188). New York: Wiley.

KOPP, C. B., & PARMELEE, A. H. (1979). Prenatal and perinatal influences on infant behavior. In J. Osofsky (Ed.), *Handbook of Infant Development* (pp. 29–75). New York: Wiley.

KOPP, C. B., & VAUGHN, B. E. (1982). Sustained attention during exploratory manipulation as a predictor of cognitive competence in preterm infants. *Child Development, 53,* 174–182.

KORNER, A. F., & THOMAN, E. B. (1972). The relative efficacy of contact and vestibular-proprioceptive stimulation in soothing neonates. *Child Development, 43,* 443–453.

KORNER, A. F., HUTCHINSON, C. A., KOPERSKI, J. A., KRAEMER, H. C., & SCHNEIDER, P. A. (1981). Stability of individual differences of neonatal motor and crying pattern. *Child Development, 52,* 83–90.

KOTELCHUK, M. (1976). The infant's relationship to the father: Experimental evidence. In M. E. Lamb (Ed.), *The role of the father in child development* (pp. 329–344). New York: Wiley.

KOUNIN, J. S. (1970). *Discipline and group management in the classroom.* New York: Holt, Rinehart & Winston.

KRAMER, M. S., BARR, R. G., LEDUC, D. G., BOISJOLY, C., & PLESS, I. B. (1985). Infant determinants of childhood weight and adiposity. *Journal of Pediatrics, 107,* 104–107.

KRANTZ, M., & BURTON, C. (1986). The development of the social cognition of social status. *Journal of Genetic Psychology, 147,* 89–95.

KREBS, D., & GILLMORE, J. (1982). The relationship among the first stages of cognitive development, role-taking abilities, and moral development. *Child Development, 53,* 877–886.

KREHBIEL, G., & MILICH, R. (1986). Issues in the assessment and treatment of socially rejected children. In R. J. Prinz (Ed.), *Advances in behavioral assessment of children and families* (pp. 249–270). Greenwich, CT: JAI Press.

KREIPE, R. E. (1983). Prevention of adolescent pregnancy: A developmental approach. In E. R. McAnarney (Ed.), *Premature adolescent pregnancy and parenthood* (pp. 37–59). New York: Grune & Stratton.

KREMENITZER, J. P., VAUGHAN, H. G., KURTZBERG, D., & DOWLING, K. (1979). Smooth-pursuit eye movements in the newborn infant. *Child Development, 50,* 441–448.

KREUTZER, M., & CHARLESWORTH, W. (1973). Infants' reactions to different expressions of emotions. Paper presented at the meeting of the Society for Research in Child Development, Philadelphia.

KREUTZER, M. A., LEONARD, C., & FLAVELL, J. H. (1975). An interview study of children's knowledge about memory. *Monographs of the Society for Research in Child Development, 40* (1, Serial No. 159).

KUCZAJ, S. A. II. (1977a). The acquisition of regular and irregular past tense forms. *Journal of Verbal Learning and Verbal Behavior, 16,* 589–600.

KUCZAJ, S. A. II. (1977b). *Old and new forms, old and new meanings: The form-function hypothesis revisited.* Paper presented at the meeting of the Society for Research in Child Development, New Orleans.

KUCZAJ, S. A. II. (1979). Evidence for a language learning strategy: On the relative ease of acquisition of prefixes and suffixes. *Child Development, 50,* 1–13.

KUCZAJ, S. A. II. (1986). Thoughts on the intentional basis of early object word extension: Evidence from comprehension and production. In S. A. Kuczaj II & M. D. Barrett (Eds.), *The development of word meaning* (pp. 99–120). New York: Springer-Verlag.

KUCZYNSKI, L., KOCHANSKA, G., RADKE-YARROW, M., & GIRNIUS-BROWN, O. (1987). A developmental interpretation of young children's noncompliance. *Developmental Psychology, 23,* 799–806.

KUCZYNSKI, L., ZAHN-WAXLER, C., & RADKE-YARROW, M. (1987). Development and content of imitation in the second and third year of life: A socialization perspective. *Developmental Psychology, 23,* 276–282.

KUHN, D. (1979). The significance of Piaget's formal operations stage in education. *Journal of Education, 161,* 34–50.

KUHN, D. (1988). Cognitive development. In M. H. Bornstein & M. E. Lamb (Eds.), *Developmental Psychology: An Advanced Textbook* (2nd ed., pp. 205–260). Hillsdale, NJ: Erlbaum.

KUHN, D., HO, V., & ADAMS, C. (1979). Formal reasoning among pre- and late adolescents. *Child Development, 50,* 1128–1135.

KUHN, D., NASH, S. C., & BRUCKEN, L. (1978). Sex role concepts of two- and three-year olds. *Child Development, 49,* 445–451.

KULIK, J. A. (1986). Evaluating the effects of teaching with computers. In P. F. Campbell & G. G. Fein (Eds.), *Young children and micro-computers* (pp. 159–169). Englewood Cliffs, NJ: Prentice-Hall.

KULL, J. A. (1986). Learning and Logo. In P. F. Campbell & G. G. Fein (Eds.), *Young children and microcomputers* (pp. 103–128). Englewood Cliffs, NJ: Prentice-Hall.

KUN, A. (1977). Development of the magnitude-covariation and compensation schemata in ability and effort attributions of performance. *Child Development, 48,* 862–872.

KURDEK, L. A. (1978). Relationship between cognitive perspective-taking and teachers' ratings of children's classroom behavior in grades one through four. *Journal of Genetic Psychology, 132,* 21–27.

KURDEK, L. A. (1980). Developmental relations among children's perspective-taking, moral judgment, and parent-rated behavior. *Merrill-Palmer Quarterly, 26,* 103–121.

LA BARRE, W. (1954). *The human animal.* Chicago: University of Chicago Press.

LA FRENIERE, P., STRAYER, F. F., & GAUTHIER, R. (1984). The emergence of same-sex affiliative preferences among preschool peers: A developmental/ethological perspective. *Child Development, 55,* 1958–1965.

Laboratory of Comparative Human Cognition. (1983). Culture and cognitive development. In P. H. Mussen (Ed.), *Handbook of child psychology: Vol. 1. History, theory, and methods* (pp. 295–356). New York: Wiley.

LACEY, J. I., & LACEY, B. C. (1970). Some autonomic-central nervous system interrelationships. In P. Black (Ed.), *Physiological correlates of emotion* (pp. 205–227). New York: Academic Press.

LADD, G. W. (1981). Effectiveness of a social learning method for enhancing children's social interaction and peer acceptance. *Child Development, 52,* 171–178.

LADD, G. W., & MIZE, J. (1983). A cognitive-social learning model of social-skill training. *Psychological Review, 90,* 127–157.

LADD, G. W., & PRICE, J. M. (1987). Predicting children's social and school adjustment following the transition from preschool to kindergarten. *Child Development, 58,* 1168–1189.

LAGERCRANTZ, H., & SLOTKIN, T. A. (1986, April). The "stress" of being born. *Scientific American, 254*(4), 100–107.

LAMAZE, F. (1958). *Painless childbirth.* London: Burke.

LAMB, M. E. (1976). Interaction between eight-month-old children and their fathers and mothers. In M. E. Lamb (Ed.), *The role of the father in child development* (pp. 307–327). New York: Wiley.

LAMB, M. E. (1977). The development of parental preferences in the first two years of life. *Sex Roles, 3,* 445–451.

LAMB, M. E., & ROOPNARINE, J. E. (1979). Peer influences on sex-role development in preschoolers. *Child Development, 50,* 1219–1222.

LAMB, M. E., THOMPSON, R. A., GARDNER, W., CHARNOV, E. L., & CONNELL, J. P. (1985). *Infant-mother attachment: The origins and developmental significance of individual differences in Strange Situation behavior.* Hillsdale, NJ: Erlbaum.

LAMB, M. E., THOMPSON, R. A., GARDNER, W., CHARNOV, E. L., & ESTES, C. (1984). Security of attachment as assessed in the Strange Situation: Its study and biological interpretation. *Behavioral and Brain Sciences, 7,* 127–147.

LAMPHEAR, V. S. (1985). The impact of maltreatment of children's psychosocial adjustment: A review of the research. *Child Abuse & Neglect, 9,* 251–263.

LANCASTER, J. B., & WHITTEN, P. (1980). Family matters. *The Sciences, 20,* 10–15.

LANDAU, R. (1982). Infant crying and fussing. *Journal of Cross-Cultural Psychology, 13,* 427–443.

LANDSBAUM, J. B., & WILLIS, R. H. (1971). Conformity in early and late adolescence. *Developmental Psychology, 4,* 334–337.

LANE, D. M., & PEARSON, D. A. (1982). The development of selective attention. *Merrill-Palmer Quarterly, 28,* 317–337.

LANGE, G. (1978). Organization-related processes in children's recall. In P. A. Ornstein (Ed.), *Memory development in children* (pp. 101–128). Hillsdale, NJ: Erlbaum.

LANGLOIS, J. H., & DOWNS, A. C. (1979). Peer relations as a function of physical attractiveness: The eye of the beholder or behavioral reality? *Child Development, 50,* 409–418.

LANGLOIS, J. H., & DOWNS, A. C. (1980). Mothers, fathers, and peers as socialization agents of sex-typed play behaviors in young children. *Child Development, 51,* 1237–1247.

LANGLOIS, J. H., ROGGMAN, L. A., CASEY, R. J., RITTER, J. M., REISER-DANNER, L. A., & JENKINS, V. Y. (1987). Infant preferences for attractive faces: Rudiments of a stereotype? *Developmental Psychology, 23,* 363–369.

LANGLOIS, J. H., & STEPHAN, C. (1977). The effects of physical attractiveness and ethnicity on children's behavioral attributions and peer preferences. *Child Development, 48,* 1694–1698

LANGLOIS, J. H., & STEPHAN, C. W. (1981). Beauty and the beast: The role of physical attraction in peer relationships and social behavior. In S. S. Brehm, S. M. Kassin, & S. X. Gibbons (Eds.), *Developmental social psychology: Theory and research* (pp. 152–168). New York: Oxford University Press.

LANGLOIS, J. H., & STYCZYNSKI, L. E. (1979). The effects of physical attractiveness on the behavioral attributions and peer preferences of acquainted children. *International Journal of Behavioral Development, 2,* 325–342.

LAOSA, L. M. (1981). Maternal behavior: Sociocultural diversity in modes of family interaction. In R. W. Henderson (Ed.), *Parent-child interaction: Theory, research, and prospects* (pp. 125–167). New York: Academic Press.

LAPSLEY, D. K. (1985). Elkind on egocentrism. *Developmental Review, 5,* 227–236.

LAPSLEY, D. K., MILSTEAD, M., QUINTANA, S. M., FLANNERY, D., & BUSS, R. R. (1986). Adolescent egocentrism and formal operations: Tests of a theoretical assumption. *Developmental Psychology, 22,* 800–807.

LAWLER, K. A., ALLEN, M. T., CRITCHER, E. C., STANDARD, B. A. (1981). The relationship of physiological responses to the coronary-prone behavior pattern in children. *Journal of Behavioral Medicine, 4,* 203–216.

LAWRENCE, R. A. (1983). Early mothering by adolescents. In E. R. McAnarney (Ed.), *Premature adolescent pregnancy and parenthood* (pp. 207–218). New York: Grune & Stratton.

LAWRENCE, R. A., MCANARNEY, E. R., ATEN, M. J., IKER, H. P., BALDWIN, C. P., & BALDWIN, A. L. (1981). Aggressive behaviors in young mothers: Markers of future morbidity? *Pediatric Research, 15,* 443.

LAZAR, I., & DARLINGTON, R. (1982). Lasting effects of early education: A report from the Consortium for Longitudinal Studies. *Monographs of the Society for Research in Child Development, 47* (2–3, Serial No. 195).

LEAHY, R. L., & EITER, M. (1980). Moral judgment and the development of real and ideal androgynous self-image during adolescence and young adulthood. *Developmental Psychology, 16,* 362–370.

LEBOYER, F. (1975). *Birth without violence.* New York: Knopf.

LEDERBERG, A. R., CHAPIN, S. L., ROSENBLATT, V., & VANDELL, D. L. (1986). Ethnic, gender, and age preferences among deaf and hearing preschool peers. *Child Development, 57,* 375–386.

LEE, C. L., & BATES, J. E. (1985). Mother-child interaction at age two years and perceived difficult temperament. *Child Development, 56,* 1314–1325.

LEETSMA, R., AUGUST, R. L., GEORGE, B., & PEAK, L. (1987). *Japanese education today: A report from the U.S. Study of Education in Japan.* Washington, DC: U.S. Government Printing Office.

LEFKOWITZ, M. M. (1981). Smoking during pregnancy: Long-term effects on offspring. *Developmental Psychology, 17,* 192–194.

LEFKOWITZ, M. M., ERON, L. D., WALDER, L. O., & HUESMANN, L. R. (1972). Television violence and child aggression: A follow-up study.

In G. A. Comstock & E. A. Rubinstein (Eds.), *Television and social behavior* (Vol. 3, pp. 35–135). Washington, DC: U.S. Government Printing Office.

LEGENDRE-BERGERON, M. F., & LAVEAULT, D. (1983). Is formal thought the final stage of cognitive development? An internal criticism of Piagetian theory. *Genetic Epistemologist, 11,* 15–20.

LEITER, M. P. (1977). A study of reciprocity in preschool play groups. *Child Development, 48,* 1288–1295.

LeMARE, L. J., & RUBIN, K. H. (1987). Perspective taking and peer interaction: Structural and developmental analyses. *Child Development, 58,* 306–315.

LEMING, J. (1978). Intrapersonal variations in stage of moral reasoning among adolescents as a function of situational context. *Journal of Youth and Adolescence, 7,* 405–416.

LEMIRE, R. J., LOESER, J. D., LEECH, R. W., & ALVORD, E. C. (1975). *Normal and abnormal development of the human nervous system.* New York: Harper & Row.

LEMPERERS, J. D., FLAVELL, E. R., & FLAVELL, J. H. (1977). The development in very young children of tacit knowledge concerning visual perception. *Genetic Psychology Monographs, 95,* 3–53.

LENNEBERG, E. H. (1967). *Biological foundations of language.* New York: Wiley.

LENNEBERG, E. H., REBELSKY, F. G., & NICHOLS, I. A. (1965). The vocalizations of infants born to deaf and hearing parents. *Human Development, 8,* 23–37.

LENNON, R. T. (1985). Group tests of intelligence. In B. B. Wolman (Ed.), *Handbook of intelligence* (pp. 825–845). New York: Wiley.

LEON, G. R., LUCAS, A. R., COLLIGAN, R. C., FERDINANCE, R. J., & KAMP, J. (1985). Sexual, body-image, and personality attitudes in anorexia nervosa. *Journal of Abnormal Child Psychology, 13,* 245–258.

LEONARD, L. B., NEWHOFF, M., & FRY, M. E. (1980). Some instances of word usage in the absence of comprehension. *Journal of Child Language, 7,* 189–196.

LEONARD, M. F., RHYMES, J. P., & SOLNIT, A. J. (1966). Failure to thrive in infants: A family problem. *American Journal of Diseases of Children, 111,* 600–612.

LEPPER, M. R. (1985). Microcomputers in education: Motivational and social issues. *American Psychologist, 40,* 1–18.

LEPPER, M. R., GREENE, D., & NISBETT, R. E. (1973). Undermining children's intrinsic interest with extrinsic rewards: A test of the overjustification hypothesis. *Journal of Personality and Social Psychology, 28,* 129–137.

LERNER, E. (1937). The problem of perspective in moral reasoning. *American Journal of Sociology, 43,* 249–269.

LERNER, R. M. (1985). Adolescent maturational changes and psychosocial development: A dynamic interactional perspective. *Journal of Youth and Adolescence, 14,* 355–372.

LERNER, R. M. (1986). *Concepts and theories of human development* (2nd ed.). New York: Random House.

LERNER, R. M., & BRACKNEY, B. (1978). The importance of inner and outer body parts attitudes in the self-concept of late adolescents. *Sex Roles, 4,* 225–238.

LERNER, R. M., & GELLERT, E. (1969). Body build identification, preference, and aversion in children. *Developmental Psychology, 1,* 456–462.

LERNER, R. M., KARABENICK, S. A., & MEISELS, M. (1975). Effects of age and sex on the development of personal space schemata towards body build. *Journal of Genetic Psychology, 127,* 151–152.

LERNER, R. M., & KORN, S. J. (1972). The development of body build stereotypes in males. *Child Development, 43,* 908–920.

LERNER, R. M., PALERMO, M., SPIRO, A., & NESSELROADE, J. (1982). Assessing the dimensions of temperamental individuality across the life-span: The Dimension of Temperament Survey (DOTS). *Child Development, 53,* 149–160.

LERNER, R. M., & SCHROEDER, C. (1971). Physique identification, preference, and aversion in kindergarten children. *Developmental Psychology, 5,* 538.

LERNER, R. M., SPANIER, G. B., & BELSKY, J. (1982). The child in the family. In C. B. Kopp & J. B. Krakow (Eds.), *The child: Development in a social context* (pp. 393–455). Reading, MA: Addison-Wesley.

LERNER, R. M., VENNING, J., & KNAPP, J. R. (1975). Age and sex effects on personal space schemata towards body build in late childhood. *Developmental Psychology, 11,* 855–856.

LESSER, G. S., FIFER, G., & CLARK, D. H. (1965). Mental abilities of children from different social-class and cultural groups. *Monographs of the Society for Research in Child Development, 30* (4, Serial No. 102).

LESTER, B. M. (1979). A synergistic process approach to the study of prenatal malnutrition. *International Journal of Behavioral Development, 2,* 377–393.

LESTER, B. M., KOTELCHUCK, M., SPELKE, E., SELLERS, M. J., & KLEIN, R. E. (1974). Separation protest in Guatemalan infants: Cross-cultural and cognitive findings. *Developmental Psychology, 10,* 79–85.

LEVENTHAL, G. S. (1970). Influence of brothers and sisters on sex role behavior. *Journal of Personality and Social Psychology, 16,* 452–465.

LEVIN, J. A., BORUTA, M. J., & VASCONELLOS, M. T. (1983). Microcomputer-based environments for writing: A writer's asssistant. In A. C. Wilkinson (Ed.), *Classroom computers and cognitive science* (pp. 219–232). New York: Academic Press.

LEVIN, J. R., McCABE, R. E., & BENDER, B. G. (1975). A note on imagery-inducing motor activity in young children. *Child Development, 56,* 263–266.

LEVIN, S. R., PETROS, T. V., & PETRELLA, F. W. (1982). Preschoolers' awareness of television advertising. *Child Development, 53,* 933–937.

LEVIN, J. R., & PRESSLEY, M. A. (1978). A test of the developmental imagery hypothesis in children's associative learning. *Journal of Educational Psychology, 70,* 691–694.

LEVINE, M. H., & SUTTON-SMITH, B. (1973). Effects of age, sex, and task on visual behavior during dyadic interaction. *Developmental Psychology, 9,* 400–405.

LEVY, D. M. (1937). Sibling rivalry. *American Orthopsychiatric Association Research Monographs* (No. 2).

LEVY, D. M. (1958). *Behavioral analysis.* Springfield, IL: Charles C. Thomas.

LEVY, H. L., KAPLAN, G. N., & ERICKSON, A. M. (1982). Comparison of treated and untreated pregnancies in a mother with phenylketonuria. *Journal of Pediatrics, 100,* 876–880.

LEWIS, C. C. (1981). The effects of parental firm control: A reinterpretation of findings. *Psychological Bulletin, 90,* 547–563.

LEWIS, M., & BROOKS, J. (1978). Self-knowledge and emotional development. In M. Lewis & L. A. Rosenblum (Eds.), *The development of affect* (pp. 205–226). New York: Plenum.

LEWIS, M., & BROOKS-GUNN, J. (1979). *Social cognition and the acquisition of self.* New York: Plenum.

LEWIS, M., & BROOKS-GUNN, J. (1981). Visual attention at three months as a predictor of cognitive functioning at two years of age. *Intelligence, 5,* 131–140.

LEWIS, M., BROOKS-GUNN, J., & JASKIR, J. (1985). Individual differences in visual self-recognition as a function of mother-infant attachment relationship. *Developmental Psychology, 21,* 1181–1187.

LEWIS, M., & FOX, N. (1983) Issues in infant assessment. In C. C. Brown (Ed.), *Childhood learning disabilities and prenatal risk: Johnson & Johnson Baby Products Co. Pediatric Roundtable* (No. 9, pp. 78–83). Urbana-Champaign, IL: University of Illinois Press.

LEWIS, M., & FREEDLE, R. (1972). *Mother-infant dyad: The cradle of meaning.* Princeton, NJ: Educational Testing Service.

LEWIS, M., & KREITZBERG, V. S. (1979). Effects of birth order and spacing on mother-infant interactions. *Developmental Psychology, 15,* 617–625.

LEWIS, M., & McGURK, H. (1972). Evaluation of infant intelligence. *Science, 178,* 1174–1177.

LEWIS, M., & MICHALSON, L. (1982). The socialization of emotions. In T. Field & A. Fogel (Eds.), *Emotion and early interaction* (pp. 189–212). Hillsdale, NJ: Erlbaum.

LEWIS, M., & MICHALSON, L. (1983). *Children's emotions and moods.* New York: Plenum.

LEWIS M., & SULLIVAN, M. W. (1985). Infant intelligence and its assessment. In B. B. Wolman (Ed.), *Handbook of infant intelligence* (pp. 505–599). New York: Wiley.

LEWIS, M., SULLIVAN, M. W., & MICHALSON, L. (1984). The cognitive-emotional fugue. In C. E. Izard, J. Kagan, & R. Zajonc (Eds.), *Emotions, cognition, and behavior* (pp. 264–288). New York: Cambridge University Press.

LEWIS, M., YOUNG, G., BROOKS, J., & MICHALSON, L. (1975). The beginning of friendship. In M. Lewis & L. A. Rosenblum (Eds.), *Friendship and peer relations* (pp. 27–66). New York: Wiley.

LEWIS, R. A. (1973). Parents and peers: Socialization agents in the coital behavior of young adults. *Journal of Sex Research, 9,* 156–190.

LEWONTIN, R. C. (1976). Race and intelligence. In N. J. Block & G. Dworkin (Eds.), *The IQ controversy* (pp. 78–92). New York: Pantheon Books.

LIBEN, L. S., & GOLBECK, S. L. (1984). Performance on Piagetian horizontality and verticality tasks: Sex-related differences in knowledge of relevant physical phenomena. *Developmental Psychology, 20,* 595–606.

LIBERTY, C., & ORNSTEIN, P. A. (1973). Age differences in organization and recall: The effects of training in categorization. *Journal of Experimental Child Psychology, 15,* 169–186.

LICKONA, T. (1976). Research on Piaget's theory of moral development. In T. Lickona (Ed.), *Moral development and behavior: Theory, research, and social issues* (pp. 219–240). New York: Holt, Rinehart and Winston.

LIEBERT, R. M. (1986). Effects of television on children and adolescents. *Developmental and Behavioral Pediatrics, 7,* 43–48.

LIEBERT, R. M., & POULOS, R. W. (1975). Television and personality development: The socializing effects of an entertainment medium. In A. Davids (Ed.), *Child personality and psychopathology: Current topics* (Vol. 2, pp. 61–97). New York: Wiley.

LIEBERT, R. M., & SPRAFKIN, J. (1988). *The early window: Effects of television on children and youth* (3rd ed.). New York: Pergamon Press.

LIEVEN, E. (1978). Conversations between mothers and young children: Individual differences and their possible implications for the study of language learning. In N. Waterson & C. Snow (Eds.), *The development of communication* (pp. 173–187). Chicester, Eng.: Wiley.

LIMBER, J. (1973). The genesis of complex sentences. In T. E. Moore (Ed.), *Cognitive development and the acquisition of language* (pp. 169–185). New York: Academic Press.

LINDBLOM, C. E. (1986). Who needs what social research for policy-making? *Knowledge: Creation, Diffusion, Utilization, 7,* 345–366.

LINN, M. C. (1985). Fostering equitable consequences from computer learning environments. *Sex Roles, 13,* 229–240.

LINN, M. C., & PETERSEN, A. C. (1985). Emergence and characterization of sex differences in spatial ability: A meta-analysis. *Child Development, 56,* 1479–1498.

LIPSCOMB, T. J., LARRIEU, J. A., MCALLISTER, H. A., & BREGMAN, N. J. (1982). Modeling and children's generosity: A developmental perspective. *Merrill-Palmer Quarterly, 28,* 275–282.

LIPSCOMB, T. J., MCALLISTER, H. A., & BREGMAN, N. J. (1985). A developmental inquiry into the effects of multiple models on children's generosity. *Merrill-Palmer Quarterly, 31,* 335–344.

LIPSITT, L. P. (1982). Infant learning. In T. M. Field, et al. (Eds.), *Review of Human Development* (pp. 62–78). New York: Wiley.

LIPSITT, L. P., ENGEN, T., & KAYE, H. (1963). Developmental changes in the olfactory threshold of the neonate. *Child Development, 34,* 371–376.

LIPSITT, L. P., REILLY, B. M., BUTCHER, M. J., & GREENWOOD, M. M. (1976). The stability and inter-relationships of newborn sucking and heart rate. *Developmental Psychobiology, 9,* 305–310.

LIPSITT, L. P., STURNER, W. Q., & BURKE, P. (1979). Perinatal indicators and subsequent crib death. *Infant Behavior and Development, 2,* 325–328.

LIPSITT, L. P., & WERNER, J. S. (1981). The infancy of human learning processes. In E. S. Gollin (Ed.), *Developmental plasticity* (pp. 101–133). New York: Academic Press.

LISS, M. B., REINHARDT, L. C., & FREDRIKSEN, S. (1983). TV heroes: The impact of rhetoric and deeds. *Journal of Applied Developmental Psychology, 4,* 175–187.

LITOWITZ, B. (1977). Learning to make definitions. *Journal of Child Language, 8,* 165–175.

LIVESLEY, W. J., & BROMLEY, D. B. (1973). *Person perception in childhood and adolescence.* London: Wiley.

LLOYD, B., & SMITH, C. (1985). The social representation of gender and young children's play. *British Journal of Developmental Psychology, 3,* 65–73.

LLOYD, P. (1983). Language and communication: Piaget's influence. In S. Modgil, C. Modgil, & G. Brown (Eds.), *Jean Piaget: An interdisciplinary critique* (pp. 105–118). London: Routledge & Kegan Paul.

LOCKE, D. (1983). Doing what comes morally. *Human Development, 26,* 11–25.

LOCKE, J. (1892). *Some thoughts concerning education.* In R. H. Quick (Ed.), *Locke on education* (pp. 1–236). Cambridge, Eng.: Cambridge University Press. (Original work published 1690)

LOCKHEED, M. E. (1985). Women, girls, and computers: A first look at the evidence. *Sex Roles, 13,* 115–122.

LOCKHEED, M. E. (1986). Reshaping the social order: The case of gender segregation. *Sex Roles, 14,* 617–628.

LOEB, R. C., HORST, L., & HORTON, P. J. (1980). Family interaction patterns associated with self-esteem in preadolescent girls and boys. *Merrill-Palmer Quarterly, 26,* 203–217.

LOEHLIN, J. C., LINDZEY, G., & SPUHLER, J. N. (1975). *Raw differences in intelligence.* San Francisco: Freeman.

LONEY, J. (1974). Intellectual functioning of hyperactive elementary school boys: A cross-sectional investigation. *American Journal of Orthopsychiatry, 44,* 754–762.

LONG, L. H. (1975). Does migration interfere with children's progress in school? *Sociology of Education, 48,* 369–381.

LONGO, L. D. (1980). Environmental pollution and pregnancy: Risks and uncertainties for the fetus and infant. *American Journal of Obstetrics and Gynecology, 137,* 162–173.

LONGSTRETH, L. E. (1981). Revisiting Skeels' final study: A critique. *Developmental Psychology, 17,* 620–625.

LONGSTRETH, L. E., DAVIS, B., CARTER, L., FLINT, D., OWEN, J., RICKERT, M., & TAYLOR, E. (1981). Separation of home intellectual environment and maternal IQ as determinants of child IQ. *Developmental Psychology, 17,* 532–541.

LORENZ, K. (1952). *King Solomon's ring.* New York: Thomas Y. Crowell.

LOUGEE, M. D., GRUENEICH, R., & HARTUP, W. W. (1977). Social interaction in same- and mixed-age dyads of preschool children. *Child Development, 48,* 1353–1361.

LOVAAS, I. (1967). A behavior therapy approach to the treatment of childhood schizophrenia. In J. P. Hill (Ed.), *Minnesota symposia on child development* (Vol. 1, pp. 108–159). Minneapolis: University of Minnesota Press.

LOVEJOY, C. O. (1981). The origin of man. *Science, 211,* 341–350.

LUCARIELLO, J., & NELSON, K. (1985). Slot-filler categories as memory organizers for young children. *Developmental Psychology, 21,* 272–282.

LUNDBERG, U. (1983). Note on type A behavior and cardiovascular responses to challenge in 3–6-yr-old children. *Journal of Psychosomatic Research, 27,* 39–42.

LURIA, A. R. (1961). *The role of speech in the regulation of normal and abnormal behavior.* New York: Pergamon Press.

LUTZ, P. (1983). The stepfamily: An adolescent perspective. *Family Relations, 32,* 367–375.

LYTTON, H. (1977). Do parents create, or respond to, differences in twins. *Developmental Psychology, 13,* 456–459.

MACCOBY, E. E., & HAGEN, J. W. (1965). Effects of distraction upon central versus incidental recall: Developmental trends. *Journal of Experimental Child Psychology, 2,* 280–289.

MACCOBY, E. E., & JACKLIN, C. N. (1974). *The psychology of sex differences.* Stanford, CA: Stanford University Press.

MACCOBY, E. E., & JACKLIN, C. N. (1980). Sex differences in aggression: A rejoinder and reprise. *Child Development, 51,* 964–980.

MACCOBY, E. E., & MARTIN, J. A. (1983). Socialization in the context of the family: Parent-child interaction. In E. M. Hetherington (Ed.),

Handbook of child psychology: Vol. 4. Socialization, personality, and social development (4th ed., pp. 1–101). New York: Wiley.

MacFarlane, A. (1975). Olfaction in the development of social preferences in the human neonate. In *Parent-infant interaction: Ciba Foundation Symposium 33* (pp. 103–117). Amsterdam: Elsevier.

MacKinnon, D. W. (1968). Selecting students with creative potential. In P. Heist (Ed.), *The creative college student: An unmet challenge* (pp. 101–116). San Francisco: Jossey-Bass.

MacKinnon, D. W., & Hall, W. B. (1973). Intelligence and creativity. In B. T. Eiduson & L. Beckman (Eds.), *Science as a career choice: Theoretical and empirical studies* (pp. 148–152). New York: Russell Sage Foundation.

Macklin, M. C., & Kolbe, R. H. (1984). Sex role stereotyping in children's advertising: Current and past trends. *Journal of Advertising, 13*(2), 34–42.

MacMillan, D. L., & Morrison, G. M. (1984). Sociometric research in special education. In R. L. Jones (Ed.), *Attitudes and attitude change in special education: Theory and practice* (pp. 93–117). Reston, VA: Council for Exceptional Children.

MacMillan, D. L., Keogh, B. K., & Jones, R. L. (1986). Special educational research on mildly handicapped learners. In M. C. Wittrock (Ed.), *Handbook of research on teaching* (3rd ed., pp. 686–724). New York: MacMillan.

Macnamara, J. (1972). Cognitive basis of language learning in infants. *Psychological Review, 79*, 1–13.

Macrides, R., Bartke, A., & Dalterio, S. (1975). Strange females increase plasma testosterone levels in male mice. *Science, 189*, 1104–1105.

Madden, N., & Slavin, R. (1983). Mainstreaming students with mild handicaps: Academic and social outcomes. *Review of Educational Research, 53*, 519–659.

Magnusson, D., Stattin, H., & Allen, V. L. (1985). Biological maturation and social development: A longitudinal study of some adjustment processes from mid-adolescence to adulthood. *Journal of Youth and Adolescence, 14*, 267–283.

Magnusson, D., Stattin, H., & Allen, V. L. (1986). Differential maturation among girls and its relation to social adjustment: A longitudinal perspective. In P. B. Baltes, D. L. Featherman, & R. M. Lerner (Eds.), *Life span development* (Vol. 7, pp. 136–172). New York: Academic Press.

Mahalski, P. A., Silva, P. A., & Spears, G. F. S. (1985). Children's attachment to soft objects at bedtime, child rearing, and child development. *Journal of the American Academy of Child Psychiatry, 24*, 442–446.

Maier, R. A., Holmes, D. L., Slaymaker, F. L., & Reich, J. N. (1984). The perceived attractiveness of preterm infants. *Infant Behavior and Development, 7*, 403–414.

Main, M., & George, C. (1985). Responses of abused and disadvantaged toddlers to distress in agemates: A study in the day care setting. *Developmental Psychology, 21*, 407–412.

Main, M., Kaplan, N., & Cassidy, J. (1985). Security in infancy, childhood, and adulthood: A move to the level of representation. *Monographs of the Society for Research in Child Development, 50* (1–2, Serial No. 209).

Malatesta, C. Z., Grigoryev, P., Lamb, C., Albin, M., & Culver, C. (1986). Emotion socialization and expressive development in preterm and full-term infants. *Child Development, 57*, 316–330.

Malatesta, C. Z., & Haviland, J. M. (1982). Learning display rules: The socialization of emotion expression in infancy. *Child Development, 53*, 991–1003.

Malina, R. M. (1975). *Growth and development: The first twenty years in man*. Minneapolis: Burgess.

Malina, R. M. (1979). Secular changes in size and maturity: Causes and effects. In A. F. Roche (Ed.), Secular trends in human growth, maturation, and development. *Monographs of the Society for Research in Child Development, 44* (3–4, Serial No. 179).

Malina, R. M. (1980). Biosocial correlates of motor development during infancy and early childhood. In L. S. Greene & F. E. Johnston (Eds.), *Social and biological predictors of nutritional status, physical growth, and neurological development* (pp. 143–171). New York: Academic Press.

Malina, R. M., Harper, A. B., & Holman, J. D. (1970). Growth status and performance relative to parental size. *Research Quarterly, 41*, 503–509.

Mallick, S. K., & McCandless, B. R. (1966). A study of catharsis of aggression. *Journal of Personality and Social Psychology, 4*, 591–596.

Mandler, J. M. (1983). Representation. In J. H. Flavell & E. M. Markman (Eds.), *Handbook of child psychology: Vol. 3. Cognitive development* (4th ed., pp. 420–494). New York: Wiley.

Mandler, J. M., & Johnson, N. S. (1977). Remembrance of things passed: Story structure and recall. *Cognitive Psychology, 9*, 111–151.

Mandler, J. M., & Robinson, C. A. (1978). Developmental changes in picture recognition. *Journal of Experimental Child Psychology, 26*, 122–136.

Maqsud, M. (1977). The influence of social heterogeneity and sentimental credibility on moral judgments of Nigerian Muslim adolescents. *Journal of Cross-Cultural Psychology, 8*, 113–122.

Marantz, S. A., & Mansfield, A. F. (1977). Maternal employment and the development of sex-role stereotyping in five- to eleven-year-old girls. *Child Development, 48*, 668–673.

Maratsos, M. (1983). Some current issues in the study of the acquisition of grammar. In J. H. Flavell & E. M. Markman (Eds.), *Handbook of child psychology: Vol 3. Cognitive development* (4th ed., pp. 707–786). New York: Wiley.

Maratsos, M. P., & Chalkley, M. A. (1980). The internal language of children's syntax. The ontogenesis and representation of syntactic categories. In K. Nelson (Ed.), *Children's language* (Vol. 2, pp. 127–214). New York: Gardner Press.

March of Dimes (1983). *PKU* (Genetic series public information health sheet). White Plains, NY: March of Dimes Birth Defects Foundation.

Marcia, J. E. (1966). Development and validation of ego identity status. *Journal of Personality and Social Psychology, 3*, 551–558.

Marcia, J. E. (1980). Identity in adolescence. In J. Adelson (Ed.), *Handbook of adolescent psychology* (pp. 159–187). New York: Wiley.

Marcus, D. E., & Overton, W. F. (1978). The development of cognitive gender constancy and sex role preferences. *Child Development, 49*, 434–444.

Marcus, J., Maccoby, E. E., Jacklin, C. N., & Doering, C. H. (1985). Individual differences in mood in early childhood: Their relation to gender and neonatal sex steroids. *Developmental Psychobiology, 18*, 327–340.

Marcus, L. C. (1983). Preventing and treating toxoplasmosis. *Drug Therapy, 13*, 129–144.

Marcus, R. F., Telleen, S., & Roke, E. J. (1979). Relation between cooperation and empathy in young children. *Developmental Psychology, 15*, 346–347.

Marion, R. W., Wiznia, A. A., Hutcheon, R. G., & Rubinstein, A. (1986). Human T-cell lymphotropic virus Type III (HTLV-III) embryopathy. *American Journal of Diseases of Children, 140*, 638–640.

Markman, E. M. (1979a). Classes and collections: Conceptual organization and numerical abilities. *Cognitive Psychology, 11*, 395–411.

Markman, E. M. (1979b). Realizing that you don't understand: Elementary school children's awareness of inconsistencies. *Child Development, 50*, 643–655.

Marsh, D. T., Serafica, F. C., & Barenboim, C. (1981). Interrelationships among perspective taking, interpersonal problem solving, and interpersonal functioning. *Journal of Genetic Psychology, 138*, 37–48

Marsh, H. W., Barnes, J., Cairns, L., & Tidman, M. (1984). Self-description questionnaire: Age and sex effects in the structure and level of self-concept for preadolescent children. *Journal of Educational Psychology, 76*, 940–956.

Marsh, H. W., Relich, J., & Smith, I. D. (1983). Self-concept: The construct validity of interpretations based upon the SDQ. *Journal of Personality and Social Psychology, 45*, 173–187.

Marsh, H. W., Smith, I. D., & Barnes, J. (1985). Multidimensional self-concepts: Relations with sex and academic achievement. *Journal of Educational Psychology, 77*, 581–596.

MARSH, R. W. (1985). Phrenoblysis: Real or chimera? *Child Development, 56*, 1059–1061.

MARSHALL, W. A. (1971). Evaluation of growth rate in height over periods of less than one year. *Archives of Disease in Childhood, 46*, 414–420.

MARSHALL, W. A. (1975). The relation of variation in children's growth rates to seasonal climatic variations. *Annals of Human Biology, 2*, 419–435.

MARSHALL, W. A., & TANNER, J. M. (1969). Variations in the pattern of pubertal changes in girls. *Archives of Disease in Childhood, 44*, 291–303.

MARTIN, C. L., & HALVERSON, C. F., JR. (1981). A schematic processing model of sex typing and stereotyping in children. *Child Development, 52*, 1119–1134.

MARTIN, C. L., & HALVERSON, C. F., JR. (1983). The effects of sex-typing schemas on young children's memory. *Child Development, 54*, 563–574.

MARTIN, G. B., & CLARK, R. D. III (1982). Distress crying in neonates: Species and peer specificity. *Developmental Psychology, 18*, 3–9.

MARTIN, J. A. (1981). A longitudinal study of the consequences of early mother-infant interaction: A microanalytic approach. *Monographs of the Society for Research in Child Development, 46* (No. 3, Serial No. 190).

MARTIN, R. M. (1975). Effects of familiar and complex stimuli on infant attention. *Developmental Psychology, 11*, 178–185.

MARTLEW, M. (1980). Mothers' control strategies in dyadic mother/child conversations. *Journal of Psycholinguistic Research, 9*, 327–347.

MARTORELL, R. (1980). Interrelationships between diet, infectious disease, and nutritional status. In L. S. Greene & F. E. Johnston (Eds.), *Social and biological predictors of nutritional status, physical growth, and neurological development* (pp. 81–106). New York: Academic Press.

MASTERS, J. C., & BINGER, C. G. (1976). *Inhibitive capability in young children: Stability and development.* Unpublished manuscript, University of Minnesota.

MASTERS, J. C., FORD, M. E., AREND, R., GROTEVANT, H. D., & CLARK, L. V. (1979). Modeling and labeling as integrated determinants of children's sex-typed imitative behavior. *Child Development, 50*, 364–371.

MASTERS, J. C., & FURMAN, W. (1981). Popularity, individual friendship selections, and specific peer interaction among children. *Developmental Psychology, 17*, 344–350.

MASUR, E. F., McINTYRE, C. W., & FLAVELL, J. H. (1973). Developmental changes in apportionment of study time among items in a multitrial free recall task. *Journal of Experimental Child Psychology, 15*, 237–246.

MATAS, L., AREND, R., & SROUFE, L. A. (1978). Continuity of adaptation in the second year: The relationship between quality of attachment and later competence. *Child Development, 49*, 547–556.

MATHENY, A. P. (1980). Bayley's Infant Behavior Record: Behavioral components and twin analyses. *Child Development, 51*, 466–475.

MATHENY, A. P., DOLAN, A., & WILSON, R. S. (1974). Bayley's Infant Behavior Record: Relations between behaviors and mental test scores. *Developmental Psychology, 10*, 696–702.

MATHENY, A. P., RIESE, M. L., & WILSON, R. S. (1985). Rudiments of infant temperament: Newborn to 9 months. *Developmental Psychology, 21*, 486–494.

MATHENY, A. P., WILSON, R. S., DOLAN, A., & KRANTZ, J. (1981). Behavioral contrasts in twinships: Stability and patterns of differences in childhood. *Child Development, 52*, 579–588.

MATTHEWS, K. A., & ANGULO, J. (1980). Measurement of the type A behavior pattern in children: Assessment of children's competitiveness, impatience-anger, and aggression. *Child Development, 51*, 466–475.

MAUDRY, M., & NEKULA, M. (1939). Social relations between children of the same age during the first two years of life. *Journal of Genetic Psychology, 54*, 193–215.

MAURER, D., & BARRERA, M. (1981). Infants' perception of natural and distorted arrangements of a schematic face. *Child Development, 52*, 196–202.

MAURO, R. J., & FEINS, R. P. (1977). *Kids, food and television: The compelling case for state action.* Albany, NY: New York State Assembly.

MAZIADE, M., BOUDREAULT, M., COTE, R., & THIVIERGE, J. (1986). Influence of gentle birth delivery procedures and other perinatal circumstances on infant temperament: Developmental and social implications. *Journal of Pediatrics, 108*, 134–136.

McANARNEY, E. R., LAWRENCE, R. A., & ATEN, M. J. (1979). Premature parenthood: A preliminary report of adolescent mother-infant interaction. *Pediatric Research, 13*, 328.

McCABE, A. E., EVELY, S., ABRAMOVITCH, R., CORTER, C. M., & PEPLER, D. J. (1983). Conditional statements in children's spontaneous speech. *Journal of Child Language, 10*, 253–258.

McCALL, R. B. (1977). Childhood IQs as predictors of adult educational and occupational status. *Science, 197*, 482–483.

McCALL, R. B. (1983). Environmental effects on intelligence: The forgotten realm of discontinuous nonshared within-family factors. *Child Development, 54*, 408–415.

McCALL, R. B. (1984). Developmental changes in mental performance: The effect of birth of a sibling. *Child Development, 55*, 1317–1321.

McCALL, R. B. (1985). The confluence model and theory. *Child Development, 56*, 217–218.

McCALL, R. B., APPELBAUM, M. I., & HOGARTY, P. S. (1973). Developmental changes in mental performance. *Monographs of the Society for Research in Child Development, 38* (3, Serial No. 150).

McCALL, R. B., EICHORN, D. H., & HOGARTY, P. S. (1977). Transitions in early mental development. *Monographs of the Society for Research in Child Development, 42* (3, Serial No. 171).

McCALL, R. B., HOGARTY, P. S., & HURLBURT, N. (1972). Transitions in sensorimotor development and the prediction of childhood IQ. *American Psychologist, 27*, 728–748.

McCALL, R. B., KENNEDY, C. B., & APPELBAUM, M. I. (1977). Magnitude of discrepancy and the distribution of attention in infants. *Child Development, 48*, 772–785.

McCALL, R. B., & McGHEE, P. E. (1977). The discrepancy hypothesis of attention and affect in infants. In F. Weizmann & I. Uzigiris (Eds.), *The structuring of experience* (pp. 179–210). New York: Plenum.

McCARTHY, D. A. (1954). Language development in children. In L. Carmichael (Ed.), *Manual of child psychology* (2nd ed., pp. 476–581). New York: Wiley.

McCARTHY, K. A., & NELSON, K. (1981). Children's use of scripts in story recall. *Discourse Processes, 4*, 59–70.

McCARTNEY, K. (1984). The effect of quality of day care environment upon children's language development. *Developmental Psychology, 20*, 244–260.

McCARTNEY, K., SCARR, S., PHILLIPS, D., & GRAJEK, S. (1985). Day care as intervention: Comparisons of varying quality programs. *Journal of Applied Developmental Psychology, 6*, 247–260.

McCAULEY, E., ITO, J., & KAY, T. (1986). Psychosocial functioning in girls with Turner syndrome and short stature. *Journal of the American Academy of Child Psychiatry, 25*, 105–112.

McCAULEY, E., KAY, T., ITO, J., & TREDER, R. (1987). The Turner Syndrome: Cognitive deficits, affective discrimination, and behavior problems. *Child Development, 58*, 464–473.

McCLELLAND, D. C., ATKINSON, J. W., CLARK, R. A., & LOWELL, E. L. (1953). *The achievement motive.* New York: Appleton-Century-Crofts.

McCONAGHY, M. J. (1979). Gender permanence and the genital basis of gender: Stages in the development of constancy of gender identity. *Child Development, 50*, 1223–1226.

McDAVID, J. W., & HARARI, H. (1966). Stereotyping of names and popularity in grade-school children. *Child Development, 37*, 453–459.

McDONALD, L., & PIEN, D. (1982). Mother conversational behaviour as a function of interactional intent. *Journal of Child Language, 9*, 337–358.

McDONALD, R. L. (1963). The role of emotional factors in obstetric complications: A review. *Psychosomatic Medicine, 30,* 222–237.

McEWEN, B. S. (1981). Neural gonadal steroid actions. *Science, 211,* 1303–1311.

McGHEE, P. E. (1974). Development of children's ability to create the joking relationship. *Child Development, 45,* 552–556.

McGHEE, P. E. (1979). *Humor: Its origin and development.* San Francisco: Freeman.

McGOWAN, R. J., & JOHNSON, D. L. (1984). The mother-child relationship and other antecedents of childhood intelligence: A causal analysis. *Child Development, 55,* 810–820.

McGREW, W. (1969). An ethological study of agonistic behaviour in preschool children. In C. R. Carpenter (Ed.), *Proceedings of the International Congress of Primatology* (Vol. 1, pp. 149–159). Basel: Karger.

McGREW, W. C. (1972). *An ethological study of children's behavior.* New York: Academic Press.

McGUIRE, K. D., & WEISZ, J. R. (1982). Social cognition and behavior correlates of preadolescent chumship. *Child Development, 53,* 1483–1484.

McKENZIE, B. E., & DAY, R. H. (1972). Distance as a determinant of visual fixation in early infancy. *Science, 178,* 1108–1110.

McKENZIE, B. E., & DAY, R. H. (1976). Infants' attention to stationary and moving objects at different distances. *Australian Journal of Psychology, 28,* 45–51.

McKENZIE, B. E., & OVER, R. (1983). Young infants fail to imitate facial and manual gestures. *Infant Behavior and Development, 6,* 85–95.

McKENZIE, B. E., TOOTELL, H. E., & DAY, R. H. (1980). Development of visual size constancy during the 1st year of human infancy. *Developmental Psychology, 16,* 163–174.

McKNIGHT, C. C., CROSSWHITE, F. J., DOSSEY, J. A., KIFER, E., SWAFFORD, J. O., TRAVERS, K. J., & COONEY, T. J. (1987). *The underachieving curriculum: Assessing U.S. school mathematics from an international perspective.* Champaign, IL: Stipes.

McKUSICK, V. A. (1983). *Mendelian inheritance in man. Catalogs of autosomal dominant, autosomal recessive, and X-linked phenotypes* (6th ed.). Baltimore: The Johns Hopkins University Press.

McLEAN, J., & SNYDER-McLEAN, L. (1978). *A transactional approach to early language training.* Columbus, OH: Merrill.

McLOYD, V. C. (1979). The effects of extrinsic rewards of differential value on high and low intrinsic interest. *Child Development, 50,* 1010–1019.

McLOYD, V. C., WARREN, D., & THOMAS, E. A. C. (1984) Anticipatory and fantastic role enactment in preschool triads. *Developmental Psychology, 20,* 807–814.

McNAMEE, S., & PETERSON, J. (1986). Young children's distributive justice reasoning, behavior, and role taking: Their consistency and relationship. *Journal of Genetic Psychology, 146,* 399–404.

McNEILL, D. (1970). The development of language. In P. H. Mussen (Ed.), *Carmichael's manual of child psychology* (3rd ed., Vol. 1, pp. 1061–1161). New York: Wiley.

McPARTLAND, J. M., & McDILL, E. L. (1977). Research on crime in schools. In J. M. McPartland & E. L. McDill (Eds.), *Violence in schools* (pp. 3–22). Lexington, MA: Lexington Books.

MEAD, G. H. (1934). *Mind, self, and society.* Chicago: University of Chicago Press.

MEAD, M. (1963). *Sex and temperament in three primitive societies.* New York: Morrow. (Originally published 1935)

MECKLENBURG, M. E., & THOMPSON, P. G. (1983). The adolescent family life program as a prevention measure. *Public Health Reports, 98,* 21–29.

MEDNICK, B. R., BAKER, R. L., & SUTTON-SMITH, B. (1979). Teenage pregnancy and perinatal mortality. *Journal of Youth and Adolescence, 8,* 343–357.

MEDRICH, E. A. (1981). *The serious business of growing up: A study of children's lives outside of school.* Berkeley: University of California Press.

MEDRICH, E. A., ROSEN, J., RUBIN, V., & BUCKLEY, S. (1982). *The serious business of growing up.* Berkeley: University of California Press.

MEDWAY, F. J., & VENINO, G. R. (1982). The effects of effort feedback and performance patterns on children's attributions and task persistence. *Contemporary Educational Psychology, 7,* 26–34.

MEECE, J. L., PARSONS, J. E., KACZALA, C. M., GOFF, S. B., & FUTTERMAN, R. (1982). Sex differences in math achievement: Toward a model of academic choice. *Psychological Bulletin, 91,* 324–348.

MEHLER, J., BERTONCINI, J., BARRIERE, M., & JASSIK-GERSCHENFELD, D. (1978). Infant recognition of mother's voice. *Perception, 7,* 491–497.

MEICHENBAUM, D., & ASARNOW, J. (1979). Cognitive behavior modification and metacognitive development: Implications for the classroom. In P. Kendall & S. Hollon (Eds.), *Cognitive behavioral interventions: Theory, research and procedure* (pp. 11–35). New York: Academic Press.

MEICHENBAUM, D. H., & GOODMAN, J. (1971). Training impulsive children to talk to themselves: A means of developing self-control. *Journal of Abnormal Psychology, 77,* 115–126.

MEILMAN, P. W. (1979). Cross-sectional age changes in ego identity status during adolescence. *Developmental Psychology, 15,* 230–231.

MEISELS, S., PLUNKETT, J., STIEFEL, G., PASICK, P., & ROLOFF, D. (1984). Patterns of attachment among preterm infants of differing biological risk. Paper presented at the International Conference on Infant Studies, New York.

MELSON, G. F., & FOGEL, A. (1988, January). Learning to care. *Psychology Today, 22*(1), 39–45.

MELTON, G. B., & DAVIDSON, H. A. (1987). Child protection and society: When should the state intervene? *American Psychologist, 42,* 172–175.

MELTON, G. B., & THOMPSON, R. A. (1987a). Getting out of a rut: Detours to less traveled paths in child-witness research. In S. J. Ceci, M. P. Toglia, & D. F. Ross (Eds.), *Children's eyewitness memory* (pp. 209–229). New York: Springer-Verlag.

MELTON, G. B., & THOMPSON, R. A. (1987b). Legislative approaches to psychological maltreatment: A social policy analysis. In M. R. Brassard, R. Germain, & S. N. Hart (Eds.), *Psychological maltreatment of children and youth* (pp. 203–216). New York: Pergamon Press.

MELTZOFF, A. N. (1988). Infant imitation and memory: Nine-month-olds in immediate and deferred tests. *Child Development, 56,* 62–72.

MELTZOFF, A. N., & BORTON, R. W. (1979). Intermodal matching by human neonates. *Nature, 282,* 403–404.

MELTZOFF, A. N., & MOORE, M. K. (1977). Imitation of facial and manual gestures by human neonates. *Science, 198,* 75–78.

MELTZOFF, A. N., & MOORE, M. K. (1983). Newborn infants imitate adult facial gestures. *Child Development, 54,* 702–709.

MENDLEWICZ, J., & RAINER, J. D. (1974). Morbidity risk and genetic transmission in manic-depressive illness. *American Journal of Human Genetics, 26,* 692–701.

MENIG-PETERSON, C. L. (1975). The modification of communicative behavior in preschool-aged children as a function of the listener's perspective. *Child Development, 46,* 1015–1018.

MENN, L. (1976). Pattern, control, and contrast in beginning speech: A case study in the development of word form and word function. *Dissertation Abstracts International, 37,* 2833A. (University Microfilms No. 76–24, 139)

MENN, L. (1985). Phonological development: Learning sounds and sound patterns. In J. Berko Gleason (Ed.), *The development of language* (pp. 61–101). Columbus, OH: Merrill.

MENYUK, P. (1977). *Language and maturation.* Cambridge, MA: MIT Press.

MENYUK, P., MENN, L., & SILBER, R. (1986). Early strategies for the perception and production of words and sounds. In P. Fletcher & M. Garman (Eds.), *Language acquisition* (2nd ed., pp. 198–222). Cambridge, Eng.: Cambridge University Press.

MERCER, J. R. (1972, September). IQ: The lethal label. *Psychology Today, 6*(4), 44–47, 95–97.

MERCER, J. R. (1975). Psychological assessment and the rights of children. In N. Hobbs (Ed.), *Issues in the classification of children* (Vol. 1, pp. 130–158). San Francisco: Jossey-Bass.

MERCER, J. R. (1979a). In defense of racially and culturally nondiscriminatory assessment. *School Psychology Digest, 8*, 89–115.

MERCER, J. R. (1979b). *System of Multicultural Pluralistic Assessment: Technical manual.* New York: Psychological Corporation.

MERCER, J. R., & LEWIS, J. F. (1978). *System of Multicultural Pluralistic Assessment.* New York: Psychological Corporation.

MERRITT, T. A. (1981). Smoking mothers affect little lives. *American Journal of Diseases of Children, 135*, 501–502.

MESSER, S. B. (1976). Reflection-impulsivity: A review. *Psychological Bulletin, 83*, 1026–1053.

MEYER, B. (1980). The development of girls' sex-role attitudes. *Child Development, 48*, 507–512.

MEYER, M. B. (1978). How does maternal smoking affect birth weight and maternal weight gain? Evidence from Ontario Perinatal Mortality Study. *American Journal of Obstetrics and Gynecology, 131*, 888–893.

MICHAELS, S. (1980). *Sharing time: An oral preparation for literacy.* Paper presented at the Ethnography in Education Research Forum, University of Pennsylvania, Philadelphia.

MIDLARSKY, E., & BRYAN, J. H. (1972). Affect expressions and children's imitative altruism. *Journal of Experimental Research in Personality, 6*, 195–203.

MILES, C. (1935). Sex in social psychology. In C. Murchison (Ed.), *Handbook of social psychology* (pp. 699–704). Worcester, MA: Clark University Press.

MILICH, R., & LANDAU, S. (1984). A comparison of the social status and social behavior of aggressive and aggressive/withdrawn boys. *Journal of Abnormal Child Psychology, 12*, 277–288.

MILICH, R., & PELHAM, W. E. (1986). The effects of sugar ingestion on the classroom and play group behavior of attention deficit disordered boys. *Journal of Consulting and Clinical Psychology, 54*, 714–718.

MILLER, G. A. (1956). The magical number seven, plus or minus two: Some limits on our capacity for processing information. *Psychological Review, 63*, 81–97.

MILLER, G. E., & EMIHOVICH, C. (1986). The effects of mediated programming instruction on preschool children's self-monitoring. *Journal of Educational Computing Research, 2*, 283–297.

MILLER, N., & MARUYAMA, G. (1976). Ordinal position and peer popularity. *Journal of Personality and Social Psychology, 33*, 123–131.

MILLER, P. H. (1983). *Theories of developmental psychology.* San Francisco, CA: Freeman.

MILLER, P. H., & BIGI, L. (1979). The development of children's understanding of attention. *Merrill-Palmer Quarterly, 25*, 235–250.

MILLER, P. H., & ZALENSKI, R. (1982). Preschoolers' knowledge about attention. *Developmental Psychology, 18*, 871–875.

MILLER, P. H., KESSEL, F. S., & FLAVELL, J. H. (1970). Thinking about people thinking about people thinking about . . . : A study of social cognitive development. *Child Development, 41*, 613–623.

MILLER, S. A. (1987). *Developmental Research methods.* Englewood Cliffs, NJ: Prentice-Hall.

MINKOFF, H., DEEPAK, N., MENEZ, R., & FIKRIG, S. (1987). Pregnancies resulting in infants with acquired immunodeficiency syndrome of AIDS-related complex: Follow-up of mothers, children, and subsequently born siblings. *Obstetrics and Gynecology, 69*, 288–291.

MINUCHIN, P., BIBER, B., SHAPIRO, E., & ZIMILES, H. (1969). *The psychological impact of school experience.* New York: Basic.

MINUCHIN, P. P., & SHAPIRO, E. K. (1983). The school as a context for social development. In E. M. Hetherington (Ed.), *Handbook of child psychology: Vol. 4. Socialization, personality, and social development* (4th ed., pp. 197–274). New York: Wiley.

MINUCHIN, S., ROSMAN, B. L., & BAKER, L. (1978). *Psychosomatic families.* Cambridge, MA: Harvard University Press.

MISCHEL, H. N. (1974). Sex bias in the evaluation of professional achievements. *Journal of Educational Psychology, 66*, 157–166.

MISCHEL, H. N., & MISCHEL, W. (1983). The development of children's knowledge of self-control strategies. *Child Development, 54*, 603–619.

MISCHEL, W. (1974). Processes in delay of gratification. In L. Berkowitz (Ed.), *Advances in experimental social psychology* (Vol. 7, pp. 249–292). New York: Academic Press.

MISCHEL, W., & BAKER, N. (1975). Cognitive appraisals and transformations in delay behavior. *Journal of Personality and Social Psychology, 31*, 254–261.

MISCHEL, W., & EBBESEN, E. B. (1970). Attention in delay of gratification. *Journal of Personality and Social Psychology, 16*, 329–337.

MISCHEL, W., & LIEBERT, R. M. (1966). Effects of discrepancies between observed and imposed reward criteria on their acquisition and transmission. *Journal of Personality and Social Psychology, 3*, 45–53.

MISCHEL, W., & METZNER, R. (1962). Preference for delayed reward as a function of age, intelligence, and length of delay interval. *Journal of Abnormal and Social Psychology, 64*, 425–431.

MISCIONE, J. L., MARVIN, R. S., O'BRIEN, R. G., & GREENBURG, M. T. (1978). A developmental study of preschool children's understanding of the words "know" and "guess." *Child Development, 48*, 1107–1113.

MITCHELL, G., & SHIVELY, C. (1984). Natural and experimental studies of nonhuman primate and other animal families. In R. D. Parke (Ed.), *Review of child development research* (Vol. 7, pp. 20–41). Chicago: University of Chicago Press.

MITCHELL, R. E., & TRICKET, E. J. (1980). An analysis of the effects and determinants of social networks. *Community Mental Health Journal, 16*, 27–44.

MIYAKE, K., CHEN, S., & CAMPOS, J. J. (1985). Infant temperament, mother's mode of interaction, and attachment in Japan: An interim report. In I. Bretherton & E. Waters (Eds.), Growing points of attachment theory and research. *Monographs of the Society for Research in Child Development, 50* (1–2, Serial No. 209).

MIYAWAKI, K., STRANGE, W., VERBRUGGE, R., LIBERMAN, A. M., JENKINS, J. J., & FUJIMURA, O. (1975). An effect of linguistic experience: The discrimination of [r] and [l] by native speakers of Japanese and English. *Perception and Psychophysics, 18*, 331–340.

MOELY, B. E. (1977). Organizational factors in the development of memory. In R. V. Kail, Jr., & J. W. Hagen (Eds.), *Perspectives on the development of memory and cognition* (pp. 203–236). Hillsdale, NJ: Erlbaum.

MOELY, B. E., OLSON, F. A., HALWES, T. G., & FLAVELL, J. H. (1969). Production deficiency in young children's clustered recall. *Developmental Psychology, 1*, 26–34.

MOERK, E. L. (1980). Relationship between parental input frequencies and children's language acquisition: A reanalysis of Brown's data. *Journal of Child Language, 7*, 105–118.

MOERK, E. L. (1983). A behavioral analysis of controversial topics in first language acquisition: Reinforcements, corrections, modeling, input frequencies, and the three-term contingency pattern. *Journal of Psycholinguistic Research, 12*, 129–155.

MOLFESE, D. L. (1977). Infant cerebral asymmetry. In S. J. Segalowitz & F. A. Gruber (Eds.), *Language development and neurological theory* (pp. 22–35). New York: Academic Press.

MOLFESE, D. L., & MOLFESE, V. J. (1979). Hemispheric and stimulus differences as reflected in the cortical responses of newborn infants to speech stimuli. *Developmental Psychology, 15*, 505–511.

MONEY, J., & EHRHARDT, A. A. (1972). *Man and woman, boy and girl.* Baltimore: Johns Hopkins University Press.

MONEY, J., & TUCKER, P. (1975). *Sexual signatures: On being a man or a woman.* Boston: Little, Brown.

MONROE, R. H., MONROE, R. L., & WHITING, B. B. (1981). *Handbook of cross-cultural human development.* New York: Garland.

MONTAGU, M. F. A. (1962). *Prenatal influences.* Springfield, IL: Thomas.

MONTEMAYOR, R. (1974). Children's performance in a game and their attraction to it as a function of sex-typed labels. *Child Development, 45*, 152–156.

MONTEMAYOR, R., & EISEN, M. (1977). The development of self-conceptions from childhood to adolescence. *Developmental Psychology, 13*, 314–319.

MOORE, K. L. (1983). *Before we are born* (2nd ed.). Philadelphia: Saunders.

MOORE, T. (1968). Language and intelligence: A longitudinal study of the first eight years, II: Environmental correlates of mental growth. *Human Development, 10,* 88–106.

MOORE, T. W. (1975). Exclusive early mothering and its alternatives. *Scandinavian Journal of Psychology, 16,* 256–272.

MORAN, G. F., & VINOVSKIS, M. A. (1986). The great care of godly parents: Early childhood in Puritan New England. *Monographs of the Society for Research in Child Development, 50* (4–5, Serial No. 211).

MORAN, J. D., MILGRAM, R. M., SAWYERS, J. K., & FU, V. R. (1983). Original thinking in preschool children. *Child Development, 54,* 921–926.

MORGAN, M. (1982). Television and adolescents' sex stereotypes: A longitudinal study. *Journal of Personality and Social Psychology, 43,* 947–955.

MORRIS, D. (1981). Attachment and intimacy. In G. Stricker (Ed.), *Intimacy* (pp. 305–323). New York: Plenum.

MORRONGIELLO, B. A., & CLIFTON, R. K. (1984). Effects of sound frequency on behavioral and cardiac orienting in newborn and five-month-old infants. *Journal of Experimental Child Psychology, 38,* 429–446.

MORRONGIELLO, B. A., CLIFTON, R. K., & KULIG, J. W. (1982). Newborn cardiac and behavioral orienting responses to sound under varying precedence-effect conditions. *Infant Behavior and Development, 5,* 249–259.

MORTIMER, J. T., & SORENSEN, G. (1984). Men, women, work, and family. In K. M. Borman, D. Quarm, & S. Gideonse (Eds.), *Women in the workplace: Effects on families* (pp. 139–167). Norwood, NJ: Ablex.

MOSER, H. W. (1975). Biochemical aspects of mental retardation. In D. B. Tower (Ed.), *The nervous system: Vol. 2. The clinical neurosciences* (pp. 369–379). New York: Raven Press.

MOSS, H. A., & ROBSON, K. S. (1970). The relation between the amount of time infants spend at various states and the development of visual behavior. *Child Development, 41,* 509–517.

MOSSBERG, N. (1948). Obesity in children: A clinical-prognostical investigation. *Acta Paediatrica, 35* (Suppl. 2), p. 1.

MOSSLER, D. G., MARVIN, R. S., & GREENBERG, M. T. (1976). Conceptual perspective-taking in 2- to 6-year-old children. *Developmental Psychology, 12,* 85–86.

MOSSMAN, K. L., & HILL, L. T. (1982). Radiation risks in pregnancy. *Obstetrics and Gynecology, 60,* 237–242.

MOWRER, O. H. (1960). *Learning theory and behavior.* New York: Wiley.

MOYNAHAN, E. D. (1973). The development of knowledge concerning the effect of categorization upon free recall. *Child Development, 44,* 238–246.

MUELLER, E. (1972). The maintenance of verbal exchanges between young children. *Child Development, 43,* 930–938.

MUELLER, E., & BRENNER, J. (1977). The origins of social skills and interaction among playgroup toddlers. *Child Development, 48,* 854–861.

MUELLER, E., & LUCAS, T. A. (1975). Developmental analysis of peer interaction among toddlers. In M. Lewis & L. A. Rosenblum (Eds.), *Friendship and peer relations* (pp. 223–257). New York: Wiley.

MUELLER, E., & RICH, A. (1976). Clustering and socially directed behaviors in a playgroup of 1-year-old-boys. *Journal of Child Psychology and Psychiatry, 17,* 315–322.

MULHERN, R. K., JR., & PASSMAN, R. H. (1981). Parental discipline as affected by sex of the parent, sex of the child, and the child's apparent responsiveness to discipline. *Developmental Psychology, 17,* 604–613.

MULLENER, N., & LAIRD, J. D. (1971). Some developmental changes in the organization of self-evaluations. *Developmental Psychology, 5,* 233–236.

MUNRO, G., & ADAMS, G. R. (1977). Ego identity formation in college students and working youth. *Developmental Psychology, 13,* 523–524.

MURDOCK, B. B. (1961). The retention of individual items. *Journal of Experimental Psychology, 62,* 618–625.

MURRAY, A. D. (1985). Aversiveness is in the mind of the beholder. In B. M. Lester & C. F. Z. Boukydis (Eds.), *Infant crying* (pp. 217–239). New York: Plenum.

MURRAY, F. B. (1978). Teaching strategies and conservation training. In A. M. Lesgold, J. W. Pellegrino, S. D. Fekkema, & R. Glaser (Eds.), *Cognitive psychology and instruction,* vol. 1 (pp. 419–428). New York: Plenum.

MUSSEN, P., & EISENBERG-BERG, N. (1977). *Roots of caring, sharing, and helping.* San Francisco: Freeman.

NADEL, L., & ZOLA-MORGAN, S. (1984). Infantile amnesia: A neurobiological perspective. In M. Moscovitch (Ed.), *Infant memory* (pp. 145–172). New York: Plenum.

NAEYE, R. L., BLANC, W., & PAUL, C. (1973). Effects of maternal nutrition on the human fetus. *Pediatrics, 52,* 494–503.

NAGEL, E. (1959). Methodological issues in psychoanalytic theory. In S. Hook (Ed.), *Psychoanalysis, scientific method, and philosophy* (pp. 38–56). New York: New York University Press.

NAPIER, J. (1970). *The roots of mankind.* Washington, DC: Smithsonian Institution Press.

National Assessment of Educational Progress (1985). *The Reading Report Card: Progress toward excellence in our schools.* Princeton, NJ: Educational Testing Service.

National Commission for the Protection of Human Subjects (1977). *Report and recommendations: Research involving children.* Washington, DC: U.S. Government Printing Office.

National Commission on Excellence in Education (1983). *A nation at risk: The imperative for educational reform.* Washington, DC: U.S. Government Printing Office.

NEAL, J. H. (1983). Children's understanding of their parents' divorces. In L. A. Kurdek (Ed.), *New Directions for Child Development* (No. 19, pp. 3–14). San Francisco: Jossey-Bass.

NEEDLEMAN, H. L., GUNNOE, C., LEVITON, A., REED, R., PERESIE, H., MAHER, C., & BARRETT, P. (1979). Deficits in psychologic and classroom performance of children with elevated dentine lead levels. *New England Journal of Medicine, 300,* 689–695.

NEIMARK, E. D. (1975). Intellectual development during adolescence. In F. Horowitz (Ed.), *Review of child development research, vol. 4* (pp. 541–594). Chicago: University of Chicago Press.

NEIMARK, E. D., SLOTNICK, N. S., & ULRICH, T. (1971). Development of memorization strategies. *Developmental Psychology, 5,* 427–432.

NEISSER, U. (1967). *Cognitive psychology.* Englewood Cliffs, NJ: Prentice-Hall.

NELSON, C. A. (1987). The recognition of facial expressions in the first two years of life: Mechanisms of development. *Child Development, 58,* 889–909.

NELSON, E. A., GRINDER, R. E., & BIAGGIO, A. M. (1969). Relationships among behavioral, cognitive-developmental, and self-support measures of morality and personality. *Multivariate Behavioral Research, 4,* 483–500.

NELSON, E. A., GRINDER, R. E., & MUTTERER, M. L. (1969). Sources of variance in behavioral measures of honesty in temptation situations: Methodological analyses. *Developmental Psychology, 1,* 265–279.

NELSON, J., & ABOUD, F. E. (1985). The resolution of social conflict between friends. *Child Development, 56,* 1009–1017.

NELSON, K. (1973). Structure and strategy in learning to talk. *Monographs of the Society for Research in Child Development, 38* (1–2, Serial No. 149).

NELSON, K. (1975). The nominal shift in semantic-syntactic development. *Cognitive Psychology, 7,* 461–479.

NELSON, K. (1976). Some attributes of adjectives used by young children. *Cognition, 4,* 13–30.

NELSON, K. (1984). The transition from infant to child memory. In M. Moscovitch (Ed.), *Infant Memory* (pp. 103–130). New York: Plenum.

NELSON, K. (1986). *Event knowledge.* Hillsdale, NJ: Erlbaum.

NELSON, K., & BROWN, A. L. (1978). The semantic-episodic distinction in memory development. In P. A. Ornstein (Ed.), *Memory development in children* (pp. 233–241). Hillsdale, NJ: Erlbaum.

NELSON, K., & GRUENDEL, J. (1981). Generalized event representations: Basic building blocks of cognitive development. In M. Lamb & A. Brown (Eds.), *Advances in developmental psychology* (Vol. 1, pp. 131–158). Hillsdale, NJ: Erlbaum.

NELSON, K., RESCORLA, L., GRUENDEL, J. M., & BENEDICT, H. (1978). Early lexicons: What do they mean? *Child Development, 49,* 960–968.

NELSON, K., & ROSS, G. (1980). The generalities and specifics of long-term memory in infants and young children. In M. Perlmutter (Ed.), *New directions for child development* (No. 10, pp. 87–101). San Francisco: Jossey-Bass.

NELSON, K. E., CARSKADDON, G., & BONVILLIAN, J. D. (1973). Syntax acquisition: Impact of experimental variation in adult verbal interaction with the child. *Child Development, 44,* 497–504.

NELSON, K. E., & KOSSLYN, S. M. (1976). Recognition of previously labeled or unlabeled pictures by 5-year-olds and adults. *Journal of Experimental Child Psychology, 21,* 40–45.

NELSON-LE GALL, S. A. (1985). Motive-outcome matching and outcome foreseeability: Effects on attribution of intentionality and moral judgments. *Developmental Psychology, 21,* 332–337.

NEMEROWICZ, G. M. (1979). *Children's perceptions of gender and work roles.* New York: Praeger.

NEUTRA, R., ET AL. (1978). Effect of fetal monitoring on neonatal death rates. *New England Journal of Medicine, 299,* 324–326.

New England primer: Or an easy and pleasant guide to the art of reading (1836). Boston: Massachusetts Sabbath School Society. (Originally published 1687)

NEWCOMB, A. F., BRADY, J. E., & HARTUP, W. W. (1979). Friendship and incentive conditions as determinants of children's task-oriented social behavior. *Child Development, 50,* 878–881.

NEWCOMB, A. F., & COLLINS, W. A. (1979). Children's comprehension of family role portrayals in televised dramas: Effects of socioeconomic status, ethnicity, and age. *Developmental Psychology, 15,* 417–423.

NEWCOMBE, N. (1982). Development of spatial cognition and cognitive development. In R. Cohen (Ed.), *Children's conceptions of spatial relationships* (pp. 65–81). San Francisco: Jossey-Bass.

NEWCOMBE, N., & DUBAS, J. S. (1987). Individual differences in cognitive ability: Are they related to timing of puberty? In R. M. Lerner & T. T. Foch (Eds.), *Biological-psychosocial interactions in early adolescence: A life-span perspective* (pp. 249–302). Hillsdale, NJ: Erlbaum.

NEWELL, A., & SIMON, H. A. (1972). *Human problem solving.* Englewood Cliffs, NJ: Prentice-Hall.

NEWPORT, E. L., GLEITMAN, H., & GLEITMAN, L. R. (1977). Mother, I'd rather do it myself: Some effects and non-effects of maternal speech style. In C. A. Ferguson & C. E. Snow (Eds.), *Talking to children* (pp. 109–149). New York: Cambridge University Press.

NEWSON, J., & NEWSON, E. (1976). *Seven years old in the home environment.* London: Allen & Unwin.

NICHOLLS, J. G. (1975). Causal attributions and other achievement related cognitions: Effects of task outcome, attainment value, and sex. *Journal of Personality and Social Psychology, 31,* 379–389.

NICHOLLS, J. G. (1976). Effort is virtuous but it's better to have ability: Evaluative responses to perceptions of effort and ability. *Journal of Research in Personality, 10,* 306–315.

NICHOLLS, J. G. (1978). The development of concepts of effort and ability, perception of academic attainment, and the understanding that difficult tasks require more ability. *Child Development, 49,* 800–814.

NICHOLLS, J. G. (1979). Development of perceptions of own attainment and causal attributions for success and failure in reading. *Journal of Educational Psychology, 71,* 94–99.

NICHOLS, R. C. (1978). Heredity and environment: Major findings from twin studies of ability, personality and interests. *Home, 29,* 158–173.

NIELSEN TELEVISION SERVICES (1985). *Nielsen report on television.* Northbrook, IL: A. C. Nielsen Co.

NIELSEN, J., NYBORG, M., & DAHL, G. (1977). Turner's syndrome. *Acta Jut Landiei, 45,* Medicare Series no. 21.

NILSSON, L. (1977). *A child is born.* New York: Delacorte.

NINIO, A., & BRUNER, J. (1978). The achievement and antecedents of labelling. *Journal of Child Language, 5,* 1–15.

NISAN, M., & KOHLBERG, L. (1982). Universality and cross-cultural variation in moral development: A longitudinal and cross-sectional study in Turkey. *Child Development, 53,* 865–876.

NORBECK, J. S., & TILDEN, V. P. (1983). Life stress, social support, and emotional disequilibrium in complications of pregnancy: A prospective, multivariate study. *Journal of Health and Social Behavior, 24,* 30–46.

NOTTELMANN, E. D. (1987). Competence and self-esteem during transition from childhood to adolescence. *Developmental Psychology, 23,* 441–450.

NOTTELMANN, E. D., SUSMAN, E. J., BLUE, J. H., INOFF-GERMAIN, G., DORN, L. D., LORIAUX, D. L., CUTLER, G. B., JR., & CHROUSOS, G. P. (1987). Gonadal and adrenal hormone correlates of adjustment in early adolescence. In R. M. Lerner & T. T. Foch (Eds.), *Biological-psychosocial interactions in early adolescence: A life-span perspective* (pp. 303–323). Hillsdale, NJ: Erlbaum.

NOWAKOWSKI, R. S. (1987). Basic concepts of CNS development. *Child Development, 58,* 568–595.

NUCCI, L. P. (1981). Conceptions of personal issues: A domain distinct from moral or societal concepts. *Child Development, 52,* 114–121.

NUCCI, L. P., & TURIEL, E. (1978). Social interactions and the development of social concepts in preschool children. *Child Development, 49,* 400–407.

NUCKOLLS, K. B., CASSEL, J., & KAPLAN, B. H. (1972). Psychosocial assets, life crisis and the prognosis of pregnancy. *American Journal of Epidemiology, 95,* 431–441.

NUNNALLY, J. C. (1982). The study of human change: Measurement, research strategies, and methods of analysis. In B. B. Wolman, (Ed.), *Handbook of developmental psychology* (pp. 133–148). Englewood Cliffs, NJ: Prentice-Hall.

OAKLAND, T. D. (1978). Predictive validity of readiness tests of middle and lower socioeconomic status Anglo, Black, and Mexican American children. *Journal of Educational Psychology, 70,* 574–582.

OAKLAND, T. D. (1979). Research on the Adaptive Behavior Inventory for Children and the Estimated Learning Potential. *School Psychology Digest, 8,* 209–213.

OAKLAND, T. D., & PARMELEE, R. (1985). Mental measurement of minority-group children. In B. B. Wolman (Ed.), *Handbook of intelligence* (pp. 699–736). New York: Wiley.

OATES, R. K. (1982). Child abuse—a community concern. In K. Oates (Ed.), *Child abuse: A community concern* (pp. 1–12). New York: Brunner/Mazel.

OATES, R. K. (1984). Similarities and differences between nonorganic failure to thrive and deprivation dwarfism. *Child Abuse and Neglect, 8,* 438–445.

OATES, R. K., PEACOCK, A., & FORREST, D. (1985). Long term effects of nonorganic failure to thrive. *Pediatrics, 75,* 36–40.

O'BRIEN, M. (1980). Sex differences in toy and activity preferences of toddlers. Unpublished master's thesis, University of Kansas.

O'BRIEN, M., & HUSTON, A. C. (1985). Development of sex-typed play behavior in toddlers. *Developmental Psychology, 21,* 866–871.

O'BRIEN, M., HUSTON, A. C., & RISLEY, T. R. (1981). Emergence and stability of sex-typed toy preferences in toddlers. Paper presented at the meeting of the Association for Behavior Analysis, Milwaukee.

O'BRIEN, M., HUSTON, A. C., & RISLEY, T. R. (1983). Sex-typed play of toddlers in a day care center. *Journal of Applied Developmental Psychology, 4,* 1–9.

OCHS, E. (1982).Talking to children in Western Samoa. *Language in Society, 11,* 77–104.

O'CONNOR, M., FOCH, T., SHERRY, T., & PLOMIN, R. (1980). A twin study of specific behavioral problems of socialization as viewed by parents. *Journal of Abnormal Child Psychology, 8,* 189–199.

O'CONNOR, R. D. (1969). Modification of social withdrawal through symbolic modeling. *Journal of Applied Behavior Analysis, 2,* 15–22.

O'CONNOR, R. D. (1972). Relative efficacy of modeling, shaping, and the combined procedures for modification of social withdrawal. *Journal of Abnormal Psychology, 79,* 327–334.

ODEN, S. L., & ASHER, S. R. (1977). Coaching children in social skills for friendship making. *Child Development, 48,* 495–506.

OETTINGEN, G. (1985). The influence of kindergarten teacher on sex differences in behavior. *International Journal of Behavioral Development, 8,* 3–13.

OFFER, D., OSTROV, E., & HOWARD, K. I. (1981). *The adolescent: A psychological self-portrait.* New York: Basic Books.

O'KEEFE, B. J., & BENOIT, P. J. (1982). Children's arguments. In J. R. Cox & C. A. Willard (Eds.), *Advances in argumentation theory and research* (pp. 154–183). Carbondale, IL: Southern Illinois University Press.

OLLER, D. K., & EILERS, R. E. (1988). The role of audition in infant babbling. *Child Development, 59,* 441–449.

OLSHO, L. W. (1984). Infant frequency discrimination. *Infant Behavior and Development, 7,* 27–35.

OLSON, C. F., & WOROBEY, J. (1984). Perceived mother-daughter relations in a pregnant and nonpregnant adolescent sample. *Adolescence, 12,* 781–794.

OLSON, G. M., & SHERMAN, T. (1983). Attention, learning and memory in infants. In M. M. Haith & J. J. Campos (Eds.), *Handbook of child psychology: Vol. 2. Infancy and developmental psychobiology* (pp. 1001–1080). New York: Wiley.

OLWEUS, D. (1979). Stability and aggressive reaction patterns in males: A review. *Psychological Bulletin, 86,* 852–875.

OLWEUS, D. (1980a). The consistency issue in personality psychology revisited—with special reference to aggression. *British Journal of Social and Clinical Psychology, 19,* 377–390.

OLWEUS, D. (1980b). Familial and temperamental determinants of aggressive behavior in adolescent boys: A causal analysis. *Developmental Psychology, 16,* 644–666.

OLWEUS, D., MATTSSON, A., SCHALLING, D., & LOW, H. (1980). Testosterone, aggression, physical, and personality dimensions in normal adolescent males. *Psychosomatic Medicine, 33,* 265–277.

O'MALLEY, J. M. (1982). *Children's English and services study: Language minority children with limited English proficiency.* Rosslyn, VA: InterAmerica Research Associates.

O'MALLEY, P. M., & BACHMAN, J. G. (1983). Self-esteem: Change and stability between ages 13 and 23. *Developmental Psychology, 19,* 257–268.

OMARK, D. R., OMARK, M., & EDELMAN, M. S. (1975). Formation of dominance hierarchies in young children: Attention and perception. In T. Williams (Ed.), *Psychological anthropology* (pp. 289–315). The Hague: Mouton.

OPENSHAW. D. K., THOMAS, D. L., & ROLLINS, B. C. (1984). Parental influences of adolescent self-esteem. *Journal of Early Adolescence, 4,* 259–274.

OPPENHEIM, D., SAGI, A., & LAMB, M. E. (1988). Infant-adult attachments on the kibbutz and their relation to socioemotional development 4 years later. *Developmental Psychology, 24,* 427–433.

ORENBERG, C. L. (1981). *DES: The complete story.* New York: St. Martin's Press.

ORNSTEIN, P. A., HALE, G. A., & MORGAN, J. S. (1977). Developmental differences in recall and output organization. *Bulletin of the Psychonomic Society, 9,* 29–32.

ORNSTEIN, P. A., MEDLIN, R. G., STONE, B. P., & NAUS, M. J. (1985). Retrieving for rehearsal: An analysis of active rehearsal in children's memory. *Developmental Psychology, 21,* 633–641.

ORNSTEIN, P. A., NAUS, M. J., & LIBERTY, C. (1975). Rehearsal and organizational processes in children's memory. *Child Development, 46,* 818–830.

ORNSTEIN, P. A., NAUS, M. J., & STONE, B. P. (1977). Rehearsal training and developmental differences in memory. *Developmental Psychology, 13,* 15–24.

O'ROURKE, D. H., GOTTESMAN, I. I., SUAREZ, B. K., RICE, J., & REICH, T. (1982). Refutation of the general single-locus model for the etiology of schizophrenia. *American Journal of Human Genetics, 34,* 630–649.

OSHERSON, D. N., & MARKMAN, E. M. (1975). Language and the ability to evaluate contradictions and tautologies. *Cognition, 2,* 213–226.

OSOFSKY, H. J., & OSOFSKY, J. D. (1983). Adolescent adaptation to pregnancy and parenthood. In E. R. McAnarney (Ed.), *Premature adolescent pregnancy and parenthood* (pp. 195–206). New York: Grune & Stratton.

OSTER, H. (1978). Facial expression and affect development. In M. Lewis & L. A. Rosenblum (Eds.), *The development of affect* (pp. 43–75). New York: Plenum.

OWEN, M. T., EASTERBROOKS, M. A., CHASE-LANSDALE, L., & GOLDBERG, W. A. (1984). The relation between maternal employment status and the stability of attachments to mother and father. *Child Development, 55,* 1894–1901.

PACK, C. (1983). Interactional synchrony as an artifact of microanalysis: An attempt to apply the discovery of interactional synchrony in neonates as an index of attachment in nonorganic failure to thrive syndrome. *Dissertation Abstracts International, 43,* 3423A. (University Microfilms No. 83-06,100)

PAGE, D. C., MOSHER, R., SIMPSON, E. M., FISHER, E. M. C., MARDON, G., POLLACK, J., McGILLIVRAY, B., DE LA CHAPELLE, A., & BROWN, L. G. (1987). The sex-determining region of the human Y chromosome encodes a finger protein. *Cell, 51,* 1091–1104.

PAGE, E. B., & GRANDON, G. M. (1979). Family configuration and mental ability: Two theories contrasted with U.S. data. *American Educational Research Journal, 16,* 257–272.

PAGET, K. F., & KRITT, D. (1986). The development of the conceptual organization of self. *Journal of Genetic Psychology, 146,* 333–341.

PAIGEN, B. (1982). Controversy at Love Canal. *Hastings Center Report, 12,* 29–37.

PALKOVITZ, R. (1984). Parental attitudes and fathers' interactions with their 5-month-old infants. *Developmental Psychology, 20,* 1054–1060.

PALLAK, S. R., COSTOMIRIS, S., SROKA, S., & PITTMAN, T. S. (1982). School experience, reward characteristics, and intrinsic motivation. *Child Development, 53,* 1382–1391.

PAPOUSEK, H. (1967). Experimental studies of appetitional behavior in newborns and infants. In H. W. Stevenson, E. H. Hess, & H. L. Rheingold (Eds.), *Early behavior* (pp. 249–277). New York: Wiley.

PAPOUSEK, H., & BERNSTEIN, P. (1969). The functions of conditioning stimulation in human neonates and infants. In A. Ambrose (Ed.), *Stimulation in early infancy* (pp. 225–252). New York: Academic Press.

PAREKH, U. C., PHERWANI, A., UDANI, P. M., & MUKHERJEE, S. (1970). Brain weight and head circumference in fetus, infant and children of different nutritional and socio-economic groups. *Indian Pediatrics, 7,* 347–358.

PARIKH, B. (1980). Development of moral judgment and its relation to family environmental factors in Indian and American families. *Child Development, 51,* 1030–1039.

PARIS, S. G. (1973). Comprehension of language connectives and propositional logical relationships. *Journal of Experimental Child Psychology, 16,* 278–291.

PARIS, S. G. (1975). Integration and inference in children's comprehension and memory. In F. Restle, R. Shiffrin, J. Castellan, H. Lindman, & D. Pisoni (Eds.), *Cognitive theory* (Vol. 1, pp. 223–246). Hillsdale, NJ: Erlbaum.

PARIS, S. G., & JACOBS, J. E. (1984). The benefits of informed instruction for children's reading awareness and comprehension skills. *Child Development, 55,* 2083–2093.

PARIS, S. G., & LINDAUER, B. K. (1977). Constructive processes in children's comprehension and memory. In R. V. Kail, Jr., & J. W. Hagen (Eds.), *Perspectives on the development of memory and cognition.* (pp. 35–60). Hillsdale, NJ: Erlbaum.

PARIS, S. G., & LINDAUER, B. K. (1982). The development of cognitive skills during childhood. In B. Wolman (Ed.), *Handbook of develop-*

mental psychology (pp. 333–349). Englewood Cliffs, NJ: Prentice-Hall.

PARKE, R. D. (1969). Effectiveness of punishment as an interaction of intensity, timing, agent nurturance and cognitive structuring. *Child Development, 40,* 213–236.

PARKE, R. D. (1977). Punishment in children: Effects, side effects and alternative strategies. In H. L. Hom, Jr. & A. Robinson (Eds.), *Psychological processes in early education* (pp. 71–97). New York: Academic Press.

PARKE, R. D., BERKOWITZ, L., LEYENS, J. P., WEST, S. G., & SEBASTIAN, R. J. (1977). Some effects of violent and nonviolent movies on the behavior of juvenile delinquents. In L. Berkowitz (Ed.), *Advances in experimental social psychology* (Vol. 10, pp. 135–172). New York: Academic Press.

PARKE, R. D., & COLLMER, C. W. (1975). *Child abuse: An interdisciplinary analysis.* (pp. 264–283). Chicago: University of Chicago Press.

PARKE, R. D., & DEUR, J. L. (1972). Schedule of punishment and inhibition of aggression in children. *Developmental Psychology, 7,* 266–269.

PARKE, R. D., MACDONALD, K. B., BEITEL, A., & BHAVNAGRI, N. (in press). The role of the family in the development of peer relations. In R. DeV. Peters & R. J. McMahan (Eds.), *Marriages and families: Behavioral treatment and processes.* New York: Brunner/Mazel.

PARKE, R. D., & SAWIN, D. B. (1976). The father's role in infancy. *Family Coordinator, 25,* 265–371.

PARKE, R. D., & SAWIN, D. B. (1980). The family in early infancy: Social interactional and attitudinal analyses. In F. A. Pedersen (Ed.), *The father-infant relationship: Observational studies in the family setting* (pp. 44–70). New York: Praeger.

PARKE, R. D., & SLABY, R. G. (1983). The development of aggression. In E. M. Hetherington (Ed.), *Handbook of child psychology: Vol. 4. Socialization, personality, and social development.* (4th ed., pp. 547–641). New York: Wiley.

PARKE, R. D., & SUOMI, S. J. (1980). Adult male-infant relationships: Human and nonprimate evidence. In K. Immelmann, G. Barlow, M. Main, & L. Petrinovitch (Eds.), *Behavioral development: The Bielefeld interdisciplinary project* (pp. 700–725). New York: Cambridge University Press.

PARKE, R. D., & TINSLEY, B. R. (1981). The father's role in infancy: Determinants of involvement in caregiving and play. In M. E. Lamb (Ed.), *The role of the father in child development* (pp. 429–458). New York: Wiley.

PARKE, R. D., & WALTERS, R. H. (1967). Some factors determining the efficacy of punishment for inducing response inhibition. *Monographs of the Society for Research in Child Development, 32* (1, Serial No. 109).

PARKER, J. G., & ASHER, S. R. (1987). Peer relations and later personal adjustment: Are low-accepted children at risk? *Psychological Bulletin, 102,* 357–389.

PARSONS, J. E. (1982). Biology, experience, and sex-dimorphic behaviors. In W. R. Gove & G. R. Carpenter (Eds.), *The fundamental connection between nature and nurture* (pp. 137–170). Lexington, MA: Lexington Books.

PARSONS, J. E. (1983). Expectancies, values and academic behaviors. In J. T. Spence (Ed.), *Achievement and achievement motives: Psychological and sociological approaches* (pp. 75–146). San Francisco: W. H. Freeman.

PARSONS, J. E., ADLER, T. F., & KACZALA, C. M. (1982). Socialization of achievement attitudes and beliefs: Parental influences. *Child Development, 53,* 310–321.

PARTEN, M. (1932). Social participation among preschool children. *Journal of Abnormal and Social Psychology, 27,* 243–269.

PASAMANICK, B., & KNOBLOCH, H. (1966). Retrospective studies on the epidemiology of reproductive casualty: Old and new. *Merrill-Palmer Quarterly, 12,* 7–26.

PASCOE, J. M., LODA, F. A., JEFFRIES, V., & EASP, J. A. (1981). The association between mothers' social support and provision of stimulation to their children. *Developmental and Behavioral Pediatrics, 2,* 15–19.

PASSMAN, R. H. (1976). Arousal reducing properties of attachment objects: Testing the functional limits of the security blanket relative to the mother. *Developmental Psychology, 12,* 468–469.

PASSMAN, R. H., & HALONEN, J. S. (1979). A developmental survey of young children's attachment to inanimate objects. *Journal of Genetic Psychology, 134,* 165–178.

PASSMAN, R. H., & WEISBERG, P. (1975). Mothers and blankets as agents for promoting play and exploration by young children in a novel environment: The effects of social and nonsocial attachment objects. *Developmental Psychology, 11,* 170–177.

PATTERSON, F. (1980). Innovative uses of language by a gorilla: A case study. In K. E. Nelson (Ed.), *Children's language* (Vol. 2, pp. 497–561). New York: Gardner Press.

PATTERSON, G. R. (1976). The aggressive child: Victim and architect of a coercive system. In L. Hammerlyck, E. Marsh, & L. Handy (Eds.), *Behavior modification and families* (pp. 267–316). New York: Brunner/Mazel.

PATTERSON, G. R. (1981). Mothers: The unacknowledged victims. *Monographs of the Society for Research in Child Development, 45* (5, Serial No. 186).

PATTERSON, G. R. (1982). *Coercive family processes.* Eugene, OR: Castilia Press.

PATTERSON, G. R. (1985). *A social learning approach to family intervention. Vol. 1, Families with aggressive children.* Eugene, OR: Castilia Press.

PATTERSON, G. R., LITTMAN, R. A., & BRICKER, W. (1967). Assertive behavior in children: A step toward a theory of aggression. *Monographs of the Society for Research in Child Development, 32* (5, Serial No. 113).

PAULSEN, K., & JOHNSON, M. (1983). Sex-role attitudes and mathematical ability in 4th, 8th, and 11th grade students from a high socioeconomic area. *Developmental Psychology, 19,* 210–214.

PEA, R. D., & KURLAND, D. M. (1984). On the cognitive effects of learning computer programming. *New Ideas in Psychology, 2,* 137–168.

PEAL, E., & LAMBERT, W. (1962). The relation of bilingualism to intelligence. *Psychological Monographs, 76* (27, Whole No. 546).

PEARLIN, L. I., YARROW, M. R., & SCARR, H. A. (1967). Unintended consequences of parental aspirations: The case of children's cheating. *American Journal of Sociology, 73,* 73–83.

PEARSON, H. A., & DIAMOND, L. K. (1971). The critically ill child: Sickle cell disease crises and their management. *Pediatrics, 48,* 629–635.

PECHMANN, T., & DEUTSCH, W. (1982). The development of verbal and nonverbal devices for reference. *Journal of Experimental Child Psychology, 34,* 330–341.

PEDERSEN, F. A. (1976). *Mother, father and infant as an interaction system.* Paper presented at the meeting of the American Psychological Association, Washington, D.C.

PEDERSEN, F. A., CAIN, R., ZAZLOW, M., & ANDERSON, B. (1980). Variation in infant experience associated with alternative family role organization. Paper presented at the International Conference on Infant Studies, New Haven, CT.

PEEPLES, D. R., & TELLER, D. Y. (1975). Color vision and brightness discrimination in two-month-old human infants. *Science, 189,* 1102–1103.

PEEVERS, B. H., & SECORD, P. F. (1973). Developmental changes in attribution of descriptive concepts and to persons. *Journal of Personality and Social Psychology, 27,* 120–128.

PENNER, S. G. (1987). Parental responses to grammatical and ungrammatical utterances. *Child Development, 58,* 376–384.

PENNINGTON, B. F., BENDER, B., PUCK, M., SALBENBLATT, J., & ROBINSON, A. (1982). Learning disabilities in children with sex chromosome anomalies. *Child Development, 53,* 1182–1192.

PEPLER, D. J., & ROSS, H. S. (1981). The effects of play on convergent and divergent problem solving. *Child Development, 52,* 1202–1210.

PERLMUTTER, M. (1984). Continuities and discontinuities in early human memory paradigms, processes, and performances. In R. V. Kail, Jr., & N. R. Spear (Eds.), *Comparative perspectives on the development of memory* (pp. 253–287). Hillsdale, NJ: Erlbaum.

PERLMUTTER, M., & LANGE, G. (1978). A developmental analysis of recall-recognition distinctions. In P. A. Ornstein (Ed.), *Memory development in children* (pp. 243–258). Hillsdale, NJ: Erlbaum.

PERRY, D. G., & BUSSEY, K. (1977). Self-reinforcement in high- and low-aggressive boys following acts of aggression. *Child Development, 48*, 653–657.

PERSELL, C. (1977). *Education and inequality: The roots and results of stratification in American schools*. New York: Free Press.

PESKIN, H. (1973). Influence of the developmental schedule of puberty on learning and ego functioning. *Journal of Youth and Adolescence, 2*, 273–290.

PETERS, D. P. (1987). The impact of naturally occurring stress on children's memory. In S. J. Ceci, M. P. Toglia, & D. F. Ross (Eds.), *Children's eyewitness memory* (pp. 122–141). New York: Springer-Verlag.

PETERSEN, A. C. (1979). Hormones and cognitive functioning in normal development. In M. A. Wittig & A. C. Petersen (Eds.), *Sex differences in cognitive functioning* (pp. 189–214). New York: Academic Press.

PETERSEN, A. C. (1983). Menarche: Meaning of measures and measuring meaning. In S. Golub (Ed.), *Menarche* (pp. 63–76). Lexington, MA: Lexington Books.

PETERSON, C., & PETERSON, R. (1986). Parent-child interaction and daycare: Does quality of daycare matter? *Journal of Applied Developmental Psychology, 7*, 1–15.

PETERSON, C. C., PETERSON, J. L., & CARROLL, J. (1986). Television viewing and imaginative problem solving during preadolescence. *Journal of Genetic Psychology, 147*, 61–67.

PETERSON, J. L., & ZILL, N. (1986). Marital disruption, parent-child relationships, and behavior problems in children. *Journal of Marriage and the Family, 48*, 295–307.

PETERSON, L. (1982). An alternative perspective to norm-based explanations of modeling and children's generosity: A reply to Lipscomb, Larrieu, McAllister, and Bregman. *Merrill-Palmer Quarterly, 28*, 283–290.

PETERSON, L., HARTMANN, D. P., & GELFAND, D. M. (1977). Developmental changes in the effects of dependency and reciprocity cues on children's moral judgments and donation rates. *Child Development, 48*, 1331–1339.

PETERSON, P. E., JEFFREY, D. G., BRIDGWATER, C. A., & DAWSON, B. (1984). How pronutrition television programming affects children's dietary habits. *Developmental Psychology, 20*, 55–63.

PETERSON, P. L. (1977). Interactive effects of student anxiety, achievement orientation, and teacher behavior on student achievement and attitude. *Journal of Educational Psychology, 69*, 779–792.

PETERSON, P. L. (1979). Direct instruction reconsidered. In P. L. Peterson & H. J. Walberg (Eds.), *Research on teaching: Concepts, findings, and implications* (pp. 57–69). Berkeley, CA: McCutchan.

PEZZULLO, T. R., THORSEN, E. E., & MADAUS, G. F. (1972). The heritability of Jensen's level I and II and divergent thinking. *American Educational Research Journal, 9*, 539–546.

PFEFFER, C. R. (1986). *The suicidal child*. New York: Guilford.

PFOUTS, J. H. (1976). The sibling relationship: A forgotten dimension. *Social Work, 21*, 200–204.

PHILLIPS, D. A. (1981). High-achieving students with low academic self-concepts: Achievement motives and orientations. *Dissertation Abstracts International, 42*, 2569B. (University Microfilms No. 81-25, 665)

PHILLIPS, D., & MCCARTNEY, K., & SCARR, S. (1987). Child-care quality and children's social development. *Developmental Psychology, 23*, 537–543.

PHILLIPS, J. C., & KELLY, D. H. (1979). School failure and delinquency: What causes which? *Criminology, 17*, 194–207.

PHILLIPS, J. L. (1975). *The origins of intellect: Piaget's theory*. San Francisco: Freeman.

PIAGET, J. (1926). *The language and thought of the child*. New York: Harcourt, Brace & World. (Original work published 1923)

PIAGET, J. (1928). *Judgment and reasoning of the child*. New York: Harcourt, Brace & World. (Original work published 1926)

PIAGET, J. (1929). *The child's conception of physical causality*. New York: Harcourt, Brace & World. (Original work published 1927)

PIAGET, J. (1930). *The child's conception of the world*. New York: Harcourt, Brace & World. (Original work published 1926)

PIAGET, J. (1950). *The psychology of intelligence*. New York: International Universities Press.

PIAGET, J. (1951a). *Play, dreams and imitation in childhood*. New York: Norton. (Original work published 1945)

PIAGET, J. (1951b). The right to education in the modern world. In UNESCO, *Freedom and culture* (pp. 67–116). New York: Columbia University Press.

PIAGET, J. (1952). *The origins of intelligence in children*. New York: International Universities Press. (Original work published 1936)

PIAGET, J. (1952a). Jean Piaget (autobiographical sketch). In E. G. Boring, H. S. Langfeld, H. Werner & R. M. Yerkes (Eds.), *A history of psychology in autobiography* (pp. 237–256). Worcester, MA: Clark University Press.

PIAGET, J. (1952b). *The origins of intelligence in children*. New York: International Universities Press. (Original work published 1936)

PIAGET, J. (1954). *The construction of reality in the child*. New York: Basic Books. (Original work published 1937)

PIAGET, J. (1965). *The moral judgment of the child*. New York: Free Press. (Originally published 1932).

PIAGET, J. (1966). Necessite et signification des recherches comparatives en psychologie genetique. *Journal International de Psychologie, 1*, 1–13.

PIAGET, J. (1968). *On the development and memory and identity*. Barre, MA: Clark University Press and Barre Publishers.

PIAGET, J. (1969). *The child's conception of time*. London: Routledge & Kegan Paul. (Original work published 1946)

PIAGET, J. (1970a). *Science of education and the psychology of the child* (from essays completed in 1935 and 1969).

PIAGET, J. (1970b). *The child's conception of movement and speed*. London: Routledge & Kegan Paul. (Original work published 1946)

PIAGET, J. (1971). *Biology and knowledge*. Chicago: University of Chicago Press.

PIAGET, J. (1978). *Success and understanding*. Cambridge, MA: Harvard University Press.

PIAGET, J., & INHELDER, B. (1956). *The child's conception of space*. London: Routledge & Kegan Paul. (Original work published 1948)

PIAGET, J., & INHELDER, B. (1969). *The psychology of the child*. London: Routledge & Kegan Paul. (Original work published 1967)

PIAGET, J., & INHELDER, B. (1973). *Memory and intelligence*. New York: Basic Books.

PIAGET, J., INHELDER, B., & SZEMINSKA, A. (1960). *The child's conception of geometry*. New York: Basic Books. (Original work published 1948)

PICK, A. D., & FRANKEL, G. W. (1974). A developmental study of strategies of visual selectivity. *Child Development, 45*, 1162–1165.

PICK, A. D., CHRISTY, M. D., & FRANKEL, G. W. (1972). A developmental study of visual selective attention. *Journal of Experimental Child Psychology, 14*, 165–175.

PICONE, T. A., ALLEN, L. H., OLSEN, P. N., SCHRAMM, M., & FERRIS, M. (1980). *The effects of maternal weight gain and smoking during pregnancy on human neonatal behavior*. Paper presented at the International Conference on Infant Studies, New Haven, CT.

PICONE, T. A., ALLEN, L. H., SCHRAMM, M. M., & OLSEN, P. N. (1982). Pregnancy outcome in North American women. 1. Effects of diet, cigarette smoking, and psychological stress on maternal weight gain. *American Journal of Clinical Nutrition, 36*, 1205–1213.

PINES, M. (1979, September). A head start in the nursery (Interview with J. McV. Hunt). *Psychology Today, 13*(9), 56–68.

PINES, M. (1984, May). In the shadow of Huntington's. *Science 84, 5*(4), 32–39.

PIPP, S., & HAITH, M. M. (1984). Infant visual responses to pattern: Which metric predicts best? *Journal of Experimental Child Psychology, 38*, 373–379.

PLOMIN, R. (1986). *Development, genetics and psychology*. Hillsdale, NJ: Erlbaum.

PLOMIN, R., & DEFRIES, J. C. (1983). The Colorado Adoption Project. *Child Development, 54*, 276–289.

PLOMIN, R., DEFRIES, J. C., & MCCLEARN, G. E. (1980). *Behavioral genetics: A primer*. San Francisco: Freeman.

PLOMIN, R., DEFRIES, J. C., & LOEHLIN, J. C. (1977). Genotype-environment interaction and correlation in the analysis of human behavior. *Psychological Bulletin, 84*, 309–322.

PLOMIN, R., & ROWE, D. C. (1979). Genetic and environmental etiology of social behavior in infancy. *Developmental Psychology, 15*, 62–72.

POLANSKY, N. A., GAUDIN, J. M., AMMONS, P. W., & DAVIS, K. B. (1985). The psychological ecology of the neglectful mother. *Child Abuse & Neglect, 9*, 265–275.

POSNER, M. I., & WARREN, R. E. (1972). Traces, concepts and conscious constructions. In A. W. Melton & E. Martin (Eds.), *Coding processes in human memory* (pp. 25–43). New York: Winston.

PRECHTL, H. F. R. (1958). The directed head turning response and allied movements of the newborn baby. *Behaviour, 13*, 212–242.

PRECHTL, H. F. R. (1965). Problems of behavioral studies in the newborn infant. In D. S. Lehrman, R. A. Hinde, & E. Shaw (Eds.), *Advances in the study of behavior* (Vol. 1, pp. 75–96). New York: Academic Press.

PRECHTL, H., & BEINTEMA, D. (1965). *The neurological examination of the full-term newborn infant*. London: William Heinemann Medical Books.

PRECHTL, H. F. R., THEORELL, K., & BLAIR, A. (1973). Behavioral state cycles in abnormal infants. *Developmental Medicine and Child Neurology, 15*, 606–615.

PREMACK, A. J. (1976). *Why chimps can read*. New York: Harper & Row.

PRESSLEY, G. M. (1979). Increasing children's self-control through cognitive interventions. *Review of Educational Research, 49*, 319–370.

PRESSLEY, M. (1982). Elaboration and memory development. *Child Development, 53*, 296–309.

PRESSLEY, M., & LEVIN, J. R. (1977a). Developmental differences in subjects' associative-learning strategies and performance: Assessing a hypothesis. *Journal of Experimental Child Psychology, 24*, 431–439.

PRESSLEY, M., & LEVIN, J. R. (1977b). Task parameters affecting the efficacy of a visual imagery learning strategy in younger and older children. *Journal of Experimental Child Psychology, 24*, 53–59.

PRESTON, R. C. (1962). Reading achievement of German and American children. *School and Society, 90*, 350–354.

PRINGLE, M. L., & BOSSIO, V. (1958). A study of deprived children. *Vita Humana, 1*, 65–91, 142–169.

PROVINE, R. R., & WESTERMAN, J. A. (1979). Crossing the midline: Limits of early eye-hand behavior. *Child Development, 50*, 437–441.

PULASKI, M. A. (1970). Play as a function of toy structure and fantasy predisposition. *Child Development, 41*, 531–537.

PULKKINEN, L. (1982). Self-control and continuity from childhood to late adolescence. In P. B. Baltes & O. G. Brim, Jr. (Eds.), *Life-span development and behavior* (Vol. 4, pp. 63–105). New York: Academic Press.

PUTALLAZ, M. (1983). Predicting children's sociometric status from their behavior. *Child Development, 54*, 1417–1426.

PUTALLAZ, M., & GOTTMAN, J. M. (1981). Social skills and group acceptance. In S. R. Asher & J. M. Gottman (Eds.), *The development of children's friendships* (pp. 116–149). New York: Cambridge University Press.

QUADAGNO, D. M., BRISCOE, R., & QUADAGNO, J. S. (1977). Effect of perinatal gonadal hormones on selected nonsexual behavior patterns: A critical assessment of the nonhuman and human literature. *Psychological Bulletin, 84*, 62–80.

QUARFOTH, J. M. (1979). Children's understanding of the nature of television characters. *Journal of Communication, 29*(2), 210–218.

QUAY, L. C. (1972). Negro dialect and Binet performance in severely disadvantaged black four-year-olds. *Child Development, 43*, 245–250.

QUAY, L. C. (1974). Language dialect, age, and intelligence-test performance in disadvantaged black children. *Child Development, 45*, 463–468.

QUAY, L. C., & JARRETT, O. S. (1986). Teachers' interactions with middle- and lower-SES preschool boys and girls. *Journal of Educational Psychology, 78*, 495–498.

RADER, N., BAUSANO, M., & RICHARDS, J. E. (1980). On the nature of the visual cliff avoidance response in human infants. *Child Development, 51*, 61–68.

RADKE-YARROW, M., CUMMINGS, E. M., KUCZYNSKI, L., & CHAPMAN, M. (1985). Patterns of attachment in two- and three-year-olds in normal families with parental depression. *Child Development, 56*, 884–893.

RADKE-YARROW, M., & ZAHN-WAXLER, C. (1984). Roots, motives and patterns in children's prosocial behavior. In J. Reykowski, J. Karylowski, D. Bar-Tel, & E. Staub (Eds.), *The development and maintenance of prosocial behaviors: International perspectives on positive mortality* (pp. 81–99). New York: Plenum Press.

RADKE-YARROW, M., ZAHN-WAXLER, C., & CHAPMAN, M. (1983). Children's prosocial dispositions and behavior. In P. H. Mussen (Ed.), *Handbook of child psychology: Vol. 4. Socialization, personality, and social development* (4th ed., pp. 469–545). New York: Wiley.

RAGOZIN, A. S., BASHAM, R. B., CRNIC, K. A., GREENBERG, M. T., & ROBINSON, N. M. (1982). Effects of maternal age on parenting role. *Developmental Psychology, 18*, 627–634.

RAMEY, C. T. (1982). Commentary on lasting effects of early education: A report from the Consortium for Longitudinal Studies. *Monographs of the Society for Research in Child Development, 47* (2–3, Serial No. 195).

RAMEY, C. T., & WATSON, J. S. (1972). Nonsocial reinforcement of infants' vocalizations. *Developmental Psychology, 6*, 538.

RAPOPORT, J. L., BUCHSBAUM, M. S., WEINGARTNER, H., ZAHN, T. P., LUDLOW, C., & MIKKELSEN, E. J. (1980). Dextroamphetamine — its cognitive and behavioral effect in normal and hyperactive boys and normal men. *Archives of General Psychiatry, 37*, 933–943.

RATNER, N., & BRUNER, J. S. (1978). Social exchange and the acquisition of language. *Journal of Child Language, 5*, 391–402.

RAYMOND, C. L., & BENBOW, C. P. (1986). Gender differences in mathematics: A function of parental support and student sex typing? *Developmental Psychology, 22*, 808–819.

READ, B. K., & CHERRY, L. J. (1978). Preschool children's production of directive forms. *Discourse Processes, 1*, 233–245.

REAVES, J. Y., & ROBERTS, A. (1983). The effect of type of information on children's attraction to peers. *Child Development, 54*, 1024–1031.

REDD, W. H., MORRIS, E. K., & MARTIN, J. A. (1975). Effects of positive and negative adult-child interaction on children's social preferences. *Journal of Experimental Child Psychology, 19*, 153–164.

REDL, F. (1966). *When we deal with children*. New York: Free Press.

REED, E. (1975). Genetic anomalies in development. In F. D. Horowitz (Ed.), *Review of Child Development Research* (Vol. 4, pp. 59–99). Chicago: University of Chicago Press.

REED, G. L., & LEIDERMAN, P. H. (1983). Is imprinting an appropriate model for human infant attachment? *International Journal of Behavioral Development, 6*, 51–69.

REES, A. N., & PALMER, F. H. (1970). Factors related to change in mental performance. *Developmental Psychology Monograph, 3* (2, Pt. 2).

REEVE, R. A., & BROWN, A. L. (1985). Metacognition reconsidered: Implications for intervention research. *Journal of Abnormal Child Psychology, 13*, 343–356.

REICH, P. A. (1986). *Language Development*. Englewood Cliffs, NJ: Prentice-Hall.

REID, J. (1982). Black America in the 1980's. *Population Bulletin, 37*(4), 1–37.

REID, J. B., TAPLIN, P. S., & LORBER, R. (1981). A social interactional approach to the treatment of abusive families. In R. B. Stuart (Ed.), *Violent behavior: Social learning approaches to prediction, management, and treatment* (pp. 83–101). New York: Brunner/Mazel.

REINISCH, J. M. (1981). Prenatal exposure to synthetic progestins increases potential for aggression in humans. *Science, 211,* 1171–1173.

REINISCH, J. M., & KAROW, W. G. (1977). Prenatal exposure to synthetic progestins and estrogens: Effects on human development. *Archives of Sexual Behavior, 6,* 257–288.

REISER, J., YONAS, A., & WIKNER, K. (1976). Radial localization of odors by human neonates. *Child Development, 47,* 856–859.

RENSHAW, P. D., & ASHER, S. R. (1983). Children's goals and strategies for social interaction. *Merrill-Palmer Quarterly, 29,* 353–374.

RESCHLY, D. J. (1978). WISC-R factor structures among Anglos, Blacks, Chicanos, and Native American Papagos. *Journal of Consulting and Clinical Psychology, 46,* 417–422.

RESCHLY, D. J. (1979). Nonbiased assessment. In G. Phye & D. Reschly (Eds.), *School psychology: Perspectives and issues* (pp. 215–253). New York: Academic Press.

RESCHLY, D. J. (1981). Psychological testing in educational classification and placement. *American Psychologist, 36,* 1094–1102.

RESCORLA, L. A. (1980). Category development in early language. *Journal of Child Language, 8,* 225–238.

REST, J. R. (1973). Patterns of preference and comprehension in moral judgment. *Journal of Personality, 41,* 86–109.

REST, J. R. (1979a). *Development in judging moral issues.* Minneapolis: University of Minnesota Press.

REST, J. R. (1979b). *Revised manual for the Defining Issues Test.* Minneapolis: Minnesota Moral Research Projects.

REST, J. R. (1983). Morality. In J. H. Flavell & E. M. Markman (Eds.), *Handbook of child psychology: Vol. 3. Cognitive development* (4th ed., pp. 556–629). New York: Wiley.

REST, J. R. (1986). *Moral development: Advances in research and theory.* New York: Praeger.

REST, J. R., DAVISON, M. L., & ROBBINS, S. (1978). Age trends in judging moral issues: A review of cross-sectional, longitudinal, and sequential studies of the Defining Issues Test. *Child Development, 49,* 263–279.

REST, J. R., & THOMA, S. J. (1985). Relation of moral judgment to formal education. *Developmental Psychology, 21,* 709–714.

REVELLE, G. L., KARABENICK, J. D., & WELLMAN, H. M. (1981). *Comprehension monitoring in preschool children.* Paper presented at the meeting of the Society for Research in Child Development, Boston.

REVILL, S. I., & DODGE, J. A. (1978). Psychological determinants of infantile pyloric stenosis. *Archives of Disease in Childhood, 53,* 66–68.

REYNOLDS, C. R., & JENSEN, A. R. (1983). WISC-R subscale patterns of abilities of blacks and whites matched on Full Scale IQ. *Journal of Educational Psychology, 75,* 207–214.

REYNOLDS, C. R., & NIGL, A. J. (1981). A regression analysis of differential validity of intelligence tests for black and for white inner city children. *Journal of Clinical Child Psychology, 10,* 176–179.

REYNOLDS, D., JONES, D., ST. LEGER, S., & MURGATROYD, S. (1980). School factors and truancy. In L. Hersov & I. Berg (Eds.), *Out of school: Modern perspectives in truancy and school refusal* (pp. 85–110). Chichester, Eng.: Wiley.

RHEINGOLD, H., & ECKERMAN, C. O. (1973). Fear of the stranger: A critical examination. In H. W. Reese (Ed.), *Advances in child development and behavior* (Vol. 8, pp. 185–222). New York: Academic Press.

RHEINGOLD, H. L., GEWIRTZ, J. L., & ROSS, H. W. (1959). Social conditioning of vocalizations in the infant. *Journal of Comparative and Physiological Psychology, 52,* 68–72.

RHODES, W. A. (1977). Generalization of attribution retraining. *Dissertation Abstracts International, 38,* 2882B. (University Microfilms No. 77-26, 737)

RHOLES, W. S., BLACKWELL, J., JORDAN, C., & WALTERS, C. (1980). A developmental study of learned helplessness. *Developmental Psychology, 16,* 616–624.

RICE, M. L., HUSTON, A. C., & WRIGHT, J. C. (1982). The forms of television: Effects on children's attention, comprehension, and social behavior. In D. Pearl, L. Bouthilet, & J. Lazar (Eds.), *Television and behavior: Ten years of scientific progress and implications for the eighties* (Vol. 2, pp. 24–38). Washington, DC: U.S. Government Printing Office.

RICE, M. L., HUSTON, A. C., & WRIGHT, J. C. (1986). Replays as repetitions: Young children's interpretation of television forms. *Journal of Applied Developmental Psychology, 7,* 61–76.

RICHARDS, J. E., & RADER, N. (1981). Crawling-onset age predicts visual cliff avoidance in infants. *Journal of Experimental Psychology, 7,* 382–387.

RICHARDSON, S. A., & BIRCH, H. G. (1973). School performance of children who were severely malnourished in infancy. *American Journal of Mental Deficiency, 77,* 623–632.

RICHARDSON, S. A., HASTORF, A. H., GOODMAN, N., & DORNBUSCH, S. M. (1961). Cultural uniformity in reaction to physical disabilities. *American Sociological Review, 26,* 241–247.

RICHARDSON, S. A., KOLLER, H., & KATZ, M. (1986). Factors leading to differences in the school performance of boys and girls. *Developmental and Behavioral Pediatrics, 7,* 49–55.

RICHMAN, N., STEVENSON, J., & GRAHAM, P. J. (1982). *Preschool to school: A behavioral study.* London: Academic Press.

RICKS, M. (1985). The social inheritance of parenting. In I. Bretherton & E. Waters (Eds.), Growing points of attachment theory and research. *Monographs of the Society for Research in Child Development, 50* (1–2, Serial No. 209).

RIDLEY, C. A., & VAUGHN, R. (1982). Interpersonal problem solving: An intervention program for preschool children. *Journal of Applied Developmental Psychology, 3,* 177–190.

RIESE, M. L. (1987). Temperament stability between the neonatal period and 24 months. *Developmental Psychology, 23,* 216–222.

RIESEN, A. H. (1966). Sensory deprivation. In E. Stellar & J. Stellar (Eds.), *Progress in physiological psychology* (pp. 117–147). New York: Academic Press.

RIM, I. J., & RIM, A. A. (1976). Association between juvenile onset obesity and severe adult obesity in 73,532 women. *American Journal of Public Health, 6,* 479.

RISMAN, B. L. (1986). Can men "mother?" Life as a single father. *Family Relations, 35,* 95–102.

ROBBINS, L. C. (1963). The accuracy of parental recall of aspects of child development and of child rearing practices. *Journal of Abnormal and Social Psychology, 66,* 261–270.

ROBBINS, W. J., BRODY, S., HOGAN, A. G., JACKSON, C. M., & GREENE, C. W. (1928). *Growth.* New Haven, CT: Yale University Press.

ROBERTS, C. (1970). The portrayal of blacks on network television. *Journal of Broadcasting, 15,* 45–53.

ROBERTS, T. (1984). Piagetian theory and the teaching of reading. *Educational Research, 26,* 77–81.

ROBINSON, B. E., & CANADAY, H. (1978). Sex-role behaviors and personality traits of male day care teachers. *Sex Roles, 4,* 853–865.

ROBINSON, B. E., ROWLAND, B. H., & COLEMAN, M. (1986). *Latchkey kids: Unlocking doors for children and their families.* Lexington, MA: Health.

ROBINSON, E. J. (1981). The child's understanding of inadequate messages and communication failure: A problem of ignorance or egocentrism? In W. P. Dickson (Ed.), *Children's oral communication skills* (pp. 167–188). New York: Academic Press.

ROCHE, A. F. (1979). Secular trends in stature, weight, and maturation. In A. F. Roche (Ed.), Secular trends in human growth, maturation, and development. *Monographs of the Society for Research in Child Development, 44* (3–4, Serial No. 179).

RODE, S. CHANGE, P., FISCH, R., & SROUFE, L. A. (1981). Attachment patterns of infants separated at birth. *Developmental Psychology, 17,* 188–191.

RODGERS, J. L. (1984). Confluence effects: Not here, not now! *Developmental Psychology, 20,* 321–331.

ROFF, M., SELLS, S. B., & GOLDEN, M. M. (1972). *Social adjustment and personality development in children.* Minneapolis: University of Minnesota Press.

ROFFWARG, H. P., MUZIO, J. N., & DEMENT, W. C. (1966). Ontogenetic development of the human sleep-dream cycle. *Science, 152,* 604–619.

ROHNER, R. P. & ROHNER, E. C. (1981). Parental acceptance-rejection and parental control: Cross-cultural codes. *Ethnology, 20,* 245–260.

ROHWER, W. D., & BEAN, J. P. (1973). Sentence effects and noun-pair learning: A developmental interaction during adolescence. *Journal of Experimental Child Psychology, 15,* 521–533.

ROHWER, W. D., & LITROWNIK, J. (1983). Age and individual differences in the learning of a memorization procedure. *Journal of Educational Psychology, 75,* 799–810.

ROMEO, F. F. (1986). *Understanding anorexia nervosa.* Springfield, IL: Thomas.

ROOPNARINE, J. L., & JOHNSON, J. E. (1984). Socialization in a mixed-age experimental program. *Developmental Psychology, 20,* 828–832.

ROOSA, M. W. (1984). Maternal age, social class, and the obstetric performance of teenagers. *Journal of Youth and Adolescence, 13,* 365–374.

ROSE, R. M., HOLADAY, J. W., & BERNSTEIN, I. S. (1976). Plasma testosterone, dominance rank and aggressive behavior in male rhesus monkeys. *Nature, 231,* 366–368.

ROSE, S. A. (1980). Enhancing visual recognition memory in preterm infants. *Developmental Psychology, 16,* 85–92.

ROSEKRANS, M. A. (1967). Imitation in children as a function of perceived similarity to a social model and vicarious reinforcement. *Journal of Personality and Social Psychology, 21,* 709–714.

ROSEN, A. C., & REKERS, G. A. (1980). Toward a taxonomic framework for variables of sex and gender. *Genetic Psychology Monographs, 102,* 191–218.

ROSEN, B. C., & D'ANDRADE, R. (1959). The psychosocial origins of achievement motivation. *Sociometry, 22,* 185–218.

ROSENBERG, L., MITCHELL, A. A., SHAPIRO, S., & SLOANE, D. (1982). Selected birth defects in relation to caffeine-containing beverages. *Journal of the American Medical Association, 247,* 1429–1432.

ROSENBERG, M. (1979). *Conceiving the self.* New York: Basic Books.

ROSENBERG, M. S., & REPPUCCI, N. D. (1985). Primary prevention of child abuse. *Journal of Consulting and Clinical Psychology, 53,* 576–585.

ROSENBERG, R. N., PETTEGREW, J. W. (1983). Genetic neurologic diseases. In R. N. Rosenberg (Ed.), *The clinical neurosciences* (pp. 33–165). New York: Churchill Livingstone.

ROSENBLITH, J. F., & SIMS-KNIGHT, J. E. (1985). *In the beginning: Development during the first two years of life.* Monterey, CA: Brooks Cole.

ROSENBLUM, L. A., COE, L. L., & BROMLEY. L. J. (1975). Peer relations in monkeys: The influence of social structure, gender and familiarity. In M. Lewis & L. A. Rosenblum (Eds.), *Friendship and peer relations* (pp. 67–98). New York: Wiley.

ROSENFIELD, P., LAMBERT, N. M., & BLACK, A. (1985). Desk arrangement effects on pupil classroom behavior. *Journal of Educational Psychology, 77,* 101–108.

ROSENHAN, D. L. (1970). The natural socialization of altruistic autonomy. In J. Macaulay & L. Berkowitz (Eds.), *Altruism and helping behavior* (pp. 251–268). New York: Academic Press.

ROSENHOLTZ, S. J., & WILSON, B. (1980). The effect of classroom structure on shared perceptions of ability. *American Educational Research Journal, 17,* 75–82.

ROSENKOETTER, L. I. (1973). Resistance to temptation: Inhibitory and disinhibitory effects of models. *Developmental Psychology, 8,* 80–84.

ROSENKRANTZ, P., VOGEL, S., BEE, H., BROVERMAN, I., & BROVERMAN, D. (1968). Sex-role stereotypes and self-concepts in college students. *Journal of Consulting and Clinical Psychology, 32,* 287–295.

ROSENTHAL, R., & FODE, K. L. (1963). The effect of experimenter bias on the performance of the albino rat. *Behavioral Science, 8,* 183–189.

ROSENTHAL, R., & JACOBSON, L. (1968). *Pygmalion in the classroom: Teacher expectations and pupils' intellectual development.* New York: Holt, Rinehart & Winston.

ROSENTHAL, R., & RUBIN, D. B. (1982). Further meta-analytic procedures for assessing cognitive gender differences. *Journal of Educational Psychology, 74,* 708–712.

ROSS, D. (1972). *G. Stanley Hall: The psychologist as prophet.* Chicago: University of Chicago Press. 1972.

ROSS, D. F., MILLER, B. S., & MORAN, P. B. (1987). The child in the eyes of the jury: Assessing mock jurors' perceptions of the child witness. In S. J. Ceci, M. P. Toglia, & D. F. Ross (Eds.), *Children's eyewitness memory* (pp. 142–154). New York: Springer-Verlag.

ROSS, G., KAGAN, J., ZELAZO, P., & KOTELCHUK, M. (1975). Separation protest in infants in home and laboratory. *Developmental Psychology, 11,* 256–257.

ROSS, G. S. (1980). Categorization in 1- to 2-year olds. *Developmental Psychology, 16,* 391–396.

ROSS, H. S., & GOLDMAN, B. D. (1977). Infants' sociability toward strangers. *Child Development, 48,* 638–642.

ROSS, R. P., CAMPBELL, T., HUSTON-STEIN, A., & WRIGHT, J. C. (1984). Nutritional misinformation of children. A developmental and experimental analysis of the effects of televised food commercials. *Journal of Applied Developmental Psychology, 1,* 329–347.

ROSSITER, J. R., & ROBERTSON, T. S. (1975). Children's television viewing: An examination of parent-child consensus. *Sociometry, 38,* 308–326.

ROTHBART, M. K. (1981). Measurement of temperament in infancy. *Child Development, 52,* 569–578.

ROTHBART, M. K., & ROTHBART, M. (1976). Birth-order, sex of child and maternal help giving. *Sex Roles, 2,* 39–46.

ROTHENBERG, B. B. (1970). Children's social sensitivity and its relationship to interpersonal competence, intrapersonal comfort, and intellectual level. *Developmental Psychology, 2,* 335–350.

ROTHENBERG, P. B., & VARGA, P. E. (1981). Relationship between age of mother and child health and development. *American Journal of Public Health, 71,* 810–817.

ROTHWELL, N. V. (1977). *Human genetics.* Englewood Cliffs, NJ: Prentice-Hall.

ROUSSEAU, J. J. (1955). *Emile.* New York: Dutton. (Originally published 1762)

ROVEE, C. K., & ROVEE, D. T. (1969). Conjugate reinforcement of infant exploratory behavior. *Journal of Experimental Child Psychology, 8,* 33–39.

ROVET, J., & NETLEY, C. (1983). The triple X chromosome syndrome in childhood: Recent empirical findings. *Child Development, 54,* 831–845.

ROWE, D. C. (1987). Resolving the person-situation debate: Invitation to an interdisciplinary dialogue. *American Psychologist, 42,* 218–227.

ROWE, D. C., & PLOMIN, R. (1981). The importance on nonshared (E_1) environmental influences on behavioral development. *Developmental Psychology, 17,* 517–531.

RUBENSTEIN, J. L., & HOWES, C. (1976). The effects of peers on toddler interaction with mothers and toys. *Child Development, 47,* 597–605.

RUBIN, J. Z., PROVENZANO, F. J., & LURIA, Z. (1974). The eye of the beholder: Parents' views on sex of newborns. *American Journal of Orthopsychiatry, 44,* 512–519.

RUBIN, K. H. (1972). Relationship between egocentric communication and popularity among peers. *Developmental Psychology, 7,* 364.

RUBIN, K. H. (1973). Egocentrism in childhood: A unitary construct? *Child Development, 44,* 102–110.

RUBIN, K. H. (1977). The social and cognitive value of preschool toys and activities. *Canadian Journal of Behavioural Science/Review of Canadian Science, 9,* 382–385.

RUBIN, K. H. (1978). Role taking in childhood: Some methodological considerations. *Child Development, 49,* 428–433.

RUBIN, K. H. (1982). Nonsocial play in preschoolers: Necessarily evil? *Child Development, 53,* 651–657.

RUBIN, K. H., & DANIELS-BEIRNESS, T. (1983). Concurrent and predictive correlates of sociometric status in kindergarten and grade one children. *Merrill-Palmer Quarterly, 29,* 337–352.

RUBIN, K. H., FEIN, G. G., & VANDENBERG, B. (1983). Play. In E. M. Hetherington (Ed.), *Handbook of child psychology: Vol. 4. Socialization, personality, and social development* (4th ed., pp. 693–774). New York: Wiley.

RUBIN, K. H., & KRASNOR, L. R. (1985). Social-cognitive and social behavioral perspectives on problem solving. In M. Perlmutter (Ed.), *Minnesota Symposia on child psychology* (Vol. 18, pp. 1–68). Hillsdale, NJ: Erlbaum.

RUBIN, K. H., LeMARE, L. J., & LOLLIS, S. (in press). Social withdrawal in childhood: Developmental pathways to peer rejection. In S. R. Asher & J. D. Coie (Eds.), *Peer rejection in childhood.* New York: Cambridge University Press.

RUBIN, K. H., & MAIONI, T. (1975). Play preference and its relationship to egocentrism, popularity, and classification skills in preschoolers. *Merrill-Palmer Quarterly, 21,* 171–180.

RUBIN, K. H., MAIONI, T. L., & HORNUNG, M. (1976). Free play behaviors in middle- and lower-class preschoolers: Parten and Piaget revisited. *Child Development, 47,* 414–419.

RUBIN, K. H., & PEPLER, D. J. (1982). Children's play: Piaget's views reconsidered. *Contemporary Educational Psychology, 7,* 289–299.

RUBIN, K. H., WATSON, K. S., & JAMBOR, T. W. (1982). Free-play behaviors in preschool and kindergarten children. *Child Development, 49,* 534–536.

RUBIN, R. T., REINISCH, J. M., & HASKETT, R. F. (1981). Postnatal gonadal steroid effects on human behavior. *Science, 211,* 1318–1324.

RUBIN, Z., & SLOMAN, J. (1984). How parents influence their children's friendship. In M. Lewis (Ed.), *Beyond the dyad* (pp. 223–250). New York: Plenum.

RUBLE, D. N. (1988). Sex-role development. In M. H. Bornstein & M. E. Lamb (Eds.), *Developmental psychology: An advanced textbook* (2nd ed., pp. 411–460). Hillsdale, NJ: Erlbaum.

RUBLE, D. N., BOGGIANO, A. K., FELDMAN, N. S., & LOEBL, J. H. (1980). Developmental analysis of the role of social comparison in self-evaluation. *Developmental Psychology, 16,* 105–115.

RUBLE, D. N., & BROOKS-GUNN, J. (1982). The experience of menarche. *Child Development, 53,* 1557–1566.

RUBLE, D. N., & RUBLE, T. L. (1982). Sex stereotypes. In A. G. Miller (Ed.), *In the eye of the beholder* (pp. 188–252). New York: Praeger.

RUBLE, T. L. (1983). Sex stereotypes: Issues of change in the 1970s. *Sex Roles, 9,* 397–402.

RUDEL, R. G., & TEUBER, H. L. (1963). Discrimination of direction of line in children. *Journal of Comparative and Physiological Psychology, 56,* 892–898.

RUFF, H. A., & HALTON, A. (1977). Is there directed reaching in the human neonate? *Developmental Psychology, 14,* 425–426.

RUGH, R., & SHETTLES, L. B. (1971). *From conception to birth: The drama of life's beginnings.* New York: Harper & Row.

RUMBAUGH, D. M. (1977). *Language learning by a chimpanzee: The Lana project.* New York: Academic Press.

RUOPP, R., TRAVERS, J., GLANTZ, F., & COELEN, C. (1979). *Children at the center: Final report of the National Day Care Study.* Cambridge, MA: Abt Books.

RUSHTON, J. P. (1980). *Altruism, socialization, and society.* Englewood Cliffs, NJ: Prentice-Hall.

RUTTER, M. (1979). Maternal deprivation 1972–1977: New findings, new concepts, new approaches. *Child Development, 50,* 283–305.

RUTTER, M. (1981). The city and the child. *American Journal of Orthopsychiatry, 51,* 610–625.

RUTTER, M., & GARMEZY, N. (1983). Developmental psychopathology. In P. H. Mussen (Ed.), *Handbook of child psychology: Vol. 4. Socialization, personality, and social development.* (pp. 775–911). New York: Wiley.

RUTTER, M., & MADGE, N. (1976). *Cycles of disadvantage.* London: Heinemann.

RUTTER, M., GRAHAM, P., CHADWICK, O. F. D., & YULE, W. (1976). Adolescent turmoil: Fact or fiction. *Journal of Child Psychology and Psychiatry, 17,* 35–56.

SAARNI, C. (1979). Children's understanding of display rules for expressive behavior. *Developmental Psychology, 15,* 424–429.

SAARNI, C. (1982). Social and affective functions of nonverbal behavior: Developmental concerns. In R. Feldman (Ed.), *Development of nonverbal behavior in children* (pp. 123–147). New York: Springer-Verlag.

SACHS, J. (1985). Prelinguistic development. In J. B. Gleason (Ed.), *The Development of Language* (pp. 37–60). Columbus, OH: Merrill.

SACKETT, G. P. (1970). Unlearned responses, differential rearing experiences, and the development of social attachments by rhesus monkeys. In L. A. Rosenblum (Ed.), *Primate behavior: Developments in field and laboratory research* (Vol. 1, pp. 111–140). New York: Academic Press.

SADEH, D., SHANNON, D. C., ABBOUD, S., SAUL, J. P., AKSELROD, S., & COHEN, R. J. (1987). Altered cardiac repolarization in some victims of sudden infant death syndrome. *New England Journal of Medicine, 317,* 1501–1505.

SAEGERT, S., & HART, R. (1976). The development of environmental competence in girls and boys. In P. Burnet (Ed.), *Women and society.* Chicago: Maaroufa Press.

SAGI, A., LAMB, M. E., LEWKOWICZ, K. S., SHOHAM, R., DVIR, R., & ESTES, D. (1985). Security of infant-mother, -father, and -metapelet attachments among kibbutz-reared Israeli children. In I. Bretherton & E. Waters (Eds.), *Monographs of the Society for Research in Child Development, 50* (1–2, Serial No. 209).

SAHLER, O. J. Z. (1983). Adolescent mothers: How nurturant is their parenting? In E. R. McAnarney (Ed.), *Premature adolescent pregnancy and parenthood* (pp. 219–230). New York: Grune and Stratton.

SALAPATEK, P. (1975). Pattern perception in early infancy. In L. B. Cohen & P. Salapatek (Eds.), *Infant perception: From sensation to cognition* (pp. 133–248). New York: Academic Press.

SALOMON, G. (1979). *Interaction of media, cognition, and learning.* San Francisco, CA: Jossey-Bass.

SALOMON, J. B., MATA, L. J., & GORDON, J. E. (1968). Malnutrition and the common communicable diseases of childhood in rural Guatemala. *American Journal of Health, 58,* 505–516.

SALTZ, E., DIXON, D., & JOHNSON, J. (1977). Training disadvantaged preschoolers on various fantasy activities: Effects on cognitive functioning and impulse control. *Child Development, 48,* 367–380.

SALTZ, E., & JOHNSON, J. (1974). Training for thematic-fantasy play in culturally disadvantaged children: Preliminary results. *Journal of Educational Psychology, 66,* 623–630.

SALTZSTEIN, H. D. (1976). Social influence and moral development: A perspective on the role of parents and peers. In T. Lickona (Ed.), *Moral development and behavior: Theory, research and social issues* (pp. 253–265). New York: Holt, Rinehart & Winston.

SAMEROFF, A. J. (1968). The components of sucking in the human newborn. *Journal of Experimental Child Psychology, 6,* 607–623.

SAMEROFF, A. J., & CAVANAUGH, P. J. (1979). Learning in infancy: A developmental perspective. In J. D. Osofsky (Ed.), *Handbook of infant development.* (pp. 344–392). New York: Wiley.

SAMEROFF, A. J., & CHANDLER, M. J. (1975). Reproductive risk and the continuum of caretaking casualty. In F. D. Horowitz (Ed.), *Review of child development research* (Vol. 4, pp. 187–244). Chicago: University of Chicago Press.

SAMUELS, M., & SAMUELS, N. (1986). *The well pregnancy book.* New York: Summit.

SANTROCK, J. W., & WARSHAK, R. A. (1979). Father custody and social development in boys and girls. *Journal of Social Issues, 35,* 112–125.

SANTROCK, J. W., WARSHAK, R. A., & ELLIOTT, G. L. (1982). Social development and parent-child interaction in father-custody and stepmother families. In M. E. Lamb (Ed.), *Nontraditional families* (pp. 289–314). Hillsdale, NJ: Erlbaum.

SARASON, I. G. (1980). *Test anxiety: Theory, research, and applications.* Hillsdale, NJ: Erlbaum.

SARNAT, H. B. (1978). Olfactory reflexes in the newborn infant. *Journal of Pediatrics, 92,* 624–626.

SATTLER, J. M. (1988). *Assessment of children's intelligence and special abilities* (3rd ed.). San Diego: Jerome M. Sattler.

SATZ, P., & BULLARD-BATES, C. (1981). Acquired aphasia in children. In M. T. Sarno (Ed.), *Acquired aphasia* (pp. 399–426). New York: Academic Press.

SAVAGE-RUMBAUGH, S. (1987). Ape language: Contrasts in symbol acquisition between Pygmee chimpanzees. Paper presented at the Society for Research in Child Development, Baltimore, MD.

SAVIC, S. (1980). *How twins learn to talk:* New York: Academic Press.

SAVIN-WILLIAMS, R. C. (1979). Dominance hierarchies in groups of early adolescents. *Child Development, 50,* 923–935.

SAVIN-WILLIAMS, R. C. (1980a). Dominance hierarchies in groups of middle to late adolescent males. *Journal of Youth and Adolescence, 9,* 75–85.

SAVIN-WILLIAMS, R. C. (1980b). Social interactions of adolescent females in natural groups. In H. C. Foot, A. J. Chapman, & J. R. Smith (Eds.), *Friendship and social relations in children* (pp. 343–364). Chichester, Eng.: Wiley.

SAVIN-WILLIAMS, R. C., & DEMO, D. H. (1984). Developmental change and stability in adolescent self-concept. *Developmental Psychology, 20,* 1100–1110.

SAXBY, L., & BRYDEN, M. P. (1984). Left-ear superiority in children for processing auditory emotional material. *Developmental Psychology, 20,* 72–80.

SAYWITZ, K. J. (1987). Children's testimony: Age-related patterns of memory errors. In S. J. Ceci, M. P. Toglia, & D. F. Ross (Eds.), *Children's eyewitness memory* (pp. 36–52). New York: Springer-Verlag.

SCARLETT, H. H., PRESS, A. N., & CROCKETT, W. H. (1971). Children's descriptions of peers: A Wernerian developmental analysis. *Child Development, 42,* 439–453.

SCARR, S. (1968). Environmental bias in twin studies. *Eugenics Quarterly, 15,* 34–40.

SCARR, S. (1985). Constructing psychology: Making facts and fables for our times. *American Psychologist, 40,* 499–512.

SCARR, S., & BARKER, W. (1981). The effects of family background: A study of cognitive differences among black and white twins. In S. Scarr (Ed.), *Race, social class, and individual differences in I.Q.* (pp. 261–315). Hillsdale, NJ: Erlbaum.

SCARR, S., & CARTER-SALTZMAN, L. (1979). Twin method: Defense of a critical assumption. *Behavior Genetics, 9,* 527–542.

SCARR, S., & KIDD, K. K. (1983). Developmental behavior genetics. In M. M. Haith & J. J. Campos (Ed.), *Handbook of child psychology: Vol. 2. Infancy and developmental psychobiology* (4th ed., pp. 345–433). New York: Wiley.

SCARR, S., & MCCARTNEY, K. (1983). How people make their own environments: A theory of genotype → environment effects. *Child Development, 54,* 424–435.

SCARR, S., PAKSTIS, A. J., KATZ, S. H., & BARKER, W. (1977). The absence of a relationship between degree of white ancestry and intellectual skills within a black population. *Human Genetics, 39,* 69–86.

SCARR, S., & WEINBERG, R. A. (1976). IQ test performance of black children adopted by white families. *American Psychologist, 31,* 726–739.

SCARR, S., & WEINBERG, R. A. (1978). The influence of "family background" on intellectual attainment. *American Sociological Review, 43,* 674–792.

SCARR, S., & WEINBERG, R. A. (1983). The Minnesota Adoption Studies. Genetic differences and malleability. *Child Development, 54,* 260–267.

SCARR, S., WEBBER, P. L., WEINBERG, R. A., & WITTIG, M. A. (1981). Personality resemblance among adolescents and their parents in biologically related and adoptive families. *Journal of Personality and Social Psychology, 40,* 885–898.

SCARR-SALAPATEK, S. (1975). Genetics and the development of intelligence. In F. D. Horowitz (Ed.), *Review of child development research* (Vol. 4, pp. 1–57). Chicago: University of Chicago Press.

SCHAB, F. (1971). Honor and dishonor in the secondary schools of three cultures. *Adolescence, 6,* 145–154.

SCHACHTEL, E. (1947). On memory and childhood amnesia. *Psychiatry, 10,* 1–26.

SCHACHTER, F. F., SHORE, E., FELDMAN-ROTMAN, S., MARQUIS, R. E., & CAMPBELL, S. (1976). Sibling deidentification. *Developmental Psychology, 12,* 418–427.

SCHACHTER, F. F., SHORE, E., HODAPP, R., CHALFIN, S., & BUNDY, C. (1978). Do girls talk earlier? Mean length utterance in toddlers. *Developmental Psychology, 14,* 388–392.

SCHACHTER, F. F., & STONE, R. K. (1985). Difficult sibling, easy sibling: Temperament and the within-family environment. *Child Development, 56,* 1335–1344.

SCHACHTER, S. (1959). *The psychology of affiliation.* Stanford, CA: Stanford University Press.

SCHACHTER, S., & RODIN, J. (Eds.) (1974). *Obese humans and rats.* Washington, DC: Erlbaum/Halsted.

SCHAEFER, E., & BAYLEY, N. (1963). Maternal behavior, child behavior and their intercorrelations from infancy through adolescence. *Monographs of the Society for Research in Child Development, 28* (3, Serial No. 87).

SCHAEFER, M., HATCHER, R. P., & BARGELOW, P. D. (1980). Prematurity and infant stimulation. *Child Psychiatry and Human Development, 10,* 199–212.

SCHAFFER, H. R. (1966). The onset of fear of strangers and the incongruity hypothesis. *Journal of Child Psychology and Psychiatry, 7,* 95–106.

SCHAFFER, H. R. (1979). Acquiring the concept of the dialogue. In M. H. Bornstein & W. Kessen (Eds.), *Psychological development from infancy: Image to intention* (pp. 279–305). Hillsdale, NJ: Erlbaum.

SCHAFFER, H. R., & EMERSON, P. E. (1964). The development of social attachments in infancy. *Monographs of the Society for Research in Child Development, 29* (3, Serial No. 94).

SCHAFFER, H. R., GREENWOOD, A., & PARRY, N. H. (1971). The onset of wariness. *Child Development, 42,* 165–176.

SCHAIE, K. W., & HERTZOG, C. (1982). Longitudinal methods. In B. B. Wolman (Ed.), *Handbook of developmental psychology* (pp. 91–115). Englewood Cliffs, NJ: Prentice-Hall.

SCHAIE, K. W., & HERTZOG, C. (1983). Fourteen-year cohort-sequential analyses of adult intellectual development. *Developmental Psychology, 19,* 531–543.

SCHAIVI, R. C., THEILGAARD, A., OWEN, D., & WHITE, D. (1984). Sex chromosome anomalies, hormones, and aggressivity. *Archives of General Psychiatry, 41,* 93–99.

SCHAIVO, R. S., & SOLOMON, S. K. (1981). The effect of summer contact on preschoolers' friendships with classmates. Paper presented at the meeting of the Eastern Psychological Association, New York.

SCHANBERG, S., & FIELD, T. M. (1987). Sensory deprivation stress and supplemental stimulation in the rat pup and preterm human neonate. *Child Development, 58,* 1431–1447.

SCHANK, R. C., & ABELSON, R. P. (1977). *Scripts, plans, goals, and understanding.* Hillsdale, NJ: Erlbaum.

SCHAU, C. G., KAHN, L., DIEPOLD, J. H., & CHERRY, F. (1980). The relationships of parental expectations and preschool children's verbal sex typing to their sex-typed toy play behavior. *Child Development, 51,* 266–271.

SCHERER, K. R. (1982). The assessment of vocal expression in infants and children. In C. E. Izard (Ed.), *Measuring emotions in infants and children* (pp. 127–163). New York: Cambridge University Press.

SCHIEFFELIN, B. B., & OCHS, E. (1983). A cultural perspective on the transition from prelinguistic to linguistic communication. In R. M. Golinkoff (Ed.), *The transition from prelinguistic to linguistic communication* (pp. 115–131). Hillsdale, NJ: Erlbaum.

SCHNEIDER, W. (1985). Developmental trends in the metamemory-memory behavior relationship: An integrative review. In D. L. Forrest-Pressley, G. E. MacKinnon, & T. G. Waller (Eds.), *Metacognition, cognition, and human performance* (Vol. 1, pp. 57–109). New York: Academic Press.

SCHNEIDER-ROSEN, K., BRAUNWALD, K. G., CARLSON, V., & CICCHETTI, D. (1985). Current perspectives in attachment theory: Illustration from the study of maltreated infants. In I. Bretherton & E. Waters (Eds.), Growing points of attachment theory and research. *Monographs of the Society for Research in Child Development, 50* (1–2, Serial No. 209).

SCHNUR, E., & SHATZ, M. (1984). The role of maternal gesturing in conversations with one-year-olds. *Journal of Child Language, 11,* 29–41.

SCHOLL, D. M., & RYAN, E. B. (1980). Development of metalinguistic performance in the early school years. *Language and Speech, 23,* 199–211.

SCHRAG, S. G., & DIXON, R. L. (1985). Occupational exposures associated with male reproductive dysfunction. *Annual Review of Pharmacology and Toxicology, 25,* 567–592.

SCHULTZ, D. P. (1975). *A history of modern psychology.* New York: Academic Press.

SCHUNK, D. H. (1981). Modeling and attributional effects on children's achievement: A self-efficacy analysis. *Journal of Educational Psychology, 73,* 93–105.

SCHUNK, D. H. (1983). Ability versus effort attributional feedback: Differential effects on self-efficacy and achievement. *Journal of Educational Psychology, 75,* 848–856.

SCHUNK, D. H., HANSON, A. R., & COX, P. D. (1987). Peer-model attributes and children's achievement behaviors. *Journal of Educational Psychology, 79,* 54–61.

SCHWARTZ, J. C. (1972). Effects of peer familiarity on the behavior of preschoolers in a novel situation. *Journal of Personality and Social Psychology, 24,* 276–284.

SCHWARTZ, P. (1983). Length of day-care attendance and attachment behavior in eighteen-month-old infants. *Child Development, 54,* 1073–1078.

SCHWARTZ, R. G., & LEONARD, L. B. (1982). Do children pick and choose? An examination of phonological selection and avoidance in early lexical acquisition. *Journal of Child Language, 9,* 319–336.

SCOTT, K. P., & SCHAU, C. G. (1985). Sex equity and sex bias in instructional materials. In S. S. Klein (Ed.), *Handbook for achieving sex equity through education* (pp. 218–232). Baltimore, MD: Johns Hopkins University Press.

SEARS, R. R. (1975). *Your ancients revisited: A history of child development.* Chicago: University of Chicago Press.

SEARS, R. R., MACCOBY, E. E., & LEVIN, H. (1957). *Patterns of child rearing.* Evanston, IL: Row, Peterson.

SEARS, R. R., RAU, L., & ALPERT, R. (1965). *Identification and child rearing.* Stanford, CA: Stanford University Press.

SEAY, B., ALEXANDER, B. K., & HARLOW, H. F. (1964). Maternal behavior of socially deprived rhesus monkeys. *Journal of Abnormal and Social Psychology, 69,* 345–354.

SEITZ, V. (1988). Methodology. In M. H. Bornstein & M. E. Lamb (Eds.), *Developmental psychology: An advanced textbook* (2nd ed., pp. 51–83). Hillsdale, NJ: Erlbaum.

SEITZ, V., ROSENBAUM, L., & APFEL, N. (1985). Effects of family support intervention: A ten year follow-up. *Child Development, 56,* 376–391.

SELKOW, P. (1984). Effects of maternal employment on kindergarten and first-grade children's vocational aspirations. *Sex Roles, 11,* 677–690.

SELLS, S. B., & ROFF, M. (1964). Peer acceptance-rejection and birth order. *Psychology in the Schools, 1,* 156–162.

SELMAN, R. L. (1976). Social-cognitive understanding: A guide to educational and clinical practice. In T. Lickona (Ed.), *Moral development and behavior: Theory, research, and social issues* (pp. 299–316). New York: Holt, Rinehart and Winston.

SELMAN, R. L. (1977). Toward a structural analysis of developing interpersonal relations concepts: Research with normal and disturbed preadolescent boys. In A. D. Pick (Ed.), *Minnesota Symposia on Child Psychology* (Vol. 10, pp. 156–200). Minneapolis: University of Minnesota Press.

SELMAN, R. L. (1980). *The growth of interpersonal understanding.* New York: Academic Press.

SELMAN, R. L. (1981). The child as a friendship philosopher. In S. R.

Asher & J. M. Gottman (Eds.), *The development of friendships* (pp. 242–272). New York: Cambridge University Press.

SELMAN, R. L., & BYRNE, D. F. (1974). A structural-developmental analysis of levels of role-taking in middle childhood. *Child Development, 45,* 803–806.

SELMAN, R. L., & DEMOREST, A. P. (1984). Observing troubled children's interpersonal negotiational strategies: Implications of and for a developmental model. *Child Development, 55,* 288–304.

SELMAN, R. L., SCHORIN, M. Z., STONE, C., & PHELPS, E. (1983). A naturalistic study of children's social understanding. *Developmental Psychology, 19,* 82–102.

SENN, M. J. E. (1975). Insights on the child development movement in the United States. *Monographs of the Society for Research in Child Development, 40* (3–4, Serial No. 161).

SERBIN, L. A., CONNOR, J. M., BURCHARDT, C. J., & CITRON, C. C. (1979). Effects of peer presence on sex-typing of children's play behavior. *Journal of Experimental Child Psychology, 27,* 303–309.

SERBIN, L. A., CONNOR, J. M., & CITRON, C. C. (1978). Environmental control of independent and dependent behaviors in preschool girls and boys: A model for early independence training. *Sex Roles, 4,* 867–875.

SERBIN, L. A., CONNOR, J. M., & CITRON, C. C. (1981). Sex-differentiated free play behavior: Effects of teacher modeling, location, and gender. *Developmental Psychology, 17,* 640–646.

SERBIN, L. A., CONNOR, J. M., & ILER, I. (1979). Sex-stereotyped and nonstereotyped introductions of new toys in the preschool classroom: An observational study of teacher behavior and its effects. *Psychology of Women Quarterly, 4,* 261–265.

SERBIN, L. A., O'LEARY, K. D., KENT, R. N., & TONICK, I. J. (1973). A comparison of teacher response to the preacademic and problem behavior of boys and girls. *Child Development, 44,* 796–804.

SERBIN, L. A., TONICK, I. J., & STERNGLANZ, S. H. (1977). Shaping cooperative cross-sex play. *Child Development, 48,* 924–929

SERPELL, R. (1979). How specific are perceptual skills? A cross-cultural study of pattern reproduction. *British Journal of Psychology, 70,* 365–380.

SEVER, J. L. (1982). Infections during pregnancy: Highlights from the collaborative perinatal project. *Teratology, 25,* 227–237.

SHAFFER, D. (1974). Suicide in childhood and early adolescence. *Journal of Child Psychology and Psychiatry, 15,* 275–291.

SHAFFER, D., & FISHER, P. (1981). The epidemiology of suicide in children and young adolescents. *Journal of the American Academy of Child Psychiatry, 20,* 545–565.

SHAFII, M., CARRIGAN, S., WHITTINGHILL, J. R., & DERRICK, A. (1985). Psychological autopsy of completed suicide in children and adolescents. *American Journal of Psychiatry, 142,* 1061–1064.

SHAINESS, N. (1961). A re-evaluation of some aspects of femininity through a study of menstruation: A preliminary report. *Comparative Psychiatry, 2,* 20–26.

SHANTZ, C. U. (1983). Social cognition. In J. H. Flavell & E. M. Markman (Eds.), *Handbook of child psychology: Vol. 3. Cognitive development* (4th ed., pp. 495–555). New York: Wiley.

SHANTZ, C. U. (1987). Conflicts between children. *Child Development, 58,* 283–305.

SHANTZ, D. W. (1986). Conflict, aggression, and peer status: An observational study. *Child Development, 57,* 1322–1332.

SHATZ, M. (1979). How to do things by asking: Form-function pairings in mothers' questions and their relation to children's responses. *Child Development, 50,* 1093–1099.

SHATZ, M. (1983). Communication. In J. H. Flavell & E. M. Markman (Eds.), *Handbook of child psychology: Vol. 3. Cognitive development* (4th ed., pp. 841–889). New York: Wiley.

SHAVELSON, R. J., & BOLUS, R. (1982). Self-concept: The interplay of theory and methods. *Journal of Educational Psychology, 74,* 3–17.

SHAVELSON, R. J., HUBNER, J. J., & STANTON, G. C. (1976). Self-concept: Validation and construct interpretations. *Review of Educational Research, 46,* 407–441.

SHENNUM, W. A., & BUGENTAL, D. B. (1982). The development of control over affective expression in nonverbal behavior. In R. Feldman (Ed.), *Development of nonverbal behavior in children* (pp. 101–121). New York: Springer-Verlag.

SHEPPARD, J. J., & MYSAK, E. D. (1984). Ontogeny of infantile oral reflexes and emerging chewing. *Child Development, 55,* 831–843.

SHERIF, M., HARVEY, O. J., WHITE, B. J., HOOD, W. R., & SHERIF, C. W. (1961). *Inter-group conflict and cooperation: The Robbers Cave experiment.* Norman: University of Oklahoma Press.

SHERMAN, J. (1980). Mathematics, spatial visualization, and related factors: Changes in girls and boys, grades 8–11. *Journal of Educational Psychology, 72,* 476–482.

SHERMAN, J., & FENNEMA, E. (1977) The study of mathematics by high school girls and boys: Related variables. *American Educational Research Journal, 14,* 159–168.

SHERMAN, M., HERTZIG, M., AUSTRIAN, R., & SHAPIRO, T. (1981). Treasured objects in school-aged children. *Pediatrics, 68,* 379–386.

SHERMAN, T. (1985). Categorization skills in infants. *Child Development, 56,* 1561–1573.

SHERRILL, D., HOROWITZ, B., FRIEDMAN, S. T., & SALISBURY, J. L. (1970). Seating aggregation as an index of contagion. *Educational and Psychological Measurement, 30, 663–668.*

SHETTLES, L. B. (1970). Factors influencing sex ratios. *International Journal of Gynaecology and Obstetrics, 8,* 643–647.

SHETTLES, L.B., & RORVIK, D. M. (1984). *How to Choose the Sex of Your Baby.* New York: Doubleday.

SHIELDS, J. W. (1972). *The trophic function of lymphoid elements.* Springfield, IL: Charles C. Thomas.

SHIFFRIN, R. M., & ATKINSON, R. C. (1969). Storage and retrieval processes in long-term memory. *Psychological Review, 76,* 179–193.

SHILLER, V., IZARD, C. E., & HEMBREE, E. A. (1986). Patterns of emotion expression during separation in the Strange Situation. *Developmental Psychology, 22,* 378–382.

SHINN, M. W. (1900). *The biography of a baby.* Boston: Houghton Mifflin.

SHIPMAN, G. (1971). The psychodynamics of sex education. In R. E. Muus (Ed.), *Adolescent behavior and society: A book of readings* (pp. 326–339). New York: Random House.

SHIRLEY, M. M. (1933). *The first two years* (Vol. 2, Institute of Child Welfare Monograph No. 7). Minneapolis: University of Minnesota Press.

SHULTZ, T. R. (1980). Development of the concept of intention. In W. A. Collins (Ed.), *Minnesota Symposia on Child Psychology* (Vol. 13, pp. 131–164). Hillsdale, NJ: Erlbaum.

SHULTZ, T. R., & HORIBE, F. (1974). Development of the appreciation of verbal jokes. *Developmental Psychology, 10,* 13–20.

SHULTZ, T. R., & PILON, R. (1973). Development of the ability to detect linguistic ambiguity. *Child Development, 44,* 728–733.

SHULTZ, T. R., & WELLS, D. (1985). Judging the intentionality of action-outcomes. *Developmental Psychology, 21,* 83–89.

SHULTZ, T. R., WELLS, D., & SARDA, M. (1980). Development of the ability to distinguish intended action from mistakes, reflexes, and passive movements. *British Journal of Social and Clinical Psychology, 19,* 301–310.

SHULTZ, T. R., & ZIGLER, E. (1970). Emotional concomitants of visual mastery in infants: The effects of stimulus movement on smiling and vocalizing. *Journal of Experimental Child Psychology, 10,* 390–402.

SHURE, M. B. (1981). Social competence as a problem-solving skill. In J. D. Wine & M. D. Smye (Eds.), *Social competence* (pp. 158–185). New York: Guilford.

SIDOROWICZ, L. S., & LUNNEY, G. S. (1980). Baby X revisited. *Sex Roles, 6,* 67–73.

SIEGAL, L. S. (1981). Infant tests as predictors of cognitive and language development at two years. *Child Development, 52,* 545–557.

SIEGAL, M., & ROBINSON, J. (1987). Order effects in children's gender-constancy responses. *Developmental Psychology, 23,* 283–286.

SIEGEL, A. W. (1981). The externalization of cognitive maps by children and adults: In search of ways to ask better questions. In L. S. Liben, A. H. Patterson, & N. Newcombe (Eds.), *Spatial representa-*

tion and behavior across the life span (pp. 167–194). New York: Academic Press.

SIEGLER, R. S. (1976). Three aspects of cognitive development. *Cognitive Psychology, 8,* 481–520.

SIEGLER, R. S. (1978). The origins of scientific reasoning. In R. S. Siegler (Ed.), *Children's thinking: What develops?* (pp. 109–149). Hillsdale, NJ: Erlbaum.

SIEGLER, R. S. (1981). Developmental sequences within and between concepts. *Monographs of the Society for Research in Child Development, 46* (2, Serial No. 189).

SIEGLER, R. S. (1983a). Information processing approaches to development. In W. Kessen (Ed.), *Handbook of child psychology: Vol. 1. History, theory, and methods* (4th ed., pp. 129–211). New York: Wiley.

SIEGLER, R. S. (1983b). Five generalizations about cognitive development. *American Psychologist, 38,* 263–277.

SIEGLER, R. S., LIEBERT, D. E., & LIEBERT, R. M. (1973). Inhelder and Piaget's pendulum problem: Teaching preadolescents as scientists. *Developmental Psychology, 9,* 97–101.

SIEGLER, R. S., & RICHARDS, D. D. (1980). *College students' prototypes of children's intelligence.* Paper presented at the meeting of the American Psychological Association, New York.

SIEGLER, R. S., & RICHARDS, D. D. (1982). The development of intelligence. In R. J. Sternberg (Ed.), *Handbook of human intelligence* (pp. 897–971). Cambridge, Eng.: Cambridge University Press.

SIEGLER, R. S., & ROBINSON, M. (1982). The development of numerical understandings. In H. W. Reese & L. P. Lipsitt (Eds.), *Advances in child development and behavior* (Vol. 16, pp. 241–312). New York: Academic Press.

SIGNORELLA, M. L., & JAMISON, W. (1986). Masculinity, femininity, androgyny, and cognitive performance: A meta-analysis. *Psychological Bulletin, 100,* 207–228.

SIGNORELLA, M. L., & LIBEN, L. S. (1984). Recall and reconstruction of gender-related pictures: Effects of attitude, task difficulty, and age. *Child Development, 55,* 393–405.

SILBERMAN, C. E. (1970). *Crisis in the classroom.* New York: Random House.

SILBERMAN, M. L. (1969). Behavioral expression of teachers' attitudes toward elementary school students. *Journal of Educational Psychology, 60,* 402–407.

SILBERMAN, M. L. (1971). Teachers' attitudes and actions toward their students. In M. Silberman (Ed.), *The experience of schooling* (pp. 86–106). New York: Holt, Rinehart & Winston.

SIMKIN, P., WHALLEY, J., & KEPPLER, A. (1984). *Pregnancy, childbirth and the newborn.* New York: Meadowbrook.

SIMMONS, R. G., BLYTH, D. A., & McKINNEY, K. L. (1983). The social and psychological effects of puberty on white females. In J. Brooks-Gunn & A. C. Petersen (Eds.), *Girls at puberty: Biological and psychosocial perspectives* (pp. 229–272). New York: Plenum.

SIMMONS, R. G., BLYTH, D. A., VAN CLEAVE, E. F., & BUSH, D. M. (1979). Entry into early adolescence: The impact of school structure, puberty and early dating on self esteem. *American Sociological Review, 44,* 948–967.

SIMMONS, R. G., BURGESON, R., CARLTON FORD, & BLYTH, D. (1987). The impact of cumulative change in early adolescence. *Child Development, 58,* 1220–1234.

SIMONS, J., & BOHEN, H. (1982). *Employed parents and their children: A data book.* Washington, DC: Children's Defense Fund.

SINGER, D. G., ZUCKERMAN, D. M., & SINGER, J. L. (1980). Helping elementary school children learn about TV. *Journal of Communication, 30*(3), 84–93.

SINGER, J. E., WESTPHAL, M., & NISWANDER, K. R. (1968). Sex differences in the incidence of neonatal abnormalities and abnormal performance in early childhood. *Child Development, 39,* 103–112.

SINGER, J. L., & SINGER, D. G. (1976). Can TV stimulate imaginative play? *Journal of Communication, 26*(3), 74–80.

SINGER, J. L., & SINGER, D. G. (1981). *Television, imagination, and aggression: A study of preschoolers.* Hillsdale, NJ: Erlbaum.

SINGER, J. L., & SINGER, D. G. (1983). Psychologists look at television. *American Psychologist, 38,* 826–834.

SINGER, J. L., SINGER, D. G., & RAPACZYNSKI, W. (1984). Family patterns and television viewing as predictors of children's beliefs and aggression. *Journal of Communication, 34*(2), 73–89.

SINGLETON, L. C., & ASHER, S. R. (1979). Racial integration and children's peer preferences: An investigation of developmental and cohort differences. *Child Development, 50,* 936–941.

SINNOTT, J. M., PISONI, D. B., & ASLIN, R. N. (1983). A comparison of pure tone auditory thresholds in human infants and adults. *Infant Behavior and Development, 6,* 3–17.

SIQUELAND, E. R., & DeLUCIA, C. A. (1969). Visual reinforcement of non-nutritive sucking in human infants. *Science, 165,* 1144–1146.

SIQUELAND, E. R., & LIPSITT, L. P. (1966). Conditioned head-turning behavior in newborns. *Journal of Experimental Child Psychology, 3,* 356–376.

SIRIGNANO, S. W., & LACHMAN, M. E. (1985). Personality change during the transition to parenthood: The role of perceived infant temperament. *Developmental Psychology, 21,* 558–567.

SIROTNIK, K. A. (1983). What you see is what you get: Consistency, persistency, and mediocrity in classrooms. *Harvard Educational Review, 53,* 16–31.

SKEELS, H. M. (1966). Adult status of children with contrasting early life experiences. *Monographs of the Society for Research in Child Development, 31*(3, Serial No. 105).

SKINNER, B. F. (1957). *Verbal behavior.* New York: Appleton-Century-Crofts.

SKINNER, B. F. (1979). *The shaping of a behaviorist.* New York: Knopf.

SKODAK, M., & SKEELS, H. M. (1945). A follow-up study of children in adoptive homes. *Journal of Genetic Psychology, 66,* 21–58.

SKODAK, M., & SKEELS, H. M. (1949). A final follow-up study of one hundred adopted children. *Journal of Genetic Psychology, 75,* 85–125.

SLABY, R. G., & FREY, K. S. (1975). Development of gender constancy and selective attention to same-sex models. *Child Development, 46,* 849–856.

SLATER, A., & MORISON, V. (1985). Shape constancy and slant perception at birth. *Perception, 14,* 337–344.

SLAVIC, S. (1980). *How twins learn to talk.* New York: Academic Press.

SLAVIN, R., MADDEN, N., & LEAVEY, M. (1984). Effects of cooperative learning and individualized instruction on mainstreamed students. *Exceptional Children, 50,* 434–443.

SLOBIN, D. I. (1973). Cognitive prerequisites for the development of grammar. In C. A. Ferguson & D. I. Slobin (Ed.), *Studies of child language development* (pp. 175–208). New York: Holt, Rinehart & Winston.

SLOBIN, D. I. (1979). *Psycholinguistics* (2nd ed.). Glenview, IL: Scott, Foresman.

SLOBIN, D. I. (1982). Universal and particular in the acquisition of language. In L. R. Gleitman & H. E. Wanner (Eds.), *Language acquisition: The state of the art* (pp. 128–170). Cambridge, Eng.: Cambridge University Press.

SLOBIN, D. I. (1985). Crosslinguistic evidence for the language-making capacity. In D. I. Slobin (Ed.), *The crosslinguistic study of language acquisition: Vol. 2. Theoretical issues* (pp. 1157–1256). Hillsdale, NJ: Erlbaum.

SLUCKIN, A. M., & SMITH, P. K. (1977). Two approaches to the concept of dominance in preschool children. *Child Development, 48,* 917–923.

SMILANSKY, S. (1968). *The effects of sociodramatic play on disadvantaged children: Preschool children.* New York: Wiley.

SMIRNOV, A. A., & ZINCHENKO, P. I. (1969). Problems in the psychology of memory. In M. Cole & L. Maltzman (Eds.), *A handbook of contemporary Soviet psychology* (pp. 452–502). New York: Basic Books.

SMITH, A. J. (1960). A developmental study of group processes. *Journal of Genetic Psychology, 97,* 29–39.

SMITH, C., & LLOYD, B. (1978). Maternal behavior and perceived sex of infant: Revisited. *Child Development, 49,* 1263–1266.

SMITH, C. L., & TAGER-FLUSBERG, H. (1982). Metalinguistic awareness and language development. *Journal of Experimental Child Psychology, 34,* 449–468.

SMITH, D. F. (1980). Adolescent suicide. In R. E. Muus (Ed.), *Adolescent behavior and society* (3rd ed., pp. 402–409). New York: Random House.

SMITH, D. W., & WILSON, A. A. (1973). *The child with Down's syndrome.* Philadelphia: Saunders.

SMITH, E. J. (1981). Adolescent suicide: A growing problem for the school and family. *Urban Education, 16,* 279–296.

SMITH, H. W. (1973). Some developmental interpersonal dynamics through childhood. *American Sociological Review, 38,* 343–352.

SMITH, J., & RUSSELL, G. (1984). Why do males and females differ? Children's beliefs about sex differences. *Sex Roles, 11,* 1111–1119.

SMITH, M. C. (1978). Cognizing the behavior stream: The recognition of intentional action. *Child Development, 49,* 736–743.

SMITH, M. L., & GLASS, G. V. (1979). *Relationship of class size to classroom processes, teacher satisfaction and pupil affect: A meta-analysis.* San Francisco: Far West Laboratory for Educational Research and Development.

SMITH, M. S., & BISSELL, J. S. (1970). Report analysis: The impact of Head Start. *Harvard Educational Review, 40,* 51–104.

SMITH, P. K. (1978). A longitudinal study of social participation in preschool children: Solitary and parallel play reexamined. *Developmental Psychology, 14,* 517–523.

SMITH, P. K., & CONNOLLY, K. J. (1972). Patterns of play and social interaction in pre-school children. In N. Blurton Jones (Ed.), *Ethological studies of child behaviour* (pp. 65–95). Cambridge, Eng.: Cambridge University Press.

SMITH, P. K., & CONNOLLY, K. J. (1980). *The ecology of preschool behaviour.* Cambridge, Eng.: Cambridge University Press.

SMITH, T. E. (1984). School grades and responsibility for younger siblings: An empirical study of the "teaching function." *American Sociological Review, 49,* 248–260.

SMOKLER, C. S. (1975). Self-esteem in pre-adolescent and adolescent females. *Dissertation Abstracts International, 35,* 3599B. (University Microfilms No. 75-00,813)

SNAREY, J. R., REIMER, J., & KOHLBERG, L. (1985). The development of social-moral reasoning among Kibbutz adolescents: A longitudinal cross-cultural study. *Developmental Psychology, 20,* 3–17.

SNOW, C. E., & HOEFNAGEL-HÖHLE, M. (1978). The critical period for language acquisition: Evidence from second language learning. *Child Development, 49,* 1114–1128.

SNOW, M. E., JACKLIN, C. N., & MACCOBY, E. E. (1981). Birth-order differences in peer sociability at thirty-three months. *Child Development, 52,* 589–596.

SOBESKY, W. E. (1983). The effects of situational factors on moral judgments. *Child Development, 54,* 575–584.

SOCIETY FOR RESEARCH IN CHILD DEVELOPMENT, ETHICAL INTEREST GROUP (1975). *Ethical standards for research with children.* Chicago, IL: Society for Research in Child Development.

SOLAN, L. (1983). *Pronominal reference: Child language and the theory of grammar.* Dordrecht, Holland: Reidel.

SOLOMON, D., & KENDALL, A. J. (1979). *Children in classrooms: An investigation of person-environment interaction.* New York: Praeger.

SOLOMON, R. L., & CORBITT, J. D. (1974). An opponent-process theory of motivation: I. Temporal dynamics of affect. *Psychological Review, 81,* 119–146.

SONG, M., & GINSBURG, H. P. (1987). The development of informal and formal mathematical thinking in Korean and U.S. Children. *Child Development, 58,* 1286–1296.

SONNENSCHEIN, S. (1986a). Development of referential communication: Deciding that a message is uninformative. *Developmental Psychology, 22,* 164–168.

SONNENSCHEIN, S. (1986b). Development of referential communication skills: How familiarity with a listener affects a speaker's production of redundant messages. *Developmental Psychology, 22,* 549–552.

SONNENSCHEIN, S., & WHITEHURST, G. J. (1983). Training referential communication skills: The limits of success. *Journal of Experimental Child Psychology, 35,* 426–436.

SONTAG, L. W. (1944). War and the fetal-maternal relationship. *Marriage and Family Living, 6,* 3–16.

SONTAG, L. W., BAKER, C. T., & NELSON, V. L. (1958). Mental growth and personality development: A longitudinal study. *Monographs of the Society for Research in Child Development, 23,* No. 2.

SORCE, J., EMDE, R. N., CAMPOS, J. J., & KLINNERT, M. (1981). Maternal emotional signaling: Its effect on the visual cliff behavior of one-year-olds. Paper presented at the meeting of the Society for Research in Child Development, Boston.

SORENSON, J., COOPER, W., & PACCIA, J. (1978). Speech timing of grammatical categories. *Cognition, 12,* 135–153.

SORRELLS-JONES, J. (1983). A comparison of the effects of Leboyer delivery and modern "routine" childbirth in a randomized sample. Unpublished doctoral dissertation, University of Chicago.

SOSA, R., KENNELL, J., KLAUS, M., ROBERTSON, S., & URRUTIA, J. (1980). The effect of a supportive companion on perinatal problems, length of labor, and mother-infant interaction. *New England Journal of Medicine, 303,* 597–600.

SPEARMAN, C. (1927). *The abilities of man: Their nature and measurement.* New York: Macmillan.

SPEECE, M. W., & BRENT, S. B. (1984). Children's understanding of death: A review of three components of a death concept. *Child Development, 55,* 1671–1686.

SPEER, J. R., & FLAVELL, J. H. (1979). Young children's knowledge of the relative difficulty of recognition and recall memory tasks. *Developmental Psychology, 15,* 214–217.

SPEIDEL, G. E., & THARP, R. (1985). Is there a comprehension problem for children who speak nonstandard English? A study of children with Hawaiian-English backgrounds. *Applied Psycholinguistics, 6,* 83–96.

SPELKE, E. S. (1985). Perception of unity, persistence, and identity: Thoughts on infants' conceptions of objects. In J. Mehler & R. Fox (Eds.), *Neonate cognition: Beyond the blooming, buzzing confusion* (pp. 89–113). Hillsdale, NJ: Erlbaum.

SPENCE, J. T., HELMREICH, R., & STAPP, J. (1975). Ratings of self and peers on sex role attributes and their relation to self-esteem and conceptions of masculinity and femininity. *Journal of Personality and Social Psychology, 32,* 29–39.

SPINETTA, J., & RIGLER, D. (1972). The child-abusing parent: A psychological review. *Psychological Bulletin, 77,* 296–304.

SPITZ, R. A. (1945). Hospitalism: An inquiry into the genesis of psychiatric conditions in early childhood. *Psychoanalytic Study of the Child, 1,* 53–74.

SPITZ, R. A. (1946). Anaclitic depression. *Psychoanalytic Study of the Child, 2,* 313–342.

SPIVACK, G., & SHURE, M. B. (1974). *Social adjustment of young children: A cognitive approach to solving real life problems.* San Francisco: Jossey-Bass.

SPOCK, B. (1946). *Commonsense book of baby and child care.* New York: Duell, Sloan & Pearce.

SPOCK, B., & ROTHENBERG, M. B. (1985). *Dr. Spock's baby and child care.* New York: Dutton.

SPRAGUE, R. L., & SLEATOR, E. K. (1975). What is the proper dose of stimulant drugs in children? *International Journal of Mental Health, 4,* 75–104.

SPREEN, O., TUPPER, D., RISSER, A., TUOKKO, H., & EDGELL, D. (1984). *Human developmental neuropsychology.* New York: Oxford University Press.

SPRIGLE, J. E., & SCHAEFER, L. (1985). Longitudinal evaluation of the effects of two compensatory preschool programs on fourth-through sixth-grade students. *Developmental Psychology, 21,* 702–708.

SROUFE, L. A. (1977). Wariness of strangers and the study of infant development. *Child Development, 48,* 731–746.

SROUFE, L. A. (1978). Attachment and the roots of competence. *Human Nature, 1*(10), 50–57.

SROUFE, L. A. (1979). Socioemotional development. In J. D. Osofsky (Ed.), *Handbook of infant development* (pp. 462–516). New York: Wiley.

SROUFE, L. A. (1983). Infant-caregiver attachment and patterns of adaptation in preschool: The roots of maladaptation. In M. Perlmutter (Ed.), *Minnesota Symposia on Child Psychology* (Vol. 16, pp. 41–83). Hillsdale, NJ: Erlbaum.

SROUFE, L. A. (1985). Attachment classification from the perspective of infant-caregiver relationships and infant temperament. *Child Development, 56,* 1–14.

SROUFE, L. A., FOX, N. E., & PANCAKE, V. R. (1983). Attachment and dependency in developmental perspective. *Child Development, 54,* 1615–1627.

SROUFE, L. A., & WATERS, E. (1976). The ontogenesis of smiling and laughter: A perspective on the organization of development in infancy. *Psychological Review, 83,* 173–189.

SROUFE, L. A., & WUNSCH, J. P. (1972). The development of laughter in the first year of life. *Child Development, 43,* 1324–1344.

ST. JOHN, N. H. (1975). *School desegregation: Outcomes for children.* New York: Wiley.

STANBURY, J. B., WYNGAARDEN, J. B., & FREDRICKSON, D. S. (1983). *The metabolic basis of inherited disease.* New York: McGraw-Hill.

STANHOPE, L., BELL, R. Q., & PARKER-COHEN, N. Y. (1987). Temperament and helping behavior in preschool children. *Developmental Psychology, 23,* 347–353.

STANKOV, L., HORN, J. L., ROY, T. (1980). On the relationship between Gf/Gc theory and Jensen's Level I/Level II theory. *Journal of Educational Psychology, 72,* 796–809.

STANLEY, J. C. (1976). The case for extreme educational acceleration of intellectually brilliant youths. *Gifted Child Quarterly, 20,* 66–75.

STANLEY, J. C. (1978). Radical acceleration: Recent educational innovation of Johns Hopkins University. *Gifted Child Quarterly, 22,* 63–67.

STARR, R. H., JR. (1979). Child abuse. *American Psychologist, 34,* 872–878.

STAUB, E. (1974). Helping a distressed person: Social, personality, and stimulus determinants. In L. Berkowitz (Ed.), *Advances in experimental social psychology* (Vol. 7, pp. 293–341). New York: Academic Press

STECHLER, G., & HALTON, A. (1982). Prenatal influences on human development. In B. B. Wolman (Ed.), *Handbook of developmental psychology* (pp. 175–189). Englewood Cliffs, NJ: Prentice-Hall.

STEIN, A. (1983). Pregnancy in gravidas over age 35 years. *Journal of Nurse-Midwifery, 28,* 17–20.

STEIN, A. H. (1967). Imitation of resistance to temptation. *Child Development, 38,* 157–169.

STEIN, A. H. (1971). The effects of sex-role standards for achievement and sex-role preference on three determinants of achievement motivation. *Developmental Psychology, 4,* 219–231.

STEIN, A. H., & SMITHELLS, J. (1969). Age and sex differences in children's sex-role standards about achievement. *Developmental Psychology, 1,* 252–259.

STEIN, Z., SUSSER, M., SAENGER, G., & MAROLLA, F. (1975). *Famine and human development: The Dutch hunger winter of 1944–1945.* New York: Oxford.

STEINBERG, L. (1986). Latchkey children and susceptibility to peer pressure: An ecological analysis. *Developmental Psychology, 22,* 433–439.

STEINBERG, L. (1988). Simple solutions to a complex problem: A response to Rodman, Pratto, & Nelson. *Developmental Psychology, 24,* 295–296.

STEINBERG, L., CATALANO, R., & DOOLEY, D. (1981). Economic antecedents of child abuse and neglect. *Child Development, 52,* 975–985.

STEINER, J. E. (1979). Human facial expression in response to taste and smell stimulation. In H. W. Reese & L. P. Lipsitt (Eds.), *Advances in child development and behavior* (Vol. 13, pp. 257–295). New York: Academic Press.

STEINMAN, S. (1981). The experience of children in a joint-custody arrangement: A report of a study. *American Journal of Orthopsychiatry, 51,* 403–414.

STEINMETZ, J. I., & BATTIG, W. F. (1969). Clustering and priority of free recall of newly learned items in children. *Developmental Psychology, 1,* 503–507.

STENBERG, C. (1982). The development of anger facial expressions in infancy. *Dissertation Abstracts International, 43,* 2359B. (University Microfilms No. 82-29,135)

STENBERG, C., CAMPOS, J., & EMDE, R. (1983). The facial expression of anger in seven-month-old infants. *Child Development, 54,* 178–184.

STENCHEVER, M. A., WILLIAMSON, R. A., LEONARD, J., KARP, L. E., LEY, B., SHY, K., & SMITH, D. (1981). Possible relationship between in utero diethylstilbesterol exposure and male infertility. *American Journal of Obstetrics and Gynecology, 140,* 186–193.

STENE, J., STENE, E., & STENGEL-RUTKOWSKI, S. (1981). Paternal age and Down's syndrome. Data from prenatal diagnosis (DFG). *Human Genetics, 59,* 119–124.

STERN, M., & HILDEBRANDT, K. A. (1986). Prematurity stereotyping: Effects on mother-infant interaction. *Child Development, 57,* 308–315.

STERNBERG, R. J. (1977). *Intelligence, information processing, and analogical reasoning: The componential analysis of human abilities.* Hillsdale, NJ: Erlbaum.

STERNBERG, R. J. (1980). Sketch of a componential subtheory of human intelligence. *Behavioral and Brain Sciences, 3,* 573–614.

STERNBERG, R. J. (1981). Testing and cognitive psychology. *American Psychologist, 36,* 1181–1189.

STERNBERG, R. J. (1982, April). Who's intelligent? *Psychology Today, 16*(4), 30–39.

STERNBERG, R. J. (1984). Evaluation of the Kaufman Assessment Battery for Children from an information processing perspective. *Journal of Special Education, 18,* 269–279.

STERNBERG, R. J. (1985a). *Beyond IQ: A triarchic theory of human intelligence.* New York: Cambridge University Press.

STERNBERG, R. J. (1985b). Cognitive approaches to intelligence. In B. B. Wolman (Ed.), *Handbook of intelligence* (pp. 59–118). New York: Wiley.

STERNBERG, R. J., CONWAY, B. E., KETRON, J. L., & BERNSTEIN, M. (1981). People's conceptions of intelligence. *Journal of Personality and Social Psychology, 41,* 37–55.

STERNBERG, R. J., & DAVIDSON, J. E. (1985). Cognitive development in the gifted and talented. In F. D. Horowitz & M. O'Brien (Eds.), *The gifted and talented: Developmental perspectives* (pp. 37–74). Washington, DC: American Psychological Association.

STEVENS, J. H. (1984). Black grandmothers' and black adolescent mothers' knowledge about parenting. *Developmental Psychology, 20,* 1017–1025.

STEVENSON, D. L., & BAKER, D. P. (1987). The family-school relation and the child's school performance. *Child Development, 58,* 1348–1357.

STEVENSON, H. (1983). How children learn—the quest for a theory. In W. Kessen (Ed.), *Handbook of child psychology: Vol. 1. History, theory, and methods* (pp. 213–236). New York: Wiley.

STEVENSON, H. W., LEE, S. Y., & STIGLER, J. W. (1986). Mathematics achievement of Chinese, Japanese, and American children. *Science, 231,* 693–699.

STEVENSON, H. W., & SIEGEL, A. E. (Eds.) (1984). *Child development research and social policy.* Chicago: University of Chicago Press.

STEVENSON, H. W., STIGLER, J. W., LEE, S., LUCKER, G. W., LITAMURA, S., & HSU, C. (1985). Cognitive performance and academic achievement of Japanese, Chinese, and American children. *Child Development, 56,* 718–734.

STEVENSON, H. W., STIGLER, J. W., LUCKER, G. W., LEE, S. Y., HSU, C. C., & KITAMURA, S. (1986). Classroom behavior and achievement of Japanese, Chinese, and American Children. In R. Glaser (Ed.), *Advances in instructional psychology* (Vol. 3, pp. 153–204). Hillsdale, NJ: Erlbaum.

STEVENSON, M. R., & BLACK, K. N. (1988). Paternal absence and sex-role development. *Child Development, 59,* 793–814.

STEWART, D. A. (1982). *Children with sex chromosome aneuploidy: Follow-up studies.* New York: Alan R. Liss.

STEWART, R. B., MOBLEY, L. A., VAN TUYL, S. S., & SALVADOR, M. A. (1987). The firstborn's adjustment to the birth of a sibling: A longitudinal assessment. *Child Development, 58,* 341–355.

STIEFVATER, K., KURDEK, L. A., & ALLIK, J. (1986). Effectiveness of a short-term social problem-solving program for popular, rejected, neglected, and average fourth-grade children. *Journal of Applied Developmental Psychology, 7,* 33–43.

STIGLER, J. W., LEE, S., & STEVENSON, H. W. (1987). Mathematics classrooms in Japan, Taiwan, and the United States, *Child Development, 58,* 1272–1285.

STILLMAN, R. J. (1982). In utero exposure to diethylstilbesterol: Adverse effects on the reproductive tract and reproductive performance in male and female offspring. *American Journal of Obstetrics and Gynecology, 142,* 905–921.

STINI, W. A., WEBER, C. W., KEMBERLING, S. R., & VAUGHAN, L. A. (1980). Lean tissue growth and disease susceptibility in bottle-fed versus breast-fed infants. In L. S. Greene & F. E. Johnston (Eds.), *Social and biological predictors of nutritional status, physical growth, and neurological development* (pp. 61–79). New York: Academic Press.

STIPEK, D. J. (1981). Children's perceptions of their own and their classmates' ability. *Journal of Educational Psychology, 73,* 404–410.

STIPEK, D. J. (1984). Sex differences in children's attributions for success and failure on math and spelling tests. *Sex Roles, 11,* 969–981.

STIPEK, D. J., & HOFFMAN, J. M. (1980). Children's achievement related expectancies as a function of academic performance histories and sex. *Journal of Educational Psychology, 72,* 861–865.

STOCH, M. B., SMYTHE, P. M., MOODIE, A. D., & BRADSHAW, D. (1982). Psychosocial outcome and CT findings after gross undernourishment during infancy: A 20-year developmental study. *Developmental Medicine and Child Neurology, 24,* 419–436.

STODDART, T., & TURIEL, E. (1985). Children's concepts of cross-gender activities. *Child Development, 56,* 1241–1252.

STODOLSKY, S. S. (1988). *The subject matters.* Chicago: University of Chicago Press.

STODOLSKY, S. S., & LESSER, G. (1967). Learning patterns in the disadvantaged. *Harvard Educational Review, 37,* 546–593.

STOEL-GAMMON, C., & OTOMO, K. (1986). Babbling development of hearing-impaired and normally hearing subjects. *Journal of Speech and Hearing Disorders, 51,* 33–41.

STOHLBERG, A. L., CULLEN, P. M., & GARRISON, K. M. (1982). The divorce adjustment project: Preventive programming for children of divorce. *Journal of Preventive Psychiatry, 1,* 365–368.

STOLZ, H. R., & STOLZ, L. M. (1971). Somatic development of adolescent boys. In M. C. Jones, N. Bayley, J. W. MacFarlane, & M. P. Honzik (Eds.), *The course of human development* (pp. 27–53). Waltham, MA: Xerox Publishing.

STONEMAN, Z., BRODY, G. H., & MACKINNON, C. E. (1986). Same-sex and cross-sex siblings: Activity choices, roles, behavior, and gender stereotypes. *Sex Roles, 15,* 495–511.

STOTLAND, E. (1969). Exploratory investigations of empathy. In L. Berkowitz (Ed.), *Advances in experimental social psychology* (Vol. 4, pp. 271–314). New York: Academic Press.

STRAIN, P. S. (1977). An experimental analysis of peer social initiation on the behavior of withdrawn preschool children: Some training and generalization effects. *Journal of Abnormal Child Psychology, 5,* 445–455.

STRAUSS, M. A., GELLES, R. J., & STEINMETZ, S. (1980). *Behind closed doors.* New York: Doubleday.

STRAUSS, S., & LEVIN, I. (1981). Commentary on Siegler's "Developmental sequences within and between concepts." *Monographs of the Society for Research in Child Development, 46* (2, Serial No. 189).

STRAYER, F. F., CHAPESKIE, T. R., & STRAYER, J. (1978). The perception of preschool social dominance. *Aggressive Behavior, 4,* 183–192.

STRAYER, F. F., & STRAYER, J. (1976). An ethological analysis of social agonism and dominance relations among preschool children. *Child Development, 47,* 980–989.

STRAYER, J. (1980). A naturalistic study of empathic behaviors and their relation to affective states and perspective-taking skills in preschoolers. *Child Development, 51,* 815–822.

STREISSGUTH, A. P., LANDESMAN-DWYER, S., MARTIN, J. C., & SMITH, D. W. (1980). Teratogenic effects of alcohol in humans and laboratory animals. *Science, 209,* 353–360.

STREISSGUTH, A. P., MARTIN, D. C., BARR, H. M., SANDMAN, B. M., KIRCHNER, G. L., & DARBY, B. L. (1984). Intrauterine alcohol and nicotine exposure: Attention and reaction time in 4-year-old children. *Developmental Psychology, 20,* 533–541.

STUNKARD, A. J. (1975). Obesity and the social environment. In A. Howard (Ed.), *Recent International Congress on Obesity* (pp. 178–190). London: Newman Publishing.

STUNKARD, A. J., D'AQUILI, E., FOX, S., & FILION, R. D. L. (1972). Influence of social class on obesity and thinness in children. *Journal of the American Medical Association, 221,* 579–584.

STYCZYNSKI, L. E., & LANGLOIS, J. H. (1977). The effects of familiarity on behavioral stereotypes associated with physical attractiveness in young children. *Child Development, 48,* 1137–1141.

SUDHALTER, V., & BRAINE, M. D. S. (1985). How does comprehension of passives develop? A comparison of actional and experiential verbs. *Journal of Child Language, 12,* 455–470.

SULLIVAN, H. S. (1953). *The interpersonal theory of psychiatry.* New York: Norton.

SULLIVAN, J. W., & HOROWITZ, F. D. (1983). The effects of intonation on infant attention: The role of the rising intonation contour. *Journal of Child Language, 10,* 521–534.

SUOMI, S. (1982). Biological foundations and developmental psychobiology. In C. B. Kopp & J. B. Krakow (Eds.), *The child: Development in a social context* (pp. 42–91). Reading, MA: Addison-Wesley.

SUOMI, S. J., & HARLOW, H. F. (1978). Production and alleviation of depressive behaviors in monkeys. In J. Maser & M. Seligman (Eds.), *Psychopathology: Experimental models* (pp. 131–173). San Francisco: W. H. Freeman.

SUPER, C. M. (1981). Behavioral development in infancy. In R. H. Monroe, R. L. Monroe, & B. B. Whiting, (Eds.), *Handbook of cross-cultural human development* (pp. 181–270). New York: Garland.

SURANSKY, V. P. (1982). *The erosion of childhood.* Chicago: University of Chicago Press.

SURGEON GENERAL'S ADVISORY ON ALCOHOL AND PREGNANCY (1981). *FDA Drug Bulletin, 11*(2), 9–10.

SUSANNE, C. (1975). Genetic and environmental influences in morphological characteristics. *Annals of Human Biology, 2,* 279–287.

SUSKIND, R. M. (1977). Characteristics and causation of protein-calorie malnutrition in the infant and preschool child. In L. S. Greene (Ed.), *Malnutrition, behavior, and social organization* (pp. 1–17). New York: Academic Press.

SUSMAN, E. J., INOFF-GERMAIN, G., NOTTELMANN, E. D., LORIAUX, D. L., CUTLER, G. B., JR., & CHROUSOS, G. P. (1987). Hormones, emotional dispositions, and aggressive attributes in young adolescents. *Child Development, 58,* 1114–1134.

SUTTON-SMITH, B. (1966). Piaget on play: A critique. *Psychological Review, 783,* 104–110.

SUTTON-SMITH, B. (1975). A developmental structural account of riddles. In B. Kirschenblatt-Gimblett (Ed.), *Speech play* (pp. 111–119). The Hague: Mouton.

SVEJDA, M., & CAMPOS, J. (1982). The mother's voice as a regulator of the infant's behavior. Paper presented at the meeting of the International Conference on Infant Studies, Austin, Texas.

SWANN, W. B., & PITTMAN, T. S. (1977). Initiating play activity of children: The moderating influence of verbal cues on intrinsic motivation. *Child Development, 48,* 1125–1132.

TAITZ, L. S. (1971). Infantile over-nutrition among artificially fed infants in the Sheffield region. *British Medical Journal, 1,* 315.

TAKANISHI, R., DELEON, P., & PALLAK, M. S. (1983). Psychology and public policy affecting children, youth, and families. *American Psychologist, 38,* 67–69.

TANGRI, S. S. (1972). Determinants of occupational role innovation among college women. *Journal of Social Issues, 28,* 177–199.

TANNER, J. M. (1962). *Growth at adolescence* (2nd ed.). Oxford: Blackwell Scientific Publications.

TANNER, J. M. (1968, January). Earlier maturation in man. *Scientific American, 218*(1), 21–27.

TANNER, J. M. (1978a). *Fetus into man.* Cambridge, MA: Harvard University Press.

TANNER, J. M. (1978b). *Education and physical growth.* New York: International Universities Press.

TANNER, J. M., & INHELDER, B. (Eds.). (1956). *Discussions on child development* (Vol. 1). London: Tavistock Publications.

TANNER, J. M., & WHITEHOUSE, R. H. (1975). Revised standards for triceps and subscapular skinfolds in British children. *Archives of Disease in Childhood, 50,* 142–145.

TANNER, J. M., WHITEHOUSE, J. H., CAMERON, N., MARSHALL, W. A., HEALEY, M. J. R., & GOLDSTEIN, H. (1983). *Assessment of skeletal maturity and prediction of adult height* (TW2 method, 2nd ed.). New York: Academic Press.

TAPLIN, J. E., STAUDENMAYER, H., & TADDONIO, J. L. (1974). Developmental changes in conditional reasoning: Logical or linguistic? *Journal of Experimental Child Psychology, 17,* 360–373.

TAUBER, M. A. (1979). Parental socialization techniques and sex differences in children's play. *Child Development, 50,* 225–234.

TAYLOR, A. R., ASHER, S. R., & WILLIAMS, G. A. (1987). The social adaptation of mainstreamed mildly retarded children. *Child Development, 58,* 1321–1334.

TAYLOR, M., & GELMAN, S. A. (1988). Adjectives and nouns: Children's strategies for learning new words. *Child Development, 59,* 411–419.

TAYLOR, M. C., & HALL, J. A. (1982). Psychological androgyny: Theories, methods, and conclusions. *Psychological Bulletin, 92,* 347–366.

TAYLOR, S. P., & LEWIT, D. W. (1966). Social comparison and deception regarding ability. *Journal of Personality, 34,* 94–104.

TEMPLIN, M. C. (1957). Certain language skills in children: Their development and interrelationships. *University of Minnesota Institute of Child Welfare Monograph, 26.*

TENNES, K., EMDE, R. N., KISLEY, A., & METCALF, D. (1972). The stimulus barrier in early infancy: An exploration of some formulations of John Benjamin. In R. Holt and E. Peterfreund (Eds.), *Psychoanalysis and contemporary science* (Vol. 1, pp. 206–234). New York: Macmillan.

TENNEY, Y. J. (1975). The child's conception of organization and recall. *Journal of Experimental Child Psychology, 19,* 100–114.

TERMAN, L. (1925). *Genetic studies of genius: Vol. 1. Mental and physical traits of a thousand gifted children.* Stanford, CA: Stanford University Press.

TERMAN, L., & ODEN, M. H. (1959). *Genetic studies of genius: Vol. 1. The gifted group at midlife.* Stanford, CA: Stanford University Press.

TERR, L. C. (1980). The child as witness. In O. H. Schetky & E. P. Benedek (Eds.), *Child psychiatry and the law* (pp. 207–221). New York: Brunner/Mazel.

TERRACE, H. S. (1979). *Nim.* New York: Knopf.

TERRACE, H. S., PETITTO, L. A., SANDERS, R. J., & BEVER, T. G. (1980). On the grammatical capacity of apes. In K. E. Nelson (Ed.), *Children's language* (Vol. 2, pp. 371–495). New York: Gardner Press.

THELEN, E. (1983). Learning to walk is still an "old" problem: A reply to Zelazo. *Journal of Motor Behavior, 15,* 139–161.

THELEN E., FISHER, D. M., & RIDLEY-JOHNSON, R. (1984). The relationship between physical growth and a newborn reflex. *Infant Behavior and Development, 7,* 479–493.

THELEN, M. H., & KIRKLAND, K. D. (1976). On status and being imitated: Effects of reciprocal imitation. *Journal of Personality and Social Psychology, 33,* 691–697.

THEORELL, K., PRECHTL, H., & VOS, J. (1974). A polygraphic study of normal and abnormal newborn infants. *Neuropaediatrie, 5,* 279–317.

THEVENIN, D. M., EILERS, R. E., OLLER, D. K., & LAVOIE, L. (1985). Where's the drift in babbling drift? A cross-linguistic study. *Applied Psycholinguistics, 6,* 3–15.

THOMA, S. J. (1986). Estimating gender differences in the comprehension and preference of moral issues. *Developmental Review, 6,* 165–180.

THOMAS, A., & CHESS, S. (1977). *Temperament and development.* New York: Brunner/Mazel.

THOMAS, A., CHESS, S., & BIRCH, H. G. (1968). *Temperament and behavior disorders in children.* New York: New York University Press.

THOMAS, A., CHESS, S., & BIRCH, H. G. (1970, August). The origins of personality. *Scientific American, 223*(2), 102–109.

THOMAS, A., CHESS, S., & KORN, S. J. (1982). The reality of difficult temperament. *Merrill Palmer Quarterly, 28,* 1–20.

THOMAS, J. R., & FRENCH, K. E. (1985). Gender differences across age in motor performance: A meta-analysis. *Psychological Bulletin, 98,* 260–282.

THOMAS, N. G., & BERK, L. E. (1981). Effects of school environments on the development of young children's creativity. *Child Development, 52,* 1152–1162.

THOMAS, R. M. (1985). *Comparing theories of child development.* Belmont, CA: Wadsworth.

THOMPSON, J. G., & MYERS, N. A. (1985). Inferences and recall at ages four and seven. *Child Development, 56,* 1134–1144.

THOMPSON, R. A. (1986). Temperament, emotionality, and infant social cognition. In J. V. Lerner & R. M. Lerner (Eds.), *New directions for child development* (No. 30, pp. 35–52). San Francisco: Jossey-Bass.

THOMPSON, R. A. (1987). Empathy and emotional understanding: The early development of empathy. In N. Eisenberg & J. Strayer (Eds.), *Empathy and its development* (pp. 119–145). Cambridge, Eng.: Cambridge University Press.

THOMPSON, R. A., & HOFFMAN, M. L. (1980). Empathy and the development of guilt in children. *Developmental Psychology, 16,* 155–156.

THOMPSON, S. K. (1975). Gender labels and early sex role development. *Child Development, 46,* 339–347.

THOMPSON, S. K., & BENTLER, P. M. (1971). The priority of cues in sex discrimination by children and adults. *Developmental Psychology, 5,* 181–185.

THORNDIKE, R. L., HAGEN, E. P., & SATTLER, J. M. (1986). *The Stanford-Binet Intelligence Scale: Guide for administering and scoring* (4th ed.). Chicago: Riverside Publishing.

THURSTONE, L. L. (1938). Primary mental abilities. *Psychometric Monographs No. 1.* Chicago: University of Chicago Press.

THURSTONE, L. L., & THURSTONE, T. G. (1953). *Examiner manual for the Primary Mental Abilities for ages 5 to 7* (3rd ed.). Chicago: Science Research Associates.

TIZARD, B., CARMICHAEL, H., HUGHES, M., & PINKERTON, G. (1980). Four-year-olds talking to mothers and teacher. In L. A. Hersov & M. Berger (Eds.), *Language and language disorders in childhood* (pp. 49–76). London: Pergamon Press.

TIZARD, B., & HODGES, J. (1978). The effect of early institutional rearing on the behaviour problems and affectional relationships of four-year-old children. *Journal of Child Psychology and Psychiatry, 19,* 99–118.

TIZARD, B., & REES, J. (1975). The effect of early institutional rearing on the behaviour problems and affectional relationships of four-year-old children. *Journal of Child Psychology and Psychiatry, 16,* 61–73.

TOBIAS, P. V. (1975). Anthropometry among disadvantaged people: Studies in Southern Africa. In E. S. Watts, F. E. Johnston, & G. W. Lasker (Eds.), *Biosocial interrelations in population adaptation: World anthropology series* (pp. 287–305). The Hague: Mouton.

TOBIN-RICHARDS, M. H., BOXER, A. M., & PETERSEN, A. C. (1983). The psychological significance of pubertal change: Sex differences in perceptions of self during early adolescence. In J. Brooks-Gunn & A. C. Petersen (Eds.), *Girls at puberty: Biological and psychosocial perspectives* (pp. 127–154). New York: Plenum.

TODD, G., & PALMER, B. (1968). Social reinforcement of infant babbling. *Child Development, 39,* 591–596.

TOMASELLO, M., MANNLE, S., & KRUGER, A. C. (1986). Linguistic environment of 1- to 2-year-old twins. *Developmental Psychology, 22,* 169–176.

TOMEH, A. K. (1979). Sex role orientation and structural correlates. *Sociological Quarterly, 20,* 333–344.

TONER, I. J., MOORE, L. P., & ASHLEY, P. K. (1978). The effect of serving as a model of self-control on subsequent resistance to deviation in children. *Journal of Experimental Child Psychology, 26,* 85–91.

TONER, I. J., MOORE, L. P., & EMMONS, B. A. (1980). The effect of being labeled on subsequent self-control in children. *Child Development, 51,* 618–621.

TONER, I. J., PARKE, R. D., & YUSSEN, S. R. (1978). The effect of observation of model behavior on establishment and stability of resistance to deviation in children. *Journal of Genetic Psychology, 132,* 283–290.

TONER, I. J., & SMITH, R. A. (1977). Age and overt verbalization in delay maintenance behavior in children. *Journal of Experimental Child Psychology, 24,* 123–128.

TONGE, W. L., JAMES, D. S., & HILLAM, S. M. (1975). *Families without hope: A controlled study of 33 problem families.* Ashford, Eng.: Headley Bros.

TORRANCE, E. P. (1966). *The Torrance tests of creative thinking: Technical-norms manual.* Lexington, MA: Personnel Press.

TORRANCE, E. P. (1976). Creativity research in education: Still alive. In I. A. Taylor & J. W. Getzels (Eds.), *Perspectives in creativity* (pp. 278–296). Chicago: Aldine.

TORRANCE, E. P. (1986). Teaching creative and gifted learners. In M. C. Wittrock (Ed.), *Handbook of research on teaching* (3rd ed., pp. 630–647). New York: Macmillan.

TOUWEN, B. (1978). Variability and stereotypy in normal and deviant development. In J. Apley (Ed.), *Care of the handicapped child* (pp. 99–110). Philadelphia: Lippincott.

TOUWEN, B. C. L. (1984). Primitive reflexes — conceptual or semantic problem? In H. F. R. Prechtl (Ed.), *Continuity of neural functions from prenatal to postnatal life* (Clinics in Developmental Medicine No. 94, pp. 115–125). Philadelphia: Lippincott.

TOVERUD, K. U., STEARNS, G., & MACY, I. G. (1950). *Maternal nutrition and child health: An interpretive review.* Washington, DC: National Research Council.

TOWBIN, A. (1978). Cerebral dysfunctions related to perinatal organic damage: Clinical-neuropathologic correlations. *Journal of Abnormal Psychology, 87,* 617–635.

TOWER, R. B., SINGER, D. G., SINGER, J. L., & BIGGS, A. (1979). Differential effects of television programming on preschoolers' cognition, imagination, and social play. *American Journal of Orthopsychiatry, 49,* 265–281.

TRAUSE, M. A. (1977). Stranger responses: Effects of familiarity, stranger's approach, and sex of infant. *Child Development, 48,* 1657–1661.

TREHUB, S. E. (1976). The discrimination of foreign speech contrasts by infants and adults. *Child Development, 47,* 466–472.

TREHUB, S. E., SCHNEIDER, B. A., & ENDMAN, M. (1980). Developmental changes in infants' sensitivity to octave-band noises. *Journal of Experimental Child Psychology, 29,* 282–293.

TRICKETT, P. K., & KUCZYNSKI, L. (1986). Children's misbehaviors and parental discipline strategies in abusive and nonabusive families. *Developmental Psychology, 22,* 115–123.

TRIOLO, S. J., McKENRY, P. C., TISHLER, C. L., & BLYTH, D. A. (1984). Social and psychological discriminants of adolescent suicide: Age and sex differences. *Journal of Early Adolescence, 4,* 239–251.

TRIVERS, R. L. (1971). The evolution of reciprocal altruism. *Quarterly Review of Biology, 46,* 35–57.

TRONICK, E. Z., ALS, H., ADAMSON, L., WISE, S., & BRAZELTON, T. B. (1978). The infant's response to entrapment between contradictory messages in face-to-face interaction. *Journal of the American Academy of Child Psychiatry, 17,* 1–13.

TULVING, E. (1972). Episodic and semantic memory. In E. Tulving & W. Donaldson (Eds.), *Organization of memory* (pp. 382–403). New York: Academic Press.

TUNMER, W. E., & BOWEY, J. A. (1984). Metalinguistic awareness and reading acquisition. In W. E. Tunmer, C. Pratt, & M. L. Herriman (Eds.), *Metalinguistic awareness in children: Theory, research, and implications* (pp. 144–168). New York: Springer-Verlag.

TUNMER, W. E., BOWEY, J. A., & GRIEVE, R. (1983). The development of young children's awareness of the word as a unit of spoken language. *Journal of Psycholinguistic Research, 12,* 567–594.

TUNMER, W. E., & NESDALE, A. R. (1982). The effects of digraphs and pseudo-words on phonemic segmentation in young children. *Journal of Applied Psycholinguistics, 3,* 299–311.

TURIEL, E. (1977). Conflict and transition in adolescent moral development. II: The resolution of disequilibrium through structural reorganization. *Child Development, 48,* 634–637.

TURIEL, E. (1983). *The development of social knowledge: Morality and convention.* New York: Cambridge University Press.

TURNER, C. W., & GOLDSMITH, D. (1976). Effects of toy guns and airplanes on children's antisocial free play behavior. *Journal of Experimental Child Psychology, 21,* 303–315.

TURNURE, C. (1971). Response to voice of mother and stranger by babies in the first year. *Developmental Psychology, 4,* 182–190.

TYACK, D., & INGRAM, D. (1977). Children's production and comprehension of questions. *Journal of Child Language, 4,* 211–224.

ULLIAN, D. Z. (1976). The development of conceptions of masculinity and femininity. In B. Lloyd & J. Archer (Eds.), *Exploring sex differences* (pp. 25–47). London: Academic Press.

UNGERER, J. A., ZELAZO, P. R., KEARSLEY, R. B., & O'LEARY, K. (1981). Developmental changes in the representation of objects in symbolic play from 19–34 months of age. *Child Development, 52,* 186–195.

URBAIN, E. S., & KENDALL, P. C. (1980). Review of social-cognitive problem-solving interventions with children. *Psychological Bulletin, 88,* 109–143.

URBERG, K. A. (1979). The development of androgynous sex-role concepts in young children. Paper presented at the meeting of the Society for Research in Child Development, San Francisco.

U.S. BUREAU OF THE CENSUS. (1987a). *Current population reports,* Series P-20. Washington, DC: U.S. Government Printing Office.

U.S. BUREAU OF THE CENSUS. (1987b). *Who's minding the kids? Current population reports,* Series P-70. Washington, DC: U.S. Government Printing Office.

U.S. DEPARTMENT OF HEALTH AND HUMAN SERVICES. (1980). *The health consequences of smoking for women: A report of the Surgeon General.* Washington, DC: U.S. Government Printing Office.

U.S. DEPARTMENT OF HEALTH AND HUMAN SERVICES, NATIONAL CENTER ON CHILD ABUSE AND NEGLECT. (1981). *Study findings: National study of the incidence and severity of child abuse and neglect.* Washington, DC: U.S. Government Printing Office.

U.S. DEPARTMENT OF HEALTH, EDUCATION, AND WELFARE. (1979). *Smoking and health: A report of the Surgeon General.* Washington, DC: U.S. Government Printing Office.

U.S. DEPARTMENT OF LABOR, BUREAU OF LABOR STATISTICS. (1986, February). *Monthly Labor Review.* Washington, DC: U.S. Government Printing Office.

U.S. DEPARTMENT OF LABOR, BUREAU OF LABOR STATISTICS. (1987, August 12). *News.* Washington, DC: U.S. Government Printing Office.

U.S. DEPARTMENT OF LABOR, BUREAU OF LABOR STATISTICS. (1988, January). *Monthly labor review.* Washington, DC: U.S. Government Printing Office.

U.S. DEPARTMENT OF LABOR, WOMEN'S BUREAU. (1982). *Employers and child care: Establishing services through the workplace. Pamphlet No. 23.* Washington, DC: U.S. Government Printing Office.

UŽGIRIS, I. C. (1964). Situational generality of conservation. *Child Development, 35,* 831–841.

UŽGIRIS, I. C. (1973). Patterns of cognitive development in infancy. *Merrill-Palmer Quarterly, 19,* 181–204.

UŽGIRIS, I. C., & HUNT, J. M. V. (1975). *Assessment in infancy: Ordinal scales of psychological development.* Urbana: University of Illinois Press.

VALIAN, V. (1986). Syntactic categories in the speech of young children. *Developmental Psychology, 22,* 562–579.

VALLIANT, G. (1977). *Adaptation to life.* Boston: Little, Brown.

VAN HEKKEN, S. M. J., VERGEER, M. M., & HARRIS, P. L. (1980). Am-

biguity of reference and listeners' reaction in a naturalistic setting. *Journal of Child Language, 7,* 555–563.

VAN IJZENDOORN, M. H., & KROONENBERG, P. M. (1988). Cross-cultural patterns of attachment: A meta-analysis of the Strange Situation. *Child Development, 59,* 147–156.

VANDELL, D. L. (1980). Sociability with peer and mother during the first year. *Developmental Psychology, 16,* 355–361.

VANDELL, D. L., & MUELLER, E. C. (1977). The effects of group size on toddler social interaction with peers. Paper presented at the meeting of the Society for Research in Child Development, New Orleans.

VANDELL, D. L., & MUELLER, E. C. (1980). Peer play and friendships during the first two years. In H. C. Foot, A. J. Chapman, & J. R. Smith (Eds.), *Friendship and social relations in children* (pp. 181–208). New York: Wiley.

VANDELL, D. L., & POWERS, C. (1983). Day care quality and children's free play activities. *American Journal of Orthopsychiatry, 53,* 493–500.

VANDELL, D. L., & WILSON, K. S. (1987). Infants' interactions with mother, sibling, and peer: Contrasts and relations between interaction systems. *Child Development, 58,* 176–186.

VANDELL, D. L., WILSON, K. S., & BUCHANAN, N. R. (1980). Peer interaction in the first year of life: An examination of its structure, content, and sensitivity to toys. *Child Development, 51,* 481–488.

VAUGHN, B., DEAN, K., & WATERS, E. (1983). The impact of out-of-home care on child-mother attachment quality: Another look at some enduring questions. Presentation to the Department of Pediatric Psychology, Rush University Medical School, Chicago.

VAUGHN, B., EGELAND, B., SROUFE, L. A., & WATERS, E. (1979). Individual differences in infant-mother attachment at twelve and eighteen months: Stability and change in families under stress. *Child Development, 50,* 971–975.

VAUGHN, B. E., GOVE, F. L., & EGELAND, B. (1980). The relationship between out-of-home care and the quality of infant-mother attachment in an economically disadvantaged population. *Child Development, 51,* 1203–1214.

VAUGHN, B. E., KOPP, C. B., & KRAKOW, J. B. (1984). The emergence and consolidation of self-control from eighteen to thirty months of age: Normative trends and individual differences. *Child Development, 55,* 990–1004.

VAUGHN, B. E., TARALDSON, B., CRICHTON, L., & EGELAND, B. (1980). Relationships between neonatal behavior organization and infant behavior during the first year of life. *Infant Behavior and Development, 3,* 78–89.

VEGA-LAHR, N., & FIELD, T. M. (1986). Type A behavior in preschool children. *Child Development, 57,* 1333–1348.

VENTURA, S. J. (1982). Trends in first births to older mothers, 1970–79. *Monthly Vital Statistics Report, 31,* 1–16.

VIANO, E. (1974). Attitudes toward child abuse among American professionals. Paper presented at the meeting of the International Society for Research on Aggression, Toronto.

VIETZE, P., FALSEY, S., O'CONNOR, S., SANDLER, H., SHERROD, K., & ALTEMEIER, W. (1980). Newborn behavioral and interactional characteristics of nonorganic failure-to-thrive infants. In T. Field, S. Goldberg, D. Stern, & A. Sostek (Eds.), *High-risk infants and children* (pp. 5–23). New York: Academic Press.

VINE, I. (1973). The role of facial visual signalling in early social development. In M. von Cranach & I. Vine (Eds.), *Social communication and movement: Studies of men and chimpanzees* (pp. 195–298). London: Academic Press.

VITRO, F. T. (1969). The effects of probability of test success, opportunity to cheat, and test importance on the incidence of cheating. Unpublished doctoral dissertation, Iowa State University, Ames.

VLIESTRA, A. G. (1982). Children's responses to task instructions: Age changes and training effects. *Child Development, 53,* 534–542.

VOGEL, S. R., BROVERMAN, I. K., BROVERMAN, D. M., CLARKSON, F., & ROSENKRANTZ, P. (1970). Maternal employment and perception of sex roles among college students. *Developmental Psychology, 3,* 384–391.

VURPILLOT, E. (1968). The development of scanning strategies and their relation to visual differentiation. *Journal of Experimental Child Psychology, 6,* 632–650.

VYGOTSKY, L. S. (1962). *Thought and language.* Cambridge, MA: MIT Press. (Original work published 1934)

VYGOTSKY, L. S. (1978). *Mind in society: The development of higher mental processes.* Cambridge, MA: Harvard University Press. (Original works published 1930, 1933, and 1935)

WABER, D. P. (1976). Sex differences in cognition: A function of maturation rate? *Science, 192,* 572–574.

WACHS, T. D. (1975). Relation of infants' performance on Piaget scales between twelve and twenty-four months and their Stanford-Binet performance at thirty-one months. *Child Development, 46,* 929–935.

WACHS, T. D., & GRUEN, G. E. (1971). The effects of chronological age, trials, and list characteristics upon children's category clustering. *Child Development, 42,* 1217–1228.

WADA, J. A., CLARK, R., & HAMM, A. (1975). Cerebral hemispheric asymmetry in humans. *Archives of Neurology, 32,* 239–246.

WADDINGTON, C. H. (1957). *The strategy of the genes.* London: Unwin & Hyman.

WADE, T. C., BAKER, T. B., MORTON, T. L., & BAKER, J. L. (1978). The status of psychological testing in clinical psychology: Relationships between test use and professional activities and orientations. *Journal of Personality Assessment, 42,* 3–10.

WAGNER, M. E., SCHUBERT, H. J. P., & SCHUBERT, D. S. P. (1985). Family size effects: A review. *Journal of Genetic Psychology, 146,* 65–78.

WAHLER, R. G. (1967). Infants' social attachments: A reinforcement theory interpretaton and investigation. *Child Development, 38,* 1079–1088.

WALBERG, H. J. (1986). Synthesis of research on teaching. In M. C. Wittrock (Ed.), *Handbook of research on teaching* (3rd ed., pp. 214–229). New York: Macmillan.

WALK, R. D., & GIBSON, E. J. (1961). A comparative and analytic study of visual depth perception. *Psychological Monographs, 75* (15, Whole No. 519).

WALKER, L. J. (1980). Cognitive and perspective-taking prerequisites for moral development. *Child Development, 51,* 131–139.

WALKER, L. J., & DE VRIES, B. (1985). Moral stages/moral orientations: Do the sexes really differ? Paper presented at the meeting of the American Psychological Association, Los Angeles.

WALKER, L. J., DE VRIES, B., & TREVETHAN, S. D. (1987). Moral stages and moral orientations in real-life and hypothetical dilemmas. *Child Development, 58,* 842–858.

WALKER, L. J., & RICHARDS, B. S. (1979). Stimulating transitions in moral reasoning as a function of stage of cognitive development. *Developmental Psychology, 15,* 95–103.

WALKER-ANDREWS, A. S. (1986). Intermodal perception of expressive behaviors: Relation of eye and voice? *Developmental Psychology, 22,* 373–377.

WALLACE, J. R., CUNNINGHAM, T. F., & DEL MONTE, V. (1984). Change and stability in self-esteem between late childhood and early adolescence. *Journal of Early Adolescence, 4,* 253–257.

WALLACH, G. P. (1984). Later language learning: Syntactic structures and strategies. In G. P. Wallach & K. G. Butler (Eds.), *Language learning disabilities in school age children* (pp. 82–102). Baltimore: Williams and Wilkins.

WALLACH, M. A. (1985). Creativity testing and giftedness. In F. D. Horowitz & M. O'Brien (Eds.), *The gifted and talented: Developmental perspectives* (pp. 99–123). Washington, DC: American Psychological Association.

WALLACH, M. A., & KOGAN, N. (1965). *Modes of thinking in young children.* New York: Holt.

WALLER, J. H. (1971). Achievement and social mobility: Relationships among IQ score, education, and occupation in two generations. *Social Biology, 18,* 252–259.

WALLERSTEIN, J. S. (1984). Children of divorce: Preliminary report of a ten-year follow-up of young children. *American Journal of Orthopsychiatry, 54,* 444–458.

WALLERSTEIN, J. S. (1985). Children of divorce: Preliminary report of a ten-year follow-up of older children and adolescents. *Journal of the American Academy of Child Psychiatry, 24,* 545–553.

WALLERSTEIN, J. S., & KELLY, J. B. (1975). The effects of parental divorce: Experiences of the preschool child. *Journal of the American Academy of Child Psychiatry, 14,* 600–616.

WALLERSTEIN, J. S., & KELLY, J. B. (1980). *Surviving the break-up: How children and parents cope with divorce.* New York: Basic Books.

WALLIS, C. (1985, December 9). Children having children. *Time, 126,* 78–82.

WALSHOK, M. L. (1978). Occupational values and family roles: A descriptive study of women working in blue-collar and service occupations. *Urban and Social Change Review, 11,* 12–20.

WALTERS, J., PEARCE, D., & DAHMS, L. (1957). Affectional and aggressive behavior of preschool children. *Child Development, 28,* 15–26.

WALTERS, R. H., & ANDRES, D. (1967). Punishment procedures and self-control. Paper presented at the meeting of the American Psychological Association, Washington, DC.

WALTERS, R. H., PARKE, R. D., & CANE, V. A. (1965). Timing of punishment and the observation of consequences to others as determinants of response inhibition. *Journal of Experimental Child Psychology, 2,* 10–30.

WANG, M. C., & BAKER, E. T. (1985–1986). Mainstreaming programs: Design features and effects. *Journal of Special Education, 19,* 503–521.

WANSKA, S. K., & BEDROSIAN, J. L. (1985). Conversational structure and topic performance in mother-child interaction. *Journal of Speech and Hearing Research, 28,* 579–584.

WARD, S., REALE, G., & LEVINSON, D. (1972). Children's perceptions, explanations, and judgments of television advertising: A further exploration. In E. A. Rubinstein, G. A. Comstock, & J. P. Murray (Eds.), *Television and social behavior* (Vol. 4, pp. 468–490). Washington, DC: U.S. Government Printing Office.

WARD, S., WACKMAN, D., & WARTELLA, E. (1977). *How children learn to buy: The development of consumer information-processing skills.* Beverly Hills, CA: Sage.

WATERMAN, A. S. (1982). Identity development from adolescence to adulthood: An extension of theory and a review of research. *Developmental Psychology, 18,* 341–358.

WATERMAN, A. S. (1984). Identity formation: Discovery or creation? *Journal of Early Adolescence, 4,* 329–341.

WATERMAN, A. S., GEARY, P. S., & WATERMAN, C. K. (1974). Longitudinal study of changes in ego identity status from the freshman to the senior year at college. *Developmental Psychology, 10,* 387–392.

WATERMAN, A. S., & GOLDMAN, A. (1976). A longitudinal study of ego identity development at a liberal arts college. *Journal of Youth and Adolescence, 5,* 361–369.

WATERMAN, A. S., & WATERMAN, C. K. (1971). A longitudinal study of changes in ego identity status during the freshman year at college. *Developmental Psychology, 5,* 167–173.

WATERS, E. (1978). The reliability and stability of individual differences in infant-mother attachment. *Child Development, 49,* 483–494.

WATERS, E., VAUGHN, B. E., & EGELAND, B. R. (1980). Individual differences in infant-mother attachment relationships at age one: Antecedents in neonatal behavior in an urban, economically disadvantaged sample. *Child Development, 51,* 208–216.

WATERS, H. S. (1982). Memory development in adolescence: Relationships between metamemory, strategy use, and performance. *Journal of Experimental Child Psychology, 33,* 183–195.

WATKINS, B., CALVERT, S., HUSTON-STEIN, A., & WRIGHT, J. C. (1980). Children's recall of television material: Effects of presentation mode and adult labeling. *Developmental Psychology, 16,* 672–674.

WATSON, J. B. (1913). Psychology as the behaviorist views it. *Psychological Review, 20,* 158–177.

WATSON, J. B. (1928). *Psychological care of infant and child.* New York: Norton.

WATSON, J. B., & RAYNOR, R. (1920). Conditioned emotional reactions. *Journal of Experimental Psychology, 3,* 1–14.

WATSON, J. D., & CRICK, F. H. C. (1953). Molecular structure of nucleic acids. *Nature, 171,* 737–738.

WATSON, J. S., & RAMEY, C. T. (1972). Reactions to response-contingent stimulation in early infancy. *Merrill-Palmer Quarterly, 18,* 219–229.

WATSON, M. W., & FISCHER, K. W. (1977). A developmental sequence of agent use in late infancy. *Child Development, 48,* 828–836.

WAXLER, C. Z., YARROW, M. R., & SMITH, J. B. (1977). Perspective-taking and prosocial behavior. *Developmental Psychology, 13,* 87–88.

WECHSLER, D. (1967). *Manual for the Wechsler Preschool and Primary Scale of Intelligence.* New York: The Psychological Corporation.

WECHSLER, D. (1974). *Manual for the Wechsler Intelligence Scale for Children — Revised.* New York: The Psychological Corporation.

WEHREN, A., DELISI, R., & ARNOLD, M. (1981). The development of noun definition. *Journal of Child Language, 8,* 165–175.

WEIL, W. B. (1975). Infantile obesity. In M. Winick (Ed.), *Childhood obesity* (pp. 61–72). New York: Wiley.

WEINER, B. (Ed.) (1974). *Achievement motivation and attribution theory.* Morristown, NJ: General Learning Press.

WEINER, B. (1987). *An attributional theory of motivation and emotion.* New York: Springer-Verlag.

WEINRAUB, M., CLEMENS, L. P., SOCKLOFF, A., ETHRIDGE, T., GRACELY, E., & MYERS, B. (1984). The development of sex role stereotypes in the third year: Relationships to gender labeling, gender identity, sex-typed toy preference, and family characteristics. *Child Development, 55,* 1493–1503.

WEINRAUB, M., & LEWIS, M. (1977). The determinants of children's responses to separation. *Monographs of the Society for Research in Child Development, 42*(4, Serial No. 172).

WEINTRAUB, K. S., & FURMAN, L. N. (December 1987). Child care: Quality, regulation, and research. *Society for Research in Child Development Social Policy Report, 2*(4).

WEISBERG, P. (1963). Social and non-social conditioning of infant vocalizations. *Child Development, 34,* 377–388.

WEISNER, T., & GALLIMORE, R. (1977). My brother's keeper: Child and sibling caretaking. *Current Anthropology, 18,* 169–190.

WEISS, G., HECHTMAN, L., PERLMAN, T., HOPKINS, J., & WENER, A. (1979). Hyperactives as young adults. A controlled prospective ten-year follow-up of 75 children. *Archives of General Psychiatry, 36,* 675–681.

WEISS, G., MINDE, K., WERRY, J. S., DOUGLAS, V. I., & NEMETH, E. (1971). Studies on the hyperactive child, VIII. Five-year follow-up. *Archives of General Psychiatry, 24,* 409–414.

WEISZ, J. R. (1978). Choosing problem-solving rewards and Halloween prizes: Delay of gratification and preference for symbolic reward as a function of development, motivation and personal investment. *Developmental Psychology, 14,* 66–78.

WEISZ, J. R., & McGUIRE, M. (1980). *Sex differences in the relation between attributions and learned helplessness in children.* Unpublished manuscript, University of North Carolina, Chapel Hill.

WEISZ, J. R., & ZIGLER, E. (1979). Cognitive development in retarded and non-retarded persons: Piagetian tests of the similar sequence hypothesis. *Psychological Bulletin, 86,* 831–851.

WEITZMAN, L. (1985). *The divorce revolution: The unexpected social and economic consequences for women and children in America.* New York: Free Press.

WELCH, R. L., HUSTON-STEIN, A., WRIGHT, J. C., & PLEHAL, R. (1979). Subtle sex-role cues in children's commercials. *Journal of Communication, 29*(3), 202–209.

WELLMAN, H. M. (1977). Preschoolers' understanding of memory relevant variables. *Child Development, 48,* 13–21.

WELLMAN, H. M. (1978). Knowledge of the interaction of memory variables: A developmental study of metamemory. *Developmental Psychology, 14,* 24–29.

WELLMAN, H. M. (1985). The child's theory of mind: The development of conceptions of cognition. In S. R. Yussen (Ed.), *The growth of reflection in children* (pp. 169–206). Orlando, FL: Academic Press.

WELLMAN, H. M., COLLINS, J., & GLIEBERMAN, J. (1981). Understanding the combination of memory variables: Developing conceptions of memory limitations. *Child Development, 52,* 1313–1317.

WELLMAN, H. M., CROSS, D., & BARTSCH, K. (1987). Infant search and object permanence: A meta-analysis of the A-not-B error. *Monographs of the Society for Research in Child Development, 51*(3, Serial No. 214).

WELLMAN, H. M., SOMERVILLE, S. C., & HAAKE, R. J. (1979). Development of search procedures in real-life spatial environments. *Developmental Psychology, 15,* 530–542.

WELLS, G. (1986). Variation in child language. In P. Fletcher & M. Garman (Eds.), *Language acquisition* (pp. 109–139). Cambridge, Eng.: Cambridge University Press.

WENGER, M. A. (1936). An investigation of conditioned responses in human infants. *University of Iowa Studies in Child Welfare, 12,* 1–90.

WERKER, J. S., & TEES, R. C. (1984). Cross-language speech perception: Evidence for perceptual reorganization during the first year of life. *Infant Behavior and Development, 7,* 49–63.

WERNER, E. E., & SMITH, R. S. (1979). An epidemiologic perspective on some antecedents and consequences of childhood mental health problems and learning disabilities. *Journal of the American Academy of Child Psychiatry, 18,* 292–306.

WERNER, E. E., & SMITH, R. S. (1982). *Vulnerable but invincible: A study of resilient children.* New York: McGraw-Hill.

WERNER, J. S, & SIQUELAND, E. R. (1978). Visual recognition memory in the preterm infant. *Infant Behavior and Development, 1,* 79–94.

WERTSCH, J. (1986). *Mind in context: A Vygotskian approach.* Paper presented at the American Educational Research Association meeting. San Francisco.

WESTOFF, C. F. (1978). Some speculations on the future of marriage and the family. *Family Planning Perspectives, 10,* 79–83.

WHALEN, C. K. (1983). Hyperactivity, learning problems, and the attention deficit disorders. In T. H. Ollendick & M. Hersen (Eds.), *Handbook of child psychopathology* (pp. 151–199). New York: Plenum.

WHEELER, M. E., & HESS, K. W. (1976). *Journal of Behavior Therapy and Experimental Psychiatry, 7,* 235–241.

WHISNANT, L., & ZEGANS, L. (1975). A study of attitudes toward menarche in white middle-class American adolescent girls. *American Journal of Psychiatry, 132,* 809–814.

WHITCOMB, D., SHAPIRO, E. R., & STELLWAGEN, L. D. (1985). *When the victim is a child: Issues for judges and prosecutors.* Washington, DC: National Institute of Justice.

WHITE, B. (1985). *The first three years of life.* Englewood Cliffs, N.J.: Prentice-Hall.

WHITE, B., & HELD, R. (1966). Plasticity of sensorimotor development in the human infant. In J. F. Rosenblith & W. Allinsmith (Eds.), *The causes of behavior* (pp. 60–70). Boston: Allyn & Bacon.

WHITE, R. W. (1959). Motivation reconsidered: The concept of competence. *Psychological Review, 66,* 297–333.

WHITE, S. H., & PILLEMER, D. B. (1979). Childhood amnesia and the development of a socially accessible memory system. In J. F. Kihlstrom & F. J. Evans (Eds.), *Functional disorders of memory* (pp. 29–73). Hillsdale, NJ: Erlbaum.

WHITEHURST, G. J. (1982). Language development. In B. B. Wolman (Ed.), *Handbook of developmental psychology* (pp. 367–386). New York: Wiley.

WHITEHURST, G. J., FISCHEL, J. E., CAULFIELD, M. B., DeBARYSHE, B. D., & VALDEZ-MENCHACA, M. C. (in press). Assessment and treatment of early expressive language delay. In P. R. Zelazo & R. Barr (Eds.), *Challenges to developmental paradigms: Implications for assessment and treatment.* Hillsdale, NJ: Erlbaum.

WHITEHURST, G. J., & VALDEZ-MENCHACA, M. C. (1988). What is the role of reinforcement in early language acquisition? *Child Development, 59,* 430–440.

WHITING, B. B., & EDWARDS, C. P. (1974). A cross-cultural analysis of sex differences in the behavior of children aged three through 11. In S. Chess & A. Thomas (Eds.), *Annual progress in child psychiatry and child development* (pp. 32–49). New York: Brunner/Mazel.

WHITING, B. B., & WHITING, J. W. M. (1975). *Children of six cultures: A psychocultural analysis*. Cambridge, MA: Harvard University Press.

WHITLEY, B. E., JR. (1983). Sex role orientation and self-esteem: A critical meta-analytic review. *Journal of Personality and Social Psychology, 44*, 765–778.

WHITLEY, B. E., JR. (1985). Children's causal attributions for success and failure in achievement settings: A meta-analysis. *Journal of Educational Psychology, 77*, 608–616.

WHITMORE, J. R., & MAKER, C. J. (1985). *Intellectual giftedness in disabled persons*. Rockville, MD: Aspen.

WICKENS, D. D., & WICKENS, C. (1940). A study of conditioning in the neonate. *Journal of Experimental Psychology, 26*, 94–102.

WIDMAYER, S., & FIELD, T. M. (1980). Effects of Brazelton demonstrations on early interactions of preterm infants and their teenage mothers. *Infant Behavior and Development, 3*, 78–89.

WIESENFELD, A. R., MALATESTA, C. Z., & DeLOACHE, J. S. (1981). Differential parental response to familiar and unfamiliar infant distress signals. *Infant Behavior and Development, 4*, 281–295.

WIKOFF, R. L. (1979). The WISC-R as a predictor of achievement. *Psychology in the Schools, 16*, 364–366.

WILLEMS, E. P. (1967). Sense of obligation to high school activities as related to school size and marginality of student. *Child Development, 38*, 1247–1260.

WILLERMAN, L. (1979). Effects of families on intellectual development. *American Psychologist, 34*, 923–929.

WILLIAMS, J. (1979). Reading instruction today. *American Psychologist, 34*, 917–922.

WILLIAMS, J. E., BENNETT, S. M., & BEST, D. L. (1975). Awareness and expression of sex stereotypes in young children. *Developmental Psychology, 11*, 635–642.

WILLIAMS, J. E., & BEST, D. L. (1982). *Measuring sex stereotypes: A thirty-nation study*. Beverly Hills, CA: Sage.

WILLIAMS, K. G., & GOULET, L. R. (1975). The effects of cuing and constraint instructions on children's free recall performance. *Journal of Experimental Child Psychology, 15*, 169–186.

WILLIAMS, T. M. (1986). *The impact of television: A natural experiment in three communities*. Orlando, FL: Academic Press.

WILSON, E. O. (1975). *Sociobiology: The new synthesis*. Cambridge, MA: Harvard University Press.

WILSON, J. G. (1973). *Environment and birth defects*. New York: Academic Press.

WILSON, M. N. (1986). The black extended family: An analytical consideration. *Developmental Psychology, 22*, 246–258.

WILSON, M. N., & TOLSON, T. F. J. (1985). An analysis of adult-child interaction patterns in three-generational black families. Charlottesville, VA: University of Virginia, Department of Psychology.

WILSON, R. S. (1976). Concordance in physical growth for monozygotic and dizygotic twins. *Annals of Human Biology, 3*, 1–10.

WILSON, R. S. (1983). The Louisville Twin Study: Developmental synchronies in behavior. *Child Development, 54*, 298–316.

WINCH, R. F. (1971). *The modern family* (3rd ed.). New York: Holt, Rinehart & Winston.

WINER, G. A., & KRONBERG, D. D. (1974). Children's responses to verbally and pictorially presented class-inclusion items and to a task of number conservation. *Journal of Genetic Psychology, 125*, 141–152.

WINICK, M., & NOBLE, A. (1966). Cellular response in rats during malnutrition at various ages. *Journal of Nutrition, 89*, 300–306.

WINICK, M., ROSSO, P., & WATERLOW, J. (1970). Cellular growth of cerebrum, cerebellum, and brain stem in normal and marasmic children. *Experimental Neurology, 26*, 393–400.

WINITZ, H. (1969). *Articulatory acquisition and behavior*. New York: Appleton-Century-Crofts.

WINNER, E. (1986, August). Where pelicans kiss seals. *Psychology Today, 20*(8), 25–35.

WINNER, E., ROSENSTIEL, A. K., & GARDNER, H. (1976). The development of metaphoric understanding. *Developmental Psychology, 12*, 289–297.

WINNICOTT, D. W. (1953). Transitional object and transitional phenomena. *International Journal of Psychoanalysis, 34*, 89–97.

WISHART, J. G., & BOWER, T. G. R. (1982). The development of spatial understanding in infancy. *Journal of Experimental Child Psychology, 33*, 363–385.

WISHART, J. G., BOWER, T. G. R., & DUNKELD, J. (1978). Reaching in the dark. *Perception, 7*, 507–512.

WISSLER, C. (1901). The correlation of mental and physical traits. *Psychological Monographs, 3* (6, Whole No. 16).

WITKIN, H. A., MEDNICK, S. A., SCHULSINGER, R., BAKKESTROM, E., CHRISTIANSEN, K. O., GOODENOUGH, D. R., HIRSCHHORN, K., LUNDSTEEN, C., OWEN, D. R., PHILIP, J., RUBIN, D. B., & STOCKING, M. (1976). Criminality in XYY and XXY men. *Science, 193*, 547–555.

WOHLWILL, J. F. (1973). *The study of behavioral development*. New York: Academic Press.

WOLFF, J. R. (1981). Some morphogenetic aspects of the development of the central nervous system. In K. Immelmann, G. W. Barlow, L. Petrinovich & M. Main (Eds.), *Behavioral development* (pp. 164–190). Cambridge, Eng.: Cambridge University Press.

WOLFF, P. H. (1963). Observations on the early development of smiling. In B. M. Foss (Ed.), *Determinants of infant behavior* (Vol. 2, pp. 113–138). London: Methuen.

WOLFF, P. H. (1966). The causes, controls and organization of behavior in the neonate. *Psychological Issues, 5*(1, Serial No. 17).

WOLFF, P. H. (1969). The natural history of crying and other vocalizations in early infancy. In B. M. Foss (Ed.), *Determinants of infant behavior* (Vol. 4, pp. 81–109). New York: Wiley.

WOODSON, E. M., WOODSON, R. H., JONES, N. G. BLURTON, POLLOCK, S. B., & EVANS, M. A. (1980). *Maternal smoking and newborn behavior*. Paper presented at the International Conference on Infant Studies, New Haven, CT.

WRIGHT, H. F. (1960). Observational child study. In P. Mussen (Ed.), *Handbook of research methods in child development* (pp. 71–139). New York: Wiley.

WRIGHT, H. F. (1967). *Recording and analyzing child behavior*. New York: Academic Press.

WRIGHT, J. C., HUSTON, A. C., ROSS, R. P., CLAVERT, S. L., ROLANDELLI, D., WEEKS, L. A., RAEISSI, P., & POTTS, R. (1984). Pace and continuity of television programs: Effects on children's attention and comprehension. *Developmental Psychology, 20*, 653–666.

WRIGHT, J. C., & VLIESTRA, A. G. (1975). The development of selective attention: From perceptual exploration to logical search. In H. W. Reese (Ed.), *Advances in child development and behavior* (Vol. 1, pp. 195–239). New York: Academic Press.

WRIGHT, P., & CROW, R. (1982). Nutrition and feeding. In P. Stratton (Ed.), *Psychobiology of the human newborn* (pp. 339–364). New York: Wiley.

WYLIE, R. (1979). *The self-concept: Theory and research on selected topics*. Lincoln, NE: University of Nebraska Press.

YANDO, R., SEITZ, V., & ZIGLER, E. (1979). *Intellectual and personality characteristics of children: Social-class and ethnic-group differences*. Hillsdale, NJ: Erlbaum.

YAP, J. N. K., & PETERS, R. DeV. (1985). An evaluation of two hypotheses concerning the dynamics of cognitive impulsivity: Anxiety-over-errors or anxiety-over-competence? *Developmental Psychology, 21*, 1055–1064.

YARROW, L. (1975). *Infant and environment: Early cognitive and motivational development*. New York: Halsted.

YARROW, M. R., CAMPBELL, J. D., & BURTON, R. V. (1970). Recollections of childhood: A study of the retrospective method. *Monographs of the Society for Research in Child Development, 35* (5, Serial No. 138).

YARROW, M. R., SCOTT, P. M., & WAXLER, C. Z. (1973). Learning concern for others. *Developmental Psychology, 8*, 240–260.

YEATES, K. O., MacPHEE, D., CAMPBELL, F. A., & RAMEY, C. T. (1983). Maternal IQ and home environment as determinants of early childhood intellectual competence: A developmental analysis. *Developmental Psychology, 19*, 731–739.

YOGMAN, M. W. (1981). Development of the father-infant relationship. In H. Fitzgerald, B. Lester, & M. W. Yogman (Eds.), *Theory and research in behavioral pediatrics* (Vol. 1, pp. 221–279). New York: Plenum.

YONAS, A., & GRANRUD, C. E. (1985). Development of visual space perception in young infants. In J. Mehler & R. Fox (Eds.), *Neonate cognition: Beyond the blooming, buzzing confusion* (pp. 45–67). Hillsdale, NJ: Erlbaum.

YONAS, A., GRANRUD, E. C., ARTERBERRY, M. E., & HANSON, B. L. (1986). Infants' distance perception from linear perspective and texture gradients. *Infant Behavior and Development, 9,* 247–256.

YONAS, A., PETTERSEN, L., & LOCKMAN, J. (1979). Young infants' sensitivity to optical information for collision. *Canadian Journal of Psychology, 33,* 268–276.

YONAS, A., PETTERSEN, L., LOCKMAN, J., & EISENBERG, P. (1980). *The perception of impending collision in 3-month-old infants.* Paper presented at the International Conference on Infant Studies, New Haven, CT.

YOUNG, G., & LEWIS, M. (1979). Effects of familiarity and maternal attention on infant peer relations. *Merrill-Palmer Quarterly, 25,* 105–119.

YOUNGER, B. A. (1985). The segregation of items into categories by ten-month-old infants. *Child Development, 56,* 1574–1583.

YOUNISS, J. (1975). Another perspective on social cognition. In A. Pick (Ed.), *Minnesota Symposia on Child Psychology* (Vol. 9, pp. 173–193). Minneapolis: University of Minnesota Press.

YOUNISS, J., & VOLPE, J. (1978). A relational analysis of children's friendships. In W. Damon (Ed.), *New directions for child development* (No. 1, pp. 1–22). San Francisco: Jossey-Bass.

ZABRUCKY, K., & RATNER, H. H. (1986). Children's comprehension monitoring and recall of inconsistent stories. *Child Development, 57,* 1401–1418.

ZAHAVI, S., & ASHER, S. R. (1978). The effect of verbal instructions on preschool children's aggressive behavior. *Journal of School Psychology, 16,* 146–153.

ZAHN-WAXLER, C., & CHAPMAN, M. (1982). Immediate antecedents of caretakers' methods of discipline. *Child Psychiatry and Human Development, 12,* 179–192.

ZAHN-WAXLER, C., CUMMINGS, E. M., MCKNEW, D. H., & RADKE-YARROW, M. (1984). Affective arousal and social interactions in young children of manic-depressive parents. *Child Development, 55,* 112–122.

ZAHN-WAXLER, C., RADKE-YARROW, M., & KING, R. A. (1979). Child-rearing and children's prosocial initiations toward victims of distress. *Child Development, 50,* 319–330.

ZAJONC, R. B. (1976). Family configuration and intelligence. *Science, 192,* 227–236.

ZAJONC, R. B., & MARKUS, G. B. (1975). Birth order and intellectual development. *Psychological Review, 82,* 74–88.

ZAJONC, R. B., MARKUS, H., & MARKUS, G. B. (1979). The birth order puzzle. *Journal of Personality and Social Psychology, 37,* 1325–1341.

ZARBATANY, L., HARTMANN, D. P., & GELFAND, D. M. (1985). Why does children's generosity increase with age: Susceptibility to experimenter influence or altruism? *Child Development, 56,* 746–756.

ZELAZO, P. R. (1972). Smiling and vocalizing: A cognitive emphasis. *Merrill-Palmer Quarterly, 18,* 350–365.

ZELAZO, P. R. (1983). The development of walking: New findings on old assumptions. *Journal of Motor Behavior, 2,* 99–137.

ZELAZO, P. R., & KOMER, M. J. (1971). Infant smiling to nonsocial stimuli and the recognition hypothesis. *Child Development, 42,* 1327–1339.

ZELAZO, P. R., ZELAZO, N. A., & KOLB, S. (1972). "Walking" in the newborn. *Science, 176,* 314–315.

ZELNICKER, T., COCHAVI, D., & YERED, J. (1974). The relationship between speed of performance and conceptual style: The effect of imposed modification of response latency. *Child Development, 45,* 779–784.

ZELNICKER, T., JEFFREY, W. E., AULT, R. L., & PARSONS, J. (1972). Analysis and modification of search strategies of impulsive and reflective children on the Matching Familiar Figures Test. *Child Development, 43,* 321–335.

ZELSON, C., LEE, S. J., & CASALINO, M. (1973). Neonatal narcotic addiction: Comparative effects of maternal intake of heroin and methadone. *New England Journal of Medicine, 289,* 1216–1220.

ZENTALL, S. S., & ZENTALL, T. R. (1983). Optimal stimulation: A model of disordered activity and performance in normal and deviant children. *Psychological Bulletin, 94,* 446–471.

ZESKIND, P. S., & LESTER, B. M. (1978). Acoustic features and auditory perception of the cries of newborns with prenatal and perinatal complications. *Child Development, 49,* 580–589.

ZESKIND, P. S., & LESTER, B. M. (1981). Analysis of cry features in newborns with differential fetal growth. *Child Development, 52,* 207–212.

ZESKIND, P. S., & RAMEY, C. T. (1978). Fetal malnutrition: An experimental study of its consequences on infant development in two caregiving environments. *Child Development, 49,* 1155–1162.

ZESKIND, P. S., & RAMEY, C. T. (1981). Preventing intellectual and interactional sequelae of fetal malnutrition: A longitudinal, transactional, and synergistic approach to development. *Child Development, 52,* 213–218.

ZIGLER, E. (1978). Controlling child abuse in America: An effort doomed to failure. In R. Bourne & E. Newberger (Eds.), *Critical perspectives on child abuse* (pp. 171–213). Lexington, MA: Heath.

ZIGLER, E. (1985). Assessing Head Start at 20: An invited commentary. *American Journal of Orthopsychiatry, 55,* 603–609.

ZIGLER, E., ABELSON, W. D., TRICKETT, P. K., & SEITZ, V. (1982). Is an intervention program necessary in order to improve economically disadvantaged children's IQ scores? *Child Development, 53,* 340–348.

ZIGLER, E., ABELSON, W. D., & SEITZ, V. (1973). Motivational factors in the performance of economically disadvantaged children on the Peabody Picture Vocabulary Test. *Child Development, 44,* 294–303.

ZIGLER, E., & BERMAN, W. (1983). Discerning the future of early childhood intervention. *American Psychologist, 38,* 894–906.

ZIGLER, E., & BUTTERFIELD, E. C. (1968). Motivational aspects of changes in IQ test performance of culturally deprived nursery school children. *Child Development, 39,* 1–14.

ZIGLER, E., & SEITZ, V. (1982). Social policy and intelligence. In R. J. Sternberg (Ed.), *Handbook of human intelligence* (pp. 586–641). Cambridge, Eng.: Cambridge University Press.

ZIGLER, E. F. (1987). Formal schooling for four-year-olds? No. *American Psychologist, 42,* 254–260.

ZIGLER, E. F., & FINN-STEVENSON, M. (1988). Applied developmental psychology. In M. H. Bornstein & M. E. Lamb (Eds.), *Developmental psychology: An advanced textbook* (2nd ed., pp. 595–634). Hillsdale, NJ: Erlbaum.

ZIMILES, H. (1985). *The role of research in an era of expanding preschool education.* Paper presented at the meeting of the American Educational Research Association, Chicago.

ZIMMERMAN, I. L., & WOO-SAM, J. M. (1978). Intelligence testing today   relevance to the school-age child. In L. Oettinger (Ed.), *The Psychologist, the school, and the child with MBD/LD* (pp. 51–69). New York: Grune & Stratton.

ZIVIN, G. (1977). On becoming subtle: Age and social rank changes in the case of social gesture. *Child Development, 48,* 1314–1321.

Name Index

Subject Index

Ability grouping, 683, 686, 690
Abortion, 89
  among teenagers, 186
Absolutism of moral perspectives, 518
Abstract thinking
  and Kohlberg's postconventional level, 525–526
  and Piaget's formal operational stage, 225, 249, 251, 252–253, 255
Abused children. *See* Maltreated children
Academic achievement
  in America, 688
  cross-national research on, 689–690
  home environment and, 688
  homework assigned and, 688, 690
  quality of instruction and, 680, 690
  racial and ethnic differences in, 688
  student body size and, 676
  time devoted to instruction and, 680, 690
  traditional versus open classrooms and, 679
  see also Education
Academic psychology, influence of, 19–29
Accelerated learning programs, 685
Accommodation, 223–224, 226, 462
Achievement motivation, 472–474, 475, 555, 683
Acquired immune deficiency syndrome (AIDS), 101
Action-consequence learning, 139
Action for Children's Television, 672
Adaptation
  and differentiation theory of perceptual development, 277
  emotions and, 416, 421, 423, 424
  evolutionary concept of, 10–11
  Piaget's concept of, 27, 220, 222, 223–224, 227, 229
Adaptive behavior inventories, 349
Adolescence
  antisocial behavior in, 659
  awareness of sex stereotypes in, 553

conformity in, 575, 661 n, 662–663
early and late maturation in, 190–192
formal operational stage (Piaget's), 253–254
friendship in, 495
identity in, 476–480, 575, 659
importance of peer evaluations in, 468
peer group norms in, 658–659
peer relations in, 647, 662–663
person perception in, 481
physical growth in, 176, 177, 179–180, 181
reaction to divorce in, 620, 621
self-concept in, 468
self-esteem in, 662
sex-role identity in, 574–575
suicide in, 478
transition to, 471
see also Puberty
Adolescent health, 14
Adoption studies
  attachment and socioemotional development 449
  heritability of intelligence, 115, 340–343, 351
  heritability of temperament and personality, 433
  heritability of weight, 209
  transracial, 343
Adrenal cortex, 195
Adrenocorticotropic hormone (ACTH), 195
Advertising, on TV, 669
Affect, expression of, 417, 426, 489
Affection, and physical growth, 212–213
African cultures
  body builds in, 211
  child rearing practices in, 33
  family traditions in, 611
  moral reasoning in, 531
  response to infant cries in, 132
Aggression
  biological influences on, 587–588

classroom crowding and, 675
development of, 585–587
environmental influences on, 588–590, 592
in families, 588–590, 591
hormone levels and, 588
hostile, 585–586
inferring others' intentions and, 483, 590
instrumental, 585
in maltreated children, 510, 634
modeling of, 53, 54–55, 510, 590, 667
predisposition for, 587
punishment and, 510, 588, 590
reinforcement of, 661
sex differences in, 566, 574, 578, 585–590
television violence and, 52–54, 666–668
treatments for, 591–592
verbal, 586
XYY syndrome and, 86
Alcohol, and pregnancy, 98, 105
Alleles, 76
Alphabet letters, discrimination of, 278–279
Altruistic behavior
  development of, 648
  empathy and, 428, 505
  in friendship, 494
  induction and, 507
  models of, 509–511
  moral reasoning and, 535
  social problem-solving and, 489
Altruistic reasoning, 539–541
Alveoli, 94
Amenorrhea, 193
American Psychological Association, ethical guidelines 64, 65
American Sign Language (ASL), 368
American society
  education in, 686–690
  violence in, 635, 636
Amnesia, infantile, 300